TORT LAW

THE AMERICAN AND LOUISIANA PERSPECTIVES

Third Revised Edition

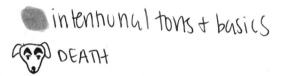 intentional torts + basics

DEATH

TORT LAW

THE AMERICAN AND LOUISIANA PERSPECTIVES

Third Revised Edition

BY

FRANK L. MARAIST, LSU LAW CENTER, EMERITUS

JOHN M. CHURCH, LSU LAW CENTER

WILLIAM R. CORBETT, LSU LAW CENTER

THOMAS C. GALLIGAN, LSU LAW CENTER

THOMAS E. RICHARD, SOUTHERN UNIVERSITY LAW CENTER, RETIRED

THOMAS M. FLANAGAN, TULANE UNIVERSITY LAW SCHOOL

VANDEPLAS PUBLISHING

UNITED STATES OF AMERICA

Tort law – The American and Louisiana Perspectives, Third Revised Edition

Frank L. Maraist, John M. Church, William R. Corbett, Thomas C. Galligan, Thomas E. Richard & Thomas M. Flanagan

Published by:

Vandeplas Publishing LLC - July 2017

801 International Parkway, 5th Floor
Lake Mary, FL. 32746 - USA

www.vandeplaspublishing.com

ISBN: 978-1-60042-290-4

ABOUT THE AUTHORS

John M. Church is the Harry S. Redmon Professor of Law and Allen L. Smith Professor of Law at the Paul M. Hebert Law Center of Louisiana State University.

William R. Corbett is the Frank L. Maraist Professor of Law and Wex S. Malone Professor of Law at the Paul M. Hebert Law Center of Louisiana State University.

Thomas M. Flanagan is an Adjunct Associate Professor of Law at Tulane University Law School.

Thomas C. Galligan is Dean and Professor at the Paul M. Hebert Law Center of Louisiana State University.

Frank L. Maraist is an Emeritus Professor of Law at the Paul M. Hebert Law Center of Louisiana State University.

Thomas E. Richard is the retired Clyde C. Tidwell Professor of Law at Southern University Law Center.

DEDICATION AND **E**XPRESSIONS OF **A**PPRECIATION

The authors dedicate this book to their colleague, mentor, and friend Professor Frank L. Maraist, LSU Law Center, who wrote the first version of this book and invited them into the project.

The authors also thank Mrs. Madeline Babin, LSU Law Center, for faithfully and conscientiously working on this book through the years on all the versions and with all the authors.

TABLE OF CONTENTS

TABLE OF CASES

CHAPTER 1

INTRODUCTION

This chapter introduces the first year law student to the law of Torts. The role that tort law plays in the law generally and in society is explained below. First, however, one must understand the basic principles about law.

Generally speaking, law is the set of rules which governs a person's conduct toward other persons. Law can be classified generally by reference to its source and to its functions.

In a democracy, the general source of law is the people. However, through constitutions, the people delegate to the legislature the power to make the general rules that govern their conduct (subject, of course, to retention of some power by the people in the form of constitutional guaranties), and delegate to the judiciary the power to interpret and, with the aid of the executive branch, to enforce those laws. In some situations, a court has jurisdiction over a case but the legislature has not provided the governing substantive law. In such cases, the court before which the matter is brought must make a determination of what law governs; this sometimes is called jurisprudential law, or common law. Any jurisprudential law is subject to subsequent modification by the legislature. Thus the relative rankings of law, based upon their sources, is as follows:

> Constitutional law
> Statutory law
> Jurisprudential (or common) law

In the United States, our unique form of federalism – "dual sovereignty" – produces additional sources of law – federal and state. Where federal law applies, it may preempt any application of state law. Thus where the matter has been delegated by the people to the federal government, the strength of the laws is accordingly

> Federal constitutional law
> Federal statutory law
> Federal jurisprudential (or common) law

A federal statute may not contravene or exceed the federal constitutional power. In some cases, the matter may be delegated to the federal sovereign by the people, but there may be no applicable federal law (Congress has not acted). In that event, state law may apply as "surrogate" federal law.

Where the matter has been delegated by the people to the state, the strength of the laws is accordingly

> State constitutional law
> State statutory law
> State jurisprudential (or common) law

Federal and state constitutions provide that the sovereign may not deprive a person of liberty or property without "due process of law." This means that a law may not be enforced against an individual unless the individual receives the procedure which is "due" him – fair notice and an opportunity to be heard. These constitutional guaranties underlie a procedural system through which the laws are enforced.

The sanctions which may be imposed as a means of enforcing the law may be a fine or imprisonment, or both. When those are the main sanctions, the law is said to be criminal substantive law, enforced by the sovereign's prosecuting attorney (usually the district attorney). In the larger number of cases, and regardless of whether the conduct also is a crime, the conduct may violate the rules designed to protect the rights of a particular individual. This is properly called civil (as opposed to criminal) law, and is enforced by the party who claims his rights have been violated, and who may institute a civil action to enforce those rights. Tort law is such law. Other kinds of civil law include law governing property rights, contracts, marriage and the family. These laws generally are state laws, although there may be some applicable federal law. An explanation of tort law and its relationship to other areas of the civil (non-criminal) law is set forth in the following article.

Excerpts from "OF ENVELOPES AND LEGENDS: REFLECTIONS ON TORT LAW"
Prof. Frank L. Maraist
61 La.L.Rev. 155 (2000)

* * * * *

"(W)hen the act of one person (the actor) causes harm to another (the victim), the first inquiry in tort law analysis is whether the legislature has made a determination of how the loss should be allocated between them. If there is a statute providing that an actor who does a particular act which causes harm to another must bear the cost ("you break, you pay"), then tort law is irrelevant. The legislature has spoken, and, given the "pecking order" of law,[1] that's it. Such statutes are rare, however.

If there is no damage-allocating statute,[2] the next inquiry is whether the parties (actor and victim) have agreed in advance how the loss should be borne. In such a case, lawyers are wont to say that the contract is the law between the parties.[3] This, of course, provokes the three questions governing contract law: Can they agree? Did they agree? What did they agree to? If the parties have not agreed, or if the law does not permit them to agree (because we need a Latin name to keep up appearances, we say the contract is *contra bones mores*),[4] then contract law is inapplicable and the next level – tort law – is reached.

This does not mean that legislation and contract law disappear from the tort process, however. A statute which does not directly impose the loss upon the actor may do so indirectly, by judicial adoption of it as the standard for tort liability.[5] Contract law also plays a major role in the configuration of tort law. One example is contractual waiver in advance of any liability for a future

---

[1] Every high school student who has not escaped a Civics course knows that legislatures make law and judges apply it. Lawyers (and, before very long, law students) know that judges make more law than do legislatures. Judges make law in interpreting and applying statutes to given fact patterns when the statutory language does not clearly dictate the result. (Sometimes judges overzealously find that the statutory language does not clearly dictate the answer, and thus seize the opportunity to make law through interpretation of an "ambiguous" statute.) Judges also make law in the many situations which arise in which there is no legislative expression on the issue. In such a case, a court with jurisdiction must either allow the matter to proceed to trial, or dismiss the case at the outset (a demurrer, a motion to dismiss for failure to state a claim upon which relief can be granted, or, in Louisiana procedure, an exception of no cause of action). Whichever way he or she goes, the judge is making substantive law.

[2] *See, e.g.,* R.S. 23:106 (an employment bureau licensee "shall pay all damages resulting in unlawful action in its capacity as an employment service"); R.S. 46:1956 (person who interferes with or injures an assistance dog "shall pay for actual damages for any economic loss to any person aggrieved thereby"). A statutory allocation of the loss may be altered by contract, although such a reallocation by the parties may in some cases be void. *See* note 6, *post.*

[3] *See, e.g., Caskey v. Kelly Oil Co.,* 737 So. 2d 1257 (La. 1999).

[4] Translated "against good morals." Such contracts are void. *See, e.g., Holliday v. Holliday,* 358 So. 2d 618 (La. 1978). Thus the law may not permit a party to "contract away" the tort-imposed duty to avoid intentionally or willfully harming another. *See, e.g.,* La. Civ. Code Art. 2004.

[5] This generally is reflected in the doctrine that the violation of a certain criminal statute is negligence per se, i.e., in and of itself without more. The result is a conversion of the negligence action into a strict liability or absolute liability action. *See, e.g., Meany v. Meany,* 639 So. 2d 229 (La. 1994).

act which may cause harm.[6] Such a waiver generally is upheld when the damages are traditional contract damages (the so called "benefit of the bargain")[7] but often is rejected as *contra bones mores* when the damages are traditional tort damages (personal injury and property damage).[8] Conversely, tort law is hesitant to provide recovery of damages where the underlying tortious conduct also involves a breach of contract.[9] Tort law may borrow contract law, such as in the development of product liability, where the underlying theory of recovery was first tort (negligence),and then contract (redhibition, or, in common laws terms, breach of implied warranty) and, finally, back to tort (strict products liability).[10] Of course, contract law makes its most pervasive foray into tort law with insurance contracts indemnifying the actor against damages which caused the actor's tortious conduct.[11]

As noted, if there is no applicable damage-allocating statute or contractual provision and the victim seeks to impose the loss upon the actor, traditional tort law rules apply. Over several hundred years and millions of cases, the common law has developed an approach to resolving tort claims which focuses upon the general risk which the actor's conduct created, and the specific risk which the victim suffered. Not surprisingly, Louisiana law, although developed from civil law traditions,[12] applies the same "general risk/special risk" concept.

The General Risks

The first inquiry in the traditional tort approach is identifying the general type of risk that may apply – is there a general principle of tort law which condemns the actor's conduct? If there is, then the other question is whether that general risk protects against the specific risk that caused the damage, i.e., should this actor be liable to this victim for these damages occurring in this particular manner? There are six types of conduct which tort law generally condemns: (1) where the actor's conduct is intentional,[13] (2) where the actor's conduct was willful or wanton (sometimes termed gross negligence or recklessness),[14] (3) where the actor's conduct was negligence,[15] (4) where the actor's

---

[6] Sometimes called express contractual assumption of the risk. The classic example is the term in a parking lot ticket by which the customer relieves the lot of liability for damage to the vehicle.

[7] *See, e.g.,* C.C. Art. 2548 (parties may agree to exclude warranty) and C.C. Art.2004 (any clause is null that in advance limits the liability of a party for intentional or gross fault). Thus a party may limit liability for economic loss caused by another's conduct which is not intentional or gross fault.

[8] *See, e.g.,* C.C. Art. 2004, providing in relevant part that "(a)ny clause is null that, in advance, excludes or limits the liability of one party for causing physical injury to the other party."

[9] *See, e.g.,* W. Page Keeton, et al, Prosser and Keeton on the Law of Torts, § 92 (5th Ed. 1984).

[10] *See, e.g.,* Dan B. Dobbs, The Law of Torts, pp 969-975 (West, 2000).

[11] Insurance is a contract by which the insurer agrees to indemnify (repay) the insured for damages sustained through the conduct of the insured or a third person. A contract may repay the insured for the damages to his person or property (examples: collision and comprehensive coverage in an auto policy, or fire and extended coverage in a homeowner's policy), and/or may indemnify the insured against his tort liability to third persons (examples: the liability coverage, usually $10/$20M, in an auto policy). The first type of insurance is sometimes called "first party" insurance, and the second type is often called "third party" or "liability" insurance. Either type of insurance is a method by which the law permits a group of persons (those insured by the same insurer against the same kind of risk) to spread their losses among themselves and reduce the impact which a particular member's loss may have upon him or her. *See* footnote 29, *post.*

[12] The "fountainhead" of Louisiana tort law is one article in the Civil Code. That article (2315) provides rather cryptically that "(e)very act whatever of man that causes damage to another obliges him by whose fault it happened to repair it." A comprehensive body of Louisiana tort law has been developed by judicial application of that 20-word legislative directive.

[13] *See e.g.,* Maraist & Galligan, Louisiana Tort Law, pp. 1-15 (Michie, 1996).
[14] *Ibid.* The most common general risks, discussed below, are that the victim will be injured by the intentional conduct or negligence of another. There is another level of egregious conduct which falls somewhere between

3

relationship to a person makes the actor liable for the wrongful conduct of that person (vicarious liability),[16] (5) where the actor's relationship to a thing makes the actor liable for the damage-causing condition of the thing (strict liability)[17] and (6) where the actor participates in an activity which subjects him or her to liability for the damages caused by that activity (absolute liability)?[18] When the actor's conduct does not fit within one of these six general risks, traditional tort law dictates that the loss should stay where it is, i.e., with the victim. At this point, one may say there is "no tort" or that the injury-causing event was "an accident," although that term is too legally imprecise to be helpful.

Each general risk is confined by an operative principle which may be precise or vague. The intentional torts, generally, are precise; a specific operative principle determines whether certain conduct is a battery, or an assault, or a false imprisonment, or an intentional infliction of emotional distress. For example, the tort of battery occurs when the actor does an act which is substantially certain to cause a harmful or offensive touching to a person of ordinary sensibilities.[19] Other general risks often have imprecise operative principles which invite more fact-specific analysis. The classic is negligence – one is negligent if he or she fails to act as a reasonably prudent person under all of the circumstances.[20] The application of the definition/operative principle of a general risk to a particular set of facts may occur often enough, and produce the same result often enough, that a "rule" of tort law develops.[21] However, one should never lose sight of the fact that it is the operative principle, and not the rule, which controls.

Nowhere is the general risk inquiry more fragmented (at least in Louisiana) than in the negligence sphere. The general risk of negligent conduct is subdivided into traditional elements of duty, breach and causation.[22] Duty, generally, asks whether the actor should have taken any care whatsoever for the safety of others. This turns upon the foreseeability of harm from conduct, i.e., could the actor foresee that his or her conduct would expose others to a risk of harm?[23] Arguably,

---

intentional and negligent conduct. While authorities generally agree that it is only one level, it may be given any one of several names by a particular jurisdiction. Other names frequently used are willful and wanton. The first thing a law student should learn is to escape the "tyranny of terminology." i.e., identify the nature of the conduct which the law proscribes, and not focus solely upon the name which the lawmaker uses.

[15] *Ibid.*

[16] *Ibid.*

[17] *Ibid.*

[18] *Ibid.*

[19] *See, e.g.,* Dobbs, note 13, *supra,* pp. 52-63; *see also,* Maraist & Galligan, note 16, *supra*, pp. 27-29.

[20] *See, e.g.,* Dobbs, note 13, *supra,* pp. 275-293; Maraist & Galligan, note 16, *supra*, pp. 75-77.

[21] The classic example is the rule that mere words do not make an assault. Ordinarily this is true, because in most cases words without some overt act will not satisfy the operative principle governing assault, i.e., an act which is substantially certain to cause apprehension of an imminent harmful or offensive touching to a person of ordinary sensibilities. But one can envision cases in which mere words alone are enough, given the particular strengths and susceptibilities of parties (such as "I'm gonna whip you" told to a child, or, for that matter, to an adult who is trapped in an elevator with the heavyweight champion).

[22] *See, e.g.,* Maraist & Galligan, note 116, *supra,* pp. 75-80; Dobbs, note, 13, *supra,* pp. 270-271.

[23] Foreseeability in fact asks whether a reasonable person, in ordering his or her daily affairs, would take this risk into consideration. For example, a reasonable person may look both ways before crossing a one-way street (it is likely enough that someone is proceeding in the wrong direction to take that into consideration); however, would he or she look skyward (although it is possible that a helicopter could be landing in the street)? It is important to draw this distinction, because foreseeability also has become a legal term of art, used in determining legal causation....

that is the end of the duty inquiry, and the reasonableness of the actor's conduct is considered at the breach level. Some, however, would add to the duty inquiry a reasonableness factor, i.e., assuming the actor could foresee that his conduct would expose others to a risk of harm, was that risk unreasonable, in the light of all of the factors (determined for the most part by balancing of the likelihood and severity of harm from the conduct against the cost to society of banning the conduct). The breach inquiry is whether the actor acted reasonably in the light of the foreseeable risk.[24] Sometimes the breach inquiry is expanded to encompass the duty inquiry, such as where a court states that the defendant owed a duty to the plaintiff to drive less than the speed limit in a rainy school zone shortly after expiration of the special zone speed limit.[25]

One might wonder why what is apparently the same operative principle is worded differently by different courts at different times, or why some legal issues are treated at different levels of analysis, i.e., as part of the general risk, or as a specific risk. For example, the operative principle of the intentional tort of battery may be defined by a court as "an act substantially certain to cause a harmful or offensive touching" or as "an act substantially certain to cause a touching which is harmful or offensive" or as "an act substantially certain to cause an unconsented to touching." Sometimes these differences are merely sloppy lawyering, but in many cases they are deliberate policy choices.[26]

How do courts formulate (and, as is frequently necessary, alter, expand or contract) these operative principles? Generally, they do the same thing a legislator does (or should do) when he or she must vote on legislation: weighing the societal good that will come from imposing liability upon the actor against the societal harm that imposition may produce. There always is some societal harm from any imposition of liability upon an actor for any conduct. One is infringement upon the freedom of that actor to do as he or she pleases, something which we all would concede is a fundamental American value. Another is proper allocation of resources: lawsuits require judges and court reporters and bailiffs and courthouses and juries, and we worry about allocating too much of our resources to the judicial resolution of controversies. Yet another evil in imposition of liability is that it may overdeter desirable conduct; one may be hesitant, for example, to impose liability upon an actor who botches a rescue, lest future rescuers would be inclined to look the other way. Still another evil in imposing liability is society's desire to encourage people to learn to live together peacefully in a now-crowded world; thus society may command that they sometime bear "the slings and arrows of outrageous fortune."

However, a reasonable person may not be willing to accept some conduct by others, and if the law does not provide such a reasonable person with a remedy, he or she is more than likely to retaliate in kind. One must never forget that a major purpose of the civil law, as with the criminal law, is to keep the peace. Thus if the conduct is such that a reasonable person cannot be expected to turn the other cheek, tort law provides substitute vengeance by permitting an award of damages to the victim. This is the deterrent effect of tort law, which, although waning in importance, still remains a valuable societal policy.

---

[24] *See* note 25, *supra.* One may discern that, depending upon the test applied to determine "duty," the "duty" and "breach" inquiries may be duplicative. This is so, but the only important distinction in such a case may be whether the judge or the jury decides the issue....

[25] *See, e.g., Posecai v. Wal-Mart* Stores, 752 So. 2d 762 (La. 1999) (in protecting patrons against criminal acts of third persons, a storeowner may owe a "duty" to post security guards, or "a duty to implement lesser security measures such as using surveillance cameras, installing improved lighting or fencing, or trimming shrubbery"); *Foster v. Conagra Poultry Co.,* 670 So. 2d 471 (La.App. 3 Cir. 1995); *Miller v. Bailey,* 621 So. 2d 1174 (La.App. 3 Cir. 1993) ("motorists have a duty to drive at a speed reasonable for the conditions of the road, the weather, the traffic and the time of day").

[26] The difference in language between the first and second definitions may produce different results on the issue of who bears the burden of a reasonable mistake by the actor. The difference between the second and third definitions may produce a variance in whether the judge or jury decides the close cases, and who bears the burden of persuading the one who decides (since consent would be an affirmative defense in the second definition but lack of consent would be an element of plaintiff's cause of action in the third).

An equally important goal of tort law is compensating the victim. We do not want to deter all accidents at any cost (if we did, we could ban automobiles, couldn't we?). So another goal of tort law is to spread the accident losses which we allow in a way that will reduce the societal impact of those losses.[27] Here, of course, the best spreaders are governments, liability insurers and manufacturers of injury-causing products, and it is not surprising that they are the most common defendants in tort litigation.

Other societal goals can be fostered by granting or withholding tort remedies. The classic nineteenth century example was the limited liability of railroads (it wouldn't make sense to give a company land to build a railroad and then impose staggering tort liability upon the company for operating the railroad, would it?). In the twentieth century, tort law was manipulated for such varying reasons as promoting the opening of private land to recreational use[28] and thwarting drug dealers. [29] There are those who hold that the prevailing societal policy motivating tort law in the second half of the twentieth century was a redistribution of the wealth by allowing unlimited tort recovery against the deepest pockets (you may not believe it, but some do, i.e., witness the tort reform of the last half of the twentieth century).

Through the years, an important societal policy fostered by tort law is satisfaction of the community's sense of justice, i.e., will it seem fair to the man (or woman) on the street if society transfers this loss from this victim to this actor?[30] Note carefully that the standard should be fairness to the disinterested man on the street, and not to the parties; the parties make up their minds as to what is fair before the litigation begins.

Accommodating these policies in the allocation of losses through tort law has led to a judicial recognition of the general risks which, if engaged in by an actor, would justify transferring the loss from the victim to that actor. The actor's conduct in exposing another to harm from a general risk may be labeled as "fault,"[31] such as where the conduct is intentional or negligent, or may be treated as liability without fault, such as where vicarious or absolute liability is imposed. As noted before, if the actor's conduct does not violate a general risk, tort law will not impose liability, although liability may be imposed on some other basis, or the loss may be redistributed through some other law, such as Social Security disability benefits.

---

[27] The law cannot make a loss "go away" but can reduce the societal impact of the loss by spreading it among a larger group. Assume, for example, that a fire destroys a law student's apartment during the first semester of law school. The student now needs $4,000 to purchase the necessities to continue law school. If, as often would be the case, the student could not come up with such funds immediately, a law career would be delayed or denied. But would an extra expense of $50 delay or defeat the pursuit of a law degree? Assuming it would not, then if each of the student fire victim's classmates chipped in $50, there would be no interruption of any legal career. The loss would remain, but its destructive impact upon the quality of human life would be eliminated.

[28] *See, e.g.,* R.S. 9:2791 and R.S. 9:2795.

[29] *See, e.g.,* R.S. 9:2800.61.

[30] This societal goal is perhaps the strongest argument for the continuation of the jury system. Jury systems are costly (both in imposition upon the citizenry and in judicial control). However, serving on a jury affords the average citizen the opportunity to participate in the governing of fellow citizens, a not unimportant goal in a democracy. More importantly, if one wants to determine the community's sense of justice, is there any better way than to submit the matter to members of the community selected in an impartial manner and presented with the relevant facts?

[31] Because of the Louisiana Civil Code constraint (C.C. Art. 2315 – liability shall be based upon fault), our courts have been compelled to define as "fault" both the traditional common law fault (intent and negligence) and the common law liability without fault, i.e., strict liability and absolute liability. Implementing the third kind of liability without fault, vicarious liability, has required the courts to tiptoe around the express language of Civil Code Article 2320, which provides that a master is liable for the damage occasioned by a servant "only...when the master...might have prevented the act which caused the damage...."

The Specific Risk

A determination that an actor's conduct falls within the scope of a general risk does not resolve the inquiry, however. The courts, and the judicial system, then must turn the inquiry to the specific risk question, i.e., assuming the actor's conduct exposes others to an impermissible general risk, do we nevertheless want to impose liability upon this actor to this victim for these damages occurring in this manner? This question must be asked to assure that transferring the loss in a particular case will achieve the best balance of the societal policies that initially led us to proscribe the general risk (condemn the actor's conduct). The specific risk question could be asked as one question, but, for a variety or reasons (some of which are purely historical) it is not. Instead, the judicial system has subdivided the question into subissues, the most important of which are causation and affirmative defenses.

Part of the "causation specific risk" inquiry is purely factual: did this actor's conduct have anything to do with this victim's loss? The answer is clearly "yes" if reasonable minds could conclude from the facts that "but for" the actor's conduct, the victim would not have suffered the loss. But in many cases (usually involving multiple actors or the coalescing improper conduct of the actor and the victim) one cannot comfortably infer causation through the use of the "but for" test. Nevertheless, where the actor's conduct could have played some part in causing the victim's harm and the actor's conduct exposed society to a prohibited general risk, it arguably is better policy (deterrence, spreading, fairness) to impose some or all of the liability upon that actor. Thus cause in fact has been expanded, for policy reasons, to include policy determinations, including a gradual alteration of the test for causation from "but for" to an inquiry into whether the actor's conduct was a "substantial factor" in bringing about the victim's harm.

The other specific risk questions may be asked at different stages of a torts analysis, including at the general risk level. Take the case of the imprudent victim. The impact of his or her conduct may defeat recovery at the general risk level, or at the specific risk level. Thus a victim who voluntarily encounters a potential batterer may be denied recovery because there was no battery (the act was not substantially certain to cause a touching which was offensive because of the consent) or could be denied recovery because of a specific risk inquiry (the victim consented to the battery, and consent is an affirmative defense defeating tort recovery.) Courts divide on the method of handling some of the specific risk inquiries.

In negligence, the "this plaintiff" specific risk inquiry may be made at the general risk duty level, the general risk breach level, or at the specific risk level. Consider, for example, the imprudent plaintiff who slides down a hill backwards on a garbage can cover and strikes a parking lot light fixture. If he or she is the last best avoider of this accident, societal policy may dictate that the loss should not be transferred from the landowner to the slider. Reaching this conclusion, a court may say that the actor did not owe a duty, or owed a duty but did not breach it, or that the actor's conduct was not the legal cause of the harm, or that the victim's recovery is barred by an affirmative defense (assumption of the risk or contributory negligence).[32]

The victim's failure to timely pursue his claim against the actor, or his unwillingness to abide by the judicial result, raise issues of judicial efficiency (how many courts will be needed) and fairness to the actor. These policies are reflected in specific risk principles that may bar the untimely[33] or repeated pursuit[34] of the victim's claim.

---

[32] At one time, the actor's recovery in such a situation would have been barred by the affirmative defense of assumption of the risk. The actor also would be contributorily negligent, and when contributory negligence also was a bar, the distinction between the two affirmative defenses rarely was made. With the advent of comparative negligence, it has become necessary to redefine the role of assumption of the risk. The Louisiana Supreme Court has abolished it. *See Murray v. Ramada Inn*, 521 So. 2d 1123 (La. 1988). Nevertheless the abolition of one specific risk category does not resolve the issue of whether the loss should be transferred to the actor from the victim, and that battle is being fought at other levels, such as duty, breach and legal cause. *See, e..g. Pitre v. Louisiana Tech University*, 673 So. 2d 585 (La. 1996).

The "this defendant" specific risk inquiry also may be made at the general risk level, but more frequently is made at the specific risk level as an affirmative defense. The most significant is so-called tort immunity, which absolves the actor from the consequences of all or part of his conduct toward a victim. The most common type of immunity is sovereign immunity, which relieves the governmental actor of liability to any person for certain activities which violate a general risk proscription and cause loss to a victim. Other immunities encompass both "this plaintiff" and "this defendant," such as the family and workplace immunities.

Both at common law and in Louisiana, the "these damages" specific risk inquiry frequently is made at the duty level. Thus one may not owe a duty to protect against harm to an unforeseeable plaintiff, or from causing mental anguish unaccompanied by contemporaneous physical injury, or from a family member's loss of society with a trauma victim. It also may be made at the causation level, a fact that has caused consternation to students of the law at every level (law school, law practice and judicial). Treating the issue at the causation level has led to the development of two separate causation elements -- causation in fact, discussed above, and legal or proximate cause. Thus a jurisdiction which determines that the better balance of societal policies (overdeterrence, fairness, interference with contract law, etc.) dictates that a victim should not recover economic loss unless his person or his tangible property is damaged may express that conclusion in terms of "no duty" to protect against certain economic harm, or may conclude that the defendant's breach of his duty was not the "legal cause" of the economic harm. In either case, the result to the litigants is the same. Not so for the judicial system, as law students and lawyers struggle to comprehend why sometimes there is no duty and sometimes there is no legal or proximate cause. This "limited duty," "duty/risk" and proximate or legal cause inquiry is the favorite of law professors,[35] probably because it affords the best opportunity to confound law students.[36]

Perhaps the easiest of the specific risk inquiries to categorize is the "this manner" risk, i.e., do we want to impose liability for damages occurring in a particular manner? When the inquiry reaches this level, the major societal policy at play is fairness (although arguably there is a deterrence/overdeterrence consideration in many of these cases). It is here that foreseeability in fact plays another important role. There is compelling logic in the argument that if we tell members of society to act reasonable in the light of the harm they can foresee, it is fundamentally unfair to hold them liable for damage occurring in a manner which they could not foresee. This has led to the emerging rule that the scope of the risks for negligent conduct is limited to the damages which the actor in fact could have foreseen when he acted. However, there are at least two problems with this conclusion. One is the fairness argument. What if the actor could not foresee the manner in which his or her conduct would cause damage, but if he had acted to avoid the harm he could foresee, it also would have avoided the unforeseeable harm that occurred? Fairness then seems to point toward imposing liability upon the actor for the unforseeable harm, particularly where the victim's conduct was not improper. The second problem is that some societal policy may dictate that there should be a limitation on damages which are foreseeable in fact, such as when a railroad engine starts a fire which spreads over a large area and causes catastrophic damages. What if, as in the 19th century, the societal policy was to limit the damages for which a railroad was responsible although such damages were foreseeable in fact when the actor (the railroad) acted? If the test in the particular jurisdiction for the scope of the risks was foreseeability, a court in denying recovery beyond the first building could state confidently that the burning of the second building was "not foreseeable." In such a case,

---

[33] A "stale claim" may be barred by the affirmative defense of laches or by a statute of limitations (in Louisiana, liberative prescription).

[34] Repeated litigation of the same issue may be barred by the doctrines of res judicata, collateral estoppel and law of the case. *See, e.g.* R.S. 13:4231, et seq.; *Lejano v. Bandak*, 705 So. 2d 158 (La. 1997).

[35] The "love affair" between law professors and proximate cause is evidenced by the length of the chapters on that subject in Torts casebooks.

[36] As Professor Bill Corbett ... so aptly puts it, "using proximate cause to baffle students is like hunting deer with a machine gun."

foreseeability becomes a term of art. Although the result may be societally acceptable, it leaves in its wake generations of law students and lawyers who are puzzled by the concept of "foreseeability."

The Bottom Line

The "bottom line" is that in every case in which an actor's conduct causes harm to another (the victim) and there is no statute or valid contractual agreement which determines where the loss should fall, the judicial system, applying "tort law," must decide whether the greatest good for the greatest number dictates that the loss should be transferred from the actor to the victim, or should stay where it is. The determination should be made by balancing the competing societal policies (values, if you will). The balancing cannot be made de novo in the resolution of every dispute in which the claim is that the actor's conduct was tortious; such a result would undercut one or more of the relevant policies. Thus without established rules, one could not predict with a reasonable amount of accuracy whether certain conduct will trigger imposition of liability for any damages it causes. Without some degree of predictability, there would be either overdeterrence or a loss of deterrence, an inability to properly spread the unavoidable losses through insurance, and, most importantly, society probably would perceive that "the law is an ass." Thus more precise guidelines have been developed by the lawmaker (which, in tort law, is primarily the jurist). Those guidelines take the shape of general risks which, if not avoided, can lead to imposition of liability. Where the actor does not avoid the general risk, tort laws makes a second inquiry into whether the better balance of societal policies dictates that a particular loss to a particular victim occurring in a particular manner should be transferred from this victim to this actor. All of this has led to operative principles such as battery, negligence, legal cause, immunity and contributory negligence. These principles, when applied to the myriad of fact patterns that emerge in a crowded society, may evolve into hard and fast rules of liability or no liability. The result is a "rule," such as one which provides that the driver of a rear-ending automobile is presumed negligent *vis a vis* the driver of the preceding vehicle. Students of the law must constantly be cognizant of the three "levels" of law – the competing societal values, the operative principles that spring from a balancing of those policies, and the rules that develop from the application of an operative principle to a frequently recurring factual scenario. The lawyer should know the operative principles and the rules, but should be ever cognizant of their origin, i.e., as a perceived proper balance of competing societal values. And the lawyer should appreciate that as society changes, its values change, and there eventually will be a concomitant change in the tort rule or the tort principle, or both.

* * * * *

For an example of how courts consider whether there is tort liability, consider the following case.

[handwritten: Q) Does La recognize tort of neg spoiliation?]

REYNOLDS
v.
BORDELON
172 So. 3d 589 (La. 2015)

[handwritten: A) NO, no COA exists in La bc no duty to preserve evi]

CLARK, J.

We granted certiorari to determine whether Louisiana recognizes the tort of negligent spoliation. For the reasons that follow, we hold that no cause of action exists for negligent spoliation of evidence. Regardless of any alleged source of the duty, whether general or specific, public policy in our state precludes the existence of a duty to preserve evidence. Thus, there is no tort. Alternative avenues of recourse are available within Louisiana's evidentiary, discovery, and contractual laws. Nonetheless, we remand for further consideration of the plaintiff's petition, finding sufficient facts were alleged by the plaintiff to state a potential breach of contract claim.

Facts and Procedural History

On March 15, 2008, a multi-vehicle accident occurred in St. Tammany Parish. The plaintiff, Richard Reynolds, sustained injuries and filed suit against Robert Bordelon, III, the driver alleged to have caused the accident. The plaintiff also asserted claims under the Louisiana Products Liability Act against Nissan North America ("Nissan"), the alleged manufacturer and distributor of the plaintiff's 2003 Infiniti G35, for failure of the airbag to deploy.[1] Additionally, the plaintiff's petition alleged that his insurer, Automobile Club Inter–Insurance Exchange ("ACIIE") and the custodian of his vehicle after the accident, Insurance Auto Auctions Corporation ("IAA"), failed to preserve his vehicle for inspection purposes to determine whether any defects existed, despite being put on notice of the need for preservation.

ACIIE and IAA each filed exceptions of no cause of action, arguing a claim of spoliation of evidence requires "an intentional destruction of evidence for the purpose of depriving opposing parties of its use" and the petition contained no allegation of an intentional act by ACIIE or IAA. The trial court sustained the exception but allowed the plaintiff to amend his petition within fifteen days to state a cause of action pursuant to La. Code Civ. P. art. 934. The plaintiff filed a First Supplemental and Amending Petition for Damages, which reads, in pertinent part:

5.

Plaintiff avers that shortly after the serious accident of March 15, 2008, giving rise to the instant matter the named defendants herein, INSURANCE AUTO AUCTIONS CORP, acting upon information and belief as the storage facility and/or as custodian of the Petitioner's vehicle on behalf of and/or in connection with AUTOMOBILE CLUB INTER–INSURANCE EXCHANGE, d/b/a "Triple A Insurance", insurer of Plaintiff, RICHARD L. REYNOLDS both respectively failed to maintain custody and/or preserve Plaintiff's vehicle despite both Defendants being on notice by Plaintiff that the vehicle was to be preserved as evidence for a lawsuit. Plaintiff avers that defendants had notice that a lawsuit was likely and was going to be pursued.

6.

Plaintiff submits that the Defendants owed certain duties to Plaintiff and are liable unto Plaintiff for their negligence resulting in damages in the following non-exclusive manners:

A.) Defendants owed a duty unto the Plaintiff pursuant to La. C.C. art. 2315, as they were respectively on notice to prudently preserve, maintain, and to refrain from any alienation or destruction of Plaintiff's vehicle to be utilized in a tort claim with Defendants agreeing and understanding that the vehicle would be maintained for purposes of litigation.

B.) Additionally, Defendants are liable unto Plaintiff as their negligent actions cause[d] impairment of the instant civil claims, as Plaintiff's right to be free from interference in pursuing and/or proving his products liability claim is prejudiced giving rise to the loss of a right and opportunity of Plaintiff.

C.) In connection with the above plead [sic] facts the Defendants are further and/or alternatively liable unto the Plaintiff for negligently spoiling the evidence as Defendants owed Plaintiff a special and/or specific duty to preserve the evidence in the following nonexclusive particulars:

(i) Pursuant to Louisiana law including La. C.C. art. 2315, and
(ii) Pursuant to an affirmative agreement/undertaking and/or understanding that the evidence be preserved after being put on notice of necessity to preserve for litigation purposes; and

---

[1] We addressed the merits of the underlying LPLA claims against Nissan in a separate opinion. *See Reynolds v. Bordelon*, 14–2371 (La.), 172 So. 3d 607, 2015 WL 3972393.

(iii) Pursuant to a special relationship as between Plaintiff and Defendants, arising through and in connection with the insurer, AUTOMOBILE CLUB INTER–INSURANCE EXCHANGE's, obligations and responsibility to their insured as set forth in section iv below; and

(iv) Pursuant to both written and verbal contractual obligations to preserve the vehicle and pursuant to the insurer's obligations to its insured per the policy of insurance as well and/or alternatively through any written and/or otherwise documented obligation arising between INSURANCE AUTO AUCTIONS CORP, acting upon information and belief as the storage facility and/or as custodian of the Petitioner's vehicle on behalf of and AUTOMOBILE CLUB INTER–INSURANCE EXCHANGE, insurer for Plaintiff.

7.

In connection with the above plead causes of action against AUTOMOBILE CLUB INTER–INSURANCE EXCHANGE and INSURANCE AUTO AUCTIONS CORP, Plaintiff seeks special damages including but not limited to past, present and future medical expenses, and past, present and future lost wages, as well as general damages for his injuries sustained including but not limited to pain and suffering, mental anguish and trauma, and disability, and all other appropriate relief including but not limited to compensatory damages that otherwise Plaintiff would have been able to present and prove but for the negligent acts of Defendants as detailed above, as Defendants' negligence results in serious prejudice to Plaintiff due to no fault of his own.

In response, ACIIE and IAA again filed exceptions of no cause of action, and ACIIE filed a motion for summary judgment, in the alternative. The trial court denied the exceptions and the motion for summary judgment in light of an opinion recently released by the First Circuit Court of Appeal, which discussed, in dicta, the theory of "negligent spoliation."[2] The court of appeal denied writs, with one judge on the panel noting the court "ha[d] not issued a studied opinion regarding whether a cause of action exists for negligent spoliation of evidence."[3] This court denied the writ application.[4]

A later decision by the First Circuit Court of Appeal was released, wherein the concept of negligent spoliation was rejected, prompting ACIIE and IAA to renew their exceptions of no cause of action.[5] Both ACIIE and IAA ultimately filed motions for summary judgment in the alternative. Based on *Clavier,* the trial court sustained ACIIE and IAA's exceptions of no cause of action. Further, the trial court declined to give leave to the plaintiff to amend the petition, finding no amendment could state a cause of action given the fact that the plaintiff conceded there were no facts to support an allegation of intentional spoliation. Additionally, the trial court denied the motions for summary judgment as moot. The court of appeal rendered an opinion, affirming the trial court's judgments, finding no cause of action exists for negligent spoliation under Louisiana law.[6] We granted certiorari to definitively rule on the viability of negligent spoliation of evidence as a cause of action in Louisiana.[7]

#conflicting 1st circuit on negligent spoiliation

---

[2] *See Dennis v. Wiley,* 09–0236 (La.App. 1 Cir. 2009), 22 So. 3d 189.

[3] *Reynolds v. Bordelon,* 10–0227 (La.App. 1 Cir. 2010), ____ So. 3d ____.

[4] *Reynolds v. Bordelon,* 10–1719 (La. 2010), 48 So. 3d 285.

[5] *See Clavier v. Our Lady of the Lake Hospital, Inc.,* 12–0560 (La.App. 1 Cir. 2012), 112 So. 3d 881, *writ denied,* 13–0264 (La. 2013), 109 So. 3d 384.

[6] *Reynolds v. Bordelon,* 13–1848 (La.App. 1 Cir. 2014), 154 So. 3d 570.

[7] *Reynolds v. Bordelon,* 14–2362 (La. 2015), 159 So. 3d 1061.

Applicable Law

[handwritten: → does law afford a remedy]

As used in the context of the peremptory exception, a "cause of action" refers to the operative facts which give rise to the plaintiff's right to judicially assert the action against the defendant.[8] The purpose of the peremptory exception of no cause of action is to test the legal sufficiency of the petition by determining whether the law affords a remedy on the facts alleged in the petition.[9] No evidence may be introduced to support or controvert the exception of no cause of action.[10] The exception is triable on the face of the pleadings, and, for purposes of resolving the issues raised by the exception, the well-pleaded facts in the petition must be accepted as true.[11] The issue at the trial of the exception is whether, on the face of the petition, the plaintiff is legally entitled to the relief sought.[12] Louisiana retains a system of fact pleading, and mere conclusions of the plaintiff unsupported by facts will not set forth a cause or right of action.[13] The burden of demonstrating that a petition fails to state a cause of action is upon the mover.[14] Because the exception of no cause of action raises a question of law and the trial court's decision is based solely on the sufficiency of the petition, review of the trial court's ruling on an exception of no cause of action is *de novo*.[15] The pertinent inquiry is whether, in the light most favorable to the plaintiff, and with every doubt resolved in the plaintiff's favor, the petition states any valid cause of action for relief.[16]

Discussion

The plaintiff contends the allegations contained in his petition are not limited to the singular cause of action of negligent spoliation of evidence and that the sufficiency of the petition should not be measured solely by the existence (or lack thereof) of that specific tort. Rather, he avers the petition sufficiently describes negligent conduct by ACIIE and IAA that is recoverable under claims ranging from (1) impairment of a civil claim; (2) loss of a right or opportunity; (3) detrimental reliance; (4) general negligence under La.Civ.Code art. 2315; and (4) breach of contract. Thus, he argues that this court's position on the viability of a negligent spoliation cause of action in Louisiana is not dispositive of the issue. We disagree with respect to his tort claims. At its heart, the petition prays for relief for third parties' acts of negligently destroying evidence. Whether the law recognizes this type of relief is not a question of semantics. Rather, it is a legal inquiry that can only be analyzed within the framework of answering the sole issue of whether Louisiana recognizes a claim for negligent spoliation.

In Louisiana, the foundation of any tort lies within the context of La.Civ.Code art. 2315, which provides, "[e]very act whatever of man that causes damage to another obliges him by whose fault it happened to repair it." Thus, while "fault" is a broader term than negligence or intent, there

---

[8] *Ramey v. DeCaire*, 03–1299, p. 7 (La. 2004), 869 So. 2d 114, 118; *Everything on Wheels Subaru, Inc. v. Subaru South, Inc.*, 616 So. 2d 1234, 1238 (La. 1993).

[9] *Ramey*, at 7, 869 So. 2d at 118; *Everything on Wheels Subaru, Inc.*, 616 So. 2d at 1235.

[10] La.Code Civ. P. art. 931.

[11] *Fink v. Bryant*, 01–0987, p. 4 (La. 2001), 801 So. 2d 346, 349; *City of New Orleans v. Board of Commissioners of Orleans Levee District*, 93–0690, p. 28 (La. 1994), 640 So. 2d 237, 253.

[12] *Ramey*, at 7, 869 So. 2d at 118.

[13] *Montalvo v. Sondes*, 93–2813, p. 6 (La. 1994), 637 So. 2d 127, 131.

[14] *Ramey*, at 7, 869 So. 2d at 119; *City of New Orleans*, at 28, 640 So. 2d at 253.

[15] *Fink*, at 4, 801 So. 2d at 349; *City of New Orleans*, at 28, 640 So. 2d at 253.

[16] *Ramey*, at 8, 869 So. 2d at 119.

still exists a limit as to actual liability. Frank Maraist and Thomas Galligan, in their treatise on tort law, explained:[17]

> All theories of recovery, or categories of tort liability, are "fault" in Louisiana, although they represent different levels of blameworthiness or culpability.... [i]t may be helpful to imagine a fault line similar to a number line.... At the left side of this line is the actor who intentionally inflicts harm upon the victim. His or her conduct is the law's most blameworthy category of fault. Moving to the right, one arrives at negligence, i.e., the actor knew or should have known that his conduct presented an unreasonable risk of harm to someone, and he or she failed to act reasonably to avoid that risk. This, too, is fault, and "blameworthy" conduct, although less "blameworthy" than the intentional tortfeasor's act. Farther to the right is the actor who could not foresee that his or her conduct would expose another to harm, or whose conduct was reasonable under the circumstances. He or she is, in the eyes of the moral philosopher, blameless. Nevertheless, society may choose to impose the cost of the harm upon the blameless actor rather than upon the victim. If so, in Louisiana, he or she was at fault, although blameless. These places along the "fault" line where the nonblameworthy actor might be or might have been liable are vicarious liability, strict liability, and absolute liability. On the far right is the actor who could not foresee harm and/or who acted reasonably, and upon whom society does not place the risk of harm caused by his conduct. This person is not at "fault" nor blameworthy. There is simply no tort, although the layman may quite incorrectly call the resulting harm a mere "accident."

[handwritten margin note: civilian concept: – society imposes liability on blameless actors → vicarious / strict / absolute]

Jurisprudentially, this civilian concept has been more readily applied within the same context as negligence claims made in common law jurisdictions, wherein the analysis is subdivided into four elements: duty, breach, causation, and damages. The duty inquiry is central to our discussion on whether Louisiana recognizes the tort of negligent spoliation of evidence.

While alternatively setting forth the general negligence theory of liability, the plaintiff asks this court to recognize the cause of action where a specific duty arose due to an agreement, contract, special relationship, or undertaking which was formed between the parties specifically for the purpose of preserving the evidence. Several appellate courts in Louisiana have followed this limited application of the tort; however, we decline to do so and expressly refuse to recognize the existence of the tort.[18] This holding applies whether under a general negligence approach or whether the source of the duty is readily apparent. Instead, we approach the duty element of the negligence analysis from a public policy perspective.

[handwritten margin note: (court approaches "duty" element from public policy perspective)]

Maraist and Galligan explain the duty element as it relates to policy:[19]

> The general duty and the specific risk inquiries both involve policy decisions on issues such as deterrence of undesirable conduct, avoiding the deterrence of desirable conduct, compensation of victims, satisfaction of the community's sense of justice, proper allocation of resources (including judicial resources), predictability, and deference to the legislative will.

The policy considerations can compel a court to simply make a categorical "no duty" rule regarding certain conduct. Examples of courts categorically excluding liability for a specific group of claims or plaintiffs are: claims for failure to act, injuries to unborn babies, negligent infliction of mental anguish, or purely economic harm unaccompanied by physical trauma to the plaintiff or his

[handwritten margin note: Ex: liability excluded by courts in these situations]

---

[17] Frank L. Maraist & Thomas C. Galligan, Jr., Louisiana Tort Law § 1.03 (2004).

[18] *See e.g., Carter v. Exide Corp.,* 661 So. 2d 698 (La.App. 2 Cir.1995).

[19] Frank L. Maraist & Thomas C. Galligan, Jr., Louisiana Tort Law § 5.02 (2004).

property.[20] This court, in *Hill v. Lundin,* expanded on its role in determining whether society is best served in recognizing a duty, and thus, a tort, stating:[21]

> The same policy considerations which would motivate a legislative body to impose duties to protect from certain risks are applied by the court in making its determination. "All rules of conduct, irrespective of whether they are the product of a legislature or are a part of the fabric of the court-made law of negligence, exist for purposes. They are designed to protect *some* persons under *some* circumstances against *some* risks. Seldom does a rule protect every victim against every risk that may befall him, merely because it is shown that the violation of the rule played a part in producing the injury. The task of defining the proper reach or thrust of a rule in its policy aspects is one that must be undertaken by the court in each case as it arises. How appropriate is the rule to the facts of this controversy? This is a question that the court cannot escape." Malone, *Ruminations on Cause–In–Fact,* 9 Stanford L.Rev. 60, 73 (1956).

Having established that the duty requirement can be analyzed in terms of policy, we turn now to those policy considerations affected by our recognition (or rejection) of the tort of negligent spoliation of evidence. As formulated by Maraist and Galligan and listed above, the first of these factors is "deterrence of undesirable conduct." We find the act of negligently spoliating evidence is so unintentional an act that any recognition of the tort by the courts would not act to deter future conduct, but would, rather, act to penalize a party who was not aware of its potential wrongdoing in the first place. This is particularly true in the case of negligent spoliation by a third party, who is not vested in the ultimate outcome of the underlying case, and thus, has no motive to destroy or make unavailable evidence that could tend to prove or disprove that unrelated claim. This factor weighs in favor of a no-duty rule.

Next, compensation of the victim is an important policy consideration. This issue is strenuously debated nationally among those states that do recognize the tort because damages are so highly speculative.[22] Determining the expected recovery in the underlying case—a case that was not fully adjudged on evidence because that evidence was discarded—leaves room for substantial guess-work. Moreover, Louisiana, as a comparative negligence jurisdiction, would also have to factor in the likelihood of success of that underlying case since that would be the measure of the proportional fault of the spoliator. Accordingly, the parties and the trier of fact would be called upon to estimate the impact of the missing evidence and guess at its ability to prove or disprove the underlying claim,

---

[20] *Id.* This rule of exclusion is not without its exceptions. *See Pitre v. Opelousas General Hospital,* 530 So. 2d 1151 (La.1988) (wherein recoverable prenatal damage claims are discussed). Moreover, the no-duty rule for failure to act claims has its own exceptions when there is a special relationship between the non-actor and the victim, such as common carriers and their passengers, innkeepers and their guests, employers and their injured employees, jailers and their prisoners, teachers and their students; and parents and their children. With regard to negligent infliction of mental distress, Louisiana law does allow "bystander" claims. Last, the categorical bar against allowing tort damages for pure economic harm has its exceptions as well, wherein appellate courts have addressed the issue on a case-by-case basis and within the confines of a standard negligence analysis.

Despite the exceptions, the inclusion in our analysis of the categorical barring of these types of claims and/or class of plaintiffs is to demonstrate the ability and the authority courts have in refusing to recognize a duty to prevent certain conduct.

[21] *Hill v. Lundin and Associates,* 260 La. 542, 256 So. 2d 620, 623.

[22] *See Smith v. Atkinson,* 771 So. 2d 429 (Ala. 2000), wherein the Alabama Supreme Court held the proper measure of damages in a negligent spoliation of evidence case is the compensatory damages that would have been awarded on the underlying cause of action, and not the probability of success in the underlying action. *Compare* to *Holmes v. Amerex Rent–A–Car,* 710 A.2d 846, 853 (D.C.1998), wherein the District of Columbia held the measure of damages in a negligent spoliation of evidence case should be compensatory damages in the underlying case adjusted by the estimated likelihood of success in the potential civil action.

14

resulting in liability based far too much on speculation. We find these hypothetical and abstract inquires weigh against recognition of the tort of negligent spoliation.

Another policy consideration is "satisfaction of the community's sense of justice." Society's sense of fairness is vital in determining whether a reasonable person should have acted or not acted in a certain manner. Because the reasonable person standard is inherent in the negligence analysis, it is prudent to ask whether reasonable persons would expect certain behavior in certain situations and, conversely, whether reasonable persons can be expected to be exposed to liability in certain situations. This question factors in squarely with another policy consideration: predictability. Thus, we will address these elements together.

Recognition of the tort of negligent spoliation would place a burden on society as a whole, causing third parties who are not even aware of litigation to adopt retention policies for potential evidence in cases, in order to reduce their exposure to liability. There is simply no predictability in requiring preservation and record keeping for unknown litigation. Moreover, broadening the delictual liability for negligent spoliation would place restrictions on the property rights of persons, both natural and juridical, insofar as the tort would act to limit the right to dispose of one's own property. These policy concerns are readily apparent in the facts before this court where ACIIE paid to the plaintiff what was owed under his policy and received the title to the totaled vehicle. Then, IAA, in the normal course of its business, received the vehicle and disposed of it by auctioning it to a salvage yard for spare parts. To impose a requirement that all potential evidence be preserved for possible future litigation would wreak havoc on an industry whose very existence is sustained by destruction of possible subjects of litigation: totaled vehicles. It is easy to imagine the trickle-down effect that a preservation policy would have on insureds themselves; the longer an insurer or auction company is required to store a vehicle, the higher the costs, and the more likely insurance premiums would be increased to absorb those costs. Moreover, the delay in proceeds being remitted to the insurer at the time of the auction prevents those funds from being immediately available to offset the total loss payout the insurer pays to the insured. Again, this practice could result in higher costs for the public. Thus, these two factors, societal justice and predictability, weigh heavily against broadening the delictual obligation for negligent spoliation.

Next, we look to the proper allocation of resources, including judicial resources. Allowing a derivative tort invites litigation and encourages parties to bring a new suit where the underlying suit was not successful. Again, this derivative litigation could open the floodgates for endless lawsuits where the loss is speculative at best. Additionally, it could create confusion for fact-finders, particularly juries, inasmuch as it allows a trial within a trial. For instance, triers of fact could be presented with the facts of the underlying case and also presented with the facts surrounding the alleged destruction of evidence, causing inconsistency and the potential for misunderstanding. Thus, this factor does not favor recognition of the tort.

Last, we are called upon to consider any deference owed to the legislature. This court, in limiting the application of the tort of interference with contractual relations, has previously held:[23]

> The framers conceived of fault as a breach of a preexisting obligation for which the law orders reparation, when it causes damage to another, and they left it to the courts to determine in each case the existence of an anterior obligation which would make an act constitute fault. 2 M. Planiol, Treatise on the Civil Law, Part 1, §§ 863–865 (1959); *Pitre v. Opelousas General Hosp.,* 530 So. 2d 1151 (La. 1988).

> ...

> Portalis, the leading drafter of the Code Napoleon, clearly foresaw that the code must constantly be applied to unexpected issues and circumstances:

---

[23] *9 to 5 Fashions, Inc. v. Spurney,* 538 So. 2d 228, 231 (La. 1989).

A code, however complete it may seem, is hardly finished before a thousand unexpected issues come to face the judge. For laws, once drafted, remain as they were written. Men, on the contrary, are never at rest; they are constantly active, and their unceasing activities, the effects of which are modified in many ways by circumstances, produce at each instant some new combination, some new fact, some new result.

A host of things is thus necessarily left to the province of custom, the discussion of learned men, and the decision of judges.

The role of legislation is to set, by taking a broad approach, the general propositions of the law, to establish principles which will be fertile in application, and not to get down to the details of questions which may arise in particular instances.

It is for the judge and the jurist, imbued with the general spirit of the laws, to direct their application. A. Levasseur, *Code Napoleon or Code Portalis?* 43 Tul.L.Rev. 762, 769 (1969) (Translation by Shael Herman)

Thus, with regard to this final policy consideration before us, we find the legislation on fault and tort law in Louisiana has left to the courts the task of determining the viability of certain causes of action. As such, we conclude that legislative will does not require recognition of the tort of negligent spoliation.

Having considered all the policy factors under the duty element of the negligence analysis in Louisiana, we reflect on one more concern, availability of other avenues of recourse. California, a state that once pioneered negligent spoliation, but subsequently reversed itself and now does not recognize the existence of the tort, stated:[24]

We do not believe that the distinction between the sanctions available to victims of first party and third party spoliation should lead us to employ the burdensome and inaccurate instrument of derivative tort litigation in the case of third party spoliation. We observe that to the extent a duty to preserve evidence is imposed by statute or regulation upon the third party, the Legislature or the regulatory body that has imposed this duty generally will possess the authority to devise an effective sanction for violations of that duty. To the extent third parties may have a contractual obligation to preserve evidence, contract remedies, including agreed-upon liquidated damages, may be available for breach of the contractual duty. Criminal sanctions, of course, also remain available.

...

In sum, we conclude that the benefits of recognizing a tort cause of action, in order to deter third party spoliation of evidence and compensate victims of such misconduct are outweighed by the burden to litigants, witnesses, and the judicial system that would be imposed by potentially endless litigation over a speculative loss, and by the cost to society of promoting onerous record and evidence retention policies.

We adopt this logic and write separately on the issue to discuss the alternative remedies plaintiffs can seek in Louisiana. Discovery sanctions and criminal sanctions are available for first-party spoliators. Additionally, Louisiana recognizes the adverse presumption against litigants who had access to evidence and did not make it available or destroyed it. Regarding negligent spoliation by third parties, the plaintiff who anticipates litigation can enter into a contract to preserve the evidence and, in the event of a breach, avail himself of those contractual remedies. Court orders for preservation

---

[24] *Temple Community Hosp. v. Superior Court,* 20 Cal.4th 464, 84 Cal.Rptr.2d 852, 976 P.2d 223 (1999).

are also obtainable. In this particular case, the plaintiff also could have retained control of his vehicle and not released it to the insurer, thereby guaranteeing its availability for inspection. Furthermore, he could have bought the vehicle back from the insurer for a nominal fee. Thus, we find the existence of alternate avenues for recovery further support our holding.

Conclusion

Our review of the policy considerations lead us to conclude that Louisiana law does not recognize a duty to preserve evidence in the context of negligent spoliation. In the absence of a duty owed, we find there is no fault under La. Civ. Code art. 2315 or under any other delictual theory in Louisiana. Furthermore, the presence of alternate remedies supports our holding that there is no tort of negligent spoliation of evidence. Accordingly, we agree with the lower courts that there is no cause of action for this tort.

* * * * *

REVERSED AND REMANDED.

NOTES

1.   As the Court explains, quoting the *Maraist* and *Galligan* treatise, intent and negligence are distinct levels of blameworthiness or fault on which tort liability is based. There are several intentional torts, including battery, assault, false imprisonment, etc.., each composed of elements required to establish a prima facie case of that tort. One might call these normative torts in that they each have a name but each one shares the necessity of proving "intent." Intentional torts are covered primarily in Chapter 2 *infra*. Negligence, on the other hand, is a broader tort theory with five elements required to establish a prima facie case: duty, breach, cause-in-fact, proximate cause or scope, and damages. Although we often refer to negligence cases by a label that identifies the breach, such as negligent spoliation, negligent entrustment, malpractice (negligent practice of ….), etc., negligence is really a broad 9and sometimes amorphous) theory of tort recovery, and the five elements change little or not at all, regardless of the type of negligence case. Negligence is covered primarily in Chapters 4, 5, and 6 *infra*. Do you think intentional torts and negligence are separate and distinct? Some courts treat them that way. Professors Maraist and Galligan, in the passage quoted by the Court in *Reynolds*, suggest that intentional torts and negligence are not different in kind, but in degree, describing a fault line like a number line. In addition to intentional torts and negligence, there are also strict and absolute liability theories, but those are, arguably, less prevalent than the "fault" based intentional torts or negligence. While all tort liability is "fault" under the Louisiana Civil Code approach and Article 2315, a common law lawyer or theorist might say strict liability and absolute liability are "no fault."

2.   In *Reynolds*, the Louisiana Supreme Court holds that the state does not recognize a "cause of action" for negligent spoliation. What is a "cause of action"? Does it differ from a "theory of recovery"?

If the Louisiana Supreme Court declares that the state does not recognize a tort, is that the end of the matter—is that conclusive?

3.   Does Louisiana recognize the tort of intentional spoliation? Does the Court address this issue in *Reynolds*?

The Louisiana Supreme Court has not ruled on whether Louisiana recognizes a cause of action for intentional spoliation. *See Rogers v. Averitt Express, Inc.*, 215 F. Supp. 3d 510 (M.D. La. 2017). However, a federal court has discerned ("*Erie* guess") that Louisiana does recognize such a

17

cause of action. *Rogers*, 215 F. Supp. 3d at 515. Moreover, some Louisiana courts of appeal so hold. *See, e.g., Tomlinson v. Landmark American Ins. Co.*, 192 So. 3d 153, 159-60 (La.App. 4 Cir. 2016); *Pham v. Contico Int'l, Inc.*, 759 So. 2d 880, 882 (La.App. 5 Cir. 2000).

How would a federal court, like the United States District Court for the Northern District of Louisiana, know the law of a state? Can a federal court simply declare state law? In *Erie R.R. v. Tompkins*, 304 U.S. 64 (1938), the U.S. Supreme Court stated as follows:

> There is no federal general common law. Congress has no power to declare substantive rules of common law applicable in a state whether they be local in their nature or 'general,' be they commercial law or a part of the law of torts. And no clause in the Constitution purports to confer such a power upon the federal courts.

Id. at 78. Does this mean that there is no federal tort law, but only state tort law? Does this mean that the tort law of Washington can differ from that of California?

4.   In the trial court, the defendants that had bought and sold the wrecked vehicle filed exceptions of no cause of action and motions for summary judgment. What are these and how are they different? The Louisiana Supreme Court holds that the issue, whether state law recognizes negligent spoliation, is an issue of law ("a legal inquiry"), and holds that lower courts correctly granted or sustained the exceptions of no cause of action. The exception of no cause of action (in federal court, a motion for failure to state a claim upon which relief can be granted) addresses only issues of law. Motions for summary judgment address the application of law to established fact.

5.   The Court notes that the plaintiffs argue that they should recover under other theories (impairment of a civil claim, loss of a right or opportunity, general negligence under C.C. Art. 2315, and breach of contract) even if the Court does not recognize a right to recover for negligent spoliation. Should the Court have recognized a right to recover for general negligence although it did not recognize a right to recover for negligent spoliation? What does that even mean? Consider again the questions and comments in note 1, *supra*.

6.   The Court draws from the Maraist and Galligan treatise several factors to be used to determine whether to recognize the existence of a duty. Stated differently, the Court uses those factors to decide whether to recognize the tort theory of negligent spoliation. Take another tort theory and apply those factors to decide whether it should be recognized—criminal conversation (the tort theory associated with adultery, in which the spurned spouse sues the third party who had sexual relations with the other spouse).

7.   The Court says, within its consideration of the factor "compensation of the victim," that it is concerned with the fact that in a negligent spoliation claim the fact finder would have to evaluate the "likelihood of success of that underlying case since that would be the measure of the proportional fault of the spoliator." That would require the fact finder "to estimate the impact of the missing evidence and guess at its ability to prove or disprove the underlying claim." This is a difficult issue of causation. This same type of inquiry must be made in legal malpractice cases--attempting to determine whether the lawyer's malpractice caused the plaintiff (former client) to lose the case in which the alleged malpractice occurred. *See* Chapter 5B *infra*. If this must be done in legal malpractice cases, why is the Court troubled by it regarding negligent spoliation?

The Court also notes that the damages for negligent spoliation would be "highly speculative" because we do not know the impact of the destroyed or missing evidence. The Court observes in FN 22 that courts that have recognized the tort have differed on the appropriate measure of damages—full compensatory damages in the underlying case or "compensatory damages in the underlying case adjusted by the estimated likelihood of success in the potential civil action." Do you understand the difference between those two measures of damages? Louisiana encountered this very issue when the Court recognized a claim for lost chance of survival (and lost chance of a better outcome) in medical malpractice. *See Smith v. State of Louisiana Dept. of Health and Hospitals*, Chapter 5B *infra*. Is the problem any more difficult with negligent spoliation claims?

8.   The Court states that there are negligence cases in which, for policy reasons, courts decide the defendant does not have a duty to exercise reasonable care. The Court notes several examples (with exceptions). These negligence cases in which there is no duty can be resolved on an exception of no cause of action or summary judgment for the defendant by the court because duty is a question of law and does not require a fact finder.

ANATOMY OF TORT LITIGATION – A PRIMER FOR BEGINNERS

Generally, a tort arises when the victim sustains damages because of the conduct of another which the law deems tortious, i.e., the actor has committed a tort. The victim, and others harmed by the injury to the victim, pursue tort claims against the actor and others who may be responsible for the actor's conduct, such as his liability insurer and, in some cases, his employer or parent.

Although the victim is not required to make a pre-suit demand upon the persons against whom he pursues the tort claim, such usually is done, and perhaps more than half of the tort claims that arise are settled without the filing of suit. The settlement, called a compromise, is effected by a written document, sometimes called a release. A valid settlement bars any subsequent action by the victim against the settling parties or those who by operation of law benefit from the settlement. Any suit brought on a claim which has been compromised is subject to immediate dismissal; because of the compromise, the matter is considered to be a "thing adjudged" – res judicata.

When a tort claim proceeds to suit, the victim files a petition (sometimes called a complaint) in a court which has jurisdiction over that type of tort claim (subject matter jurisdiction) and jurisdiction over the defendants named in the suit (jurisdiction over the person). The suit also must be filed in a court of proper venue, i.e., a court within the state to whom the legislature has allotted the particular case (the court is one of "proper venue"). For example, where Louisiana courts have jurisdiction over a tort and the alleged tortfeasor, the suit ordinarily must be filed in the parish where the tort was committed or the parish in which the defendant is domiciled.

The petition or complaint ordinarily will allege the facts the victim believes existed, the theory upon which recovery is sought (whether, for example, the actor's conduct was negligent, or intentional, or the actor is strictly or absolutely liable), and the remedy which is sought (usually the damages the victim claims he or she has sustained because of the tort).

The defendant must be served with a copy of the petition or complaint and provided with a reasonable opportunity to respond. Federal and state constitutions require that a defendant receive the procedure which is due him or her (due process), which includes, in addition to being sued in a court which has jurisdiction over his person (*see* above), the requirement that the defendant receive "fair notice" of the suit and "an opportunity to be heard." If the defendant does not answer within the time allotted, the plaintiff may obtain a judgment against him by proving his claim before the court (a default judgment).

In most cases, the defendant will respond. His first response often is that even if the plaintiff proves all of the facts he has alleged in his petition or complaint, those facts do not constitute a tort by the defendant; hence there is no need for further proceedings, and the suit should be dismissed instantly. The pleading asserting this defense is called, at common law, a demurrer; in federal court, it is a Rule 12(b)(6) motion for failure to state a claim upon which relief can be granted, and in Louisiana state court, it is the exception of no cause of action.

If the judge agrees with the defendant, the suit is dismissed, and any subsequent suit on those facts will be barred by res judicata. If the judge disagrees, he or she will overrule the motion. If the defendant is unsuccessful in obtaining dismissal through a demurrer[1] at the outset, he must file an answer in which he must admit or deny each allegation of fact made in the plaintiff's petition; the defendant also may assert an affirmative defense through which he or she contends that <u>even if the plaintiff proves the facts alleged,</u> plaintiff may not recover because of plaintiff's own conduct, the nature of the defendant, or the relationship between the parties. These affirmative defenses include prescription (the claim is barred by the statute of limitations because the plaintiff did not timely file suit) and immunity (certain defendants are immune, i.e., not subject to suit by other victims for certain claims). Thereafter, the parties are provided an opportunity to learn (through discovery) the facts and evidence bearing upon the plaintiff's claim and any affirmative defenses. Methods of discovery include propounding questions to each other (interrogatories) and taking the testimony under oath of the parties and other potential witnesses (depositions).

Usually after discovery has been completed, the defendant will contend that a trial on the merits of the claim is not necessary because although plaintiff has alleged facts which, if proven, would entitle him to recover (he survived the defendant's demurrer), one or more of those facts essential to plaintiff's recovery under that theory of law does not exist, and the defendant can establish the non-existence by written evidence (including the answers to interrogatories, depositions and affidavits[2] by witnesses). The pleading which the defendant files to accomplish this is called the motion for summary judgment. In deciding the motion, the judge must evaluate the evidence as though each witness (in his or her deposition or affidavit) is telling the truth; if the judge concludes that, even with that assumption, the plaintiff does not have sufficient evidence to support a fact essential to his or her claim, the motion will be granted and the suit will be dismissed. The dismissal also will be treated as res judicata.

Where, as is often the case, the plaintiff survives the defendant's demurrer and/or motion for summary judgment, the matter is ripe for trial on the merits. The trial usually is preceded by a pre-trial conference at which the parties identify the issues likely to arise at trial and agree (stipulate) to the existence of certain facts. The order which the judge renders after the pre-trial conference reflects the events at the pre-trial conference and generally controls all subsequent proceedings in the suit.

The suit may be tried without a jury; in such a case, the judge determines what the facts are and applies those facts to the law which he deems applicable. Based upon his conclusions, the judge enters a final judgment which may be executed (enforced) unless enforcement is suspended by appeal (see below).

Where a jury trial is available (in Louisiana, where the amount in controversy exceeds $50,000) and a party requests it, the trial begins with the selection of jurors from a panel of prospective jurors chosen at random from the community. The parties are entitled to question the jurors (called the voir dire) and to have jurors excused for cause (the juror for some reason is not impartial) or peremptorily (the party does not want this particular juror). The number of peremptory challenges allowed each party is limited, and a party may not exercise such challenges on the basis of race or gender.

After the jury has been chosen, each side presents its evidence. The plaintiff proceeds first, and in his "case in chief" must present evidence from which reasonable minds (the jury) could conclude the existence of each fact essential to his or her claim; this burden upon the plaintiff is called the burden of producing evidence. At the close of the plaintiff's case in chief, the defendant ordinarily will move for a directed verdict (which results in a dismissal of the plaintiff's case) contending that

---

[1] Demurrer is used hereafter to describe either the 12(b)(6) motion, the exception no cause of action or the demurrer, dependent upon the name ascribed to the pleading in the particular jurisdiction.

[2] An affidavit is a written statement by a witness executed before a Notary Public or other officer authorized to administer oaths.

[Margin annotations: "Affirm Ds ① RX ② immunity"; "conduct discovery"; "D files mot. S.J. → P can't meet burden of proving facts alleged."; "Pretrial conference → order guides subsequent proceedings of suit"]

the plaintiff has not met his burden of producing evidence of a fact essential to his recovery under the particular theory of law. If the judge agrees, the claim will be dismissed. If the judge disagrees and overrules the motion, the defendant presents his case. At the close of the defendant's case, both parties usually will move for a directed verdict. However, such a motion rarely is granted. At this point, the jury has heard all of the admissible evidence (evidence which is relevant and competent and is not subject to any privilege) and if there is, in the judge's view, only one rational conclusion, the jury will reach it, and if the jury does not, the judge may thereafter overturn the jury's verdict by granting a judgment notwithstanding the verdict.[3]

The jury determines the facts and applies those facts to the applicable law, which is determined by the judge and given to the jury at the close of the case (the jury "instructions" or "charges"). The judge's instructions also will inform the jury about how persuaded they must be as to the existence of the facts essential to the plaintiff's claim. This "burden of persuasion" usually is a preponderance of the evidence ("more probable than not") but in some cases may be higher (the evidence must be "clear and convincing"). The jury is provided with a verdict form which it completes in making its decision. This form usually will ask whether the defendant was negligent (or otherwise at fault) and whether the plaintiff also was negligent, and, if so, what percentage of fault (totaling 100%) is allocated to each. The jury also will be asked to determine the total amount of damages necessary to compensate the victim, i.e., "make him whole." If the judge disagrees, he may "upset" the jury verdict by granting a judgment notwithstanding the verdict or a new trial.

When the judgment is rendered after trial on the merits, or where the suit is dismissed on a demurrer or motion for summary judgment, the unsuccessful party has the right to appeal to the court of appeal. If the judgment orders a party to pay a sum of money, that party must take a "suspensive appeal," which includes posting a bond in an amount sufficient to satisfy the judgment. If he fails to do so, the successful party may execute upon (collect) the judgment while the appeal is pending. The appellate court reviews the proceedings below (a transcription of what took place at trial) and determines whether an error was committed which justifies a reversal. In the federal system, the jury's verdict is not subject to "second guessing," i.e., if reasonable minds could differ, the appellate court may not overturn the jury's verdict as erroneous. In Louisiana, the appellate courts have jurisdiction over law and facts, and theoretically can "second guess" the jury's determination of the facts; this seldom is done, however, because the Louisiana courts have imposed upon themselves the restraint of affirming a jury's decision unless it is "manifestly erroneous."

The major issue on appeal, then, is not whether the jury reached the wrong decision, but whether the judge erred in either (1) granting or refusing a demurrer, (2) granting or refusing a motion for summary judgment, (3) allowing or refusing to allow the jury to hear certain evidence, (4) providing the jury with the incorrect law through erroneous jury instructions, or (5) improperly granting a directed verdict or a judgment notwithstanding the verdict. In your study of tort law, you primarily will read, in addition to statutes, opinions written by appellate courts reviewing the actions in the trial court, and most of their decisions will turn upon whether the trial judge committed one of those errors. These decisions constitute the jurisprudential (common) law described earlier in this chapter.

The student's attention now is directed to the first and simplest of the "general risks" against which tort law protects – intentional invasion of the mind, body or property of another.

---

[3] Although state courts continue to use the "judgment notwithstanding the verdict" or JNOV label, the student should be aware that federal courts use the language "Judgment as a Matter of Law." For our purposes, the doctrines are procedurally and substantially equivalent.

CHAPTER 2

INTENTIONAL TORTS

INTRODUCTION

"Even a dog distinguishes between being stumbled over and being kicked." So said Justice Oliver Wendell Holmes in *The Common Law* (1881). This famous quote suggests that there is a clear distinction between intentional torts and negligence–so clear, in fact, that even an animal's mind can grasp it. Let us hope that we are as keen as Justice Holmes' discerning dog.

Much of our modern tort law comes from early English common law after the Norman conquest. Intentional torts and negligence trace their origins to two English common law writs.[37] Intentional torts descend from the English common law writ of trespass, which originally focused on punishment of crime rather than recovery of civil d61amages. Negligence comes from the English writ of trespass on the case, or case. The formulaic pleading rules associated with the two writs were distinct. We have clung to many of the aspects and distinctions. As you study tort law, consider the extent to which we maintain the centuries-old boundary between intentional torts and negligence. Is the distinction an anachronism?

An intentional tort is a tort theory of recovery in which the plaintiff, in order to prove his case and recover, must prove that the defendant acted with a particular mental state–intent. Tracing their origin to criminal law, intentional torts are considered to be worse than negligence; stated differently, the intentional tortfeasor is generally considered to be more blameworthy, more culpable, or more at fault than a negligent tortfeasor. After all, the intentional tortfeasor acted with a bad mental state, whereas the negligent tortfeasor merely acted without exercising reasonable care. As Holmes said, even a dog understands that it has reason to fear a malevolent kicker more than a clumsy stumbler.

It is difficult in many cases to prove an intentional tort because it is difficult to prove that a defendant acted with the intent to cause a harm. As was the case at English common law where trespass on the case eclipsed trespass, many plaintiffs simply choose to sue for negligence and do not plead or try to prove an intentional tort. Most tort lawsuits in the United States today are based on a negligence theory of recovery rather than an intentional tort theory. There are, however, reasons why a plaintiff may pursue an intentional tort theory rather than negligence. In many states, the most significant is that employers may be immune from negligence lawsuits by employees for injuries covered by workers' compensation, but not immune from intentional tort liability. *See* Chapter 11. There are other reasons, such as the dischargeability of a judgment debt in bankruptcy, availability of punitive or exemplary damages, and application of comparative fault principles or intentional tort defenses (*see* Chapters 7 and 8). There are even cases in which a plaintiff would prefer to have a defendant's harmful acts classified as negligence rather than an intentional tort. For example, some insurance policies exclude intentional acts from coverage. A plaintiff who was injured by an insured defendant more often than not is hoping to collect any judgment against the insurer of the defendant; if the acts are excluded from coverage, the plaintiff cannot collect from the insurance company. Thus, a plaintiff who sues a defendant for kicking him in the head twenty times as he lay on the ground may argue that the defendant was merely negligent and clearly did not intend to injure him, or at least not much.

This chapter first considers the meaning of intent as an element that must be proven for all intentional torts. It then considers the intentional torts that descend directly from the common law writ of trespass: battery, assault, false imprisonment and the property torts (trespass to land, trespass to chattels, and conversion). Last, the chapter considers the modern tort of intentional infliction of emotional distress, which began to be recognized by courts in the United States in the 1960s. There are other intentional torts, such as invasion of privacy and deceit, that are not covered in this chapter.

---

[37] A writ was an order compelling a person to respond to a complaint by a fellow citizen.

Of the intentional torts considered in this chapter, battery, assault, false imprisonment, and intentional infliction of emotional distress all protect interests of persons in the inviolability of their persons or personalities. They address either physical injuries, mental injuries, or both, to the person. Trespass to land, conversion, and trespass to chattels protect property interests.

A.   INTENT

Intent is the element that is common to all of the intentional torts. The definition of intent set forth in *Garratt v. Dailey*, below, is the same for all intentional torts. Thus, with all intentional torts, there must be the purpose or knowledge to a substantial certainty to cause (fill in the blank, depending on the specific intentional tort).

GARRATT
v.
DAILEY
279 P.2d 1091 (Wash. 1955)

HILL, J.

[Bench Trial]

The liability of an infant for an alleged battery is presented to this court for the first time. Brian Dailey (age five years, nine months) was visiting with Naomi Garratt, an adult and a sister of the plaintiff, Ruth Garratt, likewise an adult, in the backyard of the plaintiff's home, on July 16, 1951. It is plaintiff's contention that she came out into the backyard to talk with Naomi and that, as she started to sit down in a wood and canvas lawn chair, Brian deliberately pulled it out from under her. The only one of the three persons present so testifying was Naomi Garratt. (Ruth Garratt, the plaintiff, did not testify as to how or why she fell.)

The trial court, unwilling to accept this testimony, adopted instead Brian Dailey's version of what happened, and made the following findings:

> "III. ... that while Naomi Garratt and Brian Dailey were in the back yard the plaintiff, Ruth Garratt, came out of her house into the back yard. Some time subsequent thereto defendant, Brian Dailey, picked up a lightly built wood and canvas lawn chair which was then and there located in the back yard of the above described premises, moved it sideways a few feet and seated himself therein, at which time he discovered the plaintiff, Ruth Garratt, about to sit down at the place where the lawn chair had formerly been, at which time he hurriedly got up from the chair and attempted to move it toward Ruth Garratt to aid her in sitting down in the chair; that due to the defendant's small size and lack of dexterity he was unable to get the lawn chair under the plaintiff in time to prevent her from falling to the ground. That plaintiff fell to the ground and sustained a fracture of her hip, and other injuries and damages as hereinafter set forth.

> "IV. That the preponderance of the evidence in this case establishes that when the defendant, Brian Dailey, moved the chair in question *he did not have any wilful or unlawful purpose* in doing so; that *he did not have any intent to injure the plaintiff, or any intent to bring about any unauthorized or offensive contact with her person* or any objects appurtenant thereto; that the circumstances which immediately preceded the fall of the plaintiff established that the defendant, *Brian Dailey, did not have purpose, intent or design to perform a prank or to effect an assault and battery upon the person of the plaintiff.*" (Italics ours, for a purpose hereinafter indicated.)

It is conceded that Ruth Garratt's fall resulted in a fractured hip and other painful and serious injuries. To obviate the necessity of a retrial in the event this court determines that she was entitled to a judgment against Brian Dailey, the amount of her damage was found to be eleven thousand dollars.

Plaintiff appeals from a judgment dismissing the action and asks for the entry of a judgment in that amount or a new trial.

The authorities generally, but with certain notable exceptions ... state that, when a minor has committed a tort with force, he is liable to be proceeded against as any other person would be....

In our analysis of the applicable law, we start with the basic premise that Brian, whether five or fifty-five, must have committed some wrongful act before he could be liable for appellant's injuries.

The trial court's finding that Brian was a visitor in the Garratt backyard is supported by the evidence and negatives appellant's assertion that Brian was a trespasser and had no right to touch, move, or sit in any chair in that yard, and that contention will not receive further consideration.

It is urged that Brian's action in moving the chair constituted a battery. A definition (not all-inclusive but sufficient for our purpose) of a battery is the intentional infliction of a harmful bodily contact upon another. The rule that determines liability for battery is given in 1 Restatement, Torts, 29, § 13, as:

> "An act which, directly or indirectly, is the legal cause of a harmful contact with another's person makes the actor liable to the other, if
>
> "(a) the act is done with the intention of bringing about a harmful or offensive contact or an apprehension thereof to the other or a third person, and
>
> "(b) the contact is not consented to by the other or the other's consent thereto is procured by fraud or duress, and
>
> "c) the contact is not otherwise privileged."

We have in this case no question of consent or privilege. We therefore proceed to an immediate consideration of intent and its place in the law of battery. In the comment on clause (a), the Restatement says:

> "*Character of actor's intention.* In order that an act may be done with the intention of bringing about a harmful or offensive contact or an apprehension thereof to a particular person, either the other or a third person, the act must be done for the purpose of causing the contact or apprehension or with knowledge on the part of the actor that such contact or apprehension is substantially certain to be produced." *See, also,* Prosser on Torts 41, § 8.

We have here the conceded volitional act of Brian, *i.e.*, the moving of a chair. Had the plaintiff proved to the satisfaction of the trial court that Brian moved the chair while she was in the act of sitting down, Brian's action would patently have been for the purpose or with the intent of causing the plaintiff's bodily contact with the ground, and she would be entitled to a judgment against him for the resulting damages....

The plaintiff based her case on that theory, and the trial court held that she failed in her proof and accepted Brian's version of the facts rather than that given by the eyewitness who testified for the plaintiff. After the trial court determined that the plaintiff had not established her theory of a battery (*i.e.*, that Brian had pulled the chair out from under the plaintiff while she was in the act of sitting down), it then became concerned with whether a battery was established under the facts as it found them to be.

In this connection, we quote another portion of the comment on the "Character of actor's intention," relating to clause (a) of the rule from the Restatement heretofore set forth:

~~1. intent to contact in a defined way~~

1) voluntary act
2) intent
3) harmful or offensive contact
4) lack of consent

"It is not enough that the act itself is intentionally done and this, even though the actor realizes or should realize that it contains a very grave risk of bringing about the contact or apprehension. Such realization may make the actor's conduct negligent or even reckless but unless he realizes that to a substantial certainty, the contact or apprehension will result, the actor has not that intention which is necessary to make him liable under the rule stated in this Section."

A battery would be established if, in addition to plaintiff's fall, it was proved that, when Brian moved the chair, he knew with substantial certainty that the plaintiff would attempt to sit down where the chair had been. If Brian had any of the intents which the trial court found, in the italicized portions of the findings of fact quoted above, that he did not have, he would of course have had the knowledge to which we have referred. The mere absence of any intent to injure the plaintiff or to play a prank on her or to embarrass her, or to commit an assault and battery on her would not absolve him from liability if in fact he had such knowledge.... Without such knowledge, there would be nothing wrongful about Brian's act in moving the chair, and, there being no wrongful act, there would be no liability.

While a finding that Brian had no such knowledge can be inferred from the findings made, we believe that before the plaintiff's action in such a case should be dismissed there should be no question but that the trial court had passed upon that issue; hence, the case should be remanded for clarification of the findings to specifically cover the question of Brian's knowledge, because intent could be inferred therefrom. If the court finds that he had such knowledge, the necessary intent will be established and the plaintiff will be entitled to recover, even though there was no purpose to injure or embarrass the plaintiff.... If Brian did not have such knowledge, there was no wrongful act by him, and the basic premise of liability on the theory of a battery was not established.

It will be noted that the law of battery as we have discussed it is the law applicable to adults, and no significance has been attached to the fact that Brian was a child less than six years of age when the alleged battery occurred. The only circumstance where Brian's age is of any consequence is in determining what he knew, and there his experience, capacity, and understanding are of course material.

From what has been said, it is clear that we find no merit in plaintiff's contention that we can direct the entry of a judgment for eleven thousand dollars in her favor on the record now before us.

Nor do we find any error in the record that warrants a new trial.

* * * * *

The cause is remanded for clarification, with instructions to make definite findings on the issue of whether Brian Dailey knew with substantial certainty that the plaintiff would attempt to sit down where the chair which he moved had been, and to change the judgment if the findings warrant it.

* * * * *

REMANDED for clarification.

NOTES

1.   Was the Washington Supreme Court concerned with the lower court's findings of fact or applications of law to the facts?

What do you think the lower court decided on remand? *See Garratt v. Dailey*, 304 P.2d 681 (1956) ("superior court reviewed the evidence, listened to additional arguments and studied briefs of counsel, and entered a finding to the effect that the defendant knew, with substantial certainty, at the time he removed the chair, that the plaintiff would attempt to sit down where the chair had been, since she was in the act of seating herself when he removed the chair").

2.   The *Garratt* court's definition of "intent" in the context of intentional torts, taken from the Restatement (Second) of Torts, is the definition used by courts in every state in the nation. There are two ways to satisfy intent under the definition: one who has either purpose, or has knowledge to a substantial certainty, has intent. Why is intent defined in two different ways? Which part of the definition of intent is likely to be easier for a plaintiff to prove?

Hypothetical A: Defendant sees plaintiff, his sworn enemy, walking along the street one hundred yards away. Defendant says to people standing around, "There is no way I can hit him, but it's worth a try because I hate him." Defendant flings the rock, and against all odds, the rock strikes plaintiff, seriously injuring him. Did defendant have intent to commit a tort?

Hypothetical B: Defendant walks up to a group of acquaintances and says, "I have acid in this bucket, and I am going to throw the bucket at you. I love you all, and I sincerely hope that it does not hurt anyone." Defendant throws the acid toward the group, and several people are burned by the acid. Defendant, upon seeing that people are hurt, cries and begins trying to administer first aid. Did defendant have intent to commit a tort?

3.   Is a child capable of forming the type of intent that is required to commit an intentional tort? There is a doctrine in tort law called the "tender years doctrine" which posits that at some age and below, the law conclusively presumes (that is, it cannot be proven otherwise) that a child is not capable of negligence, which means failure to exercise reasonable care. *See Fromenthal v. Clark*, 442 So. 2d 608 (La.App. 1 Cir. 1983), *writ denied*, 444 So. 2d 1242 (La. 1984). Should the doctrine apply to intentional torts? What if a six-year old child bites a five-year old child?

4.   Poor Brian Dailey, a little boy, is found liable and must pay a judgment of $11,000 plus interest! Will his allowance be garnished (seized by the sheriff) to pay the judgment?

5.   Notice that the Washington Supreme Court focuses its analysis on the element of intent. Appellate courts have the luxury of being able to focus on one element in analyzing a tort because if the plaintiff fails to prove any element of her prima facie case, the plaintiff loses. Unlike appellate courts, litigants and law students must carefully scrutinize all elements of a tort theory.

6.   Consider the court's treatment of intent in *Hogan v. Morgan*, 960 So. 2d 1024 (La.App. 1 Cir. 2007), *writ denied*, 963 So. 2d 1000 (La. 2007). In *Hogan*, a doctor performing an independent medical examination on plaintiff was unaware of a court order restricting the examination to the shoulder area. Plaintiff mentioned the limitation to the doctor but did not resist when the doctor continued the exam. Plaintiff then sued the doctor for a battery. The court of appeal concluded that there was no evidence that the doctor intended for his examination to be harmful or offensive.

scope of the consent

27

CAUDLE
v.
BETTS
512 So. 2d 389 (La. 1981)

DENNIS, J.

This personal injury case presents the issues of whether an electrical shock administered to a worker by his employer's chief executive officer as a practical joke constitutes an intentional tort, and if so, whether the employee may recover damages for the unintended and unforeseeable impairment of his occipital nerve which resulted from the intentional tort. The trial court found that an intentional tort had not been committed because no injury was intended, held that the employee's exclusive remedy was in worker's compensation, and dismissed the damage suit. The court of appeal affirmed for the same reasons. We reverse. A harmful or offensive contact with a person, resulting from an act intended to cause him to suffer such a contact, is a battery. A defendant's liability for the harm resulting from a battery extends to consequences which the defendant did not intend and could not reasonably have foreseen.

Plaintiff, Ruben Caudle, was employed as a salesman at Betts Lincoln-Mercury in Alexandria, Louisiana. An office Christmas party was planned for the afternoon of December 23, 1983. Shortly before the party some of the employees engaged in horseplay with an electric automobile condenser. They discovered that the condenser could be charged by touching one end on a car's sparkplug wire and turning the engine over. Once charged, the condenser would deliver a slight electric shock when touched at both ends. Several employees played catch with the charged condenser. Peter Betts, the president and principal shareholder of the dealership, joined in the activity. Although the facts were disputed, the trial court found that Betts shocked the back of Caudle's neck with the charged condenser and chased Caudle with it until he escaped by locking himself in an office.

Caudle testified that following the incident he developed a headache and left the party early. In the following months Caudle had frequent and severe headaches and passed out thirty to forty times. Conservative treatment in the form of nerve blocking shots was ineffective in permanently correcting these problems. Surgery severing the occipital nerve, performed on July 23, 1984, finally alleviated plaintiff's headaches and fainting spells. The only residual effect of the surgery is a slight numbness on the right side of plaintiff's head.

Caudle filed suit against Betts individually and against Betts Lincoln-Mercury, Inc. seeking damages for past pain and suffering, lost motion and enjoyment of life, past medical expenses, loss of earnings, and future damages for the permanent paralysis in his right scalp. After a bench trial, the district court found that Mr. Betts intended to shock Mr. Caudle but did not intend to injure him beyond a momentary, unpleasant jolt. The district court dismissed the plaintiff's suit and the court of appeal affirmed 502 So. 2d 146.

The Louisiana Worker's Compensation Act provides for compensation if an employee receives personal injury by accident arising out of and in the course of his employment. La. R.S. 23:1031. As a general rule, the rights and remedies granted to an employee therein are exclusive of all rights and remedies against his employer, any officer or principal of the employer, or any co-employee. La. R.S. 23:1032.[1] However, an exception to this rule provides that nothing therein shall

---

[1] "The rights and remedies herein granted to an employee ... on account of an injury ..., shall be exclusive of all other rights and remedies ... against his employer, or any principal or any officer, director, stockholder, partner or employee of such employer or principal...

"Nothing in this chapter shall affect the liability of the employer, or any officer, director, stockholder, partner or employee of such employer or principal to a fine or penalty under any other statute or the liability, civil or criminal, resulting from an intentional act.

"The immunity from civil liability provided by this Section shall not extend to: 1) any officer, director, stockholder, partner or employee of such employer or principal who is not engaged at the time of the injury in the normal course and scope of his employment; and 2) to the liability of any partner in a partnership which has been formed for the purpose of evading any of the provisions of this Section."

affect the liability of an employer, principal, officer, or co-employee resulting from an "intentional act". *Id.*

In interpreting the statute, this court has held that compensation shall be an employee's exclusive remedy against his employer for an unintentional injury covered by the act, but that nothing shall prevent an employee from recovering from his employer under general law for an intentional tort. *Bazley v. Tortorich*, 397 So. 2d 475 (La. 1981). We concluded that in drawing a line between intentional and unintentional acts the legislative aim was to make use of the well established division between intentional torts and negligence. *Id.* at 480.

In *Bazley* this court briefly explained the basic difference between an intentional tort and a negligent act but did not profess to set forth a complete exposition of either branch of tort law. Intentional tort law encompasses far more than could be explicated reasonably in a single opinion. *See, e.g.*, Restatement (Second) of Torts, American Law Institute § 1 -- 48 (1965); W. Prosser and W. Keeton, The Law of Torts, § 8 -- 12 (5th ed. 1984); F. Harper and F. James, The Law of Torts, § 3.1 -- 3.9 (2nd ed. 1986), and, generally, Louisiana Digest Titles, Assault & Battery, False Imprisonment. Consequently, when an employee seeks to recover from his employer for an intentional tort, a court must apply the legal precepts of general tort law related to the particular intentional tort alleged in order to determine whether he has proved his cause of action and damages recoverable thereunder.

The present case is one in which the plaintiff employee sought to recover damages as the result of an intentional tort, a battery committed upon him by his employer's principal owner and chief executive officer. The trial court found that the chief executive had intentionally shocked the employee with an auto condenser as a practical joke without the employee's consent or approval but that the serious injury to the employee's occipital nerve which resulted was neither foreseeable nor intentional. From this the trial court concluded that no intentional tort occurred, and the court of appeal affirmed its judgment. Consequently, in reviewing those rulings we must decide whether a battery was committed and, if so, whether damages are recoverable under battery for the unintended and unforeseeable occipital nerve injury.

A harmful or offensive contact with a person, resulting from an act intended to cause the plaintiff to suffer such a contact, is a battery.... The intention need not be malicious nor need it be an intention to inflict actual damage. It is sufficient if the actor intends to inflict either a harmful or offensive contact without the other's consent....

The original purpose of the courts in providing the action for battery undoubtedly was to keep the peace by affording a substitute for private retribution. F. Stone, Louisiana Civil Law Treatise, Tort Doctrine, § 125 (1977). The element of personal indignity involved always has been given considerable weight. Consequently, the defendant is liable not only for contacts that do actual physical harm, but also for those relatively trivial ones which are merely offensive and insulting. W. Prosser and W. Keeton, The Law of Torts, § 9 (5th ed. 1984); *Harrigan v. Rosich*, 173 So. 2d 880 (La.App. 4 Cir. 1965).

The intent with which tort liability is concerned is not necessarily a hostile intent, or a desire to do any harm. Restatement (Second) of Torts, American Law Institute § 13, (comment e) (1965). Rather it is an intent to bring about a result which will invade the interests of another in a way that the law forbids. The defendant may be liable although intending nothing more than a good-natured practical joke, or honestly believing that the act would not injure the plaintiff, or even though seeking the plaintiff's own good....

Bodily harm is generally considered to be any physical impairment of the condition of a person's body, or physical pain or illness. Restatement (Second) of Torts, American Law Institute § 15 (1965). The defendant's liability for the resulting harm extends, as in most other cases of intentional torts, to consequences which the defendant did not intend, and could not reasonably have foreseen, upon the obvious basis that it is better for unexpected losses to fall upon the intentional wrongdoer than upon the innocent victim....

Applying these precepts to the facts found and affirmed by the lower courts, we conclude that the plaintiff employee proved that a battery had been committed on him by another employee and that he is entitled to recover for all injuries resulting therefrom including his occipital nerve impairment. It is undisputed that when Mr. Betts shocked the employee, Mr. Caudle, with the condenser, he intended the contact to be offensive and at least slightly painful or harmful. The fact that he did so as a practical joke and did not intend to inflict actual damage does not render him immune from liability. Further, as between the innocent employee victim and the wrongdoer, it is better for unexpected losses to fall upon the intentional wrongdoer. Mr. Caudle is entitled to recover for all consequences of the battery, even those that Mr. Betts did not intend and could not reasonably have foreseen.

Because the trial and appeals courts mistakenly concluded that an intentional tort had not been committed, they did not consider or award damages to the plaintiff. Consequently, the judgments below are reversed and the case is remanded to the court of appeal for further proceedings consistent with this opinion. Because we have received a copy of an order of the bankruptcy court indicating that one of the parties herein has filed a petition in bankruptcy, however, the court of appeal is instructed that upon receiving this case on remand it shall comply with 11 U.S.C. § 362(a) by staying any proceedings provided for therein.

REVERSED AND REMANDED to the court of appeal with instructions.

NOTES

1.   Does the court in *Caudle* use the same definition of "intent" as the court in *Garratt*?

2.   Intent to do what? Purpose or knowledge to a substantial certainty to cause what? 1) A contact? 2) A harmful or offensive contact? 3) The harm that occurred? Which of those three did the court in *Caudle* use to define the intent required for an intentional tort?

What if a court defined the intent required as the intent to cause a contact, be it ever so slight, which, to everyone's surprise, causes great harm? Consider *White v. Univ. of Idaho*, 797 P.2d 108 (*Id.* 1990). In *White*, one of the defendants, a professor at the University of Idaho, as a teaching device "played the piano" on the back of a student, and this action caused a serious injury to the student, who sued the professor and the university. The court defined the intent required for an intentional tort as follows: "The intent element of the tort of battery does not require a desire or purpose to bring about a specific result or injury; it is satisfied if the actor's affirmative act causes an intended contact which is unpermitted and which is harmful or offensive." Because the Idaho Supreme Court found that the professor committed an intentional tort, the University of Idaho could not be liable for his acts; the Idaho Tort Claims Act exempted the state from liability for intentional torts. A dissenting justice wrote:

> My reading of the majority opinion has little changed my own views expressed earlier, other than to note that the Court's opinion has a chilling effect on any thought of ever again tapping a dancing gent on the shoulder to ask, "May I?" Today it is learned that so doing is a battery even though no harm or offense is intended. One lives and learns. Until today it was though that "battery" had been long ago defined by the Idaho legislatures, both territorial and state, as the willful and unlawful use of force or violence upon the person of another.

3.   Based on *Caudle*, it appears that one who is merely playing a practical joke that goes badly and causes a great deal of harm can be held liable for a battery. *But see Spivey v. Battaglia*, 258 So. 2d 815 (Fla. 1972) (defendant who put his arm around coworker to embarrass her and accidentally injured her severely was negligent but did not commit intentional tort). It can make a difference in terms of magnitude of liability whether a defendant's acts are classified as an intentional tort or negligence. The extended liability principle discussed in *Caudle* imposes liability for all harm that follows from an intentional tort, no matter how unexpected that harm might be.

4.   The classification of a defendant's act as an intentional tort or negligence can have many consequences, such as applicability of workers' compensation or other immunity, which statute of limitations or prescriptive period applies, whether liability for damages is "cut off" at some point, etc. Given the importance of this classification, do you think the line between intentional torts and negligence is clear enough?

DAVIS

v.

WHITE

18 B.R. 246 (Bankr. E.D. Va. 1982)

SHELLEY, Bankruptcy Judge.

This matter comes on upon the filing of a Complaint by Ralph Edward Davis, by counsel, to determine the dischargeability of a debt of the Defendant, Walter Calvin White, Jr., pursuant to 11 U.S.C. § 523(a)(6). After the filing of an answer by the Defendant a trial was held. Upon the foregoing the Court makes the following determination.

Statement of the Facts

On September 10, 1977 Walter Calvin White, Jr. (White) shot Ralph Edward Davis (Davis) in the stomach with a handgun. White was arrested for the shooting and on November 29, 1978 the Circuit Court of the City of Richmond found him guilty of maiming Davis and sentenced him to serve five years in the state penitentiary. On February 26, 1980 Davis obtained a default judgment against White in the amount of $50,000.00 in the Circuit Court for the City of Richmond on the ground that White willfully and maliciously wounded Davis. White subsequently filed his petition in bankruptcy and Davis now asks this Court to declare White's debt on account of that judgment nondischargeable in bankruptcy.

On the day of the shooting Davis and his brother, Marvin W. Davis, were washing cars in front of their mother's house on Fairmont Avenue in Richmond, Virginia. At the same time White, a neighbor who lives less than one block away on the same street, was having a conversation with William Tipton (Tipton). In that conversation White and Tipton continued an argument which had begun approximately one week earlier. White had obtained a gun in anticipation of seeking Tipton. White was carrying the pistol in a container on his motorcycle and pulled it out of the container during the course of that argument.

When White pulled the gun Tipton mounted his motorcycle and sped away. White shot at Tipton as Tipton passed within twenty-five feet of Davis. He missed Tipton and the bullet hit Davis in the stomach. White fled the scene.

White testified at the trial that he obtained the gun with the intent of scaring Tipton. He said that he drew the gun after Tipton insulted his mother but that he did not intentionally fire the gun. He claimed the gun went off when he tripped over a rock in the street.

Davis and White did not know each other before the shooting incident. White said he pulled the gun intending to scare Tipton and that it accidently fired. This Court believes that White's testimony that the gun accidently fired when he tripped over a rock is unworthy of belief. White testified that he obtained the gun earlier that week with another meeting with Tipton in mind. Although Davis was located almost a full block from White, the bullet hit him as Tipton passed within twenty-five feet of him. White clearly intended to shoot Tipton; however, he missed and the bullet hit Davis instead.

Conclusions of Law

A debt incurred from an action based upon a willful and malicious injury by the debtor to another person may be nondischargeable in bankruptcy.[1] 11 U.S.C. § 523(a)(6). The word "willful" means deliberate or intentional.

* * * * *

White committed the wrongful act when he shot at Tipton. The act was intentional and it produced an injury although not to the person White intended to injure. White's actions cannot be excused solely because he missed his intended victim and instead hit someone else. The injury is not required to be directed against the victim, but includes any entity other than the intended victim.

Under the doctrine of transferred intent one who intends a battery is liable for that battery when he unexpectedly hits a stranger instead of the intended victim. W. Prosser, *The Law of Torts,* 33 (4th ed. 1971). If one intentionally commits an assault or battery at another and by mistake strikes a third person, he is guilty of an assault and battery of the third person if "defendant's intention, in such a case, is to strike an unlawful blow, to injure some person by his act, and it is not essential that the injury be to the one intended." *Morrow v. Flores,* 225 S.W.2d 621, 624, Tex.Civ.App. (1949), *rehearing denied* 1950.

Virginia courts have adopted the doctrine of transferred intent reasoning that "... every person is liable for the direct, natural and probable consequence of his acts, and that every one doing an unlawful act is responsible for all of the consequential results of that act." *Bannister v. Mitchell,* 127 Va. 578, 104 S.E. 800, 801 (1920). There need be no actual intent to injure the particular person who is injured. *Id.*

* * * * *

The evidence here clearly shows that the shooting was a wrongful act intentionally done and that Davis's injuries resulted from that act. White deliberately, intentionally and maliciously fired the gun and injured Davis and the debt resulting from that act is nondischargeable in bankruptcy.

* * * * *

An appropriate order will issue.

NOTES

1.   *Davis* illustrates yet another importance of a tort being classified as intentional; the judgment debt may not be extinguished in bankruptcy. *See supra* footnote in *Davis* quoting from the Bankruptcy Code.

2.   This case illustrates the doctrine of transferred intent. Two aspects of the doctrine are as follows: transfer from one tort to another and transfer from one person to another. Does the court's application of transferred intent in *Davis* illustrate both aspects or one?

3.   Should intent be transferred from all of the intentional torts to all of the other intentional torts? For example, suppose that I wish to damage your book, and in the course of doing so, I accidentally seriously injure you.

---

[1] "A discharge under section 727, 1141, or 1328(b) of this title does not discharge an individual debtor from any debt.... (6) for willful and malicious injury by the debtor to another entity or to the property of another entity...." 11 U.S.C. § 523(a)(6).

4.   Transferred intent is not a rule, and courts do not always transfer intent. *See, e.g., Citizen v. Theodore Daigle & Bro., Inc.,* 418 So. 2d 598 (La. 1982) (defendant wanted to scare co-worker with rifle that he thought was unloaded and accidentally shot coworker; court held no battery because defendant did not have intent to commit battery).

B.   BATTERY   + lack of consent

Battery is an intentional tort that protects a person's interest in being free from physical contact with his or her person. Thus, the tort of battery is said to protect one's interest in physical or bodily integrity. Like the other intentional torts, the prima facie case for battery requires a plaintiff to prove a <u>voluntary act</u> and <u>intent</u> on the part of the defendant. The voluntary act of the defendant must cause a <u>harmful or offensive contact</u> with the plaintiff. Clearly, there can be a broad range of batteries, ranging from an offensive pushing of the person that causes embarrassment, to a shooting or beating of the person that results in catastrophic injuries. Jurisdictions differ as to whether it is part of the plaintiff's prima facie case for battery to prove that the contact was unpermitted or not consented to. *See, e.g., Landry v. Bellanger,* 851 So. 2d 943 (La. 2003) ("In a suit for damages resulting from an intentional tort, the claimant must carry the burden of proving all prima facie elements of the tort, including lack of consent to the invasive conduct."). Some jurisdictions, on the other hand, treat consent as a defense to be proven by the defendant.

As with most other intentional torts, it is not necessary for a plaintiff to prove actual damages (harm) in order to establish that a battery was committed. A technical battery can be proven by proving a voluntary act, intent, and harmful or offensive contact (and, in some jurisdictions, lack of consent). Proving a technical battery will support an award of at least nominal damages (a small amount, perhaps $1.00). It should be noted, however, that if a plaintiff establishes a technical battery, a jury (or judge in a bench trial) may find the commission of the battery sufficient to award substantial damages. As with other intentional torts, punitive damages (damages which are awarded to a plaintiff in addition to those which compensate him or her for the injury, and which are designed to "punish" the actor) may be awarded in some jurisdictions.

LEICHTMAN
v.
WLW JACOR COMMUNICATIONS, INC.
634 N.E.2d 697 (Ohio App. 1994)

... Leichtman claims to be "a nationally known" antismoking advocate. Leichtman alleges that, on the date of the Great American Smokeout, he was invited to appear on the WLW Bill Cunningham radio talk show to discuss the harmful effects of smoking and breathing secondary smoke. He also alleges that, while he was in the studio, Furman, another WLW talk-show host, lit a cigar and repeatedly blew smoke in Leichtman's face "for the purpose of causing physical discomfort, humiliation and distress."

* * * * *

Leichtman contends that Furman's intentional act constituted a battery. The Restatement of the Law 2d, Torts (1965), states:
"An actor is subject to liability to another for battery if

"(a) he acts intending to cause a harmful or offensive contact with the person of the other ..., and

"(b) a harmful contact with the person of the other directly or indirectly results[; or] [footnote omitted] "c) an offensive contact with the person of the other directly or indirectly results."[2] (Footnote added.)

In determining if a person is liable for a battery, the Supreme Court has adopted the rule that "[c]ontact which is offensive to a reasonable sense of personal dignity is offensive contact." .... It has defined "offensive" to mean "disagreeable or nauseating or painful because of outrage to taste and sensibilities or affronting insultingness." .... Furthermore, tobacco smoke, as "particulate matter," has the physical properties capable of making contact....

As alleged in Leichtman's complaint, when Furman intentionally blew cigar smoke in Leichtman's face, under Ohio common law, he committed a battery. No matter how trivial the incident, a battery is actionable, even if damages are only one dollar.... The rationale is explained by Roscoe Pound in his essay "Liability": "[I]n civilized society men must be able to assume that others will do them no intentional injury -- that others will commit no intentioned aggressions upon them." Pound, An Introduction to the Philosophy of Law (1922) 169.

Other jurisdictions also have concluded that a person can commit a battery by intentionally directing tobacco smoke at another.... We do not, however, adopt or lend credence to the theory of a "smoker's battery," which imposes liability if there is substantial certainty that exhaled smoke will predictably contact a nonsmoker... Also, whether the "substantial certainty" prong of intent from the Restatement of Torts translates to liability for secondary smoke via the intentional tort doctrine . . . need not be decided here because Leichtman's claim for battery is based exclusively on Furman's commission of a deliberate act....

Neither Cunningham nor WLW is entitled to judgment on the battery claim under Civ.R. 12(B)(6). Concerning Cunningham, at common law, one who is present and encourages or incites commission of a battery by words can be equally liable as a principal.... Leichtman's complaint states, "At Defendant Cunningham's urging, Defendant Furman repeatedly blew cigar smoke in Plaintiff's face."

With regard to WLW, an employer is not legally responsible for the intentional torts of its employees that do not facilitate or promote its business.... However, whether an employer is liable under the doctrine of *respondeat superior* because its employee is acting within the scope of employment is ordinarily a question of fact.... Accordingly, Leichtman's claim for battery with the allegations against the three defendants in the second count of the complaint is sufficient to withstand a motion to dismiss under Civ.R. 12(B)(6).

* * * * *

Arguably, trivial cases are responsible for an avalanche of lawsuits in the courts. They delay cases that are important to individuals and corporations and that involve important social issues. The result is justice denied to litigants and their counsel who must wait for their day in court. However, absent circumstances that warrant sanctions for frivolous appeals ..., we refuse to limit one's right to sue. Section 16, Article I, Ohio Constitution states, "All courts shall be open, and every person, for an injury done him in his land, goods, person, or reputation, shall have remedy by due course of law, and shall have justice administered without denial or delay."

This case emphasizes the need for some form of alternative dispute resolution operating totally outside the court system as a means to provide an attentive ear to the parties and a resolution of disputes in a nominal case. Some need a forum in which they can express corrosive contempt for another without dragging their antagonist through the expense inherent in a lawsuit. Until such an

---

[2] Offensive contact: Restatement, ..., Section 18. *See, generally, Love* at 99-100, 524 N.E.2d at 167, in which the court: (1) referred to battery as "intentional, offensive touching"; (2) defined offensive contact as that which is "offensive to a reasonable sense of personal dignity"; and (3) commented that if "an arrest is made by a mere touching ... the touching is offensive and, unless privileged, is a 'battery.'"....

alternative forum is created, Leichtman's battery claim, previously knocked out by the trial judge in the first round, now survives round two to advance again through the courts into round three.

.... [W]e reverse that portion of the trial court's order that dismissed the battery claim in the second count of the complaint. This cause is remanded for further proceedings consistent with law on that claim only.

Judgment accordingly.

NOTES

1.   What element of battery caused the trial court to dismiss the battery claim in the *Leichtman* case?

2.   If the *Leichtman* case went to a jury, what damages do you think the plaintiff would recover?

3.   Did anyone make contact with the plaintiff in *Leichtman*? What or whom must make contact with what or whom for a battery to occur? Is it a battery if I push a desk against your leg? Is it a battery if I pull a book from your hand? Is it a battery if I kick a car in which you are sitting? Consider, for example, *Zimmerman v. Progressive Security Ins. Co.*, 174 So. 3d 1230 (La.App. 2 Cir. 2015), *writ denied*, 184 So. 3d 36 (La. 2015) (defendant's intent in using her vehicle to ram plaintiff's parked vehicle, in which plaintiff was sitting, three times was sufficient for a battery; evidence of defendant's intent was provided by the evidence that plaintiff and defendant had "a complicated personal relationship" before the ramming occurred).

4.   The plaintiff is suing, among others, the radio station that employs the DJ. Vicarious liability means that a person or entity is held liable for the actions of others. Consider, for example, *Garratt v. Dailey*, in which the plaintiff is seeking to hold the parents liable for the acts of their child Brian. The court in *Leichtman* explains the vicarious liability theory of *respondeat superior* ("let the master answer"), by which employers can be held liable for the acts of employees that occur within the course and scope of their employment. Vicarious liability is discussed in Chapter 12.

5.   Consider the court's lamentation regarding the crowding of court dockets with "trivial" lawsuits. The court suggests that alternative forums are needed. Is this true only for "trivial lawsuits"? What types of cases might be well-suited to alternative dispute resolution, such as arbitration (presentation to, and final determination by a non-judicial officer) or mediation (settlement negotiations supervised by a trained mediator)?

6.   Look back at the three cases in Section A above: *Garratt, Caudle,* and *Davis.* All three cases in that section involve alleged batteries. Having considered the issue of intent in each, consider whether any other elements of battery are problematic in each.

7.   What is a voluntary act? The Restatement (Second) § 2 defines "act" as "an external manifestation of the actor's will." Comment (a) states that "[t]here cannot be an act without will." Thus, involuntary and reflexive movements are not considered acts. For an interesting case on voluntary and involuntary acts, *see Dixon v. Winston*, 417 So. 2d 122 (La.App. 3 Cir. 1982), *writ denied*, 420 So. 2d 985 (La. 1983) (high school football player hit a cheerleader, who was his sometimes girlfriend, in the eye during a lunchroom argument, fracturing the bones around her eye, and court concluded that his striking her was "an involuntary reflex reaction to her attack"). A dissenting judge "perceive[d] nothing involuntary" in the striking. Also important in the *Dixon* case was the Louisiana aggressor doctrine, which was recently conclusively abrogated by the Louisiana Supreme Court. *See Landry v. Bellanger*, 851 So. 2d 943 (La. 2003). *Landry* is included *infra* Chapter 2(G)(3).

8.   Because batteries sometimes leave the victim unconscious, dazed, or otherwise impaired, a plaintiff may be able to establish a battery but have difficulty presenting evidence to establish who

committed the battery. *See, e.g., Boudreaux v. Papa Bear's Pizza, LLC*, ___So. 3d ___, 2017 WL 1532710 (La.App. 1 Cir. 2017).

C.   ASSAULT

Assault is an intentional tort theory that protects a person's interest in being free from apprehension of harmful or offensive contacts with his or her person. English common law courts explained this tort under trespass as a touching of the mind but not the body. The tort protects a mental interest, but unlike the modern tort of intentional infliction of emotional distress, it is a specific mental interest rather than a generalized fear, dread, or humiliation. One often hears reference to "assault and battery." In criminal law, assault is sometimes used interchangeably with battery. In tort law, it is important to distinguish between the two torts, although the same act may be both a battery and an assault. Some courts have said that every battery includes an assault. This is not accurate. One can suffer an assault without a battery. For example, if I swing my fist at your face and miss and you see this action, you may establish an assault, but not a battery. One also can suffer a battery without an assault. For example, if I hit you in the back with my fist and you never saw the punch coming, there is a battery but no assault. If I swing my fist at your face and hit you and you saw it coming, there is both an assault and a battery. The elements of an assault are the same as battery with the exception of the result, which is the victim being placed in apprehension of a harmful or offensive contact.

Restatement (Second) of Torts

§ 21.   Assault

(1) An actor is subject to liability to another for assault if

(a) he acts intending to cause a harmful or offensive contact with the person of the other or a third person, or an imminent apprehension of such a contact, and

(b) the other is thereby put in such imminent apprehension.

(2) An action which is not done with the intention stated in Subsection (1, a) does not make the actor liable to the other for an apprehension caused thereby although the act involves an unreasonable risk of causing it and, therefore, would be negligent or reckless if the risk threatened bodily harm.

DICKENS

v.

PURYEAR

276 S.E.2d 325 (N.C. 1981)

EXUM, J.

Plaintiff's complaint is cast as a claim for intentional infliction of mental distress. It was filed more than one year but less than three years after the incidents complained of occurred. Defendants moved for summary judgment before answer was due or filed. Much of the factual showing at the hearing on summary judgment related to assaults and batteries committed against plaintiff by defendants. Defendants' motions for summary judgment were allowed on the ground that plaintiff's claim was for assault and battery; therefore it was barred by the one-year statute of limitations applicable to assault and battery.

* * * * *

The facts brought out at the hearing on summary judgment may be briefly summarized: For a time preceding the incidents in question plaintiff Dickens, a thirty-one year old man, shared sex, alcohol and marijuana with defendant's daughter, a seventeen year old high school student. On 2

April 1975 defendants, husband and wife, lured plaintiff into rural Johnston County, North Carolina. Upon plaintiff's arrival defendant Earl Puryear, after identifying himself ... pointed a pistol between plaintiff's eyes and shouted "Ya'll come on out." Four men wearing ski masks and armed with nightsticks then approached from behind plaintiff and beat him into semi-consciousness. They handcuffed plaintiff to a piece of farm machinery and resumed striking him with nightsticks. Defendant Earl Puryear, while brandishing a knife and cutting plaintiff's hair, threatened plaintiff with castration. During four or five interruptions of the beatings defendant Earl Puryear and the others, within plaintiff's hearing, discussed and took votes on whether plaintiff should be killed or castrated. Finally, after some two hours and the conclusion of a final conference, the beatings ceased. Defendant Earl Puryear told plaintiff to go home, pull his telephone off the wall, pack his clothes, and leave the state of North Carolina; otherwise he would be killed. Plaintiff was then set free.[1]

Plaintiff filed his complaint on 31 March 1978. It alleges that defendants on the occasion just described intentionally inflicted mental distress upon him. He further alleges that as a result of defendants' acts plaintiff has suffered "severe and permanent mental and emotional distress, and physical injury to his nerves and nervous system." He alleges that he is unable to sleep, afraid to go out in the dark, afraid to meet strangers, afraid he may be killed, suffering from chronic diarrhea and a gum disorder, unable effectively to perform his job, and that he has lost $1000 per month income.

... On 7 September and 15 November 1978 defendants filed, respectively, motions for summary judgment. The motions made no reference to the statute of limitations nor did they contest plaintiff's factual allegations. Judge Braswell, after considering arguments of counsel, plaintiff's complaint, plaintiff's deposition and evidence in the criminal case arising out of this occurrence,[footnote omitted] concluded that plaintiff's claim was barred by ..., the one-year statute of limitations applicable to assault and battery. On 29 March 1979 he granted summary judgment in favor of both defendants.

* * * * *

.... Defendants contend, and the Court of Appeals agreed, that this is an action grounded in assault and battery. Although plaintiff pleads the tort of intentional infliction of mental distress, the Court of Appeals concluded that the complaint's factual allegations and the factual showing at the hearing on summary judgment support only a claim for assault and battery. The claim was, therefore, barred by the one-year period of limitations applicable to assault and battery. Plaintiff, on the other hand, argues that the factual showing on the motion supports a claim for intentional infliction of mental distress – a claim which is governed by the three-year period of limitations. [footnote omitted] At least, plaintiff argues, his factual showing is such that it cannot be said as a matter of law that he will be unable to prove such a claim at trial. We agree with plaintiff's position.

* * * * *

North Carolina follows common law principles governing assault and battery. An assault is an offer to show violence to another without striking him, and a battery is the carrying of the threat into effect by the infliction of a blow.... The interest protected by the action for battery is freedom from intentional and unpermitted contact with one's person; the interest protected by the action for assault is freedom from apprehension of a harmful or offensive contact with one's person.... The apprehension created must be one of an immediate harmful or offensive contact, as distinguished from contact in the future. As noted in *State v. Ingram,* 237 N.C. 197, 201, 74 S.E. 2d 532, 535 (1953), in order to constitute an assault there must be:

> "[A]n overt act or an attempt, or the unequivocal appearance of an attempt, with force and violence, to do some *immediate* physical injury to the person of another....

---

[1] This same occurrence gave rise to a criminal conviction of defendant Earl Puryear for conspiracy to commit simple assault. *See State v. Puryear,* 30 N.C. App. 719, 228 S.E. 2d 536, appeal dismissed, 291 N.C. 325, 230 S.E. 2d 678 (1976).

"The display of force or menace of violence must be such to cause the reasonable apprehension of *immediate* bodily harm. *Dahlin v. Fraser*, 206 Minn. 476." (Emphasis supplied.)

* * * * *

A mere threat, unaccompanied by an offer or attempt to show violence, is not an assault....

Common law principles of assault and battery as enunciated in North Carolina law are also found in the Restatement (Second) of Torts (1965) (hereinafter "the Restatement"). As noted in § 29(1) of the Restatement, "[t]o make the actor liable for an assault he must put the other in apprehension of an *imminent* contact." (Emphasis supplied.) The comment to § 29(1) states: "The apprehension created must be one of imminent contact, as distinguished from any contact in the future. 'Imminent' does not mean immediate, in the sense of instantaneous contact.... It means rather that there will be no significant delay." Similarly, § 31 of the Restatement provides that "[w]ords do not make the actor liable for assault unless together with other acts or circumstances they put the other in reasonable apprehension of an *imminent* harmful or offensive contact with his person." (Emphasis supplied.) The comment to § 31 provides, in pertinent part:

"a. Ordinarily mere words, unaccompanied by some act apparently intended to carry the threat into execution, do not put the other in apprehension of an imminent bodily contact, and so cannot make the actor liable for an assault under the rule stated in § 21 [the section which defines an assault]. For this reason it is commonly said in the decisions that mere words do not constitute an assault, or that some overt act is required. This is true even though the mental discomfort caused by a threat of serious future harm on the part of one who has the apparent intention and ability to carry out his threat may be far more emotionally disturbing than many of the attempts to inflict minor bodily contacts which are actionable as assaults. Any remedy for words which are abusive or insulting, or which create emotional distress by threats for the future, is to be found under §§ 46 and 47 (those sections dealing with the interest in freedom from emotional distress)."

Illustration

1. A, known to be a resolute and desperate character, *threatens to waylay B on his way home on a lonely road on a dark night. A is not liable to B for an assault* under the rule stated in § 21. *A may, however, be liable to B for the infliction of severe emotional distress by extreme and outrageous conduct*, under the rule stated in § 46." (Emphasis supplied.)

Again, as noted by Prosser, § 10, p. 40, "[t]hreats for the future ... are simply not present breaches of the peace, and so never have fallen within the narrow boundaries of [assault]." Thus threats for the future are actionable, if at all, not as assaults but as intentional inflictions of mental distress.

* * * * *

Although plaintiff labels his claim one for intentional infliction of mental distress, we agree with the Court of Appeals that "[t]he nature of the action is not determined by what either party calls it...." The nature of the action is determined "by the issues arising on the pleading and by the relief sought," *id.*, and by the facts which, at trial, are proved or which, on motion for summary judgment, are forecast by the evidentiary showing.

Here much of the factual showing at the hearing related to assaults and batteries committed by defendants against plaintiff. The physical beatings and the cutting of plaintiff's hair constituted batteries. The threats of castration and death, being threats which created apprehension of immediate harmful or offensive contact, were assaults. Plaintiff's recovery for injuries, mental or physical, caused by these actions would be barred by the one-year statute of limitations.

The evidentiary showing on the summary judgment motion does, however, indicate that defendant Earl Puryear threatened plaintiff with death in the future unless plaintiff went home, pulled his telephone off the wall, packed his clothes, and left the state. The Court of Appeals characterized this threat as being "an immediate threat of harmful and offensive contact. It was a present threat of harm to plaintiff...." The Court of Appeals thus concluded that this threat was also an assault barred by the one-year statute of limitations.

We disagree with the Court of Appeals' characterization of this threat. The threat was not one of imminent, or immediate, harm. It was a threat for the future apparently intended to and which allegedly did inflict serious mental distress; therefore it is actionable, if at all, as an intentional infliction of mental distress...

Having concluded, therefore, that the factual showing on the motions for summary judgment was sufficient to indicate that plaintiff may be able to prove at trial a claim for intentional infliction of mental distress, we hold that summary judgment for defendants based upon the one-year statute of limitations was error and we remand the matter for further proceedings against defendant Earl Puryear not inconsistent with this opinion.

* * * * *

NOTES

1.   Apprehension of a harmful or offensive contact is not the same as fear. Restatement (Second) § 24 defines apprehension as belief "that the act may result in imminent contact unless prevented from so resulting by the other's self-defensive action or by his flight or by the intervention of some outside force."

Suppose that you are in a crowd watching the heavyweight boxing champion of the world sign autographs. Overcome with a sense of confidence (and bad judgment), you rush forward and proclaim to the champion that you are going to knock him out with your fist in a moment. Although the champion may not fear you, he has a right to be free from apprehending such contacts, and the law does not require him to flee to avoid your threatened contact.

2.   What does "imminent" contact mean? The court in *Dickens* quotes the Restatement (Second) definition: "no significant delay." In view of that definition of "imminent," when is there an assault in the following hypothetical?

> You live in the house next door to me in a cramped suburban subdivision. You call me on the telephone and tell me that you are coming over in a moment to severely beat me, so I should stay in the house and await your arrival. Assault? I lock my doors and windows, and while I am locking my windows, I look outside and see you crossing the yard with a bat in your hand. Assault? You arrive at my front door and begin knocking on the door, and when I do not answer, beating on the door with the bat. Assault?

3.   It is often said that "words alone" are not sufficient for an assault? How often do you think there are words alone without some accompanying act?

D.   FALSE IMPRISONMENT

False imprisonment is an intentional tort theory that protects a person's interest in having one's body free from restraint or confinement. As with other intentional torts, the prima facie case includes a <u>voluntary act</u> and an <u>intent</u> to confine or restrain. Two additional elements are that the act must cause <u>complete confinement or restraint</u>, and the <u>victim must be aware of the restraint</u> or

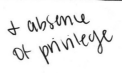
+ absence of privilege

confinement or, even if not aware of it, suffers harm as a result of it. Most false imprisonment claims in the United States today are of the false arrest variety. In a false arrest false imprisonment, the act of the defendant that causes the restraint or confinement is the assertion of legal authority to detain or confine the victim. Obviously, there is a need for law enforcement officers to be able to detain and arrest persons. Furthermore, in view of shoplifting, merchants have a need to detain persons under some circumstances for questioning and perhaps arrest. Cases of false arrest often are resolved on the basis of whether the defendant was privileged to confine or restrain the plaintiff. The following case deals with a false arrest claim.

PARVI
v.
CITY OF KINGSTON
362 N.E.2d 960 (N.Y. 1977)

FUCHSBERG, J.

.... This appeal brings up for review the dismissal, at the end of the plaintiff's case, of two causes of action, both of which arise out of the same somewhat unusual train of events. One is for false imprisonment.... The judgment of dismissal was affirmed by the Appellate Division.... The issue before us, ... is whether a prima facie case was made out. We believe it was.

Bearing in mind that, at the procedural point at which the case was decided, the plaintiff was entitled to the benefit of the most favorable inferences that were to be drawn from the record ..., we turn at once to the proof. In doing so, for the present we rely in the main on testimony plaintiff adduced from the defendant's own employees, especially since plaintiff's own recollection of the events was less than satisfactory.

Sometime after 9:00 p.m. on the evening of May 28, 1972, a date which occurred during the Memorial Day weekend, two police officers employed by the defendant City of Kingston responded in a radio patrol car to the rear of a commercial building in that city where they had been informed some individuals were acting in a boisterous manner. Upon their arrival, they found three men, one Raymond Dugan, his brother Dixie Dugan and the plaintiff, Donald C. Parvi. According to the police, it was the Dugan brothers who alone were then engaged in a noisy quarrel. When the two uniformed officers informed the three they would have to move on or be locked up, Raymond Dugan ran away; Dixie Dugan chased after him unsuccessfully and then returned to the scene in a minute or two; Parvi, who the police testimony shows had been trying to calm the Dugans, remained where he was.

In the course of their examinations before trial, read into evidence by Parvi's counsel, the officers described all three as exhibiting, in an unspecified manner, evidence that they "had been drinking" and showed "the effects of alcohol". They went on to relate how, when Parvi and Dixie Dugan said they had no place to go, the officers ordered them into the police car and, pursuing a then prevailing police "standard operating procedure", transported the two men outside the city limits to an abandoned golf course located in an unlit and isolated area known as Coleman Hill. Thereupon the officers drove off, leaving Parvi and Dugan to "dry out". This was the first time Parvi had ever been there. En route they had asked to be left off at another place, but the police refused to do so.

No more than 350 feet from the spot where they were dropped off, one of the boundaries of the property adjoins the New York State Thruway. There were no intervening fences or barriers other than the low Thruway guardrail intended to keep vehicular traffic on the road. Before they left, it is undisputed that the police made no effort to learn whether Parvi was oriented to his whereabouts, to instruct him as to the route back to Kingston, where Parvi had then lived for 12 years, or to ascertain where he would go from there. From where the men were dropped, the "humming and buzzing" of fast-traveling, holiday-bound automobile traffic was clearly audible from the Thruway; in their befuddled state, which later left Parvi with very little memory of the events, the men lost little time in responding to its siren song. For, in an apparent effort to get back, by 10:00 p.m. Parvi and Dugan had wandered onto the Thruway, where they were struck by an automobile operated by one David R. Darling. Parvi was severely injured; Dugan was killed.....

The Cause of Action for False Imprisonment

With these facts before us, we initially direct our attention to Parvi's cause of action for false imprisonment. Only recently, we had occasion to set out the four elements of that tort in *Broughton v State of New York* ... where we said that "the plaintiff must show that: (1) the defendant intended to confine him, (2) the plaintiff was conscious of the confinement, (3) the plaintiff did not consent to the confinement and (4) the confinement was not otherwise privileged".

Elements (1) and (3) present no problem here. When the plaintiff stated he had no place to go, he was faced with but one alternative – arrest. This was hardly the stuff of which consent is formed, especially in light of the fact that Parvi was, in a degree to be measured by the jury, then under the influence of alcohol. It is also of no small moment in this regard that the men's request to be released at a place they designated was refused. Moreover, one of the policemen testified that his fellow officer alone selected the location to which Parvi was taken; indeed, this was a place to which the police had had prior occasion to bring others who were being "run out of town" because they evidenced signs of intoxication. Further, putting aside for the time being the question of whether such an arrest would have been privileged, it can hardly be contended that, in view of the direct and willful nature of their actions, there was no proof that the police officers intended to confine Parvi.

Element (2), consciousness of confinement, is a more subtle and more interesting subissue in this case. On that subject, we note that, while respected authorities have divided on whether awareness of confinement by one who has been falsely imprisoned should be a *sine qua non* for making out a case .... [F]alse imprisonment, as a dignitary tort, is not suffered unless its victim knows of the dignitary invasion. Interestingly, the Restatement of Torts 2d (§ 42) too has taken the position that there is no liability for intentionally confining another unless the person physically restrained knows of the confinement or is harmed by it.

However, though correctly proceeding on that premise, the Appellate Division, in affirming the dismissal of the cause of action for false imprisonment, erroneously relied on the fact that Parvi, after having provided additional testimony in his own behalf on direct examination, had agreed on cross that he no longer had any *recollection* of his confinement. In so doing, that court failed to distinguish between a later recollection of consciousness and the existence of that consciousness at the time when the imprisonment itself took place. The latter, of course, is capable of being proved though one who suffers the consciousness can no longer personally describe it, whether by reason of lapse of memory, incompetency, death or other cause. Specifically, in this case, while it may well be that the alcohol Parvi had imbibed or the injuries he sustained, or both, had had the effect of wiping out his recollection of being in the police car against his will, that is a far cry from saying that he was not conscious of his confinement at the time when it was actually taking place. And, even if plaintiff's sentient state at the time of his imprisonment was something less than total sobriety, that does not mean that he had no conscious sense of what was then happening to him. To the contrary, there is much in the record to support a finding that the plaintiff indeed was aware of his arrest at the time it took place. By way of illustration, the officers described Parvi's responsiveness to their command that he get into the car, his colloquy while being driven to Coleman Hill and his request to be let off elsewhere. At the very least, then, it was for the jury, in the first instance, to weigh credibility, evaluate inconsistencies and determine whether the burden of proof had been met.

Passing on now to the fourth and final element, that of privilege or justification, preliminarily, and dispositively for the purpose of this appeal, it is to be noted that, since the alleged imprisonment here was without a warrant and therefore an extrajudicial act, the burden not only of proving, but of pleading legal justification was on the city, whose failure to have done so precluded it from introducing such evidence under its general denial....

Since the city nevertheless contends that as a matter of law a privilege to arrest was established in this case and since, as already indicated, in our view of the case there will have to be a new trial, raising the possibility of an amendment of the pleadings, we deem it appropriate to comment. The city's argument runs that a police officer is not required to arrest for drunkeness but may exercise discretion to take an intoxicated person home or to some other safe place as the circumstances dictate and that that was what was done here.

In *Sindle v. New York City Tr. Auth.* ..., we reflected on the scope of the privileges which constitute justification. We there said ..., "[Generally], restraint or detention, reasonable under the circumstances and in time and manner, imposed for the purpose of preventing another from inflicting personal injuries or interfering with or damaging real or personal property in one's lawful possession or custody is not unlawful". Consequently, it may be that taking a person who is in a state of intoxication to a position of greater safety would constitute justification. But it is clearly not privileged to arrest such a person for the sole purpose of running him out of town, or, as further proof at the trial here established, once having arrested such a person, to follow a practice of running him out of town to avoid guardhouse chores for the police whenever there were no other prisoners in the local jail. Such acts cannot be sanctioned with the mantle of the privilege of justification. A person who has had too much to drink is not a chattel to be transported from one locus to another at the whim or convenience of police officers.

The Restatement of Torts 2d (§ 10, Comment *d)* states it well: "Where the privilege is based upon the value attached to the interest to be protected or advanced by its exercise, the privilege protects the actor from liability only if the acts are done for the purpose of protecting or advancing the interest in question. Such privileges are often called conditional, because the act is privileged only on condition that it is done for the purpose of protecting or advancing the particular interest. They are sometimes called 'defeasible', to indicate the fact that the privilege is destroyed if the act is done for any purpose other than the protection or advancement of the interest in question." It follows that, if the conduct of the officers indeed is found to have been motivated by the desire to run the plaintiff out of town, the action for false imprisonment would not have been rebutted by the defense of legal justification. For, under plaintiff's theory, the false imprisonment count does not rest on the reasonableness of the police officers' action, but on whether the unwilling confinement of the plaintiff was the result of an arrest for a nonjustified purpose.

* * * * *

Accordingly, the order of the Appellate Division should be reversed, both causes of action reinstated and a new trial ordered, with leave to the defendant, if so advised, to move at Trial Term for leave to amend its answer to affirmatively plead a defense of justification to the cause of action for false imprisonment.

BREITEL, C.J, dissenting.

* * * * *

So long as Parvi did not remain out in public, intoxicated, creating a public nuisance, and endangering his own life, the officers had no wish to interfere with Parvi's freedom of movement. Since Parvi could suggest no suitable place where the officers might take him, the officers chose another site. Apparently, Parvi and Dugan were pleased with the choice. And it should not matter that Parvi testified, although he could recall nothing else, that he was ordered into a police car "against [his] will". (On cross-examination, he said he recalled nothing that day.) Parvi's "will" was to stay where he was, intoxicated, in public. In order to deprive him of that one choice, which the officers could do without subjecting themselves to liability for false imprisonment, the officers had to transport Parvi some place else. He was given a choice as to destination. He declined it, except for his later suggestion of an unsafe place, and the officers made the choice for him. There was no confinement, and hence no false imprisonment.

Moreover, plaintiff has failed even to make out a prima facie case that he was conscious of his purported confinement, and that he failed to consent to it. His memory of the entire incident had disappeared; at trial, Parvi admitted that he no longer had any independent recollection of what happened on the day of his accident, and that as to the circumstances surrounding his entrance into the police car, he only knew what had been suggested to him by subsequent conversations. In light of this testimony, Parvi's conclusory statement that he was ordered into the car against his will is insufficient, as a matter of law, to establish a prima facie case.

NOTES

1.   The court says that the elements of awareness of the confinement and privilege are the debatable elements in this case. When did the confinement occur?

2.   What mistake did the lower court make?

3.   Can a person be confined mentally although not confined within physical boundaries or barriers? Consider the case above and cases in which persons become members of cults that allegedly control their minds.

4.   Why does the majority say that the privilege to arrest may not prevail here?

5.   Who has the better of the arguments here–the majority or the dissent?

6.   Although we usually think of physical force or assertion of authority as being the voluntary act that accomplishes the restraint or confinement, other types of acts may do this. Threats, for example may be used. What if the store manager tells an employee that the employee is suspected of theft and must stay in an office for questioning, and if the employee attempts to leave, she will be fired? Courts are divided on whether this constitutes false imprisonment. Another type of act is called duress of goods, which involves a defendant saying, "You are free to go, but I will keep this bag of goods that I believe you stole." The plaintiff remains with her claimed property, arguing that she has a right to leave with it.

7.   Can a person be falsely imprisoned in an airplane on a runway when weather conditions do not permit takeoff? Would the conduct of the crew and the length of time make a difference? *See Perdigao v. Delta Airlines, Inc.*, 973 So. 2d 33 (La.App. 5 Cir. 2007). Would a state tort claim be preempted by federal law under such circumstances – specifically the Federal Aviation Act?

E.   INTENTIONAL INFLICTION OF EMOTIONAL DISTRESS

Intentional Infliction of Emotional Distress (IIED) was not recognized in English common law. The law was well established in the United States that, with certain limited exceptions, one could not recover for emotional damages alone, without physical harm. The exceptions were for common carriers and innkeepers (and in some jurisdictions, telegraph companies) on whom the law imposed a duty of civility with respect to their customers. In 1948, a supplement to the first Restatement of Torts included a separate tort of IIED, not tied to a requirement of physical harm. During the 1970s and 1980s, courts in most jurisdictions recognized IIED. Probably every state in the nation now recognizes this tort theory. Still, this relatively new tort theory is regarded by many courts with concern. What is an outrageous act on which an IIED claim can be predicated? It is an amorphous concept. One can readily picture acts on which a claim for battery, assault, or false imprisonment can be based; not so with IIED. Courts are solicitous to keep the bar high on outrageous conduct, often granting summary judgments for defendants because they fear a flood of litigation otherwise. Courts also are concerned about how to verify that a plaintiff has suffered severe emotional distress, and how a judge or jury is to quantify damages for such an injury.

Negligent infliction of emotional distress (NIED) is often pled as an alternative theory of recovery along with IIED. In this way, if the plaintiff is unable to prove the intent required for IIED, the plaintiff still may succeed in proving negligence. The law regarding NIED differs depending on whether the case is a bystander NIED case or a direct victim NIED case. NIED will be covered fully in Chapter 6 *infra*.

1) voluntary act
2) intent or recklessness
3) outrageous conduct
4) severe emo. distress
5) causation

43

NICKERSON
v.
HODGES
84 So. 37 (La. 1920)

DAWKINS, J.

Miss Carrie E. Nickerson brought this suit against H. R. Hayes, William or "Bud" Baker, John W. Smith, Mrs. Fannie Smith, Miss Minnie Smith, A. J. Hodges, G. G. Gatling, R. M. Coyle, Sam P. D. Coyle, and Dr. Charles Coyle, claiming $ 15,000 as damages, alleged to have been caused in the form of financial outlay, loss in business, mental and physical suffering, humiliation, and injury to reputation and social standing, all growing out of an alleged malicious deception and conspiracy with respect to the finding of a supposed pot of gold. Subsequent to the filing of the petition, and before the trial, the said Miss Nickerson died, and her legal heirs, some 10 in number, were made parties plaintiff, and now prosecute this suit.

All of the defendants, save and except Miss Minnie Smith, William or "Bud" Baker, and H. R. Hayes, filed, in effect, a general denial, denying any knowledge of or connection with the matters out of which the alleged damages arose. These three defendants filed a joint answer, in which, after denying the injuries charged, or that there was any malicious or unlawful intent, admitted that they had fixed up an old copper bucket or pot, filled with dirt and rocks, and had buried it at a point where the said Miss Carrie Nickerson and her helpers would likely dig in search of an imaginary pot of gold; that she and her said associates had been, for several months, digging over the property of defendant, John W. Smith, on information obtained from a fortune teller in the city of Shreveport, and boarding at the home of the said Smith, father of the said Minnie Smith, without paying therefor, and generally acting in such a manner as to make themselves nuisances to the community; that the course adopted by these three defendants was for the purpose of convincing the explorers of their folly; that it was intended as a practical joke, and succeeded in accomplishing the purpose mentioned.

For some reason the case was allowed to remain on the docket of the lower court for more than three years before being tried, when it was finally submitted to a jury, and resulted in a verdict in favor of the defendants. After an unsuccessful motion for a new trial, the plaintiffs prosecuted this appeal.

Statement of Facts

Miss Nickerson was a kinswoman of Burton and Lawson Deck, the exact degree of relationship not being fully shown by the record, and there had been, in the family, a tradition that these two gentlemen, who died many years ago, had prior to their deaths, buried a large amount of gold coin on the place now owned by the defendant John W. Smith, or on another near by. She was employed by the California Perfume Company to solicit orders for their wares in the towns, villages, etc., in Webster and other parishes, and on the occasion of a visit to the city of Shreveport seems to have interviewed a fortune teller, who told her that her said relatives had buried the gold, and gave her what purported to be a map or plat showing its location on the property of Smith. Thereafter, with the help of some three or four other persons, principally relatives, and one Bushong, she spent several months digging, at intervals, around the house and on the premises of Smith, who seems to have extended them a cordial welcome, and to have permitted them to dig almost without limit as to time and place, and in addition boarded the fortune hunters, while so engaged, without charge. We assume that this was due, perhaps, to the fact that he, too, had a slight hope that they might find something, and he was to receive a part thereof for his concessions. At any rate, the diggers pursued their course with such persistence and at such lengths, digging around the roots of shade trees, the pillars of his house, etc., until finally, his daughter, the said Minnie Smith, William or "Bud" Baker, and H. R. Hayes conceived the idea of themselves providing a "pot of gold" for the explorers to find. Accordingly they obtained an old copper kettle or bucket, filled it with rocks and wet dirt, and buried it in an old chimney seat on the adjoining place, where the searchers had been or were intending to also prospect for the supposed treasure. Two lids or tops were placed on the pot, the first being fastened down with hay wire; then a note was written by Hayes, dated, according to some, July 1,

1884, and, as to others, 1784, directing whoever should find the pot not to open it for three days, and to notify all the heirs. This note was wrapped in tin, placed between the first and second lids, and the latter was also securely fastened down with hay wire. This took place some time toward the latter part of March, and, according to these three defendants, was to have been an April fool; but plans miscarried somewhat, and the proper opportunity for the "find" did not present itself until April 14th. On that day Miss Nickerson and her associates were searching and digging near the point where the pot had been buried, when one Grady Hayes, a brother of H. R. Hayes, following directions from the latter, and apparently helping the explorers to hunt for the gold, dug up the pot and gave the alarm. All of those in the vicinity, of course, rushed to the spot, those who were "in" on the secret being apparently as much excited as the rest, and, after some discussion, it was decided to remove the lid. When this was done, the note was discovered, and H. R. Hayes advised Miss Nickerson that he thought it proper that its directions should be carried out, and that the bank at Cotton Valley, a few miles distant, was the best place to deposit the "gold" for safe-keeping, until the delays could run and the heirs be notified, as requested. Following this suggestion, the pot was placed in a gunny sack, tied up, and taken to the bank for deposit. Defendant Gatling was the cashier of the bank, but refused to give a receipt for the deposit as a "pot of gold," because, as he insisted, he did not know what it contained.

As might have been supposed, it did not take long for the news to spread that Miss Nickerson and her associates in the search for fortune, had found a pot of gold, and the discussion and interest in the matter became so general that defendant A. J. Hodges, vice president of the bank, went over from his place of business in Cotton Valley to the bank, and he and Gatling, after talking the matter over, decided to examine the pot, so that, in event it did contain gold, proper precautions to guard the bank might be taken, pending the return of Miss Nickerson and the appearance of those who might claim the fortune. These two undid the wire sufficiently to peep into the pot, and discovered that it apparently contained only dirt. They then replaced the lid and held their tongues until the reappearance of Miss Nickerson. However, the secret leaked out from other sources, that the whole matter was a joke, and this information too, became pretty well distributed.

After depositing the pot in the bank, Miss Nickerson went to Minden, La., and induced Judge R. C. Drew to agree to accompany her to Cotton Valley on the following Monday (the deposit at the bank having been made on Saturday) for the purpose of seeing that the ceremonies surrounding the opening of the treasure were properly conducted. Judge Drew swears that he had heard in some way that the matter was a joke, and so informed Miss Nickerson, warning her not to place too much faith in the idea that she was about to come into a fortune, but that finally, because of his friendly relations with and kindly feeling toward her, he consented and did go, mainly to gratify her wishes in the premises. Some half a dozen other relatives of Burton and Lawson Deck were notified, and either accompanied or preceded Miss Nickerson to Cotton Valley.

With the stage thus set, the parties all appeared at the bank on Monday morning at about 11 o'clock, and among the number were H. R. Hayes, one of the defendants, who seems to have been one of the guiding spirits in the scheme, and one Bushong, the latter, we infer, from intimations thrown out by witnesses in the record, being at the time either an avowed or supposed suitor of Miss Nickerson's. Judge Drew, as the spokesman for the party, approached Gatling and informed him that it was desired that the pot be produced for the purpose of opening and examining the contents for the benefit of those thus assembled. The testimony of the witnesses varies a little as to just when the storm began; some say, as soon as the sack was brought out. Miss Nickerson discovered that the string was tied near the top, instead of down low around the pot, and immediately commenced to shout that she had been robbed; others insist that she was calm until the package was opened and the mocking earth and stones met her view. Be that as it may, she flew into a rage, threw the lid of the pot at Gatling, and for some reason, not clearly explained, turned the force of her wrath upon Hayes to such an extent that he appealed for protection, and Bushong, with another, held her arms to prevent further violence.

Miss Nickerson was a maiden, nearing the age of 45 years, and some 20 years before had been an inmate of an insane asylum, to the knowledge of those who had thus deceived her. She was energetic and self-supporting in her chosen line of employment, as a soap drummer, until she met the fortune teller who gave her the "information" which she evidently firmly believed would ultimately enable her to find the fortune which the family tradition told her had been left hidden by her deceased relatives. The conspirators, no doubt, merely intended what they did as a practical joke, and had no willful intention of doing the lady any injury. However, the results were quite serious indeed, and the mental suffering and humiliation must have been quite unbearable, to say nothing of the disappointment and conviction, which she carried to her grave some two years later, that she had been robbed.

If Miss Nickerson were still living, we should be disposed to award her damages in a substantial sum, to compensate her for the wrong thus done; but as to the present plaintiffs, her legal heirs, we think that a judgment of $500 will reasonably serve the ends of justice. R. C. C. art. 2315.

The evidence fails to connect any of the defendants with the conspiracy, so as to render them liable, save and except H. R. Hayes, William or "Bud" Baker, and Miss Minnie Smith; hence the judgment will be awarded against these only.

For the reasons assigned, the judgment appealed from is annulled and reversed, and it is now ordered and decreed that the plaintiffs do have and recover judgment against the defendants H. R. Hayes, William or "Bud" Baker, and Miss Minnie Smith in the full sum of $500, and as to the other defendants the demands are rejected; the defendants so cast to pay all costs.

WHITE
v.
MONSANTO COMPANY
585 So. 2d 1205 (La. 1991)

HALL, J.

Writs were granted in this case to review a judgment of the court of appeal affirming an award of $60,000 damages to an employee against her employer and a supervisory co-employee for intentional infliction of emotional distress occasioned by the supervisor's profane outburst while dressing down the employee and two other employees for not working as he thought they should. Finding that the supervisor's conduct, although crude and uncalled for, was not of such an extreme or outrageous nature as to give rise to a cause of action for an intentional tort, we reverse and render judgment for the defendants.

I

Plaintiff, Irma White, a church-going woman in her late forties with grown children, was employed in the labor pool at Monsanto Company's refinery for several years. In the spring of 1986, she had been assigned to work in the canning department for several weeks. Defendant, Gary McDermott, a long-time Monsanto employee, was industrial foreman of that department. On the date of the incident in question, plaintiff and three other employees were assigned at the beginning of the work day to transfer a certain chemical from a large container into smaller containers. When they arrived at their work station and noticed that the container was marked "hazardous-corrosive," they requested rubber gloves and goggles before starting their assigned task. A supervisor sent for the safety equipment. Shop rules required that employees busy themselves while waiting for equipment. One of the employees went to another area to do some work. Plaintiff started doing some clean-up or pick-up work around the area. The other two employees were apparently sitting around waiting for the equipment. Someone reported to McDermott that the group was idle, causing McDermott to become angry. He went to the work station and launched a profane tirade at the three workers present, including plaintiff, referring to them as "m[_____]f[_____],'' accusing them of sitting on their "f[_____] a[____],'' and threatening to "show them to the gate." The tirade lasted for about a minute, and then McDermott left the area.

Plaintiff was upset and began to experience pain in her chest, pounding in her head, and had difficulty breathing. She went to McDermott's office to discuss the incident. He said he apologized to her; she said he did not. She went to the company nurse, who suggested that plaintiff see a doctor.

Plaintiff's family physician met her at the hospital, at which time plaintiff had chest pains, shortness of breath, and cold clammy hands. Fearing that she was having a heart attack, the doctor admitted her to the hospital. Plaintiff spent two days in the coronary care unit and another day in a regular room, during which time she had intravenous fluids, had blood drawn, and had an EKG and other tests done. A heart attack was ruled out and the doctor's diagnosis was acute anxiety reaction, a panic attack. Plaintiff was released from the hospital after three days without restriction, but with medication to take if she had further trouble.

Ms. White returned to work within a week. She was paid her regular pay while off from work, and her medical bills, totaling about $ 3,200, were paid by the company's medical benefits program. Plaintiff has continued to work at Monsanto, later transferring to McDermott's department at her own request. She occasionally becomes upset thinking about or dreaming about the incident, and has occasionally taken the prescribed medicine, but is not one to take medication.

II

Ms. White sued Monsanto and McDermott, alleging that McDermott's conduct amounted to the intentional infliction of mental anguish and emotional distress upon plaintiff for which she was entitled to recover damages. After trial, the jury awarded her $60,000. Defendants appealed to the court of appeal, which affirmed, with one judge dissenting in part as to the amount of damages....

III

LSA-R.S. 23:1032 makes worker's compensation an employee's exclusive remedy for a work-related injury caused by a co-employee, except for a suit based on an intentional act. The words "intentional act" mean the same as "intentional tort." The legislative aim was to make use of the well-established division between intentional torts and negligence in common law. The meaning of "intent" is that the person who acts either (1) consciously desires the physical result of his act, whatever the likelihood of that result happening from his conduct; or (2) knows that that result is substantially certain to follow from his conduct, whatever his desire may be as to that result. Thus, intent has reference to the consequences of an act rather than to the act itself. Only where the actor entertained a desire to bring about the consequences that followed or where the actor believed that the result was substantially certain to follow has an act been characterized as intentional. *Bazley v. Tortorich,....*

The exclusive remedy rule is inapplicable to intentional torts or offenses. The meaning of intent in this context is that the defendant either desires to bring about the physical results of his act, or believes they were substantially certain to follow from what he did. Intent is not, however, limited to consequences which are desired. If the actor knows that the consequences are certain, or substantially certain, to result from his act, and still goes ahead, he is treated by the law as if he had in fact desired to produce the result. *Bazley, supra.*

When an employee seeks to recover from his employer for an intentional tort, a court must apply the legal precepts of general tort law related to the particular intentional tort alleged in order to determine whether he has proved his cause of action and damages recoverable thereunder. *Caudle v. Betts,....*

IV

The particular intentional tort alleged in this case is the intentional infliction of emotional distress. Thus, the legal precepts of general tort law related to this tort must be applied to determine whether plaintiff has proved her cause of action and damages recoverable thereunder.

Most states now recognize intentional infliction of emotional distress as an independent tort, not "parasitic" to a physical injury or a traditional tort such as assault, battery, false imprisonment or the like.

... Discussed in the late 1930's by commentators[1] who synthesized earlier cases,[2] the tort was included in the 1948 supplement to the American Law Institute's Restatement (Second) of Torts § 46.[3] The elements of the tort as described in the text and comments of the Restatement have been widely accepted and quoted.

Several Louisiana court of appeal decisions have recognized and defined the tort, generally in accordance with the Restatement....

... [T]he Restatement is not binding on a Louisiana court, but it may be considered in determining whether liability exists under the fault-reparation principles of LSA-C.C. Art. 2315. Generally speaking, labels of specific torts and strictures attached thereto do not always coincide with Louisiana's broad and more flexible notion of fault under the Civil Code article.... Nevertheless, restrictions and guidelines established for policy reasons can give practical guidance in deciding cases, particularly those involving relatively new and developing causes of action such as those for emotional distress injuries unaccompanied by physical injury....

Drawing on the background described, including consideration of Article 2315 and duty-risk principles, we affirm the viability in Louisiana of a cause of action for intentional infliction of emotional distress, generally in accord with the legal precepts set forth in the Restatement text and comments.

One who by extreme and outrageous conduct intentionally causes severe emotional distress to another is subject to liability for such emotional distress, and if bodily harm to the other results from it, for such bodily harm.[4]

Thus, in order to recover for intentional infliction of emotional distress, a plaintiff must establish (1) that the conduct of the defendant was extreme and outrageous; (2) that the emotional distress suffered by the plaintiff was severe; and (3) that the defendant desired to inflict severe emotional distress or knew that severe emotional distress would be certain or substantially certain to result from his conduct.

The conduct must be so outrageous in character, and so extreme in degree, as to go beyond all possible bounds of decency, and to be regarded as atrocious and utterly intolerable in a civilized community. Liability does not extend to mere insults, indignities, threats, annoyances, petty oppressions, or other trivialities. Persons must necessarily be expected to be hardened to a certain amount of rough language, and to occasional acts that are definitely inconsiderate and unkind. Not every verbal encounter may be converted into a tort; on the contrary, "some safety valve must be left through which irascible tempers may blow off relatively harmless steam." Restatement, *supra*, comment d, § 46; Prosser and Keaton, The Law of Torts, § 12, p. 59 (5th ed. 1984).

---

[1] *See* Magruder, Mental and Emotional Disturbance in the Law of Torts, 49 Harvard Law Review 1033 (1936); Prosser, Intentional Infliction of Mental Suffering: A New Tort, 37 Mich. L.Rev. 874 (1939).

[2] Often mentioned was the Louisiana pot-of-gold case, *Nickerson v. Hodges,* 146 La. 735, 84 So. 37 (1920), in which nominal damages were awarded to a middle-aged mentally deficient woman who suffered severe mental distress as the result of a cruel practical joke.

[3] Restatement (Second) of Torts, § 46 (1) provides: "Outrageous Conduct Causing Severe Emotional Distress (1) One who by extreme and outrageous conduct intentionally or recklessly causes severe emotional distress to another is subject to liability for such emotional distress, and if bodily harm to the other results from it, for such bodily harm."

[4] Since the viability of plaintiff's claim in this case depends on the existence of an intentional act as distinguished from a reckless act, we do not deal with the Restatement's reference to "recklessly" causing severe emotional distress.

The extreme and outrageous character of the conduct may arise from an abuse by the actor of a position, or a relation with the other, which gives him actual or apparent authority over the other, or power to affect his interests. Restatement, supra, comment e, § 46. Thus, many of the cases have involved circumstances arising in the workplace.... A plaintiff's status as an employee may entitle him to a greater degree of protection from insult and outrage by a supervisor with authority over him than if he were a stranger....

On the other hand, conduct which may otherwise be extreme and outrageous, may be privileged under the circumstances. Liability does not attach where the actor has done no more than to insist upon his legal rights in a permissible way, even though he is aware that such insistence is certain to cause emotional stress. Restatement, *supra*, comment g, § 46. Thus, disciplinary action and conflict in a pressure-packed workplace environment, although calculated to cause some degree of mental anguish, is not ordinarily actionable. Recognition of a cause of action for intentional infliction of emotional distress in a workplace environment has usually been limited to cases involving a pattern of deliberate, repeated harassment over a period of time....

The distress suffered must be such that no reasonable person could be expected to endure it. Liability arises only where the mental suffering or anguish is extreme. Restatement, *supra*, comment j, § 46....

The defendant's knowledge that plaintiff is particularly susceptible to emotional distress is a factor to be considered. But the mere fact that the actor knows that the other will regard the conduct as insulting, or will have his feelings hurt, is not enough. Restatement, *supra*, comment f, § 46. It follows that unless the actor has knowledge of the other's particular susceptibility to emotional distress, the actor's conduct should be judged in the light of the effect such conduct would ordinarily have on a person of ordinary sensibilities.

Liability can arise only where the actor desires to inflict severe emotional distress or where he knows that such distress is certain or substantially certain to result from his conduct. Restatement, supra, comment I, § 46. The conduct must be intended or calculated to cause severe emotional distress and not just some lesser degree of fright, humiliation, embarrassment, worry, or the like.

V

Applying these precepts of law to the facts of the instant case, we find that plaintiff has failed to establish her right to recover from the defendants for an intentional tort.

The one-minute outburst of profanity directed at three employees by a supervisor in the course of dressing them down for not working as he thought they should does not amount to such extreme and outrageous conduct as to give rise to recovery for intentional infliction of emotional distress. The vile language used was not so extreme or outrageous as to go beyond all possible bounds of decency and to be regarded as utterly intolerable in a civilized community. Such conduct, although crude, rough and uncalled for, was not tortious, that is, did not give rise to a cause of action for damages under general tort law or LSA-C.C. Art. 2315. The brief, isolated instance of improper behavior by the supervisor who lost his temper was the kind of unpleasant experience persons must expect to endure from time to time. The conduct was not more than a person of ordinary sensibilities can be expected to endure. The tirade was directed to all three employees and not just to plaintiff specifically. Although the evidence certainly supports a finding that plaintiff was a decent person and a diligent employee who would not condone the use of vulgar language and who would be upset at being unjustifiably called down at her place of work, there was no evidence that she was particularly susceptible to emotional distress, or that McDermott had knowledge of any such susceptibility. It was obviously his intention to cause some degree of distress on the part of the employees, but there is no indication that his spontaneous, brief, intemperate outburst was intended to cause emotional distress of a severe nature.

The duty here was to not engage in extreme or outrageous conduct intended or calculated to cause severe emotional distress. The duty was not breached because the conduct was not extreme or outrageous to a degree calculated to cause severe emotional distress to a person of ordinary sensibilities and the supervisor did not intend to inflict emotional distress of a severe nature, nor did he believe such a result was substantially certain to follow from his conduct.

VI

For the reasons expressed in this opinion, the judgments of the district court and court of appeal are reversed, and judgment is rendered in favor of defendants dismissing plaintiff's suit, at plaintiff's cost.

REVERSED AND RENDERED.

NOTES

1. Which elements of IIED did the plaintiff fail to satisfy?

2. Why does the court state that the plaintiff was a church-going woman in her late forties with grown children?

3. The court describes a tension regarding IIED claims by employees in the workplace. As the court notes, many IIED claims are by employees or former employees. Why? The Louisiana Supreme Court continues to be reluctant to permit recovery on an IIED claim by an employee. *See Nicholas v. Allstate Ins. Co.*, 765 So. 2d 1017 (La. 2000).

4. Some characteristics of conduct that is sometimes found outrageous by courts include repetitious conduct (often increasing in severity) and an imbalance of power between the parties (or a particularly vulnerable victim, such as a child or a pregnant woman). Sexual harassment cases have been the most successful type of IIED case for plaintiffs. Why?

5. For a case involving early radio "shock jocks," *see Murray v. Schlosser*, 574 A. 2d 1339 (Conn. Super. 1990) (radio disc jockeys looked through local newspaper's wedding section photographs and picked from among the brides a "dog of the week" to whom they awarded a case of dog food).

6. A person ordinarily is not liable for intentional infliction of emotional distress for doing no more than insisting on his rights in a legal way. *See Vincent v. CSE Fed. Credit Union*, No. 15-887 (La.App. 3 Cir. 2016), 2016 WL 915062 (plaintiff made police report of threatened criminal conduct).

7. For a case involving mismanagement of a corpse, *see DuFour v. Westlawn Cemeteries, Inc.*, 639 So. 2d 843 (La.App. 5 Cir. 1994). The court discusses NIED, IIED, and "dead body" cases.

8. For a case in which a plaintiff unsuccessfully urged intentional infliction of emotional distress when his doctor expert witness changed his testimony at trial (from his deposition testimony), *see Coutee v. Beurlot*, 964 So. 2d 304 (La. 2007).

9. *Price v. Fuerst*, 24 So. 3d 289 (La.App. 3 Cir. 2009). Louisiana does not recognize a cause of action for alienation of affections, and does not permit such a claim by another name. *See infra* Chapter 2, Part G for more on alienation of affections. Plaintiff sued his wife's attorney, who engaged in an adulterous affair with her, for intentional infliction of emotional distress, claiming damages for himself and his children. Although the court condemned the attorney's conduct and suggested that it might be a basis for attorney disciplinary action, it rejected the IIED claim.

F. PROPERTY TORTS: TRESPASS TO LAND, CONVERSION, AND TRESPASS TO CHATTELS

The intentional torts discussed in earlier sections of this chapter all dealt with protecting personality interests. This section discusses three intentional torts that protect property interests. Trespass to land protects the possessory interest in real property, and conversion and trespass to chattels protect the possessory interest in personal property (chattels). For each of the property torts, the elements are an act, intent to accomplish the result, and the result. For trespass to land, the result is entry onto the land; for conversion, it is exercise of dominion and control over the personal property; and for trespass to chattels, it is interference (intermeddling) with possession of the property.

1. Trespass to Land

HERRIN
v.
SUTHERLAND
241 P.328 (Mont. 1925)

1) voluntary act
2) intent to enter
3) entry onto land

* * * * *

.... [O]n the 18th of September, 1924, the defendant, while engaged in hunting ducks and other water fowl and other migratory game birds, and while standing on the lands of another, repeatedly discharged a Winchester shotgun at water fowl in flight over plaintiff's said premises, dwelling-house and over his cattle, "thereby preventing plaintiff from the quiet, undisturbed, peaceful enjoyment of his dwelling-house, ranch and property, to plaintiff's damage in the sum of $10."

* * * * *

After defendant's general demurrer to the several causes of action was overruled he declined to answer and his default was entered. Upon the suggestion of counsel for plaintiff that only nominal damages would be demanded, the court rendered judgment in favor of the plaintiff for damages in the sum of $1 upon the eight causes of action collectively, with costs of the action. From this judgment the defendant has appealed.

MR. CHIEF JUSTICE **CALLAWAY** delivered the opinion of the court.

* * * * *

It must be held that when the defendant, although standing upon the land of another, fired a shotgun over plaintiff's premises, dwelling and cattle, he interfered with "the quiet, undisturbed, peaceful enjoyment" of the plaintiff, and thus committed a technical trespass at least. The plaintiff was the owner of the land. Land, says Blackstone, in its legal signification has an indefinite extent, upwards as well as downwards: whoever owns the land possesses all the space upwards to an indefinite extent; such is the maxim of the law....

The court of appeals of New York, in *Butler v. Frontier Telephone Co.*, 186 N.Y. 486, 116 Am. St. Rep. 563, 9 Ann. Cas. 858, 11 L.R.A. (n.s.) 920, 79 N.E. 716, had before it an ejectment case in which wire, unsupported by any structure resting upon plaintiff's land, was strung over the surface of the ground at a height of from twenty to thirty feet across the entire width of plaintiff's premises. In speaking of the extent of the operation of the ancient maxim quoted above the court said: "The surface of the ground is a guide, but not the full measure, for within reasonable limitations land includes not

51

only the surface but also the space above and the part beneath. (Co. Litt. 4a; 2 Blackstone's Com. 18; 3 Kent's Com., 14th ed.). *'Usque ad coelum'* is the upper boundary, and while this may not be taken too literally, there is no limitation within the bounds of any structure yet erected by man. So far as the case before us is concerned, the plaintiff as the owner of the soil owned upward to an indefinite extent."

Sir Frederick Pollock, in the tenth edition of his valuable work on Torts, page 363, observes that it has been doubted whether it is a trespass to pass over land without touching the soil, as one may in a balloon, or to cause a material object, as a shot fired from a gun, to pass over it. "Lord Ellensborough thought it was not in itself a trespass to 'interfere with the column of air superincumbent upon the close,' and that the remedy would be by action on the case for any actual damage: though he had no difficulty in holding that a man is a trespasser who fires a gun on his own land so that the shot fall on his neighbor's land"....

Fifty years later, says Pollock.... "As regards shooting it would be strange if we could object to shots being fired point blank across our land only in the event of actual injury being caused, and the passage of the foreign object in the air above our soil being thus a mere incident and a distinct trespass to person or property." But he concludes that when one takes into account the extreme flight of projectiles fired from modern artillery which may pass thousands of feet above the land, the subject is not without difficulty. That shortly it will become one of considerable importance is indicated by the rapid approach of the airplane as an instrumentality of commerce, as is suggested in a valuable note found in 32 Harvard Law Review, 569. However, it seems to be the consensus of the holdings of the courts in this country that the air space, at least near the ground, is almost as inviolable as the soil itself.... It is a matter of common knowledge that the shotgun is a firearm of short range. To be subjected to the danger incident to and reasonably to be anticipated from the firing of this weapon at water fowl in flight over one's dwelling-house and cattle would seem to be far from inconsequential, and, while plaintiff's allegations are very general in character, it cannot be said that a cause of action is not stated for nominal damages at least.

* * * * *

The judgment is **AFFIRMED**.

NOTES

1.   Trespass to land is an ancient tort that was used to try title to property in England. The *close* was an imaginary line that formed the boundary of a piece of real estate. The close was said to extend from the center of the earth to the heavens. One pled trespass as "trespass quare clausum fregit," meaning "wherefore, he broke the close."

The *Herrin* case illustrates the ancient notion that causing any object to enter the air space above one's land without permission is a trespass. Do you think this principle can be applied today? Consider note 2 below.

2.   The Restatement (Second) of Torts § 158 lists ways in which a trespass may occur: a) entering land in the possession of another or causing a third person or thing to enter the land; b) remaining on land after the possessor withdraws consent for one to be on the land; or c) failing to remove something from land possessed by another that one is under a duty to remove.

See, also, Restatement (Second) of Torts, Sec. 159, providing that:

(1) Except as stated in Subsection (2), a trespass may be committed on, beneath, or, above the surface of the earth.

(2) Flight by aircraft in the air space above the land of another is a trespass if, but only if,

(a) it enters into the immediate reaches of the air space next to the land, and

(b) it interferes substantially with the other's use and enjoyment of his land.

See also United States v. Causby, 328 U.S. 256 (1946) (federal government may establish minimum altitudes for air flights; flights above those altitudes are not trespasses).

3. As with most other intentional torts, there is no requirement that the plaintiff prove damages. Damages are presumed.

4. The intent required for a trespass is easily satisfied and does not necessarily involve blameworthiness: it is the intent to enter the land. Thus, if I step onto land, thinking that it belongs to my friend who would gladly receive me on his land, and it is in fact the land of another, I have trespassed, although I did not want to. Do you think that young children can form the intent to trespass? In fact, when children went onto property and were injured by equipment, structures, etc., on the land, the property owners, when sued, often defended that the children were trespassing. Should that defense be upheld if a condition on the premises was particularly attractive to young children?

5. What if defendant enters enemy's land, never meaning to harm his enemy. The two get into an argument, and enemy suffers a heart attack and dies. Enemy's wife sues defendant, claiming that defendant trespassed on the property and that enemy's death resulted from that trespass.

6. Many modern trespass cases involve improper entry onto land for the removal of timber. The following statute that provides for recovery of punitive (treble) damages for unauthorized cutting, destruction, or removal of trees.

La. R.S. 3:4278.1. Trees, cutting without consent; penalty

A. (1) It shall be unlawful for any person to cut, fell, destroy, remove, or to divert for sale or use, any trees, or to authorize or direct his agent or employee to cut, fell, destroy, remove, or to divert for sale or use, any trees, growing or lying on the land of another, without the consent of, or in accordance with the direction of, the owner or legal possessor, or in accordance with specific terms of a legal contract or agreement.

(2) It shall be unlawful for any co-owner or co-heir to cut, fell, destroy, remove, or to divert for sale or use, any trees, or to authorize or direct his agent or employee to cut, fell, destroy, remove, or to divert for sale or use, any trees, growing or lying on co-owned land, without the consent of, or in accordance with the direction of, the other co-owners or co-heirs, or in accordance with specific terms of a legal contract or agreement. The provisions of this Paragraph shall not apply to the sale of an undivided timber interest ...

B. Whoever willfully and intentionally violates the provisions of Subsection A of this Section shall be liable to the owner, co-owner, co-heir, or legal possessor of the trees for civil damages in the amount of three times the fair market value of the trees cut, felled, destroyed, removed, or diverted, plus reasonable attorney fees and costs.

C.   Whoever violates the provisions of Subsection A of this Section in good faith shall be liable to the owner, co-owner, co-heir, or legal possessor of the trees for three times the fair market value of the trees cut, felled, destroyed, removed, or diverted, if circumstances prove that the violator should have been aware that his actions were without the consent or direction of the owner, co-owner, co-heir, or legal possessor of the trees.

* * * * *

E.   The provisions of this Section shall not apply to the clearing and maintenance of rights of way or to utility service situations where a utility is acting in good faith to minimize the damage or harm occasioned by an act of God. The provisions of this Section shall not apply to land surveying by or under the direction of a registered professional land surveyor, duly registered under the laws of the state of Louisiana.

* * * * *

For cases interpreting R.S. 3:4278.1, *see Cole-Gill v. Moore*, 862 So. 2d 1197 (La.App. 2 Cir. 2003), *writ denied*, 872 So. 2d 501 (La. 2004); *Callison v. Livingston Timber, Inc.*, 849 So. 2d 649 (La.App. 1 Cir. 2003).

2.   Conversion and Trespass to Chattels

Both of these intentional torts protect the possessory interest in personal property. Historically, the personal property addressed by the torts has been tangible personal property, but that does not appear to be a limitation on the applicability of the torts. *See CompuServe Inc. v. Cyber Promotions, Inc., infra.* Whether a defendant has committed a conversion or a trespass to chattels is often a matter of degree; that is, how substantially did the defendant interfere with the plaintiff's possessory interest. For example, if I pull your dog's ear and injure it, you may recover against me for a trespass to chattels. If I take your dog and throw it from a high-rise balcony, however, I probably have converted your dog. If I take your car without permission and drive it for an hour before returning it, you may recover for a trespass to chattels. On the other hand, if I keep your car for a week, a month or a year, I probably have converted it.

The remedy for a conversion is the recovery of the full value of the property that has been essentially destroyed or stolen from the possessor. A converter is said to have "bought" the thing that he converted. With trespass to chattels, unlike most intentional torts, a plaintiff must prove that she has suffered actual damages.

The Restatement (Second) § 222A lists some factors to consider in deciding whether the interference with possessory interest is great enough to constitute a conversion: a) extent and duration of control; b) defendant's intent to claim a right to the property; c) defendant's good faith; d) harm done; and e) expense or inconvenience caused. If the interference is substantial enough to be a conversion, the defendant is said to have "exercised dominion and control" over the property. If the interference is not substantial enough to constitute a conversion, then it may be characterized as "intermeddling" with another's property, and there is a trespass to chattels.

[handwritten margin notes, top left]: Conversion: 1) act 2) intent 3) exercise of dominion or control over property — lawful recovery of destroyed or stolen

[handwritten margin notes, top right]: Chattels: 1) act 2) intent 3) interference w/ property 4) actual damages

COMPUSERVE INC.
v.
CYBER PROMOTIONS, INC.
962 F.Supp. 1015 (S.D. Ohio 1997)

GRAHAM, J.

Memorandum Opinion and Order

This case presents novel issues regarding the commercial use of the Internet, specifically the right of an online computer service to prevent a commercial enterprise from sending unsolicited electronic mail advertising to its subscribers.

Plaintiff CompuServe Incorporated ("CompuServe") is one of the major national commercial online computer services. It operates a computer communication service through a proprietary nationwide computer network. In addition to allowing access to the extensive content available within its own proprietary network, CompuServe also provides its subscribers with a link to the much larger resources of the Internet. This allows its subscribers to send and receive electronic messages, known as "e-mail," by the Internet. Defendants Cyber Promotions, Inc. and its president Sanford Wallace are in the business of sending unsolicited e-mail advertisements on behalf of themselves and their clients to hundreds of thousands of Internet users, many of whom are CompuServe subscribers. CompuServe has notified defendants that they are prohibited from using its computer equipment to process and store the unsolicited e-mail and has requested that they terminate the practice. Instead, defendants have sent an increasing volume of e-mail solicitations to CompuServe subscribers. CompuServe has attempted to employ technological means to block the flow of defendants' e-mail transmission to its computer equipment, but to no avail.

This matter is before the Court on the application of CompuServe for a preliminary injunction which would extend the duration of the temporary restraining order issued by this Court on October 24, 1996 and which would in addition prevent defendants from sending unsolicited advertisements to CompuServe subscribers.

For the reasons which follow, this Court holds that where defendants engaged in a course of conduct of transmitting a substantial volume of electronic data in the form of unsolicited e-mail to plaintiff's proprietary computer equipment, where defendants continued such practice after repeated demands to cease and desist, and where defendants deliberately evaded plaintiff's affirmative efforts to protect its computer equipment from such use, plaintiff has a viable claim for trespass to personal property and is entitled to injunctive relief to protect its property.

* * * * *

IV

This Court will now address the second aspect of plaintiff's motion in which it seeks to enjoin defendants Cyber Promotions, Inc. and its president Sanford Wallace from sending any unsolicited advertisements to any electronic mail address maintained by CompuServe.

CompuServe predicates this aspect of its motion for a preliminary injunction on the common law theory of trespass to personal property or to chattels, asserting that defendants' continued transmission of electronic messages to its computer equipment constitutes an actionable tort.

Trespass to chattels has evolved from its original common law application, concerning primarily the asportation of another's tangible property, to include the unauthorized use of personal property:

> Its chief importance now, is that there may be recovery ... for interferences with the possession of chattels which are not sufficiently important to be classed as conversion, and so to compel the defendant to pay the full value of the thing with which he has interfered. Trespass to chattels survives today, in other words, largely as a little brother of conversion.

Prosser & Keeton, Prosser and Keeton on Torts, § 14, 85-86 (1984).

The scope of an action for conversion recognized in Ohio may embrace the facts in the instant case. The Supreme Court of Ohio established the definition of conversion under Ohio law ... by stating that:

> In order to constitute a conversion, it was not necessary that there should have been an actual appropriation of the property by the defendant to its own use and benefit. It might arise from the exercise of a dominion over it in exclusion of the rights of the owner, or withholding it from his possession under a claim inconsistent with his rights. If one take the property of another, for a temporary purpose only, in disregard of the owner's right, it is a conversion. Either a wrongful taking, an assumption of ownership, an illegal use or misuse, or a wrongful detention of chattels will constitute a conversion.

* * * * *

The Restatement § 217(b) states that a trespass to chattel may be committed by intentionally using or intermeddling with the chattel in possession of another. Restatement § 217, Comment e defines physical "intermeddling" as follows:

> ... intentionally bringing about a physical contact with the chattel. The actor may commit a trespass by an act which brings him into an intended physical contact with a chattel in the possession of another[.]

Electronic signals generated and sent by computer have been held to be sufficiently physically tangible to support a trespass cause of action.... It is undisputed that plaintiff has a possessory interest in its computer systems. Further, defendants' contact with plaintiff's computers is clearly intentional. Although electronic messages may travel through the Internet over various routes, the messages are affirmatively directed to their destination.

Defendants, citing Restatement (Second) of Torts § 221, which defines "dispossession", assert that not every interference with the personal property of another is actionable and that physical dispossession or substantial interference with the chattel is required. Defendants then argue that they did not, in this case, physically dispossess plaintiff of its equipment or substantially interfere with it. However, the Restatement (Second) of Torts § 218 defines the circumstances under which a trespass to chattels may be actionable:

> One who commits a trespass to a chattel is subject to liability to the possessor of the chattel if, but only if,

(a) he dispossesses the other of the chattel, or

(b) the chattel is impaired as to its condition, quality, or value, or

(c) the possessor is deprived of the use of the chattel for a substantial time, or

(d) bodily harm is caused to the possessor, or harm is caused to some person or thing in which the possessor has a legally protected interest.

* * * * *

A plaintiff can sustain an action for trespass to chattels, as opposed to an action for conversion, without showing a substantial interference with its right to possession of that chattel.... Harm to the personal property or diminution of its quality, condition, or value as a result of defendants' use can also be the predicate for liability. Restatement § 218(b).

> An unprivileged use or other intermeddling with a chattel which results in actual impairment of its physical condition, quality or value to the possessor makes the actor liable for the loss thus caused. In the great majority of cases, the actor's intermeddling with the chattel impairs the value of it to the possessor, as distinguished from the mere affront to his dignity as possessor, only by some impairment of the physical condition of the chattel. There may, however, be situations in which the value to the owner of a particular type of chattel may be impaired by dealing with it in a manner that does not affect its physical condition. ... In such a case, the intermeddling is actionable even though the physical condition of the chattel is not impaired.

The Restatement (Second) of Torts § 218, comment h.

In the present case, any value CompuServe realizes from its computer equipment is wholly derived from the extent to which that equipment can serve its subscriber base. Michael Mangino, a software developer for CompuServe who monitors its mail processing computer equipment, states by affidavit that handling the enormous volume of mass mailings that CompuServe receives places a tremendous burden on its equipment. Defendants' more recent practice of evading CompuServe's filters by disguising the origin of their messages commandeers even more computer resources because CompuServe's computers are forced to store undeliverable e-mail messages and labor in vain to return the messages to an address that does not exist. To the extent that defendants' multitudinous electronic mailings demand the disk space and drain the processing power of plaintiff's computer equipment, those resources are not available to serve CompuServe subscribers. Therefore, the value of that equipment to CompuServe is diminished even though it is not physically damaged by defendants' conduct.

Next, plaintiff asserts that it has suffered injury aside from the physical impact of defendants' messages on its equipment. Restatement § 218(d) also indicates that recovery may be had for a trespass that causes harm to something in which the possessor has a legally protected interest. Plaintiff asserts that defendants' messages are largely unwanted by its subscribers, who pay incrementally to access their e-mail, read it, and discard it. Also, the receipt of a bundle of unsolicited messages at once can require the subscriber to sift through, at his expense, all of the messages in order to find the ones he wanted or expected to receive. These inconveniences decrease the utility of CompuServe's e-mail service and are the foremost subject in recent complaints from CompuServe subscribers. Patrick Hole, a customer service manager for plaintiff, states by affidavit that in November 1996 CompuServe received approximately 9,970 e-mail complaints from subscribers about junk e-mail, a figure up from approximately two hundred complaints the previous year. Approximately fifty such complaints per day specifically reference defendants. Defendants contend that CompuServe subscribers are provided with a simple procedure to remove themselves from the mailing list. However, the removal procedure must be performed by the e-mail recipient at his expense, and some CompuServe subscribers complain that the procedure is inadequate and ineffectual.

Many subscribers have terminated their accounts specifically because of the unwanted receipt of bulk e-mail messages. Defendants' intrusions into CompuServe's computer systems, insofar as they harm plaintiff's business reputation and goodwill with its customers, are actionable under Restatement § 218(d).

The reason that the tort of trespass to chattels requires some actual damage as a prima facie element, whereas damage is assumed where there is a trespass to real property, can be explained as follows:

> The interest of a possessor of a chattel in its inviolability, unlike the similar interest of a possessor of land, is not given legal protection by an action for nominal damages for harmless intermeddlings with the chattel. In order that an actor who interferes with another's chattel may be liable, his conduct must affect some other and more important interest of the possessor. Therefore, one who intentionally intermeddles with another's chattel is subject to liability only if his intermeddling is harmful to the possessor's materially valuable interest in the physical condition, quality, or value of the chattel, or if the possessor is deprived of the use of the chattel for a substantial time, or some other legally protected interest of the possessor is affected as stated in Clause (c). Sufficient legal protection of the possessor's interest in the mere inviolability of his chattel is afforded by his privilege to use reasonable force to protect his possession against even harmless interference.

Restatement (Second) of Torts § 218, Comment e (emphasis added).

Plaintiff CompuServe has attempted to exercise this privilege to protect its computer systems. However, defendants' persistent affirmative efforts to evade plaintiff's security measures have circumvented any protection those self-help measures might have provided. In this case CompuServe has alleged and supported by affidavit that it has suffered several types of injury as a result of defendants' conduct. The foregoing discussion simply underscores that the damage sustained by plaintiff is sufficient to sustain an action for trespass to chattels. However, this Court also notes that the implementation of technological means of self-help, to the extent that reasonable measures are effective, is particularly appropriate in this type of situation and should be exhausted before legal action is proper.

* * * * *

V

Based on the foregoing, plaintiff's motion for a preliminary injunction is GRANTED. The temporary restraining order filed on October 24, 1996 by this Court is hereby extended in duration until final judgment is entered in this case. Further, defendants Cyber Promotions, Inc. and its president Sanford Wallace are enjoined from sending any unsolicited advertisements to any electronic mail address maintained by plaintiff CompuServe during the pendency of this action.

It is so **ORDERED**.

NOTES

1.   Actual harm must be established as part of a plaintiff's prima facie case for trespass to chattels. What actual harm did the plaintiff in *CompuServe* suffer?

2.   Could the defendant's actions have risen to the level of a conversion? What would have been required?

DUAL DRILLING COMPANY
v.
MILLS EQUIPMENT INVESTMENTS, INC.
721 So. 2d 853 (La. 1998)

TRAYLOR, J.

We granted writs in this case to determine whether Louisiana law provides for a tort of conversion akin to that of the common law which imposes strict liability upon the tortfeasor....

Facts and Procedural History

In October 15, 1990, partners Travis Vollmering (Vollmering) and Atlas Iron and Metal Company (Atlas) agreed to purchase an inoperative off-shore oil rig (Rig 16) from Dual Drilling (Dual) located at the Tidex shipyard in Amelia, Louisiana. Rig 16 was comprised of three segments: an engine room, a cement room, and a pump room. The contract of sale established that Dual retained ownership of the quarters package, the derrick (complete with starting legs and storage baskets), and two National mud pumps. Vollmering reviewed the offer, blue prints of Rig 16, and inspected the rig prior to the purchase.

Subsequent to the sale, Atlas engaged Southern Scrap Recycling, Morgan City (Southern) to dismantle Rig 16 and sold the majority of the scrap metal to Southern. Southern memorialized the agreement, stating in pertinent part:

> This will confirm our conversation between your representative Mr. Travis Vollmering and the writer with reference to the Dual rigs located at the Tidewater Yard in Amelia, La. It is mutually agreed and understood that you will be responsible for removing any large items from the rig. These items will include but not be limited to the following: cranes, mud pumps, derrick base, SCR unit and transformers, rotary skid, accumulator and choke manifold, generators and engines, P Tanks. Said items being referred to herein as "retention items." ...
>
> Southern Scrap will assist you by furnishing burners to cut the retention items loose, however, Southern Scrap is not responsible for the condition of those items. The burners assigned to this task will be working under your supervision and it will be your responsibility to furnish whatever labor and equipment is necessary to remove and load the retention items.... All material left after the retention items are removed (I.E. "material to be scrapped") will become property of Southern Scrap and we will pay Atlas Iron and Metal $ 52.00 per gross (2240 #) ton for this material . . . Southern Scrap will be responsible for cutting, loading, and transporting the material

to be scrapped and shall furnish whatever personnel and equipment is necessary to accomplish this work....

Vollmering visited the shipyard with a Southern employee and identified for him each item that was to be cut. He instructed the Southern employee where to begin cutting and mistakenly identified an adjacent rig component (Rig 25) as part of his property. Vollmering marked, "Do Not Cut" on what he deemed to be salvageable items. Prior to the commencement of this project, a Dual employee, James Monnin, marked "Do Not Cut" on three sides of Rig 25 with fluorescent orange spray paint. In late February, 1991, as instructed by the partnership, Southern began cutting Rigs 16 and 25. A shipyard worker noticed Southern employees cutting Rig 25 and told them it was "not to be cut." Southern employees responded that he should not worry and should continue with his business.

On March 7, 1991, James Monnin and two other Dual employees, Khaled Farag and David Goodwill, visited the shipyard and found Rig 25 and the associated equipment missing. Two Southern employees told Farag that their supervisor, Mr. Hunter, ordered them to cut Rig 25 although it was marked, "Do Not Cut/Save XX."

At trial, Vollmering testified his impression from his dealings with Dual was that Rig 25 was part of Rig 16. He contended that the exclusion items named in the contract of sale were the only items excluded from the sale, and he prepared his bid based upon this belief. Vollmering and Southern's employees testified that all salvageable items were removed by Vollmering and that Southern never took possession of these items. The Southern employees testified that, because they did not know what a rig package was, they acted as instructed by Vollmering.

* * * * *

The trial court found that Dual was entitled to replacement cost of Rig 25 and associated equipment "less reasonable depreciation...." The trial court further found that the Defendants offered no evidence of the value of the items before the loss. Thus, Plaintiff was awarded $ 213,811 to refurbish a used cement package building, and new associated equipment was valued at $ 26,518 for the P-tank, $ 64,296 for the 500 ton swivel, $ 26,790 for the kelley spinner, and $ 4,428 for the upper kelley valve. The trial court found that because Southern was advised orally and in writing that Rig 25 was "not to be cut," it knew or should have known that Defendants were not its owners. The trial court held Defendants solidarily liable for 100% of Plaintiff's loss. The court of appeal affirmed....

Law and Analysis

The threshold issue before us is whether Louisiana law provides a strict liability remedy akin to the common law tort of conversion. We find that although conversion terminology has been borrowed from the common law, it is nonetheless securely rooted in civilian concepts of property law, offenses, and quasi-offenses. Our civilian remedies amply protect personal and real rights in movable property and should not be obscured by an application of common law conversion principles.

Principles of Civilian Conversion

The Civil Code itself does not identify causes of action for "conversion." However, causes of action for conversion have been inferred from the Codal articles providing that the right of ownership, possession, and enjoyment of movables are protected by actions for the recovery of the movables themselves, actions for restitution of their value, and actions for damages. La. Civ. Code arts. 511, 515, 521, 524, 526, and 2315. Consequently, the dispossessed owner of a corporeal movable may be accorded one of three actions to enforce his rights of ownership.

60

The first is the revendicatory action for the recovery of a movable transferred: 1) by the owner or legal possessor to a person in bad faith, 2) for less than fair value, or 3) when the movable was lost or stolen.[1] A.N. YIANNOPOULOS, LOUISIANA CIVIL LAW TREATISE § § 350-51, at 680-83 (2nd ed. 1991& Supp. 1998). The second action arises under the law of delictual obligations and exists under the theory of unjust enrichment.[2] YIANNOPOULOS, LOUISIANA CIVIL LAW TREATISE § 356, at 689-90. Because the property at issue is destroyed and no longer in the hands of the possessors, and because Plaintiff alleges a cause of action in tort rather than one for unjust enrichment, we pretermit discussion of the first two causes of action.

The third action, relevant to the instant case, is known as a delictual action. It is available to an owner dispossessed as a result of an offense or quasi-offense or, in other words, a "tort." This action is grounded on the unlawful interference with the ownership or possession of a movable and is frequently termed an action for "conversion" in Louisiana. A conversion is committed when any of the following occurs: 1) possession is acquired in an unauthorized manner; 2) the chattel is removed from one place to another with the intent to exercise control over it; 3) possession of the chattel is transferred without authority; 4) possession is withheld from the owner or possessor; 5) the chattel is altered or destroyed; 6) the chattel is used improperly; or 7) ownership is asserted over the chattel. FRANK L. MARAIST & THOMAS C. GALLIGAN, LOUISIANA TORT LAW § 1-2, at 3 (1996 & Supp. 1998); *Importsales, Inc. v. Lindeman*, 231 La. 663, 92 So. 2d 574 (La. 1957); *see also Louisiana State Bar Assoc. v. Hinrichs*, 486 So. 2d 116 (La. 1986). The conversion action is predicated on the fault of the defendant and directed to the recovery of the movable or, in the alternative, the plaintiff may demand compensation.[3]

---

[1] The revendicatory action abates when the movable is no longer in possession of the defendant. However, the plaintiff may have a personal action for damages or unjust enrichment against the former possessor of the movable.

[2] A person unjustly enriched at the expense of another is under a quasi-contractual obligation to restore the corporeal movable to the rightful owner or account for the enrichment. This cause of action traditionally lies under the code articles for a payment not yet due.

[3] Despite the use of this common law term, such actions are not to be confused with the civil law tort of conversion. In common law jurisdictions, conversion is an intentional wrong giving rise to strict liability in an action for the recovery of the value of a chattel. A.N. YIANNOPOULOS, LOUISIANA CIVIL LAW TREATISE § 357, at 690- 92. Prominent legal scholars agree that tortious activity is only established upon proof of fault under La. Civ. Code art. 2315 as opposed to the common law allowance of strict liability:

> The protection of proprietary interests in common law jurisdictions is substantially different from that accorded in civil law countries and in Louisiana. Everywhere the protection may be regarded as adequate and nearly complete.
> A word of caution may be here appropriate: due to underlying fundamental differences in conceptual technique and methodology, borrowing of common law rules for the solution of problems arising under Louisiana law is both unnecessary and confusing. The legal profession in Louisiana should look for guidance in this area to its own legal tradition and to developments in civil law countries. Particularly with respect to movable property, it ought to be remembered that the common law has never provided a real action for the revendication of chattels, that the tort of conversion dominates this area of the law, and *the absolute liability which characterizes conversion is in direct conflict with Article 2315 of the Louisiana Civil Code and the principle that liability for wrongful dispossession rests on fault.* (Emphasis added, footnote deleted). YIANNOPOULOS, LOUISIANA CIVIL LAW TREATISE § 359, at 695.
> A useful distinction may be drawn between faults that are "blameworthy" and others that are not. In this dichotomy, intentional torts and negligence would be treated as blameworthy conduct, while vicarious liability, strict liability and absolute liability would be nonblameworthy conduct that nevertheless constituted "fault" under Article 2315. Intentional torts and negligence involve the actor's actual or constructive knowledge of a risk of harm to someone, a knowledge that makes the tortfeasor morally culpable or "blameworthy." MARAIST & GALLIGAN, LOUISIANA TORT LAW § 1-2, at 3 (1996 & Supp. 1998). (Footnotes omitted)

Plaintiff herein alleged two separate acts of conversion: the first occurred when Rig 25 was dismantled, and second followed the disappearance of the associated equipment. Regarding the destruction of Rig 25, the record contains ample evidence that both Southern and the Partnership exercised dominion and control over Rig 25 which seriously interfered with Dual's property rights. It is evident that Vollmering exercised improper dominion over Rig 25 when he held himself and the Partnership out as its owner, ordered that it be demolished, and sold it as scrap metal. The Partnership asserted both dominion and a right of ownership over the rig which it did not legally possess. Likewise, Southern exercised improper dominion over Rig 25 when it carried out these orders in the face of a warning that Rig 25 was not to be cut. Furthermore, Southern should have realized Rig 25 was not part of the sale and was not to be dismantled upon seeing the fluorescent orange "Do Not Cut" markings on the rig. The trial court found Southern knew or should have known that the rig belonged to someone other than the Partnership but failed to ascertain the identity of the true owner. Southern could have acted to prevent itself from destroying the wrong rig. Instead, precautions to find the owner were not taken.

The owner of a movable wrongfully converted and subsequently destroyed certainly has the right to recover the property's value. The trial court properly determined that the Defendants were liable in solido [footnote ommitted] for the conversion of Rig 25. For these reasons, Southern and the Partnership must pay Dual for the full value of the rig at the time of the conversion. At any rate, because the trial court applied the principles of strict liability, it failed to assign a percentage of fault to each party for the conversion of Rig 25 as required by La. Civ. Code art. 2323. We remand this issue to the trial court so that fault may be properly assigned to the parties.

* * * * *

REVERSED; REMANDED.

NOTES

1.   How does the court distinguish conversion as recognized under Louisiana law from conversion as recognized in most jurisdictions? Why does it do this? What difference does it make? Would the decision in *Dual Drilling* have any effect on trespass to land or trespass to chattels? *See MCI Communications Servs., Inc. v. Hagan*, 74 So. 3d 1148 (La. 2011) (court considered question certified by Fifth Circuit whether Louisiana recognizes tort of trespass to chattels when underground cables are cut inadvertently by an intentional act; court answered that it does not, citing *Dual Drilling*).

2.   Consider the following hypotheticals:

a. I see a red sports car in the law school parking lot. It looks very much like the one that I own, and I open the unlocked door, get in, and start it with the keys which were left in the ignition. I know that I left my keys in the ignition that morning. I drive it for an hour before I realize that it is not mine. Because I am near a building where I have an important meeting, I park the car, go to the meeting, and then return the car to the same spot in the parking lot several hours later. Have I committed a conversion or trespass to chattels regarding your car?

b. Suppose instead that I know the red sports car with keys in the ignition is yours, but I have long admired it, and I decide that this is a good day to "take it for a spin." I know that you will be in class for five hours, and I know that after class you routinely spend another four hours in the law library studying. I ride in the car for several hours but bring it back before you need it to leave the school. Conversion or trespass to chattels? Suppose that I keep it until midnight and you have to get a ride home when you finish studying. Conversion or trespass to chattels? Suppose that I keep it a week. Conversion or trespass to chattels? Suppose that I keep your car only an hour, but while I have it parked at a grocery store, a grocery store buggy rolls down a hill and strikes it on the driver's side door. Conversion or trespass to chattels?

3.   Is there a tort if I pull the ear or tail of your companion pet, a poodle? If so, what could you collect in damages? Suppose that your poodle is a prize-winning show dog and I cut off its tail, and you can no longer enter it in competitions. What if the dog is not a show dog, but I intentionally run over it with my car? Tort? What damages? Some states have statutes authorizing the recovery of noneconomic damages for the killing of a pet. *See* Tenn. Code 44-17-403 (providing for up to $4,000 in noneconomic damages for the intentional or negligent killing of a pet).

G.   RELATIONAL TORTS

There are tort theories that provide recompense for damage to relationships, such as family, community, and business. These sometimes are referred to as relational torts.

One set of relational torts is for interference with family relationships. Included in these are alienation of affections (destruction of love and affection between family members), criminal conversation (sexual relations with a married person), and breach of a promise to marry. These tort theories fell into disfavor in the 1930s and again in the 1970s, with most states abolishing them either by case law or statute. A handful of states continue to recognize alienation of affections or criminal conversation or both. The Louisiana Supreme Court declared in 1927 that the state never had recognized a claim for alienation of affections. *Moulin v. Monteleone*, 115 So. 447 (La. 1927). The courts also have rejected claims pled under another theory of recovery when they appear actually to be alienation of affections. *See Mier v. Mier*, 178 So. 3d 270 (La.App. 3 Cir. 2015) (rejecting a claim for alienation of affections cast as a claim for tortious interference with contract).

Many states recognize a tort theory of intentional interference with business or contractual relations or intentional interference with economic advantage. The Louisiana Supreme Court recognized the theory in a very unusual set of facts in *9 to 5 Fashions, Inc. v. Spurney*, 538 So. 2d 228 (La. 1989). Although the Supreme Court has resisted expansions of the tort beyond the narrow facts of that case, some recent court of appeals decisions have discussed the tort. Consider, for example, the following discussion by the Second Circuit:

> Louisiana courts have recognized a cause of action for tortious interference with business. *Junior Money Bags, Ltd. v. Segal*, 970 F.2d 1 (5th Cir. 1992); *Dussouy v. Gulf Coast Inv. Corp.*, 660 F.2d 594 (5th Cir. 1981); *Bogues v. Louisiana Energy Consultants, Inc.*, 46,434 (La.App. 2 Cir. 2011), 71 So. 3d 1128. In Louisiana, the delict is based on the principle that the right to influence others not to deal is not absolute. Louisiana law protects the businessman from malicious and wanton interference, permitting only interferences designed to protect a legitimate interest of the actor. The plaintiff in a tortious interference with business suit must show by a preponderance of the evidence that the defendant improperly influenced others not to deal with the plaintiff.... It is not enough to allege that a defendant's actions affected the plaintiff's business interests; the plaintiff must allege that the defendant actually prevented the plaintiff from dealing with a third party....

> The jurisprudence has viewed this cause of action with disfavor. The plaintiff must show that the defendant acted with actual malice. Actual malice must be pleaded in the complaint. *Bogues v. Louisiana Energy Consultants, Inc.*, *supra*.

63

Henderson v. Bailey Bark Materials, 116 So. 3d 30 (La.App. 2 Cir. 2013); *see also Gulf Eng'g Co. v. Kuhn,* 209 So. 3d 1029 (La.App. 5 Cir. 2016) (rejecting expansion of *Spurney* claim based on allegations that employee had same duties as corporate officers), *writ denied,* ___ So. 3d ___, 2017 WL 1207925 (La. 2017).

H.   DEFENSES TO INTENTIONAL TORTS

1.   Consent

FRICKE

v.

OWENS-CORNING FIBERGLASS CORPORATION
571 So. 2d 130 (La. 1990)

DENNIS, J.

[Plaintiffs seek to recover damages] for intentional torts as the result of the death of one employee and the brain damage of a second which allegedly occurred when an employer's plant superintendent knowingly exposed the employees to the inhalation of toxic mustard vapors. The trial court granted defendants' motion for summary judgment, but the court of appeal reversed. *Fricke v. Owens-Corning Fiberglas,* 559 So. 2d 24 (La.App. 4 Cir. 1990). We reverse the court of appeal's judgment.

George Fricke, III, the 30 year old foreman of the mustard mill unit at Baumer Foods, Inc., looked down into an 18 foot deep mustard tank and saw Melvin Davillier, Sr. a fellow employee, lying unconscious at the bottom. He immediately fetched Roger Baumer, the 76 year old plant superintendent. Baumer started to descend a rope ladder inside the tank to rescue Davillier, but Fricke persuaded the older man to let him go instead....

* * * * *

Baumer's testimony is undisputed in the record presented for our review. During Fricke's descent Baumer went for a rope and other employees to assist in the rescue. When they returned Fricke was prostrate at the bottom of the tank beside Davillier. A rescue unit of the fire department was summoned. Baumer employees and the firemen forced an opening in the tank wall and removed the men. Tragically, however, Davillier had suffered injuries which would later prove to be fatal and Fricke had sustained severe brain damage....

[Lawsuits were instituted by Darryl Fricke (wife of George Fricke, III) individually and as the natural tutrix of Glen Henry Fricke (son of George Fricke, III), Janet Fricke and George Fricke, Jr. as curators for their injured son, George Fricke, III, and Keith Davillier, as dative curator for Melvin Davillier, Sr. (the injured employee). Subsequent to the death of Melvin Davillier, Sr., his heirs, Keith Davillier, Heath Davillier and Melvin Davillier, Jr., were substituted as plaintiffs in this action. Named as defendants were the employer, Baumer Foods, Inc., the alleged owners, Alvin Baumer, Sr. and Alvin Baumer, Jr., and Roger Baumer.]

In this court the plaintiffs argue that Baumer's acts and omissions causing Fricke to go down into the mustard tank amounted to an intentional tort because: (a) Baumer desired to cause Fricke to come into harmful or offensive contact with the vapors in the mustard tank or believed that these consequences were substantially certain to result; and, (b) Baumer and his employer therefore are subject to liability for battery or other intentional tort because he acted intending to cause a harmful or offensive contact with Fricke's person and a harmful contact resulted. *See* Restatement (Second) of Torts, American Law Institute §§ 8A & 13 (1965); *Bazley v. Tortorich*, 397 So. 2d 475 (La. 1981). Plaintiffs correctly note that in order for Baumer to be liable it is not necessary that he intend to inflict actual damage or that his intention be malicious. It is sufficient if the actor intends to inflict either a harmful or offensive contact without the other's consent. *Caudle v. Betts*, 512 So. 2d 389, 391 (La. 1987); *Karl J. Pizzalotto, M.D., Ltd. v. Wilson*, 437 So. 2d 859 (La. 1983); *Coppage v. Gamble*, 324 So. 2d 21 (La.App. 2 Cir. 1975); F. Stone, Louisiana Civil Law Treatise, Tort Doctrine § 125 (1977). Moreover, they aptly observe that when a battery has been proved, the defendant's liability for the resulting harm extends, as in most other cases of intentional torts, to consequences which the defendant did not intend, and could not reasonably have foreseen, upon the obvious basis that it is better for unexpected losses to fall upon the intentional wrongdoer than upon the innocent victim. *Caudle v. Betts*, 512 So. 2d at 392; W. Prosser and W. Keeton, The Law of Torts § 9 (5th ed. 1984); Restatement (Second) of Torts, American Law Institute § 16 (1965); 1 Harper, James and Gray, The Law of Torts § 3.3 (2d ed. 1986).

All intended wrongs, however, have in common the element that they are inflicted without the consent of the victim. 1 Harper, James and Gray, The Law of Torts § 3.10, p.298 (2d Ed. 1986). Consent therefore ordinarily bars recovery for intentional interferences with person or property. It is a fundamental principle of the common law that volenti non fit injuria – to one who is willing, no wrong is done. W. Prosser and W. Keeton, The Law of Torts § 18, p.112 (5th ed. 1984). "The absence of lawful consent," said Justice Holmes, "is part of the definition of assault." *Ford v. Ford*, 143 Mass. 577, 578, 10 N.E. 474 (1887). As remarked by Patteson, J., "An assault must be an act done against the will of the party assaulted; and therefore it cannot be said that a party has been assaulted by his own permission." *Christopherson v. Bare*, 11 Q.B. 473, 116 Eng. Rep. 554, 556 (1848). *See also Andrepont v. Naquin*, 345 So. 2d 1216, 1219 (La.App. 1 Cir. 1977); Restatement (Second) of Torts, American Law Institute § 13 (1965); R. Dias and B. Markesinis, Tort Law 174 (1984); F. Stone, Louisiana Civil Law Treatise, Tort Doctrine § 131 (1977).

From our review of the summary judgment proceeding evidence, we conclude that there is no genuine dispute of material fact and that the defendants are entitled to judgment as a matter of law. In our opinion, based on the record presented, reasonable minds must inevitably conclude that Fricke consented to whatever offensive or harmful contact that Baumer desired or believed to a substantial certainty would befall Fricke when he descended to rescue Davillier. It is uncontroverted that neither Fricke nor Baumer knew that the mustard tank contained lethal or gravely damaging vapors; and that neither knew what had felled Davillier at the bottom. The evidence indicates without dispute that, although there had been some indication that the vapors had caused breathing difficulties to a few employees, in approximately 57 years of operations prior to the accident no employee had been rendered unconscious or seriously injured by the mustard tanks' vapors.[1]

* * * * *

REVERSED; SUMMARY JUDGMENTS REINSTATED AND AFFIRMED.

---

[1] Of course, if Fricke in consenting to contact with the offensive vapors had been induced to do so by a substantial mistake as to the nature of the vapor or the extent of harm to be expected from it and the mistake had been known to Baumer or induced by Baumer's misrepresentation, Fricke's consent would not have been effective for the unexpected invasion or harm. *See* Restatement (Second) of Torts, American Law Institute § 892B (1965). However, there is nothing to indicate that Baumer had any greater knowledge of the danger than Fricke or that Baumer knew of or induced Fricke's mistake. In fact, the record is convincing beyond any reasonable doubt that both Fricke and Baumer reacted as normal, decent human beings faced with the unprecedented distress of a fellow worker in an unforeseen emergency.

NOTES

1.   Consent is assent by the subject of an offensive act, agreeing to that act. It may be communicated by language or physical act. Consent is a key defense to battery because it reflects the notion of autonomy which underlies tort law: a person enjoys the right to decide what happens to his or her own body. The problems of consent have mostly to do with locating when consent has been given, determining for what behavior consent was given, and identifying circumstances when consent, though given, was defective.

2.   Is consent a true defense? As the *Fricke* opinion relates, consent might be better regarded as an *element* of intentional torts like battery. Whether consent is an element of the tort or an affirmative defense can be a matter of great importance. How we characterize consent reflects a choice of whether the plaintiff or the defendant will be expected to show the existence or non-existence of consent. For the plaintiff to prevail in a tort case, he must prove every element of the tort in question. If he puts forth sufficient evidence that a reasonable fact finder (whether judge or jury) might determine that the element was proven, he is allowed to have the fact finder decide the case. Consequently, a defendant may defend a case by showing that the evidence used to support the plaintiff's case (to establish the elements of the cause of action) are defective or unpersuasive. On the other hand, a defendant might avail herself of an affirmative defense. This second approach of a defendant requires the defendant to establish each and every element of the affirmative defense. Therefore, if the lack of consent is an element of the tort of battery, the plaintiff must produce evidence showing that there was no consent. If it is an affirmative defense, the defendant bears the risk of nonpersuasion.

The lack of consent, though a defense, does not alone evidence a tort. In *Easter Seal Society for Crippled Children and Adults of Louisiana v. Playboy Enterprises*, 530 So. 2d 643, 648 (La.App. 4 Cir. 1988), a television station gave videotape of a staged Dixieland musical parade to a Canadian producer as stock footage. The producer used the footage in an adult film that was shown on Canadian television. Plaintiffs prevailed at the trial court in their action for false light, invasion of privacy, or defamation by plaintiffs. The Fourth Circuit reversed, arguing that:

> Plaintiffs attempt to extrapolate from the jurisprudence some rule that defendants should have obtained "consent" from each individual and represented group participating in the parade. We find neither jurisprudential nor statutory support for such a rule in these circumstances. In those cases where the courts have talked of the plaintiff's consent, either the disseminated material was clearly of a private character *or defendant relied upon consent as a defense.* The jurisprudence establishes that plaintiff's consent, properly obtained, provides a defense, but it does not establish that lack of consent translates into liability. Consent, or lack thereof, is not an element of liability; liability is determined first, consent is a defense. (Emphasis in original).

3.   Consent can be a defense to intentional torts other than battery. *See Turner v. State*, 494 So. 2d 1292 (La.App. 2 Cir. 1986) (parents cannot recover for trespass to home when daughter grants permission to defendant to enter home to conduct physical examination). Consent for purposes of criminal charges (factual consent) is generally not sufficient to show the defense of consent in tort cases. *See Brunet v. Deshotels*, 160 La. 285, 107 So. 111 (1926).

a. Establishing Consent

When considering the issue of whether consent is established, courts often refer to express and implied (or apparent) consent. Express or actual consent may be indicated by spoken or written words. Written consent forms often are referred to as waivers (of liability). Some waivers may be unenforceable as a matter of public policy. *See, e.g.,* La. Civ. Code Art. 2004 (reproduced in Chapter 7, *infra*, declaring null clauses that limit liability for 1) intentional or gross fault or 2) physical injury). The Restatement (Second) § 892(1) states that consent may be manifested by action or inaction and that "[i]f words or conduct are reasonably understood by another to be intended as consent, they constitute apparent consent and are as effective as consent in fact." *Id. § 892*(2).

Implied consent is something of a misnomer. True consent must originate with the person subjected to the offending behavior. Consent is thus not properly implied or ascribed to a person but is rather deemed to have been evidenced by the plaintiff's behavior or other evidence. Thus in contested litigation consent is often established through circumstantial evidence because a person's true state of mind cannot be directly examined.

Ultimately, the characterization of express or implied consent makes no difference because the effect of any kind of effective consent is to bar recovery.

In medical treatment cases, courts often speak of implied consent. For example, in *Douget v. Touro Infirmary*, 537 So. 2d 251, 260 (La.App. 4 Cir. 1988), the court of appeal expressly recognizes "implied consent." After describing how the consent form which the decedent, Mrs. Douget, signed referred to the possible loss of organs as a risk of the surgery, the Court opined that there existed "implied consent."

> These paragraphs clearly refer to consequences, in addition to or different from, those expressly contemplated for the anterior fusion procedure. They address risks of surgery and conditions that might arise during the anterior lumbar fusion procedure that may have been unanticipated and unforeseen at the time Mrs. Douget signed the informed consent form. Therefore, when Mrs. Douget signed the consent form, she acknowledged that her surgical risks included the possible loss of organs and she authorized her physicians to perform any additional operations beyond those contemplated which in the physicians' judgment were advisable for her well being.

> Consequently, when Dr. Ogden performed the nephrectomy and splenectomy, those procedures were performed with Mrs. Douget's *implied consent*. But, even if the procedures had not been impliedly authorized, their performance was not a battery because the record supports the jury's finding that an emergency existed so as to exempt Dr. Ogden from needing express or implied authorization for the removal of the organs. (Emphasis added.)

However, consent to medical procedures is a defense to medical malpractice, which is a negligence claim, not an intentional tort. *See* Chapter 13, Sec. A, *infra*.

1) self-defense: actual or reasonable threat to claimant's safety (tone may not exceed)
· if offender dies: belief of great injury/death (14:19)

2) necessity: ① public: complete defense (public officials)
② private: partial (risks of death, serious harm, property)

3) defense of others/property: same as self-defense (14:19)... right must be equal
no deadly tone for property

4) consent: equal to what was inflicted, can be withdrawn at any time

5) merchant's privilege: who can detain, must be reasonable belief of necessity
inquiry is mandatory, reasonable tone, reasonable time (60 min. circum.
can alter that) or police for arrest

COLE
v.
STATE OF LOUISIANA
825 So. 2d 1134 (La. 2002)

JOHNSON, J.

[Bradley Cole, a prison guard at Phelps Correctional Center in DeQuincy, LA, was a member of the prison's tactical unit. Along with other members of the Phelps tactical unit, he underwent tactical training at the Hunt Correctional Center in St. Gabriel, LA. During a training simulating a prison riot (the "angry crowd exercise"), the Phelps tactical unit "role played" as rioting prisoners. Officers from two other prisons practiced subduing them, during which time Cole sustained severe injuries. He claims that the exercise was conducted without normal safety gear (Styrofoam padding on police sticks, and padding). "Rioters" were equipped only with helmets. He also claims that the exercise continued even though he used the code word for stop (red) when his helmet fell off. Despite conflicting testimony on these key facts, it was generally agreed that the exercise "broke down," becoming "chaotic," a "free for all."]

After weighing the testimony and evidence, the trial court, without elaboration, written or oral, rendered judgment in favor of Cole, finding that Cole had established that DPSC was liable for his injuries....

The court of appeal, in an unpublished opinion, affirmed the judgment of the trial court finding no manifest error. Relying on *Rosell v. ESCO*, 549 So. 2d 840 (La. 1989), found (cq) that although the acts of DPSC employees in striking Cole were not malicious, these acts were nonetheless harmful and done with intent. The court also found that there was no manifest error in the trial court's finding that Cole received serious injuries from the battery he received, including brain trauma related injuries, headaches, and injuries to his neck and shoulder and that these injuries resulted from the intentional battery.

DPSC now appeals to this Court asserting the same assignments of error.

Discussion

Generally, any action by a worker against his employer for injuries suffered during the course and scope of employment would be exclusively through the Workers Compensation Act, La. R.S. 23:1032, which provides immunity from civil liability in favor of an employer. It is well settled that under the provisions of La. R.S. 23:1032, a worker is ordinarily limited to recovering workers' compensation benefits rather than tort damages for these injuries. However, Sec. 1032(B) provides an exception to this exclusivity when a worker is injured as a result of an employer's intentional act. *White v. Monsanto Company*, 585 So. 2d 1205 (La. 1991); *Mouton v. Blue Marlin Specialty Tools, Inc.*, 2001-648 (La.App. 3 Cir. 2001), 799 So. 2d 1215; *LaPoint v. Beaird Industries, Inc.*, 34,620 (La.App. 2 Cir. 2001), 786 So. 2d 301; *Gallant v. Transcontinental Drilling Company*, 471 So. 2d 858 (La.App. 2 Cir. 1985). When a plaintiff sustains damages as a result of an intentional battery committed by a co-employee during the course and scope of employment, the exclusivity provisions of the Louisiana Workers' Compensation Act do not apply. *See Quebedeaux v. Dow Chemical*, 2001-2297 (La. 2002), 820 So. 2d 542.

* * * * *

... we find that the lower courts did not err in finding Cole's injuries were the result of the intentional tort of battery as the evidence supports such a finding. There indeed exists a reasonable factual basis for the trial court's finding that plaintiff met his burden of proof on the elements of battery, since striking a person with a baton is at the very least a "harmful or offensive contact." Further, although the officer(s) who struck Cole with the unpadded batons may not have had malice nor intended to inflict the actual damages Cole suffered, the striking with the batons was indeed an intentional act....

Having concluded that Cole was the victim of a harmful or offensive contact, we now turn to DPSC's argument that Cole should not be allowed to recover because he consented to the battery. The defense of consent in Louisiana operates as a bar to recovery for the intentional infliction of harmful or offensive touchings of the victim. *Andrepont v. Naquin*, 345 So. 2d 1216 (La.App. 1 Cir. 1977). Consent may be expressed or implied; if implied, it must be determined on the basis of reasonable appearances. *Id.* at 1219.

As the court of appeal noted, "the record contains no consent forms, and there is no testimony that anyone specifically elicited Cole's consent or explained to him that unpadded batons or full force physical altercations would be part of the training exercise that day." DPSC maintains that Cole consented to strikes by volunteering for the tactical unit and receiving premium pay for such. However, the evidence reveals that Cole never participated in any training exercises which involved full force strikes or the use of unpadded batons. Cole testified that he did not expect a full force altercation during the angry crowd exercise and he certainly did not expect or consent to being struck with an unpadded baton at full force. Thus, the assertion that Cole consented to the battery simply because he was a member of the tactical unit is absurd. Although it is conceivable that Cole expected or even consented to possible injury during an actual riot or disturbance, it does not follow that Cole anticipated or consented to such brutality during a training session. The testimony from the participating officers reveals that this was supposed to be a low key, half speed exercise, the purpose of which was to practice formations and movement on the field. Simulated strikes were to be conducted, but no one expected a full force altercation. Accordingly, we conclude that the evidence supports the findings of the lower courts that Cole did not consent to the battery.

Even assuming arguendo that Cole did initially consent to this harmful touching during the training exercise, we find that under the circumstances of this case, any consent given by Cole was vitiated. When a person voluntarily participates in an altercation, he may not recover for the injuries which he incurs, unless force in excess of that necessary is used and its use is not reasonably anticipated. *Andrepont, supra*, citing *White v. Gill*, 309 So. 2d 744 (La.App. 4 Cir. 1975); *Buchert v. Metropolitan Life Insurance Company*, 219 So. 2d 584 (La.App. 4 Cir. 1969). The use of unnecessary and unanticipated force vitiates the consent. The court in *Andrepont* found that while the plaintiff voluntarily consented to engage in a fist fight with the defendant and his friends, the force employed by the defendant was in excess of what was reasonably necessary to repel the advances of the plaintiff and was an implementation of force to which the plaintiff did not consent.

The evidence in this case is clear and overwhelming that the force used against Cole was "unnecessary and unanticipated." As stated, Cole clearly did not anticipate being struck with unpadded batons, as evidenced by his testimony along with the testimony of other Phelps tact team members. We find that the force Cole received was also unnecessary to accomplish the goal of the training exercise. Cole's expert in field training, Ken Katsaris, testified that regular batons and full force should never be used and were unnecessary to this type of training exercise. Accordingly, we affirm the lower court's findings that Cole's injuries were a result of the intentional tort of battery; thereby, allowing him to recover damages under Louisiana tort law.

[The court went on to reverse the damage award as excessive and remanded for the lower court to recalculate]

AFFIRMED in part **REVERSED** in part. **REMANDED.**

VICTORY, J., dissenting:

While I agree with the majority that Cole failed to prove he suffered a closed head injury, I must dissent from the rest of the majority's opinion. The actions by the correctional officers during the simulated prison disturbance exercise do not fall under the very narrow intentional act exception to the exclusivity provision of the Workers' Compensation Act.

TRAYLOR, J., dissenting:

The plaintiff in this case was a member of a specialized correctional facility unit which acted in the event of prison riots and other disturbances. The training complained of by plaintiff was designed to prepare the officers for high risk purposes and necessitates intensive physical contact between the officers so that they can learn required skills in a controlled environment. Under the jurisprudence, an act such as the one complained of by plaintiff is intentional, and is drawn outside of the realm of workers' compensation, when the defendant either desires to bring about the physical results of his act or believes they were substantially certain to follow from what he did. *Bazley v. Tortorich*, 397 So. 2d 475 (La. 1981). I would not find that plaintiff's fellow officers desired to injure plaintiff as he alleges or that such alleged injuries were substantially certain to follow. Therefore, I dissent from the majority's finding that an intentional tort was committed against the plaintiff.

Furthermore, even if the tort was intentional, I would find the entirety of plaintiff's testimony to be incredible based upon the self-serving, uncorroborated testimony of plaintiff regarding his injuries, and the evidence showing that he lied about or at least exaggerated his injuries. The majority discusses that even plaintiff's own doctors stated that he exaggerated and embellished his injuries to them. Also relevant is the fact that no other officer serving the prisoner role in this exercise was injured. Based upon these points and the entirety of the evidence on the record, I would find plaintiff's testimony completely incredible and would determine that the trial court committed manifest error in finding that plaintiff was injured as a result of the tactical exercises.

Accordingly, I dissent.

KNOLL, Justice, dissenting.

* * * * *

At the time the battery occurred in the present case, Cole and his fellow correctional officers were participants in a simulated prison disturbance exercise. Contact, or battery, is inherent in this exercise, just as contact is inherent in many sport games, e.g., in football practices before the actual football game. The exercise in the present case is part of the training the officer needs to become skilled in handling a prison disturbance. Even though such training may be inherently dangerous, the use of realistic tactical training is essential for the protection of correctional officers and the prisoners they guard. *See Traweek v. LaBorde*, 30,551 (La.App. 2 Cir. 1998), 713 So. 2d 664, *writ denied*, 98-1933 (La. 1998), 727 So. 2d 449 (not an tort for a police officer to be sprayed in the face with pepper spray administered as part of his police training). Although in hindsight it may have been better to use protective styrofoam on the batons because of the attendant risks associated with this exercise, the failure to use this protective equipment does not place plaintiff's claims within the narrow intentional tort exception to workers' compensation detailed in this state's jurisprudence.

* * * * *

For these reasons, I respectfully dissent.

NOTES

1. Tort litigation often arises when plaintiffs suffer more significant injuries than they expected. That is, the plaintiff anticipated some contact, even injury, but sues when the injury suffered exceeds his expectations. This implicates the scope of consent. The *Bradley* opinion relies on *Andrepont v. Naquin*, 345 So. 2d 1216 (La.App. 1 Cir. 1977), and *White v. Gill*, 309 So. 2d 744 (La.App. 4 Cir. 1975), both cases where the injuries went beyond what the plaintiff initially anticipated. In *Andrepont*, the plaintiff went out of his way to rendevous with the defendant for a fight during which plaintiff was hit in the mouth by a baseball bat. The First Circuit, nevertheless, upheld compensation for him, arguing that the injury went beyond the consent reasonably given. In *White*, however, the Fourth Circuit found the plaintiff's injuries were within the scope of the consent inherent in his decision to meet the defendant outside a bar for a fight. In *White*, the plaintiff was hit in the mouth with a cast on defendant's hand and arm. The Court noted that the plaintiff was well aware of the cast when he went outside for the fight and rejected the plaintiff's argument that his consent to the fight was vitiated by his inebriated state.

2. Suppose A is playing football and B, a player on the opposing team, aims at and succeeds in "knocking A out of the game." Does the argument of Justice Knoll and the implication of Justice Traylor mean that consent would be found in such a case? Suppose that B's hit on A is within the rules of the game? Why and how would that matter? Would it matter if it were discovered that someone had instituted a system of rewards or bounties for producing various results, such as knocking a player out of the game?

In October of 2003, Ohio State Linebacker Robert Reynolds choked Wisconsin quarterback Jim Sorgi after tackling him. Reynolds was suspended for one game by the Big Ten Athletic Conference. If Sorgi had filed suit against Reynolds (or Ohio State), would his suit be barred by Knoll and Traylor's reading of consent?

Suppose an athlete is taking nutritional supplements that he believes are legal but which he also believes enhances his performance. The supplements are given to him by his nutritionist. It turns out the supplements contain banned performance enhancing substances. Would a suit against his nutritionist be barred by the defense of consent, assuming there was no fraud involved in the administering of the supplements?

3. Consider the court's holding that the plaintiff consented to any invasion of privacy that occurred during a medical examination in *Hogan v. Morgan*, 960 So. 2d 1024 (La. 2007).

b. Scope of Consent/Ineffective Consent

To what extent might consent be limited in time? The scope of consent given is usually express, but the duration of the consent given is rarely explicitly articulated. The First Circuit Court of Appeals confronted the duration of consent question in the 1961 case, *McAndrews v. Roy*, 131 So. 2d 256 (La.App. 1 Cir. 1961). In *McAndrews* the defendant , who operated a "health studio" in Baton Rouge, published ten year old "before and after" photographs of plaintiff, Cole McAndrews, in newspaper advertisements for his business. McAndrews, sued after he was subjected to ridicule at work and among his friends. The court found that plaintiff consented to the pictures, but also found that "it was reasonable for plaintiff to assume that since the pictures were not used shortly after they were taken that the defendant had decided not to use them." The court seemed to emphasize that the plaintiff had received nothing for the pictures and cited the defendant's admission that he probably "should not have used the pictures without again contacting the plaintiff to see if he was still willing that they should be used." While the court holds out the possibility that uncompensated consent might expire, it is not clear what other circumstance might evidence the expiration of consent. Can you imagine other circumstances?

Once consent is established, the next question is whether the consent is rendered ineffective. The Restatement (Second) §§ 892A-892B state that to be effective, the following things must be true: 1) the person giving consent must have the capacity to consent; 2) the consent must be to the conduct that occurs or to substantially similar conduct; 3) the conduct must not exceed the scope of the consent in terms of time or other restrictions; 4) the consent is not procured by either a misrepresentation or by the person giving the consent giving it while making a substantial mistake about the invasion of her interest when the actor knows of the mistake; and 5) the consent is not obtained through duress. Circumstances that render consent ineffective will be discussed further in the notes after the next case.

Sometimes, there are two analyses of consent that reach the same result of no liability. One is that consent is not established, and the other is that consent is established, but the consent is rendered ineffective. Which result did the Louisiana Supreme Court reach in *Cole, supra*?

STEPHEN K.

v.

RONI L.

105 Cal. App. 3d 640, 164 Cal. Rptr. 618 (Cal. App. 2d Dist. 1980)

BEACH, J.

* * * * *

Background

The minor child, its guardian ad litem, and its mother brought a paternity suit against Stephen K. (Stephen). After admitting paternity, Stephen filed a cross-complaint "for fraud, negligent misrepresentation and negligence." The cross-complaint alleged that Roni L. (Roni), the child's mother, had falsely represented that she was taking birth control pills and that in reliance upon such representation Stephen engaged in sexual intercourse with Roni which eventually resulted in the birth of a baby girl unwanted by Stephen. Stephen further alleged that as a "proximate result" of Roni's conduct he had become obligated to support the child financially, and had suffered "mental agony and distress all to his general damage in the amount of $ 100,000.00." Stephen also sought punitive damages of $ 100,000 against Roni for having acted "with oppression, fraud, and malice" towards him.

Roni moved for a judgment on the pleadings claiming that (1) to allow Stephen to recover damages would be against public policy, and (2) Stephen had failed to establish damages. The trial court treated Roni's motion as a general demurrer to the cross-complaint and ordered the action dismissed. Stephen appeals.

Issue on Appeal

The sole issue in this case is: As between two consenting sexual partners, may one partner hold the other liable in tort for the birth of a child conceived in an act of intercourse where the one partner relied on the other partner's false representation that contraceptive measures had been taken? We conclude that in this case Roni's conduct complained of by Stephen did not give rise to liability.

Discussion

The critical question before us is whether Roni's conduct towards Stephen is actionable at all. Stephen claims it is actionable as a tort. Neither statutory nor judicial recognition of such a claim in California or elsewhere in the United States has been brought to the attention of this court. Though the presentation of the matter as a legal issue is somewhat novel, the social conditions underlying it have existed since the advent of mankind.

Broadly speaking, the word "tort," means a civil wrong, other than a breach of contract, for which the law will provide a remedy in the form of an action for damages. It does not lie within the power of any judicial system, however, to remedy all human wrongs. There are many wrongs which in themselves are flagrant. For instance, such wrongs as betrayal, brutal words, and heartless disregard of the feelings of others are beyond any effective legal remedy and any practical administration of law. (Prosser, Torts (3d ed. 1964) ch. 1, §§ 1 and 4, pp. 1-2, 18, 21.) To attempt to correct such wrongs or give relief from their effects "may do more social damage than if the law leaves them alone." (Ploscowe, *An Action For "Wrongful Life"* (1963) 38 N.Y.U. L.Rev. 1078, 1080.) The present case falls within that category.

We are in effect asked to attach tortious liability to the natural results of consensual sexual intercourse. Stephen's claim is one of an alleged wrong to him personally and alone. Procedurally and technically it is separate and apart from any issue of either parent's obligation to raise and support the child. Although actually requiring the mother to pay Stephen monetary damages may have the effect of reducing her financial ability to support the child, we need not get into this area of discussion or resolve such problems as may exist in that area. In the posture of the case as presented to us, the state has minimal if any interest in this otherwise entirely private matter. Claims such as those presented by plaintiff Stephen in this case arise from conduct so intensely private that the courts should not be asked to nor attempt to resolve such claims. Consequently, we need not and do not reach the question of whether Stephen has established or pleaded tort liability on the part of Roni under recognized principles of tort law. In summary, although Roni may have lied and betrayed the personal confidence reposed in her by Stephen, the circumstances and the highly intimate nature of the relationship wherein the false representations may have occurred, are such that a court should not define any standard of conduct therefor.

* * * * *

The claim of Stephen is phrased in the language of the tort of misrepresentation. Despite its legalism, it is nothing more than asking the court to supervise the promises made between two consenting adults as to the circumstances of their private sexual conduct. To do so would encourage unwarranted governmental intrusion into matters affecting the individual's right to privacy....

We reject Stephen's contention that tortious liability should be imposed against Roni, and conclude that as a matter of public policy the practice of birth control, if any, engaged in by two partners in a consensual sexual relationship is best left to the individuals involved, free from any governmental interference. As to Stephen's claim that he was tricked into fathering a child he did not want, no good reason appears why he himself could not have taken any precautionary measures....

The judgment is **AFFIRMED**.

NOTES

1. On what basis did the court in the above case deny recovery? What elements of the tort theory did the plaintiff fail to establish?

2. Fraud is ordinarily a defect to consent. Consider the result in another California case, *Barbara A. v. John G.*, 193 Cal. Rptr. 422, (Ca. App. 1st Dist. 1983). In *Barbara A.* the court recognized a claim for battery against her attorney who had impregnated her after claiming falsely to have been sterile. Plaintiff had expressed that for emotional and financial reasons she did not want to become pregnant. The defendant said he could not possibly get anyone pregnant, knowing this to be a false statement. Consequently, the plaintiff consented and did engage in sexual intercourse with him twice. The result was an ectopic pregnancy, necessitating life-saving emergency surgery and leaving plaintiff sterile. The court noted that consent to an act, otherwise a battery, vitiates the wrong; however, the court found (1) that the act of impregnation exceeded the scope of the consent granted, and (2) that the consent to intercourse was fraudulently induced.

3. Louisiana courts have refused to recognize a claim for fraudulent inducement to sexual acts. *See Doe on behalf of Doe v. Cronan*, 487 So. 2d 461 (La.App. 5 Cir. 1986).

4. Consent is also defective if defendant has a duty to disclose information, in the absence of which the plaintiff would not have given consent. These duty to disclose cases are often viewed as negligence cases. Nevertheless, they can also be understood to defeat consent. In *Doe v. Johnson*, 817 F. Supp. 1382 (W.D. Mich. 1993), a federal district court denied a motion to dismiss by basketball legend Magic Johnson. The plaintiff alleged that Johnson had unprotected sexual intercourse with her despite reason to know that he had a high risk for being infected with HIV because of his promiscuous lifestyle. The court held that a person who has knowledge of his infection with a venereal disease and knows his partner does not, commits a battery by having sexual intercourse without informing his sexual partner of his infected status.

The Legislature has spoken on the subject in La. R.S. 40:1121.2:

La. R.S. 1121.2 Infection of others prohibited

> It is unlawful for any person to inoculate or infect another person in any manner with a venereal disease or to do any act which will expose another to inoculation or infection with a venereal disease.

The Louisiana Supreme Court spoke on the subject in *Meany v. Meany*, 639 So. 2d 229, 234-35 (La. 1994):

> Nationwide, courts have traditionally imposed liability for communication of harmful diseases. *Berner v. Caldwell*, 543 So. 2d 686, 688 (Ala. 1989) (citing *Crim v. International Harvester Co.*, 646 F.2d 161 (5th Cir. 1981) (valley fever); *Smith v. Baker*, 20 F. 709 (C.C.S.D.N.Y. 1884) (whooping cough); *Capelouto v. Kaiser Found. Hosp.*, 7 Cal. 3d 889, 500 P.2d 880, 103 Cal. Rptr. 856 (1972) (salmonellosis); *Hofmann v. Blackman*, 241 So. 2d 752 (Fla. Dist. Ct. App. 1970)

(tuberculosis); *Earle v. Kuklo*, 26 N.J. Super. 471, 98 A. 2d 107 (App. Div. 1953) (tuberculosis); *Jones v. Stanko*, 118 Ohio St. 147, 160 N.E. 456 (1928) (smallpox); *Franklin v. Butcher*, 144 Mo. App. 660, 129 S.W. 428 (1910) (smallpox); *Hewett v. Woman's Hospital Aid Ass'n.*, 73 N.H. 556, 64 A. 190 (1906) (diphtheria); *Edwards v. Lamb*, 69 N.H. 599, 45 A. 480 (1899) (sepsis); *Kliegel v. Aitken*, 94 Wis. 432, 69 N.W. 67 (1896) (typhoid); *Minor v. Sharon*, 112 Mass. 477 (1873) (smallpox)). The duty has been applied to both the individual who is aware of his or her infection and to third parties, such as the employer in *Crim v. International Harvester* and the landlord in *Earle v. Kuklo*, who were both aware of and in a position to prevent the spread of the disease. Note, *Interspousal Tort Liability for Infliction of a Sexually Transmitted Disease*, 29 J. FAM. L. 519, 520-1 (1990-1). Such liability imposes a great burden on the diseased person since abstinence from all social contact is required in order to prevent infection.... However, it is clear that society's interest in protecting the public health, the severity of the risk that others would be infected with diseases such as tuberculosis, diphtheria, typhoid, or smallpox, and the highly contagious nature of the diseases justify the imposition of this burden on the diseased person.

More recently, liability has been extended to the communication of sexually transmitted diseases. Furthermore, all states which have considered the issue have concluded that one spouse is liable to the other in tort for transmitting herpes. *Robert G. Spector, Tort Liability For Transmission Of A Venereal Disease*, 14 NO. 1 FAIR SHARE 23 (1994). In those cases the duty of the infected party, who knows, should know, or should suspect that he or she is infected with a sexually transmitted disease is either to abstain from sexual contact with others or, at least, to warn others of the infection prior to having contact with them. *Berner v. Caldwell*, 543 So. 2d at 689. While courts have generally required that the defendant have actual or imputed knowledge of his or her disease before liability may be assessed, a legal duty has nonetheless been imposed in a situation where a person is shown to have lacked medical confirmation that the disease had been contracted. *M.M.D. v. B.L.G.*, 467 N.W. 2d 645, 647 (Minn. App. 1991). Certainly, the presence of open, oozing genital sores indicates a serious problem, whether or not a diagnosis exists. If a defendant has experienced an attack or has sought medical advice concerning such symptoms, he would likely be deemed by the courts to possess the requisite knowledge, whether or not an actual diagnosis could be proved.... Furthermore, a defendant was not permitted to avoid liability for transmitting a sexually contagious disease because he believed that transmission was not possible as long as he was symptom free. *Doe v. Roe*, 218 Cal. App. 3d 1538, 267 Cal. Rptr. 564 (Cal. App. 1990). In balancing policy considerations, the court noted that the state's policy of preventing the spread of venereal disease is great and the burden of warning a prospective sex partner is slight, even if there is only a slight degree of foreseeability that plaintiff's injury would occur. *Id.* at 567.

Although liability has been extended to the communication of sexually transmitted diseases, courts have not adopted a policy of strict liability, or negligence per se, when the transmission of venereal disease has been statutorily prohibited. The violation of a legislative enactment commanding or prohibiting a specific act to ensure the safety of others arguably constitutes negligence per se. According to the court in *Mussivand v. David*, 45 Ohio St. 3d 314, 544 N.E. 2d 265, 271-2 (Ohio 1989), however, since the exposure of others to a dangerous disease could depend on the type of disease and the method of transmission, the relevant Ohio statute (or any other state statute concerning this issue) merely states a rule of conduct. It does not proscribe a specific act.

This Court recognizes, as a matter of public policy, that each person has a duty to use reasonable care to prevent the spread of harmful communicable diseases, including sexually transmitted diseases....

* * * * *

Suppose a person does not actually know he is infected. Can his failure to disclose be fairly considered a battery? Does he have the requisite intent? Does his sexual partner have adequate information to effectively consent?

Interpreting the Federal Tort Claims Act (FTCA), which allows suits against the United States under limited circumstances, the United States Fifth Circuit Court of appeal held that a plaintiff's claim to have been infected with herpes by a Navy recruiter amounted to an intentional tort. Intentional torts are generally not recoverable under the FTCA. The Court said:

> In essence, the complaint presents a cause of action for battery, notwithstanding [plaintiff] Leleux's protestations that the sexual intercourse between them was consensual and, therefore, not battery. Although never specifically treated by this court before, the principle that the unwanted transmission of a venereal disease during consensual sex vitiates the consent is a standard accepted by a variety of secondary sources. We hereby adopt this standard for the Fifth Circuit and hold that, where an individual fraudulently conceals the risk of sexually transmitting a disease, that action vitiates the partner's consent and transforms consensual intercourse into battery for the purposes of § 2680(h).

Leleux v. United States, 178 F.3d 750, 755 (5th Cir. 1999).

5. Excluding cases of fraud, when should the defendant's failure to disclose information invalidate consent? Consider a case where the plaintiff has consented to the harmful act, but later claims that his consent was given by mistake. Now, assume the defendant knew of plaintiff's mistaken assessment of the situation but failed to correct him? Is consent valid? Does it matter how significant the mistaken information is to the likelihood of harm resulting from the damaging act? Ordinarily two rules have guided courts in this area. First, consent grounded on mistake induced by the defendant is not a defense, but mutual, reasonable mistake does not defeat consent. Second, mistake about collateral matters does not defeat consent. Do these rules of thumb clarify consent?

Is it appropriate to read consent so as to create a law against seduction? Suppose a person consents to a sexual relationship with another because she incorrectly believes that her partner is wealthy. Should the person's consent fail because it was based on the fact that her partner dressed well, drove an expensive car, and otherwise effected a wealthy style? Suppose a person's sexual partner says falsely, in order to seduce and obtain consent, that he is the heir to the throne of a small kingdom? What if a person's consent is based on his partner's claim to have once been a famous Broadway diva with lots of money?

6. Consent is also defeated when shown it was extracted under duress. The wild tales of mobsters making someone "an offer they can't refuse" clearly illustrate the illegitimacy of consent extracted at the barrel of a gun. But when duress defeats consent is less clear if there are no obvious threats of bodily harm. The United States Supreme Court has wrestled with these issues in sexual

harassment cases where the plaintiff has engaged in sexual behavior which she claims was unwelcome but to which she consented (and which behavior could be said to have been "voluntary") because of fear of losing a job or being demoted. *See Meritor Savings Bank v. Vinson, FSB,* 477 U.S. 57 (1986).

7.   *Incapacity and Consent.* What value should be placed on the consent granted by minors? In *Doe v. Jeansonne,* 704 So. 2d 1240, 1247 (La.App. 3 Cir. 1997), *writ denied,* 718 So. 2d 433 (La. 1998), the parents of a teenaged girl sued the teenaged boy, his parents and the chaperones at the teenage party, claiming the boy impregnated her at the party. The Third Circuit reversed a summary judgment against the plaintiff because, inter alia, the girl's consent may have been vitiated by pressure from the boy and other factors:

> We have not ignored the accounts of a previous sexual encounter by this girl with another young man, and the testimony from others, as well as herself, regarding her kissing and "making out" with J. J. throughout the evening. However, we believe that her"consent," to have sex, if given, could be vitiated by factors such as the girl's age, and other factors, such as those commonly used in comparative fault determinations. *See L. K. v. Reed,* 93-659 (La.App. 3 Cir. 1994); 631 So. 2d 604, *writ denied,* 94-0544 (La. 1994); 637 So. 2d 461.

In *Doe* both children were between 13 and 16. In *L.K v. Reed.,* mentioned in *Doe,* the Third Circuit had held that a mildly retarded 13 year old's consent to have sex with an 18-year old, learning disabled classmate could not be valid. The girl's "family stress coupled with her age, intellect, and social skills, rendered her consent, from a legal standpoint, almost meaningless. *Reed,* 631 So. 2d 604. We found that she may have been unable to communicate or express her fear and lack of consent to the extent that she may have appeared to be a willing participant. The mere fact that Harry was older, bigger, stronger, and a member of the opposite sex, could have been interpreted by A. K. as force and intimidation." *John Doe,* 704 So. 2d, at 1247.

Generally, children may consent to intentional torts. *See Richard v. Mangnion,* 535 So. 2d 414 (La.App. 3 Cir. 1988) (13 year old consented to fist fight with 14 year old, barring recovery for battery), though this is likely subject to considerations related to the child's age and level of understanding. Similarly, mental disability does not completely preempt the ability to consent to a tort. In cases like *L.K. v. Reed,* however, the courts are prepared to consider mental ability and family circumstances in terms of evaluating the validity of consent given.

Several early dog bite cases focused on the ability of children to consent. *See Dotson v. Continental Insurance Co.,* 322 So. 2d 284 (La.App. 1 Cir. 1975), *writ denied,* 325 So. 2d 606 (La. 1976) (victim fault in the actions of a nine year old who proceeded into a neighbor's enclosed yard contrary to the owner's instructions and who was bitten by dog); *Parker v. Hanks,* 345 So. 2d 194 (La.App. 3 Cir. 1977), *writ denied,* 346 So. 2d 224 (La. 1977) (child victim at fault for approaching the kitchen door at the rear of the owner's house unannounced while knowing that a dog was customarily kept on a chain near the house); *Parks v. Paola,* 349 So. 2d 896 (La.App. 1 Cir. 1977), *writ denied* with Tate and Dixon, JJ. voting to grant, 350 So. 2d 1212 (La. 1977) (victim fault because nine year old who had frequently played with the dog without incident entered property uninvited, the dog was chained, and two children leaving the property warned that the dog might bite); *Duplechain v. Thibodeaux,* 359 So. 2d 1058 (La.App. 3 Cir. 1978) (victim fault in actions of a ten year old who was aware of the dog's presence, had been warned to stay away, had walked past the house with a warning sign posted, and had used a safe route the first time but chose an alternate route the second time within the dog's range). Changes in the basis for dog owner liability means that these cases would be decided differently today. *See Rozell v. Louisiana Animal Breeders Cooperative,* 469 So. 2d 269, 280 n.3 (La. 1986).

Very young children are probably not capable of consenting for legal purposes. Liability for children of "tender years" or children younger than the "age of discernment" create problems for courts searching for intent or the ability to consent. Louisiana law avoids this problem by imputing intent the child would have had if he or she were older to their parent for purposes of vicarious liability (the parent's liability for the children's wrongs). *See Turner v. Bucher*, 308 So. 2d 270 (La. 1975). However, courts have still suggested that very young children cannot form intent:

> "We are not called upon to decide in this case whether a nondiscerning minor child may also be liable for his delicts. However, it must be very apparent from our discussion of the liability of the father that it almost necessarily will follow that a nondiscerning minor child will not have delictual liability since our language has indicated that a nondiscerning minor is incapable of being legally at fault.

> We are mindful of the several articles in the Code which provide that minors are responsible for their offenses and quasi-offenses.
> Article 1785 provides:

> "* * *

> "The obligation arising from an offense or a quasi offense, is also binding on the minor."

> Article 1874 states:

> "He [a minor] is not relievable against obligations resulting from offenses or quasi offenses."

> Article 2227 states:

> "He is not restituable against the obligations resulting from his offenses or quasi offenses."

> We believe that our jurisprudence, the French jurisprudence and the French doctrine are all correct in finding that those minors incapable of discernment are immune from legal liability for delicts arising from negligence. Any basis in this opinion for concluding that there is no liability on the part of the minor for his offenses or his quasi-offenses is limited to the minor of tender age who is so incapable of discernment as to also be incapable of being legally at fault.

Id. at 276 n 14.

This same reasoning applies to persons of diminished capacity. *See von Dameck v. St. Paul Fire & Marine Ins. Co.*, 361 So. 2d 283, 287 (La.App. 1 Cir. 1978), *writs denied*, 362 So. 2d 794, 802 (La. 1978) ("If a person has such a want of reason, memory, and intelligence as prevents him from comprehending the nature and consequences of his acts, he cannot at the same time intentionally inflict injury. Though Dr. Cayer may have had the intent to shoot his wife, his insanity prevented him from having the requisite intent to inflict injury"). This would suggest that the insane may not be capable of consenting to an intentional tort.

8.   *Illegal Acts.* As the prior note suggests, consent to sexual acts by a minor might not be valid, particularly when they constitute the crime of statutory rape. It also may not be possible for a person

to consent to illegal activity such as prizefighting or gambling. However, the consequence of this general proposition is not completely clear. In the prizefighting context two common law rules have been developed. Under the first, consent to the illegal fight is rendered ineffective and cannot be used by the winner of the fight to prevent the loser from suing. The second rule does not render the consent ineffective, and thus consent to even illegal conduct bars the consenting persons from recovering. Louisiana follows the latter rule. *See White v. Gill*, 309 So. 2d 744 (La.App. 4 Cir. 1975).

conversion

Should this rule be followed in the gambling context? Suppose Plaintiff consents to gamble, loses, and pays. Allowing the defendant to keep the proceeds would allow gambling, an activity prohibited except under strict regulation. Would allowing the loser to sue, however, cast the defendant, unfairly, as though he had stolen the funds? Perhaps the question is left to criminal regulation, but imagine the following hypothetical: A is the treasurer for his church which has just held a revival. Returning home with $100,000 in cash from that event, A stops by B's bar for a high stakes poker match, hoping to win enough money to take a vacation. Instead A loses the money. Should the church be able to recover from B and others at the poker game on the theory that A could not consent to gamble? Notice that A, B, and other participants in the game might be subject to prosecution for illegal gambling. Although A is subject to severe criminal penalties for his handling of the money, and liable for conversion, it is not likely that the church will be able to recover all of its lost money from him. Does the public policy against gambling anticipate the situation of the church, allowing it to recover from B who, with A, illegally consented to an illegal activity?

What is the effect of consent to an abortion on the mother subsequently suing in tort? *See* La. R.S. 9:2800.12 ("The signing of a consent form by the mother prior to the abortion does not negate this cause of action, but rather reduces the recovery of damages to the extent that the content of the consent form informed the mother of the risk of the type of injuries or loss for which she is seeking to recover.").

2. Necessity

Necessity is an affirmative defense available where a natural event or violent act of a third person imposes on the defendant the *necessity* to harm the plaintiff. True privileges like self-defense are rooted in the ancient defense of necessity but diverge from necessity in important ways. Primarily, necessity differs from self defense (and defenses like defense of immovable and movable property) in that necessity arises from events unrelated to the behavior of the plaintiff.

There are two types of necessity, public and private necessity. Public necessity "arises when natural forces or third parties require the destruction of the property of some to save the lives or property of other people. These actions are usually undertaken by a public official charged with the welfare of the community...." Richard Epstein, Torts, § 2.16, at 65. Private necessity arises where a natural event or a violent act of a third party makes it necessary for a person to harm another to avoid harm to himself. Private necessity is limited to risks of death, serious bodily harm, or substantial property damage; "mere inconvenience or delay does not rise to the level of necessity...." *Id.*, § 2.14, at 59-60. Private necessity is distinguished from public necessity because the person responding to the necessity acts for his own exclusive benefit or for the benefit of a third party.

NOTES

1. The availability of compensation in public necessity cases is unclear. Traditionally, courts denied compensation. However, this is complicated by the United States Constitution, which commands that private property shall not be "taken for public use, without just compensation." United States Constitution, Amendment V. Similar provisions are also found in state constitutions.

See, e.g., La. Const. Art. 1, § 4. In public necessity cases where the property would have been destroyed regardless of what the public official does, compensation is ordinarily rejected. *See National Board of YMCAs v. United States*, 395 U.S. 85 (1969); *United States v. Caltex, Inc.*, 344 U.S. 149 (1952). Compensation has been allowed in cases where the "necessity" is an ordinary public goal, fulfilled through extraordinary means. Thus, in *Wagner v. Milwaukee Mutual Ins. Co.*, 479 N.W. 2d 38 (Minn. 1991), the Minnesota Supreme Court allowed compensation where private property was burned in an effort to capture a fleeing felon holed up in a third party's home. The police had shot tear gas and concussion grenades into the home in an effort to flush out the suspect. If the government's actions prevented the plaintiff from mitigating his loss, should he be able to obtain compensation? *See Surocco v. Geary*, 3 Cal. 69 (1853) (recovery rejected where plaintiffs claimed defendant's decision to explode their house in vain effort to stop the San Francisco fire deprived them of ability to remove valuables).

Should compensation be available to P from owners of homes saved when public officials blow up P's home to create a fire line? What entitles P to compensation, or makes the lucky homeowners liable to P? Are the lucky homeowners at fault? Should it matter if compensation against the state is barred?

In cases permitting compensation against the state, should compensation be had against individual officials who make the decisions? In *Bass*, should the plantation owner have an action against the contractor hired to design and build the levees? What problems follow from allowing such a cause of action?

2.   Private necessity is usually illustrated by reference to *Ploof v. Putnam*, 81 Vt. 471, 71 A. 188 (1908), or similar cases. In *Ploof*, the plaintiff, in order to avoid a violent tempest which arose on the lake on which he and his family were sailing, moored his sloop to defendant's dock. The defendant unmoored the boat and the tempest destroyed it. Plaintiff and his family were injured. Finding liability, the court held that "there are many cases on the books which hold that necessity ... will justify entries upon land and interferences with personal property that would otherwise have been trespass." The court included among these lawful entries: herded beasts which take morsels of grass or which run out the way and are quickly brought back; travelers on the highway who find it obstructed by a sudden and temporary cause and pass upon adjoining land; entrants upon land seeking to save goods which are in danger of being lost to flood or fire; and one sacrificing the property of another to save his life or that of his fellows. private necessity

3.   Private necessity is not mentioned in Louisiana's Civil Code, but the following code articles are relevant to the facts in *Ploof*.

C. C. Art. 452

Public things and common things are subject to public use in accordance with applicable laws and regulations. Everyone has the right to fish in the rivers, ports, roadsteads, and harbors, and the right to land on the seashore, to fish, to shelter himself, to moor ships, to dry nets, and the like, provided that he does not cause injury to the property of adjoining owners.

The seashore within the limits of a municipality is subject to its police power, and the public use is governed by municipal ordinances and regulations.

C. C. Art. 455

Private things may be subject to public use in accordance with law or by dedication.

C. C. Art. 456

The banks of navigable rivers or streams are private things that are subject to public use.

* * * * *

"Things are divided into common, public and private...." La. C. C. Art. 448. "Common things may not be owned by anyone. They are such as the air and the high seas...." La. C. C. Art. 449. "Public things are owned by the state or its political subdivisions ... such as running waters, the waters and bottoms of natural navigable water bodies, the territorial sea, and the seashore." La. C. C. Art. 450. "Private things are owned by individuals, other private persons, and by the state or its political subdivisions in their capacity as private persons." La. C. C. Art. 453.

4.   Compensation is usually available in private necessity cases. *See Vincent v. Lake Erie Transportation Co.*, 109 Minn. 456, 124 N.W. 221 (1910) (defendant liable for damage to dock caused by ship moored there to avoid storm). Do the above quoted Code articles imply that compensation must be paid for public use of private things?

5.   Necessity might be limited where there exists a "zero-sum game," meaning a transaction in which one person's gain is another person's loss. In cases where only one person can be rescued, the necessity defense is unavailable. "A man ought not to be stripped of his possessions against his will, if it be clear that he will once fall under the same necessity, if the possession passes to another." 2 Pufendorf, Samuel, The Law of Nature and Nations 305(1688).

3.   Self Defense

a.   Generally

In an intentional tort suit, the plaintiff normally prevails if she proves all the elements of the prima facie case. However the defendant may prevail, despite the plaintiff's showing, if she proves that she is without fault because her actions were privileged or justified. Self-defense is one such showing. In this way, self-defense is a true defense. The defense requires the showing that there was an actual or reasonably apparent threat to the claimant's safety requiring and justifying force, though the force used cannot be excessive in degree or kind. The privilege justifies protection of the defendant or certain third parties; it does not justify retaliation or revenge. It is ordinarily *not* triggered by threats and insults, though threats and insults may be part of the aggression to which self-defense responds.

SLAYTON
v.
MCDONALD
690 So. 2d 914 (La.App. 2 Cir. 1997)

WILLIAMS, J.

The plaintiff, Jimmy V. Slayton, appeals a trial court judgment rendered in favor of the defendant, A. S. McDonald, rejecting plaintiff's claim for personal injuries sustained as the result of a shooting incident. For the reasons assigned below, we affirm the trial court's judgment.

Facts

[After a disagreement on a school bus, fourteen year old plaintiff Slayton went to fourteen year old defendant McDonald's home to discuss the dispute. Junior high student McDonald believed Slayton, a high school student was perhaps 16. Slayton was definitely bigger and testimony was that Slayton had a reputation as a fighter. When McDonald saw Slayton coming, he procured his 12 gauge shotgun and confronted Slayton, telling him to leave. When Slayton did not leave, McDonald went into the house to call 911. Slayton followed him and dared him to shoot, saying McDonald "didn't have the guts" and that he was going to "kick his ass." Slayton's sister showed up and begged Slayton to return home. Shortly thereafter, McDonald shot Slayton in the knee, claiming Slayton was approaching him. There was disagreement as to whether Slayton was approaching McDonald, but prior to that point all agreed that Slayton was never more than a couple of feet in the McDonald home. The wound permanently injured Slayton's knee and caused tremendous pain and suffering. Slayton sued McDonald for the battery on him.]

Discussion

The plaintiff contends the trial court erred in finding that the defendant's son acted reasonably under the circumstances surrounding this incident, and thus, was justified in shooting the plaintiff's son in the leg. We do not find that the trial court erred.

* * * * *

LSA-C.C. Art. 2315 is the basis for tort liability in Louisiana. *See Reyes v. State of Louisiana and State Department of Transportation and Development*, 466 So. 2d 538 (La.App. 3 Cir. 1985). However, Louisiana's aggressor doctrine precludes tort recovery where the plaintiff acts in such a way to provoke a reasonable person to use physical force in fear or anticipation of further injury at the hand of the aggressor plaintiff, unless the person retaliating has used excessive force to repel the aggression. *Baugh v. Redmond*, 565 So. 2d 953, 958 (La.App. 2 Cir. 1990); *Perkins v. Certa*, 469 So. 2d 359, 361 (La.App. 2 Cir. 1985).

A plaintiff is said to be the aggressor when he is at fault in provoking the altercation in which he was injured. The question of which party is the aggressor must be decided on the peculiar facts and circumstances of each situation. *Perkins v. Certa, supra.*

Even when another party is the initial aggressor, the victim may use only so much force as is reasonably necessary to repel the attack and if the victim goes beyond that point, he is liable for damages. In determining the amount of force which is justified in repelling an attack, all facts and circumstances at the scene of the incident must be considered. *Red v. Taravella*, 530 So. 2d 1186, 1190 (La.App. 2 Cir. 1988).

Generally, one is not justified in using a dangerous weapon in self-defense if the attacking party is not armed but only commits battery with his fists or in some manner not inherently dangerous to life. However, resort to dangerous weapons to repel an attack may be justifiable in certain cases when the fear of danger of the person attacked is genuine and founded on facts likely to produce similar emotions in reasonable men. Under this rule, it is only necessary that the actor have grounds which would lead a reasonable man to believe that the employment of a dangerous weapon is necessary, and that he actually so believes. All facts and circumstances must be taken into account to determine the reasonableness of the actor's belief, but detached reflections or a pause for consideration cannot be demanded under circumstances which by their nature require split second decisions. Various factors relied upon by the courts to determine the reasonableness of the actions of the party being attacked are the character and reputation of the attacker, the belligerence of the attacker, a large difference in size and strength between the parties, an overt act by the attacker, threats of serious bodily harm, and the impossibility of a peaceful retreat. *Levesque v. Saba,* 402 So. 2d 266, 270 (La.App. 4 Cir. 1981).

In the instant case, McDonald testified that he believed that Slayton had beaten up people larger than himself, and, in essence, was capable of giving McDonald a beating as well; Slayton admitted that he had been in two fights while attending junior high school but gave no details of those altercations. Moreover, Slayton exhibited marked belligerence by refusing to leave McDonald's home despite repeated demands by McDonald while the latter was on the telephone with law enforcement authorities and was armed with a loaded twelve-gauge shotgun. This combination of reputation and belligerence evidence provides support for the trial court's conclusion that "the presence of the shotgun and defendant's threats were insufficient to thwart plaintiffs advances." It is undisputed that Slayton was considerably physically larger than McDonald, and the trial court accepted McDonald's testimony that Slayton had threatened to harm him. Indeed, Slayton himself admitted that he told McDonald that if McDonald shot him, he was going to get up and beat McDonald.

The trial court's finding that McDonald shot Slayton "to stop the plaintiff's advance" is a decision based upon the court's judgment of the credibility of the witnesses. Although both Slayton and his sister contradicted McDonald's testimony that Slayton was advancing when he was shot, Slayton's testimony that he was kneeling down when he was shot is contradicted by that of his sister and McDonald. Additionally, Slayton's testimony that he never came more than two feet into the house is contradicted by A.S. McDonald's testimony that he found blood about ten feet inside his home. Finally, the 911 tape, on which Slayton's voice became clearly audible only seconds before McDonald shot him, is further support for the conclusion that Slayton was advancing upon McDonald when shot. From its reasons for judgment, it is apparent that the trial court chose to credit McDonald's version of events over Slayton's version. Because the record supports this decision, it will not be disturbed on appeal.

Finally, it is evident that McDonald was simply unable to retreat from the encounter. While retreat is not a condition precedent for a finding of self-defense using justifiable force, in our opinion, the retreat of a lawful occupant of a home into a position in his home from which he cannot escape an attacker except by the use of force is strong evidence that the occupant's use of force to prevent the attack is proper. Although a shotgun may be a deadly weapon, McDonald used the gun in a way that he calculated would stop the attack without fatally injuring Slayton. Further, as recited above, McDonald testified that he was "afraid that if he [Slayton] came past the gun that he was crazy enough to kill me." Under these circumstances, where McDonald was on the telephone with law enforcement authorities and had repeatedly demanded that Slayton leave, and Slayton continued to advance and threaten McDonald, we cannot disagree with the trial court's conclusion that McDonald used reasonable force to repel Slayton's attack.

AFFIRMED.

NOTE

Louisiana developed a unique "aggressor doctrine" to preclude recovery where the plaintiff was the aggressor in the dispute, *see Vernon v. Bankston*, 28 La. Ann. 710 (1876); *Johns v. Bruker*, 30 La. Ann. 241 (La 1878); *Bonnaval v. American Coffee Co.*, 127 La. 57, 53 So. 426 (1910); *Hingle v. Myers*, 135 La. 383, 65 So. 549 (1914), or to reduce recovery in such disputes, especially where plaintiff's words instigated the dispute. *See Mundy v. Landry* 51 La. Ann. 303, 25 So. 66 (1899); *Richardson v. Zuntz*, 26 La. Ann. 313 (La. 1874). The doctrine, then, operated in conjunction with self-defense and other privileges to bar or limit recovery where self defense was not strictly available. This complicated the self-defense analysis and confused operation of Louisiana's comparative fault doctrine. The Louisiana Supreme Court addressed these matters in *Landry v. Bellanger*:

LANDRY

v.

BELLANGER

851 So. 2d 943 (La. 2003)

VICTORY, J.

We granted certiorari in this matter to consider whether or not the aggressor doctrine is a valid defense to an intentional tort under Louisiana's pure comparative fault regime. In addition, we are called to consider whether Section C of Civil Code Article 2323 prohibits a reduction of the plaintiff's recovery of damages for an injury partly the result of the fault of an intentional tortfeasor and partly the result of his own fault, when the plaintiff's fault amounts to more than mere negligence. For the following reasons, we conclude that the aggressor doctrine is inconsistent with Louisiana's comparative fault regime and no longer serves as a complete bar to plaintiff's recovery. However, self-defense is a valid defense to a battery, and in this case relieves the defendant of liability. We further find the prohibition of Section C is not applicable in situations where the plaintiff's conduct amounts to more than mere negligence.

Facts and Procedural History

On June 27, 1996, the plaintiff, Byron Landry ("Landry"), who had been living and working out of state, and his father, Ernest Landry, stopped at a local bar, Steve's Chevron, for a drink. While at the bar, Landry saw the defendant, Luke Bellanger, Jr. ("Bellanger"), a former high school classmate of his whom he had known for 20 years. Landry and Bellanger were both at the bar for several hours, drinking and visiting, except for a period of time when Bellanger left and returned later.

Landry's father left Steve's Chevron around 9:30 p.m., but Landry stayed behind drinking and visiting. As the evening progressed, Landry drank steadily over the next several hours, consuming approximately eight beers. Bellanger returned to the bar with his friend, Lonnie Bell, and Landry was still there. Bell, who testified by deposition, stated that he witnessed the interaction between Landry and Bellanger and that Landry appeared to be intoxicated. He testified that Landry began talking in a loud voice and became very belligerent toward Bellanger. Landry continued to harass and insult Bellanger, suggesting that he was born with a "a silver spoon in his mouth," and that he never had to work hard a day in his life. Bellanger continually asked Landry to calm down and leave him alone but Landry continued, becoming louder and more aggressive. Bell corroborated Bellanger's account of the events leading up to this point, testifying as follows: "Mr. Bellanger repeatedly ... had asked ... to please leave him alone. Asked him repeatedly ... to please calm down because he was getting a little hostile. Toward the end before they had their encounter, Mr. Landry was in Mr. Bellanger's face practically." Bell further added that at no time did Bellanger threaten Landry or say anything threatening to him.

When asked if Landry had issued a challenge to him or made any threatening comments to him, Bellanger testified that Landry walked up to him, poked him in the chest and said "if I wasn't such a f____ p____, he would take me outside [and] whip my ___." At that time, Bellanger asked Landry to step outside so they could talk, hoping he could get Landry to calm down. Landry and Bellanger then left the bar through the front door and stepped outside. Bellanger described what happened after they exited the bar, as follows:

> I got up, walked towards the bar and I walked out first. He came out behind me. I walked about 10 feet from the door, I turned around and tried to tell him, Byron, we don't need to do this, you know, this is stupid. We're friends, there's no need for us to fight. He walked up to me and started pushing me with his chest and telling me, yes, I'm going to whip your ___. I kept stepping back, I said, Byron, we don't need to do this. Well, he pushed me; when he pushed me, he kept coming. The only thing I could do was I had to defend myself.

According to Bellanger, he then struck Landry in the head with a partially closed fist, and Landry fell backwards and hit his head on the cement.

Landry's version of events is slightly different. Landry recalls that he and Bellanger argued about a woman and then Bellanger asked him to step outside. According to Landry, he walked out of the door first, but he remembers nothing about what happened in the parking lot other than being struck and falling down. The next thing Landry remembers is waking up at his parents' house the following day.

Lonnie Bell testified that he witnessed the entire incident, watching through the glass door from inside the bar. Bell indicated that prior to Landry and Bellanger going outside, it had "started to get pretty heated between the two" and Bellanger asked Landry to "step outside because he was starting to cause a scene inside of the bar." Bell reiterated that at no time did Bellanger threaten Landry. After exiting the bar, Bell saw Landry push Bellanger with his chest. Then Bell saw Bellanger hit Landry once in the head, causing him to fall to the ground and strike his head on the concrete parking lot. Bell stated that because Landry was "knocked out," they were reluctant to leave him on the ground. Thus, he and Bellanger lifted Landry into the bed of Bellanger's truck. Both Bell and Bellanger testified that although Landry was unconscious, he was still breathing and appeared to be all right. Although Landry's injury turned out to be a severe head injury, there was no evidence presented that Bellanger should have been aware that Landry had been seriously injured as a result of falling to the concrete.

Between 10 and 45 minutes after they had put Landry in the bed of the truck, Landry's father returned to the bar to check on his son. Landry's father found him passed out in the back of Bellanger's truck and assumed he had too much to drink. With the assistance of Bellanger and Bell, Landry's father put him into his vehicle and drove him home. Landry's father was unable to remove him from the vehicle so he left him there until the next morning, at which time he was able to walk with assistance. After several days of vomiting and headaches, Landry went to the emergency room at Lady of the Sea Hospital in Galliano for treatment. Tests revealed a skull fracture and a hematoma on the brain. Landry was immediately sent to Thibodaux Regional Medical Center where he underwent brain surgery for removal of the hematoma. Following surgery, he remained in the hospital for eight days and then later returned to his home in Florida with his wife.

Even after his recovery, Landry was unable to return to his former employment as an engineer in the marine industry. Landry testified that his treating neurologist advised him that he could never return to his previous employment. As a result of his brain injury, he was left with permanent neurological deficits, including loss of taste and smell, memory loss, and multiple personality changes. He also suffers from a seizure disorder and still has seizures on a daily basis. Landry sued Bellanger, claiming Bellanger committed an intentional tort, a battery, against him which caused his damages.

The trial court rendered a judgment in favor of Landry and awarded $400,000 in general damages, $320,000 in past and future loss of wages, and $24,278.41 in medical expenses, together with legal interest from the date of judicial demand and court costs. The trial court found that it was more probable than not that Landry's injury occurred when he fell onto the concrete surface in the parking lot after being struck by Bellanger and thus, his injuries were caused by a battery committed by Bellanger. In the trial court's reasons for judgment, the court found that Bellanger invited Landry outside so that he could "gain some measure of satisfaction for the verbal abuse he had endured inside of the bar for most of the evening." Accordingly, the trial court concluded that when Bellanger invited Landry outside, Bellanger became the aggressor. The trial court determined that Bellanger used force that was totally unnecessary under the circumstances and was not acting in self- defense. Additionally, the trial court noted that Landry's actions leading up to the confrontation were significant in determining the cause of his injuries and damages. The trial court recognized that prior to the amendment of Civil Code Article 2323, a plaintiff's negligence could be used to mitigate and reduce the damages resulting from an intentional tort committed by a defendant. However, it found that the amendment to Article 2323, in Paragraph C, provides that the claim for damages by a person injured partly by his own negligence and partly by an intentional tortfeasor shall not be reduced. Thus, the trial court concluded that Landry's actions can have no effect on the liability of Bellanger and the damages recovered by Landry as a result of Bellanger's liability.

On appeal, the First Circuit concluded the trial court erred in refusing to apportion fault in accordance with Article 2323. *Landry v. Bellanger*, 00-2029 (La.App. 1 Cir. 2002), 813 So. 2d 598. The court of appeal held that Article 2323(c) applies only in cases where a plaintiff's contributory fault consists of negligence and does not apply where a plaintiff's fault is intentional in nature. The court of appeal noted that the trial court acknowledged Landry's actions leading up to the confrontation were significant in determining the cause of his injuries and damages. Rejecting the trial court's conclusion that Landry's actions were negligent, the court of appeal found that these "significant" acts were intentional, not negligent, and therefore warrant a comparative fault analysis. After reviewing the evidence, the court concluded that fault should be apportioned equally between Landry and Bellanger.

Thereafter, Bellanger applied for supervisory writs in this Court, arguing that the lower courts erred in failing to properly apply the aggressor doctrine to deny a claim for damages sustained by an identified aggressor as a result of his own aggression.

We granted certiorari to consider the correctness of the court of appeal's judgment. *Landry v. Bellanger*, 02-1443 (La. 2002), 827 So. 2d 409.

Discussion

Under Louisiana Civil Code Article 2315, a person may recover damages for injuries caused by a wrongful act of another. According to that Article, "every act whatever of man that causes damage to another obliges him by whose fault it happened to repair it." La. C.C. art. 2315 (A).

Historically, fault has been the basis for tort liability in Louisiana. *Veazey v. Elmwood Plantation Association, Ltd.*, 93-2818 (La. 1994), 650 So. 2d 712, 717. Furthermore, Louisiana embraces a broad civilian concept of "fault" that encompasses any conduct falling below a proper standard, including intentional torts. *Id.* at 718. A battery is "[a] harmful or offensive contact with a person, resulting from an act intended to cause the plaintiff to suffer such a contact ..." *Caudle v. Betts,* 512 So. 2d 389, 391 (La. 1987). The defendant's intention need not be malicious nor need it be an intention to inflict actual damage. *Id.* It is sufficient if the defendant intends to inflict either a harmful or offensive contact without the other's consent. *Id.*

Under long-standing Louisiana jurisprudence, a plaintiff's recovery for damages resulting from an assault or battery would be precluded if the plaintiff's own actions were sufficient to provoke the physical retaliation. According to this "aggressor doctrine," plaintiff's recovery is precluded if the evidence establishes "he was at fault in provoking the difficulty [sic] in which he was injured, unless the person retaliating has used excessive force to repel the aggression." *See Baugh v. Redmond,* 565 So. 2d 953, 959 (La.App. 2 Cir. 1990); *Slayton v. McDonald,* 29,257 (La.App. 2 Cir. 1997), 690 So. 2d 1914 (Louisiana's aggressor doctrine precludes tort recovery where the plaintiff acts in such a way to provoke a reasonable person to use physical force in fear or anticipation of further injury at the hand of the aggressor plaintiff, unless the person retaliating has used excessive force to repel the aggressor); *Clark v. Buchaud,* 00-2750 (La.App. 4 Cir. 2001), 802 So. 2d 824; *Frazer v. St. Tammany Parish School Bd.,* 99-2017 (La.App. 1 Cir. 2000), 774 So. 2d 1227; *Duck v. McClure,* 36,045 (La.App. 2 Cir. 2002), 819 So. 2d 1070; *Frame v. Comeaux* 98-1498 (La.App. 3 Cir. 1999), 735 So. 2d 753; *Susananbadi v. Johnson,* 97-91 (La.App. 4 Cir. 1997), 700 So. 2d 886; *Minkler v. Chumley,* 32,558 (La.App. 2 Cir. 1999), 747 So. 2d 720.

The aggressor doctrine is unique to Louisiana, having evolved through decades of jurisprudence, but lacking any statutory or common law basis. However, the origin of the doctrine is possibly rooted in the legal maxim "*volenti non fit injuria,*" which provides "to one who is willing, no wrong is done." W. Page Keeton et al., Prosser & Keeton on The Law of Torts. § 18, at 112 (5th ed. 1984). The earliest Louisiana decision addressing the aggressor doctrine seems to be *Vernon v. Bankston,* 28 La.Ann. 710 (1876). Therein, the rule was stated as follows:

> One who is himself in fault cannot recover damages for a wrong resulting from such fault, although the party inflicting the injury was not justifiable under the laws.

28 La.Ann. 710, 711 (1876). The *Vernon* case asserts that this rule is well-settled in the jurisprudence of this State. However, the Court failed to cite any cases to support that the doctrine was indeed "well-settled." In fact, there does not appear to be any prior Louisiana jurisprudence asserting the aggressor doctrine principle.[1] Furthermore, in addition to the puzzling origin of the aggressor doctrine, Louisiana courts have applied the principle inconsistently, producing a rather confusing body of case law.[2]

---

[1] "The Court cited no cases from this well-settled jurisprudence, and there don't appear to be any." David W. Robertson, *The Aggressor Doctrine,* 1 S.U. L. REV. 82, 83 n.5 (1975).

[2] Professor Robertson creates a table of pre-*Morneau* jurisprudence that compares behavior held sufficiently provocative to escape battery liability with other behavior which did not justify or excuse the use of force.... there is no pattern. Robertson, "The Aggressor Doctrine" at 97; *Morneau v. American Oil Co.,* 272 So. 2d 313 (La. 1973); "The jurisprudence of Louisiana is by no means clear or settled on this point. Some judges have preferred to apply the aggressor doctrine strictly and have refused to grant any damages to the plaintiff if he were the original aggressor. Other cases have adopted a more humanitarian attitude and have attempted to give recovery by refusing to admit that the acts of the plaintiff amounted to aggression." Ferdinand F. Stone, *Tort Doctrine in Louisiana: The Aggressor Doctrine,* 21 TULANE L. REV. 362, 367 (1947).

Finally, the Court again modified the doctrine finding that mere words of provocation would not bar a plaintiff's recovery. In *Morneau v. American Oil Co.*, 272 So. 2d 313 (La. 1973), the Court concluded,

> We granted this writ primarily because, contrary to earlier Supreme Court decisions, a number of Court of Appeal decisions have followed a rule of law that words constitute provocation which excuses a battery ... The courts below erred in considering mere words as justification for a battery. The rule of law earlier adopted and followed by our court has even more merit today. The deviations in the holdings of the Courts of Appeal not only are contrary to those pronouncements but are contrary to the majority rule in this country. Moreover, they run contrary to our system of justice under law which commands the use of judicial process rather than force for the settling of disputes.... Applying the rule of law that words which are calculated to provoke and arouse to the point of physical retaliation may mitigate the damages in a civil action, we find the words used here, in the context of this incident, are insufficient to merit any mitigation of damages.

Louisiana's intentional tort doctrine has traditionally afforded an intentional tortfeasor a full defense if he can establish consent, privilege or self-defense, or enough provocation to trigger the aggressor doctrine; and a partial defense if the defendant can show a "merely verbal" provocation for a mitigation of damages. David Robertson, The Louisiana Law of Comparative Fault: A Decade of Progress, 1 Louisiana Practice Series 5 (Louisiana Judicial College, 1991).

Hence, the existence of consent means the defendant did not commit a tort and the existence of a privilege means the defendant's tort was justified. Robertson, *Louisiana's Law of Comparative Fault: A Decade of Progress,* at 6-7. Conversely, Louisiana's aggressor and mitigation doctrines are victim-fault defenses. *Id.* Neither theory implies that no tort has occurred or that the defendant's conduct was justified, but instead seek to penalize the victim. *Id.* As Robertson then points out, "On this analysis the percentage-fault approach should replace both the aggressor doctrine and the mitigation doctrine, while leaving the full defenses of consent and privilege intact. In this way the comparative fault principles will be confined to the job they were designed to do -- taking victim fault into account." Robertson, *The Louisiana Law of Comparative Fault: A Decade of Progress, supra,* at 7.

In this case, we are presented with the issue of whether the aggressor doctrine is still a valid defense that would bar the plaintiff's recovery following the 1996 amendments to Article 2323. Article 2323 provides that "in any action for damages ..., the degree or percentage of fault of all persons causing or contributing to the injury, death, or loss shall be determined, regardless of whether the person is a party to the action or a nonparty ... The [foregoing] provisions ... shall apply to any claim for recovery of damages ... asserted under any law or legal doctrine or theory of liability, regardless of the basis of liability." La. C.C. art. 2323 (A) and (B). Thus, this article clearly requires that the fault of every person responsible for a plaintiff's injuries be compared regardless of the legal theory of liability asserted against each person.[3] *Dumas v. State*, 02-0563 (La. 2002), 828 So. 2d 530.

---

[3] *See also* 2 Planiol, Civil Law Treatise no. 869c, 899 (La. St. L. Inst. Transl. 1959) *quoted in* Note, 34 La. L. Rev. 137, n. 16 (1973) ("Moreover it often happens that the fault of the victim is not the sole cause of the damage, and that the fault is shared. In that case the victim cannot be denied the right to sue under the pretext that he was at fault. The responsibility is apportioned according to the gravity of the faults committed respectfully by the author and by the victim and partial recovery takes place.")

The above provisions indicate that Louisiana employs a "pure" comparative fault system, whereby the fault of all persons causing or contributing to injury is to be compared. When it adopted the comparative fault system, Louisiana abolished the contributory negligence feature, which completely barred the recovery of injury victims because of their fault, our tort law formerly embraced prior to 1980. *See Dumas, supra,* 02-0563 at pp. 4-5, 828 So. 2d at 532-33. Applying the aggressor doctrine to bar plaintiff's recovery would reintroduce some vestige of contributory negligence law to our tort system and ignore the plain language of Article 2323(A) that directs the court to allocate a proportion of fault to every party contributing to the injury.

This court dealt with a similar proposition in *Murray v. Ramada Inns, Inc.,* 521 So. 2d 1123 (La. 1988). In that case, this Court held that the survival of assumption of risk as a total bar to plaintiff's recovery would be inconsistent with the mandate of a former version of Article 2323 stating that contributory negligence should no longer operate as a complete bar to plaintiff's recovery. Characterizing assumption of risk as a form of contributory negligence, we noted that it would be anomolous to hold that the same conduct which results only in a reduction in recovery when it is described as "comparative negligence" somehow should operate as a total bar to recovery when described as "assumption of risk." *Id.* 521 So. 2d at 1133. In *Murray,* this Court concluded that the fact that the plaintiff may have been aware of the risk created by the defendant's conduct should not operate as a total bar to recovery. Instead, comparative fault principles should apply, and the victim's "awareness of the danger" is among the factors to be considered in assessing the percentages of fault. *Id.* at 1134.

As we explained in *Murray,* the premise underlying the assumption of the risk defense was that a plaintiff who disregards a known risk has consented to his own injury and agreed to relieve the potential defendant of liability for that injury. *Id.* at 1135. Similarly, under the aggressor doctrine, the plaintiff is deemed to have consented to the physical retaliation by provoking the defendant, thereby relieving the defendant of liability for any damages that may result. Just as we did in *Murray* with respect to assumption of the risk, we find the aggressor doctrine no longer has a place in Louisiana tort law. Pursuant to the rules imposed by Article 2323, comparative fault principles should be applied to alleged plaintiff negligence, thereby eliminating the inequities inherent in the "all or nothing" recovery rules that prevailed prior to the adoption of comparative fault. We find the purpose of the aggressor doctrine, which condemns actions by barring recovery, is adequately served by the civilian concepts of comparative fault, duty/risk, and privileges.

The trial court in this case, however, relying on the provisions of La. C.C. art. 2323(C), was of the opinion that the imposition of comparative fault was inapplicable. Section C of art. 2323 provides:

does not apply to this case

C. Notwithstanding the provisions of Paragraphs A and B, if a person suffers injury, death, or loss as a result partly of his own negligence and partly as a result of the fault of an intentional tortfeasor, his claim for recovery of damages shall not be reduced. *requires negligence (vic), intentional tortfeasor*

Nothing in this section prevents the determination of the percentage of fault of all persons causing or contributing to the injury at issue. Rather, Section C provides that (when plaintiff is injured as a result of the fault of an intentional tortfeasor, his negligence shall not reduce his recovery.) Thus, reading each section of La. C.C. art. 2323 and giving effect to each portion of the Article, we find that the fault of all persons causing or contributing to injury, regardless of the basis of liability, is to be determined, and, if a negligent plaintiff is injured as a result of the fault of an intentional tortfeasor, his claim for recovery of damages shall not be reduced by his percentage of fault.

It is appropriate to consider each party's respective fault when a matter involves intentional tortfeasors. In prohibiting the reduction of a negligent plaintiff's damages, Article 2323(C) reflects a legislative determination that on the continuum of moral culpability, the act of an intentional actor should not benefit from a reduction in the damages inflicted on a less culpable negligent actor. In the face of the silence of La. C.C. art. 2323(C) regarding how to address the comparative fault of two intentional actors, we can extrapolate from paragraphs A and B of La. C.C. art. 2323 that the fault of the intentional actors can be compared. In the instant case, the plaintiff's conduct was not merely negligent, but intentional, and therefore the provisions of Section C are inapplicable.

Furthermore, the trial court found that because the plaintiff suffered an injury partly as a result of the fault of an intentional tortfeasor, Section C prevented a reduction of plaintiff's damages by the percentage of plaintiff's fault attributable to his injury. By its own terms, Section C applies only when plaintiff is injured partly by his own negligence and partly by an intentional tortfeasor. The application of Section C furthers public policy by preventing an intentional tortfeasor from using the comparative fault regime to reduce his own obligation to compensate a less culpable victim. Even before the 1996 addition of Section C, in *Veazey v. Elmwood Plantation Assoc.*, 93-2818 (La. 1994), 650 So. 2d 712, 719, we recognized this public policy and held that a negligent tortfeasor, "who by definition acted unreasonably under the circumstances in breaching their duty to plaintiff, should not be allowed to benefit at the *innocent* plaintiff's expense by an allocation of fault to the intentional tortfeasor under comparative fault principles." Therefore, the court of appeal correctly concluded that Section C applies only when plaintiff's contributory fault consists of negligence and does not apply where the plaintiff's fault is intentional.

* * * * *

In a suit for damages resulting from an intentional tort, the claimant must carry the burden of proving all prima facie elements of the tort, including lack of consent to the invasive conduct. In turn, the defendant may seek to prove that he is without fault because his actions were privileged or justified, such as self-defense. Self-defense, unlike the aggressor doctrine, is a true defense in that it operates as a privilege to committing the intentional tort. In such a case, a plaintiff's conduct must have gone beyond mere provocation under the aggressor doctrine. Under Louisiana jurisprudence, in order to succeed on a claim of self-defense (not involving deadly force), there must be an actual or reasonably apparent threat to the claimant's safety and the force employed cannot be excessive in degree or kind. Robertson, *The Aggressor Doctrine*, 1 S.U. L. REV. at 90. The privilege of self-defense is based on the prevention of harm to the actor, not on the desire for retaliation or revenge, no matter how understandable that desire. *Id.* at 84. Furthermore, the prevailing view in almost every one of our sister states is:

> Threats and insults may give color to an act of aggression, but in themselves, they do not ordinarily justify an apprehension of immediate harm, and the defendant is not privileged to vindicate his outraged personal feelings at the expense of the physical safety of another. Such provocation is considered only in mitigation of the damages.

PROSSER AND KEETON ON THE LAW OF TORTS, § 19, at 126.

Absent a qualifying privilege, any provocative or aggressive conduct on the part of the plaintiff should be incorporated into the allocation of fault by the trier of fact. However, simply because the trier of fact must consider the fault of both plaintiff and defendant, does not mean that an aggressive plaintiff can avoid responsibility for his conduct. In fact, nothing prevents a trier of fact from determining that the plaintiff's conduct was of such a provocative nature as to render it the sole cause of his injury. Thus, we must consider Landry's conduct to determine whether Bellanger was acting in self-defense, such that his conduct was justified or privileged and precludes recovery by Landry, or whether self-defense is unavailable as a complete defense, such that Landry and Bellanger's relative fault must be compared. We find, after a *de novo* review of the record, that Bellanger was acting in self-defense and is therefore without fault in causing Landry's injuries.

In the instant case, the lower court concluded that Bellanger committed a battery on the person of Landry. Clearly, by punching Landry, Bellanger perpetrated the harmful contact needed for an intentional tort and thus we find no manifest error in the trial court's conclusion that Bellanger committed a battery when he punched Landry. However, the trial court also found that in striking Landry, Bellanger was not acting in self-defense. We disagree.

* * * * *

NOTES

1.   The *Landry* court's rejection of the aggressor doctrine is not complete. The doctrine is built into several statutes, particularly La. R.S. 9:2800.10, which bars recovery of damages by a felon for injuries incurred during the commission of a felony or while fleeing from commission of a felony. R.S. 9:2800.10 provides:

> No person shall be liable for damages ... sustained by a perpetrator of a felony offense during the commission of the offense or while fleeing the scene of the offense. ... However, the provisions of this Section shall not apply if injury to or death of a perpetrator results from an intentional act involving the use of excessive force.

Landry does not alter the force of this statute.

2.   *Danger to Life or Limb Reasonably Apparent.* Self defense must be based on actual or apparent danger to life or limb. This is illustrated in the case below. As mentioned in *Landry,* self-defense cannot be based on mere words. *Morneau v. Am. Oil Co.,* 272 So. 2d 313 (La. 1973). In *Morneau* a service station customer began to argue with the station operator (Mr. Watkins) about damage to his car he claimed occurred during repair work at the station. During this argument the plaintiff used the phrase "God damm," prompting Mr. Watkins to say he didn't want plaintiff using profanity in front of his wife (who was the business manager of the station and present during the argument). When plaintiff said Ms. Watkins heard more from Mr. Watkins everyday, Mr. Watkins slapped or hit him, initiating a fight. The Supreme Court said:

> The Court of Appeal found that the use of the expression "God damn" in front of Mrs. Watkins, the request that Morneau refrain from using such language, and his response were sufficient provocation to justify the physical assault by Watkins. It held that this provocation by words which Morneau should have known would arouse resentment and possible physical retaliation barred his right to recovery. No mention was made of the property damage to Morneau's automobile.

> We granted this writ primarily because, contrary to earlier Supreme Court decisions, a number of Court of Appeal decisions have followed a rule of law that words constitute provocation which excuses a battery. This court announced in *Richardson v. Zuntz,* 26 La.Ann. 313 (1874), that mere words, no matter how calculatedly they were used to excite or irritate, cannot justify a battery. Provocation by words, however, can be considered in mitigation of damages although rejected as

justification for an unlawful act. This rule was established in a line of cases. [footnote with citations omitted] In more recent cases, however, numerous Court of Appeal decisions have recognized as our rule of law that words alone can constitute provocation to excuse or justify what would otherwise be an unlawful act.

We conclude that the courts below erred in considering mere words as justification for a battery. The rule of law earlier adopted and followed by our court has even more merit today. The deviations in the holdings of the Courts of Appeal not only are contrary to those pronouncements but are contrary to the majority rule in this country. Moreover, they run contrary to our system of justice under law which commands the use of judicial process rather than force for the settling of disputes. We reiterate the holding of *Richardson v. Zuntz, supra*, that mere words, even though designed to excite or irritate, cannot excuse a battery.

3.   *Landry, supra*, rejects the aggressor doctrine on which the mitigation of damages for provocative words was based. After *Landry* is there any ground for reducing the plaintiff's recovery if his words provoked the altercation? Is such a reduction consistent with *Morneau*?

4.   Reasonableness of a threat is issue for trier of fact. *Roberts v. Am. Employers Ins. Co.*, 221 So. 2d 550 (La.App. 3 Cir. 1969); *Robertson v. Aetna Cas. & Sur.*, 563 So. 2d 521 (La.App. 5 Cir. 1990).

5.   Suppose a man learns that another man engaged in nonconsensual sexual contact with his wife before he married her and took nude or semi-nude photos of her without her consent and then boasted of the contact and showed the photos to others. Twenty months after the incident, the husband learns about it, drives to the other man's home to discuss it with him, and eventually uses a stun gun on him multiple times. When sued, the husband claims that he is not liable for a battery under the doctrine of provocation. What result? *See Griffith v. Young*, 62 So. 3d 856 (La.App. 2 Cir. 2011).

b. Reasonable Response

What is a reasonable response in a self-defense context is often complicated by the nature of the dispute for which the defense is asserted. Sometimes self-defense and other defenses like defense of property are intermingled in a way that makes an otherwise reasonable response unreasonable or vice versa. An example of such a case is *Dean v. Nunez*, 423 So. 2d 1299 (La.App. 4 Cir. 1982), a case involving two St. Bernard Parish School Board members whose debate during a board meeting came to blows. After opposing a vote to meet in executive session, Board Member Dean made preparations to record the proceedings, despite being asked not to by fellow board members. An ensuing debate over the propriety of his recording the meeting escalated when board member Nunez insisted that the tape recorder be turned off. Nunez apparently threatened to destroy the recorder, prompting Dean to say Nunez "would be in trouble." Eventually Nunez walked over to attempt to turn the recorder off, prompting Dean to rise from his chair and, when Nunez reached for the recorder push him away with a stiff arm. Nunez responded by punching Dean, knocking him to the floor and breaking his nose.

Who should be able to employ the privilege of self-defense?

1.   *Size of aggressor is not determinative*. In *Dixon v. Winston*, 417 So. 2d 122 (La.App. 3 Cir. 1982), *writ denied*, 420 So. 2d 985 (La. 1982), a football player punched a cheerleader. The court found the punch justified:

... where there is an aggressive act, justifying a battery, the person retaliating may use only so much force as is necessary to repel the aggression; and that if he goes beyond this, he using force in excess of what would have been reasonably necessary, he is liable for damages for injury caused by the employment of such unnecessary force. *Oakes v. H. Weil Baking Company et al.*, 174 La. 770, 141 So. 456, *Whittington v. Levy* (La.App.), 184 So. 2d 577, *Bauman v. Heausler* (La.App.), 188 So. 2d 189 and *Mut v. Roy et al.* (La.App.), 185 So. 2d 639.

Of course, each case depends on its own peculiar facts and circumstances; and resort must be had to the evidence to determine who was the aggressor and whether more force than necessary was used to repel the aggression.

In rendering judgment for the defendant, the trial court had made the following factual findings:

... taking into consideration the overall posture of this situation it appears to the Court that this was a two way incident caused by the provocation of Sheila Ann Delozia and the reaction to that provocation by John Winston, Jr. I find that Sheila Ann Delozia cursed John Winston, Jr. and while not inflicting serious bodily harm did strike him with a fork in the lunch room of Natchitoches Central High School, which provocation caused John Winston, Jr. to react, striking Sheila Ann Delozia in the face. The testimony of the different witnesses to this striking and to the fork incident was rather confusing. No two persons who testified as to being eye witnesses to the incident testified identically, which is not unusual in a situation such as this type. But considering the overall picture I find that Sheila Ann Delozia provoked and participated in the incident to the extent that it acts as a bar to her right to recover in this matter – "

The appellate court noted that, before a reviewing court can disturb the factual findings of a trial court, it must conclude that such findings by the trier of fact are manifestly erroneous and have no reasonable factual basis in the record. Generally, a trial judge is in the best position to determine the credibility of witnesses and where testimony is in serious conflict and the resolution of questions necessarily depends on an evaluation of such credibility, great weight must be granted to the decision of the trial court. On this basis the Third Circuit panel concluded:

Our review of the testimony and evidence confirms as correct the trial court's conclusion that Sheila provoked the incident at issue. There is no conflict in the record regarding her instigation of the verbal altercation which culminated in her injury. In addition, we conclude, as did the trial court, that John's striking of Sheila was an involuntary reflex reaction to her attack and did not constitute the use of unreasonable force under the circumstances. There is no dispute regarding the immediacy of John's response to being struck with the fork wielded by Sheila nor is there any dispute regarding young Winston's immediate reaction of surprise and disbelief at his own actions. Also, we note that John is a scholar, athlete, class favorite, and student government officer at Natchitoches Central High School and has no past record of disciplinary problems. We find no clear error on the part of the trial court in its conclusion that Sheila's provocation of the incident bars her right of recovery for those injuries sustained as a result of the altercation.

* * * * *

The Third Circuit's analysis seems to be based on Louisiana's now rejected aggressor doctrine. Is this a case where self-defense can be sustained? Note that retaliation is never justified as self-defense and that defending party's response to the aggressor's actions must be proportional. Are these requirements met in *Dixon*?

2.   *Duty to Retreat.* The Restatement (Second) of Torts, Section 65 (2) provides that the privilege of self-defense "exists although the actor correctly or reasonably believes he can safely avoid the necessity of so defending himself by (a) retreating if he is attacked within his dwelling place, which is not also the dwelling place of the other, or (b) permitting the other to intrude upon or dispossess him of his dwelling place, or (c) abandoning an attempt to effect a lawful arrest." This provision conflicts with § 65 (3) which holds the privilege of self-defense by deadly force inapplicable if retreat is possible. In Comment g, to §65, the drafters explain:

> g. *Standing one's ground.* As stated in § 63, one whom another threatens to attack may stand his ground and repel the attack with reasonable force which does not threaten death or serious bodily harm, although he realizes that he can safely retreat and so avoid the necessity of using self-defensive force. But the interest of society in the life and efficiency of its members and in the prevention of the serious breaches of the peace involved in bloody affrays requires one attacked with a deadly weapon, except within his own dwelling place, to retreat before using force intended or likely to inflict death or serious bodily harm upon his assailant, unless he reasonably believes that there is any chance that retreat cannot be safely made. But even the slightest doubt, if reasonable is enough to justify his standing his ground, and in determining whether his doubt is reasonable every allowance must be made for the predicament in which his assailant has placed him.

In *Landry v. Bellanger*, the court adopts a similar approach. Is the court's analysis consistent with comment g?

NOTE

Preemptive action. The Louisiana Legislature responded to carjacking and other violent crime by enacting criminal statutes articulating a use of force doctrine arguably broader than recognized in tort law. The last round of amendments occurred in the 2006 legislative session.

The following statutes are Louisiana's version of the "stand-your-ground" law, which gained attention in the case of the late Trayvon Martin and George Zimmerman in Florida. The Florida statute is at Florida Statutes 776.012, 776.013, 776.031 & 776.032.

As you read the Louisiana statutes, consider the differences between tort law and criminal law. What is the effect of R.S. 9:2800.19?

La. R.S. 9:2800.19. Limitation of liability for use of force in defense of certain crimes

A.   A person who uses reasonable and apparently necessary or deadly force or violence for the purpose of preventing a forcible offense against the person or his property in accordance with R.S. 14:19 or 20 is immune from civil action for the use of reasonable and apparently necessary or deadly force or violence.

B.   The court shall award reasonable attorney fees, court costs, compensation for loss of income, and all expenses to the defendant in any civil action if the court finds that the defendant is immune from suit in accordance with Subsection A of this Section.

94

La. R.S. 14:19. Use of force or violence in defense *Slayton v. McDonald*

A.　　The use of force or violence upon the person of another is justifiable when committed for the purpose of preventing a forcible offense against the person or a forcible offense or trespass against property in a person's lawful possession, provided that the force or violence used must be reasonable and apparently necessary to prevent such offense, and that this Section shall not apply where the force or violence results in a homicide.

B.　　For the purposes of this Section, there shall be a presumption that a person lawfully inside a dwelling, place of business, or motor vehicle held a reasonable belief that the use of force or violence was necessary to prevent unlawful entry thereto, or to compel an unlawful intruder to leave the premises or motor vehicle, if both of the following occur: *presumption of reasonable force*

　　(1) The person against whom the force or violence was used was in the process of unlawfully and forcibly entering or had unlawfully and forcibly entered the dwelling, place of business, or motor vehicle.

　　(2) The person who used force or violence knew or had reason to believe that an unlawful and forcible entry was occurring or had occurred.

C.　　A person who is not engaged in unlawful activity and who is in a place where he or she has a right to be shall have no duty to retreat before using force or violence as provided for in this Section and may stand his or her ground and meet force with force.

D.　　No finder of fact shall be permitted to consider the possibility of retreat as a factor in determining whether or not the person who used force or violence in defense of his person or property had a reasonable belief that force or violence was reasonable and apparently necessary to prevent a forcible offense or to prevent the unlawful entry.

La. R.S. 14:20. Justifiable homicide

A.　　A homicide is justifiable:

　　(1) When committed in self-defense by one who reasonably believes that he is in imminent danger of losing his life or receiving great bodily harm and that the killing is necessary to save himself from that danger.

　　(2) When committed for the purpose of preventing a violent or forcible felony involving danger to life or of great bodily harm by one who reasonably believes that such an offense is about to be committed and that such action is necessary for its prevention. The circumstances must be sufficient to excite the fear of a reasonable person that there would be serious danger to his own life or person if he attempted to prevent the felony without the killing.

　　(3) When committed against a person whom one reasonably believes to be likely to use any unlawful force against a person present in a dwelling or a place of business, or when committed against a person whom one reasonably believes is attempting to use any unlawful force against a person present in a motor vehicle as defined in R.S. 32:1(40), while committing or attempting to commit a burglary or robbery of such dwelling, business, or motor vehicle.

　　(4) (a) When committed by a person lawfully inside a dwelling, a place of business, or a motor vehicle as defined in R.S. 32:1(40), against a person who is attempting to make an

95

unlawful entry into the dwelling, place of business, or motor vehicle, or who has made an unlawful entry into the dwelling, place of business, or motor vehicle, and the person committing the homicide reasonably believes that the use of deadly force is necessary to prevent the entry or to compel the intruder to leave the premises or motor vehicle.

(b) The provisions of this Paragraph shall not apply when the person committing the homicide is engaged, at the time of the homicide, in the acquisition of, the distribution of, or possession of, with intent to distribute a controlled dangerous substance in violation of the provisions of the Uniform Controlled Dangerous Substances Law.

B.   For the purposes of this Section, there shall be a presumption that a person lawfully inside a dwelling, place of business, or motor vehicle held a reasonable belief that the use of deadly force was necessary to prevent unlawful entry thereto, or to compel an unlawful intruder to leave the premises or motor vehicle, if both of the following occur:

(1) The person against whom deadly force was used was in the process of unlawfully and forcibly entering or had unlawfully and forcibly entered the dwelling, place of business, or motor vehicle.

(2) The person who used deadly force knew or had reason to believe that an unlawful and forcible entry was occurring or had occurred.

C.   A person who is not engaged in unlawful activity and who is in a place where he or she has a right to be shall have no duty to retreat before using deadly force as provided for in this Section, and may stand his or her ground and meet force with force.

D.   No finder of fact shall be permitted to consider the possibility of retreat as a factor in determining whether or not the person who used deadly force had a reasonable belief that deadly force was reasonable and apparently necessary to prevent a violent or forcible felony involving life or great bodily harm or to prevent the unlawful entry.

4. Defense of Third Parties

Use of force can be justified in the defense of third parties as well as in self-defense. This is clearly recognized in the case of defense of one's family, an issue on which the Civil Code speaks directly.

C.C. Art. 223 Parental authority includes rights and obligations of physical care, supervision, protection, discipline, and instruction of the child.

PATTERSON
v.
KUNTZ
28 So. 2d 278 (La. App. Orl. 1946)

[Defendant shot his neighbor's son whom he took to be a prowler who had been harassing his family for over a year. The trial court found for the defendant and the appellate court affirmed, reasoning that the fear for the safety of the defendant's wife and adult daughter were reasonable.]

'Where a man reasonably expects an attack from A, and in the exercise of due care mistakes B for A, and strikes B, he is, nevertheless, excused on the ground of self-defense and apparent necessity.'

* * * * *

Hence, as aforesaid, it is unimportant that we determine the intent of Patterson [Plaintiff's son] although it is apparent, from a consideration of all of the evidence in the case, that the District Judge was not at all impressed with the young man's statement.

We therefore return to a discussion of the evidence submitted by defendant in support of his plea that he was justified in shooting the young man. In view of the decision below, it is manifest to us that the District Judge reached the conclusion that the repeated harassments, intrusions and invasions of defendant's premises by the prowler were sufficient to cause a reasonably prudent man to believe that the invader intended bodily harm to his wife and daughter and that, under the peculiar circumstances of the case, he was warranted in repelling the invasion by use of a deadly weapon.

The complaint of council [sic] for plaintiff on this appeal is that the judge was in error in resolving that the shooting was justified. They maintain that defendant's fears for the safety of himself and family have been greatly exaggerated in his efforts to build up a defense and that the sum and substance of his supposed fears are founded, not upon an actual invasion of his residence, but upon undue excitement caused by mere boyish pranks, I. e., trespassers upon the premises to peep at women disrobing. Pointing to the fact that at no time did the trespasser attempt to break into or enter the house, council say that the alarm of defendant is pretended and that the truth is that defendant was unwarrantedly vexed and brutally and maliciously resorted to the use of a deadly weapon in a spirit of anger and revenge.

* * * * *

Of course, resort to the use of a dangerous weapon in order to repel a supposed attack upon a defendant's person or that of persons to whom he owes a duty to protect cannot be countenanced as justifiable save in exceptional cases where the actor's fear of the danger is not only genuine but is founded on facts which would be likely to produce similar emotions in men of reasonable prudence. Thus, in the recent case of *Bacas v. Laswell*, La.App., 22 So. 2d 591, where we had occasion to review much of the prior jurisprudence of this state on the subject, we pointed out that, while recovery in Louisiana will not be permitted in assault and battery cases where the plaintiff is the aggressor and the difficulty was brought about through his exclusive fault, this rule will not be applied where there is mutual fault respecting the difficulty which brings about the injury in cases where the defendant uses undue force (such as a dangerous weapon) not justified by the occasion.

When we apply the law, as we understand it, to the facts of the case at bar, we experience little difficulty in approving the conclusion of the judge below that the defendant was justified in believing that his wife and daughter might be attacked, and that he acted as any ordinarily prudent man would act when confronted with a like problem. In the United States, the right of a man to maintain his home free from outside interference and intrusion and to repel invasion therein by the use of force is well-recognized and generally understood. This right has always been a cherished one -- one which has been zealously guarded and protected by our basic laws. If these disturbances or attacks, treated so lightly by counsel for plaintiff, had been mere boyish pranks which occasionally occurred on the premises, there might be some room for argument that defendant was not justified in obtaining a pistol for the purpose of repelling the invader. But such was not the case, according to the undisputed evidence. The attacks were incessant and continued for a period of over a year. Defendant and his family became more and more alarmed as the nocturnal disturbances were repeated. Their anguish, we think, was natural. Protective measures, such as the lighting of his driveway, the placing of lamps at windows, summoning the police on numerous occasions, were all resorted to by defendant in vain. As time went on and the intrusions were continued, the security of defendant's home and his family

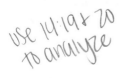

appeared to him to be in serious jeopardy. The nervous strain increased and defendant was advised by police authorities (whether rightly or wrongly is not the question) that the probabilities were that the person or persons responsible for the intrusions would some day attack his wife and daughter. Offers of the use of firearms were made to him by friends, who had observed the untenable conditions under which the family was living, and finally defendant, apparently at his wits end for protection, took the weapon and used it to repel what he believed to be an attack. Under stress of the circumstances with which defendant was confronted, we cannot say that he was not justified in shooting the intruder because the latter had never attempted to break into the house and was not effecting a felonious assault at the time the shots were fired. Nor do we think that defendant was required to wait until the transgressor exerted force to accomplish his end (which defendant believed was an attack on his womenfolk) in order to be held blameless if the feared invasions were of such a nature to impress an ordinarily prudent man that the attack would ultimately occur.

NOTES

1.   *Defense of Apartment Complex and Tenants?* In *Byrd v. Isgitt*, 338 So. 2d 374 (La.App. 3 Cir. 1976), the circuit court quoted with approval the following conclusion of the trial court in rejecting a battery claim. The plaintiff was a drunk and loud tenant whom the defendant apparently punched while trying to quiet and persuade to stop using foul language "in the presence of women."

> The Court is of the opinion that the facts establish that Mr. Isgitt, both as the Manager of the apartment complex, and as an individual, was acting to protect the premises and the interest of the other dwellers in the complex, as well as to defend his own person, and that while it appears, in retrospect, that he could have accomplished both purposes without inflicting such painful injuries on Mr. Byrd, under the pressures and heat of the occasion it cannot be found that he acted unreasonably.

Id. at 375. Does this mean that there is a right to "defend" an apartment complex from loud tenants? Is this another decision better understood as produced by Louisiana's now abandoned aggressor doctrine? Despite the court's approval of the quoted passage, its decision deemed to turn on a fact-intensive application of ordinary self-defense law. *See id.*, at 375-76. *Compare Smith v. Delery*, 238 La. 180, 114 So. 2d 857 (La. 1959) (general feeling of anxiety caused by numerous reports of prowlers in neighborhood justified shooting of newspaper boy who entered defendant's back yard to retrieve his escaped dog).

2.   *Defense of Hotel Guests.* In *Edwards v. Great Am. Ins. Co.*, 146 So. 2d 260 (La.App. 2 Cir. 1962), the Second Circuit recognized a privilege to use force in defense of a hotel, based on the innkeeper's duty to protect their guest. The court concluded:

> From a preponderance of the evidence, no conclusion could be reached other than that the youths were attempting to burglarize the tourist courts at the time one of them was shot. Under these circumstances, the defendants admit the shooting, but seek to avoid liability on the ground that the youths were prowlers or intruders with the intent to harm the guests of the tourist courts, if need be, in their attempt at burglary. In view of the surrounding facts and circumstances, notably apprehension and fear, brought about by the frequent appearances of prowlers and the actual commission of burglary in the immediate past, the conclusion is inescapable that Bullard acted as a reasonable and prudent man in the act taken to repel the invasion of the courts.

The general rule is that innkeepers or keepers of lodging houses or restaurants must protect their guests, while in their places of business, against injury by third persons, whether such third persons are guests or strangers, where it is within their power to do so. Such responsibility may be entrusted to employees or other subordinates. Although the keepers of inns, lodging houses, or restaurants are not the insurers of the safety of their guests, they are under an obligation to exercise, at least, ordinary or reasonable care to keep them from injury.

Id. at 262. As the court concluded that the defendant did not know the room being broken into was occupied, and as there was no evidence that the plaintiffs were imminent threats to harm anyone, is this result correct? Is this a defense of property case where the court justifies use of potentially deadly force? Does your opinion of the case change when you learn that the opinion describes the premises as "a motel for colored people," that all the parties are African American, and that the decision was issued in 1962?

3.   Defense of third parties might justify a bystander assisting in resistance to unlawful arrest. *State v. Lindsay*, 388 So. 2d 781 (La. 1980). *See also, Fontenot v. Fontenot*, 495 So. 2d 958 (La.App. 3 Cir. 1986); State ex rel. W. B., 461 So. 2d 366 (La.App. 2 Cir. 1984).

4.   The Restatement (Second) of Torts, Section 76 provides that:

The Actor is privileged to defend a third person from a harmful or offensive contact or invasion of his interests of personality under the same conditions and by the same means as those under and by which he is privileged to defend himself if the actor correctly or reasonably believes that

(a) the circumstances are such as to give third person a privilege of self-defense, and

(b) his intervention is necessary for the protection of the third person.

Section 77 provides:

An actor is privileged to use reasonable force, not intended or likely to cause death or serious bodily harm, to prevent or terminate another's intrusion upon the actor's land or chattels, if

(a) the intrusion is not privileged or the other intentionally or negligently causes the actor to believe that it is not privileged, and

(b) the actor reasonably believes that the intrusion can be prevented or terminated only by the force used, and

(c) the actor has first requested the other to desist and the other has disregarded the request, or the actor reasonably believes that a request will be useless or that substantial harm will be done before it can be made.

5.   Louisiana's defense of property law is similar to the Restatement; however, Louisiana's aggressor doctrine has arguably distorted the outcomes in cases involving defense of property. Consider how defense of property is analyzed in *Bray v. Isbell*, 458 So. 2d 594 (La.App. 3 Cir. 1985). Bray, his Mother and stepfather had their suit against the owner of the Sunset Motor Inn and its manager dismissed, an opinion from which they appealed and lost. Bray suffered injuries when he

broke into a vending machine on the premises of the Sunset Motor Inn and was shot by the manager's son. The Court's rendition of the facts seems to establish that Bray was armed with the tire tool he used to break into the vending machine and was running away to avoid apprehension by the motel staff when he was shot. Nevertheless, the court sustained the decision against them, seeming to invoke the aggressor doctrine:

> ... The law is well settled that a plaintiff cannot recover damages for a battery if he is at fault in provoking the difficulty in which he is injured. *Neville v. Johnson*, 398 So. 2d 111 (La.App. 3 Cir. 1981); *Levesque v. Saba*, 402 So. 2d 266 (La.App. 4 Cir. 1981); *Tripoli v. Gurry*, 253 La. 473, 218 So. 2d 563 (1969). However even where a person is the aggressor, the person retaliating may use only so much force as is reasonably necessary to repel the attack, and if he goes beyond this, he is liable for damages. *Neville, supra.* Where a person reasonably believes he is threatened with bodily harm, he may use whatever force appears reasonably necessary to protect against the threatened injury. *Byrd v. Isgitt*, 338 So. 2d 374 (La.App. 3 Cir. 1976); *Hesse v. Busby*, 379 So. 2d 25 (La.App. 3 Cir. 1979), *writ denied*, 381 So. 2d 1234 (1980). Each case is dependent on its own facts. *Roberts v. American Employers Ins. Co., Boston, Mass.*, 221 So. 2d 550 (La.App. 3 Cir. 1969).

However, this language is supplemented substantially by language suggesting the case involved self defense:

> Resort to dangerous weapons to repel an attack may be justifiable in cases when the fear of personal danger is genuine and founded on facts likely to produce similar emotions in reasonable men. *Neville, supra; Levesque, supra; McCullough v. McAnelly*, 248 So. 2d 7 (La.App. 1 Cir. 1971). It is only necessary that a person have grounds which lead a reasonable man to believe force is necessary, and that he actually so believes. Although all facts and circumstances must be taken into account to determine the reasonableness of his belief, detached reflection or a pause for consideration cannot be demanded under circumstances which require split second decisions. *Levesque, supra.*

If this characterization of the facts accurately reflects the record, is this a correct outcome in a "self defense" case?

6.   Where defendant detained suspected vandals at gunpoint, use of force was justified. *See Hesse v. Busby*, 379 So. 2d 25 (La.App. 3 Cir. 1979), *writ denied*, 381 So. 2d 1234 (La. 1980) .

7.   In the famous Iowa case, *Katko v. Briney*, 183 N.W. 2d 657 (Ia. 1971), the Iowa Supreme Court held on the following facts that excessive force had been used in defense of property. The following is an excerpt of the court's opinion:

> ... In 1957 defendant Bertha L. Briney inherited her parents' farm land in Mahaska and Monroe Counties. Included was an 80-acre tract in southwest Mahaska County where her grandparents and parents had lived. No one occupied the house thereafter. Her husband, Edward, attempted to care for the land. He kept no farm machinery thereon. The outbuildings became dilapidated.
>
> For about 10 years, 1957 to 1967, there occurred a series of trespassing and housebreaking events with loss of some household items, the breaking of windows and "messing up of the property in general." The latest occurred June 8, 1967, prior

to the event on July 16, 1967 herein involved.

Defendants through the years boarded up the windows and doors in an attempt to stop the intrusions. They had posted "no trespass" signs on the land several years before 1967. The nearest one was 35 feet from the house. On June 11, 1967 defendants set "a shotgun trap" in the north bedroom. After Mr. Briney cleaned and oiled his 20-gauge shotgun, the power of which he was well aware, defendants took it to the old house where they secured it to an iron bed with the barrel pointed at the bedroom door. It was rigged with wire from the doorknob to the gun's trigger so it would fire when the door was opened. Briney first pointed the gun so an intruder would be hit in the stomach but at Mrs. Briney's suggestion it was lowered to hit the legs. He admitted he did so "because I was mad and tired of being tormented" but "he did not intend to injure anyone". He gave no explanation of why he used a loaded shell and set it to hit a person already in the house. Tin was nailed over the bedroom window. The spring gun could not be seen from the outside. No warning of its presence was posted.

Plaintiff lived with his wife and worked regularly as a gasoline station attendant in Eddyville, seven miles from the old house. He had observed it for several years while hunting in the area and considered it as being abandoned. He knew it had long been uninhabited. In 1967 the area around the house was covered with high weeds. Prior to July 16, 1967 plaintiff and McDonough had been to the premises and found several old bottles and fruit jars which they took and added to their collection of antiques. On the latter date about 9:30 p.m. they made a second trip to the Briney property. They entered the old house by removing a board from a porch window which was without glass. While McDonough was looking around the kitchen area plaintiff went to another part of the house. As he started to open the north bedroom door the shotgun went off striking him in the right leg above the ankle bone. Much of his leg, including part of the tibia, was blown away. Only by McDonough's assistance was plaintiff able to get out of the house and after crawling some distance was put in his vehicle and rushed to a doctor and then to a hospital. He remained in the hospital 40 days.

[Testimony established the plaintiff suffered "permanent deformity, a loss of tissue, and a shortening of the leg." Plaintiff entered a plea of guilty to "larceny in the nighttime" and paid a fine of $50 and costs. He was paroled during good behavior from a 60-day jail sentence.]

The main thrust of defendants' defense in the trial court and on this appeal is that "the law permits use of a spring gun in a dwelling or warehouse for the purpose of preventing the unlawful entry of a burglar or thief". They repeated this contention in their exceptions to the trial court's instructions 2, 5 and 6. They took no exception to the trial court's statement of the issues or to other instructions.

In the statement of issues the trial court stated plaintiff and his companion committed a felony when they broke and entered defendants' house. In instruction 2 the court referred to the early case history of the use of spring guns and stated under the law their use was prohibited except to prevent the commission of felonies of violence and where human life is in danger. The instruction included a statement breaking and entering is not a felony of violence.

101

Instruction 5 stated: "You are hereby instructed that one may use reasonable force in the protection of his property, but such right is subject to the qualification that one may not use such means of force as will take human life or inflict great bodily injury. Such is the rule even though the injured party is a trespasser and is in violation of the law himself."

Instruction 6 stated: "An owner of premises is prohibited from willfully or intentionally injuring a trespasser by means of force that either takes life or inflicts great bodily injury; and therefore a person owning a premise is prohibited from setting out 'spring guns' and like dangerous devices which will likely take life or inflict great bodily injury, for the purpose of harming trespassers. The fact that the trespasser may be acting in violation of the law does not change the rule. The only time when such conduct of setting a 'spring gun' or a like dangerous device is justified would be when the trespasser was committing a felony of violence or a felony punishable by death, or where the trespasser was endangering human life by his act."

Instruction 7, to which defendants made no objection or exception stated: "To entitle the plaintiff to recover for compensatory damages, the burden of proof is upon him to establish by a preponderance of the evidence each and all of the following propositions:

"1. That defendants erected a shotgun trap in a vacant house on land owned by defendant, Bertha L. Briney, on or about June 11, 1967, which fact was known only by them, to protect household goods from trespassers and thieves.

"2. That the force used by defendants was in excess of that force reasonably necessary and which persons are entitled to use in the protection of their property.

"3. That plaintiff was injured and damaged and the amount thereof.

"4. That plaintiff's injuries and damages resulted directly from the discharge of the shotgun trap which was set and used by defendants."

The overwhelming weight of authority, both textbook and case law, supports the trial court's statement of the applicable principles of law.

Prosser on Torts, Third Edition, pages 116-118, states:

the law has always placed a higher value upon human safety than upon mere rights in property, it is the accepted rule that there is no privilege to use any force calculated to cause death or serious bodily injury to repel the threat to land or chattels, unless there is also such a threat to the defendant's personal safety as to justify self-defense. ... spring guns and other man-killing devices are not justifiable against a mere trespasser, or even a petty thief. They are privileged only against those upon whom the landowner, if he were present in person would be free to inflict injury of the same kind."

Restatement of Torts, section 85, page 180, states:

"The value of human life and limb, not only to the individual concerned but also to society, so outweighs the interest of a possessor of land in excluding from it those whom he is not willing to admit thereto that a possessor of land has, as is stated in § 79, no privilege to use force intended or likely to cause death or serious harm against another whom the possessor sees about to enter his premises or meddle with his chattel, unless the intrusion threatens death or serious bodily harm to the occupiers or users of the premises. ... A possessor of land cannot do indirectly and by a mechanical device that which, were he present, he could not do immediately and in person. Therefore, he cannot gain a privilege to install, for the purpose of protecting his land from intrusions harmless to the lives and limbs of the occupiers or users of it, a mechanical device whose only purpose is to inflict death or serious harm upon such as may intrude, by giving notice of his intention to inflict, by mechanical means and indirectly, harm which he could not, even after request, inflict directly were he present."

In Volume 2, Harper and James, The Law of Torts, section 27.3, pages 1440, 1441, this is found:

"The possessor of land may not arrange his premises intentionally so as to cause death or serious bodily harm to a trespasser. The possessor may of course take some steps to repel a trespass. If he is present he may use force to do so, but only that amount which is reasonably necessary to effect the repulse. Moreover if the trespass threatens harm to property only - even a theft of property - the possessor would not be privileged to use deadly force, he may not arrange his premises so that such force will be inflicted by mechanical means. If he does, he will be liable even to a thief who is injured by such device."

Similar statements are found in 38 Am.Jur., Negligence, section 114, pages 776, 777, and 65 C.J.S., Negligence, § 63(23), pages 678, 679; Anno. 44 A.L.R.2d 383, entitled "Trap to protect property."

* * * * *

In addition to civil liability many jurisdictions hold a land owner criminally liable for serious injuries or homicide caused by spring guns or other set devices. *See State v. Childers*, 133 Ohio St. 508, 14 N.E.2d 767 (melon thief shot by spring gun); *Pierce v. Commonwealth*, 135 Va. 635, 115 S.E. 686 (policeman killed by spring gun when he opened unlocked front door of defendant's shoe repair shop); *State v. Marfaudille*, 48 Wash. 117, 92 P. 939 (murder conviction for death from spring gun set in a trunk); *State v. Beckham*, 306 Mo. 566, 267 S.W. 817 (boy killed by spring gun attached to window of defendant's chili stand); *State v. Green*, 118 S.C. 279, 110 S.E. 145, 19 A.L.R. 1431 (intruder shot by spring gun when he broke and entered vacant house. Manslaughter conviction of owner -- affirmed); *State v. Barr*, 11 Wash. 481, 39 P. 1080 (murder conviction affirmed for death of an intruder into a boarded up cabin in which owner had set a spring gun).

In Wisconsin, Oregon and England the use of spring guns and similar devices is specifically made unlawful by statute. 44 A.L.R., section 3, pages 386, 388.

The legal principles stated by the trial court in instructions 2, 5 and 6 are well established and supported by the authorities cited and quoted supra. There is no merit in defendants' objections and exceptions thereto. Defendants' various motions based on the same reasons stated in exceptions to instructions were properly overruled.

* * * * *

Affirmed.

DISSENT: Larson, J.

I respectfully dissent, first, because the majority wrongfully assumes that by installing a spring gun in the bedroom of their unoccupied house the defendants intended to shoot any intruder who attempted to enter the room. Under the record presented here, that was a fact question. Unless it is held that these property owners are liable for any injury to an intruder from such a device regardless of the intent with which it is installed, liability under these pleadings must rest upon two definite issues of fact, i.e., did the defendants intend to shoot the invader, and if so, did they employ unnecessary and unreasonable force against him?

It is my feeling that the majority oversimplifies the impact of this case on the law, not only in this but other jurisdictions, and that it has not thought through all the ramifications of this holding.

There being no statutory provisions governing the right of an owner to defend his property by the use of a spring gun or other like device, or of a criminal invader to recover punitive damages when injured by such an instrumentality while breaking into the building of another, our interest and attention are directed to what should be the court determination of public policy in these matters. On both issues we are faced with a case of first impression. We should accept the task and clearly establish the law in this jurisdiction hereafter. I would hold there is no absolute liability for injury to a criminal intruder by setting up such a device on his property, and unless done with an intent to kill or seriously injure the intruder, I would absolve the owner from liability other than for negligence. I would also hold the court had no jurisdiction to allow punitive damages when the intruder was engaged in a serious criminal offense such as breaking and entering with intent to steal.

* * * * *

8.   Suppose plaintiff places razor wire atop the fence surrounding his home, yard and pool. Children from the neighborhood attempt to climb the fence to swim in the pool and are severely injured by the razor wire. Is the owner liable? Suppose the owner buys and trains a guard dog. Would he be liable? Notice that dogs are subject to special liability rules. *See* Chapter 10, Strict Liability, *infra*.

5.   True Privileges

Rather than recognizing traditionally accepted behavior, some privileges are created to promote public policy. These privileges literally privilege some behavior over others. Typically they license certain classes of actors to violate other's rights in specifically defined circumstances.

HARRELL
v.
DANIELS
499 So. 2d 482 (La.App. 2 Cir. 1986)

JONES, J.

This is an appeal of a judgment rejecting a claim for damages allegedly resulting from the corporal punishment of a nine year old student by a teacher. The plaintiff-appellant is Billy Joe Harrell, individually and as administrator of the estate of his minor son, William Edward Harrell. The defendants-appellees are the Bossier Parish School Board, Betty Daniels and her liability insurer, the Horace Mann Insurance Company.

We affirm.

Facts

On November 9, 1978, Betty Daniels was employed by the Bossier Parish School Board as a fourth grade teacher at Plantation Park Elementary School in Bossier City, Louisiana. William Edward Harrell, also known as Eddie Harrell, was a nine year old student in her class. At approximately 10:00 a.m. the teacher began having disciplinary problems with Eddie. The boy first slapped a female student in the face leaving a red mark upon her face. Ms. Daniels called Eddie to her desk, scolded him for his conduct and had him apologize. About ten minutes later Eddie began pulling on the hair and ears of another student. Ms. Daniels again called Eddie to her desk and warned him not to bother the student any more. Two or three minutes later Eddie slapped the student he had been warned not to molest. The teacher then called Eddie to her desk and informed him his behavior required he receive a paddling consisting of five licks. Another pupil was asked to retrieve a wooden paddle from another classroom and then the teacher escorted Eddie out into the hallway.

Betty Sue Vanderburg, a teacher in a nearby classroom, was asked to be a witness to the paddling. Ms. Daniels administered the corporal punishment and then she, Eddie and Ms. Vanderburg returned to their respective classrooms.

Eddie completed the school day without requiring further discipline and his mother, Dennie Harrell, picked him up after school and took him to a prior doctor's appointment for allergy treatment. Eddie mentioned to his mother that he had received a paddling earlier that day but he made no complaint to any school official or to the nurse who treated him at the doctor's office. Later that evening, while Eddie was preparing to take a bath and go to bed, he complained to his mother that his back hurt. His mother then removed his clothing and observed bruises on his buttocks and in an area near his left kidney. Eddie's parents then called the police who took pictures of the injured areas. The boy was then taken to the Schumpert Hospital emergency room where he was examined and released. The report described the two bluish-red bruises 2 1/2" by 3" in width, one bruise was located upon the left buttock and one bruise was located over the left flank.

Plaintiff contends Eddie soon began to manifest increased behavioral problems in the form of nightmares, altered personality and bed wetting. The boy never returned to Plantation Park Elementary School but entered a private school. He was treated by Dr. Paul Ware, a psychiatrist. Dr. Ware diagnosed Eddie's conduct as a very severe "separation anxiety" and had the boy admitted to Brentwood Hospital for one week. Dr. Ware further diagnosed the boy as suffering from "post traumatic stress disorder." Eddie was readmitted on February 27, 1979, due to increased aggressiveness toward his parents. The boy was discharged some three months later and he continued his treatment on an out-patient basis until September 15, 1983.

Eddie's father filed suit for damages and medical expenses on November 27, 1978, and the case was tried on September 25, 1985.

Eddie Harrell, age 16 at time of trial, testified that as his teacher was escorting him out into the hallway he grabbed the doorframe and asked that he not be punished. He related that Betty Daniels then pulled him from the doorway causing him to slip and fall face down a short distance away. Eddie also asserted that his teacher severely paddled him while he was in this prone position, with one blow being applied to his buttocks and six or seven blows to an area of his back near his kidneys. The boy testified teacher Betty Vanderburg, who was serving as a witness to the paddling, held his ankles to the hallway floor while Betty Daniels did the paddling. The boy concluded by relating his back was numb until later that evening when the real pain began and that no one else struck him that day. He did admit to receiving several earlier paddlings during the school year, one of which had been administered by Betty Daniels, but added that this instance was the only punishment which resulted in bruises.

Betty Daniels testified that on the date of Eddie's paddling she was 5'6" tall and weighed 135 lbs. and Eddie was about 4'5" tall and weighed about 100 lbs. She testified she administered the five blows strictly in accordance with school board policy which required using an approved wooden paddle approximately 2 1/2" wide in the presence of a witness, with the boy bent over holding his ankles while the blows were struck only on the buttocks. The policy required the filing of a written report with the principal of the school of the circumstances surrounding the paddling and Mrs. Daniels testified the report was filed. She related she was calm while the punishment was being imposed and did not use heavy force in applying the five licks as she had no desire to harm Eddie. Eddie bent over as required but stood upon receiving the first lick with the paddle. She also testified the boy stood up two other times interrupting the punishment until he could be coerced into assuming the proper position with his hands holding his ankles. After the paddling was complete Betty Daniels and Eddie returned to their classroom. Betty Daniels concluded by testifying she saw Eddie at recess and in the lunch room later in the day and he never complained to her about any type of pain.

Betty Vanderburg testified she witnessed the entire punishment and fully corroborated Betty Daniels' version of the events. Teacher Vanderburg denied that she held Eddie on the floor while the paddling was being imposed and stated that all licks were directed at his buttocks while he was standing in the required paddling posture. Another teacher, Joann Sheene, testified she had in the past witnessed a number of paddlings and that she was walking through the hallway while the punishment was being administered to Eddie and noticed nothing unusual or out of the ordinary about the way the paddling was being conducted. She related that if Eddie had been receiving his paddling while lying face down with someone holding his ankles she would have noticed such an unusual occurrence. Donna Rice, a third grade school teacher, testified she was teaching her class approximately fifteen feet from where Eddie was being punished and heard Betty Daniels tell Eddie to bend over. She also heard one lick being applied and the teacher restating her request to Eddie after this first blow. Donna Rice also related that it was not unusual to be able to hear conversations and paddlings from her classroom due to the quietness in the hallway. Betty Sue Woodall-Toms, the principal of Plantation Park Elementary School at the time of the incident, testified by deposition that Eddie had a history of behavioral problems dating back to the first grade and that she had investigated the incident and was satisfied that the punishment had been administered properly. The fact Eddie had a behavior problem is reflected in the following quote from plaintiff's brief:

"The parents of Eddie Harrell do not in any way dispute the fact that Eddie did have a behavior problem prior to this incident. There is overwhelming evidence that this child did misbehave at school and was frequently punished for that misbehavior. Thus, we do not contend that Eddie was a perfect angel prior to this incident ..."

The severity of this problem is reflected in the following quote from the defendant's brief which we find fully supported by the evidence in the record:

"Eddie's behavior at school from kindergarten until the time of the paddling can only be described as disruptive, aggressive, bizarre and pathological."

The court, in excellent written reasons, found the testimony of the teachers was more credible than that of Eddie Harrell and that the evidence did not establish the paddling was unreasonable or contributed to the boy's subsequent behavioral problems. The court acknowledged the photos showed some bruising upon the buttock and above it. The court expressed the opinion that any bruising on the boy in areas other than the buttock was caused by the boy's movements during the paddling rather than the teacher applying the licks in the wrong place.

The plaintiffs' assignment of error presents the following issues for decision: Did the trial court err in ruling that the corporal punishment was not administered in an excessive and unreasonable manner?

Law On Corporal Punishment of Students

Corporal punishment of students is permissible if reasonable in degree and administered by a teacher or school principal for disciplinary reasons. *Guillory v. Ortego*, 449 So. 2d 182 (La.App. 3 Cir. 1984); LSA-R.S. 17:223.[1] The implementation of corporal punishment is to be accomplished in accordance with rules adopted by the parish or city school board. LSA-R.S. 17:416.1.[2] Factors to be considered in determining whether a teacher's corporal punishment was reasonable are age and physical condition of student, seriousness of misconduct soliciting punishment, nature and severity of punishment, attitude and past behavior of pupil and availability of less severe but equally effective means of discipline. *LeBoyd v. Jenkins*, 381 So. 2d 1290 (La.App. 4 Cir. 1980), *writ den.*, 386 So. 2d 341 (La. 1980). A trial court's credibility evaluations in face of conflicting testimony is the province of the finder of fact and an appellate court may not reverse such findings in the absence of manifest error. *Canter v. Koehring Co.*, 283 So. 2d 716 (La. 1973). The trial court is not bound by expert testimony which is to be weighed by the court as any other evidence. *Hickman v. Hickman*, 459 So. 2d 140 (La.App. 2 Cir. 1984).

---

[1] § 223. Discipline of pupils; suspension from school:
Every teacher is authorized to hold every pupil to a strict accountability for any disorderly conduct in school or on the playground of the school, or on any school bus going to or returning from school, or during intermission or recess. *Any teacher or school principal may use corporal punishment in a reasonable manner against any pupil for good cause in order to maintain discipline and order within the public schools, subject to the provisions of R.S. 17:416.1* ... [emphasis added by court]

[2] § 416.1. Discipline of pupils; additional disciplinary authority:
A. In addition to the specific disciplinary measures authorized in R.S. 17:416 teachers, principals, and administrators of the public schools may, *subject to any rules as may be adopted by the parish or city school board, employ other reasonable disciplinary and corrective measures to maintain order in the schools;* ... [emphasis added by court]

The plaintiffs do not question the need to punish the student, or the size of the wooden paddle or the number of licks actually imposed. They do not challenge the use of corporal punishment itself or the procedures for its implementation approved by the Bossier Parish School Board and referred to by the parties but not offered into evidence. They do assert that evidence of a 2 1/2"-3" wide bruise over the boy's left kidney area is unreasonable in and of itself, as it violates the school board's own procedure of not allowing any blow above the buttocks, and that the severity of the bruises shows that the force used was excessive.

Betty Daniels testified she administered the punishment in accordance with the rules adopted by the Bossier Parish School Board. All parties agree to the substance of these rules although not offered into evidence. She further related that the blows themselves were not severe in force. This testimony was corroborated by the teacher-witness, Betty Sue Vanderburg, and by another teacher, Joann Sheene, who happened to observe the punishment as it was being administered. One other teacher also related that she heard Betty Daniels give several directions to Eddie Harrell to bend over and heard at least one lick being applied between these directions. The record also reveals that Eddie Harrell himself admitted having received several prior paddlings since the beginning of school year, one of which was given by Betty Daniels, with none resulting in bruising.

We conclude the trial court was not clearly wrong in ruling that the punishment was not conducted in an unreasonable or excessive manner and the resulting physical injuries and behavioral problems were not caused by the manner in which corporal punishment was administered. The physical characteristics of Betty Daniels and Eddie Harrell, Eddie's prior history of paddlings and behavioral problems, the testimony of witnesses to the punishment showing that it was conducted in an ordinary manner without severe force being employed and testimony showing that Eddie himself voiced no real complaint of pain to anyone until much later that evening just before bed time are circumstances which compel the conclusion that the trial court was well within its discretion in choosing to disbelieve Eddie Harrell's version of the events surrounding his corporal punishment. There is substantial evidence in the record to support the conclusion of the trial court that the paddling was imposed in accordance with regulation and that any bruises found in non-buttocks area were not caused by Betty Daniels' direction of the licks toward the boy. There is testimony from the principal of the school and other teachers who knew Eddie well that he had been a very difficult disciplinary problem in the school from his first year at the school which he had attended since his kindergarten year. This testimony supports the trial judge's conclusion that Eddie needed psychological help, the expense of which forms a substantial part of this damage suit, long before he received the paddling upon which this suit is based. Dr. Ware testified that before the paddling the child was suffering from a "behavior disorder of children." Dr. Ware testified the child's condition was aggravated by the paddling. The trial judge considered all the testimony of the principal and teachers as evidencing severe emotional problems Eddie had been experiencing for many years and rejected Dr. Ware's testimony that the paddling aggravated the boy's condition. We do not find this factual determination to be clearly wrong. The evidence fully mandates the conclusion the paddling was reasonable in degree and rendered for disciplinary reasons and imposed in accordance with the rules of the Bossier Parish School Board.

Judgment **AFFIRMED** at appellant's cost.

NOTES

1. After *Harrell*, the legislature amended R.S. 17:416.1, *see* Acts 1997, No. 619, § 1, to expand its application to suits against teachers, principals, and administrators. Additionally, Act 401 of 1997 broadly immunized school officials from suit. R.S. 17:416.11:

A. No teacher, principal, or administrator in a public school system or in an approved nonpublic school shall be personally liable for any act or failure to act in the directing of or disciplining of school children under his care and supervision, unless such act or failure to act was malicious and willfully and deliberately intended to cause bodily harm.

B. This Section shall not be applicable to the operation, use, or maintenance of any motor vehicle.

2.   School officials have an obligation to hold students accountable for their behavior, with the consequent privilege to discipline students. R.S. 17:416:

A. (1) (a) Every teacher and other school employee shall endeavor to hold every student to a strict accountability for any disorderly conduct in school or on the playgrounds of the school, on the street or road while going to or returning from school, on any school bus, during intermission or recess, or at any school-sponsored activity or function.

B. (i) Each teacher may take disciplinary action to correct a student who disrupts normal classroom activities, who is disrespectful to a teacher, who willfully disobeys a teacher, who uses abusive or foul language directed at a teacher or another student, who engages in bullying, who violates school rules, or who interferes with an orderly education process.

* * * * *

Section 416 is a detailed statute, setting out the bases and procedures for school discipline. It also prohibits discipline of students whose disruptive behavior is considered self-defense, R.S. 17:416H(1). This provision does not apply to a student who is "the aggressor," R.S. 17:416H(2), presumably preserving the relevance of the "aggressor doctrine" after *Landry, supra.*

3.   Discipline by parents is also a basis for the defense of privilege. Parents are immune from tort suits by a child during the child's minority. La. R.S. 9:571. Because the suit may be pursued after the child reaches majority, parents must resort to the defense of discipline to avoid liability. The parent's defense of discipline is not overt, however, residing apparently in Civil Code articles:

C.C. Art. 228. A child shall obey his parents in all matters not contrary to law or good morals. Parents have the right and obligation to correct and discipline the child in a reasonable manner.

C.C. Art. 232. Either parent during the marriage has parental authority over his child unless otherwise provided by law.

C.C. Art. 236. A child regardless of age owes honor and respect to his father and mother.

This defense apparently was extended to adult children in *Landry v. Himel*, 176 So. 627 (La.App. 1 Cir. 1937). There the court relied on the duty to respect one's parents, noting that such duty is greater than the parent's duty to respect one's children. Given the court's focus on the child's abusive language, which the court said constituted fighting words, it is unclear whether this holding survives the demise of Louisiana's aggressor doctrine. *See Landry v. Bellanger, supra.*

b. Shopkeeper's privilege and privilege to arrest

La. Code Cr. Proc. Article 215 provides:

A.   (1) A peace officer, merchant, or a specifically authorized employee or agent of a merchant, may use reasonable force to detain a person for questioning on the merchant's premises, for a length of time, not to exceed sixty minutes, unless it is reasonable under the circumstances that the person be detained longer, when he has reasonable cause to believe that the person has committed a theft of goods held for sale by the merchant, regardless of the actual value of the goods. The merchant or his employee or agent may also detain such a person for arrest by a peace officer. The detention shall not constitute an arrest.

(2) A peace officer may, without a warrant, arrest a person when he has reasonable grounds to believe the person has committed a theft of goods held for sale by a merchant, regardless of the actual value of the goods. A complaint made to a peace officer by a merchant or a merchant's employee or agent shall constitute reasonable cause for the officer making the arrest.

B.   If a merchant utilizes electronic devices which are designed to detect the unauthorized removal of marked merchandise form the store, and if sufficient notice has been posted to advise the patrons that such a device is being utilized, a signal from the device to the merchant or his employee or agent indicating the removal of a specially marked merchandise shall constitute a sufficient basis for reasonable cause to detain the person.

C.   As used in this Article, "reasonable under the circumstances" shall be construed in such a manner so as to include the value of the merchandise in question, the location of the store, the length of time taken for law enforcement personnel to respond, the cooperation of the person detained, and any other relevant circumstances to be considered with respect to the length of time a person is detained.

DEROUEN

v.

MILLER

614 So. 2d 1304 (La.App. 3 Cir. 1993)

THIBODEAUX, J.

Defendants, Winn Dixie Louisiana, Inc. and its employee, William Miller, appeal the trial court's decision awarding damages to the plaintiff, Sheila Lane Derouen, in the amount of $10,000.00 for an illegal detention or false imprisonment in a Winn Dixie store. Defendants raise the following two assignments of error on appeal:

(1) The trial court misinterpreted the 1983 amendment to La.C.Cr.P. art. 215 by requiring that the detention of plaintiff must be followed by reasonable questioning.

(2) The trial court awarded excessive damages to Derouen.

For the following reasons, we affirm.

Facts

On September 29, 1989, Derouen was shopping at a Winn Dixie grocery store managed by

Miller in New Iberia. Among the items selected for purchase by Derouen was a two (2) pound package of fresh shrimp which she obtained from the seafood department. The shrimp was packaged in a white bag which had a light colored design on it. Another Winn Dixie employee, Raymond Gaudet, observed Derouen being served in the seafood department. Gaudet also observed Derouen place something in her purse.

Derouen subsequently proceeded to the check-out counter. She testified that the bag of shrimp was placed in the child seat compartment of the grocery cart. Derouen stated that she removed her checkbook from her purse, which was also in the child seat compartment, to begin writing out a check for her groceries, but then remembered that she needed to purchase coke. Miller testified that after Gaudet told him what he observed, he watched Derouen as she entered the check-out line and did not see any seafood items in her basket. Derouen failed, according to Miller, to promptly return to the check-out aisle and proceeded to walk up and down several aisles until he finally confronted her in aisle seven. Derouen testified that Miller confronted her shortly after she removed the coke and bag of shrimp from the child seat compartment and placed them in the bottom of the basket. Derouen claims that she attempted to put the 2 liter coke bottle in the child seat, but that it would not stand up with the bag of shrimp and her purse already there. Miller then questioned Derouen about the shrimp by falsely claiming that he saw her take the 2-pound bag of shrimp out of her purse through a surveillance mirror. Derouen denied the allegation. Miller then asked Derouen to go to the back of the store with him. Miller asked Gaudet and another employee, Jackie, to stay in the back with Derouen while he called the police. Derouen stayed in the back of the store in the produce department for about 15 minutes before the police arrived.

Derouen was escorted by a New Iberia police officer through the front of the store and, upon reaching the outside, was put into the rear of the police vehicle. Subsequently, Derouen was taken to the police station and booked. After her mother posted a $500.00 bond, Derouen was released.

The local newspaper, The Daily Iberian, printed an item announcing the arrest of Derouen for shoplifting. Many people in her town, including friends and relatives, saw the newspaper article and questioned Derouen about the incident. Derouen testified that she was humiliated and embarrassed. Derouen, her husband, Bobby, and her friend and sometime employer, Prudence Catsulis, all testified that after the incident Derouen became emotional and cried easily. Further, Derouen and her husband testified as to her inability to sleep, her elevated blood pressure, her nail biting, development of rashes, and her change in shopping habits subsequent to the incident.

As a result of her arrest, Derouen had to defend herself in a criminal trial where she was eventually found not guilty.

The trial judge ruled in favor of Derouen, finding that Winn Dixie acted unreasonably in failing to question Derouen about the bag of shrimp before calling the police. The trial judge stated that there "may have been reasonable cause to detain but that reasonable cause could cease to exist and that the actions of the merchant may impose liability, when reasonable questioning of the suspected shoplifter is not conducted." Moreover, "[t]he limitation of liability came to an end when the merchant failed to follow the detention with reasonable questioning."

Reasonableness of the Detention

Winn Dixie argues that it should have been exempt from liability under La.C.Cr.P. art. 215 which authorizes a merchant to detain and question a person suspected of shoplifting as well as for arrest by a peace officer. The thrust of Winn Dixie's argument is that the first two sentences of LSA-C.Cr.P. art. 215(A)(1) present an either/or situation. Winn Dixie asserts that a merchant may detain a person for questioning whom they have reasonable cause to believe has shoplifted or a merchant may detain that same person for arrest by a peace officer without questioning. Counsel for Winn Dixie asserted during oral argument that a merchant is under no obligation to do any affirmative act such as questioning before detaining one for arrest. We do not agree....

LSA-C.C. art. 2315 has been interpreted to provide a cause of action in favor of those whose liberty has been interfered with in an unwarranted manner.... False imprisonment occurs when one is restrained against his or her will by another who acts without statutory authority. *Id.*

Indisputably, Derouen was detained by Miller who failed to question her about or investigate the shoplifting incident. In order for Winn Dixie to escape liability, it must prove that Derouen was detained in compliance with LSA-C.Cr.P. art. 215....

* * * * *

Winn Dixie contends that Miller had the statutory authority to detain Derouen without questioning pursuant to the second sentence of subsection (A)(1). Derouen asserts that the phrase, "such a person," in the second sentence of LSA-C.Cr.P. art. 215(A)(1) is significant. She asserts that the only possible meaning of the phrase "such a person" which would not do violence to the basic rights of individuals is that it refers to someone who has actually committed a theft of the merchant's goods. Thus, the thrust of Derouen's argument is that the statute does not give Miller authority to detain a suspected shoplifter for arrest without questioning or investigating the incident unless it is known by the merchant that the person has actually committed a theft. When Miller failed to question her before calling the police as required by the statute, he was no longer immune from civil liability due to wrongful detention. The trial court held Winn Dixie liable because Miller failed to follow the detention with reasonable questioning.

The relevancy of Article 215, above, is best explained in the Official Revision Comment (e) thereto which states:

> ".... If the detention is authorized under the first paragraph, immunity from both criminal and civil liability will naturally follow. If the peace officer, merchant, or employee does not comply with the terms of the first paragraph, the detention will not be authorized and there should be no immunity."

We agree with the trial judge. A literal reading of the statute is mandated by LSA-C.C. art. 9, i.e., when the law is clear and unambiguous and its application does not lead to absurd consequences, the law shall be applied as written and no further interpretation may be made in search of the intent of the legislature. The statute clearly bestows upon the merchant the power to detain a suspected shoplifter for arrest. However, in our view, the first and second sentences are inextricably linked in the *same* paragraph. Thus, "such a person" in the second sentence refers to a "person detained for questioning." If the legislature had intended to give merchants a choice of remedies upon suspecting a person of shoplifting, it would have written the second sentence in a separate paragraph or inserted the disjunctive "or."

The purpose of C.Cr.P. art. 215 is to provide merchants with authority to detain and question persons suspected of shoplifting without subjecting them to suits by those detained persons on the basis of false imprisonment when the merchant has reasonable cause to believe a theft of goods has occurred. The amendment protects merchants who have conducted a reasonable post-detention inquiry and held the person for arrest, when that person is subsequently found not guilty or when the shoplifting charge is dismissed. The trial court was correct in applying pre-1983 jurisprudence to the present case to determine the reasonableness of Miller's actions. Thus, the trial court did not err by requiring that Miller's detention of Derouen, based upon reasonable cause, be followed by reasonable questioning. If questioning and reasonable investigation is performed and probable cause is established, then a merchant may hold a detained person for arrest by a police officer.

* * * * *

Conclusion

Our review of the record and the reasons for judgment from the trial court convinces us that the trial court committed no error in interpreting LSA- C.Cr.P. art 215(A)(1) to require questioning of Derouen before detaining her for arrest by the police officer. Furthermore, the trial court committed no error in accepting, rejecting or in weighing the testimony as to Derouen's mental anguish and the $10,000.00 damage award was within the trial court's discretionary range. Accordingly, for the foregoing reasons, the judgment of the district court in favor of the plaintiff, Derouen, is affirmed. Costs of this appeal are assessed against the appellant.

AFFIRMED.

THOMAS
v.
SCHWEGMANN GIANT SUPERMARKET, INC.
561 So. 2d 992 (La.App. 4 Cir. 1990)

PLOTKIN, J.

* * * * *

Facts

The trial court adopted Thomas' version of the incident, although the characterization of the events differ. The two versions are particularly inconsistent concerning whether Thomas opened merchandise, removed the contents from a package of "Stick On Crazy Nails," and whether she injured her arm.

Thomas, 57, testified that she was shopping at Schwegmann on July 22, 1986 at approximately 7 p.m. She was accompanied by her two grandchildren. While shopping, Thomas said that she stopped to examine an open box of "Stick On Crazy Nails" for approximately five minutes. She put the box down, finished her shopping, and paid for her groceries. As she was about to leave, she stopped to allow her grandchildren to get balloons from a clown in the front of the store. As she waited for her grandchildren, she was approached by Albert Roger, a security guard, who asked her to come with him; she and the children complied. Roger took them to a private room where another male guard, Richard Jackson Jr., was present. Thomas was questioned about the Crazy Nails; specifically, she was asked whether she stole glue contained in the kit. Thomas testified that she became nervous and upset and denied stealing glue or anything else from the kit. Roger sent for a female employee to search Thomas. At this point, Thomas voluntarily displayed the contents of her purse, emptied her pockets, and opened her blouse to prove that she had not taken the glue. She admits that she became hysterical at this point because of the theft accusation.

Thomas testified that the guards called her "dumb" and cursed, threw her driver's license on the floor, and tried to force her to sign a confession form, but she refused. She expressed a desire to leave, along with outrage for being placed under arrest. Roger explained that she was not under arrest; however, Thomas claims that Jackson blocked the doorway so that she could not exit. Thomas testified that she walked to the door and opened it and that Jackson jerked the door closed, while her hand was on the knob, causing her serious aggravation of a pre-existing injury. Thomas was then brought to the cashier in the front of the store and forced to pay for the Crazy Nails. Upon leaving the room, Thomas encountered family acquaintances, who later drove her home because she was upset and shaking. The incident lasted 15 to 20 minutes.

The Schwegmann security guard, Roger, testified that he personally observed Thomas pick up the package of "Stick On Crazy Nails," place it in her basket, walk to another aisle, open the box of merchandise, remove the nails and try them on. Afterwards, he reportedly saw her deposit the nails on different store shelves and leave the partially empty box on another shelf. Roger then retrieved the nails and opened box. He claims that he believed that the artificial nail kit contained glue, necessary for application of the nails, which he was unable to locate on the shelves or in the box. He therefore approached Thomas, identified himself and requested that she accompany him to a private office for the purpose of paying for the merchandise.

Roger admitted that he did not closely examine the box prior to detaining Thomas. As a result, he was incorrect in his assumption that glue was a part of the contents. However, it is undisputed that his purpose in stopping Thomas was to determine whether she had stolen the glue and that he intended to request that she pay for the nails.

Both security guards maintain that Thomas was abusive and uncooperative and that for no reason, she became hysterical, threw the contents of her purse on the floor, and opened her blouse. Furthermore, they claim that Thomas' arm was not re-injured. They claim that Jackson stood with his back to the door throughout the incident and that the door was never opened until Thomas left the room to pay for the merchandise.

The trial court found that the immunity provided to store owners and operators under La. C.Cr.P. art. 215 did not apply.... On appeal, Schwegmann claims that the trial court erred in the following ways:

> (1) Finding that the detainment was not based on the reasonable belief that Mrs. Thomas had committed theft, which is protected by La. C.Cr.P. art 215,
> [three other grounds omitted]

Is Schwegmann Immune from Liability for the Detention?

Schwegmann claims civil immunity for the 15 to 20 minute detention, based on La. C.Cr.P. art. 215, which permits a merchant, or a specifically authorized employee to "use reasonable force to detain for questioning ... not to exceed 60 minutes ... when he has *reasonable cause* to believe that the person has committed a *theft of goods*."[footnote omitted] (Emphasis added.)

In passing La. C.Cr.P. art. 215, the legislature delegated quasi-police powers to a peace officer, merchant, or a specifically authorized employee or agent of a merchant to combat shoplifting. Private persons ordinarily have no authority to arrest for petty theft, which is only a misdemeanor.[2] La. C.Cr.P. art. 215 grants civil and criminal immunity from liability for malicious prosecution when

---

[2] *See* La. C.Cr.P. art. 214, which gives private persons the authority to arrest only when the person arrested has committed a felony.

the detainor has reasonable cause to believe that a theft of goods, a separate crime defined by LSA-R.S. 14:67.10,[3] has occurred. Because criminal statutes are strictly construed, LSA-R.S. 14:3, the immunity granted by La. C.Cr.P. art. 215 applies only when a person is detained on suspicion of committing a theft of goods.

The determination of whether the detention is immunized also depends upon whether "reasonable cause" exists to believe that the suspect committed a theft of goods. "Reasonable cause" is defined as "something less than probable cause; it requires that the detaining officer have articulable knowledge of particular facts sufficiently reasonable to suspect the detained person of criminal activity." *State v. Hudgins*, 400 So. 2d 889, 891 (La. 1981). The reason the legislature chose this high standard was that it does not want a citizen to be legally detained and questioned by a non-police official unless the detainor knows of facts and circumstances which warrant prudent and reasonable men to believe that a theft of goods was committed.

In order for plaintiff to recover from a merchant for the tort of false imprisonment, she must prove that a detention occurred under one or more of the following circumstances: (1) unreasonable force was used, (2) no reasonable cause to believe that that the suspect had committed a theft of goods existed, or (3) the detention lasted more than 60 minutes, unless it was reasonable under the circumstances that the suspect be detained longer.

Thomas testified that she picked up the open package of nails, examined it for five minutes, and returned it to the shelf. Roger stated that she removed the box from the shelf, placed it in her basket, walked away and opened the box. Thereafter, she placed the nails on various shelves and then deposited the box on another shelf. Roger said that he retrieved the box before he approached Thomas. The Crazy Nails package has a section marked "contains ...," followed by a list of the package contents. Glue is clearly not listed as one of the contents. Furthermore, the labeling on the package face clearly indicates in three prominent locations that the nails are applied with "stick-on" tape, not glue. Jackson, the second security guard involved in the incident, admitted at trial that he knew that no glue came with the Crazy Nails kit. Rogers could quite easily have examined the kit in his possession to determine that glue was not included in the box before he detained Thomas and accused her of stealing glue.

We conclude that Roger, a trained security guard for thirteen years at Schwegmann and a former member of the New Orleans Police Department, should have inspected or examined the Crazy Nails box in his possession before he detained, questioned, and accused Thomas of stealing the glue. He had sufficient time and opportunity to reasonably investigate the facts. Thomas made no effort to leave the premises. Roger knew or should have known that Thomas did not steal glue from the kit. We hold that Schwegmann did not have reasonable cause to detain Thomas and that the civil immunity

---

[3] La. R.S. 14:67.10 defines theft of goods as follows:

A. Theft of goods is the misappropriation or taking of anything of value which is held for sale by a merchant, either without the consent of the merchant to the misappropriation or taking, or by means of fraudulent conduct, practices, or representations. An intent to deprive the merchant permanently of whatever may be the subject of the misappropriation or taking is essential and may be inferred when a person:

(1) Intentionally conceals, on his person or otherwise, goods held for sale;
(2) Alters or transfers any price marking reflecting the actual retail price of the goods;
(3) Transfers goods from one container or package to another or places goods in any container, package, or wrapping in a manner to avoid detection;
(4) Willfully causes the cash register or other sales recording device to reflect less than the actual retail price of the goods;
(5) Removes any price marking with the intent to deceive the merchant as to the actual retail price of the goods.

from liability provided by La. C.Cr.P. art. 215 is not applicable.

Schwegmann argues that La. C.Cr.P. art. 215 provides immunity for its detention of Thomas despite the fact that Roger knew or should have known that Thomas did not steal the glue because Roger had reasonable cause to believe that Thomas had damaged merchandise. Schwegmann argues that the La. C.Cr.P. art. 215 also provides immunity from civil liability for false imprisonment when a shopper is detained and questioned on the suspicion that he damaged merchandise or opened sealed boxes and packages. The evidence indicates that one of the reasons for detaining Thomas was Roger's belief that she opened the Crazy Nails kit, thereby destroying its retail value. Schwegmann's answer to the lawsuit and Jackson's testimony indicate that he believed that Thomas had damaged merchandise and that that was the sole reason for her detention.

However, La. C.Cr.P. art. 215 refers only to the theft of goods, a crime which has been specifically defined by the legislature in LSA-R.S. 13:67.10. Theft of goods requires an intent to deprive the merchant permanently of whatever may be the subject of the misappropriation, which intent may be inferred from five explicit types of misconduct. This criminal statute unequivocally does not include damage to merchandise. We decline to extend immunity to a merchant for detention of a customer who has only damaged merchandise. We hold that Schwegmann did not have the legal authority to detain and question Thomas for damage to merchandise.

The evidence is undisputed that Thomas was physically detained. She was escorted by two male security guards, one who identified himself and led her to a small room. She was questioned and was not permitted to leave when she wanted to because Mr. Jackson blocked the door. The time element is not an issue here. Because Schwegmann failed to prove the existence of any of the circumstances which give rise to immunity under La. C.Cr.P. art. 215, we affirm the trial court's finding that Thomas was falsely detained and/or falsely imprisoned and that Schwegmann is not entitled to immunity for the detention.

* * * * *

NOTES

1.   Article 215 authorizes detention, not arrest. If a merchant seeks to benefit from the privilege to arrest, she must rely on the privilege for private citizens to effect an arrest without a warrant. Code of Criminal Procedure, Article 214, grants such authority but only for felonies: "A private person may make an arrest when the person arrested has committed a felony, whether in or out of his presence."

"A citizen may arrest on reasonable suspicion of a felony. But in such case he must not only make out a reasonable ground of suspicion, but he must prove that a felony has actually been committed. Whereas, an officer who has reasonable grounds to suspect that a felony has been committed may detain the party until inquiry may be made. Damages will not be allowed where the prosecuting officer acted in good faith and with probable cause." *Dunson v. Baker*, 144 La. 167, 172 (La. 1919).

A peace officer's grounds for arrest are more extensive. According to La. Code of Criminal Procedure, art. 213:

A peace officer may, without a warrant, arrest a person when:

(1) The person to be arrested has committed an offense in his presence; and if the arrest is for a misdemeanor, it must be made immediately or in close pursuit;

116

(2) The person to be arrested has committed a felony, although not in the presence of an officer;

(3) The peace officer has reasonable cause to believe that the person to be arrested has committed an offense, although not in the presence of the officer; or

(4) The peace officer has received positive and reliable information that another peace officer from this state holds an arrest warrant, or a peace officer of another state or the United States holds an arrest warrant for a felony offense.

A peace officer who is in close pursuit of a person to be arrested, who is making an arrest pursuant to this Article, may enter another jurisdiction in this state and make the arrest.

The circumstances for making a warrantless arrest was described in *State of Louisiana v. Phillips*, 247 So. 2d 206, 209 (La. 1977):

We have repeatedly held that a warrantless arrest must be based on the arresting officer's reasonable belief that the person to be arrested has committed or is committing an offense. Probable cause and not absolute certainty that a crime is being or has been committed is the test to be applied in judging the validity of an arrest. Probable cause exists when the facts and circumstances within the arresting officers' knowledge and as to which they have reasonably trustworthy information are sufficient to warrant a prudent man in believing that the person to be arrested has committed or is committing an offense. While the officers need not be able to negate all possible lawful explanation of a situation before making an arrest, they must have within their knowledge information upon which to reasonably base a belief that the person to be arrested is criminally connected with the circumstances. (Citations omitted)

Peace officers making an arrest supported by a warrant, valid on its face generally will not be liable for false arrest. *See* La. Code Criminal Procedure, art. 204; *Conqus v. Fuselier*, 327 So. 2d 180 (La.App. 3 Cir. 1976).

2.   Detention must be reasonable. As Article 215C reflects, the reasonableness of the detention is a fact determination. Does the statutory language suggest that an attempt to steal expensive farm equipment, in a place quite remote from the nearest police station, and where the merchant believes the suspect might try to escape, might justify tying the person to heavy equipment and leaving him in the sun for a couple of hours? Might it justify confining a person to a small room for longer then an hour if the police are late in arriving? Consider the following. Detention unreasonable: *Brasher v. Gibson's Prods. Co.*, 306 So. 2d 842 (La.App. 2 Cir. 1975) (security guard searched plaintiff for weapons, photographed him, and induced him to sign confession and waiver of right to sue merchant); *Wilde v. Schwegmann Bros. Giant Supermarkets, Inc.*, 160 So. 2d 839 (La.App. 4 Cir. 1964) (plaintiff confined in small room for thirty minutes until she signed confession). Detention reasonable: *Wilson v. Wal-Mart Stores, Inc.*, 574 So. 2d 502 (La.App. 3 Cir. 1991) (two women required, without force, to lift skirts and shirts and lower pantyhose and undergarments in front of two women employees).

Cases conflict on whether detainees must be questioned during detention. *See Brown v. Hartford Ins. Co.*, 370 So. 2d 179 (La.App. 3 Cir. 1979) (plaintiff not allowed to provide explanation of her behavior); *DeRouen v. Miller*, 614 So. 2d 1304 (La.App. 3 Cir. 1993) (detention must be followed by reasonable questioning).

c. Spousal Immunity

In Louisiana, spouses who are not judicially separated or divorced are immune from tort suits against each other, and the parent with custody of a child is immune from tort suit by the child until the child reaches majority or is emancipated. When the marriage ends the spouses may sue each other for tortious conduct occurring during the marriage. The immunity is most frequently applicable in negligence actions, and is discussed in Chapter 7. Application in an intentional tort case is possible, however. Refer to R.S. 9:291 in Chapter 7, and then read the *Duplechin* case below.

d. Parent-Child Immunity

The statutory immunity of parents is set forth in R.S. 9:571, which provides that a child who is not emancipated cannot sue 1) either parent as long as they are married and not judicially separated, or 2) the custodial parent when the marriage is dissolved or the parents are judicially separated. When the immunity no longer applies, children can sue parents for torts that occurred during the period of the immunity. In other words, the parent-child immunity is a procedural bar to a lawsuit by a child, but it does not destroy the cause of action. *See Walker v. Milton*, 268 So. 2d 654 (La. 1972). The prescriptive period begins to run generally when the immunity no longer applies to bar the action. The immunity runs only one way; parents can sue their children.

DUPLECHIN

v.

TOCE

497 So. 2d 763 (La.App. 3 Cir. 1987)

DOUCET, J.

This appeal arises from a personal injury action by a woman against her ex-husband for damages resulting from injuries inflicted during the marriage.

On August 16, 1980, an altercation occurred in the home of the parties which resulted in the hospitalization of the plaintiff for a period of 25 days.

The plaintiff first filed a petition for damages resulting from that incident on August 13, 1981. The defendant filed an Exception of No Right of Action to that suit, citing interspousal immunity as outlined in La. R.S. 9:291. The trial court granted that exception. On December 15, 1981, plaintiff was granted a divorce from the defendant. On January 5, 1982, plaintiff again filed a petition for damages resulting from the altercation of August 16, 1980. Defendant filed Exceptions of Prescription Res Judicata, No Cause, and No Right of Action, each of which was overruled in turn.

After a trial on the merits, a judgment was rendered in favor of the plaintiff and against the defendant in the amount of $12,000.00 for past and future medical expenses, and $40,000.00 in general damages, as well as for all costs of court.

The defendant's motion for new trial was denied. The defendant then filed this appeal from the trial court's ruling on the Exceptions of No Cause and No Right of Action, as well as from the judgment of the trial court on the merits.

Exceptions of No Cause And/or Right of Action

The defendant contends that the trial court erred in denying its Exceptions of No Cause or Right of Action. The defendant asserts that the provisions of La. R.S. 9:291 creates an Interspousal Immunity which prevents suit for causes of action arising during the marriage.

* * * * *

It is well settled that the interspousal immunity created by this statute does not destroy any cause of action which one spouse might have against the other. The effect of this statute is to bar the right of action which one spouse has against the other for any such cause of action. The question presented here is whether the right of action is forever barred as to causes of action arising during the marriage or whether, on the other hand, this statute merely suspends the cause of action until such time as the spouses may be judicially separated or the marriage ends in divorce. This issue was addressed only once previously by the First Circuit in *Gremillion v. Caffey*, 71 So. 2d 670 (La.App. 1 Cir. 1954). In that case, the court cited La. C.C. art. 159 and stated that:

> Under the express terms of the above cited article the judgment of absolute divorce between plaintiff and defendant rendered on February 10, 1953 removed the relative incapacity of the plaintiff to sue the defendant for the tort he committed on August 22, 1952 or, stated in another way, ended the abatement of her right of action which had existed during the continuation of the marriage, although she enjoyed a cause of action under Article 2315, LSA-C.C. By the judgment of divorce, plaintiff and defendant were placed "in the same situation with respect to each other as if no marriage had ever been contracted between them."

Suits between spouses have traditionally been prohibited on the theory that such suits disrupt domestic tranquility. However, once the marriage is ended, this would no longer seem to be a valid policy. Enforcement of Rights by Spouses, 25 La. L. Rev. 186 (1964); Family Law -- The Bar to Interspousal Suit and the Maternal Preference Rule, 52 Tul. L. Rev. 422 (1978). Accordingly, we find that it is the time of the judicial proceedings which controls the application of the Doctrine of Interspousal Immunity rather than the time of the occurrence of the tort. Further, since prescription is suspended as between spouses during the marriage, the plaintiff has both a cause and a right of action against her former husband.

* * * * *

NOTES

1.   It is important to note that interspousal immunity only bars the bringing of the suit; it does not destroy the cause of action. When the immunity abates under the terms of the statute, the cause of action may be pursued and the prescriptive period begins to run.

2.   The defense of interspousal immunity is personal to the husband and wife. Consequently, a spouse might sue their partner's insurer under the direct action statute. *See Gremillion v. State Farm Mutual Automobile Insurance Company*, 302 So. 2d 712 (La.App. 3 Cir. 1974). However, most insurance contracts by their terms bar such intra-family suits, *see Guillaume v. Guillaume*, 613 So. 2d 172 (La.App. 4 Cir. 1992), and bar recovery for intentional torts.

3.   A parent may sue his child during the child's minority. *See Deshotel v. Travelers Ind. Co.*, 243 So. 2d 259 (La. 1971).

CHAPTER 3

GROSS, WILLFUL, WANTON CONDUCT

Courts and legislatures have identified a degree of blameworthiness which falls between negligence and intent, which is variously described as "willful," "wanton," "reckless," or "gross negligence." While arguably there may be differences among the levels of culpability (for example, "willful" conduct may be more blameworthy than merely "wanton" conduct), the common law generally treats all of them as one – extreme departure from ordinary care in circumstances in which a reasonable person would exercise heightened care. *See* Note, below. *Pfister v. Shusta*, 657 N.E.2d 1013 (Ill. 1995) (willful and wanton conduct is a course of action which shows actual or deliberate intent to harm or which, if the course of action is not intentional, shows an utter indifference to or conscious disregard for a person's own safety or the safety or property of others.... Willful and wanton conduct is "a hybrid between acts considered negligent and behavior found to be intentionally tortious.... Under the facts of one case, willful and wanton misconduct may be only degrees more than ordinary negligence, while under the facts of another case, willful and wanton acts may be only degrees less than intentional wrongdoing....").

The concepts of wanton or reckless have become important in Louisiana with the passage of punitive or exemplary damage statutes imposing such damages if the specified conduct was "wanton *or* reckless" or "wanton *and* reckless," depending on the statute. *See, e.g.*, CC Art. 2315.3 (child pornography), 2315.4 (intoxication while operating a motor vehicle), and 2315.7 (criminal sexual activity with a juvenile), Chapter 8, *infra*. The terms also are used in "limited duty/immunity" statutes, such as R.S. 9:2800.4 (Chapter 7, *infra*), rendering the immunity from liability for an owner of farm or forest land inapplicable only if the landowner was guilty of an intentional act or "gross negligence"). Neither the legislation nor early cases interpreting the statutes has provided an operative test for this "intermediate" category of fault. However, the Louisiana Supreme Court apparently will adhere to the approach, discussed below, that there is only one type of wrongful conduct between intent and negligence, although it may "masquerade" under several names. *See, e.g. Ambrose v. New Orleans Police Department Ambulance Service*, 639 So. 2d 216 (La. 1994) (where the defendant's actions did not exhibit willful, wanton, or reckless conduct amounting to "complete neglect of the rights of others," or an "extreme departure from ordinary care," or the "want of even slight care," the plaintiff has failed to prove that defendant's actions constituted "gross negligence"). In *Billiot v. B.P. Oil Co.*, 645 So. 2d 604 (La. 1994), the Court held that a "wanton or reckless" standard "obliges the plaintiff to prove at least that the defendant proceeded in disregard of a high and excessive degree of danger, either known to him or apparent to a reasonable person in his position.... In other words, the 'wanton' or 'reckless' conduct that must be proved is highly unreasonable conduct, involving an extreme departure from ordinary care, in a situation where a high degree of danger is apparent." *See also Lenard v. Dilley*, 805 So. 2d 175 (La. 2002) ("reckless disregard for the safety of others," as used in a statute, is the same as gross negligence); *Falkowski v. Maurus*, 637 So. 2d 522 (La.App. 1 Cir. 1993), ("gross negligence" is "more of a willful, wanton or reckless negligence and extreme departure from ordinary care").

NOTE

Does the following excerpt from Prosser and Keeton On Torts, Fifth Edition, page 212, assist you in distinguishing between "intentional," "wanton or reckless" and merely negligent conduct?

> Willful, Wanton and Reckless. A different approach, at least in theory, looks to the actor's real or supposed state of mind. Lying between intent to do harm, which, as we have seen, includes proceeding with knowledge that the harm is substantially certain to occur, and the mere unreasonable risk of harm to another involved in ordinary negligence, there is a penumbra of what has been called "quasi-intent." To this area the words "willful," "wanton," or "reckless," are customarily applied; and sometimes, in a single sentence, all three. Although efforts have been made to distinguish them, in practice such distinctions have consistently been ignored, and

the three terms have been treated as meaning the same thing, or at least as coming out at the same legal exit. They have been grouped together as an aggravated form of negligence, differing in quality rather than in degree from ordinary lack of care. These terms are in common use in the automobile guest statutes, but even before such statutes, they represented an idea which had a legitimate place in the common law. They apply to conduct which is still, at essence, negligent, rather than actually intended to do harm, but which is so far from a proper state of mind that it is treated in many respects as if it were so intended. Thus it is held to justify an award of punitive damages, and may justify a broader duty, and more extended liability for consequences, and it will avoid the defense of ordinary contributory negligence on the part of the plaintiff.

The usual meaning assigned to "willful," "wanton," or reckless," according to taste as to the word used, is that the actor has intentionally done an act of an unreasonable character in disregard of a known or obvious risk that was so great as to make it highly probable that harm would follow, and which thus is usually accompanied by a conscious indifference to the consequences. Since, however, it is almost never admitted, and can be proved only by the conduct and the circumstances, an objective standard must of necessity in practice be applied. The "willful" requirement, therefore, breaks down and receives at best lip service, where it is clear from the facts that the defendant, whatever his state of mind, has proceeded in disregard of a high and excessive degree of danger, either known to him or apparent to a reasonable person in his position.

The result is that "willful," "wanton," or "reckless" conduct tends to take on the aspect of highly unreasonable conduct, involving an extreme departure from ordinary care, in a situation where a high degree of danger is apparent. As a result there is often no clear distinction at all between such conduct and "gross" negligence, and the two have tended to merge and take on the same meaning, of an aggravated form of negligence, differing in quality rather than in degree from ordinary lack of care. It is at least clear, however, that such aggravated negligence must be more than any mere mistake resulting from inexperience, excitement, or confusion, and more than mere thoughtlessness or inadvertence, or simple inattention, even perhaps to the extent of falling asleep at the wheel of an automobile, or even of an intentional omission to perform a statutory duty, except in those cases where a reasonable person in the actor's place would have been aware of great danger, and proceeding in the face of it is so entirely unreasonable as to amount to aggravated negligence.

burden of precaution
∠ magnitude of accident
× probability of occurrence

CHAPTER 4

NEGLIGENCE

INTRODUCTION

Negligence is the failure to exercise reasonable care under the circumstances. Technically, negligence is a tort which consists of five elements: (1) duty; (2) breach; (3) cause-in-fact; (4) proximate or legal cause (scope of duty); and (5) damages. The interrelationship of these five elements and who decides each (judge or jury) is both fascinating and vexing. In this chapter, we focus upon the first two elements – the general duty to exercise reasonable care, and what constitutes a breach of that duty.

Ever since the decision in *Vaughan v. Menlove*, 132 Eng. Rep. 490 (1837), courts have recognized that reasonable care is gauged by an objective test–what would the ordinarily prudent person do under the circumstances? The ordinary person is a hypothetical person; it is not *the* defendant, it is not *the* judge, and, it certainly is not *the* juror selected to decide the case. But, then when one considers the reasonable person under the *circumstances*, doesn't the test become more subjective? What guidelines are there? Consider the following Louisiana case.

A.   REASONABLE CARE – IN GENERAL

MISURACA → *wife of deceased brought wrongful death and survival action*
v.
CITY OF KENNER
802 So. 2d 784 (La.App. 5 Cir. 2001)

In this personal injury action, plaintiff, Daphne Husser Misuraca ("Plaintiff"), appeals a summary judgment dismissing her claims against the City of Kenner ("Kenner") and Kenner Police Officer Bryian Robson ("Robson"). We affirm.

During the early morning hours of July 27, 1996, Stephen D. Miles lost control of his vehicle while driving on West Esplanade Avenue near Williams Boulevard in Kenner. After he lost control, his car left the roadway, clipped a telephone pole guy-wire, flipped over, and landed upside-down in the adjacent drainage canal. Bystanders helped Miles and his passenger, David Hibner, out of the overturned vehicle.

Officer Bryan Robson of the Kenner Police Department was the first road officer to arrive at the accident scene. He parked his vehicle in the roadway behind another car and proceeded toward the canal. As he approached the canal, he passed two men, later identified as Frederick l. Misuraca and Davin Severa, attempting to handle the disconnected guy-wire. He instructed the men to stop handling the guy-wire, which they did. At that point, Robson touched the guy-wire himself to verify that it was not electrically charged.

Robson then proceeded to the edge of the canal where he found Miles and Hibner. After Robson began to interview the victims, Misuraca again attempted to move the disconnected guy-wire. Although Severa deterred Misuraca from wrapping the guy-wire around a metal street sign to prevent grounding, both men were electrocuted when Misuraca yanked on the guy-wire and it contacted a charged electrical line. As a result of the electrocution, Severa received burns to his hands and Misuraca died.

On July 25, 1997, plaintiff filed a wrongful death and survival action against the City of Kenner and Officer Robson among others. In her petition, she alleged that the accident that caused her husband's death was attributable to Kenner and Officer Robson for their

(a) Failure to properly secure and control the accident scene; and

123

(b) Failure to prevent civilians from participating in the accident scene; and

(c) Failure to properly train police officers to monitor and administrate over an accident of this type; and *(negligence claim against City)*

(d) Failure to take the necessary steps in order to protect the interest of the public;

(e) Failure to take precautions necessary to avoid the accident;

(f) Otherwise failing to use due care and caution commensurate with the circumstances then and there existing; and

(g) Any and all other acts of negligence proven at a trial on the merits.

On July 2, 1999, Kenner and Robson filed a peremptory exception of no cause of action, which was granted on October 27, 1999. On November 12, 1999, within the time allowed by the trial court, plaintiff filed a supplemental and amending petition alleging that Robson was negligent in allowing civilians to remain on the accident scene among downed electrical lines, failing to usher civilians from the accident scene, and failing to properly secure the accident scene to prevent civilians from contacting downed electrical lines. Plaintiff also alleged that Kenner was negligent in failing to properly train Officer Robson that downed electrical lines were dangerous to anyone on an accident scene.

On May 22, 2000, the trial judge granted Kenner and Robson's Motion to Strike Allegations, including all references to "downed power lines," "downed high voltage lines," "downed electrical power lines," or "downed electrical lines" in the plaintiff's original and supplemental petitions. Kenner and Robson filed a Motion for Summary Judgment, including a Statement of Uncontested Material Facts and Memorandum in support of the Motion. To their Motion for Summary Judgment, Kenner and Robson attached excerpts from Davin Severa's deposition and Bryian Robson's deposition, as well as copies of the Judgment sustaining their Exception of No Cause of Action and the Judgment striking the allegations.

On December 19, 2000, the day of the summary judgment hearing, the plaintiff filed an opposition to the Motion for Summary Judgment with attached deposition excerpts, which the trial court permitted the plaintiff to argue. After taking the matter under advisement, the trial court granted Kenner and Robson's Motion for Summary Judgment and dismissed the plaintiff's claim against them.

In the trial court's written reasons for judgment, it reasoned that, after the allegations of downed power lines were stricken from the pleadings, the plaintiff's only remaining claim was Officer Robson's alleged failure to secure the scene.

Under the duty-risk analysis, plaintiff must prove that the conduct in question was a cause-in-fact of the resulting harm, the defendant owed a duty of care to plaintiff, the requisite duty was breached by the defendant, and the risk of harm was within the scope of protection afforded by the duty breached. *Berry v. State, Through Department of Health and Human Resources*, 93-2748 (La. 1994), 637 So. 2d 412, 414. Whether a duty is owed is a question of law. *Id.* The inquiry is whether the plaintiff has any law--statutory, jurisprudential, or arising from general principles of fault--to support his claim. *Id.* Governmental agencies in the performance of governmental functions may be subjected to the imposition of certain duties, the breach of which may result in liability for damages to those injured by a risk contemplated by that duty. *Id.* The determination of whether a particular duty should be imposed on a particular governmental agency is a policy question. *Id.* It is our role to determine whether there is any jurisprudential or statutory rule or policy reason why, under the facts and circumstances of this case, Kenner would owe a duty to plaintiff to compensate her for her husband's death. *Id.*

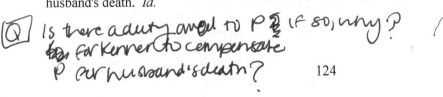
[Q] Is there a duty owed to P? If so, why? for Kenner to compensate P for husband's death?

124

In *Syrie v. Schilhab,* 96-1027 (La. 1997), 693 So. 2d 1173, the Louisiana Supreme Court enunciated the duty of law enforcement officers:

> [The] legislature has given law enforcement officers the exclusive power to regulate traffic and the public has a corresponding obligation to follow traffic regulations. Law enforcement officers are duty bound to exercise this power reasonably to protect life and limb and to refrain from causing injury or harm. When a law enforcement officer becomes aware of a dangerous traffic situation, he has the affirmative duty to see that motorists are not subjected to unreasonable risks of harm. [Further], this court stated that the scope of an officer's duty is to choose a course of action which is *reasonable* under the circumstances. In other words, the scope of an officer's duty to act reasonably under the circumstances does not extend so far as to require that the officer always choose the 'best' or even a 'better' method of approach.

Id. at 1177.

Considering all the facts and circumstances of this case, we conclude that Officer Robson had a duty to act reasonably to investigate a one-car traffic accident. When he arrived on the scene, he had the affirmative duty to choose a reasonable course of action in investigating the accident and ensure that *motorists* were not subjected to unreasonable risks of harm. Having identified the duty owed by Officer Robson, we now turn to a determination of whether that duty was breached.

Our review of the pleadings and other supporting documents supplied by both parties discloses that the following uncontested material facts regarding Robson's actions were established. Robson stated in his deposition that, after he arrived at the accident scene, his first priority was the accident victims. As he approached the accident scene, he had momentary direct contact with the men prior to their electrocution when he instructed the men to stop handling the downed guy-wire. He observed as the men stopped handling the downed guy-wire. He also immediately determined that the downed guy-wire was not electrically charged so it did not pose an immediate danger.

Severa stated in his deposition that, after Robson began his investigation of the accident scene to determine the nature of the accident and the number of victims, while Robson's back was turned, Misuraca, against Robson's previous direction began to handle the downed guy-wire again. After between one to five minutes according to the deposition testimony, while Severa held the loose end of the guy-wire, Misuraca yanked on it, which caused it to connect with a charged electrical line and electrocute them.

Considering the totality of the circumstances, the pleadings and supporting documents reveal that Officer Robson was reasonably discharging his duty when Misuraca and Severa were electrocuted. Consequently, the trial judge properly granted Kenner and Robson's Motion for Summary Judgment.

Conclusion

... Where, as here, the police officer acted reasonably under the circumstances presented, Kenner is not liable.

For the reasons stated herein, the trial court's ruling granting the City of Kenner and Officer Robson's Motion for Summary Judgment is affirmed. Costs of this appeal are assessed to the plaintiff.

AFFIRMED.

NOTES

1. Why did the court hold that the officer exercised reasonable care? How did it know? To what standard do we hold the expert? This issue is considered in more detail in the chapter on Professional Negligence. In *Oubre v. Eslaih,* 869 So. 2d 71 (La. 2004), the Louisiana Supreme Court

[handwritten annotations: "he was investigating car accident as statute requires and choose good course of action to diminish unreasonable risk to motorists" and "→ evidence"]

held that when a law enforcement officer becomes aware of a dangerous traffic situation he has an affirmative duty to protect motorists from unreasonable risks of harm. But, a plaintiff claiming a breach of that duty must prove more than just that he saw a police car pass by. He must prove that the officer, as he passed, became aware of the situation which represented an unreasonable risk of harm to the motorist and that the officer failed to act.

2.   In *Jones v. Congemi*, 848 So. 2d 41 (La.App. 5 Cir. 2003), *writ denied,* 855 So. 2d 354 (La. 2003), the court wrote:

> "[Police] regulations should indeed be followed and corrective action may be taken by the police department when an officer fails to comply with the department's regulations. However, when determining the scope of duty owed by law enforcement officers and whether such duty was breached, the legal question is whether ... a police officer's actions were reasonable, not whether he complied with departmental policies."

Is it fair to second guess police decisions made under great stress and with limited resources available? Does it matter if the decisions are policy decisions, as opposed to mere implementation of a policy? We will consider those questions in the chapter on Immunities. *See* La. R.S. 9:2798.1.

3.   In *Boyle v. Board of Supervisors,* 685 So. 2d 1080 (La. 1996), plaintiff's fall was caused by a "relatively small depression" in defendant's sidewalk which had been developing for four to ten years because of the Louisiana climate and settling soil. The depression was in a high traffic area, and plaintiff was the only person reported to have fallen there. Landowner had over 22 miles of sidewalk, and proper repair of each such depression would cost $200. *Held*, the defect causing plaintiff's fall did not present an unreasonable danger and defendant is not liable for the damages resulting therefrom.

4.   The Restatement (Second) of Torts provides:

§ 283. Conduct Of A Reasonable Man: The Standard

> Unless the actor is a child, the standard of conduct to which he must conform to avoid being negligent is that of a reasonable man under like circumstances.

§ 284. Negligent Conduct; Act Or Failure To Act

Negligent conduct may be either:

> (a) an act which the actor as a reasonable man should recognize as involving an unreasonable risk of causing an invasion of an interest of another, or

> (b) a failure to do an act which is necessary for the protection or assistance of another and which the actor is under a duty to do.

§ 289. Recognizing Existence Of Risk

> The actor is required to recognize that his conduct involves a risk of causing an invasion of another's interest if a reasonable man would do so while exercising

> (a) such attention, perception of the circumstances, memory, knowledge of other pertinent matters, intelligence, and judgment as a reasonable man would have; and

> (b) such superior attention, perception, memory, knowledge, intelligence, and judgment as the actor himself has.

§ 290. What Actor Is Required To Know

For the purpose of determining whether the actor should recognize that his conduct involves a risk, he is required to know

(a) the qualities and habits of human beings and animals and the qualities, characteristics, and capacities of things and forces in so far as they are matters of common knowledge at the time and in the community; and

(b) the common law, legislative enactments, and general customs in so far as they are likely to affect the conduct of the other or third persons.

ROBERTS
v.
STATE

396 So. 2d 566 (La.App. 3 Cir. 1981)
(Affirmed on other grounds, 440 So. 2d 1221)

LABORDE, J.

In this tort suit, William C. Roberts sued to recover damages for injuries he sustained in an accident in the lobby of the U. S. Post Office Building in Alexandria, Louisiana. Roberts fell after being bumped into by Mike Burson, the blind operator of the concession stand located in the building.

Plaintiff sued the State of Louisiana, through the Louisiana Health and Human Resources Administration, advancing two theories of liability: respondeat superior and negligent failure by the State to properly supervise and oversee the safe operation of the concession stand. The stand's blind operator, Mike Burson, is not a party to this suit although he is charged with negligence.

The trial court ordered plaintiff's suit dismissed holding that there is no respondeat superior liability without an employer-employee relationship and that there is no negligence liability without a cause in fact showing.

We affirm the trial court's decision for the reasons which follow.

On September 1, 1977, at about 12:45 in the afternoon, operator Mike Burson left his concession stand to go to the men's bathroom located in the building. As he was walking down the hall, he bumped into plaintiff who fell to the floor and injured his hip. Plaintiff was 75 years old, stood 5'6 and weighed approximately 100 pounds. Burson, on the other hand, was 25 to 26 years old, stood approximately 6' and weighed 165 pounds.

At the time of the incident, Burson was not using a cane nor was he utilizing the technique of walking with his arm or hand in front of him.

Even though Burson was not joined as a defendant, his negligence or lack thereof is crucial to a determination of the State's liability. Because of its importance, we begin with it.

Plaintiff contends that operator Mike Burson traversed the area from his concession stand to the men's bathroom in a negligent manner. To be more specific, he focuses on the operator's failure to use his cane even though he had it with him in his concession stand.

In determining an actor's negligence, various courts have imposed differing standards of care to which handicapped persons are expected to perform. Professor William L. Prosser expresses one generally recognized modern standard of care as follows:

"As to his physical characteristics, the reasonable man may be said to be identical with the actor. The man who is blind ... is entitled to live in the world and to have

127

allowance made by others for his disability, and he cannot be required to do the impossible by conforming to physical standards which he cannot meet ... At the same time, the conduct of the handicapped individual must be reasonable in the light of his knowledge of his infirmity, which is treated merely as one of the circumstances under which he acts ... It is sometimes said that a blind man must use a greater degree of care than one who can see; but it is now generally agreed that as a fixed rule this is inaccurate, and that the correct statement is merely that he must take the precautions, be they more or less, which the ordinary reasonable man would take if he were blind." W. Prosser, *The Law of Torts*, Section 32, at Page 151-52 (4th ed. 1971).

A careful review of the record in this instance reveals that Burson was acting as a reasonably prudent blind person would under these particular circumstances.

Mike Burson is totally blind. Since 1974, he has operated the concession stand located in the lobby of the post office building. It is one of twenty-three vending stands operated by blind persons under a program funded by the federal government and implemented by the State through the Blind Services Division of the Department of Health and Human Resources. Burson hired no employees, choosing instead to operate his stand on his own.

Prior to running the vending stand in Alexandria, Burson attended Arkansas Enterprises for the Blind where he received mobility training. In 1972, he took a refresher course in mobility followed by a course on vending stand training. In that same year, he operated a concession stand in Shreveport, his first under the vending stand program. He later operated a stand at Centenary before going to Alexandria in 1974 to take up operations there.

On the date of the incident in question, Mike Burson testified that he left his concession stand and was on his way to the men's bathroom when he bumped into plaintiff. He, without hesitancy, admitted that at the time he was not using his cane, explaining that he relies on his facial sense which he feels is an adequate technique for short trips inside the familiar building. Burson testified that he does use a cane to get to and from work.

Plaintiff makes much of Burson's failure to use a cane when traversing the halls of the post office building. Yet, our review of the testimony received at trial indicates that it is not uncommon for blind people to rely on other techniques when moving around in a familiar setting. For example George Marzloff, the director of the Division of Blind Services, testified that he can recommend to the blind operators that they should use a cane but he knows that when they are in a setting in which they are comfortable, he would say that nine out of ten will not use a cane and in his personal opinion, if the operator is in a relatively busy area, the cane can be more of a hazard than an asset. (Tr. 164) Mr. Marzloff further testified that he felt a reasonably functioning blind person would learn his way around his work setting as he does around his home so that he could get around without a cane. Mr. Marzloff added that he has several blind people working in his office, none of whom use a cane inside that facility. (Tr. 165)

Mr. Marzloff's testimony is similar to testimony received from Guy DiCharry, a blind business enterprise counselor with the Blind Services Division. As part of his responsibilities Mr. DiCharry supervised the Alexandria vending stand providing him with an opportunity to observe Mike Burson in a work setting. He testified that Burson knew his way around the building pretty well and that like most of his other blind operators, he did not use a cane on short trips within the building. (Tr. 132-133) He added that he discussed the use of a cane on such short trips as these with some of his other blind operators but they took offense to his suggestions, explaining that it was their choice. The only testimony in the record that suggests that Burson traversed the halls in a negligent manner was that elicited from plaintiff's expert witness, William Henry Jacobson. Jacobson is an instructor in peripathology, which he explained as the science of movement within the surroundings by visually impaired individuals. Jacobson, admitting that he conducted no study or examination of Mike Burson's mobility skills and that he was unfamiliar with the State's vending program, nonetheless testified that he would require a blind person to use a cane in traversing the areas outside the concession stand. (Tr. 200) He added that a totally blind individual probably should use a cane under

128

any situation where there in an unfamiliar environment or where a familiar environment involves a change, whether it be people moving through that environment or strangers moving through that environment or just a heavy traffic within that environment. (Tr. 202) When cross examined however, Jacobson testified:

"Q. Now, do you, in instructing blind people on their mobility skills, do you tell them to use their own judgment in which type of mobility assistance technique they're to employ?

A. Yes I do.

Q. Do you think that three (3) years is a long enough period for a person to become acquainted with an environment that he might be working with?

A. Yes I do.

Q. So you think that after a period of three (3) years an individual would probably, if he is normal ... has normal mobility skills for a blind person, would have enough adjustment time to be ... to call that environment familiar?

A. Yes.

Q. That's not including the fact that there may be people in and out of the building?

A. Right.

Q. Now is it possible that if he's familiar with the sounds of the people inside a building that he may even at some point in time become so familiar with the people in an area, regular customers or what not that you could say that the environment was familiar, including the fact that there are people there, is that possible?

A. Uh ... I would hesitate to say that, in a public facility where we could not ... uh ... control strangers coming in.

Q. Well, let's say that a business has a particular group of clients that are always there, perhaps on a daily or weekly basis. Now you've stated that a blind person sharpens his auditory skills in order to help him articulate in an area?

A. With instruction, yes.

Q. Right. Isn't is possible that if he can rely on a fixed travel of a fixed type and number of persons that it's possible that that is a familiar environment even though there are people there?

A. Only if they were the same people all the time and they know him, yes."

Upon our review of the record, we feel that plaintiff has failed to show that Burson was negligent. Burson testified that he was very familiar with his surroundings, having worked there for three and a half years. He had special mobility training and his reports introduced into evidence indicate good mobility skills. He explained his decision to rely on his facial sense instead of his cane for these short trips in a manner which convinces us that it was a reasoned decision. Not only was Burson's explanation adequate, there was additional testimony from other persons indicating that such a decision is not an unreasonable one. Also important is the total lack of any evidence in the record showing that at the time of the incident, Burson engaged in any acts which may be characterized as negligence on his part. For example, there is nothing showing that Burson was walking too fast, not paying attention, et cetera. Under all of these circumstances, we conclude that Mike Burson was not negligent.

Our determination that Mike Burson was not negligent disposes of our need to discuss liability on the part of the State.

[handwritten: But unclear... some cases say general standard if kid — some say adult standard engaging in adult activity]

[handwritten: not necessarily just age, but mental illness + disability for old folks... linked w/ aging... take it into account]

* * * * *

NOTES

1.   A child generally is held to the duty of acting as a reasonably prudent child possessing the actor's "judgmental capacity," i.e., age, intelligence, education, experience, etc. Louisiana law is unclear, partly because most of the cases involved the contributory negligence of a child at a time at which contributory negligence barred any recovery. For a general discussion of the standard presently imposed upon a child actor, *see Howard v. Allstate*, 520 So. 2d 715 (La. 1988). *See also, Johnson v. Fleet Mortgage Corp.*, 807 So. 2d 1077 (La.App. 4 Cir. 2002) (holding that although an eight year old boy may be capable of negligence, a reasonably prudent eight year old boy would not realize the danger that by jumping on some discarded plastic bottles he might cause serious chemical burns to his friend and himself; thus his mother is not liable, under C.C. Arts. 237, 2317 or 2318, for the friend's ensuing damages); *Fergins v. Caddo Parish School Board*, 736 So. 2d 943 (La.App. 2 Cir. 1999) (a child is not held to the same standard of care as that of an adult; "rather the test is whether the child, considering his age, background and inherent intelligence, indulged in gross disregard of his own safety in the face of known, understood and perceived danger). Is the child standard of care objective at all? Many courts hold the child to the standard of care of the ordinary child of like age, intelligence and experience unless the child is engaged in an adult, or inherently dangerous activity. Then, the child is held to the "adult" standard of care. *See Racine v. Moon's Towing, Inc.*, 817 So. 2d 21 (La. 2002). But what about the extremely young child? In *Jones v. Hawkins*, 708 So. 2d 749 (La.App. 2 Cir. 1998), the court held that a six year old was incapable of negligence under the circumstances.

2.   Insane persons present unique problems because imposition of liability upon one who cannot determine right from wrong equates to absolute liability. This may explain *Mathieu v. Imperial Toy Corp.*, 632 So. 2d 375 (La.App. 4 Cir. 1994), holding that where at the time of the incident the actor is a chronic paranoid schizophrenic who is delusional and unable to distinguish right from wrong, he cannot be legally at fault. The majority rule is one that who is insane must behave as a reasonable person. Is that consistent with the rule as to children? What about those who care for the mentally challenged?

The issue of negligence by an Alzheimer's patient surfaced in *Vinccinelli v. Musso*, 818 So. 2d 163 (La.App. 1 Cir. 2002). There plaintiff was for over four years a paid baby-sitter for defendant, an Alzheimer's patient. Plaintiff slipped and fell on ice cream spilled by defendant. Plaintiff knew that defendant might get ice cream on her own, and that if she spilled some, because of her disease she would not pay attention to the spill. *Held*, because of plaintiff's special status and job responsibilities, the risk from a small spill occasioned by defendant was not unreasonable vis-a-vis this particular plaintiff.

3.   What about the "sudden emergency?" The sudden emergency doctrine provides that in a sudden emergency, not of his own making, the reasonable person is held to the standard of care of a reasonable person in an emergency. But why isn't the emergency just one of the circumstances? If so, why is a special "rule" necessary? *See also* Restatement (Second) of Torts Sec. 296, which provides that:

§ 296. Emergency

(1) In determining whether conduct is negligent toward another, the fact that the actor is confronted with a sudden emergency which requires rapid decision is a factor in determining the reasonable character of his choice of action.

(2) The fact that the actor is not negligent after the emergency has arisen does not preclude his liability for his tortious conduct which has produced the emergency.

[left margin handwritten notes: generally; child = reasonable prudent child w/ actors "judgment capacity" - age - intelligence - education - experience; insane = majority rule reasonable person; Alzheimers: look at caretaker's status and job responsibility; sudden emergency doctrine - reasonable person in an emergency]

130

In one recent case, plaintiff was a passenger in a car travelling on I-10. The driver encountered zero visibility due to a combination of smoke and fog. Driver rear-ended a truck stopped in front of him. The truck had previously rear-ended a car in front of it. Subsequent collisions from behind and the side pushed the vehicle in which plaintiff was a passenger under the truck ahead, allegedly causing plaintiff to suffer serious injuries. Among others, plaintiff sued the truck with which the vehicle in which he was a passenger collided and the driver of the truck. The trial court granted the defendants' motions for summary judgment. *Held.* Affirmed. Defendants established truck driver encountered a sudden emergency which he did not create. Testimony of another driver who encountered the smoke and fog minutes before defendant driver did not establish the conditions which defendant driver encountered. *Lowe v. Noble, L.L.C.*, _____ So. 3d _____ (La.App. 1 Cir. (2017).

Defendant's vehicle strayed from the paved portion of the highway and onto the shoulder, injuring a passenger or a bystander. Defendant's contention was that he was not negligent because he suddenly became unconscious. If the loss of consciousness was foreseeable, he might have been negligent in driving, depending upon the likelihood of such an occurrence. If it was not foreseeable, then he probably was not negligent. Must plaintiff prove that defendant was unreasonable in causing an accident through his "sudden unconsciousness?" If so, how often would you expect such a defense to be urged? Louisiana treats "sudden unconsciousness" as a defense which the defendant must plead and must prove by clear and convincing evidence. *See Brannon v. Shelter Mutual Ins. Co.*, 507 So. 2d 194 (La. 1987).

What if defendant's claim is that "my brakes suddenly gave way," and he established that it was not foreseeable that the brakes would fail? What would be the outcome in Louisiana? Why? *See King v. Louviere*, 543 So. 2d 1327 (La. 1989). There, the court held that when a driver on his wrong side of the road collides with another car which is in its correct lane of traffic, the driver is required to exculpate himself of any fault, however slight, contributing to the accident. When such a trespassing motorist attempts to exonerate himself from negligence by claiming that a latent defect in the vehicle he was driving caused the accident, he bears the burden of proving: (1) the existence of such latent defect by proof so strong that it excludes any other reasonable hypothesis with reference to the cause of the accident except that it resulted solely from the alleged defect, (2) he was not aware of the defect, and (3) the defect could not reasonably have been discovered and remedied by a proper inspection. He is required to "come forward with objective and convincing evidence, other than his own testimony." He must prove that the accident "was caused exclusively by a latent defect" in the vehicle and he was not guilty even of slight negligence that "in any way contributed to the accident.")

4.   Expert witnesses often are called to testify regarding whether the defendant's conduct satisfied the standard of care (was not a breach of duty). When a witness is offered as an expert witness, the court must determine whether to accept the witness as an expert. The opposing party may challenge an expert by filing what is commonly referred to as a *Daubert* motion (from the U.S. Supreme Court's decision in *Daubert v. Merrell Dow, Inc.*, 509 U.S. 579 (1993)). The Louisiana Supreme Court adopted the *Daubert* test in *State v. Foret*, 628 So. 2d 1116 (La. 1993).

Expert witnesses are particularly important in professional malpractice cases to establish the standard of care in the profession. In most medical malpractice cases (with the exception of obvious breaches, such as a surgeon leaving a surgical implement in a patient), a plaintiff must have expert testimony that the defendant breached or the plaintiff's case will be dismissed.

B.   CUSTOM

THE T. J. HOOPER
60 F.2d 737 (2d Cir. 1932)

HAND, C. J.

The barges No. 17 and No. 30, belonging to the Northern Barge Company, had lifted cargoes of coal at Norfolk, Virginia, for New York in March, 1928. They were towed by two tugs of the petitioner, the 'Montrose' and the 'Hooper,' and were lost off the Jersey Coast on March tenth, in an easterly gale. The cargo owners sued the barges under the contracts of carriage; the owner of the barges sued the tugs under the towing contract, both for its own loss and as bailee of the cargoes; the owner of the tug filed a petition to limit its liability. All the suits were joined and heard together, and the judge found that all the vessels were unseaworthy; the tugs, because they did not carry radio receiving sets by which they could have seasonably got warnings of a change in the weather which should have caused them to seek shelter in the Delaware Breakwater en route. He therefore entered an interlocutory decree holding each tug and barge jointly liable to each cargo owner, and each tug for half damages for the loss of its barge. The petitioner appealed, and the barge owner appealed and filed assignments of error.

Each tug had three ocean going coal barges in tow, the lost barge being at the end. The 'Montrose,' which had the No. 17, took an outside course; the 'Hooper' with the No. 30, inside. The weather was fair without ominous symptoms, as the tows passed the Delaware Breakwater about midnight of March eighth, and the barges did not get into serious trouble until they were about opposite Atlantic City some sixty or seventy miles to the north. The wind began to freshen in the morning of the ninth and rose to a gale before noon; by afternoon the second barge of the Hooper's tow was out of hand and signalled the tug, which found that not only this barge needed help, but that the No. 30 was aleak. Both barges anchored and the crew of the No. 30 rode out the storm until the afternoon of the tenth, when she sank, her crew having been meanwhile taken off. The No. 17 sprang a leak about the same time; she too anchored at the Montrose's command and sank on the next morning after her crew also had been rescued. The cargoes and the tugs maintain that the barges were not fit for their service; the cargoes and the barges that the tugs should have gone into the Delaware Breakwater, and besides, did not handle their tows properly.

* * * * *

A more difficult issue is as to the tugs. We agree with the judge that once conceding the propriety of passing the Breakwater on the night of the eighth, the navigation was good enough. It might have been worse to go back when the storm broke than to keep on. The seas were from the east and southeast, breaking on the starboard quarter of the barges, which if tight and well found should have lived. True they were at the tail and this is the most trying position, but to face the seas in an attempt to return was a doubtful choice; the masters' decision is final unless they made a plain error. The evidence does not justify that conclusion; and so, the case as to them turns upon whether they should have put in at the Breakwater.

The weather bureau at Arlington broadcasts two predictions daily, at ten in the morning and ten in the evening. Apparently there are other reports floating about, which come at uncertain hours but which can also be picked up. The Arlington report of the morning read as follows: 'Moderate north, shifting to east and southeast winds, increasing Friday, fair weather to-night.' The substance of this, apparently from another source, reached a tow bound north to New York about noon, and, coupled with a falling glass, decided the master to put in to the Delaware Breakwater in the afternoon. The glass had not indeed fallen much and perhaps the tug was over cautious; nevertheless, although the appearances were all fair, he thought discretion the better part of valor. Three other tows followed him, the masters of two of which testified. Their decision was in part determined by example; but they too had received the Arlington report or its equivalent, and though it is doubtful whether alone it would have turned the scale, it is plain that it left them in an indecision which needed little to be resolved on the side of prudence; they preferred to take no chances, and chances they believed there were. Courts have not often such evidence of the opinion of impartial experts, formed in the very circumstances and confirmed by their own conduct at the time.

Moreover, the 'Montrose' and the 'Hooper' would have had the benefit of the evening report from Arlington had they had proper receiving sets. This predicted worse weather; it read: 'Increasing east and southeast winds, becoming fresh to strong, Friday night and increasing cloudiness followed by rain Friday.' The bare 'increase' of the morning had become 'fresh to strong.' To be sure this scarcely foretold a gale of from forty to fifty miles for five hours or more, rising at one time to fifty-six; but if the four tows thought the first report enough, the second ought to have laid any doubts. The master of the 'Montrose' himself, when asked what he would have done had he received a substantially similar report, said that he would certainly have put in. The master of the 'Hooper' was also asked for his opinion, and said that he would have turned back also, but this admission is somewhat vitiated by the incorporation in the question of the statement that it was a 'storm warning,' which the witness seized upon in his answer. All this seems to us to support the conclusion of the judge that prudent masters, who had received the second warning, would have found the risk more than the exigency warranted; they would have been amply vindicated by what followed. To be sure the barges would, as we have said, probably have withstood the gale, had they been well found; but a master is not justified in putting his tow to every test which she will survive, if she be fit. There is a zone in which proper caution will avoid putting her capacity to the proof; a coefficient of prudence that he should not disregard. Taking the situation as a whole, it seems to us that these masters would have taken undue chances, had they got the broadcasts.

They did not, because their private radio receiving sets, which were on board, were not in working order. These belonged to them personally, and were partly a toy, partly a part of the equipment, but neither furnished by the owner, nor supervised by it. It is not fair to say that there was a general custom among coastwise carriers so to equip their tugs. One line alone did it; as for the rest, they relied upon their crews, so far as they can be said to have relied at all. An adequate receiving set suitable for a coastwise tug can now be got at small cost and is reasonably reliable if kept up; obviously it is a source of great protection to their tows. Twice every day they can receive these predictions, based upon the widest possible information, available to every vessel within two or three hundred miles and more. Such a set is the ears of the tug to catch the spoken word, just as the master's binoculars are her eyes to see a storm signal ashore. Whatever may be said as to other vessels, tugs towing heavy coal laden barges, strung out for half a mile, have little power to manoeuver, and do not, as this case proves, expose themselves to weather which would not turn back stauncher craft. They can have at hand protection against dangers of which they can learn in no other way.

Is it then a final answer that the business had not yet generally adopted receiving sets? There are, no doubt, cases where courts seem to make the general practice of the calling the standard of proper diligence; we have indeed given some currency to the notion ourselves.... Indeed in most cases reasonable prudence is in fact common prudence; but strictly it is never its measure; a whole calling may have unduly lagged in the adoption of new and available devices. It never may set its own tests, however persuasive be its usages. Courts must in the end say what is required; there are precautions so imperative that even their universal disregard will not excuse their omission . . . . But here there was no custom at all as to receiving sets; some had them, some did not; the most that can be urged is that they had not yet become general. Certainly in such a case we need not pause; when some have thought a device necessary, at least we may say that they were right, and the others too slack. The statute (section 484, title 46, U. S. Code [46 USCA § 484]) does not bear on this situation at all. It prescribes not a receiving, but a transmitting set, and for a very different purpose; to call for help, not to get news. We hold the tugs therefore because had they been properly equipped, they would have got the Arlington reports. The injury was a direct consequence of this unseaworthiness.

DECREE AFFIRMED.

NOTE

For a Louisiana case dealing with custom, *see Johnson v. Harry Jarred, Inc.*, 391 So. 2d 898 (La.App. 2 Cir. 1980).

C.   RISK, UTILITY BALANCING AND THE REASONABLE PERSON

Louisiana uses this approach but analysis isn't strictly quantitative

UNITED STATES
v.
CARROLL TOWING CO., INC.
159 F.2d 169 (2d Cir. 1947)

HAND, J.

[During World War II in New York harbor the negligence of several persons combined to cause a barge to collide and suffer a leak. The barge sank. Several of the other negligent parties alleged that the barge sank, in part, because the bargee (a bargehand) was negligent in not being on board at the time of the collision and that the barge's negligence contributed to the sinking thereby justifying a reduction in any recovery under the applicable maritime law comparative fault scheme.]

* * * * *

It appears from the foregoing review that there is no general rule to determine when the absence of a bargee or other attendant will make the owner of the barge liable for injuries to other vessels if she breaks away from her moorings. However, in any cases where he would be so liable for injuries to others obviously he must reduce his damages proportionately, if the injury is to his own barge. It becomes apparent why there can be no such general rule, when we consider the grounds for such a liability. Since there are occasions when every vessel will break from her moorings, and since, if she does, she becomes a menace to those about her; the owner's duty, as in other similar situations, to provide against resulting injuries is a function of three variables: (1) the probability that she will break away; (2) the gravity of the resulting injury, if she does; (3) the burden of adequate precautions. Possibly it serves to bring this notion into relief to state it in algebraic terms: if the probability be called P; the injury, L; and the burden, B; liability depends upon whether B is less than L multiplied by P: i.e., whether B less than PL.

b= burden of preventing
p= probability of harm or loss
L= loss or magnitude of loss
PxL= expected accident costs

McCARTY
v.
PHEASANT RUN, INC.,
826 F.2d 1554 (7th Cir. 1987)

negligence standard

POSNER, C. J.

if B< P... precaution should be taken

* * * * *

There are various ways in which courts formulate the negligence standard. The analytically (not necessarily the operationally) most precise is that it involves determining whether the burden of precaution is less than the magnitude of the accident, if it occurs, multiplied by the probability of occurrence. (The product of this multiplication, or "discounting," is what economists call an expected accident cost.) If the burden is less, the precaution should be taken. This is the famous "Hand Formula" announced in *United States v. Carroll Towing Co.*, 159 F.2d 169, 173 (2d Cir. 1947) (L. Hand, J.), an admiralty case, and since applied in a variety of cases not limited to admiralty.

* * * * *

Unreasonable conduct is merely the failure to take precautions that would generate greater benefits in avoiding accidents than the precautions would cost.

Ordinarily, and here, the parties do not give the jury the information required to quantify the variables that the Hand Formula picks out as relevant. That is why the formula has greater analytic than operational significance. Conceptual as well as practical difficulties in monetizing personal injuries may continue to frustrate efforts to measure expected accident costs with the precision that is possible, in principle at least, in measuring the other side of the equation--the cost or burden of

negligence standard isn't 134 *actually mathematical... it's analytical + conceptual (no hard, precise #s)*

precaution. *Cf. Conway v. O'Brien*, 111 F.2d 611, 612 (2d Cir. 1940) (L. Hand, J.), rev'd on other grounds, 312 U.S. 492, 61 S. Ct. 634, 85 L. Ed. 969 (1941). For many years to come juries may be forced to make rough judgments of reasonableness, intuiting rather than measuring the factors in the Hand Formula; and so long as their judgment is reasonable, the trial judge has no right to set it aside, let alone substitute his own judgment.

[handwritten margin note: B,L, + P = not quantifiable usually so, jury makes rough, reasonable judgments]

* * * * *

NOTES

1.   Can one quantify Burden, Loss, and Probability? Do you think Judge Learned Hand contemplated quantification? Or is the formula just a guideline? Isn't that Judge Posner's point in *McCarty*? Is the formula merely a decision-making tool for people who like algebra?

2.   Recall your study of economics as an undergraduate (or do some reading today!). Recall that the efficient firm produces at that level where the marginal cost of the last unit produced equals its marginal benefit. Likewise, the efficient firm will invest in safety up to the point where the marginal benefit of the last dollar invested in safety equals its marginal cost ($1). Investing less would mean foregoing benefit. Investing more would be "overinvesting." Now, do you see why the legal economists of the late 20th century and today have championed Learned Hand's famous formula?

3.   Louisiana courts also have adopted the formula or a variation of it. *See, e.g., Sistler v. Liberty Mut. Ins. Co.*, 558 So. 2d 1106 (La. 1990); *Washington v. Louisiana Power& Light*, 555 So. 2d 1350 (La. 1990); *Levi v. SLEMCO*, 542 So. 2d 1081 (La. 1989).

4.   Sometimes, the test is restated as a risk/utility test, i.e. is the defendant's conduct more risky than it is useful. However, it is, in essence, the same "Learned Hand" test. The "risk/utility" test is a staple in products liability. *See* Chapter 17, *infra*. And, it appears in courts' statements regarding the factors of how one determines if something presents and unreasonable risk of harm. For instance, the Louisiana Supreme Court has said that the determination of whether something presents an unreasonable risk of harm involves four factors: (1) the utility of the complained-of condition; (2) the likelihood and magnitude of harm, including the obviousness and apparentness of the condition; (3) the cost of preventing the harm; and (4) the nature of the plaintiff's activities in terms of its social utility or whether it is dangerous by nature. *Broussard v. State*, 113 So. 3d 175 (La. 2013). Do you see how those factors are similar to the Learned Hand formula?

5.   The Restatement (Third) of Torts: Liability for Physical Harm (Basic Principles) § 3 provides: *[handwritten: AKA "in breach"]*

> A person acts with negligence if the person does not exercise reasonable care under all the circumstances. Primary factors to consider in ascertaining whether the person's conduct lacks reasonable care are the foreseeable likelihood that it will result in harm, the foreseeable severity of the harm that may ensue, and the burden that would be borne by the person and others if the person takes precautions that eliminate or reduce the possibility of harm.

[handwritten margin marks: L, P, B]

D.   VIOLATION OF STATUTE, A/K/A NEGLIGENCE PER SE

COMMENT

The cases we have considered so far have applied a generally articulated "reasonable care under the circumstances test;" however, sometimes a court will adopt a statute as the standard of care of the reasonable person under the circumstances. Is this because reasonable people don't violate the law? If that is the case, how fast did you drive on your last trip to New Orleans?

A court will adopt a statue as the standard of care of the reasonable person under the circumstances when (1) the plaintiff is within the class of persons the statute was enacted to protect and (2) the risk was within the class of risks the statute was enacted to guard against.

BOYER
v.
JOHNSON
360 So. 2d 1164 (La. 1979)

TATE, J.

* * * * *

"Negligence Per Se"

In holding the defendant civilly liable for his breach of a duty created by a criminal statute, we do not intend to revive the doctrine of "negligence per se." A violation of a criminal statute does not automatically create liability in a particular civil case, because the statute may have been designed to protect someone other than the plaintiff, or to protect the plaintiff from some evil other than the injury for which recovery is sought. *Laird v. Travelers Insurance Company*, cited above; *Weber v. Phoenix Assurance Co. of New York*, 273 So. 2d 30 (La. 1973).

In this sense, criminal statutes can be said to be mere guidelines for the court. Similarly, a criminal law designed to protect one person from one harm may be thus used by the court as a starting-point toward fashioning an analogical standard of conduct of due care to protect other persons subjected to generically similar risks.

Yet, where a criminal statute imposes a duty designed to protect a particular person from a particular type of injury, one who has so injured such a person by a breach of the prescribed duty cannot evade civil liability by persuading the court to disregard the clear legislative prohibition as if it were a mere discretionary "guideline."

* * * * *

NOTE

Citing *Boyer v. Johnson*, the Fourth Circuit ruled there is no negligence *per se* doctrine in Louisiana, and that to establish liability a statutory violation must be determined to be a legal cause of the accident. *Bellsouth Telecommunications, Inc. v. Eustis Engineering Co., Inc.*, 974 So. 2d 749 (La. App. 4th Cir. 2007). Note how negligence per se functions in Louisiana to affect the duty/risk analysis in determining comparative fault. In one case involving an accident between a motor vehicle and a 10-year old child on a bicycle, the court allocated 15% of the fault to the child's mother based on her violation of La. R.S. 32:199 for knowingly permitting the child, under age 12, to ride a bicycle without a helmet. "[T]here was a direct relationship between the non-use of a bicycle safety helmet and the injuries incurred." *Mitchell v. Roy*, 51 So. 3d 153 (La.App. 3 Cir. 2010), *writ denied*, 56 So. 3d 957 (La. 2011).

WRIGHT
v.
BROWN
356 A. 2d 176 (Conn. 1975)

BOGDANSKI, Asso. J.

This action seeking damages for injuries caused by a dog bite was brought by the plaintiff, Mary F. Wright, against the defendants, William Brown, the town of Plainville and Gail Litke, its dog warden. The dog warden and the town of Plainville demurred to the last four counts of the five-count complaint. The trial court sustained the demurrer to all four counts and rendered judgment on the demurrer when the plaintiff failed to plead over. From that judgment the plaintiff appealed to this court, assigning error in the sustaining of the demurrer.

The complaint alleged that a dog owned by the defendant Brown attacked and injured the plaintiff; that less than fourteen days prior to this incident, the same dog had attacked another person resulting in the quarantine of the dog by the defendant dog warden; that the dog warden released the dog prior to the expiration of the fourteen-day quarantine period required by § 22-358[38] of the General Statutes; that as a result of that premature release, the dog was placed in a situation where it attacked the plaintiff. The second and fifth counts of the complaint were based on negligence, alleging that the dog warden and the town failed to comply with the standard of conduct required by § 22-358. The third and fourth counts were based on a theory of nuisance.

The dog warden and the town demurred to the complaint as follows: (a) to the second count 'on the grounds that any purported violation of ... (§ 22-358) would not constitute negligence since the plaintiff was not within the class of persons which that statute was designed to protect'; (b) to the third and fourth counts on the ground that no positive act of the town or of its employee was alleged; and (c) to the fifth count on the grounds that (1) the plaintiff was not within the class of persons protected by § 22-358, and (2) since any act of the dog warden was governmental, the town was immune from liability.

The trial court concluded that § 22-358 was enacted to provide a period of quarantine to determine whether a person bitten by a dog required the administration of a rabies vaccine and 'to protect members of the community from being bitten by diseased dogs.' The court then concluded that the plaintiff was not within the class of persons protected by § 22-358 since she had not alleged that she was bitten by a diseased dog.

The purpose of the quarantine requirement in § 22-358 is readily ascertainable from the meaning of that word. 'Quarantine' means to isolate as a precaution against contagious disease or a detainment to prevent exposure of others to disease. Webster's Third New International Dictionary 1859; 39 C.J.S., Health, s 15a. *See In re Halco*, 246 Cal.App.2d 553, 557, 54 Cal.Rptr. 661; *Daniel v. Putnam County*, 113 Ga. 570, 572, 38 S.E. 980; 3A C.J.S., Animals, § 73. While the specific concern of the legislature may have been to protect the victim of a dog bite from the threat of rabies,[39] that

---

[38] '(General Statutes) Sec. 22-358. ... Quarantine of biting dogs. ... (b) Any person who is bitten, or shows visible evidence of attack by any dog, when such person is not upon the premises of the owner or keeper of such dog, may kill such dog during such attack or make complaint to the chief canine control officer, any canine control officer or the warden or regional canine control officer of the town wherein such dog is owned or kept; and such chief canine control officer, canine control officer, warden or regional canine control officer shall immediately make an investigation of such complaint. If such warden, chief canine control officer, canine control officer, or regional canine control officer finds that such person has been bitten or so attacked by such dog when such person was not upon the premises of the owner or keeper of such dog, such warden, chief canine control officer, canine control officer, or regional canine control officer shall quarantine such dog in a public pound or order the owner to quarantine it in a veterinary hospital or a kennel approved by the commissioner for such purpose; ... and the commissioner, the chief canine control officer, any canine control officer, any warden or any regional canine control officer may make any order concerning the restraint or disposal of any biting dog as he deems necessary.... On the fourteenth day of such quarantine said dog shall be examined by the commissioner or someone designated by him to determine whether such quarantine shall be continued or removed....'

[39] *See* 13 H.R.Proc., Pt. 2, 1969 Sess., p. 928, wherein Representative Stewart B. McKinney commented during debate of an amendment (H.B. 5522, Public Acts 1969, No. 35) to § 22-358 on the need to quarantine a biting dog in order to detect the presence of rabies. *See also* 2 Gray, Attorneys' Textbook of Medicine (3d Ed.) 40.27(3) wherein it is noted that if a dog lives and is well at the end of ten quarantine days, a rabies vaccine need not be given to the bitten victim.

restricted purpose is not expressed in the language of § 22- 358. Nowhere is the control of rabies mentioned. The intent expressed in the language of the statute is the controlling factor. *Kellems v. Brown*, 163 Conn. 478, 515, 313 A.2d 53; *United Aircraft Corporation v. Fusari*, 163 Conn. 401, 410, 311 A.2d 65. The trial court correctly concluded that § 22- 358 was intended not only to protect persons bitten by a dog from the threat of rabies, but also to protect the general public from contact with diseased dogs.

'Where a statute is designed to protect persons against injury, one who has, as a result of its violation, suffered such an injury as the statute was intended to guard against has a good ground of recovery.' *Knybel v. Cramer*, 129 Conn. 439, 443, 29 A.2d 576, 577; *Coughlin v. Peters*, 153 Conn. 99, 102, 214 A.2d 127. That principle of the law sets forth two conditions which must coexist before statutory negligence can be actionable. First, the plaintiff must be within the class of persons protected by the statute. *Id.*, 153 Conn. 101, 214 A.2d 127; *Hassett v. Palmer*, 126 Conn. 468, 473, 12 A.2d 646; *Monroe v. Hartford Street Ry. Co.*, 76 Conn. 201, 207, 56 A. 498. Second, the injury must be of the type which the statute was intended to prevent. *Toomey v. Danaher*, 161 Conn. 204, 212, 286 A.2d 293; *Longstean v. McCaffrey's Sons*, 95 Conn. 486, 493, 111 A. 788. *See* Prosser, Torts (4th Ed.) s 36; Restatement (Second), 2 Torts §§ 286, 288.

If we apply these principles to the purpose of § 22-358, it becomes clear that the class of persons protected is not limited; rather the statute was intended to protect the general public or, as stated by the trial court, 'members of the community.'

Since the demurrer to the second and fifth counts was addressed only to the class of persons protected by sec. 22-358, and since the plaintiff, as a member of the general public, is within that class, the demurrer should not have been sustained on that ground. *See Stradmore Development Corporation v. Commissioners*, 164 Conn. 548, 551, 324 A.2d 919; *Ross Realty Corporation v. Surkis*, 163 Conn. 388, 391, 311 A.2d 74; *Covino v. Pfeffer*, 160 Conn. 212, 213, 276 A.2d 895.

Although we have concluded that the second and fifth counts are not insufficient for the reason specified in the defendants' demurrer, we are not to be understood as holding that those counts can successfully withstand a claim that the plaintiff's injuries were not of the type which sec. 22-358 was intended to prevent. The second and fifth counts allege only that the plaintiff was attacked and injured by a dog that was prematurely released from quarantine. That allegation does not claim an injury of the type sec. 22-358 was intended to prevent. *Cf. Stiebitz v. Mahoney*, 144 Conn. 443, 448, 134 A.2d 71.

* * * * *

NOTE

In *Ducote v. Boleware*, 216 So. 3d 934 (La.App. 4 Cir. 2016), defendant's cat attacked and bit plaintiff. Defendant testified that the cat had been vaccinated for rabies but he could not establish proof of that fact, as required by a New Orleans ordinance. He was cited for violating the failure to prove vaccination ordinance. Plaintiff opted to have anti--rabies vaccine. *Held*. The violation of the ordinance did not constitute negligence per se and, under the circumstances (the cat did not have rabies which was confirmed after quarantine and observation), the defendant is not liable.

RAINS
v.
BEND OF THE RIVER
124 S.W.3d 580 (Tenn. Ct. App. 2003)

KOCH, J.

This appeal involves an eighteen year old who committed suicide with his parents' .25 caliber handgun. The parents filed suit in the Circuit Court for Putnam County against the retailer who sold their son ammunition for the handgun shortly before his death. They later amended the complaint to seek loss of consortium damages for themselves and their son's surviving siblings. The trial court denied the retailer's motion for summary judgment regarding the wrongful death claims.... We granted permission to appeal and have now determined that the trial court erred by denying the retailer's Tenn. R. Civ. P. 56 and 12.02(6) motions because, based on the undisputed facts, the suicide was not reasonably foreseeable and was the independent, intervening cause of the young man's death.

* * * * *

Mr. Rains turned eighteen in mid-January 1997. At some point on July 16, 1997, Mr. Rains found the key to his father's gun case and removed the .25 caliber handgun. He closed and locked the case and then returned the key to his mother's jewelry box where he had found it. Then, he set out to find ammunition for the pistol because his father did not have any ammunition in the house. His first stop was the sporting goods department at a local K-Mart. He inquired about the minimum age for purchasing .25 caliber ammunition and was told that buyers of that ammunition must be at least twenty-one years old. Mr. Rains showed the clerk his driver's license and commented, "Oh, I'm only eighteen." Rather than purchasing the ammunition, Mr. Rains purchased a package of BBs and left K-Mart.

After leaving K-Mart, Mr. Rains drove to Bend of the River Shooting Supplies, a store in Cookeville selling firearms, shooting supplies, and ammunition. While at Bend of the River, Mr. Rains purchased a box of Winchester .25 ACP automatic caliber 50 gr. full metal jacket cartridges. The store clerk did not ask Mr. Rains for proof of his age and accepted Mr. Rains's personal check in the amount of $11.85 in payment for the ammunition. There is no evidence that Mr. Rains's conduct and demeanor while he was at Bend of the River were out of the ordinary.

Sometime later, either on July 16, 1997 or early July 17, 1997, Mr. Rains drove his car to Walker Hollow Road and parked. He loaded his parents' pistol with the ammunition he had purchased at Bend of the River and fatally shot himself. The box of ammunition bearing Bend of the River's price tag was found in his car. It is undisputed that Mr. Rains used the .25 caliber handgun and ammunition to commit suicide. It is equally undisputed that neither Mr. Rains's parents nor any other family members had any sort of warning that Mr. Rains was planning to take his own life. From all outward signs, he was a happy, well-adjusted young man.

* * * * *

The Negligence Per Se Claim

In Tennessee, the common-law standard of conduct to which a person must conform to avoid being negligent is the familiar "reasonable person under similar circumstances" standard. As a general matter, this standard requires a person to exercise reasonable care under the circumstances to refrain from conduct that could foreseeably injure others. This standard is flexible, and its contours are inherently fact-sensitive. Therefore, determinations regarding whether particular conduct conforms to the common-law standard of conduct are made on a case-by-case basis.

However, the common law is not the only source of legal duties or standards of conduct in negligence cases. In addition to the general duty to act reasonably to avoid harming others, more specific duties governing particular situations and relationships may be imposed by the General Assembly. Legislatively created legal duties arise in two ways. First, the General Assembly may create a legal duty and then provide a civil cause of action for its breach.[40] Second, the General Assembly may enact a penal statute that does not explicitly provide a civil remedy,[41] and the courts may then derive a civil legal duty from the penal statute. "Negligence per se" is the term used to describe one of the two doctrines associated with the latter process.[42]

The negligence per se doctrine enables the courts to mold standards of conduct in penal statutes into rules of civil liability. The process has been analogized to "judicial legislation,"[43] and its governing principles and their application vary considerably from jurisdiction to jurisdiction.[44] Still, a consensus exists regarding many of the doctrine's basic precepts.

The negligence per se doctrine does not create a new cause of action. Rather, it is a form of ordinary negligence, that enables the courts to use a penal statute to define a reasonably prudent person's standard of care. Negligence per se arises when a legislative body pronounces in a penal statute what the conduct of a reasonable person must be, whether or not the common law would require similar conduct.

The negligence per se doctrine is not a magic transformational formula that automatically creates a private negligence cause of action for the violation of every statute. Not every statutory violation amounts to negligence per se. To trigger the doctrine, the statute must establish a specific standard of conduct. Restatement (Second) of Torts § 286 cmt. d; Restatement (Second) of Torts § 874A cmt. e ("The common law tort of negligence is not changed, but the expression of the standard

---

[40] For example, the Tennessee Consumer Protection Act of 1977 imposes on merchants the duty to refrain from engaging in defined unfair and deceptive trade practices, Tenn.Code Ann. § 47-18-104 (Supp.2002), and provides for a private cause of action for the breach of this statutory obligation. Tenn.Code Ann. § 47-18-109(a)(1) (2001).

[41] For example, motorists must stop in response to an illuminated flashing red traffic signal. Tenn.Code Ann. §§ 55-8-112(a)(1), -145(a)(1) (1998). Failure to obey these rules of the road is a Class C misdemeanor, but neither statute contains a provision explicitly authorizing a civil action for damages against persons who violate the statute.

[42] In addition to the negligence per se doctrine, courts may also infer new private rights of action from a penal statute. *Compare* Restatement (Second) of Torts §§ 286, 288 (1965) *with* Restatement (Second) of Torts § 874A (1979). These two doctrines are analytically related but legally distinct. *See Pratico v. Portland Terminal Co.,* 783 F.2d 255, 265-67 (1st Cir. 1985); Restatement (Second) of Torts § 874A cmt. e. However, many of the same considerations that are relevant to determining whether to identify a new private right of action are also relevant to determining whether a specific statutory standard of conduct should be imported into a negligence action.

[43] W. Page Keeton, Prosser and Keeton on the Law of Torts § 36, at 222 (5th ed. 1984) ("Prosser & Keeton"). Deciding whether to invoke the negligence per se doctrine requires the courts to make policy decisions. The courts are not required to provide these civil remedies, and the decision to do so is a judicial act, not a legislative act. Restatement (Second) of Torts § 286 cmt. d.

[44] 2 Stuart M. Speiser, et al., The American Law of Torts § 9:8, at 1023-24 (1985) (noting that "[t]his area of the effect of the violation of a statute, ordinance or administrative regulation in the law of negligence is one in which, indeed, angels fear to tread. Overbroad language and sweeping statements can be found in decisions to support virtually any position as to the effect of such violation.").

of care in certain fact situations is modified; it is changed from a general standard to a specific rule of conduct."). Many states require the statutory standard of conduct to differ from the ordinary prudent person standard of conduct. Invoking the negligence per se doctrine is unnecessary and redundant if the statute requires only the ordinary reasonable person standard of conduct.[45]

The effect of declaring conduct negligent per se is to render the conduct negligent as a matter of law.[46] Thus, a person whose conduct is negligent per se cannot escape liability by attempting to prove that he or she acted reasonably under the circumstances. However, a finding of negligence per se is not equivalent to a finding of liability per se. Plaintiffs in negligence per se cases must still establish causation in fact, legal cause, and damages.

The fact that the General Assembly has enacted a statute defining criminal conduct does not necessarily mean that the courts must adopt it as a standard of civil liability. Decisions regarding the proper civil standard of conduct rest with the courts. Thus, the courts must ultimately decide whether they will adopt a statutory standard to define the standard of conduct of reasonable persons in specific circumstances. Restatement (Second) of Torts § 874A cmt. e ("[I]t is the court that adopts and utilizes the statutory rule in substitution for the general standard and ⋯ [the court] may exercise its sound discretion as to when this should be done.").

The courts consider a number of factors to determine whether the violation of a statute should trigger the negligence per se doctrine. The two threshold questions in every negligence per se case are whether the plaintiff belongs to the class of persons the statute was designed to protect and whether the plaintiff's injury is of the type that the statute was designed to prevent. Restatement (Second) of Torts § 286.[47] Affirmative answers to these questions do not end the inquiry. Courts also consider (1) whether the statute is the sole source of the defendant's duty to the plaintiff, (2) whether the statute clearly defines the prohibited or required conduct, (3) whether the statute would impose liability without fault, (4) whether invoking the negligence per se doctrine would result in damage awards disproportionate to the statutory violation, and (5) whether the plaintiff's injury is a direct or indirect result of the violation of the statute. Restatement (Second) of Torts § 874A cmt. h(1). *read through it,*

court is reasoning here ... they're just reading it ⋯ think it out, not really a right or wrong

We have substantial doubt that the illegal sale of handgun ammunition to an eighteen-year-old purchaser who used it to commit suicide should trigger the negligence per se doctrine. Congress did not undertake to create a private, civil cause of action for these sorts of violations of the Gun Control Act of 1968.[48] In addition, the Act does not contain a clearly defined standard of conduct

---

[45] For example, Tenn.Code Ann. § 55-8-112(a)(2) requires drivers to proceed with caution when confronted with an illuminated flashing yellow caution signal. This statute requires the driver to exercise his or her judgment and reflects a standard of care that is no different from the ordinary prudent person standard of conduct. It differs from Tenn.Code Ann. § 55-8-112(a)(1) which requires motorists to stop at flashing red warning lights without exercising their judgment regarding the necessity of stopping.

[46] *See also* Prosser & Keeton § 36, at 230 ("The effect of such a rule is to stamp the defendant's conduct as negligence, with all the effects of common law negligence, but no greater effect.").

[47] The Restatement points out that the courts should not adopt a standard of conduct defined by legislation if the legislation's exclusive purpose is (1) to protect a class of persons other than the one whose interests are invaded, (2) to protect an interest other than the one invaded, (3) to protect against other harm than that which has resulted, or (4) to protect against other hazards than that from which the harm has resulted. Restatement (Second) of Torts § 288(d) - (g).

[48] Since the Act's original enactment, there have been several unsuccessful attempts to amend the Gun Control Act of 1968 to expressly provide a civil cause of action for negligent handgun and ammunition sale. Kennedy-Rodino Handgun Crime Control Act of 1983, S.511 § 105(d), 98th Cong., 1st Sess., 129 Cong. Rec. S1315, at S1319 (proposed amendment to Section 924(e)) (daily ed., Feb. 17, 1983)

with regard to the sale of ammunition to persons who may be intending to use it for self-destructive purposes. Finally, it is far from clear that Congress intended to protect adults from self-destructive acts when it enacted the Gun Control Act.[49]

The courts that have addressed the question of whether various violations of the Gun Control Act of 1968 trigger liability under the negligence per se doctrine have reached inconsistent results. [footnote omitted] However, the Tennessee Supreme Court has, over the years, been quick to invoke the negligence per se doctrine with regard to violations of penal statutes designed to protect the public[50] Prosser & Keeton § 36, at 227. In addition, another panel of this court has implied that the sale of handgun ammunition to a person under twenty-one years of age is negligence per se under Tennessee law. Accordingly, for the purpose of reviewing the trial court's denial of Bend of the River's motion for summary judgment, we will presume that the sale of handgun ammunition to an eighteen year old purchaser in violation of 18 U.S.C. § 922(b)(1) is negligence per se.

Concluding that Bend of the River was negligent per se for its violation of 18 U.S.C. § 922(b)(1) does not end the inquiry. To maintain a successful negligence per se action, Mr. Rains's parents must prove not only that Bend of the River violated a penal statute designed to protect the public but also that the violation of the statute was the legal cause of Mr. Rains's death.

[The court goes on to hold that the decedent's act of suicide was "an independent, intervening cause that insulates Bend of the River from liability on his parents' negligence per se claim."]

NOTES

1. The Restatement (Second) of Torts provides:

§ 285. How Standard Of Conduct Is Determined

The standard of conduct of a reasonable man may be

(a) established by a legislative enactment or administrative regulation which so provides, or

(b) adopted by the court from a legislative enactment or an administrative regulation which does not so provide, or
(c) established by judicial decision, or

(d) applied to the facts of the case by the trial judge or the jury, if there is no such enactment, regulation, or decision.

§ 286. When Standard Of Conduct Defined By Legislation Or Regulation Will Be Adopted

---

[49] The United States Supreme Court has explained that the "principal purpose of the federal gun control legislation ⋯ was to curb crime by keeping 'firearms out of the hands of those not legally entitled to possess them because of age, criminal background, or incompetency.'" *Huddleston v. United States*, 415 U.S. 814, 824, 94 S.Ct. 1262, 1268-69, 39 L.Ed.2d 782 (1974). Even courts that have given the Gun Control Act of 1968 a most expansive reading have pointed out that its purpose is to address the prevalence of lawlessness and violent crime in the United States.

[50] The Tennessee General Assembly later restricted the scope of the court's negligence per se holding in this case.

142

The court may adopt as the standard of conduct of a reasonable man the requirements of a legislative enactment or an administrative regulation whose purpose is found to be exclusively or in part

       (a) to protect a class of persons which includes the one whose interest is invaded, and

       (b) to protect the particular interest which is invaded, and

       (c) to protect that interest against the kind of harm which has resulted, and

       (d) to protect that interest against the particular hazard from which the harm results. *circumstances*

[handwritten margin notes: negligence per se analysis: NOT IN LA: statute analysis — A. #1: helpful? (specific instructions) #2: class of persons? #3: this kind of harm? — B. what effect? #1: establishes breach per se #2: rebuttable presumption of breach #3: goes to jury]

2.   Is the decision in *Wright* on class of persons helpful at all? Doesn't it impose a duty to the world? Reconsider this question after you read Judge Andrew's dissent in *Palsgraf, infra*, at 183.

3.   With the legislature increasingly regulating the details of our day-to-day conduct and lives, would you expect the negligence per se approach to negligence to become more important? Reconsider this issue after you have studied the chapter on legal cause.

4.   Once the court has adopted the statute as the standard of care of the reasonable person under the circumstances, what affect does the statute have? Is the jury bound by it? That is, does the jury lose its power to decide if the victim behaved as a reasonable person under the circumstances? Is it limited to simply deciding whether defendant violated the statute as a matter of fact? That effect is sometimes called negligence per se. Or, does the violation of the statute create a presumption of negligence which defendant must rebut by proving that it exercised reasonable care under the circumstances. Under that effect it is said that the violation of the statute created a rebuttable presumption of negligence. Finally, the violation may simply be treated as some evidence of negligence which the jury may put into the hopper with all the other evidence of negligence with the plaintiff keeping the burden of proof. This third procedural affect of violation of statute seems to be the Louisiana approach. But, as you continue to study torts you will become increasingly comfortable (or frustrated) with the answer–the law is confused and unsettled.

5.   Sometimes, courts neither ask the jury to decide whether the defendant acted as a reasonable person under circumstances nor adopt a statute as the standard of care of the reasonable person under the circumstances. Instead, the court articulates a "rule of law." It articulates what it determines was reasonable care under the circumstances. Justice Oliver Wendell Holmes, Jr. was a champion of this approach, believing that as trial judges became more familiar with recurring factual situations they were in a better position than a jury to decide what was reasonable care. *See, e.g.,* Oliver Wendell Holmes, Jr., The Common Law 122-24 (1881). As an appellate judge, he articulated one of the most famous of these rules of law in *B. & O.R. Co. v. Goodman*, 275 U.S. 66 (1927), holding that when a vehicle approached a railroad crossing the driver was negligent as a matter of law if she failed to "stop, look, and listen." Predictably, such rules lead to exceptions, and Holmes' "stop, look, and listen" rule was limited in *Pokora v. Wabash Ry. Co.*, 292 U.S. 98 (1934), an opinion written by Justice Cardozo. Another famous "rule of law" case is *Helling v. Carey*, 83 Wash. 2d 514, 519 P. 2d 981 (1974). There, the Washington Supreme Court held that it was negligence for an ophthalmologist to fail to give a glaucoma test to a patient who was under 40, even though the risk of disease was generally slight.

6.   How different are the cases discussed in the next section?

7. Consider the statute below, La. R.S. 32:292.1. What effect will the statute have on negligence cases in terms of imposing liability and in terms of creating an immunity from liability?

§ 292.1. Transportation and storage of firearms in privately owned motor vehicles;

A. Except as provided in Subsection D of this Section, a person who lawfully possesses a firearm may transport or store such firearm in a locked, privately-owned motor vehicle in any parking lot, parking garage, or other designated parking area.

B. No property owner, tenant, public or private employer, or business entity or their agent or employee shall be liable in any civil action for damages resulting from or arising out of an occurrence involving a firearm transported or stored pursuant to this Section, other than for a violation of Subsection C of this Section.

C. No property owner, tenant, public or private employer, or business entity shall prohibit any person from transporting or storing a firearm pursuant to Subsection A of this Section. However, nothing in this Section shall prohibit an employer or business entity from adopting policies specifying that firearms stored in locked, privately-owned motor vehicles on property controlled by an employer or business entity be hidden from plain view or within a locked case or container within the vehicle.

D. This Section shall not apply to:

(1) Any property where the possession of firearms is prohibited under state or federal law.

(2) Any vehicle owned or leased by a public or private employer or business entity and used by an employee in the course of his employment, except for those employees who are required to transport or store a firearm in the official discharge of their duties.

(3) Any vehicle on property controlled by a public or private employer or business entity if access is restricted or limited through the use of a fence, gate, security station, signage, or other means of restricting or limiting general public access onto the parking area, and if one of the following conditions applies:

(a) The employer or business entity provides facilities for the temporary storage of unloaded firearms.

(b) The employer or business entity provides an alternative parking area reasonably close to the main parking area in which employees and other persons may transport or store firearms in locked, privately-owned motor vehicles.

8. What about La. R.S. 32:71, which provides that 1) on a multi-lane highway, no vehicle shall be driven in the left hand lane except when a) preparing for a left turn, b) overtaking or passing a vehicle, or c) the right lanes are congested; 2) no vehicle driven in the left lane shall impede another vehicle in that lane except when preparing for a proper left turn; and 3) no vehicle traveling in a left lane shall be driven at a speed slower than any vehicle to its right on the same road.

9. Or, La. R.S. 22:1338. The Act prohibits an insurer from cancelling or failing to renew homeowners' insurance merely because the property had or has Chinese drywall which was installed before December 31, 2009 or the insured made a claim based upon Chinese drywall installed before

that date. An insurer who cancels or fails to renew after the insured has made a claim has thirty days to reinstate the policy or else may be subject to penalties, attorney fees, and court costs.

How would this act change the duty/risk analysis outside of the insurance context? Would homeowners who were aware of the presence of the faulty drywall as evidenced by their reliance on this statute to preserve coverage be subject to a concurrent increase in their own duty to prevent or mitigate harm caused by the product? Reliance on this statute might be a double-edged sword if it were used in a negligence action to prove the homeowner was aware of an increased risk and failed to take increased precautions to prevent or mitigate accidents.

E. SPECIAL DUTIES

(handwritten: ① high degree of care → innkeeper cases → common carrier)

In some circumstances, courts will state that a defendant owes a "high" or "the highest" degree of care to the plaintiff. The circumstances usually include some of the following: (1) the plaintiff has little choice in whether to enter into a relationship with defendant, (2) the defendant's activity involves an unusually high risk of harm, (3) the defendant has superior control, viz a viz the plaintiff, over the risk of harm, and (4) the better societal policy is to spread the harm among those who participate in or benefit from the defendant's activity. Other courts reject the "high degree of care" terminology, concluding merely that under the circumstances, a reasonably prudent person, exercising ordinary care, would be extremely cautious. One example of a "high degree of care" can be seen in the "innkeeper" cases. *See, e.g., Laubie v. Sonesta International Hotel Corp.,* 398 So. 2d 1374 (La. 1981). Another is the "common carrier." In *Galland v. NOPSI,* 377 So. 2d 84 (La. 1979), the Supreme Court held that the mere showing of an injury to a fare-paying passenger on a public conveyance and his failure to reach his destination safely establishes a prima facie case of negligence and imposes on the carrier the burden of exculpating itself of negligence. The court held that the appellate court had erred in holding that before the presumption arises, the plaintiff must not merely prove that the injury occurred, but must also prove that the injury was caused by an incident, occurrence or condition attributable to the carrier. Subsequently, in *Rodriguez v. NOPSI,* 400 So. 2d 884 (La. 1981), the court clarified its position. It stated that a carrier of passengers is required to exercise the highest degree of care and is liable for the slightest negligence; the reason for the rule is the notion that one who is in the business of providing transportation for a fee should be a more professional transporter than the "reasonably prudent" driver with respect to hazards associated with the transportation of passengers. However, injury to a passenger resulting from a battery committed by another passenger is totally unconnected with the hazards generally associated with transportation. In such a case the carrier does not owe the "highest degree" duty, but only the duty owed by a business which permits the public to enter its premises, i.e., reasonable care under the circumstances.

(handwritten: private carrier → guard against predictable assault)

In *Luckette v. Bart's On The Lake, Ltd.,* 602 So. 2d 108 (La.App. 4 Cir. 1992), the court held that the law applicable to a private business enterprise, and not the high degree of care imposed on public common carriers, applies to a private carrier. However, a private carrier has a general duty to "guard against the predictable risk of assaults" related to the operation of its business enterprise, even though the victim is not a paying customer. A private carrier which knowingly undertakes the transportation of intoxicated persons has a duty to protect third parties from risks occurring or connected with the transportation, such as an assault or molestation of a third person in the conveyance.

(handwritten: → maintenance of power lines / utility company)

In *Levi v. Slemco,* 542 So. 2d 1081 (La. 1989), the court held that a company which maintains and employs high power lines is required to exercise the "utmost care" to reduce hazards to life as far as practicable. In *Perkins v. Entergy Corp.,* 756 So. 2d 388 (La.App. 1 Cir. 1999) the court said that the appropriate duty of a utility company is "utmost care" when someone is directly injured because of the dangerous nature of electricity, such as when someone is electrocuted by coming into contact with a high voltage line in the possession and control of the utility company. However, in cases which involve accidents other than electrocution which occur on the customer's property but which allegedly are caused by some action or inaction on the part of the utility company, the utility's duty is to use reasonable care.

[handwritten: → elevator owners & operators]

In *Broussard v. State,* 113 So. 3d 175 (La. 2013), the court stated that elevator owners and operators owe a high degree of care.

A significant number of cases explore and sometimes impose upon actors a "fiduciary duty" to a tort victim. *See, e.g. Wadsworth v. ABC Ins. Co.,* 732 So. 2d 56 (La.App. 4 Cir. 1998). In most of these cases the court may be concluding either (1) the actor owed a tort duty to protect the victim from harm by third persons, or a duty to disclose information to the victim, or (2) because of the relationship between them and the nature of the activity, the actor's duty of reasonable care required extreme caution (the "high degree of care" concept). It does not appear that much is accomplished by adding to such determinations a conclusion that one owes a "fiduciary duty" in a tort case.

[handwritten margin note: Fiduciary duty to tort victim]

F. RES IPSA LOQUITUR

[handwritten: (THA BOP) = Prepord evi → More likely than not]

COMMENT

Ordinarily, the plaintiff in a tort case must prove each element and his cause of action by a preponderance of the evidence, i. e., "more probable than not." However, there are really two things being proven, the facts, and whether the facts give rise to a tort. At the first level (proof of facts), the plaintiff must present evidence from which reasonable minds could conclude (usually by the "probability" test) the existence of the facts which he contends give him a cause of action. Thus plaintiff must first show "what happened." Proof may be by direct evidence (the witness has first hand knowledge of the fact) or by circumstantial evidence (no first hand knowledge of the fact, but knowledge of the circumstances from which, when combined with other circumstances, one reasonably could infer the existence of the fact). Because credibility is for the jury, direct evidence satisfies the plaintiff's burden of producing evidence as to that fact. If plaintiff offers only circumstantial evidence as to the existence of the fact, the judge first must determine whether reasonable minds could conclude the existence of the fact from the circumstances.

The second level of proof is that the facts constitute "fault," *i.e.,* could reasonable minds conclude from the circumstances that the defendant acted unreasonably, or the defendant did an act which was substantially certain to invade a protected interest? This is sometimes called a "mixed question law and fact." The judge's control over jury determinations of fact and mixed questions of law and fact is provided through the directed verdict (*see, e.g.,* CCP Art. 1810) and the judgment notwithstanding the verdict (*see, e.g,* CCP Art. 1811).

There are cases in which the plaintiff cannot prove "what happened," but he can prove circumstances from which reasonable minds could infer and conclude that the defendant acted unreasonably or that the "thing" presented an unreasonable risk of harm. Put another way, although plaintiff cannot prove exactly what happened, he can prove that circumstances existed from which reasonable minds could conclude that the defendant was at fault and that fault caused plaintiff's damage.

This common sense evaluation of the strength of circumstantial evidence sometimes is called *res ipsa loquitur* or "the thing speaks for itself." Consider the following two cases discussing *res ipsa loquitur.*

TATE, J.

[handwritten: – circ. evi doesn't have to negate all other possibilities, just needs to be more probable than not that harm was caused by D]

* * * * *

The decedent Boudreaux was suffocated in the early hours as he lay asleep in his attic apartment in premises adjacent to the steak house. His suffocation was the result of a major fire which originated in the kitchen of the restaurant shortly after it had closed.

* * * * *

Because of the lack of proof as to what had caused the fire, both the trial and the intermediate court held that the plaintiffs had not proved by a preponderance of the evidence that the insured's negligence was the cause of their decedent's wrongful death. We granted certiorari because of our doubt that these courts had correctly applied this burden of proof required in civil cases.

Recently, in *Jordan v. Travelers Insurance Co.*, 257 La. 995, 245 So. 2d 151, 155 (1971), we summarized the several judicial formulations of this burden of proof in civil cases and concluded:

"In describing this burden of proof, the courts sometimes speak of proof to a 'reasonable certainty' or to a 'legal certainty'; or of proof by evidence which is of 'greater weight' or 'more convincing' than that offered to the contrary; or (in the case of circumstantial evidence) of proof which excludes other reasonable hypotheses than the defendant's tort with 'a fair amount of certainty'. Whatever the descriptive term used, however, proof by direct or circumstantial evidence is sufficient to constitute a preponderance, when, taking the evidence as a whole, such proof shows that the fact or causation sought to be proved is more probable than not."

Further, as we specifically held in *Naquin v. Marquette Casualty Co.*, 244 La. 569, 153 So. 2d 395 (1963), by this burden of proof, the circumstantial evidence requisite in civil negligence cases need not negate *all* other *possible* causes of injury, as the opinions of the previous courts seemed to hold. It suffices if the circumstantial proof excludes other reasonable hypotheses only with a fair amount of certainty, so that it be more probable than not that the harm was caused by the tortious conduct of the defendant. 153 So. 2d 396--397.

[handwritten: → neg. inferred based on facts that make it more prob than not]

In this respect, the principle of *"res ipsa loquitur"* (the thing speaks for itself) sometimes comes into play as a rule of circumstantial evidence, whereby negligence is inferred on the part of a defendant because the facts indicate this to be the more probable cause of injury *in the absence of other as- plausible explanation* by witnesses found credible.[6] *Pilie v. National Food Stores of*

---

[6] *King v. King*, 253 La. 270, 217 So. 2d 395, 397 (1968): "*Res ipsa loquitur* is a rule of circumstantial evidence. Its applicability is determined at the conclusion of the trial. The rule applies when the facts shown suggest the negligence of the defendant as the most plausible explanation of the accident." (Italics ours.)

In addition to describing this principle of circumstantial evidence, the term "*res ipsa loquitur*" is also sometimes used to describe the burden to prove themselves *not* negligent required of those using dangerous substances or engaging in dangerous activities which injure others or of those under some special relationship of care to others injured through their activity. In this type of situation, the effect of the doctrine is not only to supply an element of proof but also to shift the burden onto such type of defendant to explain or pay. Malone, Res Ipsa Loquitur, 4 La.L.Rev. 70, 95–99, 103 (1941); Prosser on Torts, pp. 213, 223, 228--30 (4th ed. 1971).

Louisiana, 245 La. 276, 158 So. 2d 162 (1963); *Larkin v. State Farm Mutual Auto. Ins. Co.*, 233 La. 544, 97 So. 2d 389 (1957); Malone, Res Ipsa Loquitur and Proof by Inference, 4 La.L.Rev. 70 (1941); Comment, 25 La.L.Rev. 748 (1965). Thus, by this principle where properly applied, the circumstantial evidence indicates that the injury was caused by some negligence on the part of the defendant, without necessarily proving just what negligent act caused the injury.

We noted in *Larkin v. State Farm Mutual Automobile Ins. Co.*, 233 La. 544, 97 So. 2d 389, 391 (1957): "... the maxim (*res ipsa loquitur*) means only that the facts of the occurrence warrant the inference of negligence, not that they compel such an inference.... The application of the rule does not, therefore, dispense with the necessity that the plaintiff prove negligence, but is simply a step in the process of such proof, permitting the plaintiff, in a proper case, to place in the scales, along with proof of the accident and enough of the attending circumstances to invoke the rule, an inference of negligence.... When all the evidence is in, the question is still whether the preponderance is with the plaintiff."

Nevertheless, when all the evidence is in and the question is whether, by reason of the *res ipsa loquitur* rule, the plaintiff has preponderantly proved that the defendant is responsible in tort for his injury, we have in our most recent decision on the issue noted that the real test of applying *res ipsa loquitur* to be as follows: Do the facts of the controversy suggest negligence of the defendant, rather than some other factors, as the *most plausible* explanation of the accident? *Pilie v. National Food Store*, 245 La. 276, 158 So. 2d 162, 165 (1963). (Italics ours.) On the other hand, application of the principle is defeated if "an inference that the accident was due to a cause other than defendant's negligence could be drawn *as reasonably* as one that it was due to his negligence." 158 So. 2d 165 (Italics ours.) *See also* Comment, 25 La.L.Rev. 748, 764 (1965). This is simply another formulation of the burden of a plaintiff in a tort action to prove that, more probably than not, his injury was caused by the negligence of the defendant.

* * * * *

LINNEAR
v.
CENTERPOINT ENERGY ENTEX/RELIANT ENERGY
966 So. 2d 36 (La. 2007)

VICTORY, J.

We granted this writ application to determine whether the court of appeal properly applied the doctrine of *res ipsa loquitur* to this negligence case. After reviewing the record and the applicable law, we find that the doctrine does not apply. Accordingly, we reverse the judgment of the court of appeal and reinstate the jury verdict and trial court judgment in favor of the defendant.

Facts and Procedural History

Plaintiffs, Charles and Dronzy Linnear, allege that on the morning of July 16, 2002, Mrs. Linnear stepped into a sinkhole next to her driveway as she was placing items in the backseat of her car. The Linnears sued CenterPoint Energy Entex/Reliant Energy ("CenterPoint") alleging that Mrs. Linnear's fall was caused by CenterPoint's negligence. Eleven days before the accident, CenterPoint was dispatched to investigate a gas leak at the Linnear residence. After locating the leak, turning off the gas, and installing a temporary line to maintain service, CenterPoint returned a few days later to install a new gas line. The crew dug a trench four inches wide and eighteen inches deep running parallel to the Linnear's driveway, with approximately two to three feet between the trench and the driveway. They installed an 80 to 90 foot gas line from the meter located in the back of the house to the street in the front of the house. The Linnears used the area alongside the driveway as a path for walking to and from their vehicles and there is no dispute that the accident occurred in the general area where the trench was dug. The Linnears alleged that CenterPoint negligently filled the trench and failed to resod the area, resulting in the sinkhole that caused Mrs. Linnear to fall.

At trial, Mrs. Linnear testified that in the early morning hours of July 19 it had rained but was no longer raining at 9:30 a.m., the time of the accident. She testified that she and her three-year-old granddaughter were preparing to take some items to church. While her granddaughter stayed on the porch, Mrs. Linnear walked with the items to the car and placed them in the backseat behind the driver's seat. She testified that when she stepped backwards from the open rear door, her right foot sank into a sinkhole and that her right leg sank into the ground up to her knee. She fell forwards and felt a sharp pain in her back. She was able to pull herself up using the door handle and then got her granddaughter from the front porch and continued on her errand. She was later diagnosed with a herniated disk and underwent surgery in December of 2003. She testified that the area where the accident occurred was wet because it had rained that morning but it was not muddy and appeared stable.

Mr. Linnear testified that Mrs. Linnear called him after the accident and he returned home at around 11:30 a.m. to find her in pain. He took photographs of the accident scene, one of which showed a muddy area with an indentation of a footprint in the mud. The Linnears testified that it had rained early in the morning of July 19, was not raining at the time of the accident, but had rained again between the time of the accident and the time the photograph was taken. He testified that they had lived in the house for 23 years and used that area of the yard often and no one had ever fallen in that area.

Workers for CenterPoint testified as to the work done at the Linnear's residence. Herbert Burkins, the crew leader, testified the trench was back-filled by adding up to four inches of dirt at a time and stepping on the area using body weight after each addition to compact the dirt. The crew then took turns using a 30-pound steel tamper to tamp down and harden the dirt. A backhoe was then used over some of the area to further harden the dirt. After a visual check, Burkins inserted a screwdriver into the ground to check the compaction and the entire area was fully compacted. He testified that the crew did not use any extra dirt in the trench, nor did they add any sod on top. Thomas Salter gave testimony consistent with Burkins regarding the methods of compaction used. Specifically, he testified that he weighed 230 pounds and that he personally compacted the soil by putting two to three inches of soil in the trench and then compacting it as follows: "One foot is placed inside the trench, the other foot on the actual shift, which would be the ground level, and you actually just walk in there, almost like a bunny hop, and push your weight up and down on the actual pipe itself to compact the soil." He repeated the process of adding soil and walking over it until the soil was level. Once the soil was level, they used a six by six inch 30-pound steel tamper to manually tamp down the soil, then "we take the piece of equipment, run it over with the tires, and-to make sure that the ground is level and compact." He testified that based on the way they compacted the trench, it was not possible that someone Mrs. Linnear's size could step in the trench and sink to a point just below her knee. In addition, he testified that he had seen sinkholes before and they appear in a circular pattern, not as depicted in the photograph showing an imprint of Mrs. Linnear's footprint as alleged by plaintiffs. He further testified that the area alongside the driveway where the accident occurred was not covered in grass before they dug the trench, and similarly they did not place any sod over that area afterwards. He testified that the yard was in good condition after they completed the job and that the soil covering the trench was sturdy and uniform. Salter testified that he had done hundreds of jobs and they were all done this same way. After the accident, Salter testified, he returned to the property and distributed about half a wheelbarrow of dirt throughout the area and sodded the area as requested. He did not recall filling any holes in the area.

The photographs that Mr. Linnear had taken after the accident were also introduced into evidence. The photographs depict an indentation of a footprint in a muddy area and a garden hose in the area which was not there when the trench was filled. Based on these photographs, the defense argued that Mrs. Linnear simply stepped into an open and obvious muddy area and slipped; had she stepped into a sink hole, the footprint in the mud would have gone down much deeper than depicted in the photograph. The defense also argued that the plaintiffs failed to bring in expert testimony to prove their case by way of soil borings.

Prior to the case being sent to the jury, the plaintiffs requested a jury instruction on the doctrine of *res ipsa loquitur,* which the trial court rejected. After a three-day jury trial, the jury returned a verdict in favor of CenterPoint, giving a negative answer to the first question on the jury verdict form, which was "Does the preponderance of the evidence establish that CenterPoint Energy or any of its employees were negligent and that their negligence caused or contributed to the accident on July 16, 2002?"

* * * * *

The Linnears appealed to the Second Circuit,.... On appeal, the court of appeal concluded that the trial judge's refusal to give a *res ipsa loquitur* instruction constituted legal error which "impeded" the fact-finding process of the jury. Accordingly, the court conducted a *de novo* review of the record and found liability on the part of CenterPoint, awarding a judgment in the amount of $273,032.74....

Discussion

Analysis of the doctrine of *res ipsa loquitur* reveals that the court of appeal erred in applying that doctrine to this case. As explained below, the appellate court's errors were its misapplication of *res ipsa loquitur* to a case involving direct evidence and its misinterpretation of language from *Cangelosi v. Our Lady of the Lake Regional Medical Center,* 564 So. 2d 654 (La. 1989) (on rehearing) regarding the standard to be used by the trial court in determining whether to give a *res ipsa loquitur* instruction to the jury.

The court of appeal began its analysis of *res ipsa loquitur* on the right track, stating the law as follows:

> The doctrine of *res ipsa loquitur* applies in cases where the plaintiff uses circumstantial evidence alone to prove negligence by the defendant. *Cangelosi, supra.* The doctrine, meaning "the thing speaks for itself," permits the inference of negligence on the part of the defendant from the circumstances surrounding the injury. *Id.* As explained in *Cangelosi, supra,* the doctrine applies when three criteria are met. First, the injury is the kind which ordinarily does not occur in the absence of negligence. While the plaintiff does not have to eliminate all other possible causes, he must present evidence indicating at least a probability that the accident would not have occurred absent negligence. Second, the evidence must sufficiently eliminate other more probable causes of the injury, such as the conduct of the plaintiff or a third person. The circumstances must warrant an inference of negligence. Third, the negligence of the defendant must fall within the scope of his duty to plaintiff. This

150

may, but not necessarily, be proved in instances where the defendant had exclusive control of the thing that caused the injury.

945 So.2d at 8. This is indeed a correct statement of the well-known requirements of the *res ipsa loquitur* doctrine. We further explained in *Cangelosi* that "[t]he doctrine of *res ipsa loquitur* involves the simple matter of a plaintiff's using circumstantial evidence to meet the burden of proof by a preponderance of the evidence" and "merely assists the plaintiff in presenting a prima facie case of negligence when direct evidence is not available." *Cangelosi, supra* at 665.[4] As early as 1957, this Court noted that "it is the lack of direct evidence indicating negligence on the part of the defendant as the responsible human cause of the particular accident which actually furnishes the occasion and necessity for invoking the rule in its strict and distinctive sense." *Larkin v. State Farm Mut. Auto. Ins. Co.*, 233 La. 544, 97 So. 2d 389 (1957); *see also Walker v. Union Oil Mill, Inc.*, 369 So. 2d 1043, 1048 (La. 1979) ("*Res ipsa loquitur* does not apply if there is sufficient direct evidence explaining the occurrence and establishing the details of the negligence charged.") Most recently, in *Lawson v. Mitsubishi Motor Sales of America*, 05-257 (La. 2006), 938 So. 2d 35, 51, we held that a plaintiff cannot take advantage of the doctrine where direct evidence of defendant's possible negligence is available, but could not be considered because the plaintiffs had tampered with the evidence before the defendants could examine it.

Although the court of appeal correctly recognized that *res ipsa loquitur* is only applicable where the plaintiff offers only circumstantial evidence from which negligence might be inferred, it went on to apply this doctrine in a case where direct evidence was not only available, but was presented by both parties. The plaintiffs used the testimony of Mrs. Linnear, who gave her eyewitness account of how the accident happened. Both Linnears testified as to the condition of the yard after CenterPoint finished installing the new gas line in an attempt to show that CenterPoint installed the gas line and filled the trench in a negligent manner. The defendant presented the testimony of two workers who actually installed the gas line and filled the trench in an attempt to show that their performance was not negligent. Although some circumstantial evidence was presented, including photographs showing an indented footprint in a muddy area where the trench was dug and showing the area with a garden hose nearby, this was not a "circumstantial evidence only" case, where direct evidence was unavailable to the plaintiff such that he was forced to rely on circumstantial evidence. This was a case where there was competing direct evidence, along with some circumstantial evidence presented by plaintiffs (which did not aide their case), and the jury was forced to make a credibility call. As we stated in *Cangelosi*, and as recognized by the court of appeal in this case, *res ipsa loquitur* only applies where direct evidence of defendant's negligence is not available to assist the plaintiff to present a prima facie case of negligence. In this case, not only was it available, but it was presented to and considered by the jury.

The court of appeal's next error was in the methodology it used in determining that a *res ipsa loquitur* instruction should have been given and was based on a misinterpretation of language from *Cangelosi*. The court of appeal reasoned as follows:

> In deciding whether to instruct the jury on *res ipsa loquitur*, the trial court employs a standard similar to that for directed verdicts. *Id.* The trial court determines whether the facts and inferences point so strongly and overwhelmingly in favor of one party

---

[4] "A fact established by direct evidence is one which has been testified to by witnesses as having come under the cognizance of their senses." *Cangelosi, supra* at 664 (citing J. Wigmore, *Evidence,* § 25, at 954 (1983)). Circumstantial evidence on the other hand, is "evidence of one fact, or of a set of facts, from which the existence of the fact to be determined may reasonably be inferred." *Id.* at 664-665 (citing W. Prosser & W. Keeton, *The Law of Torts,* § 39, at 242 (5th ed. 1984)).

that reasonable persons could not arrive at a contrary verdict. If reasonable minds could reach different conclusions as to whether the defendant's negligence caused the plaintiff's injury, then the trial court must instruct the jury on *res ipsa loquitur*. *Cangelosi, supra; Smith v. Bundrick,* 27,552 (La.App. 2 Cir. 1995), 663 So. 2d 554. The jury then decides whether to infer negligence on the part of the defendant from the circumstances of the case.

From our review of the record, we find that the trial court erred in not instructing the jury on *res ipsa loquitur* at the close of the case. The trial testimony included Mrs. Linnear's account of how the accident happened, her assertion that she fell in a sinkhole, and testimony that no such accidents had ever happened in their yard before CenterPoint dug the trench and that none have happened since CenterPoint returned to restore the property to its pre-repair condition. The trial testimony also included the description of how CenterPoint's crew refilled the trench, compacted the soil, and left the yard in good condition. The testimony was such that reasonable minds could reach different conclusions as to whether CenterPoint's negligence caused Mrs. Linnear's injury. The trial court recognized as much in denying CenterPoint's motion for involuntary dismissal at the close of the plaintiffs' case after all witnesses had testified, except for Salter, who was called back on direct for CenterPoint. Moreover, we find that the failure to instruct the jury on *res ipsa loquitur* precluded the jury from rendering a verdict based on the law and the facts. This case turned on circumstantial evidence, but the jury was not even instructed on that aspect of the law. The jury should have been given instruction on circumstantial evidence and *res ipsa loquitur* to be allowed to evaluate the evidence and determine whether the circumstances warranted the inference that the defendant's negligence caused the plaintiff's injury. Thus, we find that the *res ipsa loquitur* instruction should have been included by the trial court. Having recognized the error of law, we are charged to conduct a de novo review of this complete record and render judgment.

945 So.2d at 8-9.

This analysis goes far astray of the intent of *Cangelosi* in setting out the trial court's standard of review in determining whether a *res ipsa loquitur* instruction is warranted. First of all, as stated above, the court of appeal never should have reached this determination as *res ipsa loquitur* does not apply where direct evidence is used to explain the accident or injury. Secondly, the standard set out by *Cangelosi* does not mean that a trial judge must give a *res ipsa loquitur* instruction anytime the parties present conflicting evidence of negligence and reasonable minds could reach different conclusions as to whether the defendant's negligence caused the plaintiff's injury. If that were the case, the trial judge would have only two choices in every negligence case: either grant a directed verdict or give a *res ipsa loquitur* instruction.

However, we recognize that the language in *Cangelosi* is not quite as clear as it could be and evidently led to confusion in this case. Thus, some clarification is necessary. *Cangelosi* simply requires the trial judge to undertake the following analysis. In cases involving only circumstantial evidence, *res ipsa loquitur* may be applicable, if the trial judge sequentially determines that the three criteria for its use are satisfied. The three criteria are: (1) the injury is of the kind which does not ordinarily occur in the absence of negligence on someone's part; (2) the evidence sufficiently eliminates other more probable causes of the injury, such as the conduct of the plaintiff or of a third person; and (3) the alleged negligence of the defendant must be within the scope of the defendant's duty to the plaintiff. As *Cangelosi* instructs, the trial judge determines whether reasonable minds could differ on the presence of **all three criteria.** If reasonable minds could not conclude that all three criteria are satisfied, then the legal requirements for the use of *res ipsa loquitur* are not met. Consequently, the jury should not be instructed on the doctrine. If reasonable minds could differ as to all three criteria, then the law permits the use of *res ipsa loquitur* to allow the jury to infer negligence if it chooses to do so from all the circumstances presented, including the incident itself.[5]

Using the correct analysis, this case does not pass the first requirement, as this injury was of the kind which can ordinarily occur in the absence of negligence on someone's part. In *Cangelosi*, we explained that "the event must be such that in light of ordinary experience it gives rise to an inference that someone *must* have been negligent." *Cangelosi, supra* at 666 (emphasis added). People fall in their yards and injure themselves all the time without any third party involvement at all. We have long held that "[r]es ipsa loquitur, as 'a qualification of the general rule that negligence is not to be presumed,' must be sparingly applied." *Spott v. Otis Elevator Co.*, 601 So. 2d 1355, 1362 (La. 1992) (citing *Day v. National U.S. Radiator Corp.*, 241 La. 288, 128 So. 2d 660, 665 (1961)). The doctrine only applies "when the circumstances surrounding an accident are so unusual" as to give rise to an inference of negligence. *Id.* It does not apply to cases involving ordinary accidents or injuries that often occur in the absence of negligence, such as this one. Thus, the court of appeal erred in failing to consider this requirement. It is clear that reasonable minds could not differ on this point. That being the case, there is no need to consider the other two requirements.

* * * * *

Conclusion

Res ipsa loquitur is a rule of circumstantial evidence which allows an inference of negligence on the part of the defendant if the facts indicate the defendant's negligence, more probably than not, caused the injury. It applies in cases involving circumstantial evidence, rather than direct evidence, provided the plaintiff establishes the following foundation of facts: (1) the injury is of the kind which does not ordinarily occur in the absence of negligence; (2) the evidence sufficiently eliminates other possible causes of the injury, such as the plaintiff's own responsibility or the responsibility of others; and (3) the alleged negligence of the defendant must fall within the scope of his duty to the plaintiff, which will often be the case if the defendant had exclusive control of the thing or situation that caused the injury to the plaintiff. After all the evidence has been presented, the trial judge must determine whether to give the instruction, which would allow the jury to infer the defendant's negligence. In order to give the instruction, he must satisfy himself that reasonable minds could differ as to the presence of each of the three requirements. In this case, the court of appeal misinterpreted our prior case law to mean that, regardless of whether direct or circumstantial evidence is presented and disregarding the three requirements, if reasonable minds could differ as to whether defendant's negligence caused plaintiff's injury, the instruction must be given. As explained above, this was clear error.

Decree

For the reasons stated herein, the judgment of the court of appeal is reversed and the jury verdict and trial court judgment in favor of the defendant is reinstated.

---

[5] *Cangelosi* stated the standard as "whether the facts and inferences point so strongly and overwhelmingly in favor of one party that reasonable men could not arrive at a contrary verdict." 564 So. 2d at 667. What that really means is that if the facts and inferences point so strongly and overwhelmingly in favor of the defendant on those three points, then the instruction should not be given. For if the trial judge finds that reasonable minds could only find that a particular requirement has been met, which is stronger than finding that reasonable minds could differ, then of course that requirement is met and the trial judge moves on to analyze the next requirement.

NOTES

1.   Why did the Louisiana Supreme Court restrict the use of *res ipsa loquitur* in *Linnear*? How useful will *res ipsa loquitur* be to plaintiffs in future cases?

2.   For the lawyer and student results in *res ipsa* cases may be more useful than attempts at logical explanation.

no res ipsa this BC prong #1

    In *Benjamin v. Housing Authority of New Orleans*, 893 So. 2d 1 (La. 2004), a two and half year old child fell out of the second floor window of her apartment building; a few days earlier, the owner's employee had installed window screens in the apartment. There was no evidence that the screen was negligently installed and there was no evidence that the screen failed to withstand "the slight use of force." *Held*, the lower court erred in applying *res ipsa*; "it was just as likely" that the screen was properly installed but that someone unlocked the screen, or that the child accidently fell on the screen.

    Reaching a different conclusion regarding the application of *res ipsa* the court in *Perkins v. Wurster Oil Corp.*, 886 So. 2d 229 (La.App. 3 Cir. 2004) considered a case in which plaintiff alleged that he began pumping gasoline at a convenience store; while the gas was pumping, he reentered the cab of his truck, and then he got out of the vehicle to stop the pumping, touching the bed of the truck as he did so. Static electricity ignited the fuel vapors and burned plaintiff. *Held, res ipsa* applies; the injury does not occur in the absence of negligence, and plaintiff's testimony that he touched the bed sufficiently excluded his own responsibility for the accident. In addition, the *res ipsa* inference was appropriate since defendant destroyed or discarded some of the physical evidence bearing on the case.

    Likewise, in *Honeycutt v. State Farm Fire & Cas. Co.*, 890 So. 2d 756 (La.App. 2 Cir. 2004), plaintiff's vehicle struck defendant's cow, which was blocking plaintiff's lane of traffic on a highway. The cow had been quartered in defendant's adjoining fenced property. *Held,* res ipsa applies in plaintiff's claim against defendant; "[a]bsent negligence, a cow confined within fencing of proper height and maintenance will not wander into the center of the roadway in the middle of the night, endangering motorists." *See also, Lawson v. Mitsubishi Motor Sales of America, Inc.*, 938 So. 2d 35 (La. 2006) (holding that res ipsa can be applied in a products liability case, but refusing to apply it in case involving discharge of airbag).

    But, in *Escobar v. Cajun Operating Co.*, 209 So. 3d 198 (La.App. 1 Cir. 2016) plaintiff was injured when her finger was caught on the underside of a chair at a restaurant. The district court awarded damages, applying the doctrine of res ipsa loquitur to infer negligence on the part of the restaurant. Court of appeal found the district court erred in applying res ipsa loquitur to satisfy the element of constructive notice because the facts did not suggest that the negligence of the restaurant, rather than some other factor, was the most plausible explanation for plaintiff's injuries. It was possible that a design defect caused plaintiff's injuries.

res ipsa w/ multiple Ds

3.   For a case applying *res ipsa* under Louisiana law to multiple defendants, *see Winans v. Rockwell International Corp.*, 705 F.2d 1449 (5th Cir. 1983). *See, also, National Union Fire Ins. Co. of La. v. Harrington*, 854 So. 2d 880 (La.App. 3 Cir. 2003) (Louisiana courts do not refuse to apply the doctrine of *res ipsa* simply because there is more than one defendant; rather, courts refuse to apply the doctrine where a possible tortfeasor is not joined; the court does not err in applying *res ipsa* where the only possible tortfeasors (the manufacturer and user of a product) are before the jury at trial, and the only other alleged possible tortfeasor was previously dismissed on summary judgment.

courts refuse to potentially use it potential tortfeasor NOT joined in suit

154

4.   When the ceiling of a building collapses upon the tenant, must he offer proof of a "defect," or can it be inferred from the collapse? *See, e.g., Hughes v. Green*, 612 So. 2d 82 (La.App. 4 Cir. 1992).

5.   Numerous "presumptions," of varying weight, apply in auto accident cases. *See, e.g., Brannon v. Shelter Mut. Ins. Co.*, 507 So. 2d 194 (La. 1987), and *King v. Louviere*, 543 So. 2d 1327 (La. 1989). *See, also, Ferrell v. Fireman's Fund Ins. Co.*, 650 So. 2d 742 (La. 1995) – when a driver's vehicle leaves its traffic lane and collides with the bridge railing, the burden of proof is on the driver to show that she was not guilty of any dereliction, however slight, that caused the subsequent accidents (collisions by oncoming motorists with the police car parked to investigate the driver's accident, and with vehicles disabled after colliding with the police car).

Presumptions may be of varying force. A presumption may be so strong that, once the predicate facts are established, the opponent cannot rebut the presumption. In such a case, the "presumption" is a rule of law (such as an "irrebuttable" presumption that the husband of the mother is the father of the child). On the other end of the spectrum, the presumption may be so weak that it merely permits the jury to infer the fact, but the jury is free to reject that inference. In the middle are those presumptions that are of such strength that they come forward with evidence that establishes that the presumed fact is probably not true. *See also*, note 4 following the *Roberts* case, *supra*.

Presumptions

Irrebuttable = strong presump.
⟶ presumption becomes rule of law

Rebuttable
⟶ Middle presump. = good enough to show that fact was prob untrue
⟶ weak presump = just allows jury to infer fact, BUT jury can reject inference

(summary judgment 1st)

Louisiana Analysis of Negligence:

1) Rule d Law
2) Cause-in-fact
court 3) Duty — reasonable person
question 4) Breach   customary (experts)
                   risk-utility
5) Scope   statutes (neg. per se)
6) ease of association test   foreseeable?
     a) class of plaintiffs
     b) type of harm
         >damages

open + obvious doctrine?

[Handwritten top margin: but-for: fact-finder... no summ. judgment]

[Handwritten: substantial factor: less than but-for knife v. fists take out knife]

CHAPTER 5

CAUSE IN FACT

[Handwritten arrow pointing to CHAPTER 5: La begins neg analysis w/ this element.]

[Handwritten arrow pointing to CAUSE IN FACT: one can fail to use reasonable care BUT unreasonable act does not cause harm]

INTRODUCTION

Causation is an element of the prima facie case of negligence.[51] One may have a duty to exercise reasonable care toward others and may fail to exercise reasonable care, but the unreasonable act does not cause harm. For example, one may run through a crowd of people swinging a sword, but strike no one and cause no physical injuries. Assuming no emotional distress injuries, a negligence lawsuit will fail. The basic proposition is that one who does not cause harm is not liable. The requirement of causation is so fundamental to the negligence analysis that some jurisdictions, including Louisiana, begin the analysis with cause in fact. *See, e.g., Breithaupt v. Sellers, infra.*

[Handwritten arrow: Q of fact (usually not policy Q)]

Cause in fact is generally said to be a question of fact that does not involve policy decisions, but it is by no means clear that this is true in all cases. Cause in fact can raise some difficult questions because it requires that we suppose the counterfactual. In its most basic "but-for" formulation, the question may be stated as follows: Is it more probable than not (the burden of persuasion) that but for the breach of duty by the defendant the harm would not have occurred? What this question requires is that we identify the unreasonable act(s) or omission(s) of the defendant, take that conduct out of the fact situation and replace it with reasonable conduct (nonbreach) and speculate whether the harm would have occurred if the defendant had acted reasonably. It should be obvious that this can raise numerous problems. There may be numerous alternatives to the defendant's breach. We may conclude that the alternatives most likely would have caused some harm, but not the same harm. When there are multiple defendants who breached the standard of care and the victim suffered multiple injuries, how do we know which act by which defendant caused which injury? For example, suppose there is a multi-car collision. The plaintiff is in a car in the middle of the collision, and she suffers a broken arm, a whiplash, a collapsed lung, and other injuries. She sues the drivers of the other cars, some in front of her car and some behind. How do we know which drivers caused which injuries? If we could go back and evaluate plaintiff's injuries after each impact, we might have evidence to divide the injuries among the defendants who caused them, but such evidence is rarely available.

[Handwritten right margin: but-for]

The line between cause in fact and proximate cause also is not so clear. Suppose that I drive on an interstate for fifty miles, speeding the entire way. I am stopped by police who use a radar to determine my speed shortly before I reach my destination. When I arrive at the exit and drive into the city which is my destination, I carefully adhere to the speed limit. I have a collision with another car when I am exercising utmost care. The driver of the other car sues me for negligence, asserting that if I had not sped on the interstate, I would not have arrived at the point where the collision occurred at the time that he arrived there. Plaintiff is correct that my speeding did cause me to arrive at that place at that time, but no court is going to hold me liable when I was exercising care at the time of the accident. Why? Was my speeding a cause in fact of the accident? Is this an issue of cause or an issue of proximate or legal cause?

Although we do not address allocation of fault between the participants in a traumatic event until Chapter 10, you will begin to see some allocation issues in this chapter. Bear in mind that there is a difference between allocation of harm caused and allocation of the fault which caused that harm.

[Handwritten: Remember: diff btw allocation of harm caused AND allocation of fault that caused harm]

---

[51] Some speak of causation as including cause in fact and proximate or legal cause. This book separates the two elements. Proximate or legal causation is discussed in Chapter 6.

A.   **BUT-FOR CAUSATION**

PERKINS

v.

TEXAS AND NEW ORLEANS RAILROAD COMPANY
147 So. 2d 646 (La. 1962)

SANDERS, J.

This is a tort action. Plaintiff, the 67-year-old widow of Tanner Perkins, seeks damages for the death of her husband in the collision of an automobile, in which he was riding, with a train of the defendant railroad. The district court awarded damages. The Court of Appeal affirmed. We granted certiorari to review the judgment of the Court of Appeal.

The tragic accident which gave rise to this litigation occurred at the intersection of Eddy Street and The Texas and New Orleans Railroad Company track in the town of Vinton, Louisiana, at approximately 6:02 a. m., after daylight, on September 28, 1959. At this crossing Eddy Street runs north and south, and the railroad track, east and west. Involved was a 113-car freight train pulled by four diesel engines traveling east and a Dodge automobile driven by Joe Foreman in a southerly direction on Eddy Street. Tanner Perkins, a guest passenger, was riding in the front seat of the automobile with the driver.

Located in the northwest quadrant of the intersection of the railroad track and Eddy Street was a warehouse five hundred feet long. A "house track" paralleled the main track on the north to serve the warehouse. This warehouse obstructed the view to the west of an automobile driver approaching the railroad crossing from the north on Eddy Street. It likewise obstructed the view to the north of trainmen approaching the crossing from the west. Having previously served on this route, the engineer and brakeman were aware of this obstruction.

To warn the public of the approach of trains, the defendant railroad had installed at the crossing an automatic signal device consisting of a swinging red light and a bell. At the time of the accident, this signal was operating. A standard Louisiana railroad stop sign and an intersection stop sign were also located at the crossing.

Proceeding east, the train approached the intersection with its headlight burning, its bell ringing, and its whistle blowing.

The engineer, brakeman, and fireman were stationed in the forward engine of the train. The engineer was seated on the right or south side, where he was unable to observe an automobile approaching from the left of the engine. The brakeman and fireman, who were seated on the left or north side of the engine, were looking forward as the train approached the intersection. These two crewmen saw the automobile emerge from behind the warehouse. At that time the front wheels of the automobile were on or across the north rail of the house track. The fireman estimated that the train was approximately 60 feet from the crossing when the automobile emerged from behind the warehouse. The brakeman, however, estimated that the train was 30 to 40 feet from the crossing at the time the automobile came into view. Both crewmen immediately shouted a warning to the engineer, who applied the emergency brakes. The train struck the right side of the automobile and carried it approximately 1250 feet. The two occupants were inside the automobile when it came to rest. Both were killed.

The speed of the automobile in which Tanner Perkins was riding was variously estimated from 3-4 miles per hour to 20-25 miles per hour.

The plaintiff and defendant railroad concede in their pleadings that Joe Foreman, the driver of the automobile, was negligent in driving upon the track in front of the train and that his negligence was a proximate cause of the death of Tanner Perkins.

Parties concede that auto driver's negligence = legal cause of P's death

158

It is conceded that the railroad's safety regulations imposed a speed limit of 25 miles per hour on trains in the town of Vinton. The plaintiff has conceded in this Court that this self-imposed speed limit was a safe speed at the crossing. The train was in fact traveling at a speed of 37 miles per hour.

Applicable here is the rule that the violation by trainmen of the railroad's own speed regulations adopted in the interest of safety is evidence of negligence. The rule has special force in the instant case because of the unusually hazardous nature of the crossing. We find, as did the Court of Appeal, that the trainmen were negligent in operating the train 12 miles per hour in excess of the speed limit.

As one of several defenses, the defendant railroad strenuously contends that the excessive speed of the train was not a proximate cause of the collision for the reason that the accident would not have been averted even had the train been traveling at the prescribed speed of 25 miles per hour. Contrariwise, the plaintiff contends that the speed of the train constituted a "proximate, direct and contributing cause" of the accident.

Thus presented, the prime issue in this case is whether the excessive speed of the train was a cause in fact[4] of the fatal collision.

It is fundamental that negligence is not actionable unless it is a cause in fact of the harm for which recovery is sought. It need not, of course, be the sole cause. Negligence is a cause in fact of the harm to another if it was a substantial factor in bringing about that harm. Under the circumstances of the instant case, the excessive speed was undoubtedly a substantial factor in bringing about the collision if the collision would not have occurred without it. On the other hand, if the collision would have occurred irrespective of such negligence, then it was not a substantial factor.

The burden of proving this causal link is upon the plaintiff. Recognizing that the fact of causation is not susceptible of proof to a mathematical certainty, the law requires only that the evidence show that it is more probable than not that the harm was caused by the tortious conduct of the defendant. Stated differently, it must appear that it is more likely than not that the harm would have been averted but for the negligence of the defendant.

In the instant case the train engineer testified that at a speed of 25 miles per hour he would have been unable to stop the train in time to avoid the accident. Other facts of record support his testimony in this regard. With efficient brakes, the mile-long train required 1250 feet to stop at a speed of 37 miles per hour. It is clear, then, that even at the concededly safe speed of 25 miles per hour, the momentum of the train would have, under the circumstances, carried it well beyond the crossing. This finding, of course, does not fully determine whether the collision would have been averted at the slower speed. The automobile was also in motion during the crucial period. This necessitates the further inquiry of whether the automobile would have cleared the track and evaded the impact had the train been moving at a proper speed at the time the trainmen observed the automobile emerge from behind the warehouse. Basic to this inquiry are the speed of the automobile and the driving distance between it and a position of safety.

The testimony of the witnesses is in hopeless conflict as to the speed of the automobile at the time of the collision. The estimates range from a low of 3 miles per hour to a high of 25 miles per hour. Both the district court and Court of Appeal concluded that the speed of the automobile had not been definitely established. Each of these courts found only that the automobile was proceeding at "a slow speed." In her brief the plaintiff states: "The speed of the automobile cannot be determined, at least by the testimony." We conclude that the evidence fails to establish the speed of the automobile with reasonable certainty.

---

[4] The term "cause in fact," is used in preference to "proximate cause" because it brings the issue in the instant case into sharper focus.

Although the record discloses that the train struck the automobile broadside, it does not reflect the driving distance required to propel the vehicle from the danger zone.

Finally, we also note that the defendant railroad produced testimony, which is the only testimony of record on this point, that the deceased made no attempt to leave the moving automobile. That he was in the vehicle when it came to rest is undisputed. Moreover, the record fails to reflect the distance required for the deceased to scramble past the diesel engine to a place of safety, had he succeeded in getting out of the automobile.

Despite these deficiencies in the evidence, the plaintiff argues that had the train been traveling at a proper speed the driver of the automobile would "conceivably" have had some additional time to take measures to avert disaster and the deceased would have had some additional time to extricate himself from danger. Hence, the plaintiff reasons, the collision and loss of life "might not" have occurred.

On the facts of this case, we must reject the escape theory advanced in this argument. Because of the deficiencies in the evidence which we have already noted, it is devoid of evidentiary support. The record contains no probative facts from which the Court can draw a reasonable inference of causation under this theory. In essence the argument is pure conjecture.

Based upon the evidence of record, it appears almost certain that the fatal accident would have occurred irrespective of the excessive speed of the train. It follows that this speed was not a substantial factor in bringing about the accident.

We conclude that the plaintiff has failed to discharge the burden of proving that the negligence of the defendant was a cause in fact of the tragic death. The judgment in favor of plaintiff is manifestly erroneous.

For the reasons assigned, the judgment of the Court of Appeal is reversed, and the plaintiff's suit is dismissed at her cost.

HAMLIN, Justice (dissenting).

I am compelled to agree with the Court of Appeal that in view of the blind crossing the overspeeding by the employees of the Railroad Company was negligence, which was a proximate cause of the accident.

It is my opinion that this train (approximately one mile long, made up of one hundred and thirteen cars and four diesels) should not have entered the Town of Vinton at thirty-seven miles per hour, its speed at the time of the accident. Notwithstanding the rules of the Railroad Company that its speed in Vinton should not have exceeded twenty-five miles per hour, even this speed, under the circumstances found by the Court of Appeal, would be excessive.

I respectfully dissent.

NOTES

1.   Could the plaintiff have argued that if the train had been traveling at a slower speed, the motorist would have had an enhanced opportunity to observe its approach and avoid the collision? If so, could one say that the train's speed was a substantial factor in the collision? *See Thomas v. Missouri Pacific R.R. Co.*, 466 So. 2d 1280 (La. 1985).

2.   To prove cause in fact, what must a plaintiff do? Take out the breach by the defendant, replace it with conduct which is a nonbreach and determine whether the harm would have occurred? What are the possible results in this case if the defendant had not breached?

3.   Consider the fact situation from *Ford v. Trident Fisheries*, 122 N.E. 389 (Mass. 1919). A ship mate fell overboard and immediately disappeared beneath the water. A rescue boat was launched to look for the mate, but because the boat was not suspended from davits but lashed to the ship with rope that had to be cut, there was a delay in launching. Moreover, when the rescue boat was launched, it was discovered that it was equipped with only one oar. Mate's spouse brought wrongful death action alleging the manner of securing the rescue boat and equipping with one oar as breaches. Evaluate cause in fact.

SALINETRO

v.

NYSTROM

341 So. 2d 1059 (Fla. App. 1977)

PER CURIAM.

Anna Salinetro sustained back injuries in an automobile accident and applied for personal injury benefits from her insurer, State Farm Mutual Automobile Insurance Company. State Farm required Anna to submit to a medical examination and on December 10 x-rays were taken by Dr. Nystrom of her lower back and abdominal area. Although unknown to her, Anna was approximately four-six weeks pregnant at the time; however, neither Dr. Nystrom nor his receptionist or his x-ray technician inquired whether or not she was pregnant or the date of her last menstrual period. Thereafter, upon suspecting she was pregnant, on December 12 Anna visited her gynecologist, Dr. Emilio Aldereguia, who, after running some tests, confirmed her pregnancy. In January Dr. Aldereguia learned that Dr. Nystrom had taken x-rays of Anna's pelvis and advised her to terminate her pregnancy because of possible damage to the fetus by the x-rays. Anna underwent a therapeutic abortion and the pathology report stated that the fetus was dead at the time of the abortion. Thereafter, Anna filed the instant lawsuit against Dr. Nystrom for medical malpractice. During the jury trial, Dr. Aldereguia was called as a witness for the plaintiff but the trial judge refused to allow him to testify as an expert with respect to whether or not the conduct of Dr. Nystrom fell below the standard of medical care on the ground that Dr. Aldereguia was a specialist in obstetrics and gynecology, not radiology, and, therefore, he was not qualified to pass upon the standard of care required of Dr. Nystrom, an orthopedic specialist. After the presentation of all the evidence on Anna's behalf, Dr. Nystrom moved for a directed verdict on the ground she failed to make a prima facie case of medical malpractice. The trial judge granted the motion and entered judgment for Dr. Nystrom.

Anna first contends that the record contains sufficient evidence to present to the jury a prima facie case of malpractice.

Liability for negligence depends on a showing that the injury suffered by plaintiff was caused by the alleged wrongful act or omission to act by the defendant. Merely to show a connection between the negligence and the injury is sufficient to establish liability....

Assuming arguendo that Dr. Nystrom's conduct fell below the standard of care in failing to inquire of Anna whether she was pregnant or not on the date of her last menstrual period, this omission was not the cause of her injury. Anna herself testified that even if asked about being pregnant, she would have answered in the negative. Anna further testified to the effect that being a few days late with her menstrual period was not unusual and did not indicate to her that she may have been pregnant at the time she went to Dr. Nystrom; that six days prior thereto she had visited Dr. Aldereguia, and he had found no evidence that she was pregnant. We further note that simply because Anna was late with her menstrual period would not in and of itself mean that she was pregnant because further tests were required to ascertain whether she was pregnant. Thus, this point is without merit.

* * * * *

AFFIRMED.

NOTES

1.	What is the alleged breach in this case?

2.	The court assumes, for purposes of argument, that the doctor breached the standard of care. Why, then, does the plaintiff lose?

3.	Can you think of other possible breaches by the doctor for which causation might be established?

4.	Both *Perkins* and *Salinetro* involve a counterfactual. This is commonly referred to as the "but for" test. That is, "but for" the breach would the injury have occurred? If the answer is no, then the causation element is enough.

5.	Restatement (Third) of Torts, § 26 provides that, "[c]onduct is factual cause of harm when the harm would not have occurred absent the conduct."

BREITHAUPT
v.
SELLERS
390 So. 2d 870 (La. 1980)

DIXON, C. J.

Robert Breithaupt, Jr. was the victim of a hunting accident. Breithaupt, who had himself been hunting deer, was shot in the left thigh by another hunter. He contends that Luke Sellers is the man who shot him, and has instituted this tort action against Sellers. After the close of the plaintiff's case, the trial judge directed a verdict for the defendant, ruling as a matter of law that plaintiff's contributory negligence barred his recovery.[1] The Court of Appeal affirmed.... Both the trial court and the Court of Appeal reasoned that, inasmuch as R.S. 56:143 requires hunters to wear fluorescent material known as "Hunter orange,"[2] a victim of a hunting accident is barred from recovering for his injuries if he was a hunter who was not wearing "Hunter orange." Because we disagree with this reasoning, we reverse.

---

[1] The presentation of plaintiff's case in chief lasted five days and consisted of seventeen witnesses and a jury view of the scene. At the close of plaintiff's case, the defense moved for a directed verdict on the theory that plaintiff was contributorily negligent as a matter of law because of his failure to wear "Hunter orange." Prior to oral argument, the trial judge was unreceptive to the motion, because he believed that "... the real issue is not, whether failure to wear hunter's orange is negligence or not. It's a question of whether or not that caused the accident." Defense counsel then argued that under *Tolbert v. Ryder*, 345 So. 2d 548 (La.App. 3 Cir. 1977), violation of a statute creates a presumption of negligence, and the burden of proof shifts to that party to exculpate himself. Defense counsel pointed out that in the instant case, plaintiff had not carried his burden because he had shown neither that "Hunter orange" was unavailable to him, nor that the accident would have occurred anyway. Plaintiff's attorney responded:

> "That's right Your Honor, there was no testimony on that point. I will agree with him that the testimony on that part of it, uh, just wasn't there. And, I'm not joining in this motion, but that testimony was awful, awful weak, I remember that, it wasn't in there."

After hearing additional argument, the trial judge granted the motion, announcing to the jury that "(t)his Court will not be placed in a position of being the only lawyer in the courtroom who disagrees with (defense counsel's) arguments." The trial judge's initial reaction was correct.

[2] R.S. 56:143 entitled "'Hunter orange' display by deer hunters with guns," is a criminal statute found in title 56, "Wild Life, Fisheries, and Forestry." It provides:

> "Any person hunting deer shall display on his head or chest, and/or back a total of not less than four hundred square inches of material of daylight fluorescent orange color known as "Hunter orange'. These provisions shall not apply to persons hunting deer on property which is privately owned and legally posted, or to archery deer hunters except when bow and arrow are used to hunt deer on wildlife management areas where a gun season for deer is in progress.

Whoever violates the provision of this section shall be fined not more than $ 100 or imprisoned for not more than ninety days, or both."

[handwritten margin notes: "neg per se = presumption of neg w/ violation of statute"; "here, statute required P to wear orange"]

162

The motion for directed verdict, a new device in Louisiana, was first made available in civil jury trials in 1977. C.C.P. 1810, added by 1977 La. Acts, No. 699. Although it created the device, the legislature did not provide the standard of proof by which the judge must decide whether or not to grant the motion, and the judges of this state have undertaken the task of formulating the appropriate standard....

In the instant case, the Court of Appeal adopted the following test:

"... could reasonable persons, viewing all the evidence in a light most favorable to plaintiff, have reached different conclusions as to whether plaintiff was contributorily negligent." 380 So. 2d at 1259.

Utilizing the standard adopted by the Court of Appeal, and viewing the evidence in the light most favorable to the plaintiff, the accident occurred in the following manner:

On the afternoon of November 30, 1977, plaintiff went deer hunting at the South Olla Oil Field near Jena. The land, although privately owned, was not posted. Thus, plaintiff violated R.S. 56:143 when he did not wear "Hunter orange." After sitting at his stand for approximately one hour, he spotted another hunter from a distance later determined to be 833 feet. The man momentarily disappeared into the woods. When the man reappeared, the plaintiff stood up, waved his rifle over his head, and, believing the man had seen him, began walking toward the figure. After another brief disappearance, the man dropped to one knee, aimed at the plaintiff, and fired. At some point prior to the accident, the plaintiff says he looked at the man through the scope of his own rifle, and saw a man with a narrow lined face, light grey hair, wearing camouflage coveralls and a "Hunter orange" vest. Additionally, Breithaupt noticed that the weapon was a bolt action rifle with a scope and a sling. Breithaupt later identified Sellers as the man he had seen.

On the face of the record, a major obstacle to the plaintiff's credibility is the fact that, until this trial, he apparently never told anyone that he had "scoped" the hunter who shot him.[3] Furthermore, plaintiff at trial "forgot" his prior testimony that he had initially accused his friend Grayson Walpole of having shot him.[4] Nonetheless, it is not the function of this court to judge the credibility of the plaintiff's story. Credibility determinations are within the province of the trier of fact. We accept the facts in a light most favorable to plaintiff in order to assess the propriety of the trial judge's ruling granting the motion for directed verdict. When the evidence is viewed in this manner, this court cannot accept the Court of Appeal's conclusion that plaintiff was contributorily negligent as a matter of law.

Even assuming that Breithaupt was negligent in failing to wear "Hunter orange,"[5] plaintiff's conduct could not constitute contributory negligence unless such negligence also was a legal cause of

---

[3] Prior to this tort action, there had been an unsuccessful criminal prosecution against Sellers. The record is unclear regarding the specific criminal statute alleged to have been violated by Sellers. Breithaupt testified at the criminal trial that he "could make out his features." He did not, however, indicate that the basis of his identification was anything other than what he had seen with his unaided eyes.

[4] Grayson Walpole, a friend of plaintiff, was the first person who came to Breithaupt's rescue. At the criminal trial Breithaupt testified that the first thing he told Walpole was: "Damn, Walpole, I think you shot me." During cross-examination in the tort action, he testified that he did not remember making such a statement.

[5] In order to bar a plaintiff's recovery because of his contributory negligence, a court must find both that the plaintiff was negligent and that the negligence was a legal cause of his injury. The plaintiff's attorney in brief has argued that plaintiff was not negligent in failing to wear "Hunter orange" since he had terminated his hunting activities and thus no longer required to wear "Hunter orange." Alternatively, the plaintiff's attorney argued that the accident occurred after legal hunting hours so the statute was inapplicable. As a final argument, the plaintiff's

To find P contributory neg, must find:
① P was negligent, AND
② neg was legal cause of P's injury

his accident. *Weber v. Phoenix Assurance Co. of New York*, 273 So. 2d 30 (La. 1973). The threshold inquiry in the determination of legal cause is whether the act was a substantial factor in causing the injury. As stated by this court in *Dixie Drive It Yourself System New Orleans co. v. American Beverage Co.*, 242 La. 471, 137 So. 2d 298 (1962):

> "Negligent conduct is a cause-in-fact of harm to another if it was a substantial factor in bringing about that harm. Under the circumstances of this case, the negligent conduct is undoubtedly a substantial factor in bringing about the collision if the collision would not have occurred without it. A cause-in-fact is a necessary antecedent. If the collision would have occurred irrespective of the negligence of the driver of the R C Cola Truck, then his negligence was not a substantial factor or cause-in-fact...." 242 La. at 482, 137 So. 2d at 302. (Footnotes omitted).

In determining Breithaupt's conduct to be a cause-in-fact of his injury, the Court of Appeal reasoned:

> "We do not believe we are assuming too much in believing plaintiff would not have been shot had he been properly attired. The evidence clearly established conditions of visibility such that, had plaintiff been attired with "hunter's orange', any hunter would have noted this fact. We feel that we can assume that reasonable persons would have responded properly by concluding that plaintiff was a human being and not a game animal-a deer. Such a reasonable person would not have fired at plaintiff. The assumption that whoever shot plaintiff was a reasonable person is warranted because we are dealing with the question of plaintiff's negligence. If plaintiff had been clothed in "hunter's orange' but had nevertheless been shot, the inquiry then would be whether the shooter acted unreasonably, and contributory negligence on plaintiff's part would not have been a factor." 380 So. 2d at 1260.

We disagree with this reasoning. As we stated in *Dixie Drive It Yourself System*, the inquiry is whether the accident would have occurred regardless of whether Breithaupt wore "Hunter orange." If Breithaupt's story is believed, then the jury might be willing to infer that, since plaintiff could discern the hunter's facial features, the hunter should have been able to detect that plaintiff was a man and not a deer. The jury might have been willing to believe that the hunter fired without adequately looking at his target and that the accident would have happened regardless of whether Breithaupt wore "Hunter orange." Whether plaintiff's conduct was a cause-in-fact of his injury is a question of fact appropriate for the jury's consideration. The Court of Appeal, in assessing the causative role of plaintiff's negligence, assumed that the other hunter acted reasonably. In so doing, the Court of Appeal has assumed the most difficult factual issue presented by this case. If one assumes that the hunter acted reasonably, then one is led to the inescapable conclusion that the only cause of the injury was plaintiff's own negligence.

If the other hunter, through the use of reasonable care, could have detected that plaintiff was a man and not a deer, then he had a duty to refrain from shooting regardless of whether his victim was an innocent picnicker or a fellow hunter who has violated R.S. 56:143. We note that this statute is of limited utility, since it does not apply if an individual is not hunting deer, or if he is hunting on private, posted land. Had the statute been inapplicable, then under the reasoning of the Court of Appeal, the plaintiff could have recovered. This would mean that hunters who shoot men in the woods are free from liability only when they shoot fellow hunters who violate R.S. 56:143. Hunters who violate R.S. 56:143 do not, for that reason alone, deserve to be shot.

---

counsel argued that R.S. 56:143 is not an appropriate standard of care in a civil case inasmuch as it is not designed to promote safety but is designed to enable game wardens to spot hunters. Because this court has found that a factual issue exists regarding whether plaintiff's conduct was a legal cause of his injury, we pretermit the issue of whether plaintiff's conduct was negligent. We assume for purposes of this opinion that plaintiff was negligent in failing to wear "Hunter orange."

A motion for directed verdict would have been appropriate only if reasonable men could not have disagreed on the issue of plaintiff's contributory negligence. Whether this plaintiff's conduct contributed to his injury is a factual issue that should have been presented to the jury. For the foregoing reasons, a directed verdict was inappropriate in this case.

The judgment of the Court of Appeal is reversed, and the case is remanded to the trial court for a new trial. Allocation of costs is to await final judgment.

NOTES

[handwritten: means that injury would not have occurred without the negligent conduct]

1.   What does the court mean by "substantial factor"?

2.   Take a close look at the argument before the judge on the motion for directed verdict recorded in footnote 1. Why did the court grant the motion? *[handwritten: bc P failed to rebut presumption that he was contributorily negligent in case and chief]*

3.   According to the Supreme Court, what mistake did the court of appeals make in its analysis? *[handwritten: that other hunter acted reasonably — assumed that ... P's failure to wear orange was C1 F of ...]*

4.   *Breithaupt* involves not just a claim of primary negligence but also contributory negligence on the part of the plaintiff. As you can see, each element of negligence must be evaluated on each claim. The case also demonstrates that you cannot evaluate cause in fact until you identify the alleged breach. *[handwritten: why P bc it assumed, then only answer is that P's own negligence was only thing that caused injury]*

5.   *Breithaupt* states the basic general test of causation in Louisiana. There are, however, cases that apply a "lighter" standard of causation. *See, e.g., Faucheaux v. Terrebone Consol. Gov't,* 615 So. 2d 289, 292 (La.App. 1 Cir. 1993) ("To the extent that the defendant's actions had something to do with the injury the plaintiff sustained, the test of a factual, causal relationship is met."); *Roberts v. Benoit,* 605 So. 2d 1032, 1052 (La. 1992) ("[I]nasmuch as the sheriff's actions can be said to have appreciably enhanced the chance of the accident occurring, they are a cause-in-fact of the accident"). Is this another way of saying that the sheriff's actions were a substantial or material factor in causing the accident?

B.   OTHER STANDARDS OF CAUSATION

Restatement (Second) of Torts,

§ 432   Negligent Conduct as Necessary Antecedent of Harm

(1) Except as stated in Subsection (2), the actor's negligent conduct is not a substantial factor in bringing about harm to another if the harm would have been sustained even if the actor had not been negligent.

(2) If two forces are actively operating, one because of the actor's negligence, the other not because of any misconduct on his part, and each of itself is sufficient to bring about harm to another, the actor's negligence may be found to be a substantial factor in bringing it about.

ANDERSON
v.
MINNEAPOLIS, ST. PAUL & SAULT STE. MARIE RAILWAY CO.
179 N.W. 45 (Minn. 1920)

LEES, J.

This is a fire case brought against the defendant railway company and the Director General of Railroads. For convenience, we shall refer to the railway company, throughout this opinion, as the defendant. Plaintiff had a verdict. The appeal is from an order denying a motion in the alternative for judgment notwithstanding the verdict or for a new trial. The complaint alleged, that early in August,

1918, sparks from one of defendant's locomotive engines set a fire on or near the right of way, and that this fire spread until it finally reached plaintiff's land, where it destroyed some of his property.

The answer was a general denial followed by an allegation that, if plaintiff was damaged by fire, the fire was not due to any act of defendant, was of unknown origin, and, by reason of extraordinary weather conditions, became a huge conflagration.

The reply put these allegations in issue.

Plaintiff's case in chief was directed to proving that in August, 1918, one of defendant's engines started a fire in a bog near the west side of plaintiff's land; that it smoldered there until October 12, 1918, when it flared up and burned his property shortly before it was reached by one of the great fires which swept through northeastern Minnesota at the close of that day.

Defendant introduced evidence to show that on and prior to October 12 fires were burning west and northwest of and were swept by the wind towards plaintiff's premises. It did not show how such fires originated, neither did it clearly and certainly trace the destruction of plaintiff's property to them.

By cross-examination of defendant's witnesses and by his rebuttal evidence, plaintiff made a showing which would have justified the jury in finding that the fires proved by defendant were started by its locomotive on or near its right of way in the vicinity of Kettle river.

* * * * *

The following proposition is stated in defendant's brief and relied on for a reversal:

"If plaintiff's property was damaged by a number of fires combining, one ... being the fire pleaded ... the others being of no responsible origin, but of such sufficient or such superior force that they would have produced the damage to plaintiff's property regardless of the fire pleaded, then defendant was not liable."

This proposition is based upon *Cook v. Minneapolis, St. P. & S.S.M. Ry. Co....* In *Farrell v. Minneapolis & R.R. Ry. Co....*, this court considered the Cook case, but refrained from expressing approval or disapproval of its doctrine. The supreme court of Michigan has referred to it as good law. *Pluchak v. Crawford,....* The supreme court of Idaho says the opinion is logical and well reasoned, but the discussion is in a large measure theoretical and academic. *Miller v. N.P. Ry. Co. 24 Idaho,....* Judge Thompson in his work on Negligence, Vol. 1, § 739, says that the conclusion reached is so clearly wrong as not to deserve discussion. If the Cook case merely decides that one who negligently sets a fire is not liable if another's property is damaged, unless it is made to appear that the fire was a material element in the destruction of the property, there can be no question about the soundness of the decision. But if it decides that if such fire combines with another of no responsible origin, and after the union of the two fires they destroy the property, and either fire independently of the other would have destroyed it, then, irrespective of whether the first fire was or was not a material factor in the destruction of the property, there is no liability, we are not prepared to adopt the doctrine as the law of this state. If a fire set by the engine of one railroad company unites with a fire set by the engine of another company, there is joint and several liability, even though either fire would have destroyed plaintiff's property. But if the doctrine of the Cook case is applied and one of the fires is of unknown origin, there is no liability. G.S. 1913, § 4426, leaves no room for the application of a rule which would relieve a railroad company from liability under such circumstances. Moreover the reasoning of the court in *McClellan v. St. Paul, M. & M. Ry. Co....*, leads to the conclusion that, regardless of the statute, there would be liability in such a case. We, therefore, hold that the trial court did not err in refusing to instruct the jury in accordance with the rule laid down in the Cook case.

In the foregoing discussion we have assumed, although it is doubtful, that the evidence was such that a foundation was laid for the application of the rule if it was otherwise applicable.

* * * * *

We find no error requiring a reversal, and hence the order appealed from is affirmed.

NOTES

1.   Why doesn't the court apply a "but-for" causation test in *Anderson*?

2.   How is the substantial factor test stated in Restatement (Second) § 432 and illustrated by the *Anderson* case different from "but for" causation?

3.   Note that when Louisiana courts use the term "substantial factor," as in *Breithaupt, supra*, they usually mean "but-for" causation. But where the "but for" test does not eliminate the actor as a factor in the accident at suit, is it error for the court to give a "but for" instruction? The Louisiana Supreme Court explained the relationship between the two tests of causation in *Perkins v. Entergy Corp.*, 782 So. 2d 606 (La. 2001):

> ... Cause-in-fact usually is a "but for" inquiry, which tests whether the accident would or would not have happened but for the defendant's substandard conduct. Where there are concurrent causes of an accident, the proper inquiry is whether the conduct in question was a substantial factor in bringing about the accident. *Id.* at 612.

The *Perkins* court then pointed out that "our case law is clear that the substantial factor test is the preferred test for causation when there are multiple causes.... "*Id.* at 612 n.4. *See also Scott v. Dauterive Hospital Corp.*, 851 So. 2d 1152 (La.App. 3 Cir. 2003), *writ denied*, 857 So. 2d 487 (La. 2003), where the trial court instructed the jury as to causation with statements regarding both the "substantial factor" and the "but for" inquiries. The appellate court concluded that "the jury was advised of the substantial factor test and we do not find that the inclusion of the 'but for' information 'misled the jury to the extent it was prevented from dispensing justice.' "

4.   When two or more forces or actors cause harm, it may be difficult or impossible to determine whether the harm was caused by one, the other, or all of the forces or actors. Even if it can be determined that two or more caused the harm, a second issue is how much of the harm did each cause. These issues are present in *Anderson, supra*, but there is only one actor that can be identified and held liable. The Texas Supreme Court dealt with those issues in *Landers v. East Texas Salt Water Disposal Co.*, 248 S.W. 2d 731 (Tex. 1952). In *Landers*, plaintiff owned a lake that he had spent a considerable sum to stock with fish. On about the same day, a salt water disposal company's pipelines broke, emptying thousands of barrels of salt water onto plaintiff's land and into his lake, and an oil company caused salt water and oil to be discharged into plaintiff's lake. All of the fish were killed. With no way to determine which defendant's actions had killed the fish, or how many each defendant had killed, the court characterized it as practically "a single indivisible injury." The court's solution was to hold the two defendants jointly and severally liable, meaning that the plaintiff could collect the entire judgment from either defendant.

The California Supreme Court encountered some of these causation issues in *Summers v. Tice*, 199 P.2d 1 (Calif. 1948). Three men were hunting, and plaintiff was shot in the eye. Plaintiff flushed some quail, and the other two men shot their shotguns in plaintiff's direction, with shot striking plaintiff in the eye and lip. Most of the damages awarded were based on the eye injury, and only one of the defendants caused that injury, but the plaintiff could not prove which of the two caused it. The California Supreme Court addressed the problem of the plaintiff being unable to prove causation by shifting the burden on causation to the two defendants, requiring each to prove that he did not cause the harm. Because both were unable to prove they did not cause the harm, they were held jointly and severally liable.

5.   The Restatement (Third) of Torts: Liability for Physical and Emotional Harm (2010) jettisons the "substantial factor" label and provides a dramatically altered version of the test:

§27 Multiple Sufficient Causes

If multiple acts occur, each of which alone would have been a factual cause under §26 [setting forth the but-for test] of the physical harm at the same time in the absence of the other act(s), each act is regarded as a factual cause of the harm.

How would *Anderson* be decided if §27 were the standard?

[handwritten: CAUSATION]

[handwritten: → legal malpractice case]

[handwritten: (a) Did Ps have to prove that attys negligence caused P damages AND prove amount of the damages?]

JENKINS
v.
ST. PAUL FIRE & MARINE INSURANCE CO.
422 So. 2d 1109 (La. 1982)

[handwritten: → NO, BC:]

LEMMON, J.

[handwritten: P: loss of opp to assert claim BC attys failed to file w/in Rx period]

This is a legal malpractice action brought against plaintiff's two former attorneys, who allegedly allowed prescription to run before filing suit on plaintiff's claim for damages for personal injuries sustained in a truck-train collision. The trial court, after a jury trial and verdict in favor of plaintiff, rendered judgment against both attorneys in the sum of $87,000. The court of appeal reversed, holding that plaintiff's negligence was a contributing cause of the collision and would have barred his recovery against the railroad company. 393 So. 2d 851. We granted certiorari to review that judgment.... The grant was prompted to some extent by the concern over the "case within a case" approach used by the court of appeal in this case and by other courts in earlier decisions. Under that approach a plaintiff in legal malpractice litigation must prove not only that the attorney was negligent in handling the client's claim or litigation, but also that the claim or litigation would have been successful but for the attorney's negligence....

[handwritten: "case within a case"]

[handwritten: legal malpractice cases]

I

[handwritten: (1) neg of attys (2) causation]

In the present case, the attorneys concede that they were negligent in not filing suit until two days after prescription had run. . The remaining question is whether the client, after proving the attorneys' negligence, must also establish the validity of the underlying claim by proving that the attorneys' negligence caused him damages and by further proving the amount of the damages.

[handwritten: → BUT FOR atty's neg Ps claim would have been successful]

Plaintiff contends that, once the client has established negligence on the part of the attorney, the burden should be placed on the negligent attorney to prove that the mishandled claim or litigation would have been unsuccessful.

Causation, of course, is an essential element of any tort claim. However, once the client has proved that his former attorney accepted employment and failed to assert the claim timely, then the client has established a prima facie case that the attorney's negligence caused him some loss, since it is unlikely the attorney would have agreed to handle a claim completely devoid of merit. In such a situation, a rule which requires the client to prove the amount of damages by trying the "case within a case" simply imposes too great a standard of certainty of proof. Rather, the more logical approach is to impose on the negligent attorney, at this point in the trial, the burden of going forward with evidence to overcome the client's prima facie case by proving that the client could not have succeeded on the original claim, and the causation and damage questions are then up to the jury to decide. Otherwise, there is an undue burden on an aggrieved client, who can prove negligence and causation of some damages, when he has been relegated to seeking relief by the only remedy available after his attorney's negligence precluded relief by means of the original claim.[2]

Accordingly, when the plaintiff (as in this case) proves that negligence on the part of his former attorney has caused the loss of the opportunity to assert a claim and thus establishes the inference of causation of damages resulting from the lost opportunity for recovery, an appellate court

---

[2] The client's problem is frequently compounded when the attorney's negligence and the lapse of time has left a new attorney to search for stale evidence and has prevented or severely hampered thorough and effective preparation of the claim for trial.

(viewing the evidence on the merits of the original claim in the light most favorable to the prevailing party in the trial court) must determine whether the negligent attorney met his burden of producing sufficient proof to overcome plaintiff's prima facie case.

Accordingly, the judgment of the court of appeal is **AFFIRMED**.

MARCUS, Justice (concurring).

I agree with the result reached in this case but adhere to the rule that in a legal malpractice case plaintiff must prove not only that the attorney was negligent in handling his client's claim or litigation but also that the claim or litigation would have been successful but for the attorney's negligence. Accordingly, I respectfully concur.

WATSON, Justice, dissenting.

* * * * *

The reversal of burden of proof espoused by the majority opinion has no significance. If this is a contributory negligence case, as held by the Court of Appeal, then the burden of proof, at least to the resolutory issue of contributory negligence, was already on the defendant lawyers.

I would hold plaintiff could have recovered from the railroad, if his case had not prescribed. Therefore, I respectfully dissent.

DENNIS, Justice, dissenting.

I commend the plurality for its improvement in the law by modifying the "case within a case" requirement by placing the burden of going forward with the evidence upon the defendant attorney once his malpractice has been established. This is certainly more just than the former rule of law. However, I think our civil code and justice require that a person whose legal rights have been permanently prejudiced by the wrongful acts of his attorney be afforded a more complete remedy. La. Civ. Code art. 2315 ("Every act whatever of man that caused damage to another obliges him by whose fault it happened to repair it.") La. Civ. Code art. 2316 ("Every person is responsible for the damage he occasions not merely by his act, but by his negligence, his imprudence, or his want of skill.").

Although the plaintiff's rights were litigious, they surely had some value before they were allowed to prescribe by his attorney. The plaintiff should be allowed to recover for the loss of this value regardless of whether he would have triumphed in a full-scale hypothetical trial....

Accordingly, in the interest of justice and the faithful application of our civil code, I would jettison the case within a case requirement. I would require that the party guilty of malpractice repair the wrong he has done to his client by paying him an amount equal to the value of the right destroyed.

With this approach, we would reach a result under our code similar to that adopted by jurisdictions which have abandoned the case within a case requirement in favor of more modern rules. ... Additional proposed approaches include the "lost substantial possibility" test suggested by cases in the medical malpractice arena, ..., or the award of damages based upon "reasonable settlement value." This last approach has considerable logical appeal, since as many as 92.9% of personal injury suits are settled prior to trial. Bridgman, Legal Malpractice--A Consideration of the Elements of a Strong Plaintiff's Case, *30 S.C.L.R. 213, 234 (1979)*.

Because the plurality fails to resolve the major legal issue which is presented by this case in a manner which I find faithful to the precepts of our civil code and to a sense of justice, I respectfully dissent.

169

NOTES

1.   *Jenkins* is a legal malpractice case. Malpractice is the name given to negligence in the performance of professional work. You are of course familiar with medical malpractice. Consider accountant malpractice. What about educational malpractice? *See Miller v. Loyola Univ. of New Orleans*, 829 So. 2d 1057 (La.App. 4 Cir. 2002), *writ denied*, 839 So. 2d 38 (La. 2003). What could constitute a breach of the duty of reasonable care by an attorney other than letting a claim prescribe? What if the attorney failed to know the applicable law?

2.   Would an attorney's violation of an ethical rule constitute a breach in a legal malpractice analysis? *See Leonard v. Reeves*, 82 So. 3d 1250, 1257 (La.App. 1 Cir. 2012) ("standing alone, does not constitute actionable legal malpractice *per se* or proof of factual causation"). Is violation of an ethical rule relevant to the issue of breach in a legal malpractice analysis? *Id.* (Usually yes).

3.   Is expert testimony required in legal malpractice cases to establish a breach? Does the jury need to hear expert testimony regarding the standard of care for attorneys and whether the acts at issue fell below that standard of care? The Louisiana Supreme Court's answer is "not necessarily." The Court explained that for some acts of legal malpractice, the breach may be so obvious that expert testimony is not required. *See MB Indus., LLC v. CNA Ins. Co.*, 74 So. 3d 1173, 1184-85 (La. 2011). Compare the treatment of expert testimony in legal malpractice cases with the treatment of expert testimony in medical malpractice cases. *See* Chapter 12, Part A, *infra.*

4.   Does *Jenkins* eliminate the "case-within-a-case" approach in legal malpractice actions?

5.   The burden of production of evidence is usually on the plaintiff to prove each element of the prima facie case for negligence. What is the justification for shifting the burden in a legal malpractice case?

6.   Under *Jenkins*, what happens if the defendant attorney satisfies the burden of production on causation? How would an attorney satisfy the burden of production on causation? What happens if the defendant attorney fails to satisfy the burden of production?

7.   How is *Jenkins* like the California case, *Summers v. Tice*, discussed in note 4 after *Anderson*, *supra*? How is it different?

8.   Note how Justice Dennis in dissent would have changed the analysis in legal malpractice cases. Keep this in mind as you read the next case, *Smith*, on lost chance of survival.

9.   *Jenkins* involved a specific act of attorney malpractice–failing to file a petition within the prescriptive period. Do you think the *Jenkins* "framework" with the shifting burden of persuasion applies to other acts of alleged legal malpractice? The First Circuit addressed this issue, stating as follows:

> By its own terms, the *Jenkins* rationale is applicable only to "such a situation" as was involved in that case, *i.e.,* the final or complete loss of an opportunity to assert a legal claim (or, conversely, to present a defense) caused by an attorney's negligent failure to comply with the applicable procedural standards or constraints.... The *Jenkins* rule does not necessarily apply to all situations of alleged legal malpractice, as confirmed by subsequent jurisprudence.... In *Teague,* we held that the *Jenkins* rule did not apply in the specific context of that case, *i.e.,* "where the [client], an insured, is claiming the loss of an opportunity to *defend* a monetary claim, the immediate cause of such lost opportunity being the independent decision of the [client's] insurer to settle the adverse claim within its policy's monetary liability limits [.]"

Leonard v. Reeves, 82 So. 3d 1250, 1259 (La.App. 1 Cir. 2012).

10.   If a client failed to file an appeal of the unfavorable result allegedly resulting from the attorney's malpractice (did not appeal the case within the case), would the failure to appeal preclude the client from suing for legal malpractice? *See MB Indus., LLC v. CNA* Ins. *Co.*, 74 So. 3d 1173, 1183 (La. 2011) (not necessarily; standard is whether "a reasonably prudent party would have filed an appeal, given the facts known at the time and avoiding the temptation to view the case through hindsight").

11.   For a case examining the issue of when peremption begins to run on a legal malpractice claim, *see Teague v. St. Paul Fire & Marine Ins. Co.*, 974 So. 2d 1266 (La. 2008) (holding that "knowledge alone of a bad result is not sufficient to trigger the running of peremption").

On remand in the *Teague* case, the First Circuit Court of Appeal held that the attorney was not liable for legal malpractice. *Teague v. St. Paul Fire & Marine Ins. Co.*, 10 So. 3d 806 (La.App. 1 Cir. 2009), *writ denied*, 10 So. 3d 722 (La. 2009). One of the court's significant holdings was that "proof of the violation of an ethical rule by an attorney, standing alone, does not constitute *actionable* legal malpractice *per se.*" *Id.* at 825. The court also explained why the burden of persuasion never shifted to the defendant under the *Jenkins* analysis:

> In the present case, we conclude that the mere failure of the defendants to timely post the jury bond, or to notify Dr. Teague of the mediation, given all the circumstances, did not establish a *prima facie* case of "some loss" on the part of Dr. Teague (as opposed to St. Paul) applicable to the monetary claim being defended. Thus, Dr. Teague at all times retained the burden of proof that he in fact sustained damages caused by the defendants' omissions, and the nature and extent of his claimed damages.

Id. at 827.

The Louisiana Supreme Court held that the continuous representation rule (i.e., prescription on an act of legal malpractice does not begin to run while the attorney continues to represent the client and attempts to remedy the act of malpractice) does not suspend the one-year peremptive period for legal malpractice actions (La. R.S. 9:5605) in *Jenkins v. Starns*, 85 So. 3d 612 (La. 2012).

12.   For a line of cases reducing and shifting the burden of proving that an accident caused an injury, *see Housley v. Cerise*, 579 So. 2d 973, 980 (La. 1991):

[handwritten: → presumption of causation]

In *Lukas v. Insurance Company of North America*, 342 So. 2d 591 (La. 1977), this Court stated:

> [a] claimant's disability is presumed to have resulted from an accident, if before the accident the injured person was in good health, but commencing with the accident the symptoms of the disabling condition appear and continuously manifest themselves afterwards, providing that the medical evidence shows there to be a reasonable possibility of causal connection between the accident and the disabling condition.

Id. at 596.

SMITH
v.
STATE OF LOUISIANA DEPARTMENT OF HEALTH AND HOSPITALS
676 So. 2d 543 (La. 1996)

LEMMON, J.

On several occasions, this court has recognized the right to recover damages in medical malpractice cases for the loss of a chance of survival.... In *Ambrose v. New Orleans Police Dept.*

Ambulance Serv., 93-3099, 93-3110, 93-3112, p. 4 (La. 1994); 639 So. 2d 216, 219 n.4, we noted that this court has not yet addressed the method of valuation of the damages recoverable for the loss of a chance of survival. We granted certiorari in the instant medical malpractice case to address that issue.

I

In August 1987, Benjamin Smith went to E. A. Conway Memorial Hospital, complaining of a sore on top of his right foot. The attending physician diagnosed cellulitis with lymphangitis, and Smith underwent minor surgery to drain the fluid from his foot.

Smith's five-day hospitalization included a routine chest x-ray which the staff radiologist reported as showing "a mediastinal mass projected to the right of the trachea." The doctor stated that "lymphoma must be considered in the differential diagnosis" and recommended a CT scan of the thoracic area. The hospital staff failed to inform Smith or his family of the x-ray results or to recommend further testing. Smith was simply discharged from the hospital without any information about the mass in his chest.

Almost fifteen months later, Smith returned to E. A. Conway, complaining of a three-week history of "left pleuritic chest pain, fever, and chills." A second chest x-ray on October 31, 1988, compared with the August 1987 x-ray, revealed that the mass had doubled in size. Smith and his family then learned for the first time of the August 1987 x-ray report.

Further testing confirmed the diagnosis of small cell carcinoma of the lungs, a fast-acting and lethal cancer. By this time, Smith's cancer had progressed to the "extensive" stage, in that the cancer was present in both lungs and was non-operable.[1] Despite aggressive drug treatment and chemotherapy, Smith died on March 16, 1989, nineteen months after the initial x-ray. He was forty-five years old at his death.

Smith's wife and their two minor children petitioned for a medical review panel. The Louisiana Department of Health and Hospitals, which operated E. A. Conway Hospital, stipulated to its breach of the standard of care and waived the panel. In the stipulation, the Department "admitted that its employees and/or physicians for whom it is responsible pursuant to La. Rev. Stat. 40:1299.39 were at fault and breached the standard of reasonable care in failing to render follow-up testing and/or treatment in connection with the x-ray of August 14, 1987." However, the Department expressly reserved the right to contest causation and damages. This action followed, seeking both survival and wrongful death damages.[2]

The Department answered, reiterating its stipulation that its employees and physicians had breached the standard of care for medical treatment under the circumstances, but contesting whether the delay in treatment had caused any damages. Alternatively, the Department asserted that if the delay in treatment caused any diminution in Smith's reasonable life expectancy, then only a reduced amount of the normal survival and wrongful death damages should be awarded.

At trial, the parties presented evidence by several doctors relating to the percentage chance of survival for certain periods of time after discovery of small cell carcinoma of the lung at various stages of progression of the disease. The trial court ruled that plaintiffs had not met their burden of proving that the fifteen-month delay in treatment resulting from the State's admitted negligence had caused Smith to die or to lose a chance of survival. The judge noted that Smith actually "lived his

---

[1] The experts contrasted "extensive" stage with "limited" stage, in which the cancer is limited to one side of the thorax or treatable by one radiation point. Smith apparently was in the "limited" stage at the time of the first x-ray.

[2] While plaintiffs' petition asserts the unconstitutionality of the cap on medical malpractice damages set forth in La. Rev. Stat 40:1299.39, this issue was bifurcated by joint agreement between the parties. This issue is thus not before us.

expected life span" after the 1987 x-ray, referring to the estimated length of time Smith would have been expected to survive, according to statistical averages, if he had received treatment immediately after the x-ray. Accordingly, the judge dismissed plaintiffs' action.

The court of appeal reversed, concluding that the trial court was plainly wrong in failing to find the loss of a chance of survival.... Although Smith arguably lived without treatment as long as the average life span of a patient who underwent treatment, the court stated that every expert testified Smith had lost some chance of surviving the disease because of the Department's negligence. Supported by excellent analytical reasoning, the court held that plaintiffs were entitled to recover damages for Smith's loss of a chance of survival.

As to the method of measuring those damages, the intermediate court rejected plaintiffs' contention that they were entitled to full damages for the death, noting that plaintiffs failed to prove, more probably than not, that Smith would have survived but for the Department's malpractice. Drawing heavily on Joseph H. King, Jr., Causation, Valuation and Chance in Personal Injury Torts Involving Preexisting Conditions and Future Consequences, 90 Yale L. J. 1353 (1981), the court reasoned that granting recovery upon lesser proof than the more-probable-than-not rule should be balanced by a concomitant reduction of the potential damages for a case where the tort victim's death probably would not have occurred but for the defendant's fault. However, the court pointed out that the plaintiff in a loss of a chance of survival case still retains the burden of proving by a preponderance of the evidence that the defendant's negligence caused the loss of a chance.

Accordingly, the court held that "the percentage probability of loss, if less than 50%, is the proper measure of the plaintiff's damages in a case of wrongful death due to medical malpractice." 26,280, p. 11, 647 So. 2d at 662. Referring to expert evidence that recurrence of cancer after five years is rare, the court then reviewed other expert testimony as to the chance of survival for five years. Four doctors testified that the chance of survival, at the stage of the disease when the initial x-ray was taken, was one to twelve percent, ten to fifteen percent, five percent, and seven to twenty-five percent respectively.[3] The experts further agreed that Smith's chance of survival at the time of the October 1988 x-ray was less than one percent. Analyzing this evidence de novo, the court concluded that the evidence preponderated to show that the Department's negligence was a substantial factor in depriving Smith of a ten percent chance of surviving for five years. Fixing the total damages at $764,347,[4] the court reduced this amount proportionate to the lost ten percent chance of survival and awarded a total of $ 76,434 to Mrs. Smith and her two minor children.

On plaintiffs' application, we granted certiorari, primarily to address the method of measuring the damages caused by the deprivation of a chance of survival of less than fifty percent. 95-0038 (La. 3/10/95); 650 So. 2d 1167.

II

The court of appeal was correct in holding that plaintiff proved by a preponderance of the evidence that the negligence of the Department's physicians and employees deprived Smith of a chance of survival, a loss for which the Department must respond in damages. *Hastings v. Baton Rouge Gen. Hosp.*, 498 So. 2d 713 (La. 1986). The court of appeal was also correct in holding that the plaintiffs were not required to prove a "reasonable" or "substantial" chance of survival. The issues in

---

[3] From this testimony, the court concluded that a range of seven to twelve percent encompasses most of the experts' estimates.

[4] The court fixed the total damages as follows:

Wrongful death damage (one-third each)	$450,000.00
Funeral expenses	$4,004.00
Future lost earnings and value of household services	$250,343.00
Survival action damages	$60,000.00
	$764,347.00

173

loss of a chance of survival cases are whether the tort victim lost any chance of survival because of the defendant's negligence[5] and the value of that loss. The question of degree may be pertinent to the issue of whether the defendant's negligence caused or contributed to the loss, but such a tort-caused loss in any degree is compensable in damages.[6]

Allowing recovery for the loss of a chance of survival is not, as the court of appeal suggested, a change or a relaxation of the usual burden of proof by a preponderance of the evidence. Rather, allowing such recovery is a recognition of the loss of a chance of survival as a distinct compensable injury caused by the defendant's negligence, to be distinguished from the loss of life in wrongful death cases, and there is no variance from the usual burden in proving that distinct loss.

Thus, in a medical malpractice case[7] seeking damages for the loss of a less-than-even chance of survival because of negligent treatment of a pre-existing condition, the plaintiff must prove by a preponderance of the evidence that the tort victim had a chance of survival at the time of the professional negligence and that the tortfeasor's action or inaction deprived the victim of all or part of that chance, and must further prove the value of the lost chance, which is the only item of damages at issue in such a case.

All experts testified that Smith had some chance of survival if he had been treated immediately after the August 1987 x-ray, and that he had virtually no chance of survival in October 1988 after he went almost fifteen months without treatment because of the Department's negligence. Smith's chance of survival in August 1987, though not better than even, was still a chance that was denied him as a result of the Department's failure to meet its standard of care. That chance had some value when viewed from the standpoint of the tort victim and his heirs, and that value is the appropriate focus of the analysis in this case.

III

Courts and commentators have recognized three possible methods of valuation of the loss of a chance of survival in professional malpractice cases.[8]

The first, and the method we adopt today in this decision, is for the factfinder – judge or jury - - to focus on the chance of survival lost on account of malpractice as a distinct compensable injury and to value the lost chance as a lump sum award based on all the evidence in the record, as is done for any other item of general damages.

The second method, as advocated by plaintiffs, is to allow full survival and wrongful death damages for the loss of life partially caused by malpractice, without regard to the chance of survival. We reject this argument, agreeing with the court of appeal that full recovery is not available for

---

[5] The pre-existing condition causes the conceptual problem. The jury should focus on the damages that the defendant caused -the loss of a chance of avoiding a death that might not have occurred if the health care provider had performed properly. The court should instruct the jury to determine the amount of damages for this specific loss on the basis of all the evidence.

[6] *Contrast Pfiffner v. Correa*, 94-0992 (La. 1994); 643 So. 2d 1228, in which the plaintiffs failed to prove there was any chance of survival at the time of the alleged malpractice.

[7] This decision only addresses damages in a medical malpractice case and does not consider damages for loss of a chance of survival in cases against other types of tortfeasors. *See Hardy v. Southwestern Bell Tel. Co.*, 910 P.2d 1024 (Okla. 1996). That decision is left for another day.

[8] While the loss of a chance of survival doctrine has spawned a plethora of commentary and has been recognized by a majority of the states, John D. Hodson, Medical Malpractice: "Loss of Chance" Causality, 54 A.L.R. 4th 10 (1987); Martin J. McMahon, Medical Malpractice: Measure and Elements of Damages in Actions Based on Loss of Chance, 81 A.L.R. 4th 485 (1987), little attention has been given to the complex issue we focus on today of the appropriate methodology for calculating the value of the loss of a chance of survival.

174

deprivation of a chance of survival of less than fifty percent. To allow full recovery would ignore the claimants' inability to prove by a preponderance of the evidence that the malpractice victim would have survived but for the malpractice, which is a requirement for full recovery.

percentage prob of loss

The third method, and the method adopted by the court of appeal in this case, is to compute the compensable chance as "the percentage probability by which the defendant's tortious conduct diminished the likelihood of achieving some more favorable outcome." Joseph H. King, Jr., *Causation, Valuation and Chance in Personal Injury Torts Involving Preexisting Conditions and Future Consequences*, 90 Yale L. J. 1353, 1382 (1981). Professor King's percentage-probability-of-loss theory estimates "the compensable value of the victim's life if he survived" and reduced that estimate according to the percentage chance of survival at the time of the malpractice. Id. This method has gained acceptance by the courts and commentators because of its pragmatic appeal, providing concrete guidelines for calculating damages and alleviating the perceived "pulling out of the hat problem" allegedly associated with the method that we adopt today. *See Borgren v. United States*, 723 F.Supp. 581, 582-83 (D. Kan. 1989).

Our point of disagreement with the court of appeal's method of computing damages for the loss of a chance of survival is its rigid use of a precise mathematical formula, based on imprecise percentage chance estimates applied to estimates of general damages that never occurred, to arrive at a figure for an item of general damages that this court has long recognized cannot be calculated with mathematical precision. *See Boutte v. Hargrove*, 290 So. 2d 319, 322 (La. 1974); *Walton v. William Wolf Baking Co.*, 406 So. 2d 168, 175 (La. 1981). When these total hypothetical damages are reduced by a numerical factor determined from evidence of percentage rates of survival for certain periods after discovery of the disease at various stages of the disease, the uncertainty progresses geometrically.

→ general damages

The starting point of our analysis is to recognize that the loss of a less-than-even chance of survival is a distinct injury compensable as general damages which cannot be calculated with mathematical certainty. Next, we recognize that the factfinder should make a subjective determination of the value of that loss, fixing the amount of money that would adequately compensate the claimants for that particular cognizable loss. On the other hand, the approach of the court of appeal requires the factfinder first to make a hypothetical determination of the value of survival and wrongful death claims that are not really at issue and then to discount that value mathematically. This mathematical discounting of the subjective valuation of inapplicable claims does not magically make that approach more precise or more accurate than simply allowing the factfinder to value directly the loss of a chance of survival that is the sole item of damages at issue in the case. *Borgren*, 723 F.Supp. at 583.

The lost chance of survival in professional malpractice cases has a value in and of itself that is different from the value of a wrongful death or survival claim.[9] The jury can calculate the lost chance

---

[9] Valuation of the loss of a chance of survival in this medical malpractice case is similar to the valuation of the loss of a chance of recovery by judgment or settlement in a legal malpractice action in which a lawyer lets a case prescribe and the tort victim sues the lawyer for malpractice. In the early cases, a plaintiff could only recover by trying a "case-within-a-case" -- that is, by proving that he or she would have prevailed on the underlying cause of action. If not, the plaintiff could not recover. (The parallel in the medical malpractice area is the jurisprudence that rejects entirely the loss of a chance of survival doctrine.) Recognizing the unfairness to tort victims who had a chance of recovery and lost it because of legal malpractice, the courts, including this one, modified the case-within-a-case doctrine somewhat by shifting the burden of proof to the negligent attorney. *See Jenkins v. St. Paul Fire & Marine Ins. Co.*, 422 So. 2d 1109 (La. 1982). Even under this approach, however, the jury must engage in a pretend exercise of measuring damages based on events that never in reality occurred or can occur. The preferable approach in legal malpractice cases (although not yet adopted by a holding of this court) is to let the jury value the lost chance of recovery based on the value of the claim before prescription. *See Jenkins v. St. Paul Fire & Marine Ins. Co.*, 422 So. 2d 1109, 1114-15 (La. 1982) (Dennis, J., dissenting). Indeed, one commentator criticized the case-within-a-case approach as "speculative" and suggested it would be preferable just to let the jury value the lost chance of recovery. Richard G. Coggin, *Attorney Negligence ... A Suit Within a Suit*, 60 W. Va. L. Rev. 225, 234-35 (1965). As this commentator aptly noted, "the major objection which has been raised to [the case-within-a-case] mode of proof is that it will require the present jury to 'speculate' as to the amount of damages which the first jury, had it heard the case, would have assessed, thus bringing the question

of survival without going through the illusory exercise of setting a value for the wrongful death or survival claims and then mechanically reducing that amount by some consensus of the expert estimates of the percentage chance of survival. The methodology for fixing damages attributable to the loss of a chance of survival should not be so mechanistic as to require the jury merely to fill in the blanks on a verdict sheet with a consensus number for the percentage chance of survival and the total amount of damages, and then have the judge perform the multiplication task.

The calculation of damages for the loss of a chance of survival is not like the calculation of comparative fault damages. In the comparative fault context, the jury determines the entire amount of general and special damages actually sustained by the tort victim, which is an amount that would be awarded in the absence of contributory negligence. The percentage reduction merely implements the law of comparative fault in fixing the tortfeasor's total obligation. But in the loss of a chance of survival context, the award of damages for this particular loss is the "bottom line" figure. Any theoretical figure representing the amount the claimants would have been awarded if they had been successful in proving the defendant's fault more probably than not caused the loss of the tort victim's life is not a concrete figure that can properly be subjected to a reduction because of plaintiffs' failure of proof. Rather, the jury in a loss of a chance of survival case merely considers the same evidence considered by a jury in a survival and wrongful death action, and the loss-of-chance jury then reaches its general damages award for that loss on that evidence as well as other relevant evidence in the record.[10]

This approach for valuation of the loss of a chance of survival is more appropriate than the method used by the court of appeal in that it allows the jury to render a verdict in the lump sum amount of damages attributable only to the lost chance of survival. This is a valuation of the only damages at issue – the lost chance – which is based on all of the relevant evidence in the record, as is done for any other measurement of general damages. Allowing the jury to consider all the evidence, including expert medical testimony regarding the percentage chances of survival, and to value directly the lost chance is more logical than requiring the jury to calculate damages for wrongful death when the physician's negligence was not the more probable cause of the death.

The method we adopt today will not leave the jury without any guidance or any factors to consider. The jury will be allowed to consider an abundance of evidence and factors, including evidence of percentages of chance of survival along with evidence such as loss of support and loss of love and affection, and any other evidence bearing on the value of the lost chance. The jury's verdict of a lump sum amount of damages can be tested on appeal for support in the record by reviewing the percentage chances and the losses incurred by the tort victim and his or her heirs, and any other relevant evidence, thus providing assurance against speculative verdicts.

* * * * *

For these reasons, the judgment of the court of appeal is set aside, and the case is remanded to the district court for further proceedings in accordance with this opinion.

---

within the familiar 'rule of certainty'" which permits recovery of only damages that are susceptible of determination with a reasonable degree of certainty. *Id.* at 234. Continuing, this commentator made the suggestion that the preferable methodology would be to present all relevant issues to the jury for its exclusive determination and noted that "no substantial right of the defendant would be violated by such a course of action." *Id.* at 235. This commentator further noted that this approach would be consistent with the policy that "no wrong shall be without a remedy." *Id.*

[10] Evidence of loss of support, loss of love and affection and other wrongful death damages is relevant, but not mathematically determinative, in loss of a chance of survival cases, as is evidence of the percentage chance of survival at the time of the malpractice. The plaintiff may also present evidence of, and argue, other factors to the jury, such as that a ten percent chance of survival may be more significant when reduced from ten percent to zero than when reduced from forty to thirty percent. The jury may also consider such factors as that the victim, although not likely to survive, would have lived longer but for the malpractice.

VICTORY and MARCUS, JUSTICES, dissenting.

NOTES

1.   Do you agree with the Court that, in recognizing a lost chance claim, it has not changed the burden of proof with respect to cause in fact? According to the Court, what has changed? If that is true, then can a person who has lost a quantifiable chance of survival and yet survived recover for the chance lost? *See Claudet v. Weyrich*, 662 So. 2d 131 (La.App. 4 Cir. 1995).

What if the evidence showed that because of a pre-existing condition the victim probably would have required a hip transplant by age 60, but because of the accident, the transplant probably would be required by age 55? Or what if the accident increased by 10% the likelihood that the victim would be required to have the transplant at any time?

2.   For a court rejecting the lost chance claim, see *Kramer v. Lewisville Memorial Hospital*, 858 S.W.2d 397 (Tex. 1993).

Unless courts are going to compensate patients who "beat the odds" and make full recovery, the lost chance cannot be proven unless and until the ultimate harm occurs. ... Hence, legal responsibility under the loss of chance doctrine is in reality assigned based on the mere possibility that a tortfeasor's negligence was a cause of the ultimate harm.... That damages for loss of chance may be reduced to some degree is ultimately beside the point.

* * * * *

Furthermore, assuming we adopt the loss of chance doctrine in the context of this medical malpractice action, it is doubtful that there is any principled way we could prevent its application to similar actions involving other professions.

3.   Is a lost chance case simply a wrongful death case in which there are problems proving that the breach caused the death? When does a wrongful death case become a lost chance case?

4.   How is the *Smith* case different from the *Jenkins* case in terms of causation standards?

5.   Do you think that awards in lost chance cases differ significantly from awards in wrongful death cases? *See Stroud v. Golson*, 744 So. 2d 1286 (La. 1999) (Victory, J. dissenting from denial of writ).

6.   Would you allow recovery for lost chance in the following fact situation: 82-year old woman having annual check up had chest x-ray and doctor did not look at it that day; she died of severe bilateral pneumonia several days later; none of the doctors would assess percentage chance of survival, and one characterized chance as "small" or "very low." *See Lovelace v. Giddens*, 740 So. 2d 652 (La.App. 2 Cir. 1999), *writ denied*, 750 So. 2d 987 (La. 1999).

7.   Lost chance cases sometimes vary from lost chance of survival, encompassing lost chance of better outcomes. *See, e.g., Coody v. Barraza*, 111 So. 3d 485 (La.App. 2 Cir. 2013) (lost chance of achieving a second remission of ovarian cancer). The court stated as follows: "[C]uring the disease is not a requirement. Achieving a second remission would have been a better medical outcome. It could have prolonged Mrs. Coody's life, if only briefly, and possibly have granted her a reprieve from the chemotherapy that was causing her and her family added pain and suffering." *Id.* at 492. The court listed the elements a plaintiff must prove in a loss of chance claim (taken from *Smith*): 1) the victim had a chance to survive at the time of malpractice; 2) malpractice deprived the victim of all or part of that chance; and, 3) value of that lost chance. *Id.* at 490. The Louisiana Supreme Court has not yet recognized lost chance of a better outcome.

BLACK
v.
ABEX CORP.
603 NW.2d 182 (N.D. 1999)

KAPSNER, J.

Rochelle Black appeals from a summary judgment dismissing her wrongful death and survival claims premised upon market share or alternative liability against numerous asbestos manufacturers. Concluding Black has failed to raise a genuine issue of material fact which would preclude summary judgment, we affirm.

I

Rochelle Black's husband, Markus, served in the Air Force as an auto mechanic from 1971 to 1986. He died of lung cancer in 1991. Black sued forty-eight asbestos manufacturers, alleging her husband's death had been caused by his occupational exposure to asbestos-containing products. Included in her complaint were claims based upon market share and alternative liability.

The defendants moved for partial summary judgment requesting dismissal of the market share and alternative liability claims. The court granted the motion for partial summary judgment and dismissed those claims in its Pretrial Order dated August 29, 1995.

Subsequently, all remaining claims against the defendants were either settled or voluntarily dismissed prior to the scheduled trial. On February 25, 1999, the court entered a "Concluding Order" covering this and several other consolidated asbestos cases, indicating all of the cases had been "fully and finally disposed of and the time for all appeals of this Court's orders and judgments in those cases has run." Black filed a notice of appeal from the Concluding Order and from the 1995 Pretrial Order granting the motion for summary judgment.[1]

* * * * *

III

Black asserts the district court erred in dismissing her claims based upon market share liability. She argues market share liability is a viable tort theory under North Dakota law and its application is appropriate under the facts of this case.

A

The genesis of market share liability lies in the California Supreme Court's decision in *Sindell v. Abbott Laboratories,* 26 Cal.3d 588, 163 Cal.Rptr. 132, 607 P.2d 924 (1980). In *Sindell,* the court held that women who suffered injuries resulting from their mothers' ingestion of the drug DES during pregnancy could sue DES manufacturers, even though the plaintiffs could not identify the specific manufacturer of the DES each of their respective mothers had taken. The court fashioned a new form of liability which relaxed traditional causation requirements, allowing a plaintiff to recover upon showing that she could not identify the specific manufacturer of the DES which caused her injury, that the defendants produced DES from an identical formula, and that the defendants manufactured a "substantial share" of the DES the plaintiff's mother might have taken. *Id.* at 936-37. The court held each defendant would be liable for a proportionate share of the judgment based upon its share of the relevant market, unless it demonstrated it could not have made the product which caused the plaintiff's injury. *Id.* at 937.

---

[1] Black has settled with or dismissed all claims against forty-four of the defendants. The only defendants remaining as appellees are Chrysler Corporation, General Motors Corporation, Borg Warner, and Allied Signal.

The essential elements of market share liability are summarized in W. Page Keeton et al., *Prosser and Keeton on the Law of Torts*, § 103, at 714 (5th ed.1984):

> The requirements for market-share liability seem to be: (1) injury or illness occasioned by a fungible product (identical-type product) made by all of the defendants joined in the lawsuit; (2) injury or illness due to a design hazard, with each having been found to have sold the same type product in a manner that made it unreasonably dangerous; (3) inability to identify the specific manufacturer of the product or products that brought about the plaintiff's injury or illness; and (4) joinder of enough of the manufacturers of the fungible or identical product to represent a substantial share of the market.

The overwhelming majority of courts which have addressed the issue have held market share liability is inappropriate in cases alleging injury from exposure to asbestos.... The leading treatise recognizes:

> [I]t can reasonably be argued that it would not be appropriate to apply this fungible product concept to asbestos-containing products because they are by no means identical since they contain widely varying amounts of asbestos.

Prosser, *supra,* § 103, at 714.

Black essentially concedes market share liability is inappropriate in a "shotgun" asbestos case, where the plaintiff is alleging injury from exposure to many different types of asbestos products. Black asserts, however, market share liability may be appropriate when the plaintiff seeks to hold liable only manufacturers of one type of asbestos-containing product. Relying upon *Wheeler v. Raybestos-Manhattan,* 8 Cal.App.4th 1152, 11 Cal.Rptr.2d 109 (1992), Black asserts she should be allowed to proceed in her market share claims against the manufacturers of asbestos-containing "friction products," including brake and clutch products. In *Wheeler,* the California Court of Appeal held a plaintiff could proceed on a market share theory against manufacturers of asbestos-containing brake pads. The court overturned the trial court's order granting a nonsuit in favor of the manufacturers, concluding the plaintiff's offer of proof sufficiently alleged that the brake pads, although not identical, were "fungible" because they contained percentages of asbestos within a "restricted range" of between forty and sixty percent and posed nearly equivalent risks of harm....

Black requests that we recognize market share liability as a viable tort theory under North Dakota law. Black further requests that we follow *Wheeler* and hold that automotive "friction products," including asbestos- containing brake and clutch products, are sufficiently fungible to support a market share claim.

* * * * *

C

This Court has never addressed whether market share liability is recognized under North Dakota tort law. Other courts faced with the question have reached varying conclusions on the general availability of this novel remedy. *See* 1 Louis R. Frumer & Melvin I. Friedman, *Products Liability* § 3.06 [5] (1999); Richard E. Kaye, Annotation, *"Concert of Activity," "Alternate Liability," "Enterprise Liability," or Similar Theory as Basis for Imposing Liability Upon One or More Manufacturers of Defective Uniform Product, in Absence of Identification of Manufacturer or Precise Unit or Batch Causing Injury,* 63 A.L.R.5th 195 at § 4 (1998), and cases collected therein. We find it unnecessary to resolve this general issue because we conclude, assuming market share liability were recognized in this state, summary judgment was still appropriate based upon the record in this case.

The dispositive question presented is whether Black has raised a genuine issue of material fact on the issue of fungibility. Market share liability is premised upon the fact that the defendants have produced identical (or virtually identical) defective products which carry equivalent risks of harm. Accordingly, under the market share theory, it is considered equitable to apportion liability based upon the percentage of products each defendant contributed to the entire relevant market.

This reasoning hinges, however, upon each defendant's product carrying an equal degree of risk. As the Supreme Court of Oklahoma explained in *Case,* 743 P.2d at 1066:

> In the *Sindell* case, and those following it, it was determined that public policy considerations supporting recovery in favor of an innocent plaintiff against negligent defendants would allow the application of a theory of liability which shifted the burden of proof of causation from plaintiff to defendants. However, as previously stated, that theory was crafted in a situation where each potential defendant shared responsibility for producing a product which carried with it a singular risk factor. The theory further provided that each potential defendant's liability would be proportional to that defendant's contribution of risk to the market in which the plaintiff was injured. This situation thus provided a balance between the rights of the defendants and the rights of the plaintiffs. A balance being achieved, public policy considerations were sufficient to justify the application of the market share theory of liability.

Similar reasoning was employed by the Supreme Court of Ohio in *Goldman,* 514 N.E.2d at 701:

> Crucial to the *Sindell* court's reasoning was this fact: there was no difference between the risks associated with the drug as marketed by one company or another, and as all DES sold presented the same risk of harm, there was no inherent unfairness in holding the companies accountable based on their share of the DES market.

Numerous other courts have stressed the importance of a singular risk factor in market share cases. *See, e.g., King v. Cutter Laboratories,* 714 So. 2d 351, 354-55 (Fla. 1998); *Leng,* 143 Ill.Dec. 533, 554 N.E.2d at 471; *Becker v. Baron Bros.,* 138 N.J. 145, 649 A.2d 613, 620-21 (1994).

Unless the plaintiff can demonstrate that the defendants' products created a "singular risk factor," the balance between the rights of plaintiffs and defendants evaporates and it is no longer fair nor equitable to base liability upon each defendant's share of the relevant market. The rationale underlying market share liability, as developed in *Sindell,* is that it did not matter which manufacturer's product the plaintiff's mother actually ingested; because all DES was chemically identical, the same harm would have occurred. Thus, any individual manufacturer's product would have caused the identical injury, and it was through mere fortuity that any one manufacturer did not produce the actual product ingested. Under these circumstances, viewing the overall DES market and all injuries caused thereby, it may be presumed each manufacturer's products will produce a percentage of those injuries roughly equivalent to its percentage of the total DES market. As the *Sindell* court recognized, "[u]nder this approach, each manufacturer's liability would approximate its responsibility for the injuries caused by its own products." *Sindell,* 163 Cal.Rptr. 132, 607 P.2d at 937.

In order to prevail on its market share claims, Black would therefore have to demonstrate that the asbestos-containing "friction products" her husband was exposed to carried equivalent degrees of risk. Black asserts this problem has been "disposed of" by the holding in *Wheeler.* Although *Wheeler* recognized that non-identical products may give rise to market share liability if they contain roughly equivalent quantities of a single type of asbestos fiber, the court did not hold that all asbestos-containing friction brake products in all cases will be considered fungible. In fact, the court in *Wheeler* indicated that such products must carry a nearly equivalent risk of harm to support market share liability. *Wheeler,* 11 Cal.Rptr.2d at 111- 12. Furthermore, *Wheeler* was a reversal of a nonsuit based upon an offer of proof made by the plaintiff. The court stressed its holding was narrow: the plaintiffs had not proven the elements of a market share case, but were merely being afforded the opportunity to prove it. *Id.* at 113. Clearly, *Wheeler* does not serve as evidence of fungibility and equivalent risks of harm of the products in this case.

Black points to uncontroverted evidence in this record that the four remaining defendants produced friction products which contained between seven and seventy-five percent asbestos fibers. This is a far greater range than the forty to sixty percent the *Wheeler* court considered "roughly comparable" for purposes of fungibility under *Sindell*.[3] *Wheeler*, 11 Cal.Rptr. 2d at 111. It is closer to the fifteen to one-hundred percent range which the Supreme Court of Ohio held precluded market share liability as a matter of law. *See Goldman*, 514 N.E.2d at 697, 701. It seems obvious that a product which contains seventy-five percent asbestos would create a greater risk of harm than one which contains only seven percent. *See, e.g., Leng*, 143 Ill.Dec. 533, 554 N.E.2d at 471 (toxicity of an asbestos product varies with percentage of asbestos fiber, and "products with high concentrations of asbestos fibers have a correspondingly high potential for inducing disease"). Absent introduction of expert evidence demonstrating that in spite of the differences the products would produce equivalent risks of harm, application of market share liability would be inappropriate.

Black failed to present competent, admissible evidence from which a fact finder could determine the "friction products" her husband was exposed to carried equivalent risks of harm and were fungible under *Sindell*. Accordingly, summary judgment was appropriate.

IV

Black asserts the district court erred in dismissing her claims based upon alternative liability.

Alternative liability was first recognized by the Supreme Court of California in *Summers v. Tice*, 33 Cal.2d 80, 199 P.2d 1 (1948). In *Summers,* the plaintiff was struck by a shot fired by one of the defendants, who had simultaneously fired at a quail near the plaintiff. When the plaintiff could not prove which of the two negligently fired shots had struck him, the court shifted the burden of proving causation to the defendants. *Id.* at 3-4; *see also* W. Page Keeton et al., *Prosser and Keeton on the Law of Torts,* § 41 (5th ed.1984). The rule of *Summers* has been adopted in the Restatement (Second) of Torts § 433B(3):

> Where the conduct of two or more actors is tortious, and it is proved that harm has been caused to the plaintiff by only one of them, but there is uncertainty as to which one has caused it, the burden is upon each such actor to prove that he has not caused the harm.

This Court has not previously addressed whether alternative liability, as embodied in *Summers* and Section 433B(3), is recognized under North Dakota law. Courts addressing the issue have reached varying results. *See* Richard E. Kaye, Annotation, *"Concert of Activity," "Alternate Liability," "Enterprise Liability," or Similar Theory as Basis for Imposing Liability Upon One or More Manufacturers of Defective Uniform Product, In Absence of Identification of Manufacturer of Precise Unit or Batch Causing Injury,* 63 A.L.R.5th 195 at § 3 (1998), and cases collected therein. We find it unnecessary to resolve this general issue because we conclude, assuming alternative liability were recognized in this state, summary judgment was appropriate under the facts of this case.

As recognized by the Supreme Court of Texas in *Gaulding v. Celotex Corp.,* 772 S.W.2d 66, 69 (Tex.1989), "[a] crucial element to alternative liability is that *all* possible wrongdoers must be brought before the court." Thus, most courts addressing the issue have rejected application of alternative liability in asbestos cases. *See, e.g., Vigiolto v. Johns- Manville Corp.,* 643 F.Supp. 1454, 1457 (W.D.Pa.1986); *Rutherford v. Owens- Illinois, Inc.,* 16 Cal.4th 953, 67 Cal.Rptr.2d 16, 941 P.2d 1203, 1216-21 (1997); *Goldman v. Johns-Manville Sales Corp.,* 33 Ohio St.3d 40, 514 N.E.2d 691, 696-99 (1987); *Gaulding,* 772 S.W.2d at 68-69. As the court explained in *Lineaweaver v. Plant*

---

[3] We also note the holding in *Wheeler* was limited to asbestos-containing brake pads. Black seeks to include a broader range of products--brake and clutch "friction products"--in her market share claims. Black has not drawn our attention to any evidence in this record demonstrating how, or if, the different nature and function of brake and clutch products affects their relative degree of risk.

Insulation Co., 31 Cal.App.4th 1409, 37 Cal.Rptr.2d 902, 907 (1995) (quoted in *Rutherford*, 67 Cal.Rptr.2d 16, 941 P.2d at 1220-21):

> Unlike *Summers*, there are hundreds of possible tortfeasors among the multitude of asbestos suppliers. As our Supreme Court has recognized, the probability that any one defendant is responsible for plaintiff's injury decreases with an increase in the number of possible tortfeasors. When there are hundreds of suppliers of an injury-producing product, the probability that any of a handful of joined defendants is responsible for plaintiff's injury becomes so remote that it is unfair to require defendants to exonerate themselves. The probability that an individual asbestos supplier is responsible for plaintiff's injury may also be decreased by the nature of the particular product. Asbestos products have widely divergent toxicities. Unlike the negligent hunters of *Summers,* all asbestos suppliers did not fire the same shot. Yet, under a burden shifting rule, all suppliers would be treated as if they subjected plaintiff to a hazard identical to that posed by other asbestos products. [Citations omitted].

Black does not assert she has included as defendants all possible manufacturers of the asbestos-containing brake and clutch "friction products" which her husband was exposed to during his lengthy career as a mechanic. Accordingly, alternative liability is inapplicable in this case.

V

The summary judgment dismissal of Black's market share and alternative liability claims is **AFFIRMED**.

NOTES

1.   Louisiana does not have any reported decisions adopting market share or enterprise liability. The federal Fifth Circuit in a diversity case stated that market share and enterprise liability "represent radical departures from traditional theories of tort liability." *Thompson v. Johns-Manville Sales Corp.*, 714 F.2d 581 (5th Cir. 1983), *cert. denied*, 465 U.S. 1102 (1984). The Fifth Circuit refused to adopt those theories for Louisiana, saying such a decision is for the Louisiana courts. *See also Cimino v. Raymack Indus., Inc.*, 151 F.3d 297 (5th Cir. 1998).

2.   In *George v. Housing Authority of New Orleans*, the Court observed that there is no Louisiana case adopting the "market share" theory of causation in product liability cases, and that the theory would not apply in a claim against two manufacturers of smoke alarms, because the products of different manufacturers have different qualities and "cannot be deemed fungible products." 906 So. 2d 1282 (La.App. 4 Cir. 2005).

CHAPTER 6

LEGAL CAUSE/SCOPE OF THE DUTY

INTRODUCTORY NOTE

No area of torts has baffled students, professors, practitioners and judges more than the question of "proximate cause" or "scope of the risk." Proximate cause is laden with policy considerations, although those policy considerations are sometimes hidden behind the language of "foreseeable risk" or "ease of association." Complicating the area even further is the fact that jurisdictions often use different language to describe exactly the same considerations. There are several key concepts that you should consider in the following materials.

1.   What is the question? It doesn't really matter whether we call this "proximate cause," "legal cause," "scope of the risk," "scope of the duty," or whether we are applying principles from the common law or sections of a Civil Code. The fundamental question is the same. Should "this" defendant be responsible in "this" case? One of your authors has described legal cause as a series of "this" questions: Should "this" defendant be responsible to "this" plaintiff who was harmed by "this" instrumentality, in "this" manner, at "this" location, at "this" time, etc... Or: should this defendant (and similarly situated individuals) be liable to this plaintiff (or similarly situated individuals) for this injury (and injuries like it) which occur under these circumstances (or similar circumstances). Ask yourselves why the parentheticals! However you ask the scope of liability question, it is inherently a policy question.

2.   What are the policies? As you will soon discover, most Louisiana cases are decided by application of a "risk rule" which asks whether the injury to this plaintiff was reasonably foreseeable. However, there are many other policy considerations which are important as well. Go back to the *Bordelon* negligent spoliation case in Chapter 1 and review the "tort" policies the court considered.

3.   Who decides? One important question in the legal cause/scope of the duty inquiry is whether the policy issues are matters for the judge or jury. The dispute is often couched in terms of whether the policy issues are analyzed as questions of duty or causation.

In the final analysis, perhaps the best way to think about the problem is to treat legal cause/scope of the duty as a fifth and independent element of the negligence theory. This fifth element involves applying policy factors to determine whether the defendant should be responsible to this plaintiff. The policy analysis includes a broad range of factors and may be performed by the judge or jury or both.

Although the lack of concrete standards may be frustrating, you should try to see the uncertainty as an opportunity. Proximate cause/scope of the duty questions can be complex, and good lawyers are able to bring clarity and sanity to seemingly unsolvable polycentric problems. Your task, as a law student, is to begin to discover the various and competing policy considerations which are at stake.

A.   THE CONCEPT OF LEGAL CAUSE

To introduce the concept of legal cause, we turn to the noted legal commentator, Mother Goose.

For Want of a Nail

For want of a nail, the shoe was lost;
For want of the shoe, the horse was lost;
For want of the horse, the rider was lost;
For want of the rider, the battle was lost;

For want of the battle, the kingdom was lost,
And all for the want of a horseshoe nail.

NOTES

1.   How would you define the duty of the manufacturer/supplier of the horseshoe nail in a negligence case?

2.   Assuming that the manufacturer of the nail owes a duty, was the breach of that duty an actual cause of the lost kingdom? What standard did you apply?

3.   Should we hold the nail manufacturer liable for the lost kingdom? Why or why not?

4.   The question in Note 3 represents the question of this chapter and the subject matter of the legal cause/scope of the duty inquiry.

B.   INTRODUCTION TO THE RISK RULE

1.   Foreseeable Plaintiff

PALSGRAF
v.
LONG ISLAND R. CO.
248 N.Y. 339 (N.Y. 1928)

CARDOZO, C. J.

Plaintiff was standing on a platform of defendant's railroad after buying a ticket to go to Rockaway Beach. A train stopped at the station, bound for another place. Two men ran forward to catch it. One of the men reached the platform of the car without mishap, though the train was already moving. The other man, carrying a package, jumped aboard the car, but seemed unsteady as if about to fall. A guard on the car, who had held the door open, reached forward to help him in, and another guard on the platform pushed him from behind. In this act, the package was dislodged, and fell upon the rails. It was a package of small size, about fifteen inches long, and was covered by a newspaper. In fact it contained fireworks, but there was nothing in its appearance to give notice of its contents. The fireworks when they fell exploded. The shock of the explosion threw down some scales at the other end of the platform, many feet away. The scales struck the plaintiff, causing injuries for which she sues.

The conduct of the defendant's guard, if a wrong in its relation to the holder of the package, was not a wrong in its relation to the plaintiff, standing far away. Relatively to her it was not negligence at all. Nothing in the situation gave notice that the falling package had in it the potency of peril to persons thus removed. Negligence is not actionable unless it involves the invasion of a legally protected interest, the violation of a right. "Proof of negligence in the air, so to speak, will not do." "Negligence is the absence of care, according to the circumstances."

The plaintiff as she stood upon the platform of the station might claim to be protected against intentional invasion of her bodily security. Such invasion is not charged. She might claim to be protected against unintentional invasion by conduct involving in the thought of reasonable men an unreasonable hazard that such invasion would ensue. These, from the point of view of the law, were the bounds of her immunity, with perhaps some rare exceptions, survivals for the most part of ancient forms of liability, where conduct is held to be at the peril of the actor. If no hazard was apparent to the eye of ordinary vigilance, an act innocent and harmless, at least to outward seeming, with reference to her, did not take to itself the quality of a tort because it happened to be a wrong, though apparently not one involving the risk of bodily insecurity, with reference to some one else. "In every instance, before negligence can be predicated of a given act, back of the act must be sought and found a duty to the individual complaining, the observance of which would have averted or avoided the injury." "The ideas of negligence and duty are strictly correlative." The plaintiff sues in her own right for a wrong personal to her, and not as the vicarious beneficiary of a breach of duty to another.

A different conclusion will involve us, and swiftly too, in a maze of contradictions. A guard stumbles over a package which has been left upon a platform. It seems to be a bundle of newspapers. It turns out to be a can of dynamite. To the eye of ordinary vigilance, the bundle is abandoned waste, which may be kicked or trod on with impunity. Is a passenger at the other end of the platform protected by the law against the unsuspected hazard concealed beneath the waste? If not, is the result to be any different, so far as the distant passenger is concerned, when the guard stumbles over a valise which a truckman or a porter has left upon the walk? The passenger far away, if the victim of a wrong at all, has a cause of action, not derivative, but original and primary. His claim to be protected against invasion of his bodily security is neither greater nor less because the act resulting in the invasion is a wrong to another far removed.

In this case, the rights that are said to have been violated, the interests said to have been invaded, are not even of the same order. The man was not injured in his person nor even put in danger. The purpose of the act, as well as its effect, was to make his person safe. If there was a wrong to him at all, which may very well be doubted, it was a wrong to a property interest only, the safety of his package. Out of this wrong to property, which threatened injury to nothing else, there has passed, we are told, to the plaintiff by derivation or succession a right of action for the invasion of an interest of another order, the right to bodily security. The diversity of interests emphasizes the futility of the effort to build the plaintiff's right upon the basis of a wrong to some one else. The gain is one of emphasis, for a like result would follow if the interests were the same. Even then, the orbit of the danger as disclosed to the eye of reasonable vigilance would be the orbit of the duty. One who jostles one's neighbor in a crowd does not invade the rights of others standing at the outer fringe when the unintended contact casts a bomb upon the ground. The wrongdoer as to them is the man who carries the bomb, not the one who explodes it without suspicion of the danger. Life will have to be made over, and human nature transformed, before prevision so extravagant can be accepted as the norm of conduct, the customary standard to which behavior must conform.

The argument for the plaintiff is built upon the shifting meanings of such words as "wrong" and "wrongful," and shares their instability. What the plaintiff must show is "a wrong" to herself, i. e., a violation of her own right, and not merely a wrong to some one else, nor conduct "wrongful" because unsocial, but not "a wrong" to any one. We are told that one who drives at reckless speed through a crowded city street is guilty of a negligent act and, therefore, of a wrongful one irrespective of the consequences. Negligent the act is, and wrongful in the sense that it is unsocial, but wrongful and unsocial in relation to other travelers, only because the eye of vigilance perceives the risk of damage. If the same act were to be committed on a speedway or a race course, it would lose its wrongful quality. The risk reasonably to be perceived defines the duty to be obeyed, and risk imports relation; it is risk to another or to others within the range of apprehension. This does not mean, of course, that one who launches a destructive force is always relieved of liability if the force, though known to be destructive, pursues an unexpected path. "It was not necessary that the defendant should have had notice of the particular method in which an accident would occur, if the possibility of an accident was clear to the ordinarily prudent eye." Some acts, such as shooting, are so imminently dangerous to any one who may come within reach of the missile, however unexpectedly, as to impose a duty of prevision not far from that of an insurer. Even today, and much oftener in earlier stages of the law, one acts sometimes at one's peril. Under this head, it may be, fall certain cases of what is known as transferred intent, an act willfully dangerous to A resulting by misadventure in injury to B. These cases aside, wrong is defined in terms of the natural or probable, at least when unintentional. The range of reasonable apprehension is at times a question for the court, and at times, if varying inferences are possible, a question for the jury.

Here, by concession, there was nothing in the situation to suggest to the most cautious mind that the parcel wrapped in newspaper would spread wreckage through the station. If the guard had thrown it down knowingly and willfully, he would not have threatened the plaintiff's safety, so far as appearances could warn him. His conduct would not have involved, even then, an unreasonable probability of invasion of her bodily security. Liability can be no greater where the act is inadvertent.

Negligence, like risk, is thus a term of relation. Negligence in the abstract, apart from things related, is surely not a tort, if indeed it is understandable at all. Negligence is not a tort unless it results in the commission of a wrong, and the commission of a wrong imports the violation of a right, in this case, we are told, the right to be protected against interference with one's bodily security. But bodily security is protected, not against all forms of interference or aggression, but only against some. One who seeks redress at law does not make out a cause of action by showing without more that there has been damage to his person. If the harm was not willful, he must show that the act as to him had possibilities of danger so many and apparent as to entitle him to be protected against the doing of it though the harm was unintended. Affront to personality is still the keynote of the wrong. Confirmation of this view will be found in the history and development of the action on the case. Negligence as a basis of civil liability was unknown to mediaeval law. For damage to the person, the sole remedy was trespass, and trespass did not lie in the absence of aggression, and that direct and personal. Liability for other damage, as where a servant without orders from the master does or omits something to the damage of another, is a plant of later growth. When it emerged out of the legal soil, it was thought of as a variant of trespass, an offshoot of the parent stock. This appears in the form of action, which was known as trespass on the case. The victim does not sue derivatively, or by right of subrogation, to vindicate an interest invaded in the person of another. Thus to view his cause of action is to ignore the fundamental difference between tort and crime. He sues for breach of a duty owing to himself.

The law of causation, remote or proximate, is thus foreign to the case before us. The question of liability is always anterior to the question of the measure of the consequences that go with liability. If there is no tort to be redressed, there is no occasion to consider what damage might be recovered if there were a finding of a tort. We may assume, without deciding, that negligence, not at large or in the abstract, but in relation to the plaintiff, would entail liability for any and all consequences, however novel or extraordinary. There is room for argument that a distinction is to be drawn according to the diversity of interests invaded by the act, as where conduct negligent in that it threatens an insignificant invasion of an interest in property results in an unforseeable invasion of an interest of another order, as, e. g., one of bodily security. Perhaps other distinctions may be necessary. We do not go into the question now. The consequences to be followed must first be rooted in a wrong.

The judgment of the Appellate Division and that of the Trial Term should be reversed, and the complaint dismissed, with costs in all courts.

ANDREWS, J. (dissenting).

* * * * *

Upon these facts may she [plaintiff] recover the damages she has suffered in an action brought against the master? The result we shall reach depends upon our theory as to the nature of negligence. Is it a relative concept--the breach of some duty owing to a particular person or to particular persons? Or where there is an act which unreasonably threatens the safety of others, is the doer liable for all its proximate consequences, even where they result in injury to one who would generally be thought to be outside the radius of danger? This is not a mere dispute as to words. We might not believe that to the average mind the dropping of the bundle would seem to involve the probability of harm to the plaintiff standing many feet away whatever might be the case as to the owner or to one so near as to be likely to be struck by its fall. If, however, we adopt the second hypothesis we have to inquire only as to the relation between cause and effect. We deal in terms of proximate cause, not of negligence.

* * * * *

But we are told that "there is no negligence unless there is in the particular case a legal duty to take care, and this duty must be one which is owed to the plaintiff himself and not merely to others." This, I think too narrow a conception. Where there is the unreasonable act, and some right that may be affected there is negligence whether damage does or does not result. That is immaterial. Should we drive down Broadway at a reckless speed, we are negligent whether we strike an approaching car or miss it by an inch. The act itself is wrongful. It is a wrong not only to those who happen to be within the radius of danger but to all who might have been there-- a wrong to the public at large. Such is the language of the street. Such the language of the courts when speaking of contributory negligence. Such again and again their language in speaking of the duty of some defendant and discussing proximate cause in cases where such a discussion is wholly irrelevant on any other theory. As was said by Mr. Justice HOLMES many years ago, "the measure of the defendant's duty in determining whether a wrong has been committed is one thing, the measure of liability when a wrong has been committed is another." Due care is a duty imposed on each one of us to protect society from unnecessary danger, not to protect A, B or C alone.

* * * * *

In the well-known *Polemis* case (1921, 3 K. B. 560), SCRUTTON, L. J., said that the dropping of a plank was negligent for it might injure "workman or cargo or ship." Because of either possibility the owner of the vessel was to be made good for his loss. The act being wrongful the doer was liable for its proximate results. Criticized and explained as this statement may have been, I think it states the law as it should be and as it is.

The proposition is this. Every one owes to the world at large the duty of refraining from those acts that may unreasonably threaten the safety of others. Such an act occurs. Not only is he wronged to whom harm might reasonably be expected to result, but he also who is in fact injured, even if he be outside what would generally be thought the danger zone. There needs be duty due the one complaining but this is not a duty to a particular individual because as to him harm might be expected. Harm to some one being the natural result of the act, not only that one alone, but all those in fact injured may complain. We did not limit this statement to those who might be expected to be exposed to danger. Unreasonable risk being taken, its consequences are not confined to those who might probably be hurt. If this be so, we do not have a plaintiff suing by "derivation or succession." Her action is original and primary. Her claim is for a breach of duty to herself--not that she is subrogated to any right of action of the owner of the parcel or of a passenger standing at the scene of the explosion.

The right to recover damages rests on additional considerations. The plaintiff's rights must be injured, and this injury must be caused by the negligence. We build a dam, but are negligent as to its foundations. Breaking, it injures property down stream. We are not liable if all this happened because of some reason other than the insecure foundation. But when injuries do result from our unlawful act we are liable for the consequences. It does not matter that they are unusual, unexpected, unforeseen and unforseeable. But there is one limitation. The damages must be so connected with the negligence that the latter may be said to be the proximate cause of the former.

These two words have never been given an inclusive definition. What is a cause in a legal sense, still more what is a proximate cause, depend in each case upon many considerations, as does the existence of negligence itself. Any philosophical doctrine of causation does not help us. A boy throws a stone into a pond. The ripples spread. The water level rises. The history of that pond is altered to all eternity. It will be altered by other causes also. Yet it will be forever the resultant of all causes combined. Each one will have an influence. How great only omniscience can say. You may speak of a chain, or if you please, a net. An analogy is of little aid. Each cause brings about future events. Without each the future would not be the same. Each is proximate in the sense it is essential. But that is not what we mean by the word. Nor on the other hand do we mean sole cause. There is no such thing.

* * * * *

It is all a question of expediency. There are no fixed rules to govern our judgment. There are simply matters of which we may take account. We have in a somewhat different connection spoken of "the stream of events." We have asked whether that stream was deflected--whether it was forced into new and unexpected channels. This is rather rhetoric than law. There is in truth little to guide us other than common sense.

There are some hints that may help us. The proximate cause, involved as it may be with many other causes, must be, at the least, something without which the event would not happen. The court must ask itself whether there was a natural and continuous sequence between cause and effect. Was the one a substantial factor in producing the other? Was there a direct connection between them, without too many intervening causes? Is the effect of cause on result not too attenuated? Is the cause likely, in the usual judgment of mankind, to produce the result? Or by the exercise of prudent foresight could the result be foreseen? Is the result too remote from the cause, and here we consider remoteness in time and space. Clearly we must so consider, for the greater the distance either in time or space, the more surely do other causes intervene to affect the result. When a lantern is overturned the firing of a shed is a fairly direct consequence. Many things contribute to the spread of the conflagration--the force of the wind, the direction and width of streets, the character of intervening structures, other factors. We draw an uncertain and wavering line, but draw it we must as best we can. Once again, it is all a question of fair judgment, always keeping in mind the fact that we endeavor to make a rule in each case that will be practical and in keeping with the general understanding of mankind.

Here another question must be answered. In the case supposed it is said, and said correctly, that the chauffeur is liable for the direct effect of the explosion although he had no reason to suppose it would follow a collision. "The fact that the injury occurred in a different manner than that which might have been expected does not prevent the chauffeur's negligence from being in law the cause of the injury." But the natural results of a negligent act--the results which a prudent man would or should foresee--do have a bearing upon the decision as to proximate cause. We have said so repeatedly. What should be foreseen? No human foresight would suggest that a collision itself might injure one a block away. On the contrary, given an explosion, such a possibility might be reasonably expected. I think the direct connection, the foresight of which the courts speak, assumes prevision of the explosion, for the immediate results of which, at least, the chauffeur is responsible.

It may be said this is unjust. Why? In fairness he should make good every injury flowing from his negligence. Not because of tenderness toward him we say he need not answer for all that follows his wrong. We look back to the catastrophe, the fire kindled by the spark, or the explosion. We trace the consequences--not indefinitely, but to a certain point. And to aid us in fixing that point we ask what might ordinarily be expected to follow the fire or the explosion.

This last suggestion is the factor which must determine the case before us. The act upon which defendant's liability rests is knocking an apparently harmless package onto the platform. The act was negligent. For its proximate consequences the defendant is liable. If its contents were broken, to the owner; if it fell upon and crushed a passenger's foot, then to him. If it exploded and injured one in the immediate vicinity, to him also as to A in the illustration. Mrs. Palsgraf was standing some distance away. How far cannot be told from the record--apparently twenty-five or thirty feet. Perhaps less. Except for the explosion, she would not have been injured. We are told by the appellant in his brief "it cannot be denied that the explosion was the direct cause of the plaintiff's injuries." So it was a substantial factor in producing the result--there was here a natural and continuous sequence--direct connection. The only intervening cause was that instead of blowing her to the ground the concussion smashed the weighing machine which in turn fell upon her. There was no remoteness in time, little in space. And surely, given such an explosion as here it needed no great foresight to predict that the natural result would be to injure one on the platform at no greater distance from its scene than was the plaintiff. Just how no one might be able to predict. Whether by flying fragments, by broken glass, by wreckage of machines or structures no one could say. But injury in some form was most probable.

Under these circumstances I cannot say as a matter of law that the plaintiff's injuries were not the proximate result of the negligence. That is all we have before us. The court refused to so charge. No request was made to submit the matter to the jury as a question of fact, even would that have been proper upon the record before us.

The judgment appealed from should be affirmed, with costs.

1.   Why does the majority relieve the defendant of liability? What does Justice Cardozo mean when he says, "the orbit of the danger as disclosed to the eye of reasonable vigilance would be the orbit of the duty"?

2.   According to Justice Cardozo, is the policy analysis a part of the duty or part of causation? Does Justice Andrews agree? What difference does it make?

3.   What standard does Justice Andrews apply to determine whether the negligence is the "proximate cause" of the injury?

4.   Note that the defendant in *Palsgraf* is the railroad. Would it make any difference if the man carrying the fireworks was the defendant? Why or Why not?

2.   Foreseeable Risk

OVERSEAS TANKSHIP (U.K.) LIMITED
v.
MORTS DOCK & ENGINEERING CO., LIMITED (THE WAGON MOUND)
A.C. 388 (Privy Council 1961)

Appeal from an order of the Full Court of the Supreme Court of New South Wales. In the action the respondents sought to recover from the appellants compensation for the damage which its property known as the Sheerlegs Wharf, in Sydney Harbour, and the equipment thereon had suffered by reason of fire which broke out on November 1, 1951. For that damage they claimed that the respondents were in law responsible.

The respondents at the relevant time carried on the business of ship-building, ship-repairing and general engineering at Morts Bay, Balmain, in the Port of Sydney. They owned and used for their business the Sheerlegs Wharf, a timber wharf about 400 feet in length and 40 feet wide, where there was a quantity of tools and equipment. In October and November, 1951, a vessel known as the Corrimel was moored alongside the wharf and was being refitted by the respondents. Her mast was lying on the wharf and a number of the respondents' employees were working both upon it and upon the vessel itself, using for that purpose electric and oxy-acetylene welding equipment.

At the same time the appellants were charterers by demise of the S.S. Wagon Mound, an oil-burning vessel, which was moored at the Caltex Wharf on the northern shore of the harbour at a distance of about 600 feet from the Sheerlegs Wharf. She was there from about 9 a.m. on October 29 until 11 a.m. on October 30, 1951, for the purpose of discharging gasoline products and taking in bunkering oil.

During the early hours of October 30, 1951, a large quantity of bunkering oil was, through the carelessness of the appellants servants, allowed to spill into the bay, and by 10:30 on the morning of that day it had spread over a considerable part of the bay, being thickly concentrated in some places and particularly along the foreshore near the respondents' property. The appellants made no attempt to disperse the oil. The Wagon Mound unberthed and set sail very shortly after.

When the respondents' works manager became aware of the condition of things in the vicinity of the wharf he instructed their workmen that no welding or burning was to be carried on until further orders. He inquired of the manager of the Caltex Oil Company, at whose wharf the Wagon Mound was then still berthed, whether they could safely continue their operations on the wharf or upon the Corrimel. The results of the inquiry coupled with his own belief as to the inflammability of furnace oil in the open led him to think that the respondents could safely carry on their operations. He gave instructions accordingly, but directed that all safety precautions should be taken to prevent inflammable material falling off the wharf into the oil.

For the remainder of October 30 and until about 2 p.m. on November 1 work was carried on as usual, the condition and congestion of the oil remaining substantially unaltered. But at about that time the oil under or near the wharf was ignited and a fire, fed initially by the oil, spread rapidly and burned with great intensity. The wharf and the Corrimel caught fire and considerable damage was done to the wharf and the equipment upon it. The outbreak of fire was due, as the judge found, to the fact that there was floating in the oil underneath the wharf a piece of debris on which lay some smouldering cotton waste or rag which had been set on fire by molten metal falling from the wharf: that the cotton waste or rag burst into flames: that they flames from the cotton waste set the floating oil afire either directly or by first setting fire to a wooden pile coated with oil, and that after the floating oil became ignited the flames spread rapidly over the surface of the oil and quickly developed into a conflagration which severely damaged the wharf.

The trial judge found that the appellants did not know and could not reasonably be expected to have known that the oil on the water was capable of being set on fire. That is a very important finding and it was not challenged on appeal. The only other finding to which reference should be made was that some of this oil had congealed on the respondents' slipways and interfered with their use. It is the appellants' contention that this fact is irrelevant. It is further to be observed that no claim against the appellants was raised in respect of it, and there was no proof of the respondents having thereby suffered any damage. The judge concluded that on the basis of the decision in *In re Polemis* the appellants were on the facts guilty of negligence. What constitutes negligence is the first major point of this case.

The present case is of some general importance and interest since it raises directly, and for the first time, the question whether *Polemis* was rightly decided. On the second point there are two heads; namely, if Polemis is right: (1) Was the damage by fire the direct consequence of the spilling of the oil? (2) Was it due to independent causes?

Negligence involves breach of duty causing the damage. There is no actionable breach of duty unless it can be shown that at the time of the act the consequences of the act were reasonably foreseeable. The test is objective, the requisite foresight being that of the reasonable man.

There can be no doubt that the decision of the Court of Appeal of *Polemis* plainly asserts that, if the defendant is guilty of negligence, he is responsible for all the consequences whether reasonably foreseeable or not. The generality of the proposition is perhaps qualified by the fact that each of the Lords Justices refers to the outbreak of fire as the direct result of the negligent act. There is thus introduced the conception that the negligent actor is not responsible for consequences which are not "direct," whatever that may mean. It has to be asked, then, why this conclusion should have been reached. The answer appears to be that it was reached upon a consideration of certain authorities, comparatively few in number, that were cited to the court.

Enough has been said to show that the authority of *Polemis* has been severely shaken though lip-service has from time to time been paid to it. In their Lordships' opinion it should no longer be regarded as good law. It is not probable that many cases will for that reason have a different result, though it is hoped that the law will be thereby simplified, and that in some cases, at least, palpable injustice will be avoided. For it does not seem consonant with current ideas of justice or morality that for an act of negligence, however slight or venial, which results in some trivial foreseeable damage the actor should be liable for all consequences however unforeseeable and however grave, so long as they can be said to be "direct." It is a principle of civil liability, subject only to qualifications which have no present relevance, that a man must be considered to be responsible for the probable consequences of his act. To demand more of him is too harsh a rule, to demand less is to ignore that civilized order requires the observance of a minimum standard of behaviour.

This concept applied to the slowly developing law of negligence has led to a great variety of expressions which can, as it appears to their Lordships, be harmonized with little difficulty with the single exception of the so-called rule in *Polemis*. For, if it is asked why a man should be responsible for the natural or necessary or probable consequences of his act (or any other similar description of them) the answer is that it is not because they are natural or necessary or probable, but because, since

190

they have this quality, it is judged by the standard of the reasonable man that he ought to have foreseen them. Thus it is that over and over again is has happened that in different judgments in the same case, and sometimes in a single judgment, liability for a consequence has been imposed on the ground that it was reasonably foreseeable or, alternatively, on the ground that it was natural or necessary or probable. The two grounds have been treated as coterminous, and so they largely are. But, where they are not, the question arises to which the wrong answer was given in *Polemis*. For, if some limitation must be imposed upon the consequences for which the negligent actor is to be held responsible – and all are agreed that some limitation there must be – why should that test (reasonable foreseeability) be rejected which, since he is judged by what the reasonable man ought to foresee, corresponds with the common conscience of mankind, and a test (the "direct" consequence_) be substituted which leads to nowhere but the never-ending and insoluble problems of causation. "The lawyer," said Sir Frederick Pollock, "cannot afford to adventure himself with philosophers in the logical and metaphysical controversies that beset the idea of cause." Yet this is just what he has most unfortunately done and must continue to do if the rule in *Polemis* is to prevail.

The validity of a rule or principle can sometimes be tested by observing it in operation. Let the rule in Polemis be tested in this way. [The court then considered cases in which applying the *Polemis* rule created difficulties.]

* * * * *

In the same connection may be mentioned the conclusion to which the Full Court finally came in the present case. Applying the rule in *Polemis* and holding therefore that the unforeseeability of the damage by fire afforded no defense, they went on to consider the remaining question. Was it a "direct" consequence? Upon this Manning J. said: "Notwithstanding that, if regard is had separately to each individual occurrence in the chain of events that led to this fire, each occurrence was improbable and, in one sense, improbability was heaped upon improbability, I cannot escape from the conclusion that if the ordinary man in the street had been asked, as a matter of common sense, without any detailed analysis of the circumstances, to state the cause of the fire any detailed analysis of the circumstances, to state the cause of the fire at Mort's Dock, he would unhesitatingly have assigned such cause to spillage of oil by the appellant's employees." Perhaps he would, and probably he would have added: "I never should have thought it possible." But with great respect to the Full Court this is surely irrelevant, or, if it is relevant, only serves to show that the Polemis rule works in a very strange way. After the event even a fool is wise. But it is not the hindsight of a fool; it is the foresight of the reasonable man which alone can determine responsibility. The *Polemis* rule by substituting "direct" for "reasonably foreseeable" consequence leads to a conclusion equally illogical and unjust.

It is not the act but the consequences on which tortious liability is founded. Just as (as it has been said) there is no such thing as negligence in the air, so there is no such thing as liability in the air. Suppose an action brought by A for damage caused by the carelessness (a neutral word) of B, for example, a fire caused by the careless spillage of oil. It may, of course, become relevant to know what duty B owed to A, but the only liability that is in question is the liability for damage by fire. It is vain to isolate the liability from its context and to say that B is or is not liable, and then to ask for what damage he is liable. For his liability is in respect of that damage and no other. If, as admittedly it is, B's liability (culpability) depends on the reasonable foreseeability of the consequent damage, how is that to be determined except by the foreseeability of the damage which in fact happened – the damage in suit? And, if that damage is unforeseeable so as to displace liability at large, how can the liability be restored so as to make compensation payable?

But, it is said, a different position arises if B's careless act has been shown to be negligent and has caused some foreseeable damage to A. Their Lordships have already observed that to hold B liable for consequences however unforeseeable of a careless act, if, but only if, he is at the same time liable for some other damage however trivial, appears to be neither logical nor just. This becomes more clear if it is supposed that similar unforeseeable damage is suffered by A and C but other foreseeable damage, for which B is liable, by A only. A system of law which would hold B liable to A but not to C for the similar damage suffered by each of them could not easily be defended. Fortunately, the attempt is not necessary. For the same fallacy is at the root of the proposition. It is irrelevant to the question whether B is liable for unforeseeable damage that he is liable for foreseeable damage, as irrelevant as would the fact that he had trespassed on Whiteacre be to the question whether he has trespassed on Blackacre. Again, suppose a claim by A for damage by fire by the careless act of B. Of what relevance is it to that claim that he has another claim arising out of the same careless act? It would surely not prejudice his claim if that other claim failed: it cannot assist if it succeeds. Each of them rests on its own bottom, and will fail if it can be established that the damage could not reasonably be foreseen.

Their Lordships conclude this part of the case with some general observations. They have been concerned primarily to displace the proposition that unforeseeability is irrelevant if damage is "direct." In doing so they have inevitably insisted that the essential factor in determining liability is whether the damage is of such a kind as the reasonable man should have foreseen.

Their Lordships will humbly advise Her Majesty that this appeal should be allowed, and the respondents' action so far as it related to damage caused by the negligence of the appellants be dismissed with costs, but that the action so far as it related to damage caused by nuisance should be remitted to the Full Court to be dealt with as that court may think fit. The respondents must pay the costs of the appellants of this appeal and in the courts below.

NOTES

1.   What standard does this case establish for proximate cause? How does it differ from that established in *Palsgraf*? How is it similar?

2.   *In re Polemis*, 3 K.B. 560, 90 L.S.K.B. 1353, 126 L.T. 154 (1921) is cited in both *Palsgraf* and *Wagon Mound*. What standard for proximate cause did *Polemis* adopt? How does it differ from the risk rule?

3.   What is the underlying rationale for the risk rule? Why shouldn't we hold negligent actors responsible for remote or unforeseeable consequences?

4.   Every jurisdiction must ask how precisely to draw the standard of "foreseeability." Must the defendant be able to foresee the risk to the particular plaintiff or merely a class of plaintiffs? Must the defendant be able to foresee the specific mechanism or manner of harm, or is foreseeability of the general hazard sufficient? Must the defendant foresee the harm or merely the hazard? Most jurisdictions adopt a flexible, but uncertain approach to the problem. Consider the following cases.

A.   *Hughes v. Lord Advocate*, A.C. 837 (H.L. 1962), involved the question of the liability of the Post Office of Scotland for burn-related injuries to an eight-year old boy. Employees of the Post Office were working on an underground telephone line which they left unguarded during a tea break. The eight-year old plaintiff and a ten-year old companion descended through the manhole and then came back to the surface without incident. Once at the surface, however, the boys dropped the lantern into the hole and, unforeseeably, some kerosene ignited and created an explosion and fire. The plaintiff fell into the hole and suffered severe burns. The lower court found that burns were foreseeable, but the vaporization of the kerosene and resulting explosion were not, and relieved the Post Office of liability.

On appeal, the panel of judges found that the fact that the explosion was unforeseeable was not important because "[a]n explosion is only one way in which burning can be caused. Burning can also be caused by the contact between liquid paraffin and a naked flame…. Upon this view the explosion was an immaterial event in the chain of causation. It was simply one way in which the burning might be caused by the potentially dangerous paraffin lamp…"

B.   In *Doughty v. Turner Manufacturing Co., Limited*, 1 Q.B. 518 (C.A. 1963), the defendant's manufacturing process involved the use of two vats of molten liquid maintained at 800 degrees centigrade. A worker knocked a cover into one of the vats. The cover sank without a splash. One or two minutes later, the liquid erupted and burned the plaintiff. Investigation revealed that components in the cover would undergo a chemical change at 500 degrees centigrade to create water. At high temperature, the water would turn to steam and produce an explosion.

The court found for the defendant. "The evidence showed that splashes caused by sudden immersion … were a foreseeable danger…" Therefore, plaintiff's counsel argued that the accident was "merely a variant of foreseeable accidents by splashing… [I]t would be quite unrealistic to describe this accident as a variant of the perils from splashing. The cause of the accident … was the intrusion of a new and unexpected factor … [T]he reasoning in *Hughes v. Lord Advocate* cannot be extended far enough to cover this case."

How would you reconcile these cases?

5.   As you read the remainder of the cases in this section, ask whether Louisiana requires foreseeability of general classes of plaintiffs/risks or specific plaintiffs/mechanism of harm. You should also ask whether foreseeability is the only consideration or whether there are other policy factors which help to explain the results in the particular cases.

6.   Consider the following sections of the Restatement (Second) of Torts governing legal or proximate cause:

§ 431. What Constitutes Legal Cause

The actor's negligent conduct is a legal cause of harm to another if

(a) his conduct is a substantial factor in bringing about the harm, and

(b) there is no rule of law relieving the actor from liability because of the manner in which his negligence has resulted in the harm.

§ 435. Foreseeability Of Harm Or Manner Of Its Occurrence

(1) If the actor's conduct is a substantial factor in bringing about harm to another, the fact that the actor neither foresaw nor should have foreseen the extent of the harm or the manner in which it occurred does not prevent him from being liable.

(2) The actor's conduct may be held not to be a legal cause of harm to another where after the event and looking back from the harm to the actor's negligent conduct, it appears to the court highly extraordinary that it should have brought about the harm.

§ 437. Actor's Subsequent Efforts To Prevent His Negligence From Causing Harm

If the actor's negligent conduct is a substantial factor in bringing about harm to another, the fact that after the risk has been created by his negligence the actor has exercised reasonable care to prevent it from taking effect in harm does not prevent him from being liable for the harm.

§ 440. Superseding Cause Defined

A superseding cause is an act of a third person or other force which by its intervention prevents the actor from being liable for harm to another which his antecedent negligence is a substantial factor in bringing about.

§ 441. Intervening Force Defined

(1) An intervening force is one which actively operates in producing harm to another after the actor's negligent act or omission has been committed.

(2) Whether the active operation of an intervening force prevents the actor's antecedent negligence from being a legal cause in bringing about harm to another is determined by the rules stated in §§ 442-453.

§ 442. Considerations Important In Determining Whether An Intervening Force Is A Superseding Cause

The following considerations are of importance in determining whether an intervening force is a superseding cause of harm to another:

(a) the fact that its intervention brings about harm different in kind from that which would otherwise have resulted from the actor's negligence;

(b) the fact that its operation or the consequences thereof appear after the event to be extraordinary rather than normal in view of the circumstances existing at the time of its operation;

(c) the fact that the intervening force is operating independently of any situation created by the actor's negligence, or, on the other hand, is or is not a normal result of such a situation;

(d) the fact that the operation of the intervening force is due to a third person's act or to his failure to act;

(e) the fact that the intervening force is due to an act of a third person which is wrongful toward the other and as such subjects the third person to liability to him;

(f) the degree of culpability of a wrongful act of a third person which sets the intervening force in motion.

§ 443. Normal Intervening Force

The intervention of a force which is a normal consequence of a situation created by the actor's negligent conduct is not a superseding cause of harm which such conduct has been a substantial factor in bringing about.

7.   Restatement (Third) Physical & Emotional Harm (2010) abandons the term "proximate cause:"

§ 29 Limitations On Liability For Tortious Conduct

An actor's liability is limited to those harms that result from the risks that made the actor's conduct tortious.

The Comment to § 29 succinctly explains the abandonment:

As mentioned in the Special Note at the outset of this Chapter, the term "proximate cause" is a poor one to describe limits on the scope of liability. It is also an unfortunate term to employ for factual cause or the combination of factual cause and scope of liability. Even if lawyers and judges understand the term, it is confusing for a jury. Courts should craft instructions that inform the jury that, for liability to be imposed, the harm that occurred must be one that results from the hazards that made the defendant's conduct tortious in the first place. Employing the term "proximate cause" implies that there is but one cause—the cause nearest in time or geography to the plaintiff's harm—and that factual causation bears on the issue of scope of liability. Neither of those implications is correct. Multiple factual causes always exist, see § 26, Comment c, and multiple proximate causes are often present. An actor's tortious conduct need not be close in space or time to the plaintiff's harm to be a proximate cause. And proximate cause is only remotely related to factual causation. Thus, the term "causation" should not be employed when explaining this concept to a jury.

Restatement (Third) § 29 Cmt. b.

The Comments also further develop the scope of risk concept adopted by Restatement (Third) in place of "proximate cause":

> *d. Harm different from the harms risked by the tortious conduct.* Central to the limitation on liability of this Section is the idea that an actor should be held liable only for harm that was among the potential harms—the risks—that made the actor's conduct tortious. The term "scope of liability" is employed to distinguish those harms that fall within this standard and, thus, for which the defendant is subject to liability and, on the other hand, those harms for which the defendant is not liable. This limit on liability serves the purpose of avoiding what might be unjustified or enormous liability by confining liability's scope to the reasons for holding the actor liable in the first place. To apply this rule requires consideration, at an appropriate level of generality, see Comment *l*, of: (a) the risks that made the actor's conduct tortious, and (b) whether the harm for which recovery is sought was a result of any of those risks. Risk is explained in § 3, Comment *e*, as consisting of harm occurring with some probability. The magnitude of the risk is the severity of the harm discounted by the probability that it will occur. For purposes of negligence, which requires foreseeability, risk is evaluated by reference to the foreseeable (if indefinite) probability of harm of a foreseeable severity. If a strict-liability claim does not require foreseeability, the concept of risk can be determined by examining the severity and probability in retrospect. *See* Comment *j*.

> Thus, the jury should be told that, in deciding whether the plaintiff's harm is within the scope of liability, it should go back to the reasons for finding the defendant engaged in negligent or other tortious conduct. If the harms risked by that tortious conduct include the general sort of harm suffered by the plaintiff, the defendant is subject to liability for the plaintiff's harm. When defendants move for a determination that the plaintiff's harm is beyond the scope of liability as a matter of law, courts must initially consider all of the range of harms risked by the defendant's conduct that the jury *could* find as the basis for determining that conduct tortious. Then, the court can compare the plaintiff's harm with the range of harms risked by the defendant to determine whether a reasonable jury might find the former among the latter.

> The standard imposed by this Section is often referred to as the requirement that the harm be "within the scope of the risk," or some similar phrase, for liability to be imposed. For the sake of convenience, this limitation on liability is referred to in the remainder of this Chapter as the "risk standard."

Restatement § 29 Cmt. d.

8.   As you study Louisiana's duty-risk analysis of negligence in the section below, the development of which began in *Dixie Drive It Yourself v. American Beverage Co.,* consider whether the Restatement (Third) has more or less adopted the Louisiana approach to "proximate cause"/scope of the risk.

1.   **Development of the Duty-Risk Approach**

DIXIE DRIVE IT YOURSELF SYSTEM NEW ORLEANS CO.
v.
AMERICAN BEVERAGE CO.
137 So. 2d 298 (La. 1962)

SANDERS, J.

This is a tort action. The plaintiff, Dixie Drive It Yourself System New Orleans Co., Inc., seeks to recover from the defendants, American Beverage Company and its insurer, Northern Insurance Company of New York, the sum of $2,665.49 for property damage to an International stake-body truck and the loss of income sustained by its withdrawal from use.

In the operation of its business, Dixie leased the truck to Gulf States Screw Products Company. On June 3, 1957, an employee of Gulf, Paul Langtre, was operating it in a southerly direction toward New Orleans on U.S. Highway 61 (the Airline Highway). At about 12:45 p.m. he collided with an R C Cola beverage truck (a tractortrailer type) owned by the defendant, American Beverage Company, and driven by its employee, which was stopped on the highway about three miles north of Kenner.

The highway at this point embraces two roadways divided by a neutral ground. The roadway on each side of the neutral ground consists of two twelve-foot traffic lanes. The shoulders on each side of the highway are fifteen feet wide. It had been raining heavily prior to the collision, and the highway was wet. At the time of the accident, it was drizzling or misting. Before the collision the R C Cola truck was also proceeding in the direction of New Orleans. A coil wire to the distributor became disconnected and killed the motor. The driver brought the vehicle to a stop in the right-hand traffic lane, leaving a clearance of less than fifteen feet in the left lane. It remained in this position from eight to ten minutes prior to the collision. The driver did not display signal flags on the highway or take any other action to protect approaching traffic. Langtre, the driver of the Dixie truck, was proceeding in the right-hand lane at a speed of about forty-five miles per hour. His windshield wiper was operating, and his headlights were on. Langtre testified that he was following an unidentified truck which moved into the left lane and passed the R C Cola truck. Two other witnesses did not recall seeing the unidentified truck. Langtre estimated that he first observed the R C Cola truck at a distance of about a quarter of a block, or about 200 feet. At that time it appeared to him to be moving. When he reached a point estimated by him to be eighty-five feet away, he perceived that it was stationary. He immediately started pulling into the left lane to pass, but was prevented from doing so by an overtaking automobile operated by Dr. Frank B. Wheeler in the left traffic lane at a speed of fifty-five or sixty miles per hour. Langtre applied his brakes, but was unable to avoid colliding with the rear end of the R C Cola truck. Dr. Wheeler, who perceived that the R C Cola truck was stopped at approximately the same time as Langtre, likewise applied his brakes. His automobile crossed the highway and came to rest on the left side of the road.

For recovery the plaintiff relies principally upon the following complaints of negligence against the driver of the obstructing R C Cola truck:

> 1. Stopping and parking the truck upon the main travelled portion of the highway and leaving less than fifteen feet of the highway unobstructed in violation of LSA-R.S. 32:241.

> 2. Failing to display signal flags or other warning devices on the highway at a distance of one hundred feet behind and in front of the truck to protect approaching traffic as required by LSA-R.S. 32:442.

> 3. Taking no action to warn approaching traffic of the stalled vehicle.

The defendants denied that the driver of the R C Cola truck was guilty of any negligence and assert that the sole cause of the accident was the negligence of the driver of the Dixie truck (who is not a party to the suit) in driving at an excessive rate of speed under the prevailing conditions, in failing to keep a proper lookout, and in failing to have his truck under sufficient control to avoid the accident. In the alternative, the defendants contend that the negligence of Langtre is imputable to plaintiff and plead contributory negligence.

The district court rejected the demands of plaintiff. On appeal the Court of Appeal affirmed the judgment. The Court of Appeal found that the driver of the obstructing R C Cola truck was negligent in failing to place signal flags behind and in front of the truck as required by LSA-R.S. 32:442 and, for purposes of the decision, in stopping the truck on the main travelled portion of the highway and leaving less than fifteen feet clearance in violation of LSA-R.S. 32:241(A). The court held, however, that the negligence of the driver in these respects was not a proximate cause of the collision. *See* La.App., 128 So.2d 841. We granted certiorari to review this judgment.

The principal question presented for decision is whether the driver of the obstructing truck was guilty of negligence and, if so, whether that negligence was a legal cause of the collision.

Preliminarily, we consider the contention that the alleged negligence of the driver of the Dixie truck is imputable to the plaintiff. For this determination it is of importance that the plaintiff had leased the truck to Gulf States Screw Products Company. The vehicle was under the exclusive control of Gulf and was operated by its employee. The relationship between plaintiff and Gulf was one of bailment.

It is well established that the negligence of a bailee cannot be imputed to the bailor. It follows that the defendants are liable if the driver of the obstructing R C Cola truck was negligent and that negligence was a legal cause of the collision. When the actionable negligence of two tort feasors contributes in causing harm to a third party, each of them is responsible for the damage. They are solidarily liable.

The Louisiana Highway Regulatory Act imposes upon the driver of a vehicle disabled on the highway a 'responsibility to protect traffic', and during the daytime he is required to place a red signal flag one hundred feet behind and in front of the vehicle 'in such position as to be visible to all approaching traffic.'

The evidence in the instant case discloses that the driver of the R C Cola truck stopped it squarely in the lane of traffic. He had a companion in the truck with him. Inasmuch as eight to ten minutes elapsed prior to the collision, the driver had ample time to take precautions. Despite this, he did not position the signal flags, warn approaching drivers, or take any action to discharge his responsibility to protect traffic. He remained in the truck. We conclude that the driver violated the statute by failing to display the red signal flags and to reasonably discharge his responsibility to protect traffic.

The statute was designed to protect life and property on the highways. It is a safety measure. The violation of its provisions is negligence Per Se, and this negligence is actionable if it was a legal cause of the collision.

There is no universal formula for the determination of legal cause. In the instant case it bifurcates into two distinct inquiries: whether the negligence of the obstructing driver was a cause-in-fact of the collision; and whether the defendants should be relieved of liability because of the intervening negligence of the driver of the Dixie truck. It is clear that more than one legally responsible cause can, and frequently does, contribute to a vehicular collision.

Negligent conduct is a cause-in-fact of harm to another if it was a substantial factor in bringing about that harm. Under the circumstances of this case, the negligent conduct is undoubtedly a substantial factor in bringing about the collision if the collision would not have occurred without it. A cause-in-fact is a necessary antecedent. If the collision would have occurred irrespective of the negligence of the driver of the R C Cola truck, then his negligence was not a substantial factor or cause-in-fact. The question is not free from difficulty. A brief review of the circumstances surrounding the accident is essential. For the purpose of this review we accept the finding of the district court that there was no intervening truck preceding the Dixie truck prior to the collision. This circumstance is not crucial to the decision.

The evidence discloses that the weather was rainy, and the highway was wet. It was drizzling or misting at the time. Langtre, the driver of the Dixie truck, was using his windshield wiper. He was also driving with his lights on. Although he had seen the R C Cola truck a moment earlier, he did not perceive that it was stationary until he was rather close to it. He estimated the distance at eighty-five feet. Dr. Wheeler, the other overtaking driver, observed that the truck was stopped at approximately the same time.

Upon first observing that the truck was stationary, Langtre commenced moving into the left lane of traffic to pass the truck. The overtaking automobile of Dr. Wheeler, approaching from the rear in the left lane, thwarted this maneuver and trapped the Dixie truck in the right lane behind the stalled truck. Langtre applied his brakes immediately, but was unable to avoid striking the truck.

* * * * *

Considering the maneuver to the left and the normal reaction time to apply the brakes, … the record fully supports the finding of both the district court and the Court of Appeal that the driver of the Dixie truck was negligent in that he: '. . . failed to see . . . (the obstructing truck), and failed to realize it was stopped on the highway, in time to avoid the collision.' We adopt this finding of fact.

The display of the signal flags at a specified distance from the vehicle is designed not only to warn of the presence of a vehicle on the highway, but also to give notice to all approaching traffic that the vehicle is stationary. A stationary vehicle and a moving one require different driving actions by an overtaking motorist. A momentary delay in the recognition that a vehicle is stationary may create a dangerous traffic situation. The signal is designed to arrest the attention of all approaching drivers-- even an inattentive one.

The display of the red signal flag one hundred feet behind the R C Cola truck would have served as an advance warning to both the driver of the Dixie truck and Dr. Wheeler that a stationary vehicle was ahead. Furthermore, the discharge of the driver's responsibility to protect traffic would have of necessity included a hand or other signal at a reasonable distance from the truck, a clear warning of the stationary vehicle. If either or both of the approaching drivers had seen the flag or signal, the accident would have been averted. We can reasonably infer that the collision would not have occurred if the statutory precautions to protect approaching traffic had been taken. The mere possibility that the accident would have occurred despite the required precautions does not break the chain of causation.

We conclude that the negligence of the obstructing driver was a substantial factor in bringing about the collision, or a cause-in-fact.

The inquiry as to whether a defendant should be relieved of liability because of the intervening negligence of another is frequently couched in terms of proximate cause. In the instant case the Court of Appeal concluded that the defendants should be relieved of liability based upon the following statement of law:

Whatever negligence may have been involved on the part of the driver of the defendant vehicle had become passive and too remote to be a contributing cause of the accident. The sole proximate cause thereof was the negligence of the driver of the plaintiff truck. The defendant is not liable because the negligence of its employee-driver was not a proximate cause of the accident.

The thrust of this formulation of law is toward relieving all but the last wrongdoer of liability to an innocent victim in torts involving intervening negligence. This restrictive doctrine finds little support in legal theory. We do not subscribe to the formulation as applied in this case.

The essence of the present inquiry is whether the risk and harm encountered by the plaintiff fall within the scope of protection of the statute. It is a hazard problem. Specifically, it involves a determination of whether the statutory duty of displaying signal flags and responsibility for protecting traffic were designed, at least in part, to afford protection to the class of claimants of which plaintiff is a member from the hazard of confused or inattentive drivers colliding with stationary vehicles on the highway.

* * * * *

In a scholarly article entitled 'Proximate Cause in Louisiana' by Jesse D. McDonald, 16 Louisiana Law Review 391, the principle is stated as follows:

'... Since the law never gives absolute protection to any interest, recovery will be allowed only if the rule of law on which plaintiff relies includes within its limits protection against the particular risk that plaintiff's interests encountered. This determination of the particular risks to plaintiff that fall within the ambit of protection of the rule of law on which plaintiff relies is the determination of the issue of proximate cause.

'The presence of causes intervening subsequent to defendant's act which brings about injury presents no special problem. In such cases, the inquiry of the court is simply whether the risk produced by the combination of defendant's act and the intervening cause is one which is within the scope of protection of the rule of law upon which plaintiff relies.'

To the same effect *see* Green, Rationale of Proximate Cause, pp. 142--144. The inattention or confusion of motor vehicle drivers is not a highly extraordinary occurrence. The objective of the statutory provisions violated in the instant case was to protect against the likelihood that an oncoming motorist, whether cautious, confused or inattentive, would fail to timely perceive the vehicle or that it was stationary and become involved in an accident. The law was designed to protect the plaintiff (and any member of its class) against such an accident as occurred in this case. To deny recovery because of the plaintiff's exposure to the risk from which it was the purpose of the law to protect him would nullify the statutory duty and render its protection meaningless. The negligence of the driver of the Dixie truck was responsive to that of the driver of the R C Cola truck. It was dependent upon it. The negligence of the two combined to bring about harm to the plaintiff. Law and reason support a conclusion that the defendants should not be relieved of liability. .

It appears futile to attempt a reconciliation of these and other cases dealing with actions by third parties arising from collisions between a moving and stationary vehicle. This is rendered difficult by the ambiguity of the language of proximate cause. As employed by courts, proximate cause is a legal concept without fixed content. It is used indiscriminately to refer to cause-in-fact, the scope of liability, and other negligence factors.

The obstruction of a main artery of traffic without statutory precautions is fraught with danger to motorist. The traffic congestion and advancing speed of recent years have added to that danger.

We hold that the defendants are liable to the plaintiff for the damages sustained by it.

* * * * *

BARHAM, J.

This is an action ex delicto for damages for injuries the plaintiff received when she tripped and fell over a metal ladder lying on the ground. The plaintiff, Celeste Hill, was working as a maid and babysitter for one of the defendants, Mrs. Rosemary Delouise, when the accident happened, and the ladder over which she tripped had been left on the Delouise premises by the other defendant, Lundin & Associates, Inc., a home repair contractor. Mrs. Delouise had employed Lundin to repair damage to her house caused by Hurricane Betsy. Because of the unusual number of repair jobs necessitated by hurricane damage, the urgency of making repairs immediately so that further damage would not result, and the shortage of equipment and men, Lundin organized his contracts for maximum speed and efficiency. The materials and equipment were delivered to the various job sites by truck, the repairmen for a particular job came at the first opportunity in automobiles, and after completion of a job a company truck returned when possible to pick up the equipment and any materials left over.

After the repairs to the Delouise house had been finished, among Lundin's property remaining on the premises was a metal ladder left standing in an upright position against the side of the house. At some time before the accident, which occurred a few days after completion, someone (not an employee of the defendant Lundin) moved the ladder and laid it in the yard. The plaintiff was well aware of the position of the ladder on the ground. On the day of the accident she was caring for the youngest Delouise child, who was two or three years old, and doing the family wash. She left the house through the back door to hang the wash on the clothesline in the yard. Going from the back door to the clothesline, the plaintiff had to walk past the ladder, which she observed lying on the ground. As she was hanging up the wash, she heard the door of the house slam, and turned and saw the young child running to her, directly toward the ladder. Hurrying in his direction to stop him from falling over the ladder, she tripped on the ladder, fell, and was hurt.

The plaintiff brought this suit against Mrs. Delouise, her employer, and Lundin, the contractor, alleging the negligence of both. Both defendants in answer denied negligence and alternatively pleaded the contributory negligence of the plaintiff. The trial judge found Mrs. Delouise free from negligence and, pretermitting the question of Lundin's negligence, held that the contributory negligence of the plaintiff barred her recovery from that defendant.

On the plaintiff's appeal from these adverse holdings, the appellate court affirmed the finding of the trial court that Mrs. Delouise was not negligent but reversed the decision of that court as to the plaintiff's claim against Lundin. *See* 243 So.2d 121. The following is the Court of Appeal's total finding of negligence of Lundin: '... We find that Lundin & Associates, Inc. was negligent in leaving this ladder on the job site, unattended, for two or three days after the work had been completed, Where it was foreseeable that someone could be injured by the ladder....' (Emphasis supplied.) The appellate court then applied the so-called 'momentary forgetfulness' doctrine to excuse the plaintiff's conduct which otherwise would have constituted contributory negligence.

Only the defendant Lundin applied for writs. Therefore the denial of plaintiff's claim against Mrs. Delouise is final, and the sole issue before us is the question of Lundin's liability to the plaintiff. We are of the opinion that the plaintiff has failed to establish actionable negligence on Lundin's part, and we reverse.

The accident in this case occurred because the plaintiff fell over a ladder lying on the ground. We first inquire whether any causal relationship existed between the harm to the plaintiff and the defendant's allegedly negligent conduct. If the defendant had not left the ladder on the premises, it could not have later been placed on the ground in the yard. To this extent it may be said that the defendant's act had something to do with the harm.

200

However, if the defendant's conduct of which the plaintiff complains is a cause in fact of the harm, we are then required in a determination of negligence to ascertain whether the defendant breached a legal duty imposed to protect against the particular risk involved.

The Court of Appeal's holding implies that a ladder is a dangerous instrumentality or that simply leaving a ladder unattended is negligence per se. We reject this reasoning as being totally unsound in law. It is only that conduct which creates an appreciable range of risk for causing harm that is prohibited. Leaving a ladder unattended under certain conditions may create an unreasonable risk of harm to others which would impose a reciprocal duty upon the actor. If we assume that the defendant was under a duty not to leave the ladder leaning against the house because of an unreasonable risk of harm, the breach of that duty does not necessarily give rise to liability in this case. Although the defendant would owe a duty to protect certain persons under certain circumstances from this risk, it is not an insurer against every risk of harm which is encountered in connection with the ladder.

Here a third party had moved the ladder to the ground, and the plaintiff was injured as she sought to prevent the child from tripping on the ladder. The basic question, then, is whether the risk of injury from a ladder lying on the ground, produced by a combination of defendant's act and that of a third party, is within the scope of protection of a rule of law which would prohibit leaving a ladder leaning against the house.

Foreseeability is not always a reliable guide, and certainly it is not the only criterion for determining whether there is a duty-risk relationship. Just because a risk may foreseeably arise by reason of conduct, it is not necessarily within the scope of the duty owed because of that conduct. Neither are all risks excluded from the scope of duty simply because they are unforeseeable. The ease of association of the injury with the rule relied upon, however, is always a proper inquiry.

Where the rule of law upon which a plaintiff relies for imposing a duty is based upon a statute, the court attempts to interpret legislative intent as to the risk contemplated by the legal duty, which is often a resort to the court's own judgment of the scope of protection intended by the Legislature. Where the rule of law is jurisprudential and the court is without the aid of legislative intent, the process of determining the risk encompassed within the rule of law is nevertheless similar. The same policy considerations which would motivate a legislative body to impose duties to protect from certain risks are applied by the court in making its determination. All rules of conduct, irrespective of whether they are the product of a legislature or are a part of the fabric of the court-made law of negligence, exist for purposes. They are designed to protect some persons under some circumstances against some risks. Seldom does a rule protect every victim against every risk that may befall him, merely because it is shown that the violation of the rule played a part in producing the injury. The task of defining the proper reach or thrust of a rule in its policy aspects is one that must be undertaken by the court in each case as it arises. How appropriate is the rule to the facts of this controversy? This is a question that the court cannot escape.'

This defendant's alleged misconduct, its alleged breach of duty, was in leaving the ladder leaning against the house unattended. The risk encountered by the plaintiff which caused her harm was the ladder lying on the ground where it was placed by another, over which she tripped as she moved to protect the child. The record is devoid of any evidence tending to establish that the defendant could have reasonably anticipated that a third person would move the ladder and put it in the position which created this risk, or that such a 'naked possibility' was an unreasonable risk of harm.

A rule of law which would impose a duty upon one not to leave a ladder standing against a house does not encompass the risk here encountered. We are of the opinion that the defendant was under no duty to protect this plaintiff from the risk which gave rise to her injuries. The plaintiff has failed to establish legal and actionable negligence on the part of the defendant.

The judgment of the Court of Appeal is reversed, and plaintiff's suit is dismissed at her costs.

NOTES

1.   Although "duty/risk" became the prevailing standard in Louisiana courts following *Hill*, the legislature thereafter adopted legislation requiring the courts to determine whether certain conduct was the proximate or legal cause of certain damages. *See, e.g.*, La. Rev. Stat. 9:2800.1 (1988); 9:2800.54 (1991); La. Code of Civ. Proc. Art. 1812.

2.   What are the primary differences between the traditional common law negligence approach and Louisiana's duty/risk approach? Why does it matter?

3.   Common law states which turn to the Restatement (Third) in order to untangle the confusion surrounding "Products Liability" or "Liability for Physical or Emotional Harm", will find themselves using a framework of liability that is surprisingly similar to the familiar duty/risk analysis that Louisiana has been using to allocate liability since the early 1970's. For example, the Restatement (Third) imposes a duty if the actors conduct creates a risk of physical harm, but does not impose such a duty if the actor's conduct does not create such a risk.[52] This mirrors a basic requirement and duty of Louisiana courts, which had been adopted by the courts as case law as early as 1972 in the case above, *Hall v. Lundin & Associates*, in which the courts manifestly stated that "It is only that conduct which creates an appreciable range of risk for causing harm that is prohibited ... although a defendant would owe a duty to protect certain persons under certain circumstances from this risk, it is not an insurer against every risk of harm which is encountered in [connection]..." with the risk.[53] The court is essentially saying that only a small subset of risks that are encountered, the risks that are foreseeable, are subject to a duty under the analysis, which at its most basic level, attempts to explore the boundaries of foresight.

JONES

v.

ROBBINS

289 So. 2d 104 (La. 1974)

BARHAM, J.

The plaintiff, Willie Leon Jones, is the father of the minor child, Candy Jones. The defendants, Henry Robbins and George Robbins, are the owner and the manager, respectively, of Robbins Gulf Service Station in Mansfield, Louisiana. This delictual action has been instituted to recover damages incurred when four year old Candy suffered burns caused by gasoline she ignited, gasoline which had been obtained from George Robbins at the Robbins Station by her half-sister.

At three o'clock on the afternoon of June 9, 1971, Penny Wyatt, the half-sister of the child who was badly burned, went to the Robbins Service Station and attempted to obtain, in a small glass container, a small quantity of coal oil or gasoline. She was told that gasoline could not be placed in the glass container. The number of return trips by Penny to the station is disputed, but, at any rate, upon the second or third visit to the service station, the six year old Penny carried a plastic container. Penny either purchased four cents worth of gasoline from George Robbins, or was given a small quantity of gasoline which was placed in the plastic container. The defendant, George Robbins, says that, at the time, Penny told him that her mother wanted the gasoline. The child disputes this.

Penny took the plastic container of gasoline back to her yard, where she and other children in the family played, and placed it on the rim of a well. She claimed that she had paint on her hands and that she had obtained the gasoline to wash the paint from her hands. After she had completed her hand-washing with the gasoline, her nine year old sister, Zelma Wyatt, came out of the house nearby and washed her hands in the gasoline, pretending that she had paint on her hands. At about this time (approximately an hour and a half had elapsed from the first attempt to obtain the gasoline) the four

---

[52] Restatement (Third) of Torts: Liability for Physical Harm §§7, 37 (1998).

[53] *Hill v. Lundlin & Assoc. Inc.*, 256 So. 2d 620 (La. 1972).

year old half-sister of these two children, Penny and Zelma, approached the well where the children had been washing their hands in the gasoline. The four year old half-sister, Candy, had found a match previously. She struck it and threw it into the gasoline, whereupon the contents of the plastic container burst into flame and, as one of the children described it, the flames grabbed Candy's legs and her dress was ignited. Candy ran towards the street, and a young male neighbor, Wayne Howard, and a mature female neighbor, Roxy Ann Brown, caught the child and extinguished the fire by throwing dirt on the burning dress. Roxy Ann Brown then carried Candy to her mother in the house. It was apparent that she was badly burned. The child's father returned from work almost immediately after the occurrence and the child was hurriedly carried to the hospital for treatment. It was then approximately five o'clock.

Under this set of facts, we are required to determine whether the defendants should respond in damages for the injury suffered by the four year old child, who was badly burned when she ignited the gasoline obtained from the defendants by her six year old half-sister.

We first inquire whether there is a causal relationship between the burning of the child, Candy, and the sale of the gasoline by one of the defendants to the six year old half-sister. Was the sale of the gasoline by George Robbins a cause in fact of the burns received by Candy? Did the defendant's act in making a sale of gasoline to a six year old child have something to do with the harm that was suffered by her four year old half-sister? Quickly, and without difficulty, we find that the sale of gasoline by George Robbins to the six year old Penny was a cause in fact of the injuries suffered by Candy. It was this defendant who placed the gasoline in Penny's possession and it was that gasoline which burst into flame and burned the four year old Candy when she threw a match into it.

Next, we are required, before making a determination of negligence and liability, to ascertain whether the defendants owed a legal duty which encompassed the particular risk that caused the harm to Candy. *Hill v. Lundin*, 260 La. 542, 256 So.2d 620 (1972); *Pierre v. Allstate Insurance Co.*, 257 La. 471, 242 so.2d 821 (1970). Our inquiry in this case is bifurcated. We must first determine if the defendants owed a particular duty not to sell gasoline to a six year old child under the particular facts of this case. Gasoline, while not classified as an ultra hazardous substance, is still a dangerous, highly inflammable, and explosive substance. Even when handled by knowledgeable people, it often causes harm because the special care required with its use is not taken. There is little reason to believe that incompetent persons would treat gasoline differently than they would treat water, milk or other liquids which have no dangerous propensities for exploding or becoming ignited. As a general statement, it may be said that the vendor of gasoline has the duty not to place it in the hands of those who, by reason of age or other disabilities, are unaware of the special propensities of the material, and of the precautionary measures which must be taken when using or storing it. Under the particular facts of this case, when a six year old child comes alone to a service station attendant and procures gasoline, without any adult solicitation or any adult supervision, it may be said that the attendant has breached a duty imposed by a standard of care owed to at least the one to whom he has dispensed the gasoline.

The second part of the question, and the more serious issue, is whether or not this duty not to place gasoline in the hands of an incompetent six year old child encompassed the risk of harm which came to her four year old half-sister. More simply stated, is the risk that Penny's four year old half-sister would throw a lighted match into the gasoline, encompassed within the duty of the attendant not to place the gasoline in the hands of the six year old?

One of the reasons for imposing a duty that gasoline should not be placed in the hands of a child of tender age is the knowledge that such a person is likely to engage in play with the highly flammable and explosive substance. Children have a great propensity for engaging in group play. A small child of six routinely engages in play with children of her own age, or those slightly younger or older. It is a breach of duty to permit another person to use a thing or engage in an activity which originally was controlled by the actor if the actor knows, or should know, that the third person is likely to use the thing or to engage in conduct with it in such a manner as to create an unreasonable risk of harm to others. Restatement of Torts, Second, § 308. Thus, it is a breach of duty to others to place loaded firearms, poisons, or explosive substances in the hands of young children or other mental incompetents. The act of placing the gasoline in the hands of this incompetent child carried with it full realization, or at least a requirement to realize, that the conduct of the small child with the dangerous substance involved an unreasonable risk of harm to others. Particularly included within the risk of harm to others is the fact that, with the expectation of child group play, an easily associated risk is that some other incompetent, by reason of tender age, would misbehave or would misuse the gasoline.[1]

It was totally within the range of the attendant's realization of the consequences of his act that not only might harm result from misuse of the gasoline by the six year old Penny, but that other children of tender age might engage in conduct while playing around and with the gasoline so as to cause it to ignite or explode. The risk that the four year old half-sister would be injured through the possession of the gasoline by the incompetent six year old is exactly the kind of risk which the legal duty we have imposed on the attendant was designed to protect against. The duty not to place gasoline in the hands of an unsupervised incompetent six year old was designed not only to protect that child, but also to protect those whom she would likely expose to the danger of the highly flammable substance. Moreover, it included the risk that another incompetent of tender age might engage in an activity of misuse which would actually ignite the gasoline and create the harm which the four year old Candy here suffered. The defendant, George Robbins, breached the legal duty which was designed to protect against the risk of harm which Candy encountered. He is liable under Civil Code Articles 2315 and 2316 for the damages caused by his fault. Henry Robbins is liable under Civil Code Article 2320 for the damage occasioned by his servant, George Robbins, in the exercise of the function for which he was employed.

The judgments of the district court and the court of appeal are reversed and set aside. The case is remanded to the Court of Appeal for assessment of damages. All costs are cast against the defendants.

SUMMERS, J., dissents and assigns reasons.

CULPEPPER, J., dissents.

SUMMERS, Justice (dissenting).

* * * * *

We have no difficulty in finding that the sale of the gasoline by Robbins to the child Penny was a link in the chain of causation leading to Candy's injury and the ensuing damage. The gasoline was placed in Penny's possession, and it was that gasoline which burst into flame and burned Candy when she threw a match into it. But for the sale of the gasoline, the injury would not have occurred.

However, the mere existence of a causal relationship does not establish legal liability for ensuing harm. The question remains whether the conduct has been so significant and important a cause that the defendant should be legally liable. Essentially, the question becomes whether the policy of the law will extend responsibility for the conduct to the consequences which have in fact occurred. Prosser, The Law of Torts, 41, 42 (4th ed. 1971).

---

[1] There are particular facts in this case which are not necessary to determination of the issue of breach of duty. George Robbins testified that he knew these children well. The house in which they lived and the yard in which they played were near the service station where he worked. He knew there were several children in the family and was familiar with their play activity. He was aware that all of the children, including the four year old Candy, played without adult supervision much of the time. He complained rather bitterly in his testimony that he believed that the mother did not properly supervise the children, therefore, he knew that Penny's activities, as well as those of her playmates, were not under the constant surveillance of a knowledgeable adult. By his own testimony he knew that Penny had young sisters with whom she was in constant contact and with whom she played. The reality of the projected realization, which we have stated should have been in George's mind, is clearly established under the facts and circumstances of this particular case, though not necessary for the determination of the legal issue.

It is not enough, therefore, to show that Candy was injured by the gasoline fire. If the harm was not willful, and it was not in this case, to allow recovery we must find as a prerequisite that there had existed a duty owed by Henry Robbins to the injured child. *Hill v. Lundin & Associates, Inc.*, 260 La. 542, 256 So.2d 620 (1972). The injured child was not the child to whom the gasoline was sold and to whom a direct duty was owed. Robbins sold no gas to Candy. In fact, the record does not indicate he was aware of her existence. Even so, if it was reasonably foreseeable on the part of Robbins that these consequences might result to this plaintiff, liability would result.

In my view there is no liability, because there was no negligence toward the injured plaintiff. Negligence is a matter of relation between the parties which must be founded upon the foreseeability of harm to the person in fact injured. Robbins' conduct was not a wrong toward Candy merely because it may have been negligence toward Penny. Candy cannot sue as the vicarious beneficiary of a breach of duty to Penny. *Palsgraf v. Long Island R.R.*, 248 N.Y. 339, 162 N.E. 99 (1928); *Blum v. Weatherford & Cary Bros.*, 121 La. 298, 46 So. 317 (1908).

Nor is it reasonable to suppose that Robbins should be called upon to take precautions for the safety of other neighborhood children. To the contrary, he was free to anticipate that Alberta Jones, the mother, would be fully responsible for the use to which the gasoline was put once Penny returned, especially since he understood it was Alberta who sent the child for the gasoline. And if this is true as to Penny, it was an even more valid assumption as to Alberta's other children, including Candy. *Lopes v. Sahuque*, 114 La. 1004, 38 So. 810 (1905); *Sherman v. Parish of Vermilion*, 51 La.Ann. 880, 25 So. 538 (1899).

There is a time factor, too, which further insulates this defendant from legal responsibility. At least one and a half, perhaps two, hours elapsed from the time the gasoline was sold to the moment when Candy threw the match into the container. Assuming the mother did not send the child for the gasoline, there was nevertheless ample opportunity in this time interval for the mother, by the exercise of reasonable diligence and proper supervision over these children of tender years, to discover the gasoline in plain view a few feet from her door, and to protect the children from harm. This inaction and omission on her part, as the party most duty-bound to protect and supervise the children, was an intervening cause shifting the responsibility for the harm from Robbins to Alberta Jones.

This Court should not hold defendant responsible, an hour and a half after he sold the gasoline, for the improper supervision and care of children of tender years a block and a half away at their dwelling where the mother and other family members were present and able to exercise the needed supervision but did not. The trial judge and the Court of Appeal refused to impose this liability. I agree with the result reached by those courts. There is nothing in this record to warrant overturning their carefully considered judgments. The limits of liability are often difficult to find, but there are limits.

I respectfully dissent.

2.   A Return to Proximate Cause and Variations of the Risk Rule

PITRE
v.
OPELOUSAS GENERAL HOSP.
530 So. 2d 1151 (La. 1988)

DENNIS, J.

This medical malpractice suit filed by parents of an albino child, seeking damages for themselves and the child, arises out of a surgeon's alleged negligence which caused the failure of a bilateral tubal ligation to sterilize the mother, resulting in the unplanned and unwanted birth of the child. We granted a writ to review the pretrial ruling by the court of appeal under its supervisory jurisdiction dismissing the child's suit for failure to state a cause of action and striking all of the parents' individual claims except for expenses associated with pregnancy and delivery and for the husband's loss of consortium. The primary questions presented for our consideration are (1) whether the physician owed a duty to the parents to exercise reasonable care in performing the operation or to advise the parents that the operation had failed, and, if so, what are the kinds and the extent of damages for which the physician may be held accountable; (2) whether the physician owed a duty to the unconceived child to avoid acts or omissions foreseeably likely to cause the child to be born with a congenital defect, and if so, whether under the facts alleged in this case the physician's duty encompassed the risk that the child would be born with albinism.

Facts and Procedural History

Tammy Pitre underwent a bilateral tubal ligation on April 25, 1984 at Opelousas General Hospital. The surgery was performed by Dr. John Kempf in conjunction with the delivery of the Pitres' second child. A pathology report dated April 30, 1984 indicated that Dr. Kempf severed fibro muscular vascular tissue rather than fallopian tissue during the surgical procedure. The petitioners Tammy & Dwain Pitre were not informed of this finding. Mrs. Pitre later became pregnant and gave birth to their third child, Hannah. Hannah was born with the congenital defect known as albinism.

The Pitres filed suit naming Opelousas General Hospital and Dr. John Kempf as defendants. The petition alleges that as a result of the failure of Dr. Kempf to properly perform the bilateral tubal ligation and the failure of either Opelousas General Hospital or Dr. Kempf to inform Tammy Pitre that the operation had been unsuccessful, she became pregnant. Petitioners also allege that Hannah Pitre was born with a physical deformity, albinism, which will require medical attention for the rest of her natural life, that she has severe problems with visual acuity, cannot see in bright light and will have permanent visual problems.

The claim of the parents includes damages for expenses incurred as a result of the pregnancy and delivery or birth as well as a general demand for emotional and mental distress, past, present and future. They ask for costs of rearing the child, special expenses for the child's deformity, expenses for the change in family status including extra money to compensate for the fact that their society, comfort, care, protection and support must be spread over a larger group, and money to replenish the "family exchequer" so that Hannah's needs will not deprive other members of the family. Additionally, Tammy Pitre seeks damages for her physical pain and suffering and Dwain Pitre seeks damages for loss of consortium, service and society.

On behalf of their minor child, Tammy & Dwain Pitre seek damages for the "wrongful life" of Hannah Pitre in that she was born with a physical deformity, namely albinism, future medical expenses, past, present, and future, emotional and mental hardship, pain and suffering.

The trial court overruled the various motions and exceptions filed by the three defendants including exceptions of no cause of action, motions for summary judgment and a motion to strike those portions of the petition concerning the "wrongful life" action and certain damages alleged by Tammy and Dwain Pitre individually. The court of appeal granted Dr. Kempf's pretrial writ application to consider the validity of the asserted causes of action. Although Dr. Kempf was the only party to apply for writs, the court of appeal ordered a stay of all further proceedings in this case.

After considering written and oral arguments, the court of appeal sustained the exception of no cause of action as to the "wrongful life" claim of Hannah Pitre. The court of appeal found it would be improper to grant Dr. Kempf's exception of no cause of action regarding the parents' claim. However, by granting a motion to strike, the court of appeal limited the elements of damages possibly recoverable by Tammy Pitre to expenses incurred during pregnancy and delivery and limited those of Dwain Pitre to loss of consortium, service, and society and expenses incurred during pregnancy, delivery, and post delivery. *Pitre v. Opelousas General Hospital*, 517 So.2d 1019 (La.App. 3 Cir.1987). This court granted a writ to review the court of appeal decision. *Pitre v. Opelousas General Hospital*, 519 So.2d 105 (La.1987).

Similar Tort Claims in Other States

Recent decades have produced a variety of tort claims arising when a member of the medical profession's negligence results in the birth of an unwanted child. The various causes of actions have been defined and distinguished to help clarify precisely what issues are involved in the case.

In wrongful birth actions, parents claim they would have avoided conception or terminated the pregnancy if they had been informed of the risk of birth defects to the child. Whereas a wrongful birth action is brought by the parents, a wrongful life action is brought by or on behalf of the child for having to endure life in the afflicted condition. There is no allegation that the physician's negligence directly caused the defect. Rather, it is alleged that the physician's negligent practice or failure to properly advise the parents has led to the birth of the child in the afflicted condition. A wrongful pregnancy or wrongful conception action involves a suit brought by the parents of a child, usually born healthy. The parents allege that the negligent performance of a sterilization technique caused the conception of the unplanned child.

A study of other jurisdictions reveals a myriad of answers to the problem. The recognition or denial of particular causes of actions, and the respective reasons offered by various courts, may promote a clearer understanding of the issues. In 1967, New Jersey handed down the landmark decision of *Gleitman v. Cosgrove*, 49 N.J. 22, 227 A.2d 689 (1967). The mother claimed the doctor had negligently assured her that the disease contracted during her pregnancy would not affect the child. Moreover, the mother claimed that if she had been adequately informed she may have procurred an abortion. The court denied recovery finding it impossible to measure the difference between life with defects against nonlife. In addition, there were the practical difficulties of calculating damages and the fear by the court that allowing such an action would be tantamount to sanctioning abortion. Both the wrongful life and the wrongful birth actions were denied by the court.

The years following *Gleitman* witnessed the legalization of abortion and many jurisdictions became receptive to parents' wrongful birth claims. On the other hand, all jurisdictions that have confronted the issue have denied the child's wrongful life cause of action for general damages for the suffering of being born in an afflicted condition. Finally, a great majority of courts allow recovery to the parents for their wrongful conception or wrongful pregnancy claims. However, the courts disagree on the amount of damages that should be recoverable. Of the courts recognizing the cause of action, most allow expenses directly associated with the pregnancy and delivery. Although some award child-rearing expenses, this figure is usually reduced by the "benefit" the parents receive by being blessed with this child.

Elements of Delictual Responsibility

Under one analytical approach, in order for a defendant to be held liable for damages caused another by his negligence, affirmative answers must be given to these questions: (1) given the relationship and circumstances of the parties, does the law impose upon the defendant a duty of reasonable conduct for the benefit of the plaintiff, the violation of which is considered to be fault? (2) If the defendant owed such a duty, did his conduct fall short of the standard and come within the scope set by law? (3) Did the defendant's negligence in fact cause damage to the plaintiff ('cause in fact')? (4) Should any of the damage to the plaintiff be ascribed in law to the defendant, and, if so, should the defendant be held liable for every kind of damage done to each of plaintiff's interests ('legal cause')?

For the purpose of determining the validity of the defendant's motion and exception, all well pleaded allegations of fact are accepted as true. Accordingly, we accept as true the plaintiff's allegations that defendant was guilty of negligence that in fact caused the damages. Thus, the only issues present for our consideration are whether defendant owed a duty of reasonable care to the plaintiffs and whether his negligence was a legal cause of the damage done to each of the plaintiffs' interests that was injured.

The legal cause of the damage in question could be stated as part of the duty inquiry: was the defendant under a duty to protect each of the plaintiff's interests affected against the type of damage that did in fact occur? Such a form of statement is sometimes helpful because it is less likely than "proximate cause" to be interpreted as if it were policy free fact finding; thus, "duty" is more apt to direct attention to the policy issues which determine the extent of the original obligation and its continuance, rather than to the mechanical sequence of events which goes to make up causation in fact. The duty risk approach is most helpful, however, in cases where the only issue is in reality whether the defendant stands in any relationship to the plaintiff as to create any legally recognized obligation of conduct for the plaintiff's benefit. Terms such as "duty" are merely verbal expressions of policy decisions and do not explain them. Allusions to policy should not be made a substitute for more determinate legal principles when they may be utilized. It is the task of the bench and the bar not only to ensure that justice is done, but also to demonstrate that it is being done according to law, which is essential to preserving public confidence. Policy considerations do indeed shape one's sense of the right decision, but whenever possible these should be given effect through the indispensable minimum of principles of liability in negligence, nebulous though they may be in themselves. Accordingly, we conclude that, when the case presents difficult issues as to the nature and extent of damages ascribed to the defendant, once it has been decided that the defendant's breach of a duty in fact caused damage to the plaintiff, it may be helpful to use a "legal cause" analysis which affords the application of "foreseeability" rules and other concepts of limitation. Although indistinct, these rules and concepts are more determinate than the abstract idea of a "duty" based on various "policy considerations" and may prove more helpful to triers of the facts, at least as starting points for legal reasoning.

Duty of Care–In General

In Louisiana, "[e]very act whatever of man that causes damage to another obliges him by whose fault it happened to repair it." This fundamental principle tells us that he who causes a damage to another, by his fault, is obliged to repair it, but does not tell us, and can not tell us, when the author of the damage is at fault. When they spoke of "any act", the authors of the Code had in mind the repression of the innumerable acts which constituted faults under whatever form they appeared. The framers conceived of fault as a breach of a preexisting obligation, for which the law orders reparation, when it causes damage to another, and they left it to the court to determine in each case the existence of an anterior obligation which would make an act constitute fault.

A physician has special legal obligations in connection with his profession. As any person, he "is responsible for the damage he occasions not merely by his act, but by his negligence, his imprudence, or his want of skill." Additionally, a general practitioner is obliged to possess the degree of knowledge or skill possessed, and to exercise the degree of care ordinarily exercised, by physicians actually practicing in a similar community under similar circumstances; a physician practicing in a specialty is required to exercise the degree of care ordinarily practiced by doctors in that specialty. The violation of these obligations constitutes a fault which must be evaluated, taking into account the professional practices and customs by comparing the conduct of the author of the damage with the normal and regular activity of a person exercising the same profession.

Duty of Care–Parents' Claim

Plaintiffs allege that the defendant physician negligently performed a bilateral tubal ligation on Tammy Pitre and failed to inform her that the operation had been improperly performed. Consequently, they contend, she became pregnant and gave birth to a child with a birth defect. Clearly, under the circumstances, the doctor owed a duty to the Pitres to exercise the degree of care ordinarily exercised by surgeons performing such operations in that specialty. Moreover, if he was aware of the failure of the operation, he owed them the duty to inform them that the object of sterilization had not been attained. Virtually all of the important policy considerations affecting tort liability demand recognition of such a duty: e.g., the moral aspect of defendant's conduct, the need for compensation, the need for incentive to prevent future harm, the relative ability of each class of litigants to bear or distribute losses. Furthermore, there is now quite general agreement that a doctor who negligently fails directly to prevent the conception or birth of an unwanted child, as by negligently performing a sterilization or abortion procedure, or by failing to diagnose or inform the parents that the child might be born with a birth defect--because of a disease or genetic condition--breaches his duty of care owed to the parents.

Duty of Care–Child's Claim

The plaintiffs allege that the defendant's negligent surgery and failure to warn the parents caused the child to be born with albinism. Apparently they do not contend that the malpractice directly caused the birth defect, but their petition implies that the doctor's carelessness caused the child's birth and thereby made it possible for the congenital defect to occur.

Although we conclude provisionally that under the facts alleged in the petition the doctor did not owe a duty to protect the child from the risk of albinism, we reject defendant's arguments calling for a categorical denial of any duty on the part of a physician to protect an unconceived child from being born with a birth defect. When a physician knows or should know of the existence of an unreasonable risk that a child will be born with a birth defect, he owes a duty to the unconceived child as well as to its parents to exercise reasonable care in warning the potential parents and in assisting them to avoid the conception of the deformed child. The time has come when we can and should say that each person owes a duty to take reasonable care to avoid acts or omissions which he can reasonably foresee would be likely to injure a present or future member of society unless there is some justification or valid explanation for its exclusion. Although there may be good reason in a particular case to limit liabiity for breach of this duty under concepts of legal cause, everything in the Code, the statutes and the underlying policy considerations encourages the recognition of such a duty as a prima facie obligation.

The persons at whose disposal society has placed the potent implements of technology owe a heavy moral obligation to use them carefully and to avoid foreseeable harm to present or future generations. In the field of medicine, as in that of manufacturing, the need for compensation of innocent victims of defective products and negligently delivered services is a powerful factor influencing tort law. Typically in these areas also the defendants' capacity to bear and distribute the losses is far superior to that of consumers. Additionally these defendants are in a much better position than the victims to analyze the risks involved in the defendants' activities and to either take precautions to avoid them or to insure against them. Consequently, a much stronger and more effective incentive to prevent the occurrence of future harm will be created by placing the burden of foreseeable losses on the defendants than upon the disorganized, uninformed victims.

Logic and sound policy require a recognition of a legal duty to a child not yet conceived but foreseeably harmed by the negligent delivery of health care services to the child's parents. Although this view has not yet been widely adopted, several courts have held that it is not necessary that the legal duty be owed to one in existence at the time of the wrongful act.

Actually these cases do not present a significant extension of the principles of liability for prenatal injuries. Moreover, it has long been recognized that a duty may exist to one foreseeably harmed though he be unknown and remote in time and place.

That the duty of care, the breach of which will create liability, should not depend on the physical existence of the individual plaintiff at the moment of the defendant's wrongful act is most aptly illustrated by the frequently used hypothetical examples of defective baby food manufactured before the child who consumed it was born, and of the dangerous apparatus installed in the home before the child injured by it was born. If recovery depended on the baby being alive at the time of manufacture, then such a child would be without a remedy. A wrong without a remedy could easily occur in any products liability case involving a young child victim.

Nevertheless, we conclude that in the present case the physician did not owe a duty to the unconceived child to protect her from the risk of being born with albinism. Our brief study of some of the literature on this congenital disorder indicates that it cannot be easily predicted or foreseen by a treating physician. The plaintiffs' petition does not contain any allegation that the defendant physician knew or should have known of the risk of this abnormality. The policy considerations affecting tort law do not impel the recognition of a duty when the doctor had no reason to suspect that the danger existed and did not have reasonable means of detecting its potentiality. In the event that our appreciation of the nature of the birth defect or of the precautions available to the medical profession is in error, however, the child's petition shall be dismissed provisionally only, with leave to amend the petition within thirty days of the finality of this decision.

Legal Cause–In General

We have concluded that the law recognizes a duty by a physician in this kind of situation to potential parents to take reasonable care to avoid acts or omissions which he can reasonably foresee would be likely to lead to the birth of a child. According to the pleadings, which must be accepted as true for purposes of the exception and motion, the doctor violated his duty of care and thereby in fact caused damage to the parents. Consequently, we are concerned here with whether the doctor's negligence was a legal cause of the parents' damage and, if so, the kind and the extent of damage to be attributed to the physician.

Because the civil code does not define legal causation any better than it defines fault or damage, our courts have had to fill in the content of this notion. In doing so, this court has relied heavily on the works of Professors Green and Malone in developing a duty risk approach that incorporates the consideration of policy factors involved in a legal cause analysis elsewhere. While this single case could be decided adequately on duty alone, we feel that more is called for here because of the complexity of the issues and the newly emerging legal duties involved. Rather than merely deciding that the defendant's duty does or does not cover certain types of damage after reflecting on appropriate policy considerations, we will not only engage fully in that judicial process but we will also attempt to articulate auxiliary rules for determining the extent and nature of damages ascribable to the defendant that will be helpful to triers of fact in future cases. These rules should be considered as general principles that can and should be expanded or contracted according to the relevance of certain policy considerations in a particular case. Furthermore, in formulating and applying these auxiliary rules or principles it may be helpful to compare some of the legal cause concepts that have developed in both the civil and the common law.

Legal Cause–Civil Law

Several restrictive theories have evolved in the civil law which tend to impose limits on causation for legal purposes. The theory of adequate cause was formulated by the German Von Kries at the end of the nineteenth century. In practice, adequate cause has been defined as "the fact or event which is normally calculated to produce harm of the kind in question, in a given situation, as distinct from the cause which produces such harm only by reason of extraordinary circumstances."

Although the theory of adequate cause and even that of reasonable foreseeability have had a perceptible influence, modern French law is not committed to any particular restrictive theory. Article 1150 of the French Civil Code limits the damages payable in the case of breach of contract to the amount foreseeable at the time the contract was made. But this article applies only in the law of contract: It has no direct application to delictual responsibility. In regard to delictual responsibility, French law rejects the subjective approach to the notion of reasonable foresight. At present, no kind of "systemization" is possible, but certain observable tendencies do exist.

The moral factor is important in the appreciation of causation. There is a clear tendency to give greater causal effect to an intentional fault than to a merely negligent fault, and to a negligent fault than to an act or circumstance where the element of fault is altogether absent. Another tendency is that of distinguishing between the consequences of a harmful act that are immediate in time, and the more remote consequences of the same act. A still further, and doubtless clearer, trend consists in distinguishing between physical harms and other forms of damage, which may be described as economic harms. Compensation for the immediate physical consequences of a harmful act extends well beyond the limits suggested by the criterion of reasonable foresight.

Thus, legal causation is influenced by the other two elements of civil responsibility, fault and damage. The moral element in the harmful act weighs very heavily on the thinking of the court in determining the question of causation. The court is necessarily less exigent in requiring proof of causation where great fault has been established. The influence of damage on the causation problem is less obvious but no less probable: According to the particular facts of each case, the court takes into account the nature of the interest affected (physical, material or moral), that is to say the nature of the damage. Being only human, there is no doubt that the judges pay more or less attention, as the case may be, to the need for compensation.

Legal Cause–Common Law Approaches

Even where the defendant's conduct has in fact been one of the causes of the plaintiff's injury, the question of legal cause remains, i.e., where the policy of the law will extend responsibility for the conduct to the consequences which have in fact occurred. It would not be possible or useful for us to examine in detail the countless variations of legal or proximate cause theory. But it may be helpful to restate some of the recognized generalizations about this area of legal doctrine.

There are two contrasting theories of legal cause which recur throughout the cases and account for most of the conflict with respect to the choice of a basic theory: (a) The foreseeable risk theory--the scope of liability should ordinarily extend to but not beyond the scope of the "foreseeable risks"--that is, the risks by reason of which the actor's conduct is held to be negligent. (b) The direct consequences theory--the scope of liability should ordinarily extend to but not beyond all "direct" (or "directly traceable") consequences and those indirect consequences that are foreseeable. Results are reached in certain types of fact situations that are more accurately characterized as exceptions to these basic rules, but often these outcomes are explained as if they were routine applications of the basic rule. This outcome is accomplished by expansive or narrow application of such flexible concepts as "foreseeable" and "direct." For example, some courts have thrown over the language of foreseeability, and have said outright that it becomes a matter of hindsight, by relating the consequences backward to the original negligence after they have occurred. The Restatement of Torts has in a limited way adopted this approach by saying that the defendant is not to be liable for consequences which, looking backward after the event with full knowledge of all that has occurred, would appear to be "highly extraordinary".

In English law many tests are used for determining whether damage is to be legally attributable to the defendant, but the one which predominates in the terminology of the courts is foreseeability of damage. The test, be it noted, is foreseeability in the sense of hindsight, not foresight; it is what a court, reviewing an event later, considers to have been foreseeable in order to do justice in the case before it.

A minority view holds that a defendant who is negligent must take existing circumstances as they are, and may be liable for consequences brought about by the defendant's acts, even though they were not reasonably to be anticipated. This view becomes a majority position by almost universal agreement, however, when unforeseeable harm to a plaintiff follows an impact upon his person. For example, the defendant is held liable when his negligence operates on a concealed physical condition, such as pregnancy, or a latent disease, or susceptibility to disease, to produce consequences which the defendant could not reasonably anticipate.

The "scope of the foreseeable risk" is on its way to ultimate victory as the criterion of what is legal cause, but the triumph has been both more easily achieved and less clearly significant because the concept of foreseeability so completely lacks all clarity and precision; it amounts to little more than a convenient formula for disposing of the case-- usually leaving it to the jury under instructions calling for "foreseeable", or "natural and probable" consequences.

Legal Cause–Underlying Policy Considerations

What are the underlying policy considerations that have caused both civilian and common law courts to expand or contract the concepts of "foreseeability" in particular cases and to grope from time to time for some more precise methods of limiting liability? Inspired by both Geny and Cardoza, this court has identified the policy sources informing the conception of the duty in a tort case to be those moral, social and economic considerations that a conscientious, objective policy maker would advert to in formulating a rule to govern the case. Common law scholars have singled out for special mention various factors affecting tort liability: the need for compensation of losses; the historical development of precedents; the moral aspects of the defendant's conduct; the efficient administration of the law; the deterrence of future harmful conduct; the capacity to bear or distribute losses.

Legal Cause–Louisiana Civil Code

Although the articles in the Code on damages under Title IV on conventional obligations or contracts are primarily intended to govern contractual liability, our objective search for rules to govern a tort case may involve looking for an analogy among codal rules, principles, concepts or statutory doctrines. Under these articles, damages are measured by the loss sustained by the obligee and the profit of which he has been deprived. An obligor in good faith is liable only for the damages that were foreseeable at the time the contract was made. An obligor in bad faith is liable for all the damages, foreseeable or not, that are a direct consequence of his failure to perform. An obligor is in bad faith if he intentionally or maliciously fails to perform his obligation. When damages are insusceptible of precise measurement, much discretion shall be left to the court for the reasonable assessment of these damages.

Formulation and Application of Precepts

After considering the foregoing rules and policy considerations, we conclude that as a general principle that the same criterion of foreseeability and risk of harm which determined whether a physician in this kind of situation was negligent in the first instance should determine the extent of his liability for that negligence; and that the doctor should not be held liable for consequences which no reasonable practitioner would expect to follow from the conduct. In accordance with the almost universal rule, however, the physician shall be liable for all resulting harm to the person caused by a negligent physical impact upon the person of the plaintiff. Likewise, in accordance with the general rule, and by analogy to our civil code articles governing contractual damages, a physician who intentionally, recklessly or in bad faith violates his legal duty shall be liable for all damages, foreseeable or not, that are a direct consequence of his breach of obligation.

We reject as a general rule the test of foreseeability in the sense of hindsight, not foresight, as being inappropriate when the doctor has been guilty only of ordinary negligence in this kind of medical malpractice case. If the trier of fact is required to attribute the knowledge of hindsight to the practitioner, the doctor may be held unfairly to a standard of knowledge or information impossible in daily practice and attainable only by the research scientist or the analytical pathologist looking backward reflectively at the particular case. "[T]o one gifted with ominisence as to all existing circumstances, no result could appear remarkable, or indeed anything but inevitable, as a matter of hindsight."

Applying these precepts to the facts alleged in the petition, we conclude that the parents upon proper proof may recover for the expenses incurred during pregnancy and delivery, the mother's pain and suffering, the father's loss of consortium, service and society, and their emotional and mental distress associated with the birth of an unplanned and unwanted child and the unexpected restriction upon their freedom to plan their family. These damages were foreseeable consequences of the doctor's alleged negligent acts and omissions.

The parents may not recover for the special expenses regarding the child's deformity, or for emotional and mental distress associated with the child's deformity. These are not consequences which were caused by an impact on the person of the mother or which a reasonable practitioner would expect to follow from the conduct as alleged in the petition. Based on our present knowledge of the congenital disorder of albinism and methods of predicting its occurrence we cannot infer that the doctor reasonably could have foreseen an unreasonable risk of a birth defect in this case. As in the child's action, however, the parents will be permitted to amend their petition in good faith to remove this deficiency.

The plaintiffs cannot recover for the economic costs of rearing an unplanned and unwanted child, expenses of the change in family status, including extra money to compensate for the fact that the mother must spread her society, comfort, care, protection and support over a larger group, money to replenish the "family exchequer" so that the child will not deprive the other family members. These are the ordinary vicissitudes that befall any family with the birth of a healthy, normal child. Absent unusual circumstances, a child is presumed to be a blessing not offset by the inconvenience of redistributing the family income and patrimony which he or she may occasion. Unfortunately, the child in this case may represent a greater burden than a healthy offspring but that is a result of her albinism which we have determined is not a legal consequence of the conduct alleged. Therefore, proof of the ordinary economic impact of an additional child would not constitute proof of a loss to the parents or the family.

Procedural Issues

The defendant's exception of no cause of action to the child's claim was correctly sustained by the court of appeal. In the interests of justice, however, the plaintiffs will be granted thirty days from the finality of this decision within which to amend the petition, if they can, to remove the grounds of the objection noted in this opinion.

When a petition states a cause of action as to any ground or portion of the demand, the exception of no cause of action must be overruled. The trial court should exclude evidence at trial pertaining to those elements of damages which, under this opinion, are not recoverable based on the present allegations of facts. The court of appeal correctly applied this rule in overruling the defendant's exception of no cause of action as to the parents' claim. In the interests of justice, the plaintiffs will be granted thirty days from the finality of this decision to amend their petition to remove the grounds of the objection.

The court of appeal erred in granting the defendant's motion to strike and in striking portions of plaintiff's petition. A motion to strike is not an authorized or proper way to procure the dismissal of a complaint or a cause of action. Moreover, the granting of a motion to strike rests in the sound discretion of the trial court. The trial court refused to grant the motion in this case. There being no showing or indication in the record of an abuse of discretion, the trial court's decision should be affirmed.

Decree

The court of appeal's judgment granting the motion to strike is reversed. The court of appeal's judgment sustaining the exception as to the child's claim and overruling the exception as to the parents' claims is affirmed, except that the plaintiffs are granted leave and time to amend the petition to remove the objections. The case is remanded to the trial court for these purposes and for further proceedings.

REVERSED IN PART; AFFIRMED IN PART; AMENDED AND REMANDED to trial court.

NOTES

1.   In *Pitre* does Justice Dennis treat the policy issues as questions of duty or questions of causation? Does your answer differ depending on whether we are asking the "this person", "this manner" or "these damages" question?

2.   *Pitre* may have appeared to be a retreat from duty/risk analysis, but subsequent Louisiana cases have applied duty/risk. *Cay v. State, infra* is representative of these cases. *See also Brooks v. State ex rel. Dept. of Transp. and Development*, 74 So. 3d 187, 195-96 (La. 2011) (Knoll, J., concurring).

3.   Must the plaintiff foresee the full extent of the harm or merely the general nature of the harm? Generally speaking, the defendant will be subject to liability if he could reasonably foresee the nature

of the harm done, even if he could not reasonably foresee the extent of the damage. For example, the "eggshell" or "thinskull" rule refers to an imagined situation where the plaintiff has an unusually thin skull and is uniquely susceptible to injury. A defendant who negligently injures the plaintiff's head is responsible for all injuries, even those which might not be foreseeable to a normal-skulled plaintiff. The defendant is said to take the plaintiff as he finds him. *E.g., David v. DeLeon*, 250 Neb. 109, 547 N.W. 2d 726 (1996).

CAY
v.
STATE DEPT. OF TRANSP. AND DEVELOPMENT
631 So. 2d 393 (La. 1994)

LEMMON, J

This is a wrongful death action filed by the parents of Keith Cay, who was killed in a fall from a bridge constructed and maintained by the Department of Transportation and Development (DOTD). The principal issues are (1) whether plaintiffs proved that DOTD's construction of the bridge railing at a height lower than the minimum standard for pedestrian traffic was a cause-in- fact of Cay's fall from the bridge, and (2) if so, whether Cay's fall was a risk that was within the scope of DOTD's duty to construct a higher railing.

Facts

Cay, a twenty-seven year-old single offshore worker, returned to his home in Sandy Lake from a seven-day work shift on November 3, 1987. Later that afternoon his sister drove him to Jonesville, thirteen miles from his home, to obtain a hunting license and shotgun shells for a hunting trip the next day. Cay cashed a check for $60.00 and paid for the hunting items, but remained in Jonesville when his sister returned to Sandy Lake about 7:00 p.m. Around 10:00 p.m. Cay entered a barroom and stayed until about 11:00 p.m., when he left the barroom on foot after declining an offer for a ride to his home. He carried an opened beer with him. Five days later, Cay's body was discovered on a rock bank of the Little River, thirty-five feet below the bridge across the river. Cay would have had to cross the bridge in order to travel from Jonesville to his home. Cay's body was found in a thicket of brambles and brush. The broken brush above the body and the lack of a path through the brush at ground level indicated that Cay had fallen from the bridge. There was no evidence suggesting suicide or foul play. There was evidence, however, that Cay, who was wearing dark clothes, was walking on the wrong side of the road for pedestrian traffic and was intoxicated.

The bridge, built in 1978, was forty feet wide, with two twelve-foot lanes of travel and an eight-foot shoulder on each side. The side railings were thirty-two inches high, the minimum height under existing standards for bridges designed for vehicular traffic. There were no curbs, sidewalks or separate railings for pedestrian traffic, although it was well known that many pedestrians had used the old bridge to cross the river to communities and recreation areas on the other side.

Cay's parents filed this action against DOTD, seeking recovery on the basis that the guard railings on the sides of the bridge were too low and therefore unsafe for pedestrians whom DOTD knew were using the bridge and that DOTD failed to provide pedestrian walkways or signs warning pedestrians about the hazardous conditions.

The trial court rendered judgment for plaintiffs, concluding that Cay accidently fell from the bridge. The court held that the fall was caused in part by the inadequate railing and in part by Cay's intoxicated condition. Pointing out that DOTD had closed the old bridge to both vehicular and pedestrian traffic and should have been aware that numerous pedestrians would use the new bridge to reach a recreational park, the Trinity community and other points across the river from Jonesville, the court found that DOTD breached its duty to pedestrians by failing to build the side railings to a height of thirty-six inches, as required by the American Association of State Highway and Transportation Officials (AASHTO) standards for pedestrian railings. The court concluded that this construction deficiency was a cause of the accident in that "a higher rail would have prevented the fall." Noting that there was no evidence establishing what actually caused the incident, the court surmised that Cay was "startled by oncoming traffic, moved quickly to avoid perceived danger, tripped over the low rail, lost his balance, and with nothing to prevent the fall, fell from the Little River Bridge." The court apportioned fault sixty percent to DOTD and forty percent to Cay.

The court of appeal affirmed. The court concluded that the inadequate railing was a cause-in-fact of the accident, stating, "It is true that the accident might have occurred had the railing been higher. However, it is also true that the accident might not have happened had the railing been higher." The court further stated, "Had the railing been higher, the decedent might have been able to avoid the accident."

Because these statements are an incorrect articulation of the preponderance of the evidence standard for the plaintiffs' burden of proof in circumstantial evidence cases, we granted certiorari.

Burden of Proof

In a negligence action, the plaintiff has the burden of proving negligence and causation by a preponderance of the evidence. Proof is sufficient to constitute a preponderance when the entirety of the evidence, both direct and circumstantial, establishes that the fact or causation sought to be proved is more probable than not.

One critical issue in the present case is causation, and the entirety of the evidence bearing on that issue is circumstantial. For the plaintiff to prevail in this type of case, the inferences drawn from the circumstantial evidence must establish all the necessary elements of a negligence action, including causation, and the plaintiff must sustain the burden of proving that the injuries were more likely than not the result of the particular defendant's negligence. The plaintiff must present evidence of circumstances surrounding the incident from which the factfinder may reasonably conclude that the particuar defendant's negligence caused the plaintiff's injuries.

Cause-in-Fact

Cause-in-fact is the initial inquiry in a duty-risk analysis. Cause-in-fact is usually a "but for" inquiry which tests whether the injury would not have occurred but for the defendant's substandard conduct. The cause-in-fact issue is usually a jury question unless reasonable minds could not differ.

The principal negligence attributed to DOTD in the present case is the failure to build the bridge railings to the height required in the AASHTO standards. The causation inquiry is whether that failure caused Cay's fall or, conversely, whether the fall would have been prevented if DOTD had constructed the railing at least thirty-six inches high.

The determination of whether a higher railing would have prevented Cay's fall depends on how the accident occurred. Plaintiffs had the burden to prove that a higher railing would have prevented Cay's fall in the manner in which the accident occurred. Two civil engineers testified as expert witnesses regarding the design and safety of the bridge for pedestrian use. DOTD's expert, Dr. Olan Dart, stated that the bridge was designed for vehicular use and met all safety standards for vehicular traffic, but that the design did not prohibit pedestrian use or pose an unreasonable risk or hazard to pedestrians. He stated without explanation that a pedestrian railing is not required for this particular bridge. Dart concluded that the eight-foot shoulders provided sufficient space for pedestrians to cross the bridge safely and indicated that pedestrians who were crossing the bridge in a normal manner would not likely fall from the bridge. He noted that the alcohol-impaired victim was crossing on the wrong side of the road while wearing dark clothing and carrying no flashlight. Dart speculated as to Cay's jumping, being pushed and other possible causes of the accident, finally suggesting that a vehicle approaching Cay from the rear may have frightened him with lights or a horn, causing him to move toward the rail and fall over. He stated that he could not determine exactly how the accident occurred, but noted that a pedestrian would have to approach the rail at a sharp angle to fall over the side.

Plaintiffs' expert, Larry Jones of H & H Engineering, testified that the bridge was designed solely for vehicular use and was clearly hazardous for pedestrians. According to Jones, the low railing was insufficient to protect pedestrians who might stumble and fall against the railing, since the forty-two-inch minimum height standard is designed to keep the top of the railing above the center of gravity of an average person and thereby prevent a fall over the railing. Jones stated that this railing's New Jersey parapet design, which has a three-inch high vertical base that projects nine inches into the shoulder and slopes upward and inward to the top of the railing, was intended to protect vehicular traffic, but presents a stumbling hazard for pedestrians who, upon hitting the toe area, would fall nine more inches before hitting the top of the rail. He opined that a bridge intended for pedestrian use should have curbs and a sidewalk with railings of adequate height, noting that shoulders are primarily designed for emergency use by vehicles. Jones further observed that the bridge lacked any type of barrier or signs which should be utilized to prohibit pedestrian traffic on bridges which are not intended for pedestrian use.

The circumstantial evidence did not establish the exact cause of Cay's fall from the bridge, but it is more likely than not that Cay's going over the side was not intentional, either on his part or of the part of a third party. More probably than not, Cay did not commit suicide, as evidence of plans and preparation for a hunting trip minimize this possibility. More probably than not, he was not pushed, as he had little money or valuables on his person, and the evidence from barroom patrons does not suggest any hostility toward or by him during the evening. More likely than not, he was not struck by a vehicle and knocked over the railing. It is therefore most likely that he accidently fell over the railing.

The evidence suggests that Cay moved at a sharp angle toward the railing, for some unknown reason, and stumbled over. For purposes of the cause-in-fact analysis, it matters little whether his movement toward the railing was prompted by perceived danger of an approaching automobile or by staggering in an intoxicated condition or for some other reason. Whatever the cause of Cay's movement toward the railing at a sharp angle, the cause-in-fact inquiry is whether a higher railing would have prevented the accidental fall.

The trial judge's finding that a higher railing would have prevented the fall is supported by expert testimony that the very reason for the minimum height requirement for railing on bridges intended for pedestrian use is to have a railing above the center of gravity of most persons using the bridge so that the users will not fall over.

A cause-in-fact determination is one of fact on which appellate courts must accord great deference to the trial court. We cannot say that the trial court erred manifestly in determining that a railing built to AASHTO minimum specifications would have prevented Cay's fall when he approached the railing at a sharp angle, although the exact cause of Cay's approaching the railing at a sharp angle is not known. While a higher rail would not have prevented Cay from jumping or a third party from throwing Cay over the rail, one could reasonably conclude that a rail above Cay's center of gravity would have prevented an accidental fall. The absence of a higher railing materially increased the risk and was a substantial factor in DOTD's failure to prevent Cay's accidental fall.

Duty

The next inquiry in the duty-risk analysis is whether there was a duty imposed by statute or rule of law on DOTD to construct a bridge that provided adequate safety for pedestrians who were expected to cross the Little River Bridge. DOTD knew that there would be considerable pedestrian traffic on the bridge, and DOTD clearly had the duty to construct railings of sufficient height to provide safe crossing for pedestrians or to prohibit pedestrian traffic by signs or access limitations.

Breach of Duty

The third inquiry involves breach of the duty. The height of the railing constructed by DOTD was below the minimum safety standard for bridges intended for pedestrian use. This construction deficiency constituted a breach of DOTD's duty.

216

DOTD argues, however, that the wide shoulder on the bridge fulfilled its duty to provide safe crossing for pedestrians. The wide shoulder provided additional safety from the danger of being hit by automobiles, but did little to lessen the risk of an accidental fall over the railing by a pedestrian walking as far as possible from vehicular traffic. We conclude that the wide shoulder bears more on Cay's contributory negligence than on DOTD's fulfillment of duty.

Scope of Duty

The critical inquiry in the duty-risk analysis is whether the risk of the injury sustained by Cay was within the ambit of the duty imposed on DOTD. The duty to build a bridge railing higher than the center of gravity of most pedestrians is designed to prevent the risk that a pedestrian will accidently stumble and fall over a low railing. However, there must be an ease of association between the injury and the rule of law giving rise to the duty. Here, the general manner of harm was foreseeable. The fact that the precise manner of harm (an intoxicated person's staggering or being frightened toward a bridge railing) may not have been anticipated does not break the claim of causation. There is an ease of association between an accidental fall over the railing of a bridge and the failure to build the railing to a height above an average person's center of gravity.

In summary, DOTD built a new bridge in 1978 with the knowledge that pedestrians were going to use the bridge and the knowledge that AASHTO standards required a minimum height for railings on bridges to be used by pedestrians, and DOTD simply failed to build the bridge in accordance with those minimum standards, a failure which was a cause-in-fact of the accidental fall. Accordingly, DOTD's concurrent fault in causing the accident renders DOTD liable for plaintiffs' damages, subject to a reduction for contributory negligence.

Contributory Negligence

The evidence established that Cay was intoxicated and was wearing dark clothes at the time of his death which, more probably than not, occurred during darkness, within a few hours after he left the barroom. The position of his body below the bridge indicates that he was improperly walking with traffic approaching from his rear (since he was probably crossing in the direction from Jonesville to Trinity).

Cay's voluntary intoxication and his negligence in following rules for pedestrian travel at night were significant factors in his fall. While DOTD had a duty to protect intoxicated or careless pedestrians who stumbled into the bridge railing from falling off the bridge, Cay's fault was far greater in causing this accident. The degree of the risk created by Cay's conduct and his far superior capacity to avoid the accident require that a much higher degree of blame be attributed to him in the causation of this accident.

We conclude that the trial judge erred manifestly in allocating sixty percent of the fault to DOTD. Accordingly, we amend the judgment to quantify Cay's fault at ninety percent and DOTD's fault at ten percent.

Decree

For these reasons, the judgments of the lower courts are amended, and the comparative fault of Keith Cay is fixed at ninety percent, while the fault of the Department of Transportation and Development is fixed at ten percent. As amended, the judgment is affirmed.

NOTES

1.   *Cay* represents one of the clearest applications of the duty/risk formulation. But hidden within the precise application are many unasked and unanswered questions. For example, doesn't the scope of the DOTD's duty extend to guard against inebriated pedestrians? Why or why not? If it does, then why reduce the plaintiff's recovery by the fault associated with his inebriation? You will learn more about comparative fault in Chapter 7, *infra*.

2.　　　In *Doucet v. Alleman*, 175 So. 3d 1107 (La.App. 3 Cir. 2015), *writ denied*, 179 So. 3d 609 (La. 2015), Doucet was killed in a collision when Alleman was distracted by a motorcycle procession, veered off the road, overcorrected, and crashed into Doucet. Doucet's survivors sued the Louisiana Department of Public Safety and Corrections based on its failure to revoke Doucet's parole prior to the accident even though Doucet had failed numerous drug tests in the months leading up to the accident. LDPSC filed a motion for summary judgment, which the trial court granted. *Held*, the duty of probation officer to protect the public from foreseeable consequences does not include the risk Alleman would become distracted by a motorcycle procession, veer off the road, overcorrect, and suffer a head-on collision. Further, whether instituting termination of probation would have prevented the injury was speculative.

　　　In *Hayes v. Sheraton Operating Corp.*, 195 So. 3d 563 (La.App. 4 Cir. 2016) the court held that despite allegations that the plaintiff had been bullied at school during the school year and had complained to no avail to the administration about her mistreatment, the school owed no duty to the plaintiff for a rape that occurred at a private party away from campus after the school year had concluded.

TYSON
v.
KING
29 So. 3d 719 (La.App. 3 Cir. 2010)

In this suit for personal injuries, Plaintiffs appeal the trial court's grant of summary judgment in favor of Defendants. For the following reasons, we reverse and remand with instructions.

Facts

On November 16, 2006, Darlene Kay Tyson was operating a motor vehicle southbound on Louisiana Highway 3225 (Highway 3225), a two-lane roadway in Rapides Parish, Louisiana, approaching its intersection with Ates Road. Simultaneously, Floyd King was proceeding northbound on Highway 3225. As Mr. King passed the intersection of Highway 3225 and Ates Road, he "blacked out" and crossed into the southbound lane of travel on Highway 3225. Mrs. Tyson, in an effort to avoid a collision with Mr. King, applied her brakes and lost control of her vehicle before coming to a stop on the roadway. As a result of her having to take this evasive action, Mrs. Tyson allegedly sustained personal injury. There was no impact between the Tyson vehicle and the King vehicle, nor was there any impact with the Tyson vehicle and any other vehicle or object.

Plaintiffs, Mrs. Tyson and her spouse, William Tom Tyson, Jr., filed suit against Defendants, Mr. King and his automobile liability insurer, Property and Casualty Insurance Company of Hartford (Hartford). Mr. King and Hartford filed a Motion for Summary Judgment which was heard by the trial court on September 22, 2008. At the conclusion of that hearing, the trial court deferred making a ruling "without further evidence." Following additional discovery, Defendants reurged their Motion for Summary Judgment which came before the trial court on June 1, 2009. The trial court orally granted Defendants' motion and signed a judgment consistent therewith dismissing the claims of Mrs. Tyson, with prejudice. Mrs. Tyson appeals.

Issues

Mrs. Tyson presents the following issues for our review:

1. Did the trial court err in finding that [Mrs.] Tyson was no more than a "witness" to the accident because there was no physical impact between her vehicle and the King vehicle?

2. Did the trial court err in failing to use a duty-risk analysis in deciding the [M]otion for [S]ummary [J]udgment?

Law and Discussion

* * * * *

Based upon the record of these proceedings, we find that the material facts are not in dispute. Accordingly, we must determine whether the trial court's grant of summary judgment constituted legal error.

In her first issue presented for our review, Mrs. Tyson asserts that the trial court erroneously classified her as a "witness" to the subject accident given the absence of physical contact between her vehicle and Mr. King's vehicle. She contends that "[a]s a result of [Mr. King's] breach of [the] duty owed to her, she became a participant in the accident, even though there was no direct impact between the vehicles." Mrs. Tyson argues that "[s]he does not seek to recover as a result of witnessing an injury to another; she seeks to recover because she was involved in a traumatic accident as a result of the defendant's negligence." Mrs. Tyson concludes that "[s]ince she was a participant in the accident[,] she is entitled to recover." Because we find Mrs. Tyson's second issue to be inclusive of this argument, we will address both of these issues together.

Mrs. Tyson asserts on appeal that the trial court erred in not applying a duty-risk analysis to the facts of this case. She argues that Mr. King's actions, in crossing over the center line into her lane of travel, violated the provisions of La. R.S. 32:79.[2] Mrs. Tyson contends that this statutory duty "was imposed to protect against the risk of injuries such as that suffered by [her]" and that Mr. "King breached this duty by [his] failure to abide by [La. R.S. 32:79]." Continuing with the duty-risk analysis, Mrs. Tyson, concludes that "[t]he breach of the duty by [Mr.] King resulted in injuries to [her]." Moreover, "[t]he mere fact that the vehicles of [Mr.] King and [Mrs.] Tyson did not physically collide does not excuse the breach of the duty by [Mr.] King, nor does it absolve [him] or [Hartford] of liability."

To the contrary, Mr. King and Hartford classify the present matter as one involving a "non-accident." In their words, under the duty/risk analysis, it presents "[t]he broader legal issue [of] whether the risk of a person being allegedly injured by bringing their vehicle to a stop without any impact or trauma to the vehicle is within the scope of protection afforded by a motorist's duty to maintain control of their vehicle." They conclude that the requisite element of "legal or proximate cause" which "considers whether the risk of harm was within the scope of protection afforded by the duty breached" is lacking in the present case.

We find that the transcript of the hearing on the Motion for Summary Judgment reveals that the trial court granted the motion solely on the basis of a lack of physical contact between the vehicles. At the hearing on the Motion for Summary Judgment, the trial court stated the following:

> Okay. All right, I was interested in finding out if there were any cases,-I looked, too,-Counselor, if there were any involving a personal injury where there was no contact. I could not find any either. So, the Motion for Summary Judgment is granted and you will have to take it up with [the] Third Circuit.

However, this ruling of the trial court constituted legal error as there is no statutory or jurisprudential requisite of a physical impact between vehicles for the imposition of liability in a

---

[2] Louisiana Revised Statutes 32:79 provides as follows:
Whenever any roadway has been divided into two or more clearly marked lanes for traffic, the following rules, in addition to all others consistent herewith, shall apply.
(1) A vehicle shall be driven as nearly as practicable entirely within a single lane and shall not be moved from such lane until the driver has first ascertained that such movement can be made with safety.
(2) The department may erect signs directing slow moving traffic to use a designated lane or designating those lanes to be used by traffic moving in a particular direction, and drivers of vehicles shall obey the directions of such signs.

personal injury case arising out of a motor vehicle accident. Rather, the proper analysis in this negligence action is the duty/risk analysis.[3] This court has recently explained the duty/risk analysis as follows:

> [I]n order for liability to attach under a duty/risk analysis, a plaintiff must prove five separate elements: (1) the defendant had a duty to conform his or her conduct to a specific standard of care (the duty element); (2) the defendant failed to conform his or her conduct to the appropriate standard (the breach of duty element); (3) the defendant's substandard conduct was a cause-in-fact of the plaintiff's injuries (the cause-in-fact element); (4) the defendant's substandard conduct was a legal cause of the plaintiff's injuries (the scope of liability or scope of protection element); and, (5) actual damages (the damages element)....

According to the record, and specifically the trial court's reasons for judgment, the trial court granted summary judgment in favor of Defendants based solely upon the fact that "there was no contact." We find that there is no statutory or jurisprudential requisite of a physical impact or contact between vehicles for the imposition of liability in a motor vehicle accident. The absence of physical contact between Mrs. Tyson's vehicle and Mr. King's vehicle does not necessarily absolve Mr. King from liability. The trial court committed legal error in granting Defendants' Motion for Summary Judgment without due consideration of a duty/risk analysis.

Consequently, we reverse the trial court's grant of summary judgment in this case and remand the case to the trial court with instructions that it address Defendants' Motion for Summary Judgment pursuant to a duty/risk analysis.

Decree

The judgment of the trial court granting summary judgment in favor of Floyd King and Property and Casualty Insurance Company of Hartford and dismissing the claims of Darlene Kay Tyson and William Tom Tyson, Jr., is reversed. The matter is remanded for further proceedings with instructions to the trial court that it address Defendants' Motion for Summary Judgment pursuant to a duty/risk analysis. Costs of this appeal are assessed against Defendants/Appellees, Floyd King and Property and Casualty Insurance Company of Hartford.

NOTES

1.   Schools have a duty of reasonable supervision over students. Should a school board be liable when a student is kept after school and misses a bus, walks home, and is sexually assaulted? *See S. J. v. Lafayette Parish School Bd.*, 959 So. 2d 884 (La. 2007) (holding the school board liable).

Also, the Court recently held that La. R.S. 17:158(A)(1), which provides that a school board shall provide for transportation for a student who resides more than one mile from the school, does not expand the scope of the board's duty of reasonable supervision of students within its care. The statute is not designed to prevent injury or the assault of a student once that student leaves the school. *S.J. v Lafayette Parish School Board*, 41 So. 3d 1119 (La. 2010).

2.   It is important that you distinguish scope of the risk from allocation of fault among defendants. Scope of the risk asks whether this defendant's duty extends to this particular injury to this plaintiff. A finding that the scope of the risk does not encompass this injury results in a finding of no liability.

---

[3] "The standard negligence analysis we employ in determining whether to impose liability under La.Civ.Code art. 2315 is the duty/risk analysis...." *Rando v. Anco Insulations, Inc.*, 08-1163, 08-1169, p. 26 (La. 5/22/09), 16 So.3d 1065, 1085.

In contrast, allocation of fault among defendants concerns the percentage share of fault assigned to each defendant. Third party crime cases provide a good illustration. In *Veazey v. Elmwood Plantation Associates, Ltd.*, 650 So. 2d 712 (La. 1994), the Louisiana Supreme Court found that the duty of an apartment owner extended to protect tenants from the foreseeable criminal acts of third parties. In *Veazey*, the intervening criminal act was a phantom rapist who was never found and whose identity was unknown. The court took the analysis further and found that because the apartment complex's duty included the criminal act of the phantom rapist, the apartment complex was allocated 100% of the fault and was responsible for all damages.

Veazey was legislatively overruled in 1996, when La. C.C. Arts. 2323 and 2324 were amended to require the allocation of fault among all defendants. For more on allocation, *see* Chapter 7.

D. SOME SPECIFIC PROXIMATE CAUSE/LEGAL CAUSE/DUTY RISK ISSUES

1. Controlling Third Parties

[handwritten: duty = ✓ if, negligently endanger, try to help them to rescue, try to help but leave them worse, relationship]

Generally, courts do not impose a duty upon a person to act to either help a person or to control the conduct of a third person actor to prevent tortious conduct by that actor unless the person has a "special relationship" with either the actor or the actor's potential victim. Consider the following sections of the Restatement (Second) of Torts:

§ 314. Duty To Act For Protection Of Others

The fact that the actor realizes or should realize that action on his part is necessary for another's aid or protection does not of itself impose upon him a duty to take such action.

§ 314A. Special Relations Giving Rise To Duty To Aid Or Protect

(1) A common carrier is under a duty to its passengers to take reasonable action

(a) to protect them against unreasonable risk of physical harm, and

(b) to give them first aid after it knows or has reason to know that they are ill or injured, and to care for them until they can be cared for by others.

(2) An innkeeper is under a similar duty to his guests.

(3) A possessor of land who holds it open to the public is under a similar duty to members of the public who enter in response to his invitation.

(4) One who is required by law to take or who voluntarily takes the custody of another under circumstances such as to deprive the other of his normal opportunities for protection is under a similar duty to the other.

§ 315. General Principle

There is no duty so to control the conduct of a third person as to prevent him from causing physical harm to another unless

(a) a special relation exists between the actor and the third person which imposes a duty upon the actor to control the third person's conduct, or

(b) a special relation exists between the actor and the other which gives to the other a right to protection.

[handwritten: third-party crim: duty = ✓ if history of crime or place assumes duty]

221

§ 316. Duty Of Parent To Control Conduct Of Child

A parent is under a duty to exercise reasonable care so to control his minor child as to prevent it from intentionally harming others or from so conducting itself as to create an unreasonable risk of bodily harm to them, if the parent

(a) knows or has reason to know that he has the ability to control his child, and

(b) knows or should know of the necessity and opportunity for exercising such control.

§ 317. Duty Of Master To Control Conduct Of Servant

A master is under a duty to exercise reasonable care so to control his servant while acting outside the scope of his employment as to prevent him from intentionally harming others or from so conducting himself as to create an unreasonable risk of bodily harm to them, if

(a) the servant

(i) is upon the premises in possession of the master or upon which the servant is privileged to enter only as his servant, or

(ii) is using a chattel of the master, and

(b) the master

(i) knows or has reason to know that he has the ability to control his servant, and

(ii) knows or should know of the necessity and opportunity for exercising such control.

§ 319. Duty Of Those In Charge Of Person Having Dangerous Propensities

One who takes charge of a third person whom he knows or should know to be likely to cause bodily harm to others if not controlled is under a duty to exercise reasonable care to control the third person to prevent him from doing such harm.

§ 320. Duty Of Person Having Custody Of Another To Control Conduct Of Third Persons

One who is required by law to take or who voluntarily takes the custody of another under circumstances such as to deprive the other of his normal power of self-protection or to subject him to association with persons likely to harm him, is under a duty to exercise reasonable care so to control the conduct of third persons as to prevent them from intentionally harming the other or so conducting themselves as to create an unreasonable risk of harm to him, if the actor

(a) knows or has reason to know that he has the ability to control the conduct of the third persons, and

(b) knows or should know of the necessity and opportunity for exercising such control.

Some Louisiana applications follow:

222

1.   *Hackett v. Schmidt*, 630 So. 2d 1324 (La.App. 4 Cir. 1993), *writ denied*, 635 So. 2d 1123 (La. 1994) – Husband allegedly sexually molested plaintiff's minor daughter in wife's house at a time at which plaintiff, the minor's father and other relatives were at the house. The minor visited wife's house only in company of minor's mother or grandmother. Wife knew of her husband's propensity for sexual misconduct with minor females, but because of therapy and lapse of time (15 years) she believed that the problem had been resolved. Plaintiff knew of husband's propensities to molest minor females. *Held*, under the circumstances, wife did not owe a duty to warn plaintiff about, or protect the minor child from husband's improper sexual advances.

      See, also, West v. Hilton Hotels Corp., 714 So. 2d 179 (La.App. 4 Cir. 1998), holding that a spouse does not owe a duty to prevent the intoxication of the other spouse or to warn third persons of the spouse's intoxicated condition, nor is there any legal basis "for the imposition of a duty on one spouse to supervise the other spouse to prevent that spouse from being harmed by the negligence of a third person."

      But, in *Toups v. Dantin*, 182 So. 3d 36 (La. 2016), husband had an extensive history of driving while intoxicated and was not allowed to operate a car without an ignition interlock device. While he had alcohol and drugs in his system, A operated his wife's car, which did not have an ignition control device; husband was involved in a rear end collision, which resulted in A's death; held: summary judgment was not appropriate; issues of fact remained concerning what spouse knew or should have known whether her husband, husband, was likely to driver her vehicle in an impaired, negligent and/or intoxicated state

      A chaperone must exercise reasonable supervision of teenagers attending a teenage party, and may be liable for damages where negligent supervision contributes to teenage sex at the party, and one of the teenagers did not "freely consent to the sexual encounter." *Doe v. Jeansonne*, 704 So. 2d 1240 (La.App. 3 Cir. 1997), *writ denied*, 718 So. 2d 433 (La. 1998). *See, also, Frederick v. Vermilion Parish School Board*, 772 So. 2d 208 (La.App. 3 Cir. 2000), *writ denied*, 781 So. 2d 561 (La. 2001), holding that the negligence of the school in failing to inform students about the cancellation of an after-hours campus activity does not encompass the risk that a student remaining on the campus for the activity will willingly accept a ride with a male student she knew and would become the victim of a brutal sexual assault at his hands.

2.   The jailer's duty encompasses the risk that the prisoner will escape and harm a third person. But how far does the duty extend? *See, e.g., Wilson v. State*, 576 So. 2d 490 (La. 1991). *See, also, Marceaux v. Gibbs*, 699 So. 2d 1065 (La. 1997), where the court ruled that if negligence of the custodian of an inmate facilitates the escape, the custodian is liable for damages to a third person injured in a collision with the escapee, who, 15 minutes after the escape, is driving the custodian's vehicle and is being pursued by law enforcement officers. In *Harris v. Stimac*, 653 So. 2d 15 (La.App. 1 Cir. 1994), *writ denied*, 660 So. 2d 460 (La. 1995) the court held that the state may be liable for tort committed by child where state was negligent in failing to properly supervise and place child after adjudication as a child in need of supervision and commitment to the state's custody.

3.   In *Posecai v. Wal-Mart Stores, Inc.*, 752 So. 2d 762 (La. 1999), Mrs. Posecai was robbed at gunpoint in the parking lot of a Sam's Wholesale Club located in Kenner, Louisiana. In the lawsuit against Sam's, the Supreme Court said

      With the foregoing considerations in mind, we adopt the following balancing test to be used in deciding whether a business owes a duty of care to protect its customers from the criminal acts of third parties. The foreseeability of the crime risk on the defendant's property and the gravity of the risk determine the existence and the extent of the defendant's duty. The greater the foreseeability and gravity of the risk of the harm, the greater the duty of care that will be imposed on the business. A very high degree of foreseeability is required to give rise to a duty to post security guards, but a lower degree of foreseeability may support a duty to implement lesser security measures such as using surveillance cameras, installing improved lighting or fencing, or trimming shrubbery. The plaintiff has the burden of establishing the duty the defendant owed under the circumstances.

On the facts, the Court found that three predatory offenses over a six and a half year period, when two of the offenses did not occur in the parking lot against Sam's customers, did not create a foreseeable risk of crime. As a result, Sam's owed no duty to Mrs. Posecai.

Could it be said that the merchant is in a "special relationship" with the customer who is injured by the criminal act? With the actor who causes the injury? Who is in a best position to (a) avoid the harm or (b) spread the harm?

With *Posecai, compare St. Peters v. Hackbarth Delivery Service Inc and Walgreen Co.*, 204 So. 3d 1157 (La.App. 5 Cir. 2016). There, plaintiff, a commercial driver transporting a load of pharmaceutical goods, was attacked by robbers when he arrived at a warehouse owned by defendant, Hackbarth, a company specializing in the movement of customer goods while providing warehousing for those goods when necessary. District court granted summary judgment in favor of Hackbarth, finding that Hackbarth had no duty to protect plaintiff from the criminal acts of third parties. The court of appeal found that the district court erred as a matter of law in its application of the balancing test adopted by the Supreme Court in *Posecai* when it failed to adequately consider the compelling evidence presented by plaintiff concerning whether Hackbarth should have reasonably foreseen the occurrence of the criminal acts in question in determining whether Hackbarth had a duty to protect plaintiff from such third-party criminal conduct, given a similar incident at Tuscaloosa, Alabama Hackbarth facility and the detailed procedures Hackbrath adopted thereafter concerning communication with drivers and deliveries—which procedures may not have been followed in the Louisiana incident. Accordingly, the court of appeal found that Hackbarth was not entitled to summary judgment.

4.   *Meany v. Meany*, 639 So. 2d 229 (La. 1994) – Each person has a duty to use reasonable care to prevent the spread of harmful communicable diseases, including sexually transmitted diseases. This rule is intended to protect a plaintiff from infection by a defendant who knows or should know that he or she is infected with a sexually transmitted disease. "It is only necessary that defendant know or suspect that he had symptoms suggesting any kind of venereal disease in order for the duty to be imposed that he either refrain from sexual contact with his wife or warn her of his symptoms."

5.   *Penton v. Clarkson*, 633 So. 2d 918 (La.App. 1 Cir. 1994) – Defendant was sharing an apartment with decedent; they had been dating for approximately two years. After an argument which lasted several hours, decedent was injured by, and later died from a self-inflicted gunshot wound. Decedent had threatened or attempted suicide on numerous prior occasions, and on the fatal evening, he threatened defendant with physical violence, and she feared he might shoot her with the gun. *Held*, under these circumstances, defendant did not owe a duty to take action to prevent the self-inflicted injury and resulting death.

6.   Under a negligence standard, a hospital owes a duty to its visitors to exercise reasonable care for their safety, commensurate with the particular circumstances involved, but the duty owed is less than that owed by a merchant. In any slip-and-fall case against a hospital, the plaintiff must show that she slipped, fell and was injured because of a foreign substance on the hospital's premises. The burden then shifts to the hospital to exculpate itself from the presumption of negligence. The hospital must show that it acted reasonably to discover and correct the dangerous condition reasonably anticipated in its business activity. The trial court must consider the relationship between the risk of a fall and the reasonableness of the measures taken by the hospital to eliminate the risk. *Terrance v. Baton Rouge General Medical Center*, 39 So. 3d 842 (La.App. 1 Cir. 2010), *writ denied*, 46 So. 3d 1271 (La. 2010).

7.   For a case in which a business sued a casino for the embezzlement by one of the business's employees who was a compulsive gambler, *see NOLA 180 v. Treasure Chest Casino, LLC*, 90 So. 3d

1066 (La.App. 5 Cir. 2012). The court began by stating that "[g]enerally, there is no duty to protect others from the criminal activities of third persons.... It is well settled that there is no duty to control the actions of a third person and thereby prevent him from causing harm to another unless some special relationship exists to give rise to such a duty." *Id.* at 452. Finding no special relationship between the plaintiff business and the casino, the court held that the casino had no duty.

A casino does not have a duty to identify a compulsive gambler *in NOLA 180 v. Harrah's Operating Co., Inc.*, 94 So. 3d 886 (La.App. 4 Cir. 2012), *writ denied*, 98 So. 3d 855 (La. 2012). "The law provides that a casino must disseminate information regarding programs to assist persons who recognize themselves as problem gamblers, and to allow those persons to self-report. Once the gambler self-reports and is placed on a list maintained by the casino, only then can a casino be held liable should a compulsive gambler be allowed to patronize that establishment." *Id.* at 889.

8.   Consider a case in which a gas company discontinued the supply of natural gas to nonpaying customer's house, notifying customer that it was doing so, and customer illegally used own wrench to restart supply of natural gas, and forgetting to shut off open line in house after illegally restarting gas, suffered explosions in house from natural gas escaping into house. Plaintiff's family members who were injured by explosion and fire sued power company. *See Jones v. Centerpoint Energy Entex,* 66 So. 3d 539 (La.App. 3 Cir. 2011), *writ denied*, 75 So. 3d 946 (La. 2011).

2.   The Employment Relationship

Businesses are sued by employees for injuries they sustain while working. Businesses also are sued by non-employees, such as customers, for injuries caused by employees of the business. Workers' compensation, a no-fault system of compensation for workplace injuries of employees, plays a significant role in the first situation but not in the second. Thus, it is important to identify who is bringing a negligence claim against a business – an employee of the business or a third party, such as a customer.

Negligence claims by employee against employer and/or co-employees: If an employee is suing her employer for negligence of the employer or negligence of a co-employee, the employer and the co-employee are immune if the injury is covered by workers' compensation. Workers' compensation provides the exclusive remedy if the injury is covered unless the plaintiff employee was injured by an intentional tort of the employer or a co-employee. However, not all workplace injuries resulting from negligence are covered by workers' compensation. Consider for example, *Mundy v. Dept. of Health & Human Resources, infra* Chapter 7 (nurse's injuries at hospital not covered by workers' compensation, so she could sue employer for negligent provision of security). The topic of what is required for coverage under workers' compensation is discussed in Chapter 7. If workers' compensation does not provide a remedy for the employee's injury, the employee can sue for negligence based onan employer's duty to protect an employee from a dangerous condition or person on his premises. *See, e.g., Carr v. Sanderson Farms, Inc.,* 215 So. 3d 437 (La.App. 1 Cir. 2017); *Martin v. Bigner*, 665 So. 2d 709 (La.App. 2d Cir. 1995). Furthermore, an employee owes a duty of reasonable care to a co-employee. Negligence claims against co-employees, like negligence claims against the employer, are barred by the workers' compensation immunity if the injury is covered by workers' compensation.

Negligence claims against a business by a third party, such as a customer: Workers' compensation has no applicability to claims of non-employee third parties, such as customers. If a customer is injured at a business by an employee of the business, the plaintiff typically will sue the business for vicarious liability for the tort of the employee (alleging the employee was in the course and scope of employment) and for negligence of the business. For example, if an employee of a business carelessly ran into a customer, knocking him down and injuring him, the customer could sue the business vicariously for the employee's negligence and for the negligence of the business in training or supervising the employee.

3. Duty to Rescuers

When addressing a rescue situation, you must distinguish between the duty to rescue and the duty to the rescuer. In this subsection, we address the scope of the duty owed by a negligent party to a rescuer. The scope is different depending on whether the rescuer is an amateur or a professional rescuer.

The amateur rescuer is usually within the scope of the risks of the negligent defendant's conduct. One of the leading cases is *Inseco v. Cambridge Mut. Fire Ins. Co.*, 447 So. 2d 606 (La.App. 3 Cir. 1984). Allowing recovery by a visitor injured while assisting in the extinguishment of a house fire, the court made these observations:

> "(T)he special treatment afforded the rescuer does not arise out of legal considerations but out of moral considerations.[1]

> 'Where the argument is made that a party, plaintiff or defendant, could have ignored all cries for help or dictates of humanity and remained safe and sound, courts have a distinct tendency to look with favor on "white knights," provided their conduct is not too quixotic. The moral answer is clear: it is good that he went to the rescue even though he had no duty to do so. The legal position to a large extent reflects morality. The rescuer is not to be viewed as an officious intermeddler nor as one who assumed a risk.' La. Civil Law Treatise, 12 § 282.

> We find that there is an ease of association between defective electrical wiring and the risk of fire and the additional risk that an invitee will be injured in attempting to preserve the lives and property endangered by that fire.[2]

> The remaining question is whether the plaintiff in this case was injured as the result of encountering the risk posed by the defect or whether he was injured as the result of his own fault. This inquiry encompasses the question often posed as part of the rescuer doctrine, that is, whether the actions of the rescuer are wanton or must be condemned by reason.

> On this issue, this defendant has the burden of proof to show fault on the part of plaintiff. We find that the defendant failed in that burden. We believe that plaintiff's actions, when viewed in light of the emergency and thus the necessity for quick action, which was the result of the risk posed by the defect, were prudent. Plaintiff's actions were justified by the fact that he acted for the purpose of saving property and life from imminent danger."

For professional rescuers, consider the following:

---

[1] Indeed, the existence of a legal duty on the tort of the rescuer, such as in the case of a fireman, involves altogether different moral, social and economic considerations which may compel a different result. *See Thompson v. Warehouse Corporation of American, Inc.*, 337 So. 2d 572 (La.App. 4 Cir. 1976).

[2] "The risk of rescue if only it be not wanton, is born of the occasion. The emergency begets the man ... Danger invites rescue. The cry of distress is the summons to relief. The law does not ignore these reactions of the mind in tracing conduct to its consequences. It recognizes them as normal. It places their effects within the range of the natural and probable." Cardozo, C.J., in *Wagner v. International R. Cor.* (1921), 232 N.Y. 176, 133 N.E. 137, 19 A.L.R. 1.

GANN
v.
MATTHEWS
873 So. 2d 701 (La.App. 1 Cir. 2004)
writ denied, 876 So. 2d 804 (La. 2004)

GAIDRY, J.

On this case involving injuries sustained by a police officer while attempting to handcuff an arrestee, the trial court awarded damages to the plaintiffs for these injuries and defendants appealed. For the following reasons, we reverse.

Facts and Procedural History

On June 28, 1998, Officer Brenda Gann responded to a call regarding a disturbance at the home of Tammie Matthews. Tammie Matthews had previously obtained a restraining order against her estranged husband, Terrance Matthews, giving her temporary use of the family home and ordering Terrance to stay away from her. On the night of June 28, Tammie called the police after Terrance came to the family home and slashed the tires on Tammie's car and broke windows on the house. Officer Gann arrived at the scene as Terrance was backing out of the driveway. Officer Gann blocked him in and turned on her lights and Terrance parked his car. Terrance then exited the car from the passenger side, holding a young child. Officer Gann had been out to the Matthews' residence before, and was aware of other officers going out for similar domestic disturbances. She testified that Terrance was always drunk, and that was what usually caused the disturbance. Officer Gann testified that Terrance's speech was very slurred, he was staggering, and when she got closer to him, she noticed a strong odor of alcohol. He told Officer Gann to back off because he might have a gun, and Officer Gann drew her own weapon. Mr. Matthews then reached behind his back and pulled out a box cutter. Officer Gann ordered him to drop the box cutter, and he cooperated by tossing the box cutter onto the back of Tammie's car. Officer Gann then ordered him to let go of the child and to put his hands on the car. He did not comply right away, but Officer Gann could see that he didn't have anything else in his hands, so she holstered her weapon and grabbed him by the back of the pants and pulled the child away from him. At this point, she attempted to handcuff him and was holding him by his right arm. She testified that Terrance was facing the car and was not resisting, but did not put his hands behind his back. She decided to try a distractionary technique called a common peroneal strike, which would momentarily stun Terrance so that she could handcuff him easily without fighting with him. To accomplish this surprise maneuver, she stood behind Terrance and stepped back with her left leg and then attempted to hit Terrance above the back of the knee with her left knee. She was not directly behind Terrance as she needed to be to properly perform this maneuver, but instead was slightly to one side. Right before she made contact, Terrance, who had been staggering and unable to stand still, moved slightly, causing Officer Gann to strike her knee on the bumper of the car. Officer Gann testified that Terrance was drunk and "off balance" and had no idea that she was attempting to strike him from behind. She also testified that she did not expect a drunk person to stand perfectly still. Terrance was not charged with resisting arrest.

Officer Gann initially thought she had bruised her knee, but after experiencing increasing pain, she sought medical attention and it was ultimately determined that she had a deep hairline fracture that irritated the fat pad.

Officer Gann and her husband filed suit against Terrance Matthews, Tammie Matthews, and Allstate, both as Tammie's homeowners' insurer and her automobile insurer. Tammie Matthews was voluntarily dismissed during trial. After a bench trial before the Honorable Janice Clark, judgment was rendered in favor of the Ganns and against Terrance Matthews and Allstate in the amount of $38,180.19....

* * * * *

Discussion

Professional Rescuer's Doctrine

The trial court did not address the applicability of the Professional Rescuer's Doctrine. The Professional Rescuer's Doctrine is a jurisprudential rule that essentially states that a professional rescuer, such as a fireman or a policeman, who is injured in the performance of his duties, "assumes the risk" of such an injury and is not entitled to damages. *Mullins v. State Farm Fire and Casualty Co.*, 96-0629 p. 3 (La.App. 1 Cir. 1997), 697 So. 2d 750, 752. However, firemen, police officers, and others who, in their professions of protecting life and property, necessarily endanger their safety do not assume the risk of *all* injury without recourse against others. *Id.*

A professional rescuer may recover for an injury caused by a risk that is independent of the emergency or problem he has assumed the risk to remedy. A risk is independent of the task, and the assumption of the risk rationale does not bar recovery, if the risk-generating object could pose the risk to the rescuer in the absence of the emergency or specific problem undertaken. On the other hand, "dependent" risks arise from the very emergency that the professional rescuer was hired to remedy. The assumption rationale bars recovery from most dependent risks except when (1) the dependent risks encountered by the professional rescuer are so extraordinary that it cannot be said that the parties intended the rescuers to assume them, or (2) the conduct of the defendant may be so blameworthy that tort recovery should be imposed for the purposes of punishment or deterrence. *Mullins,* 96-0629 pp. 3-4, 697 So. 2d at 752-53.

Police officers are hired to protect others from criminal activities, are expected to effect arrests as part of their duties, and could expect a criminal to resist arrest. Accordingly, the risk of being injured while carrying out an arrest is a dependent risk, arising out of the specific problem which the police officer was hired to remedy. Therefore, in order for a police officer to recover for injuries received while attempting to arrest a criminal who is resisting, the risk created by the arrestee's conduct must either be so extraordinary that it cannot be said that the parties intended the police officer to assume them, or the conduct of the arrestee in resisting must be so blameworthy that tort recovery should be imposed for purposes of punishment or deterrence. *Worley v. Winston,* 550 So. 2d 694 (La.App. 2 Cir. 1989), *writ denied,* 551 So. 2d 1342 (La. 1989).

In *Worley v. Winston,* the plaintiff, a police officer, was injured when he and his partner attempted to arrest a "peeping tom." Plaintiff's partner approached defendant and shouted, "Police. Freeze." The defendant jumped up and ran away and climbed over a fence. Plaintiff joined the pursuit and eventually approached the defendant, identified himself as a police officer, and told him to stop twice. The defendant did not stop. Plaintiff began to struggle with defendant, and plaintiff's little finger and his watch were broken during the struggle. The court found that while the risk of being injured while effecting an arrest is a dependent risk, under the circumstances plaintiff should recover damages because defendant's conduct in resisting arrest was not only highly blameworthy, but also criminal.

In the present case, Officer Gann testified that although Terrance was not fully cooperative, he was not resisting arrest. Terrance was not charged with resisting arrest. Furthermore, Officer Gann was aware that Terrance was drunk and did not expect him to stand perfectly still. Therefore, his act in swaying or staggering while she attempted to perform a surprise knee strike from behind cannot be said to create such an extraordinary risk that she cannot expect to have encountered it, nor is it so blameworthy that tort recovery should be allowed as a punishment or deterrence. Therefore, recovery for these injuries is barred by the Professional Rescuer's Doctrine.

Based on our finding that Officer Gann's recovery is barred by the Professional Rescuer's Doctrine, we pretermit discussion of the remaining assignments of error.

For the above assigned reasons, the trial court judgment is reversed. Costs of this appeal are assessed to plaintiffs.

REVERSED.

GONZALES
v.
KISSNER
24 So. 3d 214 (La.App. 1 Cir. 2009)

This is an action for personal injuries sustained by an animal control officer who was mauled by defendants' dog while investigating a complaint of an attack by the dog the day before. Following the trial court's grant of plaintiff's motion for a partial summary judgment as to the liability of the dog's owners, the dog's owners have appealed. For the reasons that follow, we reverse in part, affirm in part, and remand.

Facts

On or about March 20, 2006, plaintiff, Iberville Parish Animal Control Officer Toni Gonzales, was attacked repeatedly by a 100-pound German shepherd owned by defendants, John Q. Kissner, Jr. and his wife, Elena Kissner, at the Kissner residence, located at 7095 Bayou Paul Road in St. Gabriel, Louisiana. Ms. Gonzales had gone to the Kissner residence on the aforementioned date in the course of her employment to investigate a complaint that a 13-year-old boy had been bitten by the Kissners' dog the day before.

Upon Ms. Gonzales' arrival at the Kissner home, Elena Kissner came outside via the back door, leaving the dog in the kitchen. As the two women began talking alongside Ms. Gonzales' truck, the dog managed to escape from the house after apparently forcing open the back door. The dog lunged at Ms. Gonzales and began to maul her about the head, face, and neck. Grabbing the dog's collar, Elena Kissner was able to physically pull the dog off of Ms. Gonzales. The dog thereafter forcibly extricated itself from its collar and began to chase Ms. Gonzales around her truck, attacking her from behind and knocking her to the ground. Only by thrusting her elbow into the dog's mouth was Ms. Gonzales able to ward off further attacks until Elena Kissner could restrain the dog. After the arrival of emergency response personnel, the dog was put down by Mr. Kissner.

* * * * *

The Professional Rescuer's Doctrine, sometimes referred to as the "fireman's rule," is a jurisprudential rule that essentially states, a professional rescuer injured in the performance of his professional duties "assumes the risk" of such an injury and is not entitled to damages. *See, Mullins v. State Farm Fire and Casualty Co....* However, firemen, police officers, and others who, in their professions of protecting life and property, necessarily endanger their safety; however, do not assume the risk of all injury without recourse against others. *Id....* Louisiana courts have recognized two exceptions.

A professional rescuer may recover for an injury caused by a risk that is independent of the emergency or problem he has assumed the duty to remedy.... A risk is independent of the task, if the risk-generating object could pose the risk to the rescuer in the absence of the emergency or specific problem undertaken....

On the other hand, a "dependent" risk arises from the very emergency that the rescuer was hired to remedy.... The assumption rationale bars recovery from most dependent risks except when: (1) the dependent risks encountered by the professional rescuer are so extraordinary that it cannot be said that the parties intended the rescuers to assume them; or (2) the conduct of the defendant may be so blameworthy that tort recovery should be imposed for the purposes of punishment or deterrence. *Gann v. Matthews.*

Assuming for purposes of argument that the duties of an animal control officer, such as the plaintiff in the present case, fall within the ambit of a professional rescuer, it could be further argued animal control officers are hired to protect the public from harm occasioned by animals. As part of their duties, animal control officers are expected to investigate complaints by the public and also take control of animals causing injuries to people. Animal control officers could reasonably expect in the course of apprehending a dangerous animal that the animal would respond aggressively. Accordingly, the risk of being bitten while apprehending a dangerous animal is a dependent risk, arising out of the specific problem which the animal control officer was hired to remedy. Therefore, in order for an animal control officer to recover for injuries received while attempting to apprehend a dangerous animal, the risks created by the conduct of the animal or its owner, who is vicariously liable, must either be so extraordinary that it cannot be said that the parties intended the animal control officer to assume such risks, or so blameworthy that tort recovery should be imposed for purposes of punishment or deterrence....

In the case presently before us, Elena Kissner testified in her deposition that upon learning of Ms. Gonzales' arrival at her home, she left the dog in the kitchen and walked outside, closing the door behind her. Elena Kissner also conceded that she and her husband never locked their home even though the dog had inexplicably escaped on two prior occasions. As the two women spoke outside in the driveway, the dog escaped from the confines of the house and, without provocation or warning, mauled Ms. Gonzales. In view of the fact the dog had similarly attacked a neighbor's child the day before, it is our belief Ms. Gonzales had every reason to expect the dog to be restrained. It is the opinion of this court that Elena Kissner's failure to properly confine or restrain their dog and/or lock their home despite knowledge of the dog's dangerous propensities, coupled with their knowledge that the dog had escaped from their house on two previous occasions, constitutes conduct so blameworthy that tort recovery should be allowed under these facts as a punishment or deterrence. Therefore, we hold that under the facts presented in this case, Ms. Gonzales' recovery for injuries sustained in this manner is not barred by the Professional Rescuer's Doctrine. This assignment is also without merit.

The third and final assignment raised by John and Elena Kissner is that the trial court erred in failing to apply the doctrines of assumption of risk and comparative negligence. Based upon our review of the record in this matter, and our holdings above, we can find no basis for application of said doctrines and, accordingly, decline to do so. This assignment is similarly without merit.

Conclusion

Thus, based upon the record before this court, we find no error on the part of the trial court that would warrant reversal of Ms. Gonzales' motion for a partial summary judgment as to the liability of the dog's owners, John and Elena Kissner. We note however that the trial court's revised judgment of February 19, 2009, mistakenly granted a partial summary judgment as to the concurrent liability of the property owner defendant Catherine Kissner. Accordingly, the trial court's judgment of February 19, 2009, is reversed as to the liability of defendant Catherine Kissner, and affirmed in all other respects. This matter is hereafter remanded to the trial court for further proceedings consistent with this opinion. All costs associated with this appeal shall be assessed against defendants John and Elena Kissner.

NOTES

1. Why treat professional rescuers differently from amateur rescuers?

2. A volunteer fireman is injured when a loaded gun overheats and discharges. Should the fireman be allowed to recover against the landowner? *See Bourgeois v. Duplessis*, 540 So. 2d 397 (La.App. 1 Cir. 1989), *writ denied*, 541 So. 2d 1392 (La. 1989).

3. The previous case turns on foreseeability. The defendants argue that the risks of being bitten

by an animal are foreseeable and so an animal control officer "assumes the risk" of this possibility. The Court phrases the holding in terms of foreseeability also: that the animal control officer had "every reason to expect the dog to be restrained…" and that based on the dog's escape from the house on two previous occasions, coupled with the dog's aggressive nature, it was foreseeable that the dog would escape and maul someone, as it had only the day before. Because of this clear foreseeability, the Court seems to suggest that the conduct of the defendant in not taking precautions to prevent the attack was particularly egregious, and constituted "conduct so blameworthy that tort recovery should be allowed under these facts as a punishment or deterrence." Should foreseeability have been such an issue in determining liability? If a person owes a duty that is breached, liability will attach to the conduct. Should liability be more severe if it can be shown that the injury could be expected or would be more "likely"? Can you see how foreseeability removes the analysis from being a binary determination (either a duty exists or not) to a realm of speculation based on hypothetical possibilities, and how this might lead to wildly varying results?

Perhaps in an effort to provide more cohesive results, the role of foreseeability of risk in the assessment of duty in negligence actions has recently been revisited by drafters of the Restatement (Third) of Torts. "An actor ordinarily has a duty to exercise reasonable care when the actor's conduct creates a risk of physical harm."[10] Thus, in most cases involving physical harm, courts "need not concern themselves with the existence or content of this ordinary duty," but instead may proceed directly to the elements of liability set forth in section 6.[11] The general duty of reasonable care will apply in most cases, and thus courts "can rely directly on § 6 and need not refer to duty on a case-by-case basis."[12] Like Louisiana, the drafters of the latest Restatement have shifted the focus to the duty-risk approach, under which "an actor owes a general duty to exercise reasonable care when the actor's conduct creates a risk of physical harm" except in exceptional cases, when an articulated countervailing principle or policy warrants denying or limiting liability, in which a court may decide that the defendant has no duty or that the ordinary duty of reasonable care requires modification.[13] The foreseeability of physical injury to a third party is not considered in determining whether an actor owes a general duty to exercise reasonable care.[14] Instead, it is used to define the boundaries of the duty if one is established. The Restatement (Second) rarely used the term "proximate cause," but instead used "legal cause" as an umbrella term to address both concepts of factual cause and proximate cause.[15] However, the drafters of the Restatement (Third) have abandoned the use of the term "legal cause" because, like "proximate cause," it "contributes to the misleading impression that limitations on liability somehow are about factual cause" and the term has never become widely accepted and utilized in tort law.[16]

In effect, the Sections of Restatement (Third) of Torts governing scope of liability provide that an actor's liability should be limited to those physical harms that result from the risks that made the actor's conduct tortious, and therefore should not be determined by whether the actor's conduct was a "substantial factor" in causing the harm at issue. This has the effect of removing foreseeability from the equation.

4.   Consider foreseeability in the context of the following case absolving a hotel in a claim by a pedestrian who was injured when the body of a suicide victim fell on him outside the hotel, *see Keller*

---

[10] Restatement (Third) of Torts: Liab. for Physical Harm § 7(a).

[11] *Id.* § 6 comment F, at 81.

[12] *Id.* § 7 comment A, at 90.

[13] Restatement (Third) of Torts: Liab. for Physical Harm § 7.

[14] *Id.*

[15] Ch. 6 Special Note on Proximate Cause, at 574.

[16] *Id.* at 575.

v. Monteleone Hotel, 43 So. 3d 1041 (La.App. 4 Cir. 2010). Here, is it foreseeable that a suicide victim would fall onto a person walking by the front of the hotel? Not that this is a separate question of whether or not the hotel has a responsibility to protect against the possibility that suicide victims would attempt to access high spaces to jump. This analysis would look at the presence of railings, and possibly whether hotel guests had attempted to jump from the roof in the past. Should something as aberrant and random as suicide ever come into play as part of a duty/risk analysis in designing high spaces in a construction setting?

What about the foreseeability of someone seeing the "donkey" pumps at an oil rig site and deciding to "ride" one like a bucking bronco? Surprisingly, the Third Circuit held that this was entirely within the range of foreseeable responses that someone might have upon seeing the oil pump and that the manufacturer had a duty to guard against this. Reversing the Third Circuit, the Supreme Court ruled that the manufacturer of a pumping unit on an oil well pump should not have reasonably anticipated that a 13-year-old boy would climb onto the moving pendulum of the pump and attempt to ride the pendulum; thus the manufacturer was not liable because the damage did not arise out of a "reasonably anticipated use" of the product. *Payne v. Gardner*, 56 So. 3d 229 (La. 2011), *reh'g denied*, 62 So. 3d 104, 2010-2627 (La. 2011).

4.   Duty to Rescue

Under what circumstances might an actor be under a duty to rescue? If there is a duty to rescue, what injuries will be within the scope of the duty if the rescue is performed negligently? Consider the following sections from the Restatement (Second) of Torts:

§ 321.   Duty To Act When Prior Conduct Is Found To Be Dangerous

(1) If the actor does an act, and subsequently realizes or should realize that it has created an unreasonable risk of causing physical harm to another, he is under a duty to exercise reasonable care to prevent the risk from taking effect.

(2) The rule stated in Subsection (1) applies even though at the time of the act the actor has no reason to believe that it will involve such a risk.

§ 322.   Duty To Aid Another Harmed By Actor's Conduct

If the actor knows or has reason to know that by his conduct, whether tortious or innocent, he has caused such bodily harm to another as to make him helpless and in danger of further harm, the actor is under a duty to exercise reasonable care to prevent such further harm.

§ 323.   Negligent Performance Of Undertaking To Render Services

One who undertakes, gratuitously or for consideration, to render services to another which he should recognize as necessary for the protection of the other's person or things, is subject to liability to the other for physical harm resulting from his failure to exercise reasonable care to perform his undertaking, if

(a) his failure to exercise such care increases the risk of such harm, or

(b) the harm is suffered because of the other's reliance upon the undertaking.

§ 324. Duty Of One Who Takes Charge Of Another Who Is Helpless

One who, being under no duty to do so, takes charge of another who is helpless adequately to aid or protect himself is subject to liability to the other for any bodily harm caused to him by

(a) the failure of the actor to exercise reasonable care to secure the safety of the

232

other while within the actor's charge, or

> (b) the actor's discontinuing his aid or protection, if by so doing he leaves the other in a worse position than when the actor took charge of him.

One might conclude that there is a duty to rescue if there is a special relationship between the defendant and the person in need to rescue. Special relationships imposing a duty to rescue or a duty to act may include parent and child, spouses, teacher and student or someone else taking control of a child and the child, employer and employee, jailer and prisoner, common carrier and passenger, innkeeper and guest, and possibly more. Alternatively, one may assume a duty to act. Once one begins to act to help another, there may be a duty to exercise reasonable care to continue to help. Consider the above quoted Restatement (Second) sections. *See also, Kadlec Medical Center v. Lakeview Anesthesia Associates* 527 F.3d 412 (5th Cir. 2008) (a person who writes a referral letter about a former employee assumes a duty not to make affirmativemisrepresentations; however, in the absence of a fiduciary or contractual duty, a person does not have an affirmative duty to disclose negative information).

5. Slip and Fall

[handwritten: statute only applies to merchants ↓ defined in (c)(2)]

La. R.S. 9:2800.6. Burden of proof in claims against merchants

A. A merchant owes a duty to persons who use his premises to exercise reasonable care to keep his aisles, passageways, and floors in a reasonably safe condition. This duty includes a reasonable effort to keep the premises free of any hazardous conditions which reasonably might give rise to damage.

[handwritten: Typical Slip & fall → special duty = reasonable care to keep reasonable safe condition]

B. In a negligence claim brought against a merchant by a person lawfully on the merchant's premises for damages as a result of an injury, death, or loss sustained because of a fall due to a condition existing in or on a merchant's premises, the claimant shall have the burden of proving, in addition to all other elements of his cause of action, all of the following:

> (1) The condition presented an unreasonable risk of harm to the claimant and that risk of harm was reasonably foreseeable.

> (2) The merchant either created or had actual or constructive notice of the condition which caused the damage, prior to the occurrence.

> (3) The merchant failed to exercise reasonable care. In determining reasonable care, the absence of a written or verbal uniform cleanup or safety procedure is insufficient, alone, to prove failure to exercise reasonable care.

[handwritten: → no safety procedure is in itself NOT enough to met burden on this element]

C. Definitions:

> (1) "Constructive notice" means the claimant has proven that the condition existed for such a period of time that it would have been discovered if the merchant had exercised reasonable care. The presence of an employee of the merchant in the vicinity in which the condition exists does not, alone, constitute constructive notice, unless it is shown that the employee knew, or in the exercise of reasonable care should have known, of the condition.

[handwritten: → one who sells things at fixed place of biz.]

> (2) "Merchant" means one whose business is to sell goods, foods, wares, or merchandise at a fixed place of business. For purposes of this Section, a merchant includes an innkeeper with respect to those areas or aspects of the premises which are similar to those of a merchant, including but not limited to shops, restaurants, and lobby areas of or within the hotel, motel, or inn. *[handwritten: parking lots]*

D. Nothing herein shall affect any liability which a merchant may have under Civil Code Arts. 660, 667, 669, 2317, 2322, or 2695.

[handwritten: should have cleaned — but-for
① merchant
② rule of law
③ cause in fact
④ duty
⑤ breach
⑥ created condition
⑦ actual know.
⑧ const. know.
⑨ scope
⑩ ease of assoc.
⑪ damages]

233

skipped.... just tell
us that statute
applied to bar

BALLAS
v.
KENNY'S KEY WEST, INC.
836 So. 2d 289 (La.App. 5 Cir. 2002)

DALEY, J.

The plaintiff, Keith Ballas, has appealed the trial court judgment in favor of the defendant, Kenny's Key West, Inc. For the reasons that follow, we affirm.

Facts

Plaintiff filed suit against the defendant alleging that he slipped and fell in a puddle of water that was leaking from a container used by defendant to cool beer. He alleged strict liability on the part of defendant. Defendant answered with a general denial and claimed plaintiff's injuries were caused by his own negligence. The plaintiff was an engineer and subcontractor for The Sound Source, a concert production company that was contracted to provide sound for music at defendant's place of business, a lounge in Jefferson Parish. Part of plaintiff's responsibilities in preparation for a concert were to bring in and set up all sound equipment and dismantle and remove the equipment after the concert. Plaintiff testified that on the night of August 20, 1997, as he was taking down a speaker cabinet with the help of a co-employee, his right leg slipped out from under him causing him to fall on his left knee. When asked what may have caused his accident, plaintiff testified that he noticed water on the floor. He explained that his pants were damp and there was water on his boots. Plaintiff testified that there was a large metal tub from which the defendant was selling cold beer about six to eight feet from the location of the speaker cabinet. He testified that he never saw anyone mop or inspect the area around the tub during the entire night. He further testified that there was no non-skid material around the tub, nor was he given any warning of a dangerous condition by the defendant's employees. Plaintiff testified that he reported the accident to Linda Milto, a manager of Kenney's Key West, on the night of the accident. He sought medical treatment and was diagnosed as having a partially torn ligament in his knee.

On cross-examination, plaintiff testified that he did not recall looking around before taking down the speaker. He further testified that he had no idea how long the water had been on the floor. He explained that had he looked down he would not have been able to see the water because it was too dark.

Linda Milto testified that she had worked at Kenney's Key West for eight and a half years. She explained that the policy at the lounge regarding spills was for all employees to report any spills. There are mops, as well as wet floor signs, to be used in the event of a spill. She testified that there are two employees stationed in the concert room and it is their job to constantly walk the floor. Ms. Milto was not aware of any spills on the night of August 20, 1997. She testified that the beer tubs did not leak that night. She testified that the beer tub sits on a wooden block that sits on top of carpet. Ms. Milto testified that the person working the beer tub would call management or the bar back if there was a problem with condensation around the floor of the beer tub. She denied that plaintiff reported his accident to her on the night that it occurred; rather she stated that she became aware of plaintiff's accident at a later date.

At the conclusion of the trial, the trial judge found no liability on the part of defendant. This timely appeal followed.

Law and Discussion

On appeal, the plaintiff argues that the trial court erred in applying R.S. 9:2800.6 to this case because the defendant's establishment does not fit the definition of "merchant" within the statute.

R.S. 9:2800.6 sets forth plaintiff's burden of proof in order to recover for injuries sustained in a slip and fall accident ...

234

[*see* 9:2800.6 *supra*]

Plaintiff contends that the defendant's establishment does not sell goods, food, wares, or merchandise, like a typical retailer or restaurant, and that the conditions inside the establishment on the night of the accident were not similar to those inside of a retailer or restaurant. While we agree with plaintiff that the conditions inside defendant's establishment are not similar to those of a typical retailer, we nevertheless find that R.S. 9:2800.6 does apply to this situation. Under the broad definition of merchant, defendant's establishment sells goods and food at a fixed place of business. Additionally, in *Nuccio v. Robert,* 99-1327 (La.App. 5 Cir. 2000), 761 So. 2d 84, this court analyzed the plaintiff's burden of proof in a slip and fall that occurred at a bar under the provisions of R.S. 9:2800.6.

Plaintiff next argues that if R.S. 9:2800.6 applies, he met his burden of proof. In support of his position, plaintiff states that defendant served beer from tubs in a manner that created a dangerous condition that would reasonably be expected to cause injury to plaintiff. Plaintiff contends that the tubs leaked and/or there was no provision for preventing liquids accumulating from this method of selling beer from falling to the floor. He submits that his testimony established that no one inspected the floor for liquid during the concert. Plaintiff further contends that he could not have seen the liquid on the floor because it was too dark.

In his reasons for finding there was no liability on the part of defendants, the trial judge stated that there was no testimony or evidence that there was a puddle on the floor. A close reading of the transcript indicates that plaintiff never testified that he slipped in a puddle of water or that there was water on the floor. Rather, he testified:

Q: Was there anything--was there anything on you to indicate what you may have fallen on or in?

A: Yes, there was, you know, my pants--my seat pants were damp and I had water on my boots.

The trial court obviously concluded that this single reference to damp pants and water on plaintiff's boots did not establish to the trial court's satisfaction that a puddle caused plaintiff's fall. Further, Ms. Milto testified that two employees were stationed in this room to constantly walk the floors and there were no reports of spills or puddles on the night of the accident. Ms. Milto further testified that the beer tubs were elevated 15 to 18 inches above the dance floor and that a carpet was placed under the tubs.

Given this testimony, we cannot say that the trial judge erred in concluding that plaintiff failed to carry his burden of proving that the selling of beer from the tubs created an unreasonable risk of harm to the claimant, that the risk of harm was reasonably foreseeable, and that the defendant had constructive notice of this condition.

The plaintiff further argues that Ms. Milto was a surprise witness and should not have been allowed to testify. The record indicates that Ms. Milto's name did not appear on defendant's witness list or on defendant's pre-trial order. However, plaintiff knew that he reported this accident to Ms. Milto and in Answers to Interrogatories, defendant stated that a statement had been taken from Ms. Milto. Additionally, defendant's witness list stated that a representative from Kenny's Key West would be called to testify. While we agree with the trial judge that Ms. Milto's name should have been listed on the witness list or pre-trial order by defendant, it is clear from the record that plaintiff knew who Ms. Milto was. It is unclear from the record why plaintiff chose not to depose Ms. Milto prior to trial. We do not find the trial judge erred in allowing Ms. Milto to testify. Moreover, plaintiff failed to carry his burden of proof even in the absence of Ms. Milto's testimony.

For the foregoing reasons, the judgment of the trial court is **AFFIRMED**.

Under R.S. 9:2800.6, a person allegedly injured because of a condition on a merchant's premises must make a positive showing of the existence of the condition prior to the fall. A claimant who simply shows that the condition existed, without an additional showing that the condition existed for some time before the fall, does not carry the burden of proving constructive notice as mandated by the statute. The absence of repair or maintenance for a period of three years prior to the incident does not prove that the merchant had constructive notice of the condition at the time of the fall. *Glass v. Home Depot U.S.A., Inc.,* 50 So. 3d 832 (La.App. 5 Cir. 2010).

NOTES

1.   Does a merchant's failure to comply with its own inspection procedures establish constructive notice of an unreasonably dangerous condition? *See Luft v. Winn-Dixie Montgomery, LLC,* ____ So. 3d____(La.App. 5 Cir. 2017) (no).

2.   Regarding proof of constructive notice, consider:

> A defendant merchant does not have to make a positive showing of the absence of the existence of the condition prior to the fall.... A claimant who simply shows that the condition existed without an additional showing that the condition existed for some time before the fall has not carried the burden of proving constructive notice as mandated by the statute.... Though the time period need not be specific in minutes or hours, constructive notice requires that the claimant prove the condition existed for some time period prior to the fall.

White v. Wal-Mart Stores, Inc., 699 So. 2d 1081, 1084-85 (La. 1997).

3.   Do you think that comparative fault should apply in slip-and-fall cases? The Louisiana Supreme Court held that it does, rejecting an argument that the statute imposes a nondelegable duty on a merchant that precludes the application of comparative fault. *Thompson v. Winn-Dixie Montgomery, Inc.,* 181 So. 3d 656 (La. 2015).

4.   Falling merchandise cases are governed by 9:2800.6(A), but not (B):

> This court has held in *Smith v. Toys "R" Us, Inc., et al.,* 98-2085 (La. 1999), 754 So. 2d 209, *writ denied,* 772 So. 2d 652 (La. 2000), that the heightened burden under R.S. 9:2800.6(B) is applicable only in situations where a customer "falls" on a merchant's premises. In a "falling merchandise" case under R.S. 9:2800.6(A), as in the present case, the standard is that the merchant must use reasonable care to keep its aisles, passageways and floors in a reasonably safe condition and free of hazards which may cause injury. Further, a plaintiff who is injured by falling merchandise must prove, even by circumstantial evidence, that a premise hazard existed. *Id.* Once a plaintiff proves a prima facie premise hazard, the defendant has the burden to exculpate itself from fault by showing that it used reasonable care to avoid such hazards by means such as periodic clean up and inspection procedures. *Id.*

Davis v. Wal-Mart Stores, Inc., 774 So. 2d 84, 90 (La. 2000), *reh'g denied,* 785 So.2d 819, 2000-0445 (La. 2001).

5.   Should placement of a three-foot-high yellow warning cone be adequate for merchant to avoid liability if the floor is wet where cone is placed? *Bertaut v. Corral Gulfsouth, Inc.,* 209 So. 3d 352 (La.App. 5 Cir. 2016) (yes).

6.   **Grossly Negligent Actors**

A grossly negligent actor's conduct may bar or reduce his recovery from a defendant. *See* Chapter 7. But does it break the chain of causation between the original actor and a third person injured by a combination of the original act and the intervening grossly negligent actor? *See, e.g.,*

Curry v. Johnson, 590 So. 2d 1213 (La.App. 1 Cir. 1991) – the scope of the highway department's duty to construct and maintain highways in a safe manner does not include the risk of injury or death caused by the gross negligence of a third party motorist. *See also, Tassin v. State Farm Ins. Co.*, 692 So. 2d 604 (La.App. 3 Cir. 1997) – the state's duty to maintain highway shoulders does not extend to the risk that (1) a motorist would become stuck in the mud on the shoulder, (2) a "good Samaritan," attempting to extricate the motorist, would block the highway, and (3) plaintiff, driving under the influence of alcohol, would fail to heed the warnings of flagmen and collide with the "good Samaritan's " truck.

In *Graves v. Page*, motorist, injured when a felon fleeing police pursuit lost control of his automobile and crossed into motorist's lane of traffic, sought damages against the DOTD because vegetation growing within the highway right of way obscured motorist's view of oncoming traffic. The Supreme Court reversed an assessment of 10% fault against the DOTD, the lead opinion observing that the DOTD's duty to maintain the roadways and shoulders does not encompass the risk that an intoxicated oncoming driver, traveling at a high rate of speed, will cross over into a motorist's lane of travel. 688 So. 2d 1061 (La. 1997).

An actor's conduct may be so grossly negligent that it is not "foreseeable" to a negligent actor whose fault coalesces with the grossly negligent conduct to cause harm. In such a case, a Louisiana court may hold that the grossly negligent conduct is not within the scope of the risks created by the negligent actor. *See, e.g., Davis v. Witt*, 851 So. 2d 1119 (La. 2003) (professional truck driver's conduct was reckless and unreasonable when, with full knowledge of the perils to the motoring public, he backed his tractor trailer with an unlighted, dangerous load across the highway at night; such conduct was unforeseeable, thus relieving law enforcement officers of any liability to the third party victims).

In *Netecke v. State*, 747 So. 2d 489 (La. 1999), defendant driver, allegedly to avoid hitting a cat: (1) steered her car on to the paved shoulder and then on to the adjacent unpaved grassy area, and (2) while so traveling, allegedly perceived a "brown embankment" that caused her to oversteer her car back onto the highway and injure plaintiff. The jury assessed DOTD with 98% of the fault and defendant driver with 2%; the appellate court reduced DOTD's percentage to 50%. Relieving the DOTD of any liability, the Supreme Court remarks that "DOTD's legal duty did not encompass the risk that a driver, in an effort to avoid a cat in the opposite lane of travel, will intentionally drive her vehicle out of her travel lane and paved shoulder and onto the adjacent grassy area without stopping or significantly slowing her vehicle and then overcorrect her mistake when she perceives something that was not there."

The state has no duty to bring old highways up to current safety standards, unless the highway has undergone major reconstruction. The state does have a duty to correct conditions existing on old highways that are unreasonably dangerous. However, the state's duty to maintain old highways does not include the risk that an intoxicated driver will fall asleep and drive off the road at a sharp angle, failing to see a clearly visible roadside obstacle 17 feet from the shoulder, i.e., the back slope of the ditch. *Cormier v. Comeaux*, 748 So. 2d 1123 (La. 1999).

A manufacturer's liability for making a product with an unreasonably dangerous characteristic extends to the risk that the dealer who discovers the defect may fail to notify the buyer and provide safety instructions, where the dealer's conduct is not deliberate, wanton, willful or extraordinary in character. *Masters v. Courtesy Ford Company, Inc.*, 758 So. 2d 171 (La.App. 2 Cir. 2000).

7.   **Providers of Alcohol**

La. R.S. 9:2800.1. Limitation of liability for loss connected with sale, serving, or furnishing of alcoholic beverages

A.   The legislature finds and declares that the consumption of intoxicating beverages, rather than the sale or serving or furnishing of such beverages, is the proximate cause of any injury, including death and property damage, inflicted by an intoxicated person upon himself or upon another person.

B. Notwithstanding any other law to the contrary, no person holding a permit under either Chapter 1 or Chapter 2 of Title 26 of the Louisiana Revised Statutes of 1950, nor any agent, servant, or employee of such a person, who sells or serves intoxicating beverages of either high or low alcoholic content to a person over the age for the lawful purchase thereof, shall be liable to such person or to any other person or to the estate, successors, or survivors of either for any injury suffered off the premises, including wrongful death and property damage, because of the intoxication of the person to whom the intoxicating beverages were sold or served.

C. (1) Notwithstanding any other law to the contrary, no social host who serves or furnishes any intoxicating beverage of either high or low alcoholic content to a person over the age for the lawful purchase thereof shall be liable to such person or to any other person or to the estate, successors, or survivors of either for any injury suffered off the premises, including wrongful death and property damage, because of the intoxication of the person to whom the intoxicating beverages were served or furnished.

(2) No social host who owns, leases, or otherwise lawfully occupies premises on which, in his absence and without his consent, intoxicating beverages of either high or low alcoholic content are consumed by a person over the age for the lawful purchase thereof shall be liable to such person or to any other person or to the estate, successors, or survivors of either for any injury suffered off the premises, including wrongful death and property damage, because of the intoxication of the person who consumed the intoxicating beverages.

D. The insurer of the intoxicated person shall be primarily liable with respect to injuries suffered by third persons.

E. The limitation of liability provided by this Section shall not apply to any person who causes or contributes to the consumption of alcoholic beverages by force or by falsely representing that a beverage contains no alcohol.

BERG
v.
ZUMMO
786 So. 2d 708 (La. 2001)

VICTORY, J.

We granted this writ to determine whether the court of appeal erred in reversing a jury verdict against the defendant, LMJD, Inc., (the "Boot"), upon finding (1) that liability cannot be imposed against a bar owner who serves alcohol to a minor who becomes intoxicated and causes injury to others, and (2), that punitive damages cannot be assessed against a bar owner under La. Civ. Code art. 2315.4. After reviewing the record and the applicable law, we reverse the appellate court's finding that merely serving alcohol to a minor can never result in liability; however, we affirm the appellate court's ruling that the punitive damages statute does not allow the imposition of punitive damages against those who have contributed to the driver's intoxication.

Facts and Procedural History

Plaintiff, Matthew Berg ("Berg"), filed a negligence action against Philip Zummo ("Zummo"), several of his companions, and Zummo's insurance company, alleging that on June 15, 1994, at approximately 1:30 a.m., as Berg approached the intersection of Audubon Street and Zimple Street in New Orleans, Zummo and four companions, approached him, and, with no warning, accosted and beat him. Then, in leaving the scene, Zummo hit Berg with his truck, causing him serious bodily injury.

Zummo was criminally charged with aggravated battery as a result of this incident. At his criminal trial, which resulted in a not guilty verdict, Zummo testified that he was only 17 years old at the time of the incident and that he had been drinking beer inside The Boot, a bar in the university area, immediately before the incident. Based on this testimony, Berg amended his petition to name The Boot as a defendant and alleged that The Boot's negligence in serving Zummo alcohol was a proximate cause of his injuries. All of the parties except The Boot reached a settlement with Berg. On May 12, 1998, a four day trial commenced with The Boot as the only remaining defendant.

* * * * *

After a four day jury trial, the jury rendered a verdict in favor of Berg. In response to Special Jury Interrogatories, the jury found that the actions of The Boot "in serving alcoholic beverages to Philip Zummo was a cause in fact although it may not be the only cause in fact of the damages suffered by Matthew Berg as a result of the incident of June 5, 1994." Pursuant to this finding, they awarded general damages in the amount of $50,000.00 and past medical expenses in the amount of $3,600.00, and attributed fault in the following percentages: 40% to The Boot; 25% to Berg; 30% to Zummo, 2% to Madigans, and 1.5% each to two of Zummo's friends. Next, the jury found that Zummo exhibited a wanton or reckless disregard for the rights and safety of Berg and that he was intoxicated when he drove away from the scene of the incident in his truck. Further, the jury found that the intoxication of Zummo and his wanton or reckless disregard for the rights and safety of Berg was a proximate cause of the damages suffered by Berg. The jury found that The Boot was 45% responsible for Zummo's intoxication, Madigan's was 15% responsible, and Zummo was 40% responsible, and fixed punitive damages at $50,000.00. The trial court entered judgment in accordance with the verdict.

The Fourth Circuit reversed, finding as a matter of law that "merely serving alcohol to an underage person who becomes intoxicated and causes injury to others or to himself is not an 'affirmative act' which can result in liability of the bar." *Berg v. Zummo*, 99-CA-0974 (La. App. 4 Cir. 5/10/00), 763 So. 2d 57. In addition, the court of appeal reversed the punitive damages award, finding, as a matter of law, that the punitive damages statute does not allow the imposition of punitive damages against persons who have allegedly contributed to the driver's intoxication. *Id.* We granted Berg's writ to consider these two legal issues. *Berg v. Zummo*, 00-1699 (La. 10/22/00), 767 So. 2d 710.

Discussion

This Court first addressed the imposition of liability on a seller of alcoholic beverages for damages in *Lee v. Peerless Ins. Co.*, 248 La. 982, 183 So. 2d 328 (1966). In that case, we held that a vendor was not liable for damages incurred by an intoxicated patron who was injured when he was hit by a car after being ejected from a nightclub next to a busy highway. This holding was based on the fact that Louisiana had never had a "dramshop"[1] law and that under our jurisprudence, "the proximate cause of the injury is the act of the purchaser in drinking the liquor and not the act of the vendor in selling it." 183 So. 2d at 330. Ten years later, in a factually similar case, this Court overruled *Lee* and held that a vender could be liable for the breach of two duties: (1) the statutory duty imposed on retailers to refrain from serving alcoholic beverages to an intoxicated person under La. R.S. 26:88(2); and (2) the duty of the vendor under La. C.C. arts. 2315 and 2316 as a business invitor to conform their conduct to that of a reasonable man under like circumstances, which duty requires that they refrain from affirmative acts which increase the peril to the intoxicated person. *Pence v. Ketchum*, 326 So. 2d 831,835 (La. 1976). Three years later, in a case where an intoxicated adult patron was injured when he was ejected from a bar, this Court overruled *Pence* in part, holding that:

---

[1] The term "dram shop" is derived from the fact that commercial establishments typically sold liquor by the dram, a unit of measurement less than a gallon, in the 1800's when "Dram Shop" Acts were first introduced in this country. *Godfrey v. Boston Old Colony Ins. Co.*, 97-2568 (La. App. 4 Cir. 1998), 718 So. 2d 441, n. 2, *writ denied*, 98-2487 (La. 1998). In those states which have enacted "Dram Shop" Acts, strict liability, irrespective of negligence, is imposed upon the seller of intoxicating liquors because of the purchaser's intoxication. Prosser, Law of Torts, § 81.

There is, and should be, no absolute liability imposed upon an alcoholic beverage retailer for the consequence of a patron's intoxication. As this Court observed in *Lee*, Louisiana has never had a civil damage or "dramshop" statute. Regardless of whether the prohibition of R.S. 26:88(2) is purely and simply criminal in nature or has attendant civil consequences the cause more proximate to an injury to an inebriated patron which results from his intoxication is the consumption of the alcohol and not the sale.

Thrasher v. Leggett, 373 So. 2d 494, 496 (La. 1979). However, this Court held that *"Pence* was correct in finding that Article 2315 imposes upon a bar owner a duty to avoid affirmative acts which increase the peril to an intoxicated person" and that "it is not inappropriate as in *Pence* to find that a proprietor who closes his establishment and puts an intoxicated patron out on a busy highway breaches his duty not to increase his patron's peril." *Id.* at 497. We held that "[u]nder Article 2315 the proper standard to determine whether a bar owner has breached his duty to an intoxicated patron is whether his conduct was that generally required of a reasonable man under like circumstances." *Id.* Applying the reasonable man standard under La. C.C. art. 2315, we concluded that "the defendant is not responsible for the ensuing harm to this patron caused, not by any affirmative act of defendant's, but simply by plaintiff's inebriated condition" because the defendant's bouncer had a right and duty to remove the disruptive plaintiff from the premises using reasonable force under the circumstances. *Id.*

In this Court's first case dealing with liability arising from the service of alcohol to a minor, we rejected the plaintiffs' contention that absolute liability should be imposed on a minor social host who serves intoxicating liquor to another minor. *Gresham v. Davenport*, 537 So. 2d 1144, 148 (La. 1989) (applying pre-1986 law). We explained that this State has never implemented dramshop liability statutes against providers of alcoholic beverages and that instead, "we have chosen to apply the well accepted duty risk analysis to claims of injuries caused by effects of alcoholic beverages." *Id.*[2] Likewise, in *St. Hill v. Tabor*, we applied the duty-risk analysis to determine that an adult social host was negligent for serving alcohol to a minor who drowned during a large and raucous swimming party at her home, allowing the pool to become so cloudy that it was impossible to see to the bottom of the pool, and not having a life guard to supervise the swimmers. *St. Hill v. Tabor*, 542 So. 2d 499 (La. 1989). In these two social host cases involving the provision of alcohol to minors, this Court applied the basic duty-risk analysis, e.g., that the conduct of which the plaintiff complains must be a cause-in-fact of the harm, and that, after determining causation, the court must also determine what was the duty imposed on defendant, and whether the risk which caused the accident was within the scope of the duty. In these two cases involving minors, there was no requirement of an "affirmative act" on the part of the social host that increased the minor's risk of harm.

In 1986, the Louisiana Legislature enacted La. R.S. 9:2800.1, entitled "Limitation of Liability for loss connected with sale, serving, or furnishing of alcoholic beverages" which provides as follows:

> A.   The Legislature finds and declares that the consumption of intoxicating beverages, rather than the sale or serving or furnishing of such beverages, is the proximate cause of any injury, including death and property damage, inflicted by an intoxicated person upon himself or upon another person.
>
> B.   Notwithstanding any other law to the contrary, no person holding a permit under either Chapter 1 or Chapter 2 of Title 26 of the Louisiana Revised Statutes of 1950, nor any agent, servant, or employee of such a person, who sells or serves intoxicating beverages of either high or low alcohol content <u>to a person over the age for the lawful purchase thereof</u>, shall be liable to such person or to any other person or to the estate, successors, or survivors of either for any injury suffered off the

---

[2] In *Gresham*, we found that although the alcohol provided by the minor social host was a cause-in-fact of the minor's automobile accident, the minor social host had no duty not to provide alcohol to another minor, and, even if she did have such a duty, the risk that the minor she served, who was a passenger in the vehicle, would grab the steering wheel and cause an accident did not fall within the scope of the duty.

premises, including wrongful death and property damage, because of the intoxication of the person to whom the intoxicating beverages were sold or served. (Emphasis added.)

La. R.S. 9:2800.1(A) places the responsibility for the consequences of intoxication on the intoxicated person by providing that it is the consumption of alcohol, rather than the sale, service or furnishing of alcohol, that is the proximate cause of any injury inflicted by an intoxicated person. In furtherance of La. R.S. 9:2800.1(A), subsection (B) provides immunity to vendors of alcoholic beverages who sell or serve alcohol to persons "over the age for the lawful purpose thereof."[3]

However, this immunity is only provided for damages resulting from the sale or service of alcohol to persons over the age for the lawful purchase of alcohol. Although La. R.S. 9:2800.1(A) has no specific language limiting its application to persons over the age for the lawful purchase of alcohol, it must be read *in pari materia* with La. R.S. 9:2800.1(B), which does have such language. La. R.S. 9:2800.1(B) would be superfluous if La. R.S. 9:2800.1(A) was meant to provide across the board immunity for damages resulting from the service of alcohol to minors and adults. La. R.S. 9:2800.1(C), which provides the same immunity for social hosts who provide alcohol to persons 21 years or older, would likewise be superfluous. If the Legislature intended that bar owners be absolutely immune from liability for the sale or service of alcoholic beverages to persons under 21 years of age who cause damage because of their intoxication, it would not have limited the immunity in La. R.S. 9:2800.1(B) to the sale or service of such beverages "to a person over the age for the lawful purchase thereof."

As every court of appeal that has considered this issue has recognized, when a bar serves alcohol to a minor and that minor causes damage to another because of his intoxication, La. R.S. 9:2800.1 does not immunize it from liability, nor is it absolutely liable; instead, the court must determine whether the vendor violated general negligence principles, applying the traditional duty/risk analysis. *See Godfrey v. Boston Old Colony Ins. Co., supra; Hopkins v. Sovereign Fire & Cas. Ins. Co.,* 626 So. 2d 880 (La.App. 3 Cir. 1993), *writ denied,* 634 So. 2d 390 (La. 1994); *Mills v. Harris,* 615 So. 2d 533 (La.App. 3 Cir. 1993); *Edson v. Walker,* 573 So. 2d 545 (La.App. 1 Cir. 1991), *writ denied,* 576 So. 2d 34 (La. 1991). However, the Fourth Circuit in *Godfrey* held that under the duty/risk analysis, the alcoholic beverage vendor's duty includes: (1) a duty to act as a reasonable person under the circumstances of the case, and (2) a duty not to commit any affirmative acts which increase the peril caused by the intoxication. *Godfrey, supra* at 454. In *Mills,* the Third Circuit, as part of its duty/risk analysis, cited *Thrasher* for the legal proposition that "merely serving alcoholic drinks to an intoxicated person is not an affirmative act which would impose liability under LSA-C.C. 2315." *Mills, supra* at 535. The courts in *Edson* and *Hopkins* mentioned no such "affirmative act" requirement.

In this case, the Fourth Circuit applied the standard set out by *Godfrey,* that "in cases in which a bar has sold alcohol to an underage person, and the underage person has then been involved in a tort as a result of intoxication, the application of general negligence principles and the duty/risk analysis required that, before the bar can be held liable, it must be proven that (1) the bar failed to exercise the care of a reasonable person under the circumstances and (2) the bar committed some 'affirmative act'

---

[3] This Court has never addressed, nor do we address today, whether the bar owner can be liable in spite of La. R.S. 9:2800.1 for taking an affirmative act which increases the peril to an intoxicated adult patron under the pre-La. R.S. 9:2800.1 reasoning of *Thrasher v. Leggett.* In *Mayo v. Hyatt Corp.,* 898 F. 2d 47 (5th Cir. 1990), the United States Fifth Circuit Court of Appeal held that under La. R.S. 9:2800.1, "the sole duty of a seller of alcoholic beverages is to avoid taking "affirmative acts which increase the peril to an intoxicated person." 898 F. 2d at 49 (citing *Thrasher v. Leggett, supra*).

which 'increased the peril' posed by the minor's intoxication." Slip Op. at 5. Then, relying on the holding in *Mills*, the court of appeal held that "[m]erely serving alcohol to an underage person who becomes intoxicated and causes injury to others or to himself is not an 'affirmative act' which can result in liability to the bar." *Id.* The court equated an "affirmative act" with ejectment from the premises and found that because Zummo "simply left The Boot in an ordinary way," there was a complete absence of any basis to impose liability on The Boot.

The "affirmative act" requirement, specifically unreasonable ejectment from the premises, was put into place by this Court in *Thrasher*, as a requirement to impose liability on an alcoholic beverage vendor who serves alcohol to an intoxicated <u>adult</u>. However, the difference between selling and serving alcohol to an adult and a minor is tremendous. Legislation has been enacted specifically pertaining to the sale of alcohol to minors,[4] and although those statutes impose criminal, rather than civil, responsibility, they serve as guidelines for the determination of an alcoholic beverage vendor's duty to refrain from selling or serving alcohol to minors. It further evidences the public policy of this state to prohibit the sale of alcohol to minors and to protect minors and the general public from the effects of a minor's intoxication, particularly when the minor is operating an automobile. The court of appeal's holding that serving alcohol to a minor is not an affirmative act which can result in liability would allow alcoholic beverage vendors throughout the state to sell and serve alcohol to minors in violation of state law without fear of civil liability and, thus, we reject that holding.

As we stated in *Gresham*, a suit involving a minor social host providing alcohol to another minor, this Court has "chosen to apply the well accepted duty risk analysis to claims of injuries caused by the effects of alcoholic beverages." Thus under the duty/risk analysis, the plaintiff must prove five separate elements: (1) the defendant had a duty to conform his conduct to a specific standard (the duty element); (2) the defendant failed to conform his conduct to the appropriate standard (the breach of duty element); (3) the defendant's substandard conduct was a cause-in-fact of the plaintiff's injuries (the cause-in-fact element); (4) the defendant's substandard conduct was a legal cause of the plaintiff's injuries (the scope of liability or scope of protection element; and, (5) actual damages (the damage element). *Roberts v. Benoit*, 605 So. 2d 1032, 1051 (La. 1991) (on rehearing).

First, it must be determined what duty was imposed on The Boot and whether The Boot breached that duty. We find that a vendor of alcoholic beverages has a duty to refrain from selling or serving alcohol to minors. Moreover, it is illegal. The Boot clearly breached that duty by serving alcohol to Zummo, a seventeen year old. The jury heard testimony from Zummo that his identification was not checked when he entered The Boot or when he purchased the pitcher of beer.

Next, it must be determined if the conduct of which the plaintiff complains is a cause-in-fact of the harm. "Negligent conduct is a cause-in-fact of harm to another if it was a substantial factor in bringing about that harm." *Gresham, supra* at 1147. The jury in this case heard four days of testimony and answered a special jury interrogatory finding that the actions of The Boot in serving alcoholic beverages to Zummo was a cause in fact, although it might not have been the only cause in fact, of the damages suffered by Berg (the jury assessed 60% of the fault to others). The jury heard testimony from Berg that as he approached Zummo and his four friends that they appeared intoxicated and they attacked him for no apparent reason, and then Zummo ran over him in his truck in his attempt to quickly leave the scene, going the wrong way down a one way street. Further, the jury heard the testimony of Jill McCoy who witnessed Zummo and his friends beating up Berg, one friend throwing a drink on Berg from the back of the truck, and then Zummo's truck screeching out of its

---

[4] In 1994, La. R.S. 14:91 applied, making it illegal to sell alcohol to anyone under the age of 18. Today, La. R.S. 14:93.11 makes the sale or delivery of alcohol to a person under the age of 21 illegal. Likewise, La. R.S. 14:93.12 makes the purchase or possession of alcohol by anyone under the age of 21 illegal.

parking spot, striking Berg, fishtailing, and then speeding the wrong way down a one-way street. It also heard Zummo testify that he drank as much as a half a pitcher of beer at The Boot. The jury clearly believed Berg's evidence, and not the testimony of Zummo and his friends who testified they were not intoxicated and that the beer they drank at The Boot played no part in their conduct. We cannot say that the jury finding was manifestly erroneous.

Next, it must be determined whether the risk that caused the accident was within the scope of the duty. We find that the risk that a minor who is served alcohol might become intoxicated and get into a fight and injure someone with his car is clearly within the scope of the duty of The Boot not to serve alcohol to a minor. Finally, actual damages were proven.

Thus, we find that the jury's finding that The Boot was liable for general damages to Berg for its negligence in serving alcohol to Zummo was not manifestly erroneous and we reinstate the jury verdict in this regard.

We also granted this writ to determine whether the court of appeal erred in overturning the jury's verdict assessing a percentage of punitive damages against The Boot under La. C.C. art. 2315.4. La. C.C. art. 2315.4 provides:

> In addition to general and special damages, exemplary damages may be awarded upon proof that the injuries on which the action is based were caused by a wanton or reckless disregard for the rights and safety of others by a defendant whose intoxication while operating a motor vehicle was a cause in fact of the resulting injuries.

The court of appeal held that the punitive damages statute does not allow the imposition of punitive damages against persons who have allegedly contributed to the driver's intoxication. Slip Op. at 6. This issue is *res nova* before this Court although courts of appeal have considered whether punitive damages can be awarded against a party other than the intoxicated driver of the motor vehicle.

The Fourth Circuit Court of Appeal has held on two occasions that an intoxicated driver's employer, when held vicariously liable for damages caused by the driver, may be cast for exemplary damages under article 2315.4. *Lacoste v. Crochet,* 99-0602 (La.App. 4 Cir. 2000), 751 So. 2d 998; *Curtis v. Rome,* 98-0966-98-0970 (La.App. 4 Cir. 1999), 735 So. 2d 822. However, in a case involving vendors of alcoholic beverages, the Third Circuit has held that La. C.C. Art. 2315.4 limits those against whom punitive damages can be assessed to the intoxicated driver of the vehicle. *Bourque v. Bailey,* 93-1657 (La.App. 3 Cir. 1994), 643 So. 2d 236, *writ denied,* 94-2619 (La. 1994), 648 So. 2d 392. In holding that punitive damages could not be assessed against the store which sold alcohol to a minor who then provided it to another minor who caused an automobile accident, nor a bar which sold alcohol to an unnamed third party of legal age who then provided it the minor driver, the court relied in part on the legislative history of La. C.C. art. 2314.5. *Id.* at 239.

We have examined the legislative history of La. C.C. art. 2315.4, which was enacted by Acts 1984, No. 511, Section 1, and originated as House Bill 1051. The Minutes from the House Committee on Civil Law and Procedure clearly indicate that the bill was "targeted" at intoxicated drivers and was intended "to punish the intoxicated defendant ... [to] punish him financially the way he should be punished by paying additional damages." (Minutes from the House Committee on Civil Law and Procedure, June 4, 1984). Although there was some discussion about insurance coverage for such damages, there was no discussion that the bill would penalize anyone but the intoxicated driver.

We find that the legislative history reflects the legislature's intent to penalize only the intoxicated driver of motor vehicle and is in line with the narrow construction that this Court gives to penal statutes.[5] Thus, we affirm the court of appeal's holding that La. C.C. art. 2315.4 does not allow the imposition of punitive damages against persons who have allegedly contributed to the driver's intoxication.

Conclusion

The liability of a vender of alcoholic beverages who sells or serves alcohol to a person under the legal drinking age is determined under La. C.C. arts. 2315 and 2316 using the traditional duty/risk analysis on a case by case basis. Under this analysis, the vendor has the duty to refrain from selling or serving alcohol to a minor, and if the other requirements of breach of duty, causation and damages are proven, the vendor will be liable for damages. It is not necessary that the vendor commit an additional "affirmative act," such as ejecting the minor patron from the premises, that increases the peril of the intoxicated patron, in order for liability to be imposed.

However, under the punitive damages statute, La. C.C. art. 2315.4, punitive damages cannot be assessed against a vendor of alcoholic beverages for selling or serving alcohol to an intoxicated person whose intoxication while operating a motor vehicle causes injury.

* * * * *

CALOGERO, Chief Justice dissents and assigns reasons.

I would hold that, applying La.Rev.Stat. 9:2800.1(A) under our duty/risk analysis, the sale, serving, or furnishing of alcoholic beverages to a person under the age for lawful purchase, without any other act or omission on the part of the person selling, serving, or furnishing the alcoholic beverages that could be the legal cause of any injury inflicted by the intoxicated person, is not sufficient to impose liability on the person selling, serving, or furnishing the alcoholic beverage. Here, the plaintiff has not alleged that any other act of The Boot or breach of any other duty, other than selling Zummo a pitcher of beer, caused his damages. Consequently, I would affirm the appellate court's holding that The Boot is not liable for general damages under La.Civ.Code arts. 2315 or 2316.

MORRIS
v.
BULLDOG BR, LLC
147 So. 3d 1122 (La.App. 1 Cir. 2014)

McCLENDON, J.

The plaintiff appeals the judgment of the trial court, granting the defendant's peremptory exception raising the objection of no cause of action and dismissing his suit with prejudice. For the reasons that follow, we affirm.

Factual and Procedural History

On January 21, 2012, Daniel Morris and Nathaniel Crowson were riding their bicycles on Perkins Road in Baton Rouge, when they were struck from behind by a vehicle driven by Joseph Branch. Tragically, Mr. Crowson was killed, and Mr. Morris was severely injured. Mr. Morris filed suit on January 17, 2013, seeking to recover the damages he suffered. In his petition, Mr. Morris alleged that Mr. Branch was operating a motor vehicle, under the influence of alcohol, when the vehicle struck him and Mr. Crowson, causing his injuries and damages and causing the death of Mr. Crowson. Mr. Morris further alleged that prior to the subject accident, Mr. Branch was a patron at The Bulldog BR, LLC (The Bulldog), a Baton Rouge bar, where he drank a number of alcoholic beverages and was visibly intoxicated. Mr. Morris also asserted that The Bulldog "engaged in affirmative acts

---

[5] We express no view on whether punitive damages can be imposed against a party who is vicariously liable for general damages resulting from the conduct of an intoxicated person, such as an employer.

that increased the peril to [Mr. Branch], ultimately resulting in the subject incident."[1]

In response to the petition, The Bulldog filed a peremptory exception raising the objection of no cause of action, contending that it was immune from civil liability under LSA–R.S. 9:2800.1, Louisiana's "anti-dram shop" statute. A hearing on the exception was held on April 29, 2013. On June 21, 2013, the trial court issued its ruling sustaining the exception. On July 9, 2013, the trial court signed a judgment, dismissing The Bulldog from the proceeding with prejudice. Mr. **Morris** has appealed.

Standard of Review

* * * * *

Discussion

Prior to 1986, Louisiana did not have a "dramshop" law, and the imposition of liability on a seller of alcoholic beverages for damages sustained or caused by an intoxicated patron was determined by the application of general negligence principles (duty-risk analysis) under the "reasonable man" standard. *Aucoin v. Rochel*, 08–1180 (La.App. 1 Cir. 2008), 5 So. 3d 197, 200, *writ denied*, 09–0122 (La. 2009), 5 So. 3d 143. Moreover, Louisiana jurisprudence consistently opposed the application of absolute liability on an alcoholic beverage retailer for the consequences of a patron's intoxication. *See Thrasher v. Leggett*, 373 So. 2d 494, 496 (La. 1979).

Thereafter, in 1986, the Louisiana Legislature enacted LSA–R.S. 9:2800.1, entitled "Limitation of liability for loss connected with sale, serving, or furnishing of alcoholic beverages," with the express purpose of placing the responsibility for consequences of intoxication on the intoxicated person, rather than the server of the alcohol. *Aucoin*, 5 So. 3d at 201; *Berg v. Zummo*, 2000–1699 (La. 2001), 786 So. 2d 708, 713–14. Subsection A of LSA–R.S. 9:2800.1 provides specifically that "the *consumption* of intoxicating beverages, rather than the sale or serving or furnishing of such beverages *is the proximate cause of any injury*, ... inflicted by an intoxicated person upon himself or upon another person." (Emphasis added.) In furtherance of this stated goal, LSA–R.S. 9:2800.1B provides:

> Notwithstanding any other law to the contrary, *no person*.... nor any agent, servant, or employee of such a person, *who sells or serves intoxicating beverages* ... to a person over the age for the lawful purchase thereof, *shall be liable* to such person *or to any other person* ... for any injury suffered off the premises, including wrongful death and property damage, *because of the intoxication of the person to whom the intoxicating beverages were sold or served.* (Emphasis added.)

The only exceptions to the limitation of liability expressly provided by the statute are when alcoholic beverages are sold or served to minors (by omission under Subsection B) and to any person who causes or contributes to the consumption of alcoholic beverages by force or by falsely representing that a beverage contains no alcohol. LSA–R.S. 9:2800.1E;[2] *Aucoin*, 5 So. 3d at 201.

In this case, Mr. Morris argues, as did the plaintiff in the *Aucoin* case, that notwithstanding the clear wording of the statute, the pre-Statute reasoning of *Thrasher v. Legget* should apply to impose liability when the bar owner takes affirmative action that increases the peril of an intoxicated

---

[1] In the petition, The Bulldog was named a defendant, along with Mr. Branch; State Farm Insurance Company, Mr. Branch's insurer; and ABC Insurance Company, identified as The Bulldog's insurer.

[2] Subsection E provides:
The limitation of liability provided by this Section shall not apply to any person who causes or contributes to the consumption of alcoholic beverages by force or by falsely representing that a beverage contains no alcohol.

patron. Mr. Morris, like Mr. Aucoin, relies on dicta by the supreme court in the *Berg* case, wherein the court stated in a footnote that "[t]his [c]ourt has never addressed, nor do we address today, whether the bar owner can be liable in spite of La. R.S. 9:2800.1 for taking an affirmative act which increases the peril to an intoxicated *adult* patron under the pre-La. R.S. 9:2800.1 reasoning of *Thrasher v. Leggett.*" *Berg,* 786 So.2d at 714 n. 3. However, *Berg* involved damages resulting from the sale of alcohol to a minor and accordingly, was clearly outside the scope of immunity provided by the statute. Moreover, this statement simply acknowledged that the issue was not directly before the court.

We find the statutory language of LSA–R.S. 9:2800.1 to be clear and unambiguous, leaving no room for interpretation beyond the ordinary meaning of the words employed. *See Aucoin,* 5 So.3d at 203. Additionally, the statute itself provides exceptions, which have not been pled in this case. Accordingly, we are constrained to hold that the clear language of the statute provides immunity to The Bulldog for the injuries caused by the intoxication of Mr. Branch, when the only act alleged to have been committed by The Bulldog was serving alcohol to the intoxicated tortfeasor, who was of legal age.[3] As the trial court stated: "Other than an allegation that The Bulldog engaged in 'affirmative acts' there are no allegations against The Bulldog that would fall under the exceptions to the immunity statute.... There is no allegation that would result in liability. Thus, the exception of no cause of action is sustained."

We further find that the basis for the peremptory exception raising the objection of no cause of action cannot be removed by amendment of the petition. *See* LSA–C.C.P. art. 934. Based on the undisputed facts before us, neither exception to LSA–R.S. 9:2800.1 is applicable herein. Therefore, we cannot say that the trial court abused its discretion in failing to allow Mr. **Morris** the opportunity to amend his petition to remove the grounds of the objection.

Conclusion

Because The Bulldog is entitled to the immunity provided by LSA–R.S. 9:2800.1 for the acts of negligence alleged against it, we find that the trial court correctly sustained The Bulldog's peremptory exception raising the objection of no cause of action. Therefore, we affirm the July 9, 2013 judgment of the trial court, sustaining the exception and dismissing Mr. Morris's suit with prejudice. The costs of this appeal are assessed to Daniel Morris.

AFFIRMED.

NOTES

1.   In *Gresham v. Davenport*, the Supreme Court reviewed the liability of a minor for providing intoxicating beverages to another minor. The 15-year-old girl, hosting a party at her parent's house, provided beer to her 16-year-old boyfriend. Neither was a "novice to beer drinking." The boyfriend left the party with plaintiff and others; plaintiff was injured when boyfriend, a passenger in a vehicle, grabbed the steering wheel and caused an accident. The Court ruled that the minor was not absolutely liable for injuries caused by providing the intoxicating beverage to the minor. Turning to the negligence theory, the Court observed that "it would be doubtful that (the 15-year-old girl) had a duty not to serve beer to (the 16-year-old boyfriend). This is not to say that there could never be a case in which a minor may owe a duty to another minor not to provide him or her with alcoholic beverages." However, any duty which the minor may have owed did not encompass the risk that the boyfriend, a passenger in a vehicle, would grab the steering wheel and cause an accident. 537 So. 2d 1144 (La.

---

[3] In *Zapata v. Cormier,* 02–1801 (La.App. 1 Cir. 2003), 858 So. 2d 601, we applied the clear language of LSA–R.S. 9:2800.1 and held that several requirements must be met for the statutory immunity to apply: 1) the bar owner must hold a permit under either Chapter 1 or Chapter 2 of Title 26 of Louisiana Revised Statutes of 1950; 2) the bar owner, its agent and servants or employees, sell or serve intoxicating beverages of either high or low alcoholic content to a person over the age for a lawful purchase thereof; 3) the purchaser thereof suffers an injury off the premises including wrongful death and property damage; and 4) this injury or accident was caused by the intoxication of the person to whom the intoxicating beverages were sold or served. *Aucoin,* 5 So.3d at 203; *Zapata,* 858 So. 2d at 606–07. In this matter, no one has alleged that the requirements were not met.

1989). *See also, Hopkins v. Sovereign Fire & Cas. Ins.*, 626 So. 2d 880 (La.App. 3 Cir. 1993), *writ denied*, 634 So. 2d 390 (La. 1994) – La. R.S. 14:91.1, making it unlawful for a minor to "possess" any alcoholic beverage, does not impose a duty on the minor not to share the beverage with a friend, and a minor's providing another with wine does not encompass the risk that the recipient, an unlicensed driver, subsequently would drive while intoxicated. *See, also, Guy v. State Farm Mut. Ins. Co.*, 725 So. 2d 39 (La.App. 3 Cir. 1998), *writ denied*, 739 So. 2d 203 (La. 1999) (minor who obtains alcohol and furnishes it to another person who is under the legal drinking age is not liable for the tortious behavior of that person resulting from his or her consumption of the alcohol).

2.   In *Boudreaux v. Delchamps, Inc.*, 567 So. 2d 700 (La.App. 3 Cir. 1990), *writ denied*, 571 So. 2d 629 (La. 1990), the court held that a storeowner does not owe a duty to refrain from selling alcohol to a major when the major is accompanied by minors, or to inquire of a major lawfully purchasing beer whether he planned to violate the law by providing the alcohol to the minors.

3.   In *Kramer v. Continental Casualty Co.*, 641 So. 2d 557 (La.App. 3 Cir. 1994), *writ denied*, 648 So. 2d 402 (La. 1994), off-duty police officers, employed by motel as security guards, became aware that underage persons were possessing and consuming alcohol on the motel premises. The officers did not confiscate the beverages or halt the drinking, but ordered the youths to leave the premises. One of the youths was injured while a guest passenger of another of the youths in an auto accident which occurred minutes after they left the motel and which was caused in part by the host driver's intoxication. *Held*, the motel is liable through respondeat superior for the actions of the security guards, who owed a "special duty" (*see Stewart v. Schmieder*, 386 So. 2d 1351 (La. 1980)) to enforce R.S. 14:91.1.2 (unlawful for minors to possess alcoholic beverages).

4.   In *Vaughan v. Hair*, 645 So. 2d 1177 (La.App. 3 Cir. 1994), *writ denied*, 650 So. 2d 1186 (La. 1995), the court held that an employer which allows its employees to consume alcoholic beverages on its premises after they finish working for the day is a "social host" entitled to the protection of R.S. 9:2800.1.

5.   Does a bar operator lose the immunity provided by La. R.S. 9:2800.1 by serving alcohol after legally mandated closing hour to an intoxicated patron who is subsequently killed in a motor vehicle accident? *See Roy v. Kryles, Inc.*, 983 So. 2d 975 (La.App. 3 Cir. 2008).

6.   For an excellent duty-risk analysis of the potential liability of a vendor of alcoholic beverages to underage persons who subsequently injure third parties, *see Brodnax v. Foster*, 92 So. 3d 427 (La.App. 2 Cir. 2012). There, defendant convenience store owner's duty not to sell alcoholic beverages to a 19 year old did not encompass the risk that the young man would, after several hours of drinking, severely burn a friend by throwing gasoline onto a fire. The court stated as follows:

> A primary policy underlying the duty of the alcohol vendor is to prevent the societal risk of the impaired driving of underage persons. Importantly, however, a violation of that policy in this case was not a cause of the accident. Instead, there were two intervening factors. The trial court weighed the facts concerning the other adults' responsibility for Nolan's drinking. Brodnax and Foster were obviously aware of the younger Nolan's inebriated state. Their decisions were to not discourage his conduct, but to participate with him in what Brodnax now asserts as Nolan's misuse of alcohol. The second intervening factor was the participants' choice to mix gasoline with the fire. This use of gasoline on that evening was not a one-time accidental occurrence with a sudden ignition that surprised the participants. There was a continuous pattern of horseplay lighting the gasoline on and around the bonfire, and those actions had occurred for some time before the final fire consumed Brodnax. The trial court could consider the timing and the facts of the prior accident with the smaller gasoline can which caused Foster's clothing to catch on fire. The court could reasonably conclude that the prior event should have served as an immediate warning that the recklessness of the men's actions must end.

Id. at ____.

8. Unborn Children

The seminal case on the duty to an unborn child is *Pitre* v. *Opelousas General Hosp., supra.* It was preceded by *Danos v. St. Pierre,* 402 So. 2d 633 (La. 1981), holding that parents may recover the damages they sustain when tortfeasor fault causes a prenatal injury to a fetus who is subsequently born dead because of the injury. La. Civ. Code art. 26 provides that "[a]n unborn child shall be considered as a natural person for whatever relates to its interests from the moment of conception. If the child is born dead, it shall be considered never to have existed as a person, except for purposes of actions resulting from its wrongful death."

Cox v. Gaylord Container Corp., 897 So. 2d 1 (La.App. 1 Cir. 2004), *writ denied,* 901 So. 2d 1102 (La. 2005), presents a rather unique case. Laura Cox was a pregnant employee of Gaylord container Corporation and was injured on the job when she ran a forklift into a steel I-beam. Laura was examined and released the same day. Four months later, Olivia Cox was born with cerebral palsy.

In Olivia's action against Gaylord, the court seemed to recognize that Gaylord could be vicariously liable for injury to Olivia, but that vicarious liability was inappropriate because "responsibility attaches only when the employer might have prevented the act that caused the damage, and did not do so" and Gaylord was required to allow Laura to continue to work because of the Pregnancy Discrimination Act. As a result "Gaylord had no choice but to keep Laura working ... and had no way to protect itself from Olivia being negligently injured on the job by her mother."

There are a couple of other interesting questions raised in this case. First, could Olivia sue Laura (her mother) for negligence, or is the parent immune? The court found that the parent's immunity suspended or delayed the child's right to sue, but that the right was not extinguished. Second, does the worker's compensation immunity apply to a child's injury when the injury occurred *in utero*? The court did not answer the question.

9. Mental Anguish

a. Introduction

When a plaintiff is able to show physical injury, courts typically allow the injured party to recover mental anguish associated with the injury; such mental anguish damages are often said to be "parasitic" to the physical injury.

In this section, we explore when mental anguish may, in the absence of physical injury, satisfy the requirements of the tort of negligence. At common law, there was no duty to protect against negligently inflicted emotional distress in the absence of physical injury. Slowly, the courts began to recognize exceptions, such as where there was some impact, no matter how slight, with the person of the plaintiff. Later, the courts expanded the right to recover to those in the zone of physical danger from defendant's conduct even if there was no injury or no impact. *See generally, CONRAIL v. Gottshall*, 512 U.S. 532, 114 S. Ct. 2396, 129 L. Ed. 2d 427 (1994). Interestingly,in *Gaynor v. State Farm Mut. Auto Ins. Co.,* 727 So. 2d 1279 (La.App. 4 Cir. 1999), plaintiff, after her vehicle stalled on an interstate highway, left the scene to seek assistance. When she was approximately 100 feet away, she heard a crash, turned and saw that her vehicle had been heavily damaged by defendant's vehicle. *Held,* plaintiff may not recover mental anguish damages. She was not in the "zone of danger;" "[t]he zone of danger theory of recovery is employed in situations where the plaintiff has an impending fear of death or injury due to his proximity to an actual or near accident. We are reticent to expand this definition." In addition, plaintiff sought to recover for the emotional distress she suffered when her property was destroyed, a valid claim under Louisiana law. *See, In re Air Crash Disaster Near New Orleans v. Turgeau,* 764 F. 2d 1084 (5th Cir. 1985). However, she was unsuccessful on that theory as well because (1) she did not witness the actual collision but only saw the effect, (2) her concern over the damages was "mere worry or inconvenience over the consequences of property damage," and (3) the medical testimony failed to establish the causal relationship between the property damage and the complained of mental anguish.

Further development of the Louisiana negligent infliction of emotional distress experience is set forth in the following materials.

b. "Direct" Mental Anguish Victims ← *fear of contracting is a subset*

MORESI
v.
STATE DEPARTMENT OF WILDLIFE AND FISHERIES
567 So. 2d 1081 (La. 1990)

DENNIS, J.

In this civil rights action by the plaintiff duck hunters against the state and its game agents for damages caused by unconstitutional arrests, searches and seizures, the principal questions are whether the agents' conduct violated clearly established constitutional rights in (1) stopping duck hunters for questioning in their mudboat, (2) searching ice chests and a boat compartment, (3) arresting hunters for failing to comply with duck tagging regulations, (4) seizing untagged game in the hunters' possession, and (5) detaining the arrested hunters 45 to 60 minutes and requiring them to take two of the officers in the mudboat to the hunters' duck camp. After a bench trial, the district court entered judgment in favor of the hunters against the state and the game officers for actual damages, punitive damages, and attorneys' fees. The court of appeal affirmed in the main but vacated the punitive damage award and reduced the attorneys' fees. *Moresi v. Dept. of Wildlife & Fisheries*, 552 So. 2d 1259 (La.App. 3 Cir. 1989). We reverse the judgment entirely and dismiss the plaintiffs' suit.

On January 11, 1986, the last day of duck hunting season in Louisiana's western zone, four game agents of the state Wildlife and Fisheries Commission converged on Stelly's Landing and Little Prairie Landing in Vermilion Parish to watch for game violators. Several of these state game agents were also commissioned as deputy federal agents. The agents were acting on a tip that a duck hunter named "Byron Begnaud" would be transporting a large quantity of illegally taken ducks--as much as a freezer chest full--via one of the landings. In connection with the investigation, it was decided that the agents would check all boats that came into the landings. Agents Breaux and Vaughn were stationed at Stelly's Landing. After checking the first two boats to come in that morning, they saw two youthful hunters, Patrick Damas Moresi and Kern Alleman, approach the landing in a mudboat towing a flatboat. The flatboat contained equipment and supplies. A large number of slain ducks and a large ice chest were fully visible on the bow and deck of the mudboat. After the mudboat landed, one of the agents boarded the vessel and inspected the ducks in sight. Three daily bag limits of the ducks bore tags with the names of "Paul Moresi," "Dr. Howard Alleman" and "John W. Darby" inscribed on them. Two daily bag limits of the ducks were untagged. The agent asked the hunters what was in the ice chest. One of the young hunters replied "Ducks from yesterday." The agent opened the ice chest and found three more daily limits of ducks, two of which were untagged. Agent Breaux summoned two other agents, Jukes and Schreifer, who had been stationed at Little Prairie Landing. When he arrived Agent Jukes asked to see the hunters' life jackets and was told that they were in a locked compartment in the bow. Jukes took the key from the boat's ignition, unlocked the compartment, and inspected the life preservers.

Patrick Moresi and Kern Alleman, then ages 18 and 21, told the agents that they had just left their fathers, Paul Moresi, Jr., a lawyer, and Dr. Howard K. Alleman, a doctor, at their duck camp approximately two miles away in the marsh. Agent Breaux testified that he told the young men that some of the agents would return to the camp with them to complete the investigation. Two of the agents went with the young hunters in their mudboat to the duck camp to verify that the tagged ducks had been taken by the persons named on the tags and to insure that the tags were not being used as a ruse to smuggle out the ducks supposedly stockpiled at a camp in the marsh by Byron Begnaud. After the agents discussed the violations with the fathers of the young hunters and verified the proper tagging of the limits of birds found in the boat, Agent Jukes lifted the lid of an empty ice chest sitting in front of the camp and glanced inside. The entire group returned to Stelly's landing where Patrick Moresi and Kern Alleman were issued citations for violating the federal game law and regulations by their failure to properly tag ducks killed the previous day. The agents released the young hunters but confiscated the ducks in the ice chest. Approximately 45 minutes to one hour elapsed during the detention. After reviewing the charges, the United States Attorney refused to prosecute.

Patrick Moresi and Kern Alleman returned to the duck camp on March 25, 1986. On the door they discovered a business card of Scott Guillory, Louisiana Wildlife Enforcement Agent, with a handwritten inscription on its back: "We missed you this time but look out next time!!" [Signed] "Jimmie and Scott".

Paul Moresi, Jr., Howard K. Alleman, Patrick Moresi and Kern Alleman filed a civil damage suit against the State of Louisiana and its game agents under 42 U.S.C. 1983, Article I, § 5 of the 1974 Louisiana Constitution, and La. Civil Code art. 2315 for deprivation of their rights secured by the Constitutions and laws in connection with the incidents. Kern Alleman died before trial, and his legal successors were substituted for him. After a bench trial, the district court rendered judgment in favor of the plaintiffs against all of the defendants except for one of the game agents, awarding plaintiffs actual damages of $ 43,000, punitive damages of $ 4,000, and attorneys' fees of $ 32,939.10.

In its oral reasons for judgment the trial court made the following findings of fact and conclusions of law: The agents did not have reasonable cause to detain Patrick Moresi and Kern Alleman on January 11, 1986 or to conduct any of the searches or seizures. Moresi and Alleman in fact had not committed any offense. Although the agents honestly believed they were following the law as they understood it, they were in fact ignorant of the correct interpretation of the law. Therefore, they legally were not in good faith. The two agents who left the business card at the duck camp on March 25, 1986 did so by mistake, having confused the Moresi-Alleman camp with that of another. Therefore, these two agents are liable only for their negligence under state law.

The Court of Appeal, a panel of three judges, with one judge dissenting and one judge concurring in the result affirmed the trial court judgment, except for the punitive damage award which was reversed, and the attorneys' fees award which was reduced. *Moresi v. Dept. of Wildlife & Fisheries*, 552 So. 2d 1259 (La.App. 3 Cir. 1989). We granted certiorari to review the decisions below for possible errors in the selection and application of legal precepts. 558 So. 2d 592 (1990).

* * * * *

Infliction of Mental Distress

We are called upon to decide whether the trial court properly awarded the plaintiffs' damages for negligently inflicted mental distress based on state law. On March 25, 1986, over two months after the searches, seizures and arrests that had occurred on January 11, 1986, the plaintiffs discovered that state game agents had left a message on their camphouse door. The message, hand written on the reverse side of Agent Scott Guillory's business card, read: "We missed you this time but look out next time" [signed] "Jimmie and Scott." Neither Guillory nor the other signatory agent, Jimmie Meaux, were involved in the arrests or other events involving the Moresis and Allemans on January 11th. Furthermore, the trial judge's uncontested factual finding was that Guillory and Meaux had left the message at the Moresi-Alleman camp by mistake. Originally, the agents intended to leave the message at the nearby camp of their friend, Dr. Clyde Prejean, but misinterpreted his directions to the camp. Neither agent had ever been to Dr. Prejean's camp, and at the time of the occurrence both thought that they had left the card on his door. Upon learning of the message found at his camp, Mr. Moresi immediately contacted Dr. Jack C. Cappel, a member of the State Wildlife and Fisheries Commission, and voiced a complaint. Later, he sent Dr. Cappel a letter containing a copy of the note left at the camp. Two days later Guillory called upon Mr. Moresi at his office to explain the mistake and to apologize. Two weeks later the Secretary of the Department of Wildlife and Fisheries had hand-delivered to Moresi a letter containing statements from the agents explaining the mix-up. Several days later Dr. PreJean called Mr. Moresi, confirming that Guillory and Meaux were personal friends and that the note was intended for him. The plaintiffs testified that following these events their enjoyment of the camp was diminished because of their fear of further harassment. However, despite their contention plaintiffs continued to use their camp and improved it by adding air conditioning. The trial court awarded each plaintiff $ 1,000.00 for his mental distress resulting from the errant message.

This case does not present a situation in which recovery for mental distress may be based upon a breach of contract or a separate tort such as assault, battery, false imprisonment, trespass to land, nuisance, or invasion of the right to privacy. *See* Prosser & Keeton § 12 at p.60. Nor do the facts of the present case come within the general rule of recovery for the independent tort of intentional infliction of mental distress, the elements of which, according to the Restatement 2d, are: "One who by extreme and outrageous conduct intentionally or recklessly causes severe emotional distress to another is subject to liability for such emotional distress, and if bodily harm to the other result from it, for such bodily harm." Restatement of Torts (2d) § 46(1); *See Nickerson v. Hodges*, 146 La. 735, 84 So. 37 (1920); *Steadman v. So. Cent. Bell Tel. Co.*, 362 So. 2d 1144 (La.App. 2 Cir. 1978); *Todd v. Aetna Casualty & Surety Co.*, 219 So. 2d 538 (La.App. 3 Cir. 1969); *Boudoin v. Bradley*, 549 So. 2d 1265 (La.App. 3 Cir. 1989); Prosser & Keeton, § 12 at p.60; F. Stone, Tort Doctrine § 168, in 12 La. Civil Law Treatise (1977); D. Robertson, Intervening Negligence--Proximate Cause, 23 La.L.Rev. 281 (1963); Note, Damages For Emotional Distress Caused by Intentional Injury to Chattels, 23 La.L.Rev. 805 (1963).

Furthermore, the plaintiffs have not alleged or proved that they suffered any bodily harm or property damage as the result of the agents' negligence in missending the message. Consequently, they are seeking to recover on the basis that defendants' ordinary negligence caused them only mental disturbance. Under the general rule followed by the great majority of jurisdictions, if the defendant's conduct is merely negligent and causes only mental disturbance, without accompanying physical injury, illness or other physical consequences, the defendant is not liable for such emotional disturbance. Prosser & Keeton § 54 at p.361; Restatement of Torts (2d) § 436A; *Eastern Airlines, Inc. v. King*, 557 So. 2d 574 (Fla. 1990); *Czaplicki v. Gooding Joint School Dist.*, 775 P.2d 640 (Idaho 1989); *Niblo v. Parr Mfg., Inc.*, 445 N.W.2d 351, 354 (Iowa 1989), citing *Wanbsgans v. Price*, 274 N.W.2d 362, 365; *Decker v. Princeton Packet, Inc.*, 561 A.2d 1122 (N.J. 1989).

In our jurisprudence, there have been deviations from the general rule. A number of courts have allowed recovery against a telegraph company for the negligent transmission of a message, especially one announcing death, indicating on its face a potential for mental distress. *E.g., Graham v. Western Union*, 109 La. 1069, 34 So. 91 (1930) Some others have allowed similar recovery for the mishandling of corpses, *see French v. Ochsner Clinic*, 200 So. 2d 371 (La.App. 4 Cir. 1967); *Blanchard v. Brawley*, 75 So. 2d 891 (La.App. 1 Cir. 1954); *Morgan v. Richmond*, 336 So. 2d 342 (La.App. 1 Cir. 1976); *Shelmire v. Linton*, 343 So. 2d 301 (La.App. 1 Cir. 1977); failure to install, maintain or repair consumer products, *Pike v. Stephens Imports, Inc.*, 448 So. 2d 738 (La.App. 4 Cir. 1984); failure to take photographs or develop film, *Grather v. Tipery Studios, Inc.*, 334 So. 2d 758 (La.App. 4 Cir. 1976); negligent damage to one's property while the plaintiffs were present and saw their property damaged, *Holmes v. Le Cour Corp.*, 99 So. 2d 467 (Orl. La. App. 1958); *Lambert v. Allstate Insurance Co.*, 195 So. 2d 698 (La.App. 1 Cir. 1967); and in cases allowing damages for fright or nervous shock, where the plaintiff was actually in great fear for his personal safety. *Pecoraro v. Kopanica*, 173 So. 203 (Orl. La. App. 1937); *Klein v. Medical Building Realty Co., Inc.*, 147 So. 122 (Orl. La. App. 1933); *Laird v. Natchitoches Oil Mill, Inc.*, 10 La.App. 191, 120 So. 692 (2 Cir. 1929); *Cooper v. Christensen*, 212 So. 2d 154 (La.App. 4 Cir. 1968). There may be other cases, but all of these categories have in common the especial likelihood of genuine and serious mental distress, arising from the special circumstances, which serves as a guarantee that the claim is not spurious. Prosser & Keeton § 54 at p.362; W. Malone & L. Guerry, Studies in Louisiana Tort Law, 45 (1970); *Robertson, supra* at 292.

Applying these precepts to the present case, we conclude that Agents Guillory and Meaux should not be held liable for the plaintiffs' mental disturbance caused by the agents' negligence. The agents' acts were not intentional, outrageous or related to another tort. In addition, the plaintiffs' mental disturbance was not severe, or related to personal injury or property damage, and the plaintiffs were not in great fear for their personal safety. Therefore, this case does not fall within any category having an especial likelihood of genuine and serious mental distress, and thus lacks any recognized elements guaranteeing the genuineness of the injury claimed. *Id.*

Conclusion

For the reasons assigned, the judgments of the court of appeal and the trial court are reversed and plaintiffs' suit is dismissed.

NOTES

1.　*Vallery v. Southern Baptist Hospital*, 630 So. 2d 861 (La.App. 4 Cir. 1993), *writ denied*, 634 So. 3d 860 (La. 1994) – A victim may recover for negligently inflicted fear of contracting AIDS if she establishes (1) the presence of HIV and (2) a "channel" to the plaintiff for infection. A hospital which negligently exposes its security guard to HIV owes a duty to the guard's wife to warn her of the exposure; if it breaches the duty, the wife's mental anguish claim, unlike her consortium claim, is not barred by the hospital's worker compensation tort immunity. *See, also, Boutin v. Oakwood Village Nursing Home*, 692 So. 2d 1289 (La.App. 3 Cir. 1997), *writ denied*, 695 So. 2d 1358 (La. 1997), holding that a claimant may not recover for negligent infliction of mental distress because of exposure to a bacterial infection (MRSA) unless he can show a "channel" for the infection from the carrier to claimant, such as direct contact with the infected part of the carrier or the carrier's body fluids, or some alternative means of infection; *Vallier v. Louisiana Health Systems, Inc.*, 722 So. 2d 418 (La.App. 3 Cir. 1998), *writ denied*, 738 So. 2d 587 (La. 1999) (defendant hospital used an improperly disinfected instrument on plaintiff; defendant did not perform any tests to determine if there were any contagions present in the instrument, and plaintiff was required to undergo testing for hepatitis and HIV; *held*, these circumstances rise "to the level of guaranteeing that the claim is not spurious" as required by *Moresi;* accordingly, plaintiff has stated a cause of action for negligent infliction of emotion distress); *Falcon v. Our Lady of the Lake Hospital, Inc.*, 729 So. 2d 1169 (La.App. 1 Cir. 1999) (a person may maintain a cause of action for mental anguish from fear of contracting a disease such as AIDS if he can establish the presence of HIV or another blood-borne and/or contagious disease and a "channel" of exposure or infection; thus where the blood which plaintiff was given from the hospital blood bank inventory tested negative, and there is no controverting evidence, she may not recover mental anguish because the hospital failed to use her "directed donor" blood).

2.　In *Raney v. Walter O. Moss Regional Hospital*, 629 So. 2d 485 (La.App. 3 Cir. 1993), *writ denied*, 635 So. 2d 1134 (La. 1994), the court held that a person's fear of acquiring a disease is compensable if there is any possibility, no matter how remote, of acquiring that disease. *Compare Walker v. Allen Parish Health Unit*, 711 So. 2d 734 (La.App. 3 Cir. 1998), *writ denied*, 727 So. 2d 440 (La. 1998). There, claimant brought an action for negligent infliction of the mental distress she suffered after her 28 month old child was pricked by a used needle while at the Parish Health Unit. Child was immediately, and thereafter periodically, tested for hepatitis and AIDS; all tests were negative. Claimant "felt nervous and upset about the incident" and "might have developed stomach problems for a few months for which she saw a physician and was successfully treated..." There was expert testimony that "it was not reasonable to fear that a person stuck by a needle used for immunization of a member of the general public not known to be infected with HIV" would contact AIDS "because the chances of acquiring the disease from the stick are so very small." *Held*, the Health Unit owed claimant an independent duty, but the trial court properly dismissed claimant's suit; the emotional distress did not reach the level of seriousness contemplated by *Moresi*. In *Lilley v. Louisiana State University*, 735 So. 2d 696 (La.App. 3 Cir. 1999), *writ denied*, 744 So. 2d 629 (La. 1999), plaintiff established that he was exposed to asbestos-containing matter and that he now may have a slightly increased risk of asbestos-related disease, and that the increase, however slight, has caused him concern. *Held*, plaintiff has established an "especial likelihood of genuine and serious mental distress" which permits recovery for mental anguish unaccompanied by physical injury under *Moresi*. However, the minimal increase in the risk of disease does not satisfy the "significant increased risk" required for medical monitoring damages under *Bourgeois*; "compensable mental injuries do not necessarily have to exist with a proven need for medical monitoring."

3.   "Cancerphobia" is a "special circumstance ... (which) guarantee(s) that the claim (for mental disturbance without physical consequences) is not spurious." *Straughan v. Ahmed*, 618 So. 2d 1225 (La.App. 5 Cir. 1993), *writ denied*, 625 So. 2d 1033 (La. 1993).

4.   The federal rule in cases involving railroad workers and seamen requires that the plaintiff either sustained a physical impact or was in immediate risk of physical impact ("zone of danger"), thus precluding *LeJeune*-type damages. *See, e.g., Consolidated Rail Corp. v. Gottshall*, 512 U.S. 532, 114 S. Ct. 2396, 129 L Ed. 2d 427 (1994). However, simple physical contact with a substance that might cause a disease at a substantially later time, and threatens no harm other than that disease-related risk (such as in the case before the court, physical contact with insulation dust) does not amount to "physical impact" so as to permit recovery. *Metro-North Commuter Railroad Co. v. Buckley*, 521 US 424, 117 S. Ct. 2113, 138 L.Ed 2d 560 (1997).

c.   Bystander Emotional Distress

Lejune claim

C.C. Art. 2315.6   Liability for damages caused by injury to another

A.   The following persons who view an event causing injury to another person, or who come upon the scene of the event soon thereafter, may recover damages for mental anguish or emotional distress that they suffer as a result of the other person's injury:

(1)   The spouse, child or children, and grandchild or grandchildren of the injured person, or either the spouse, the child or children, or the grandchild or grandchildren of the injured person;

(2)   The father and mother of the injured person, or either or them;

(3)   The brothers and sisters of the injured person or any of them;

(4)   The grandfather and grandmother of the injured person, or either of them.

B.   To recover for mental anguish or emotional distress under this Article, the injured person must suffer such harm that one can reasonably expect a person in the claimant's position to suffer serious mental anguish or emotional distress from the experience, and the claimant's mental anguish or emotional distress must be severe, debilitating, and foreseeable. Damages suffered as a result of mental anguish or emotional distress for injury to another shall be recovered only in accordance with this Article.

TRAHAN

v.

MCMANUS

728 So. 2d 1273 (La. 1999)

LEMMON, J.

The parents of Terry Trahan filed this action to recover damages under La. Civ.Code art. 2315.6 for their mental anguish and emotional distress resulting from their son's injury and death. The principal issues are (1) whether this action falls within the limitations of the Medical Malpractice Act, and (2) whether "bystander damages" are recoverable when the "event" observed by the plaintiffs that allegedly caused their mental anguish was the negligent omission of the doctor who failed to treat their son in the hospital emergency room for serious injuries sustained in an automobile accident.

Facts

253

Plaintiff Marie Trahan received a telephone message that her thirty-six-year-old son, who was living with his parents at the time, had been injured in a one-vehicle accident. She went to the hospital emergency room, where her son appeared to be in pain. However, the doctor relieved Mrs. Trahan's anxiety by assuring her that her son was not seriously injured and simply needed bed rest. The doctor discharged the son about two and one-half hours after he had entered the hospital.

Unfortunately, the doctor had read the wrong chart, and Terry Trahan, as suggested by the vital signs on his chart, was suffering from shock and internal bleeding. At home, Terry Trahan complained of severe pain to both of his parents, and his condition continued to worsen. He died in the presence of his parents about seven hours after his discharge from the hospital.

Two separate actions arose from the alleged malpractice. Terry Trahan's widow, from whom he was separated at the time of his death, filed a survival and wrongful death action under La. Civ.Code arts. 2315.1 and 2315.2 against the doctor and the hospital on behalf of herself and their children....

Terry Trahan's parents separately filed the present action under La. Civ.Code art.2315.6 against the doctor and his insurer.[2] Defendants responded with (1) an exception of no right of action, contending that plaintiffs were not within the category of persons entitled to emotional distress under Article 2315.6, since Terry Trahan was survived by a spouse and children; and (2) an exception of no cause of action, contending that the law did not authorize recovery of bystander damages under Article 2315.6 under the facts of this case, since plaintiffs did not witness the event that caused the injury to their son. The trial court maintained the exceptions, but the court of appeal reversed and remanded the case for trial on the merits.

After trial, the jury, although finding the doctor was negligent, returned a verdict in favor of defendants, based on the additional finding that Terry Trahan did not suffer, as a result of the doctor's negligence, any "injury that would not otherwise have been incurred." The jury thus apparently accepted defendants' argument that Terry Trahan would have died from the automobile accident injuries, even if he had been treated at the hospital.

The court of appeal reversed, with one judge dissenting. First reiterating its earlier decision that plaintiffs had a cause of action for Article 2315.6 damages,[3] the court noted that the injury-causing event was the doctor's negligent discharge of the patient, which was viewed by the mother and which caused her severe and debilitating anguish. As to the father, the court stated that "the continuing event was visited almost instantaneously" on the father who was compelled to witness the distressing events of the final seven hours of his son's life.

The intermediate court further held that the trial judge erred in instructing the jury on the law and burdens of proof in a medical malpractice case, because this case did not fall under the Medical Malpractice Act. The court concluded that the Act only applies to a claim by the patient against a qualified health care provider.

The court then reviewed the record de novo, concluding that the doctor's negligence was a cause-in-fact of Terry Trahan's death.[4] The court determined from the record that plaintiffs had

---

[2] Plaintiffs had no right of action under Articles 2315.1 and 2315.2 because their son was survived by a spouse and children.

[3] Plaintiffs clearly had a right of action under Article 2315.6, which lists the tort victim's parents among the persons entitled to recover emotional distress damages. Unlike Articles 2315.1 and 2315.2, Article 2315.6 does not exclude parents from recovery when the tort victim is survived by a spouse or child.

[4] The court of appeal incorrectly applied the "law of the case" doctrine as an alternative basis for reversing the jury's factual determination regarding cause-in-fact. The earlier pronouncement by the court of appeal that the doctor's malpractice was a cause-in-fact of Terry Trahans death did not result from reviewing the evidence produced at a trial on the merits, but rather involved a review of a judgment on an exception of no cause of action

proved Terry Trahan would have survived if the doctor had rendered proper care timely. Further determining that plaintiffs had proved their emotional distress was serious, severe and debilitating, the court awarded damages of $100,000 to each plaintiff.

On defendants' application, this court granted certiorari.

Action for Article 2315.6 Damages under Medical Malpractice Act

The outset complaint to this court by defendants and amici relates to the holding by the court of appeal that this is not a medical malpractice action. The intermediate court made that ruling in the context of its determination that the trial judge erred when he instructed the jury on La. Rev. Stat. 9:2794 pertaining to the required elements of proof and the burden of proof in a medical malpractice action. Reasoning that plaintiffs were not patients of the defendant doctor and were not parties to a health care contract, the court held that the Medical Malpractice Act does not apply to an action by a third party for the mental anguish damages resulting from a patient's injury or death caused by the negligence of the patient's health care provider. We disagree.

The cause of action for damages resulting from an injury to or death of a patient caused by a doctor is provided by Civil Code Articles 2315, 2315.1 and 2315.2. The Medical Malpractice Act simply provides procedures for and limitations on such causes of action when the doctor is a qualified health care provider. Similarly, Article 2315.6 provides a cause of action to specified persons for mental anguish damages resulting from an injury to or death of a patient caused by a doctor, subject to the procedures and limitations of the Medical Malpractice Act, when the specified relatives of the patient incur the mental anguish within the circumstances outlined in Article 2315.6.

The Act defines "malpractice" as follows:

> "Malpractice" means any unintentional tort or any breach of contract based on health care or professional services rendered, by a health care provider, to a patient, including failure to render services timely and the handling of a patient, and also includes all legal responsibility of a health care provider arising from defects in blood, tissue, transplants, drugs and medicines, or from defects in or failures of prosthetic devices, implanted in or used on or in the person of a patient.

La.Rev.Stat. 40:129941A(8) (emphasis added).

The conduct complained of in the present case was an unintentional tort arising out of a qualified health care provider's failure to render professional services which should have been rendered to a patient. Each of the patient's parents was a "person having a claim under this Part for bodily injuries to or death of a patient on account of malpractice...." La. Rev. Stat. 40:1299.41E(1).

In *Hutchinson v. Patel*, 637 So. 2d 415, 428 (La. 1994), a case in which a health care provider committed a tort against a person who was not his patient, this court noted that while the Medical Malpractice Act applies exclusively to claims arising from injury to or death of a patient, the claimant need not be a patient, and non-patient claimants may include representatives of a patient acting on the patient's behalf and "other persons with claims arising from injuries to or death of a patient." That language applies to the facts of the present case.

In summary, nothing in the Medical Malpractice Act distinguishes between damage claims by the patient under Article 2315, damage claims by statutory survivors of the patient under Articles 2315.1 and 2315.2, and damage claims by statutorily-limited relatives of the patient under Article 2315.6. The fact that the damages recoverable under Article 2315.6 are limited to mental anguish

---

for which the allegations of the petition were accepted as true only for the purpose of the exception. The jury's subsequent determination regarding cause-in-fact was based on evidence presented at trial, and the intermediate court's earlier pre-trial decision with respect to cause-in-fact did not constitute "the law of the case" in the review of the subsequent judgment on the merits.

damages and to specifically required facts and circumstances does not serve to remove Article 2315.6 claims from the applicability of the Medical Malpractice act, as long as the mental anguish arises from the injury to or death of a patient caused by the negligence of a qualified health care provider.

Recovery of Damages under Article 2315.6

For many years, Louisiana and other jurisdictions declined to recognize a cause of action for recovery of mental anguish damages based on negligent infliction of emotional distress when the claimant's mental anguish resulted from a tort-caused physical injury to another. *See, e.g., Black v. Carrollton RR Co.*, 10 La.Ann 33 (1855). Recovery in early cases was allowed only for mental anguish that was "parasitic" to a physical injury, when the claimant could show some sort of "impact," however slight, upon his person. *See* W. Page Keeton et al., Prosser & Keeton on Torts, 363 (5th ed.1984). Later cases allowed recovery for mental anguish when there was physical injury to a person other than the plaintiff, if the plaintiff was in the "zone of danger" of the harm that befell the other person. *Id.* at 365. The common rationale for limiting recovery to these situations was that, absent impact or a near miss, the defendant could not reasonably have anticipated any harm to the plaintiff and therefore should not be held liable for such harm. *Id.*

Probably the first reported modern case to allow a claim for bystander damages beyond the limits of the impact or zone of danger rules was *Dillon v. Legg*, 441 P.2d 912 (Cal. 1968). In *Dillon*, the California Supreme Court allowed a claim for emotional distress damages by a mother who saw her young daughter run over and killed by an automobile. The court stated that the mother's "shock resulted from a direct emotional impact upon plaintiff from the sensory and contemporaneous observance of the accident." *Id.* at 920 (emphasis added).

Prior to 1990, Louisiana followed the pre-*Dillon* common law jurisprudence, even though mental anguish damages resulting from injury to another person literally fell within the scope of La. Civ.Code art.2315. This court reconsidered that position in *Lejeune v. Rayne Memorial Hosp.*, 556 So. 2d 559 (La. 1990), in which the plaintiff's husband was hospitalized in a comatose condition. The plaintiff entered the hospital room and observed her husband shortly after a nurse had cleaned some of the blood from wounds caused by rats chewing on her husband's face, neck and legs. Although the plaintiff was neither physically injured nor exposed to the physical injury that befell her husband, this court, applying the duty-risk analysis, held that the risk of a person of mental anguish damages occasioned by the negligent infliction of injury to a third person may, under certain circumstances, fall within the scope of the hospital's duty under Article 2315. The decision outlined four circumstances under which mental anguish damages may be recovered, the one pertinent to the present case being: A claimant need not be physically injured, nor suffer physical impact in the same accident in order to be awarded mental pain and anguish damages arising out of injury to another. Nor need he be in the zone of danger to which the directly injured party is exposed. He must, however, either view the accident or injury-causing event or come upon the accident scene soon thereafter and before substantial change has occurred in the victim's condition.[5] *Id.* at 569-70 (emphasis added).

The following year, the Legislature codified the *Lejeune* decision by enacting La. Civ. Code art. 2315.6, which allows certain "persons who view an event causing injury to another person, or who come upon the scene of the event soon thereafter [to] recover damages for mental anguish or emotional distress that they suffer as a result of the other person's injury..."[6] La. Civ. Code art.

---

[5] The other three circumstances listed by the court were: The direct victim of the traumatic injury must suffer such harm that it can reasonably be expected that one in the plaintiff's position would suffer serious mental anguish from the experience. The emotional distress sustained must be both serious and reasonably foreseeable to allow recovery. There must be a close relationship between the claimant and the direct victim. *Id.* at 569-70.

[6] Other requirements for recovery under Article 2315.6 are that the harm to the injured person must be severe enough that one could reasonably expect the observer to suffer serious mental distress; the plaintiff must suffer emotional distress that is "severe, debilitating, and foreseeable"; and the plaintiff must have a specifically enumerated relationship with the injured person. The Legislature thus defined the "close relationship" that had been left as an open question in *Lejeune*.

If recovery of mental anguish damages resulting from negligently caused physical injury to another person had been allowed prior to the *Lejeune* decision, a tortfeasor, under the literal terms of Article 2315, might have been held liable to repair any damages remotely caused by his or her fault. However, liability for fault does not extend to all damages the result from that fault. *Hill v. Lundin & Assoc.*, 260 La. 542, 256 So. 2d 620 (1972). As a matter of policy, the courts, under the scope of duty element of the duty-risk analysis, have established limitations on the extent of damages for which a tortfeasor is liable. *See, e.g., PPG Industries v. Bean Dredging Co.*, 447 So. 2d 1058 (La. 1984), in which this court held that the liability of a dredging contractor who negligently damaged a natural gas pipeline does not extend to the economic losses incurred by the pipeline owner's contract customer who was required to obtain gas at a higher price from another source during the period of repair of the damaged pipeline. This court noted that the list of possible victims and the extent of economic damages might be extended indefinitely unless the court made a policy decision placing some limitation on the recovery of damages.

The *Lejeune* decision, while recognizing for the first time a claimant's right to recover mental anguish damages resulting from negligently caused physical injury to another, carefully delineated limitations on bystander recovery. But for this limitation, liability might have extended, under the literal terms of Article 2315, to allow recovery of mental anguish damages by an acquaintance of the tort victim who learned of the injury by telephone call several days after the injury-causing event. The Legislature, in codifying the *Lejeune* decision, placed further limitations by specifying the category of persons who may recover. More significantly, the Legislature prohibited any recovery of mental anguish damages resulting from the negligent infliction of injury to another, except under the circumstances outlined in Article 2315.6.[7] Accordingly, this right of recovery has been recognized jurisprudentially and legislatively to exist only under very limited circumstances. Article 2315.6

Article 2315.6 Damages in the Present Case

In the *Dillon* and *Lejeune* cases, the plaintiffs suffered mental distress contemporaneously with observing the event that immediately caused observable injury to another person. Emotional distress usually occurs contemporaneously with the observance of the event when the event is a negligent act by the tortfeasor. However, when the act is a negligent omission by the tortfeasor, such as frequently occurs in medical malpractice cases, the applicability of Article 2315.6 becomes more problematic for recovery of damages for mental distress resulting from observing an injury-causing event or arriving on the scene of the injury soon after the event while the victim is still in the condition, caused by the event, that creates emotional distress in the observer.

A historical review of cases allowing recovery of bystander damages shows that bystander damages are intended to provide a remedy when severe mental distress arises directly and immediately from the claimant's observing a traumatic injury-causing event to the direct victim. In order to recover, the claimant who observes the injury-causing event (or soon thereafter comes upon the scene of the injury) must be contemporaneously aware that the event has caused harm to the direct victim. The requirement of temporal proximity has always been at the root of allowing recovery for emotional distress caused by an injury to another, *see* Prosser & Keeton at 366, whether recovery is limited to one who actually witnessed a traumatic injury (as in *Dillon*), or whether recovery is extended to one coming soon upon the traumatic injury, as under the Louisiana rule. Recovery of damages for mental anguish has almost never been extended to one who observed the victim's suffering at a place other than where the injury-causing event occurred or at a time not closely connected to the event.

The requirements of Article 2315.6, when read together, suggest a need for temporal proximity between the tortious event, the victim's observable harm, and the plaintiff's mental distress

---

[7] Article 2315.6B provides in part that "[d]amages suffered as a result of mental anguish or emotional distress for injury to another shall be recovered only in accordance with this Article." (emphasis added).

arising from an awareness of the harm caused by the event.[8] The Legislature apparently intended to allow recovery of bystander damages to compensate for the immediate shock of witnessing a traumatic event which caused the direct victim immediate harm that is severe and apparent,[9] but not to compensate for the anguish and distress that normally accompany an injury to a loved one under all circumstances.[10]

The present case is complicated by the fact that the event which caused the injury and death was the automobile accident. The doctor's negligence was failing to read the correct chart and to provide treatment to the patient based on the data on the chart, which arguably caused the patient to lose his chance of surviving the automobile accident injuries. This negligence of omission, while a concurrent cause of the death (if plaintiffs proved cause-in-fact, an issue we do not reach), was not an injury-causing event in which the claimant was contemporaneously aware that the event had caused harm to the direct victim, as required for recovery of Article 2315.6 damages.

Even under the view of the court of appeal that the injury-causing event was the doctor's negligent discharge of the patient, that event was not a traumatic event likely to cause severe contemporaneous mental anguish to an observer, even though the ultimate consequences were tragic indeed. There was no observable harm to the direct victim that arose at the time of the negligent failure to treat, and no contemporaneous awareness of harm caused by the negligence. The doctor's negligent discharge of the patient, accompanied by mistaken assurances that the patient would soon recover, was not itself an emotionally shocking event. Similarly, the father's witnessing his son's arrival home from the hospital was not the witnessing of an injury-causing event, or the coming soon after upon the scene of an injury-causing event, for which bystander damages may be awarded under the strict limitations of Article 2315.6.

Furthermore, the observance of the injury-causing event in the present case can hardly be compared to witnessing the car crash that caused the decedent's injuries in the first place. Nor can it even compare to the situation in *Wartelle v. Women's and Children's Hosp.*, 97-9744 (La. 1997); 704

---

[8] This approach is consistent with the duty-risk considerations articulated in *Lejeune*, where this court recognized the need to proceed somewhat conservatively in what is still a relatively new area of tort law. *Lejeune*, 556 So. 2d at 568-69. In *Lejeune*, this court stated that "the essence of the tort is the shock caused by the perception of the especially horrendous event.... The emotional injury must be directly attributable to the emotional impact of the plaintiff's observation or contemporaneous sensory perception of the accident and immediate viewing of the accident victim." 556 So. 2d at 570, n.11 (internal quotations and citations omitted). For the same reasons, recovery is not permitted when the plaintiff has merely been informed of the accident. *See, e.g., Chamberlain v. State, D.O.T.D.*, 624 So. 2d 874 (La. 1993) (no recovery when victim's parents learned of accident from others). A non-contemporaneous onset of mental distress is not within the scope of the tortfeasor's liability, as limited by this court in *LeJeune* and by the Legislature in Article 2315.6, particularly when the tortious event was not itself shocking when it happened.

[9] This was the view taken by the dissenting judge in the first appeal in the present case. 653 So. 2d at 94. *See also Simmons v. Hartford Ins. Co.*, 786 F.Supp. 574 (E.D.LA. 1992), in which the court, applying Louisiana law as it stood after the *Lejeune* decision but before the enactment of Article 2315.6, stated:

> For purposes of this action, the Court need not address whether [the victim's father] experienced such distress from the entire experience surrounding his daughter's death. Instead, our focus is on whether he experienced severe and debilitating distress specifically from "the shock caused by the perception of the especially horrendous event." That is, did [the father] suffer severe and debilitating distress solely as a result of his initial perception of the aftermath of the accident? It follows that "the claimant must realize, at the time he witnesses the event, that the injuries are serious." Otherwise, the distress would not arise from the perception of the event, but rather from being told of the seriousness of the event at some future time. *Id.* at 578 (emphasis added).

[10] The damages awarded to plaintiffs in this case were really more like the damages commonly awarded in a wrongful death action. But wrongful death damages cannot be awarded under the guise of bystander damages when the claimant did not experience shock or other emotional distress contemporaneously with viewing a traumatic injury to the victim. *Cf. Lloyd v. State*, 395 So. 2d 1385 (La. App. 1 Cir. 1981) (plaintiff's were allowed mental distress damages for their mother's wrongful death, but were not allowed bystander damages for finding her mutilated body).

So. 2d 778, where the medical malpractice, the awareness of harm, and the ensuing mental anguish were all very close in time.[11]

We are aware of the decisions in *Ochoa v. Superior Court (Santa Clara County)*, 703 P.2d 1 (Cal. 1985)[12] and *Love v. Cramer*, 606 A.2d 1175 (Pa.Super.Ct. 1992),[13] which argue favorable to the initial decision by the court of appeal in the present case that overruled the exception of no cause of action. First, even if *Ochoa* and *Love* expanded the circumstances under which bystander damages may be recovered in accordance with *Dillon v. Legg*, those were jurisprudential expansions of prior case law. The courts in *Ochoa* and *Love* were not limited, as Louisiana courts are, by a legislative edict that allows recovery only under specified circumstances and prohibits recovery under any other circumstances.

Second, it is doubtful that plaintiffs in the second case could recover even if this court adopted the jurisprudence expansion of bystander damages expressed in *Ochoa*. The court in *Ochoa* recognized that while the doctor's negligent failure to render treatment was not itself traumatic, bystander damages were recoverable because the plaintiff observed the doctor's conduct and was contemporaneously aware that the conduct was causing harm to the patient. Contemporaneous awareness of harm caused by the event has been a critical factor for recover in almost all bystander damages cases, and there was no such contemporaneous awareness in the present case.

We accordingly conclude that the severe mental anguish undoubtedly experienced by plaintiffs in this case did not occur within the limited circumstances prescribed by Article 2315.6 as the sole basis for awarding damages for mental anguish caused by negligent injury inflicted upon another person.

Decree

The judgment of the court of appeal is **REVERSED**, and plaintiffs' action is dismissed.

---

[11] Today's decision should not be read as necessarily precluding recovery of bystander damages in all medical malpractice contexts. In *Wartelle v. Women's and Children's Hosp.*, 97-9744 (La. 1997); 704 So. 2d 778, the court did not reach the issue raised in the present case, recovery of bystander damages having been denied based on the "non-person" status of the stillborn child. 704 So. 2d 15 784-85. However, the plaintiffs in that case not only witnessed the defendant's negligent act and the stillbirth that immediately resulted, but they also suffered mental anguish from contemporaneous awareness of the harm to the direct victim.

[12] In *Ochoa*, the plaintiffs witnessed their thirteen-year-old son's dying of pneumonia in juvenile custody because the authorities refused to provide adequate care or to let the parents take their son to a private doctor.

[13] In *Love*, the plaintiff witnessed the misdiagnosis of her mother's heart disease, and her mother died of congestive heart failure seven weeks later. Focusing on negligence by omission, the court allowed recovery of bystander damages because the plaintiff witnessed both the negligent omission and the injurious consequences which eventually occurred, reasoning that "[i]t is enough if the negligence constituted the proximate cause of the injury, and of the resulting emotional trauma." *Id.* at 1177.

PER CURIAM.

We granted certiorari in this matter to determine whether the Court of Appeal, Third Circuit, erred in reversing the trial court's judgment which sustained the defendants' Exception of No Cause of Action and dismissed the plaintiffs' claims and lawsuit with prejudice. For the reasons that follow, we reverse the court of appeal's ruling and reinstate the judgment of the trial court.

Facts and Procedural History

On July 4, 2005, Joshua Paul Veroline (hereinafter referred to as "plaintiff") and his sister Heather were spending time with friends at Toledo Bend Lake. Heather Veroline injured her knee when she was tossed into the air by a friend. Priority One received a call from the Sabine County's Sheriff's Department and dispatched an ambulance to the scene of the accident. Joshua witnessed the emergency medical technicians (hereinafter referred to as "EMTs") place her in the ambulance that was to bring her to the hospital. Joshua and two friends left for the hospital in Heather's vehicle but stopped several times on the way. Soon after, the ambulance embarked to the hospital. At some point during the twenty mile trip to the hospital, the ambulance, with its lights on and traveling fast, passed Joshua, causing him to believe that Heather (who had recently been diagnosed with reactive airway disease and developed new allergies) had taken a turn for the worse. By the time Joshua reached the hospital, Heather had been taken to the emergency room. She died before he could see her alive.

The plaintiffs filed a Petition for Damages on June 2, 2006, and it was amended several times. In the last amended petition, which was filed on February 7, 2007, Joshua alleges that he is entitled to damages for emotional distress as a result of the defendants' negligent treatment of his sister while she was in their care in the ambulance. The defendants subsequently filed a pleading titled "Peremptory Exception of No Right of Action and No Cause of Action, Alternatively Motion for Summary Judgment." A hearing was held on the defendants' exception on February 7, 2008, and the judgment was signed on March 27, 2008.

The trial court sustained the defendants' Exception of No Cause of Action and dismissed the plaintiffs' claims and lawsuit with prejudice, though it did not address the defendants' Motion for Summary Judgment. The trial court reviewed the elements of a bystander claim as set out in *Lejeune v. Rayne Branch Hospital*...stating that Joshua must meet those elements to have a cause of action under La. Civ.Code art. 2315.6. According to *Lejeune*, 1) the plaintiff must either view the accident or come upon the accident scene soon after it has occurred and before any substantial change has taken place in the victim's condition; 2) the victim must have suffered such harm that it can be reasonably expected that someone in the plaintiff's position would suffer serious mental anguish; and 3) the emotional distress must be serious and reasonably foreseeable, meaning it goes beyond mental pain and anguish and is both severe and debilitating. The trial court specifically found that the plaintiff could not establish the first element of Article 2315.6 because he did not view the accident or come upon the scene soon after it occurred.

The Court of Appeal, Third Circuit, reversed and remanded, stating that all well-pled allegations of fact found in the pleadings must be treated as true. Finding persuasive the plaintiffs' argument that Joshua observed the ambulance switch to emergency mode en route to the hospital, came upon the event[2] immediately after it happened, and observed the result (his deceased sister), the court of appeal explained that the trial court wrongly dismissed the petition for damages based on Joshua's absence in the ambulance when the injury-causing event occurred. The court concluded that

---

[2] The "event," as discussed by the court of appeal here, is the event that occurred in the ambulance that caused Heather's death and not the knee injury.

the plaintiffs do have a cause of action under La. Civ.Code art. 2315.6 because, as the petition alleges, Joshua arrived at the scene soon after the injury-causing event occurred.

The defendants' writ application to this court asserts that the court of appeal erred in reversing the decision of the trial court sustaining the defendants' Exception of No Cause of Action and dismissing the claims and lawsuit with prejudice. The defendants argue that the trial court correctly granted their Exception of No Cause of Action because Joshua did not witness either the injury-causing event or arrive at the scene soon thereafter in the manner required to maintain a cause of action under La. Civ.Code art. 2315.6. In addition, the defendants ask this court to grant their Motion for Summary Judgment, which was not addressed by the trial court, for the sake of judicial economy and because justice so requires on the undisputed facts.

* * * * *

La. Civ.Code art. 2315.6 requires, among other things, that the plaintiff either view the accident or come upon the accident scene soon after it has occurred and before any substantial change has taken place in the victim's condition. The trial court determined that the plaintiff did not satisfy this requirement because he could not establish that he viewed the accident or came upon the scene soon after it occurred. We agree. Although the court of appeal found that the plaintiff arrived at the scene immediately after the injury-causing event occurred, we find that the trial court correctly determined the plaintiff did not arrive "soon thereafter" in the sense that this court and the legislature intended. As noted by the trial court, this court in *Trahan v. McManus* stated that the legislature's purpose in enacting La. Civ.Code art. 2315.6 was "to compensate for the immediate shock of witnessing a traumatic event which caused the direct victim harm that is severe and apparent, but not to compensate for the anguish and distress that normally accompany an injury to a loved one under all circumstances."

Although the court of appeal found that the plaintiff arrived at the scene immediately after the injury-causing event occurred, accepting the plaintiffs' facts alleged as true, we do not find that the plaintiff has satisfied the temporal proximity requirement of La. Civ.Code art. 2315.6. The plaintiff in his petition states, "Joshua Paul Veroline went to the hospital immediately upon discovering that his sister had been transported there. Upon arriving, he suffered immediate pain and suffering as a result of viewing his deceased sister." The plaintiff has not alleged that he suffered "immediate shock from witnessing a traumatic event which caused the direct victim harm that is severe and apparent." He did not actually view the event that caused his sister's death, nor did he come upon the accident scene soon after it had occurred and before any substantial change had taken place in the victim's condition, as required by Article 2315.6. At most, in seeing his deceased sister when he arrived at the hospital, the plaintiff endured "anguish and distress that normally accompanies an injury to a loved one under all circumstances." As explained by this court in *Trahan*, the legislature did not intend such scenarios to be encompassed by La. Civ.Code art. 2315.6

Consequently, we find the court of appeal was in error, as the plaintiff has not satisfied the first prong of La. Civ.Code art. 2315.6, and therefore, the trial court did not err in granting the defendants' Exception of No Cause of Action and dismissing the claims and lawsuit with prejudice.

Decree

For all of the foregoing reasons, we find that the Court of Appeal, Third Circuit, erred in reversing the judgment of the trial court sustaining the defendants' Exception of No Cause of Action and dismissing the plaintiffs' claims and lawsuit with prejudice. Accordingly, we grant the defendant's writ application, reverse the court of appeal's decision, and reinstate the trial court's judgment.

NOTES

1.   In *Labouisse v. Orleans Parish School Board*, 757 So. 2d 866 (La.App. 4 Cir. 2000), child suffered a large bruise to his forehead after being struck by a tether ball pole; he was unconscious for five minutes or less, and was treated at an emergency room and released. Mother did not witness the

accident, a substantial amount of time transpired before she arrived at the school and personally transported child to the hospital, and there was no evidence to indicate mother's mental anguish upon arriving at school was "severe or debilitating." *Held*, the trial court did not err in refusing to award *Lejeune* (C.C. Art. 2315.6) damages.

2.   Wife and son may not recover mental anguish damages under C.C. Art. 2315.6 caused by the termination of husband-father's employment contract, where they were not at the scene of the event-causing injury (the termination). *Kipps v. Callier*, 197 F.3d 765 (5th Cir. 1999), *cert denied*, 531 U.S. 816 (2000).

3.   In a post-*Lejeune*, pre-CC Art. 2315.6 case, plaintiff, upon arriving at a nursing home, noticed a strong odor emanating from her mother's room. She demanded that the bandage on her mother's foot be removed, and when it was, plaintiff viewed the "severely deteriorated condition" of her mother's heel. She then called her son to come and photograph the condition of the heel. Although son described his mother as "very upset," there was no testimony that she was thereafter unable to function or that she required any psychological counseling. *Held*, plaintiff has not established an emotional injury that is both severe and debilitating; thus the jury was clearly wrong in awarding mental anguish damages. *Nelson v. Ruston Longleaf Nurse Care Center*, 751 So. 2d 436 (La.App. 2 Cir. 2000), *writ denied*, 760 So. 2d 1175 (La. 2000).

4.   Plaintiff wife, pregnant, went to the scene of her husband's auto accident; subsequently, the couple's child was stillborn. *Held*, in the couple's suit for the wrongful death of the child brought against the offending motorist, they must meet the requirements of CC Art. 2315.6, restricting recovery for damages stemming from injury to another. *Martinez v. Shelter Mut. Ins. Co.*, 771 So. 2d 793 (La.App. 3 Cir. 2000), *writ denied*, 778 So. 2d 1144 (La. 2001).

5.   In *Guillot v. Doe*, 879 So. 2d 374 (La.App. 3 Cir. 2004), a mother arrived on the scene shortly after her son, a guest at a birthday party, was shot in the head with a pellet gun. The son was not seriously injured, but did suffer some long-term psychological injury for which he recovered. His mother, upon seeing her son, "broke down and began to cry hysterically" and was eventually sedated. The court found that the minor physical wound was not the type of "horrendous event" justifying recovery for the mother under La. Civil Code art. 2315.6.

6.   In *Wartelle v. Women's and Children's Hosp., Inc.* 704 So. 2d 778 (La. 1997), the parents of a stillborn child sought 2315.6 bystander damages. Finding that a stillborn fetus is not a *person*, the claim was denied. Justice Lemmon dissented, arguing that the mother should be entitled to emotional distress damages because but-for the tort, the fetus would have been born alive. Which position is appropriate? Why? For a case distinguishing *Wartelle*, *see Guillot v. Daimlerchrysler Corp.*, 50 So. 3d 173 (La.App. 3 Cir. 2010), *writ denied*, 58 So. 3d 461 (La. 2011) (child born and lived 17 days).

7.   In *Crockett v. Cardona*, 713 So. 2d 802 (La.App. 4 Cir. 1998), groom was injured in an auto accident while driving to his home to prepare for his wedding, scheduled to begin an hour and a half later. Because of the injury, groom arrived about two hours late for the wedding. *Held*, the bride may not recover mental anguish damages caused by worry about groom and the "utter ... ruin" of her wedding day because of the delay. The car accident was not the "legal cause" of the damages, and the bride may not recover under CC Art. 2315.6 (they were not yet married) or *Moresi*.

8.   Unlike its predecessor, the Restatement (Third): Liability for Physical and Emotional Harm (Tentative Draft No. 5) directly addresses the basic elements of liability for third-person NIED.

§ 47.   Negligent Infliction of Emotional Disturbance Resulting From Bodily Harm To A Third Person

An actor who negligently causes serious bodily injury to a third person is subject to liability for serious emotional disturbance thereby caused to a person who:

(a) perceives the event contemporaneously, and

(b) is a close family member of the person suffering the bodily injury.

d. "Participants" in the Tort

In *Clomon v. Monroe City School Board*, 572 So. 2d 571 (La. 1990), a majority of the Court permitted recovery by a young woman against a school board for damages because of the severe emotional distress she sustained without contemporaneous physical injury when her automobile struck and killed a four year old school boy. The boy darted into the woman's path after the board's bus driver and bus attendant discharged the boy from the bus, prematurely deactivated the bus warning devices and drove away, leaving the boy alone to cross the street to his home. The Court observed that the plaintiff could not recover under the "bystander" rule set out in *LeJeune* because she did not have a close relationship with the trauma victim. However, "the *LeJeune* court did not intend to modify or interrupt the development of rules or decisions permitting recovery for emotional distress from a tortfeasor who owed the plaintiff a special direct duty created by law, contract or special relationship...(B)y vesting the bus driver with authority similar to that of a policeman to direct the motorist's use of the highway under pain of criminal penalty the legislature has imposed upon the bus driver the duty to perform his role properly for the benefit of the motorist...(I)n the narrow class of cases involving the direct, special statutory duty owed to the motorist, there is no justification for the creation of juristic limitations upon the principle of reparation underlying Civil Code Article 2315." The motorist's contributory negligence reduced but did not bar her claim for emotional distress.

Does C.C. Art. 2315.6 eliminate the "Clomon-type" plaintiff? In *Pourciau v. Allstate Ins. Co.*, 712 So. 2d 250 (La.App. 3 Cir. 1998), where plaintiff was roller skating with decedent when decedent was struck and killed by defendant's vehicle; plaintiff avoided the collision by swerving and allegedly falling to the ground. The appellate court allowed plaintiff to recover injury, reasoning that because of the "near miss", plaintiff was involved in this accident." However, the Supreme Court reversed, per curiam, observing that "(p)laintiff ... is not one of the classes of persons under La. Civ. Code art. 2315.6 who may recover mental anguish damages for the injury to another. Accordingly, insofar as plaintiff attempts to recover damages other than those arising from her own mental anguish caused by the accident, the partial exception of no right of action is hereby granted." 805 So. 2d 184 (La. 1998).

10.   Misrepresentation

Intentional misrepresentation constitutes fraud, and is actionable, whether it causes personal injury or only economic harm. *See, e.g., America's Favorite Chicken Co. v. Cajun Enterprises, Inc.*, 130 F.3d 180 (5th Cir. 1997). Negligent misrepresentation which causes personal injury also is compensable, if personal injury was foreseeable (a truck driver negligently signals a following driver that it is safe to pass on a curve?). Where negligent misrepresentation causes only economic harm, courts are hesitant to allow recovery. The policy reasons are obvious; the "floodgates" and "overdeterrence" arguments are most obvious. Nevertheless, the desire to compensate victims of undesirable conduct has led courts to permit some recovery. The *Barrie* case is the leading Louisiana authority on the point.

ORTIQUE, J.

At issue is whether the lower courts erred in finding the petition of plaintiffs, purchasers of a dwelling, fails to state a cause of action in tort against the termite inspector who issued a wood destroying insect report to the vendor of the dwelling in prospect of the sale, when the inspector knew the report would be given to them, the prospective purchasers to facilitate the sale, and its contents which allegedly negligently concluded the premises had "no physical evidence of active and/or old infestation from subterranean termites," would influence their decision to purchase, when they suffered pecuniary loss as a result. The trial court sustained the peremptory exceptions of no cause of action filed by the termite inspector, his company and his insurer. Their motions for summary judgment, dismissing plaintiffs' suit as to them, were also granted. The appellate court affirmed, indicating plaintiffs' action for negligent misrepresentation could not lie against these defendants because there was no privity between them.

We granted certiorari to determine whether a termite inspector has a duty to exercise reasonable care and competence in obtaining and communicating information in a termite inspection report, so as to protect third persons for whose benefit and guidance the information was sought and supplied, and who may detrimentally rely on its contents thereby suffering pecuniary loss. We conclude Louisiana law provides such a duty. Our general tort principles provide a cause of action against a termite inspector who, in the course of his business, allegedly fails to exercise reasonable care, competence or skill in ascertaining facts and/or in communicating the facts or opinion in a termite inspection report which was contracted for and supplied to another, a vendor, to facilitate a sale of real estate, in favor of the purchasers of the property who suffered foreseeable pecuniary loss because they detrimentally relied upon the contents of the report, even though the purchasers are not a party to the contract and have had no direct or indirect contact with the termite inspector, when the termite inspector supplied it to facilitate the sale so as to make the purchasers intended users of the report. Therefore, we reverse. The judgments of the lower courts are vacated and the case remanded to the trial court for further proceedings in keeping with the legal principles set forth herein.

* * * * *

The common law tort of misrepresentation is generally separated into three tort classifications: intentional, negligent, and strict liability. Prosser and Keeton, The Law of Torts, § 107, p. 745 (5th ed. 1984). Pertinent to this case is the classification of negligent misrepresentation, specifically, representations made in the course of rendering service pursuant to a contract, when made with an honest belief in its truth, but because of lack of reasonable care or an absence of skill or competence in ascertaining the facts or making the opinion, and/or in the manner of communicating the facts or opinion, the representation causes economic loss to be suffered by a third party, but an intended user of the information, who relies on the information to their detriment. *See id.*, pp. 745, 746. It is distinguished from actions for intentional fraud or deceit, warranty actions and actions where plaintiff has suffered physical harm.

* * * * *

Despite Cardozo's "assault on the citadel of privity" by recognizing a tort duty owed under certain circumstances to a third party to a contract who relies on negligent misinformation, some states have continued to adhere to the traditional common law view that economic losses cannot be recovered in tort in the absence of privity of contract.... Nevertheless, in the states which recognize a tort duty where privity is absent, three standards[10] have developed since the venerable Justice Cardozo authored these two hallmark cases: the "akin to privity" view, the foreseeability view and the

---

[10] Some courts maintain there are four standards, the last standard being a balancing test....

Restatement (2d) of Torts § 552 view....

The "akin to privity" view is the restrictive minority view. It extends liability for economic loss only to those persons with whom defendant is in a relationship "akin to privity." ... The rule defines and limits the scope of the defendant's duty according to the defendant's state of mind and the agreed upon expectations of the parties of the underlying contract....

The foreseeability view is an expansive view because it allows recovery to third parties "to the extent that damages incurred by non-clients are reasonably foreseeable." ... Liability under this rule extends to all reasonably foreseeable plaintiffs who, as a result of their actual and justifiable reliance on negligently made representations, suffer economic damages.... It dispenses with privity notions altogether....

The Restatement (2d) of Torts § 552 view[12] is considered a majority rule as it has been embraced by at least nineteen states.... It is an adaptation of Glanzer's intended beneficiary doctrine.... § 552 allows a restricted group of third parties to a contract to recover for pecuniary losses attributable to misinformation.... Where the "akin to privity" rule requires that the precise identity of the informational consumer be foreseen by defendants, "the Restatement contemplates identification of a narrow group, not necessarily the specific membership within that group.".... The view expressly limits liability to a select group of non-clients who the misinformer actually knows will receive inaccurate information principally because the misinformer knows the client will channel the work product to that restricted group. *Id.*... Direct communication of the information from the misinformer to the person acting in reliance upon it, therefore, is not necessary. § 552, comment G. The misinformer need only know its client intends to use the inaccurate information to influence a particular business transaction, or a "substantially similar" transaction to follow.... It is not required that plaintiff be identified or known to the misinformer as an individual when the information is supplied. § 552, comment H.

III

Louisiana is a jurisdiction which allows recovery in tort for purely economic loss caused by negligent misrepresentation where privity of contract is absent. *Pastor v. Lafayette Bldg. Ass'n.*, 567 So.2d 793 (La.App. 3d Cir.1990); *Payne v. O'Quinn*, 565 So. 2d 1049 (La.App. 3 Cir. 1990); *Cypress Oilfield Contractors, Inc. v. McGoldrick Oil Co., Inc.*, 525 So. 2d 1157 (La.App. 3 Cir. 1988), *writ den.*, 530 So. 2d 570 (La.1988). Thus far, the tort theory has developed case by case. Our courts have not subscribed to any one of the three common law standards. *See* Section II, *supra*.

The seminal Louisiana case on the topic, *Devore v. Hobart Mfg. Co.*, 367 So. 2d 836, 839 (La. 1979), acknowledged that LSA-C.C. arts. 2315 and 2316 are sufficiently broad to encompass a cause of action for negligent misrepresentation. While Devore recited Restatement (2d) of Torts § 552 in a footnote when recapitulating the arguments urged by the plaintiff, it did not adopt the

---

[12] Section 552 of the Restatement (2d) of Torts, provides as follows:
   § 552. INFORMATION NEGLIGENTLY SUPPLIED FOR THE GUIDANCE OF OTHERS
      (1) One who, in the course of his business, profession or employment, or in any other transaction in which he has a pecuniary interest, supplies false information for the guidance of others in their business transactions, is subject to liability for pecuniary loss caused to them by their justifiable reliance upon the information, if he fails to exercise reasonable care or competence in obtaining or communicating the information.
      (2) Except as stated in Subsection (3), the liability stated in Subsection (1) is limited to loss suffered (a) by the person or one of a limited group of persons for whose benefit and guidance he intends to supply the information or knows that the recipient intends to supply it; and (b) through reliance upon it in a transaction that he intends the information to influence or knows that the recipient so intends or in a substantially similar transaction.
      (3) The liability of one who is under a public duty to give the information extends to loss suffered by any of the class of persons for whose benefit the duty is created, in any of the transactions in which it is intended to protect them.

Restatement's view. The holding in Devore, nevertheless, was consistent with the Restatement (and the other two common law standards) as defendant was found to have no affirmative duty to supply correct information merely from gratuitously providing plaintiff with requested information.[15] *See* § 552, comment C.

* * * * *

Whether a duty is owed is a question of law. *Harris v. Pizza Hut of Louisiana, Inc.*, 455 So. 2d at 1371. Where there is privity of contract or a fiduciary relationship, our appellate courts have found a duty owed to the tort victim under factual scenarios of both non-disclosure and misinformation. For example: *Ernestine v. Baker, supra* [realtor has a duty to disclose to purchasers defects of which he has knowledge]; *Braydon v. Melancon, supra* [realtor has a duty to relay accurate information concerning the property]; *Dousson v. South Central Bell, supra* [under § 552 of the Restatement, SCB had a tort duty to exercise reasonable care when it informed Plaintiff of the steps necessary to obtain the same telephone number of a service station he was purchasing]; *Woods v. Integon Life Ins. Corp.*, 507 So. 2d 259 (La.App. 3 Cir. 1987), *writ den.*, 512 So. 2d 461 (La. 1978) [insurer had duty to supply correct information which was breached when insurer failed to inform the prospective insureds that it converted their joint application into an individual application for the wife only]; *Josephs v. Austin, supra* [realtor has a duty to relay accurate information since both vendor and vendee rely on his honesty, access to information, knowledge and expertise]; *Beal v. Lomas and Nettleton Co., supra* [mortgagee, who collected insurance premium from mortgagor, has a duty to correctly convey information to mortgagor on the substitution of one insurer's policy for another with respect to new coverage].

More pertinently, in cases where privity of contract is absent but there is communication of the misinformation by the tortfeasor directly to the user or the user's agent, they have also found the user is owed a tort duty. *See Payne v. O'Quinn*, 565 So. 2d at 1054 [where termite inspector delivered a wood destroying insect report to the realtor representing both vendor and vendee (under the assumption that the exterminator had no contractual relationship with vendee), *held*: the exterminator "assumed a duty to insure the information it provided as part of its stated obligation as well as that which it volunteered to provide was correct. Furthermore, that duty encompassed the risk that a prospective purchaser (Payne) would rely upon the misrepresentation provided to the realtor, and suffer the damages sustained."]; *Pastor v. Lafayette Bldg. Ass'n.*, 567 So. 2d at 796 [where a second mortgagee sued the first mortgagee in connection with the subordination of an additional amount at the time of the sale of the property, held: the first mortgagee had no duty to supply any information to the second mortgagee, a non-client; however, "once it volunteered the information [directly to plaintiff], it assumed a duty to insure that the information volunteered was correct."]; *Cypress Oilfield Contractors, Inc. v. McGoldrick Oil Co., Inc.*, 525 So. 2d at 1162 [when bank wrote to plaintiff, a non-

---

[15] The petition of plaintiff, Annie Devore, alleged she was a Rapides Parish School Board employee who was injured by boiling water when it spewed out of a double boiler in the school kitchen. Her attorney wrote to the school board to learn the name of the manufacturer of the double boiler. The school board, through its Director of Food Services, negligently advised Devore's attorney that the manufacturer was Cleveland Manufacturing Company rather than Cleveland Range Company. As a result, Devore's attorney sued the wrong manufacturing company. More than a year after the anniversary of Devore's injury, the correct manufacturer was named as a defendant and, in the alternative, so was the Rapides Parish School Board and its Director of Food Services for supplying the misinformation. The correct manufacturer was dismissed by the trial court on the peremptory exception of prescription. The trial court also dismissed the school board and its director on a peremptory exception of no cause of action. The court of appeal affirmed, as did this court. While this court recognized that LSA-C.C. arts. 2315 and 2316 are sufficiently broad to encompass a cause of action for negligent misrepresentation we, nevertheless, found plaintiff's petition failed to state a cause of action under that tort theory because there was no duty on the part of defendants to supply the correct information. 367 So. 2d at 839. We stated that defendants did not have an affirmative duty to supply correct information merely because it had gratuitously provided plaintiff with the information requested, especially as it had not apprised the school board of the high degree of reliance she would place upon the information. *Id.* We further found there was no duty on the part of defendants to supply the correct information because plaintiff did not allege defendants had actual knowledge of the use plaintiff intended or defendants' exclusive control over the information. *Id.*

customer, stating clearly that the financial condition of one of the bank's customers to whom it had extended credit was not in jeopardy, held: the bank "assumed a duty to insure that the information volunteered was correct"].[16]

In sum, Louisiana's case by case development of the tort of negligent misrepresentation has not been restricted to a set theory. It has been broadly used to encompass situations of non-disclosure in fiduciary relationships, to situations of direct disclosure to non-clients. Adopting one of the common law standards as the sole method for determining liability for this tort is not necessary. The case by case application of the duty/risk analysis, presently employed by our courts, adequately protects the misinformer and the misinformed because the initial inquiry is whether, as a matter of law, a duty is owed to this particular plaintiff to protect him from this particular harm.

IV

The scope of the duty that V.P. and its owner/agent/employee, Palumbo, owed to the Barries was to use reasonable care and competence in obtaining or ascertaining facts for and/or in communicating the facts or opinion in the wood destroying insect report. The duty was owed to the Barries even though they were a third party to V.P., without privity of contract or direct or indirect contact, because they were known to V.P. as the intended users of the report. The Barries were members of the limited group for whose benefit and guidance the report was contracted and supplied. V.P. owed the duty to the Barries because of its knowledge that the ultimate purpose for the report, and its employment, was to facilitate the sale of the dwelling it inspected. The Barries' expected use of the report made the magnitude of their loss a foreseeable probability. The obligation for the liability is imposed by law based upon policy considerations due to the tortfeasor's knowledge of the prospective use of the information which expands the bounds of his duty of reasonable care to encompass the intended user. *See Glanzer v. Shepard, supra.* The duty of care owed by V.P., encompassed by LSA-C.C. arts. 2315 and 2316, is compatible with the one stated in the Restatement (2d) of Torts, § 552. Liability is not confined by the limitations of the third-party beneficiary/stipulation pour autrui contact theory. *See* LSA-C.C. art. 1978 et seq.

* * * * *

Unlike the plaintiff in Devore who was owed no duty, V.P. did not perform its services gratuitously. Palumbo gathered and conveyed the information in the context of a business transaction for which V.P. received compensation. *See* § 552, comment C, D. Thus, in contrast to the school board in Devore which undertook only the general obligation of honesty when it gratuitously provided the plaintiff the requested information, due to V.P.'s pecuniary interest in supplying the information, the duty arose to exercise reasonable care and competence in obtaining the information for the wood destroying insect report and communicating it to the intended users, which group included the Barries. *See* § 552, comments A, D, E.

For V.P. and Palumbo to be obligated in tort to the Barries, it was not necessary for the Barries to employ V.P., or for Palumbo to directly communicate with them or indirectly communicate with them through their agent.... The duty of care attached to the plaintiffs' identity not because Palumbo knew them as individuals but because he knew Secor intended to transmit the report to its prospective purchasers. *See* § 552, comments H, J.

Defendants, as licensed structural pest control operators under LSA-R.S. 3:3361 et seq. issuing a wood destroying insect report as required by LSA-R.S. 3:3370(C), by implication, held themselves out as specialists. The Barries, as intended recipients of the wood destroying insect report,

---

[16] *See also Mills v. Ganucheau*, 416 So. 2d at 365 [although plaintiff was not the user of the misinformation, the Clerk of Court was found to have a duty to properly check the records of the court before replying to a letter from the Los Angeles Police Department, when he knew the possibility of criminal actions against plaintiff was dependent on his response; the Clerk of Court was found liable for damages plaintiff suffered when he was extradited and incarcerated].

were entitled to expect that a structural pest control operator licensed by this state would perform its investigation with reasonable care and competence, exercising normal professional competence when issuing its written report. *See* § 552, comments E, F.

Tort liability extending to third persons for whose benefit and guidance the wood destroying insect report is supplied, promotes the maintenance of a high quality of services by the licensed structural pest control operator and imparts confidence in those services to the contracting party and to those persons who, due to current business practices, are expected to receive and rely upon the contents of the report. Therefore, the duty to use reasonable care and competence in obtaining the information for the wood destroying insect report and communicating it to the prospective buyers of the dwelling existed as a matter of law.

* * * * *

NOTES

1. Note that the theory of recovery is the tort of negligence, not contract theory. There is no contract between the plaintiff (Barrie) and the defendant (V.P. Exterminators). How does the tort theory differ from a contract theory?

2. *Venture Associates Inc. of Louisiana v. Transportation Underwriters of La.*, 634 So. 2d 4 (La.App. 3 Cir. 1994), *writ denied*, 639 So. 2d 1165 (La. 1994) – An agent who supplies a third party with incorrect information about agent's principal may owe a duty to subsequently supply the third party with the correct information, although in the interim the agency relationship has terminated.

3. The elements of a claim for negligent misrepresentation are (1) the existence of a legal duty on the part of the defendant to supply correct information or to refrain from supplying incorrect information, (2) breach of that duty, and (3) damages caused to the plaintiff as a result of that breach. An attorney has a legal duty to supply correct information such that he is liable to a non-client for malpractice if the non-client shows that the attorney provided legal services and that the attorney knew that the non-client intended to rely upon those legal services. An attorney's liability to the third party flows from the code provision establishing liability for a stipulation pour autrui. Where an attorney contracts to provide a professional opinion for the benefit of a third person, privity of contract results. *Trust Company of Louisiana v. N.N.P., Inc.*, 92 F.3d 341 (5th Cir. 1996). *See, also, Hardy v. Hartford*, 236 F.3d 287 (5th Cir. 2001) – a negligent misrepresentation claim is made out when a person, in the course of his business or other matters in which he has a pecuniary interest, supplies false information without exercising reasonable care, for the guidance of others, who justifiably and detrimentally rely on such information and thereby suffer a pecuniary loss.

4. A related claim is for the tort of spoliation (intentional destruction or negligent failure to preserve evidence). Usually, spoliation is committed by a litigant, and the penalty is procedural, i.e., the jury is told it must presume that the evidence would have been unfavorable to the spoliator or, in extreme cases, default judgment is rendered against the spoliator. In *Reynolds v. Bordelon*, 172 So. 3d 607 (La. 2015), the Louisiana Supreme Court held that no private cause of action exists for negligent spoliation. An excerpt from *Reynolds* is reprinted in Chapter 1.

5. Defendant, a subcontractor of an independent contractor engaged by employer, allegedly was negligent in handling a urine sample submitted by plaintiff, a prospective employee, for a required pre-employment drug screen. As a result, the employment was delayed, which caused a delay in the commencement of employee's coverage in employer's health benefits program. After he began his employment but before his health benefits coverage began, employee was severely injured. *Held*, defendant is not liable in tort or in contract to employee; employee was not a third party beneficiary to employer's subcontract with defendant, and defendant's alleged negligence did not encompass the risk that occurred. *Paul v. Louisiana State Employees' Group Benefit Program*, 762 So. 2d 136 (La.App. 1 Cir. 2000).

6. In *Guidry v. U.S. Tobacco Co.*, 188 F.3d 619 (5th Cir. 1999), the court, noting the distinction

between intentional misrepresentation involving the risk of physical harm and such misrepresentation involving only the risk of economic harm, concludes that Louisiana courts would use as the standard for intentional misrepresentation involving physical harm one similar to Restatement (Second) of Torts, Sec. 310, which provides that an actor who makes a misrepresentation is subject to liability for physical harm to another which results from an act done by the other or a third person in reliance upon the truth of the representation, if the actor (a) intends his statement to induce or should realize that it is likely to induce action by the other, or by a third person, which involves an unreasonable risk of harm to the other, and (b) knows (i) that the statement is false, or (ii) that he has not the knowledge which he professes. *See also*, Chapter 12, Sec. B(2), *infra*.

7. A federal district court, applying Louisiana law, stated the rule of *Barrie* as follows:

> *Barrie* extended the duty scenario slightly. Although *Barrie* was a case of misinformation (as opposed to non-disclosure), the defendant had not delivered the report directly to the plaintiff or the plaintiff's agent or otherwise had contact with the plaintiffs, as had been the case in previous scenarios where courts had extended a contractual duty beyond the contract (absent a fiduciary or confidential relationship). The court concluded that the inspector nevertheless owed a duty to the plaintiffs "because they were known to [the inspector] as the intended users of the report." 625 So. 2d at 1016. The purchaser's "use of the termite inspection report was not merely one possibility among many, but the end and aim of the ... transaction." *Id.* at 1016-17 (internal quotations omitted). The seller had contracted for the report solely for the purpose of providing it to the buyers to give them assurance regarding the condition of the dwelling, and the inspector knew this. In reaching its holding, the court emphasized that Louisiana's approach to negligent misrepresentation has been and continues to be a "case by case application of the duty/risk analysis." *Id.* at 1016.

In re FEMA Trailer Formaldehyde Products Liability Litigation, 838 F. Supp. 2d 497, 2012 WL 137803 (E.D.La. 2012).

8.   Consider these sections of the Restatement (Second) of Torts:

§ 304. Negligent Misrepresentation Affecting Conduct Of Others

A misrepresentation of fact or law may be negligent conduct.

§ 310. Conscious Misrepresentation Involving Risk Of Physical Harm

An actor who makes a misrepresentation is subject to liability to another for physical harm which results from an act done by the other or a third person in reliance upon the truth of the representation, if the actor

(a) intends his statement to induce or should realize that it is likely to induce action by the other, or a third person, which involves an unreasonable risk of physical harm to the other, and

(b) knows

(i) that the statement is false, or

(ii) that he has not the knowledge which he professes.

§ 311. Negligent Misrepresentation Involving Risk Of Physical Harm

(1) One who negligently gives false information to another is subject to liability for physical harm caused by action taken by the other in reasonable reliance upon such information, where such harm results

269

(a) to the other, or

(b) to such third persons as the actor should expect to be put in peril by the action taken.

(2) Such negligence may consist of failure to exercise reasonable care

(a) in ascertaining the accuracy of the information, or

(b) in the manner in which it is communicated.

11. Economic Loss

The "economic loss" doctrine is the label for a principle that denies recovery in tort caused by injury to the person or property of another. The leading case is *Robin's Dry Dock & Repair Company v. Flint*, 275 U.S. 303 (1927), where the Supreme Court held that to recover for a maritime casualty such as a collision, the plaintiff must suffer physical damage to some property in which the plaintiff has a "proprietary interest."

For example, consider the facts of In re Bertucci Contracting Co., L.L.C., 712 F.3d 245 (5th Cir. 2013), the vessel *Julie Marie* ran into a bridge that connected the communities of Lafitte and Barataria, Louisiana. This inconvenienced the residents of Barataria who had to take the long way around to New Orleans. Residents brought a class action for lost use of property, lost business revenue, and other similar damage. The U.S. Fifth Circuit affirmed the dismissal of the case because the plaintiffs did not suffer injury to their own property. Rather, the injury occurred to the bridge and plaintiffs only suffered economic loss that resulted from injury to the property of another.

The economic loss rule is applied in admiralty cases like *Robins* and *Bertucci* and has been adopted by many, but not all states. In Louisiana, any blanket "rule" has been rejected.

PPG INDUSTRIES, INC.
v.
BEAN DREDGING
447 So. 2d 1058 (La. 1984)

LEMMON, J.

The issue in this case is whether a dredging contractor who negligently damaged a natural gas pipeline may be held liable for the economic losses incurred by the pipeline owner's contract customer who was required to seek and obtain gas from another source during the period of repair. Thus, this case brings into focus the broad question of recovery of an indirect economic loss incurred by a party who had a contractual relationship with the owner of property negligently damaged by a tortfeasor.[1] We conclude that while the situation giving rise to the question in this case falls literally within the expansive terms of La.C.C.Art. 2315, in that the dredging contractor's "act ... cause[d] damage to another", the customer cannot recover his indirect economic loss.[2] For the policy reasons hereinafter

---

[1] Recovery of economic losses for *negligent* interference with contractual relations is almost uniformly denied in other jurisdictions. See Restatement (Second) of Torts § 766 C comment a (1977). On the other hand, recovery for *intentional* interference with contractual relations has been permitted in every jurisdiction in this country except Louisiana. Malone, The Work of the Louisiana Appellate Courts for the 1963-1964 Term-Torts, 25 La.L.Rev. 341 (1965). *See also* W. Prosser, Law of Torts § 129 at 930 (4th Ed.1971). There is considerable sentiment for permitting recovery in Louisiana for intentional interference with contracts, such as by the deliberate inducing of breach of contract. However, that issue is not presented in this case.

[2] La.C.C.Art. 2315 provides in pertinent part:
"Every act whatever of man that causes damage to another obliges him by whose fault it happened to repair it."

stated in a duty-risk analysis, we hold that the damages to the economic interest of the contract purchaser of natural gas, caused by a dredging contractor's negligent injury to property which prevents the pipeline owner's performance of the contract to supply natural gas to the purchaser, do not fall within the scope of the protection intended by the law's imposition of a duty on dredging contractors not to damage pipelines negligently.

Bean Dredging Company's dredging operations in the Calcasieu River caused damage to Texaco's natural gas pipeline. As a result, Texaco was unable to fulfill its contract to supply natural gas to PPG Industries for operation of its manufacturing plant, and PPG had to obtain fuel from another source at an increased cost. PPG filed this suit against Bean, seeking to recover the increased cost of obtaining natural gas. Bean filed an exception of no cause of action, contending that Louisiana has never recognized the right of recovery for negligent interference with contractual relations.

The trial court sustained Bean's exception of no cause of action. The court of appeal affirmed, relying on *Forcum-James Co. v. Duke Transportation Co.,* 231 La. 953, 93 So. 2d 228 (1957). 419 So. 2d 23. We granted certiorari. 422 So. 2d 151.

When the question of recovery of indirect economic losses caused by a negligent injury to property that interferes with contractual relations has been presented in previous cases, the courts of this state have generally denied recovery without analyzing the problem, taking a mechanical approach to the unreasoned conclusion that the petition fails to state a cause of action for which relief can be granted. Most cases have cited *Robins Dry Dock & Repair Co. v. Flint,* 275 U.S. 303, 48 S.Ct. 134, 72 L.Ed. 290 (1927), and *Forcum-James Co. v. Duke Transportation Co.,* above, which were relied on by the court of appeal in the present case. *See*, for example, *Desormeaux v. Central Industries, Inc.,* 333 So. 2d 431 (La.App. 3 Cir. 1976), *cert. denied* 337 So. 2d 225 (La. 1976); *Messina v. Sheraton Corporation of America,* 291 So. 2d 829 (La.App. 4 Cir.1974).

In *Robins,* an admiralty case, the charterer of a vessel sought recovery of damages for its loss of use while the vessel was out of service after the dry dock operator negligently damaged its propeller. The Supreme Court denied recovery on the basis that the negligent repairer, who acted unintentionally while unaware of the contract of charter, cannot be held liable unless the party seeking damages had a proprietary interest in the damaged property.

Although knowledge does not seem to be a relevant factor to the determination of the defendant's liability to the charterer, the case has been cited countless times for the proposition that recovery is generally denied for negligent interference with contractual relations.[3] A better reasoned explanation for the *Robins* decision was suggested in F. Harper & F. James, The Law of Torts § 6.10

---

[3] The Supreme Court of Louisiana relied on *Robins* in deciding the *Forcum-James* case. The plaintiff in *Forcum-James* was a contractor who was required by a contract with the Department of Highways to repair a state-owned bridge that had been damaged by the tortfeasor. Plaintiff sued the tortfeasor to recover the cost of the repairs. The court held that the state, as owner, was the proper party to sue for the damage to the bridge and maintained an exception of no *right* of action as to plaintiff's suit against the tortfeasor. As to plaintiff's damages sustained by reason of having to repair the bridge, the court, relying on *Robins,* stated that "where a third person suffers damage by reason of a contractual obligation to the injured party, such damage is too remote and indirect to become the subject of a direct action ex delicto, in the absence of subrogation". 93 So. 2d at 230.

The obvious purpose of the *Forcum-James* decision was to prevent the tortfeasor from having to pay twice for the same damage, and the court in effect required that suit for the damage to the bridge be filed by either the owner of the bridge or a party subrogated to the rights of the owner. Because evidence of subrogation had been excluded in the trial court, the court remanded for introduction of such evidence.

The instant case presents a different, but related, problem. In *Forcum-James,* the cost of repairing the bridge was a loss to be recovered by either one party or the other, but not both. Here, only one party was entitled to recover the cost of repairing the pipeline, but both Texaco and PPG (and perhaps other parties) incurred economic losses during the period of repair that would not have been incurred *but for* the tortfeasor's negligence.

(1956), as follows:

> "It is the reluctance of the Court to hold the tort-feasor liable, in addition to the physical damage to the vessel, for the value of *two* bargains. Under the contract with the owners, the charterers were excused from paying rent while the ship was laid up for repairs. This loss was included in the settlement between the defendants and the owners. Having made good one bargain, the tort-feasor is now asked to make good the still better bargain of the charterer. This, conceivably, *could go on and on. The Court drew the line after the first.* The *multiplicity of actions* and the *unforeseeable extension of liability* may well have influenced the Court in denying the charterer's claim, as a *matter of policy.*" (Emphasis supplied.)

Similar policy considerations lead to our decision in the present case. Under the alleged facts, there appears to be no question that Bean is liable to Texaco for the costs of repairing the pipeline and for the direct economic losses sustained by Texaco during the period of repair.[4] However, the rule of law which prohibits negligent damage to property does not necessarily require that a party who negligently causes injury to property must be held legally responsible to *all* persons for *all* damages flowing in a "but for" sequence from the negligent conduct.

Rules of conduct are designed to protect *some* persons under *some* circumstances against *some* risks. Malone, Ruminations on Cause-in-Fact, 9 Stan.L.Rev. 60 (1956). Policy considerations determine the reach of the rule, and there must be an ease of association between the rule of conduct, the risk of injury, and the loss sought to be recovered. *Hill v. Lundin & Assoc., Inc.,* 260 La. 542, 256 So.2d 620 (1972). A judge, when determining whether the interest of the party seeking recovery of damages is one that falls within the intended protection of the rule of law whose violation gave rise to the damages, should consider the particular case in the terms of the moral, social and economic values involved, as well as with a view toward the ideal of justice. *See Entrevia v. Hood,* 427 So.2d 1146 (La.1983).

There is clearly an ease of association in the present case between the rule of law which imposes a duty not to negligently damage property belonging to another and the risk of injury sustained by Texaco because of the damage to its property. As noted, however, a rule of law is seldom intended to protect *every* person against *every* risk. It is much more difficult to associate the same rule of law, in terms of the moral, social and economic values involved, with the risk of injury and the economic loss sustained by the person whose only interest in the pipeline damaged by the tortfeasor's negligence arose from a contract to purchase gas from the pipeline owner. It is highly unlikely that the moral, social and economic considerations underlying the imposition of a duty not to negligently injure property encompass the risk that a third party who has contracted with the owner of the injured property will thereby suffer an economic loss.

Moreover, imposition of responsibility on the tortfeasor for such damages could create liability "in an indeterminate amount for an indeterminate time to an indeterminate class". *Ultramares Corp. v. Touche,* 255 N.Y. 170, 179, 174 N.E. 441, 444 (1931). If any of PPG's employees were laid off while PPG sought to obtain another source of fuel for its plant, they arguably sustained damages which in all likelihood would not have occurred *but for* defendant's negligence. If any of PPG's customers had contracted to purchase products that PPG could not produce and deliver because of the accident, perhaps they sustained damages which in all likelihood would not have occurred *but for* defendant's negligence. Because the list of possible victims and the extent of economic damages might be expanded indefinitely, the court necessarily makes a policy decision on the limitation of recovery of damages. *See* James, Limitations on Liability for Economic Loss Caused by Negligence; A Pragmatic Approach, 25 Vand.L.Rev. 43 (1972).[5]

---

[4] For purposes of the exception of no cause of action, the court must accept as proved facts the allegations of the petition that Bean negligently damaged the pipeline, that as a result of the accident Texaco was unable to deliver natural gas to PPG in accordance with their contract, and that PPG thereby sustained economic losses.

[5] In the article Professor James argues that *Robins* was illogical in denying recovery for the charterer for lost

272

We conclude that the duty allegedly violated in the present case did not encompass the particular risk of injury sustained by PPG and did not intend protection from the particular loss for which recovery is sought in PPG's petition.

Accordingly, the judgments of the lower courts are affirmed.

DIXON, C.J., concurs.

CALOGERO, J., dissents and assigns reasons.

CALOGERO, Justice, dissenting.

I applaud the majority's applying a duty risk analysis in the consideration of tort recovery for negligent interference with contractual relations, and its abandoning the per se exclusion of such damages which our courts have heretofore adopted on the heels of *Robins* and *Forcum-James.*[1]

Where I disagree, is in the majority's determination that PPG's economic loss, from added fuel cost, is not a risk encompassed within the duty not to negligently injure Texaco's pipelines. PPG's loss of profits; PPG's employees' loss of jobs and income; PPG's customers' losses, because PPG could not produce and deliver; are all economic losses which might properly be determined to fall outside the scope of the protection intended by the law's imposing a duty on dredging contractors not to damage pipelines negligently. The same cannot be said for PPG's added fuel cost.

Bean was dredging the waterway that ran right along the side of PPG's plant. There were signs along the waterway warning of the existence of the gas pipeline and cautioning against dredging in the area. There were also maps of the water bottom showing the pipelines. At the time Bean negligently dredged through the waterway, there could have been no doubt to anyone that the pipeline in question was providing PPG with its fuel to run its plant. The damages suffered by PPG were *not unforeseen,* at least as far as the added fuel costs go.

If PPG is to be denied its added fuel cost I can perceive no instance in which a nonowner of negligently damaged property may recover from a tortfeasor. In light of the result here it would probably have been better if the majority had simply affirmed the jurisprudential rule established in *Robins* and *Forcum-James* which has prevailed so long.

NOTE

We have already seen examples of the Louisiana approach applied to negligent misrepresentation and spoliation. What policies justify the economic loss doctrine?

---

business resulting from boat damage simply because the charterer did not own the boat. He points out that the injury was neither unforeseeable nor unlimited, that the damages would have been determined had plaintiff been the owner, and that questions of multiple liability, proper plaintiffs, and protection of settlements could be handled by regular procedural devices. *Id.* at 56.

[1] *Robins Dry Dock & Repair Co. v. Flint,* 275 U.S. 303, 48 S.Ct. 134, 72 L.Ed. 290 (1927); *Forcum-James Co. v. Duke Transportation Co.,* 231 La. 953, 93 So. 2d 228 (1957).

12. Negligent Hiring, Training, Retaining and Supervising

ROBERTS
v.
BENOIT
605 So. 2d 1032 (La. 1992) (on rehearing)

HALL, J.

This is a suit for damages sustained by plaintiff, Bobby Ray Roberts, Jr., as a result of the accidental discharge of a gun owned and possessed by Joseph T. Benoit, a commissioned deputy sheriff with the Orleans Parish Criminal Sheriff's Office. Plaintiff sued Benoit, the State of Louisiana, the City of New Orleans, the Parish of Orleans, the Criminal Sheriff for the Parish of Orleans, Sheriff Charles Foti, Jr., individually, and Southern American Insurance Company, the insurer for the Criminal Sheriff's Office.[1] Plaintiff's wife, Kathy Roberts, intervened in this suit on behalf of herself and plaintiff's three minor children. The trial court found that plaintiff established the negligence of Benoit and Sheriff Foti, and awarded damages in the amount of $785,000 to plaintiff, $25,000 to plaintiff's wife, and $ 10,000 to each of plaintiff's three minor children. The court of appeal, finding that plaintiff established Sheriff Foti's negligence in hiring, commissioning and failing to adequately train Benoit, affirmed the trial court's judgment, with one judge dissenting in part.[2] *Roberts v. Benoit*, 574 So. 2d 1256 (La.App. 4 Cir. 1991). Having granted Sheriff Foti's writ application, 575 So. 2d 816 (La. 1991), we now reverse in part and render judgment rejecting the demands against the sheriff.

Facts

In March 1979, Sheriff Foti hired the defendant Benoit as a cook. In January 1981, Sheriff Foti commissioned the kitchen workers, including Benoit, as deputy sheriffs, enabling them to receive state supplemental pay. Before being commissioned, the kitchen workers completed a training course. Training was given on an intermittent basis over a six-week period and included only one day (eight hours) of firearm training.

During the training course, the trainees were instructed that while off duty, it was better to have a gun and not need it than to need a gun and not have it, thereby impliedly encouraging deputies to carry a gun while off duty. The trainees were also given a copy of department regulations stating that when engaged in recreational activities which include the consumption of alcohol, a deputy should in all cases remove his firearm to a safe place, or leave it at home, before commencing with such activities. The regulations also stated that a weapon should be drawn only when one's life is in danger, or the use of deadly force is anticipated.

On October 25, 1981, the day of the accident, Benoit completed his regular kitchen duties at 2:30 p.m. After work, Benoit went home, bathed, changed clothes and went to his mother-in-law's home. Benoit then went to the home of his brother-in-law, Merlin Fontenette. While at Fontenette's home, Benoit drank a beer. Benoit and Fontenette then went to plaintiff's home to have plaintiff repair a broken light in Benoit's car. When they arrived at plaintiff's home, plaintiff was installing a stereo in another vehicle, and Benoit was drinking another beer. While there, Benoit drank a glass of wine and, by this time, was staggering a little.[4]

---

[1] Before trial, the City of New Orleans and the State of Louisiana were dismissed. Also, Southern went bankrupt and the Insurance Guaranty Association assumed the defense on behalf of Southern and the Sheriff's Office.

[2] Judge Plotkin disagreed with the finding of liability based on the direct negligence of the sheriff, but would have found the sheriff vicariously liable under master-servant principles. He considered the amount of damages awarded inadequate.

[4] Based on the evidence presented, the trial court concluded that Benoit was unquestionably intoxicated at the time of the accident.

Benoit had in his possession two weapons: a M1 carbine rifle which was in the trunk of his car, and a .38 caliber Charter Arms revolver purchased by him after he was commissioned as a deputy which was in an ankle holster on his leg. While at plaintiff's home, Benoit removed the revolver from the holster and played with the revolver for a period of almost forty-five minutes before the accident occurred. During this period, Benoit handed the revolver to Fontenette, who handed it back to Benoit; and, at one point, when the bullets fell from the revolver, plaintiff picked them off of the floor and handed them back to Benoit. Benoit cocked and uncocked the gun. During this period, plaintiff asked Benoit to put the gun away several times. Thereafter, the revolver discharged severely injuring plaintiff.

* * * * *

Law

At the outset, we identify two potential codal bases for imposing legal responsibility on Sheriff Foti: (1) primary liability under Civil Code Article 2315 and (2) vicarious liability under Civil Code Article 2320. In applying these general codal provisions to concrete master-servant problems, we have recognized the appropriateness of drawing freely from the common law jurisprudence. *Ermert, supra*. As the precise questions posed by the master-servant problem presented in the instant case have not previously been considered by the courts of this state, we begin by discussing the jurisprudence of other jurisdictions that have considered similar claims.

Similar Torts in Other States

Under the common law jurisprudence, a third party injured by an off-duty deputy's negligent handling of a firearm has been recognized as having two potential theories for holding the deputy's municipal employer liable: (1) the common law doctrine of respondeat superior and (2) the tort of negligent hiring.[6] The former is based on the deputy's negligence, which is imputed to the municipal employer; the latter is based upon the employer's independent negligence in hiring, commissioning, training and/or retaining the deputy. These two theories of liability are separate and independent.... The major difference between them is that the tort of negligent hiring is not cabined to the narrow confines imposed by the respondeat superior's "scope of employment" limitation.... A similar limitation, however, is imposed on the negligent hiring cause of action. This limitation is that the deputy in some respect be engaged in furthering the employer's business -- law enforcement -- when he "stepped beyond the line of duty." ... Thus, the considerations relied upon by courts in imposing liability under the two doctrines are similar.

First, under the respondeat superior doctrine, a municipal employer has been held vicariously liable for the tortious acts of its deputy when the deputy, albeit technically "off duty," is acting within the scope of his employment.

* * * * *

In sum, every conceivable discharge of a gun in an off-duty deputy's possession will not be found to be within the scope of employment.... The following cases are illustrative of the type of conduct that has been found sufficient to take off-duty deputies outside the scope of employment: *Fitzgerald v. McCutcheon*, 270 Pa. Super. 102, 410 A. 2d 1270 (1979) (intoxicated off-duty deputy shooting neighbor during dispute over deputy's car keys); *Dzing v. City of Chicago*, 84 Ill.App.3d 704, 40 Ill.Dec. 420, 406 N.E.2d 121 (Ill. App. 1 Dist. 1980) (intoxicated off-duty deputy shooting his way into victim's apartment, believing he was confronting an intruder in his own apartment); *Strachan v. Kitsap County*, 27 Wash. App. 271, 616 P.2d 1251, review denied, 94 Wash. App. 1025 (1980) (accidental shooting by off-duty deputy engaged in horseplay with loaded gun); *Nishan v. Godsey*, 166 F. Supp. 6 (E.D. Tenn. 1958) (reckless horseplay with loaded gun); ... *Olson v. Staggs-Bilt*

---

[6] The term "deputy" as used herein refers to any law enforcement officer and the term "municipal" refers to any governmental employer. Negligent "hiring" refers to hiring, training and retention of employees.

Homes, Inc., 23 Ariz. App. 574, 534 P.2d 1073 (1975) (security guard engaged in horseplay was outside scope of employment).

We turn now to the tort of negligent hiring. Under this tort, a duty is imposed on a municipal employer in arming deputies to exercise reasonable care in hiring, training and retaining such deputies. *McAndrew v. Mularchuk*, 33 N.J. 172, 162 A. 2d 820 (1960); *Marusa v. District of Columbia*, 484 F. 2d 828, 831 (D.C. Cir 1973); *Kull, supra*; *McQuillan, supra*; Greenstone, Liability of Police Officers for Misuse of Their Weapons, 16 Clev.-Mar. L.Rev. 397, 410-11 (1967). The rationale impelling the recognition of a negligent hiring cause of action was clearly articulated by the New Jersey Supreme Court in *McAndrew, supra*:

> Municipal entities must take cognizance of the hazard of sidearms. That knowledge casts an obligation on them when they arm or sanction the arming of reserve patrolmen for active police duty. The obligation is to use care commensurate with the risk to see to it that such persons are adequately trained or experienced in the proper handling and use of the weapons they are to carry. If the official in general authority in the police department sends or permits a reserve officer to go out on police duty without such training or experience, his action is one of negligent commission -- of active wrongdoing --, and if an injury results from an unjustified or negligent shooting by that officer in the course of performance of his duty, which is chargeable to the lack of training or experience, the municipality is liable.

162 A. 2d at 827 (emphasis added)....

From the ... language in *McAndrew* quoted above can be gleaned a limitation on the negligent hiring theory that the deputy, while not necessarily within the "scope of employment," be engaged in some respect in furthering the employer's business of law enforcement...

Similar to the cases in which respondeat superior liability has been imposed, the courts in imposing negligent hiring liability have generally relied heavily upon the presence of a requirement that the deputy be armed at all times....

Thus, the courts in other jurisdictions that have addressed this issue have concluded that a municipal employer who negligently either hires, commissions, trains or retains an incompetent or unfit deputy may be liable to a third party injured as a proximate result of the employer's negligence.... Simply stated, the municipal employer is said to have a duty to exercise reasonable care in hiring, commissioning and training its deputies. This duty is not unique to sheriffs, but rather is common to all employers....

In determining the exact risks anticipated by the imposition of the duty to use care in employing others, it has been suggested that this duty should be confined to cases in which three factors are present:

> (1) the employee and the plaintiff have been in places where each had a right to be when the wrongful act occurred;

> (2) the plaintiff met the employee as a direct result of the employment; and

> (3) the employer would receive some benefit from the meeting had the wrongful act not occurred.

Note, The Responsibility of Employers for the Actions of Their Employees: The Negligent Hiring Theory of Liability, 53 Chi.-Kent L. Rev. 717, 730 (1977). These factors serve to balance the interests of all the parties -- the employer, employee and public. *Id.* Overall, the most important element is establishing a connection between the employment and the plaintiff. *Id.* at 721. *See also* Speiser, Krause and Gans, The American Law of Torts § 4:8 (1983).

* * * * *

Louisiana Law – Negligence Liability

While the facts of this case present a novel issue in this state, we do not view this case as presenting a novel concept in our negligence law. Rather, we view this case as calling for the application of our standard negligence analysis. The standard negligence analysis we employ in determining whether to impose liability under Civil Code Article 2315 is the duty-risk analysis, which consists of the following four-prong inquiry: *[handwritten: cause-in-fact]*

I. Was the conduct in question a substantial factor *[handwritten: cause-in-fact]* in bringing about the harm to the plaintiff, i.e., was it a cause-in-fact of the harm which occurred?

II. Did the defendant owe a duty *[handwritten: duty]* to the plaintiff?

III. Was the duty breached? *[handwritten: breach]*

IV. Was the risk, and harm caused, within the scope of protection *[handwritten: legal cause]* afforded by the duty breached?

* * * * *

For a plaintiff to recover on a negligence theory, all four inquiries must be affirmatively answered. Based on the facts of this case, we conclude that all four inquiries cannot be answered affirmatively.

Cause in Fact

In the instant case, the first inquiry is whether the sheriff's conduct complained of was a cause in fact of plaintiff's injuries. The trial court answered this inquiry in the affirmative, finding that Sheriff Foti's negligence in commissioning Benoit as a deputy was a cause in fact of plaintiff's injuries. In affirming, the court of appeal found that "the failure to adequately train Deputy Benoit clearly was a cause in fact of plaintiff's injuries. But for his commission as a deputy sheriff, defendant Benoit would not have been carrying the weapon which caused plaintiff's injuries." 574 So. 2d at 1263. The court of appeal also found that Sheriff Foti was negligent in hiring Benoit in the first place.

* * * * *

Cause in fact is generally a "but for" inquiry; if the plaintiff probably would have not sustained the injuries but for the defendant's substandard conduct, such conduct is a cause in fact. *Fowler v. Roberts*, 556 So. 2d 1, 5 (La. 1989); Malone, Ruminations on *Dixie Drive It Yourself Versus American Beverage Company*, 30 La. L.Rev. 363, 370 (1970)....

An alternative method for determining cause in fact, which is generally used when multiple causes are present, is the "substantial factor" test. Fowler, *supra*. Under this test, cause in fact is found to exist when the defendant's conduct was a "substantial factor" in bringing about plaintiff's harm. *Dixie Drive It Yourself System v. American Beverage Co.*, 242 La. 471, 137 So. 2d 298 (1962). Under either method, it is irrelevant in determining cause in fact whether the defendant's actions were "lawful, unlawful, intentional, unintentional, negligent or non-negligent." Green, The Causal Relation Issue in Negligence Law, 60 Mich. L.Rev. 543, 549 (1962). Rather, the cause in fact inquiry is a neutral one, free of the entanglements of policy considerations -- morality, culpability or responsibility -- involved in the duty-risk analysis. *Shelton v. Aetna Casualty & Surety Co.*, 334 So. 2d 406, 409 (La. 1976).

We recognized the very limited scope of the cause in fact inquiry in *Hill v. Lundin & Associates, Inc.*, 260 La. 542, 256 So. 2d 620 (1972). There, we held that to the extent the defendant's actions had something to do with the injury the plaintiff sustained, the test of a factual, causal relationship is met. 256 So. 2d at 622. Applying these principles to the instant case, although the cause in fact determination is not without difficulty, we cannot find that the court of appeal erred in affirming the trial court's finding that Sheriff Foti's alleged negligence in hiring, training and/or commissioning Benoit as a deputy had something to do with -- was a cause in fact of -- plaintiff's injuries.

Both lower courts found that Benoit lacked basic qualifications for commissioning as a law enforcement officer and that his training, especially in the use of firearms, was inadequate. More probably than not, this accident would not have happened if Benoit had possessed the basic qualifications of education, experience, intelligence and reliability, and if he had been adequately trained in the safe, responsible use of firearms.

Duty

Duty is a question of law. Simply put, the inquiry is whether the plaintiff has any law -- statutory or jurisprudential -- to support his claim.

* * * * *

Louisiana courts first recognized this duty of an employer to exercise reasonable care in hiring employees who in the performance of their duties are likely to subject third parties to serious risk of harm in *Lou-Con, Inc. v. Gulf Building Services, Inc.*, 287 So. 2d 192 (La.App. 4 Cir. 1973), *writ denied*, 290 So. 2d 899 and 901 (La. 1974). *Cf. Morse v. Jones*, 223 La. 212, 65 So. 2d 317, 320 (1953) (finding that employer had no duty to investigate employee's background); *See also, Smith v. Orkin Exterminating Co., Inc.*, 540 So. 2d 363 (La.App. 1 Cir. 1989) (holding an employer liable for failure to exercise reasonable care in hiring and retaining employees it sends into customers' homes). We now expressly recognize the tort of negligent hiring as cognizable under Louisiana fault principles embodied in LSA-C.C. Art. 2315.

Our conclusion that Sheriff Foti had a duty to exercise reasonable care in hiring, commissioning and training Benoit, however, is only the initial step of the duty-risk analysis. As noted, a fundamental flaw in the court of appeal's analysis is that it stops at this point, leaving the more difficult legal causation questions unanswered; as the dissent aptly observed, "the legal causation issue is not directly addressed." 574 So. 2d at 1264. This flaw illustrates a common confusion, which we discussed in *Fowler v. Roberts*, 556 So. 2d 1, 6 (La. 1989), between the duty inquiry and the scope of protection (or scope of liability) inquiry. While the former questions the existence of a duty, the latter assumes a duty exists and questions whether the injury the plaintiff suffered is one of the risks encompassed by the rule of law that imposed the duty. Id. As our resolution of the scope of protection issue below is dispositive of this case, we pretermit the breach of duty analysis that is usually done at this point.[7]

Scope of Protection of Duty

The most critical issue in the instant case is whether the injury plaintiff sustained was within the contemplation of the duty discussed above. There is no "rule" for determining the scope of the duty. Regardless if stated in terms of proximate cause, legal cause, or duty, the scope of the duty inquiry is ultimately a question of policy as to whether the particular risk falls within the scope of the duty. *Edwards v. State*, 556 So. 2d 644, 648-49 (La.App. 2 Cir. 1990). In making this policy determination, this court has previously quoted the following language from Malone, Ruminations on Cause-In-Fact, 9 Stan. L.Rev. 60, 73 (1956), which is worthy of repetition.

> All rules of conduct, irrespective of whether they are the product of a legislature or are a part of the fabric of the court-made law of negligence, exist for purposes. They are designed to protect some persons under some circumstances

---

[7] We add, however, that there is substantial evidence supporting the lower courts' findings of breach of duty. Benoit lacked basic qualifications for commissioning as a deputy sheriff and his training was inadequate for that position, even though his regular duties did not encompass the usual full gamut of law enforcement duties.

against some risks. Seldom does a rule protect every victim against every risk that may befall him, merely because it is shown that the violation of the rule played a part in producing the injury. The task of defining the proper reach or thrust of a rule in its policy aspects is one that must be undertaken by the court in each case as it arises. How appropriate is the rule to the facts of this controversy? This is a question that the court cannot escape.

* * * * *

Generally, the scope of protection inquiry becomes significant in "fact-sensitive" cases in which a limitation of the "but for" consequences of the defendant's substandard conduct is warranted. *Fowler*, 556 So. 2d at 6. These cases require logic, reasoning and policy decisions be employed to determine whether liability should be imposed under the particular factual circumstances presented. This is such a case. Particularly, the court of appeal's "but for" conclusion is that had Benoit not been commissioned as a deputy he would not have been carrying the gun that caused plaintiff's injuries. *Roberts*, 574 So. 2d at 1263.

In determining the limitation to be placed on liability for a defendant's substandard conduct -- i.e., whether there is a duty-risk relationship -- we have found the proper inquiry to be how easily the risk of injury to plaintiff can be associated with the duty sought to be enforced. Hill, *supra*. Restated, the ease of association inquiry is simply: "How easily does one associate the plaintiff's complained-of harm with the defendant's conduct? ...."

In the instant case, we find the ease of association between Sheriff Foti's alleged negligence in hiring, commissioning and inadequately training Benoit and the risk of injury to this plaintiff under the circumstances and in the manner the injury occurred is, at best, attenuated. Particularly, enforcement of Sheriff Foti's duty is attenuated by several factors. First, Sheriff Foti had no requirement that Benoit carry a gun on or off duty, although carrying a gun off duty by deputies was, in general, authorized and encouraged. Second, Benoit's actions in carrying a gun on the day of the accident were in violation of Sheriff Foti's written regulation prohibiting carrying firearms while drinking. Finally, Benoit's actions in engaging in horseplay with a loaded gun while intoxicated were in violation of common sense. In spite of Benoit's lack of basic qualifications and inadequate training, nothing in his employment record indicated any likelihood that he would engage in such foolhardy conduct. In sum, we find foreseeability lacking, as "we do not believe that [the sheriff] can be expected to foresee that one of his officers would violate, not only the . . . regulation [regarding the handling of firearms while intoxicated], but also elementary standards of conduct relative to the use of firearms which are within the common knowledge and experience of everyone." *Martin v. Garlotte*, 270 So. 2d 252, 254-55 (La.App. 1 Cir. 1972), *writ refused*, 272 So. 2d 376 (1973).

We noted previously that in determining the exact risks anticipated by the imposition of the duty to use care in employing others, other courts have generally confined this duty to cases where there is a connection between the employment and the plaintiff, that is, where the plaintiff met the employee as a result of the employment and the employer would receive some benefit from the meeting had the wrongful act not occurred.

These factors are lacking in this case. Plaintiff met Benoit in a purely personal context, wholly unrelated to Benoit's employment. While it is suggested that Sheriff Foti derived some potential benefit from Benoit's choice to arm himself, as discussed above, we reject that suggestion. *See Fitzgerald*, *supra*. Thus, application of these factors reveals that the record is totally devoid of any connection between the plaintiff and Benoit's employment.

After carefully delineating the duty, it is evident that the primary purpose for imposing the duty to exercise reasonable care in hiring, commissioning and training deputies is to ensure effective and efficient law enforcement, and also to protect the public from injury caused by a deputy's negligent use of firearms while engaged in his law enforcement duties. The risk that a deputy while off duty and under no requirement to carry a gun would engage in horseplay with a loaded revolver while intoxicated, an action in violation of the Sheriff's regulations, and cause injury to plaintiff is clearly outside the ambit of protection contemplated by the imposition of that duty.

Accordingly, we find that the court of appeal erred in affirming the trial court's finding of liability on the part of Sheriff Foti. The judgment of the district court as affirmed by the court of appeal is reversed in so far as it finds Sheriff Foti liable, and the demands of plaintiff and intervenors against the sheriff are rejected.

REVERSED IN PART AND RENDERED.

CALOGERO, CJ, and WATSON, J, dissent.

On Rehearing

COLE, J.

To prevail on a negligence claim under La. Civ. Code arts. 2315 and 2316, a plaintiff must prove five separate elements: (1) the defendant had a duty to conform his conduct to a specific standard (the duty element); (2) the defendant failed to conform his conduct to the appropriate standard (the breach of duty element); (3) the defendant's substandard conduct was a cause-in-fact of the plaintiff's injuries (the cause-in-fact element); (4) the defendant's substandard conduct was a legal cause of the plaintiff's injuries (the scope of liability or scope of protection element); and, (5) actual damages (the damages element). *Fowler v. Roberts*, 556 So. 2d 1, 4 (La. 1989). In our original opinion we found the plaintiff had proven all elements except the fourth, legal cause. We adhere to that basic position.

However, we clarify the cause-in-fact element in one respect. This case appears to be a close one on the issue of cause-in-fact. It is likely that this accident might have occurred had Benoit, who already owned a weapon, never been commissioned. Thus, it is impossible to say with any degree of certainty, "but for" the sheriff's conduct, this accident would not have happened. Nonetheless, inasmuch as the Sheriff's actions can be said to have appreciably enhanced the chance of the accident's occurring, they are a cause-in-fact of the accident. *Pierre v. Allstate Insurance Co.*, 257 La. 471, 242 So. 2d 821, 831 (1970), on rehearing; *see also*, Wex Malone, Ruminations on Cause-in-Fact, 9 Stan.L.Rev. 60, 74 (1956).

Legal Cause: the Theory

As we stated in our original opinion: "Regardless if stated in terms of proximate cause, legal cause, or duty, the scope of the duty inquiry is ultimately a question of policy ... " 586 So. 2d at 142.[5] While we maintain the truth of this assertion, we feel an in-depth analysis of legal cause would be helpful.

* * * * *

In our original opinion we stated the sheriff has a duty to commission as deputies only competent law enforcement officers. Upon reconsideration, we find that the duty implicated by this case is actually much narrower, viz., the duty not to promote a cook to deputy in name alone, that is, not to engage in ersatz promotions. Hence, though we conclude that the sheriff may have acted in a suspect manner in finessing supplemental pay for kitchen workers by titularly promoting cooks to deputies, the duty to refrain from so doing does not stem from the risk that such a cook might harm someone as a result of this paper-promotion. Such a duty not to play havoc with the public fisc has, as its primary goal, the integrity of pay scales, not the safety of the public encountering cooks who are paid as deputies. Ultimately, however, whether the duty is characterized broadly or narrowly, the

---

[5] Of course, in Louisiana, we are most familiar with legal cause when stated in terms of the scope of the risk, due to the "inherent flexibility [of] the duty-risk methodology." Timothy J. McNamara, The Duties and Risks of the Duty-Risk Analysis, 44 La.L.Rev. 1227, 1236 (1984).

outcome in this case remains the same. We do not quibble with the opinion on original hearing, we simply feel it was generous in its characterization of the duty.

* * * * *

Legal Cause: the Practice in Louisiana

The cases on legal cause are many and diverse. Our modern jurisprudence begins with the seminal duty-risk case, *Dixie Drive It Yourself System New Orleans Co. v. American Beverage Co.*, 242 La. 471, 137 So. 2d 298 (1962), in which this Court held:

> The essence of the [legal cause] inquiry is whether the risk and harm encountered by the plaintiff fall within the scope of protection of the [duty].

* * * * *

Id. at 304. In this case, the inquiry becomes whether the duty not to promote a cook to deputy, in name only, is meant to protect the class of claimants, of which plaintiff is a member, from the risk that the cook will: acquire, of his own accord, the trappings of a deputy; while off-duty, become intoxicated; play games with his loaded gun; and, in the process, inadvertently shoot someone. We do not think the duty encompasses such a far-flung hazard, dependent as it is on the unpredictable and idiosyncratic foibles of one person. While it is not necessary that the exact risk encountered be foreseeable, it is unrealistic to expect the sheriff, who promoted Benoit simply to put him on the supplemental pay rolls, could have expected any harm to result from this maneuver. The facts indicate that what little training Benoit received, he received as a matter of form alone.

* * * * *

The courts of this state have had three decades since *Dixie Drive It Yourself, supra*, was handed down to hone the duty-risk analysis. In light of the jurisprudence on legal cause, it is our considered judgment that the ambit of the duty not to manipulate classifications, not to promote a cook to a deputy, solely to enable the cook to receive supplemental pay, cannot be cast so broadly as to encompass the risk that the titular deputy might harm someone. Although *LeJeune* and *Clomon, supra*, decimated the class of plaintiffs who would otherwise be *Palsgraf*-plaintiffs and *Ermert, supra*, swelled the ranks of those engaged in business pursuits, the facts of this case leave little room for further expanding liability.

Much has been made in this case about the sheriff's including in his training of the kitchen workers the epigram: it is better to have a gun and not need it than to need a gun and not have it. The plaintiff contends this suggestion is tantamount to entrusting a gun to Benoit, though Benoit was never required to have, nor was he issued, a gun. We do not believe a passing remark about the advisability of possessing a weapon amounts to constructive entrustment. In brief, the plaintiff argues that Benoit, as a deputy, was allowed to carry a concealed weapon. Because concealment of the weapon had nothing to do with the accident in this case, however, we find the argument unpersuasive.

Moreover, the spectrum of liability appears to us to be this: at the no-liability end of the scale is entrusting a gun to a well-trained and qualified officer; at the certain-liability end of the scale is entrusting a gun to a child,[11] – with "entrustment" to Benoit lying somewhere between the two. The

---

[11] *See Watson v. State Farm Fire and Cas. Ins. Co.*, 469 So. 2d 967 (La. 1985), in which a father gave his twelve-year old a weapon without adequately schooling him in its use. In Watson, the Court assumed a twelve-year-old can be properly trained to use a gun: Although he had owned a 'child's model .22' caliber rifle since the age of ten, and had been allowed to shoot since he was nine, Shane had until then merely hunted small game. He had, however, admired his father's Marlin 30-30 rifle, and the gun was presented to him on his twelfth birthday (just twelve weeks before the ill fated deer hunting trip).... Shane himself testified that he had only twice fired this weapon. Perhaps more significantly, the boy lacked familiarity with the use of the scope attached to the rifle. *Id.* at 969. (Emphasis added)

plaintiff argues entrustment to Benoit is more akin to entrusting a gun to a child. Were we to agree with the plaintiffs, virtually anyone who was actually responsible for putting a lethal weapon in the hands of an adult who was not well-trained with the weapon would be negligent. Interestingly, Professor Robertson, in his Reason Versus Rule in Louisiana Tort Law: Dialogues on *Hill v. Lundin & Associates, Inc.*, 34 La.L.Rev. 1 (1973), once posed the following hypothetical: "If I hand an eight-year-old child a loaded shotgun; if he takes it home and gives it to his father; if that night his father gets drunk and kills your prize heifer, ... [the odds are] nine to one that I escape liability to you, even though: (1) I was negligent ... [and] (2) my conduct a cause of your loss." *Id.* Robertson concludes the initial giver's negligence was not a proximate cause of the loss, that "too much else has intervened--time, space, people, and bizarreness." To hold the Sheriff's Office liable here would be to succumb to the notion that Benoit is but an empty vessel, suggestible and devoid of personal responsibility. Although a cook with a ninth-grade education, Benoit was an average, functioning member of society, acting on his own initiative, off-duty, on business far-removed from anything which could be even remotely associated with the work of the Sheriff's Office. Although more training might have made a marksmen of Benoit, the accident occurred because he played with a gun while intoxicated.

As noted earlier, negligent hiring has also been put forth as a theory of liability. Once again, however, because Benoit's titular promotion did not in any way give him an opportunity he did not otherwise have, to engage in the conduct which lead to this accident, we find no merit in this theory. *Cf. Smith v. Orkin Exterminating Co.*, 540 So. 2d 363 (La.App. 1 Cir. 1989) (in which an exterminator, while on the job, unlatched windows, so that he could return later to rape a customer).

* * * * *

NOTES

1.   Cases involving negligent hiring, training, retaining, or supervising do not vary the negligence analysis at all. The label after "negligent" indicates the alleged breach by the business.

2.   Nonemployees, such as customers, injured by an employee of a business typically will sue the business for (1) vicarious liability (respondeat superior) for the tort of the employee, alleging that the employee was in the course and scope of her employment, and for (2) the business's own negligence in hiring, training, retaining, or supervising the employee. Consider for example, *Griffin v. Kmart Corp.*, 776 So. 2d 1226 (La.App. 5 Cir. 2000). The defendant store hired employee to work in its sporting goods department, from which it sold firearms. Defendant did not make any provision for gun-safety training of employees, and no one explained gun safety procedures to employee. While waiting upon two customers whom he did not otherwise know, employee fired an air pistol at each of them, creating a loud noise and fear among the customers that they had been shot. Held, defendant was negligent in not adequately training employee in handling the weapons he was responsible for selling and in appropriate behavior with customers regarding guns. In addition, defendant was vicariously liable for employee's conduct; although defendant presumably would not have condoned employee's conduct, such conduct was connected closely enough to his employment to make it fair that the loss be borne by the enterprise. For a case distinguishing *Griffin* on the ground that its imposition of liability is based on the job giving the employee "unique opportunities to commit a tort", see *Kelley v. Dyson*, 10 So. 3d 283 (La. App. 5 Cir. 2009).

A hotel was not held liable under either vicarious liability or negligence for a sexual assault perpetrated by a hotel employee on a hotel guest away from the hotel and not during the employee's working hours in *Jackson v. Ferrand*, 658 So. 2d 691 (La.App. 4 Cir. 1994), *writ denied*, 659 So. 2d 496 (La. 1995).

It is difficult to square the Court's assumption in Watson that a twelve-year-old, not yet in the eighth grade presumably, may be taught to hunt with sophisticated weapons, with the contention that an adult, because of his educational level and concealed DWI, cannot be imputed with knowledge of the most rudimentary tenets of gun-handling, such as: loaded guns should not be played with, especially by intoxicated people.

3.   If the plaintiff is an employee of the business injured by a co-employee and his injury is covered by workers' compensation, the employer and co-employee usually are immune from negligence claims.

4.   La. R.S. 23:291 immunizes a prospective employer from civil liability, including liability for negligent hiring or retention, if he hires or retains in reasonable reliance upon information pertaining to the employee's job performance or reasons for separation which is disclosed to him by a former employer. The employer is not immune if further investigation (including a criminal background check) was required by law. The act immunizes an employer who, upon request by a prospective employer or current or former employee, provides accurate information about the employee's job performance or reasons for separation, unless the employer is acting in bad faith. *See also, Jackson v. Ferrand*, 658 So. 2d 691 (La.App. 4 Cir. 1994), *writ denied*, 659 So. 2d 496 (La. 1995).

5.   Although not required to do so by employer, employee worked a 21-hour shift and then attempted to drive home; he was involved in an accident en route which injured plaintiff. *Held*, plaintiff may not maintain a direct negligence action against employer; employer is not liable "to public highway users for failing to prevent its employees from driving home after working a twenty-one-hour shift or for failing to keep its employees from working twenty-one-hour shifts at all." *Baggett v. Brumfield*, 758 So. 2d 332 (La.App. 3 Cir. 2000), *writ denied*, 761 So. 2d 1292 (La. 2000).

6.   A trial judge does not err in refusing to charge the jury on employer's negligent hiring and training, where the injuring employee was in the course and scope of his employment at the time of the accident. If the employee breached a duty to plaintiff, employer is liable under respondeat superior, and if the employee did not breach a duty to plaintiff, then no degree of negligence on the part of the employer in hiring or training employee would make employer liable to plaintiff. *Libersat v. J & K Trucking, Inc.*, 772 So. 2d 173 (La.App. 3 Cir. 2000), *writ denied*, 789 So. 2d 598 (La. 2001).

7.   The theory of negligent supervision also can be applied to parents and children. Under what circumstances do parents have a duty to supervise children? What is required of parents to satisfy that duty? *Compare Otillio v. Entergy La., Inc.*, 836 So. 2d 293 (La.App. 5 Cir. 2002) (parents required to use reasonable precautions in supervision child), with *Rideau v. State Farm Mut. Auto Ins. Co.*, 970 So. 2d 564 (La.App. 1 Cir. 2007), *writ denied*, 972 So. 2d 1168 (La. 2008) (parents have no duty to supervise when child reaches age of discernment). Note that both of these cases involve injured children and defendants arguing that parents were contributorily negligent. *See* Chapter 9.c, *infra*, regarding parents' vicarious liability for damage caused by children.

13.   Negligent Entrustment

JOSEPH
v.
DICKERSON
754 So. 2d 912 (La. 2000)

CALOGERO, C. J.

This case arises out of an automobile collision between a car owned by plaintiff Linda Joseph, driven by her son, plaintiff Andrew Joseph, and a car owned by defendant Judith Dickerson, driven by her daughter, defendant Christina Dickerson. At the time of the accident, Christina was nineteen years old and lived with her mother and baby in New Orleans. The vehicles collided at the intersection of North Miro Street and A.P. Tureaud Avenue in New Orleans. We granted writs in this case to determine whether the court of appeal was correct in finding Judith liable because she loaned or entrusted her car to her daughter, Christina, whose negligence caused the accident, knowing that Christina was an excluded driver under a policy Judith had procured from Midland Risk Insurance Company.

This case presents three significant issues. First, we must determine whether the court of appeal was correct in finding Judith negligent for entrusting her vehicle to Christina, a competent, but policy-excluded, driver. As is indicated hereinafter, we hold that the court of appeal incorrectly found Judith liable for lending her car to an otherwise competent driver known by Judith to be excluded from coverage under her liability policy. A person who loans or entrusts an automobile to another can be found liable for the borrower's causing damages to a third person if the circumstances show the lender to be negligent in loaning or entrusting the vehicle. Restatement (Second) of Torts § 390 (1965). A lender cannot be found liable for loaning the car to a competent driver, or to a driver not known to be a risk or threat to other persons, as was the case here, simply for the reason that she knew or should have known that her own liability insurance policy, by its terms, would not cover the driver's liability for negligently causing injury.

The second issue in this case requires us to determine independently whether Judith is vicariously liable to the plaintiffs for Christina's acts while Christina performed a family chore at Judith's request. Is Judith responsible for Christina's negligence because Judith asked Christina to take Christina's great-grandmother, in Judith's car, to a doctor's appointment? We find that Judith is not vicariously liable under a "mission" theory of liability for her daughter's negligent conduct. As a consequence, our conclusion obviates the need to decide whether the endorsement provision offends public policy, which denies coverage to the insured for imputed negligence arising out of the excluded driver's use of the car.

Finally, we must resolve whether the named driver exclusion endorsement is even applicable in light of the statutory requirement that the excluded person be a resident of the same household in order to bypass the omnibus coverage requirement of La.Rev.Stat. 32:861 and La.Rev.Stat. 32:900. We find that the exclusion endorsement does apply. The record supports the finding that Christina was a resident of the same household as the named insured, Judith. La.Rev.Stat. 32:900(L) has been satisfied. Thus, plaintiffs are precluded from recovering from Midland Risk.

For the reasons that follow, we thus reverse the court of appeal's casting Judith Dickerson in damages to the plaintiffs. Furthermore, we affirm the judgment of the court of appeal insofar as it dismissed the plaintiffs' claims against the automobile liability insurer, Midland Risk.

On June 19, 1996, Christina Dickerson broadsided Andrew Joseph at the intersection of North Miro Street and A.P. Tureaud Avenue. Andrew was driving his mother's car west on North Miro Street. Christina was driving her mother's car north on A.P. Tureaud Avenue. At the time of the accident, Christina was an adult. The Joseph vehicle was struck in the middle of the driver's side. The impact caused the vehicle to spin three hundred and sixty degrees. Andrew Joseph was injured and Linda Joseph's car was damaged.

At the time of the accident, Christina, who had taken her great-grandmother to the doctor, was returning the great-grandmother to the latter's home. Ordinarily, Judith would have accompanied the patient, her own grandmother, to the doctor's appointment. However, Judith was unable to leave her job. Judith had therefore asked her daughter Christina to drive the patient, in Judith's car, to the medical appointment.

Alleging property damage and multiple injuries to Andrew, the plaintiffs, Linda Joseph and her son Andrew, filed a petition in First City Court, Parish of Orleans, against Judith, Christina, and Midland Risk Insurance Company, Judith's automobile liability insurer. The plaintiffs asserted negligence and vicarious liability claims. In response, Midland Risk denied coverage, arguing that Judith had signed, and thus put into place, a policy endorsement specifically excluding Christina from coverage. Further, Midland Risk denied coverage for any possible liability of Judith Dickerson because of the policy provision that denies coverage for negligence that may be imputed by law to the named insured arising out of the use of the car by the excluded driver, Christina.

The city court dismissed the action against Midland Risk, finding that the insurance policy excluded coverage for Christina and otherwise did not provide relevant coverage for Judith. The city court judge did, however, cast both Christina and Judith in judgment in solido for damages, and awarded $1,500.00 to Linda Joseph for property damages and $4,368.00 to Andrew Joseph for compensatory damages.

The plaintiffs and Judith Dickerson appealed the city court's judgment. The court of appeal affirmed. Joseph v. Dickerson, 98-1013 (La.App. 4 Cir. 1999), 728 So. 2d 1066. The court of appeal found no manifest error in the city court's finding that Christina Dickerson was a resident of her mother's household, not rated on the policy, and specifically excluded, by name, from coverage. In addition, the court of appeal found that Christina was not on a mission for her mother, such as would cause her mother to be held vicariously liable. In so finding, the appellate court stated that the act of driving her great-grandmother to a doctor's appointment is both a natural obligation and a typical favor, not a mission for which the car-owning mother might be exposed to vicarious liability. Nevertheless, the court of appeal panel, in a two-to-one decision, did find Judith negligent for entrusting her vehicle to a driver she knew was not covered by the liability insurance policy on her automobile, and who negligently caused harm to the plaintiffs.

In this Court, the plaintiffs seek a judgment against the liability insurer, Midland Risk, arguing that the insurance policy requires the insurer to pay all damages that its named insured causes or for which the named insured is responsible. Additionally, the plaintiffs argue that the named driver exclusion does not bar coverage in this case, because the insurer has not sufficiently proven that Christina resided in the same household as Judith. Defendant Judith Dickerson is seeking to overturn the majority's finding that she is liable solely because she had entrusted her car to her competent, licensed, but policy-excluded, daughter, who subsequently caused the accident.

In light of the reason for granting writs in this case, and as a matter of sequencing, we will discuss in turn: negligent entrustment, vicarious liability, the exclusion provision, and the residency requirement.

We first consider the issue that prompted us to grant Judith Dickerson's writ application: whether the court of appeal was correct in determining that Judith is liable for negligently entrusting her automobile to her policy-excluded major daughter whose negligence harmed the plaintiffs.

Negligence claims under La. Civ. Code art. 2315 are examined using a Duty/Risk analysis. The Duty/Risk analysis is a set of five separate elements that takes into account the conduct of each party and the peculiar circumstances of each case. The plaintiffs bear the burden of proving each of the following elements: (1) the defendants' conduct was a cause-in-fact of the plaintiffs' injuries, (2) the defendants had a duty to conform their conduct to a specific standard, (3) the defendants breached that duty to conform their conduct to a specific standard, (4) the defendants' conduct was the legal cause of the plaintiffs' injuries, and (5) actual damages. Teel v. State, DOTD, 96- 0592, pp. 9-10 (La. 1996), 681 So. 2d 340, 343; Roberts v. Benoit, 605 So. 2d 1032, 1041-42 (La. 1991). A negative answer to any of the elements of the Duty/Risk analysis prompts a no-liability determination. Stroik v. Ponseti, 96-2897, pp. 6-7 (La. 1997), 699 So. 2d 1072, 1077.

One of the necessary considerations in the Duty/Risk analysis is to determine what, if any, duties were owed by the respective parties. Mart v. Hill, 505 So. 2d 1120, 1122 (La. 1987). Generally, there is an almost universal legal duty on the part of a defendant in a negligence case to conform to the standard of conduct of a reasonable person in like circumstances. Boykin v. Louisiana Transit Co., 96-1932, p. 10 (La. 1998), 707 So. 2d 1225, 1231. Whether a legal duty exists, and the extent of that duty, depends on the facts and circumstances of the case, and the relationship of the parties. Socorro v. City of New Orleans, 579 So. 2d 931, 938 (La. 1991). Judith, as a lending car owner, has a duty to not entrust her car to another, when Judith knows or has reason to know that the borrower is likely to use the car in a manner involving an unreasonable risk of physical harm, because of the borrower's youth, inexperience, intoxication, incompetence, or otherwise. Restatement (Second) of Torts § 390 (1965).

duty

Having established that Judith Dickerson owed a duty, the question then becomes whether Judith breached that duty by failing to act in a reasonable and prudent manner. We find that Judith did not breach her duty to exercise reasonable care in lending her car to Christina. At the time of the accident, Christina was not a minor; nor was she intoxicated or incompetent. Judith is not liable for entrusting her car to her daughter merely because Judith knew that her own liability insurance policy would not cover Christina's liability for negligently causing injury. Accordingly, the plaintiffs' claim is without merit because, under the traditional Duty/Risk analysis, Judith did not breach her duty owed to these plaintiffs. Thus, Judith is not liable for the plaintiffs' injuries. We find that the court of appeal erred in finding Judith Dickerson liable for loaning her car to her daughter, an ostensibly competent, yet policy-excluded, driver.

The second issue before the Court is whether Christina Dickerson's performance of a family chore, prompted by Judith Dickerson's request, renders Judith vicariously liable for Christina's negligence. A principal is not liable for the torts of a non-servant mandatary. *Blanchard v. Ogima*, 253 La. 34, 215 So. 2d 902, 906 (1968). The imputation of liability to a principal for the negligent or tortious acts of a mandatary requires a relationship between the parties that is more than merely principal-mandatary. *Blanchard*, 215 So. 2d at 904. For example, our law dictates that a master or employer is vicariously liable for the tortious conduct of a servant or employee who acts within the scope of employment. La. Civ.Code art. 2320. Liability is imputed in this close relationship because the master or employer has the right of control of the servant's or employee's time and activities. Blanchard, 215 So. 2d at 905. Likewise, parents and tutors are responsible for the damages caused by their minor or unemancipated children. La. Civ.Code art. 2318. This form of vicarious liability arises out of the parent-child relationship and is statutorily imposed.

In this case, Judith Dickerson is not vicariously liable for the collision-causing negligence of Christina Dickerson. At the time of the accident, Christina was neither a minor residing with her mother nor an employee of her mother. At most, Christina was a non-servant mandatary, whose fault cannot be vicariously visited upon the principal, Christina's car-owning mother. This gratuitously performed family service is an insufficient ground to impute Christina's fault to her mother.

* * * * *

JOHNSON, J., dissenting.

An owner of a vehicle is liable for the driver's fault where the driver is on a mission for the owner or when the driver is an agent of the owner. *Talamo v. Shad*, 92-1085, 92-1086 (La.App. 4 Cir. 1993), 619 So. 2d 699. This court and the court of appeal failed to recognize what I see as an agency relationship between Judith Dickerson, the owner of the vehicle, and Christina Dickerson, the driver. According to testimony presented at trial, Christina was not ordinarily allowed to drive her mother's vehicle. However, on the day of the accident, Judith instructed Christina to take her great-grandmother to the doctor because Judith had to go to work. Because Christina was acting on behalf of Judith, I believe that Judith should be vicariously liable for the damages caused by Christina.

* * * * *

NOTES

1.   *Brooks v. Minnieweather*, 16 So. 3d 1244, 1250 (La.App. 2 Cir. 2009):
     Under the negligent entrustment theory, the lender of a vehicle is not responsible for the negligence of the borrower unless he knew or should have known that the borrower was physically or mentally incompetent to drive; if the lender knew or should have known of the borrower's incompetency then he is responsible for the harm resulting from the incompetent operation of the vehicle.

2.   The Louisiana Supreme Court reversed a summary judgment for a defendant in a case in which a man who was prohibited from driving a car not equipped with an ignition interlock device drove his wife's car (not so equipped) while under the influence of drugs and alcohol and had an accident. The Court found a genuine issue of fact as to whether the wife knew or should have known that her husband would drive the car in an intoxicated or impaired state. *Toups v. Dantin*, 182 So. 3d 36 (La. 2015).

14.   Subsequent Injury

Prior to 1996, the duty of a tortfeasor to refrain from causing injury to another through negligence encompassed the risk that the victim's injuries might be worsened by the treatment for those injuries. *Weber v. Charity Hospital of Louisiana*, 475 So. 2d 1047 (La. 1985). *See also, Jones v. St. Francis Cabrini Hospital*, 638 So. 2d 673 (La. 1995), where defendant's negligent treatment was the cause in fact of decedent's foreseeable and "not unreasonable" decision to undergo a corrective (although not essential) surgery; decedent died as a result of the corrective surgery. *Held*, defendant is liable for the decedent's death; the duty not to injure decedent encompassed the risk that she would undergo the corrective surgery. Louisiana also followed the "weakened condition" theory -- the duty of a tortfeasor not to injure a victim included the risk that due to his weakened physical condition, the victim would require the assistance of a medical device or appliance to accomplish his daily tasks, and that such device might be defective, further injuring the victim. *Younger v. Marshall Industries, Inc.*, 618 So. 2d 866 (La. 1993).

The "subsequent injury" case must be distinguished from the "second accident" injury case, i.e., a defect in machinery is not a cause in fact of the accident but enhances the injury. Courts generally permit recovery in "second accident" cases. *See, e.g., Craft v. Allstate Ins. Co.*, 663 So. 2d 116 (La.App. 3 Cir. 1995), *writ denied*, 664 So. 2d 454 (La. 1995) (plaintiff whose injuries were caused or enhanced by his inability to wear a seat belt has a cause of action against the owner of the vehicle in which he was injured who allegedly negligently removed the seat belt). With the demise of solidarity, a court may be required to fix the damages attributable to the "second accident" (either those damages caused solely by the "second accident" or the extent to which the damages were enhanced by the "second accident.")

See, also, Jenkins v. Lindsey, 693 So. 2d 238 (La.App. 4 Cir. 1997). There plaintiff, injured in a motor vehicle accident, brought a claim against her UM carrier, which thereafter brought a third party demand against defendant grocery, alleging a subsequent accident inside the grocery aggravated plaintiff's injury from the motor vehicle accident. *Held*, UM carrier does not have a cause of action against grocery. Where an injury occurs through the negligent act of one party and is aggravated by a separate negligent act of another party, the original negligent party is only responsible for the damages caused by his own fault.

Query: what is the effect of Act 3 of the 1996 Special Session, amending C.C. Art. 2324(B) to provide that "(a) joint tortfeasor shall not be liable for more than his degree of fault," upon the "subsequent injury" and "second accident" cases described above? *See Dumas v. State*, 828 So. 2d 530 (La. 2002), reproduced in Chapter 7.

CHAPTER 7

GENERAL DEFENSES

INTRODUCTION

In this chapter we explore those situations in which the victim's recovery is barred or reduced because of his or her conduct, or because of the nature of the injury-causing actor or the relationship of that actor with the victim. In Chapter 2, we looked at victim conduct which barred or reduced recovery where the other actor's wrongful conduct was deemed an intentional tort. Where the actor's wrongful conduct is negligence (including gross negligence), or liability is imposed without fault (strict or absolute liability), the victim's recovery may be barred or reduced because of his or her pre or post-accident conduct or because of the status of the actor or the actor's relationship with the victim. The circumstances in which victim conduct bars or reduces recovery include the victim's own unreasonably risky conduct (contributory negligence, assumption of the risk and failure to mitigate), encountering a known risk, or his agreement in advance that the other actor need not protect the victim from certain harm (waiver), or the failure to timely pursue the claim (prescription and peremption). All of these circumstances are discussed Section A.

Even where the victim's conduct is not blameworthy, his or her recovery against the actor may be barred because the actor occupies such a position in society, or such a relationship with the victim, that the actor is deemed immune from tort liability to the victim. The immunity may be total or may be partial, i.e., the actor is immune from some types of claims but not others. The immunity defenses are discussed in Section B.

An actor seeking to avoid liability for his or her wrongful conduct under the circumstances discussed above normally bears the burden of pleading and proving the existence of the circumstances that avoid liability. Thus, a defendant in a negligence action who believes that the plaintiff's own negligence contributed to his harm must plead the affirmative defense of contributory negligence. In addition, the defendant also may contend that the plaintiff's conduct was so foolhardy that the defendant did not owe a duty to protect him from harm.

As you read these materials, consider what societal values justify the end result of barring or reducing the recovery of a victim against an actor whose conduct has been deemed societally undesirable, and ask whether those values justify the result which the law has reached.

A.   VICTIM MISCONDUCT

1.   Contributory Negligence/Comparative Fault

LI
v.
YELLOW CAB COMPANY OF CALIFORNIA
13 Cal.3d 804, 532 P.2d 1226, 119 Cal.Rptr. 858 (1975)

SULLIVAN, J.

In this case we address the grave and recurrent question whether we should judicially declare no longer applicable in California courts the doctrine of contributory negligence, which bars all recovery when the plaintiff's negligent conduct has contributed as a legal cause in any degree to the harm suffered by him, and hold that it must give way to a system of comparative negligence, which assesses liability in direct proportion to fault. As we explain in detail *infra*, we conclude that we should. In the course of reaching our ultimate decision we conclude that: (1) The doctrine of comparative negligence is preferable to the 'all-or-nothing' doctrine of contributory negligence from the point of view of logic, practical experience, and fundamental justice; (2) judicial action in this area is not precluded by the presence of section 1714 of the Civil Code, which has been said to 'codify' the 'all-or-nothing' rule and to render it immune from attack in the courts except on constitutional grounds; (3) given the possibility of judicial action, certain practical difficulties attendant upon the adoption of comparative negligence should not dissuade us from charting a new course--leaving the resolution of some of these problems to future judicial or legislative action; (4) the doctrine of comparative negligence should be applied in this state in its so-called 'pure' form under which the assessment of liability in proportion to fault proceeds in spite of the fact that the plaintiff is equally at fault as or more at fault than the defendant; and finally (5) this new rule should be given a limited retrospective application.

The accident here in question occurred near the intersection of Alvarado Street and Third Street in Los Angeles. At this intersection Third Street runs in a generally east-west direction along the crest of a hill, and Alvarado Street, running generally north and south, rises gently to the crest from either direction. At approximately 9 p.m. on November 21, 1968, plaintiff Nga Li was proceeding northbound on Alvarado in her 1967 Oldsmobile. She was in the inside lane, and about 70 feet before she reached the Third Street intersection she stopped and then began a left turn across the three southbound lanes of Alvarado, intending to enter the driveway of a service station. At this time defendant Robert Phillips, an employee of defendant Yellow Cab Company, was driving a company-owned taxicab southbound in the middle lane on Alvarado. He came over the crest of the hill, passed through the intersection, and collided with the right rear portion of plaintiff's automobile, resulting in personal injuries to plaintiff as well as considerable damage to the automobile.

The court, sitting without a jury, found as facts that defendant Phillips was traveling at approximately 30 miles per hour when he entered the intersection, that such speed was unsafe at that time and place, and that the traffic light controlling southbound traffic at the intersection was yellow when defendant Phillips drove into the intersection. It also found, however, that plaintiff's left turn across the southbound lanes of Alvarado 'was made at a time when a vehicle was approaching from the opposite direction so close as to constitute an immediate hazard.' The dispositive conclusion of law was as follows: 'That the driving of NGA LI was negligent, that such negligence was a proximate cause of the collision, and that she is barred from recovery by reason of such contributory negligence.' Judgment for defendants was entered accordingly.

I

Contributory negligence is conduct on the part of the plaintiff which falls below the standard to which he should conform for his own protection, and which is a legally contributing cause cooperating with the negligence of the defendant in bringing about the plaintiff's harm.' (Rest.2d Torts, § 463.) Thus the American Law Institute, in its second restatement of the law, describes the kind of conduct on the part of one seeking recovery for damage caused by negligence which renders him subject to the doctrine of contributory negligence. What the effect of such conduct will be is left to a further section, which states the doctrine in its clearest essence: 'Except where the defendant has the last clear chance, the plaintiff's contributory negligence bars recovery against a defendant whose negligent conduct would otherwise make him liable to the plaintiff for the harm sustained by him.' (Rest.2d Torts, § 467.) (Italics added.)

This rule, rooted in the long-standing principle that one should not recover from another for damages brought upon oneself (see Baltimore & P.R. Co. v. Jones (1877) 95 U.S. 439, 442, 24 L.Ed. 506; Buckley v. Chadwick (1955) 45 Cal.2d 183, 192, 288 P.2d 12, 289 P.2d 242), has been the law of this state from its beginning.... Although criticized almost from the outset for the harshness of its operation, it has weathered numerous attacks, in both the legislative and the judicial arenas, seeking its amelioration or repudiation. We have undertaken a thorough reexamination of the matter, giving particular attention to the common law and statutory sources of the subject doctrine in this state. As we have indicated, this reexamination leads us to the conclusion that the 'all-or-nothing' rule of contributory negligence can be and ought to be superseded by a rule which assesses liability in proportion to fault.

It is unnecessary for us to catalogue the enormous amount of critical comment that has been directed over the years against the 'all-or-nothing' approach of the doctrine of contributory negligence.

The essence of that criticism has been constant and clear: the doctrine is inequitable in its operation because it fails to distribute responsibility in proportion to fault.[54] Against this have been raised several arguments in justification, but none have proved even remotely adequate to the task.[55] The basic objection to the doctrine--grounded in the primal concept that in a system in which liability is based on fault, the extent of fault should govern the extent of liability – remains irresistible to reason and all intelligent notions of fairness.

Furthermore, practical experience with the application by juries of the doctrine of contributory negligence has added its weight to analyses of its inherent shortcomings: 'Every trial lawyer is well aware that juries often do in fact allow recovery in cases of contributory negligence, and that the compromise in the jury room does result in some diminution of the damages because of the plaintiff's fault. But the process is at best a haphazard and most unsatisfactory one.' (Prosser, Comparative Negligence, *supra*, p. 4; fn. omitted.).... It is manifest that this state of affairs, viewed from the standpoint of the health and vitality of the legal process, can only detract from public confidence in the ability of law and legal institutions to assign liability on a just and consistent basis....

It is in view of these theoretical and practical considerations that to this date 25 states,[6] have abrogated the 'all or nothing' rule of contributory negligence and have enacted in its place general

---

[54] Dean Prosser states the kernel of critical comment in these terms: 'It (the rule) places upon one party the entire burden of a loss for which two are, by hypothesis, responsible.' (Prosser, Torts (4th ed. 1971) § 67, p. 433.) Harper and James express the same basic idea: '(T)here is no justification--in either policy or doctrine--for the rule of contributory negligence, except for the feeling that if one man is to be held liable because of his fault, then the fault of him who seeks to enforce that liability should also be considered. But this notion does not require the all-or-nothing rule, which would exonerate a very negligent defendant for even the slight fault of his victim. The logical corollary of the fault principle would be a rule of comparative or proportional negligence, not the present rule.' (2 Harper & James, The Law of Torts (1956) § 22.3, p. 1207.)

[55] Dean Prosser, in a 1953 law review article on the subject which still enjoys considerable influence, addressed himself to the commonly advanced justificatory arguments in the following terms: 'There has been much speculation as to why the rule thus declared found such ready acceptance in later decisions, both in England and in the United States. The explanations given by the courts themselves never have carried much conviction. Most of the decisions have talked about 'proximate cause,' saying that the plaintiff's negligence is an intervening, insulating cause between the defendant's negligence and the injury. But this cannot be supported unless a meaning is assigned to proximate cause which is found nowhere else. If two automobiles collide and injure a bystander, the negligence of one driver is not held to be a superseding cause which relieves the other of liability; and there is no visible reason for any different conclusion when the action is by one driver against the other. It has been said that the defense has a penal basis, and is intended to punish the plaintiff for his own misconduct; or that the court will not aid one who is himself at fault, and he must come into court with clean hands. But this is no explanation of the many cases, particularly those of the last clear chance, in which a plaintiff clearly at fault is permitted to recover. It has been said that the rule is intended to discourage accidents, by denying recovery to those who fail to use proper care for their own safety; but the assumption that the speeding motorist is, or should be, meditating on the possible failure of a lawsuit for his possible injuries lacks all reality, and it is quite as reasonable to say that the rule promotes accidents by encouraging the negligent defendant. Probably the true explanation lies merely in the highly individualistic attitude of the common law of the early nineteenth century. The period of development of contributory negligence was that of the industrial revolution, and there is reason to think that the courts found in this defense, along with the concepts of duty and proximate cause, a convenient instrument of control over the jury, by which the liabilities of rapidly growing industry were curbed and kept within bounds.' (Prosser, Comparative Negligence (1953) 41 Cal.L.Rev. 1, 3--4; fns. omitted. For a more extensive consideration of the same subject, *see* 2 Harper & James, *supra*, § 22.2, pp. 1199--1207.)

To be distinguished from arguments raised in justification of the 'all or nothing' rule are practical considerations which have been said to counsel against the adoption of a fairer and more logical alternative. The latter considerations will be discussed in a subsequent portion of this opinion.

[6] Arkansas, Colorado, Connecticut, Georgia, Hawaii, Idaho, Maine, Massachusetts, Minnesota, Mississippi, Nebraska, Nevada, New Hampshire, New Jersey, North Dakota, Oklahoma, Oregon, Rhode Island, South Dakota, Texas, Utah, Vermont, Washington, Wisconsin, Wyoming. (Schwartz, Comparative Negligence (1974), Appendix A, pp. 367--369.)

apportionment Statutes calculated in one manner or another to assess liability in proportion to fault. In 1973 these states were joined by Florida, which effected the same result by Judicial decision. (*Hoffman v. Jones* (Fla. 1973) 280 So. 2d 431.) We are likewise persuaded that logic, practical experience, and fundamental justice counsel against the retention of the doctrine rendering contributory negligence a complete bar to recovery--and that it should be replaced in this state by a system under which liability for damage will be borne by those whose negligence caused it in direct proportion to their respective fault.[56a]

The foregoing conclusion, however, clearly takes us only part of the way. It is strenuously and ably urged by defendants and two of the amici curiae that whatever our views on the relative merits of contributory and comparative negligence, we are precluded from making those views the law of the state by judicial decision. Moreover, it is contended, even if we are not so precluded, there exist considerations of a practical nature which should dissuade us from embarking upon the course which we have indicated. We proceed to take up these two objections in order.

II

It is urged that any change in the law of contributory negligence must be made by the Legislature, not by this court. Although the doctrine of contributory negligence is of judicial origin-- its genesis being traditionally attributed to the opinion of Lord Ellenborough in Butterfield v. Forrester (K.B.1809) 103 Eng.Rep. 926 – the enactment of section 1714 of the Civil Code[57] in 1872 codified the doctrine as it stood at that date and, the argument continues, rendered it invulnerable to attack in the courts except on constitutional grounds. Subsequent cases of this court, it is pointed out, have unanimously affirmed that--barring the appearance of some constitutional infirmity--the 'all-or-nothing' rule is the law of this state and shall remain so until the Legislature directs otherwise. The fundamental constitutional doctrine of separation of powers, the argument concludes, requires judicial abstention.

We are further urged to observe that a basic distinction exists between the situation obtaining in Florida prior to the decision of that state's Supreme Court abrogating the doctrine (*Hoffman v. Jones, supra*, 280 So. 2d 431), and the situation now confronting this court. There, to be sure, the Florida court was also faced with a statute, and the dissenting justice considered that fact sufficient to bar judicial change of the rule. The statute there in question, however, merely declared that the general English common and statute law in effect on July 4, 1776, was to be in force in Florida except to the extent it was inconsistent with federal constitutional and statutory law and acts of the state Legislature. (Fla.Stat., § 2.01, F.S.A.) The majority simply concluded that there was no clearcut common law rule of contributory negligence prior to the 1809 *Butterfield* decision,... and that therefore that rule was not made a part of Florida law by the statute.... In the instant case, defendants and the amici curiae who support them point out, the situation is quite different: here the Legislature has specifically enacted the rule of contributory negligence as the law of this state. In these circumstances, it is urged, the doctrine of separation of powers requires that any change must come from the Legislature.

We have concluded that the foregoing argument, in spite of its superficial appeal, is fundamentally misguided. As we proceed to point out and elaborate below, it was not the intention of

---

In the federal sphere, comparative negligence of the 'pure' type (*see infra*) has been the rule since 1908 in cases arising under the Federal Employers' Liability Act (*see* 45 U.S.C. § 53) and since 1920 in cases arising under the Jones Act (*see* 46 U.S.C. § 688) and the Death on the High Seas Act (*see* 46 U.S.C. § 766.)

[56a] In employing the generic term 'fault' throughout this opinion we follow a usage common to the literature on the subject of comparative negligence. In all cases, however, we intend the term to import nothing more than 'negligence' in the accepted legal sense.

[57] Section 1714 of the Civil Code has never been amended. It provides as follows: 'Everyone is responsible, not only for the result of his willful acts, but also for an injury occasioned to another by his want of ordinary care or skill in the management of his property or person, Except so far as the latter has, willfully or by want of ordinary care, brought the injury upon himself. The extent of liability in such cases is defined by the Title on Compensatory Relief.' (Italics added.)

the Legislature in enacting section 1714 of the Civil Code, as well as other sections of that code declarative of the common law, to insulate the matters therein expressed from further judicial development; rather it was the intention of the Legislature to announce and formulate existing common law principles and definitions for purposes of orderly and concise presentation and with a distinct view toward continuing judicial evolution.

* * * * *

The resources of the common law at that time (in 1872) did not include techniques for the apportionment of damages strictly according to fault--a fact which this court had lamented three years earlier (*see* fn. 17, *ante*). They did, however, include the nascent doctrine of last clear chance which, while it too was burdened by an 'all-or-nothing' approach, at least to some extent avoided the often unconscionable results which could and did occur under the old rule precluding recovery when any negligence on the part of the plaintiff contributed in any degree to the harm suffered by him. Accordingly the Legislature sought to include the concept of last clear chance in its formulation of a rule of responsibility. We are convinced, however, as we have indicated, that in so doing the Legislature in no way intended to thwart future judicial progress toward the humane goal which it had embraced. Therefore, and for all of the foregoing reasons, we hold that section 1714 of the Civil Code was not intended to and does not preclude present judicial action in furtherance of the purposes underlying it.

III

We are thus brought to the second group of arguments which have been advanced by defendants and the amici curiae supporting their position. Generally speaking, such arguments expose considerations of a practical nature which, it is urged, counsel against the adoption of a rule of comparative negligence in this state even if such adoption is possible by judicial means.

The most serious of these considerations are those attendant upon the administration of a rule of comparative negligence in cases involving multiple parties. One such problem may arise when all responsible parties are not brought before the court: it may be difficult for the jury to evaluate relative negligence in such circumstances, and to compound this difficulty such an evaluation would not be res judicata in a subsequent suit against the absent wrongdoer. Problems of contribution and indemnity among joint tortfeasors lurk in the background....

A second and related major area of concern involves the administration of the actual process of fact-finding in a comparative negligence system. The assigning of a specific percentage factor to the amount of negligence attributable to a particular party, while in theory a matter of little difficulty, can become a matter of perplexity in the face of hard facts. The temptation for the jury to resort to a quotient verdict in such circumstances can be great.... These inherent difficulties are not, however, insurmountable. Guidelines might be provided the jury which will assist it in keeping focused upon the true inquiry, ... and the utilization of special verdicts or jury interrogatories can be of invaluable assistance in assuring that the jury has approached its sensitive and often complex task with proper standards and appropriate reverence....

The third area of concern, the status of the doctrines of last clear chance and assumption of risk, involves less the practical problems of administering a particular form of comparative negligence than it does a definition of the theoretical outline of the specific form to be adopted. Although several states which apply comparative negligence concepts retain the last clear chance doctrine, ... the better reasoned position seems to be that when true comparative negligence is adopted, the need for last clear chance as a palliative of the hardships of the 'all-or-nothing' rule disappears and its retention results only in a windfall to the plaintiff in direct contravention of the principle of liability in proportion to fault.... As for assumption of risk, we have recognized in this state that this defense overlaps that of contributory negligence to some extent and in fact is made up of at least two distinct defenses. 'To simplify greatly, it has been observed ... that in one kind of situation, to wit, where a plaintiff unreasonably undertakes to encounter a specific known risk imposed by a defendant's negligence, plaintiff's conduct, although he may encounter that risk in a prudent manner, is in reality a form of contributory negligence.... Other kinds of situations within the doctrine of assumption of risk are those, for example, where plaintiff is held to agree to relieve defendant of an obligation of reasonable conduct toward him. Such a situation would not involve contributory negligence, but rather a reduction of defendant's duty of care....' We think it clear that the adoption of a system of comparative negligence should entail the merger of the defense of assumption of risk into the general scheme of assessment of liability in proportion to fault in those particular cases in which the form of assumption of risk involved is no more than a variant of contributory negligence....

Finally there is the problem of the treatment of willful misconduct under a system of comparative negligence. In jurisdictions following the 'all-or- nothing' rule, contributory negligence is no defense to an action based upon a claim of willful misconduct (*see* Rest.2d Torts, § 503; Prosser, Torts, *supra*, § 65, p. 426), and this is the present rule in California.... As Dean Prosser has observed, '(this) is in reality a rule of comparative fault which is being applied, and the court is refusing to set up the lesser fault against the greater.' (Prosser, Torts, *supra*, § 65, p. 426.) The thought is that the difference between willful and wanton misconduct and ordinary negligence is one of kind rather than degree in that the former involves conduct of an entirely different order,[20] and under this conception it might well be urged that comparative negligence concepts should have no application when one of the parties has been guilty of willful and wanton misconduct. In has been persuasively argued, however, that the loss of deterrent effect that would occur upon application of comparative fault concepts to willful and wanton misconduct as well as ordinary negligence would be slight, and that a comprehensive system of comparative negligence should allow for the apportionment of damages in all cases involving misconduct which falls short of being intentional.... The law of punitive damages remains a separate consideration....

The existence of the foregoing areas of difficulty and uncertainty (as well as others which we have not here mentioned--*see generally* Schwartz, *supra*, § 21.1, pp. 335--339) has not diminished our conviction that the time for a revision of the means for dealing with contributory fault in this state is long past due and that it lies within the province of this court to initiate the needed change by our decision in this case. Two of the indicated areas (i.e., multiple parties and willful misconduct) are not involved in the case before us, and we consider it neither necessary nor wise to address ourselves to specific problems of this nature which might be expected to arise. As the Florida court stated with respect to the same subject, 'it is not the proper function of this Court to decide unripe issues, without the benefit of adequate briefing, not involving an actual controversy, and unrelated to a specific factual situation.' (*Hoffman v. Jones, supra,280* So. 2d 431, 439.)

Our previous comments relating to the remaining two areas of concern (i.e., the status of the doctrines of last clear chance and assumption of risk, and the matter of judicial supervision of the finder of fact) have provided sufficient guidance to enable the trial courts of this state to meet and resolve particular problems in this area as they arise. As we have indicated, last clear chance and assumption of risk (insofar as the latter doctrine is but a variant of contributory negligence) are to be subsumed under the general process of assessing liability in proportion to fault, and the matter of jury supervision we leave for the moment within the broad discretion of the trial courts.

Our decision in this case is to be viewed as a first step in what we deem to be a proper and just direction, not as a compendium containing the answers to all questions that may be expected to arise. Pending future judicial or legislative developments, we are content for the present to assume the position taken by the Florida court in this matter: 'We feel the trial judges of this State are capable of applying (a) comparative negligence rule without our setting guidelines in anticipation of expected problems. The problems are more appropriately resolved at the trial level in a practical manner instead of theoretical solution at the appellate level. The trial judges are granted broad discretion in adopting

---

[20] 'Disallowing the contributory negligence defense in this context is different from last clear chance; the defense is denied not because defendant had the last opportunity to avoid the accident but rather because defendant's conduct was so culpable it was different in 'kind' from the plaintiff's. The basis is culpability rather than causation.' (Schwartz, *supra*, § 5.1, p. 100; fn. omitted.)

such procedures as may accomplish the objectives and purposes expressed in this opinion.' (280 So. 2d at pp. 439–440.)

It remains to identify the precise form of comparative negligence which we now adopt for application in this state. Although there are many variants, only the two basic forms need be considered here. The first of these, the so-called 'pure' form of comparative negligence, apportions liability in direct proportion to fault in all cases. This was the form adopted by the Supreme Court of Florida in *Hoffman v. Jones, supra*, and it applies by statute in Mississippi, Rhode Island, and Washington. Moreover it is the form favored by most scholars and commentators.... The second basic form of comparative negligence, of which there are several variants, applies apportionment based on fault up to the point at which the plaintiff's negligence is equal to or greater than that of the defendant – when that point is reached, plaintiff is barred from recovery. Nineteen states have adopted this form or one of its variants by statute. The principal argument advanced in its favor is moral in nature: that it is not morally right to permit one more at fault in an accident to recover from one less at fault. Other arguments assert the probability of increased insurance, administrative, and judicial costs if a 'pure' rather than a '50 percent' system is adopted, but this has been seriously questioned....

We have concluded that the 'pure' form of comparative negligence is that which should be adopted in this state. In our view the '50 percent' system simply shifts the lottery aspect of the contributory negligence rule[21] to a different ground. As Dean Prosser has noted, under such a system '(i)t is obvious that a slight difference in the proportionate fault may permit a recovery; and there has been much justified criticism of a rule under which a plaintiff who is charged with 49 percent of a total negligence recovers 51 percent of his damages, while one who is charged with 50 percent recovers nothing at all.'[22] Prosser, Comparative Negligence, *supra*, 41 Cal.L.Rev. 1, 25; fns. omitted.) In effect 'such a rule distorts the very principle it recognizes, i.e., that persons are responsible for their acts to the extent their fault contributes to an injurious result. The partial rule simply lowers, but does not eliminate, the bar of contributory negligence.' (Juenger, Brief for Negligence Law Section of the State Bar of Michigan in Support of Comparative Negligence as Amicus Curiae, Parsonson v. Construction Equipment Company, *supra*, 18 Wayne L.Rev. 3, 50; *see also* Schwartz, *supra*, § 21.3, p. 347.)

* * * * *

For all of the foregoing reasons we conclude that the 'all-or-nothing' rule of contributory negligence as it presently exists in this state should be and is herewith superseded by a system of 'pure' comparative negligence, the fundamental purpose of which shall be to assign responsibility and liability for damage in direct proportion to the amount of negligence of each of the parties. Therefore, in all actions for negligence resulting in injury to person or property, the contributory negligence of the person injured in person or property shall not bar recovery, but the damages awarded shall be diminished in proportion to the amount of negligence attributable to the person recovering. The doctrine of last clear chance is abolished, and the defense of assumption of risk is also abolished to the extent that it is merely a variant of the former doctrine of contributory negligence; both of these are to be subsumed under the general process of assessing liability in proportion to negligence. Pending future judicial or legislative developments, the trial courts of this state are to use broad discretion in seeking to assure that the principle stated is applied in the interest of justice and in furtherance of the purposes and objectives set forth in this opinion.

---

[21] 'The rule that contributory fault bars completely is a curious departure from the central principle of nineteenth century Anglo-American tort law--that wrongdoers should bear the losses they cause. Comparative negligence more faithfully serves that central principle by causing the wrongdoers to share the burden of resulting losses in reasonable relation to their wrongdoing, rather than allocating the heavier burden to the one who, as luck would have it, happened to be more seriously injured.' (Comments on *Maki v. Frelk, supra*, 21 Vand.L.Rev. 889, Comment by Keeton, pp. 912--913.)

[22] This problem is compounded when the injurious result is produced by the combined negligence of several parties. For example in a three-car collision a plaintiff whose negligence amounts to one-third or more recovers nothing; in a four-car collision the plaintiff is barred if his negligence is only one-quarter of the total....

* * * * *

The judgment is **REVERSED**.

* * * * *

CLARK, Justice (dissenting).

I dissent.

For over a century this court has consistently and unanimously held that Civil Code section 1714 codifies the defense of contributory negligence. Suddenly--after 103 years--the court declares section 1714 shall provide for comparative negligence instead. In my view, this action constitutes a gross departure from established judicial rules and role.

First, the majority's decision deviates from settled rules of statutory construction. A cardinal rule of construction is to effect the intent of the Legislature. The majority concedes 'the intention of the Legislature in enacting section 1714 of the Civil Code was to state the basic rule of negligence together with the defense of contributory negligence modified by the emerging doctrine of last clear chance.' (*Ante*, p. 870 of 119 Cal.Rptr., p. 1238 of 532 P.2d.) Yet the majority refuses to honor this acknowledged intention--violating established principle.

The majority decision also departs significantly from the recognized limitation upon judicial action--encroaching on the powers constitutionally entrusted to the Legislature. The power to enact and amend our statutes is vested exclusively in the Legislature. (Cal.Const., art. III, § 3; art. IV, § 1.) 'This court may not usurp the legislative function to change the statutory law which has been uniformly construed by a long line of judicial decisions.' (Estate of Calhoun (1955) 44 Cal.2d 378, 387, 282 P.2d 880, 886.) The majority's altering the meaning of section 1714, notwithstanding the original intent of the framers and the century-old judicial interpretation of the statute, represents no less than amendment by judicial fiat. Although the Legislature intended the courts to develop the working details of the defense of contributory negligence enacted in section 1714 (*see generally*, Commentary, Arvo Van Alstyne, the California Civil Code, 6 West Civ.Code (1954) pp. 1–43), no basis exists--either in history or in logic--to conclude the Legislature intended to authorize judicial repudiation of the basic defense itself at any point we might decide the doctrine no longer serves us.

I dispute the need for judicial – instead of legislative – action in this area. The majority is clearly correct in its observation that our society has changed significantly during the 103-year existence of section 1714. But this social change has been neither recent nor traumatic, and the criticisms leveled by the majority at the present operation of contributory negligence are not new. I cannot conclude our society's evolution has now rendered the normal legislative process inadequate.

Further, the Legislature is the branch best able to effect transition from contributory to comparative or some other doctrine of negligence. Numerous and differing negligence systems have been urged over the years, yet there remains widespread disagreement among both the commentators and the states as to which one is best. (*See* Schwartz, Comparative Negligence (1974) Appendix A, pp. 367--369 and § 21.3, fn. 40, pp. 341--342, and authorities cited therein.) This court is not an investigatory body, and we lack the means of fairly appraising the merits of these competing systems. Constrained by settled rules of judicial review, we must consider only matters within the record or susceptible to judicial notice. That this court is inadequate to the task of carefully selecting the best replacement system is reflected in the majority's summary manner of eliminating from consideration All but two of the many competing proposals--including models adopted by some of our sister states.

Contrary to the majority's assertions of judicial adequacy, the courts of other states--with near unanimity--have conceded their inability to determine the best system for replacing contributory negligence, concluding instead that the legislative branch is best able to resolve the issue.

By abolishing this century old doctrine today, the majority seriously erodes our constitutional function. We are again guilty of judicial chauvinism.

McCOMB, J., concurs.

COMMENT

Initially, Louisiana applied contributory negligence as a bar to recovery, although the language of the Civil Code did not necessarily dictate that result. Louisiana has joined the overwhelming number of states which now provide that plaintiff's negligence does not necessarily bar recovery. The Louisiana version applies "pure" comparative fault. The applicable statute was amended in 1996 and is reproduced below. Note that comparative "fault" is used rather than comparative negligence because, according to paragraph B, the allocation of fault applies to all theories of tort liability–not just negligence. About five states cling to the contributory negligence bar: Alabama, Maryland, North Carolina, Virginia, and the District of Columbia. *See* William E. Westerbeke, *In Praise of Arbitrariness: The Proposed 83.7% Rule of Modified Comparative Fault*, 59 U. Kan. L. Rev. 991, 991-92 (2011).

Although the term "contributory negligence" often is used to refer to a regime in which any allocation of fault to a plaintiff for the plaintiff's own negligence bars the plaintiff's recovery, the term also refers to negligent conduct by the plaintiff. Thus, it is still appropriate under a comparative fault regime, like the one Louisiana now has, to refer to a plaintiff's contributory negligence. One simply has to recognize that the effect of such contributory negligence is, in most cases, to reduce recovery rather than bar recovery.

Note that the legislature provided in paragraph 2323C for a particular situation in which fault allocated to a plaintiff for her negligence will not reduce her recovery: when the plaintiff is merely negligent and the defendant commits an intentional tort against the plaintiff. Recall that 2323C was implicated in *Landry v. Bellanger, supra* Chapter 2.

La. Civil Code Article 2323.   Comparative fault

A.   In any action for damages where a person suffers injury, death, or loss, the degree or percentage of fault of all persons causing or contributing to the injury, death, or loss shall be determined, regardless of whether the person is a party to the action or a nonparty, and regardless of the person's insolvency, ability to pay, immunity by statute, including but not limited to the provisions of R.S. 23:1032, or that the other person's identity is not known or reasonably ascertainable. If a person suffers injury, death, or loss as the result partly of his own negligence and partly as a result of the fault of another person or persons, the amount of damages recoverable shall be reduced in proportion to the degree or percentage of negligence attributable to the person suffering the injury, death, or loss.

B.   The provisions of Paragraph A shall apply to any claim for recovery of damages for injury, death, or loss asserted under any law or legal doctrine or theory of liability, regardless of the basis of liability.

C.   Notwithstanding the provisions of Paragraphs A and B, if a person suffers injury, death, or loss as a result partly of his own negligence and partly as a result of the fault of an intentional tortfeasor, his claim for recovery of damages shall not be reduced.

Watson factors:
1. who had better knowledge of the danger.
2. how great was the risk of each actor's conduct
3. how useful was conduct
4. who had better capacity?
5. is anyone under circum.
cause to act & who had

COMMENT

An issue that is implicated with allocation of fault is, once percentages of fault are allocated, how much can the plaintiff collect from each person allocated fault. The answer may seem obvious: if on a $100,000 judgment, Defendant A is allocated 40% of the fault, Defendant B is allocated 20%, plaintiff is allocated 20%, and a nonparty is allocated 20%, then plaintiff presumably could collect $40,000 from Defendant A and $20,000 from Defendant B. The rest of the judgment would be uncollectible. In a pure comparative fault regime, that is a likely result. Two caveats are necessary. First, not all jurisdictions are pure comparative fault. Some "modified comparative fault" jurisdictions bar a plaintiff from recovering from a defendant whose allocation of fault is equal to or less than that of a plaintiff. A majority of U.S. states and territories have adopted a modified comparative fault system, some requiring that a plaintiff's fault be less than a defendant's to recover and others requiring that a plaintiff's fault not be greater. *See generally* Westerbeke, *supra*, at 993.

A second consideration that affects how much and from whom a plaintiff can recover once percentages are allocated is indicated in Art. 2323 paragraph A: some people allocated fault either cannot pay or are not required to pay. If fault is allocated to a nonparty, that person is not required to pay because he or she was not sued. A subsequent lawsuit against such a person probably would be barred by res judicata. If fault is allocated to an immune person, such as a plaintiff's employer (immune from negligence liability under workers compensation law), the plaintiff cannot collect from the immune person. A person who settles the claim against him may be allocated fault, but he already has paid a sum in settlement and has been released from further liability. *See*, for example, *Watson v. State Farm Fire & Casualty Ins. Co.*, *infra*, in which the insurer for the boy's mother settles the claim based on the boy's negligence. Some people are allocated fault but never identified—so-called "phantom tortfeasors." Some parties are allocated fault but are insolvent. Plaintiffs try to avoid allocations of fault to themselves and to persons who cannot pay or are not required to pay.

A final consideration in how much plaintiff can collect from whom once percentages are allocated is whether a jurisdiction recognizes joint and several liability or solidary liability, as it is called in Louisiana. This topic will be explored in more detail in Chapter 15, *infra*, but it is important to be aware of it here regarding collecting judgments after allocation of fault. Some jurisdictions follow full joint and several liability, which means that if a defendant is allocated any percentage of fault, that defendant can be required to pay the entire collectible judgment (not including fault allocated to plaintiff), and that defendant, which paid more than its allocated percentage, may sue codefendants for contribution of their shares. Louisiana has largely abrogated joint and several or solidary liability, leaving each defendant to pay only its own share. Civil Code Art. 2324, also amended in 1996, is reproduced below. You will see in 2324 paragraph A the very limited circumstances in which it preserves solidary liability.

La. Civil Code Article 2324.   Liability as solidary or joint and divisible obligation

A.   He who conspires with another person to commit an intentional or willful act is answerable, in solido, with that person, for the damage caused by such act.

B.   If liability is not solidary pursuant to Paragraph A, then liability for damages caused by two or more persons shall be a joint and divisible obligation. A joint tortfeasor shall not be liable for more than his degree of fault and shall not be solidarily liable with any other person for damages attributable to the fault of such other person, including the person suffering injury, death, or loss, regardless of such other person's insolvency, ability to pay, degree of fault, immunity by statute or otherwise, including but not limited to immunity as provided in R.S. 23:1032, or that the other person's identity is not known or reasonably ascertainable.

C.   Interruption of prescription against one joint tortfeasor is effective against all joint tortfeasors.

The *Dumas* case, *infra*, discusses some of the recent history of Articles 2323 and 2324, whereby Louisiana changed to a pure comparative fault regime. As you will read, this has not been a smooth transition.

298

KIMBALL, J.

This is a wrongful death and survival action brought to recover damages sustained when the victim was injured in a bicycle accident and subsequently died while being treated for those injuries in a hospital. We granted certiorari in this case to consider whether the 1996 amendments to La. C.C. arts. 2323 and 2324(B) allow the initial tortfeasor to present, as an affirmative defense, evidence relating to alleged malpractice on the part of the health care providers. For the reasons that follow, we conclude that the 1996 amendments allow the initial tortfeasor to present such evidence. Furthermore, we conclude that the amendments effected a change in Louisiana's tort policies such that our pre-1996 opinions holding that an original tortfeasor may be held liable for the victim's injuries caused by negligent medical treatment do not serve to bar the initial tortfeasor from presenting evidence relating to the alleged malpractice of the treating health care providers.

Facts and Procedural History

On April 22, 1996, George Dumas was riding a bicycle in Chemin-a-Haut State Park near Bastrop, Louisiana, when he allegedly hit a pothole in the park road. As a result of the alleged accident, Mr. Dumas was thrown from his bicycle and sustained a large laceration to his right forehead and scalp. Mr. Dumas was transported to Morehouse General Hospital where he received medical treatment for his wounds. Several hours after arriving at the hospital, Mr. Dumas died.

On April 21, 1997, Mr. Dumas's wife and three adult children filed a wrongful death and survival action against the State of Louisiana through its Department of Culture, Recreation and Tourism and its Department of Transportation and Development (collectively referred to as the "State"), alleging the pothole presented an unreasonable risk of harm, the State had both constructive and actual knowledge of the defect, and the State failed to cure the defect in the road or warn of its presence. Plaintiffs further alleged this failure was the cause of Mr. Dumas's death. The State filed an answer denying liability and alleging fault on the part of Mr. Dumas. Subsequently, on May 15, 2001, the State filed an amended answer alleging as an affirmative defense that the death of Mr. Dumas resulted solely from the medical negligence of physicians and staff at Morehouse General Hospital, particularly in the administration and maintenance of anesthesia services following a routine surgical procedure to repair a scalp laceration. The amended answer asserted that the negligent medical treatment caused Mr. Dumas to aspirate his stomach contents, which ultimately lead to cardiac arrest. The amended answer further stated:

17 (d).

The State affirmatively pleads, in defense to the claims asserted, the fault of third parties in the medical treatment of George Dumas, as described above, as the cause of the death of plaintiffs' decedent, for which the State is not jointly liable.

17 (e).

The State further pleads, in affirmative defense, the applicability of Louisiana's law of comparative fault, particularly the law of joint and divisible liability as enunciated in Louisiana Civil Code Articles 2323 A & B, and 2324 B.

In response to the State's amended answer, plaintiffs filed a motion to strike on grounds that the allegations added therein were immaterial, irrelevant, and insufficient. Specifically, plaintiffs argued that the amended answer sought to introduce factual allegations and evidence of medical malpractice in violation of the jurisprudential rules set forth in *Weber v. Charity Hosp. of La.,* 475 So. 2d 1047 (La.1985) and *Lambert v. United States Fidelity & Guar. Co.,* 629 So. 2d 328 (La.1993), that, as a matter of policy, the original tortfeasor is the legal cause of any subsequent injury which might result from inadequate medical treatment.

In opposition, the State argued the 1996 legislative changes to La. C.C. arts. 2323 and 2324 abolished solidary liability in cases involving negligent acts and, with it, abolished the action for contribution among joint tortfeasors. The State contended the analysis underlying the *Weber* and *Lambert* cases was no longer applicable in light of the 1996 amendments.

After a hearing, the trial court granted the motion to strike, reasoning that the analysis set forth in *Weber* and *Lambert* is still viable in the context of subsequent medical malpractice after the 1996 amendments to La. C.C. arts. 2323 and 2324. The State applied to the second circuit court of appeal for a writ of certiorari to review the trial court's judgment. The intermediate court granted supervisory review and affirmed the trial court's judgment granting plaintiffs' motion to strike. *Dumas v. State ex rel. Dept. of Culture, Recreation & Tourism*, 35,492 (La.App. 2 Cir. 2001), 804 So. 2d 813. The majority of the court of appeal concluded that the 1996 amendments to Articles 2323 and 2324 did not change the rule of *Weber* and *Lambert* because the rule of those cases is based upon legal cause such that, as a matter of policy, when the duty breached by a tortfeasor includes the risk that a victim's injuries might be worsened by subsequent medical treatment, the initial tortfeasor is liable for 100% of the damages. The court further determined that because the original tortfeasor is liable for 100% of the damages, there is no additional percentage of fault by the medical provider to quantify. Finally, the court of appeal noted that its ruling did not prohibit the State from filing a third-party demand for contribution pursuant to La. C.C. arts. 1804 and 1805.

We granted the State's application for certiorari to consider whether the lower courts properly granted plaintiffs' motion to strike the State's amended answer on the basis of the *Weber/Lambert* rationale in light of the 1996 amendments to La. C.C. arts. 2323 and 2324(B). *Dumas v. State ex rel. Dept. of Culture, Recreation & Tourism*, 02-0563 (La. 2002), 816 So. 2d 860.

Discussion

Prior to 1980, Louisiana courts applied a judicially-created rule based on common-law precedents under which a plaintiff's contributory negligence barred any recovery in a negligence action. *Rozell v. Louisiana Animal Breeders Co-op., Inc.*, 496 So. 2d 275, 279 (La. 1986); *Bell v. Jet Wheel Blast*, 462 So. 2d 166, 169 (La. 1985). The first Louisiana case that clearly adopted the doctrine of contributory negligence was *Fleytas v. Pontchartrain Railroad Co.*, 18 La. 339 (1841), which was decided at a time when there was no organized body of civilian doctrine on the issue of comparative fault. *Bell*, 462 So. 2d at 169. Effective August 1, 1980, the legislature amended La. C.C. art. 2323 to eliminate the doctrine of contributory negligence and to provide a procedure by which a plaintiff's negligence would operate only to reduce his recovery in proportion to his fault. *Murray v. Ramada Inns, Inc.*, 521 So. 2d 1123, 1132 (La. 1988); *Bell*, 462 So. 2d at 170. As amended by Act No. 431 of 1979, La. C.C. art. 2323, entitled "Computation of damages," provided:

> When contributory negligence is applicable to a claim for damages, its effect shall be as follows: If a person suffers injury, death or loss as the result partly of his own negligence and partly as a result of the fault of another person or persons, the claim for damages shall not thereby be defeated, but the amount of damages recoverable shall be reduced in proportion to the degree or percentage of negligence attributable to the person suffering the injury, death or loss.

The amendment, the effect of which was to prevent courts from applying any rule more damaging to plaintiff's case than comparative negligence, *Bell*, 462 So. 2d at 170, was beneficial to plaintiffs in that it increased the probability that they would be compensated, at least in part, for their injuries.

Act No. 431 of 1979 also revised La. C.C. art. 2324 to reaffirm the principle of solidary liability among joint tortfeasors, a principle that had been a part of Louisiana's civil tradition for more than 150 years. *See Touchard v. Williams*, 617 So. 2d 885 (La. 1993). As amended by this Act, La. C.C. art. 2324, entitled "Liability for assisting or encouraging wrongful act," provided:

He who causes another person to do an unlawful act, or assists or encourages in the commission of it, is answerable, in solido, with that person, for the damage caused by such act.

Persons whose concurring fault has caused injury, death or loss to another are also answerable, in solido; provided, however, when the amount of recovery has been reduced in accordance with the preceding article, a judgment debtor shall not be liable for more than the degree of his fault to a judgment creditor to whom a greater degree of negligence has been attributed, reserving to all parties their respective rights of indemnity and contribution.

One of the underlying policies of solidary liability, as well as tort law as a whole, is victim compensation. *Touchard,* 617 So. 2d at 889. The imposition of the principle of solidarity among joint tortfeasors " 'espouse[s] a theory that it is better to allocate damages to the injurers, even in greater portions than their respective degrees of fault, than have victims suffer a reduced recovery.' " *Id.* at 890 (quoting M. Kevin Queenan, *Civil Code Article 2324: A Broken Path to Limited Solidary Liability,* 49 La. L.Rev. 1351, 1356 (1989)). That is, the modern justification for solidary liability is founded on the belief that the innocent plaintiff should have the opportunity to obtain full compensation from any person whose fault was an indispensable factor in producing the harm. *Touchard,* 617 So. 2d at 890. Thus, the primary effect of solidary liability is that any tortfeasor may be made to pay the judgment in full for other defendants who are insolvent, unknown, or absent. *Id.*

In 1987, the legislature confronted the problem of compelling solvent defendants who were not 100% at fault to pay for 100% of plaintiffs' damages by enacting compromise legislation that attempted to balance the competing interests of judgment creditors and judgment debtors.[1] *Id.* By Act No. 373 of 1987, the legislature amended La. C.C. art. 2324, newly entitled "Liability as solidary or joint and divisible obligation," to provide:

A. He who conspires with another person to commit an intentional or willful act is answerable, in solido, with that person, for the damage caused by such act.

B. If liability is not solidary pursuant to Paragraph A, or as otherwise provided by law, then liability for damages caused by two or more persons shall be solidary only to the extent necessary for the person suffering injury, death, or loss to recover fifty percent of his recoverable damages; however, when the amount of recovery has been reduced in accordance with the preceding article, a judgment debtor shall not be liable for more than the degree of his fault to a judgment creditor to whom a greater degree of fault has been attributed. Under the provisions of this Article, all parties shall enjoy their respective rights of indemnity and contribution. Except as provided in Paragraph A of this Article, or as otherwise provided by law, and hereinabove, the liability for damages caused by two or more persons shall be a joint, divisible obligation, and a joint tortfeasor shall not be solidarily liable with any other person for damages attributable to the fault of such other person, including the person suffering injury, death, or loss, regardless of such other person's insolvency, ability to pay, degree of fault, or immunity by statute or otherwise.

This amendment balanced the risks of insolvent, incapable of paying, unknown, and absent tortfeasors among plaintiffs and known, solvent defendants. *Touchard,* 617 So. 2d at 892.

In a case arising prior to the 1987 amendment, *Weber v. Charity Hosp. of La. at New Orleans,* 475 So. 2d 1047 (La. 1985), this court was presented with the issue of whether a compromise with and release of an initial tortfeasor discharged a hospital and a blood supplier that gave the victim unwholesome blood during treatment for injuries she sustained in the original accident from any

---

[1] The original bill initiating this legislation would have wholly eliminated solidary liability among joint tortfeasors, except for those cases involving willful or intentional acts. *See Touchard,* 617 So. 2d at 890.

obligation relating to the blood transfusion. To answer this question, we were required to determine whether the original tortfeasor was solidarily liable for the damages resulting from the transfusion since the release of one solidary obligor discharged other solidary obligors. We concluded that an initial tortfeasor may be liable for the injuries he directly caused to the tort victim as well as for the victim's additional suffering caused by inappropriate treatment by a health care provider who treated the original injuries and characterized this inquiry as one of legal causation which should be addressed under a duty-risk analysis. We then determined that the initial tortfeasor's negligence was a cause in fact of the injuries the victim received as a result of inappropriate medical care, and that the initial tortfeasor's duty to refrain from negligently harming others encompassed the risk that the victim's injuries might be worsened by the treatment for those injuries. Consequently, we found that, as a matter of policy, the initial tortfeasor's negligence was the legal cause of the injuries arising from the subsequent medical treatment and the initial tortfeasor could therefore be held liable for any damages resulting from that treatment. Finally, we concluded that the initial tortfeasor's liability for any damages arising out of the medical treatment was solidary with any liability found to exist on the part of the hospital and the blood supplier.

After the 1987 amendment of Article 2324, an issue arose concerning the effect of the amendment on this court's holding in *Weber*. In *Lambert v. United States Fidelity & Guar. Co.,* 629 So. 2d 328 (La. 1993), a per curiam opinion, we determined that the amendment reducing solidarity among solidary obligors to only the extent necessary for the tort victim to recover fifty percent of his recoverable damages did not change the principle announced in *Weber* that the initial tortfeasor could be held liable for any damages arising out of medical treatment necessitated by the original accident. We stated that the initial tortfeasor's liability was based on the fact that he was the legal cause of 100% of the victim's harm as well as on the imposition of a solidary obligation between joint tortfeasors. We determined that the 1987 amendment to La. C.C. art. 2324 did not change the *Weber* principle, in part because an apportionment of fault between the original tortfeasor and the subsequently treating health care provider could result in the victim receiving less than the full amount of the judgment. We went on to note, however, that even under the *Weber* rationale that remained valid despite the 1987 amendment, the original tortfeasor would not ultimately bear the cost of the entire tort judgment because he had the right to seek contribution from the health care provider. We explained this result relieved the victim of having to prove which of the two tortfeasors caused what injuries and, instead, properly placed this burden on the original tortfeasor.

Several years after this court's opinion in *Lambert,* the legislature again amended La. C.C. arts. 2323 and 2324(B), this time to abolish solidary liability among non-intentional tortfeasors and to place Louisiana in a pure comparative fault system. Amended by Act 3 of the 1st Ex.Sess. of 1996, La. C.C. art. 2323, entitled "Comparative fault," now provides:

A. In any action for damages where a person suffers injury, death, or loss, the degree or percentage of fault of all persons causing or contributing to the injury, death, or loss shall be determined, regardless of whether the person is a party to the action or a nonparty, and regardless of the person's insolvency, ability to pay, immunity by statute, including but not limited to the provisions of R.S. 23:1032, or that the other person's identity is not known or reasonably ascertainable. If a person suffers injury, death, or loss as the result partly of his own negligence and partly as a result of the fault of another person or persons, the amount of damages recoverable shall be reduced in proportion to the degree or percentage of negligence attributable to the person suffering the injury, death, or loss.

B. The provisions of Paragraph A shall apply to any claim for recovery of damages for injury, death, or loss asserted under any law or legal doctrine or theory of liability, regardless of the basis of liability.

C. Notwithstanding the provisions of Paragraphs A and B, if a person suffers injury, death, or loss as a result partly of his own negligence and partly as a result of the fault of an intentional tortfeasor, his claim for recovery of damages shall not be reduced.

In addition to Article 2323, Act 3 also amended La. C.C. art. 2324 to provide:

A. He who conspires with another person to commit an intentional or willful act is answerable, in solido, with that person, for the damage caused by such act.

B. If liability is not solidary pursuant to Paragraph A, then liability for damages caused by two or more persons shall be a joint and divisible obligation. A joint tortfeasor shall not be liable for more than his degree of fault and shall not be solidarily liable with any other person for damages attributable to the fault of such other person, including the person suffering injury, death, or loss, regardless of such other person's insolvency, ability to pay, degree of fault, immunity by statute or otherwise, including but not limited to immunity as provided in R.S. 23:1032, or that the other person's identity is not known or reasonably ascertainable.

C. Interruption of prescription against one joint tortfeasor is effective against all joint tortfeasors.

The Act was effective April 16, 1996.[2]

In this case, the State contends Article 2323(A) and (B) and Article 2324(B), as amended in 1996, abolished solidary liability in civil cases involving negligent acts and therefore this court's analysis in *Weber* and *Lambert* is no longer applicable to prevent it from arguing the fault of a subsequent health care provider as an affirmative defense at trial. The State further supports its analysis by pointing out that there is no longer an action for contribution among joint tortfeasors, a possibility it contends underlies the *Lambert* decision, because those joint tortfeasors are no longer solidarily liable with any other person. The State also argues that the 1996 amendment to La. C.C. art. 2324(B) not only eliminated solidarity between non-intentional tortfeasors, but also eliminated the solidarity "otherwise provided by law," including that law enunciated in *Weber* and *Lambert*. Based on these arguments, the State concludes a legal basis for this court's decisions in *Weber* and *Lambert* no longer exists. Plaintiffs, on the other hand, contend the result urged by the State is not required by the amended statutes because the amendments do not clearly provide that they apply to medical malpractice claims and because such a result would be contrary to the legislative policies found in the Medical Malpractice Act. According to plaintiffs, allowing tortfeasors to question the medical care rendered to their victims will necessarily cause a large increase in the number of medical malpractice claims, which in turn will increase medical malpractice insurance premiums and will have a direct negative effect on the legislative goals underlying the Medical Malpractice Act.

When a law is clear and unambiguous and the application of the law does not lead to absurd consequences, the law must be applied as written without any further interpretation of the intent of the legislature. La. C.C. art. 9. Accordingly, the starting point for the interpretation of any statute is the language of the statute itself. *Riddle v. Bickford,* 00-2408, p. 9-10 (La. 2001), 785 So. 2d 795, 802.

We find the language of Articles 2323 and 2324(B), as amended by Act 3, is clear, unambiguous, and does not lead to absurd consequences. Article 2323 provides that "[i]n *any action for damages* ..., the degree of percentage of fault of *all persons* causing or contributing to the injury, death or loss *shall* be determined, regardless of whether the person is a party to the action or a nonparty.... The [foregoing] provisions ... *shall* apply to *any claim* ... asserted under *any law or legal doctrine or theory of liability, regardless of the basis of liability.*" (Emphasis added.) Thus, this article clearly requires that the fault of every person responsible for a plaintiff's injuries be compared, whether or not they are parties, regardless of the legal theory of liability asserted against each person.

Likewise, the language of Article 2324(B) is equally clear. It provides that in non-intentional cases, liability for damages caused by two or more persons *shall* be a joint and divisible obligation.[3]

---

[2] There is no question that the provisions of Act 3 of the 1st Ex.Sess. of 1996 are applicable in the case at bar as the accident occurred on April 22, 1996, six days after the effective date of the Act.

Each joint tortfeasor *shall not* be liable for more than his degree of fault and *shall not* be solidarily liable with any other person for damages attributable to the fault of that other person. This provision abolishes solidarity among non-intentional tortfeasors,[4] and makes each non-intentional tortfeasor liable only for his own share of the fault, which must be quantified pursuant to Article 2323.

In this case, the State alleges that a portion of the damages sought by plaintiffs was caused by medical malpractice on the part of the health care providers treating Mr. Dumas for the injuries he sustained in the bicycle accident. Pursuant to Article 2323, the fault of both the State and the allegedly negligent health care providers should be determined notwithstanding the fact that the health care providers are nonparties. Under Article 2324(B), if a jury determines that both the State and the health care providers negligently injured Mr. Dumas and plaintiffs, then the liability between them will be a joint and divisible obligation, they will not be solidarily liable, and each joint tortfeasor will be liable only for his portion of fault. The comparative fault article, La. C.C. art. 2323, makes no exceptions for liability based on medical malpractice; on the contrary, it clearly applies to any claim asserted under any theory of liability, regardless of the basis of liability. There is no conflict between either Article 2323 or Article 2324(B) and the Medical Malpractice Act that could be fairly classified as "absurd." Accordingly, we find the clear language of Articles 2323 and 2324(B), applied as written, leads to the inescapable conclusion that the State in this case must be allowed to put on evidence related to the health care provider's alleged fault as part of its defense. While we recognize that these articles, which substantially impede the ability of an injured party to obtain full recovery of his damages, are in derogation of established rights and are to be strictly construed, *Touchard,* 617 So. 2d at 892, we simply cannot construe their unmistakably clear language in a contrary manner without overstepping our role as jurists.

Plaintiffs' reliance on this court's prior holdings in *Weber* and *Lambert* to justify the opposite result is misplaced. The principle of *Weber* and *Lambert* can be characterized as one of policy formulated by this court in terms of legal cause under the then-prevailing rule of solidarity and in the absence of a contrary legislative expression. "Regardless if stated in terms of proximate cause, legal cause, or duty, the scope of the duty inquiry is ultimately a question of policy." *Roberts v. Benoit,* 605 So. 2d 1032, 1052 (1991) (on rehearing). This inquiry "is a policy question in purest form." *Id.* As explained earlier in this opinion, the policy behind solidarity is one of victim compensation. By imposing solidarity among joint tortfeasors, Louisiana subscribed to a theory that it was more desirable to force a tortfeasor to pay damages in greater proportion than the degree of fault allocated to him than to have an innocent victim suffer less than full recovery. Our holdings in *Weber* and *Lambert* effectuated this policy. In those cases, we did not find that the subsequently negligent health care provider did not cause some portion of plaintiff's injuries or that those providers were not liable; rather, the determination that, as a matter of policy, the initial tortfeasor was the legal cause of 100% of plaintiff's harm allowed plaintiff to seek the entirety of his damages caused by the subsequent tortfeasor from either the initial or the subsequent tortfeasor. Thereafter, because of the imposition of solidarity between the initial and subsequent tortfeasors, the initial tortfeasor who paid the entire judgment could seek contribution from the health care provider.[5] This result furthered Louisiana's policy of full victim compensation by placing the burden of recovery from the subsequent tortfeasor on the initial tortfeasor. In fact, we noted in *Lambert* that a contrary resolution would be undesirable on policy grounds because it could result in the victim receiving less than the full amount of the judgment.

---

[3] La. C.C. art. 1788 provides:
>   When different obligors owe together just one performance to one obligee, but neither is bound for the whole, the obligation is joint for the obligors.

[4] La. C.C. art. 1796 provides:
>   Solidarity of obligation shall not be presumed. A solidary obligation arises from a clear expression of the parties' intent or from the law.

[5] Prior to the 1996 amendments, La. C.C. art. 2324(B) specifically reserved the rights of indemnity and contribution among co- tortfeasors.

With the 1996 amendments to Articles 2323 and 2324(B), however, the legislature has effected a total shift in tort policy. Prior to the enactment of the amendments, the policy behind Louisiana's tort law was ensuring that innocent victims received full compensation for their injuries. Now, however, Louisiana's policy is that each tortfeasor pays only for that portion of the damage he has caused and the tortfeasor shall not be solidarily liable with any other person for damages attributable to the fault of that other person. With the advent of this new policy, the right of contribution among solidary tortfeasors also disappeared since it is no longer necessary in light of the abolishment of solidarity. The legislature has struck a new balance in favor of known, present and solvent tortfeasors instead of the previous priority that fully compensated injured victims. While one may question the advisability of this shift in policy, we are bound to follow it. *See Soloco v. Dupree,* 97-1256 (La. 1998), 707 So. 2d 12, 17 ("It is not the prerogative of the judiciary to disregard public policy decisions underlying legislation or to reweigh balances of interests and policy considerations already struck by the legislature.").

The policies upon which *Weber* and *Lambert* were based have simply been changed by the legislature. Because it is error for a court to allow "its own policy determination to override the policy determination made by the legislature," *Id.,* we cannot allow the policy-based rule of *Weber* and *Lambert* to prevent the State from presenting a defense to which it is clearly entitled under the amendments to La. C.C. arts. 2323 and 2324(B). The factfinder in the instant case is required to determine the percentage of fault of all persons causing injury to plaintiffs. If the factfinder concludes that plaintiffs' damages were caused by more than one person, then each joint tortfeasor is only liable for his degree of fault and cannot be held solidarily liable with another tortfeasor for damages attributable to that other tortfeasor's fault. The State in this case is therefore entitled to present, as an affirmative defense, evidence relating to the fault of another person it believes caused injury to plaintiffs. Consequently, we find that plaintiffs' motion to strike the State's amended answer on the basis that it is immaterial, irrelevant, and insufficient should be denied.

Accordingly, the judgments of the lower courts granting plaintiffs' motion to strike are reversed, and the case is remanded to the district court for further proceedings not inconsistent with this opinion.

REVERSED and **REMANDED.**

CALOGERO, Chief Justice, dissents and assigns reasons.

I disagree that the legislature by the 1996 amendments to La. Civ.Code arts. 2323 and 2324(B) overruled the reasoning of this state's courts that an original tortfeasor may be held liable for the victim's injuries caused by subsequent, negligent medical treatment. Such a policy was recognized in Louisiana as early as 1962 in *Hudgens v. Mayeaux,* 143 So. 2d 606 (La.App. 3 Cir. 1962), and by this court in 1985 in *Weber v. Charity Hospital of Louisiana,* 475 So. 2d 1047 (La. 1985). In *Weber,* we reasoned that the duty of the negligent driver to refrain from causing injury to another encompassed the risk that the tort victim's injuries might be worsened by subsequent, negligent medical treatment for those injuries. 475 So. 2d at 1050. We iterated that principle more recently in *Lambert v. U.S. Fidelity & Guaranty Co.,* 629 So. 2d 328 (La. 1993), in which we reasoned that "in *Weber*-like cases, the original tortfeasor's liability for 100% of the tort victim's injuries is based on more than the imposition of a solidary obligation between joint tortfeasors; his liability for 100% of the victim's damages results because he is the legal cause of 100% of the victim's harm." 629 So. 2d at 329. In *Weber,* we explained that "[i]t is the coextensiveness of the obligations for the same debt, and not the source of liability, which determines the solidarity of the obligation." 475 So. 2d at 1051.

The two courts of appeal that have considered whether the 1996 amendments have overruled *Weber* and *Lambert* have both answered in the negative. *Dumas v. State, Dep't of Culture, Recreation & Tourism,* 35,492 (La.App. 2 Cir. 2001), 804 So. 2d 813; *Knabel v. Lewis,* 00-1464 (La.App. 1 Cir. 2001), 809 So. 2d 314. As the court of appeal below explained:

> When the duty breached by a tortfeasor includes the risk that a plaintiff's injuries might be worsened by subsequent medical treatment, the tortfeasor is liable for 100%

of the damages. The rule is based upon legal cause. When a tort victim takes reasonable steps to secure medical treatment, the original tortfeasor may also be liable for subsequent medical malpractice. That a tort victim will seek medical care when injured and thus, be subject to further risk and damages, is foreseeable and easily associated with the original injury. This is not a divisible obligation. There is no additional percentage of fault by the medical care provider to quantify.

Dumas, 35,492, pp. 6-7, 804 So. 2d at 817.

La. Civ.Code art. 2324(B) states that a "joint tortfeasor shall not be liable for more than his degree of fault and shall not be solidarily liable with any other person for damages attributable to the fault of such other person...." Applying that language to *Weber*-type cases, it is my view that the original tortfeasor's fault includes damages that may arise from subsequent, negligent medical treatment of the original injury, because he is the legal cause of the victim's injuries, and thus there is no fault to apportion to the negligent medical provider in a suit against the original tortfeasor. Accordingly, I do not believe that the legislature, which more likely intended to preclude original tortfeasors from seeking contribution from subsequent negligent medical providers, thereby protecting medical care providers from liability, instead overruled the *Weber/Lambert* rule to place innocent Louisiana victims at risk of not being able to be completely compensated for their tort injuries.

* * * * *

COMMENT

Even in a comparative fault regime, a plaintiff's contributory negligence may act as a complete bar in some circumstances. One such case is when the plaintiff's contributory negligence is deemed the sole "legal cause" of the accident. *See, e.g., Exxon Company, U.S.A. v. Sofec, Inc.,* 517 U.S. 830 (1996). In other cases, a statute may bar recovery. Consider the following three statutes that bar a plaintiff's recovery in various circumstances where the plaintiff is at fault. Do the statutes, which essentially reinstitute contributory negligence by statute in specified circumstances, reflect the legislature's dissatisfaction with pure comparative fault? *See generally,* Frank L. Maraist, H. Alston Johnson III, Thomas C. Galligan, Jr. & William R. Corbett, *Answering a Fool According to His Folly: Ruminations on Comparative Fault Thirty Years On,* 70 La. L. Rev. 1105 (2010).

La. R.S. 14:63. **Criminal trespass**

* * * * *

H. The provisions of any other law notwithstanding, owners, lessees, and custodians of structures, watercraft, movable or immovable property shall not be answerable for damages sustained by any person who enters upon the structure, watercraft, movable or immovable property without express, legal or implied authorization, or who without legal authorization, remains upon the structure, watercraft, movable or immovable property after being forbidden by the owner, or other person with authority to do so; however, the owner, lessee or custodian of the property may be answerable for damages only upon a showing that the damages sustained were the result of the intentional acts or gross negligence of the owner, lessee or custodian.

La. R.S. 9:2800.10. Immunity from liability for injuries sustained while committing a felony offense

A. No person shall be liable for damages for injury, death, or loss sustained by a perpetrator of a felony offense during the commission of the offense or while fleeing the scene of the offense.

B. The provisions of this Section shall apply regardless of whether the injury, death, or loss was caused by an intentional or unintentional act or omission or a condition of property or a building. However, the provisions of this Section shall not apply if injury to or death of a perpetrator results from an intentional act involving the use of excessive force.

C.   For purposes of this Section "damages" includes all general and special damages which may be recoverable for personal injury, death, or loss of or damage to property, including those otherwise recoverable in a survival or wrongful death action.

La. R.S. 9:2798.4.   Immunity from liability; injuries sustained by persons driving under the influence of alcoholic beverages or drugs

A.   Neither the state, a state agency, or a political subdivision of the state nor any person shall be liable for damages, including those available under Civil Code Article 2315.1 or 2315.2, for injury, death, or loss of the operator of a motor vehicle, aircraft, watercraft, or vessel who:

(1)   Was operating a motor vehicle, aircraft, watercraft, or vessel while his blood alcohol concentration of 0.08 percent or more by weight based on grams of alcohol per one hundred cubic centimeters of blood; or

(2)   Was operating a motor vehicle, aircraft, watercraft, or vessel while he was under the influence of any controlled dangerous substance described in R.S. 14:98(A)(1)(c) or R.S. 40:964.

B.   The provisions of this Section shall not apply unless:

(1)   The operator is found to be in excess of twenty-five percent negligent as a result of a blood alcohol concentration in excess of the limits provided in R.S. 14:98(A)(1)(b), or the operator is found to be in excess of twenty-five percent negligent as a result of being under the influence of a controlled dangerous substance described in R.S. 14:98(A)(1)(c); and

(2)   This negligence was a contributing factor causing the damage.

C.   For purposes of this Section, "damages" include all general damages, including those otherwise recoverable in a survival or wrongful death action, which may be recoverable for personal injury, death or loss, or damage to property by the operator of a motor vehicle, aircraft, watercraft, or vessel or the category of persons who would have a cause of action for the operator's wrongful death.

D.   The provisions of this Section shall not apply if the operator tests positive for any controlled dangerous substance covered by the provisions of R.S. 14:98(A)(1)(c) or R.S. 40:964 and the operator is taking that substance pursuant to a valid prescription for the identified substance or a health care provider verifies that he has prescribed or furnished the operator with that particular substance.

E.   Unless the operator's insurance policy provides otherwise, nothing in this Section shall be construed to preclude the operator from making a claim under his or her own policy for first party indemnity coverages.

NOTE

La. R.S. 9:2798.4 is not the only Louisiana statute addressing damages that may be attributable to alcohol consumption. How would that statute interact with La. R.S. 9:2800.1, *supra* Chapter 6 Part 7, which generally provides that sellers and social hosts are not liable for damages caused by those who consume alcohol that the sellers or hosts provide. The immunity of 9:2800.1 does not apply, however, if the person to whom the alcohol is provided is underage. What would happen if such an underage drinker sued the provider of the alcohol, who would not benefit from the immunity of 9:2800.1, but the provider claimed the benefit of immunity under 9:2798.4? *Compare Stead v. Swanner*, 52 So. 3d 1149 (La.App. 5 Cir. 2010), *writ denied*, 61 So. 3d 684 (La. 2011) *with Stewart v. Daiquiri Affair, Inc.*, 20 So. 3d 1041 (La.App. 1 Cir. 2009), *writ denied*, 19 So. 3d 477 (La. 2009).

CALOGERO, J.

A lawsuit was brought by Ora Watson, individually and as tutrix of her minor child, and six major Watson children, against Earl Creel and his insurer, State Farm Fire and Casualty Insurance Co., for the wrongful death of Ora's husband and the children's father, Doyle Watson. The claim arose out of a hunting accident in which Earl Creel's minor son, Shane, shot and killed the fifty-three year old Watson with a high-powered rifle. A trial jury rendered a verdict in favor of defendants, finding decedent Watson 100% at fault in connection with the accident. The First Circuit Court of Appeal, 459 So. 2d 1235, affirmed.

We granted writs in this essentially factual dispute because we perceived the Court of Appeal to have applied an inappropriate standard of review. The Court of Appeal found that the jury's verdict was "based upon a reasonable evaluation of credibility," an applied review standard which seemed quite similar to the "reasonable basis for (a trial court's) finding" test which this Court found insufficient in *Arceneaux v. Domingue*, 365 So. 2d 1330, 1333 (La. 1978). In fact the appropriate standard is that a finding of fact by the trial court should be upheld "unless it is *clearly wrong*," or manifestly erroneous. Furthermore, it just seemed so *clearly wrong* for the lower courts to have determined that the victim of this accidental shooting by a deer hunter was the only party at fault, especially inasmuch as comparative fault, rather than the bar of contributory negligence, prevailed in the law when the shooting took place.

The accident occurred on the Watson farm in Mt. Hermon, a community located in Washington Parish, in the early evening hours of December 29, 1981.[1] The Creel family had been invited to hunt deer on the Watson property by the victim, Doyle Watson, since deer had been decimating the vegetable garden on Watson's farm.[2] (In fact, each hunter was later positioned on the edge of a field to cover as much of the farm as possible and each was instructed as to the most likely approaches of the deer as they prepared to feed.) After meeting at the farmhouse, the group of hunters traveled on a field road in Earl Creel's truck to the positions pointed out by Mr. Watson. Earl Creel's sixteen year old stepson was dropped off first, then Shane. Shane was placed on a tree stand at the edge of an oval field, which was surrounded by woods. Some bales of hay were located near the tree stand and Shane was offered this location as an alternative should he become too cold in the tree stand. He did move to the bales, and it was from this spot that he later fired the fatal shot. Earl Creel was also placed in a tree stand, out of sight of the boys. Willie Creel drove the truck another 150 yards from Earl and used the truck itself as a stand. Mr. Watson proceeded into the swamp on foot in search of a large buck. He planned to hunt until dark before walking home, and the position of his body on the road, as well as his footprints, indicated that he had in fact been returning home at the time of the accident.

Shane Creel ... was just twelve years old and in the seventh grade when he fatally shot Doyle Watson.... Shane lacked experience in firing the rifle. Shane himself testified that he had only twice

---

[1] Earl Creel testified that he heard the report of the Marlin 30-30 rifle at approximately 5:25 P.M. He had begun to get off his stand in anticipation of the group's departure. He noted that the sun had set but there was still sufficient light for the hunters to drive their truck without the use of headlights and that they were able to locate Mr. Watson's body without the use of a flashlight.

[2] The hunting party included, besides young Shane Creel, his father Earl Creel, his grandfather Willie Creel and his stepbrother Tony Lala. Mr. Watson and Willie Creel were acquaintances of long standing, but Mr. Watson met the other family members for the first time on the day of the accident. He had no knowledge of their hunting experience or expertise.

fired this weapon.[4] Perhaps more significantly, the boy lacked familiarity with the use of the scope attached to the rifle.... Shane had had no formal instruction of any kind in the use of firearms.

On this occasion, Shane had been alone either on the stand or near the bales for about two hours before he noticed a moving object which, in the light of dusk, he thought was a deer. In recalling its location in the field, the boy's testimony indicated uncertainty, perhaps because the scope altered his perspective. He stated:

> It was out in the edge of the woods, I guess, or it could have been in the center of the field.

He also testified that the view was about the same from either on top of the four foot high bales of hay or from the twenty-five foot high tree stand. At any rate, he described an object moving back and forth in front of him and occasionally dropping its head from view, presumably to either eat or drink. He claimed to have followed visually the object's movements through the scope for several minutes, "to be sure what I was shooting at" before firing. In deposition, read at trial, Shane stated, "I kept on studying it for a little while and then I presumed that it was a deer and I fired at it." He proceeded to search for the fallen deer, but without success. He could not find any tracks, much less a deer.

A single shot had been fired, and 461 feet away Doyle Watson sustained a large wound in the right front portion of his head. His death was apparently immediate. Watson *was* wearing black work boots, a dark baseball cap with a white front displaying an advertisement of some kind, gray work pants, a green-colored camouflaged hunting jacket, and partially visible white insulated underclothing. Although the Creels all wore the "Hunter orange" vests and offered one to Mr. Watson, he declined the offer.[5] Furthermore, although Watson had, himself, placed Shane at the stand, and had directed the boy's attention for hunting to the very area in which he was later shot, he apparently made no effort to call to Shane or otherwise alert the boy to his presence in the same area shortly before the accident. Of course, it is possible that he assumed that the Creels had already left the farm. He had earlier told them not to wait for him, and apparently anticipated that their departure would precede his own.

Plaintiffs' attorney sought to establish the negligence of Earl Creel, Shane's father,[6] on several bases: (1) giving his son Shane a high-powered rifle on the child's twelfth birthday; (2) not properly

---

[4] Shane testified that he "shot two different bullets in it on the same day."

[5] La.Rev.Stat.Ann. § 56:143 provides:
> Any person hunting deer shall display on his head or chest, and/or back a total of not less than four hundred square inches of material of daylight fluorescent orange color known as "hunter orange." These provisions shall not apply to persons hunting deer on property which is privately owned and legally posted, or to archery deer hunters except when bow and arrow are used to hunt deer on wildlife management areas where a gun season for deer is in progress.
> Whoever violates the provision of this section shall be fined not more than $100 or imprisoned for not more than ninety days, or both.

Watson was hunting deer on his own privately owned farm. Nonetheless, since his property was not legally posted, he was technically in violation of the statute. However, this court in *Breithaupt v. Sellers*, 390 So. 2d 870 (La. 1980), decided, when contributory negligence was the prevailing law, that a hunter/victim in violation of R.S. 56:143 (the Hunter orange requirement) was not necessarily contributorily negligent, that causation was for the factfinder, and that thus a directed verdict had improperly been granted.

[6] Under La.Civ.Code Ann. art. 2318, parents "are responsible for the damage occasioned by their minor or unemancipated children residing with them, ..." In this case, Janice R. Creel and Earl Creel, Shane's parents, were divorced, and Shane generally resided with his mother Janice, who had been awarded his custody. Since she was vicariously liable for Shane's negligence under art. 2318 and the jurisprudence under that article (and perhaps because Shane himself was an insured under his mother's homeowner's policy because an occupant of the home), Janice's homeowner's liability insurer, Farm Bureau, settled with the Watsons by paying $85,000, 85% of the policy limits. Coincident therewith, the Watsons executed a release of Janice Creel and Farm Bureau from all claims as a result of the accident and executed also a covenant with Mrs. Creel and Shane to desist from asserting

instructing Shane in the use of that weapon; (3) not adequately supervising Shane at the time of the accident, particularly in failing to show him how to sight game with the rifle's scope. On the other hand, plaintiffs' counsel attempted in his opening statement to the jury to minimize Shane's fault, which he described as "very slight, if any." Counsel for the defense countered that the accident would not have occurred had Mr. Watson worn the "Hunter orange" vest, or signified his presence when he walked in the area which he had personally designated for hunting.

We agree with the lower courts to this extent. Watson was not without fault in this accidental shooting. However, the concept of comparative negligence, written into La.Civ.Code Ann. art. 2323,[7] permits a plaintiff such as Mr. Watson (or his wife and children) to recover damages, notwithstanding his own negligence.

A pure comparative fault system was adopted in Louisiana in 1979 by Act No. 431. That act became effective only on August 1, 1980.[8] It was specifically designed to ameliorate the harshness of the contributory negligence doctrine by apportioning losses between the plaintiff and defendant when both are negligent.[9] This allocation of shares of negligence, however, is not an easy task for the factfinder, and the Louisiana statute does not describe with particularity how it should be accomplished.[10]

---

against Shane any claim in this regard. Liability on the part of Mr. Creel, the non-custodial parent, is predicated on proof of his own negligence.

[7] La.Civ.Code Ann. art. 2323 provides:
> When contributory negligence is applicable to a claim for damages, its effect shall be as follows: If a person suffers injury, death or loss as the result partly of his own negligence and partly as a result of the fault of another person or persons, the claim for damages shall not thereby by defeated, but the amount of damages recoverable shall be reduced in proportion to the degree or percentage of negligence attributable to the person suffering the injury, death or loss.

[8] The effective date was postponed while the Legislature authorized a thorough study of comparative negligence, indicating a legislative willingness to reconsider the issues presented by the concept of comparative negligence before the scheduled effective date of the statute. R. Pearson, Apportionment of Losses Under Comparative Fault Laws--An Analysis of the Alternatives, 40 La.L.Rev. 343, 343-44 (1980).

[9] The apportionment of losses, however, may be accomplished by either of two systems, pure comparative fault or modified comparative fault (the latter not being the type in effect in Louisiana.) Both are based upon the principle that liability should be proportionally related to negligence. This includes an apportionment between plaintiff and defendant, as well as among defendants. Under modified comparative negligence, the plaintiff will not recover in some instances where less than all of the negligence is allocated to him. Under the pure comparative fault system, adopted by the Louisiana legislature in 1980, plaintiff's negligence will only diminish, not defeat, recovery as long as plaintiff's negligence is less than 100%. See R. Pearson, Apportionment of Losses, 40 La.L.Rev. 343, 344 (1980). Thus, in at least negligence cases, as opposed to those involving strict liability, the application of the comparative fault system is straight forward. Legal scholars have enumerated the basic elements: (1) the plaintiff's negligence, even if it comprises 99% of the total fault, only diminishes his recovery according to the percent of negligence found against him by the trier of fact; (2) although tortfeasors obligated for the same injuries continue to be solidarily liable, under La.Civ.Code Ann. art. 2324, that defendant whose fault is less than the plaintiff's owes only his percentage of plaintiff's damages; (3) the defendants' percentages of fault determine their contribution rights; (4) a tortfeasor who settles is insulated against claims for contribution, as well as liability to the plaintiff; and (5) although the nonsettling tortfeasor's contribution rights are defeated by the settlement, he has the right to have the plaintiff's recovery against him reduced in proportion to the percentage of fault assigned to the settling tortfeasor. D. Robertson, Ruminations on Comparative Fault, Duty-Risk Analysis, Affirmative Defenses, and Defensive Doctrines in Negligence and Strict Liability Litigation in Louisiana, 44 La.L.Rev. 1341, 1345 (1984).

[10] A "fault line" has been suggested as a method of conceptualizing the share of negligence attributable to each party. One end, designated with a value of zero, would indicate the absence of fault; at the other end, a value of ten would indicate deliberate wrongdoing. The factfinder can then designate on the line where the conduct of each party falls. From the scale, the various allocations of fault can be converted to percentages. R. Pearson, Apportionment of Losses Under Comparative Fault Laws, 40 La.L.Rev. at 348-49.

Clearly, however, the concept of comparative negligence is not applicable when the victim alone is the party at fault. In this case, the jury in response to interrogatories found that Earl Creel was not at fault in causing the accident, that Shane Creel was not at fault in causing the accident,[11] and that Doyle Watson *was* at fault. Expressed in terms of a percent, the jury answered that Watson's degree of fault was "100%."

* * * * *

Here, the jury was clearly wrong, considering all the evidence, in deciding that Earl Creel and his twelve year old son Shane were each without fault in the accidental death of Doyle Watson. It is incomprehensible that no negligence was involved in Earl Creel's arming an untrained twelve year old boy with a high-powered rifle, from which the boy had had occasion to fire previously only two shells, and leaving him alone in the woods to hunt a species of animal which he had never seen. So too, it is incomprehensible that the boy did not share some fault in this tragic accident, for it surely constitutes negligence to fire a rifle at a moving object without ascertaining with certainty that it is not a human being.

The Court of Appeal stated that they were required to uphold the finding of a jury when "based upon a reasonable evaluation of credibility." Shane's testimony about sighting a deer and firing at it after properly identifying his target, the Court of Appeal considered quite positive testimony. And they held that the jury could reasonably have concluded that Shane had exercised reasonable care and had in fact identified a deer before firing. As noted at the outset of this opinion, the Court of Appeal's upholding the jury verdict upon finding it "based upon a reasonable evaluation of credibility" is the application of a standard of review quite similar to the test rejected in *Arceneaux, supra*. It is not enough to sustain the determination of the district court when "there is some reasonable evidence to support the finding." Rather, the appropriate question is, was that finding clearly wrong or manifestly erroneous. Our answer to this question is that it *was* clearly wrong.

Shane's testimony regarding the sighting of the deer was quite equivocal.[12] Even his statement quoted by the Court of Appeal clearly progresses, with the benefit of leading questions, from an expression of doubt, to assurance concerning the object sighted. Shane initially responded that "I thought I saw something," explained that "[t]o the best of my knowledge, I saw a deer," and finally asserted in answer to a direct question that there was no doubt in his mind that he was looking at a deer when he fired. And, since it is highly unlikely that a deer would have been meandering across a field, drinking water in close proximity to a man walking in the open along a nearby field road, it is much more likely, if not entirely certain, that there was no deer, and that Shane was following the

---

[11] La.Code Civ.Pro.Ann. art. 1812 provides in pertinent part:
   C.   In cases to recover damages for injury, death, or loss, the court may submit to the jury, unless waived by all parties, special written questions inquiring as to:
      * * * * *
      (2)   If appropriate, whether another person, whether party or not, other than the person suffering injury, death, or loss, was at fault, and, if so:
         (a) Whether such fault was a legal cause of the damages, and, if so:
         (b) The degree of such fault, expressed in percentage.
   Thus, although Shane is not a party to this suit, "the factfinder may assign a percentage of fault to every person involved in the accident, presumably including those persons who have been released by the plaintiff." M. Chamallas, "Comparative Fault and Multiple Party Litigation in Louisiana, 40 La.L.Rev. 373, 374 (1980).
   For a recent case of this court where art. 1812 was discussed, *see Lemire v. New Orleans Public Service, Inc.*, 458 So. 2d 1308 (La. 1984).

[12] A review of the record also discloses some very questionable testimony by Shane. In one instance, Shane testified that he had sighted a deer and fired the rifle earlier in the afternoon. Since the distinctive report, clearly heard by Earl Creel when Shane fired the fatal shot, had not been heard earlier, Shane's testimony in this regard seems suspect.

movements of Doyle Watson as he was walking along a rutted road, partially obscured by a knoll in the center of the field and grass about two feet high.[13]

Although the accident might have been avoided had Mr. Watson worn the "Hunter orange" vest or called out to Shane on entering the field, it seems equally likely that an experienced hunter, such as Earl Creel, would have correctly interpreted the moving object as a man rather than a deer. We believe that Earl Creel's negligence in either failing to provide his young son with a supervised experience in sighting large game through a scope and firing this high-powered rifle, or closely supervising him on this occasion was a cause in fact of Mr. Watson's accidental death. We also believe that causation for the accident must be attributed to Shane as well as to his father. The twelve year old must share some responsibility for this death in view of his own negligence in firing a dangerous weapon at a man he *presumed* to be a deer.

Having determined that the jury's allocation of 100% fault to the plaintiff was against the weight of the evidence, and was clearly wrong, we are empowered by La.Code Civ.Pro.Ann. art. 2164 to "render any judgment which is just, legal, and proper upon the record on appeal."[14] We recognize that a standard for determining percentages of fault has not been provided by the Legislature, and we are therefore presented with an opportunity to offer guidelines as we apportion fault in this instance.[15] In so doing we have looked to the Uniform Comparative Fault Act, 2(b) and Comment (as revised in 1979),[16] which incorporates direction for the trier of fact. Section 2(b) provides:

> In determining the percentages of fault, the trier of fact shall consider both the nature of the conduct of each party at fault and the extent of the causal relation between the conduct and the damages claimed.

In assessing the nature of the conduct of the parties, various factors may influence the degree of fault assigned, including: (1) whether the conduct resulted from inadvertence or involved an awareness of the danger, (2) how great a risk was created by the conduct, (3) the significance of what was sought by the conduct, (4) the capacities of the actor, whether superior or inferior, and (5) any extenuating circumstances which might require the actor to proceed in haste, without proper thought. And, of course, as evidenced by concepts such as last clear chance, the relationship between the fault/negligent conduct and the harm to the plaintiff are considerations in determining the relative fault of the parties.

---

[13] Jack Underwood, the investigating detective from the Washington Parish Sheriff's Department testified that the field road had potholes and an up and down motion in it. He noted that "at some points, you could see a subject and some points you couldn't walking down the road."

[14] According to Comment (a), "(t)he purpose of this article is to give the appellate court complete freedom to do justice on the record."

[15] Although our apportionment is admittedly somewhat inexact, it is certainly superior to the "all-or-nothing position" imposed by the theory of contributory negligence. *See* J. Wade, Comparative Negligence--Its Development in the United States and Its Present Status in Louisiana, 40 La.L.Rev. 299, 314 (1980).

[16] Uniform Acts are drafted by the National Conference of Commissioners on Uniform State Laws, composed of representatives, termed Commissioners, from within the legal profession of each of the fifty states as well as the District of Columbia and Puerto Rico. In order "to promote uniformity in state law on all subjects where uniformity is deemed desirable and practical," the Conference recommends acts for general adoption throughout the jurisdiction of the United States. While Louisiana has adopted some twenty-two of the one hundred twenty-five uniform laws, such as the Child Custody Jurisdiction Act, articles 1, 3, 4, 5, 7 and 8 of the Commercial Code, the Criminal Extradiction Act, the Gifts to Minors Act, and the Trade Secrets Act, it has not incorporated the entirety of the Uniform Comparative Fault Act into its law. Several matters such as set-off, the effect of the release of one tortfeasor on the contribution rights of others, as well as the standard to be used in apportioning percentages of fault, have by the Louisiana Legislature apparently been left for Louisiana courts to resolve. The Uniform Act, however, benefiting from the comments of many sources during its special committee's five years of consideration, addressed all potential problems and attempted to provide the best solutions for them.

Our consideration of these factors suggest that the majority of the fault must rest with the Creels. The causal relation between negligently firing a dangerous weapon and/or negligently failing to instruct or supervise a minor child in the use of the weapon, and plaintiff's death, is a direct one. On the other hand, plaintiff's failure to wear Hunter orange or signify his presence may have contributed to the youth's fatal error in identifying his target. But it was not as directly related to the plaintiff's demise as was the conduct of the Creels.

Furthermore, the factors suggested in evaluating the conduct of the parties indicate that a lesser degree of fault should be attributed to plaintiff. His conduct, at least in walking along the field road within the boy's rifle range, was inadvertent. His failure to don the bright hunting vest, however, was a conscious action which necessarily involved adverting to, or consciously considering the risk, or possible danger. Nevertheless, plaintiff's omissions at worse had only an indirect causative impact on the accident. In contrast, none of the actions of Shane or his father Earl Creel can be considered inadvertent. They were aware that the high-powered rifle was deadly and that it was imperative to discern a target with certainty before firing. In a similar vein, the risk of firing or failing to train and supervise the firing of such a weapon had a direct potential for fatal consequences. And, in considering possible mitigating factors, the Creels had no higher motive than sport when their acts of negligence occurred, and their actions were not dictated by any emergency or other circumstance which could lessen the fault attributed to this poor judgment. Finally, with regard to capacity, the age and experience of Watson and Earl Creel would require a greater imposition of fault on them for their negligent conduct, in comparison to that of the twelve year old youth, Shane.

After weighing the factors discussed hereinabove, we apportion the fault as follows. To plaintiff, we assign 20% of the fault in this fatal accident. We find further that Earl Creel and his son, Shane Creel, were each also at fault, and the degree or percentage of negligence attributable to them was 40% each.

* * * * *

2. Encountering a Known Risk

[handwritten: how aware of the danger? — great of risk?]

This section examines the circumstances where plaintiff's actions in encountering a known risk will act as a complete bar to recovery. Under a contributory negligence regime, the plaintiff was said to have "assumed the risk." As jurisdictions evolved to comparative fault, the doctrine of assumption of the risk must be evaluated. The following sections from the Restatement (Second) of Torts provide the general statement of assumption of the risk, while *Murray* represents the Louisiana approach to the doctrine in a comparative fault regime.

[handwritten: — significance of conduct?]

Restatement (Second) of Torts

§ 496A. General Principle

A plaintiff who voluntarily assumes a risk of harm arising from the negligent or reckless conduct of the defendant cannot recover for such harm.

§ 496C. Implied Assumption of Risk

(1) Except as stated in Subsection (2), a plaintiff who fully understands a risk of harm to himself or his things caused by the defendant's conduct or by the condition of the defendant's land or chattels, and who nevertheless voluntarily chooses to enter or remain, or to permit his things to enter or remain within the area of that risk, under circumstances that manifest his willingness to accept it, is not entitled to recover for harm within that risk.

(2) The rule stated in Subsection (1) does not apply in any situation in which an express agreement to accept the risk would be invalid as contrary to public policy.

§ 496D. Knowledge and Appreciation of Risk

Except where he expressly so agrees, a plaintiff does not assume a risk of harm arising from the defendant's conduct unless he then knows of the existence of the risk and appreciates its unreasonable character.

§ 496E. Necessity of Voluntary Assumption

(1) A plaintiff does not assume a risk of harm unless he voluntarily accepts the risk.

(2) The plaintiff's acceptance of a risk is not voluntary if the defendant's tortious conduct has left him no reasonable alternative course of conduct in order to

(a) avert harm to himself or another, or

(b) exercise or protect a right or privilege of which the defendant has no right to deprive him.

§ 496F. Violation of Statute

The plaintiff's assumption of risk bars his recovery for the defendant's violation of a statute, unless such a result would defeat a policy of the statute to place the entire responsibility for such harm as has occurred upon the defendant.

§ 496G. Burden of Proof

If the defendant would otherwise be subject to liability to the plaintiff, the burden of proof of the plaintiff's assumption of risk is upon the defendant.

MURRAY
v.
RAMADA INNS, INC.
521 So. 2d 1123 (La. 1988)

CALOGERO, J.

Today we are called upon to resolve the role, if any, which the assumption of risk defense continues to play in Louisiana tort law, given the legislature's adoption of a comparative fault system. The issue has presented itself in a case certified to us by the United States Court of Appeals for the Fifth Circuit, *Murray v. Ramada Inn, Inc.*, 821 F.2d 272 (1987). The certified question is as follows:

> Does assumption of risk serve as a total bar to recovery by a plaintiff in a negligence case, or does it only result in a reduction of recovery under the Louisiana comparative negligence statute?

We accepted certification, 514 So. 2d 21 (La. 1987), and now answer that assumption of risk does not serve as a total bar to a plaintiff's recovery in a negligence case.

We also note at the outset that the certified question comes to us in a case where the defendants were found strictly liable under La.Civ.Code Ann. art. 2317 (West, 1979), the jury having been instructed by the trial judge to apply the provisions of that article when determining whether or not the defendants were liable. Because of that fact, and in order to provide an unambiguous response to the certified question, we further answer that assumption of risk should not operate as a total bar to recovery regardless of whether the defendant is found negligent or strictly liable.

Assumption of risk terminology has been utilized to describe three basic types of plaintiff conduct. In the vast majority of cases that have involved the assertion of the defense, the plaintiff conduct at issue was in reality a form of contributory negligence. Such conduct henceforth should be exclusively adjudged by the comparative fault principles set forth in La.Civ.Code Ann. art 2323. (West Supp. 1988). In a relative handful of other cases, the assumption of risk defense has been used to deny recovery on the ground that the plaintiff expressly agreed to release the defendant from liability. Our decision here does not require a different result in such cases, which may be resolved in favor of a defendant without resort to assumption of risk. Finally, the defense has been used in a few cases to bar recovery by plaintiffs who have opted to place themselves in situations which involve virtually unpreventable risks, the textbook example being the sports spectator who has the misfortune of being hit by an errant ball. Our decision also does not necessarily call for a different outcome in cases of this type, which may be resolved in appropriate cases on the simple ground that the defendant is not negligent.

Regardless of the context in which it has been utilized, the assumption of risk defense has produced confusion and conceptual difficulties. The doctrine is easily replaceable by other established principles of tort law which more readily comport with civilian tradition, such as comparative fault and duty/risk analysis. Accordingly, and given the Legislature's adoption of a comparative fault system, we conclude that the assumption of risk defense no longer has a place in Louisiana tort law.

I

Facts and Proceedings in Federal Court

On July 30, 1983, Gregory Murray and two of his brothers began doing shallow water dives in the pool at a Ramada Inn Motel in Shreveport. After making two dives without incident, Murray made a third dive and struck his head on the bottom of the pool. Murray suffered instant paralysis, from which he never recovered. He died of his injuries five months later, and his wife and son subsequently brought this wrongful death action in federal district court against the companies which franchised, owned and operated the motel, as well as their respective liability insurers.

At trial, it was established that no lifeguard was on duty at the time of the accident, and that the absence of a guard was a violation of the Louisiana Sanitary Code. It was further established that there were no signs in the area which warned against diving into the shallow end of the pool, even though other Ramada Inn pools had signs which prohibited diving. Other testimony indicated that the motel had previously removed the diving board from the pool, in order to curtail diving.

Gregory knew how to dive, his brother Carl testified, for Gregory had told him that shallow water diving was dangerous. He further stated that shortly before the accident, Gregory had warned his brothers to "be careful" while diving into the pool. There was also a sign near the pool which stated "NO LIFE GUARD-SWIM AT OWN RISK."

At the close of the evidence, the defendants asked the trial judge to instruct the jury on the elements of assumption of risk. They also urged that assumption of risk, if found applicable by the jury, should act as a complete bar to the plaintiffs' recovery. The trial judge denied the request and refused to instruct the jury on assumption of risk, concluding that the defense has been replaced by comparative negligence. The jury's verdict was returned in the form of responses to special interrogatories, the pertinent interrogatories and responses being as follows:

(1) Under the circumstances and facts of this case, did the swimming pool as it was being operated present an unreasonable risk of harm which was approximate because of Gregory Murray's injury and death?

Answer: Yes.

(2) Do you find that Gregory Murray was himself negligent and that such negligence was a proximate cause of his own injury or death?

Answer: Yes.

The jury further assessed Murray's negligence at 50%, and awarded $250,000 in damages (before reduction for comparative negligence) to each plaintiff.

On appeal to the United States Fifth Circuit, the defendants argued that the trial judge erred by refusing to instruct the jury on assumption of risk, and by failing to hold that that defense, distinct from comparative negligence, was available as a total bar to recovery. Reviewing the evidence, the Fifth Circuit concluded that "testimony supports *the jury's conclusion* that Murray knew, appreciated, and voluntarily exposed himself to the risk of diving into the shallow end of the swimming pool." 821 F.2d at 276 (emphasis added). With due respect to our Fifth Circuit brethren, the jury did not make such a specific finding, at least not as is evident from the record. Instead, the jury responded in the affirmative to an interrogatory which asked whether Murray was *negligent*. However, we take this language in the opinion to mean simply that the Fifth Circuit panel, after reviewing the evidence, concluded that Murray assumed the risk of his injury and subsequent death.

However, the Fifth Circuit also noted that the impact of an assumption of risk finding is "unsettled" in Louisiana in light of the Legislature's adoption of a comparative fault system. 821 F.2d at 274. Thus, they have asked us to decide on certification whether the defense serves "as a total bar to recovery in a negligence case,"[1] or results only "in a reduction of recovery under the Louisiana comparative negligence statute." *Id.* at 276.

II

The Origins and Evolution of the Assumption of Risk Defense

(A) Development at Common Law

Assumption of risk is a common law doctrine "not well developed in Louisiana," *Rozell v. Louisiana Animal Breeders Cooperative, Inc.*, 496 So. 2d 275, 278 (La. 1986), and has been described as a concept "more difficult to understand and apply than almost any other in the law of torts." Mansfield, *Informed Choice in the Law of Torts*, 22 La.L.Rev. 17, 17 (1961). In its various attempts to interpret and explain the supposedly distinct nature of the defense, this Court has usually turned to non-civilian sources, such as the Restatement (Second) of Torts. *See, e.g., Dorry v. Lafleur*, 399 So. 2d 559, 560-61 (La. 1981); *Langlois v. Allied Chemical Corp.*, 258 La. 1067, 1087, 249 So. 2d 133, 141 (La. 1971). Accordingly, we will preface our analysis of the certified question with a discussion of the development of the defense at common law, and the subsequent attempts of Louisiana courts to incorporate the doctrine into civilian jurisprudence.

(1) Contractual Roots

The original premise of the assumption of risk defense appears to have been contractual rather than delictual. Early assumption of risk cases were based on the theory that the plaintiff could not recover because he had *actually consented* to undertake the risk of injury posed by a given situation, and therefore could not be heard to complain when such an injury occurred. *See generally, Wade, The Place of Assumption of Risk in the Law of Negligence*, 22 La.L.Rev. 5 (1961). The doctrine was described by the maxim "volenti non fit injuria," meaning "no wrong is done to one who is willing." W. Prosser & J. Wade, Cases and Materials on Torts 534 (5th ed. 1971).

---

[1] Although the Fifth Circuit phrases the question in terms of a "negligence case," we note that the parties assert in brief that the defendants were found strictly liable under article 2317, as custodians of a pool that was unreasonably dangerous because of the absence of appropriate warning signs and a lifeguard. Further, the record reflects that the trial judge instructed the jury to assess the liability issue under the strict liability provisions of civil code article 2317. On the other hand, the jury found that the pool was "operated" in an unreasonably dangerous manner, which perhaps led the Fifth Circuit to conclude that the basis of liability was negligence. In any event, our answer to the certified question would be the same regardless of whether the jury's finding was based on negligence or strict liability. For reasons set forth in the body of the opinion, assumption of risk should not be available as a total bar to recovery in either instance.

Thus, the defense appeared frequently in early common law cases which involved servants or employees who were injured while performing their employment duties. The right of such employees to recover damages from their employers was barred under the rationale that, as an implied provision of the employment contract, the servant assumed all risks incidental to his normal employment duties. *See, e.g., Thomas v. Quartermaine*, 18 Q.B.D. 685 (1887); *Saxton v. Hawksworth*, 26 L.T. 851, 853 (Ex.Ch. 1872); *Farwell v. Boston & Worcester R.R.*, 4 Metc. 49 (Mass. 1842). *See also, Wade, supra*, 22 La.L.Rev. at 8; V. Schwariz, Comparative Negligence § 9.1 at 154-55 (1974).

The philosophy of the defense, premised on the idea that a plaintiff who confronts a known danger necessarily must have chosen to do so, was "a terse expression of the individualistic tendency of the common law," which regarded "freedom of individual action as the keystone of the whole [legal] structure." Bohlen, *Voluntary Assumption of Risk*, 20 Harv.L.Rev. 14, 14 (1906). Consequently, assumption of risk was thereafter extended in application far beyond the master-servant relationship. On the theory that "[a] true contract may be indicated by conduct as well as by express language," courts *presumed* that plaintiffs in certain situations had agreed to accept the risk of injury, even though actual consent was a fiction. *Wade, supra*, 22 La.L.Rev. at 8.

For example, a plaintiff who accepted an invitation to a party at the defendant's home could not recover for an injury he suffered on the premises because he was "presumed to accept such generous entertainment with an understanding that he accommodates himself to the conditions of his host." *Comeau v. Comeau*, 285 Mass. 578, 579, 189 N.E. 588, 589-90 (1934). Similarly, the baseball fan who purchased tickets to a ballgame was usually presumed to have accepted responsibility for the risks inherent in watching a game, including the possibility of being struck by an errant ball. *See Kavafian v. Seattle Baseball Club*, 105 Wash. 219, 181 P. 679 (1919). As this contractual doctrine began to acquire a separate identity as a tort defense, the need arose to distinguish the assumed risk concept from another tort defense, contributory negligence.

(2) Similarity to Contributory Negligence

As early as 1906, a distinguished commentator expressed the view that it was "essential" that contributory negligence and assumption of risk "should be kept quite distinct." *Bohlen, supra*, 20. Harv. L.Rev. at 18. But at an even earlier date, there were indications that Professor Bohlen's hopes in this regard were in vain. In *Eckert v. Long Island R.R.*, 43 N.Y. 502, 3 Am.Rep.721 (1871), plaintiffs sued the railroad company after their decedent was killed in the process of removing a small child from the path of an oncoming train. The New York Court of Appeal affirmed the trial court's judgment in favor of the plaintiffs, but there were two dissenting opinions. One dissent urged that the plaintiff should not recover on the ground that he was contributorily negligent; the other dissenting opinion posited that the plaintiff should not recover because he had assumed the risk. Neither of the dissenting opinions discussed the other, nor attempted to distinguish between the two defenses.

Nonetheless, other courts insisted that there was a distinction between the two doctrines. Contributory negligence was described as the inadvertent or unintentional failure of the plaintiff to exercise due care for his own safety. *See James, Contributory Negligence*, 62 Yale L.J. 691, 723 (1953). The defense called for an objective inquiry into whether the plaintiff's conduct fell below the standard required of a "reasonable man of ordinary prudence" under the circumstances. W. Prosser & J. Wade, Cases and Materials on Torts, *supra* at 505 n.6.

The first category has been called "express assumption of risk," and it includes those cases, infrequent in occurrence, where the plaintiff "expressly contracts with another not to sue for any future injuries which may be caused by that person's negligence." *Anderson v. Ceccardi*, 6 Ohio St.3d 110, 451 N.E.2d 780, 783 (1983). *See also* V. Schwartz, *Comparative Negligence, supra* at 154; *Keegan v. Anchors Inns, Inc.*, 606 F.2d 35, 37-38 (3rd Cir. 1979). Express consent, which might also be called "waiver" or "release," will usually bar recovery by the plaintiff "unless there is a statute or established public policy against it." *Wade, supra*, 22 La.L, Rev. at 8.

A second category of cases involves what has been called "implied primary" assumption of risk. In such cases, the plaintiff has made no express agreement to release the defendant from future liability, but he is presumed to have consented to such a release because he has voluntarily participated in a "particular activity or situation" which involves inherent and well known risks. *Duffy v. Midlothian Country Club*, 135 Ill. App. 429, 90 Ill. Dec. 237, 241, 481 N.E. 1037, 1041 (1985). Implied primary assumption of risk has been described as "an alternate expression of the proposition that the defendant was not negligent", i.e., either owed no duty or did not breach the duty owed. *Meistrich v. Casino Arena Attraction, Inc.*, 31 N.J. 44, 155 A.2d 90, 93 (1959).

The third and largest category of assumption of risk cases are those in which the plaintiff is said to assume the risk of defendant's negligence. Even though the defendant in such cases is found to be at fault, the plaintiff is barred from recovery on the ground that he knew of the unreasonable risk created by the defendant's conduct and voluntarily chose to encounter that risk. The plaintiff conduct at issue has been labeled "implied secondary" assumption of risk. However, most common law courts now agree that the plaintiff conduct involved in these cases is nothing more and nothing less than contributory negligence. *See* Duffy, 90 Ill.Dec. at 241-42, 481 N.E.2d at 1041-42 and authorities cited therein; *Meistrich*, 155 A.2d at 93-96.

Abandonment of Assumption of Risk

The high courts in a number of states lost patience with the assumption of risk doctrine and abolished it even prior to the widespread adoption of comparative negligence.... In those states, conduct which previously had been described as assumption of risk was re-classified as contributory negligence.

Many other states were spurred to eliminate the assumption of risk doctrine by the adoption of a comparative fault system. In some of these states, the comparative fault statute enacted by the legislature specifically indicates that conduct which had been described by assumed risk terminology should be re-classified as comparative fault (and should thereby operate only as a comparative reduction of the plaintiffs recovery, rather than a complete bar). *See, e.g.,* Ariz.Rev.Stat.Ann. § 12-2505 (Supp. 1987); Mass.Gen.Laws Ann. ch. 231 § 85 (West 1985). In other jurisdictions which have adopted comparative fault statutes that do not expressly refer to assumption of risk, the courts have subsequently determined that assumption of risk should not survive as a distinct defense that totally bars recovery. *See, e.g., Mizushima v. Sunset Ranch, Inc.*, 737. P.2d 1158, 1161 (Nev. 1987); *Salinas v. Vierstra*, 107 Idaho 984, 695 P.2d 369, 372-75 (1985); *Wilson v. Gordon*, 354 A.2d 398, 401-03 (Me. 1976).

Some states have retained assumption of risk terminology only for the purpose of referring to "express" or "contractual" consent cases. *See, e.g., Mizushima*, 737 P.2d at 1161; Wilson, 354 A 2d at 401-03; *Segoviano v. Housing Auth. of Stanislaus City*, 143 Cal.App.3d 162, 191 Cal.Rptr. 578, 583 (1983). Other jurisdictions have insisted on the total elimination of the defense, most notably New Jersey in *McGrath v. American Cyanamid Co.*, 41 N.J. 272, 196 A.2d 238, 240-41 (1963). There, the court stated that the term assumption of risk is "so apt to create mist that it is better banished from the scene. We hope we have heard the last of it." *Id.*

All told, it appears that sixteen states have totally abolished the defense, and seventeen more have eliminated the use of assumption of risk terminology in all cases except those involving express or contractual consent by the plaintiff. *See* H. Woods, Comparative Fault §§ 6.1-6.8. (2d ed. 1987). After long ago arriving in the torts arena as a refugee from contract law, assumption of the risk now appears to be passing from the scene in most common law jurisdictions.

(B) Civil Law Development

While the rough equivalent of an assumption of risk defense may have been recognized at Roman law, *see* F. Stone, 12 Louisiana Civil Law Treatise, Tort Doctrine, § 293 (West 1977), there is little evidence of any "organized body of civilian doctrine" on the subject. *Bell v. Jet Wheel Blast, Division of Ervin Industries*, 462 So. 2d 166, 169 (La. 1985) (discussing the similar absence of early civilian authority on comparative fault). Louisiana courts appear simply to have borrowed the assumption of risk doctrine from the common law, part and parcel with the analytical problems that have confronted courts in other states.

* * * * *

This Court attempted to maintain the same distinction between the defenses that had been utilized at common law. We have held on numerous occasions that assumption of risk turns on the plaintiff's actual knowledge of the danger, and whether he has voluntarily encountered a known risk, whereas contributory negligence is governed by the objective standard of whether the plaintiff knew or should have known of the risk. *Bass v. Aetna Ins. Co.*, 370 So. 2d 511 (La. 1979); *Prestenbach v. Sentry Ins. Co.*, 340 So. 2d 1331 (La. 1976); *McInnis v. Fireman's Fund Ins. Co.*, 322 So. 2d 155 (La. 1975); *Langlois v. Allied Chemical Corp.*, 258 La. 1067, 249 So. 2d 133 (1971).

However, even as we held that assumption of risk involves a purely subjective standard and turns on whether the plaintiff actually knew of the risk, we were willing to impute such knowledge to the plaintiff whenever it could be *assumed* from the given facts that he *must have known* of the danger. *See Dorry v. Lafleur*, 399 So. 2d 559, 561-63 (La. 1981) and authorities cited therein. Such analysis made the distinction between contributory negligence and assumption of risk all the more obscure. *See, e.g., Bass v. Aetna Ins. Co.*, 370 So. 2d at 515 (Blanche, J., dissenting on the ground that plaintiff assumed the risk because she "knew, or reasonably should have known" of the risk of injury, based upon "her own personal experience...."); *Prestenbach v. Sentry Ins. Co.*, 340 So. 2d at 1335 (assumption of risk applies when, based upon certain observations, the plaintiff "should reasonably have known that a risk was involved.")

Louisiana courts have not followed the common law tradition of dividing assumption of risk into various categories, such as "express," "implied primary," and "implied secondary." Nonetheless, assumption of risk terminology has been applied by our courts to identifiable classes of plaintiff conduct, which can be analyzed in a manner similar to that used at common law.

In a limited number of cases, assumption of risk terminology has been used to defeat recovery where the plaintiff has expressly agreed with the defendant, in writing, to accept the risk of injury. *See, e.g., Robillard v. P & R Racetracks, Inc.*, 405 So. 2d 1203 (La.App. 1 Cir. 1981); *Forsyth v. Jefferson Downs, Inc.*, 152 So. 2d 369 (La. App. 4 Cir. 1962), *writ refused*, 244 La. 895, 154 So. 2d 767 (1963). *Robillard* and *Forsyth* would probably be classified at common law as "express consent" cases.

In another identifiable but small class of cases, similar to the "implied primary" category used at common law, assumption of risk has been employed to deny recovery where the plaintiffs have participated in certain activities, or placed themselves in situations which involve inherent and well known risks. *See, e.g., Bonanno v. Continental Casualty Co.*, 285 So. 2d 591 (La. App. 4 Cir. 1973) (plaintiff assumed risk of injury suffered in haunted house exhibit); *Colclough v. Orleans Parish School Board*, 166 So. 2d 647 (La.App. 4 Cir. 1964) (plaintiff assumed risk of injury by standing on sidelines of a football game); *Lorino v. New Orleans Baseball & Amusement Co.*, 16 La.App. 95, 133 So. 408 (Orl.Cir. 1931) (baseball spectator who elected to sit in area where balls are known to fly into stands assumed risk of injury).

Most Louisiana decisions which involve the assertion of the assumption of risk defense, however, are cases in which the plaintiff was found to have disregarded a risk created by the defendant's fault (called "implied secondary" assumption of risk at common law). In these cases, it is not realistically possible to distinguish the plaintiff conduct at issue from contributory negligence. *See, e.g., Richards v. Marlow*, 347 So. 2d 281 (La.App. 2 Cir. 1977), *writ denied*, 350 So. 2d 676 (La. 1977) (regardless of defendant's negligence, plaintiff could not recover because she assumed the risk of trying to walk on a wet pipe); *Giovingo v. Cochiara*, 449 So. 2d 699 (La.App. 5 Cir. 1984), *writ denied*, 456 So. 2d 165 (La. 1984) (plaintiff who slipped on concrete boat ramp assumed the risk of injury because he knew that the ramp was slippery); *Passman v. Allstate Ins. Co.*, 208 So. 2d 386 (La.App. 1 Cir. 1968), *application denied* 252 La. 265, 210 So. 2d 507 (1968) (plaintiff who had been warned of tractor driver's inexperience assumed the risk of injury by riding on a wagon attached to the tractor). It is a fiction to say that plaintiffs in cases such as these actually consented to, or assumed, the risk of injury. It is much more accurate to conclude that such plaintiffs negligently disregarded a known risk, or, in other words, were contributorily negligent.

However, when the plaintiff's cause of action sounded in negligence, there was often no need for courts to dwell upon whether the plaintiffs conduct constituted assumption of risk, contributory negligence or both. Prior to the adoption of comparative fault, the result was the same regardless of the "technical label" chosen to describe the plaintiff's conduct; the successful assertion of either defense meant no recovery for the plaintiff. *See Passman v. Allstate Ins. Co.*, 204 So. 2d at 387-88. On the other hand, in strict liability cases which arose prior to the adoption of comparative fault, and in which contributory negligence was held to be legally unavailable as a defense, we indicated that assumption of risk could nonetheless be urged as a total bar to the plaintiff's recovery. *See, e.g., Dorry v. Lafleur*, 399 So. 2d at 561; *Langlois v. Allied Chemical Corp.*, 258 La. at 1086; 249 So. 2d at 140.

Thus, by 1980, when the comparative fault system adopted by the legislature became effective, the status of the law of assumption of risk could charitably be described as confusing. As discussed above, the defense seemed indistinguishable from contributory negligence in most cases, yet could be asserted in strict liability cases even when the defense of contributory negligence was legally unavailable. This case squarely presents the issue of whether the assumption of risk doctrine should have continuing viability now that Louisiana is a comparative fault jurisdiction.[2]

III

Answer to the Certified Question

In 1979, Louisiana Civil Code article 2323 was rewritten to eliminate the judicially created rule that contributory negligence was a complete bar to the plaintiff's recovery, and to substitute a procedure by which any negligence on the part of the plaintiff would operate as a percentage reduction of his recovery...

One question which this change in the law presented was whether assumption of risk should continue to operate as a complete bar to the plaintiff's recovery, even though contributory negligence no longer constitutes such a bar. Noting that Louisiana courts of appeal have taken "divergent views" on this issue,[3] the Fifth Circuit certified to us the question of whether assumption of risk bars recovery totally, or only results in a reduction of recovery under article 2323.

Our response is that the common law doctrine of assumption of risk no longer has a place in Louisiana tort law. The types of plaintiff conduct which the defense has been used to describe are governed by civilian concepts of comparative fault and duty/risk. Assumption of risk should not survive as a distinct legal concept for any purpose, and certainly can no longer be utilized as a complete bar to the plaintiff's recovery.

---

[2] In cases arising prior to the adoption of comparative fault, this Court did not have occasion to decide whether assumption of risk should have continuing viability. Instead, we frequently and repeatedly found that the defense could not be successfully asserted based upon the facts of the case before us. See *Rozell v. Louisiana Animal Breeders Co-Op*, 496 So. 2d at 278-79 (plaintiff did not assume an unreasonable risk of injury by entering pen where bull was kept); *Bass v. Aetna Ins. Co.*, 370 So. 2d at 514-15 (plaintiff did not subjectively comprehend any risk of injury associated with praying in church aisle); *Dorry v. Lafleur*, 399 So. 2d at 561-63 (plaintiff was not aware before the accident of the puddle in which he slipped while skating); *Dofflemyer v. Gilley*, 384 So. 2d 435, 438-39 (La. 1980) (no proof in record that plaintiff actually knew or understood the risk of being struck by a car); *Prestenbach v. Sentry Ins. Co.*, 340 So. 2d at 1335-36 (no proof that passenger actually knew driver was intoxicated); *McInnis v. Fireman's Fund Ins. Co.*, 322 So. 2d at 157 (no proof that plaintiff knew of risk associated with lifting certain equipment); *Langlois v. Allied Chemical Corp.*, 258 La. at 1088-89, 249 So. 2d at 133 (plaintiff fireman may have assumed certain risks, but not the risk created by the defendant's conduct).

[3] Footnote omitted.

Because the term "assumption of risk" is almost always used to describe plaintiff conduct that is indistinguishable from contributory negligence, it would make no sense for us to hold otherwise. Under article 2323, plaintiff negligence results only in a comparative reduction of recovery, and it would be anamolous for us to hold that the same conduct which results only in a reduction of recovery when it is described as "comparative negligence" somehow should operate as a total bar to recovery when described as "assumption of risk." As another state supreme court considering this issue has concluded, "it would be the ultimate legal inconsistency to reject contributory negligence as an absolute defense yet at the same time allow its effect to continue under the guise of assumption of risk." *Salinas v. Vierstra*, 107 Idaho 984, 695 P.2d 369, 374 (1985).

Defendants argue that because article 2323 does not expressly mention assumption of risk, the legislature intended that the defense would survive the adoption of comparative fault as a complete bar to recovery. Their reasoning is that the legislature had to be aware of the existence of the defense at the time article 2323 was enacted, and if the Legislature had intended to alter the application of the doctrine, it would have expressly referred to assumption of risk in the code article. Instead, the article simply states it is applicable "[w]hen contributory negligence is applicable to a claim for damages," and does not refer to assumption of risk.

However, the fact that article 2323 does not contain the words "assumption of risk" is not dispositive of the issue. As we have noted elsewhere, it is equally plausible to argue that if the Legislature had intended to preserve the defense as a total bar to recovery, it could have easily and expressly stated that intention in article 2323. *Turner v. New Orleans Public Service, Inc.*, 476 So. 2d 800, 804 (La. 1985). The dispositive factor here should be that there is no doubt that the Legislature intended by article 2323 to eliminate contributory negligence as a complete bar to recovery and to make comparative fault applicable to those cases in which the plaintiff's conduct may result in a reduction of recovery. *Bell v. Jet Wheel Blast*, 462 So. 2d 166, 171 (La. 1985). Beyond that clearly expressed intention, we have observed that the legislature left the "tough details" regarding the scope and application of article 2323 "for the courts to decide." *Turner*, 476 So. 2d at 804. The issue we are called upon to decide here is whether the survival of assumption of risk as a defense which totally bars recovery would be consistent with the Legislature's expressed intention of eliminating the total bar of contributory negligence.

The answer is that the survival of assumption of risk as a total bar to recovery would be inconsistent with article 2323's mandate that contributory negligence should no longer operate as such a bar to recovery. The arguments raised by the defendants in support of a rigid construction of the wording of article 2323 do not take into consideration the fact that, in all but a relative handful of cases (the express and implied primary assumption of risk cases, which are affected by this opinion in the manner discussed below), "assumption of risk" is simply a term that has been used to describe a form of contributory negligence. The statute clearly dictates that contributory negligence shall no longer operate as a complete bar to recovery, and the intent of the statute should not be frustrated by the unfortunate practice of describing certain plaintiff conduct as "assumption of the risk." To the contrary, the true intent of the statute will be fulfilled by the application of comparative fault principles to such alleged plaintiff negligence, thereby eliminating the inequities inherent in the "all or nothing" recovery rules that prevailed prior to the adoption of comparative fault. *Turner* 476 So. 2d at 800. As we stated in *Bell v. Jet Wheel Blast*, "the adoption of a system of comparative fault should, where it applies, entail the merger of the defenses of misuse and assumption of risk into the general scheme of assessment of liability in proportion to fault." 462 So. 2d at 172.

Thus, in any case where the defendant would otherwise be liable to the plaintiff under a negligence or strict liability theory, the fact that the plaintiff may have been aware of the risk created by the defendant's conduct should not operate as a total bar to recovery. Instead, comparative fault principles should apply, and the victim's "awareness of the danger" is among the factors to be considered in assessing percentages of fault. *Watson v. State Farm Fire & Cas. Ins. Co.*, 469 So. 2d 967, 974 (La. 1985).[4]

In order to avoid further confusion in this area of the law, we believe that the courts, lawyers and litigants would best be served by no longer utilizing the term assumption of risk to refer to plaintiff conduct. We belatedly join the New Jersey Supreme Court in expressing our view that assumption of risk terminology "is better banished from the scene." *McGrath v. American Cyanamid Co.*, 196 A.2d at 240-41.

However, our answer to the certified question does not change the law in those cases where the plaintiff, by oral or written agreement, expressly waives or releases a future right to recover damages from the defendant.[5] Assuming that the existence of a voluntary and express pre-accident agreement is proven, and that no public policy concerns would invalidate such a waiver (*see also* La.Civil Code art. 2004), the plaintiff's right to recover damages may be barred on a release theory. Applying duty/risk analysis to this situation, it can be concluded that the defendant has been relieved by contract of the duty that he otherwise may have owed to the plaintiff.

Nor does our decision today mean that the *result* reached in the sports spectator or amusement park cases (common law's "implied primary" assumption of risk cases) was incorrect. However, rather than relying on the fiction that the plaintiffs in such cases implicitly consented to their injuries, the sounder reasoning is that the defendants were not liable because they did not breach any duty owed to the plaintiffs.

For example, in the classical baseball spectator setting, the case for negligence may often fall short on the question of whether the defendant breached a duty owed to the plaintiff. While a stadium operator may owe a duty to spectators to provide them with a reasonably safe area from which they can watch the game, it is generally not considered reasonable to require the stadium operator to screen all spectator areas from flying baseballs. Even while applying assumption of risk terminology to these types of cases, courts have simultaneously recognized that the defendant was not negligent because his conduct vis-a-vis the plaintiff was not unreasonable. *See Lorino v. New Orleans Baseball & Amusement Co.*, 16 La.App. at 96, 133 So. at 408 ("It is well known ... that it is not possible ... for the ball to be kept at all times within the confines of the playing field.") On the other hand, the failure to protect spectator areas into which balls are frequently hit, such as the area behind home plate, might well constitute a breach of duty. These types of cases will turn on their particular facts and may be analyzed in terms of duty/risk. The same analysis applies in other cases where it may not be reasonable to require the defendant to protect the plaintiff from all of the risks associated with a particular activity. *See, e.g., Bonanno v. Continental Casualty Co.*, 285 So. 2d at 592 (operator of haunted house provided adequate supervision and space for patrons, and therefore was not negligent).

---

[4] Of course, we have recognized that there are some strict liability cases in which comparative fault principles may not be employed to reduce the plaintiff's recovery, *Bell*, 462 So. 2d at 171-73, and this opinion does not change the jurisprudence in that respect.

[5] The case on certification does not fall into either the express or implied primary assumption of risk categories, as the decedent's conduct is indistinguishable from contributory negligence, see Section (IV) of this opinion, *infra*, and thus would be categorized as implied secondary assumption of risk at common law. However, because the term assumption of risk has been different meanings in different contexts, the certified question "cannot be answered with a single, all-encompassing statement on `assumption of risk' for all instances." Amicus Curiae Brief of Louisiana Association of Defense Counsel (LADC) at 12. The LADC acknowledges in its brief that secondary assumption of risk should be "relegated to treatment as with other forms of contributory negligence," but argues that the defense should be retained in express consent and implied primary situations. Id. We accordingly give separate attention in our answer to the certified question to the impact which our decision should have on those occasional cases which would be categorized at common law under the express or implied primary assumption of risk labels.

IV

Application of the Answer to the Certified Question to the Facts of this Case

Having reviewed the impact that our answer to the certified question will have on the different types of cases in which courts have relied on assumption of risk terminology, we return to the facts of this case. The defendants urge that the plaintiffs' decedent assumed the risk of his injuries by diving into the shallow end of a swimming pool, even though, according to the evidence, he had actual knowledge of the dangers associated with that activity. The same conduct which is described by the defendants as assumption of risk, however, also constitutes contributory negligence, since it may be said that a reasonable, prudent person exercising due care for his own safety would not have engaged in shallow water diving. While defendants concede that the successful assertion of the contributory negligence argument can only result in a percentage reduction of recovery under article 2323, they argue that the same evidence used by the jury to assess comparative negligence at 50% should be used to bar recovery under the assumption of risk doctrine. For reasons previously discussed, the law cannot allow such an anomaly. The plaintiffs should be entitled to recover the full amount of their damages, minus a percentage assessed as comparative fault.

An attempt to analyze this plaintiff's conduct in terms of assumption of risk highlights the weakness of the underlying premise of the defense: the fiction that the plaintiff who disregards a known risk necessarily has consented to his own injury and agreed to relieve the potential defendant of liability for that injury. It cannot be seriously contended that Murray, by attempting to dive into the shallow end of the pool, consented to the risk that he would suffer a fatal blow to his head on the bottom of the pool, and thus agreed in advance to relieve the defendants from liability for his injury. To the contrary, it is obvious from the record that Murray thought that he could safely dive into the shallow end of the pool, an assumption on his part which turned out to be a grave mistake. As Prosser has noted, a miscalculation of the risk constitutes contributory negligence:

> Suppose ... that the plaintiff dashes into the street in the middle of the block, in the path of a stream of automobiles driven in excess of the speed limit. Given these facts, the ordinary entering law student would immediately say that he has of course assumed the risk. Yet by no stretch of the imagination can such conduct be regarded as manifesting consent that the drivers shall be relieved of the obligation of care for the plaintiffs safety. Rather it clearly indicates a demand, and an insistence, that they shall look out for him and, use all reasonable care to protect him. No consent that they shall not is implied on any rational basis. This is an ordinary case of contributory negligence, and not assumption of risk at all.

W. Prosser & J. Wade, Cases and Materials on Torts, *supra*, at 535.

Another argument raised by the defendants deserves attention here, because in light of our holding today, similar arguments might arise in future cases. Defendants suggest that, leaving aside the doctrine of assumption of risk, they should not be liable because they had *no duty* to protect the decedent from a danger of which he had knowledge. In essence, defendants contend here that they were *not negligent* because the plaintiff voluntarily encountered the risk.

The Fifth Circuit wisely rejected this contention. 821 F.2d at 276. If accepted, defendants' argument would inject the assumption of risk doctrine into duty/risk analysis "through the back door." By that, we mean that the argument attempts to define the defendant's initial duty in terms of the plaintiff's actual knowledge, and thereby seeks to achieve the same result which would be reached if assumption of risk were retained as a defense, i.e., a total bar to the plaintiff's recovery.

A defendant's duty should not turn on a particular plaintiff's state of mind, but instead should be determined by the standard of care which the defendant owes to all potential plaintiffs. *See Robertson, supra*, 44 La.L.Rev. at 1378. Here, for example, the defendants owed a duty to all potential users of the pool to operate that facility in a reasonably safe fashion. Further, the defendants faced strict liability under civil code article 2317 if the pool constituted an unreasonably dangerous thing over which they had custody and control.

The jury found that the pool was operated in an unreasonably dangerous manner after hearing evidence on the absence of warning signs regarding diving, the removal of the diving board and the absence of a lifeguard. The jury further determined that the unreasonably dangerous manner in which the pool was operated was a cause of the decedent's injuries and subsequent death. Once these determinations were made, it was then proper for the jury to consider the decedent's alleged fault. It would not have been proper for the jury to turn this analytical process on its head by finding, as urged by the defendants, that this particular plaintiff's knowledge of the risk rendered the pool operator free from fault. If such a finding were allowed to stand, the decedent's negligent disregard for the risk, i.e., his contributory negligence, would bar recovery despite defendants' fault, and the comparative fault rules of article 2323 would be circumvented.

Again, this is not to say that a duty is owed or breached in all situations that involve injury. We have held, for example, that the duty which a landowner owes to persons entering his property is governed by a standard of reasonableness, and that a potentially dangerous condition that should be obvious to all comers is not, in all instances, *unreasonably dangerous. See, e.g., Shelton v. Aetna Casualty & Surety Co.*, 334 So. 2d 406, 410-11 (La. 1976). However, the key to a finding of no liability in such cases is not the plaintiff's subjective awareness of the risk, but the determination that the defendant did not act unreasonably vis-a-vis the plaintiff, or injure the plaintiff through the instrumentality of an unreasonably dangerous thing in his custody. The determination of what the plaintiff knew regarding the risk of injury is made after fault on the part of the defendant has been established, and is governed by the comparative fault principles enunciated in La.Civ.Code art. 2323.

CERTIFIED QUESTION ANSWERED.

COMMENT

Murray v. Ramada Inns is the case in which the Louisiana Supreme Court stated that Louisiana, as a pure comparative fault jurisdiction, no longer recognizes implied assumption of the risk. Do you understand why the Court reached that result? In light of the result in *Murray*, what do you make of the following case?

PITRE
v.
LOUISIANA TECH UNIVERSITY
673 So. 2d 585 (La. 1996)

VICTORY, J.

This personal injury case based upon alleged negligence arises out of a sledding accident that occurred on the campus of Louisiana Tech University ("Tech") during a rare winter ice and snow storm. The plaintiff, Earl Garland Pitre, Jr., sustained serious spinal injuries and paralysis when the plastic garbage can lid that he was sledding upon collided with the concrete base of a light pole located in a campus parking lot. We granted writs to examine whether Tech had a duty to warn of the associated risks and/or to protect against injury. Under the circumstances, we find that Tech had no duty since the light pole was obvious and apparent and the risks of colliding with it while sledding are known to everyone.

Facts

In early January of 1988 a winter storm was forecast for northeast Louisiana. In anticipation of the storm, the Housing Department at Tech distributed the following bulletin to all of its dormitory residents:[1]

Winter Storms and Louisiana Tech

The Housing Office would like to pass on to each resident some helpful information all students should find beneficial during winter storm conditions on campus.

We encourage all students to dress warmly when ice or snow is on the ground. We discourage hypothermia, frostbite, etc., all realities during winter storms, but not pleasant realities.

We encourage snowmen, sledding, etc., in proper areas and using good judgement. We discourage sledding down the hills along Tech Drive into the path of oncoming cars--not good judgement--nor is being dragged behind a moving vehicle considered using good judgement. Fifteen reported personal injuries were associated with such behavior during the last snow.

We encourage students to get outdoors and enjoy these rare occasions on Tech Campus when everything is blanketed in white. We discourage rowdy and disruptive behavior such as throwing snow/ice balls at passing cars and dorm windows. We had numerous broken car windshields and residence hall windows during our last snow--damages which cost all students.

We encourage groups of students or even entire halls to walk around the campus and surrounding area to view the beauty and spectacle. We discourage students driving during this time. Our accident rate on campus was up several hundred percent during our last snow.

We encourage students to be particularly aware of the special conditions existing during winter storms--e.g., hazardous driving conditions; certain streets and roads closed due to icy conditions; and ice on steps and sidewalks making footing precarious. We discourage any and all behavior unbecoming of a college student--

In addition we encourage students who must drive or walk during winter storm conditions to note the following tips:

How to Go in Snow

Skids--Take your foot off the gas; do not brake. For rear-wheel skids, turn the steering wheel in the same direction as the skid. For front-wheel skids, do not turn the steering wheel until traction is regained and you regain control.

Stopping Suddenly--Slow gradually by pumping the brakes several times; do not brake sharply.

Stuck in Snow--Clear snow from around all tires and find something to help traction. It's good to carry traction mats or some wire mesh for this purpose. Or you can use dry sand, or ashes.

Icy Hills--Going up: maintain a steady speed. If wheels begin to spin, ease up on the gas pedal, then reaccelerate slowly. Going down: brake gently to reduce speed.

Using Snow Tires and Chains--Keep snow tires inflated to the recommended maximum. For best results, place snow tires or chains on all four wheels.

---

[1] Hereinafter referred to as the "Winter Storms Bulletin."

When Walking--Use warm shoes or boots which repel water and have good grips/soles. (Underline in original. Bold added.)

As predicted, a rare winter storm did occur on January 6-7, 1988. The entire Tech campus was covered with ice and snow, and classes scheduled for January 7 were canceled. Because of the conditions, many of the 3,406 students residing in Tech dormitories were unable to leave the campus. A number of these students took advantage of the unique opportunity by engaging in sledding, an infrequent activity on Tech's campus and for most Louisiana residents.

Among those was 20-year-old Earl Garland Pitre, Jr. ("Pitre"), a native of Lake Charles, Louisiana, who was in his third year at Tech. On the evening of January 7, 1988, Pitre walked from his room at Neilson Dormitory through a parking lot between the Thomas Assembly Center and the Joseph Aillet Football Stadium to attend a Tech basketball game at the Assembly Center. When the game ended at approximately 9:00 p.m., Pitre walked back through the same parking lot to his room and made a few telephone calls. After visiting with fellow dormitory resident, Todd Efird, the two walked back to the Assembly Center where they gathered to sled with friends, Paul McCarver, Mark White and David White.

The Assembly Center is located on a hill near the football stadium. At the east and northeast entrances of the Assembly Center, the hill (approximately 15 feet high and 85 feet long from its crest to its base) slopes into the stadium parking lot. At the other end of the parking lot is the football stadium, which is surrounded by a road and is approximately 143 feet from the base of the hill. Several light poles, spaced about 150 feet apart, are located throughout the parking lot. The poles are secured with concrete bases approximately 1 foot 10 inches in height and 2 feet in diameter.

When Pitre arrived at approximately 11:00 p.m., there were several students sledding down the hill into the stadium parking lot using various devices, including, (cq) cardboard, a toilet seat, plastic advertising signs, food trays, baking trays, part of a rocking chair, and homemade sleds. Initially, Pitre made three trips down the hill on a piece of cardboard. He then began sledding on a large plastic garbage can lid approximately five to six feet wide, which had been brought from off-campus. The lid was more desirable because it held up to four riders, and went faster and farther than any of the other devices. On several occasions the lid traveled as far as the stadium, over 224 feet.

This tragic accident occurred during Pitre's eighth trip down the hill on the lid. Pitre mounted the lid with three other individuals, Allyson Hines, Johanna Broussard and John Dumond. These riders (including Pitre) described their assumed positions as lying side-by-side on their backs with their feet facing uphill and their heads facing downhill. The lid was then pushed from the top of the hill by Paul McCarver. As it proceeded down the hill into the football stadium parking lot, the lid collided with the concrete base of one of the light poles. As a result, Pitre sustained head and back injuries resulting in permanent paralysis from the mid-chest down.

Procedural History

On December 30, 1988, Pitre and his parents, Earl G. Pitre, Sr. and Joan Pitre, filed suit against Tech and the State of Louisiana. They alleged that Tech was negligent in the following respects: (1) encouraging students, by way of the Winter Storms Bulletin, to engage in sledding activities in areas which Tech knew or should have known were hazardous; (2) failing to erect cushions around solid objects to prevent sledding injuries; (3) failing to warn students of the hazards which might be encountered in the area in which sledding took place; and (4) failing to prohibit sledding in the area where the accident occurred.

On November 28, 1990, the defendants moved for summary judgment claiming that Tech had no duty to Pitre. On December 5, 1990, the plaintiffs also moved for summary judgment. The trial court granted the defendants' motion, finding that the danger of striking a fixed object while sledding was obvious and apparent. Accordingly, the trial court held that Tech had no duty to warn, that the Winter Storms Bulletin did not create an affirmative duty, and that there was no duty to place cushions around the light poles.

On appeal, a narrow majority of the Louisiana Second Circuit Court of Appeal reversed and remanded. *Pitre v. Louisiana Tech University*, 596 So. 2d 1324 (La.App. 2 Cir. 1991). According to the court of appeal, Tech's general duty as a landowner, to discover unreasonably dangerous conditions or uses of its premises and to either correct or warn of their existence, was heightened by its relationship with Pitre as a dormitory resident and student. Relying upon *Fox v. Board of Supervisors of Louisiana State University*, 576 So. 2d 978 (La. 1991), the court of appeal acknowledged that adult students must be held responsible for their own conduct, and that Tech could not practically control all on-campus activities. However, the court of appeal concluded that Tech could not "abandon all efforts to insure the physical safety of its students" because "parents, students and the general community have some expectations that reasonable care will be exercised to protect students from foreseeable harm." Citing *Socorro v. City of New Orleans*, 579 So. 2d 931 (La. 1991), the court of appeal also reasoned that it was not proper to focus solely upon Pitre's knowledge and conduct when examining whether Tech had a duty.

The court of appeal found that Tech knew that the students would be using this hill for sledding; that Tech was aware, through the campus Police Department which had stopped sledding on campus hills, of the specific danger presented by the light poles; and that through the Winter Storms Bulletin, Tech "encouraged" Pitre, a 20-year-old student without prior sledding experience, to undertake the risk. According to the court of appeal, these circumstances created "an illusion of safety" which removed or lessened Pitre's reality of the actual danger, and gave Tech the duty to protect or warn against this unreasonably dangerous activity.

The defendants requested review of the court of appeal's decision, which this Court denied, stating: "Review of the court of appeal's denial of defendant's motion for summary judgment is not warranted at this state of the proceeding." *Pitre v. Louisiana Tech University*, 604 So. 2d 998 (La. 1992).

After trial on the merits, the trial court issued a lengthy opinion wherein it again found that Tech owed no duty to Pitre. On appeal, the trial court's decision was reversed. *Pitre v. Louisiana Tech University*, 26388 (La.App. 2 Cir. 1995); 655 So. 2d 659 (Hightower, J., dissenting). The court of appeal refused to address the duty issue, finding that its prior decision was law-of-the-case and that the trial court legally erred by revisiting the duty issue on remand. The court of appeal found that the duty issue became final when this Court denied writs. Upon considering the elements of breach and causation, the court of appeal concluded that Pitre was 75% at fault in causing the accident. Pitre was awarded the following damages, subject to reduction: $2,500,000.00 in general damages; $128,770.87 in past medical expenses; and $1,163,831.00 in future medical expenses. Pitre's parents were each awarded $35,000.00 (subject to reduction) for loss of consortium.

We granted the plaintiffs' and the defendants' respective applications for writs of certiorari. Under the facts presented, we find that sledding is not inherently dangerous, the light pole was patently obvious and apparent to all, and that the hazards of colliding with fixed objects while sledding are well- known. As such, the light pole did not present an unreasonably dangerous condition, and Tech had no duty to warn of the condition or protect against the obvious risks associated with sledding down a hill in the direction of a light pole.

* * * * *

Negligence & Duty-risk Analysis

Tech's potential liability is predicated upon the concepts of fault and negligence under La. Civ.Code arts. 2315 and 2316, which make all persons responsible for damages caused by their "negligence." In order to determine whether liability exists under the facts of a particular case, this Court has adopted a duty-risk analysis.[2] This analysis takes into account the conduct of each

---

[2] *See Hill v. Lundin & Associates, Inc.*, 260 La. 542, 256 So. 2d 620 (1972); *Dixie Drive It Yourself System v. American Beverage Company*, 242 La. 471, 137 So. 2d 298 (1962). *See also,* Robertson, Reason Versus Rule in Louisiana Tort Law: Dialogues on *Hill v. Lundin & Associates, Inc.*, 34 La. L.Rev. 1 (1973); Crowe, Anatomy

individual party and the peculiar circumstances of each case. *Socorro*, 579 So. 2d at 938. The relevant inquiries are: (1) Was the conduct of which the plaintiff complains a cause-in-fact of the resulting harm? (2) What, if any, duties were owed by the respective parties? (3) Whether the requisite duties were breached? (4) Was the risk, and, harm caused, within the scope of protection afforded by the duty breached? (5) Were actual damages sustained? *Socorro*, 579 So. 2d at 938-39 (citations omitted).

If the plaintiff fails to satisfy one of the elements of duty-risk, the defendant is not liable. Because we find that Tech had no duty under the facts of this case, we pretermit discussion and consideration of the remaining elements.

Duty

A landowner owes a plaintiff a duty to discover any unreasonably dangerous condition and to either correct the condition or warn of its existence. *Socorro*, 579 So. 2d at 939, *citing Shelton v. Aetna Casualty & Surety Company*, 334 So. 2d 406, 410 (La. 1976). It is the court's obligation to decide which risks are unreasonable, based upon the facts and circumstances of each case. *Harris v. Pizza Hut of Louisiana, Inc.*, 455 So. 2d 1364, 1371 (La. 1984). Whether a particular risk is unreasonable is a difficult question which requires a balance of the intended benefit of the thing with its potential for harm and the cost of prevention. *Socorro*, 579 So. 2d at 939, citing *Landry v. State*, 495 So. 2d 1284, 1288 (La. 1986); *Entrevia v. Hood*, 427 So. 2d 1146 (La. 1983).

In making this determination in negligence actions, the "obviousness" and "apparentness" of the complained of condition have historically been taken into consideration.[3] In *Shelton, supra*, the plaintiff sought damages for injuries she sustained after slipping in the yard of her son's property. Pursuant to a usufruct granted to them by their son, the plaintiff and her husband lived in an apartment adjacent to the son's home. On the morning of the accident the plaintiff's son washed a garage on the property, using a mixture of lime, baking soda and water. Later that evening, the plaintiff slipped upon a small residual patch of the mixture as she was walking from the apartment to a nearby swing. She sued her son's homeowner's liability insurer, claiming negligence. This Court found that no duty existed because the residual mixture did not present an unreasonable risk of harm. In so finding, the Court observed:

> [T]he proper test to be applied in determining a landowner's liability under articles 2315 and 2316 of the Civil Code is "'whether in the management of his property he has acted as a reasonable man in view of the probability of injury to others,'".... The duty of a landowner is not to insure against the possibility of an accident on his premises, but rather to act reasonably in view of the probability of injury to others. Thus the landowner is not liable for an injury resulting from a condition which should have been observed by an individual in the exercise of reasonable care or which was as obvious to a visitor as to the landowner. *Shelton*, 334 So. 2d at 410 (citations omitted).

This test was reaffirmed in *Murray v. Ramada Inns, Inc.*, 521 So. 2d 1123 (La. 1988). There, the decedent sustained fatal injuries after striking his head upon the bottom of a Ramada Inn swimming pool while diving. His wife and children instituted a wrongful death action against the companies that franchised, owned and operated the motel, and their respective liability insurers, alleging liability based on negligence and strict liability. Upon certification from the U.S. Fifth Circuit Court of Appeal, this Court held that the absolute defenses of assumption of the risk and

---

of a Tort--Greenian, As Interpreted by Crowe Who Has Been Influenced by Malone--A Primer, 22 Loy. L.Rev. 903 (1976).

[3] These considerations are also relevant in products liability actions. La. R.S. 9:2800.57(B). *See also Maehler, Note, Glittenberg v. Doughboy Recreational Industries*: The "Open and Obvious Danger" Rule, 1993 Det. C.L.Rev. 1357 (Fall, 1993).

contributory negligence were no longer viable as they had been subsumed by comparative fault principles.

The defendants raised a subsidiary argument independent of the defenses of assumption of the risk and contributory negligence. They contended that they were not liable to the plaintiffs because they had no duty to protect the decedent from a danger of which he had knowledge (i.e., diving into shallow water). The Court rejected the defendants' argument finding:

> If accepted, defendants' argument would inject the assumption of risk doctrine into duty/risk analysis "through the back door." By that, we mean that the argument attempts to define the defendant's initial duty in terms of the plaintiff's actual knowledge, and thereby seeks to achieve the same result which would be reached if assumption of risk were retained as a defense, i.e., a total bar to the plaintiffs recovery. A defendant's duty should not turn on a particular plaintiffs state of mind, but instead should be determined by the standard of care which the defendant owes to all potential plaintiffs. *See Robertson, supra*, 44 La. L.Rev. at 1378. *Murray*, 521 So. 2d at 1136.

Continuing, the Court differentiated between the defendants' argument regarding the plaintiff's subjective knowledge of the danger, and the potential argument that a duty is not owed when the complained of condition is obvious and apparent to all:

> Again, this is not to say that a duty is owed or breached in all situations that involve injury. We have held, for example, that the duty which a landowner owes to persons entering his property is governed by a standard of reasonableness, and that a potentially dangerous condition that should be obvious to all comers is not, in all instances, unreasonably dangerous. *See, e.g., Shelton v. Aetna Casualty & Surety Co.*, 334 So. 2d 406, 410-11 (La. 1976). However, the key to a finding of no liability in such cases is not the plaintiff's subjective awareness of the risk, but the determination that the defendant did not act unreasonably vis-a-vis the plaintiff, or injure the plaintiff through the instrumentality of an unreasonably dangerous thing in his custody. The determination of what the plaintiff knew regarding the risk of injury is made after fault on the part of the defendant has been established, and is governed by the comparative fault principles enunciated [sic] in La. Civ.Code art. 2323. (Italics in original.) *Murray*, 521 So. 2d at 1136.

Thus, the obviousness and apparentness of a potentially dangerous condition are relevant factors to be considered under the duty-risk analysis. If the facts of a particular case show that the complained of condition should be obvious to all, the condition may not be unreasonably dangerous and the defendant may owe no duty to the plaintiff. *Socorro*, 579 So. 2d at 942, citing *Murray*, 521 So. 2d at 1137.

Application of the Law to the Facts

Utility of the Light Pole

We begin our analysis by examining the utility of the light pole. Clearly, the poles were erected to support the lights that illuminated the stadium parking lot. By necessity, the poles were systematically spaced throughout the parking lot to provide uniform lighting throughout. The affidavit of Bill Cox, the Director of Athletic Facilities, indicates that the parking lot lights were automatically programmed to turn on every evening at 7:00 p.m. and off every morning at 1:00 a.m. For evident safety reasons, providing adequate lighting for users of the parking lot, including both pedestrians and motorists, is of great interest to Tech and the public at large. As such, we find that the light poles serve an important public interest and are of great utility.

With this in mind, we next study the likelihood and magnitude of the harm. It is here that the obviousness and apparentness of the complained of condition should be considered, since it is improbable that a potentially dangerous condition which is observable to all will cause injuries to an individual who exercises reasonable care.

The trial court decided on two separate occasions (the motion for summary judgment and the trial on the merits) that the area was well-lit on the evening of the accident, and that the light pole was "readily observable" or "clearly visible" by those engaged in sledding that night. After examining the evidence, we conclude that the trial court was correct in this determination.

* * * * *

This evidence overwhelmingly demonstrates that the parking lot was well- lit, and as the trial court found, that the light pole should have been readily apparent and observable to anyone sledding on the Assembly Center hill on the evening of the accident. Thus, the likelihood of harm was slim to anyone exercising reasonable care.

In brief, the plaintiffs claim that this case is similar to *Socorro, supra,* wherein this Court held that the defendant had a duty to warn the plaintiff not to dive into a particular area of Lake Ponchartrain because rip rap was shallowly located under the water. The plaintiffs argue that the danger there was no less obvious than here. We disagree. The dangerous condition in *Socorro*, the rip rap, was concealed by water and was not obvious and apparent to all. Here, the dangerous condition was in plain view and should have been seen by all.

Cost to Prevent Harm

The plaintiffs argue that there were numerous methods that Tech could have employed to prevent this accident, including placing warning signs on the hill, posting an officer on the hill and erecting barriers around the light poles (e.g., bales of hay or cushions).

While these proposed means for preventing sledding and protecting against the accident are feasible, they were not necessary in light of the low likelihood of injury if sledders used good judgment and exercised reasonable care. Again, the potential for injury by sledding into a fixed object is obvious and apparent. The most effective means of preventing this accident rested with Pitre. To require Tech to take the proposed measures to protect from this obvious and apparent danger would place a huge burden upon the University by requiring it to warn and/or protect against all risks (e.g., buildings, signs, fences, trees, etc.) associated with sledding on campus. The cost to prevent potential harm by posting signs, officers and/or barriers at every object on campus that one might slide into would be enormous.

Nature of Activity

Finally, we end our inquiry by examining the activity, particularly its social utility and whether it is dangerous by nature. The recreational activity of sledding, while fun, is of minimal social utility. Although it is gratifying to participants, it is voluntary and does not generally benefit society in any substantial way.

Furthermore, the record supports the trial court's conclusion that sledding is not dangerous by nature. Dr. David Nichols, the defendant's expert in campus public safety and law enforcement, compared sledding to skateboarding or biking. In each of these activities it is the manner in which the activity is undertaken that determines the degree of dangerousness.

It is common knowledge that one must be able to steer to avoid colliding with fixed objects while sledding. Despite his familiarity with the campus and the parking lot, Pitre chose to sled, on his back, head first, down a hill on a device over which he had no control. While Pitre claims not to have perceived the danger, if true, he clearly was unreasonable in not doing so and taking simple measures, such as sledding feet first and on a sled not so slippery, to protect himself.

In sum, the light pole is of great social utility, as it serves important safety interests by providing lighting to pedestrians and users of the parking lot. Furthermore, the likelihood of the harm was minimal since the light pole was obvious and apparent to those sledding on the hill that evening, and the associated risks of colliding with it while sledding were well-known.

The cost of prevention would have been great to Tech. The obviousness and apparentness of the condition made it easy for Pitre to avoid the accident simply by exercising reasonable care to protect himself.

For these reasons, we conclude that the trial court was correct in finding that the condition was not unreasonably dangerous and that Tech had no duty to Pitre.

* * * * *

Conclusion

When deciding whether a condition is unreasonably dangerous, the obviousness or apparentness of the complained of condition is a factor to be considered as part of the likelihood of the harm element. Under the facts of this case, we find that sledding is not inherently dangerous and that the light pole and the danger of sledding down the hill into the pole were obvious and apparent to all on the evening of the accident. Thus, the light pole did not present an unreasonably dangerous condition and Tech had no duty to warn of the apparent danger or take steps to protect against injury. Further, the Tech Police Department's unwritten policy of stopping dangerous sledding, the Housing Department's Winter Storms Bulletin, and the plaintiff's relationship with Tech do not change this conclusion. Since Tech had no duty to Pitre under these facts, the defendants can not be held liable.

* * * * *

REVERSED.

LEMMON, Judge, concurring.

In my view, the pivotal issue in the duty-risk analysis in this case is not the existence of a duty, but the breach of duty.

The duty-risk analysis usually focuses on the general duty imposed upon the defendant by statute or rule of law, according to the relationship between the parties and the circumstances of the particular case, and then determines whether there was a breach of that general duty. The statement that "the defendant had no duty," as noted in Professor David W. Robertson et al, Cases and Materials on Torts 161 (1989), should be reserved for those "situations controlled by a rule of law of enough breadth and clarity to permit the trial judge in most cases raising the problem to dismiss the complaint or award summary judgment for defendant on the basis of the rule." Thus, a "no duty" defense generally applies when there is a categorical rule excluding liability as to whole categories of claimants or of claims under any circumstances. In the usual case where the duty owed depends upon the circumstances of the particular case, analysis of the defendant's conduct should be done in terms of "no liability" or "no breach of duty."

Here, the defendant had a duty to act reasonably in view of the foreseeable risks of danger to students resulting from the winter storm. As noted by the majority, the defendant did act reasonably under the circumstances. The defendant warned students by means of the Winter Storms Bulletin that sledding, while fun, can be dangerous unless limited to proper areas and accompanied by the use of good judgment. The bulletin provided several examples of bad judgment that had led to injuries in the past. Furthermore, the campus police halted any unsafe sledding and other dangerous activities that the officers observed. Because the particular risk in this case of colliding with the light poles was obvious and apparent to everyone, including the plaintiff and his companions, no warning was required, and the defendant did not breach its duty of reasonable care by failing to warn of that particular risk or by failing to erect protective barriers.

WATSON, Justice, dissenting.

* * * * *

The court of appeal correctly held: Defendants knew that the hill at the Assembly Center was utilized by sledders. They knew that the last snow resulted in fifteen personal injuries associated with student play in the snow and icy conditions. Furthermore, the danger presented by the light poles in the parking lot at the Assembly Center was such that serious injury was likely to occur should a sledder strike one of the posts.... (T)he burden of prevention was minimal to the university; there were several inexpensive measures that could have been implemented to either warn students of the danger presented or to make the hill safe. The only positive action taken by the university was to place a bulletin on each dorm student's bed encouraging sledding. Defendants breached the duty owed to Earl by failing to correct or warn of the danger presented by the light poles at the bottom of the Assembly Center hill.

* * * * *

The majority opinion seeks to renew the doctrines of assumption of the risk and contributory negligence. Even so, the majority is wrong. This writer does not believe for one moment that young Pitre said to himself: "I am going to slide down the hill and take the risk of hitting one of those poles." Simply put, he foolishly ignored the poles and the danger, just as did Tech. Their negligence was properly compared.

I respectfully dissent.

NOTES

1.   In a number of cases, Louisiana courts struggled to find a workable application of the "no duty for open and obvious risks" doctrine. For example, the Supreme Court in *Hutchison v. Knights of Columbus, Council No. 5747*, 866 So. 2d 228 (La. 2004), wrote:

> "(D)efendants generally have no duty to protect against an open and obvious hazard. If the facts ... show that the complained of condition should be obvious to all, the condition may not be unreasonably dangerous and the defendant may owe no duty to the plaintiff.... Specifically, in a trip and fall case, the duty is not solely with the landowner. A pedestrian has a duty to see that which should be seen and is bound to observe whether the pathway is clear.... The degree to which a danger may be observed by a potential victim is one factor in the determination of whether the condition is unreasonably dangerous. A landowner is not liable for an injury which results from a condition which should have been observed by the individual in the exercise of reasonable care or which was as obvious to a visitor as it was to the landowner."

Similarly, in *Pryor v. Iberia Parish School Board*, the Supreme Court in a per curiam ruling, reversed the Third Circuit's decision allowing recovery to a 69-year-old plaintiff who fell while traversing bleacher steps containing an 18-inch gap; holding that the "plaintiff was aware of the open and obvious risk. She could have easily avoided any risk by using additional care, as she did when she first ascended the bleachers, or by choosing to sit on the west side of the stadium where suitable accommodations for persons with physical impairments were provided." 60 So. 3d 594 (La. 2011). *See also Jimenez v. Omni Royal Orleans Hotel*, 66 So. 3d 528, 2010-1647 (La.App. 4 Cir. 2011), *writ denied*, 73 So. 3d 385 (La. 2011) (uncovered manhole on sidewalk was open and obvious).

(Storekeeper exercised reasonable care by placing two different ("wet floor") signs to alert customers that the floor had been mopped.) *Melancon v. Popeye's Famous Fried Chicken*, 59 So. 3d 513 (La.App. 3 Cir. 2011).

2. Note that where a duty is owed, comparative fault also may come into the analysis. In one case, comparative fault of 75% (reduced from 100%) allocated to the city which had notice of the large hole for at least a year and failed to make simple and inexpensive repair, and 25% to victim, who could have seen the broken area had he been looking down at that particular time. *Matlock v. City of Shreveport*, 58 So. 3d 1131 (La.App. 2 Cir. 2011).

3. In 2012, the Louisiana Supreme Court rejected an argument that a casino was negligent in the fall of a patron in the casino. Responding to the argument that flashing lights on the steps may have contributed to the fall, the Court states as follows:

> [A]ssuming the flashing lights created a hazard, such a condition is open and obvious. A landowner is not liable for an injury which results from a condition which should have been observed by the individual in the exercise of reasonable care, or which was as obvious to a visitor as it was to the landowner. *Dauzat v. Curnest Guillot Logging, Inc.*, 08–0528 (La. 2008), 995 So. 2d 1184; *Hutchinson v. Knights of Columbus*, 03–1533 at p. 9 (La. 2004), 866 So. 2d 228, 234; *Pitre v. Louisiana Tech University*, 95–1466, 95–1487 at p. 11 (La. 1996), 673 So. 2d 585, 591.

Mansoor v. Jazz Casino Co., LLC, 98 So. 3d 795, 795 (La. 2012). Is this really a case where the casino owes no duty, or is it a case for comparative fault? Perhaps because of this uncertainty, the Louisiana Supreme Court has recently addressed this issue.

4. Louisiana has struggled with the "no duty" question. There are two relevant questions to consider. First, should the open and obvious nature of the defect be considered as part of the duty element or as part of the breach element? As a corollary, you should ask why it matters. Second, what is the standard? That is, how would you define the "no liability" standard?

Pitre provides one answer to these questions, but in 2013, 2014 and 2015 Louisiana revisited the questions. In a rather stunning set of cases, the Supreme Court significantly altered the "open and obvious" doctrine.

BROUSSARD

v.

STATE EX REL. OFFICE OF STATE BUILDINGS
113 So. 3d 175 (La. 2013)

KNOLL, Justice.

In this personal injury case, we must determine whether a one and one-half to three inch misalignment between the floors of an elevator and a building's lobby created an unreasonable risk of harm as found by the jury, or whether the elevator's defective condition presented an open and obvious hazard as determined by the Court of Appeal. Plaintiff, Paul Broussard, filed this suit against the State of Louisiana ("the State") for damages he sustained from an accident caused by the misaligned elevator. Upon conclusion of a three-day trial, a jury returned a verdict in Broussard's favor, finding the offset between the elevator and lobby floors presented an unreasonable risk of harm. After reducing Broussard's damages in proportion to his assigned percentage of fault, the District Court entered a judgment consistent with the jury verdict in the amount of $985,732.56. The First Circuit Court of Appeal held the jury's factual determination that the elevator's defective condition presented an unreasonable risk of harm was manifestly erroneous because the defect was open and obvious, and reversed. We granted Broussard's writ to further examine, under the manifest error doctrine, whether a defective condition is more properly considered an open and obvious hazard where no duty is owed, rather than an unreasonably dangerous condition where comparative fault is applicable.

After reviewing the applicable law and the record in its entirety, we find the jury's unreasonable risk of harm determination was not manifestly erroneous. The record contains a reasonable factual basis to support the jury's finding the misaligned elevator created an unreasonable risk of harm to Broussard and the State breached its duty to maintain its property in a reasonably safe condition by failing to remedy this defect or warn of its existence. Accordingly, we reverse the Court of Appeal and reinstate in its entirety the judgment of the District Court rendered in conformity with the jury's verdict.

Facts and Procedural History

The Wooddale Tower ("the Tower") is a twelve-story, State-owned office building located in Baton Rouge. There are two elevators in the Tower's lobby. Sometime in 1998, the State contracted to have the Tower's roof repaired. This roofing project generated a large amount of dust and debris, which eventually settled and accumulated on the elevators' relay contacts, causing the elevators to operate erratically for several years. Most significantly, the Tower's elevators would often stop in a position uneven with floors of the building. These misalignments would create an offset between the elevator floor and the building floor ranging anywhere from a few inches to several feet. Between 1999 and 2000, the State received multiple complaints from the Tower's tenants expressing their concern the malfunctioning elevators would eventually cause a serious accident.... Although the State planned to modernize the elevators and, in response to the reported problems, advanced the project's start date from 2001 to 1999, it was unable to successfully bid out the repair contract until June 20, 2001, almost five months after Broussard's accident.

On January 23, 2001, Broussard, a United Parcel Service ("UPS") delivery driver, sustained a serious back injury while maneuvering a loaded dolly into one of the Tower's misaligned elevators. Before this incident, Broussard worked for UPS eleven years, seven of which were as a delivery driver. During his tenure as a UPS driver, Broussard delivered parcels to the Tower on a daily basis. He was, therefore, familiar with the building and knew its elevators intermittently stopped at a level uneven with the building's floors.

* * * * *

Broussard subsequently sued the State of Louisiana through the Office of State Buildings for the damages he suffered as a result of the accident. In his petition, Broussard alleged the State was negligent in failing to properly maintain and adequately repair a defective thing within its custody and care, thereby creating an unreasonable risk of harm. The case proceeded to trial and was tried to a jury on August 23–26, 2010. At the conclusion of trial, the jury returned a verdict in favor of Broussard, specifically finding (1) the offset between the elevator and lobby floors created an unreasonable risk of harm, (2) the State had a reasonable opportunity to remedy the defect but failed to do so, and (3) the defect was the proximate cause of Broussard's injuries. The jury then found Broussard 38% at fault in causing the accident and apportioned the remaining 62% to the State. Ultimately, the jury awarded Broussard $1,589,890.23 in damages. After reducing these damages in proportion to Broussard's assigned percentage of fault, the District Court rendered a judgment consistent with the jury verdict in the amount of $985,732.56.

* * * * *

Discussion

Broussard's claims against the State are rooted in La. Civ.Code arts. 2317 and 2322. A public entity's liability for a defective thing within its custody or care is ordinarily analyzed under La.Rev.Stat. § 9:2800(C). La.Rev.Stat. § 9:2800(A), however, exempts buildings from the scope of § 9:2800(C), stating "[a] public entity is responsible under Civil Code Article 2317 for damages caused by the condition of buildings within its care and custody." Therefore, § 9:2800(A) directs us to Article 2317 to determine a public entity's liability for the damages caused by the condition of a building within its custody and care. In this case, the State is the owner of two defective elevators. These elevators, while not "buildings," are, under Louisiana law, component parts of a building. We have previously stated that "necessary appurtenances to structures and movables made immovable by attachment, which are defective or have fallen into ruin, also may be included within that term 'building' for purposes of the building-owner's delictual responsibility under Article 2322."... There is no set test for determining whether a thing attached to a building, such as an elevator, is part of the building for purposes of the building-owner's delictual liability. Various courts, however, have found the following factors persuasive: (1) how securely the thing is attached to the building, ... ; (2) the permanence of the attachment, ... (transitorily attached panel and enclosure system not necessary appurtenance to or component part of a building); and (3) whether the attachment would be considered permanent under the Civil Code articles regulating property rights, ... (Civil Code articles defining component parts provide sole framework for determining whether an attachment to a building is part of that building for purposes of assessing liability under Article 2322). We find the elevators in this case are properly considered part of the Tower for purposes of the State's liability under Article 2322, as they were permanently attached to the building....

Because these elevators are component parts of the Tower, Broussard's claims are properly analyzed under La. Civ.Code art. 2317, as directed by La.Rev.Stat. § 9:2800(A). Article 2317 states "[w]e are responsible, not only for the damage occasioned by our own act, but for that which is caused by ... the things we have in our custody." La. Civ.Code art. 2322 specifically modifies liability under Article 2317 with respect to the owner of a ruinous building or a defective component part of that building. Article 2322 provides, in pertinent part:

> The owner of a building is answerable for the damage occasioned by its ruin, when this is caused by neglect to repair it, or when it is the result of a vice or defect in its original construction. However, he is answerable for damages only upon a showing that he knew or, in the exercise of reasonable care, should have known of the vice or defect which caused the damage, that the damage could have been prevented by the exercise of reasonable care, and that he failed to exercise such reasonable care....

Under Article 2322, a plaintiff must prove the following elements to hold the owner of a building liable for the damages caused by the building's ruin or a defective component: (1) ownership of the building; (2) the owner knew or, in the exercise of reasonable care, should have known of the ruin or defect; (3) the damage could have been prevented by the exercise of reasonable care; (4) the defendant failed to exercise such reasonable care; and (5) causation. La. Civ.Code art. 2322. Additionally, our jurisprudence requires that the ruinous building or its defective component part create an unreasonable risk of harm....[4] The sole issue we must address here is whether the defect in the Tower's elevators created an unreasonable risk of harm, thereby subjecting the State to liability under Article 2322.

The owner of a building is not responsible for all injuries resulting from any risk posed by the building.... Rather, the owner is only responsible for those injuries caused by a ruinous condition or defective component part that presents an unreasonable risk of harm to others.... We have described the question of whether a defect presents an unreasonable risk of harm as "a disputed issue of mixed fact and law or policy that is peculiarly a question for the jury or trier of the facts."...[5] As a mixed

---

[4] In brief and oral argument, the State argues its potential liability should be analyzed under La.Rev.Stat. § 9:2800(C). We note the elements of a claim under § 9:2800(C) closely parallel the elements of a claim under Article 2322. In order to hold a public entity liable under § 9:2800(C), a plaintiff must prove the following: (1) custody or ownership of the defective thing by the public entity, i.e., garde; (2) the defect created an unreasonable risk of harm; (3) the public entity had actual or constructive knowledge of the defect; (4) the public entity failed to take corrective action within a reasonable time; and (5) causation. *Chambers v. Vill. of Moreauville*, 11–898, p. 5 (La. 2012), 85 So. 3d 593, 597; *Dupree v. City of New Orleans*, 99–3651, p. 6 (La. 2000), 765 So. 2d 1002, 1008 n. 6. Our analysis would, therefore, be substantially the same, regardless of whether we apply Article 2322 or § 9:2800(C). The sole, dispositive issue we must address is whether the elevators' defective condition presented an unreasonable risk of harm—an issue we would analyze in the same manner under both provisions.

[5] We have also made the seemingly contradictory statement that "[i]t is the court's obligation to decide which risks are unreasonable based on the facts and circumstances of each case." *Pryor*, 10–1683 at p. 4, 60 So. 3d at

question of law and fact, it is the fact-finder's role—either the jury or the court in a bench trial—to determine whether a defect is unreasonably dangerous. Thus, whether a defect presents an unreasonable risk of harm is "a matter wed to the facts" and must be determined in light of facts and circumstances of each particular case....

To aid the trier-of-fact in making this unscientific, factual determination, this Court has adopted a risk-utility balancing test, wherein the fact-finder must balance the gravity and risk of harm against individual societal rights and obligations, the social utility of the thing, and the cost and feasibility of repair.... Specifically, we have synthesized this risk-utility balancing test to a consideration of four pertinent factors: (1) the utility of the complained-of condition; (2) the likelihood and magnitude of harm, including the obviousness and apparentness of the condition; (3) the cost of preventing the harm; and (4) the nature of the plaintiff's activities in terms of its social utility or whether it is dangerous by nature....

The second prong of this risk-utility inquiry focuses on whether the dangerous or defective condition is obvious and apparent. Under Louisiana law, a defendant generally does not have a duty to protect against an open and obvious hazard. *See, e.g., Hutchinson*, 03–1533 at p. 9, 866 So. 2d at 234. In order for a hazard to be considered open and obvious, this Court has consistently stated the hazard should be one that is open and obvious to all, i.e., everyone who may potentially encounter it. *E.g., Caserta v. Wal–Mart Stores, Inc.*, 12–0853, p. 1 (La.6/22/12), 90 So. 3d 1042, 1043 (per curiam); *Dauzat*, 08–0528 at p. 3, 995 So. 2d at 1186; *Hutchinson*, 03–1533 at p. 9, 866 So. 2d at 234; *Pitre*, 95–1466 at p. 11, 673 So. 2d at 591; *Murray v. Ramada Inns, Inc.*, 521 So. 2d 1123, 1136 (La.1988) ("[A] potentially dangerous condition that should be obvious to all comers is not, in all instances, unreasonably dangerous."). Although the "open and obvious" argument suggests a disguised application of contributory negligence or assumption of the risk, when the risk is open and obvious to everyone, the probability of injury is low and the thing's utility may outweigh the risks caused by its defective condition. MARAIST & GALLIGAN, LOUISIANA TORT LAW § 14.03, p. 14–9. *See also* Frank L. Maraist, H. Alston Johnson III, Thomas C. Galligan, Jr., & William R. Corbett, *Answering a Fool According to His Folly: Ruminations on Comparative Fault Thirty Years On*, 70 LA. L.REV. 1105, 1107 (2011) ("The [C]ourt, however, has recognized ... situations in which conduct falls within traditional assumption of the risk principles but does not overlap with conduct that customarily is considered contributory negligence ... [one of which is where] the victim voluntarily encounters a known risk that is 'obvious to all comers,' sometimes also referred to as 'open and obvious risk.' ").

We have stated that if the facts and circumstances of a particular case show a dangerous condition should be open and obvious to all who encounter it, then the condition may not be unreasonably dangerous and the defendant may owe no duty to the plaintiff. *E.g., Caserta*, 12–0853 at p. 1, 90 So. 3d at 1043; *Dauzat*, 08–0528 at p. 4, 995 So. 2d at 1186; *Hutchinson*, 03–1533 at p. 9, 866 So. 2d at 234; *Pitre*, 95–1466 at p. 7, 673 So. 2d at 589; *Socorro v. City of New Orleans*, 579 So. 2d 931, 942 (La. 1991). While this statement is consistent with our "open and obvious to all" doctrine, by tethering the existence of a duty to a determination of whether a risk is unreasonable, our prior decisions have admittedly conflated the duty and breach elements of our negligence analysis. *See* Maraist, et. al., *Answering a Fool*, 70 LA. L.REV. at 1121–22, 1124. This conflation, in turn, has confused the role of judge and jury in the unreasonable risk of harm inquiry and arguably transferred "the jury's power to determine breach to the court to determine duty or no duty." *Id.* at 1124, 1132–33.

596; *Pitre v. Louisiana Tech. Univ.*, 95–1466, p. 9 (La. 1996), 673 So. 2d 585, 590; *Socorro v. City of New Orleans*, 579 So. 2d 931, 940 (La. 1991). However, *Pryor* and *Socorro* involved bench trials. 10–1683 at p. 2, 60 So. 3d at 596, 579 So. 2d at 934. As such, "the court," acting as trier-of-fact, was responsible for making the factual determination of whether the defects in *Pryor* and *Socorro* presented an unreasonable risk of harm. Likewise, *Pitre* was decided on a motion for summary judgment filed by the defendants. 95–1466 at p. 5, 673 So. 2d at 588. In this procedural posture, it was the court's obligation in *Pitre* to decide if there was a genuine issue of material fact as to whether concrete light poles at the base of a hill created an unreasonable risk of harm to college students sledding down that hill.

Additionally, our courts of appeal have followed *Reed* and *Tillman*, characterizing the unreasonable risk harm inquiry as a mixed question of law and fact....

In order to avoid further overlap between the jury's role as fact-finder and the judge's role as lawgiver, we find the analytic framework for evaluating an unreasonable risk of harm is properly classified as a determination of whether a defendant breached a duty owed, rather than a determination of whether a duty is owed ab initio. It is axiomatic that the issue of whether a duty is owed is a question of law, and the issue of whether a defendant has breached a duty owed is a question of fact. . . . The judge decides the former, and the fact-finder—judge or jury—decides the latter. "In the usual case where the duty owed depends upon the circumstances of the particular case, analysis of the defendant's conduct should be done in terms of 'no liability' or 'no breach of duty.' " *Pitre*, 95–1466 at p. 22, 673 So. 2d at 596 (Lemmon, J., concurring). Because the determination of whether a defect is unreasonably dangerous necessarily involves a myriad of factual considerations, varying from case to case, ... , the cost-benefit analysis employed by the fact-finder in making this determination is more properly associated with the breach, rather than the duty, element of our duty-risk analysis.[6] *See* Maraist, et. al., *Answering a Fool*, 70 LA. L.REV. at 1120 ("[O]ne might persuasively argue that the cost-benefit analysis used to determine whether a risk is reasonable or unreasonable is the heart of the breach decision and is one that should be conducted by the fact-finder, rather than by the court...."). Thus, while a defendant only has a duty to protect against unreasonable risks that are not obvious or apparent, the fact-finder, employing a risk-utility balancing test, determines which risks are unreasonable and whether those risks pose an open and obvious hazard. In other words, the fact-finder determines whether defendant has breached a duty to keep its property in a reasonably safe condition by failing to discover, obviate, or warn of a defect that presents an unreasonable risk of harm.

Because the determination of whether a defective thing presents an unreasonable risk of harm "encompasses an abundance of factual findings, which differ greatly from case to case, followed by an application of those facts to a less-than scientific standard, a reviewing court is in no better position to make the determination than the jury or trial court." ... Accordingly, the fact-finder's unreasonable risk of harm determination is subject to the manifest error standard of review and should be afforded deference on appeal.... Under the manifest error standard of review, a court of appeal may not set aside a jury's finding of fact unless it is manifestly erroneous or clearly wrong.... The reviewing court must only decide whether the fact-finder's conclusion was reasonable, not whether it was right or wrong.... In order to reverse a jury's factual finding as manifestly erroneous, an appellate court must find the record, when reviewed in its entirety, (1) contains no reasonable factual basis for the jury's finding and (2) establishes the finding is clearly wrong.... The court of appeal must always be mindful that if the jury's findings "are reasonable in light of the record reviewed in its entirety ... [it] may not reverse even though convinced that had it been sitting as the trier of fact, it would have weighed the evidence differently." ...

Applying these precepts to the case sub judice, we conclude the record contains a reasonable factual basis to support the jury's determination the offset presented an unreasonable risk of harm to Broussard. Moreover, the record supports a finding that the elevator's defective condition was not an open and obvious hazard, as the defect was not readily apparent to all who encountered it. As can be seen from the following application of our risk-utility balancing test, the risk of harm created by the defect was significant when weighed against the elevators' social utility and the cost of preventing the harm.

Utility of the Elevators

First, we address the utility of the Tower's elevators. Broussard does not dispute the Tower's elevators serve a valuable, perhaps indispensable, societal function. The Tower is a multi-story office building, housing numerous State agencies and approximately 250 State employees. It is necessary for this building to have elevators so these employees can get to and from their offices in an efficient manner and carry on the important business of our State's government. These elevators, therefore,

---

[6] In cases addressing the State's liability for unreasonably dangerous conditions on public roadways, we have stated that the determination of whether a defect presents an unreasonable risk of harm is analogous to the breach element of our duty-risk analysis.... Louisiana appellate courts have also made this comparison....

serve a valuable societal function by quickly shuttling State employees to and from their offices in a large, multi-story office tower.

Likelihood and Magnitude of Harm: Open and Obvious

The elevators' utility, however, must be balanced against the likelihood and magnitude of the harm presented by their defective condition, including whether the defect was open and obvious. In this case, the State is postured as the owner of a malfunctioning elevator. Because a malfunctioning elevator can quickly become a dangerous instrumentality, Louisiana law places "a high degree of care" upon elevator owners analogous to the degree of care imposed upon common carriers....

In light of this heightened standard, an elevator owner, like any property owner, would invariably be required to maintain its elevator in a reasonably safe condition.... Included in the owner's duty to keep its elevator in a reasonably safe condition are the related obligations to discover if the elevator is in an unreasonably dangerous condition and, if so, to either correct the condition or warn of its existence.... Furthermore, an owner of an unreasonably dangerous thing has a duty to label or mark the thing so as to provide adequate and reasonable warning to individuals using or attempting to use the thing....

The Tower's malfunctioning elevators presented a significant and likely risk of harm. The State had a heightened degree of care precisely because these elevators were malfunctioning and had become dangerous instrumentalities.... Indeed, the public does not ordinarily anticipate offsets between the floors of elevators and buildings—a point the State's expert safety consultant, Michael Frenzel, conceded on cross examination. Thus, in this regard, we are not addressing an ordinary trip-and-fall case, wherein we generally state pedestrians must exercise ordinary care, keeping in mind irregularities frequently exist in sidewalks.... We find the elevators' frequent failure to stop at a level flush with the building's floors presented a significant and likely risk of harm, which was further exacerbated by the fact pedestrians do not ordinarily anticipate irregularities, such as the offset in question, when entering and exiting elevators....

An elevator owner, being akin to a common carrier, does not, however, insure the safety of every individual who may happen to ride its elevator.... If the elevator's defective condition is open and obvious to all who encountered it, then the defect may not be unreasonably dangerous. The Court of Appeal reached this conclusion, finding the one and one-half to three inch offset was open and obvious.... On this point, we find the Court of Appeal supplanted its own judgment for that of the jury.... Instead, we find the record clearly supports a finding the offset was not, under our jurisprudence, an open and obvious defect.

To be sure, we have consistently echoed one central theme throughout our open and obvious jurisprudence: If the complained-of condition should be obvious to all, then it may not be unreasonably dangerous. *E.g., Pitre*, 95–1466 at p. 11, 673 So. 2d at 591; *Socorro*, 579 So. 2d at 942; *Murray*, 521 So. 2d at 1136. Thus, in order to be open and obvious, the risk of harm should be apparent to all who encounter the dangerous condition. *See, e.g., Pitre*, 95–1466 at p. 11, 673 So. 2d at 591–92 (light poles in the area where college students were sledding were visible to everyone and thus open and obvious); *Oster v. Dep't. of Transp. & Dev., State of La.*, 582 So. 2d 1285, 1288 (La.1991) (ditch on shoulder of road readily discernable from a considerable distance and thus not unreasonably dangerous). Our "open and obvious to all" principle is not a hollow maxim. Rather, it serves an invaluable function, preventing concepts such as assumption of the risk from infiltrating our jurisprudence. Over 25 years ago in *Murray*, we recognized that defining a defendant's initial duty in terms of a plaintiff's, versus everyone's, knowledge of a dangerous condition would preserve assumption of the risk as a defense and undermine Louisiana's pure comparative fault regime:

If accepted, defendants' argument would inject the assumption of risk doctrine into duty/risk analysis "through the back door." By that, we mean that the argument attempts to define the defendant's initial duty in terms of the plaintiff's actual knowledge, and thereby seeks to achieve the same result which would be reached if assumption of risk were retained as a defense, i.e., a total bar to the plaintiff's recovery. A defendant's duty should not turn on a particular plaintiff's state of mind, but instead should be determined by the standard of care which the defendant owes to all potential plaintiffs.

> 521 So. 2d at 1136. In contrast, the "open and obvious to all" rule is "sensible ... and does not undermine the comparative fault regime by allowing a plaintiff's negligence to operate as a bar to recovery in a case where the defendant's conduct poses a risk of harm to the hypothetical blameless plaintiff." Maraist, et. al., *Answering a Fool*, 70 LA. L.REV. at 1130. The open and obvious inquiry thus focuses on the global knowledge of everyone who encounters the defective thing or dangerous condition, not the victim's actual or potentially ascertainable knowledge. Simply put, we would undermine our comparative fault principles if we allowed the fact-finder to characterize a risk as open and obvious based solely on the plaintiff's awareness of that risk. The plaintiff's knowledge or awareness of the risk created by the defendant's conduct should not operate as a total bar to recovery in a case where the defendant would otherwise be liable to the plaintiff. *Murray*, 521 So. 2d at 1134. Instead, comparative fault principles should apply, and the plaintiff's "awareness of the danger" is but one factor to consider when assigning fault to all responsible parties under La. Civ.Code art. 2323. *Id.* (citing *Watson v. State Farm Fire & Cas. Ins. Co.*, 469 So. 2d 967, 974 (La. 1985)).[8]

> In this case, there was a reasonable basis upon which the jury could conclude the defect in the Tower's elevators, while apparent to Broussard, was not "open and obvious to all." There is no dispute that Broussard was aware of the offset after it impeded his initial attempt to push the dolly onto the elevator. Moreover, Tammy Loupe, the woman who entered the elevator before Broussard, testified she too was aware of the offset. The record, however, contains numerous exhibits highlighting instances of State employees either tripping or falling on the elevators after failing to notice they were misaligned. For example, Steve Bowers, a state loss prevention officer, sent a memorandum to his supervisor on October 13, 1999, wherein he reported a dramatic increase in complaints about the Tower's elevators. In the memo, Bowers recalled an incident where a handicapped employee almost fell while exiting one of the elevators, which had stopped approximately a foot and a half above the building floor. The record also contains a letter dated February 2, 1999, from Richie Dorian, owner of the maintenance company serving the Tower's elevators, to the State. In his letter, Dorian states his company received multiple reports of passengers tripping on the Tower's misaligned elevators. Finally, the jury examined the July 10, 2000 tenant memo, in which concerned employees from the Department of Social Services recalled numerous instances of employees tripping while entering or exiting the misaligned elevators. As numerous individuals—including those most familiar with the elevators, i.e., State employees working at the Tower—failed to notice and tripped over the misaligned elevators, a fact-finder could reasonably infer the defect, while apparent to Broussard, was not open and obvious to all who encountered it.

---

[8] Our "open and obvious to all" rule is also mandated by the policy of legislative supremacy. In 1979, the Legislature adopted a pure comparative fault regime, which became effective in 1980, and in 1996, it modified this regime by extending comparative fault principles to virtually all negligent parties. *See* La. Civ.Code. art. 2323; Acts 1996, 1st Ex.Sess., No. 3, § 1; Acts 1979, No. 431, § 1. As a civil law jurisdiction, we must give deference to the acts and policy choices of the Legislature. See La. Civ.Code arts. 1 and 2 ("The sources of law are legislation and custom," and "[l]egislation is a solemn expression of legislative will.").... "Thus, any rule or system of rules that tends to undermine comparative fault principles to either allow the ... [negligent] plaintiff to recover 100% ... or allow the faulty defendant to escape liability must be viewed with some skepticism and, if allowed to exist at all, must be kept in relative check." Maraist, et. al., *Answering a Fool*, 70 LA. L.REV. at 1132. Again, the "open and obvious to all" doctrine keeps principles such as assumption of the risk and contributory negligence "in relative check."

Notably, the phrase "unreasonable risk of harm" is not used in any of the statutes governing premises liability or governmental entity liability. *See* La. Civ.Code arts. 2317, 2317.1, & 2322 and La.Rev.Stat. § 9:2800. However, Louisiana courts have consistently applied this test in premises liability cases for over 35 years, and the doctrine has attained the status of jurisprudence constante. *See, e.g., Dupree*, 99–3651 at p. 5, 765 So.d at 1008; *Jones v. Hawkins*, 98–1259 (La. 1999), 731 So. 2d 216, 218; *Oster*, 582 So.d at 1288; *Landry v. State*, 495 So. 2d 1284, 1287 (La. 1986); *Loescher v. Parr*, 324 So. 2d 441, 446 (La. 1975). The phrase "open and obvious" is also notably absent from any of the premises liability statutes. These concepts—embodied in our risk-utility analysis—are thus strictly jurisprudential doctrines and cannot undermine or trump the Legislature's will in enacting a pure comparative fault regime.

The State relies heavily on several of this Court's recent per curiam opinions. *See Pryor*, 10–138, 60 So. 3d 594; *Eisenhardt v. Snook*, 08–1287 (La. 2009), 8 So. 3d 541 (per curiam); *Dauzat*, 08–0528, 995 So. 2d 1184. It argues these cases support the position Broussard should not recover because his awareness of the offset made the defect an open and obvious danger. We disagree....

[The court discusses and distinguishes each of the cases.]

Admittedly, it appears our recent per curiam opinions have produced a patchwork of inconsistent jurisprudence. However, we emphasize again that each case involving an unreasonable risk of harm analysis must be judged under its own unique set of facts and circumstances ... There is no bright-line rule. The fact-intensive nature of our risk-utility analysis will inevitably lead to divergent results. Moreover, each defect is equally unique, requiring the fact-finder to place more or less weight on different considerations depending on the specific defect under consideration. What may compel a trier-of-fact to determine one defect does not present an unreasonable risk of harm may carry little weight in the trier-of-fact's consideration of another defect. For instance, a fact-finder analyzing a defective sidewalk may find the cost and feasibility of repair to the city or municipality outweighs all other considerations. *See, e.g., Chambers*, 11–898 at pp. 9–10, 85 So. 3d at 600; *Reed*, 708 So. 2d at 366. In contrast, the inherently dangerous nature of the plaintiff's activity may persuade the trier-of-fact to conclude a defective logging road, for example, is not unreasonably dangerous. And here, a defective component part may lead the fact-finder to employ a different weighing and balancing of the unreasonable risk of harm criteria. In short, while the unreasonable risk of harm calculus will remain amorphous, one variable must remain constant: In order for a defect to be considered open and obvious, the danger created by that defect must be apparent to all comers.

Cost of Preventing Harm

The third prong of our risk-utility balancing test requires the fact-finder to balance the risk of harm against the cost and feasibility of repair.... The State set a $275,000 budget for the contract to modernize the Tower's elevators. While certainly not inexpensive, the price of modernization, when weighed against the gravity of harm created by a malfunctioning elevator, was not inordinate or cost-prohibitive. *Compare with Chambers*, 11–898 at pp. 9–10, 85 So. 3d at 600 (cost of repairing every minor sidewalk deviation substantial); *Reed*, 97–1174 at p. 7, 708 So. 2d at 366 (substantial cost of repairing every minor deviation in concrete parking lot prohibitive); *Boyle*, 685 So. 2d at 1083 (not feasible to repair every minor deviation in 22–plus miles of sidewalk on LSU's campus).... While the State's hands were tied during the bidding process, there were other inexpensive, interim steps it could have taken to warn employees and visitors of the hazard posed by the Tower's elevators. Again, the owner of an elevator, like any property owner, has a duty to discover if its elevator is in an unreasonably dangerous condition and, if so, to either correct such condition or warn of its existence.... Although the State was limited in its ability to correct the elevators' condition, it certainly could have warned employees and visitors until the condition could be corrected by placing visible signs at or near the elevators' entrances....

Nature of Plaintiff's Activity

Finally, the fact-finder must analyze the nature of the plaintiff's activity in terms of its social utility or whether it is dangerous by nature.... As the Court of Appeal correctly noted, the activity Broussard was engaged in, delivering office supplies, is highly useful to society. Just as an office building cannot function effectively without elevators, it is equally unlikely it could function in our modern business world without high-speed delivery companies such as UPS and its competitors. The State argues Broussard's act of pulling the dolly over the offset was inherently dangerous. We find there is a reasonable basis in the record upon which the jury could reach the opposite conclusion. First, Broussard testified he encountered and successfully maneuvered his dolly over offsets and curbs on a daily basis, suggesting it was not unreasonable for him to believe he could maneuver his dolly over the minor offset between the elevator and lobby floors. Second, the dolly was not overloaded, as it had a capacity of 500 lbs. and was loaded with only 300 lbs....

In sum, we find the District Court properly instructed the jury to balance the gravity and risk of harm created by the offset against the elevators' social utility, as well as the cost and feasibility of repair. Our review of the record in its entirety reveals this balancing weighs in favor of finding the offset presented an unreasonable risk of harm. Under this risk-utility balancing, the elevator's defective condition was not open and obvious to all, and thus the risk of harm created by this condition was significant in comparison to the elevators' social utility and the relatively low cost to the State of preventing the harm. In light of these findings, we conclude the Court of Appeal fell into error by substituting its own judgment of whether the defect presented an unreasonable risk of harm for that of the jury. Under our manifest error review, we find the record clearly supports a reasonable basis for the jury's findings.

Conclusion

After considering the record in its entirety under the manifest error doctrine, we hold a reasonable basis exists to support the jury's factual determination that a one and one-half to three inch offset between the floor of the elevator and the floor of the Tower's lobby presented an unreasonable risk of harm. We further find a reasonable factual basis exists to support a finding the elevator's defective condition was not an open and obvious hazard, as the defect was not readily apparent to all who encountered it. The State, therefore, breached its duty of care by failing to remedy the defect or warn of its existence until the defect could be remedied. Accordingly, we reverse the judgment of the Court of Appeal and reinstate the judgment of the District Court rendered in conformity with the jury's verdict.

Decree

For the foregoing reasons, we hereby render judgment reversing the judgment of the Court of Appeal. The District Court's judgment entered in conformity with the jury's verdict is hereby reinstated in its entirety. REVERSED AND RENDERED; DISTRICT COURT JUDGMENT REINSTATED IN ITS ENTIRETY.

VICTORY, Justice, dissents and assigns reasons. GUIDRY, Justice, dissents and assigns reasons.

NOTES

1.   How does the Court majority describe the open-and-obvious principle? Why does the defendant not prevail under the principle as articulated and applied by the Court?

2.   Is the open-and-obvious doctrine, as articulated by the Court, a clear one? Will we readily know when we encounter a case involving an open-and-obvious risk of harm? How does a defendant prove that a risk is open and obvious under the Court's standard? Why was the proof in this case not sufficient?

3.   Does the Court majority effectively distinguish the open-and-obvious principle from implied assumption of the risk, which was abrogated in *Murray v. Ramada Inns*?

4.   The Court recognizes that what is really at stake is the allocation of functions between the judge and jury. The majority allows the jury to allocate fault, while the dissent would take the issue away from the jury. Do you think that trust or lack of trust in the jury system could explain the result?

5.   In 2014, the Louisiana Supreme Court revisited the open and obvious doctrine in the following case.

BUFKIN
v.
FELIPE'S LOUISIANA, LLC
171 So. 3d 851 (La. 2014)

HUGHES, J.

This writ presents the issue of whether a building contractor breached any legal duty owed to a pedestrian crossing a street next to the contractor's dumpster, who was struck by an oncoming bicyclist. After a thorough review of the record presented, we conclude that the dumpster was obvious and apparent, and not unreasonably dangerous; thus, there was no duty to warn of the clearly visible obstruction, and the district court erred in failing to grant summary judgment dismissing the contractor. Therefore, we reverse the district court judgment, render summary judgment in favor of the defendant/contractor, and remand to the district court for further proceedings.

Facts and Procedural History

This personal injury action arose on December 2, 2011, at approximately 4:30 in the afternoon, when Royce Bufkin, Jr. was walking through the French Quarter from a jewelry store on Royal Street to a wine shop on Chartres Street, via Conti Street. Outside a building under renovation at 622 Conti Street, Mr. Bufkin encountered a construction barrier blocking the sidewalk, which directed pedestrians to use the sidewalk on the other side of the street. At this location, there was also a large construction dumpster placed on several adjacent on-street parking spaces by Shamrock Construction Co., Inc. ("Shamrock"), in connection with renovations it had contracted to make at 622 Conti Street. While attempting to cross the street by the dumpster, Mr. Bufkin was hit by a bicyclist and injured.

At the time of the accident, Mr. Bufkin was walking toward the Mississippi River down Conti Street, which is a one-way street in the same direction. The bicyclist, who was working in the course and scope of his employment as a deliveryman for Felipe's Louisiana, LLC d/b/a Felipe's Taqueria Restaurant ("Felipe's"), was traveling in the wrong direction (away from the river) on Conti Street. Mr. Bufkin had stopped before crossing Conti, next to the dumpster, to allow two cars to pass (approaching from the direction of Lake Ponchartrain), but he failed to look to his right (in the direction of the river) before crossing the street, and he did not see the bicyclist approaching.

Mr. Bufkin filed the instant suit on March 6, 2012, naming as defendants: Felipe's; Felipe's insurer, Maryland Casualty Company; Shamrock; Lewis C. Ramel, Jr., the alleged owner of 622 Conti Street; and "Any Unidentified Owners of 622 Conti Street."

Shamrock's argument

On November 20, 2013 Shamrock filed a motion for summary judgment, contending that it was not negligent and that the plaintiff would be unable to establish that it owed a duty, as alleged. Following a December 13, 2013 hearing on Shamrock's motion for summary judgment, the district court denied the motion for summary judgment, reasoning that whether Shamrock posted a warning on its sidewalk-closure sign sufficient to notify the plaintiff of the "existence of problems" was a question of fact that precluded summary judgment.

The appellate court denied Shamrock's subsequent writ application. *See Bufkin v. Felipe's Louisiana*, LLC, 14–0051 (La.App. 4 Cir. 2014) (unpublished). Thereafter, this court granted Shamrock's writ application. *See Bufkin v. Felipe's Louisiana, LLC,* 14–0288 (La. 2014), 141 So. 3d 276. We conclude that the condition presented by the presence of Shamrock's clearly marked and visible construction dumpster, adjacent to a one-way French Quarter street, was obvious, apparent, and did not create an unreasonable risk of harm; thus, no duty was owed.

Law and Analysis

This court applies a de novo standard of review in considering lower court rulings on summary judgment motions. Thus, we use the same criteria that govern the district court's consideration of whether summary judgment is appropriate. A court must grant a motion for summary judgment if the pleadings, depositions, answers to interrogatories, and admissions, together with the affidavits, if any, show that there is no genuine issue as to material fact, and that the mover is entitled to judgment as a matter of law, pursuant to LSA–C.C.P. art. 966(B). *See Catahoula Parish School Board v. Louisiana Machinery Rentals, LLC,* 12–2504 (La. 2013), 124 So. 3d 1065, 1071.

On motion for summary judgment, the burden of proof remains with the movant. However, if the moving party will not bear the burden of proof on the issue at trial and points out that there is an absence of factual support for one or more elements essential to the adverse party's claim, action, or defense, then the non-moving party must produce factual support sufficient to establish that he will be able to satisfy his evidentiary burden of proof at trial. If the opponent of the motion fails to do so, there is no genuine issue of material fact and summary judgment will be granted. *See* LSA–C.C.P. art. 966(C)(2); *Schultz v. Guoth,* 10–0343 (La. 2011), 57 So. 3d 1002, 1006.

In its motion for summary judgment, Shamrock asserted that the plaintiff would be unable to establish the duty element of his negligence action. Shamrock argued that since the duty element is an essential element of the plaintiff's negligence action and there was no genuine issue of material fact, it was entitled to a judgment of dismissal as a matter of law. Shamrock asserted that it had no duty to warn the plaintiff to look both ways before crossing the street.

The plaintiff maintained that Shamrock was liable for his injuries because Shamrock had negligently created an unreasonable risk of harm to pedestrians by setting up a "blind spot" that prevented pedestrians from seeing oncoming traffic when crossing the street near Shamrock's dumpster. The plaintiff argued that Shamrock's sidewalk closure funneled pedestrians into crossing the street by the dumpster, and Shamrock's placement of the large dumpster immediately next to the street, without a buffer zone, created a line-of-sight obstruction for pedestrians of traffic on the street. The plaintiff further asserted that Shamrock's sign, which advised that the sidewalk was closed and that the sidewalk on the other side of the street should be used, should also have advised pedestrians that the dumpster created a blind spot and that the street should be crossed at the corner. Further, the plaintiff contended that Shamrock should have placed "fences or buffers around [the dumpster] as is customarily placed around such dumpsters," contending that such a "buffer" would have "eliminated that blind spot had it been properly placed at that area of the construction site."

The issue thus framed is whether the sidewalk condition, created by Shamrock's allegedly insufficient posted warnings and the placement of the large curbside dumpster, produced a vision obstruction for pedestrians crossing the street at that location that was unreasonably dangerous, and, if so, whether Shamrock owed a duty to place additional warnings on its signage and/or to construct a buffer zone that would mitigate against any vision obstruction created.

As we stated in *Christy v. McCalla,* 11–0366 (La. 2011), 79 So. 3d 293, Louisiana courts have adopted a duty-risk analysis in determining whether liability exists under the facts of a particular case. Under this analysis, a plaintiff must prove five separate elements: (1) the defendant had a duty to conform his or her conduct to a specific standard of care; (2) the defendant failed to conform his or her conduct to the appropriate standard of care; (3) the defendant's substandard conduct was a cause-in-fact of the plaintiff's injuries; (4) the defendant's substandard conduct was a legal cause of the plaintiff's injuries; and (5) actual damages. *Christy v. McCalla,* 79 So. 3d at 299 (citing *Pinsonneault v. Merchants & Farmers Bank & Trust Company,* 01–2217 (La. 2002), 816 So .2d 270, 275–76).

The threshold issue in any negligence action is whether the defendant owed the plaintiff a duty, and whether a duty is owed is a question of law. *Milbert v. Answering Bureau, Inc.,* 13–0022 (La. 2013), 120 So. 3d 678, 687–88.

In the instant case, by closing the sidewalk adjoining 622 Conti Street for its construction/renovation activities, which also extended into the abutting parking spaces where it placed its dumpster, Shamrock, acting on behalf of the building owner, effectively assumed custody of the sidewalk and abutting parking spaces. Thus, LSA–C.C. art. 2317 and 2317.1 are relevant to this proceeding, and provide:

Art. 2317. Acts of others and of things in custody

We are responsible, not only for the damage occasioned by our own act, but for that which is caused by the act of persons for whom we are answerable, or of the things which we have in our custody. This, however, is to be understood with the following modifications.

Art. 2317.1. Damage caused by ruin, vice, or defect in things

The owner or custodian of a thing is answerable for damage occasioned by its ruin, vice, or defect, only upon a showing that he knew or, in the exercise of reasonable care, should have known of the ruin, vice, or defect which caused the damage, that the damage could have been prevented by the exercise of reasonable care, and that he failed to exercise such reasonable care. Nothing in this Article shall preclude the court from the application of the doctrine of res ipsa loquitur in an appropriate case.

The burden for tort liability arising from a defect in a public sidewalk is generally with the municipality, not the adjoining landowner, unless the abutting property owner negligently caused a defect in the sidewalk. *See Randall v. Feducia,* 507 So. 2d 1237, 1239 (La. 1987); *Arata v. Orleans Capitol Stores,* 219 La. 1045, 1058–60, 55 So. 2d 239, 244 (La. 1951); *Stern v. Davies,* 128 La. 182, 54 So. 712 (La. 1911). Notwithstanding, a pedestrian has a duty to see that which should be seen and is bound to observe his course to see if his pathway is clear. *Hutchinson v. Knights of Columbus, Council No. 5747,* 03–1533 (La. 2004), 866 So. 2d 228, 234; *Williams v. Leonard Chabert Medical Center,* 98–1029 (La.App. 1 Cir. 1999), 744 So. 2d 206, 211, *writ denied,* 00–0011 (La. 2000), 754 So. 2d 974.

When evaluating the duty owed relative to a sidewalk condition, the facts and surrounding circumstances of each case control and the test applied requires the consideration of whether the sidewalk was maintained in a reasonably safe condition for persons exercising ordinary care and prudence. Courts have adopted a risk-utility balancing test to determine whether such a condition is unreasonably dangerous, wherein the trier of fact balances the gravity and the risk of harm against the individual and societal utility and the cost and feasibility of repair. *See Chambers v. Village of Moreauville,* 11–0898 (La. 2012), 85 So. 3d 593, 597–98.

This court has synthesized the risk-utility balancing test to a consideration of four pertinent factors: (1) the utility of the complained-of condition; (2) the likelihood and magnitude of harm, including the obviousness and apparentness of the condition; (3) the cost of preventing the harm; and (4) the nature of the plaintiff's activities in terms of social utility or whether the activities were dangerous by nature. *Broussard v. State ex rel. Office of State Buildings,* 12–1238 (La. 2013), 113 So. 3d 175, 184; *Dauzat v. Curnest Guillot Logging, Inc.,* 08–0528 (La. 2008), 995 So. 2d 1184, 1186–87 (per curiam); *Hutchinson v. Knights of Columbus, Council No. 5747,* 03–1533 (La. 2004), 866 So. 2d 228, 235; *Pitre v. Louisiana Tech University,* 95–1466 (La. 1996), 673 So. 2d 585, 591–93.

Regarding the first prong of this test, the utility of the defendant's activities in this case is not disputed. Conducting repairs and renovations to aging French Quarter buildings is not only desirable but necessary.

The second prong of this risk-utility inquiry focuses on whether the allegedly dangerous or defective condition was obvious and apparent. Under Louisiana law, a defendant generally does not have a duty to protect against that which is obvious and apparent. In order for an alleged hazard to be considered obvious and apparent, this court has consistently stated the hazard should be one that is open and obvious to everyone who may potentially encounter it. *Broussard v. State ex rel. Office of State Buildings,* 113 So. 3d at 184; *Hutchinson v. Knights of Columbus, Council No. 5747,* 866 So. 2d at 234.

* * * * *

344

In accordance with the law and jurisprudence cited hereinabove, Shamrock, having assumed custody of the sidewalk and abutting parking spaces outside of 622 Conti Street during the pertinent time period, would have been liable for any unreasonably dangerous condition it created. However, the evidence presented on motion for summary judgment established that any vision obstruction, ②caused by the dumpster, to a pedestrian crossing Conti Street at that mid-block location was obvious and apparent, and reasonably safe for persons exercising ordinary care and prudence. Moreover, because the size of the dumpster was comparable to a pick-up truck, this particular situation was of the type any pedestrian might encounter on a regular basis. Thus, we conclude that Shamrock had no duty to warn of the obstruction presented to pedestrians by its pick-up-truck-sized dumpster, a large inanimate object visible to all.

Once Shamrock demonstrated that the plaintiff would be unable to bear his burden to prove an essential element of his negligence action, that a duty was owed by Shamrock to him, then the burden shifted to the plaintiff to demonstrate that he would be able to meet the burden at trial. *See Schultz v. Guoth,* 57 So. 3d at 1006. Yet the plaintiff failed to produce any affidavit, deposition, or other evidence admissible on motion for summary judgment to show that Shamrock did have a duty to warn pedestrians of the obstruction or take extra measures to aid pedestrians to see around the obstruction.[1]

* * * * *

Conclusion

In this case, Shamrock met its burden of producing evidence, on motion for summary judgment, to point out the lack of factual support for an essential element in the plaintiff's case, demonstrating that because the condition complained of by the plaintiff was obvious and apparent and was reasonably safe for pedestrians exercising ordinary care and prudence, it had no duty to extend additional warnings to pedestrians or to create a buffer zone around its dumpster. The burden then shifted to the plaintiff to come forward with evidence (by affidavit, deposition, discovery response, or other form sanctioned by LSA–C.C.P. arts. 966 and 967) to demonstrate that he would be able to meet his burden at trial to show a duty on the party of Shamrock. The plaintiff failed to meet this burden; therefore, the district court erred in failing to grant summary judgment in Shamrock's favor.

Decree

Accordingly, the judgment of the district court is reversed, and summary judgment is hereby entered in favor of Shamrock Construction Co., Inc., dismissing this defendant from this action, with prejudice. We remand this matter to the district court for further proceedings consistent with the foregoing.

REVERSED; JUDGMENT RENDERED; REMANDED.

JOHNSON, Chief Justice, dissents.

GUIDRY, Justice, concurs and assigns reasons.

NOTES

1. How does the *Bufkin* court distinguish *Broussard*? (Hint: This is a trick question.)

  → could have easily said "no breach of duty" bc doesnt matter for MSJ.

---
[1] Subject to a trial court's *Daubert–Foret* review, expert opinion evidence, in the form prescribed by LSA–C.C.P. arts. 966(B) and 967, may be considered on motion for summary judgment. *See Independent Fire Insurance Company v. Sunbeam Corporation,* 99–2181 (La. 2000), 755 So. 2d 226, 231–36. *See also Daubert v. Merrell Dow Pharmaceuticals, Inc.,* 509 U.S. 579, 113 S.Ct. 2786, 125 L.Ed.2d 469 (1993), and *State v. Foret,* 628 So. 2d 1116 (La. 1993).

2.   Four months after *Bufkin*, the Louisiana Supreme Court visited the open and obvious doctrine once again in *Allen v. Lockwood*, 156 So. 3d 650 (La. 2015).

ALLEN
v.
LOCKWOOD
156 So. 3d 650 (La. 2015)

Opinion

PER CURIAM.

The narrow issue presented in this writ is whether defendants are entitled to summary judgment when plaintiff is unable to produce any evidence supporting her contention their parking lot was unreasonably dangerous. We granted this writ not only to reverse the district court's denial of summary judgment, but also to provide much needed guidance to both the practitioners and the Judiciary of this State on the proper interpretation and application of our holding in *Broussard v. State Ex Rel. Office of State Buildings*, 12–1238 (La. 2013), 113 So. 3d 175, when addressing motions for summary judgment on the issue of whether an alleged defect presents an unreasonable risk of harm.

Facts and Procedural History

This matter arises from an accident, which took place in the parking area of the Wesley Chapel United Methodist Church. The church sits in a small patch of partially cleared woods in a rural area of St. Helena Parish, off Louisiana Highway 448. Congregants attending services at the church typically pull in among the trees and unpaved grassy areas on the church grounds to park their vehicles. The accident occurred when an elderly church member, Hattie Lockwood, entered her vehicle following services. Ms. Lockwood reversed her car at a high rate of speed, striking plaintiff as she was walking.

As a result of the accident, plaintiff filed suit against several defendants, including Wesley Chapel United Methodist Church and its insurer, GuideOne Specialty Mutual Insurance Company (hereinafter referred to collectively as the "church defendants"). With regard to the church defendants, plaintiff alleged they were responsible for all or part of the accident based on various defects in the premises, including defective design of the parking area, improper markings in the parking lot, and improper safety barriers and/or improper safety measures.

The church defendants filed a motion for summary judgment, arguing plaintiff was unable to establish the accident resulted from any negligence in the design or maintenance of the parking area. In support, they relied on plaintiff's deposition, in which she admitted she was unable to say what the church did wrong to cause the accident. Plaintiff was asked, "[c]an you tell me what it was factually that you feel like the Wesley Chapel did wrong that caused this accident?" Plaintiff replied, "[n]ot really." The church defendants also introduced an affidavit from Mack Cornet, a member of the church's congregation for fifty-one years. Mr. Cornet averred the grassy areas surrounding the church were routinely used by congregants to park. According to Mr. Cornet, "on no occasion other than this one or since has there ever been any accidents or issues with congregants parking in such a fashion." Finally, the church defendants introduced photographs showing the parking area.

Plaintiff opposed the motion, arguing genuine issues of material fact as to the cause of the accident exist. However, plaintiff did not support her opposition with any evidence.

After a hearing, the district court denied the motion for summary judgment, explaining:

Well, quite frankly, I think that both sides could have done a wee bit better job on summary judgment. Telling me what the outlining duties are. I suspect that as a matter of general contracting law, that there is some kind of duty to have a parking lot, even in the absence of building codes. I don't know what the code is here in St.

346

Helena Parish, but I think that the allegation of obstacles in the parking lot and the fact that the parking lot either wasn't laid out at all or was half hazardly laid out, is some evidence of negligence. So, for that reason, I'm going to deny your motion. But, it's thin. I don't mind telling you, it's thin.

The court of appeal denied defendants' application for supervisory writs, stating:

> Whether a defect presents an unreasonable risk of harm must be determined in light of facts and circumstances of each particular case. The supreme court has held that the question of whether a defect presents an unreasonable risk of harm is a mixed question of law and fact and, accordingly, should be determined by the fact-finder. *Broussard v. State Ex Rel. Office of State Buildings*, 2012–1238 (La. 2013), 113 So. 3d 175, 183.

Allen v. Lockwood, 14–0518 (La.App. 1 Cir. 2014). Judge Welch dissented, reasoning: "There is no way a rational trier of fact could find that a rural church in Greensburg, Louisiana, that has a cleared wooded area for a parking lot, was in any way negligent or a cause in fact of the accident sued upon." Based on the evidence presented or lack thereof, we agree.

We first note the Court of Appeal misinterpreted our holding in *Broussard* by concluding "[t]he supreme court has held that the question of whether a defect presents an unreasonable risk of harm is a mixed question of law and fact and, accordingly, should be determined by the fact-finder," which would preclude summary judgment on these issues. In *Broussard*, which involved *a full jury trial, not a motion for summary judgment*, we held the determination of whether a defect constituted an unreasonable risk of harm was a question for the trier of fact:

> In order to avoid further overlap between the jury's role as fact-finder and the judge's role as lawgiver, we find the analytic framework for evaluating an unreasonable risk of harm is properly classified as a determination of whether a defendant breached a duty owed, rather than a determination of whether a duty is owed *ab initio*. It is axiomatic that the issue of whether a duty is owed is a question of law, and the issue of whether a defendant has breached a duty owed is a question of fact. *E.g., Brewer v. J.B. Hunt Transp., Inc.*, 09–1408, p. 14 (La. 2010), 35 So. 3d 230, 240 (citing *Mundy v. Dep't of Health and Human Res.*, 620 So. 2d 811, 813 (La. 1993)). The judge decides the former, and the fact-finder—judge or jury—decides the latter.

Broussard, 12–1238 at pp. 11–12, 113 So. 3d at 185.

Notably, *Broussard* was a three-day jury trial involving a fact-intensive determination as to whether the defect posed an unreasonable risk of harm or constituted an open and obvious defect. The jury returned a verdict in favor of Broussard. The First Circuit Court of Appeal reversed on grounds of manifest error because it found the defect was open and obvious. This Court reversed finding no manifest error in the jury's determination. We resolved the issue under the risk-utility balancing test. Our comments under this discussion clearly pertained to cases that were tried either by judge or jury. *Broussard* did not involve summary judgment practice nor did our discussion infer that issues of this nature must be determined by a trial. Any reading of *Broussard* interpreting it as a limit on summary judgment practice involving issues of unreasonable risk of harm is a misinterpretation of the *Broussard* case.

In another recent case, *Bufkin v. Felipe's Louisiana, LLC*, 14–0288, p. 12, n. 3 (La. 2014), ____ So. 3d ____, 2014 WL 5394087, which involved the issue of whether a construction dumpster was open and obvious or posed an unreasonable risk of harm, we found defendants were entitled to summary judgment as a matter of law. In *Bufkin*, we clarified our holding in *Broussard*, stating "[*Broussard*] should not be construed as precluding summary judgment when no legal duty is owed because the condition encountered is obvious and apparent to all and not unreasonably dangerous." Further we explained that once a defendant points out a lack of factual support for an essential element in the plaintiff's case, the burden then shifts to the plaintiff to come forward with evidence (by affidavit, deposition, discovery response, or other form sanctioned by La.Code Civ. P. arts. 966 and 967) to demonstrate that he or she would be able to meet his or her burden at trial. As *Bufkin* demonstrated, "our jurisprudence does not preclude the granting of a motion for summary judgment in cases where the plaintiff is unable to produce factual support for his or her claim that a complained-of condition or things is unreasonably dangerous." *Bufkin,* ____ So. 3d at ____ – ____, 2014 WL 5394087, at pp. *7–8 (Guidry, J., concurring); *see also Reagan v. Recreation and Park Com'n for Parish of East Baton Rouge,* 13–2761 (La. 2014), 135 So. 3d 1175 (Guidry, J., dissenting in writ denial). Rather, in such a procedural posture, the court's obligation is to decide "if there [is] a genuine issue of material fact as to whether the [complained-of condition or thing] created an unreasonable risk of harm...." *Broussard,* 12–1238 at p. 9, n. 5, 113 So. 3d at 184, n. 5.

Turning to the instant case, the church defendants produced evidence, through affidavits, depositions, and photographs, that the parking area had been used by congregants for decades without incident and the complained-of condition—the unpaved grassy parking area—was obvious and apparent to anyone who may potentially encounter it. Plaintiff then failed to produce *any* evidence to rebut their evidence or demonstrate how the alleged defects caused the accident. Moreover, she could not even say what the church defendants did to cause the accident. Therefore, as there is no genuine issue as to whether the parking area was unreasonably dangerous, the church defendants are entitled summary judgment in their favor as a matter of law.

Accordingly, the writ is granted. The judgment of the district court is reversed. Summary judgment is granted in favor of Wesley Chapel United Methodist Church and GuideOne Specialty Mutual Insurance Company, dismissing plaintiff's claims against them with prejudice.

NOTES

1.   Are you satisfied with the distinction between *Broussard* and *Bufkin/Allen*?

2.   Is the open and obvious nature of the defect considered as part of the duty element or as part of the breach element?

3.   Other jurisdictions have struggled with the open and obvious doctrine reaching varied results. Several jurisdictions distinguish a duty to warn of a defect from a duty to remedy a defect, finding that the "open and obvious" nature of the defect is a defense to the former, but merely a non-dispositive factor in the determination of the unreasonable nature of the risk for the latter. *See, e.g., Kentucky River Medical Center v. McIntosh,* 319 S.W.3d 385 (Ken. 2010); *Donohue v. San Francisco Housing Authority,* 16 Cal.App.4th 658, 665 (1993); *City of Winder v. Girone,* 462 S.E.2d 704 (Ga. 1995). Similarly, several jurisdictions have adopted the approach of §343(A) of the Second Restatement which provides that "[a] possessor of land is not liable to his invitees for physical harm caused to them by any activity or condition on the land whose danger is known or obvious to them, unless the possessor should anticipate the harm despite such knowledge or obviousness." *Wilmington Country Club v. Cowee,* 747 A.2d 1087 (Del. 2000); *Coffin v. Lariat Associates,* 766 A.2d 1018 (Me. 2001) (citing *Williams v. Boise Cascade Corp.,* 507 A.2d 576, 577 (Me.1986) (citing the Restatement (Second) of Torts § 343A(1) (1965))). Finally, it is noteworthy that , if there is any discernable trend, jurisdictions tend to be abandoning the "open and obvious" defense in lieu of an approach that treats the open and obvious nature of the defect as either a factor in determining duty or breach or as a fact that goes to comparative fault. *Cummings v. Prater,* 95 Ariz. 20, 27, 386 P.2d 27, 31 (1963); *Gargano v. Azpiri,* 955 A.2d 593 (2008). For example, Texas has "expressly abolished a 'no-duty' doctrine previously applicable to open and obvious dangers known to the invitee. Instead, a plaintiff's knowledge of a dangerous condition is relevant to determining his comparative negligence but does not operate as a complete bar to recovery as a matter of law by relieving the defendant of its duty to reduce or eliminate the unreasonable risk of harm." *Del Lago Partners, Inc. v. Smith,* 307 S.W.3d 762 (Tx. 2010) (citing *Parker v. Highland Park, Inc.,* 565 S.W.2d 512, 516–17 (Tex. 1978)).

However, there are states that continue to treat the open and obvious nature of the hazard as a complete defense, usually treating the issue as part of the duty element. For example, the Ohio Supreme Court recently ruled that "[w]here a danger is open and obvious, a landowner owes no duty of care to individuals lawfully on the premises." *Lang v. Holly Hill Motel, Inc.*, 909 N.E.2d 120 (Oh. 2009). "'he owner or occupier may reasonably expect that persons entering the premises will discover open and obvious dangers and take appropriate measures to protect themselves. When a plaintiff is injured by an open and obvious danger, summary judgment is generally appropriate because the duty of care necessary to establish negligence does not exist as a matter of law." *Id.*

3.   Waiver

Restatement (Second) of Torts, Sec. 496B: Express Assumption Of Risk

A plaintiff who by contract or otherwise expressly agrees to accept a risk of harm arising from the defendant's negligent or reckless conduct cannot recover for such harm, unless the agreement is invalid as contrary to public policy.

WOLF

v.

FORD

335 Md. 525, 644 A.2d 522 (1994)

KARWACKI, J.

In this case we focus upon the enforceability of an exculpatory clause in an agreement between an investor and a securities investment firm. The clause at issue provides that the investment firm will not be liable for losses to the investor resulting from the firm's negligence, but only for those losses resulting from its gross negligence or wilful misconduct. Under the circumstances of the instant case, we shall enforce the exculpatory clause. Viewing the evidence and all inferences therefrom in a light most favorable to Elizabeth Wolf, the appellant, the following facts were established at trial.

* * * * *

I

Before this Court, Wolf argues that the exculpatory clause contained in the Discretionary Account Agreement is void as against public policy and that the case should therefore be remanded for a determination of the existence of simple negligence on the part of Ford or Legg Mason. We disagree.

The late Judge Charles E. Orth, Jr., writing for the Court of Special Appeals, discussed the validity of exculpatory clauses at length in *Winterstein v. Wilcom,* 16 Md.App. 130, 293 A.2d 821, *cert. denied,* 266 Md. 744 (1972). In the absence of legislation to the contrary, exculpatory clauses are generally valid, and the public policy of freedom of contract is best served by enforcing the provisions of the clause. *Id.* at 135, 293 A.2d at 824; 57A Am.Jur.2d, Negligence § 53, at 112 (1989). The rule has also been explained thus:

> "It is quite possible for the parties expressly to agree in advance that the defendant is under no obligation of care for the benefit of the plaintiff, and shall not be liable for the consequences of conduct which would otherwise be negligent. There is in the ordinary case no public policy which prevents the parties from contracting as they see fit...."

W. Page Keeton, et al., Prosser and Keeton on the Law of Torts, § 68, at 482 (5th ed. 1984). *See also* Comment (a), Restatement, Second, Contracts § 195 (1981) ("a party to a contract can ordinarily exempt himself from liability for harm caused by his failure to observe the standard of reasonable care imposed by the law of negligence").

There are circumstances, however, under which the public interest will not permit an exculpatory clause in a contract; these have often been grouped into three general exceptions to the rule. First, a party will not be permitted to excuse its liability for intentional harms or for the more extreme forms of negligence, i.e., reckless, wanton, or gross.... Second, the contract cannot be the product of grossly unequal bargaining power. "When one party is at such an obvious disadvantage in bargaining power that the effect of the contract is to put him at the mercy of the other's negligence, the agreement is void as against public policy."... Third, public policy will not permit exculpatory agreements in transactions affecting the public interest.... This last category includes the performance of a public service obligation, e.g., public utilities, common carriers, innkeepers, and public warehousemen. It also includes those transactions, not readily susceptible to definition or broad categorization, that are so important to the public good that an exculpatory clause would be "patently offensive," such that " 'the common sense of the entire community would ... pronounce it' invalid."... This standard is a strict one, in keeping with our general reluctance to invoke the nebulous public interest to disturb private contracts....

* * * * *

Because the concept of the "public interest" is amorphous, it is difficult to apply. Courts, therefore, have struggled to refine and narrow the definition in an attempt to make the concept more concrete. *Winterstein* referred to a six-factor test developed by the Supreme Court of California in *Tunkl v. Regents of the Univ. of Calif.,* 60 Cal.2d 92, 383 P.2d 441, 32 Cal.Rptr. 33 (1963) that was intended to determine which exculpatory agreements affect the "public interest" and which do not. *Winterstein* quoted the following passage from *Tunkl,* noting that it is to be used as a rough outline of that type of transaction in which exculpatory provisions will be held invalid:

> " 'Thus the attempted but invalid exemption involves a transaction which exhibits some or all of the following characteristics. It concerns a business of a type generally thought suitable for public regulation. The party seeking exculpation is engaged in performing a service of great importance to the public, which is often a matter of practical necessity for some members of the public. The party holds himself out as willing to perform this service for any member of the public who seeks it, or at least for any member coming within certain established standards. As a result of the essential nature of the service, in the economic setting of the transaction, the party invoking exculpation possesses a decisive advantage of bargaining strength against any member of the public who seeks his services. In exercising a superior bargaining power the party confronts the public with a standardized adhesion contract of exculpation, and makes no provision whereby a purchaser may pay additional reasonable fees and obtain protection against negligence. Finally, as a result of the transaction, the person or property of the purchaser is placed under the control of the seller, subject to the risk of carelessness by the seller or his agents.' "

Winterstein, 16 Md.App. at 137, 293 A.2d at 825, quoting *Tunkl,* 60 Cal.2d at 98-101, 383 P.2d at 445-46, 32 Cal.Rptr. at 37-38 (footnotes omitted).

* * * * *

Even though these cases have not found an activity that is sufficiently connected to the "public interest" so as to invalidate the exculpatory clause, we are concerned that the six-factor test of *Tunkl,* originally intended to be a rough outline in guiding a court's determination as to whether a given transaction affects the public interest, may become too rigid a measuring stick. Because of the fluid nature of the "public interest," strict reliance on the presence or absence of six fixed factors may be arbitrary. The *Tunkl* court itself recognized that the public interest does not--and cannot--lend itself easily to definition, because "the social forces that have led to such characterization [of the public interest] are volatile and dynamic. No definition of the concept of public interest can be contained within the four corners of a formula." *Tunkl,* 60 Cal.2d at 98, 383 P.2d at 444, 32 Cal.Rptr. at 36.

We expressly decline, therefore, to adopt the six-factor test set forth in *Tunkl* and relied upon, to varying degrees, by the Court of Special Appeals in the exculpatory clause cases mentioned above.

This is not to say that the factors listed cannot be considered by a court in determining whether a given transaction involves the public interest, but the six factors are not conclusive. The ultimate determination of what constitutes the public interest must be made considering the totality of the circumstances of any given case against the backdrop of current societal expectations.

II

Turning to the merits of the case *sub judice,* we perceive no reason why the exculpatory clause should not be enforced. None of the three exceptions to the general rule permitting exculpatory clauses is applicable here.

First, there has been no allegation of fraud or willful misconduct, and Wolf concedes that there is no evidence of gross negligence.... Second, contrary to Wolf's assertion, we do not believe that there was any disparate bargaining advantage. Wolf claims that the very fact that she was eighteen years old and an unsophisticated investor renders the relationship so lopsided as to impose an extraordinary duty upon Ford. We do not accept that notion. Although young, she had attained her legal majority at the time. She was not solicited by Legg Mason; rather, she initiated contact with Ford. Wolf was under no compulsion, economic or otherwise, to invest her money in the stock market with Legg Mason or any other securities investment firm....

Third, a stockbroker-client relationship is not one that so affects the public interest that we should disturb the parties' ability to contractually exempt a party from liability for negligence. Wolf argues that we should adopt the six-factor *Tunkl* test for defining the public interest, and that under that test, a stockbroker-client relationship is affected with public interest. We have stated above, however, that we do not adopt the six-factor test as conclusive, and we will not invalidate a private contract on grounds of public policy unless the clause at issue is patently offensive. This clause does not meet that test. Individuals who choose freely to invest their money in the stock market understand that there is some risk involved; such is the nature of the securities industry. If the parties to a contract determine that one party will bear the burden of the other party's simple negligence, they are entitled to do just that. This is particularly important where an account is accepted on a discretionary basis, as in the instant case, and the investor asks the broker to purchase stocks using the broker's best judgment. This is not a case in which an investment is made based upon a broker's misrepresentation.... Rather, the possibility of poor performance of the securities chosen is precisely the sort of harm that is within the contemplation of the parties at the time they entered the agreement. Because of the volatile nature of financial markets, what may appear to be negligence in the purchase of securities one year may eventually turn out to be a stroke of genius in following years, and vice versa. Thus, the allocation of risk of negligence between parties to a private contract is not patently offensive; rather, it is part and parcel of the freedom to contract in private matters.

* * * * *

We hold, therefore, that the exculpatory clause in the Discretionary Account Agreement between Wolf and Ford is valid and enforceable.

JUDGMENT AFFIRMED, WITH COSTS.

La. Civil Code Article 2004.   Clause that excludes or limits liability

(1) Any clause is null that, in advance, excludes or limits the liability of one party for intentional or gross fault that causes damage to the other party. → just pecuniary / prop damage. Not physical injury.

(2) Any clause is null that, in advance, excludes or limits the liability of one party for causing physical injury to the other party.

RAMIREZ → K clause void that
v.   says you wont
FAIR GROUNDS CORPORATION sue if injured
575 So. 2d 811 (La. 1991)

DENNIS, J.

In this case plaintiff seeks to recover damages for severe permanently disabling physical injuries he suffered when he fell from a loft in a building owned by defendant. Defendant moved for summary judgment on the basis of clauses in a previously entered into stall-space agreement with plaintiff which, in advance, released defendant from any and all liability for damages suffered by plaintiff. The trial court granted defendant's motion for summary judgment. The court of appeal affirmed. *Ramirez v. Fair Grounds Corporation*, 563 So. 2d 570 (La.App. 4 Cir. 1990). We granted Ramirez's writ application. 567 So. 2d 1111 La.1990). We reverse, deciding that the clauses in the agreement are null because "[a]ny clause is null that, in advance, excludes or limits the liability of one party for causing physical injury to the other party." La. Civ. Code art. 2004.

On February 10, 1985, Henry Ramirez, a licensed racehorse trainer with over 25 years of experience, was injured when he fell from a 12-foot high loft in a stall which is part of a stable owned by the Fair Grounds Corporation (hereinafter "Fair Grounds"). *Ramirez* filed suit against the Fair Grounds alleging that he suffered extensive damage to both feet and legs and that the cause of the fall was the lack of hand rails or banisters on the loft, in violation of applicable building codes, for which defendant is strictly liable pursuant to La. Civ. Code arts. 2317 and 2322.

On September 30, 1984, approximately 4 months before the accident, *Ramirez* signed an application for stall space and use of the Fair Ground facilities. This application acts as a license or permit to use the stall space and facilities free of charge. The clauses in paragraphs 8 and 9 of the application provide as follows:

> 8.   It is agreed that neither Fair Grounds Corp., nor any of its officers or agents shall be in any way liable for any loss, damage, death or injury of any kind to any person, animal, vehicle or other property arising out of or connected with the presence on or use of Fair Grounds premises by said Applicant and all employees, agents, jockeys, members of the families, property and animals of said Applicant, whether such injury, loss, death or damage is claimed to be caused by the condition of said premises or any act or negligence or omissions to act of Fair Grounds or of its agents or servants or from any cause, and the undersigned Applicant hereby specifically assumes all such risks fully and completely.

> 9.   The undersigned Applicant hereby agrees to indemnify and save harmless Fair Grounds Corp., and its respective officers, employees and agents from any and all liabilities, claims and demands for damages, injuries, deaths, or losses or costs or expenses of any kind resulting from or arising out of or claimed to result from or arise out of the presence on or use of said premises at Fair Grounds by said Applicant and all employees, agents, jockeys, members of the families, property and animals of Applicant and Applicant agrees to defend any claim or suit which may arise from the foregoing and to pay all attorneys fees and costs thereof.

Fair Grounds filed a motion for summary judgment based on the above quoted terms of the contract. The trial court granted the motion for summary judgment and dismissed Ramirez's suit. The court of appeal affirmed, concluding that Ramirez's agreement to release the Fair Grounds from any and all liability barred his recovery and that the agreement was not prohibited by Article 2004. *Ramirez v. Fair Grounds Corporation*, 563 So. 2d 570 (La.App. 4 Cir. 1990).

(The court reproduced C.C. Art. 2004, *supra*.)

352

The clauses in the application are null because they, in advance, exclude the liability of Fair Grounds for causing physical injury to Ramirez. *Id.*

Fair Grounds acknowledges in its brief that "if one takes this article at face value, it would appear that it does render the indemnity and hold harmless clause null." But defendant argues that the words of the statute are qualified by the comments thereunder. Defendant specifically relies on comment (a) which states that Article 2004 "does not change the law" and comment (e) which states that the article "does not govern 'indemnity' clauses, 'hold harmless' agreements, or other agreements where parties allocate between themselves the risk of potential liability towards third persons."

We need not determine whether the comments were intended to convey a meaning contrary to the plain words of the statute. Article 2004 of the Louisiana Civil Code was enacted by Louisiana Act 331 of 1984. Section 9 of Act 331 specifically provides that "[t]he headings and comments in this Act are not part of the law and are not enacted into law by virtue of their inclusion in this Act." 1984 La. Acts No. 331, § 9. Consequently, even if the comments were to be interpreted so as to express a meaning different from the statute, they have no legislative effect on the statute because they are not part of the law.

Furthermore, because the statute is clear and unambiguous with respect to the issue in this case, and its application does not lead to absurd consequences, it shall be applied as written and no further interpretation may be made of it in search of the intent of the legislature. La. Civ. Code art. 9. Accordingly, there is no justification for our considering the comments even as persuasive sources or interpretive aids in the present case.

For the reasons assigned, the judgment of the court of appeal is reversed, defendant's motion for summary judgment is denied, and the case is remanded to the trial court for further proceedings consistent with this opinion.

REVERSED and **REMANDED** to the trial court.

4.   Mitigation   → D can't say P failed to mitigate damages by not wearing seatbeat...

a.   Pre-Accident Conduct

La. R.S. 32:295.1   Safety belt use

A. (1) Each driver of a passenger car, van, or truck having a gross weight of six thousand pounds or less, commonly referred to as a pickup truck, in this state shall have a safety belt properly fastened about his or her body at all times when the vehicle is in forward motion. The provisions of this Section shall not apply to those cars, vans, or pickups manufactured prior to January 1, 1981.

B. Except as provided by R.S. 32:295 for children under the age of thirteen or as otherwise provided by law, each occupant of a passenger car, van, or truck having a gross weight of ten thousand pounds or less, commonly referred to as a pickup truck, in this state shall have a safety belt properly fastened about his or her body at all times when the vehicle is in forward motion, if a belt for his seating space has been provided by the manufacturer.

* * * * *

E. In any action to recover damages arising out of the ownership, common maintenance, or operation of a motor vehicle, failure to wear a safety belt in violation of this Section shall not be considered evidence of comparative negligence. Failure to wear a safety belt in violation of this Section shall not be admitted to mitigate damages.

NOTES

1.   La. R.S. 32:190 previously allowed motorcycle, motor driven cycle, and motorized bicycle operators and riders age eighteen or older the choice of not wearing a safety helmet provided they were insured by a health insurance policy with at least ten thousand dollars of medical benefits for bodily injuries. In 2004, the Louisiana legislature amended the statute to require all operators and riders of these conveyances to wear a safety helmet meeting certain statutory and administrative specifications. Can the failure to wear a safety helmet in violation of this statute be considered as evidence of either comparative negligence or mitigation of damages?

2.   *Young v. Joy*, 30 So. 3d 1116 (La.App. 3 Cir. 2010). Evidence of a plaintiff's serious and long-term pre-accident substance abuse is relevant to her claims of pain after the accident.

3.   Act 166 of 2009 amended La. R.S. 32:295.1 to provide that generally (with some statutory exceptions) each occupant of a passenger car, truck, or pickup truck must have a safety belt properly fastened at all times that the vehicle is in motion. *See* paragraph B, *supra*.

b.   Post-Accident Conduct

JACOBS
v.
NEW ORLEANS PUBLIC SERVICE, INC.
432 So. 2d 843 (La. 1983)

DENNIS, J.

* * * * *

The trial court rejected a claim for loss of future earnings because it found plaintiff had unreasonably failed to undertake continued psychotherapy to mitigate her emotional disorder. The court of appeal reversed this finding on appeal and amended the judgment to add $158,471 for plaintiff's lost future earnings. This amendment forms the basis of defendant's second assignment of error.

Our law seeks to fully repair injuries which arise from a legal wrong. However, an accident victim has a duty to exercise reasonable diligence and ordinary care to minimize his damages after the injury has been inflicted.... He need not make extraordinary or impractical efforts, but he must undertake those which would be pursued by a man of ordinary prudence under the circumstances.... Thus, his recovery will not be limited because of a refusal to undergo medical treatment that holds little promise for successful recovery.... The expense and inconvenience of treatment are also proper considerations in determining the reasonableness of a person's refusal to submit to treatment.... Moreover, an unreasonable refusal of medical treatment which does not aggravate his injury will not restrict a victim's recovery.... The tortfeasor has the burden of showing both the unreasonableness of the victim's refusal of treatment and the consequent aggravation of the injury....

* * * * *

NOTE

Alexander v. Tate, 30 So. 3d 1122 (La.App. 3 Cir. 2010). Evidence of plaintiff's settlement of a subsequent accident and the amount of that settlement are relevant to proving that plaintiff was not seriously injured in that subsequent accident. *But see Deville v. Frey*, 63 So. 3d 435 (La.App. 3 Cir. 2011), *writ denied*, 69 So. 3d 1158 (La. 2011) (reversible error to admit settlement per Code Evid. Art. 413).

B. **Stale Claims**

[handwritten margin note: if you wait too long, you can lose asserting your claim. BUT La doesn't apply Laches... La applies Rx period, which depends on type of claim...]

1. **Laches and Statutes of Limitations**

Unfairness to the potential defendant, and the judicial inefficiency in resolving cases on the basis of stale evidence, dictates that a party must pursue a claim within a reasonable time. If there is no state statute barring a claim because it was not pursued timely, the equitable doctrine of laches applies. Under laches a claim is barred if the plaintiff failed to pursue the remedy judicially within a reasonable time, and the defendant was prejudiced thereby.

In nearly every jurisdiction, however, the legislature has substituted a statutory time bar. At common law, this is called a statute of limitations; in the civil law, it is a prescriptive statute. This subsection focuses upon the Louisiana prescriptive statutes for tort claims. Subsection b introduces one to the Louisiana statutory scheme governing prescription. Because Louisiana generally has a relatively "short" statute of limitations on tort claims, much jurisprudence has developed on the issues of when a time period provided by the statute commences and when, after the statute has begun to run, it is "tolled," i.e., suspended. The important cases on this issue are discussed in subsection c.

Ordinarily, a statute of limitations (prescriptive statute) begins to run when the damage is done. Legislatures have determined that in some cases this may not be the best societal policy, and have provided in those cases that the claim is barred after the passage of a certain period of time after the wrongful act is performed, even though the damage occurs later. Louisiana's foray into this field, called "statutes of repose" at common law and "peremption" at civil law, are discussed in subsection d.

The following material first presents the language of the relevant code articles. Second, cases discussing potential exceptions to prescription are presented; followed by a discussion of peremption.

2. **General Statutes of Limitations (Prescriptive Statutes)**

La. Civil Code Article 3492. **Delictual actions** *(tort)*

Delictual actions are subject to a liberative prescription of one year. This prescription commences to run from the day injury or damage is sustained. It does not run against minors or interdicts in actions involving permanent disability and brought pursuant to the Louisiana Products Liability Act or state law governing product liability actions in effect at the time of the injury or damage. *[handwritten margin note: ONE YEAR]* *[handwritten note: → extremely narrow exception.]*

La. Civil Code Article 3493.1 **Delictual actions; two-year prescription; criminal act** *[handwritten note: → La state criminal code]*

Delictual actions which arise due to damages sustained as a result of an act defined as a crime of violence under Chapter 1 of Title 14 of the Louisiana Revised Statutes of 1950 are subject to a liberative prescription of two years. This prescription commences to run from the day injury or damage is sustained.

La. Civil Code Article 3496.1. **Action against a person for abuse of a minor** *[handwritten: X]*

An action against a person for abuse of a minor, or for physical abuse of a minor resulting in permanent impairment or permanent physical injury or scarring, is subject to a liberative prescriptive period of three years. This prescription commences to run from the day the minor attains majority, and this prescription, for all purposes, shall be suspended until the minor reaches the age of majority. This prescriptive period shall be subject to any exception of peremption provided by law.

La. R.S. 9:2800.9. **Action against a person for abuse of a minor** *[handwritten: X]*

A. An action against a person for sexual abuse of a minor, or for physical abuse of a minor resulting in permanent impairment or permanent physical injury or scarring, is subject to a liberative prescriptive period of ten years. This prescription commences to run from the day the minor attains majority, and this prescription for all purposes shall be suspended until the minor reaches the age of majority. Abuse has the same meaning as provided in Louisiana Children's Code Article 603. This prescriptive period shall be subject to any exception of peremption provided by law.

B. Every plaintiff twenty-one years of age or older at the time the action is filed shall file certificates of merit executed by the attorney for the plaintiff and by a licensed mental health practitioner selected by the plaintiff declaring, respectively, as follows:

(1) That the attorney has reviewed the facts of the case, that the attorney has consulted with at least one licensed mental health practitioner who is licensed to practice and practices in this state and who the attorney reasonably believes is knowledgeable of the relevant facts and issues involved in the particular action, and that the attorney has concluded on the basis of that review and consultation that there is reasonable and meritorious cause for the filing of the petition. The person consulted may not be a party to the litigation.

(2) That the mental health practitioner consulted is licensed to practice and practices in this state and is not a party to the action, has interviewed the plaintiff and is knowledgeable of the relevant facts and issues involved in the particular action, and has concluded, on the basis of his knowledge of the facts and issues, that in his professional opinion there is a reasonable basis to believe that the plaintiff has been subject to criminal sexual activity during their childhood as defined in this Article.

(3) That the attorney was unable to obtain the consultation required by Subparagraph (1) because a statute of limitations would impair the action and that the certificates required by Subparagraphs (1) and (2) could not be obtained before the impairment of the action. If a certificate is executed pursuant to this Subparagraph, the certificates required by Subparagraph (1) and (2) shall be filed within sixty days after filing the petition.

C. Where certificates are required pursuant to Paragraph B of this Article, separate certificates shall be filed for each defendant named in the complaint.

D. A petition filed pursuant to paragraph B of this Article may not name the defendant or defendants until the court has reviewed the certificates of merit filed and has determined, in camera, based solely on those certificates of merit, that there is reasonable and meritorious cause for filing of the action. At that time, the petition may be amended to name the defendant or defendants. The duty to give notice to the defendant or defendants shall not attach until that time.

E. A violation of paragraph B of this Article may constitute unprofessional conduct and may be the grounds for discipline against the attorney.

La. Civil Code Article 3456.   Computation of time by years

If a prescriptive period consists of one or more years, prescription accrues upon the expiration of the day of the last year that corresponds with the date of the commencement of prescription.

3.   Suspension and Interruption of Prescription

La. Civil Code Article 3462.   Interruption by filing of suit or by service or process

Prescription is interrupted when the owner commences action against the possessor, or when the obligee commences action against the obligor, in a court of competent jurisdiction and venue. If action is commenced in an incompetent court, or in an improper venue, prescription is interrupted only as to a defendant served by process within the prescriptive period.

La. Civil Code Article 3463. **Duration of interruption; abandonment or discontinuance of suit**

An interruption of prescription resulting from the filing of a suit in a competent court and in the proper venue or from service of process within the prescriptive period continues as long as the suit is pending. Interruption is considered never to have occurred if the plaintiff abandons, voluntarily dismisses, or fails to prosecute the suit at the trial.

NOTE

The most common type of abandonment is the failure of a party to take a "step" in the prosecution or defense of a pending lawsuit for a period of three years. C.C.P. Art. 561. Dismissal for abandonment is without prejudice, i.e., the plaintiff is not precluded through res judicata from refiling the suit. However, since the suit was abandoned, it is considered as not having been filed, and the successor suit will nearly always be barred by the statute of limitations, i.e., prescribed.

La. Civil Code Article 3464. **Interruption by acknowledgment**

Prescription is interrupted when one acknowledges the right of the person against whom he had commenced to prescribe.

La. Civil Code Article 3468. **Incompetents**

Prescription runs against absentees and incompetents, including minors and interdicts, unless exception is established by legislation.

La. Civil Code Article 3469. **Suspension of prescription**

Prescription is suspended as between: the spouses during marriage, parents and children during minority, tutors and minors during tutorship, and curators and interdicts during interdiction.

La. Civil Code Article 3503. **Solidary obligors**

When prescription is interrupted against a solidary obligor, the interruption is effective against all solidary obligors and their successors.

When prescription is interrupted against a successor of a solidary obligor, the interruption is effective against other successors if the obligation is indivisible. If the obligation is divisible, the interruption is effective against other successors only for the portions for which they are bound.

La. Civil Code Article 2324. **Liability as solidary or joint and divisible obligation**

*(handwritten) → not as broad** as it seems...*

C. Interruption of prescription against one joint tortfeasor, whether the obligation is considered joint and divisible or solidary, is effective against all joint tortfeasors. Nothing in this Subsection shall be construed to affect in any manner the application of the provisions of R.S. 40:1299.41(G).

* * * * *

(handwritten) → played some role in fault, BUT not co-conspirators...

NOTE

There are many complex issues surrounding the prescriptive period. The following cases raise two of the important considerations: contra non valentem and the doctrine of "relation back."

CORSEY
v.
STATE DEPARTMENT OF CORRECTIONS
375 So. 2d 1319 (La. 1979)

TATE, J.

The plaintiff Corsey was a prisoner at the state penitentiary. He sues the state department of corrections for personal injuries sustained on June 18, 1972. He did not file suit so as to interrupt prescription until June 25, 1974.[1] Since this legal demand was made more than one year after the tortious injury was sustained, La.Civ.C. arts. 3536, 3537, his suit was dismissed as prescribed. 366 So. 2d 964 (La.App. 1 Cir. 1978).

We granted certiorari, 368 So. 2d 127 (February 23, 1979). We desired to consider whether prescription could run against the plaintiff (a prisoner within the total control of the defendant state agency) when, due solely to the defendant's negligence, the tort-caused physical and mental (brain) injuries to the plaintiff so mentally incapacitated him that he lacked any understanding of what had happened to him and of his possible legal remedies until July 1973, when he began to recover an awareness of the events and of his condition.[2]

For the reasons set forth more fully below, we hold that, under these facts, prescription did not begin to run against the plaintiff until July 1973. Therefore, his legal demand of June 1974 was timely. In so holding, we rely upon the principle that prescription does not run against a party who is unable to act (a principle often denoted by the maxim *contra non valentem agere nulla currit praescriptio*). The principle is especially applicable in the present instance, where the plaintiff's inability to act is due to the defendant's willful or negligent conduct.

I

The specific issue before us[3] is whether the year within which the plaintiff must bring his tort action for personal injuries negligently caused by the defendant, La.Civ.C. arts. 3536, 3537, is interrupted or suspended during the period in which, due to the defendant's negligent conduct, the plaintiff had incurred such mental incapacity as to be unable to assert a legal demand to recover for such injuries.

Article 3521 of our Civil Code provides, "Prescription runs against all persons, unless they are included in some exception established by Law (i.e., legislation)." (Italics ours.) Despite the express statutory provision, our Louisiana jurisprudence has recognized a limited exception where in fact and for good cause a plaintiff is unable to exercise his cause of action when it accrues. French jurisprudence (despite an identical provision in the French Civil Code) likewise recognizes this exception. Comment, The Scope of the Maxim Contra Non Valentem in Louisiana, 12 Tul.L.Rev. 244 (1938); Planiol, Civil Law Treatise, Volume 1, Section 2704-05, Volume 2, Section 678 (LSLI translation, 1959).

The exception is founded on the ancient civilian doctrine of Contra non valentem agere nulla currit praescriptio, predating and within the penumbras of modern civilian codes, and it has been

---

[1] Footnote omitted.

[2] The defendants stipulated, for purposes of determining this question of law with respect to prescription, that plaintiff was mentally incapacitated until July 1973, due to defendant's negligence. They have reserved the right to introduce evidence on the question of plaintiff's actual mental capacity during this time, should their exception of prescription be overruled.

[3] A factor in our decision, however, is that under the showing the plaintiff was in the custody of the defendant agency during the entire period prescription was suspended, so that no one else was aware of the plaintiff's cause of action or could assert it on his behalf.

recognized from Louisiana's earliest jurisprudence.[4] Comment, 12 Tul.L.Rev. 244, cited above; *Henson v. St. Paul Fire & Marine Ins. Co.*, 363 So. 2d 711 (La. 1978); *Hyman v. Hibernia Bank & Trust Co.*, 139 La. 411, 71 So. 598 (1916); *McKnight v. Calhoun*, 36 La.Ann. 408 (1884); Quierry's Ex'r & Faussier's Ex'rs, 4 Mart. (O.S.) 609 (1817).

II   *"contra non valentem" exceptions to presumption*

As the cited comment notes, 12 Tul.L.Rev. at 253-54, this court in *Reynolds v. Batson*, 11 La.Ann. 729, 730-31 (1856), authoritatively lays down the three categories of situations in which our early jurisprudence held that the principle *contra non valentem* applied so as to prevent the running of liberative prescription: (1) Where there was some legal cause which prevented the courts or their officers from taking cognizance of or acting on the plaintiff's action[5]; (2) Where there was some condition coupled with the contract or connected with the proceedings which prevented the creditor from suing or acting[6]; and (3) *Where the debtor himself has done some act effectually to prevent the creditor from availing himself of his cause of action.*[7]

Modern jurisprudence also recognizes a fourth type of situation where contra non valentem applies so that prescription does not run: Where the cause of action is not known or reasonably knowable by the plaintiff, even though his ignorance is not induced by the defendant. (This principle will not except the plaintiff's claim from the running of prescription if his ignorance is attributable to his own willfulness or neglect; that is, a plaintiff will be deemed to know what he could by reasonable diligence have learned. *Cartwright v. Chrysler Corporation*, 255 La. 597, 598, 232 So. 2d 285 (1970); *Sumerall v. St. Paul Fire & Marine Ins. Co.*, 366 So. 2d 213 (La.App. 2 Cir. 1978).)

* * * * *

This fourth or more modern situation, which has been judicially characterized as a *contra non valentem* exception to the running of prescription, is generically similar to instances provided by statute where prescription does not begin to run until the claimant has knowledge of his cause of action.[8] In these, the cause of action does not mature (so prescription does not begin to run) until it is known or at least knowable.

The fourth situation is thus generically somewhat distinguishable from the earlier three situations first recognized to justify exceptions to prescription on the basis of *contra non valentem*. In them (as in the present case, as we will show), the cause of action had accrued, but nevertheless the

---

[4] The cited Comment notes that, based on the Code article now found as Article 3521 of the 1870 Civil Code, this court overruled or ignored decisions recognizing the *contra non valentem* exception to prescription from 1867 until 1881, until these decisions were themselves overruled. See 12 Tul.L.Rev. at 250. The *contra non valentem* principle, although exceptional in nature, has been consistently recognized in Louisiana except during this interval.

[5] *See, e. g., Quierry's Ex'r v. Faussier's Ex'rs*, 4 Mart. (O.S.) 609 (1817).

[6] *See, e. g., Orleans Parish School Board v. Pittman Construction Co.*, 261 La. 665, 260 So. 2d 661 (1972); *Dalton v. Plumbers and Steamfitters Local Union No. 60*, 240 La. 246, 122 So. 2d 88 (1960).

[7] *See, e. g., Hyman v. Hibernia Bank & Trust Co.*, 139 La. 411, 71 So. 598 (1916). Ultimately, we will rest our decision on the last (above italicized) reason for application of *contra non valentem* to the present facts–that prescription cannot run against a plaintiff who is prevented by the debtor's conduct from knowing of or acting upon his cause of action.

[8] Our statutory law provides the same rule in certain explicit situations. For example, prescription runs in an action for damage to land, timber or property from "the date knowledge of such damage is received by the owner thereof." La.Civ.C. art. 3537. Medical malpractice actions must be brought within one year of "the alleged act, omission or neglect, or within one year from the date of discovery of the alleged act, omission or neglect." La.R.S. 9:5628. A disavowal of paternity suit "must be filed within one hundred eighty days after the husband learned or should have learned of the birth of the child;" La.Civ.C. art. 189 (1976).

plaintiff was prevented from enforcing it by some reason external to his own will--the courts closed by wartime conditions, some contract or administrative condition preventing his access to the courts, or some conduct of the defendant which prevented him from availing himself of his judicial remedy.

In concluding our general discussion of the application of *contra non valentem*, we should finally note that the Louisiana jurisprudence, as does the French,[9] distinguishes between personal disabilities of the plaintiff (which do *not* prevent prescription from running) and an inability to bring suit for some cause foreign to the person of the plaintiff (which does suspend its running).

Thus, a person whose ignorance of his cause of action or inability to assert it is the result of his own mental incapacity cannot claim the benefits of this rule unless he has been interdicted.[10] *Israel v. Smith*, 302 So. 2d 392 (La.App. 3 Cir. 1974), *cert. denied*, 303 So. 2d 183 (La. 1974);[11]*Buvens v. Buvens*, 286 So. 2d 144 (La.App. 3 Cir. 1973), *Lassere v. Lassere*, 255 So. 2d 794 (La.App. 4 Cir. 1972), *cert. denied*, 257 So. 2d 434 (La. 1972). *Perrodin v. Clement*, 254 So. 2d 704 (La.App. 3 Cir. 1971). *Cf., Vance v. Ellerbe*, 150 La. 388, 90 So. 735 (1922).

Likewise, a plaintiff cannot invoke *contra non valentem* to escape the running of prescription based merely upon his inability to attend to his affairs because of his personal illness, *Ayres v. New York Life Ins. Co.*, 219 La. 945, 54 So. 2d 409 (1951) at least when this illness arises independently of any fault on the part of the defendant.

III

In the present instance, we are not, strictly speaking, concerned with whether the plaintiff Corsey's cause of action had accrued or matured at the time of the incident, for it had: the damage was immediately discernible to a person of ordinary diligence and capacity. Nor are we concerned with his mental competency *per se*, since (as he was not interdicted) he is a person subject to having prescription run against his cause of action.

Here, however, unlike mere mental incompetency (which will not suspend prescription), the defendant's own tort has produced the plaintiff's mental and physical inability to file suit during the period of tort-caused incompetency. The values at issue are not similar to those which control in cases of mere mental incompetency; they are more analogous to those which permit invocation of *contra non valentem* to suspend prescription because the defendant has concealed information or has otherwise prevented the plaintiff from bringing the action within the prescriptive delay.

Due to the defendant's wrongful conduct, until July 1973 the plaintiff was unable because of the tort-caused mental incompetency to know he had a cause of action or to have the mental ability to pursue it. We hold that, consequently, prescription did not begin to run against the plaintiff (under the facts stipulated for purpose of the exception pleading prescription) until July, 1973.

---

[9] The Comment, cited above, at 12 Tul.L.Rev. 245 summarizes the French holdings: "(A) disability which is personal to the individual who is being prescribed against, such as feeblemindedness, prodigality, insanity which has not been established by interdiction, absence, or even ignorance of the cause of action, will not arrest the course of prescription. *However, if the ignorance of the creditor or owner is due to the fault of the adverse party, the latter is not permitted to avail himself of the prescription which has run."* (Italics ours.)

[10] If the plaintiff has been interdicted, however, he is not really invoking the jurisprudential exception, in being freed from the effects of prescription. Rather he is enjoying the protection of La.Civ.C. arts. 3522 and 3554 which provide that persons under interdiction cannot be prescribed against.

[11] This is the only case found in which a plaintiff made the claim that the plaintiff Corsey makes today--that the defendant's negligently injurious behavior left him mentally incapacitated to bring suit. The court of appeal rejected the proposed application of *contra non valentem*, citing various cases in which (unlike the present) the plaintiff's mental incapacity was totally unrelated to the actions of the defendant. This decision was relied upon by the First Circuit in upholding the defendants' exception of prescription in the action before us. 366 So. 2d 964, 966 (1978). The decision is overruled to the extent that it is inconsistent with the views we express today.

The fault or wrongful conduct of the defendant which prevents the plaintiff from suing timely is a traditional *contra non valentem* reason to except the plaintiff's claim from prescriptive extinguishment (see footnotes 7 and 11 above). We find this principle here applicable.

It is true that the usual case in which *contra non valentem* was applied on this ground has involved conduct of the defendant preventing the plaintiff's pursuit of his claim--conduct separate from the wrongful conduct giving rise to the claim itself. We have not previously been confronted by a case in which the same wrongdoing that gave rise to the cause of action also made it impossible for the plaintiff to avail himself of his legal remedy because of the tort-caused mental incapacity. Nevertheless, we can discern no rational distinction which would justify us to apply *contra non valentem* in the former case, but not in the latter.

As Justice Provosty stated for this court in the *Hyman v. Hibernia Bank & Trust*, 139 La. 411, 417, 71 So. 598, 600 (1916), an "exception must be recognized, we think, in a case like the present, where the inability of the plaintiff to act was brought about by the practice of the defendant. Otherwise, the defendants would be profiting by their own wrong--a thing inadmissible in law."

To permit prescription to run under the present facts would permit a defendant with custody and control over a person he had tortiously injured to profit by his subsequent laxity in medical treatment, when (as here stipulated) the injured person's recovery of mental faculties was retarded beyond the prescriptive period. The plaintiff in these circumstances is doubly helpless to file suit by virtue both of his mental incapacity and also of his removal from the solicitous attention of relatives and friends who might act in his stead.

* * * * *

REVERSED and **REMANDED.**

RENFROE
v.
STATE
809 So. 2d 947 (La. 2002)

VICTORY, J.

At issue in this case is whether the plaintiff's supplemental and amending petitions, which added Road District No. 1 of the Parish of Jefferson ("Road District No. 1") and the Greater New Orleans Expressway Commission ("GNOEC") as defendants outside of the one-year prescriptive period, relates back to an earlier timely filed petition against the State of Louisiana through the Department of Transportation and Development ("DOTD"). After reviewing the record and the applicable law, we reverse the judgments of the lower courts and hold that plaintiff's action has prescribed.

Facts and Procedural History

On April 28, 1998, as Rose Renfroe was driving south on Causeway Boulevard approximately two-tenths of a mile before reaching the overpass over U.S. Highway 61 (Airline Highway), her vehicle crossed the concrete median on Causeway Boulevard and collided with a pickup truck and a tractor trailer, both of which were proceeding north on Causeway Boulevard. Mrs. Renfroe was pronounced dead at the scene.

On April 22, 1999, Mrs. Renfroe's husband, Lonnie Renfroe, filed a petition for damages individually, and on behalf of the estate Rose Renfroe and Judith Renfroe Prince, against the DOTD. Plaintiff alleged that the DOTD was liable for Mrs. Renfroe's death under Louisiana Civil Code articles 2315 and 2317 due to improper construction, maintenance, and design of Causeway

361

Boulevard. Plaintiff named the DOTD as defendant based on signs along parts of Causeway Boulevard designating it as "LA 3046" and also because the State Police investigated the accident.

On July 19, 1999, the DOTD filed a motion for summary judgment alleging that, although another part of Causeway Boulevard is a state highway, the state highway begins at Jefferson Highway to the south and ends at its junction with the south right of way line with Airline Highway, which does not include the portion of Causeway Boulevard where the accident occurred.[1] Accordingly, on September 20, 1999, plaintiff filed its first supplemental and amending petition adding Jefferson Parish and the GNOEC as defendants as the proper owners of the portion of Causeway Boulevard where the accident occurred. On October 5, 1999, Jefferson Parish filed an exception of misjoinder and nonjoinder of an indispensible party, Road District No. 1, a separate legal entity, created and governed by Jefferson Parish. Thereafter, on October 15, 1999, plaintiff filed its second supplemental and amending petition, substituting Road District No. 1 as a defendant in place of Jefferson Parish.[2]

On December 14, 1999, the trial court granted partial summary judgment in favor of the DOTD, dismissing the plaintiff's action against the DOTD on all matters connected with the ownership and maintenance of the accident location, finding that the DOTD did not own or maintain that portion of Causeway Boulevard, and leaving the remaining issue against the DOTD that of defective design. On June 30, 2000, the trial court granted the DOTD's exception of peremption on the design defect claim under La. R.S. 9:2772, which provides a seven-year peremptive period for actions involving deficiencies in design. Thus, the DOTD was dismissed from the suit with prejudice.

On August 18, 2000, and October 23, 2000, respectively, Road District No. 1 and the GNOEC filed exceptions of prescription, claiming that the release of the timely sued solidary obligor, the DOTD, caused the case against them to prescribe. The trial court denied the defendants' motions, finding that the suit against Road District No. 1 and the GNOEC related back to plaintiff's suit against the DOTD, and therefore was timely. The court of appeal agreed and denied the defendants' writ application. *Renfroe v. State of Louisiana through the DOTD, et al.*, 01-0292 (3/15/01). We granted the defendants' writ application to determine whether the plaintiff's supplemental and amending petitions relate back to the timely filed suit against the DOTD. *Renfroe v. State of Louisiana through the DOTD, et al.*, 01-1646 (La. 2001), 798 So. 2d 952.

Discussion

Delictual actions are subject to a liberative prescriptive period of one year, which commences to run from the date the injury is sustained. La. C.C. art. 3492. The delictual action against Road District No. 1 and the GNOEC was not filed during the one-year prescriptive period, although suit was timely filed against the DOTD. Under La. C.C. art. 3462, prescription is interrupted by the commencement of suit against the obligor in a court of competent jurisdiction and venue. Further, the interruption of prescription by suit against one solidary obligor is effective as to all solidary obligors. La. C.C. arts. 1799 and 3503. The same principle is applicable to joint tortfeasors. La. C.C. art. 2324C. However, a suit timely filed against one defendant does not interrupt prescription as against other defendants not timely sued, where the timely sued defendant is ultimately found not liable to plaintiffs, since no joint or solidary obligation would exist. *Spott v. Otis Elevator Co.*, 601 So. 2d 1355 (La.1992). Because the timely sued defendant, the DOTD, was dismissed from the suit,

---

[1] At some point north of the accident scene, Causeway Boulevard again becomes a state highway.

[2] According to Jefferson Parish's exception of misjoinder and nonjoinder of an indispensable party, the accident site is located within the geographic boundaries of Road District No. 1, which was created pursuant to La. R.S. 48:571 and 582 for the purpose of, among other things, constructing, maintaining, and improving public roads, highways, and bridges within its territorial limits. According to Jefferson Parish's exception, Jefferson Parish functions only in a representative capacity as the governing authority of Road District No. 1. For the purposes of determining whether prescription has run against Road District No. 1 in this case, we will treat Jefferson Parish and Road District No. 1 as the same party, as did the trial court.

prescription against Road District No. 1 and the GNOEC is not interrupted and plaintiff's suit against them has prescribed, unless some other basis to revive this suit is found.

Plaintiff argues that the untimely supplemental and amending petitions relate back to the timely filed petition against the DOTD under La. C.C.P. art. 1153. La. C.C.P. art. 1153 provides:

> When the action or defense asserted in the amended petition or answer arises out of the conduct, transaction, or occurrence set forth or attempted to be set forth in the original pleading, the amendment relates back to the date of filing the original pleading.

In *Ray v. Alexandria Mall, Through St. Paul Property & Liability Ins.*, 434 So. 2d 1083, 1087 (La.1983), this Court established the following criteria for determining whether art. 1153 allows an amendment which changes the identity of the party or parties sued to relate back to the date of filing of the original petition:

> (1) The amended claim must arise out of the same transaction or occurrence set forth in the original petition;

> (2) The purported substitute defendant must have received notice of the institution of the action such that he will not be prejudiced in maintaining a defense on the merits;

> (3) The purported substitute defendant must know or should have known that but for a mistake concerning the identity of the proper party defendant, the action would have been brought against him;

> (4) The purported substitute defendant must not be a wholly new or unrelated defendant, since this would be tantamount to assertion of a new cause of action which would have otherwise prescribed.

Plaintiff argues that all of the criteria of *Ray* have been met; we disagree. The second *Ray* criteria is very clear--the purported substitute defendants, in this case Road District No. 1 and the GNOEC, "must have received notice of the institution of the action such that he will not be prejudiced in maintaining a defense on the merits." *Ray, supra* at 1087. In this case, there is no evidence in the record, and plaintiff makes no contention, that either of these entities "received notice of the institution of the action." While plaintiff argues that Jefferson Parish received *notice of the accident* because Jefferson Parish deputies responded to the accident, this is not the same as receiving *notice of the institution of the lawsuit.* As we stated in *Giroir v. South Louisiana Medical Center, Div. of Hospitals,* 475 So. 2d 1040 (La. 1985):

> The fundamental purpose of prescription statutes is only to afford a defendant economic and psychological security if no claim is made timely, and to protect him from stale claims and from the loss of non-preservation of relevant proof. They are designed to protect him against lack of notification of a formal claim within the prescriptive period, not against pleading mistakes that his opponent makes in filing the formal claim within the period.

There is no doubt that neither Road District No. 1 nor the GNOEC received notice of the institution of the suit within the prescriptive period. However, plaintiff claims that under *Findley v. Baton Rouge,* 570 So. 2d 1168 (La. 1990), notice is not technically necessary, and that the real issue is whether the defendants would be prejudiced by the lack of notice. In *Findley,* plaintiff timely filed suit against the City of Baton Rouge for an accident that occurred in a public park, but, upon learning that the park was actually owned by the Recreation and Park Commission of East Baton Rouge Parish ("BREC"), filed an untimely amended petition adding BREC as a defendant. This Court held that the amended petition against the new defendant related back to the original petition, even though BREC may not have received formal notice of the institution of the lawsuit. *Findley, supra.* The basis of that holding, however, was that "when there is an identity of interest between the originally named defendant and

363

the party the plaintiff actually intended to sue, the amendment may relate back, in the absence of prejudice, on the basis that institution of the action against one serves to provide notice of the litigation to the other." *Findley, supra* at 1171 (citing 6A Charles Alan Wright, Arthur R. Miller & Mary Kay Kane, *Federal Practice and Procedure,* § 1499 (1990); 3 *Moore's Federal Practice and Procedure* ¶ 15.08[5] (2d ed. 1989)). We held that "[s]ufficiency of the identity of interests depends upon the closeness of the relationship between the parties in their business operations and other activities,...." *Id.* After analyzing the relationship between the City of Baton Rouge and BREC, we found that it was much the same as that between a parent corporation and a subsidiary, and that, as "Rule 15(c)[3] was amended for the purpose of preventing unjust results when a plaintiff, confronted with a maze of closely related corporate or governmental entities, initially chooses the wrong one to sue, unless prejudice exists," "institution of the suit against the City served to provide 'such notice of the institution of the action that [BREC] will not be prejudiced in maintaining [its] defense on the merits.'" *Id.* at 1172 (citing Fed. R. Civ. Proc. 15(c)).[4]

Unlike in *Findley,* in this case there is no "identity of interests" between the DOTD and Road District No. 1 or the GNOEC such that notice of the suit to the DOTD would serve as notice to Road District No. 1 or the GNOEC. The relationship between the DOTD and these other defendants has none of the components of a parent corporation and wholly owned subsidiary relationship as was found to be present in *Findley. See West v. Parish of Jefferson,* 96-530 (La.App. 5 Cir. 1996), 685 So. 2d 371 (finding that the City of Kenner and the Parish of Jefferson did not have a sufficient connexity of relationship to make them related parties, such that institution of the suit against one would not serve to provide notice of the litigation to the other). Thus, we find that the second criteria of *Ray* was not met, as neither Road District No. 1, nor the GNOEC received notice of the institution of the lawsuit within the prescriptive period.

Likewise, we find that the fourth criteria of *Ray,* that "the purported substitute defendant must not be a wholly new or unrelated defendant, since this would be tantamount to assertion of a new cause of action which would have otherwise prescribed," was not met either. In *Ray,* the plaintiff merely made a mistake as to the proper name of the defendant, naming as the defendant the "Alexandria Mall," rather than the "Alexandria Mall Company." In this case, the plaintiff clearly intended to name the DOTD as the proper defendant, as the plaintiff thought that the DOTD owned and maintained that portion of Causeway Boulevard. When plaintiff later learned that a wholly new defendant, either Road District No. 1 or the GNOEC, owned and maintained that portion of the road, he filed supplemental and amending petitions against them after the prescriptive period. As we held in *Findley,* the *Ray* criteria seek "to prevent injustice to plaintiffs who mistakenly named an incorrect defendant, at least when there was no prejudice to the subsequently named correct defendant ... [;] the rule however [does] not apply when the amendment sought to name a new and unrelated defendant." *Findley, supra* at 1170 (citing *Giroir, supra*); *see also Newton v. Ouachita Parish School Bd.,* 624 So. 2d 44 (La.App. 2 Cir. 1993) (holding that where plaintiff timely sued the Ouachita Parish School Board ("OPSB"), mistakenly believing that OPSB supervised and controlled the school where the

---

[3] This Court has looked to commentary and jurisprudence under Federal Rule of Civil Procedure 15(c), upon which La. C.C. art. 1153 was based, for the proper interpretation of La. C.C. art. 1153. *See Giroir, supra; Ray, supra; Allen v. Smith,* 390 So. 2d 1300 (La. 1980); Tate, *Amendment of Pleadings in Louisiana,* 43 Tul. L.Rev. 211 (1969).

[4] In analyzing the relationship between the City of Baton Rouge and BREC, we considered the following: The City's governing body and its chief executive appoint seven of the nine members of BREC, indicating an element of control similar to that existing between corporations with interlocking officers and directors; BREC uses many properties owned by the City, and the City, although retaining ownership, cannot sell or alienate as long as the recreational use continues; the city council makes appropriations for BREC's support; BREC uses the accounting services of the City's finance department, as well as the services of the City's engineering, building maintenance, central garage and purchasing divisions; BREC is part of and subject to the personnel system for City employees; BREC prepares and presents a capital budget annually to the City's planning commission, which has the power to approve or disapprove each item; the City's planning commission also must approve BREC's issuance of bonds and certificates of indebtedness, as well as appropriations for purchases of land and construction of buildings. *Findley, supra* at 1171.

tortious incident occurred, and then filed an untimely petition naming the Monroe City School Board ("MCSB") as the proper party, the court held that the purpose of plaintiff's amended petition was to name a wholly new defendant and not to merely correct a misnomer, such that suit against the MCSB had prescribed under *Ray*).

Thus, we find that plaintiff's supplemental and amending petitions against Road District No. 1 and the GNOEC fail to meet the second and fourth criteria set out in *Ray* for relation back to the original timely filed petition against the DOTD under La. C.C. P. art. 1153.

Plaintiff also argues that the doctrine of *contra non valentem* operates to interrupt prescription against the two belatedly sued defendants in this case. La. C.C. art. 3467 states that "prescription runs against all persons unless exception is established by legislation." In spite of the clear language of La. C.C. art. 3467, the jurisprudential doctrine of *contra non valentem* remains a viable exception to this rule. *Plaquemines Parish Comm. Council v. Delta Dev. Co.,* 502 So. 2d 1034 (La.1987); *see also* La. C.C. art. 3467, Official Revision Comment (d). This Court has recognized four factual situations in which the doctrine of *contra non valentem* applies so as to prevent the running of liberative prescription:

> (1) where there was some legal cause which prevented the courts or their officers from taking cognizance of or acting on the plaintiff's action;

> (2) where there was some condition coupled with the contract or connected with the proceedings which prevented the creditor from suing or acting;

> (3) where the debtor himself has done some act effectually to prevent the creditor from availing himself of his cause of action; or

> (4) where the cause of action is neither known nor reasonably knowable by the plaintiff even though plaintiff's ignorance is not induced by the defendant. (discovery doctrine)

Id.

Plaintiff argues that the fourth application of *contra non valentem* applies in this case because the fact that some party other than the DOTD owned or maintained the small stretch of Causeway Boulevard was not reasonably knowable to the plaintiff. The plaintiff claims that he exercised reasonable diligence in ascertaining the proper party defendants and was reasonable in believing that the portion of the roadway was owned and maintained by the DOTD, due to the investigation by State Police at the scene of the accident, and signage on parts of the roadway designating it as a state highway.

However, the doctrine of *contra non valentem* only applies in "exceptional circumstances." La. C.C. art. 3467, Official Revision Comment (d); *State ex rel. Div. of Admin. v. McInnis Brothers Construction, Inc.,* 97- 0742 (La. 1997), 701 So. 2d 937, 940. In fact, when this Court first officially recognized this fourth type of situation where *contra non valentem* applies, we specifically clarified that "[t]his principle will not exempt the plaintiff's claim from the running of prescription if his ignorance is attributable to his own wilfulness or neglect; that is, a plaintiff will be deemed to know what he could by reasonable diligence have learned." *Corsey v. State of Louisiana, Through the Department of Corrections,* 375 So. 2d 1319, 1322 (La. 1979) (citing *Cartwright v. Chrysler Corp.,* 255 La. 597, 598, 232 So. 2d 285 (1970); *Sumerall v. St. Paul Fire & Marine Ins. Co.,* 366 So. 2d 213 (La.App. 2 Cir. 1978)).

While it is indeed unusual that different unrelated parties would own and maintain different portions of one roadway, the fact that the portion of the roadway was owned by some party other that the DOTD was "reasonably knowable" by the plaintiff within the prescriptive period. Thus, the doctrine of *contra non valentem* does not apply in this case.

* * * * *

365

REVERSED and **REMANDED.**

KNOLL, J., dissenting.

Although I agree that the majority properly applies *Ray v. Alexandria Mall, Through St. Paul Property & Liability Ins.,* 434 So. 2d 1083 (La. 1983), the first mode of analysis utilized in the opinion, I disagree with the majority's rejection of the fourth application of *contra non valentem* to the facts of this case. As observed in the majority opinion, we have consistently stated that the doctrine of *contra non valentem* is applicable only in exceptional circumstances. In my view, the facts of this case, as found by the trial court, provide just such an exceptional circumstance.

* * * * *

NOTES

1. Article 1067 of the Louisiana Code of Civil Procedure provides that "an incidental demand is not barred by prescription or peremption if it was not barred at the time the main demand was filed and is filed within ninety days of date of service of main demand or in the case of a third party defendant within ninety days from service of process of the third party demand."

2. Incidental demands include cross-claims, interventions, reconventional demands, and third party demands. For example, in *Renfroe v. State*, suppose that within ninety days of being served with plaintiffs' petition and all amending supplemental petitions, GNOEC filed a reconventional demand against plaintiffs based upon a claim that prescribed one day after filing of plaintiffs' main demand. Has GNOEC's cause of action prescribed?

3. The specific legislation of La. R.S. 9:5822 and 5824 which suspended and/or extended prescription in cases arising as a result of Hurricanes Katrina and Rita supersedes the general jurisprudential exception of *contra non valentem*. *Harris v. Stogner*, 967 So. 2d 1151 (La. 2007).

4. *See Le v. The Bradford Group, LLC,* 105 So. 3d 186 (La.App. 3 Cir. 2012), *writ denied* 109 So. 3d 367 (La. 2013) for a discussion of the discovery rule of the doctrine of *contra non valentem*.

4. Statutes of Repose (Peremption)

As the foregoing section illustrates, a statute of limitations does not commence to run until the victim sustains damage as a result of the actor's wrongful act. Even where the victim has sustained damage, the statute of limitations may not commence to accrue until the victim knows or reasonably should know that he has been damaged by the actor's wrongful act. As a result, the statute of limitations may not bar some claims until years after the wrongful act has occurred. To alleviate a perceived unfairness to the actor in such circumstances, some jurisdictions adopt statutes which bar recovery if an action is not instituted within a fixed period of time after the alleged wrongful act, regardless of whether the victim has yet sustained damages or could reasonably know about the claim. These are called statutes of repose or, in the civil law, peremption. The two most common in Louisiana are the peremptive statutes for legal and medical malpractice, reproduced below. There are similar statutes of repose for accountants (R.S. 9:5604) and for "deficiencies in surveying, design, supervision or construction of immovables or improvements thereon" (R.S. 9:2772).

La. R.S. 9:5628. Actions for medical malpractice

A. No action for damages for injury or death against any physician, chiropractor, dentist, hospital or nursing home duly licensed under the laws of this state, whether based upon tort, or breach of contract, or otherwise, arising out of patient care shall be brought unless filed within one year from the date of the alleged act, omission or neglect, or within one year from the date of discovery of the alleged act, omission or neglect; provided, however, that even as to claims filed within one year from the date of such discovery, in all events such claims must be filed at the latest within a period of three years from the date of the alleged act, omission or neglect.

B.   The provisions of this Section shall apply to all persons whether or not infirm or under disability of any kind and including minors and interdicts.

C.   The provisions of this Section shall apply to all healthcare providers listed herein or defined in R.S. 40:1299.41 regardless of whether the health care provider avails itself of the protections and provisions of R.S. 40:1299.41 et seq, by fulfilling the requirements necessary to qualify as listed in R.S. 40:1299.42 and 1299.44.

BOREL

v.

YOUNG

989 So. 2d 42 (La. 2008)

On Rehearing

WEIMER, Justice.

This court granted plaintiffs' application for rehearing because of concern about the correctness of the conclusion that the amendment and re-enactment of LSA-R.S. 9:5628 by 1987 La. Acts No. 915, § 1 effected a substantive change in the statute, transforming the three-year limitation period set forth therein from a prescriptive period to one of peremption. The determination in the original opinion that the three-year time period in LSA-R.S. 9:5628 is peremptive is based on an interpretation of 1987 La. Acts No. 915, § 1, which changed the language as to the three-year period from "**provided, however, that** even as to claims filed within one year from the date of such discovery, in all events such claims **must** be filed at the latest within a period of three years from the date of the alleged act, omission, or neglect" to read "**however,** even as to claims filed within one year from the date of such discovery, in all events such claims **shall** be filed at the latest within a period of three years from the date of the alleged act, omission, or neglect." It was reasoned that this change in language indicated an intent to change the law and, accordingly, to express the Legislature's intent that the three-year time period be peremptive. *Borel v. Young*, 989 So. 2d at 47-48.

In their application for rehearing, plaintiffs challenged the holding that the three-year period set forth in LSA-R.S. 9:5628 is peremptive, contending that the changes effected to the statute by 1987 La. Acts No. 915, § 1 were stylistic changes that did not change the character of the three-year limitations period as a prescriptive period. Plaintiffs argued that nothing in the 1987 Act indicated an intent to legislatively overrule this court's decision in *Hebert v. Doctors Memorial Hospital,* 486 So. 2d 717 (La. 1986), which held that both the one-year and three-year periods set forth in LSA-R.S. 9:5628 are prescriptive periods. Further, they pointed out that the peremption issue was not briefed by the parties, who, as did the court of appeal, relied on *Hebert* as the settled law on this issue. Accordingly, they requested an opportunity to address the continued viability of *Hebert* in this court.

Following a careful review of our original decision in this case, in light of the parties' supplemental arguments on rehearing, we reinstate our original judgment affirming the decision of the court of appeal; however, we do so on different grounds. On rehearing, we find, contrary to our original decision, that 1987 La. Acts. No. 915, § 1 did not change the character of the three-year limitation period in LSA-R.S. 9:5628 from a prescriptive period to one of peremption. We therefore reaffirm our holding in *Hebert* that both the one-year and the three-year periods set forth in LSA-R.S. 9:5628 are prescriptive. However, we also find, consistent with our opinion in *LeBreton v. Rabito,* 97-2221 (La. 1998), 714 So. 2d 1226, that the more specific provisions of the Medical Malpractice Act regarding suspension of prescription against joint tortfeasors apply in this case to the exclusion of the general code articles on interruption of prescription against joint tortfeasors, and in particular LSA-C.C. art. 2324(C). As a result, we hold that plaintiffs' suit against Dr. Young and his insurer, filed well beyond the time period designated by LSA-R.S. 40:1299.47(A)(2)(a), is barred by prescription.

Facts and Procedural History

In April 1999, an ultrasound disclosed the presence of a mass in the left lower abdomen of Mary Borel. Mrs. Borel's internist, Dr. Clinton Young, referred her to Dr. Aldy Castor, an OB/GYN, for surgical evaluation. Dr. Castor recommended surgery. Mrs. Borel was admitted to Lafayette General Medical Center ("LGMC") on August 18, 1999. The following day, August 19, 1999, Dr. Castor performed a left ovarian cystectomy and appendectomy. Mrs. Borel tolerated the procedure well, but her condition began to deteriorate rapidly the next day. By late afternoon, August 20, 1999, Mrs. Borel's oxygen saturation had dropped, her pulse was elevated, and her temperature had spiked to 103.8 degrees. She was moved to ICU, intubated and placed on a ventilator.

Mrs. Borel was diagnosed with congestive heart failure of unknown cause. On August 21, 1999, Drs. Castor and Kinchen performed an exploratory laparotomy for possible pelvic abscess. Mrs. Borel was placed on antibiotics, and Dr. Gary Guidry was consulted for pulmonary management. Her condition did not improve. On August 25, 1999, after developing multi-organ failure, Mrs. Borel was returned to surgery. Thereafter, she remained on antibiotic therapy, but continued to have difficulty oxygenating and remained unresponsive. On October 15, 1999, she was transferred to St. Brendan's Long Term Care Facility, where she remained until her death on May 23, 2000.

On August 14, 2000, Minos Borel, Mrs. Borel's husband, and their adult children filed a medical malpractice claim with the Patient Compensation Fund against Dr. Young, Dr. Castor, and LGMC. On January 17, 2002, the medical review panel rendered an opinion finding no breach in the standard of care by Dr. Young, Dr. Castor, or LGMC. Plaintiffs received the opinion on January 22, 2002.

On March 28, 2002, plaintiffs filed suit in district court against LGMC. Neither Dr. Young nor Dr. Castor was named as a defendant. On April 24, 2002, LGMC answered the plaintiffs' petition asserting the comparative negligence or fault of parties not made defendants to the lawsuit. Two years later, in January 2004, plaintiffs learned that Dr. James Falterman would testify as an expert for LGMC. On February 17, 2005, during the course of Dr. Falterman's deposition, plaintiffs contend they discovered, for the first time, that Dr. Falterman would testify that Drs. Young and Castor's treatment of Mrs. Borel fell below the applicable standard of care. Prior to this date, plaintiffs claim they had no reasonable cause to believe, from any source qualified to testify as to the standard of care required of an internist or OB/GYN, that there was negligence on the part of Dr. Young or Dr. Castor.

Plaintiffs attempted to amend their original petition to add Dr. Young, Dr. Castor, and the physicians' insurer, Louisiana Medical Mutual Insurance Company ("LAMMICO"), as defendants. When their efforts were rebuffed, they filed a separate suit for malpractice in the district court, naming Dr. Young, Dr. Castor, and LAMMICO as defendants, and alleging the joint, several and in solido liability of these defendants with LGMC. The second suit was consolidated with the pending lawsuit against LGMC.

Dr. Young and LAMMICO filed a peremptory exception of prescription. Following a hearing on August 22, 2005, the district court granted the exception, finding that plaintiffs' suit, filed in district court on March 15, 2005, more than three years from the date of the alleged malpractice, was barred by peremption, pursuant to LSA-R.S. 9:5628(A). Plaintiffs appealed.

On December 29, 2006, the Court of Appeal, Third Circuit rendered its decision. The court of appeal affirmed the decision of the district court, but for different reasons. Relying on *Hebert, supra,* the court determined that LSA-R.S. 9:5628(A) is prescriptive in nature, not peremptive. Examining the exception of prescription in light of *LeBreton, supra,* the appellate court found that the more specific provisions of the Medical Malpractice Act control the time in which suit must be filed against health care providers covered by the Act, rather than the general codal articles on interruption and suspension of prescription. Finding LSA-R.S. 40:1299.47(A)(2)(a), regarding the suspension of prescription against joint tortfeasors in the medical malpractice setting, to be controlling over the general codal article on interruption of prescription against joint tortfeasors found in LSA-C.C. 2324(c), the court of appeal concluded that plaintiffs' suit against Dr. Young is barred by prescription:

The alleged malpractice occurred on May 23, 2000, and a timely medical review proceeding was filed against Dr. Young and LGMC, joint tortfeasors, on August 14, 2000. The medical review panel proceedings extended for a period of two years following the alleged date of malpractice. During the pendency of the proceedings, the prescription was suspended. The Plaintiffs were notified of the medical review panel decision on January 22, 2002. Accordingly, we find under La. R.S. 40:1299.47(A)(2)(a), Plaintiffs had until January 29, 2003, to bring Dr. Young, who had been previously named in the medical review panel, into the suit. Their attempt to bring him into the suit on March 15, 2005, was well beyond the time period designated by the statute.

Borel v. Young, 06-0352, 06-0353, p. 16-17 (La.App. 3 Cir. 2006), 947 So. 2d 824, 835. On plaintiffs' application, we granted certiorari to review the correctness of the court of appeal's decision. Borel v. Young, 07-0419 (La. 2007), 956 So. 2d 617.

On original hearing, we did not reach the issue addressed by the court of appeal-whether the specific provisions in the Medical Malpractice Act regarding suspension of prescription against joint tortfeasors apply to the exclusion of the general codal articles on interruption of prescription against joint tortfeasors found in LSA-C.C. 2324(c). Instead, we found that plaintiffs' suit was extinguished by peremption. Borel v. Young, supra, 989 So. 2d at 51. We granted a rehearing to consider whether the determination that the three-year time limitation contained in LSA-R.S. 9:5628 is peremptive is a correct interpretation of Louisiana law.

Law and Analysis

Prescription v. Peremption in LSA-R.S. 9:5628

In 1975, the legislature passed 1975 La. Acts No. 808, § 1, enacting La. R.S. 9:5628, a statute governing the time in which a medical malpractice action must be filed. The Act provides, in relevant part:

AN ACT

To amend Code Title XXIII of Title 9 of the Louisiana Revised Statutes of 1950 by adding thereto a new Section to be designated as Section 5628, to provide for a maximum prescriptive period and abandonment with respect to medical malpractice claims.

Be it enacted by the Legislature of Louisiana:

Section 1. Section 5628 of Title 9 of the Louisiana Revised Statutes of 1950 is hereby enacted to read as follows:

§ 5628. Actions for medical malpractice

A. No action for damages for injury or death against any physician, dentist, or hospital duly licensed under the laws of this state, whether based upon tort, or breach of contract, or otherwise, arising out of patient care shall be brought unless filed within one year from the date of the alleged act, omission or neglect, or within one year from the date of discovery of the alleged act, ommission [sic] or neglect; provided, however, that even as to claims filed within one year from the date of such discovery, in all events such claims must be filed at the latest within a period of three years from the date of the alleged act, omission or neglect.

In Hebert, supra, this court was called upon to determine whether, in passing 1975 La. Acts No. 808, § 1, the legislature intended to enact a prescriptive statute or a peremptive statute. Noting that the ultimate test for distinguishing between prescriptive and peremptive periods is the legislative intent, we pointed out that the title of the Act describes its object: "to provide for a maximum prescriptive period and abandonment with respect to medical malpractice claims" (emphasis added).

Finding no other indicators to suggest that the legislature intended to deviate from this stated purpose and enact a peremptive period, this court concluded:

> La.Rev.Stat. § 9:5628 sets forth more than one time period. Initially, it coincides with La. Civ.Code art. 3492's basic one year prescriptive period for delictual actions, coupled with the "discovery" exception of our jurisprudential doctrine of *contra non valentem* ("within one year from the date of the alleged act, omission or neglect, or within one year from the date of discovery of the alleged act, omission or neglect"). A separate and independent feature, or provision, of § 9:5628 is contained in the following clause:
>
>> provided, however, that even as to claims filed within one year from the date of discovery, in all events such claims must be filed at the latest within a period of three years from the date of the alleged act, omission or neglect.
>
> ....
>
> When we examine the evolution of the theory of peremption and the considerations which bear on the distinction between peremption and prescription, we conclude that La.Rev.Stat. § 9:5628 is in both of its features noted above a prescription statute, with only the single qualification that the discovery rule is expressly made inapplicable after three years from the act, omission or neglect.

Hebert, 486 So. 2d at 723-724. Our holding in *Hebert* that LSA-R.S. 9:5628 is, in both of its features, a prescriptive statute, was reiterated that same year in *Crier v. Whitecloud,* 486 So. 2d at 714,*on reh'g,* 496 So. 2d at 307 (La. 1986).

Since the date of the *Hebert* opinion, LSA-R.S. 9:5628 has been amended five times, each time for the primary purpose of adding to the list of healthcare practitioners included in its provisions. *See,* 1990 La. Acts No. 501, § 1 (adding "community blood center or tissue bank as defined in R.S. 40:1299.41(A)"); 1995 La. Acts. No. 818, § 1 (adding "optometrist"); 1995 La. Acts No. 983, § 1 (adding "nurse, licensed midwife practitioner"); 2001 La. Acts No. 95, § 1 (adding "nursing home" and present section C which extends the statute to "apply to all healthcare providers listed herein or defined in R.S. 40:1299.41 regardless of whether the healthcare provider avails itself of the protections and provisions of R.S. 40:1299.41 et seq., by fulfilling the requirements necessary to qualify as listed in R.S. 40:1299.42 and 1299.44."). Indeed, that was the primary focus of a 1987 amendment to the statute, which was enacted as part of a comprehensive bill providing for the licensure and regulation of psychologists.[17]

In addition to revising the provisions of Chapter 28 of Title 37, relative to the licensure and regulation of psychologists, 1987 La. Acts. No. 915, § 1 amended LSA-R.S. 9:5628(A) to insert the word "psychologist" after "dentist," thereby including psychologists in the enumerated list of healthcare providers covered by the provisions of LSA-R.S. 9:5628, and providing a specific limitations period for actions for damages against psychologists.

---

[17] As set forth in its title, the purpose of 1987 La. Acts No. 915, § 1 is as follows:

To amend and reenact R.S. 9:5628(A) and Chapter 28 of Title 37 of the Louisiana Revised Statutes, to be comprised of R.S. 37:2351 through 2366, relative to licensing of psychologists, to provide for definitions; to provide with respect to the State Board of Examiners of Psychologists, and its organization, duties, powers, membership, and members' terms of office; to provide for judicial review; to provide for fees; to provide with respect to licensure, including provisions for requirements therefor, for renewal of licenses; for filing copies of licenses with the office of the secretary of state; to provide with respect to the denial, revocation, or suspension of licenses; to provide with respect to offenses and for disciplinary action and for violations and penalties; to provide for injunctive proceedings; to provide with respect to the protection of privileged information; to provide exceptions; to provide with respect to the scope of the Chapter, to provide for time limitations applicable to actions for damages against psychologists, and to provide for related matters.

In the process of adding psychologists to the list of healthcare providers covered by LSA-R.S. 9:5628, the Act made one further change to LSA-R.S. 9:5628(A). It struck out the words "provided" and "that" in the phrase "provided, however, that" and it substituted the word "shall" for "must" in the phrase "in all events such claims must be filed at the latest within a period of three years from the date of the alleged act, omission, or neglect."

In our original opinion, the majority drew upon the change in language and the presumption that, where a new statute is worded differently from a preceding statute, the legislature is presumed to have intended to change the law, *Brown v. Texas-LA Cartage, Inc.*, 98-1063, p. 7 (La. 1998), 721 So. 2d 885, 889, to conclude that "[t]he plain language of La.Rev.Stat. § 9:5628 as reenacted by 1987 La. Acts No. 915, § 1 does clearly indicate the Legislature's intent that the three-year time period is peremptive." *Borel*, at 50. Upon further reflection and study, we find that the interpretation of the effect of 1987 La. Acts No. 915, amending and reenacting LSA-R.S. 9:5628, was incorrect, and that the Act did not, by changing the word "must" to "shall," change the character of the three-year time period from a prescriptive period to one of peremption.

Our finding in this regard is based on several considerations. First, prior to the passage of 1987 La. Acts No. 915, § 1, the jurisprudence interpreting LSA-R.S. 9:5628 had consistently held that LSA-R.S. 9:5628 is a prescriptive statute in both its features. *Hebert*, 486 So. 2d at 723; *Crier*, 486 So. 2d at 714, *on reh'g*, 496 So. 2d at 307; *Chalstrom v. Desselles*, 433 So. 2d 866 (La.App. 4 Cir. 1983), *writ denied*, 438 So. 2d 215 (La.1983). According to our well-settled rules of statutory construction, we presume that the legislature was aware of the interpretation that had been given to the statute by the jurisprudence. *State, Dept. of Public Safety and Corrections, Office of State Police, Riverboat Gaming Division v. Louisiana Riverboat Gaming Commission and Horseshoe Entertainment*, 94-1872, 94-1914, p. 17 (La. 1995), 655 So. 2d 292, 301 n. 10 (noting that those who enact statutory provisions are presumed to act deliberately and with full knowledge of existing laws on the same subject, with awareness of court cases and well-established principles of statutory construction, and with knowledge of the effect of their acts and a purpose in view). Yet, in the twenty-two years since the <u>Hebert</u> decision was issued, the only change that the legislature has effected to the relevant portion of the statute is the substitution of the word "shall" for "must" in the 1987 Act, and the deletion of the words "provided" and "that."

There is no indication in the 1987 Act that the legislature, in substituting the word "shall" for "must," intended to change the law as interpreted by this court.[18] In fact, the words, in both their ordinary and legal usage, are virtually synonymous:

> **Must.** This word, like the word "shall," is primarily of mandatory effect; and in that sense is used in antithesis to "may."

> ....

> **Shall.** As used in statutes, contracts, or the like, this word is generally imperative or mandatory. In common or ordinary parlance, and in its ordinary signification, the term "shall" is a word of command, and one which has always or which must be given a compulsory meaning; as denoting obligation. The word in ordinary usage means "must" and is inconsistent with a concept of discretion.

BLACK'S LAW DICTIONARY, 1019, 1375 (6th ed. 1990). *See also, Pittman Construction Co. v. Housing Authority of Opelousas*, 167 F.Supp. 517 n. 38 (W.D.La.1958), aff'd, 264 F.2d 695 (5th Cir. 1959) ("The word 'shall' is ordinarily imperative, of similar effect and import with the word 'must,' and inconsistent with the idea of discretion.").

---

[18] To the contrary, the Digest to the Engrossed and Re-Engrossed versions of House Bill No. 1035, the origin of 1987 La. Acts. No. 915, § 1 explains: "*Proposed law* adds licensed psychologists to the enumeration of those against whom actions for damages arising out of patient care must be brought within the stated time limits and otherwise retains *present law.*" (Emphasis added.)

Since the words "shall" and "must" carry virtually the same legal signification, it is apparent that the amendment effected by the 1987 Act produced only a stylistic change to the statute's text: the word "must" in the phrase "in all events such claims **must** be filed at the latest within a period of three years from the date of the alleged act, omission, or neglect" was changed to "shall" to make the language consistent with that of the preceding clause: "No action for damages for injury or death ... arising out of patient care **shall** be brought unless filed within one year from the date of the alleged act, omission or neglect, or within one year from the date of discovery of the alleged act, omission or neglect," and the words "provided" and "that" in the phrase "provided, however, that" were omitted as unnecessary surplusage. The change in language did not effect, nor was it intended to effect, a substantive change in the law.

As we explained in our original opinion, it is not always easy to determine whether a particular time limitation is prescriptive or peremptive, and the civil code gives no guidance on how to make such a determination. *Borel,* at 47-48. As a result, "this court has resorted to an exploration of the legislative intent and public policy underlying a particular time limitation, for it is primarily whether the legislature intended a particular time period to be prescriptive or peremptive that is the deciding factor in such a case." *State, Division of Administration v. McInnis Brothers Construction,* 97-0742, p. 4 (La. 1997), 701 So. 2d 937, 940. Typically, courts look to the language of the statute, the purpose behind the statute, and the public policy mitigating for or against suspension, interruption or renunciation of that time limit to determine whether a time limitation is prescriptive or peremptive. *State Board of Ethics v. Ourso,* 02-1978, p. 5 (La. 2003), 842 So. 2d 346, 349. An examination of each of these factors in the present case reveals that 1987 La. Acts No. 915, § 1, amending and re-enacting LSA-R.S. 9:5628, does not evidence a legislative intent to change the result of *Hebert* and make the statute's three-year period peremptive.

Because what the legislature says in the text of a statute is considered the best evidence of legislative intent, *State v. Williams,* 00-1725, p. 13 (La. 2001), 800 So. 2d 790, 800, we begin with an examination of the language of LSA-R.S. 9:5628. Clearly, there is no language in LSA-R. S. 9:5628, as amended and re-enacted by 1987 La. Acts. No. 915, § 1, which indicates the legislature's intent that the three-year time period is peremptive. While we have held that it is not necessary for the legislature to state in a statute that it is peremptive in order for this court to hold that it is in fact peremptive, *State Board of Ethics v. Ourso,* 02-1978 at 5, 842 So. 2d at 349, in some cases where this court has found a time period to be peremptive, specific language in the statute clearly indicated the legislature's intent in that regard. *See, e.g., Reeder v. North,* 97-0239, p. 9 (La. 1997), 701 So. 2d 1291, 1297 ("The legal malpractice statute of limitations ... La. R.S. 9:5605 expressly states that the period is 'peremptive' and 'in accordance with Civil Code Article 3461, may not be renounced, interrupted, or suspended.' "). When the legislature wishes to enact a peremptive period, it certainly knows how to make that intention manifest. *See,* LSA-R.S. 9:5604, 9:5605 and 9:5606, quoted at n. 4, *infra,* establishing peremptive periods for actions for damages against accountants, attorneys, and insurance agents. Moreover, an examination of the statutes which, like LSA-R.S. 9:5628, establish limitation periods for negligence actions against professionals, reveals that where the legislature has chosen to enact a peremptive period, it has specifically stated its intent and, in addition, it has also specially exempted claims for fraud, a characteristic which is not present in LSA-R.S. 9:5628.[19] *See, e.g.,* LSA-R.S. 9:5605(E) ("The peremptive period provided in Subsection A of the Sections shall not apply in cases of fraud, as defined in Civil Code Article 1953.")

In our original opinion, we relied almost exclusively on the legislature's use of the word "shall" in the statute as indicative of its intent to create a peremptive period. *Borel,* at 50. However, if, as originally opined, the substitution of the word "shall" for "must" indicates a legislative intent to change the law and create a peremptive period, then we would be compelled to conclude that not only the three-year period, but also the one-year period, is peremptive, because the statute clearly states that

---

[19] Presumably, by exempting claims of fraud, the legislature intended to restore the third category of *contra non valentem* so as to prevent a potential defendant from benefitting from the effects of peremption by intentionally concealing his or her wrongdoing.

"[n]o action ... **shall** be brought unless filed within one year." LSA-R.S. 9:5628 (emphasis added).[20] Such an interpretation of LSA-R.S. 9:5628, would produce an irreconcilable conflict between the statute and the provisions of the Medical Malpractice Act, a result clearly not intended by the legislature.

The laws of statutory construction require that laws on the same subject matter be interpreted in reference to each other. LSA-C.C. art. 13; *Louisiana Municipal Association v. State*, 04-0227, p. 36 (La. 2005), 893 So. 2d 809, 837. Where it is possible, courts have a duty in the interpretation of a statute to adopt a construction which harmonizes and reconciles it with other provisions dealing with the same subject matter. *Id.; Hollingsworth v. City of Minden,* 01-2658, p. 4 (La. 2002), 828 So. 2d 514, 517.

Louisiana Revised Statutes 9:5628 cannot be examined alone, but must be interpreted in conjunction with the provisions of the Medical Malpractice Act, codified in LSA-R.S. 40:1299.41, et

---

[20] *See also* and *compare,* LSA-R.S. 9:5604, 9:5605, and 9:5606, which govern actions for professional accounting liability, legal malpractice, and professional insurance agent liability, respectively. Therein, the legislature utilizes essentially identical language to that contained in *both* time periods of LSA-R. S. 9:5628, including the mandatory "shall," and then expressly declares that the "one-year and three-year periods of limitation provided in Subsection A of this Section are peremptive periods within the meaning of Civil Code Article 3458 and, in accordance with Civil Code Article 3461, may not be renounced, interrupted, or suspended."

LSA-R.S. 9:5604 provides, in relevant part:
    A. No action for damages against any accountant duly licensed under the laws of this state, or any firm as defined in R.S. 37:71, whether based upon tort, or breach of contract, or otherwise, arising out of an engagement to provide professional accounting service shall be brought unless filed in a court of competent jurisdiction and proper venue within one year from the date of the alleged act, omission or neglect, or within one year from the date that the alleged act, omission, or neglect is discovered or should have been discovered; however, even as to actions filed within one year from the date of such discovery, in all events such actions shall be filed at the latest within three years from the date of the alleged act, omission, or neglect.
    B. ... The one-year and three-year periods of limitation provided in Subsection A of this Section are peremptive periods within the meaning of Civil Code Article 3458 and, in accordance with Civil Code Article 3461, may not be renounced, interrupted, or suspended. [Emphasis added.]

LSA-R.S. 9:5605 similarly provides, in relevant part:
    A. No action for damages against any attorney at law duly admitted to practice in this state, any partnership of such attorneys at law, or any professional corporation, company, organization, association, enterprise, or other commercial business or professional combination authorized by the laws of this state to engage in the practice of law, whether based upon tort, or breach of contract, or otherwise, arising out of an engagement to provide legal services shall be brought unless filed in a court of competent jurisdiction and proper venue within one year from the date of the alleged act, omission, or neglect, or within one year from the date that the alleged act, omission, or neglect is discovered or should have been discovered; however, even as to actions filed within one year from the date of such discovery, in all events such actions shall be filed at the latest within three years from the date of the alleged act, omission, or neglect.
    B. ... The one-year and three-year periods of limitation provided in Subsection A of this Section are peremptive periods within the meaning of Civil Code Article 3458 and, in accordance with Civil Code Article 3461, may not be renounced, interrupted, or suspended. [Emphasis added.]

LSA-R.S. 9:5606 provides, in relevant part:
    A. No action for damages against any insurance agent, broker, solicitor, or other similar licensee under this state, whether based upon tort, or breach of contract, or otherwise, arising out of an engagement to provide insurance services shall be brought unless filed in a court of competent jurisdiction and venue within one year from the date of the alleged act, omission, or neglect, or within one year from the date that the alleged act, omission, or neglect is discovered or should have been discovered. However, even as to actions filed within one year from the date of such discovery, in all events such actions shall be filed at the latest within three years from the date of the alleged act, omission, or neglect.
    ....
    D. The one-year and three-year periods of limitation provided in Subsection A of this Section are peremptive periods within the meaning of Civil Code Article 3458 and, in accordance with Civil Code Article 3461, may not be renounced, interrupted, or suspended. [Emphasis added.]

seq.[21] As we explained in *LeBreton*, the Medical Malpractice Act prohibits the filing of a medical malpractice claim against a qualified health care provider prior to presenting the complaint to a medical review panel. The legislature, in enacting this legislation, took special cognizance of the need to fully protect plaintiffs from the detrimental effect of liberative prescription; the legislature provides for suspension of the time within which suit must be filed during the pendency of the review process and for ninety days following notification to the claimant or his or her attorney of the panel opinion. *LeBreton*, 97-2221 at 10, 714 So. 2d at 1230-1231; LSA-R.S. 40:1299.47(A)(2)(a) and (c). Indeed, the Medical Malpractice Act is replete with provisions respecting the operation and effect of this suspension.[22] Suspension, as we have explained, applies only to prescription; a peremptive period, by definition, is not subject to interruption, suspension or renunciation. LSA-C.C. art. 3461; *Hebert*, 486 So. 2d at 723. To suggest that the language of LSA-R.S. 9:5628 and, in particular, the use of the word "shall," indicates an intent to establish a peremptive period would be to render the provisions of the Medical Malpractice Act relative to suspension meaningless, a result we cannot condone. *Hollingsworth*, 01-2658 at 5, 828 So. 2d at 517 ("[C]ourts are bound to give effect to all parts of a statute and cannot give a statute an interpretation that makes any part superfluous or meaningless, if that result can be avoided.").[23]

As to the purpose behind the statute, we find it significant, as we did in *Hebert*, that the title to 1987 Acts. No. 915, § 1, which amended and re-enacted LSA-R.S. 9:5628, states that its purpose is

---

[21] "Actions for medical malpractice against certain health care providers, such as the defendants herein, are governed by special laws, Part XXIII of Chapter 5, Miscellaneous Health Provisions of La. R.S. 40:1299.41, et seq., and La. R.S. 9:5628, which delineate the liberative prescription applicable to actions for medical malpractice under Title 40." *LeBreton*, 97-2221 at 7-8, 714 So. 2d at 1229.

[22] *See, e.g.,* LSA-R.S. 40:1299.41(D) ("If a health care provider does not so qualify, the patient's remedy will not be affected by the terms and provisions of this Part, except as hereinafter provided with respect to the suspension and the running of prescription of actions against a health care provider who has not qualified under this Part when a claim has been filed against the health care provider for review under this Part."); LSA-R. S. 40:1299.41(F) ("The provisions of this Part that provide for the suspension and the running of prescription with respect to a health care provider who has not qualified under the Part, but against whom a claim has been filed under this Part, do not apply to any act of malpractice which occurred before September 1, 1981."); LSA-R.S. 40:1299.41(G) ("Notwithstanding the provisions of Subsection D, the running of prescription against a health care provider who is answerable in solido with a qualified health care provider against whom a claim has been filed for review under this Part shall be suspended in accordance with the provisions of R.S. 40:1299.47(A)(2)(a)."); LSA-R. S. 40:1299.47(A)(2)(a) ("The filing of a request for a review of a claim shall suspend the time within which suit must be instituted, in accordance with this Part, until ninety days following notification, by certified mail."); LSA-R. S. 40:1299.47(A)(2)(c) ("The filing of a request for a medical review panel shall suspend the time within which suit must be filed until ninety days after the claim has been dismissed in accordance with this Section.")

[23] Throughout its provisions, the Medical Malpractice Act contains repeated references to the "suspension and running of prescription" against healthcare providers, references that are consistent with the conclusion that LSA-R.S. 9:5628 is in both its features a prescriptive statute. *See,* n. 6, *supra.* In only one of its provisions is there a reference to peremption. LSA-R. S. 40:1299.47(B)(2) provides that a health care provider against whom a claim has been filed may raise any exception or defenses available pursuant to R.S. 9:5628 in a court of competent jurisdiction and venue at any time without need for completion of the review process, and "[i]f the court finds that the claim had prescribed or otherwise was perempted prior to being filed, the panel, if established, shall be dissolved." Because the word "perempted" appears in the provision, it is suggested that the legislature must have intended the three-year period in LSA-R. S. 9:5628 to be peremptive; otherwise there would be no reason for the legislature to have included the word. However, this language was in the provision at the time of the *Hebert* decision, having been added by 1984 La. Acts No. 435, § 5, and since *Hebert*, there has been no attempt by the legislature to amend the core language of LSA-R. S. 9:5628 to specify a peremptive period. Moreover, the phrase "otherwise was perempted" in the statute clearly suggests peremption occurring "otherwise" than through LSA-R.S. 9:5628; for example, through a statute like R.S. 9:5628.1, which contains a three-year peremptive period. If that had not been the intention, the statute would simply read: "[i]f the court finds that the claim had prescribed or was perempted." Such a construction of this statute comports with the fundamental principle that "prescriptive statutes are strictly construed against prescription and in favor of the obligation sought to be extinguished; ... of two possible constructions, that which favors maintaining, as opposed to barring, an action should be adopted." *Lima v. Schmidt*, 595 So. 2d 624, 629 (La. 1992). It also harmonizes and gives effect to all provisions of the Act.

"to provide for time limitations applicable to actions for damages against psychologists." Had the Legislature intended the "time limitations" to be peremptive, it could very easily have so indicated in the title of the act. *Compare,* 1990 La. Acts No. 683, § 1, which states as its purpose: "To enact 9:5604 and 5605, relative to limitations of actions, to provide for liberative prescription and for peremption of actions against accountants and attorneys." It did not do so, despite its presumed knowledge of the jurisprudence construing the "time limitations" in LSA-R.S. 9:5628 as prescriptive periods.

In short, there is nothing in the language of the amended and re-enacted statute, or in the title or history of 1987 La. Acts No. 915, § 1 to indicate the legislature's intent that the three-year time period of LSA-R.S. 9:5628 be peremptive. Had the Legislature meant for the time period to be peremptive, it could have expressed its intent in the title or text of the act, or in the language of the statute itself. *Conerly v. State, Louisiana State Penitentiary and the Department of Corrections,* 02-1852, p. 8 (La.App. 1 Cir. 2003), 858 So. 2d 636, 644, *writ denied,* 03-2121 (La. 2003), 858 So. 2d 432. The legislature would not "hint" about peremption when it clearly knows how to specify its intention in this regard, (*see and compare,* LSA-R.S. 9:5628.1)[24] especially given its presumed knowledge of the jurisprudence interpreting the statute as prescriptive.

As to the public policy concerns which underlie the enactment of LSA-R.S. 9:5628, and mitigate for or against suspension, interruption, or renunciation of its time limits, *Hebert* explains that the statute is a prescription statute with a qualification, that is, the *contra non valentem* type exception to prescription embodied in the discovery rule is expressly made inapplicable after three years from the act, omission, or neglect, and that:

> [t]his legislative limitation to a maximum of three years on the application of the discovery rule for a tort action involving medical malpractice-the discovery rule is an embodiment of *contra non valentem*-was purportedly a response to the problem of sharp increases in medical malpractice insurance rates.... It was believed that lengthy periods for filing suit brought about by the discovery rule (a mechanism by which the statute of limitations commenced running only upon discovery of an injury rather than upon perpetration of the tort) had contributed to the increasing number of malpractice claims and that, if the number of suits brought were restricted, insurance risks would be reduced and rates would decline. [Citations omitted.]

Hebert, 486 So. 2d at 722 n. 9. The public interest in controlling insurance costs to ensure the availability of health care is not thwarted or undermined by creating a hybrid prescriptive statute which expressly limits application of the discovery rule in an action for medical malpractice to a maximum of three years in lieu of creating a strict peremptive period requiring that an action be commenced within three years or forever lost. Clearly, the legislature intended that some type of suspension would operate, as it made a provision for such in the Medical Malpractice Act itself, recognizing the need to fully protect plaintiffs who would otherwise suffer the detrimental effect of liberative prescription during the panel review process that is required before an action can be filed. *LeBreton,* 97-2221 at 10, 714 So. 2d at 1230-1231; LSA-R.S. 40:1299.47(A)(2)(a). Thus, public

---

[24] LSA-R.S. 9:5628.1, enacted in 1999, provides, in relevant part:
  A. No action for damages against any healthcare provider as defined in this Section, whether based upon negligence, products liability, strict liability, tort, breach of contract, or otherwise, arising out of the use of blood or tissue as defined in this Section shall be brought unless filed in a court of competent jurisdiction within one year from the date of the alleged cause of action or other act, omission, or neglect, or within one year from the date that the alleged cause of action or other act, omission, or neglect is discovered or should have been discovered; however, except as provided in Subsection B, even as to actions filed within one year from the date of such discovery, in all events such actions shall be filed at the latest within three years form the date of the act, omission, or neglect.
  B. ...The three-year period of limitation provided in Subsection A of this Section is a peremptive period within the meaning of Civil Code Article 3458 and, in accordance with Civil Code Article 3461, shall not be renounced, interrupted, or suspended.[Emphasis added.]

policy mitigates in favor of some type of limited suspension such as that created in the provisions of the Medical Malpractice Act.[25]

In summary, there is no indication in the language, purpose, or public policy surrounding 1987 La. Acts No. 915, § 1 of the legislature's intent to legislatively overrule this court's holding in *Hebert* that both the one-year and three-year periods in LSA-R. S. 9:5628 are prescriptive. The stylistic substitution of the word "shall" for "must" is simply not sufficient to indicate an intent to change the three-year period in the statute from a prescriptive period to one of peremption. With the exception of this minor change in language, all other indicators relied upon in *Hebert* to find the existence of a prescriptive statute remain intact: (1) peremption statutes generally create the right of action and stipulate the delay during which the right must be exercised, but LSA-R.S. 9:5628 does not create the right to file suit in a tort action; (2) peremptive statutes often involve claims of a public law nature, but a suit for damages against a health care provider is a matter of private rather than public law; and (3) peremptive periods are generally less than one year, but the period in LSA-R.S. 9:5628 is not. *Hebert,* 486 So. 2d at 724.

* * * * *

Accordingly, we find that we erred in our original opinion in concluding that LSA-R.S. 9:5628 establishes a peremptive time period and that plaintiffs' action against Dr. Young, filed over three years after the alleged act of malpractice, is extinguished by peremption.

Prescription-Medical Malpractice Act v. Civil Code Articles on Interruption of Prescription

The finding that plaintiffs' suit is not barred by peremption does not end our inquiry. We must next consider the issue that was pretermitted by our opinion on original hearing: whether the court of appeal erred in relying on our decision in *LeBreton, supra,* to find that plaintiffs' action against Dr. Young has prescribed. For the following reasons, we find that the court of appeal did not err.

Mrs. Borel died on May 23, 2000. On August 14, 2000, plaintiffs filed a malpractice complaint with the Patient Compensation Fund against Dr. Young, Dr. Castor, and LGMC, thereby satisfying the requirements of LSA-R.S. 40:1299.47(B)(1)(a)(i).[26] This timely request for a medical review panel suspended prescription until ninety days following notification of the panel's issuance of an opinion. LSA-R.S. 40:1299.47(A)(2)(a). Plaintiffs were notified of the panel's opinion on January 22, 2002. Within ninety days of that notification, plaintiffs filed suit in district court against LGMC, an alleged joint tortfeasor.

On appeal, plaintiffs asserted that the timely filed suit against LGMC interrupted prescription as to Dr. Young, a joint tortfeasor, pursuant to the provisions of LSA-C.C. art. 2324(C),[27] and this court's decision in *Hebert,* which, in holding that LSA-R.S. 9:5628 is a prescription statute, relied upon the general Civil Code articles regarding interruption of prescription to find that a timely filed suit against a solidary obligor interrupts the prescription set forth in LSA-R.S. 9:5628. *Hebert,* 486 So. 2d at 725.

---

[25] Any other interpretation of the three-year time period could, in some instances, produce the anomalous result that claims timely presented to the medical review panel might be perempted before the required review process is completed and an opinion rendered, an absurd consequence that the legislature clearly did not intend.

[26] LSA-R.S. 40:1299.47(B)(1)(a)(i) provides:
    No action against a health care provided covered by this Part, or his insurer, may be commenced in any court before the claimant's proposed complaint has been presented to a medical review panel established pursuant to this Section.

[27] LSA-C.C. art. 2324(C) states:
    Interruption of prescription against one joint tortfeasor is effective against all joint tortfeasors.

The court of appeal rejected plaintiffs' argument, finding that this court's decision in *LeBreton* "clearly overruled the prior jurisprudence which applied the general provisions on interruption of prescription to a medical malpractice case and held the more specific provision found in the MMA controls the time in which suit must be filed against health care providers covered by the Act." *Borel*, 06-0352 at 9, 947 So. 2d at 830. Plaintiffs dispute this finding, arguing that *LeBreton* is limited to its unique facts and was never intended to interfere with the line of jurisprudence, pre-dating its issuance, permitting the addition of a solidary obligor to a pending, timely filed lawsuit, even if the addition occurred more than three years from the date of the alleged medical malpractice.

Plaintiffs are correct in their assertion that *LeBreton* does not present the exact factual scenario presented here. *LeBreton* addressed the effect of filing a medical malpractice suit in district court before submitting the claim to a medical review panel, as required by LSA-R. S. 40:1299.47(B)(1)(a)(i). Prior to *LeBreton*, a medical malpractice plaintiff could interrupt prescription by filing suit in district court against a health care provider within one year of the malpractice. The defendant would typically respond by filing an exception of prematurity seeking dismissal of the lawsuit for the plaintiff's failure to first file a request for a medical review panel. The plaintiff would then file a complaint with the Patient Compensation Fund. Following the rendition of the panel decision, prescription would commence to run anew, thereby allowing plaintiff as much as an additional year within which to file suit in district court.

LeBreton specifically addressed, and sought to rectify, the "anachronistic benefit" afforded to those litigants who, in failing to follow the proper procedural sequence in medical malpractice litigation, were able to simultaneously utilize the civil code articles on interruption of prescription with the specific provisions regarding suspension of prescription found in LSA-R.S. 40:1299.47(A)(2)(a) of the Medical Malpractice Act to prolong their malpractice claim. *LeBreton*, 97-2221 at 11, 714 So. 2d at 1231. Nevertheless, in analyzing the interplay between the general codal articles on interruption of prescription and the statutes specifically providing for suspension of prescription in the context of the Medical Malpractice Act, this court set forth general principles applicable to all actions brought pursuant to the Act.

In *LeBreton*, we pointed out that actions for medical malpractice against certain health care providers, such as defendants herein, are governed by special laws which delineate the applicable liberative prescription. Relying on the rules of statutory construction, we pointed out that although statutes dealing with the same subject matter should be harmonized if possible, where there is a conflict, the statute specifically directed to the matter at issue must prevail as an exception to the statute more general in character. *LeBreton*, 97-2221 at 7; 714 So. 2d at 1229. We further recognized that, in the civil law, suspension exists as an equalizer to litigants who find themselves in situations where interruption of prescription is not available, and that, by including special provisions regarding suspension of prescription in the medical malpractice statutes, the legislature excluded the applicability of interruption of prescription. *LeBreton*, 97-2221 at 9-10, 714 So. 2d at 1230. We reasoned:

> [I]t is evident that the Louisiana Medical Malpractice Act took cognizance of the need to suspend prescription and fully protects plaintiffs who would otherwise suffer the detrimental effect of liberative prescription. Because the Medical Malpractice Act prohibits the filing of a medical malpractice claim against a qualified health care provider prior to panel review, the act specifies that the filing of a request for review before a panel suspends prescription. La. R.S. 40:1299.47(A)(2)(a). Moreover, as provided by statute, the filing of the complaint prevents prescription from lapsing during the pendency of the review process and further suspends prescription from the time of filing until ninety-days following notification to the claimant or his attorney of the panel opinion. *Id.* After reviewing these special provisions, it is clear that the legislature has equitably provided for suspension to aid the plaintiff in the medical malpractice arena who is prevented by law from the outset from filing suit against the qualified health care provider.... Thus, considering the doctrinal underpinnings for the existence of the rules of suspension, it is evident that there is no need for the

general rules of interruption of prescription to combine with suspension to synergistically benefit the plaintiff.

LeBreton, 97-2221 at 10, 714 So. 2d at 1230-1231 (footnote omitted). Although issued in the context of a case presenting itself in a different factual and procedural posture from the instant one, our holding in *LeBreton* clearly stands for the principle that medical malpractice claims are governed by the specific provisions of the Medical Malpractice Act regarding suspension of prescription, to the exclusion of the general codal articles on interruption of prescription. That holding is broad enough to extend to the instant case.

In fact, jurisprudence subsequent to *LeBreton* has applied its principles to joint tortfeasor situations, such as presented in this case. *Richard v. Tenet Health Systems, Inc.*, 03-1933(La.App. 4 Cir. 2004), 871 So. 2d 671, *writ denied*, 04-1521 (La. 2004), 885 So. 2d 587. In *Richard*, the court of appeal addressed the issue of whether a timely filed suit against one health care provider interrupted prescription as to other health care providers, not previously named in the panel request, who were alleged to be jointly liable with the named defendants. In answering this inquiry in the negative, the court of appeal applied the principles articulated in *LeBreton* to conclude that the specific provisions of the Medical Malpractice Act applied to the exclusion of the general code articles on interruption of prescription. The court expressly rejected any reliance on *Hebert* for the proposition that the general civil code articles on interruption of prescription apply in the medical malpractice setting, finding that *Hebert* was decided before *LeBreton*, which effectively "changed the way courts analyze prescription issues in medical malpractice cases." *Richard*, 03-1933 at 3, 871 So. 2d at 673 n. 1. The appellate court explained: " *LeBreton* and the cases following it recognize that the legislature has established special rules for prescription under the Medical Malpractice Act. Consequently, the general rules of prescription do not apply." *Id.* Accordingly, the court held that the initial request for a medical review panel suspended prescription as to the health care providers alleged to be joint tortfeasors and/or solidary obligors with the named health care providers; however, pursuant to LSA-R.S. 40:1299.41(G) and LSA-R.S. 40:1299.47(A)(2)(a), that prescription was suspended for only 90 days following notification, by certified mail, of the issuance of the medical review panel's opinion. Plaintiffs waited for over five years after the opinion of the medical review panel to name as additional defendants those previously unnamed health care providers who were alleged to be joint and/or solidary obligors. Therefore, the court found that plaintiffs' claim as to these defendants had prescribed.

The reasoning applied by the appellate court in *Richard* applies with equal force to this case, in which plaintiffs sought to add Dr. Young, an alleged joint tortfeasor, to a pending medical malpractice action more than 90 days after the receipt of the medical review panel's decision finding that his conduct did not fall below the applicable standard of care and more than three years from the date of the alleged malpractice. Pursuant to *LeBreton*, and the cases following it, the specific provisions of the Medical Malpractice Act regarding the suspension of prescription against joint tortfeasors apply to the exclusion of the general code article on interruption of prescription against joint tortfeasors, LSA-C.C. 2324(c).[28] The specific provisions of the Medical Malpractice Act are found in LSA-R.S. 40:1299.41(G) and LSA-R.S. 40:1299.47(A)(2)(a).

Louisiana Revised Statutes 40:1299.41(G) states:

> Notwithstanding the provisions of Subsection D, the running of prescription against a health care provider who is answerable in solido with a qualified health care provider against whom a claim has been filed for review under this Part shall be suspended in accordance with the provisions of R.S. 40:1299.47(A)(2)(a).

Louisiana Revised Statutes 40:1299.47(A)(2)(a) provides, in relevant part:

---

[28] A contrary holding would potentially subject a health care provider to an indefinite period of prescription, even after the claim has been evaluated by a medical review panel, a result clearly at odds with the purpose of the Medical Malpractice Act, which as discussed, *infra*, was to curtail lengthy periods for filing malpractice suits by limiting application of the discovery rule of *contra non valentem* to a maximum of three years.

The filing of the request for a review of a claim shall suspend the time within suit must be instituted, in accordance with this Part, until ninety days following notification, by certified mail, as provided in Subsection J of this Section, to the claimant or his attorney of the issuance of the opinion by the medical review panel, in the case of those health care providers covered by this Part, or in the case of a health care provider against whom a claim has been filed under the provisions of this Part, but who has not qualified under this Part, until ninety days following notification by certified mail to the claimant or his attorney by the board that the health care provider is not covered by this Part. The filing of a request for review of a claim shall suspend the running of prescription against all joint and solidary obligors, and all joint tortfeasors, including but not limited to health care providers, both qualified and not qualified, to the same extent that prescription is suspended against the party or parties that are the subject of the request for review.

Applying these provisions to the facts of the instant case, it becomes apparent that plaintiffs' claims against Dr. Young were properly dismissed. The alleged malpractice occurred on May 23, 2000. On August 14, 2000, a request for a medical review panel was filed against Dr. Young, Dr. Castor and LGMC, as joint tortfeasors. During the pendency of the panel proceedings, prescription was suspended as to all joint and solidary obligors, and all joint tortfeasors, including but not limited to health care providers, both qualified and not qualified. Plaintiffs were notified of the medical review panel decision on January 22, 2002. Thereafter, they had 90 days, plus the remainder of the one-year prescriptive period that was unused at the time the request for a medical review panel was filed (282 days), or until January 29, 2003,[29] to bring Dr. Young, who had been previously named in the medical review panel, into the suit.[30] Their attempt to bring him into the lawsuit on March 15, 2005, came too late. The district court correctly sustained the peremptory exception of prescription.

Conclusion

In conclusion, for the reasons expressed, we find that 1987 Acts No. 915, § 1 did not change the character of the three-year limitation period in LSA-R.S. 9:5628 from a prescriptive period to one of peremption. We therefore reaffirm our holding in *Hebert* that both the one-year and three-year periods set forth in LSA-R.S. 9:5628 are prescriptive, with the qualification that the *contra non valentem* type exception to prescription embodied in the discovery rule is expressly made inapplicable after three years from the act, omission, or neglect.

We additionally find that the rule of *LeBreton* extends to this case, and that the more specific provisions of the Medical Malpractice Act regarding suspension of prescription against joint tortfeasors apply to the exclusion of the general code article on interruption of prescription against joint tortfeasors, LSA-C.C. art. 2324(C). Applying those provisions to the facts of this case, we find that plaintiffs' suit against Dr. Young and his insurer, filed well beyond the time period designated by

---

[29] In *Guitreau v. Kucharchuk,* 99-2570 (La. 2000), 763 So. 2d 575, we held that when the ninety-day period of suspension after the decision of the medical review panel is completed, the medical malpractice victim is entitled to the remainder of the one-year prescriptive period that was unused at the time the request for the medical review panel was filed.

[30] Plaintiffs assert that prescription could not have "continued" to run against Dr. Young after the period of suspension ceased because they had no reasonable cause to believe, from any source qualified to testify as to the standard of care required of an internist, that there was negligence on the part of Dr. Young. They argue that prescription could not commence until they "discovered" that he may have been negligent. The court of appeal correctly disposed of this argument: Dr. Young was not an unknown party, but was actually named in plaintiffs' request for a medical review panel, alleging that he breached the applicable standard of care in his treatment of Mrs. Borel. Further, when LGMC answered the plaintiffs' petition in April 2002, it asserted the "comparative negligence and/or fault of third parties not made defendants," alerting plaintiffs of the potential negligence of persons other than LGMC. *Borel,* 06-0352 at 15-16, 947 So. 2d at 834.

LSA-R.S. 40:1299.47(A)(2)(a), is barred by prescription. The judgment of the court of appeal is affirmed.

AFFIRMED.

CALOGERO, C.J., concurs in part, dissents in part and assigns reasons on rehearing.

Johnson, J., dissents on rehearing.

TRAYLOR, J., concurs with reasons in the result only on rehearing.

KNOLL, J., concurs in result only and assigns reasons on rehearing. CALOGERO, Chief Justice, concurring in part and dissenting in part and assigning reasons.

WARREN

v.

LOUISIANA MEDICAL MUTUAL INSURANCE COMPANY
21 So. 3d 186 (La. 2009)

On Rehearing

VICTORY, J.

We granted an application for rehearing in this case to consider whether our holding on original hearing conflicts with our decision in *Borel v. Young*, 07-0419 (La. 2007), 989 So. 2d 42 (on rehearing). On original hearing, this Court held that an amended pleading adding a new plaintiff's wrongful death claim after the medical malpractice action prescribed related back to the timely filing of the original petition pursuant to La. C.C.P. art. 1153 and the analysis set forth in *Giroir v. South La. Med. Ctr., Div. of Hospitals*, 475 So. 2d 1040 (La. 1985). Further, we held that the new plaintiff was entitled to the benefit of the interruption of prescription on her survival action such that the amended petition adding her as a plaintiff to that cause of action was timely filed under the reasoning of *Williams v. Sewerage & Water Bd. of New Orleans*, 611 So. 2d 1383 (La. 1993). After reconsidering the record and the applicable law, we find that we erred on original hearing and now hold that the newly added plaintiff's claims have prescribed under the provisions of the Medical Malpractice Act (the "Act"). We therefore vacate our decision on original hearing, reverse the judgment of the court of appeal, and order that the case be remanded to the district court to grant defendants' exception of prescription.

Facts and Procedural History

On October 10, 12, and 13, 2000, Terry Warren received medical treatment from various health care providers, and, on October 13, 2000, he died. Alleging that his death was caused by substandard medical care which led to a delay in diagnosing and treating a heart attack, on September 11, 2001, Pamela Warren and Theresa Rene Warren filed a medical malpractice complaint with the Louisiana Patient's Compensation Fund. Pamela and Theresa Warren are the wife and daughter of the decedent. At the time the PCF complaint was filed, the decedent's other daughter, Sarah Warren Jimenez ("Sarah"), was aware of the filing but consciously chose not to be involved in the matter. On August 27, 2002, a medical review panel issued an opinion stating that there was no breach of the standard of care, and the opinion was received by counsel for plaintiffs on September 19, 2002. On November 25, 2002, Pamela Warren and Theresa Warren timely filed suit against defendants[1] in the Nineteenth Judicial District Court alleging wrongful death and survival actions. Again, Sarah chose not to join in the suit. On July 6, 2004, plaintiffs filed a First Supplemental and Amending petition adding Sarah as a plaintiff asserting survival and wrongful death claims.

---

[1] The defendants are Louisiana Medical Mutual Insurance Company, Jeffrey A. Lamp, M.D., Robyn B. Germany, M.D., Sandra Moody, NP-C, and Family Health of Louisiana, Inc.

Defendants filed an exception of prescription arguing that Sarah's claims had prescribed because she did not file her action within the time periods provided by the Act. Defendants asserted that Sarah testified in deposition that she was aware of the filing of the medical review complaint and the instant lawsuit but chose not to participate. However, after she became aware that she might be called by plaintiffs as a witness, she determined that she might as well be part of the lawsuit. Defendants argued that these facts did not allow the relation back of her claims to the original petition under *Giroir* and that they were prejudiced by the addition of a new plaintiff nearly three years after the request for a medical review panel and nineteen months after the lawsuit was filed.

The trial court overruled the defendants' exception of prescription and the court of appeal denied the defendants' writ, citing La. C.C.P. art. 1153 and *Giroir. Warren v. Louisiana Medical Mut. Ins. Co.,* 06-412 (La.App. 1 Cir. 2006). This Court then remanded the case to the court of appeal for briefing, argument and opinion. *Warren v. Louisiana Medical Mut. Ins. Co.,* 06-1547 (La. 2006), 938 So. 2d 693. Again, the court of appeal denied the writ relying on *Giroir. Warren v. Louisiana Medical Mut. Ins. Co.,* 06-412 (La.App. 1 Cir. 2007). This Court granted the defendants' writ application, *Warren v. Louisiana Medical Mut. Ins. Co.,* 07-492 (La. 2007), 955 So. 2d 670, and affirmed the judgment of the court of appeal. *Warren v. Louisiana Medical Mut. Ins. Co.,* 07-0492 (La. 2008), ____ So. 2d ____. On February 13, 2009, we granted the defendants' application for rehearing.

Discussion

La. R.S. 9:5628(A) provides the time periods in which medical malpractice actions must be filed, as follows:

> A. No action for damages for injury or death against any physician, chiropractor, nurse, licensed midwife practitioner, dentist, psychologist, optometrist, hospital or nursing home duly licensed under the laws of this state, or community blood center or tissue bank as defined in R.S. 40:1299.41(A), whether based upon tort, or breach of contract, or otherwise, arising out of patient care shall be brought unless filed within one year from the date of the alleged act, omission, or neglect, or within one year from the date of discovery of the alleged act, omission, or neglect; however, even as to claims filed within one year from the date of such discovery, in all events such claims shall be filed at the latest within a period of three years from the date of the alleged act, omission, or neglect.

In order to file a medical malpractice action, a party must first present his proposed complaint to a medical review panel for review.La.R.S.40:1299.47(B)(1)(a)(i). La. R.S. 40:1299.47(A)(2)(a) provides for the suspension of the period provided in La. R.S. 9:5628 during the time the complaint is pending before the medical review panel, as follows:

> The filing of the request for a review of a claim shall suspend the time within which suit must be instituted, in accordance with this Part, until ninety days following notification, by certified mail, as provided in Subsection J of this Section, to the claimant or his attorney of the issuance of the opinion by the medical review panel, in the case of those health care providers covered by this Part, or in the case of a health care provider against whom a claim has been filed under the provisions of this Part, but who has not qualified under this Part, until ninety days following notification by certified mail to the claimant or his attorney by the board that the health care provider is not covered by this Part. The filing of a request for review of a claim shall suspend the running of prescription against all joint and solidary obligors, and all joint tortfeasors, including but not limited to health care providers, both qualified and not qualified, to the same extent that prescription is suspended against the party or parties that are the subject of the request for review....[2]

---

[2] In *LeBreton v. Rabito,* 97-2221 (La. 1998), 714 So. 2d 1226, 1230-31, we explained this suspensive period as follows:

Recently, in *Borel, supra,* four members of this Court held that the three year time period in La. R.S. 9:5628 was prescriptive, rather than peremptive.[3] In so doing, we reaffirmed our prior holding in *Hebert v. Doctors Memorial Hospital,* 486 So. 2d 717, 723-24 (La. 1986), which had held that the one and three year periods were prescriptive "with only the single qualification that the discovery rule is expressly made inapplicable after three years from the act, omission or neglect."

In *Borel,* the plaintiffs timely filed a malpractice complaint with the Louisiana Patient's Compensation Fund against two doctors and a hospital, thereby satisfying the requirements of La. R.S. 40:1299.47(B)(1)(a)(i) that no action may be filed against a health care provider before a claimant's proposed complaint has been presented to a medical review panel. This timely request suspended prescription until ninety days following notification of the panel's issuance of an opinion against all parties named in the complaint and all joint and solidary obligors and all jointfeasors. La. R.S. 40:1299.47(A)(2)(a). Within 90 days of being notified of the panel's opinion, the plaintiffs filed suit in district court against the hospital, but not against the two doctors. After the three year period provided in La. R.S. 9:5628, plaintiffs attempted to amend their petition to add the doctors and their insurer, and when this failed, they filed a separate lawsuit against them which was later consolidated with the original suit. In response, the defendants filed an exception of prescription. Plaintiffs contested, arguing that La. C.C. art. 2324(C), providing that "[i]nterruption of prescription against one joint tortfeasor is effective against all joint tortfeasors," applied such that their timely suit against the hospital interrupted prescription against the other joint tortfeasors. In *Borel,* we disagreed and held that "the more specific provisions of the Medical Malpractice Act regarding suspension of prescription against joint tortfeasors apply to the exclusion of the general code article on interruption of prescription against joint tortfeasors, LSA-C.C. art. 2324(C)."*Borel, supra* at 69.

In reaching this conclusion, we relied on our earlier decision in *LeBreton, supra.* In *LeBreton,* the plaintiffs filed their medical malpractice action in the district court before filing their request for review before a medical review panel as required by La. R.S. 40:1299.47(B)(1)(a)(i). The plaintiffs' district court suit was dismissed without prejudice as premature. Several years later, the medical review panel notified plaintiffs of its opinion, but plaintiffs did not file suit within 90 days as required by La. R.S. 40:1299.47(A)(2). Plaintiffs argued that its suit was not prescribed because the filing of suit in district court prior to filing the medical review panel complaint interrupted prescription under La. C.C. art. 3466 and 3472. Because prescription was interrupted at the time their medical review request was filed and because that filing suspended prescription until 90 days after being notified of the panel decision, plaintiffs argued that prescription began again at that time and they had one year

---

Keeping in mind Plainiol's explanation for the underlying need for the principle of suspension, it is evident that the Louisiana Medical Malpractice Act took cognizance of the need to suspend prescription and fully protects plaintiffs who would otherwise suffer the detrimental effect of liberative prescription. Because the Medical Malpractice Act prohibits the filing of a medical malpractice claim against a qualified health care provider prior to panel review, the act specifies that the filing of a request for review before a panel suspends prescription.La.R.S. 40:1299.47(A)(2)(a). Moreover, as provided by statute, the filing of the complaint prevents prescription from lapsing during the pendency of the review process and further suspends prescription from the time of filing until ninety-days following notification to the claimant or his attorney of the panel opinion. *Id.* After reviewing these special provisions, it is clear that the legislature has equitably provided for suspension to aid the plaintiff in the medical malpractice arena who is prevented by law from the outset from filing suit against the qualified health care provider.... Thus, considering the doctrinal underpinnings for the existence of the rules of suspension, it is evident that there is no need for the general rules of interruption of prescription to combine with suspension to synergistically benefit the plaintiff.

[3] However, our further holding in *Borel* lessens the impact of this distinction. As explained in this opinion, by ruling that specific provisions of the Act applied to the exclusion of the general codal articles on interruption of prescription, *Borel* held that only the suspensive periods provided for in the Act can apply to suspend the prescriptive period of La. R.S. 9:5628. So, although the three year period is prescriptive, it is so only in a limited sense because the general codal articles allowing interruption or suspension of that prescriptive period do not apply.

after the expiration of the suspensive period of La. R.S. 40:1299.47(A)(2) in which to file suit. This Court disagreed, holding as follows:

> Actions for medical malpractice against certain health care providers, such as the defendants herein, are governed by special laws, Part XXIII of Chapter 5, Miscellaneous Health Provisions of La. R.S. 40:1299.41, *et seq.,* and La. R.S. 9:5628, which delineate the liberative prescription applicable to actions for medical malpractice under Title 40. It specifically provides, inter alia, that the filing of a medical malpractice claim with the board only suspends the time within which suit must be instituted in a district court. On the other hand, *if the general codal articles of 3466 and 3472 apply ... then the prescription and suspension provisions provided in the Medical Malpractice Act will be written out. Therein lies the conflict.* If we let this ruling stand, we will condone and encourage the technique of unnecessarily prolonging malpractice litigation by a lesser standard. The party who improperly files a premature medical malpractice suit without first filing the claim with the board for a medical review panel, and whose suit is subsequently dismissed without prejudice, gains an additional year of prescription in addition to the suspended time provided by the Medical Malpractice Act, within which to file the suit anew.

714 So. 2d at 1229-30. Thus, we held that the general provisions on interruption of prescription found in La. C.C. art. 3462 could not be simultaneously applied with the specific provision on suspension of prescription contained in La. R.S. 40:1299.47(A)(2)(a) to defeat the defendants' exception of prescription.

In relying on *LeBreton* in *Borel,* we held although *LeBreton* was presented in a different factual and procedural posture, the "holding in *LeBreton* clearly stands for the principle that medical malpractice claims are governed by the specific provisions of the Medical Malpractice Act regarding suspension of prescription to the exclusion of the general codal articles on interruption of prescription," and "that holding is broad enough to extend to the instant case." *Borel, supra* at 67. We noted in *Borel* that a contrary holding applying La. C.C. art. 2324(C) "would potentially subject a health care provider to an indefinite period of prescription, even after the claim has been evaluated by a medical review panel, a result clearly at odds with the purpose of the [Act], which ... was to curtail lengthy periods for filing malpractice suits ..." *Id.* at 68, n. 12.

In reviewing our opinion on original hearing, we see that it is contrary to *Borel* in two respects. First, on original hearing this Court relied on *Williams, supra,* to hold that because Sarah shared her survival cause of action with her mother and sister, prescription on that cause of action was interrupted when Sarah's mother and sister timely filed suit. However, while *Williams* held that the general codal articles on interruption of prescription, La. C.C. art. 3462,[4] 1799,[5] and 3503,[6] applied such that suit against one solidary obligor interrupted prescription against another solidary obligor, *Williams* was not a medical malpractice action. For had it been a medical malpractice action, *Borel* would dictate that the specific provisions of the Act apply to the exclusion of the general code articles on interruption of prescription against solidary obligors, just as the specific provisions of the Act regarding suspension of prescription applied to the exclusion of the general code article on interruption of prescription against joint tortfeasors under *Borel.* Because the holding of *Williams* has no application in the medical malpractice area and its application in that area is contrary to *Borel,* we erred in relying on *Williams* on original hearing to hold that Sarah's survival claim had not prescribed.

---

[4] La. C.C. art. 3462 provides that prescription is interrupted when the obligee commences an action against the obligor in a court of competent jurisdiction and venue.

[5] La. C.C. art. 1799 provides that the "interruption of prescription against one solidary obligor is effective against all solidary obligors, and their heirs."

[6] La. C.C. art. 3503 provides that "[w]hen prescription is interrupted against a solidary obligor, the interruption is effective against all solidary obligors and their successors."

Secondly, our holding on original hearing that the amended pleading adding a new plaintiff after the expiration of the prescriptive period related back to the timely filing of the original petition pursuant to La. C.C.P. art. 1153 is contrary to *Borel,* as well as to *LeBreton.* La. C.C.P. art. 1153 provides that "[w]hen the action or defense asserted in the amended petition or answer arises out of the conduct, transaction, or occurrence set forth or attempted to be set forth in the original pleading, the amendment relates back to the date of filing the original pleading." *LeBreton* and *Borel* stand for the proposition that medical malpractice claims are governed by the specific provisions of the Medical Malpractice Act regarding suspension of prescription to the exclusion of the general codal articles on interruption of prescription. These cases are equally applicable here. The expressed reasoning behind the holding in *LeBreton* was that if the general rules on interruption were to apply to a medical malpractice action, "then the prescription and suspension provisions provided in the Medical Malpractice Act will be written out," and "[t]herein lies the conflict." *LeBreton, supra* at 1230.Although La. C.C.P. art. 1153 does not "interrupt" prescription as did the general codal articles in *LeBreton* and *Borel,* "relation back" of an untimely filed amended petition directly avoids the application of prescription by allowing a claim that would have otherwise prescribed to proceed. The effect of this interference is that if relation back is allowed, the "prescription and suspension provisions provided in the Medical Malpractice Act will be written out," which, as we recognized in *LeBreton,* presents "a conflict." *LeBreton, supra* at 1230.Further, the application of La. C.C.P. art. 1153"would potentially subject a health care provider to an indefinite period of prescription, ... a result clearly at odds with the purpose of the [Act]."*Borel, supra* at 68, n. 12.Because medical malpractice actions are governed by the specific provisions of the Act regarding prescription and suspension of prescription, under *Borel,* we find that any general codal article which conflicts with these provisions may not be applied to such actions in the absence of specific legislative authorization in the Act. The Act has no rules allowing relation back of pleadings for medical malpractice claims. The application of Article 1153 would permit the adding of an plaintiff subsequent to the expiration of the three-year period provided for in La, R.S. 9:5628, and would read out of the statute the prescription and suspension period provisions by La. R.S. 9:5628 and La. R.S. 40:1299.47; therefore, La. C.C.P. art. 1153 may not be applied to the medical malpractice action under the reasoning of *LeBreton* and *Borel.*[7]

Conclusion

We erred on original hearing allowing relation back of a pleading adding a plaintiff after the prescriptive period provided by the Act had run. Our prior jurisprudence holds that medical malpractice claims are governed exclusively by the specific provisions of the Act regarding prescription and suspension of prescription. For that reason, our holding on original hearing that a general codal article providing for interruption of prescription applied to defeat prescription on Sarah's survival claim under the Act was error. Further, because any general codal article which conflicts with the operation of prescription under the Act cannot be applied in a medical malpractice case, we erred in allowing a general codal article allowing relation back of a pleading to defeat prescription on Sarah's wrongful death claim under the Act.[8]

---

[7] This case is not governed by *Guitreau v. Kucharchuk.,* 99-2570 (La. 2000), 763 So. 2d 575, which specifically found that there was no conflict between La. R.S. 40:1299.47 and La. C.C. art. 3472, and thus applied art. 3472 to the medical malpractice action. La. C.C. art. 3472 simply provides that a period of suspension is not counted toward accrual of prescription and that prescription commences to run again upon the termination of the suspensive period. The Court in *Guitreau* applied those guidelines to the suspension of prescription provided for in La. R.S. 40:1299.47, and held that after the ninety-day period was completed, the plaintiffs were entitled to the period of time under La. R.S. 9:5628 that remained unused at the time the request for a medical review panel is filed. There was no conflict as the application of La. C.C. art. 3472 did nothing to interfere with prescription and suspension of prescription provided for under the Act.

[8] Because of our decision on these issues, any discussion of the issue of whether relation back of a pleading belatedly adding a plaintiff under La. C.C.P. art. 1153 is allowed in the absence of a pleading mistake would be dicta. However, we note that our opinion on original hearing addressing the requirements for adding a plaintiff under La. C.C.P. art. 1153 has been vacated.

Decree

For the reasons expressed herein, the judgment of the court of appeal is reversed and the matter is remanded to the trial court to grant defendants' exception of prescription.

REVERSED AND REMANDED.

JOHNSON, J., dissents and assigns reasons.

KNOLL, J., concurs in the result and assigns reasons.

GUIDRY, J., concurs in the result.

WEIMER, J., dissents and assigns reasons.

WILLIAMSON
v.
HEBERT
31 So. 3d 1047 (La. 2010)

PER CURIAM.

Based on the facts of this case, we find defendant failed to establish plaintiff had constructive knowledge of the alleged medical malpractice more than one year prior to the filing of her August 16, 2002 complaint. In *Campo v. Correa*, 01-2707 (La. 2002), 828 So. 2d 502, 511, we explained "a plaintiff's mere apprehension that something may be wrong is insufficient to commence the running of prescription, unless the plaintiff knew or should have known through the exercise of reasonable diligence that his problem may have been caused by acts of malpractice." Plaintiff in the instant case clearly had some apprehension something was wrong following her surgery, as she consulted two different doctors regarding her condition. However, both of these doctors assured plaintiff her condition would continue to improve, with one of the doctors indicating her symptoms might take two years to resolve. When plaintiff's symptoms failed to improve by August 2002 (two years after the August 3, 2000 surgery), plaintiff performed computer research, and learned for the first time her symptoms may have been caused by malpractice. Plaintiff's August 16, 2002 complaint was filed within one year of her discovery of this alleged malpractice.

Accordingly, the writ is granted. The judgment of the court of appeal is reversed, and the judgment of the district court denying defendant's exception of prescription is reinstated. The case is remanded to the district court for further proceedings.

COMMENT

In contrast to the very complex prescription and peremption provisions for medical malpractice, the applicable statute for attorneys is quite simple.

La. R.S. 9:5605.   Actions for legal malpractice

A.   No action for damages against any attorney at law duly admitted to practice in this state, any partnership of such attorneys at law, or any professional corporation, company, organization, association, enterprise, or other commercial business or professional combination authorized by the laws of this state to engage in the practice of law, whether based upon tort, or breach of contract, or otherwise, arising out of an engagement to provide legal services shall be brought unless filed in a court of competent jurisdiction and proper venue within one year from the date of the alleged act, omission, or neglect, or within one year from the date that the alleged act, omission, or neglect is discovered or should have been discovered; however, even as to actions filed within one year from the date of such discovery, in all events such actions shall be filed at the latest within three years from the date of the alleged act, omission or neglect.

B.   The provisions of this Section are remedial and apply to all causes of action without regard to the date when the alleged act, omission, or neglect occurred. However, with respect to any alleged act, omission, or neglect occurring prior to September 7, 1990, actions must, in all events, be filed in a court of competent jurisdiction and proper venue on or before September 7, 1993, without regard to the date of discovery of the alleged act, omission, or neglect. The one-year and three-year periods of limitation provided in Subsection A of this Section are peremptive periods within the meaning of Civil Code Article 3458 and, in accordance with Civil Code Article 3461, may not be renounced, interrupted, or suspended.

C.   Notwithstanding any other law to the contrary, in all actions brought in this state against any attorney at law duly admitted to practice in this state, any partnership of such attorneys at law, or any professional law corporation, company, organization, association, enterprise, or other commercial business or professional combination authorized by the laws of this state to engage in the practice of law, the prescriptive and peremptive period shall be governed exclusively by this Section.

D.   The provisions of this Section shall apply to all persons whether or not infirm or under disability of any kind and including minors and interdicts.

E.   The peremptive period provided in Subsection A of this Section shall not apply in cases of fraud, as defined in Civil Code Art. 1953.

NOTES

1.   C.C. Article 1953 provides that "fraud is a misrepresentation or a suppression of the truth made with the intention either to obtain an unjust advantage for one party or to cause a loss or inconvenience to the other. Fraud may also result from silence or inaction," and C.C. Article 1954 provides that "fraud does not vitiate consent when the party against whom the fraud was directed could have ascertained the truth without difficulty, inconvenience, or special skill. This exception does not apply when a relation of confidence has reasonably induced a party to rely on the other's assertions or representations."

2.   In *Hebert v. Doctors Memorial Hospital*, 486 So. 2d 717 (La. 1986), the court ruled that a timely filed suit (within one year of "discovery," and three years of the "act") against a joint tortfeasor will interrupt the running of the three year statute as to another medical malpractice joint tortfeasor. Does this make sense? Why?

3.   Does R.S. 9:5628 differ from R.S. 9:5605? How? Should it make any difference?

4.   The Louisiana Supreme Court considered the issue of relation back in the context of legal malpractice claims in *Naghi v. Brenner:*

NAGHI
v.
BRENER
17 So. 3d 919 (La. 2009)

VICTORY, J.

We granted this writ application to determine whether Louisiana Code of Civil Procedure Article 1153, allowing an amended petition to relate back to the time of filing of the original petition, applies to the one-year peremptive period to bring legal malpractice actions under La. R.S. 9:5605. Because nothing may interfere with the running of a peremptive period, we hold that an amended and supplemental petition adding a plaintiff cannot relate back to the original petition in this case; therefore, we reverse the judgments of the lower courts and remand the case to the district court to grant the defendant's exception of peremption.

Facts and Procedural History

Plaintiffs, Benny and Ephraim Naghi, were represented by Lisa Brener in connection with a claim for damages which arose on October 26, 2005 when their property was damaged by fire. According to the plaintiffs, Ms. Brener failed to pursue the claim timely, resulting in prescription of their claim on October 26, 2006. On December 7, 2006, the plaintiffs filed the instant legal malpractice suit against Lisa Brener and her professional law corporation. The named plaintiffs were Benny and Ephraim Naghi. In response, Ms. Brener filed a partial exception of no right of action and motion for summary judgment, asserting that the property was actually owned by Mohtaram, Inc., and not by the Naghis personally, and that therefore, the Naghis had no right of action for damage to the property. The Naghis are directors and shareholders of Mohtaram, Inc. The trial court granted the exception and allowed plaintiffs ten days to amend their petition. On March 12, 2008, plaintiffs filed a "First Supplemental/Amending Petition," to "add and designate proper party plaintiff, Mohtaram, Inc." Ms. Brener then filed an "Exception of No Cause of Action, Exception of Prescription, Exception of Peremption, Exception of No Right of Action and Motion for Summary Judgment,"[4] essentially arguing that the claims asserted in the First Supplemental/Amending Petition were perempted under La. R.S. 9:5605.

The trial court denied the Exception of Peremption and Motion for Summary Judgment. In written reasons for judgment, the court found that the Supplemental/Amending petition was filed within the three-year peremptive period provided by La. R.S. 9:5605. However, although that petition was not filed within the one-year period, the trial court found that period to be prescriptive, and held that, therefore, the petition would relate back to the original petition if the factors set forth in *Giroir v. South Louisiana Medical Center, Div. of Hospitals*, ..., were met.[6] The court found the *Giroir* factors were met, stating as follows:

* * * * *

Discussion

La. R.S. 9:5605 provides for the time limits in which to file legal malpractice actions:

> A. No action for damages against any attorney at law duly admitted to practice in this state ... whether based upon tort, or breach of contract, or otherwise, arising out of an engagement to provide legal services shall be brought unless filed in a court of competent jurisdiction and proper venue within one year from the date of

---

[2] In 2008, La. C.C.P. art. 927 was amended to add peremption as an objection that may be raised by peremptory exception. La. C.C.P. art. 927(A)(2), added by Acts 2008, No. 824, § 1, eff. Jan. 1, 2009. Prior to that date, the proper procedural vehicle to bring an exception relating to peremption was, as a general rule, the exception of no cause of action. *Coffey v. Block*, 99-1221 (La.App. 1 Cir. 2000), 762 So. 2d 1181, 1186, *writ denied*, 00-2226 (La. 2000), 772 So. 2d 651; *Dowell v. Hollingsworth*, 94-0171 (La.App. 1 Cir. 1994), 649 So. 2d 65, *writ denied*, 95-0573 (La. 1995), 653 So. 2d 572. As Ms. Brener brought the objection on peremption grounds by both an exception of peremption and an exception of no cause of action, she has utilized the proper procedure under Article 927 both prior to, and after, 2008. The basis for these exceptions was La. R.S. 9:5605, providing for peremptive periods for actions against attorneys.

[4] The basis for the motion for summary judgment was that there were no material facts in dispute that the action was perempted and that Mohtaram has been fully compensated for the damages asserted and its insurer is subrogated to such claims.

[6] In *Giroir*, this Court allowed a petition adding a plaintiff to relate back to the original petition under La. C.C.P. art. 1153 if the following criteria were met:
> [A]n amendment adding or substituting a plaintiff should be allowed to relate back if (1) the amended claim arises out of the same conduct, transaction, or occurrence set forth in the original pleading; (2) the defendant either knew or should have known of the existence and involvement of the new plaintiff; (3) the new and the old plaintiffs are sufficiently related so that the added of substituted party is not wholly new or unrelated; (4) the defendant will not be prejudiced in preparing and conducting his defense.
475 So. 2d at 1044.

the alleged act, omission, or neglect, or within one year from the date that the alleged act, omission, or neglect is discovered or should have been discovered; however, even as to actions filed within one year from the date of such discovery, in all event such actions shall be filed at the latest within three years from the date of the alleged act, omission, or neglect.

B. The provisions of this Section are remedial and apply to all causes of action without regard to the date when the alleged act, omission, or neglect occurred.... The one-year and three-year periods of limitation provided in Subsection A of this Section are peremptive periods within the meaning of Civil Code Article 3458 and, in accordance with Civil Code Article 3461, may not be renounced, interrupted, or suspended.

...

* * * * * *Return to the statute*

This case involves the interaction of La. C.C.P. art. 1153 and the one-year peremptive period of La. R.S. 9:5605. The Naghis discovered the alleged malpractice when their claim for damages prescribed on October 26, 2006. While the original petition filed on behalf of "Benny and Ephraim Naghi" was timely filed within one year, on December 7, 2006, that petition was brought on behalf of parties that had no right of action to bring the property damages claim as the Naghis did not own the property individually. After the one-year period had run, the petition was supplemented and amended to name the owner of the property, Mohtaram, Inc., as proper party plaintiff. The plaintiffs allege that the Supplemental/Amending Petition was timely filed because it relates back to the filing of the original petition pursuant to La. C.C.P. art. 1153.

La. C.C.P. art. 1153 provides:

When the action or defense asserted in the amended petition or answer arises out of the conduct, transaction, or occurrence set forth or attempted to be set forth in the original pleading, the amendment relates back to the date of filing of the original pleading.

Although this article speaks only to the relation back of an "action or defense," this Court has applied this article to allow the relation back of pleadings adding a defendant, *Ray v. Alexandria Mall, Through St. Paul Property & Liability Ins.*, 434 So. 2d 1083 (1983), or adding a plaintiff, *Giroir, supra*, if certain conditions are satisfied. Plaintiffs assert that the amended petition meets the requirements set forth in *Giroir*, and that, therefore, it should be allowed to relate back to the original timely filed petition. Plaintiffs argue that relation back under this article does not interrupt or suspend the peremptive time period, it merely applies the date of the original petition to the amended petition. We disagree.

"The primary importance of [La. C.C.P. art. 1153] is the avoidance of prescription by amending to add an overlooked defendant or cause of action or to join a tardy plaintiff." Frank L. Maraist, 1 Louisiana Civil Law Treatise: Civil Procedure, § 6:10, p. 224 (2nd Ed. 2008) (emphasis added); *see also Ray, supra* at 1086 (holding that an amended petition may not add a wholly new and unrelated defendant, "since this would be tantamount to asserting a new cause of action which would have been otherwise prescribed"). While Article 1153 does not specifically refer to its effect on statutory time limitations for filing suit, there can be no question but that "relation back" of an untimely filed amended petition directly interferes with the application of prescription or preemption by allowing a claim that would have otherwise prescribed or been preempted to proceed. Thus, we cannot consider Article 1153 in a vacuum without considering whether it has a prohibitive effect on the operation of preemption.

This Court has never directly addressed whether an amended petition adding a plaintiff will related back to the original timely filed petition under Article 1153 where the time period for filing suit is peremptive, rather than prescription. However, in *Naquin v. Lafayette City-Parish Consol. Government*, 06-2227 (La. 2007), 950 So. 2d 657, we held that new claims added by an amended pleading after the peremptive period provided in La. Const. art. 6, § 35 had expired were perempted and could not be considered. Although the plaintiffs in that case argued that no new issues were raised in the supplemental pleading, we carefully analyzed whether the claims presented in the supplemental pleading were also raised in the original, and timely filed, pleading and held that any claims not raised in the original pleading were perempted. We held that the peremptive period in that case was "intended to limit the rights of parties who have timely raised challenges to expand their pleadings to raise new issues after the passage of the constitutional peremptive period, even if the expansion is presented in the guise of supplemental argument." 950 So. 2d at 669. While we did not specifically refer to Art. 1153 in that case, we relied on a court of appeal case that held that "a supplemental challenge ... that was filed by plaintiffs after the peremptive period did not relate back to the date of the filing of the original petition that did not state a cause of action." *Id.* at 668 (citing *Lege v. Vermillion Parish School Bd.*, 360 So. 2d 664 (La.App. 3 Cir. 1978)).

* * * * *

Conclusion

The one and three-year periods for filing a legal malpractice suit under La. R.S. 9:5605 are peremptive time periods. Peremption differs from prescriptive in two respects: (1) the expiration of the peremptive time period destroys the cause of action itself; and (2) nothing may interfere with the running of a peremptive time period. La. C.C. P. art. 1153 would avoid the operation of the peremptive time period by allowing a pleading filed after the expiration of the period to relate back to the filing of an original and timely filed petition. Because the avoidance of the time period interferes with the running of that time period, relation back of a petition adding a new plaintiff is not permitted where the time period involved is peremptive. Further, because the expiration of a peremptive time period destroys the cause of action, there is nothing for an amended or supplemental petition to relate back to under La. C.C.P. art. 1153. Because the plaintiffs in this case did not file suit in the name of the proper party plaintiff before the peremptive time period of La. R.S. 9:5605 had expired, the First Supplemental/Amending Petition attempting to do so cannot relate back to the original petition under La. C.C.P. art. 1153. Therefore, the defendants' exception of peremption should have been granted.

Decree

For the reasons stated herein, the judgments of the lower courts are reversed and the case is remanded to the trial court to grant the defendants' exception of peremption.

REVERSED AND REMANDED.

KIMBALL, C.J., dissents and assigns reasons.

JOHNSON, J., dissents.

KNOLL and WEIMER, JJ., concur in the result.

C.   IMMUNITY: DEFENDANT'S STATUS OR RELATIONSHIP TO VICTIM

1.   Defendant's Status (Sovereign Immunity)

A tort suit may be barred because the tort defendant's status or relationship to the victim makes it poor policy to allow recovery. While such a policy choice may be expressed in terms of "scope of the risk" or "legal cause," it usually is treated as an affirmative defense called "immunity." One of the dominant immunities is that generally a sovereign is immune from suits in its own courts. The doctrine had an interesting historical birth. At early common law all potential litigants were required to obtain the permission of the sovereign to pursue claims judicially, and the sovereign could refuse to permit itself to be sued. The doctrine generally has been carried over into modern times.

Can you think of any societal policies which justify making the sovereign immune from tort liability for the same kind of conduct for which it imposes tort liability upon its subjects?

Most jurisdictions have partially or fully waived sovereign immunity from tort claims. The waiver by the federal sovereign is contained generally in the Federal Tort Claims Act, 28 U.S.C. § 2674. The Louisiana waiver, in the state's constitution, is reproduced below.

Article 12, Section 10, Louisiana Constitution (prior to 1995 amendment)

§ 10. Suits Against the State

(A) **No Immunity in Contract and Tort**. Neither the state, a state agency, nor a political subdivision shall be immune from suit and liability in contract or for injury to person or property.

(B) **Waiver in Other Suits**. The legislature may authorize other suits against the state, a state agency, or a political subdivision. A measure authorizing suit shall waive immunity from suit and liability.

(C) **Procedure; Judgments**. The legislature shall provide a procedure for suits against the state, a state agency, or a political subdivision. It shall provide for the effect of a judgment, but no public property or public funds shall be subject to seizure. No judgment against the state, a state agency, or a political subdivision shall be eligible, payable, or paid except from funds appropriated therefor by the legislature or by the political subdivision against which judgment is rendered.

COMMENT

In Louisiana, prior to 1974, there was no general waiver of sovereign immunity. Waiver was on a "case by case" basis, with the prospective plaintiff first obtaining a legislative act authorizing him to sue the state and obtain judgment, and, if successful, returning for another act authorizing payment of the judgment. Article 12, Section 10 of the 1974 Constitution waived immunity from suit and judgment in some kinds of cases (including tort claims), but did not waive the restriction against seizure of public property. Thus, today the successful claimant nevertheless must return to the legislature to obtain an act directing payment of a judgment against the state. Similar provisions apply to state agencies and political subdivisions.

In *Chamberlain v. State*, 624 So. 2d 874 (La. 1993), the Supreme Court ruled that R.S. 13:5106(B)(1), which imposed a $500,000 ceiling on general damages recoverable in a personal injury suit against the state, its agencies or its subdivisions, contravened the constitutional proscription against sovereign immunity contained in Art. XII, Sec. 10 of the Constitution. In *Rick v. State*, 630 So. 2d 1271 (La. 1994), the Court held that R.S. 13:5112(C), limiting pre-judgment interest against the state, was unconstitutional. Then in 1995 Section C of Section 10 of Article 12 was amended to read as follows:

"(C) **Limitations; Procedure; Judgments**. Notwithstanding Paragraph (A) or (B) or any other provision of this constitution, the legislature by law may limit or provide for the extent of liability of the state, a state agency, or a political subdivision in all cases, including the circumstances giving rise to liability and the kinds and amounts of recoverable damages. It shall provide a procedure for suits against the state, a state agency, or a political subdivision and provide for the effect of a judgment, but no public property or public funds shall be subject to seizure. The legislature may provide that such limitations, procedures, and effects of judgments shall be applicable to existing as well as future claims. No judgment against the state, a state agency, or a political subdivision shall be exigible, payable, or paid except from funds appropriated therefor by the legislature or by the political subdivision against which the judgment is rendered."

The federal sovereign has waived tort immunity generally in the Federal Tort Claims Act, 28 USC §§ 1346, 2671-80. The waiver does not apply to certain intentional torts. *See, e.g., Truman v. United States*, 26 F.3d 592 (5th Cir. 1994). A negligence claim related to the employee's intentional tort may proceed only where the negligence arises out of an independent, antecedent duty unrelated to the employment relationship between the tortfeasor and the United States. "Only negligent conduct, undertaken within the scope of employment and unrelated to an excluded tort...may form the basis of a cause of action." *Leleux v. U.S.,* 178 F.3d 750 (5th Cir. 1999).

A state may not be sued in federal court for money damages, except that an individual may sue a state in federal court where Congress has authorized suit in the exercise of its power to enforce the Fourteenth Amendment, or where a state has waived its sovereign immunity by consenting to suit. A state waives its immunity from suit in federal court only if it voluntarily invokes or clearly declares that it intends to submit itself to the jurisdiction of the federal court. A state does not impliedly waive its immunity from suit in federal court by participating in a federally regulated activity, even one that traditionally is performed by private entities, and even when supplemented by an unambiguous statement of congressional intent to subject the states to suit. *College Savings Bank v. Florida Prepaid Postsecondary Education Expense Board*, 527 U. S. 627 (1999).

In addition, Congress may not subject a nonconsenting state to a private suit for damages in the state's own courts. *Alden v. Maine*, 527 U. S. 706 (1999). However, a state may not be immune from suit in the courts of another state.

a.   The Louisiana Governmental Claims Act, R.S. 13:5101, et. seq.

La. R.S. 13:5101.   **Title and Application**

B.   This Part applies to any suit in contract or for injury to person or property against the state, a state agency, an officer or employee of the state or a state agency arising out of the discharge of his official duties or within the course and scope of his employment, or a political subdivision of the state, as defined herein, or against an officer or employee of a political subdivision arising out of the discharge of his official duties or within the course and scope of his employment. The provisions of this Part shall not supersede the provisions of R.S. 15:1171 et seq or R.S. 15:1181 et seq.

La. R.S. 13:5102. Definitions

A.   As used in this Part, "state agency" means any board, commission, department, agency, special district, authority, or other entity of the state and, as used in R.S. 13:5106, any nonpublic, nonprofit agency, person, firm, or corporation which has qualified with the United States Internal Revenue Service for an exemption from federal income tax under Section 501(c)(3), (4), (7), (8), (10), or (19) of the Internal Revenue Code, and which, through contract with the state, provides services for the treatment, care, custody, control, or supervision of persons placed or referred to such agency, person, firm, or corporation by any agency or department of the state in connection with programs for treatment or services involving residential or day care for adults and children, foster care, rehabilitation, shelter, or counseling; however, the term "state agency" shall include such nonpublic, nonprofit agency, person, firm, or corporation only as it renders services to a person or persons on behalf of the state pursuant to a contract with the state. The term "state agency" shall not include a nonpublic, nonprofit agency, person, firm or corporation that commits a willful or wanton, or grossly negligent, act or omission. A nonpublic, nonprofit agency, person, firm or corporation otherwise included under the provisions of this Subsection shall not be deemed a "state agency" for the purpose of prohibiting trial by jury under R.S. 13:5105, and a suit against such agency, person, firm or corporation may be tried by jury as provided by law. "State agency" does not include any political subdivision or any agency of a political subdivision.

B.   As the term is used in this Part, "political subdivision" means:

(1)   Any parish, municipality, special district, school board, sheriff, public board, institution, department, commission, district, corporation, agency, authority, or an agency or subdivision of any of these, and other public or governmental body of any kind which is not a state agency.

(2)   Any private entity, such as Transit Management of Southeast Louisiana, Inc. (TMSEL), including its employees, which on the behalf of a public transit authority was created as a result of Section 13(c) of the Urban Mass Transportation Act, requiring the terms of transit workers' collective bargaining agreements to be honored and provides management and administrative duties of such agency or authority and such entity is employed by no other agency or authority, whether public or private.

* * * * *

La. R.S. 13:5105. Jury trial prohibited

A.   No suit against a political subdivision of the state shall be tried by jury. Except upon a demand for jury trial timely filed in accordance with law by the state or a state agency or the plaintiff in a lawsuit against the state or state agency, no suit against the state or a state agency shall be tried by jury.

* * * * *

D.   Notwithstanding the provisions of Subsection A, a political subdivision, by general ordinance or resolution, may waive the prohibition against a jury trial provided in Subsection A of this Section. Whenever the jury trial prohibition is waived by a political subdivision, and a jury trial is demanded by the political subdivision or the plaintiff in a suit against the political subdivision or against an officer or employee of the political subdivision, the demand for a jury trial shall be timely filed in accordance with law. The rights to and limitations upon a jury trial shall be as provided in Code of Civil Procedure Articles 1731 and 1732.

* * * * *

La. R.S. 13:5106. Limitations

A.   No suit against the state or a state agency or political subdivision shall be instituted in any court other than a Louisiana state court.

B.   (1)   The total liability of the state and political subdivisions for all damages for personal injury to any one person, including all claims and derivative claims, exclusive of property damages, medical care and related benefits and loss of earnings, and loss of future earnings, as provided in this Section, shall not exceed five hundred thousand dollars, regardless of the number of suits filed or claims made for the personal injury to that person.

(2)   The total liability of the state and political subdivisions for all damages for wrongful death of any one person, including all claims and derivative claims, exclusive of property damages, medical care and related benefits and loss of earnings or loss of support, and loss of future support, as provided in this Section, shall not exceed five hundred thousand dollars, regardless of the number of suits filed or claims made for the wrongful death of that person.

(3)(a)   In any suit for personal injury against a political subdivision wherein the court, pursuant to judgment, determines that the claimant is entitled to medical care and related benefits that may be incurred subsequent to judgment, the court shall order that a reversionary trust be established for the benefit of the claimant and that all medical care and related benefits incurred subsequent to judgment be paid pursuant to the reversionary trust instrument. The reversionary trust instrument shall provide that such medical care and related benefits be paid directly to the provider as they are incurred. Nothing in this Paragraph shall be construed to prevent the parties from entering into a settlement or compromise at any time whereby medical care and related benefits shall be provided, but with the requirement of establishing a reversionary trust.

(b) Any funds remaining in a reversionary trust that is created pursuant to Subparagraph (3)(a) of this Subsection shall revert to the political subdivision that established the trust, upon the death of the claimant or upon the termination of the trust as provided in the trust instrument. The trustee may obtain the services of an administrator to assist in the administration of the trust. All costs, fees, taxes, or other charges imposed on the funds in the trust shall be paid by the trust. The trust agreement may impose such other reasonable duties, powers, provisions, and dispute resolution clauses as may be deemed necessary or appropriate. Disputes as to the administration of the trust can be appealed to the district court. Nothing in this Paragraph shall preclude the political subdivision from establishing other alternative funding mechanisms for the exclusive benefit of the claimant. The terms and conditions of the reversionary trust instrument or other alternative funding mechanism, prior to its implementation, must be approved by the court. The parties to the case may present recommendations to the court for the terms and conditions of the trust instrument or other funding mechanism to be included in the order. Upon request of either party, the court shall hold a contradictory hearing before granting a final order implementing the reversionary trust or the alternative funding mechanism.

(c) In any suit for personal injury against the state or a state agency wherein the court pursuant to judgment determines that the claimant is entitled to medical care and related benefits that may be incurred subsequent to judgment, the court shall order that all medical care and related benefits incurred subsequent to judgment be paid from the Future Medical Care Fund as provided in R.S. 39:1533.2. Medical care and related benefits shall be paid directly to the provider as they are incurred. Nothing in this Subparagraph shall be construed to prevent the parties from entering into a settlement or compromise at any time whereby medical care and related benefits shall be provided but with the requirement that they shall be paid in accordance with this Subparagraph.

* * * * *

La. R.S. 13:5107. Service of citation and process

A. (1) In all suits filed against the state of Louisiana or a state agency, citation and service may be obtained by citation and service on the attorney general of Louisiana, or on any employee in his office above the age of sixteen years, or any other proper officer or person, depending upon the identity of the named defendant and in accordance with the laws of this state, and on the department, board, commission, or agency head or person, depending upon the identity of the named defendant and in accordance with the laws of this state, and on the department, board, commission, or agency head or person, depending upon the identity of the named defendant and the identity of the named board, commission, department, agency, or officer through which or through whom suit is to be filed against.

(2) Service shall be requested upon the attorney general within ninety days of filing suit. This shall be sufficient to comply with the requirements of Subsection D of this Section and also Code of Civil Procedure Article 1201(C). However, the duty of the defendant served through the attorney general to answer the suit or file other responsive pleadings does not commence to run until the additional service required upon the department, board, commission, or agency head has been made.

B. In all suits filed against a political subdivision of the state, or any of its departments, offices, boards, commissions, agencies or instrumentalities, citation and service may be obtained on any proper agent or agents designated by the local governing authority and in accordance with the laws of the state provided that the authority has filed notice of the designation of agent for service of process with and paid a fee of ten dollars to the secretary of state, who shall maintain such information with the information on agents for service of process for corporations. If no agent or agents are designated for service of process, as shown by the lack of such designation in the records of the secretary of state, citation and service may be obtained on the district attorney, parish attorney, city attorney, or any other proper officer or person, depending upon the identity of the named defendant and in accordance with the laws of the state, and on the department, board, commission, or agency head or person, depending upon the identity of the named defendant and the identity of the named board, commission, department, agency, or officer through which or through whom suit is to be filed against.

* * * * *

D. (1)   In all suits in which the state, a state agency, or political subdivision, or any officer or employee thereof is named as a party, service of citation shall be requested within ninety days of the commencement of the action or the filing of a supplemental or amended petition which initially names the state, a state agency, or political subdivision or any officer or employee thereof as a party. This requirement may be expressly waived by the defendant in such action by any written waiver. If not waived, a request for service of citation upon a defendant shall be considered timely if requested on the defendant within the time period provided by this Section, notwithstanding insufficient or erroneous service.

(2)   If service is not requested by the party filing the action within the period required in Paragraph (1) of this Subsection, the action shall be dismissed without prejudice, after contradictory motion as provided in Code of Civil Procedure Article 1672(C), as to the state, state agency, or political subdivision, or any officer or employee thereof, upon whom service was not requested within the period required by Paragraph (1) of this Subsection.

(3)   When the state, a state agency, or a political subdivision, or any officer or employee thereof, is dismissed as a party pursuant to this Section, the filing of the action, even as against other defendants, shall not interrupt or suspend the running of prescription as to the state, state agency, or political subdivision, or any officer or employee thereof; however, the effect of interruption of prescription as to other persons shall continue.

COMMENT

The Louisiana Supreme Court interpreted La. R.S. 13:5107(D)(2) in *Tranchant v. State*, 5 So. 3d 832 (La. 2009). The issue was what satisfies the statutory language "[i]f service is not requested by the party filing the action." The Court presented the issue this way:

> "Specifically, we are called to determine whether a request for service is deemed made when a letter containing service instructions is mailed or when it is received by the clerk's office." *Id.* at 832-33. The court held that "request" usually means a two-party transaction wherein one party asks that something be done and the other party acts in response. Thus, service is requested within the meaning of the statute when the clerk of court receives the service instructions. Because the letter to the clerk with the service instructions was mailed by the plaintiff's attorney on the 90th day, the service request was untimely, and the defendant's declinatory exception of insufficiency of service of process was granted without prejudice.

La. R.S. 13:5108. Prescription, immunity; pleas

The defendant in any suit filed against the state of Louisiana, a state agency or a political subdivision of the state shall not be entitled to file a plea of prescription or peremption barring such suit or the liability of the entity instituting the suit if the suit in contract or for injury to person or property is filed within the time fixed by law for such suits against private persons, or in other suits authorized by the legislature if the suit is filed within one year after the date on which the resolution authorizing it was adopted or within one year after the date on which the law authorizing it becomes effective.

b.   Claims Against Public Entities For Defective Conditions

In many cases plaintiffs argue that the government has created an unreasonable risk by failing to properly maintain roads or neglecting repairs of buildings. In such cases, Louisiana, and many states, apply what is known as the "public duty" doctrine. The public duty doctrine in Louisiana is contained in La. R.S. 9:2800.

La. R.S. 9:2800. Limitation of liability for public bodies

A. A public entity is responsible under Civil Code Article 2317 for damages caused by the condition of buildings within its care and custody.

B. Where other constructions are placed upon state property by someone other than the state, and the right to keep the improvements on the property has expired, the state shall not be responsible for any damages caused thereby unless the state affirmatively takes control of and utilizes the improvement for the state's benefit and use.

C. Except as provided for in Subsections A and B of this Section, no person shall have a cause of action based solely upon liability imposed under Civil Code Article 2317 against a public entity for damages caused by the condition of things within its care and custody unless the public entity had actual or constructive notice of the particular vice or defect which caused the damage prior to the occurrence, and the public entity has had a reasonable opportunity to remedy the defect and has failed to do so.

D. Constructive notice shall mean the existence of facts which infer actual knowledge.

E. A public entity that responds to or makes an examination or inspection of any public site or area in response to reports or complaints of a defective condition on property of which the entity has no ownership or control and that takes steps to forewarn or alert the public of such defective condition, such as erecting barricades or warning devices in or adjacent to an area, does not thereby gain custody, control, or garde of the area or assume a duty to prevent personal injury, wrongful death, property damage, or other loss as to render the public entity liable unless it is shown that the entity failed to notify the public entity which does have care and custody of the property of the defect within a reasonable length of time.

F. A violation of the rules and regulations promulgated by a public entity is not negligence per se.

G. (1) "Public entity" means and includes the state and any of its branches, departments, offices, agencies, boards, commissions, instrumentalities, officers, officials, employees, and political subdivisions and the departments, offices, agencies, boards, commissions, instrumentalities, officers, officials, and employees of such political subdivisions. Public entity also includes housing authorities, as defined in R.S. 40:384(15), and their commissioners and other officers and employees and sewerage and water boards and their employees, servants, agents, or subcontractors.

(2) "Public site or area" means any publicly owned or common thing, or any privately owned property over which the public's access is not prohibited, limited, or restricted in some manner including those areas of unrestricted access such as streets, sidewalks, parks, or public squares.

COMMENT

The Louisiana Supreme Court explained what a plaintiff must prove to recover against a public entity for defective roads or other conditions:

> Accordingly, for a plaintiff to successfully recover against a public entity for damages due to road defects, he must prove: (1) the thing that caused his damages was in the defendant's custody; (2) the thing was defective due to a condition that created an unreasonable risk of harm; (3) the defendant had actual or constructive notice of the defect, yet did not take steps to correct it within a reasonable period of

time; and (4) the defect was a cause in fact of the plaintiff's harm. *Jones v. Hawkins*, 731 So. 2d 216, 218 (La. 1999).

For recent cases finding the public entities not liable because the conditions did not constitute an unreasonable risk of harm, *see Chambers v. Village of Moreauville,* 85 So. 3d 593 (La. 2012) (one-and-one-quarter to one-and-one-half inch deviation in sidewalk); *Pryor v. Iberville Parish School Board*, 60 So. 3d 594 (La. 2011) (eighteen inch gap in bleacher seat boards).

In another case, *Casborn v. Jefferson Parish Hosp. Dist. No. 1*, 96 So. 3d 540 (La.App. 5 Cir. 2012), the public entity, a parish hospital, was sued when plaintiff, who was visiting someone at the hospital, caught her foot on an uneven concrete section of walkway next to a parking garage. The court held that plaintiff could not prove defendant's actual or constructive knowledge of the defect. The court explained that there are two theories under which a public entity may be held liable for damages, but the analysis is now the same for each. Explaining the convergence of the two theories, the court stated as follows:

> Traditionally, these theories could be distinguished, because under strict liability, a plaintiff was relieved of proving that the owner or custodian of a thing which caused damage knew or should have known of the risk involved. However, with the enactment of La. R.S. 9:2800, the legislature has eviscerated this distinction in claims against public entities by requiring proof of actual or constructive knowledge of the defect which causes the damage under either theory. Thus, with respect to public entities, the burden of proof is the same under either theory.

Id. at 543-44.

c. Policy-Making or Discretionary Acts or Omissions of Public Entities, Officers, and Employees

Related to the public duty doctrine is the issue of liability of public entities or their officers and employees based upon their discretionary acts or omissions. The Louisiana Legislature has enacted La. R.S. 9:2798.1 as guidance in this area.

La. R.S. 9:2798.1.   Policy-making or discretionary acts or omissions of public entities or their officers or employees

A.   As used in this Section, "public entity" means and includes the state and any of its branches, departments, offices, agencies, boards, commissions, instrumentalities, officers, officials, employees, and political subdivisions and the departments, offices, agencies, boards, commissions, instrumentalities, officers, officials, and employees of such political subdivisions.

B.   Liability shall not be imposed on public entities or their officers or employees based upon the exercise or performance or the failure to exercise or perform their policy-making or discretionary acts when such acts are within the course and scope of their lawful powers and duties.

C.   The provisions of Subsection B of this Section are not applicable:

(1) To acts or omissions which are not reasonably related to the legitimate governmental objective for which the policy-making or discretionary power exists; or

(2) To acts or omissions which constitute criminal, fraudulent, malicious, intentional, willful, outrageous, reckless, or flagrant misconduct.

* * * * *

COMMENT

The immunity here, though similar to qualified immunity, turns on the officer's discretion to make the decision at issue. The immunity does not apply when a statute, regulation, or policy specifically prescribes a course of action where there is no element of choice or discretion involved; also, it only confers immunity where the discretionary action involves the permissible exercise of a policy judgment grounded in social, economic or public policy. *Williams v. Galliano,* 697 So. 2d 294 (La.App. 1 Cir. 1997). In many cases, this amounts to much the same as the federal "clearly established law" requirement, since officers have no discretion to violate clearly established law. *See Tenhaaf v. Quenqui,* 571 So. 2d 898 (La.App. 5 Cir. 1990) (municipality cannot benefit from immunity because it has no discretion to violate applicable law). Significantly, the statute seems to exclude intentional torts. However, many "intentional" acts are really policy judgments or discretionary decisions that might fall under the act.

At common law, government officials have traditionally been afforded immunity from suits for damages caused by their exercise of governmental power. One court described the immunity of judges from liability for actions in their judicial capacity as one which "obtains in all countries where there is any well-ordered system of jurisprudence. It has been the settled doctrine of the English courts for many centuries, and has never been denied, that we are aware of, in the courts of this country. It has, as Chancellor Kent observes, 'a deep root in the common law.'" *Bradley v. Fisher*, 80 U.S. 335, 347 (1871) (judge immune from suit by attorney for defendant in Lincoln assassination trial for summarily disbarring him), *citing Yates v. Lansing*, 5 Johnson, 291. Ordinarily this immunity is divided between "absolute" or "qualified" immunity. The latter is sometimes called discretionary or good faith immunity.

Absolute immunity applies only to certain public officials, typically judges, *see McCoy v. City of Monroe*, 747 So. 2d 1234 (La.App. 2 Cir. 1999), non-party witnesses in court proceedings, *Genovese v. Usner*, 602 So. 2d 1084 (La.App. 1 Cir. 1992), legislators, and prosecutors in their prosecutorial capacity. *See Knapper v. Connick*, 681 So. 2d 944 (La. 1996). Absolute immunity has also been extended to officers exercising quasi-judicial authority, such as members of boards, commissions, and non-judicial adjudicatory boards that decide disputes in prisons. *Cf. Durousseau v. State*, 724 So. 2d 844 (La.App. 4 Cir. 1998) (extending such immunity to boards and commissions on same ground as their members).

Qualified immunity is available to all government officials, but attaches only where the officer's behavior was consistent with what a reasonable officer would have believed permissible. In federal law, this immunity is assumed unless the plaintiff can show that the officer violated a legal right clearly established at the time of which a reasonable person would have known. The purpose of the qualified immunity is to ensure that officers are on notice of the illegality of their conduct before they are subjected to suit. *See Hope v. Peltzer*, 536 U.S. 730 (2002); *Saucier v. Katz*, 533 U.S. 194 (2001). Louisiana statutory law is discussed more extensively, in negligence defenses, *infra*. It generally provides the same immunities for individuals as for public entities. *See* R.S. 9:2798.1.

2.   Defendant's Relationship to Victim

a.   Family Immunities

In every jurisdiction, certain family members are immune from suits by other family members. The immunity varies. In some cases the immunity does not extend to the insurer of the family members whose conduct otherwise would have been wrongful to another family member. In such cases, the immunity is said to be "personal. The leading family immunities in Louisiana are parent and child and spouses.

La. R.S. 9:291. Suits between spouses

Spouses may not sue each other except for causes of action pertaining to contracts or arising out of the provisions of Book III, Title VI of the Civil Code; for restitution of separate property; for divorce or declaration of nullity of the marriage; and for causes of action pertaining to spousal support or the support or custody of a child while the spouses are living separate and apart.

La. R.S. 9:571. Actions between parent, person having parental authority, or tutor and child

A. No parent may sue his unemancipated minor child. No other person having parental authority over the minor may sue him.

B. An unemancipated minor may not sue any person having parental authority over him.

C. An unemancipated minor may not sue his tutor. The tutor may not sue the minor.

GUILLOT

v.

TRAVELERS INDEM. CO.
338 So. 2d 334 (La.App. 3 Cir. 1977)

DOMENGEAUX, J.

Defendant, The Travelers Indemnity Company, appeals from a judgment awarding $12,500.00 to plaintiff, Leontine Guillot, for personal injuries sustained by the latter. Plaintiff has answered the appeal seeking an increase in the award. We affirm the judgment of the district court.

On May 5, 1975, plaintiff was a passenger in an automobile owned and driven by her husband, Irvin Joseph Guillot, in the town of Marksville, Avoyelles Parish, Louisiana.

The Guillot vehicle was involved in an accident with another automobile, the causation of which was determined to be the sole negligence of Mr. Guillot. Plaintiff sought to recover from her husband's insurer, defendant, under the liability and uninsured motorist provisions of the policy issued to the former.[1]

Defendant-insurer did not contest the issue of Mr. Guillot's liability for the injuries sustained by his wife as a result of the accident. Travelers paid $10,000.00 (policy limits) under the liability portions of the insurance contract but contended that Mrs. Guillot's injuries were not covered under the uninsured motorist provisions due to certain exclusionary clauses contained in the policy. The trial judge disagreed with the defendant's position and awarded Mrs. Guillot $10,000.00 under the liability provisions of the policy and an additional $2,500.00 under the uninsured motorist provisions of said policy.

Defendant's appeal is directed toward the following specifications of error: (1) The trial court erred in allowing the tort victim to recover uninsured motorist benefits from insurer where the victim was not legally entitled to recover from the uninsured motorist, her husband; (2) The trial court erred in holding that a tort victim who was a passenger in a tortfeasor's vehicle could recover from the tortfeasor's insurer under both liability and uninsured motorist provisions of said vehicle, despite the terms and conditions of insurer's policy.

'Legally Entitled to Recover'

The statute applicable to the instant case is LSA-R.S. 22:1406. LSA-R.S. 22:1406(D)(1) provides:

No automobile liability insurance covering liability arising out of the ownership, maintenance, or use of any motor vehicle shall be delivered or issued for delivery in this state with respect to any motor vehicle registered or principally garaged in this

---

[1] On the date of the accident Mr. Guillot had in effect a policy with the defendant providing coverage of $10,000/$20,000 for liability and like amounts for uninsured motorist protection.

state unless coverage is provided therein or supplemental thereto, in not less than the limits of bodily injury liability provided by the policy, under provisions filed with and approved by the commissioner of insurance, for the protection of persons insured thereunder who are legally entitled to recover damages from owners or operators of uninsured or underinsured motor vehicles because of bodily injury, sickness, or disease, including death, resulting therefrom.... (Emphasis added).

Defendant contends that plaintiff is not 'legally entitled to recover' damages from her husband's insurer due to the doctrine of interspousal immunity embodied in LSA-R.S. 9:291. This issue was previously considered by this court in the case of *Gremillion v. State Farm Mutual Automobile Insurance Company*, 302 So. 2d 712 (La.App. 3 Cir. 1974), *writ refused*, 305 So. 2d 134. In *Gremillion* we held that the defense of interspousal immunity is personal to the husband or wife and cannot be raised by an insurer in a direct action against same.

In *Gremillion* we quoted extensively from *Booth v. Fireman's Fund Insurance Company*, 253 La. 521, 218 So. 2d 580 (1968) as follows:

... the insurer does not stand in the shoes of the uninsured motorist who is the tort feasor.

We interpret the words 'legally entitled to recover' to mean simply that the plaintiff must be able to establish fault on the part of the uninsured motorist which gives rise to damages and prove the extent of those damages.

See also Deshotels v. Travelers Indemnity Company, 257 La. 567, 243 So. 2d 259 (La. 1971).

Defendant urges this court to reconsider our decision in *Gremillion* and reverse the holding therein. We are of the opinion that the *Gremillion* case was correctly decided and are inclined to adhere to its holding. Accordingly we find that the trial judge correctly ruled that plaintiff was 'legally entitled to recover' under the provisions of LSA-R.S. 22:1406(D)(1)(a).

* * * * *

NOTES

1.   These immunities exist to promote family stability during the marriage and child rearing years. Because they are personal, these immunities do not prevent a direct action against the immune individual's liability insurer. Frank L. Maraist and Thomas C. Galligan, Jr., *Louisiana Tort Law*, § 11.02, (perm. ed., rev. vol., 2013).

2.   In *Deshotel v. Travelers Indemnity Co.*, 243 So. 2d 259 (La. 1971), the Court concluded that the father has a cause of action against his minor son for damages resulting from the minor's delictual acts. Is this case still valid after the revision of R.S. 9:571 effective January 1, 2016? Can a tutor of the minor sue a custodial parent? *See, Walker v. State Farm Mutual Auto Ins. Co.*, 765 So. 2d 1224 (La.App. 2 Cir. 2000).

3.   While some immunities preclude any tort recovery, the family immunities merely bar enforcement during the existence of the relationship. Accordingly, one spouse may not sue the other spouse in tort during the existence of the marriage. Also, during the marriage, an unemancipated child born of the marriage cannot sue either parent in tort. If the marriage has terminated, the child may sue the noncustodial parent, but she may not sue the parent entitled to her custody and control. Upon reaching majority the child may sue the custodial parent. *See, Duplechin v. Toce*, 497 So. 2d 763 (La.App. 3 Cir. 1986); *see also* Maraist and Galligan, *Louisiana Tort Law*, § 11.02 (perm. ed., rev. vol., 2013).

3.   Defendant's Activities

a. Use of Land

La. R.S. 9:2795 **Limitation of liability of landowner of property used for recreational purposes; property owned by the Department of Wildlife and Fisheries; parks owned by public entities**

A.   As used in this Section:

(1)   "Land" means urban or rural land, roads, water, watercourses, private ways or buildings, structures, and machinery or equipment when attached to the realty.

(2)   "Owner" means the possessor of a fee interest, a tenant, lessee, occupant or person in control of the premises.

(3)   "Recreational purposes" includes but is not limited to any of the following, or any combination thereof: hunting, fishing, trapping, swimming, boating, camping, picnicking, hiking, horseback riding, bicycle riding, motorized, or nonmotorized vehicle operation for recreation purposes, nature study, water skiing, ice skating, roller skating, roller blading, skate boarding, sledding, snowmobiling, snow skiing, summer and winter sports, or viewing or enjoying historical, archaeological, scenic, or scientific sites.

(4)   "Charge" means the admission price or fee asked in return for permission to use lands.

(5)   "Person" means individuals regardless of age.

B.   (1)   Except for willful or malicious failure to warn against a dangerous condition, use, structure, or activity, an owner of land, except an owner of commercial recreational developments or facilities, who permits with or without charge any person to use his land for recreational purposes as herein defined does not thereby:

(a)   Extend any assurance that the premises are safe for any purposes.

(b)   Constitute such person the legal status of an invitee or licensee to whom a duty of care is owed.

(c)   Incur liability for any injury to person or property caused by any defect in the land regardless of whether naturally occurring or man-made.

(2)   The provisions of this Subsection shall apply to owners of commercial recreational developments or facilities for injury to persons or property arising out of the commercial recreational activity permitted at the recreational development or facility that occurs on land which does not comprise the commercial recreational development or facility and over which the owner has no control when the recreational activity commences, occurs, or terminates on the commercial recreational development or facility.

C.   Unless otherwise agreed in writing, the provisions of Subsection B shall be deemed applicable to the duties and liability of an owner of land leased for recreational purposes to the federal government or any state or political subdivision thereof or private persons.

D.   Nothing in this Section shall be construed to relieve any person using the land of another for recreational purposes from any obligation which he may have in the absence of this Section to exercise care in his use of such land and in his activities thereon, or from the legal consequences of failure to employ such care.

E.   (1)   The limitation of liability provided in this Section shall apply to any lands or water bottoms owned, leased, or managed by the Department of Wildlife and Fisheries, regardless of the purposes for which the land or water bottoms are used, and whether they are used for recreational or nonrecreational purposes.

        (2)   (a)   The limitation of liability provided in this Section shall apply to any lands, whether urban or rural, which are owned, leased, or managed as a public park by the state or any of its political subdivisions and which are used for recreational purposes.

* * * * *

        (c)   For purposes of the limitation of liability afforded to parks pursuant to this Section this limitation does not apply to playground equipment or stands which are defective.

        (d)   The limitation of liability as extended to parks in this Section shall not apply to intentional or grossly negligent acts by an employee of the public entity.

F.   The limitation of liability extended by this Section to the owner, lessee, or occupant of premises shall not be affected by the granting of a lease, right of use, or right of occupancy for any recreational purpose which may limit the use of the premises to persons other than the entire public or by the posting of the premises so as to limit the use of the premises to persons other than the entire public.

La. R.S. 9:2800.4.   **Limitation of liability of owner of farm or forest land; owner of oil, gas, or mineral property**

A.   As used in this Section:

        (1)   "Owner" means the owner and also a tenant, lessee, occupant, or person in control of any farm or forest land or in control of any oil, gas, or mineral property.

        (2)   "Farm land or forest land" shall mean bona fide agricultural or timberland assessed as such for parish ad valorem taxes.

        (3)   "Gleaning" means gathering the residue of a crop left in the fields to waste after harvesting is completed.

        (4)   "Oil, gas, or mineral property" shall mean any land leased for the development and production of oil, gas, or minerals.

B.   An owner of farm or forest land shall not be liable to any person, who unlawfully enters upon his farm or forest land, for damages for any injury, death, or loss which occurs while on the farm or forest land of the owner, unless such damage, injury, or death was caused by the intentional act or gross negligence of the owner.

C.   An owner of farm or forest land, who allows his land to be used as a landing strip for aerial applications for agricultural purposes, shall not be liable to any person for damages for any injury, death, or loss which occurs during or in connection with such application while on the land of the owner, unless such damage, injury, or death was caused by the intentional act or negligence of the owner.

D.   An owner of farm or forest land, who allows his land to be used by a group or individuals for the purpose of gleaning, without compensation to the landowner from the group or individuals, shall not be liable to any person for damages for any injury, death, or loss which occurs during or in connection with such gleaning while on the land of the owner, unless such damage, injury, or death was caused by the intentional act or negligence of the owner.

E.   An owner of oil, gas, or mineral property shall not be liable to any person who unlawfully enters upon his oil, gas, or mineral property, for damages for any injury, death, or loss which occurs while on the oil, gas, or mineral property of the owner, unless such damage, injury, or death was caused by the intentional act or gross negligence of the owner.

NOTES

1.   For a thorough analysis of the recreational use immunity statutes, *see, Richard v. Hall*, in Chapter 12. In *Richard*, the Louisiana Supreme Court determined that insofar as La. R.S. 9: 2791 conflicts with La. R.S. 9:2795, the latter is controlling, and held that a lessee who does not use the leased premises for commercial profit from recreational activities is entitled to assert the statutory immunity despite the owner-lessor having leased the property as part of a commercial recreational venture.

2.   For an expansive interpretation and application of the recreational immunity statute, see *Richard v. Louisiana Newpack Shrimping Co., Inc.*, 82 So. 3d 541 (La.App. 5 Cir. 2011).

> We hold that the levee was recreational within the meaning of the Immunity Act. Because of the expansive definition of "recreational purpose", we find that the levee itself need not be recreational in character. Although the levee walkway adjacent to Bayou Segnette might not be primarily recreational in character, boating in the bayou is certainly recreational and the levee walkway allowed boaters the ability to reach their boats. Taken as a whole, we find that the bayou and its adjacent levee walkway were intended or permitted to be used for recreational purposes.

Id. at 548.

b.   Charitable and Public Service Activities

COMMENT

The Louisiana legislature has enacted a multitude of statutes designed to limit the liability of individuals, organizations, and associations from alleged negligent behavior. These statutes are not true "limited liability" statutes because they actually limit the duty that must be breached for liability to attach. Rather than assessing liability for mere negligence, these statutes preclude liability unless the actor's conduct is intentional, willful or wanton, or grossly negligent. A small sampling of these statutes is provided below.

La. R.S. 9:2793   "Amateur"   "Doctrine"

§ 2793. Gratuitous service at scene of emergency; limitation on liability

A.   No person who in good faith gratuitously renders emergency care, first aid or rescue at the scene of an emergency, or moves a person receiving such care, first aid or rescue to a hospital or other place of medical care shall be liable for any civil damages as a result of any act or omission in rendering the care or services or as a result of any act or failure to act to provide or arrange for further medical treatment or care for the person involved in the said emergency; provided, however, such care or services or transportation shall not be considered gratuitous, and this Section shall not apply when rendered incidental to a business relationship, including but not limited to that of employer-employee, existing between the person rendering such care or service or transportation and the person receiving the same, or when incidental to a business relationship existing between the employer or principal of the person rendering such care, service or transportation and the employer or principal of the person receiving such care, service or transportation. This Section shall not exempt from liability those individuals who intentionally or by grossly negligent acts or omissions cause damages to another individual.

B.   The immunity herein granted shall be personal to the individual rendering such care or service or furnishing such transportation and shall not inure to the benefit of any employer or other person legally responsible for the acts or omissions of such individual, nor shall it inure to the benefit of any insurer.

C. For purposes of this Section, rendering emergency care, first aid, or rescue shall include the use of an automated external defibrillator as defined by R.S. 40:1137.2.

La. R.S. 9:2796.1   **Limitation of liability for loss connected with St. Patrick's Day parades or any ethnic parade**

Notwithstanding any other law to the contrary, no person shall have a cause of action against any organization which presents St. Patrick's Day parades or other street parades connected with any ethnic celebration, or against any nonprofit organization chartered under the laws of this state, or any member thereof, which sponsors fairs or festivals that present parades, for any loss or damage caused by any member thereof or related to the parades presented by such organization, unless said loss or damage was caused by the deliberate and wanton act or gross negligence of the organization. The provisions of this Section shall not be intended to limit the liability of a compensated employee of such organization for his individual acts of negligence.

NOTES

1.   For a listing of other specialized immunities and a discussion of the wisdom and constitutionality of some of these special immunities *see* Maraist and Galligan, *Louisiana Tort Law* § 11.03 (perm. ed., rev. vol., 2013).

2.   If a float rider in a St. Patrick's Day parade is struck on the head by an audio speaker knocked from its mooring atop the float by an overhanging tree branch, will the parade sponsor who was aware of need for care and who attempted to comply with float height restrictions be immune from liability under La. R.S. 9:2796.1? Will your answer be the same if evidence is adduced that a similar accident occurred on the same float in the preceding year? *See, Tauzier v. St. Patrick Parade Committee of Jefferson, Inc.*, 807 So. 2d 1106 (La.App. 5 Cir. 2002).

3.   La. R.S. 9:2800.2 provides immunity to a psychologist, psychiatrist, marriage and family therapist, licensed professional counselor, or social worker against liability or a cause of action arising from an invasion of privacy or breach of confidentiality associated with disclosures made in warning potential victims that a patient or client has threatened physical violence toward that individual. The statute also imposes a duty on these mental health professionals to warn the potential victim of the threat or to take reasonable measures to provide protection from the patient or client's violent behavior, if the threat of violence is deemed to be significant in the professional's clinical opinion and the patient has the apparent intent and ability to carry out the threat.

This law is primarily a codification of the holding in *Tarasoff v. Regents of the University of California,* 17 Cal.3d 425 (Cal. 1976). In *Tarasoff,* a patient at a university health facility communicated to a mental health professional a threat to a female. Taking no protective measures, the professional allowed the patient to leave the facility, and the female was murdered by the patient. The California Supreme Court held that a duty was owed to the victim.

In determining, pursuant to La.R.S. 9:2800.2, whether the threat of violence is significant in the professional's clinical judgment, should the standard be objective or subjective?

If a paranoid schizophrenic diagnosed by a psychiatrist as having suicidal and homicidal tendencies is discharged from psychiatric care and later attacks and stabs a third person, will the psychiatrist be immune from liability pursuant to La. R.S. 9:2800.2 if the stabbing victim files suit? Will the hospital also be immune? *See, Durapau v. Jenkins*, 656 So. 2d 1057 (La.App. 5 Cir. 1995).

4.   Dr. E. works as an emergency room physician on an independent contract basis at General Hospital. Dr. E. is employed by his professional medical corporation. A serious pedestrian-ambulance accident occurs in the driveway entrance to General Hospital. Dr. E. runs to render emergency medical care, but does so negligently. Is Dr. E.'s professional medical corporation entitled to Dr. E.'s immunity under La. R.S. 9:2793?

5.   For a discussion of the applicability of the Equine Immunity Statute, La. R.S. 9:2795.3, to a

case where plaintiff lost a thumb feeding carrots to a pony, *see Larson v. XYZ Insurance Company*, 2016-C-0745 (La. 2017).

4. Workplace Immunity

a. Introduction

At the beginning of the twentieth century, as the industrial revolution was proceeding apace, workers were being maimed and killed on a daily basis. There was no Occupational Health and Safety Act to require businesses to make workplaces safer, and there was no Americans with Disabilities Act to require employers to make reasonable accommodations to enable disabled workers to continue doing their jobs after their injuries. Consequently, the body and injury count mounted with no reason to believe the situation would change and no provision of compensation or benefits for the injured workers and their dependents. The typical scenario involved a worker being injured in an accident involving machinery or a condition of the premises in the workplace. Thus, there was an identifiable single accident resulting in a physical injury. The injured workers and their families turned to the only means of compensation they had–tort lawsuits. Very few recovered anything, however, because tort law favored the defendant businesses. One or more of three tort defenses almost always applied to bar recovery: assumption of the risk, contributory negligence, or the fellow servant rule.

This situation of leaving workers disabled and uncompensated obviously was intolerable. With political pressure at both the federal and state levels, state legislatures began enacting workers' compensation laws. Eventually, every state adopted a law. Louisiana passed its workers' compensation act in 1914. Although the various state laws differ in several respects, all provide for compensation benefits for workers who are injured at work. The types of benefits typically provided are medical expenses and disability benefits, which provide partial wage replacement during a period of time during which the worker is unable to work or to work at his regular job; injured workers sometimes return to work in light-duty jobs for a period of time until they are able to resume their regular jobs. Employers pay workers' compensation benefits either by obtaining a workers' compensation insurance policy or by self insuring (paying the benefits without insurance).

The most significant aspect of workers' compensation for tort law is the workers' compensation immunity or exclusivity. Workers' compensation laws provide no-fault compensation; that is, as long as the employer, employee, and accident-causing injury are covered under the workers' compensation act, the worker does not have to prove that the employer or a co-employee negligently or intentionally caused the injury, or otherwise was at fault. In exchange for providing workers' compensation benefits without proof of fault, employers received something in the workers' compensation acts: immunity from tort lawsuits; in other words, an employer that is liable for workers' compensation benefits cannot be held liable in most tort lawsuits. Workers' compensation is said to be the worker's exclusive remedy for his injury. This often is referred to as workers' compensation immunity, or workers' compensation exclusivity, or the exclusive remedy rule of workers' compensation. In a typical case in which an injured worker sues his employer in tort, the employer files a motion to dismiss on the ground that workers' compensation renders the employer immune from negligence lawsuits.

The most significant exception to workers' compensation immunity is for intentional acts. Different state workers' compensation laws deal with this issue differently. Some provide for enhanced benefits, such as three times the usual benefits. Others, including Louisiana, provide that the immunity or exclusivity rule does not apply to intentional torts. Thus, an employee who is injured at work as a result of an intentional act by his employer or a co-employee can sue the employer in tort, and the suit is not barred by the workers' compensation immunity. The employee can recover workers' compensation benefits and then sue his employer for the intentional tort. If the intentional tort was committed by a co-employee, the plaintiff must prove that the employee was in the course and scope of his employment in order for the employer to held vicariously liable for the intentional tort of the employee. If the employee recovers both workers' compensation benefits and an award of damages for an intentional tort, the court will credit the employer in the tort lawsuit with sums paid in workers' compensation benefits and does not permit double recovery. *Gagnard v. Baldridge*, 612 So. 2d 732 (La. 1993).

The two sections of the workers' compensation act that are relevant to immunity are La. R.S. 23:1031, which sets forth the requirements for workers' compensation coverage, and La. R.S. 23:1032, which provides the exclusivity rule.

WORKERS COMP!

La. R.S. 23:1031. **Employee's right of action; joint employers, extent of liability; borrowed employees** *(not vic. liab.)*

A. If an employee not otherwise eliminated from the benefits of this Chapter receives personal injury by accident arising out of and in the course of his employment, his employer shall pay compensation in the amounts, on the conditions, and to the person or persons hereinafter designated.

* * * * *

course = time
scope = employment — reasonable duties

C. In the case of any employee for whose injury or death payments are due and who is, at the time of the injury, employed by a borrowing employer in this Section referred to as a "special employer", and is under the control and direction of the special employer in the performance of the work, both the special employer and the immediate employer, referred to in this Section as a "general employer", shall be liable jointly and in solido to pay benefits as provided under this Chapter. As between the special and general employers, each shall have the right to seek contribution from the other for any payments made on behalf of the employee unless there is a contract between them expressing a different method of sharing the liability. Where compensation is claimed from, or proceedings are taken against, the special employer, then, in the application of this Chapter, reference to the special employer shall be substituted for reference to the employer, except that the amount of compensation shall be calculated with reference to the earnings of the employee under the general employer by whom he is immediately employed. The special and the general employers shall be entitled to the exclusive remedy protections provided in R.S. 23:1032.

D. An injury by accident shall not be considered as having arisen out of the employment and is thereby not covered by the provisions of this Chapter if the injured employee was engaged in horseplay at the time of the injury.

E. An injury by accident should not be considered as having arisen out of the employment and thereby not covered by the provisions of this Chapter if the employer can establish that the injury arose out of a dispute with another person or employee over matters unrelated to the injured employee's employment.

INTENTIONAL TORT or NO COVERAGE

La. R.S. 23:1032. **Exclusiveness of rights and remedies; employer's liability to prosecution under other laws**

UNDER WORKERS COMP.

A. (1) (a) Except for intentional acts provided for in Subsection B, the rights and remedies herein granted to an employee or his dependent on account of an injury, or compensable sickness or disease for which he is entitled to compensation under this Chapter, shall be exclusive of all other rights, remedies, and claims for damages, including but not limited to punitive or exemplary damages, unless such rights, remedies, and damages are created by a statute, whether now existing or created in the future, expressly establishing same as available to such employee, his personal representatives, dependents, or relations, as against his employer, or any principal or any officer, director, stockholder, partner, or employee of such employer or principal, for said injury, or compensable sickness or disease.

(b) This exclusive remedy is exclusive of all claims, including any claims that might arise against his employer, or any principal or any officer, director, stockholder, partner, or employee of such employer or principal under any dual capacity theory or doctrine.

1) employer) employee relationship
2) injury by accident
3) occupational illness

405

(2)   For purposes of this Section, the word "principal" shall be defined as any person who undertakes to execute any work which is a part of his trade, business, or occupation in which he was engaged at the time of the injury, or which he had contracted to perform and contracts with any person for the execution thereof.

B.   Nothing in this Chapter shall affect the liability of the employer, or any officer, director, stockholder, partner, or employee of such employer or principal to a fine or penalty under any other statute or the liability, civil or criminal, resulting from an intentional act.

C.   The immunity from civil liability provided by this Section shall not extend to such employer or principal who is not engaged at the time of the injury in the normal course and scope of his employment; and

(1)   Any officer, director, stockholder, partner, or employee of such employer or principal who is not engaged at the time of the injury in the normal course and scope of his employment; and

(2)   To the liability of any partner in a partnership which has been formed for the purpose of evading any of the provisions of this Section.

COMMENT

There are two situations involving injured workers in which workers are not barred from pursuing a tort lawsuit. The first situation is that in which the intentional act exception applies, which is addressed in section b below. The second situation is that in which workers' compensation does not provide coverage, and thus exclusivity does not apply, covered in section c below; in other words, if workers' compensation provides no remedy at all, the exclusive remedy rule is not applicable, and the injured employee can recover from the employer for negligence of the employer or a co-employee.

In both situations, plaintiff employees can sue their employers in tort and the exclusivity rule does not bar recovery. One difference between these two situations, however, is that when a plaintiff sues for an intentional act, he also may recover workers' compensation benefits from the employer if the coverage requirements are satisfied.

b.   **Intentional Acts**

CLARK
v.
DIVISION SEVEN, INC.
776 So. 2d 1262 (La.App. 4 Cir. 2001)
writ denied, **787 So. 2d 318 (La. 2001)**

KIRBY, J.

Defendant Division Seven, Inc. appeals the trial court's judgment in favor of plaintiff Gary Clark following the liability phase of this bifurcated trial.[1] The sole issue on appeal is whether plaintiff's injuries resulted from an intentional act under the exception to the exclusivity provision of the Louisiana Workers' Compensation Act. After review of the record and the applicable law, we affirm the trial court's judgment.

The only witnesses called to testify at trial were plaintiff and his co-worker, Robert Naquin. Their testimony revealed that on February 15, 1995, they were performing roofing work at a church

---

[1] Trial in this matter was bifurcated into liability and damages phases. The judgment appealed from is on the issue of liability only. Under La. C.C. P. art. 1915A(5), this judgment is final and appealable, and the certification requirements of La. C.C. P. art. 1915B(1) do not apply in this situation.

located near Picayune, Mississippi for their employer, the defendant in this case. The foreman on this job was Sandroz Ray. On the date of the accident, there was light rain with occasionally heavy showers. Each time the rain became heavy, the three men came down off of the roof. According to the uncontroverted testimony of plaintiff and Naquin, Ray ordered them to return to their roofing work after each heavy shower lightened up. Both men protested to Ray several times that it was too dangerous to resume work on the slanted roof due to its wet and slippery condition following the rainfall. According to plaintiff and Naquin, Ray told them to return to their roofing work after the rain stopped or they would be fired. After returning to the roof several times after heavy rain stopped, Naquin slipped on the roof and almost fell to the ground. Naquin's body from the chest down was off of the roof when he managed to grab on to a wooden block near the edge of the roof and avoid falling to the ground. The height of the church that was the site of the roofing job was described as almost that of a three story building. Following his narrowly averted fall, Naquin again complained to Ray of the danger of working on the wet, slippery roof. Ray reiterated to both men that they had the choice of returning to work or being fired. At that point, Naquin chose to be fired and left the work site.

Plaintiff remained at the site and continued his roofing work. Shortly after Naquin left the work site, plaintiff slipped on the wet roof and fell to the ground, sustaining serious injuries.

Plaintiff filed a petition for damages against defendant, alleging that the actions of his employer were intentional so as to allow him to sue his employer in tort. In its answer, defendant asserted that plaintiff's exclusive remedy as to defendant is under the Louisiana Workers' Compensation Act, and argued that plaintiff's tort claim should be dismissed.

By agreement of the parties, trial in this matter was bifurcated into liability and damages phases. Following trial on the liability issue, the trial judge rendered judgment in favor of plaintiff, finding that the actions of defendant's agent, Sandroz Ray, constituted an intentional act and that the intentional act of requiring plaintiff to work on a wet, slippery roof was the cause of plaintiff's injuries. Defendant appeals.

On appeal, the defendant argues that the trial court erred in finding that an intentional tort occurred such as to exempt the plaintiff from the exclusive remedy of the Louisiana Workers' Compensation Act. In the case of *Gallon v. Vaughan Contractors, Inc.*, ..., this Court set forth the law regarding the intentional act exception to the exclusivity provision of the Louisiana Workers' Compensation Act as follows:

> Under the worker's compensation scheme, employees have an exclusive remedy against employers for personal injuries arising out of and in the course of their employment. LSA-R.S. 23:1032. However, there is an exception to the exclusive remedy of worker's compensation when the employee's injury was caused by an "intentional act." LSA-R.S. 23:1031(B). "Intentional act," as used in the statute, means "intentional tort." "Intent," has been defined by the Louisiana Supreme Court, to mean "that the defendant either desired to bring about the physical results of his act or believed they were substantially certain to follow from what he did." *Bazley v. Tortorich,....* Since the inception of the intentional act exception, Louisiana courts have respected the underlying legislative policy, and thus, narrowly interpreted the exception.

To meet the criteria of the "substantially certain" prong of the *Bazley* test, jurisprudence requires more than a reasonable probability that an injury will occur; this term has been interpreted as being equivalent to "inevitable," "virtually sure," and "incapable of failing." Additionally, even where a defendant's conduct is grossly negligent, this fact alone will not allow the imputation of intent....

In the instant case, the defendant's agent, Sandroz Ray, ignored repeated reports from plaintiff and Naquin that the slanted portion of the roof that they were working on was wet and slippery. The uncontroverted testimony was that Ray continued to demand that plaintiff and Naquin return to the their roofing duties after each hard rainfall or they would be fired. When Ray ordered plaintiff to return to the wet, slippery roof shortly after Naquin slipped and narrowly avoided falling to the ground, the circumstances indicated that injury to the plaintiff was inevitable or substantially certain to occur. Based on the record before us, we conclude that the trial court did not err in finding that the conduct of the defendant's agent constituted an intentional act that was the cause of plaintiff's injuries.

For these reasons, we affirm the trial court judgment.

AFFIRMED.

NOTES

1.   What intentional tort could the foreman have committed by ordering the plaintiff to return to work on the roof? Was it a battery? A false imprisonment? Is it necessary to satisfy the intentional act requirement of La. R.S. 23:1032 that a plaintiff prove a specific intentional tort?

2.   Plaintiffs often sue in tort and attempt to avoid workers' compensation exclusivity by alleging that the employer acted with intent. The two-pronged definition of intent from *Garratt v. Daley*, *supra*, comes in handy in this context.

3.   For a case reaching a different result from *Clark* on the intentional act argument, *see Lapoint v. Beaird Indus., Inc.*, 786 So. 2d 301 (La.App. 2 Cir. 2001), *writ denied*, 796 So. 2d 686 (La. 2001).

The Louisiana Supreme Court denied recovery under the intentional act exception in *Reeves v. Structural Preservation Systems*, 731 So. 2d 208 (La. 1999). In *Reeves* a supervisor directed an employee to move manually a sandblasting pot. The direction violated an OSHA guideline, and the plaintiff employee alleged that the supervisor gave the direction although he feared that someone would get hurt if the pot was moved manually. The Court held that the intentional act exception was not satisfied: "The employer's conduct in this case, while negligent or perhaps even grossly negligent, does not meet the 'substantial certainty' requirement of the intentional act exception to the Workers' Compensation Act...." *Id.* at 213.

4.   A plaintiff suing an employer for the intentional act of a co-employee often faces the significant burden of proving that the employer should be held vicariously liable for the acts of the co-employee. To do so, the plaintiff must prove that the co-employee was in the course and scope of his employment at the time of the acts. *See infra* Chapter 11 on respondeat superior. On a related point, it is not enough that an intentional act was committed; it must have been committed by someone for whom the employer can be held vicariously liable. For example, in *Mundy, infra,* the intruder in the hospital that stabbed the plaintiff nurse with a knife committed a battery, but she sues her employer, the hospital, for negligence in providing security because the hospital could not be held vicariously liable for the acts of the intruder.

c.   Lack of Workers' Compensation Coverage

When workers' compensation laws were enacted at the beginning of the twentieth century, injured employees needed a compensation system because the vast majority had little to no chance of recovering in a tort lawsuit. Tort law, with the three defenses of contributory negligence, assumption of the risk, and the fellow servant rule, favored defendants. As tort law has evolved, and these defenses have changed or been abrogated, tort law now provides a more level playing field. Consequently, many injured employees now prefer filing tort lawsuits to recovering workers' compensation benefits. Here's the problem for injured employees: Most accidents at work that can be said to be cause by an employer's fault are based on the employer's negligence; rarely can an injured employee prove an intentional act for which the employer will be held liable. How then does a plaintiff, suing his employer for negligence in causing his workplace injury, avoid the exclusivity of workers' compensation? The answer is to establish that the injury is not covered by workers' compensation. There are three basic requirements for workers' compensation coverage (set forth in La. R.S. 23:1031, *supra*): 1) employer-employee relationship; 2) personal injury by accident (or occupational illness); and 3) occurring in the course of and arising out of employment. If any one of these three requirements is not satisfied, workers' compensation does not provide coverage, and if it does not provide coverage, the exclusivity rule does not apply.

MUNDY

v.

DEPARTMENT OF HEALTH AND HUMAN RESOURCES
593 So. 2d 346 (La. 1992)

LEMMON, J.

Plaintiff filed this tort action against her employer to recover damages for injuries sustained when she was stabbed by an unknown assailant in an elevator at Charity Hospital in New Orleans en route to report for the evening shift at her work station on the eleventh floor. The issue is whether La. Rev. Stat. 23:1032 restricts plaintiff to worker's compensation benefits as her exclusive remedy against her employer. We hold that under an analysis of the "course of employment" and "arising out of employment" requirements of the Worker's Compensation Act, in light of the facts of this case, the employer failed to carry its burden of proving its entitlement to tort immunity.

Plaintiff had been employed by the Department of Health and Human Resources as a licensed practical nurse for eleven years. At the time of the incident she was working the evening shift in the dialysis department located on the eleventh floor of Charity Hospital. Evening shift employees in that department were expected to report to work at 11:15 p.m. and were considered to be late at 11:20 p.m., although the afternoon shift did not end until 11:30 p.m.

On November 13, 1986, plaintiff arrived at the hospital at approximately 11:17 p.m. and proceeded to the east elevators. She noticed that the two guards usually stationed at those elevators were not present at the time. After plaintiff entered the elevator on her way to work on the eleventh floor, a man jumped into the elevator as the doors closed and pressed the second floor button. When the elevator stopped at the second floor, the man began to leave the elevator, but turned suddenly and attacked plaintiff with a knife. Plaintiff pressed the emergency button on the elevator panel, hoping that the alarm would scare off the assailant or attract assistance. However, the button was not in working order, and the alarm did not sound. The assailant stabbed plaintiff repeatedly while standing in the elevator door before losing his balance and falling backward, allowing the doors to close. Plaintiff then sought assistance on an upper floor.

Plaintiff filed this tort action against her employer based on the employer's negligence in failing to provide adequate security in the hospital and to maintain procedures for the safety of patients, visitors and employees. The trial court rendered judgment in favor of plaintiff in the amount of $125,000, subject to a credit of $6,338.61 for compensation benefits paid by the employer. The judge, accepting plaintiff's testimony completely, found that plaintiff "had not come under the control or supervision of Charity Hospital at the time when the incident occurred." He accordingly ruled that plaintiff was not in the course of her employment at the time of the incident and therefore was not restricted to compensation as her exclusive remedy. The judge further found that plaintiff's employer was negligent in the maintenance and operation of the hospital premises.

The court of appeal reversed. 580 So. 2d 493. Reasoning that the beneficial purpose of the compensation remedy requires a claimant to be brought under worker's compensation in any manner reasonably possible, the court concluded that plaintiff was injured during the course of her employment because both elements of time and place were present.[1] The court further reasoned that plaintiff's injury arose out of her employment because the necessities of her employer's business required her to be at the place of the incident at the time it occurred.

This court then granted plaintiff's application for certiorari. 586 So. 2d 519.

---

[1] The court noted that plaintiff's work shift, scheduled to commence at 11:15 p.m., had in fact begun at the time of the incident. However, the incident occurred before the time for late arrival, and plaintiff had not yet reached her work station or begun her employment duties.

The employer is responsible for compensation benefits to an employee who is injured by an accident which occurs in the course of the employment and arises out of the employment. *La. Rev. Stat. 23:1031*. Compensation benefits are the employee's exclusive remedy against his employer for such an injury. *La. Rev. Stat. 23:1032*. When the employer seeks to avail itself of tort immunity under Section 1032, the employer has the burden of proving entitlement to immunity.

An accident occurs in the course of employment when the employee sustains an injury while actively engaged in the performance of his duties during working hours, either on the employer's premises or at other places where employment activities take the employee. *Kern v. Southport Mill*, ...; W. Malone & H. Johnson, 13 Louisiana Civil Law Treatise - Worker's Compensation § 161 (2d ed. 1980). While coverage has been extended in some cases to include accidents during times for rest or lunch periods or before and after work on the employer's premises, or to include accidents at places where employment duties are performed off the employer's premises, the principal criteria for determining course of employment are time, place and employment activity.

The determination of whether an accident arises out of employment focuses on the character or source of the risk which gives rise to the injury and on the relationship of the risk to the nature of the employment. An accident arises out of employment if the risk from which the injury resulted was greater for the employee than for a person not engaged in the employment. *Myers v. Louisiana Railway and Navigation Co.,....* Moreover, an accident has also been held to arise out of employment if the conditions or obligations of the employment caused the employee in the course of employment to be at the place of the accident at the time the accident occurred, ... Thus, when the employee is squarely within the course of his employment, virtually any risk (whether an increased risk or not) has been considered as arising out of employment. W. Malone & H. Johnson, *supra* at § 193.

The principal objective of the "arising out of employment" requirement is to separate accidents attributable to employment risks, which form the basis of the employer's obligation under the compensation system, from accidents attributable to personal risks, for which the employer should normally not be responsible. 1 A. Larson, Workmen's Compensation § 7.00 (1990). The risks which have caused the greatest difficulty are those that have neither a particular employment character nor a particular personal character. *Id.*

This court has declined to view the "course of employment" and "arising out of employment" requirements as separate and unrelated concepts. Rather, this court has recognized the mutual interdependence of the two concepts in determining the relationship of the injury to the employment. *See* W. Malone & H. Johnson, supra at § 144; 1 A. Larson, *supra* at § 29.00, 29.10. In a close case a strong showing of "course of employment" has been held to counterbalance a relatively weak showing of "arising out of employment." *See Raybol v. Louisiana State University,* ... (a custodial employee of a university, assaulted by a jilted lover while performing her regular employment duties during regular working hours in an unoccupied portion of a dormitory, was entitled to compensation because the "course of employment" showing was clear, and the employee was so totally innocent of causing or inviting the attack that the assault could be viewed as perpetrated by a total stranger). When the accident occurs at such a time or place or during such an activity so that the employee is barely within the outer boundary of the "course of employment" inquiry, a very strong showing by the employee that the risk arose out of the employment is necessary to establish the relationship between the injury and the employment necessary for entitlement to compensation....

In the present case the "arising out of employment" inquiry reveals that the risk which gave rise to the injury was not greater for plaintiff than for a person not so employed. Moreover, while the conditions of the employment arguably caused plaintiff to be at the place of the attack at the time the attack occurred, there were other alternative routes for her to reach her work station.[2] Inasmuch as the risk which gave rise to the injury was a neutral risk that was not related either to plaintiff's employment or to her personal life, the "arising out of employment" showing by the employer, while

---

[2] There were two other banks of elevators, as well as stairs.

not particularly strong, could be considered sufficient if there was a strong "course of employment" showing.

As to the "course of employment" inquiry, plaintiff was attacked before she arrived at her work station and before she began her employment duties. Although she had entered the building in which her work station was located, she was in the public area of the building open to the public, on an elevator used by patients and visitors as well as employees. She had never performed employment duties on the first or second floor, or on the elevator between those floors, and was not doing so at the time of the assault. She clearly had not yet reached the place where she would be under the supervision and control of her employer. *Templet v. Intracoastal Truck Line, Inc.*,..... Under the circumstances one could hardly say that there was a strong "course of employment" showing.

The employer contends, however, that the threshold doctrine establishes a more solid showing of "course of employment." Generally, an accident that occurs while the employee is going to or returning from work does not occur in the course of the employment.[3] W. Malone & H. Johnson, *supra*, at § 168. An exception, known as the threshold doctrine, has been recognized when an accident occurs at a place with an unusually hazardous travel risk which is immediately adjacent to, but not on, the employer's premises. The threshold doctrine generally involves a special risk, attributable to the location of the work premises, that is different from the risks to which the general traveling public is exposed or that is more aggravated in the area adjacent to the employer's premises than elsewhere. W. Malone & H. Johnson, *supra*, at § 169; ...

The threshold doctrine is not applicable here. Even if the risk which gave rise to the injury could be considered as a defect hazardous to travelers immediately adjacent to the employer's premises, the risk was no more dangerous in the immediate vicinity of the employer's premises than elsewhere along her route of travel to work.

Because the neutral nature of the risk from which the injury arose required a strong showing of "course of employment," and because the evidence relative to time, place and employment activity provided only a relatively weak showing of "course of employment," we conclude the employer failed to meet its burden of proving entitlement to tort immunity.

Accordingly, the judgment of the court of appeal is reversed. The case is remanded to the court of appeal for review of the remaining issues not reached in its original decision.

NOTES

1.   In *Mundy*, it is the defendant employer that is arguing for workers' compensation coverage; the employer bases its motion for summary judgment on the exclusivity of workers' compensation. Note that when the employer raises workers' compensation exclusivity as a defense in a tort lawsuit, the burden is on the defendant employer to prove that all of the coverage requirements of 23:1031 are satisfied.

2.   The *Mundy* case provides as complete and succinct a discussion of the in the course/arises out of tests as will be found in Louisiana jurisprudence.

Consider the similarity between the standard for workers' compensation coverage, the statutory language--"arising out of and in the course of his employment"--and the test for vicarious liability of an employer for the torts of an employee (respondeat superior)—course and scope of employment. The terms have very similar meanings, but consider the different purposes served by the two tests. Would you expect courts to apply the two tests the same? If a court applied one test more expansively (found it satisfied more broadly), which of the two would you expect it to be? Can you

---

[3] If the employee is actually performing services for the employer when an accident occurs while going to or returning from work, the accident is viewed as occurring in the course of employment because of the employment activity.

create a hypothetical that calls for application of both tests?

3.   In the past contested workers' compensation claims were tried in the state district courts in Louisiana. Then the legislature established the Office of Workers Compensation Administration. The OWCA now has jurisdiction over workers' compensation claims, and the cases are heard by workers' compensation judges within the OWCA. Appeals of OWCA decisions go to the state courts of appeals. What issues are raised by having workers' compensation claims and lawsuits against employers for workplace injuries tried by different tribunals? Suppose a case in which an injured employee files a workers' compensation claim and sues his employer for negligence.

Workers' compensation acts include a number of exclusions from coverage. For example, in 1989 the Louisiana legislature amended the workers' compensation act to exclude from coverage injuries resulting from horseplay and personal disputes unrelated to employment. *See* paragraphs D and E of La. R.S. 23:1031 above. Businesses supported these amendments to avoid paying workers' compensation benefits. Can you see the problem that such exclusions created for businesses? Read *Holliday*.

HOLLIDAY
v.
STATE OF LOUISIANA
747 So. 2d 755 (La.App. 1 Cir. 1999)
writ denied, **758 So. 2d 154 (La. 2000)**

FOIL, J.

At issue in this case is whether an employer is entitled to invoke the immunity provision of the workers' compensation law, where the incident giving rise to a tort suit is specifically excluded from coverage by the compensation law. We hold the trial court properly found that the employer is not immune from tort suit, and we affirm.

Background

This tort litigation arises from a shooting incident at a workplace. Andrea Wright, an employee of the State of Louisiana, Office of Financial Assistance (state), was working at her office in the Wooddale State Office Building in Baton Rouge when her husband, Donald Ray Wright, walked into her office and shot her six times. Andrea died as a result. This tort lawsuit, filed by her mother, Lottie Holliday, followed. Named as defendants were the state, the City of Baton Rouge through its police department, Vinson Guard Service, Inc., and Vinson's insurer, National Union Fire Insurance Company of Louisiana.

The allegations of plaintiff's petition can be summarized as follows: Several days before the fatal shooting, Andrea asked her supervisor for time off to obtain a restraining order against her husband because they were involved in an ongoing personal dispute, unrelated to her employment, and because her husband threatened to kill her. On November 29, 1996, Donald Ray Wright telephoned Andrea at work and told her he was coming to the office to kill her. Andrea told her supervisor, who escorted her to an office where Andrea telephoned the police. At approximately 1:58 p.m., she spoke with an officer and beseeched him to send someone to help her because her husband threatened to kill her. A sergeant informed her the police could not respond to her call unless she had a restraining order in her possession.

Andrea telephoned plaintiff to bring the restraining order to the building. At approximately 2:20 p.m., Donald Ray Wright arrived at the Wooddale office building and proceeded without delay to the fifth floor, where Andrea worked, sought Andrea out and began shooting her. Plaintiff arrived at the building with the restraining order while the shooting was in progress.

At the time Andrea was killed, she was four months pregnant. Plaintiff sought wrongful death damages for the death of Andrea and the unborn fetus on behalf of Andrea's four surviving children.

Additionally, plaintiff sought to recover her own LeJuene-type damages based on her presence at the scene when the fatal shooting occurred, and made a claim for these type of damages on behalf of one of the minor children who was also at the scene at the time of the shooting.

Plaintiff averred the state was negligent for, among other things, failing to provide adequate security and failing to protect Andrea from the criminal attack despite the knowledge of her supervisors of the impending nature of the attack. She also alleged that the state was liable for the failure of its employees to inform the security guard on duty of the impending criminal attack.

The state filed a motion for summary judgment claiming plaintiff is precluded from pursuing a tort remedy against the state pursuant to the exclusivity provision of the Louisiana Workers' Compensation Act, La. R.S. 23:1032. Plaintiff filed a motion for partial summary judgment, asserting La. R.S. 23:1032 does not bar this tort suit against the state because the injury to Andrea Wright is not compensable under the workers' compensation law.

The trial judge granted plaintiff's motion for partial summary judgment and denied the state's motion for summary judgment. The judge held that La. R.S. 23:1032 does not bar plaintiff from bringing this tort suit. The trial court designated the judgment as a final judgment for the purposes of appeal, finding no just reason for delay pursuant to La. Code Civ. P. art. 1915B. This appeal, taken by the state, followed.

Discussion

* * * * *

The facts crucial to the issue presented on the motion for summary judgment are not disputed. It is undisputed that Andrea was shot by her husband during the course of her employment. There has been no suggestion by the state that this shooting was in any way related to Andrea's employment other than the fact it occurred at the workplace. This shooting clearly arose from a personal dispute between Andrea and Donald Ray Wright. Thus, we must decide whether under these undisputed facts the exclusivity provision of the workers' compensation scheme precludes a tort suit against the employer based on the workplace shooting incident.

La. R.S. 23:1032A(1)(a) provides that except for "intentional acts" the rights and remedies granted to an employee or his dependent "on account of an injury or compensable sickness or disease for which he is entitled to compensation" under the compensation law, shall be exclusive of all other rights, remedies and claims for damages against his or her employer. (emphasis added). The state argues that as the employer of Andrea Wright, it can be sued in tort only if the plaintiff's suit is based on an intentional tort. It contends that plaintiff's allegations all sound in negligence, and therefore, workers' compensation is plaintiff's exclusive remedy.

Plaintiff relies on the language "for which he is entitled to compensation" found in La. R.S. 23:1032. She posits that the immunity provision does not apply by its literal terms because the compensation act specifically excludes Andrea Wright from coverage. Plaintiff relies on La. R.S. 23:1031E which provides:

> An injury by accident should not be considered as having arisen out of the employment and thereby not covered by the provisions of this Chapter if the employer can establish that the injury arose out of a dispute with another person or employee over matters unrelated to the injured employee's employment.

Plaintiff points to the case of *Guillory v. Interstate Gas Station*, ..., in which the Louisiana Supreme Court held that a shooting of a worker by her estranged husband at her place of work fell under the scope of La. R.S. 23:1031E.[1] In that case, the worker made a claim for compensation benefits. The employer and insurer sought to deny benefits on the basis of La. R.S. 23:1031E. The Supreme Court held that the attack on the employee was the result of an ongoing "dispute" between the couple and was in no way related to the plaintiff's employment except for the fact that the injury arose at her place of employment. The court held that injuries arising from a dispute with another person which is unrelated to the plaintiff's employment do not "arise out of the employment" and are therefore not covered by the workers' compensation remedy. *Guillory....*

As noted earlier, the state does not suggest that the shooting of Andrea Wright was related to her employment. Instead, the state argues the term "dispute" used in La. R.S. 23:1031E does not include general attacks by an aggressor against a passive victim. The state posits that since Andrea was not involved in a "dispute" but was "attacked" at work, La. R.S. 23:1031E does not preclude workers' compensation coverage.

The argument advanced by the state was clearly rejected in *Guillory*. We conclude in light of La. R.S. 23:1031E and the *Guillory* decision, the compensation act specifically excluded the shooting of Andrea Wright from the scope of its coverage as it arose from a dispute between Andrea and Donald Ray Wright that was unrelated to Andrea's employment.

As the compensation act itself did not cover the shooting death of Andrea Wright, we find plaintiff is not barred from bringing this tort suit against her employer. The exclusivity provision makes the compensation remedy exclusive only with respect to those injuries for which an employee is entitled to workers' compensation benefits. In *O'Regan v. Preferred Enterprises, Inc.,* ..., the Louisiana Supreme Court discussed the concept of an employee's entitlement to benefits for the purpose of the exclusivity provision. In that case, an employee filed a claim seeking compensation benefits against her employer claiming her employment caused her to contract an occupational disease. The workers' compensation judge ruled that she failed to carry her burden of proving she contracted the disease as a result of her employment. Thereafter, she filed a tort suit against her employer claiming her employer's negligence caused her to contract the disease. She theorized that since her claim for compensation benefits had been rejected, she was not "entitled" to such benefits and she was therefore free to sue her employer in tort, as only employees who are "entitled" to benefits are precluded from pursuing a tort remedy against their employer.

The Supreme Court disagreed, holding that the compensation act provided the plaintiff's exclusive remedy. In so doing, the court distinguished between a compensation claim that fails for lack of proof, and a claim that is not covered under the compensation scheme. The court stated:

> Entitlement to a remedy under the act is not synonymous with ultimate success on the merits in an individual case. Every employee who has a remedy under the compensation act does not recover. If failure to succeed on the merits in a compensation case resulted in the right to pursue a tort claim, the immunity granted employers under the act would be largely illusory. A plaintiff who cannot prove a case for compensation benefits does not by that failure get a second bite at the apple--an arguably more lucrative tort remedy. The distinction between a claim for disease or injury not covered under the act, in which case a tort recovery is allowed, and a claim that fails for want of proof, in which case no tort remedy may be pursued, is well illustrated in 6 Larson's Workers' Compensation Law § 65.40 (1999) wherein Professor Larsen explains:
>
> > A distinction must be drawn ... between an injury which does not come within the fundamental coverage provisions of the act, and an injury which is in itself covered but for which, under the facts of the

---

[1] At the time *Guillory* was decided, the pertinent provision was designated La. R.S. 23:1031D. Without changing the wording of the cited provision, in 1997, by Act 315, the legislature redesignated subsection D as subsection E.

particular case, no compensation is payable.

The exclusive remedy feature of our workers' compensation scheme is an essential element of its operation. Where the act covers an accidental injury or occupational disease, it is the employee's exclusive remedy; the employer's immunity from tort suits extends to all but intentional torts.

O'Regan v. Preferred Enterprises, Inc., ...

In light of the above, we hold that where an injury is specifically excluded from the scope of the compensation scheme, the exclusivity provision of the compensation law does not apply, and the employer is not immune from a tort suit based on that injury. As the compensation statute specifically excluded any claims arising out of the workplace attack on Andrea Wright by her husband, the state is not immune from tort suit arising out of that shooting death, and the trial court correctly held that La. R.S. 23:1032 does not bar plaintiff from pursuing a tort remedy against the state.

Conclusion

Based on the foregoing, the judgment appealed from is affirmed. All costs of this appeal are assessed to appellant, State of Louisiana, in the amount of $364.87. The case is hereby remanded to the trial court to conduct proceedings consistent with this opinion.

AFFIRMED and **REMANDED.**

NOTES

1.   Can you see why business support of legislative removal of workers' compensation coverage can result in employers being "hoisted with their own petard"?

2.   Notice that *Holliday* involves a wrongful death claim by the mother of an employee killed at work. The court holds that the negligence lawsuit is not barred because there was no workers' compensation coverage. Because the person bringing the claim is not the employee, why would it even be possible that workers' compensation would apply to bar a negligence claim? The answer is that one of the benefits provided under workers' compensation is a death benefit to specified surviving dependent family members.

3.   In *O'Regan v. Preferred Enterprises*, discussed in *Holliday*, the Louisiana Supreme Court considered a provision in the Workers' Compensation Act that did not remove occupational illnesses from workers' compensation coverage, but instead created more burdensome procedural and evidentiary requirements for a person claiming benefits for an occupational disease when the person was employed by the employer for less than 12 months. Because of the more burdensome requirements to prove workers' compensation coverage, the court held that workers' compensation exclusivity did apply. Subsequently, in *Deshotel v. Guichard Operating Co., Inc.* 916 So. 2d 72 (La. 2004), the Court ruled that non-dependent, adult children of an employee killed in an accident arising out of and in the course of employment are barred from bringing a tort claim, pursuant to the exclusivity provisions of the Comp Act, and that those provisions do not violate the "open court" provision in Art. 1, Sec. 22 of the Louisiana Constitution. The Court distinguished *O'Regan* as a case in which the claimant's injuries were not covered by the Comp Act, as opposed to one in which the injury is covered but no compensation is payable.

d.   Statutory Employer

In enacting workers' compensation laws, legislatures recognized a potential gap in workers' compensation coverage in situations in which some businesses had their employees perform work for other businesses. The Louisiana Supreme Court explained the legislative impetus for creating "statutory employers:"

The legislatures that adopted the early workers' compensation acts feared that employers would attempt to circumvent the absolute liability those statutes imposed by interjecting between themselves and their workers intermediary entities which would fail to meet workers' compensation obligations. Frank L. Maraist and Thomas C. Galligan, Jr., *The Employer's Tort Immunity: A Case Study in Post-Modern Immunity*, 57 La.L.Rev. 467, 488 (1997). To assure a compensation remedy to injured workers, these legislatures provided that some principals were by statute deemed, for purposes of liability for workers' compensation benefits, the employers of employees of other entities. *Id.* The legislative approaches to what is commonly referred to as the "statutory employer" doctrine varied.

Allen v. State, 842 So. 2d 373 (La. 2003).

Thus was born the concept of statutory employer. A business which is not the regular payroll employer of an employee can be deemed a statutory employer for purposes of workers' compensation liability. Although originally intended by the legislature as a gap filler for workers' compensation coverage, statutory employer has come to be used by businesses as a defense to negligence lawsuits. In the typical scenario, an injured plaintiff employee sues a business that is not his payroll employer for negligence. The defendant business files a motion for summary judgment arguing that it is the plaintiff's statutory employer. Although a statutory employer is, like a regular employer, liable for workers' compensation benefits, they seldom pay them, as the regular payroll employer usually has insurance and pays the workers' compensation benefits. However, a business that is responsible for workers' compensation benefits does not actually have to pay them to be entitled to the immunity (workers' compensation exclusivity) of 23:1032. Thus, the defendant business is claiming that, as a statutory employer, it is immune from the employee's negligence lawsuit.

There are two ways in which a business may be a statutory employer. One is referred to as the two-contract theory. Under this version, a general contractor enters into subcontracts for performance of parts of work in a general contract. The general contractor becomes the statutory employer of the subcontractor's employees performing the work. The two-contract theory is codified in 23:1061(A)(2), *infra*.

For the other version of statutory employer, which lacks a name, the Louisiana courts and legislature have sparred over the proper test for whether a defendant business is a statutory employer. The current test is set forth in 23:1061(A)(3). This statutory test requires a written contract with a provision stating the statutory employer test, which creates a rebuttable presumption of statutory employer status.

La. R.S. 23:1061.   Principal contractors; liability

A.   (1)   Subject to the provisions of Paragraphs (2) and (3) of this Subsection, when any "principal" as defined in R.S. 23:1032(A)(2), undertakes to execute any work, which is a part of his trade, business, or occupation and contracts with any person, in this Section referred to as the "contractor", for the execution by or under the contractor of the whole or any part of the work undertaken by the principal, the principal, as a statutory employer, shall be granted the exclusive remedy protections of R.S. 23:1032 and shall be liable to pay to any employee employed in the execution of the work or to his dependent, any compensation under this Chapter which he would have been liable to pay if the employee had been immediately employed by him; and where compensation is claimed from, or proceedings are taken against, the principal, then, in the application of this Chapter reference to the principal shall be substituted for reference to the employer, except that the amount of compensation shall be calculated with reference to the earnings of the employee under the employer by whom he is immediately employed. For purposes of this Section, work shall be considered part of the principal's trade, business, or occupation if it is an integral part of or essential to the ability of the principal to generate that individual principal's goods, products, or services.

(2)   A statutory employer relationship shall exist whenever the services or work provided by the immediate employer is contemplated by or included in a contract between the principal and any

person or entity other than the employee's immediate employer.

(3)   Except in those instances covered by Paragraph (2) of this Subsection, a statutory employer relationship shall not exist between the principal and the contractor's employees, whether they are direct employees or statutory employees, unless there is a written contract between the principal and a contractor which is the employee's immediate employer or his statutory employer, which recognizes the principal as a statutory employer. When the contract recognizes a statutory employer relationship, there shall be a rebuttable presumption of a statutory employer relationship between the principal and the contractor's employees, whether direct or statutory employees. This presumption may be overcome only by showing that the work is not an integral part of or essential to the ability of the principal to generate that individual principal's goods, products, or services.

B.   When the principal is liable to pay compensation under this Section, he shall be entitled to indemnity from any person who independently of this Section would have been liable to pay compensation to the employee or his dependent, and shall have a cause of action therefor.

* * * * *

NOTES

1.   For a recent interpretation of the statutory employer statute, *see Prejean v. Maintenance Enters., Inc.*, 8 So. 3d 766 (La.App. 4 Cir. 2009), *writ denied*, 11 So. 3d 496 (La. 2009). The court held that a contract provision which provided that the principal was the statutory employer and it would be liable for workers compensation benefits *if* the contractor or subcontractors were unable to meet their workers' compensation obligations to their employees did not satisfy the requirements of 23:1061 because the workers' compensation obligation was made conditional. The court stated as follows: "Because [defendant] did not accept unconditionally, implicitly or explicitly, the *obligation* of a statutory employer, it cannot obtain the *benefit* of a statutory employer, which is tort immunity." *Id.* at 776. The Fifth Circuit rejected the argument of a business that it was a statutory employer because it was not listed as a statutory employer in the procurement agreement between other parties. *See Louque v. Scott Equipment Co., LLC*, 170 So. 3d 335 (La.App. 5 Cir. 2015), *writ denied*, ___ So. 3d ___, 2017 WL 1534865 (La. 2017). Although the agreement referred to subsidiaries or affiliates of the buyer as statutory employers, the defendant was not listed as an affiliate, subsidiary, or buyer but rather as a location for services.

2. In *Rainey v. Entergy Gulf States, Inc.*, 35 So. 3d 215 (La. 2010), there was a contract addendum providing that principal was statutory employer bore typewritten signature of principal's representative. This was sufficient where it was authorized and intended to constitute a signature. Additionally, the addendum was effective based on the signature of the employer, as the principal was the party that prepared and presented the addendum to the employer.

e.   A Summary

As the foregoing materials reflect, the claim against his employer by a person injured in a workplace accident may be limited to worker compensation benefits and, concomitantly, the worker may be barred from pursuing a tort claim against his employer if

(1)   there is an employer-employee relationship between them, and

(2)   the injury occurred in the course and scope of that relationship.

An employer may be either a general employer (one who hires and fires and directly supervises the employee) or a special employer, i.e., a borrowing employer or a "statutory" employer.

Even if there is an employment relationship and the injury arises out of that relationship, the employee may pursue a tort claim against the employer if certain exclusions apply, such as an intentional tort or horseplay, or if the claim arises out of a non-employment-related dispute.

417

CHAPTER 8

DAMAGES

A. GENERALLY

COMMENT

The recoverability of certain types of damages for certain conduct generally is part of the "duty/risk/legal cause" inquiry, i.e., do we want to impose liability upon this faulty defendant for this particular type of damage occurring in this particular manner? Most of those issues are discussed in Chapter 6. This chapter covers some of these issues, such as punitive damages and damages for loss of consortium. The other thrust of this chapter is to provide some framework for determining how recoverable damages are proved and calculated. That issue generally is left to the factfinder, with some judicial control.

Generally, there are three types of damages: nominal, compensatory, and punitive. Nominal damages are awarded where plaintiff establishes the invasion of a right but no real damages. Nominal damages were once important in cases where what was really sought was a declaration of the parties' rights. Today, with declaratory judgment actions and other procedural devices, nominal damages are much less important. The most important type of damages are compensatory damages–the amount designed to place the plaintiff in the position she would have been in if the tort had never occurred. The most controversial category of damages is punitive damages–an amount, in addition to compensatory damages, that is designed to punish and deter the defendant and others like her. Recently, punitive damages have come under Constitutional attack; that attack and the most recent U.S. Supreme Court case on the subject are set forth below.

While this chapter focuses on damages, a tort victim might seek recovery based on unjust enrichment. In such a case the plaintiff's recovery might be measured not by the plaintiff's loss but by the defendant's gain. Will traditional tort recovery be limited by Code of Criminal Procedure Article 895.1(A), which provides that (1) a "judicially determined" award of restitution to a victim or his family is a civil money judgement, and (2) "(t)he amount of any (restitution) judgment . . . shall be credited against the amount of any subsequent civil judgment against the defendant and in favor of the victim . . . which arises out of the same . . . acts which are the subject of the criminal offense. . . .?"

Alternatively, or in addition to any other relief sought, a tort plaintiff might seek an injunction ordering defendant to stop engaging in a certain activity.

La. Civil Code Art. 2324.1. Damages: discretion of judge or jury

In the assessment of damages in cases of offenses, quasi offenses, and quasi contracts, much discretion must be left to the judge or jury.

NOTE

1. How "much" is the "much discretion" left to the judge or jury? Concluding that the appellate court abused its discretion in reducing a $1.4 million general damages award to a seaman whose leg injury left him disabled and with a "grotesque disfigurement," the Supreme Court reminded that the trier of fact's discretion in the amount of an award of general damages is "great, and even vast, so that an appellate court should rarely disturb ... (such) an award." *Youn v. Maritime Overseas Corp.*, 623 So. 2d 1257 (La. 1993).

B. PERSONAL INJURY DAMAGES

In Louisiana Tort Law, § 7.02, Maraist, Galligan, Maraist & Corbett note:

Compensatory damages are divided into two broad categories: special damages and general damages. Special damages are those which either must be specially pled or have a "ready market value," i.e., the amount of the damage supposedly can be determined with relative certainty.

In personal injury cases, special damages include past and future medical expenses, loss of earnings or earning capacity, and loss of services. Maraist and Galligan continue:

General damages are those which are inherently speculative in nature and cannot be fixed with mathematical certainty. These include pain and suffering, mental anguish, and loss of enjoyment of life....

1. Special Damages

Past lost earnings do not present particular problems. The loss is added up and awarded. But future lost earnings or earning capacity are more problematic because courts in tort cases do not award periodic payments. Rather the award is made in a lump sum. Thus, the factfinder must determine if the injury will reduce future earnings or earning capacity and, if so, by how much. This will require the factfinder to make difficult decisions about an unknown future. Then, the factfinder must consider the reality that an award made today to compensate for $150,000 in lost earnings fifteen years from now will, if invested prudently, be worth more than $150,000 in fifteen years. Since that would make the plaintiff more than whole, the factfinder must "discount" the future lost earnings award to present value. It must calculate an amount that, if awarded today and prudently invested, would yield $150,000 in year fifteen. This task usually requires expert testimony and consideration of personal, industry, and even national productivity, as well as, inflation, deflation, and safe investment rates.

FOLSE
v.
FAKOURI
371 So. 2d 1120 (La. 1979)

award for lost earning capacity

SUMMERS, C. J.

* * * * *

Many factors could have entered into the jury's deliberations on the question of plaintiff's loss of the capacity to earn more during the four year-eight month period prior to trial. He was fifty years old at the time of the accident. He was apparently vigorous and industrious and had been steadily employed. The actuary who testified for plaintiff stated that the average salary of bus drivers throughout the United States in 1964 as determined by the Department of Labor was $10,174. Inflation and the additional employment opportunities created by a burgeoning economy after his injury and before trial may also have played a part in the jury's deliberations and the unarticulated reasons for their award.

The jury was entitled to determine from these and other factors in the record the probabilities and estimates of plaintiff's ability to earn money. What plaintiff earned before and after the injury does not constitute the measure. Even if he had been unemployed at the time of the injury he is entitled to an award for impairment or diminution of earning power. And while his earning capacity at the time of the injury is relevant, it is not necessarily determinative of his future ability to earn. *Coco v. Winston Industries, Inc.*, 341 So. 2d 332 (La.1976). Damages should be estimated on the injured person's ability to earn money, rather than what he actually earned before the injury.

* * * * *

Earning capacity in itself is not necessarily determined by actual loss; damages may be assessed for the deprivation of what the injured plaintiff could have earned despite the fact that he may never have seen fit to take advantage of that capacity. The theory is that the injury done him has deprived him of a capacity he would have been entitled to enjoy even though he never profited from it monetarily.

* * * * *

NOTES

1.   The court of appeals, reversing a jury verdict, awarded plaintiff damages for lost wages because "there is an absence of evidence indicating that he would not have continued to work absent his injury." *Held*, the court of appeals erred. The proof established that plaintiff's job was eliminated by his employer for reasons completely unrelated to his injuries and there was no objective proof that plaintiff could not continue to work because of the accident. A plaintiff may not obtain an award for lost wages unless he proves positively that he would have been earning the wages but for the accident in question. The appellate court "erroneously switched the burden away from the plaintiff." *Boyette v. United Services Automobile Assoc.*, 783 So. 2d 1276 (La. 2001).

2.   In *Bowens v. Patterson*, 716 So. 2d 69 (La.App. 3 Cir. 1998), a high school senior was rendered a quadriplegic in an auto accident. At trial he presented unrefuted testimony (parents, coach and part time employer) that but for the accident, he would have more probably than not gone to college and graduated in computer science. The evidence included his long range plans, his ability and grades, and that he and others, acting on his behalf, had actually taken steps towards his going to college. *Held*, the trial court abused its "vast discretion" in ignoring this evidence and refusing to award damages for future lost wages based upon plaintiff's future employment as a computer science graduate. But in *Woods v. Hall*, 194 So. 3d 689 (La.App. 1 Cir. 2016), the court did not permit recovery of diminished earning capacity or loss of future wages to a plaintiff who was a semi-professional opera singer before a car accident. Plaintiff claimed that as a result of the accident she was unable to attend a particular opera audition in New York (she said it was comparable to the "NFL Combine"), and that missing that audition left her unable to work the entire opera season, reducing her earning potential. However, plaintiff was paid for some opera singing engagements after the accident, she was not guaranteed work from the New York audition, she had not purchased tickets to the audition at the time of the accident, she had no evidence that she had registered for the audition, and she did not attend the audition the two years following the accident. Essentially, the only evidence plaintiff produced regarding lost income from the missed audition was "her own speculative, conjectural, and self-serving testimony."

3.   The award of medical expenses, particularly if extensive treatment or care is anticipated in the future, can be just as complex. In reference to medical expenses, Maraist and Galligan state:

> A victim may recover past (from injury to trial) and future (post trial) medical expenses caused by tortious conduct. He must establish that he incurred past medical expenses in good faith as a result of his injury, and must show that future medical expenses probably will be incurred.

Maraist, Galligan, Maraist, & Corbett, Louisiana Tort Law, § 7.02 [1] at 7-4 – 7-5. A tortfeasor must pay for the cost of overtreatment or unnecessary medical treatment, unless the overtreatment was incurred in bad faith. *Jones v. Super One Foods/Brookshires Grocery Co.*, 774 So. 2d 200 (La.App. 2 Cir. 2000). To state the obvious, the medical expenses must be related to the injury. *Johnson v. Tregre*, 726 So. 2d 1105 (La.App. 5 Cir. 1999). Difficult factual and legal issues can arise where the injury aggravates a pre-existing injury.

5.   A 1999 amendment to C.C. Art. 2315 provides:

> A. Every act whatever of man that causes damage to another obliges him by whose fault it happened to repair it.

B. Damages may include loss of consortium, service, and society, and shall be recoverable by the same respective categories of persons who would have had a cause of action for wrongful death of an injured person. Damages do not include costs for future medical treatment, services, surveillance, or procedures of any kind unless such treatment, services, surveillance, or procedures are directly related to a manifest physical or mental injury or disease. Damages shall include any sales taxes paid by the owner on the repair or replacement of the property damaged.

MARTINEZ
v.
U.S. FIDELITY AND GUAR. CO.
423 So. 2d 1088 (La. 1982)

* * * * *

In passing, we note that this court has never decided whether income taxes may be considered at all in formulating damage awards, and that our courts of appeal are divided on the issue. *Reeve v. Louisiana Arkansas Railway Co.*, 304 So. 2d 370 (La.App. 1st Cir.) *cert denied*, 305 So. 2d 123 (La.1974); *Menard v. Travelers Ins. Co.*, 240 So. 2d 390 (La.App. 3rd Cir.1970); *Teal v. Allstate Ins. Co.*, 348 So. 2d 83 (La.App. 4th Cir.) *cert denied*, 351 So. 2d 164 (La.1977); Annot, 16 A.L.R 4th 589, 614 (1982). The parties in this case have not addressed the merits of this question, however, and we decline to consider this important issue on the record and briefs before us, since we have found that in the context of this case it is unnecessary for us to do so.

* * * * * *

NOTES

1.   The court has still not decided. The issue is critical and troublesome because personal injury awards (other than punitive damages) are *not* taxable. *See* 26 U.S.C. § 104 (a) (2). Thus, defendants argue that because personal injury awards are *not* taxable, awarding gross lost wages makes the plaintiff more than whole. Consequently, defendants seek to be able to inform the jury about the "non-taxability" of the award and to urge the jury to reduce the lost earnings recovery to avoid overcompensation. Plaintiffs argue that reduction of awards for "tax" effects is contrary to Congress' intent and will under-deter defendants.

2.   In *Harris v. Tenneco*, 563 So. 2d 317 (La.App. 4 Cir. 1990), the court adopted gross wages as the test, overruled prior cases, and discussed the split among the circuits. *See also, Masters v. Courtesy Ford Co., Inc.*, 758 So. 2d 171 (La.App. 2 Cir. 2000) (gross income should be used in determining a loss of earnings and earning capacity in a wrongful death suit, and future growth should be factored into the assessment.)

3.   When the injuries are catastrophic, the dollar award may exceed millions of dollars.

2.   General Damages

NOTES

1.   How does a court or jury award or "value" general damages? Since each case and each person is different, how does a court value pain and suffering or mental anguish? Is it possible to do so? Is it fair? Is it fair not to?

Recall the wide discretion the factfinder has in awarding damages? Lawyers cannot make a "golden rule" argument–"Ladies and gentlemen of the jury, put yourself in the plaintiff's position." That argument is deemed too prejudicial. How about a "per diem" argument? That argument poses a limited time period, such as one minute, one day, or one year; suggests a dollar value to compensate for the pain for that limited time period, and then multiplies the value by the expected duration of the injury's effect. The end product emanating from a modest initial value can be quite staggering and quite persuasive.

Plaintiff's lawyers frequently present "day in the life" videos showing how seriously injured people spend a day. As a defense lawyer, why might you want to be extremely familiar with the production process of the film? Alternatively, defendants might present filmed surveillance evidence of plaintiff engaged in activities he claims he can no longer engage in.

In some cases defendants have objected to the presence of seriously injured plaintiffs in the courtroom, alleging that the very sight of the plaintiff in the courtroom might prejudice the jury. If you were defense counsel, would you want to make that objection in the presence or hearing of the jury? Why not?

2.   A particularly perplexing and tragic issue which has arisen involves the injury victim who is in a coma. Should he be able to recover for pain and suffering? In *McDougald v. Garber*, 73 N.Y. 2d 246, 538 N.Y. S. 2d 937, 536 N.E. 3d 372 (1989), the court held that the comatose plaintiff cannot recover pain and suffering damages. Should the issue be decided as a matter of law or should it depend upon the particular plaintiff and the particular expert testimony?

3.   The plaintiff may seek damages for loss of enjoyment of life (sometimes called "hedonic") damages. The Louisiana Supreme Court approved of hedonic damages as a separate element of damages in *McGee v. A. C. and S., Inc.*, 933 So. 2d 770 (La. 2006). However, the trauma victim's family members may not recover for their loss of enjoyment of life due to the trauma. One of the concerns expressed is that lost enjoyment of life damages may duplicate damages for pain, suffering or emotional distress. Do you see why?

An award for scarring and disfigurement may be duplicative of an award for mental pain and anguish that accompanies such disfigurement and scarring. Are these questions of duplicative recovery appropriate for the judge, or should we trust the jury to avoid such dupicative recovery?

4.   Should damages for future pain and suffering be reduced to present value? *Compare Mentz v. United Technologies*, 754 F.2d 63 (2d Cir. 1985), with *In Re Air Crash Disaster Near New Orleans*, 764 F.2d 1084 (5th Cir. 1986).

5.   Events after an accident that affect a plaintiff's life span can and should be taken into account in determining future damages. The plaintiff bears the burden of proving his damages, including proof that "more probably than not" he will sustain the future damages, based upon a normal life expectancy. Thus where plaintiff was suffering from cancer and all doctors who testified agreed that he had a 30-40% chance of surviving five years, the lower court erred in requiring defendant to prove with a "reasonable degree of medical certainty" that the plaintiff would not live more than five years." *Degruise v. Houma Courier Newspaper Corp.*, 683 So. 2d 689 (La. 1996).

6.   May a jury make an award of the cost of the plaintiff's medical treatment, but "zero" her on general damages, i.e., pain and suffering? In *Wainwright v. Fontenot*, 774 So. 2d 70 (La. 2000), the Court concluded that a factfinder does not err as a matter of law when it declines to award general damages after finding defendant at fault for plaintiff's injuries and awarding special damages for plaintiff's medical expenses. As a general proposition, such a determination may be illogical or inconsistent, but in some cases the factfinder can reasonably reach the conclusion that a plaintiff has proven entitlement to recovery of certain medical costs, yet has failed to prove that he endured compensable pain and suffering. The issue on appeal in such a case is whether the factfinder abused its discretion. There is no abuse of discretion where the jury could conclude that the plaintiff did not suffer any compensable pain or suffering but that placing him in a hospital overnight was a reasonable precaution under the circumstances.

7.   A plaintiff may recover future medical expenses without being awarded future general damages if the plaintiff has made a decision not to ask for future general damages in *Averette v. Phillips*, 185 So. 3d 16 (La.App. 1 Cir. 2015). Usually, a court will find that an award of future

medical expenses without future general damages for pain and suffering is inconsistent. However, there are circumstances in which the evidence of record supports such an award.

C.   PROPERTY DAMAGES

ROMAN CATHOLIC CHURCH
v.
LOUISIANA GAS SERVICE COMPANY
618 So. 2d 874 (La. 1993)

* * * * *

As a general rule of thumb, when a person sustains property damage due to the fault of another, he is entitled to recover damages including the cost of restoration that has been or may be reasonably incurred, or, at his election, the difference between the value of the property before and after the harm.   If, however, the cost of restoring the property in its original condition is disproportionate to the value of the property or economically wasteful, unless there is a reason personal to the owner for restoring the original condition or there is a reason to believe that the plaintiff will, in fact, make the repairs, damages are measured only by the difference between the value of the property before and after the harm.   Consequently, if a building such as a homestead is used for a purpose personal to the owner, the damages ordinarily include an amount for repairs, even though this might be greater than the entire value of the building.

* * * * *

NOTES

1.   The rule enunciated in *Roman Catholic Church* above applies where plaintiff whose marsh lands were damaged had demonstrated a genuine interest in the health of the marsh, lived adjacent to it and used it for recreational purposes for a considerable period of time, attempted unsuccessfully to repair the damaged marsh, and undertook other restorative projects. *St. Martin v. Mobil Exploration & Producing U.S. Inc.,* 234 F. 3d 31 (La. App. 5th Cir. 2000).   In *Hornsby v. Bayou Jack Logging,* 902 So. 2d 361 (La. 2005), the Supreme Court allowed a landowner treble damages under La. R.S. 3:4278.1 for the unlawful cutting and removal of trees without the landowner's consent, but denied the landowner restoration costs under La. Civ. Code art. 2315 which were disproportionate to the value of the property because the evidence did not establish the landowner's intent to restore the land; "[u]nder the precepts enunciated in *Roman Catholic* restoration costs which exceed the value of the property, are justifiable only when there are 'reasons personal to the owner.' "   The Court apparently also concluded that plaintiff's contributory negligence would not reduce the treble damage award.   If a court is considering restoration damages, why not just order defendant to fix it?

2.   If a vehicle is a total loss (the cost to repair exceeds the value), plaintiff is limited to the total value of the vehicle prior to the accident, less the salvage value if plaintiff elects to keep the vehicle. If plaintiff elects to transfer the vehicle to the defendant, defendant must pay the pre-accident value of the vehicle, but may retain the vehicle.   If the vehicle is not a total loss, the owner is entitled to repair costs and, in some factual situations, depreciation (as where the repaired vehicle decreases in value, despite a quality repair job, solely because it was involved in the accident). *Davies v. Automotive Cas. Ins.,* 647 So. 2d 419 (La.App. 2 Cir. 1994).   Who bears the burden of proving that a vehicle is a total loss?   Who should?

3.   A victim may recover damages for loss of use of damaged property during the period of repair.   Damages for loss of use of a "totaled" car are recoverable only for a reasonable time after the plaintiff learns that the car is a total loss. *See, e.g., Bonner v. Louisiana Indemnity Co.,* 607 So. 2d 915 (La.App. 2 Cir. 1992).

4.   After a fire loss, plaintiff reopened her business in a new location.   She was serving a different market, and the good-will she acquired at the old business was not transferable to the new

one. Plaintiff operated the new business under a newly formed corporate entity with a new trade name. *Held*, the judge did not err in determining that plaintiff's original business was destroyed rather than interrupted, and that the appropriate measure of damages was for destruction of the business. *Achee v. National Tea Co.*, 686 So. 2d 121 (La.App. 1 Cir. 1996).

5.   Under La. Civ. Code art. 2315, "damages shall include any sales tax paid by the owner on the repair or replacement of the property damaged."

6.   Act 716 of 2008 amended several articles of the Code of Civil Procedure, including Art. 4272, 4521, and 4522 to provide that when money is paid to a minor as a result of a judgment or a settlement, the court may order that "the money be paid under a structured settlement agreement which provides for periodic payments and is underwritten by a financially responsible entity that assumes responsibility for future payments." La. Civ. Code art. 42722. The article also lists factors that a court must consider in making that determination.

D.   INTEREST AND COURT COSTS

COMMENT

A breach of contract can also be a tort, i.e., the contracting party failed to act reasonably and could have foreseen that his conduct would cause harm to the other contracting party. This "overlap" is important in certain areas, such as recovery of mental anguish damages, economic harm unaccompanied by physical damage to person or property, venue and prescription. To this list, add interest. Under La. Civ. Code art. 2000, interest on a cause of action arising from a breach of contract generally begins to run "from the time it is due," pursuant to La. Civ. Code art. 2000. However, when the cause of action arises from a breach of duty growing out of the contract (such as failure to perform the construction in a workmanlike manner), it is "ex delicto" and interest is due from date of judicial demand, pursuant to La. R.S. 13:4203. *Nicholson & Loup, Inc. v. Carl E. Woodward, Inc.*, 596 So. 2d 374 (La.App. 4 Cir. 1992). La. Civ. Code art. 2924 provides a procedure by which the commissioner of financial institutions computes, from the average of the prime or reference rates of certain leading financial institutions, a prime rate, and establishes the effective judicial interest rate for the following calendar year as one percentage point above that prime rate. This variable interest rate under La. Civ. Code art. 2924 was established in 1987; prior to that time, the rate was fixed (12% in the years immediately preceding the 1987 act). Does a judgment rendered before the effective date of the amendment establishing the variable rate bear interest thereafter at the fixed rate in effect when it was rendered, or at the variable rate thereafter? *Compare Matthias v. Brown*, 599 So. 2d 495 (La.App. 3 Cir. 1992), with *State v. Dietrich*, 598 So. 2d 649 (La.App. 3 Cir. 1992). The judicial interest rate has fluctuated significantly since the variable rate was established.

The prevailing rule is that a court is mandated under La. R.S. 13:4203 to award prejudgment legal interest from date of judicial demand on a lump sum award for future economic damages. *See, e.g., Edwards v. Daugherty*, 848 So. 2d 787 (La.App. 3 Cir. 2003), *writ denied*, 863 So. 2d 607 (La. 2003), and the cases cited therein. Prejudgment interest is due on awards for future damages in tort cases. *Edwards v. Daugherty*, 863 So. 2d 932 (La. 2004). However, in addition to discounting the award for post-judgment periods, the court may reduce the award to adjust for the legal interest which will be applied from date of judicial demand until date of judgment. *Doss v. Second Chance Body Armor, Inc.*, 794 So. 2d 97 (La.App. 2 Cir. 2001). A court should not award pre-judgment interest on punitive damages. In Re: New Orleans Train Car Leakage Fire Litigation, 794 So. 2d 955 (La.App. 4 Cir. 2001).

In state court, the prevailing party usually is awarded court costs, although the judge has discretion. *See, e.g.*, La. Code of Civ. Pro. art. 1920. La. Code of Civ. Pro. art.. 970 provides an "offer of judgment" procedure containing these provisions: (1) the offer must settle all claims between offeror and offeree; (2) the offer must be in writing, must specify amounts and whether it includes costs, interest, attorney's fees, etc., and is confidential unless accepted; (3) the offer is withdrawn unless it is accepted in writing within ten days; (4) if the offer is accepted, either party may move for judgment on the offer, which is a final judgment which cannot be appealed by a party who has consented to the judgment, and (5) if the offer is not accepted and the final judgment obtained by or against the offeree is 25% more or less (depending upon whether he is plaintiff or defendant) than the offer, the offeree must pay the offeror's costs (which does not include attorney fees) incurred after the offer was made.

E.   LOSS OF CONSORTIUM DAMAGES

When A suffers personal injury, her spouse, B, may suffer various losses. These may be recovered under the heading of loss of consortium. Recovery for loss of consortium with a tort victim presents three difficult problems: can anybody recover, and, if so, who should recover, and how much? The first two problems have been legislatively resolved. La. Civ. Code art. 2315 provides that "(d)amages may include loss of consortium, service, and society, and shall be recoverable by the same respective categories of persons who would have had a cause of action for wrongful death of an injured person." The third issue is being resolved by the courts. Generally courts reduce the consortium plaintiff's recovery by the contributory negligence of the trauma victim. *See, e.g., Crane v. Exxon Corp.*, U.S.A., 633 So. 2d 636 (La.App. 1 Cir. 1993). The claims of the consortium plaintiff and the trauma victim generally may be treated together as injury to one person for the purposes of insurance and statutory "per person" limits. *See Ferrell v. Fireman's Fund Ins. Co.*, 696 So. 2d 569 (La. 1997). Other judicial approaches are presented in the following cases and notes.

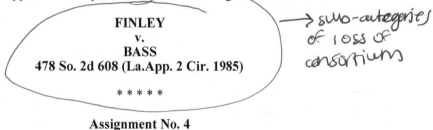

FINLEY

v.

BASS

478 So. 2d 608 (La.App. 2 Cir. 1985)

→ sub-categories of loss of consortium

* * * * *

Assignment No. 4

In this assignment, appellants claim the trial court erred in awarding damages to Mrs. Finley for loss of consortium; the Finleys answered, seeking an increase in this award from $5,000 to $30,000. The thrust of appellants' argument is that the Finleys failed to present any evidence of the value of the services allegedly lost. The entitlement to these damages is accorded by statute. LSA--C.C. art. 2315 B provides:

> Damages may include loss of consortium, service, and society, and shall be recoverable by the same respective categories of persons who would have had a cause of action for wrongful death of an injured person.

This paragraph, added by Acts of 1982, No. 202, creates, defines and regulates a cause of action for certain relations of a tort victim who does not die from his injuries. *Ferguson v. Burkett*, 454 So. 2d 413 (La.App. 3d Cir. 1984). Because of the recentness of this amendment, there is no jurisprudential guidance for the assessment of damages. We have no difficulty, however, dismissing appellants' argument that the Finleys proved no damages. It is quite plain from the circumstances that Mrs. Finley has suffered and is entitled to an award under the provisions of the statute.

Because of the dearth of jurisprudence, it is more difficult to analyze the Finleys' contention that the damages are insufficient. They urge that we break down the concept of "consortium" into seven component parts. We have done so, for lack of any other approach, and find that even under this analysis the damages do not appear to be abusively low.

The first element of loss is love and affection. There is no allegation that Mrs. Finley stopped loving her husband as a result of the accident. We can appreciate that the events surrounding the accident may have placed some strain on their relationship. Second is society and companionship. There is no doubt that Mrs. Finley misses her husband when he must retire early due to pain and discomfort. On the other hand, Mr. Finley will spend much more time at home with her now that ambulation is a problem for him. This will provide them with more togetherness than they used to

426

enjoy when Mr. Finley was away in Baton Rouge at the Exxon Plant. Third is sexual relations. Mrs. Finley testified that the frequency had decreased by seventy percent; this is undisputed. The loss should be considered against the age and general health of Mr. Finley. Fourth is the right of performance of material services. Mrs. Finley testified that she and her son must now perform numerous household and farming chores that Mr. Finley used to do. She did not testify, however, that she would not have engaged in these tasks but for the accident, nor did she allege that she was forced to hire extra help, thereby incurring a financial loss. Since material services are susceptible to reasonably certain proof, some evidence should have been offered. *Cf. Edwards v. Lewis Grocer Co.*, 391 So. 2d 13 (La.App. 2d Cir. 1980). Fifth is the right of support from her husband. We construe this to mean financial support. The trial court awarded Mr. Finley $178,000 to compensate him for lost wages and earning potential. This is equivalent to the salary or commissions he would have taken home to support himself and his wife, so the loss here is not great. Sixth is aid and assistance, which Mrs. Finley has not sufficiently distinguished from "material services." The quantum of this loss was not proved. Finally is the loss of felicity. Mrs. Finley has not elaborated on this element of damages. We think that every personal injury tends to decrease the parties' overall happiness but Mrs. Finley has not shown any particular losses distinct from the other elements enumerated. In sum, Mrs. Finley has proved a definite loss on only one element, sexual relations, and a potential loss of material services.

The trial court has great discretion to assess damages that cannot be calculated with certainty. LSA--C.C. arts. 1999, 2324.1. His formulation of damages is enhanced by his personal observation of the parties' demeanor. We will not adjust the award unless there is an obvious abuse of discretion. Mrs. Finley's award of $5,000 is probably on the lower end of the discretionary scale, but it is not abusively low in light of the elements we have outlined. The part of the judgment awarding damages for lost consortium is affirmed.

* * * * *

NOTES

1.   Are the spouse and children entitled to some damages upon establishing some (however minimal) loss of society with the injured spouse? *See Boudreaux v. Murray*, 489 So. 2d 948 (La.App. 5 Cir. 1986).

2.   What if the trauma victim does not suffer trauma, but only injured feelings, such as a victim of malicious prosecution or defamation? Can his Article 2315 beneficiaries recover for any loss of consortium resulting therefrom? *See Minion v. Gaylord's International Corp.*, 541 So. 2d 209 (La.App. 4 Cir. 1989).

3.   Can one "marry a cause of action," i.e., recover damages for loss of consortium resulting from the spouse's pre-marital injury? *Compare Leckelt v. Eunice Superette, Inc.*, 555 So. 2d 11 (La.App. 3 Cir. 1989) and *Morales v. Davis Bros. Construction Co., Inc.*, 706 So. 2d 1048 (La. App. 4 Cir. 1998), with *Aldredge v. Whitney*, 591 So. 2d 1201 (La.App. 2 Cir. 1991). *See, also, Herndon v. Southwestern Elec. Power Co.*, 655 So. 2d 678 (La.App. 2 Cir. 1995). There, wife married husband after his accident and subsequently filed a claim against the tortfeasor for loss of consortium. However, she could not show that she reasonably believed that husband had fully recovered from the known and apparent initial injuries before the marriage and that he had experienced a new, different, unforeseen and more serious injury after the marriage. *Held*, wife does not have a claim for loss of consortium.

4.   Sometimes a court or factfinder will deny an award for loss of consortium because after the accident the trauma victim was able to spend more time with the consortium plaintiff.

5.   In *Fils v. Allstate Ins. Co.*, 186 So. 3d 152 (La.App. 1 Cir. 2015) an aunt who had legal and physical custody of a minor child and who was judicially appointed as the child's tutor sought loss of consortium damages for the child's injuries The aunt argued that she had become the parent of the child. Because no definition of "father" or "mother" is provided by La. Cov. Code art. 2315.2, the court looked to the Children's Code (quoting La. Children's Code Art. 116(17)), which defines

"parent" as "any living person who is presumed to be a parent under the Civil Code or a biological or adoptive mother or father of a child." The court found no authority for the proposition that one who is appointed as tutor and given custody of a child can bring an action for wrongful death or loss of consortium of the child.

6.   The trauma victim also loses "consortium" with his spouse and family. This usually is compensated in an award to him of "hedonic" damages, i.e., loss of enjoyment of life. *See, e.g., Lougon v. Era Aviation, Inc.*, 609 So. 2d 330 (La.App. 3 Cir. 1992); *Foster v. Trafalgar House Oil & Gas*, 603 So. 2d 284 (La. App. 2 Cir. 1992).

7.   A difficult question arises when a spouse suffers loss of earnings when he or she "nurses" the victim spouse. *See, e.g, Morgan v. Cenac*, 634 So. 2d 60 (La.App. 4 Cir. 1994) -- Plaintiffs (husband and wife) alleged that husband took early retirement to care for ailing wife, the tort victim, and sought damages for his loss of earning capacity and early retirement. *Held*, plaintiffs did not have a cause of action for such damages; however, wife is entitled to recover the cost of services required as a result of her injuries, and husband is entitled to recover for the loss of his wife's services and support to the community.

Courts have upheld awards for loss of household services although the trauma victim did not actually hire help to perform the services. *See Varnell v. Louisiana Tech University, supra; Creel v. St. Charles Gaming Co., Inc.,* 707 So. 2d 475 (La.App. 3 Cir. 1998).

8.   A needy adult child may be entitled to recover from a tortfeasor for the loss of services which the parent would have been able to provide to the child if the parent had not been injured by the tortfeasor. *Sebastien v. McKay,* 649 So. 2d 711 (La.App. 3 Cir. 1994).

F.   PUNITIVE DAMAGES

As noted, punitive damages are awarded over and above compensatory damages to punish and deter the defendant and others like him, her, or it. In all jurisdictions something more than mere negligence is required. In Louisiana, consistently with the Civil Law tradition, punitive damages are generally *not* available. There are certain statutes under which treble damages may be recovered, *see, e.g.*, La. R.S. 3:4278.1 (timber cutting), and two code articles allowing recovery of punitive damages, La. Civ. Code art. 2315.4, involving drunk driving, and La. Civ. Code art. 2315.7, involving criminal sexual activity with a minor. Additionally, La. R. S. 9:2800.61 (The Louisiana Drug Dealer Liability Act) creates a cause of action against persons furnishing drugs. Under that act designated persons (including, in some circumstances, the user) may recover compensatory and punitive damages against the provider of drugs and certain convicted drug dealers.

1.   La. Civil Code Art. 2315.3.

Former Article 2315.3 provided:

In addition to general and special damages, exemplary damages may be awarded, if it is proved that plaintiff's injuries were caused by the defendant's wanton or reckless disregard for public safety in the storage, handling, or transportation of hazardous or toxic substances.

Act 2 of the 1996 Special Session repealed La. Civ. Code art. 2315.3. The repeal "shall only be applicable to causes of action which arise on or after the effective date," which is April 16, 1996.

Critically, in *Bujol v. Entergy Services, Inc.*, 922 So. 2d 1113 (La. 2004), the Supreme Court held that a plaintiff was *not* entitled to punitive damages unless he also is entitled to compensatory damages. This general rule probably applies to all Louisiana punitive damage articles and statutes.

2.   La. Civil Code Article 2315.4

Art. 2315.4. Additional damages; intoxicated defendant

In addition to general and special damages, exemplary damages may be awarded upon proof that the injuries on which the action is based were caused by a wanton or reckless disregard for the rights and safety of others by a defendant whose intoxication while operating a motor vehicle was a cause in fact of the resulting injuries. For a case imposing exemplary damages under La. Civ. Code art. 2315.4, *see Berg v. Zummo, supra* Chapter 6.

MYRES

v.

NUNSETT

511 So. 2d 1287 (La.App. 2 Cir. 1987)

JONES, J.

Plaintiff, injured in a rear-end automobile accident appealed a lower court judgment awarding him $1750 ($1000 in general damages and $750 in special damages), and failing to award exemplary damages under La.C.C. Art. 2315.4. We affirm.

On September 29, 1984, at 1:20 a.m., Myres was driving his vehicle West on Milam Street in Shreveport. Myres stopped his vehicle in the 2500 block of Milam near its intersection with Kenneth Street and waited for a person who had flagged him down for a ride about two blocks before. While stopped, the Myres vehicle was rear-ended by a pickup truck driven by Horace Nunsett (Nunsett subsequently pled guilty to driving while intoxicated).

* * * * *

A number of other states take the position that operating a motor vehicle on the public road after voluntary intoxication in and of itself constitutes sufficient reckless disregard to warrant an award of exemplary damages. Our codal article requires an additional showing that the accident resulting in injury was caused by the voluntary intoxication of a defendant.

In the instant case, Nunsett testified that he pled guilty to DWI on the advice of counsel as it was the most expedient and inexpensive way to dispose of the matter. There was no showing that anything but Nunsett's failure to observe the stopped vehicle caused this rear-end collision. No evidence was presented that indicates Nunsett's drinking was a cause-in-fact of this accident.

For the foregoing reasons we affirm the district court judgment, at appellant's cost.

NOTES

1.   In *Bourgeois v. State Farm Mut. Auto. Ins. Co.*, 562 So. 2d 1177 (La.App. 4 Cir. 1990), the court held that (1) punitive damages were recoverable by a plaintiff who sustained only property damage as a result of the wrongful conduct; (2) to recover, plaintiff must establish three elements (DWI, cause in fact, and wanton and reckless disregard); (3) mere influence and impairment does not necessarily establish wanton or reckless disregard, but (4) a blood alcohol level of .227 does.

2.   *Clifton v. Collins*, 563 So. 2d 408 (La.App. 1 Cir. 1990) -- if jury could have found that factors other than intoxication caused the accident, it was not manifest error to deny punitive damages. (Defendant, truckdriver, returned from long distance run to attend funeral; returning from funeral, he failed to completely return to correct lane after passing.) *See also, Aycock v. Jenkins Tile Co.*, 703 So. 2d 117 (La.App. 1 Cir. 1997). There a guest passenger, who was injured when the host driver, his twin brother, turned left in front of an oncoming vehicle, sought punitive damages from host driver's employer. Host driver's BAL was .33; however, both brothers testified they had not been drinking any alcohol on the day of the accident, although they drank the night before. *Held*, the trial judge did not

abuse his discretion in refusing to award exemplary damages; "This was not a situation in which a person stumbled out of a bar and got behind the wheel.... Nor was (guest passenger) ... a totally innocent victim.... (He) knew when and how much his twin brother had been drinking and was in a position to assess his condition on the day of the accident." *See also, Davis v. Fenerty*, 892 So. 2d 55 (La.App. 5 Cir. 2004) (trial judge erred in granting a JNOV and awarding punitive damages against an intoxicated driver who was at fault in the accident, where the jury refused to award such damages and the plaintiff failed to prove that the intoxication was the cause in fact of the plaintiff's injuries). *Compare, Branan v. Allstate Ins. Co.*, 761 So. 2d 612 (La.App. 5 Cir. 2000) (drinking beer sufficient to raise one's alcohol level almost twice the legal limit and getting behind a wheel of an automobile is precisely the type of activity article 2315.4 was enacted to deter).

3.   A jury may exercise its discretion not to award exemplary damages, although it determines that the plaintiff has established all of the elements necessary for imposition of such damages. *Boulmay v. Dubois*, 593 So. 2d 769 (La.App. 4 Cir. 1992).

4.   In *Hill v. Sampson*, 628 So. 2d 81 (La.App. 2 Cir. 1993), the court held that proof that injuries were caused by wanton or reckless disregard of the rights and safety of others does not require evidence of a specific action on the defendant's part; plaintiff must only prove a general state of mind and a conscious indifference to the consequences. Conscious indifference can be found where the actor knows or should know his actions will cause harm and proceeds anyway; it is determined by the facts and circumstances of each case, including (in a claim for punitive damages under La. Civ. Code art. 2315.4) the blood alcohol level, evidence of the effect of alcohol on the specific defendant, and the consequences of alcohol consumption.

5.   In *Berg v. Zummo*, 786 So. 2d 708 (La. 2001), the Supreme Court decided that punitive damages under Article 2315.4 could not be recovered from a vendor of alcoholic beverages for selling or serving alcohol to an intoxicated person whose intoxication while driving caused injury.

3.   La. Civil Code Article 2315.7

Art. 2315.7.   Liability for damages caused by criminal sexual activity occurring during childhood

> In addition to general and special damages, exemplary damages may be awarded upon proof that the injuries on which the action is based were caused by a wanton and reckless disregard for the rights and safety of the person through criminal sexual activity which occurred when the victim was seventeen years old or younger, regardless of whether the defendant was prosecuted for his or her acts. The provisions of this Article shall be applicable only to the perpetrator of the criminal sexual activity.

The Louisiana Third Circuit has addressed the issue of vicarious liability for punitive damages in *Gillespie v. Calcasieu Parish School Bd.*, 179 So. 3d 966 (La.App. 3 Cir. 2015), *writ denied*, 187 So. 3d 470 (La. 2016). In *Gillespie*, a high school student and her parents recovered punitive damages under Article 2315.3 against a teacher for sexual conduct with a minor child. The court rejected the argument that the school board could be vicariously liable for punitive damages under Article 2320.

4.   Some General Concerns

As noted, punitive damages raise peculiar and particular issues. Some of these are discussed in the following passage from Galligan, *Augmented Awards: The Efficient Evolution of Punitive Damages*, 51 La. L. Rev. 3, 32-34 (1990) (footnotes omitted).

A.   The Punitive Hornbook of Punitive Damages

Just as many of the philosophical questions surrounding punitive damages have not changed, the law has similarly been relatively static until very recently. Certainly mass tort cases and the recent efforts of tort reformers have led to some new problems and peculiar twists.... The law, like the philosophical debate, has been grounded in punitive or penal concerns. For instance, in most states, the plaintiff in order to recover punitive damages must show the defendant engaged in worse activity than mere negligence. The defendant must have committed an intentional tort or otherwise acted wilfully, wantonly, maliciously, recklessly, or outrageously. In order to be liable for punitive damages, a defendant must have engaged in some morally blameworthy conduct deserving of punishment. In instructing juries on the proper amount to award as punitive damages, courts typically advise them to award an amount sufficient to punish the defendant and to deter the defendant and others like him from engaging in similar conduct in the future. This deterrence is punishment oriented. Courts also tell juries to consider the wealth of the defendant, the severity of harm with which the plaintiff was threatened, the relationship between the harm that the plaintiff suffered or with which he was threatened, the amount of compensatory damages awarded, the egregiousness of the defendant's conduct, the amount of any other punitive damages awards the defendant had to pay or is threatened with paying, and any criminal punishment the defendant suffered or may suffer as a result of the same conduct forming the basis of the plaintiff's tort suit. Most of these factors are designed and discussed in reference to how much punishment is needed, not in reference to efficiency and accident avoidance. Appellate courts have traditionally reversed punitive damage assessments only if they "shocked the conscience." Recently courts have grown more willing to review and reverse, or revise downward, punitive damage awards. Still, there are cries for greater reform. Aside from the shock the conscience standard, appellate courts have traditionally relied upon the oft-cited rule that punitive damages must bear a reasonable relationship to compensatory damages or else they will be reduced. There is an aspect of the "punishment must fit the crime" to this reasonable relationship rule.

5.   The Constitutionality of Punitive Damages

1.   In *Galjour v. General American Tank Corp.*, 764 F. Supp. 1093 (ED La. 1991), the court held that CC Art. 2315.3 did not violate due process or equal protection, and required proof of punitive damages only by a preponderance of the evidence. Consider the next case.

STATE FARM MUTUAL AUTOMOBILE INSURANCE COMPANY
v.
CAMPBELL
538 U.S. 408, 123 S.Ct. 1523 (2003)

KENNEDY, J.

We address once again the measure of punishment, by means of punitive damages, a State may impose upon a defendant in a civil case. The question is whether, in the circumstances we shall recount, an award of $145 million in punitive damages, where full compensatory damages are $1 million, is excessive and in violation of the Due Process Clause of the Fourteenth Amendment to the Constitution of the United States.

I

In 1981, Curtis Campbell (Campbell) was driving with his wife, Inez Preece Campbell, in Cache County, Utah. He decided to pass six vans traveling ahead of them on a two-lane highway. Todd Ospital was driving a small car approaching from the opposite direction. To avoid a head-on collision with Campbell, who by then was driving on the wrong side of the highway and toward oncoming traffic, Ospital swerved onto the shoulder, lost control of his automobile, and collided with a vehicle driven by Robert G. Slusher. Ospital was killed, and Slusher was rendered permanently disabled. The Campbells escaped unscathed.

In the ensuing wrongful death and tort action, Campbell insisted he was not at fault. Early investigations did support differing conclusions as to who caused the accident, but "a consensus was reached early on by the investigators and witnesses that Mr. Campbell's unsafe pass had indeed caused the crash." 65 P.3d at 1141 (Utah 2001). Campbell's insurance company, petitioner State Farm Mutual Automobile Insurance Company (State Farm), nonetheless decided to contest liability and declined offers by Slusher and Ospital's estate (Ospital) to settle the claims for the policy limit of

$50,000 ($25,000 per claimant). State Farm also ignored the advice of one of its own investigators and took the case to trial, assuring the Campbells that "their assets were safe, that they had no liability for the accident, that [State Farm] would represent their interests, and that they did not need to procure separate counsel." *Id.,* at 1142. To the contrary, a jury determined that Campbell was 100 percent at fault, and a judgment was returned for $185,849, far more than the amount offered in settlement.

At first State Farm refused to cover the $135,849 in excess liability. Its counsel made this clear to the Campbells: " 'You may want to put for sale signs on your property to get things moving.' " *Ibid.* Nor was State Farm willing to post a supersedeas bond to allow Campbell to appeal the judgment against him. Campbell obtained his own counsel to appeal the verdict. During the pendency of the appeal, in late 1984, Slusher, Ospital, and the Campbells reached an agreement whereby Slusher and Ospital agreed not to seek satisfaction of their claims against the Campbells. In exchange the Campbells agreed to pursue a bad faith action against State Farm and to be represented by Slusher's and Ospital's attorneys. The Campbells also agreed that Slusher and Ospital would have a right to play a part in all major decisions concerning the bad faith action. No settlement could be concluded without Slusher's and Ospital's approval, and Slusher and Ospital would receive 90 percent of any verdict against State Farm.

In 1989, the Utah Supreme Court denied Campbell's appeal in the wrongful death and tort actions. *Slusher v. Ospital,* 777 P.2d 437 (Utah 1989). State Farm then paid the entire judgment, including the amounts in excess of the policy limits. The Campbells nonetheless filed a complaint against State Farm alleging bad faith, fraud, and intentional infliction of emotional distress. The trial court initially granted State Farm's motion for summary judgment because State Farm had paid the excess verdict, but that ruling was reversed on appeal. 840 P.2d 130 (Utah App. 1992). On remand State Farm moved *in limine* to exclude evidence of alleged conduct that occurred in unrelated cases outside of Utah, but the trial court denied the motion. At State Farm's request the trial court bifurcated the trial into two phases conducted before different juries. In the first phase the jury determined that State Farm's decision not to settle was unreasonable because there was a substantial likelihood of an excess verdict.

Before the second phase of the action against State Farm we decided *BMW of North America, Inc. v. Gore,* 517 U.S. 559, 116 S.Ct. 1589, 134 L.Ed.2d 809 (1996), and refused to sustain a $2 million punitive damages award which accompanied a verdict of only $4,000 in compensatory damages. Based on that decision, State Farm again moved for the exclusion of evidence of dissimilar out-of-state conduct. App. to Pet. for Cert. 168a-172a. The trial court denied State Farm's motion. *Id.,* at 189a.

The second phase addressed State Farm's liability for fraud and intentional infliction of emotional distress, as well as compensatory and punitive damages. The Utah Supreme Court aptly characterized this phase of the trial:

> "State Farm argued during phase II that its decision to take the case to trial was an 'honest mistake' that did not warrant punitive damages. In contrast, the Campbells introduced evidence that State Farm's decision to take the case to trial was a result of a national scheme to meet corporate fiscal goals by capping payouts on claims company wide. This scheme was referred to as State Farm's 'Performance, Planning and Review,' or PP & R, policy. To prove the existence of this scheme, the trial court allowed the Campbells to introduce extensive expert testimony regarding fraudulent practices by State Farm in its nation-wide operations. Although State Farm moved prior to phase II of the trial for the exclusion of such evidence and continued to object to it at trial, the trial court ruled that such evidence was admissible to determine whether State Farm's conduct in the Campbell case was indeed intentional and sufficiently egregious to warrant punitive damages." 65 P.3d at 1143.

Evidence pertaining to the PP & R policy concerned State Farm's business practices for over 20 years in numerous States. Most of these practices bore no relation to third-party automobile insurance claims, the type of claim underlying the Campbells' complaint against the company. The jury awarded the Campbells $2.6 million in compensatory damages and $145 million in punitive damages, which the trial court reduced to $1 million and $25 million respectively. Both parties appealed.

The Utah Supreme Court sought to apply the three guideposts we identified in *Gore, supra,* at 574-575, 116 S.Ct. 1589, and it reinstated the $145 million punitive damages award. Relying in large part on the extensive evidence concerning the PP & R policy, the court concluded State Farm's conduct was reprehensible. The court also relied upon State Farm's "massive wealth" and on testimony indicating that "State Farm's actions, because of their clandestine nature, will be punished at most in one out of every 50,000 cases as a matter of statistical probability," 65 P.3d at 1153, and concluded that the ratio between punitive and compensatory damages was not unwarranted. Finally, the court noted that the punitive damages award was not excessive when compared to various civil and criminal penalties State Farm could have faced, including $10,000 for each act of fraud, the suspension of its license to conduct business in Utah, the disgorgement of profits, and imprisonment. *Id.,* at 1154. We granted certiorari. 535 U.S. 1111, 122 S.Ct. 2326, 153 L.Ed.2d 158 (2002).

II

We recognized in *Cooper Industries, Inc. v. Leatherman Tool Group, Inc.,* 532 U.S. 424, 121 S.Ct. 1678, 149 L.Ed.2d 674 (2001), that in our judicial system compensatory and punitive damages, although usually awarded at the same time by the same decisionmaker, serve different purposes. *Id.,* at 432, 121 S.Ct. 1678. Compensatory damages "are intended to redress the concrete loss that the plaintiff has suffered by reason of the defendant's wrongful conduct." *Ibid.* (citing Restatement (Second) of Torts § 903, pp. 453-454 (1979)). By contrast, punitive damages serve a broader function; they are aimed at deterrence and retribution. *Cooper Industries, supra,* at 432, 121 S.Ct. 1678; *see also Gore, supra,* at 568, 116 S.Ct. 1589 ("Punitive damages may properly be imposed to further a State's legitimate interests in punishing unlawful conduct and deterring its repetition"); *Pacific Mut. Life Ins. Co. v. Haslip,* 499 U.S. 1, 19, 111 S.Ct. 1032, 113 L.Ed.2d 1 (1991) ("[P]unitive damages are imposed for purposes of retribution and deterrence").

While States possess discretion over the imposition of punitive damages, it is well established that there are procedural and substantive constitutional limitations on these awards. *Cooper Industries, supra; Gore,* 517 U.S., at 559, 116 S.Ct. 1589; *Honda Motor Co. v. Oberg,* 512 U.S. 415, 114 S.Ct. 2331, 129 L.Ed.2d 336 (1994); *TXO Production Corp. v. Alliance Resources Corp.,* 509 U.S. 443, 113 S.Ct. 2711, 125 L.Ed.2d 366 (1993); *Haslip, supra.* The Due Process Clause of the Fourteenth Amendment prohibits the imposition of grossly excessive or arbitrary punishments on a tortfeasor. *Cooper Industries, supra,* at 433, 121 S.Ct. 1678; *Gore,* 517 U.S., at 562, 116 S.Ct. 1589; see also *id.,* at 587, 116 S.Ct. 1589 (Breyer, J., concurring) ("This constitutional concern, itself harkening back to the Magna Carta, arises out of the basic unfairness of depriving citizens of life, liberty, or property, through the application, not of law and legal processes, but of arbitrary coercion"). The reason is that "[e]lementary notions of fairness enshrined in our constitutional jurisprudence dictate that a person receive fair notice not only of the conduct that will subject him to punishment, but also of the severity of the penalty that a State may impose." *Id.,* at 574, 116 S.Ct. 1589; *Cooper Industries, supra,* at 433, 121 S.Ct. 1678 ("Despite the broad discretion that States possess with respect to the imposition of criminal penalties and punitive damages, the Due Process Clause of the Fourteenth Amendment to the Federal Constitution imposes substantive limits on that discretion"). To the extent an award is grossly excessive, it furthers no legitimate purpose and constitutes an arbitrary deprivation of property. *Haslip, supra,* at 42, 111 S.Ct. 1032 (O'Connor, J., dissenting) ("Punitive damages are a powerful weapon. Imposed wisely and with restraint, they have the potential to advance legitimate state interests. Imposed indiscriminately, however, they have a devastating potential for harm. Regrettably, common-law procedures for awarding punitive damages fall into the latter category").

Although these awards serve the same purposes as criminal penalties, defendants subjected to punitive damages in civil cases have not been accorded the protections applicable in a criminal proceeding. This increases our concerns over the imprecise manner in which punitive damages systems are administered. We have admonished that "[p]unitive damages pose an acute danger of

433

arbitrary deprivation of property. Jury instructions typically leave the jury with wide discretion in choosing amounts, and the presentation of evidence of a defendant's net worth creates the potential that juries will use their verdicts to express biases against big businesses, particularly those without strong local presences." *Honda Motor, supra,* at 432, 114 S.Ct. 2331; *see also Haslip, supra,* at 59, 111 S.Ct. 1032 (O'Connor, J., dissenting) ("[T]he Due Process Clause does not permit a State to classify arbitrariness as a virtue. Indeed, the point of due process--of the law in general--is to allow citizens to order their behavior. A State can have no legitimate interest in deliberately making the law so arbitrary that citizens will be unable to avoid punishment based solely upon bias or whim"). Our concerns are heightened when the decisionmaker is presented, as we shall discuss, with evidence that has little bearing as to the amount of punitive damages that should be awarded. Vague instructions, or those that merely inform the jury to avoid "passion or prejudice," App. to Pet. for Cert. 108a-109a, do little to aid the decisionmaker in its task of assigning appropriate weight to evidence that is relevant and evidence that is tangential or only inflammatory.

In light of these concerns, in *Gore, supra,* we instructed courts reviewing punitive damages to consider three guideposts: (1) the degree of reprehensibility of the defendant's misconduct; (2) the disparity between the actual or potential harm suffered by the plaintiff and the punitive damages award; and (3) the difference between the punitive damages awarded by the jury and the civil penalties authorized or imposed in comparable cases. *Id.,* at 575, 116 S.Ct. 1589. We reiterated the importance of these three guideposts in *Cooper Industries* and mandated appellate courts to conduct *de novo* review of a trial court's application of them to the jury's award. 532 U.S., at 424, 121 S.Ct. 1678. Exacting appellate review ensures that an award of punitive damages is based upon an " 'application of law, rather than a decisionmaker's caprice.' " *Id.,* at 436, 121 S.Ct. 1678 (quoting *Gore, supra,* at 587, 116 S.Ct. 1589 (Breyer, J., concurring)).

III

Under the principles outlined in *BMW of North America, Inc. v. Gore,* this case is neither close nor difficult. It was error to reinstate the jury's $145 million punitive damages award. We address each guidepost of *Gore* in some detail.

A

"[T]he most important indicium of the reasonableness of a punitive damages award is the degree of reprehensibility of the defendant's conduct." *Gore, supra,* at 575, 116 S.Ct. 1589. We have instructed courts to determine the reprehensibility of a defendant by considering whether: the harm caused was physical as opposed to economic; the tortious conduct evinced an indifference to or a reckless disregard of the health or safety of others; the target of the conduct had financial vulnerability; the conduct involved repeated actions or was an isolated incident; and the harm was the result of intentional malice, trickery, or deceit, or mere accident. 517 U.S., at 576-577, 116 S.Ct. 1589. The existence of any one of these factors weighing in favor of a plaintiff may not be sufficient to sustain a punitive damages award; and the absence of all of them renders any award suspect. It should be presumed a plaintiff has been made whole for his injuries by compensatory damages, so punitive damages should only be awarded if the defendant's culpability, after having paid compensatory damages, is so reprehensible as to warrant the imposition of further sanctions to achieve punishment or deterrence. *Id.,* at 575, 116 S.Ct. 1589.

Applying these factors in the instant case, we must acknowledge that State Farm's handling of the claims against the Campbells merits no praise. The trial court found that State Farm's employees altered the company's records to make Campbell appear less culpable. State Farm disregarded the overwhelming likelihood of liability and the near-certain probability that, by taking the case to trial, a judgment in excess of the policy limits would be awarded. State Farm amplified the harm by at first assuring the Campbells their assets would be safe from any verdict and by later telling them, postjudgment, to put a for-sale sign on their house. While we do not suggest there was error in awarding punitive damages based upon State Farm's conduct toward the Campbells, a more modest punishment for this reprehensible conduct could have satisfied the State's legitimate objectives, and the Utah courts should have gone no further.

This case, instead, was used as a platform to expose, and punish, the perceived deficiencies of State Farm's operations throughout the country. The Utah Supreme Court's opinion makes explicit that State Farm was being condemned for its nationwide policies rather than for the conduct direct toward the Campbells. 65 P.3d at 1143 ("[T]he Campbells introduced evidence that State Farm's decision to take the case to trial was a result of a national scheme to meet corporate fiscal goals by capping payouts on claims company wide"). This was, as well, an explicit rationale of the trial court's decision in approving the award, though reduced from $145 million to $25 million. App. to Pet. for Cert. 120a ("[T]he Campbells demonstrated, through the testimony of State Farm employees who had worked outside of Utah, and through expert testimony, that this pattern of claims adjustment under the PP & R program was not a local anomaly, but was a consistent, nationwide feature of State Farm's business operations, orchestrated from the highest levels of corporate management").

The Campbells contend that State Farm has only itself to blame for the reliance upon dissimilar and out-of-state conduct evidence. The record does not support this contention. From their opening statements onward the Campbells framed this case as a chance to rebuke State Farm for its nationwide activities. App. 208 ("You're going to hear evidence that even the insurance commission in Utah and around the country are unwilling or inept at protecting people against abuses"); *id.,* at 242 ("[T]his is a very important case.... [I]t transcends the Campbell file. It involves a nationwide practice. And you, here, are going to be evaluating and assessing, and hopefully requiring State Farm to stand accountable for what it's doing across the country, which is the purpose of punitive damages"). This was a position maintained throughout the litigation. In opposing State Farm's motion to exclude such evidence under *Gore,* the Campbells' counsel convinced the trial court that there was no limitation on the scope of evidence that could be considered under our precedents. App. to Pet. for Cert. 172a ("As I read the case [*Gore*], I was struck with the fact that a clear message in the case ... seems to be that courts in punitive damages cases should receive more evidence, not less. And that the court seems to be inviting an even broader area of evidence than the current rulings of the court would indicate"); *id.,* at 189a (trial court ruling).

A State cannot punish a defendant for conduct that may have been lawful where it occurred. *Gore, supra,* at 572, 116 S.Ct. 1589; *Bigelow v. Virginia,* 421 U.S. 809, 824, 95 S.Ct. 2222, 44 L.Ed.2d 600 (1975) ("A State does not acquire power or supervision over the internal affairs of another State merely because the welfare and health of its own citizens may be affected when they travel to that State"); *New York Life Ins. Co. v. Head,* 234 U.S. 149, 161, 34 S.Ct. 879, 58 L.Ed. 1259 (1914) ("[I]t would be impossible to permit the statutes of Missouri to operate beyond the jurisdiction of that State ... without throwing down the constitutional barriers by which all the States are restricted within the orbits of their lawful authority and upon the preservation of which the Government under the Constitution depends. This is so obviously the necessary result of the Constitution that it has rarely been called in question and hence authorities directly dealing with it do not abound"); *Huntington v. Attrill,* 146 U.S. 657, 669, 13 S.Ct. 224, 36 L.Ed. 1123 (1892) ("Laws have no force of themselves beyond the jurisdiction of the State which enacts them, and can have extra-territorial effect only by the comity of other States"). Nor, as a general rule, does a State have a legitimate concern in imposing punitive damages to punish a defendant for unlawful acts committed outside of the State's jurisdiction. Any proper adjudication of conduct that occurred outside Utah to other persons would require their inclusion, and, to those parties, the Utah courts, in the usual case, would need to apply the laws of their relevant jurisdiction. *Phillips Petroleum Co. v. Shutts,* 472 U.S. 797, 821-822, 105 S.Ct. 2965, 86 L.Ed.2d 628 (1985).

Here, the Campbells do not dispute that much of the out-of-state conduct was lawful where it occurred. They argue, however, that such evidence was not the primary basis for the punitive damages award and was relevant to the extent it demonstrated, in a general sense, State Farm's motive against its insured. Brief for Respondents 46-47 ("[E]ven if the practices described by State Farm were not malum in se or malum prohibitum, they became relevant to punitive damages to the extent they were used as tools to implement State Farm's wrongful PP & R policy"). This argument misses the mark. Lawful out-of-state conduct may be probative when it demonstrates the deliberateness and culpability of the defendant's action in the State where it is tortious, but that conduct must have a nexus to the specific harm suffered by the plaintiff. A jury must be instructed, furthermore, that it may not use evidence of out-of-state conduct to punish a defendant for action that was lawful in the jurisdiction where it occurred. *Gore,* 517 U.S., at 572-573, 116 S.Ct. 1589 (noting that a State "does not have the power ... to punish [a defendant] for conduct that was lawful where it occurred and that had no impact on [the State] or its residents"). A basic principle of federalism is that each State may make its own reasoned judgment about what conduct is permitted or proscribed within its borders, and each State alone can determine what measure of punishment, if any, to impose on a defendant who acts within its jurisdiction. *Id.,* at 569, 116 S.Ct. 1589 ("[T]he States need not, and in fact do not, provide such protection in a uniform manner").

For a more fundamental reason, however, the Utah courts erred in relying upon this and other evidence: The courts awarded punitive damages to punish and deter conduct that bore no relation to the Campbells' harm. A defendant's dissimilar acts, independent from the acts upon which liability was premised, may not serve as the basis for punitive damages. A defendant should be punished for the conduct that harmed the plaintiff, not for being an unsavory individual or business. Due process does not permit courts, in the calculation of punitive damages, to adjudicate the merits of other parties' hypothetical claims against a defendant under the guise of the reprehensibility analysis, but we have no doubt the Utah Supreme Court did that here. 65 P.3d at 1149 ("Even if the harm to the Campbells can be appropriately characterized as minimal, the trial court's assessment of the situation is on target: 'The harm is minor to the individual but massive in the aggregate' "). Punishment on these bases creates the possibility of multiple punitive damages awards for the same conduct; for in the usual case nonparties are not bound by the judgment some other plaintiff obtains. *Gore, supra,* at 593, 116 S.Ct. 1589 (Breyer, J., concurring) ("Larger damages might also 'double count' by including in the punitive damages award some of the compensatory, or punitive, damages that subsequent plaintiffs would also recover").

The same reasons lead us to conclude the Utah Supreme Court's decision cannot be justified on the grounds that State Farm was a recidivist. Although "[o]ur holdings that a recidivist may be punished more severely than a first offender recognize that repeated misconduct is more reprehensible than an individual instance of malfeasance," *Gore, supra,* at 577, 116 S.Ct. 1589, in the context of civil actions courts must ensure the conduct in question replicates the prior transgressions. *TXO,* 509 U.S., at 462, n. 28, 113 S.Ct. 2711 (noting that courts should look to " 'the existence and frequency of similar past conduct' ") (quoting *Haslip,* 499 U.S., at 21-22, 111 S.Ct. 1032).

The Campbells have identified scant evidence of repeated misconduct of the sort that injured them. Nor does our review of the Utah courts' decisions convince us that State Farm was only punished for its actions toward the Campbells. Although evidence of other acts need not be identical to have relevance in the calculation of punitive damages, the Utah court erred here because evidence pertaining to claims that had nothing to do with a third-party lawsuit was introduced at length. Other evidence concerning reprehensibility was even more tangential. For example, the Utah Supreme Court criticized State Farm's investigation into the personal life of one of its employees and, in a broader approach, the manner in which State Farm's policies corrupted its employees. 65 P.3d at 1148; *id.,* at 1150. The Campbells attempt to justify the courts' reliance upon this unrelated testimony on the theory that each dollar of profit made by underpaying a third-party claimant is the same as a dollar made by underpaying a first-party one. Brief for Respondents 45; *see also* 65 P.3d at 1150 ("State Farm's continuing illicit practice created market disadvantages for other honest insurance companies because these practices increased profits. As plaintiffs' expert witnesses established, such wrongfully obtained competitive advantages have the potential to pressure other companies to adopt similar fraudulent tactics, or to force them out of business. Thus, such actions cause distortions throughout the insurance market and ultimately hurt all consumers"). For the reasons already stated, this argument is unconvincing. The reprehensibility guidepost does not permit courts to expand the scope of the case so that a defendant may be punished for any malfeasance, which in this case extended for a 20-year period. In this case, because the Campbells have shown no conduct by State Farm similar to that which harmed them, the conduct that harmed them is the only conduct relevant to the reprehensibility analysis.

Turning to the second *Gore* guidepost, we have been reluctant to identify concrete constitutional limits on the ratio between harm, or potential harm, to the plaintiff and the punitive damages award. *Gore, supra,* at 582, 116 S.Ct. 1589 ("[W]e have consistently rejected the notion that the constitutional line is marked by a simple mathematical formula, even one that compares actual *and potential* damages to the punitive award"); *TXO, supra,* at 458, 113 S.Ct. 2711. We decline again to impose a bright-line ratio which a punitive damages award cannot exceed. Our jurisprudence and the principles it has now established demonstrate, however, that, in practice, few awards exceeding a single-digit ratio between punitive and compensatory damages, to a significant degree, will satisfy due process. In *Haslip,* in upholding a punitive damages award, we concluded that an award of more than four times the amount of compensatory damages might be close to the line of constitutional impropriety. 499 U.S., at 23-24, 111 S.Ct. 1032. We cited that 4-to-1 ratio again in *Gore.* 517 U.S., at 581, 116 S.Ct. 1589. The Court further referenced a long legislative history, dating back over 700 years and going forward to today, providing for sanctions of double, treble, or quadruple damages to deter and punish. *Id.,* at 581, and n. 33, 116 S.Ct. 1589. While these ratios are not binding, they are instructive. They demonstrate what should be obvious: Single-digit multipliers are more likely to comport with due process, while still achieving the State's goals of deterrence and retribution, than awards with ratios in range of 500 to 1, *id.,* at 582, 116 S.Ct. 1589, or, in this case, of 145 to 1.

Nonetheless, because there are no rigid benchmarks that a punitive damages award may not surpass, ratios greater than those we have previously upheld may comport with due process where "a particularly egregious act has resulted in only a small amount of economic damages." *Ibid.; see also ibid.* (positing that a higher ratio *might* be necessary where "the injury is hard to detect or the monetary value of noneconomic harm might have been difficult to determine"). The converse is also true, however. When compensatory damages are substantial, then a lesser ratio, perhaps only equal to compensatory damages, can reach the outermost limit of the due process guarantee. The precise award in any case, of course, must be based upon the facts and circumstances of the defendant's conduct and the harm to the plaintiff.

In sum, courts must ensure that the measure of punishment is both reasonable and proportionate to the amount of harm to the plaintiff and to the general damages recovered. In the context of this case, we have no doubt that there is a presumption against an award that has a 145-to-1 ratio. The compensatory award in this case was substantial; the Campbells were awarded $1 million for a year and a half of emotional distress. This was complete compensation. The harm arose from a transaction in the economic realm, not from some physical assault or trauma; there were no physical injuries; and State Farm paid the excess verdict before the complaint was filed, so the Campbells suffered only minor economic injuries for the 18-month period in which State Farm refused to resolve the claim against them. The compensatory damages for the injury suffered here, moreover, likely were based on a component which was duplicated in the punitive award. Much of the distress was caused by the outrage and humiliation the Campbells suffered at the actions of their insurer; and it is a major role of punitive damages to condemn such conduct. Compensatory damages, however, already contain this punitive element. *See* Restatement (Second) of Torts § 908, Comment *c,* p. 466 (1977) ("In many cases in which compensatory damages include an amount for emotional distress, such as humiliation or indignation aroused by the defendant's act, there is no clear line of demarcation between punishment and compensation and a verdict for a specified amount frequently includes elements of both").

The Utah Supreme Court sought to justify the massive award by pointing to State Farm's purported failure to report a prior $100 million punitive damages award in Texas to its corporate headquarters; the fact that State Farm's policies have affected numerous Utah consumers; the fact that State Farm will only be punished in one out of every 50,000 cases as a matter of statistical probability; and State Farm's enormous wealth. 65 P.3d at 1152. Since the Supreme Court of Utah discussed the Texas award when applying the ratio guidepost, we discuss it here. The Texas award, however, should have been analyzed in the context of the reprehensibility guidepost only. The failure of the company to report the Texas award is out-of-state conduct that, if the conduct were similar, might have had some bearing on the degree of reprehensibility, subject to the limitations we have described.

Here, it was dissimilar, and of such marginal relevance that it should have been accorded little or no weight. The award was rendered in a first-party lawsuit; no judgment was entered in the case; and it was later settled for a fraction of the verdict. With respect to the Utah Supreme Court's second justification, the Campbells' inability to direct us to testimony demonstrating harm to the people of Utah (other than those directly involved in this case) indicates that the adverse effect on the State's general population was in fact minor.

The remaining premises for the Utah Supreme Court's decision bear no relation to the award's reasonableness or proportionality to the harm. They are, rather, arguments that seek to defend a departure from well-established constraints on punitive damages. While States enjoy considerable discretion in deducing when punitive damages are warranted, each award must comport with the principles set forth in *Gore*. Here the argument that State Farm will be punished in only the rare case, coupled with reference to its assets (which, of course, are what other insured parties in Utah and other States must rely upon for payment of claims) had little to do with the actual harm sustained by the Campbells. The wealth of a defendant cannot justify an otherwise unconstitutional punitive damages award. *Gore,* 517 U.S., at 585, 116 S.Ct. 1589 ("The fact that BMW is a large corporation rather than an impecunious individual does not diminish its entitlement to fair notice of the demands that the several States impose on the conduct of its business"); *see also id.,* at 591, 116 S.Ct. 1589 (Breyer, J., concurring) ("[Wealth] provides an open-ended basis for inflating awards when the defendant is wealthy.... That does not make its use unlawful or inappropriate; it simply means that this factor cannot make up for the failure of other factors, such as 'reprehensibility,' to constrain significantly an award that purports to punish a defendant's conduct"). The principles set forth in *Gore* must be implemented with care, to ensure both reasonableness and proportionality.

C

The third guidepost in *Gore* is the disparity between the punitive damages award and the "civil penalties authorized or imposed in comparable cases." *Id.,* at 575, 116 S.Ct. 1589. We note that, in the past, we have also looked to criminal penalties that could be imposed. *Id.,* at 583, 116 S.Ct. 1589; *Haslip,* 499 U.S., at 23, 111 S.Ct. 1032. The existence of a criminal penalty does have bearing on the seriousness with which a State views the wrongful action. When used to determine the dollar amount of the award, however, the criminal penalty has less utility. Great care must be taken to avoid use of the civil process to assess criminal penalties that can be imposed only after the heightened protections of a criminal trial have been observed, including, of course, its higher standards of proof. Punitive damages are not a substitute for the criminal process, and the remote possibility of a criminal sanction does not automatically sustain a punitive damages award.

Here, we need not dwell long on this guidepost. The most relevant civil sanction under Utah state law for the wrong done to the Campbells appears to be a $10,000 fine for an act of fraud, 65 P.3d at 1154, an amount dwarfed by the $145 million punitive damages award. The Supreme Court of Utah speculated about the loss of State Farm's business license, the disgorgement of profits, and possible imprisonment, but here again its references were to the broad fraudulent scheme drawn from evidence of out-of-state and dissimilar conduct. This analysis was insufficient to justify the award.

IV

An application of the *Gore* guideposts to the facts of this case, especially in light of the substantial compensatory damages awarded (a portion of which contained a punitive element), likely would justify a punitive damages award at or near the amount of compensatory damages. The punitive award of $145 million, therefore, was neither reasonable nor proportionate to the wrong committed, and it was an irrational and arbitrary deprivation of the property of the defendant. The proper calculation of punitive damages under the principles we have discussed should be resolved, in the first instance, by the Utah courts.

The judgment of the Utah Supreme Court is reversed, and the case is remanded for proceedings not inconsistent with this opinion.

IT IS SO ORDERED.

Justice Scalia, dissenting.

I adhere to the view expressed in my dissenting opinion in *BMW of North America, Inc. v. Gore,* 517 U.S. 559, 598-99, 116 S.Ct. 1589, 134 L.Ed.2d 809 (1996), that the Due Process Clause provides no substantive protections against "excessive" or " 'unreasonable' " awards of punitive damages. I am also of the view that the punitive damages jurisprudence which has sprung forth from *BMW v. Gore* is insusceptible of principled application; accordingly, I do not feel justified in giving the case *stare decisis* effect. *See id.,* at 599, 116 S.Ct. 1589. I would affirm the judgment of the Utah Supreme Court.

Justice Thomas, dissenting.

I would affirm the judgment below because "I continue to believe that the Constitution does not constrain the size of punitive damages awards." *Cooper Industries, Inc. v. Leatherman Tool Group, Inc.,* 532 U.S. 424, 443, 121 S.Ct. 1678, 149 L.Ed.2d 674 (2001) (Thomas, J., concurring) (citing *BMW of North America, Inc. v. Gore,* 517 U.S. 559, 599, 116 S.Ct. 1589, 134 L.Ed.2d 809 (1996) (Scalia, J., joined by Thomas, J., dissenting)). Accordingly, I respectfully dissent.

Justice Ginsburg, dissenting.

Not long ago, this Court was hesitant to impose a federal check on state-court judgments awarding punitive damages. In *Browning-Ferris Industries of Vt., Inc. v. Kelco Disposal, Inc.,* 492 U.S. 257, 109 S.Ct. 2909, 106 L.Ed.2d 219 (1989), the Court held that neither the Excessive Fines Clause of the Eighth Amendment nor federal common law circumscribed awards of punitive damages in civil cases between private parties. *Id.,* at 262-276, 277-280, 109 S.Ct. 2909. Two years later, in *Pacific Mut. Life Ins. Co. v. Haslip,* 499 U.S. 1, 111 S.Ct. 1032, 113 L.Ed.2d 1 (1991), the Court observed that "unlimited jury [or judicial] discretion ... in the fixing of punitive damages may invite extreme results that jar one's constitutional sensibilities," *id.,* at 18, 111 S.Ct. 1032; the Due Process Clause, the Court suggested, would attend to those sensibilities and guard against unreasonable awards, *id.,* at 17-24, 111 S.Ct. 1032. Nevertheless, the Court upheld a punitive damages award in *Haslip* "more than 4 times the amount of compensatory damages, ... more than 200 times [the plaintiff's] out-of-pocket expenses," and "much in excess of the fine that could be imposed." *Id.,* at 23, 111 S.Ct. 1032. And in *TXO Production Corp. v. Alliance Resources Corp.,* 509 U.S. 443, 113 S.Ct. 2711, 125 L.Ed.2d 366 (1993), the Court affirmed a state-court award "526 times greater than the actual damages awarded by the jury." *Id.,* at 453, 113 S.Ct. 2711;[58] *cf. Browning-Ferris,* 492 U.S., at 262, 109 S.Ct. 2909 (ratio of punitive to compensatory damages over 100 to 1).

It was not until 1996, in *BMW of North America, Inc. v. Gore,* 517 U.S. 559, 116 S.Ct. 1589, 134 L.Ed.2d 809 (1996), that the Court, for the first time, invalidated a state-court punitive damages assessment as unreasonably large. *See id.,* at 599, 116 S.Ct. 1589 (Scalia, J., dissenting). If our activity in this domain is now "well-established," *see ante,* at 1519, 1525, it takes place on ground not long held.

In *Gore,* I stated why I resisted the Court's foray into punitive damages "territory traditionally within the States' domain." 517 U.S., at 612, 116 S.Ct. 1589 (dissenting opinion). I adhere to those views, and note again that, unlike federal habeas corpus review of state-court convictions under 28 U.S.C. § 2254, the Court "work[s] at this business [of checking state courts] alone," unaided by the participation of federal district courts and courts of appeals. 517 U.S., at 613, 116 S.Ct. 1589. It was once recognized that "the laws of the particular State must suffice [to superintend punitive damages

---

[58] By switching the focus from the ratio of punitive to compensatory damages to the potential loss to the plaintiffs had the defendant succeeded in its illicit scheme, the Court could describe the relevant ratio in *TXO* as 10 to 1. *See BMW of North America, Inc. v. Gore,* 517 U.S. 559, 581, and n. 34, 116 S.Ct. 1589, 134 L.Ed.2d 809 (1996).

awards] until judges or legislators authorized to do so initiate system-wide change." *Haslip,* 499 U.S., at 42, 111 S.Ct. 1032 (Kennedy, J., concurring in judgment). I would adhere to that traditional view.

* * * * *

NOTES

1.   In the *Cooper Industries* case described in *Campbell*, the U.S. Supreme Court held that where a punitive damages award is challenged as unconstitutional, the appellate court must conduct a *de novo* review. However, in *Mosing v. Domas*, 830 So. 2d 967 (La. 2002), the Louisiana Supreme Court held that where a punitive damages award is *not* attacked on constitutional grounds, the standard of review is manifest error.

2.   In *Mosing v. Domas*, note 1, *supra*, the Court held that if no constitutional claim is raised, the determination of whether an exemplary damage award is excessive under Louisiana law is determined by an application of the BMW guideposts, and the court also should consider the wealth of the defendant.

3.   Although a multiplier based on compensatory damages is used in determining on appeal whether a punitive damage award is excessive, the trial judge should not instruct the jury that it may use such a multiplier in determining punitive damages. The judge should instruct the jury to determine the amount of punitive damages by consideration of all relevant factors. *In Re New Orleans Train Car Leakage Fire Litigation*, 690 So. 2d 255 (La. 1997).

4.   Many states have instituted various levels of punitive damages reform, as set forth below in Galligan, *Augmented Awards: The Efficient Evolution of Punitive Damages*, 51 La. L. Rev. 3, 34-35 (1990).

6.   Insurability of Punitive Damages

CREECH
v.
AETNA CAS. & SUR. CO.
516 So. 2d 1168 (La.App. 2 Cir. 1987)

HALL, C. J.

In this personal injury action seeking both compensatory and exemplary damages, the plaintiffs John R. and Denice S. Creech and defendants Curtis Bay Rawkins and Hawkins Painters & Decorators, Inc. appealed the trial court's granting of a motion for partial summary judgment in favor of Aetna Casualty & Surety Company denying insurance coverage for exemplary damages.

* * * * *

Aetna contends that the language of the policies does not cover "exemplary damages" and that insurance coverage for exemplary damages would violate the public policy of Louisiana. Appellants argue that the policies provide for payment of all damages, whether compensatory or exemplary, and that there is no public policy which precludes insurance coverage for exemplary damages.

Thus, the issues are: (1) Do the liability policies provide coverage for exemplary damages awarded under LSA--C.C. Art. 2915.4, and (2) If so, does Louisiana public policy preclude such coverage. These issues have never been decided by a state court in Louisiana where exemplary or punitive damages have not historically been available, but the issues have been presented to and decided by the courts of many other states. Most courts have rejected the contention that the usual language of liability insurance policies does not provide coverage for exemplary or punitive damages. The majority of courts of other states have also rejected the contention that such insurance coverage violates public policy, although there is substantial authority to the contrary. *See* Annot., 16 A.L.R. 4th 11 (1982); Bolin, *Enter Exemplary Damages*, 32 La.Bar Journal 216 (1984). We are in accord with the majority view on both issues and hold that (1) the policies provide coverage of exemplary damages, and (2) public policy does not prohibit insurance coverage for exemplary damages.

The Insurance Policies Issued by Aetna Provide Coverage for Exemplary Damages

The business automobile policy provides in pertinent part:

"Part IV--Liability Insurance.

A.   WE WILL PAY.

1.   We will pay *all sums the insured legally must pay as damages because of bodily injury or property damage* to which this insurance applies, caused by an accident and resulting from the ownership, maintenance or use of a covered auto." (emphasis added)

The excess indemnity (umbrella) policy provides in pertinent part:

"Section 2. INSURING AGREEMENTS

2.1   COVERAGE. The Company will indemnify the insured for ultimate net loss in excess of the applicable underlying limit *which the insured shall become legally obligated to pay as damages because of*

A.   *Personal injury,*

B.   *Property Damage, or*

C.   Advertising Offense

to which this policy applies, caused by an occurrence anywhere in the world, provided that:..." (Emphasis added)

In the policies the insurer promises to pay all sums or indemnify for ultimate net loss which the insured legally must pay or shall become legally obligated to pay as damages *because of* bodily injury or property damage. There no doubt that the exemplary damages contemplated by C.C. Art 2315.4 are awarded because of injuries. "Injuries" is a predicate for the article to become applicable. If there is no injury then no exemplary damages may be awarded. If exemplary damages are due because of injury caused by the conduct described in the Article, then the insured is legally obligated to pay them.

There is no language in the policies distinguishing between compensatory and exemplary damages. Neither of Aetna's policies contains an exclusion of exemplary or punitive damages (see Part IV, Section C, Exclusions of the Business Automobile Policy and Section 2, Part 2.2, Exclusions of the Excess Indemnity (Umbrella) Policy).

A majority of the courts of other states which have considered the issue hold that insurance policies with similar language afford coverage for exemplary damages.[4] Most policies contain such

---

[4] *Hensley v. Eric Insurance Co.*, 168 W.Va. 172, 283 S.E.2d 227 (1981) [Intoxicated driver]. *Anthony v. Frith*, 394 S.2d 867 (Miss. 1981) [Intoxicated driver], *Michael v. Cola*, 122 450, 595 P.2d 995 (1979) [automobile accident]. *Price v. Hartford Accident & Indemnity Co.*, 108 Ariz. 485, 502 P.2d 522 (1972) [Reckless driver engaged in a drag race]. *First National Bank of St. Mary's v. Fidelity & Deposit Co.*, 283 Md. 228, 389 A.2d 359 (1978) [Declaratory judgment sought by insured bank for a determination that its liability insurer should have

language as the obligation to pay "all sums ... the insured shall become legally obligated to pay" or to pay "damages for bodily injury or property damage for which the law holds you responsible" without specifically excluding exemplary damages. The courts reason that such language is broad enough to include exemplary damages and further that the average premium paying insured contemplates protection against claims of any character not intentionally inflicted. The insurer designed the policy in question. As stated in *Insurance Company of North America v. Solari Parking, Inc.*, 370 So. 2d 503 (La. 1979), "It is settled jurisprudence that policy language is to be read broadly in favor of coverage, *Kendrick v. Mason*, 234 La. 271, 99 So. 2d 108 (1958); *Craft v. Trahan*, 351 So. 2d 277 (La.App. 3 Cir. 1977), and that ambiguities are to be construed against the insurer. *Hendrick v. Mason, supra; Ory v. Louisiana and Southern Life Insurance Co.*, 352 So. 2d 308 (La.App. 4 Cir. 1977)." Even if the language was ambiguous it should be construed toward coverage. Aetna could have changed the policy language. The company could easily have provided for exclusion. Since Aetna specified the terms of the contract it is bound by them.

Some recent decisions of federal district courts in Louisiana have held that liability insurance policies do not provide coverage for punitive damages awarded under maritime law. *Daughdrill v. Ocean Drilling and Exploration Co.*, 665 F.Supp. 477 (E.D.La. 1987); *Dubois v. Arkansas Valley Dredging, Inc.*, 651 F.Supp. 299 (W.D.La. 1987); *Smith v. Front Lawn Enterprises, Inc.*, No. 83-5147 (E.D.La. September 29, 1986). *But see* and *compare Fagot v. Ciravola*, 445 F.Supp. 342 (E.D.La. 1978). While authoritative, we do not regard those decisions as controlling under Louisiana law, and we reach a contrary result.

We hold that the provisions of the liability insurance policies issued by Aetna provide coverage for exemplary damages awarded under LSA--C.C. Art- 2315.4.

Insurance Coverage of Exemplary Damages Is Not Against Public Policy

The contract of insurance, like any other agreement, is the law between the parties. *Wiley v. Louisiana & Southern Life Insurance Co.*, 302 So. 2d 704 (La.App. 3 Cir. 1974) *writ denied* 305 So. 2d 540 and 305 So. 2d 541 (La.1975). The provisions of the insurance policy should be given effect except to the extent they conflict with law or public policy. *O'Donnell v. Fidelity General Insurance Co.*, 344 So. 2d 91 (La.App. 2 Cir. 1977).

Aetna contends that even if the policies provide coverage for exemplary damages this court should preclude coverage as void against public policy. Many courts have denied coverage.[5]

---

been obligated to defend the bank in a prior malicious prosecution action and pay exemplary damages awarded therein]. *Harrell v. Travelers Indemnity Co.*, Or. 199, 567 P.2d 1013 (1977) [Reckless Driver]. *Abbie Uriguen Oldsmobile Buick, Inc. v. United States Fire Insurance Co.*, 95 Idaho 501, 511 P.2d 783 (1973) [Intoxicated driver]. *Dairyland County Mutual Insurance Co. v. Wallgren*, 477 S.W.2d 341 (Tex. Civ. App. 1972) [Grossly negligent operation of an automobile]. *Scott v. Instant Parking Inc.*, 105 Ill.App.2d 133, 245 N.E.2d 124 (1969) [General liability policy]. *Lazenby v. Universal Underwriters Insurance Co.*, 214 Tenn. 639, 383 S.W.2d 1 (1964) [Intoxicated driver]. *Carroway v. Johnson*, 245 S.C. 200, 139 S.E.2d 908 (1965) [automobile accident]. *Ridgeway v. Gulf Life Insurance Co.*, 578 F.2d 1026 (5th Cir.1978) [Texas law]. *Travelers Insurance Co. v. Wilson*, 261 So. 2d 545 (4th Dist.Ct.App. 1972) [vicarious liability]. *American Fidelity & Casualty Co. v. Werfel*, 231 Ala. 285, 164 So. 383 (1935). *Southern Farm Bureau Casualty Insurance Co. v. Daniel*, 246 Ark. 849, 440 S.W.2d 582 (1969). *Continental Insurance Cos. v. Hancock*, 507 S.W.2d 146 (Ct.of App.Ky 1973). *Cedar Rapids v. Northwestern National Insurance Co. of Milwaukee Wisconsin*, 304 N.W.2d 228 (Iowa 1981). *Morrell v. LaLonde*, 45 R.I. 112. 120 A. 435 (1923). *Concord General Mutual Insurance Co. v. Hills*, 345 F.Supp. 1090 (S.D.Maine 1972).

[5] These authorities may be divided into four categories:

    1. The language of the policy does not provide coverage: *Smith v. Front Lawn Enterprises, Inc.*, No. 83-5147 (E.D.La. September 29, 1986); *California State Automobile Association Inter-Insurance Bureau v. Carter*, 164 Cal.App.3d 257, 210 Cal.Rptr. 140 (5th Dist.1985) construed statutory language of uninsured motorist provision and policy coverage in the same manner;

    2. Public policy precludes coverage: *Daughdrill v. Ocean Drilling and Exploration Co.*, 665 F.Supp. 477 (E.D.La.1987); *Dubois v. Arkansas Valley Dredging*, 651 F.Supp. 299 (W.D.La.1987); *Northwestern National Casualty Co v. McNulty*, 307 F.2d 432 (5th Cir.1962) drunk driving case utilizing Florida and

Aetna suggests that by allowing exemplary damages under LSA--C.C. 2315.4, the legislature intended to punish and/or deter the drunken driver, and by allowing insurance coverage this deterrence would be eviscerated. While we agree with appellee that this article was enacted to deter drunk driving, it does not necessarily follow that insurance coverage for exemplary damages would be against public policy.

The leading case holding that public policy precludes insuring against punitive damages is *Northwestern National Casualty Co. v. McNulty*, cited in footnote 5, which involved punitive damages under Virginia and Florida law for the gross negligence of a drunken driver. The rationale of *McNulty* was that punitive damages are meant to punish and deter the wrongdoer and to allow these damages to be passed along to an insurance company would undermine the purpose of the law.

Leading cases taking the contrary view are *Lazenby v. Universal Underwriters Insurance Co.*, *Harrell v. Travelers Indemnity Co.* and *Hensley v. Erie Insurance Co.*, cited in footnote 4. Courts rejecting the public policy preclusion argument have recognized that a substantial distinction exists in degree of culpability between intentional acts and wantonly reckless acts such as drunk driving. Permitting insurance coverage for such acts will not likely increase the frequency of such acts any more than permitting insurance coverage for ordinary negligent acts increases their frequency. Wanton negligence is still negligence and from a public policy standpoint should not be precluded from insurance coverage. Permitting coverage does not automatically shift the burden of payment. The insurance company can charge the insured a premium for coverage of exemplary damages. To the extent that such damages exceed the policy limits, there is no shift in the payment of damages. Although the purpose of punitive damages is to punish and deter, the injured party receives the benefit of such payment and from the plaintiff's standpoint, punitive damages are additional compensation for the egregious conduct inflicted upon him.

It is true that the purpose of punitive damages is to discourage egregious conduct. However, deterrence is one of the complex of purposes that is said to lie at the heart of all tort law, not merely that aspect labeled "punitive". *Fagot v. Ciravola, supra.* Whether precluding insurance coverage of exemplary damages assessed against drunk drivers will have a greater deterrent effect on wrongdoing than holding their insurers liable as well is a matter better left to legislative investigation than judicial speculation.

As stated in *Harrell v. Travelers Indemnity Co.*, cited in footnote 4:
"It has long been recognized that there is no empirical evidence that contracts of insurance to protect against liability for negligent conduct are invalid, as a matter of public policy, because of any 'evil tendency' to make negligent conduct 'more probable' or because there is any 'substantial relationship' between the fact of

---

Virginia law; *American Surety Co. of New York v. Gold*, 375 F.2d 523 (10th Cir. 1966) Kansas law; *Ford Motor Co. v. Home Insurance Co.*, 116 Cal.App.3d 374 172 Cal.Rptr. 59 (2nd Dist.1981); *City Products Corp. v. Globe Indemnity Co.*, 88 Cal.App.3d 31, 151 Cal.Rptr. 494 (2nd Dist.1979); *U.S. Concrete Co. v. Bould*, 437 So. 2d 1061 (Fla.1983) public policy precludes coverage of one's own wrongful conduct but not one vicariously liable; *Nicholson v. American Fire and Casualty Insurance Co.*, 1775 So. 2d 52 (Fla. 2nd Dist.Ct.App. 1965); *Beaver v. Country Mutual Insurance Co.*, 95 Ill.App.3d 1122. 51 Ill. Dec. 500, 420 N.E.2d 1058 (5th Dist. 1981) public policy precludes coverage for one's own misconduct; *Variety Farms, Inc v. New Jersey Manufacturers Insurance Co.*, 172 NJ.Super. 10, 410 A.2d 696 (1980); *Hartford Accident and Indemnity Co. v. Hempstead*, 48 N.Y.2d 218, 422 N.Y.5.2d 47. 397 N.E 2d 737 (1979); *Universal Indemnity Insurance Co. v. Tenery*, 96 Colo. 10, 39 P.2d 776 (1934);

3. Policy language provides coverage but public policy precludes coverage: *Dayton Hudson Corp. v. American Mutual Liability Insurance Co.*, 621 P.2d 1155 (Okla.1980); court recognized exception to allow coverage for one vicariously liable;

4. Policy language does not provide coverage and public policy precludes coverage: Guardianship of Estate of *Smith v. Merchants Mutual Bonding Co.*, 211 Kan. 397, 507 P.2d 189 (1973) bond does not cover punitive damages without an express statutory provision and public policy precludes coverage; *Crull v. Gleb*, 382 S.W.2d 17 (Mo.App.1964); *Lo Rocco v. N.J. Manufactures Indemnity Insurance Co.*, 197 A.2d 591 (N.J. 1964); *Esmond v. Liscio*, 209 Pa.Super. 200, 224 A2d 793 (1966); intentional tort excluded from coverage.

insurance and such negligent conduct. Neither is there any such evidence that contracts of insurance to protect against liability for punitive damages have such an 'evil tendency' to make reckless conduct 'more probable' or that there is any 'substantial relationship' between the fact of such insurance and such misconduct. Conversely, neither is there any such evidence that to invalidate insurance contract provisions to protect against liability for punitive damages on grounds of public policy would have any substantial 'tendency' to make such conduct 'less probable,' i.e., that to do so would have any 'deterrent effect' whatever upon such conduct."

It has been said of public policy as a ground for invalidation by the courts of private contracts that "those two alliterative words are often used as if they had a magic quality and were self-explanatory ..." and that for a court to undertake to invalidate private contracts upon the ground of "public policy" is to mount "a very unruly horse, and when you once get astride it you never know where it will carry you" *Id.* at 1016; 6A Cortin on Contracts 10, § 1375 (1962); 14 Williston on Contracts 7-8, § 1629 (3d 1972).

Nowhere in LSA--C.C. Art. 2315.4 does the legislature prohibit insurance coverage of exemplary damages. The legislature is well aware that motorists are required to have automobile insurance and that these policies generally provide protection against claims of any character not intentionally inflicted. The legislature could easily have provided that no insurance coverage shall be allowed to cover exemplary damages, but did not do so.

There is more than one public policy. One such policy is that an insurance company which accepts a premium for covering all liability for damages should honor its obligation. We have already mentioned the policy that favors coverage, both for the benefit of the insured and the injured person. *See* LSA--R.S. 22:655, last paragraph. Public policy is better served by giving effect to the insurance contract rather than by creating an exclusion based on a judicial perception of public policy not expressed by the legislature. We hold that public policy does not preclude insurance coverage of exemplary damage awards under LSA--C.C. Art. 2315.4.

Aetna further contends that imposition of exemplary damages as to them would be a denial of due process. Aetna suggests that it is being penalized by the imposition of exemplary damages under LSA--C.C Art. 2315.4 and that there is no limit to the amount of exemplary damages that may be awarded under the article. This argument has no merit since there is nothing fundamentally unfair and no penalty is being imposed by requiring a party to a contract to comply with its terms. The amount of damages awarded may be limited by judicial process and by the terms of the insurance contacts.

Decree

For the reasons assigned, the judgment of the district court is reversed and set aside and the motion for partial summary judgment is overruled. The case is remanded to the district court for further proceedings in accordance with law. Costs of this appeal are assessed to appellee.

REVERSED AND REMANDED.

Sexton, Judge, additionally concurring.

The concept of exemplary damages is strongly adverse to the civil law in general, and the law of Louisiana in particular. 12 F. Stone, Louisiana Civil Treatise § 12 (1977). Thus, on first impression an observer is likely to assume that the legislature's only purpose in enacting LSA--C.C. Art. 2315.4 was to penalize an intoxicated driver who causes personal injury. But if so, why didn't the legislature preclude insurance coverage for such damages. They did not and we should not, as this opinion correctly points out.

Thus, I write not to indicate a difference of opinion regarding the rationale herein, but to emphasize that the statute, without exempting such damages from insurance coverage, serves no purpose other than to placate those who inveigh against the drinking driver and to reward the victim of the drinking driver (and his attorney) beyond the measure of that victim's actual damages. However, there are even more important negative aspects to the legislation, to include the legal problems created with respect to uninsured motorist coverage and settlements. The legislature should repeal the act or amend out insurance coverage at its first opportunity.

NOTE

The underlying purposes allegedly served by punitive damages awards remain controversial today. In many states, and also at the federal level, punitive damages are the target of tort reformers. Recent legislation has made certain changes in rules governing the recoverability of punitive damages. Some states now require that the plaintiff establish his or her right to recover punitives by clear and convincing evidence. Other states achieved the same result judicially. Colorado has gone so far as to require that the plaintiff prove his or her right to punitive damages beyond a reasonable doubt, an obvious analogue to the punishment aspects of the doctrine. Other states have placed caps on the amount of recoverable punitive damages. Some states have passed legislation authorizing the bifurcation of punitive damages cases separating the liability/compensatory damages aspects of the case from the punitive damages aspect.

G. THE COLLATERAL SOURCE RULE

LOUISIANA DEPARTMENT OF TRANSPORTATION AND DEVELOPMENT
v.
KANSAS CITY SOUTHERN RAILWAY CO.
846 So. 2d 734 (La. 2003)

CALOGERO, C. J.

Louisiana Department of Transportation and Development ("DOTD") expended several million dollars to remove environmental pollution at a construction site for Interstate 49 in Shreveport, Louisiana. The United States government, through the Federal Highway Administration ("FHWA"), thereafter reimbursed DOTD ninety percent of the remediation costs. DOTD sued, among other defendants, Kansas City Southern Railway Co. ("KCS") under the Louisiana Environmental Quality Act ("LEQA") to recover the clean-up costs, alleging that KCS polluted the site. The courts below held that DOTD's action was limited to the ten percent of clean-up costs it had actually incurred, and that DOTD could not recover the portion of the costs reimbursed to DOTD by the FHWA. We reverse the lower courts and conclude that DOTD may seek judgment against KCS for the full measure of damages caused by its pollution.

Facts and Procedural History

Each year, Congress appropriates billions of dollars to subsidize state highway construction projects, and the FHWA apportions these funds among the states. 23 U.S.C. § § 104(b), 118. States become eligible for their allotted federal funds by obtaining FHWA approval for a project, signing a project agreement with the FHWA, paying the full cost of construction from state funds, and, finally, requesting reimbursement from the FHWA for the federal share of the cost, which is ninety percent on interstate projects. In completing these federally funded highway projects, states must closely adhere to FHWA standards and procedures.

On June 2, 1989, DOTD entered into a project agreement with FHWA to construct a segment of Interstate 49 in Shreveport. During construction, DOTD discovered environmental contamination at the site.... DOTD paid the full costs of clean-up from state funds, and was thereafter reimbursed by FHWA the ninety percent federal share. DOTD filed suit to recover the cost of eliminating the pollution, naming several defendants ... KCS is the only defendant remaining in this litigation.

In its petition, DOTD alleged that KCS's responsibility for the contamination arises out of a March 31, 1966 train derailment which occurred at or near the property in question. The contents of the derailed train cars were destroyed or disposed of at the scene of the accident. The train had allegedly been carrying hazardous materials, and the materials were buried at or near the site. DOTD brought its action under the LEQA, La.Rev.Stat. 30:2271, *et seq.,* specifically citing La.Rev.Stat. 30:2276(G)(3), which provides that a party who has incurred remedial costs in responding to a discharge or disposal of a hazardous substance covered by the Act may sue to recover such remedial costs.... In support of its Motion in Limine, DOTD argued that the collateral source rule prevented defendants from receiving a reduction in their liability simply because DOTD received funding for the remediation from an independent source. DOTD further stated that its relationship with FHWA was analogous to a partnership, giving DOTD authority to recover the full amount of damages on the partnership's behalf. DOTD pointed out that FHWA was paying, as well, ninety percent of the attorney's fees to pursue this action....

(DOTD) argued that DOTD had no standing or other legal authority to recover on behalf of the FHWA the ninety percent of the damages reimbursed by FHWA. ... (because) allowing DOTD to seek the entire amount of incurred clean-up costs would constitute an impermissible double recovery by DOTD of the identical remediation costs.... DOTD re-urged the applicability of the collateral source rule. Alternatively, DOTD asserted that FHWA had specifically authorized DOTD to act on its behalf to recover the federal portion of the clean-up costs. DOTD relied on affidavits, as well as on four documents prepared by FHWA in an attempt to prove this agency relationship.

The district court ... found that DOTD would receive a double recovery if it were allowed to recover the ninety percent federal share of the clean-up costs after having the same costs funded by the federal government. The trial court further found insufficient evidence to indicate that a partnership existed between DOTD and FHWA or that DOTD was specifically authorized by FHWA to recover the federal money expended....

* * * * *

The court of Appeal affirmed the district court's grant of partial summary judgment, finding that allowing DOTD to recover the entire amount of remediation costs incurred would constitute an impermissible double recovery. The court of appeal held that the collateral source rule was not applicable in this action under the LEQA. Furthermore, the court found that DOTD supplied no evidence containing any special authorization from FHWA enabling DOTD to sue on its behalf to recover the federal portion of the remediation costs. We granted certiorari to review the correctness of the court of appeal's decision.

Law and Analysis

DOTD urges this court to reverse the court of appeal and find that it has standing to seek a judgment against KCS for the entire amount of expenses made necessary by the contamination at the construction site. DOTD primarily argues that, pursuant to authority granted by the FHWA, it is suing the alleged polluter on FHWA's behalf; thus, it will not receive a double recovery. DOTD alternatively contends that the collateral source rule prevents KCS from obtaining a reduction in liability for the DOTD's removal costs, in large measure funded by FHWA.

* * * * *

Under the collateral source rule, a tortfeasor may not benefit, and an injured plaintiff's tort recovery may not be reduced, because of monies received by the plaintiff from sources independent of the tortfeasor's procuration or contribution. *Warren v. Fidelity Mut. Ins. Co.,* 99 So. 2d 382, 385 (La.App. 1 Cir. 1957); *Williamson v. St. Francis Med. Ctr., Inc.,* 559 So. 2d 929, 934 (La.App. 2 Cir. 1990); *Griffin v. The Louisiana Sheriff's Auto Risk Assoc.,* 99-2944, p. 34 (La.App. 1 Cir. 2001), 802 So. 2d 691, 713. Under this well-established doctrine, the payments received from the independent source are not deducted from the award the aggrieved party would otherwise receive from the wrongdoer. *Terrell v. Nanda,* 33,242, p. 3 (La.App. 2 Cir. 2000), 759 So. 2d 1026, 1028.

The collateral source rule is of common law origin, Restatement (Second) of Torts § 920A (1979), yet well-established in the jurisprudence of this state, *see Warren,* 99 So. 2d at 385; *Doerle v. State, DOTD,* 147 So. 2d 776, 782 (La.App. 3 Cir. 1962); *Thomas v. Paper Haulers,* 165 So. 2d 61,

63 (La.App. 2 Cir. 1964). And, it has not been altered statutorily. In fact, early Louisiana cases cite legal encyclopedias and other common law reference sources as the basis for application of the collateral source rule. *See Warren,* 99 So. 2d at 385 (citing 25 C.J.S. Damages, § 99); *see also Doerle,* 147 So. 2d at 782 (citing 25 C.J.S. Damages, § 99; 15 Am.Jur. Damages, § 201).

Several public policy concerns support the collateral source rule generally. The reason most often stated is that the defendant should not gain an advantage from outside benefits provided to the plaintiff independently of any act of the defendant. *Bryant v. New Orleans Public Service, Inc.,* 406 So. 2d 767, 768 (La.App. 4 Cir. 1981), *affirmed,* 414 So. 2d 322 (La. 1982). It is also clear that the collateral source rule promotes tort deterrence and accident prevention. *Suhor v. Lagasse,* 00-1628, p. 3 (La.App. 4 Cir. 2000), 770 So. 2d 422, 424. Moreover, absent the collateral source rule, victims would be dissuaded from purchasing insurance or pursuing other forms of reimbursement available to them. *Bryant,* 406 So. 2d at 769.

In support of its contention that its otherwise applicable recovery under the LEQA should not be reduced by the amount of federal reimbursement, DOTD argues that the collateral source rule must be given a broad application to further the public policy considerations supporting it. DOTD notes that the "polluter pays" principle, a fundamental aspect of the public policy embodied in environmental law, seeks to deter environmental contamination by placing the burden of that contamination on the polluter. *Joslyn Mfg. Co. v. Koppers Co., Inc.,* 40 F.3d 750, 762 (5th Cir. 1994). DOTD alleges that the elements of the collateral source rule are present in this case: KCS is not entitled to a credit for payments to DOTD provided independently of KCS's procuration or contribution.

KCS, on the other hand, asserts that courts have applied the collateral source rule only in limited contexts, specifically, in tort situations involving insurance and other proceeds procurable by the victim. KCS further argues that the LEQA is a penal statute, and that the collateral source rule cannot be applied in this case, as penal statutes must be strictly construed, citing *Goodwin v. Agrilite,* 26,601, p. 7 (La.App. 2 Cir. 1994), 643 So. 2d 249, 254.

Both courts below agreed with KCS. The court of appeal found that the collateral source rule, a tort-based concept with a limited application, did not apply in this environmental clean-up dispute, which "does not involve insurance, tort deterrence, or accident prevention," according to them. *Louisiana Department of Transportation & Development v. Kansas City Southern Ry.,* 30,002, p. 36 (La.App. 2 Cir. 2002), 827 So. 2d 443, 461.

We reverse the court of appeal and hold that the collateral source rule applies in cases arising under the LEQA, at least where a damaged party is seeking reimbursement only for remediation expenses. If, after a trial on the merits, it is found to be legally responsible for some portion of the contamination present at the construction site, KCS cannot be exonerated from paying the full consequences of its act simply because DOTD independently obtained reimbursement in large part from FHWA for the clean-up costs incurred. This holding is not contrary to the existing jurisprudence of this state, and is consistent with the case law of numerous federal and state jurisdictions. Finally, our holding today is commanded by the paramount public interest in ensuring that those persons or entities responsible for harming our environment and the welfare of our citizens be held fully responsible for the consequences of their actions, and deterred from committing future violations of the LEQA.

We recognize that the collateral source rule is most commonly applied to insurance proceeds. Under this general rule, a tortfeasor's liability to an injured plaintiff should be the same, regardless of whether or not that plaintiff had the foresight to obtain insurance. *Wooten v. Central Mut. Ins. Co.,* 182 So. 2d 146, 148 (La.App. 3 Cir. 1966). However, our courts have applied the doctrine to a range of situations where the collateral source is provided to the plaintiff by a government agency or even a gratuitous source.

For example, a tortfeasor's liability may not be reduced by the amount of a victim's medical expenses paid by Medicare. *Womack v. Travelers Ins. Co.,* 258 So. 2d 562, 568 (La.App. 1 Cir. 1972); *Weir v. Gasper,* 459 So. 2d 655, 658 (La.App. 4 Cir. 1984); *Cooper v. Borden,* 709 So. 2d 878,

882 (La.App. 2 Cir. 1998). In *Francis v. Brown,* 671 So. 2d 1041, 1046-47 (La.App. 3 Cir. 1996), the court applied the collateral source rule and required the defendant to pay the full amount of the plaintiff's medical bills, including those amounts which had been paid by plaintiff's attorney. Additionally, a plaintiff's recovery is not reduced by the welfare payments received during period she did not work. *Bonnet For and Behalf of Bonnet v. Slaughter,* 422 So. 2d 499, 502 (La.App. 4 Cir. 1982).

In each of the above-cited cases, the courts focused their analysis on the fact that a wrongdoer may not benefit, and an injured party's recovery may not be diminished, because of benefits received by the plaintiff from sources independent of the wrongdoer's procuration or contribution. As one court described the collateral source rule, "only payments already made by the tortfeasor can be used to grant the tortfeasor a credit towards the amount of the ... award." *Coscino v. Wolfley,* 696 So. 2d 257, 264 (La.App. 4 Cir. 1997).

We additionally believe it is mere happenstance that the collateral source rule has been applied chiefly in the context of a conventional La. Civ.Code art. 2315 tort. The court of appeal's finding that the collateral source rule is inapplicable to this "environmental clean-up dispute" because it "does not involve insurance, tort deterrence, or accident prevention" is erroneous. Because the particular concerns presented through application of environmental law have arisen relatively recently, Louisiana courts have not had the opportunity to address the impact of statutes that impose duties affecting the environment on the collateral source rule. Like conventional tort cases, environmental law statutory remedies involve claims to recover damages for harm caused by a defendant's acts.[7] For the following reasons, the logic supporting application of the collateral source rule is equally persuasive whether we are dealing with a defendant polluter under the LEQA, or a traditional "tortfeasor" whose liability arises under La. Civ.Code art. 2315, or other general tort law.

A cause of action arising under an environmental statute, such as the LEQA, presents compelling public policy reasons supporting application of the collateral source rule. Louisiana citizens, speaking through the drafters of our 1974 Constitution, have established environmental preservation as a preeminent public policy concern:

> The natural resources of the state, including air and water, and the healthful, scenic, historic, and esthetic quality of the environment shall be protected, conserved, and replenished insofar as possible and consistent with the health, safety, and welfare of the people. The legislature shall enact laws to implement this policy.

La. Const. art. IX, § 1 (1974). When applying environmental laws, the concern prompting the collateral source rule's goals of tort deterrence and accident prevention is especially implicated, although in the context of deterring future acts in violation of the LEQA. *See Suhor,* 00-1628, p. 3, 770 So. 2d at 424. The welfare of our environment and the health of our citizens command that those persons or entities which are found to have polluted our state pay full restitution for the consequences of their acts. Violators of the LEQA should not be allowed to escape the consequences of their actions because the federal government chooses to provide financial assistance to states in essential and time-sensitive clean-up operations.

As we noted previously, Louisiana derives its collateral source rule from the common law; thus, we find persuasive other U.S. jurisdictions' application and interpretation of the collateral source rule. A review of the relevant case law indicates that courts do not restrict application of the collateral source rule to cases involving insurance payments and other benefits purchased by the injured party. To begin, the Restatement (Second) of Torts, § 920A provides:

---

[7] One court has analogized the citizen suit cause of action under the LEQA to a tort cause of action, and applied the one-year prescription applicable to torts. *See Morris & Dickson Co. v. Jones Bros. Co.,* 29, 379, p. 24 (La.App. 2 Cir. 1997), 691 So. 2d 882, 895 (citing Kenneth M. Murchison, *Enforcing Environmental Standards Under State Law: The Louisiana Environmental Quality Act,* 57 La. L.Rev. 497, 555 (1997)).

(1) A payment made by a tortfeasor or by a person acting for him to a person he has injured is credited against his tort liability, as are payments made by another who is, or believes he is, subject to the same tort liability.

(2) Payments made to or benefits conferred on the injured party from other sources are not credited against the tortfeasor's liability, although they cover all or a part of the harm for which the tortfeasor is liable.

(Emphasis added). The comments to § 920A specifically note that social legislation benefits, such as social security and welfare payments, are subject to the collateral source rule.

* * * * *

The overwhelming authority, therefore, supports our holding today in this case that the collateral source rule applies to the reimbursement DOTD received from FHWA. A wrongdoer's liability should not be reduced by the amount of collateral source payments to an injured plaintiff, even where the nature of the collateral source is a public relief provided to the plaintiff by application of federal or state law. The court of appeal and KCS erroneously focus the analysis on whether DOTD will receive a windfall if allowed to recover the full measure of damages from KCS after having been previously reimbursed by FHWA. Other state and federal jurisdictions, however, have generally not been concerned with allowing a plaintiff to receive a windfall as a result of the collateral source rule. *See e.g., Town of East Troy,* 653 F.2d at 1132; *Hall,* 465 A.2d at 226.[8] The federal Second Circuit Court of Appeals, in applying the collateral source rule to an action brought under the Carriage of Goods by Sea Act, aptly noted that "the question is not whether a windfall is to be conferred, but rather who shall receive the benefit of a windfall which already exists.... This may permit a double recovery, but it does not impose a double burden. The tortfeasor bears only the single burden for his wrong." *Thyssen, Inc. v. S/S Eurounity,* 21 F.3d 533, 538 (2d Cir. 1994) (citing *Gypsum Carrier, Inc. v. Handelsman,* 307 F.2d 525, 534 (9th Cir. 1962)).

Similarly, in the present case, we must choose between allowing DOTD a possible windfall,[9] or allowing the liability of potential wrongdoer under the LEQA to be reduced by the 90 percent federal share. We find that the former option is preferable and is not inconsistent with existing Louisiana jurisprudence. As the court in *Griffin* determined:

the focus of the collateral source rule is that a tortfeasor should not be allowed to benefit from the victim's foresight and prudence in securing insurance and other benefits. Thus, the focus of our analysis should be on the nature of the write-offs *vis-a-vis* the tortfeasor, rather than *vis-a-vis* the tort victim.... To allow such a reduction in the tortfeasor's liability would indeed be a "windfall"--inuring to the benefit of the tortfeasor! This is precisely what the collateral source rule is designed to prevent.

Griffin, 99-2944, p. 36, 802 So. 2d at 714-15 (emphasis added). Although the *Griffin* court was discussing the collateral source rule's most common application to insurance payments in tort cases, the logic applies with equal force to the facts and circumstances at hand. The Fourth Circuit Court of Appeal, in discussing the collateral source rule generally, has also noted that, for policy reasons, "double recovery is justified in some cases because the tortfeasor should not receive the benefits of the victim's thrift, employment benefits, or special services rendered by a third party." *Suhor,* 00-1628, p. 3, 770 So. 2d at 424.

---

[8] The comments to Restatement (Second) of Torts § 920A (1979) state "to the extent that the defendant is required to pay the total amount there may be a double compensation for a part of the plaintiff's injury."

[9] It is not likely that DOTD will actually enjoy a double recovery in light of its representation to this court and the lower courts that it will repay FHWA the ninety percent federal share of any judgment obtained.

It is important to note that if DOTD eventually obtains a judgment against KCS after a full merits trial, FHWA may later seek, and indeed is likely to collect, a portion of this judgment from DOTD as reimbursement for the clean-up costs it provided.[10] Actual ownership or utilization of the proceeds from any judgment which may be rendered against KCS is an issue for another day. Therefore, it speculative at this point whether DOTD will actually receive a windfall or double recovery by being allowed to receive a judgment against KCS for the entirety of the remediation costs.

Finally, we address KCS's contention that the LEQA is a penal statute, and thus should not implicate the collateral source rule. We take KCS's argument to be that the collateral source rule, as a permissible facilitation of multiple recovery, is defensible only if what the tortfeasor pays is the actual remedial cost imposed upon the victim by the tortfeasor's conduct. According to KCS, a statute that is penal in nature, and which imposes a greater penalty than mere remediation is not an appropriate application or extension of the collateral source rule. KCS cites *Goodwin,* 26,601, p. 7, 643 So. 2d at 254, which noted that LEQA § 30:2276(G) is penal and must be strictly construed.

* * * * *

Conclusion

We hold today that the collateral source rule applies to DOTD's action against KCS for the costs incurred to clean-up the highway construction site. Any judgment to be rendered by the district court against KCS should not be reduced by the ninety percent federal share of the remediation funded by FHWA. This holding is commanded by Louisiana's unique constitutionally enunciated public policy of environmental protection and preservation, coupled with the public policy supporting the collateral source rule. Persons or entities found to have violated the LEQA must pay the full measure of damages they caused, and cannot escape liability because our state is independently entitled to reimbursement of ninety percent of remediation costs from a federal agency.

We emphasize that our holding today is a narrow one addressing the applicability of the collateral source rule in the circumstances of this case. The resolution of the discrete legal issue posed at this juncture should have no bearing on whether KCS is either actually responsible for some part of the contamination, or whether it is legally bound to pay for all or part of the remediation. In fact, KCS has vehemently denied that the 1966 train derailment contributed in any way to the site's pollution. The issue of liability is to be resolved by the district court after a trial on the merits.

* * * * *

The judgment is **AFFIRMED**.

NOTES

1. The "collateral source" rule prevents the admission of evidence that plaintiff's attorney provided the funds for plaintiff's medical expenses. *Francis v. Brown*, 671 So. 2d 1041 (La.App. 3 Cir. 1996). But, in *Hoffman v. 21st Century North America Ins. Co.*, 209 So. 3d 702 (La. 2015), the Louisiana Supreme Court addressed the issue of whether the collateral source rule applies to a write-off (reduction in price) for medical procedures performed on a plaintiff when the write-offs are negotiated by the plaintiff's attorney. The Court held that the collateral source rule did not apply to an attorney-negotiated medical write-off because the plaintiff suffered no diminution of his patrimony to obtain the write-off. Thus, to permit a recovery of the written-off amount would be a windfall to the plaintiff. Later, the Fifth Circuit distinguished *Hoffman* and found the collateral source rule applicable to a reduction in medical expenses negotiated by the plaintiff with her medical providers in *Lockett v. UV Ins. Risk Retention Group, Inc.*, 80 So. 3d 557 (La.App. 5 Cir. 2015). The court explained that "Plaintiff negotiated, and paid for, the reduction through her own efforts and with her own funds,

---

[10] DOTD asserts that it will reimburse FHWA on its own, but, even if it does not, DOTD contends that FHWA will nonetheless seek recovery of its ninety percent participation from any judgment DOTD obtains.

450

without the involvement of her attorneys." *Id.* at 571. Thus, applying the collateral source rule, the court permitted plaintiff to recover from the defendants the medical expense reduction that she had negotiated. *See also, Royer v. State of Louisiana, DOTD,* 210 So. 3d 910 (La.App. 3 Cir. 2017).

2.   The collateral source rule precludes a defendant from benefitting from the PPO discounts which the plaintiff obtains through his own insurer. *LeBlanc v. Acadian Ambulance Service, Inc.,* 746 So. 2d 665 (La.App. 3 Cir. 1999). *See also, Griffin v. The Louisiana Sheriff's Auto Risk Assoc.,* 802 So. 2d 691 (La.App. 1 Cir. 2002) (the collateral source rule applies to contractual write-offs procured by an insurance company in exchange for providing a volume of business; evidence of such write-offs should be excluded from a jury's consideration in determining an award for medical expenses to the insured who purchased coverage from the insurer). However, in *Bozeman v. State,* 879 So. 2d 692 (La. 2004), the court held that under the collateral source rule, a tortfeasor may not benefit, and an injured plaintiff's tort recovery may not be reduced, because of monies received by the plaintiff from sources independent of the tortfeasor's procuration or contribution. However, the plaintiff may not recover such expenses if plaintiff does not pay an enrollment fee, does not have any wages deducted, and does not otherwise provide any consideration for the collateral source benefits he receives. Thus, the plaintiff may not recover his medical expenses which are "written off" by the health care provider in compliance with the federal Medicaid program. In those instances where the plaintiff's patrimony has been diminished in some way in order to obtain the collateral source benefits (such as Medicare or private insurance benefits), plaintiff may recover the full value of his medical services, including the "write off" amount.

H.   MITIGATION OF DAMAGES

An injured plaintiff must act reasonably to avoid or mitigate her damages. The defendant bears the burden of proving that the plaintiff failed to mitigate her damages. The extent to which the plaintiff has satisfied that obligation normally is a question for the factfinder. The "mitigation" rule is also often referred to as the rule of avoidable consequences. The key, of course, is reasonableness. It is one thing to leave a wrecked automobile on a highway shoulder for several weeks; it is another to undergo an operation which has a probability of reducing the consequences of a personal injury.

I.   RESTITUTION

There are criminal law statutes providing for victims of crimes to receive restitution. Consider, for example, the following general provision from the Code of Criminal Procedure:

La. Code Cr. Proc. Article 883.2. Restitution to victim

A.   In all cases in which the court finds an actual pecuniary loss to a victim, or in any case where the court finds that costs have been incurred by the victim in connection with a criminal prosecution, the trial court shall order the defendant to provide restitution to the victim as a part of any sentence that the court shall impose.

B.   Additionally, if the defendant agrees as a term of a plea agreement, the court shall order the defendant to provide restitution to other victims of the defendant's criminal conduct, although those persons are not the victim of the criminal charge to which the defendant pleads. Such restitution to other persons may be ordered pursuant to Article 895 or 895.1 or any other provision of law permitting or requiring restitution to victims.

C.   The court shall order that all restitution payments be made by the defendant to the victim through the court's designated intermediary, and in no case shall the court order the defendant to deliver or send a restitution payment directly to a victim, unless the victim consents.

A more specific restitution provision is found in Act 429 of 2013:

La. R.S. 15:539.3 Mandatory restitution

A.   A person convicted of a violation of R.S. 14:46.2 (human trafficking) or R.S. 14:46.3 (trafficking of children for sexual purposes) shall be ordered to pay mandatory restitution to the victim, with the proceeds from property forfeited under R.S. 15:539.1 applied first to payment of restitution, after the costs of the public sale or auction, court costs, and fees related to seizure and storage have been satisfied. Restitution under this Section shall include any of the following:

(1)   Costs of medical and psychological treatment.

(2)   Costs of necessary transportation and temporary housing.

(3)   The greater of (a) the value of the victim's labor as guaranteed under the minimum wage and overtime provisions of the federal Fair Labor Standards Act; or (b) the gross income or value to the defendant of the victim's labor or services engaged in by the victim while in the human trafficking situation. In the case of sex trafficking, the victim shall be entitled to restitution for the income he would have earned, had he not been victimized, as guaranteed under the minimum wage and overtime provisions of the federal Fair Labor Standards Act.

(4)   Return of property, cost of damage to property, or full value of property if destroyed or damaged beyond repair.

(5)   Expenses incurred by the victim and any household members or other family members in relocating away from the defendant or the defendant's associates, including but not limited to deposits for utilities and telephone service, deposits for rental housing, temporary lodging and food expenses, clothing, and personal items. Expenses incurred pursuant to this Section shall be verified by law enforcement to be necessary for the personal safety of the victim or household or family members, or by a mental health treatment provider to be necessary for the emotional well-being of the victim.

B.   For purposes of this Section, the return of the victim to the victim's home country or other absence of the victim from the jurisdiction shall not prevent the victim from receiving restitution.

CHAPTER 9

WRONGFUL DEATH AND SURVIVAL ACTIONS AND LOSS OF CONSORTIUM

At common law in England, when a person was injured through the fault of others and subsequently died, the tort claims that the decedent could have asserted died with her. English legislation eventually changed that common law result. Although American courts followed the common law principle for some time, states eventually enacted statutes, as England did, that changed that rule. Now, all states have statutes creating either or both survival actions or wrongful death actions. The two actions are different, although they often are brought by the same person(s). Survival actions reverse the common law rule and provide that an injured person's tort claim survives her death and is passed on to some survivor. A survival action is the tort claim that the dead person could have brought against a defendant for the damages she could have recovered. In contrast, a wrongful death action is a new and wholly independent action that arises on the death of a person in favor of certain designated beneficiaries for what they lost when the injured person died. A wrongful death action is like a loss of consortium claim when the injured person dies.

Louisiana statutorily provides for both survival actions and wrongful death actions. The beneficiaries who can bring the actions are the same, except the survival action article provides a last category not included in the wrongful death article—the succession representative of the dead person. Do you understand why the succession representative is listed in only the survival action article? It is important to understand that the lists in C.C. Arts. 2315.1 and 2315.2 are hierarchical or preemptive and a higher category precludes a lower category from bringing an action. For example, if a spouse and child survive, they alone can bring the survival and wrongful death actions; all lower classes are precluded even if the spouse and child choose not to pursue a wrongful death and survival action.

It is important to understand that one must have a tort theory on which to sue a defendant in wrongful death and survival actions. For example, was the decedent injured by the negligent acts or intentional torts of the defendant? Obviously, most wrongful death and survival actions are based on negligence.

The key issues with wrongful death and survival actions are who can assert them, when the prescriptive period accrues, and what damages can be recovered.

Damages in a survival action are the damages that the decedent could have recovered if she had survived, such as loss of earnings from time of injury to death, general damages including pain and suffering, medical expenses, and funeral expenses. Damages in wrongful death are for the loss suffered by the beneficiary, including support, services, society, love and affection, and sex (for spouses).

The prescriptive period for wrongful death does not begin to run until the person dies because a wrongful death claim does not arise until the person dies. In contrast, the prescriptive period for a survival action begins to run typically when the tort occurs, subject to contra non valentem. However, if the tort claim has not prescribed when the person dies, C.C. Art. 2315.1 provides a "bonus"—the survival action prescribes one year from the date of death.

Do not confuse survival actions with claims for loss of a chance of survival. *See supra* Chapter 5.

La. Civil Code Article 2315.1.   Survival action

A.   If a person who has been injured by an offense or quasi offense dies, the right to recover all damages for injury to that person, his property or otherwise, caused by the offense or quasi offense, shall survive for a period of one year from the death of the deceased in favor of:

(1)   The surviving spouse and child or children of the deceased, or either the spouse or the child or children.

(2)   The surviving father and mother of the deceased, or either of them if he left no spouse or child surviving.

(3)   The surviving brothers and sisters of the deceased, or any of them, if he left no spouse, child, or parent surviving.

(4)   The surviving grandfathers and grandmothers of the deceased, or any of them, if he left no spouse, child, parent, or sibling surviving.

B.   In addition, the right to recover all damages for injury to the deceased, his property or otherwise, caused by the offense or quasi offense, may be urged by the deceased's succession representative in the absence of any class of beneficiary set out in Paragraph A.

C.   The right of action granted under this Article is heritable, but the inheritance of it neither interrupts nor prolongs the prescriptive period defined in this Article.

D.   As used in this Article, the words "child", "brother", "sister", "father", "mother", "grandfather", and "grandmother" include a child, brother, sister, father, mother, grandfather, and grandmother by adoption, respectively.

E.   For purposes of this Article, a father or mother who has abandoned the deceased during his minority is deemed not to have survived him.

La. Civil Code Article 2315.2.   Wrongful death action

A.   If a person dies due to the fault of another, suit may be brought by the following persons to recover damages which they sustained as a result of the death:

(1)   The surviving spouse and child or children of the deceased, or either the spouse or the child or children.

(2)   The surviving father and mother of the deceased, or either of them if he left no spouse or child surviving.

(3)   The surviving brothers and sisters of the deceased, or any of them, if he left no spouse, child, or parent surviving.

(4)   The surviving grandfathers and grandmothers of the deceased, or any of them, if he left no spouse, child, parent, or sibling surviving.

B.   The right of action granted by this Article prescribes one year from the death of the deceased.

C.   The right of action granted under this Article is heritable, but the inheritance of it neither interrupts nor prolongs the prescriptive period defined in this Article.

D.   As used in this Article, the words "child", "brother", "sister", "father", "mother", "grandfather", and "grandmother" include a child, brother, sister, father, mother, grandfather, and grandmother by adoption, respectively.

E.   For purposes of this Article, a father or mother who has abandoned the deceased during his minority is deemed not to have survived him.

theory of recovery
support, society, services, sex
        ↑
    love & affection

454

La. Civil Code Article 2315.5.   Wrongful death and survival action; exception

Notwithstanding any other provision of law to the contrary, the surviving spouse, parent, or child of a deceased, who has been convicted of a crime involving the intentional killing or attempted killing of the deceased, or, if not convicted, who has been judicially determined to have participated in the intentional, unjustified killing or attempted killing of the deceased, shall not be entitled to any damages or proceeds in a survival action or an action for wrongful death of the deceased, or to any proceeds distributed in settlement of any such cause of action. In such case, the other child or children of the deceased, or if the deceased left no other child surviving, the other survivors enumerated in the applicable provisions of Articles 2315.1(A) and 2315.2(A), in order of preference stated, may bring a survival action against such surviving spouse, parent, or child, or an action against such surviving spouse, parent, or child for the wrongful death of the deceased.

An executive pardon shall not restore the surviving spouse's, parent's, or child's right to any damages or proceeds in a survival action or an action for wrongful death of the deceased.

La. Civil Code Art. 197. Child's action to establish paternity; proof; time period

A child may institute an action to prove paternity even though he is presumed to be the child of another man. If the action is instituted after the death of the alleged father, a child shall prove paternity by clear and convincing evidence.

For purposes of succession only, this action is subject to a peremptive period of one year. This peremptive period commences to run from the day of the death of the alleged father.

* * * * *

BLANCHARD
v.
TINSMAN
445 So. 2d 149 (La.App. 3 Cir. 1984)

STOKER, J.

The parents of Michael Lawrence Blanchard brought a wrongful death action and a survival action arising from his death. Among others that suit was brought against Richard T. Tinsman, driver of a tractor-trailer unit which jackknifed on the highway and collided with a vehicle driven by Michael Lawrence Blanchard (Michael). Michael died instantly as a result of injuries received in the collision. Michael's wife, Cheryl Verret Blanchard, also died as a result of injuries sustained in the collision, but she exhibited some sign of life, a heartbeat, for a period of time after Michael's death. There were no children of the marriage of Michael and Cheryl.

Various other defendants, who would be legally liable for the alleged negligence of Richard Tinsman, filed exceptions of no right of action grounded on the contention that plaintiffs have no right of action under LSA-C.C. art. 2315 under the circumstances. The circumstances relied upon by exceptors are that Michael's wife survived him; she therefore acquired the right to assert a survival action for his death and a wrongful death action for her personal damages sustained from his loss; and, finally that these rights passed to Cheryl Verret Blanchard's parents by inheritance when she died some minutes after Michael.

The trial court sustained the exception and, as to exceptors, dismissed the action of Michael's parents, William Blanchard, individually and as administrator of Michael's estate, and Sherry Blanchard. In a separate judgment the trial court additionally dismissed Richard T. Tinsman and other defendants. The plaintiffs appeal. We affirm.

The appellants urge equitable considerations, but unfortunately the case must be decided against them. The trial court's ruling was correct. LSA-C.C. art. 2315; *Haas v. Baton Rouge General*

Hospital, 364 So. 2d 944 (La. 1978); *Simmons v. Brooks,* 342 So. 2d 236 (La.App. 4 Cir.1977); *Walker v. St. Paul Ins. Companies,* 339 So. 2d 441 (La.App. 1 Cir. 1976), *writ granted,* 341 So. 2d 554 (La. 1977), on remand 343 So. 2d 251 (La.App. 1 Cir. 1977), *writ denied* 345 So. 2d 61 (La. 1977).

Preliminarily the appellants urge that because Cheryl never regained consciousness and never was aware of Michael's death, she did not acquire an action under Article 2315 and, therefore, she had no action which passed to her parents. Such an argument can only relate to the elements of damage which may be recovered and not to the question of right of action under Article 2315. In the matter now before us, we decide only that the parents of Michael have no right of action under the circumstances. Whether Michael suffered any conscious pain and suffering and whether Cheryl was conscious so as to experience any loss of love, affection and companionship are questions of fact and relate to the elements of damage for which a recovery in this case can be had. At this point we confine ourselves to affirming the exception. If on trial of any action by Cheryl's parents it should be decided that there could be no recovery for the elements of damage mentioned above, that would not shift any right of action to the parents of Michael.

In appellants' principal contention and argument, they urge that we give a broad interpretation to the word "surviving" as used in LSA-C.C. art. 2315. They contend that we should not consider Cheryl to be the survivor merely because she survived in the technical sense. The collision rendered Cheryl unconscious and she remained in the throes of certain death which did occur within a short period of time. In fact, the only life sign she showed was a heartbeat. She was not breathing. Efforts at resuscitation were unsuccessful. Cheryl's heartbeat ceased in the ambulance on the way to the hospital and she did not respond to chest compressions. In view of these facts and circumstances appellants urge that, under a common sense interpretation of Article 2315, they are the true survivors.

* * * * *

As we interpret the article the term "surviving" has reference to survival in fact, in point of actual time, not survival of the accident. As harsh as the result seems to be, that is the result dictated by the clear meaning of the article. The jurisprudence cited above has so interpreted the article.

For reasons that are not entirely clear the appellants cite and discuss at length the case of *Collins v. Becnel,* 297 So. 2d 506 (La.App. 4 Cir. 1974). Appellants urge that *Collins v. Becnel* gives an "ordinary, common sense definition of 'surviving' " as employed in Article 2315. They urge that a common and ordinary interpretation be given the article here and urge that we not adopt a technical and narrow interpretation of the word "surviving." We cannot find that *Collins v. Becnel, supra,* has any application to this case. The decision and reasoning of the court in that case may have given a common sense and ordinary meaning to the word "surviving" as it applied to the facts of that case. However, the opinion in that case does not influence the decision here.

The facts of the case of *Collins v. Becnel, supra,* are altogether different from the facts before us. In Collins the deaths of a mother and her only child occurred simultaneously and instantaneously. The defendants sought to defend against an action by the mother's brothers and sisters, the claimants next in line under Article 2315. The defendants sought to invoke the presumptions of survivorship of commorientes set forth in LSA-C.C. arts. 936-939 to determine beneficiaries of wrongful death claims under Article 2315. The defendants in Collins contended that under Article 939 there was a presumption that the daughter survived the mother. The Court of Appeal for the Fourth Circuit held in Collins that the presumptions sought to be invoked, applicable in succession law, are not applicable, and did not apply, to actions for wrongful death under Article 2315. The Court of Appeal held that the law of torts made the mother's brothers and sisters "the wrongful death action beneficiaries ... where in actual fact the victim 'left no spouse, child, or parents surviving.' "

By holding that the presumptions of survivorship applicable in succession law did not apply, and "in actual fact" the mother could not be said to have left her deceased only child (who died simultaneously with her), the brothers and sisters were the next in line to assert the Article 2315 action.

456

We do not interpret appellants' arguments contained in their brief relative to *Collins v. Becnel, supra*, as urging that we adopt the presumptions of survivorship contained in the Civil Code articles. Appellants appear to concede their inapplicability. They quote from a law review note in 50 Tul.L.Rev. 441 at pages 449-450, entitled "Tort-Wrongful Death" which treats the Collins case, in which the writer states that the court in *Collins* employed the word "surviving" in its ordinary sense and meant surviving in actual fact. Appellants then argue that if we should follow *Collins v. Becnel,* "the ordinary, common sense definition of 'surviving' allows Michael's parents a right of action for their loss of love and affection, and Cheryl's parents the same right for the loss of their daughter." Appellants further suggest that this would be the just and equitable solution. We are inclined to agree that such would be a just and equitable solution. Nevertheless, in this case we are compelled to conclude that, *in actual fact,* Cheryl survived Michael. Therefore, Cheryl was the surviving beneficiary under Article 2315 in the first instance.

If this result is unjust and inequitable, as we are inclined to think it is, it is a matter for legislative correction. We feel bound by the decision and holding in *Haas v. Baton Rouge General Hospital, supra*; *Simmons v. Brooks, supra*, and *Walker v. St. Paul Ins. Companies, supra*, and the clear meaning of Article 2315.

* * * * *

NOTES

1.   For the historical development of Louisiana wrongful death and survival actions, *see* Johnson, "Death and Survival Actions," 37 La. L. Rev. 1 (1976). Louisiana, despite its civilian heritage, followed the general common law rule that tort claims were personal, and therefore, were extinguished upon the death of either the victim or the tortfeasor. *See, Hugh v. New Orleans and Carrollton Railroad*, 6 La. Ann. 495 (1851). Shortly thereafter in 1855 the Louisiana legislature enacted a survival action and later passed a wrongful death action in 1884. These provisions have been amended over time to their current state.

2.   Beneficiaries for Louisiana survival and wrongful death actions are identical, with one minor exception. In a survival action, if there are no surviving beneficiaries, the succession representative of the victim may institute the survival action. Despite the similarity of these categories of beneficiaries, determination of who fits into each classification has been the subject of frequent litigation.

   a.   Spouse and Children. Does the term "spouse" include:

      i.   a judicially or physically separated spouse?;
      ii.   a spouse living with another lover?;
      iii.   a spouse who remarried after the victims injury?;
      iv.   a spouse who married the victim subsequent to the injury?;
      v.   a putative spouse?

   Does the term "child" include either an adopted child or an illegitimate child? *See*, Johnson, *supra* note 1 at 15-16. In *Guidry v. Coregis Ins. Co.*, 896 So. 2d 164 (La.App. 3 Cir. 2004) the trial testimony revealed that plaintiff was not decedent's biological daughter, although his signature appeared on her birth certificate and he had executed an act of acknowledgment of paternity. *Held,* plaintiff may not recover as a wrongful death beneficiary. A C.C. Art. 203 formal acknowledgment, absent a biological relationship, is a nullity; the acknowledgment by signing the birth certificate and the execution of the act of acknowledgment are both forms of Article 203 formal acknowledgment and are nullities.

   b.   Parents. The term "parents" includes parents by blood and by adoption. Does it include stepparents? *See*, Johnson, *supra* note 1 at 18-19.

   c.   Siblings. The term "siblings" includes half-siblings. Does it also include illegitimate siblings? *See*, Johnson, *supra* note 1 at 20-21.

d.   Grandparents. In *Baudoin v. Acadia Parish Police Jury*, 620 So. 2d 453 (La.App. 3 Cir. 1993), *writ denied*, 626 So. 2d 1166 (La. 1993), a surviving grandparent who reared a grandchild killed in an accident was precluded from recovering survival and wrongful death damages. Would the same result hold true under present Louisiana Law? C.C. Arts. 2315.1 and 2315.2 were amended in 1997.

3.   Where the victim dies, punitive damages, where appropriate, are recoverable under the victim's survival action but not in the beneficiaries' wrongful death action. *Bulot v. Intracoastal Tubular Services, Inc.*, 888 So. 2d 1017 (La.App. 4 Cir. 2004), *writ denied as premature*, 888 So. 2d 877 (La. 2004).

4.   When does prescription begin to run in a survival action? A wrongful death action? Assume victim is injured in an accident. Although competent, victim does not file a personal injury claim within a year of the accident. Victim subsequently dies. Has the survival action prescribed? Has the wrongful death action prescribed? *See*, La. C.C. Arts. 2315.1 and 2315.2; *Guidry v. Theriot, supra*; and *Dunn v. North Community Hospital*, 545 So. 2d 1267 (La. App. 2 Cir. 1989), *writ denied*, 550 So. 2d 633 (La. 1989).

5.   Assume Pete and Repeat are twins who have no other living relatives. If Repeat is convicted of conspiring to murder Pete, does La. C.C. Art 2315.5 preclude Repeat from recovering damages in a wrongful death action against his co-conspirators? Would your response be the same if Repeat is the father of Pete?

6.   Can parents recover wrongful death damages for the death of an unborn fetus? *See*, La. C.C. Arts. 25 and 26, *Danos v. St. Pierre*, 402 So. 2d 633 (La. 1981), and *Bellard v. South Central Bell Telephone Co.*, 702 So. 2d 695 (La.App. 3 Cir. 1997). Is this consistent with *Wartelle*, Chapter 6?

7.   Act 477 of 2007 enacted La. R.S. 40:1061.27 and created a cause of action to be maintained under certain circumstances for injuries and wrongful death for partial birth abortions.

8.   Comparative fault applies in wrongful death and survival actions. Fault of the decedent may reduce the plaintiffs' recovery in these actions.

9.   If an employee is injured at work and dies as a result of an event that is covered by workers' compensation, both the survival action and the wrongful death action, if not based on an intentional tort, are barred by the workers' compensation immunity. It should be obvious why the survival action is barred because it is the tort claim of the injured employee. It is not as obvious why the wrongful death action is barred. The Workers' Compensation Act provides for payment of a death benefit.

CHAPTER 10

STRICT LIABILITY

COMMENT

This chapter explores strict liability in Louisiana before and after the adoption of tort reform legislation in 1996. That legislation replaced much strict liability with liability based upon negligence (e.g., liability of owners and/or custodians of things, buildings, and animals, except dogs); however, some vestiges of strict liability remain either unchanged (e.g., nondiscerning children) or altered to some extent (e.g., dogs).

A. THINGS

Prior to 1996, liability for "things" was governed by C.C. Article 2317, which reads as follows:

La. Civil Code Article 2317. Acts of others and of things in custody

We are responsible, not only for the damage occasioned by our own act, but for that which is caused by the act of persons for whom we are answerable, or of the things which we have in our custody. This, however, is to be understood with the following modifications.

The 1996 "tort reform" legislation retained Article 2317 but added 2317.1, which reads as follows:

La. Civil Code Article 2317.1. Damage caused by ruin, vice, or defect in things

The owner or custodian of a thing is answerable for damage occasioned by its ruin, vice, or defect, only upon a showing that he knew or, in the exercise of reasonable care, should have known of the ruin, vice, or defect which caused the damage, that the damage could have been prevented by the exercise of reasonable care, and that he failed to exercise such reasonable care. Nothing in this Article shall preclude the court from the application of the doctrine of res ipsa loquitur in an appropriate case.

Prior to 1996, Article 2317 was interpreted as imposing strict liability. The seminal case is *Loescher v. Parr*, reproduced below.

LOESCHER
v.
PARR
324 So. 2d 441 (La. 1976)

TATE, J.

The plaintiff Loescher's automobile was demolished when a tree from a neighboring lot fell across it. He sues Parr, the owner of the neighboring lot, and Parr's homeowner's liability insurer (State Farm).

The court of appeal affirmed the district court's dismissal of the suit, holding that no negligence on Parr's part is proven. 312 So. 2d 347 (La.App. 1 Cir. 1975). We granted certiorari, 313 So. 2d 833 (La.1975), to consider the correctness of the holding that the owner of a diseased tree cannot be held for damage caused to a neighbor (who is himself without fault) by the fall of the tree because of its diseased condition.

The Facts

The tree which fell was a magnolia tree some sixty feet high. From the outside, the tree did not appear to be obviously diseased. However, in fact, the magnolia was 90% rotted out and hollow beneath its outside structure of the bottom portion of the trunk. The tree was situated on the defendant Parr's home lot six feet from his home.

At 3:00 a.m. the tree fell across the property line and onto the plaintiff Loescher's Cadillac on the neighboring lot. The vehicle was parked in the parking lot of the apartment house into which Loescher had moved three weeks earlier.

The primary cause of the fall was the diseased condition of the tree. The weather was windy, of a nature that occurs in the vicinity about thirty times a year; but the wind was not even of storm nature. The only tree that was damaged or fell in the town was the present one.

The Legal Issue

The trial and intermediate courts held that Parr could not be held liable for the fall of his diseased tree in the absence of proven negligence on his part. These previous courts accepted his testimony that, from the outside, the tree did not appear to be diseased. They rejected testimony, as mistaken, of a tree surgeon that, shortly before the accident, he had warned the defendant's wife of the defective condition of the tree and recommended its removal.

We are not prepared to hold that the trial court committed error in its appreciation of the facts. *Canter v. Koehring*, 283 So. 2d 716 (La. 1973). Thus, we accept the factual holding that the tree was internally diseased but that the owner could not reasonably realize its defective condition, although such defect of the tree constituted an unreasonable hazard of injury to those upon whom it might foreseeably fall.

The issue remains whether, nevertheless, the owner of a tree with such a defect may be held liable to others injured by reason of such defect, even in the absence of negligent conduct or inattention on his part.

The plaintiff argues that the owner is liable for damage caused by the defect of a thing in his custody. Civil Code Article 2317. The plaintiff further contends that, at any rate, the owner should be held liable for the fall of a diseased tree, analogously to the strict liability of an owner of a building for its fall due to a structural defect or to his neglect to repair it. Civil Code Articles 670, 2322.

Liability of an Owner for the Fall of His 'Building'

At the least, the liability of an owner for harm caused because of a defect in his building is illustrative of the strict liability here sought to be imposed upon the owner of a tree for harm caused through its defect.

Under Louisiana law, founded on Articles 670[59] and 2322,[60] the owner of a building is liable to a neighbor or passer-by injured through the fall of his building due either to a vice in its original construction or to his neglect to repair it. His fault is founded upon the breach of his obligation to maintain or repair his building so as to avoid creation of risk of undue injury to others.

---

[59] Article 670 provides: "Every one is bound to keep his buildings in repair, so that neither their fall, nor that of any part of the materials composing them, may injure the neighbors or passengers (passers-by), under the penalty of all losses and damages, which may result from the neglect of the owner in that respect."

[60] Article 2322 provides: "The owner of a building is answerable for the damage occasioned by its ruin, when this is caused by neglect to repair it, or when it is the result of a vice in its original construction."

460

Neither ignorance of the condition of the building, nor circumstances that the defect could not easily be detected, absolve the owner from his liability for damages so caused. He is absolved from such liability only if the thing owned by him falls, not because of its defect, but rather because of the fault of some third person or of the person injured thereby, or because the fault is caused by an irresistible cause or force not usually foreseeable, Article 3556(14), (15) (usually, an act occasioned exclusively by violence of nature without the interference of or contribution by any human agency).

* * * * *

In arguing for similar liability here, the plaintiff Loescher points out that a tree is an immovable thing considered as part of the land to which it is attached. Articles 462, 465.

If the tree can be considered a 'building', its fall is within the strict liability envisioned by Articles 670, 2322. *Davis v. Royal-Globe Insurance Companies*, 257 La. 523, 242 So. 2d 839 (1970). *See also Cothern v. LaRocca*, 255 La. 673, 232 So. 2d 473 (1970). However, as the reasoning of the latter decision indicates, under our jurisprudence there is substantial doubt as to whether a tree can be considered a 'building' for purposes of the owner's strict liability under Articles 670, 2322.

Nevertheless, as will be set forth more fully below, Article 2317 (to be quoted below) provides for the liability of an owner of things for damages caused through their defect. In the scheme of the Civil Code of Louisiana, which is based upon the scheme of the French Civil Code, this article rather than Articles 670 and 2322 is the code basis of the fault of an owner in possessing and failing to properly maintain a tree on his property which, through its defect, falls and causes injury to a neighbor or passer-by who is himself without fault.

We pretermit, therefore, whether by analogy the strict liability of an owner for damages caused through a defect of buildings on his premises might not also include a liability for damages caused by fault or ruin of any other immovable part of his premises, such as a tree. But *see Langlois v. Allied Chemical Corporation*, 258 La. 1067, 249 So. 2d 133 (1971).

The 'Fault' Scheme of the Civil Code

Articles 2315 through 2324 of the Louisiana Civil Code comprise the code's entire chapter of legal principle regulating offenses and quasi- offenses.

The underlying principle is provided by Article 2315: 'Every act whatever of man that causes damage to another obliges him by whose Fault it happened to repair it....' The remaining articles constitute amplifications as to what constitutes 'fault' and under what circumstances a defendant may be held liable for his act or that of a person or thing for which he is responsible.

Article 2316 provides for delictual (tort) responsibility for negligent acts or omissions: 'Every person is responsible for the damage he occasions not merely by his act, but his negligence, his imprudence, or his want of skill.' However, negligence is not necessarily a basis for the obligation to respond in damages for harm caused by persons or things for which we are responsible as provided by the subsequent Articles 2317 through 2322.[61]

We have already noted that the owner of a building is held to strict liability under Article 2322 for damage caused by a defect in his building, without regard to his own personal negligence. Likewise, under Article 2320 it has long been settled that a master (employer) is liable for the harm

---

[61] Article 2317 provides for liability for damages caused by a person for whom we are responsible or by a thing in our custody. Article 2318 provides for liability of a parent or tutor for acts done by a minor for whom he is responsible. Article 2319 provides for liability of a curator for damage done by his interdict. Article 2320 provides for the liability of an employer for the act of his employee in the exercise of the employment. Article 2321 provides for the liability of an owner of an animal for harm done by it. Article 2322 provides for the liability of an owner of a building for damage occasioned by its fall.

caused through his servant's (employee's) unreasonable creation of risk of injury to others (negligence), despite the freedom from personal negligence of the master thus vicariously held liable. *See Blanchard v. Ogima*, 253 La. 34, 215 So. 2d 902 (1968), citing long-established jurisprudence.

Recently, upon examination of the code scheme of fault liability, we held that under Article 2318 the parent of a minor child is liable for the damage caused by the child's conduct which creates an unreasonable risk of injury to others, even though the parent himself is not personally negligent and the child is too young to be personally negligent. *Turner v. Bucher*, 308 So. 2d 270 (La. 1975), following *Mullins v. Blaise*, 37 La.Ann. 92 (1885) and overruling intervening jurisprudence. Likewise reverting to earlier jurisprudence, in *Holland v. Buckley*, 305 So. 2d 113 (La. 1974) we held that under Article 2321 the owner of an animal which creates an unreasonable risk of injury to others is liable for the harm done by that animal because of its deficient conduct, even though the owner himself was not personally negligent.

The principle of legal fault thus recognized under Articles 2318, 2320, 2321, and 2322--and indicated as applicable under Article 2319[62], it is argued, should also be held to apply to the liability under Article 2317 of the guardian (in this case, the owner) of a thing for damages caused by its defect.

Summary of Principles of Legal Fault Under Articles 2318, 2320, 2321 and 2322

To summarize the principle of legal fault thus already recognized in favor of an injured person himself without fault:

> When harm results from the conduct or defect of a person or thing which creates an unreasonable risk of harm to others, a person legally responsible under these code articles for the supervision, care, or guardianship of the person or thing may be held liable for the damage thus caused, despite the fact that no personal negligent act or inattention on the former's part is proved. The liability arises from his legal relationship to the person or thing whose conduct or defect creates an unreasonable risk of injuries to others.

The Fault of the person thus liable is based upon his failure to prevent the person or thing for whom he is responsible from causing such unreasonable risk of injury to others. Thus, the person to whom society allots the supervision, care, or guardianship (custody) of the risk-creating person or thing bears the loss resulting from creation of the risk, rather than some innocent third person harmed as a consequence of his failure to prevent the risk. His fault rests upon his failure to prevent the risk-creating harm and upon his obligation to guard against the condition or activity (by the person or thing for which he is responsible) which creates the unreasonable risk of harm to others.

This jurisprudence recognizes that the injured person must prove the vice (i.e., unreasonable risk of injury to another) in the person or thing whose act causes the damage, and that the damage resulted from this vice. Once this is proved, the owner or guardian responsible for the person or thing can escape liability only if he shows the harm was caused by the fault of the victim, by the fault of a third person, or by an irresistible force.

The legal fault thus arising from our code provisions has sometimes been referred to as strict liability.

The plaintiff argues that Article 2317 by its express terms statutorily mandates these principles of legal fault as applicable when an innocent neighbor or bystander is damaged because of

---

[62] This concerns the liability of a curator for the act of an insane person under his care. *See*: *Turner v. Bucher*, 308 So. 2d 270, 275--76 (1975); *Scott v. McCrocklin*, 29 So. 2d 619 (La.App. 2 Cir. 1947), Noted, 8 La.L.Rev. 144 (1947); *Yancey v. Maestri*, 155 So. 509 (La.App.Orl. 1934); Stone, Tort Doctrine in Louisiana, 17 Tul.L.Rev. 159, 189--92.

the vice or defect of a thing (the tree); just as we have already recognized these principles of legal fault as applicable and mandated by the companion articles (2318, 2320, 2321, 2322) in the series mandating legal fault for the acts of persons or things for which we are responsible.

Liability of the Owner-Guardian of a Thing under Article 2317

Article 2317 provides: 'We are responsible, not only for the damage occasioned by our own act, but for that which is caused by the act of persons for whom we are answerable, or of things which we have in our custody. This however, is to be understood with the following modifications.'[63]

This provision of our 1870 civil code was also found in our civil codes of 1808 and 1825. Civil Code 1808, p. 320, Art. 20, par. 1; Civil Code of 1825, Article 2296. In French text, it is identical to French Civil Code Article 1384(1) (which, however, does not contain the last sentence).

The provision that one is responsible for damage 'which is caused by the act ... of things which we have in our custody' is a translation of the provision of the French article, taken verbatim from the French Civil Code, that one is responsible for damage 'qui est cause par le fait ... des choses que l'on a sous sa garde.' See Article 2317 La.C.C.Comp.Ed. in 17 West's LSA-C.C. p. 17 (1972).[64]

Articles 2315 through 2322 express the same concepts and represent the same scheme as French Civil Code Articles 1382 through 1386, of which they are to a large part verbatim translations. See Articles 2315--17 La.C.C.Comp.Ed. in 17 West's LSA-C.C. pp. 14--21 (1972). In this context, in applying the French verbatim counterpart code provision, the liability of the guardian of a thing for damages caused through the vice or defect of the thing has been interpreted as providing for liability of the guardian without personal negligence on his part, his legal fault (as also in the case of the owner of a building or of an animal) being based upon the breach of his legal obligation to keep his thing in such condition or in such control that it does no damage to others. These interpretations have been reached not only in France but also in Belgium and in Quebec, which like Louisiana adopted a civil code scheme of articles and concepts based almost verbatim on the articles of the French Civil Code.

* * * * *

We find no reason why Civil Code Article 2317 should not be interpreted as incorporating a similar concept of legal fault. As with the French, Canadian, and Belgian counterparts--each found in the same code scheme of delictual liability--, the code provision for the liability of the owner of a thing for damages caused by its vice would be unnecessary if the basis of code liability thus expressly provided were only for negligence, a basis already provided by the preceding Article 2316 (and its preceding counterparts in the French, Canadian, and Belgian codes).

---

[63] The "modifications" are set forth by the "following" Articles 2317--2322. Thus, an employer is answerable for the damage occasioned by his servants "in the exercise of the functions in which employed."Article 2320. The owner of an animal is answerable for the damage it causes, unless "the animal had been lost, or had strayed more than a day" in which case a different measure of responsibility is provided. Article 2321. The owner of a building is reponsible for the damage caused "by its ruin." Article 2322. The other articles in the series do not provide any other modification of the liability of the owner of other things for the damage they cause.

[64] At this point, however, we should note that the English translation of 'sous sa garde' as 'in our custody' does not fully express the concept of the 'garde' of a thing--the legal responsibility for its care of keeping--, so that one may lose the custody of a thing without losing its 'garde'. H.L. & J. Mazeaud, Traite The orique et Pratique de la Responsabilite Civile, Volume 2, No. 1160 (6th ed. 1970); Verlander, We are Responsible ..., 2 Tulane Civil Law Forum No. 2, p. 61 (1974).

At Note, Things in One's Custody, 43 Tul.L.Rev. 907, 912 (1969), a French legal dictionary is quoted as defining 'garde' as: 'Obligation imposed by the law on the proprietor of a thing or of an animal or on the one who avails himself of it to prevent this thing or this animal from causing damage to others.' It is there noted that French doctrinal writers afford the term an even broader definition.

Further, as noted, we have previously adopted the concept of legal fault without personal negligence of a parent for the deficient act of his child (Article 2318), of an employer for the deficient act of his employee (Article 2320), of an owner for the damage caused through the deficient act of his animal (Article 2321), and of an owner for the damage caused by the defect of his building (Article 2322). It is logically consistent and in accord with the scheme of delictual responsibility represented by these companion code articles to hold that, similarly, Article 2317 embodies the concept of the legal fault of the guardian of a thing for the damage caused by the defect of his thing.

The implication to the contrary in *Cartwright v. Fireman's Insurance Co.*, 254 La. 330, 223 So. 2d 822 (1969) is inconsistent with the earlier jurisprudence interpreting Articles 2320 and 2322, cited above, and with the later jurisprudence interpreting Articles 2318 and 2321, also cited above (as well as with the interpretations by other civilian jurisdictions of comparable provisions of their civil codes set in similar code context as Louisiana's Article 2317). The interpretation of Article 2317 we reach today is more in accord with jurisprudence interpreting companion code articles and with the functional intent of Article 2317 within our Civil Code's general scheme of fault liability.

The Fall of a Tree

With regard to liability for the fall, the tree, is a thing, *see* Civil Code Articles 462, 465. In civilian jurisdictions, such as France, Belgium, and Spain, the owner of a tree is liable for the fall of a tree due to its disease or decay, without negligence on the owner's part. Stone, cited above, Nos. 81--89. Mazeaud, cited above, No. 1269. *See also* Demogue, Responsabilite pour la chute d'un arbe, Rev.Trim.Dr.Civ. 345 (1936). These authorities note that the owner may be liable, though the tree's fall results also from an external force such as a wind or an accident in the course of felling it.

* * * * *

Our brothers of the Second Circuit analogously have held a landlord liable to his tenant for damages caused by the fall of a tree, although it fell without negligence on the landlord's part. *Pollard v. Roberts*, 306 So. 2d 801 (La.App. 2 Cir. 1975). The liability imposed was essentially founded upon the strict liability of an owner-landlord to his tenant for vices or defects in the premises, Civil Code Articles 2692, 2695, a liability similar in nature to the strict liability of an owner to a neighbor or passerby for damage caused by vices or defects of his building.

Application of these Principles to the Present Facts

In the present case, the plaintiff neighbor has proved (a) that the thing (tree) which caused the damage was in the care (custody) of the defendant owner,[65] (b) the defect or vice of the tree, and (c) that his damage occurred through this defect or vice. The owner-guardian of the defective tree is therefore liable for his legal fault in maintaining the defective tree and in preventing its vice from causing injury, unless he prove that the damage was caused by the fault of the victim, by the fault of a third person, or by an irresistible force.

The owner contends that the high wind of the night constituted such an intervening force exculpating him from liability. However, the force contemplated by the jurisprudence is an event which happens from an irresistible cause or force not foreseeable, usually a vis major or act occasioned exclusively by the violence of nature without the contribution by legal fault of any human.

---

[65] In Verlander, We are Responsible ..., 2 Tulane Civil Law Forum, No. 2, p. 64 (1974), which contains a perceptive and thorough analysis of the French, Quebecois, and Louisiana interpretations, it is suggested: "(T)he things in one's care are those things to which one bears such a relationship as to have the right of direction and control over them, and to draw some kind of benefit from them. This relationship will ordinarily be associated with ownership, but the guardianship will also belong to the bailee, the lessee, the usufructuary, the borrower for use and the repairmen, among others. It will not belong to the agent or the mandatory, the employee or the servant, or to anyone else for whom there is a responsible principal. The owner may transfer the guardianship by transferring the thing to another who will bear such a relationship to the thing as to himself have the care of it. He may also lose the care of this thing, principally by the theft of the thing."

Article 3556(14), (15); *Thompson v. Commercial National Bank*, 156 La. 479, 100 So. 688 (1924); *Barnes v. Beirne*, 38 La.Ann. 280 (1886).

Here, the wind, although high and gusty, was not so abnormal as to be unforeseeable. The wind was not, for instance, of hurricane force, so as to permit its being classified as a reasonably unforeseeable violent manifestation of nature causing the damage independent of any defect of the tree, since a healthy tree as well as a diseased one might be overblown.

The defendant owner-guardian of the tree, therefore, is not exculpated of liability, for the wind was not under our code a fortuitous event. The gust of wind which contributed to the fall of the diseased tree was not unforeseeable in the vicinity, nor was it of irresistible force. No showing is made that the fault of the victim or of any third person contributed to (i.e., was a substantial factor in) the fall of the tree.

* * * * *

NOTES & QUESTIONS

1.   What is the prima facie case for an action under 2317? How does this differ from a negligence action?

2.   What does it mean to require that the "thing" pose an unreasonable risk of harm? How do you determine whether the risk is reasonable or unreasonable?

3.   *Compare* the approach in the primary case with the approach in a case applying the amended version of La. Civ. Code arts. 2317, 2317.1, reprinted immediately below.

MONSON
v.
TRAVELERS PROPERTY & CASUALTY INSURANCE COMPANY
955 So. 2d 758, 06-921 (La.App. 5 Cir. 2007)

WICKER, J.

The judgment before this court is a grant of a defense motion for summary judgment in which the trial court dismissed plaintiff's action. We affirm.

Plaintiff, Nancy Monson, filed this action against several defendants, including Toys "R" Us-Delaware, Inc. (Toys "R" Us) and the Parish of Jefferson (Parish), for injuries sustained when she stepped in a hole in a grassy area between the Toys "R" Us parking lot curbing and the sidewalk. The matter was joined and discovery ensued. Subsequently, both Toys "R" Us and the Parish filed motions for summary judgment. After a hearing, the trial court granted both motions finding that, as a matter of law, neither Toy "R" Us nor the Parish owed a duty to plaintiff, and further, that the Parish had no notice of the defect. Those rulings are the subject of this appeal filed by plaintiff.

Initially we note that, although the appeal is from the grant of summary judgment in favor of both the Parish and Toys "R" Us, in brief to this court plaintiff only addresses issues regarding Toys "R" Us. Assignments of error not briefed or argued before this court are deemed abandoned. *Milton v. Elmwood Care, Inc.,* 95-442 (La.App. 5 Cir. 1995), 664 So. 2d 503. Consequently, in this opinion we will only consider the propriety of the grant of summary judgment in favor of Toys "R" Us.

The facts surrounding the incident are undisputed. Plaintiff drove to Toys "R" Us to purchase a birthday gift. After she completed that task, she decided to meet her daughter for a meal at a restaurant across the street. She moved her car to the edge of the Toys "R" Us parking lot that was closest to the Hessmer Street Restaurant. As she stepped over the parking lot curbing onto the grassy area to reach the sidewalk, she stepped in a hole and fell, causing injuries to her ankle and leg. In her deposition, Ms. Monson testified that she did not move her car to the restaurant parking lot even though parking spaces were available there because she "didn't want her car hit."

Toys "R" Us admitted it was responsible for maintaining the grassy area pursuant to its lease with the owner of the property. However, counsel for Toys "R" Us argued successfully in the trial court that no duty was owed to the plaintiff because adequate pedestrian walkways were provided and maintained, but plaintiff chose instead to use an area which was never intended to be a pedestrian walkway to get to a restaurant across the street.

A summary judgment is appropriate "only if the pleadings, depositions, answers to interrogatories, and admissions on file, together with affidavits, show that there is no genuine issue as to material fact and that the mover is entitled to judgment as a matter of law." La. C.C.P. art. 966(B). The mover bears the initial burden of proof. However, if the mover will not bear the burden of proof at trial, it is not necessary for the mover to negate all essential elements of the adverse party's claim, action, or defense, but rather to point out to the court that there is an absence of factual support for one or more elements essential to the adverse party's claim, action, or defense. Thereafter, if the adverse party fails to produce factual support sufficient to establish that he will be able to satisfy his evidentiary burden of proof at trial, there is no genuine issue of material fact. La. C.C.P. art. 966 C(2).

To impose liability for an unreasonably dangerous defect a plaintiff has the burden to show that the thing was in the custodian's custody or control, it had a vice or defect that presented an unreasonable risk of harm, the defendant knew or should have known of the unreasonable risk of harm, and that the damage was caused by the defect. La. C.C. art. 2317.1; *Dauzat v. Thompson Const. Co., Inc.,* 02-989 (La.App. 5 Cir. 2003), 839 So. 2d 319. The addition of the element of knowledge to article 2317.1 has effectively turned it from strict liability to a negligence claim. *Leonard v. Parish of Jefferson,* 05-32 (La.App. 5 Cir. 2005), 902 So. 2d 502.

A threshold issue in any negligence action is whether the defendant owed the plaintiff a duty. *Verdin v. Rogers,* 05-664 (La.App. 5 Cir. 2006), 926 So. 2d 603. Whether a duty is owed is a question of law. However, whether defendant has breached a duty owed is a question of fact. *Mundy v. Department of Health and Human Resources,* 620 So. 2d 811 (La.1993). The inquiry is whether the plaintiff has any law, statutory, jurisprudential, or arising from general principles of fault, to support his claim. *Verdin v. Rogers, supra.* Thus, plaintiff must show that Toys "R" Us had a duty to her to make sure the grassy area in which she fell was free from holes and safe for pedestrians.

While an owner and occupier of land has a duty to discover any unreasonably dangerous conditions existing on his premises and to either correct those conditions or to warn of their existence, an owner is not the insurer of the safety of visitors. The duty of a property owner is to keep their premises in a safe condition for use in a manner consistent with the purposes for which they are intended. *Dingler v. Zurich Commercial Ins. Co.,* 02-674 (La.App. 3 Cir. 2002), 833 So. 2d 524.

Not every defect gives rise to liability. The defect must be of such a nature to constitute a dangerous condition, which would reasonably be expected to cause injury to a prudent person using ordinary care under the circumstances. *Amest v. City of Breaux Bridge,* 01-1034 (La.App. 3 Cir. 2001), 801 So. 2d 582.

As this court has explained in *Stone v. Hebert,* 99-1394 (La.App. 5 Cir. 2000), 762 So. 2d 220 at 222. A landowner owes a plaintiff a duty to discover any unreasonably dangerous condition and to either correct the condition or warn of its existence. It is the court's obligation to decide which risks are unreasonable, based upon the facts and circumstances of each case. In determining whether a given condition is unreasonably dangerous, the degree to which the damage may be observed by a potential victim, who may then provide self-protection, is a major factor. *Id.* (Citations omitted)

In our *de novo* review[1] of the issue of whether the condition of the grassy area presented an unreasonable risk of harm we are mindful of the fact that the criterion for this decision is "not a simple rule of law which can be applied mechanically. It requires a balancing of claims and interests, a weighing of the risk and the gravity of harm, and the consideration of individual and societal rights and obligations." *Bell v. State of La., et al.,* 553 So. 2d 902, 907 (La.App. 4 Cir. 1989) (Citations omitted).

While a landowner has an obligation to maintain lawns and other grassy areas, that obligation does not require a "table-top" smooth surface. *Wood v. Cambridge Mut. Fire Ins. Co.* (La.App. 2 Cir. 1986), 486 So. 2d 1129. It is inherent in grassy areas that are not intended or designed for use as a walkway, that they present minor hazards such as uneven ground or holes which could cause a person to trip and fall. Such conditions do not amount to defects that present an unreasonable risk of injury to tenants. *Id.*

In the matter before us, plaintiff argues the trial court erred in granting the motion for summary judgment because Toy "R" Us knew or should have known that the area was used by pedestrians, and caused several holes to be dug in the area after the removal of trees and shrubs, making the area unreasonably dangerous. To support this claim, plaintiff presented photos which show two plastic cups, and holes under the grassy cover of the area. Plaintiff asserts the cups are from patrons of a nearby bar using the area to their vehicles parked in the Toys "R" Us parking lot. Plaintiff also asserts that Toys "R" Us had actual knowledge of the holes it created. Additionally, plaintiff testified that she returned to the area a week and a half after her fall and photographed three holes in a relatively straight line which were about equidistant from each other. Plaintiff also offered photographs of the area to show that some shrubs still remain in the area. While plaintiff asserts that Acadian, a former company contracted by Toys "R" Us to keep the area mowed and maintained, dug the holes to remove trees, there is no evidence of that in the record. If, in fact, Toys "R" Us had created the holes by the removal of trees, and failed to cover the holes, the condition which caused plaintiff's fall may have given rise to an unreasonable risk of harm under the circumstances. In that case Toy "R" Us would have a duty to correct the condition it created. However, the assertion that Toys "R" Us created the condition and that the area was used by bar patrons is merely a speculation by plaintiff and is unsupported.

Knowledge of the condition is an essential element for finding liability. Given the "circumstantial evidence" plaintiff presents, we cannot find she can meet her burden of proof on that essential issue.

While we do not agree with the conclusive statement made by the trial court that there is no duty owed by Toys "R" Us to maintain the grassy area, we do agree with the trial court that the summary judgment should be granted. We believe holes created in the area where plaintiff fell could give rise to the level of unreasonable risk of harm under the reasonable person standard. However, the plaintiff failed in her burden of proof that the holes were created by Toys "R" Us, or that Toys "R" Us had any knowledge of the holes. Thus, plaintiff has failed to show that, as a matter of law, Toys "R" Us owes her a duty that has been breached.

For the foregoing reasons, we affirm the judgment of the trial court and assess costs of this appeal to plaintiff.

AFFIRMED.

---

[1] The appellate review of a grant of a summary judgment is *de novo*. *Prince v. K-Mart Corp.,* 99-253 (La.App. 5 Cir. 1999), 742 So. 2d 718.

NOTE

1.   Article 2317 imposed liability for things in our "custody," a mistranslation of "garde" contained in the French version of the article. The Louisiana Supreme Court had developed a number of cases involving the concept of garde. *See, Ross v. La Coste de Monterville*, 502 So. 2d 1026 (La. 1987); *King v. Louviere*, 543 So. 2d 1327 (La. 1989), and *Doughty v. Insured Lloyds Insurance Co.*, 576 So. 2d 461 (La.1991). Should the concept of garde be carried over into the cases interpreting Article 2317.1? When does one have garde of a thing? *See Spott v. Otis Elevator Co.*, 601 So. 2d 1355 (La. 1992). Can the presumption of garde be rebutted? *See Doughty v. Insured Lloyd's Insurance Co.*, *supra*. Can two or more people simultaneously have garde of a thing? *See, King v. Louviere, supra.*

B.   CHILDREN

La. Civil Code Article 2318.   Acts of minors

The father and the mother and, after the decease of either, the surviving parent, are responsible for the damage occasioned by their minor or unemancipated children, residing with them, or placed by them under the care of other persons, reserving to them recourse against those persons.

The same responsibility attaches to the tutors of minors.

TURNER

v.

BUCHER

308 So. 2d 270 (La. 1975)

BARHAM, J.

The precise question presented for our determination in this suit is whether the father of a six-year-old child is liable for damages which arose when the child struck one of the plaintiffs with his bicycle on a city sidewalk. The activity causing plaintiff's injury would have been sufficiently negligent, imprudent and careless to constitute civil negligence if the child had been a person of discernment. The court of appeal denied recovery. 293 So. 2d 535 (La.App. 4 Cir. 1974). We granted certiorari to review that judgment. 295 So. 2d 808 (La. 1974). We reverse the judgment of the court of appeal.

Laura Wallace Turner, a sixty-two-year-old woman, was walking on a sidewalk in the city of New Orleans when she was struck from the rear and injured by a bicycle ridden by six-year-old Gregory Bucher. In their trial court petition, the plaintiffs alleged the child's independent negligence. It is not disputed that if gauged by the usual standards of conduct, the actions of Gregory Bucher would have constituted negligence on his part. However, plaintiffs conceded that under the jurisprudence, a six-year-old child could not be capable of fault or negligence.

On appeal, plaintiffs urged only the personal negligence of the parents in their supervison of the child as the basis of liability of the father for the injury caused by the child. Before this Court, the plaintiffs have broadened their theory for recovery in writ application, in brief, and in argument; and we must properly resolve the case before us under the applicable law. *See* La.C.C.P. art. 2164.

The court of appeal found no independent negligence by the father; nor do we. Therefore, we must resolve the issue of his liability under the Civil Code articles relating to paternal responsibility. Article 237 of the Louisiana Civil Code provides:

> 'Fathers and mothers are answerable for the offenses or quasi-offenses committed by their children, in the cases prescribed under the title: Of Quasi-Contracts, and of Offenses and Quasi-Offences.'

Under the title Of Offenses and Quasi-Offenses, Article 2318 provides:

'The father, or (and)[1] after his decease, the mother, are responsible for the damage occasioned by their minor (or)[2] unemancipated children, residing with them, or placed by them under the care of other persons, reserving to them recourse against those persons.

'The same responsibility attaches to the tutors of minors.'

The original source of our Article 2318 was Paragraph 2, Art. 20, Title III, Book III of the Projet du Gouvernement (1800). In Article 20 of the Projet, the drafters placed several paragraphs outlining the various aspects of delictual responsibility for other persons, things, and animals under one's control. When the Code Napoleon was adopted in 1804, it followed the format of the Projet by listing the many facets of delictual responsibility under a single article, Article 1384. However, the French Code did not follow the precise language of the Projet and it departed in substance in some instances.

When we adopted our Code of 1808, we followed the Projet du Gouvernement of 1800 rather than the Code Napoleon. We also utilized the French method of placing many facets of delictual responsibility under one article, our Article 20. Paragraph 2 of that article at pages 320--322, Title 4, § 2, related to paternal liability and it was a literal translation of the source paragraph in the Projet du Gouvernement. It read:

'The father, and after the death of the husband, the mother is responsible for the delinquency (de lits) of their minor children.'

In the Projet du Gouvernement and in our Code of 1808, the liability of 'parents, Masters, or principals' was imposed only if they 'could have prevented the delinquency (de lits) and have failed to do it.' (Emphasis here and elsewhere supplied). In the Code Napoleon, only fathers, mothers, Tutors and artisans were excused from responsibility if '... they were not able to prevent the act which gives rise to such responsibility.'

In the Louisiana Projet of 1825, as well as in the Code of 1825, the single long article delineating the liability of persons occupying positions of responsibility for others was broken into several articles. When this was done, a drastic change was made in the conditions for culpability. We then provided in Article 2299 of the Code of 1825 that responsibility of masters, employers, Teachers and artisans attached only when they '... might have prevented the act which caused the damage, and have not done it.' However, very significantly Under Article 2297 the father and the mother were assigned the responsibility for the damage caused by the minor children and were denied any conditions releasing them from their paternal liability.

For the first time in Louisiana, teachers and artisans were permitted an opportunity to escape responsibility for acts of their students and apprentices; and, More importantly for the case at bar, Parents were for the first time placed in a position of strict responsibility for the acts of their children. Another very important change occurred in the transition from the 1808 Code to the 1825 Code. In 1808, the parents' responsibility was for the 'delinquency' or 'delicts' of their minor children. From 1825 through subsequent revisions, the parents were responsible '... for the Damage occasioned by their minor or unemancipated children'. This change in language, though now coinciding with Article 1384 of the Code Napoleon as well as with the Code Civil[3] in effect in France today, is significant in

---

[1] The original French in Article 2297 of our Civil Code of 1825, which became Article 2318 in the 1870 Civil Code, did not contain the French word "ou," which is translated "or," but rather "et," which is translated "and." Art. 2318, La.C.C. Comp.Ed., in 17 West's LSA-C.C. 17–18 (Dainow ed. 1973).

[2] The "or" is not part of the original French in the Civil Code of 1825, Art. 2297. The original French would translate better if the comma as well as the "or" were omitted. *Id.*

[3] In this opinion, when "Code Civil" is used in reference to the Code Napoleon of 1804, it is followed by the date, i.e., (1804). In all other instances it refers to the Code Civil presently in effect in France.

Louisiana for a reason other than this similarity. 'Damage,' when substituted for 'delicts,' indicates a possible lack of legal liability in some cases on the part of the minor child. Thus, liability may attach to a parent even though the child is incapable of legal liability.

The French Code Civil and the Louisiana Civil Code are thus dissimilar in their treatment of paternal responsibility for damage caused by minor children. These differences began with the adoption of the original codes in each jurisdiction and persists in the present provisions of the two codes. In France, an act of a minor child which causes damage raises a rebuttable presumption that the parent was negligent or imprudent in the 'garde'[4] or care of the child. 2 M. Planiol, Treatise on the Civil Law 507--08, 510, Nos. 909, 910B (L.S.L.I. transl. 1939). The parents' liability is thus modified to the extent that the '... father and mother ... can prove that they were not able to prevent the act which gives rise to such responsibility.' Code Civil art. 1384 (1804). When Code Civil art. 1384 was considered for adoption, it was said that the impossibility of the parent to prevent the act was the equivalent of a 'force majeure,' i.e., a fortuitous event. 13 P. Fenet, Recueil Complet des Travaux Pre paratoires du Code Civil 476 (1836); 13 Locre , La Legislation Civile, commercials et Criminally de la France 42, No. 13 (1828). Tailor was of the opinion that '(i)n order to be relieved of responsibility, the father ... has to prove nothing else but that his child was of too tender an age to act with discernment.' 11 C. Tailor, Le Droit Civil Francais--Suivant l'ordre du Code, No. 270 (1832), cited in *Johnson v. Butterworth*, 180 La. 586, 602, 606, 157 So. 121, 126, 127 (1934). Laurent, Marcade , and other French doctrinal writers, however, were of the opinion that since the responsibility imposed by French law depended upon the fault or negligence of the parents, the age of the children or their ability to discern were immaterial and irrelevant.[5]

Louisiana Civil Code art. 2318 is contrary to the French concept of a rebuttable presumption; in the former, the language is clear and unambiguous that it was the legislative intent to impose a sort of strict liability upon parents as a responsibility flowing from paternal authority. That liability is considerably stronger than the presumption at French law as it does not permit parents to escape responsibility by showing an absence of negligence on their part with regard to the 'garde' or care of minor children. However, the Louisiana and French concepts coincide in holding that nondiscerning persons do not possess the capability of knowing the consequences of their conduct; they lack the moral guilt usually associated with delictual responsibility and, therefore, they should not be legally liable for acts under an objective standard designed for normal reasoning persons[6]. Nevertheless, an innocent victim should not be denied reparation if there exists a source of financial responsibility; therefore, the parent of an infant of tender years and the curator of an insane person, who are charged with the legal 'garde' or care of these persons who cannot care for themselves, should be required to respond for the acts of those within their 'garde' because of their legal relation to and legal responsibility for these nondiscerning persons.

The leading case on this issue is *Johnson v. Butterworth*, 180 La. 586, 157 So. 121 (1934). The holding in this case, which has been much relied upon in subsequent jurisprudence, is that a parent is not responsible for the damage caused by a minor of tender years who lacks the capacity for discernment. The writer of that opinion appears to reason that the original source of Article 2318 was the French Code article 1384. 180 La. at 592, 157 So. at 123. He then rationalizes that even if there were pertinent differences between the French and the Louisiana provisions, they '... resulted merely from the arranging of the several paragraphs of article 1384 of the French Code into separate articles in the Louisiana Code (of 1825); and it is possible that this result, although of some effect, was accidental, as we shall proceed to explain.' In the several pages following the writer discusses his

---

[4] The word "garde," as used in this opinion, is the French word for safekeeping, care, protection, custody, charge, watch, heed, attention. See Cassell's French-English, English-French Dictionary 365 (Baker ed. 1951). This word is used in lieu of the English "guard" because the French "garde" better connotes the meaning of protecting others from potential harm by the child as well as protecting the child from harm.

[5] 20 F. Laurent, Principes de Droit Civil Francais 594 (1869--78); 5 V. Marcade , Revue Critique de Le gislation et de Jurisprudence 287 (1854) (hereinafter cited as Marcade).

[6] 2 M. Planiol, Treatise on the Civil Law 490--491, Nos. 879, 880 (L.S.L.I. transl. 1939).

belief that the omission from the 1825 Code of the exemption from paternal liability for those delicts of their minor children which the parents could not have prevented was accidental. We are of the opinion that the direct and original source of Article 2318 of our Code is the Projet du Gouvernement.[7] We are also of the opinion that the change in exemptions from liability of different parties in the 1825 Code was a result of specific legislative intent.

The earliest case in Louisiana interpreting our present provision for paternal delictual responsibility is *Mullins v. Blaise*, 37 La.Ann. 92 (1885).[8] In that case the court said that a six-year-old boy's act of pointing a blazing roman candle in the direction of other children and injuring one of them:

> '... was a fault of the most culpable character. It is true that by reason of the tender years and lack of discernment of the minor, this fault may not be, in a legal sense, imputable to him. But the exploded vagary of *Toullier* that this is a reason for exempting the Father from liability can find no recognition at our hands. The law itself imputes the fault to the father. It presumes that it resulted from lack of sufficient care, watchfulness and discipline on his part, in the exercise of the paternal authority. This is the very reason and foundation of the rule.'

The opinion further stated that for a similar reason, the law imposes similar responsibility upon the owner for damage occasioned by his animals which certainly have no greater power of discernment than an infant of tender years.[9]

* * * * *

In 1825, Louisiana made substantial changes in the liability for damage caused by the acts of persons for whom one is answerable or for things which one has in his custody; it is most obvious that this was done with the specific intent to realign and reassess delictual liability in this area. For example, when we adopted Civil Code Article 2318, we not only omitted the exculpating clause for parents who could not have prevented the 'delinquency,' but we also amended the article to make parents responsible for 'the damage' occasioned by their children instead of 'the delinquency' of their children. Moreover, for the first time, we introduced a new class of persons responsible for those in their custody. The article immediately following paternal liability, Article 2319, reads:

> 'The curators of insane persons are answerable for the damage occasioned by those under their care.'[13]

Our redactors apparently adopted the distinction made by Pothier between the interdicted 'insane' person and the person interdicted for other reasons. It is only the curator of the insane person to whom we have attached delictual liability. The legislature of 1825 was obviously aware that there should be a distinction in attaching responsibility for delictual acts between those who were capable of discernment and those who were not. It also seems readily apparent that those legislators did not intend persons incapable of discernment to be liable for their delicts. As it was said in *Mullins v. Blaise*, 37 La.Ann. at 93: '... this fault may not be, in a legal sense imputable to him (one incapable of discernment).' Nevertheless, the legislature very wisely chose to cast someone in damages for the

---

[7] Paragraph 2, Art. 20, Title III, Book III (1800).

[8] In an earlier case, *Marionneaux v. Brugier*, 35 La.Ann. 13 (1883) a thirteen-year-old child accidentally shot a nine-year-old child and contributory negligence was pleaded. The court actually found, as a matter of fact, that the act of the nine-year-old did not constitute contributory negligence, and did not discuss the legal aspects of contributory negligence for children.

[9] The opinion cites 5 Marcade at 270, and 2 F. Mourlon, Repetitions Ecrites sur le Code Civil 888 (11 ed. 1878-81).

[13] This is the only article concerning either curators or interdicts which is limited to the 'insane' alone.

delictual harms visited upon others by the nondiscerning. For the insane person, the law automatically imputes the fault to the curator. For the child too young to reason or have intellectual discernment, '... (t)he law itself imputes the fault to the father.'[14]

In the recent case of *Holland v. Buckley*, 305 So. 2d 113 (La. 1974), this Court reappraised the liability of the owner of an animal for damages caused by the animal. That case contains an excellent discussion of French authorities interpreting Article 1385 of the French Civil Code, which is comparable to our Civil Code Article 2321. This Court there found that our Article 2321 is a Verbatim reenactment of the equivalent article of the Projet du Gouvernement (1800). We held, in respect to the liability of the master for the harm caused by his animal, that the master is presumed to be at fault, that the fault is in the nature of strict liability, and that the owner may exculpate himself from this presumed fault only by showing that the harm was caused by the fault of the victim, the fault of a third person, or by a fortuitous event. We rejected the concept that the owner of an animal could absolve himself of fault 'by showing that he himself did not contribute to the accident by some lack of care on his part.'

Thus, in *Holland v. Buckley* we overruled jurisprudence which, according to *Johnson v. Butterworth, supra*, had held the owner of an animal answerable for the damage he has caused '... Only when the act of the animal that caused the damage is attributable to some fault or imprudence on the part of the owner of the animal.' *Johnson v. Butterworth* analogized the responsibility of an owner of an animal to the responsibility of parents for their children. That analogy is no longer applicable. A preferable analogy is to the responsibility of the curator who has the care of an insane person. La.Civil Code art. 2319.

We are of the opinion that *Johnson v. Butterworth* and other jurisprudence relieving parents from liability for the delicts of infant children who lack discernment are erroneous in their conclusions. We specifically overrule such holdings. In so doing, we reinstate the holding in *Mullins v. Blaise*, 37 La.Ann. 92 (1885) and the reasoning therein. Thus, our holding in the case before us merely constitutes a return to earlier jurisprudence which we now consider to have been correct in its interpretation of the Code. This opinion in no way affects the long line of jurisprudence which holds that certain minor children are incapable of contributory negligence. We do not here set the standard of care to which a victim is subject with regard to such a nondiscerning person. Our holding in this case is limited to a situation such as the one before us where the victim is unwarned and unsuspecting of any impending harm from the acts of a child.

We conclude that although a child of tender years may be incapable of committing a legal delict because of his lack of capacity to discern the consequences of his act, nevertheless, if the act of a child would be delictual except for this disability, the parent with whom he resides is legally at fault and, therefore, liable for the damage occasioned by the child's act. This legal fault is determined without regard to whether the parent could or could not have prevented the act of the child, i.e., without regard to the parent's negligence. It is legally imposed strict liability. This liability may be

---

[14] We are not called upon to decide in this case whether a nondiscerning minor child may also be liable for his delicts. However, it must be very apparent from our discussion of the liability of the father that it almost necessarily will follow that a nondiscerning minor child will not have delictual liability since our language has indicated that a nondiscerning minor is incapable of being legally at fault.

We are mindful of the several articles in the Code which provide that minors are responsible for their offenses and quasi-offenses. Article 1785 provides: 'The obligation arising from an offense or a quasi offense, is also binding on the minor.' Article 1874 states: 'He (a minor) is not relievable against obligations resulting from offenses or quasi offenses.' Article 2227 states: 'He is not restituable against the obligations resulting from his offenses or quasi offenses.'

We believe that our jurisprudence, the French jurisprudence and the French doctrine are all correct in finding that those minors incapable of discernment are immune from legal liability for delicts arising from negligence. Any basis in this opinion for concluding that there is no liability on the part of the minor for his offenses or his quasi-offenses is limited to the minor of tender age who is so incapable of discernment as to also be incapable of being legally at fault.

escaped when a parent shows the harm was caused by the fault of the victim, by the fault of a third person, or by a fortuitous event.

Having made the threshold determination that a father is responsible for the delicts of his minor child whether or not the child is of sufficient age to be capable of discerning the consequences of his acts, we need not determine whether this particular child, Gregory Bucher, was possessed of the requisite age and capacity to know the consequences of his act. Such an inquiry would be irrelevant and immaterial in answering the issue before us. The fact that the conduct was tortious when measured by normal standards is enough to render the father liable therefore.

Thus, we decide in this case that the father is responsible for damages to the plaintiff for the harm occasioned by the act of his child, Gregory Bucher, under Louisiana Civil Code Article 2318. Zurich Insurance Company, as insurer of the father is, of course, also liable. Since the court of appeal has not yet reviewed the case for damages, we, in keeping with our usual practice, remand the case to that court for the assessment of damages.

For the reasons assigned, judgment is rendered in favor of plaintiffs, Laura Wallace Turner and August Turner, against the defendants, Francis Bucher and Zurich Insurance Company, for such amounts as may hereinafter be assessed by the court of appeal. All costs of court are assessed against the defendants.

It is further ordered, adjudged and decreed that the case be remanded to the court of appeal for the assessment of damages.

REVERSED and **REMANDED**.

SANDERS, Chief Justice (dissenting).

Recently, in *Holland v. Buckley*, ... overruling long-established jurisprudence interpreting our code articles, the majority held that owners are strictly liable for the damage caused by domestic animals. Today, further expanding the scope of strict liability, the majority holds that parents are strictly liable for damage caused by their young children below the age of discernment. The holding creates a new no-fault liability. Under our law, parents have always been liable for damage caused by the fault of their minor children.

In so holding, the majority overrules a long line of decisions, which have carefully reviewed every aspect of our code articles.

* * * * *

The majority opinion throws no new light on the Louisiana Civil Code articles. The variance between our articles and those of the Code Napoleon was noted long ago and carefully considered in the decisions. Nonetheless, the majority declines to give effect to the explicit language of Article 237, which reads:

> 'Fathers and mothers are answerable for the offenses or quasi-offenses committed by their children, in the cases prescribed under the title: Of Quasi- Contracts, and of Offenses and Quasi-Offenses.'

The article clearly limits the vicarious liability of parents to 'the offenses and quasi-offenses committed by their children'. Article 2318, though phrased in general terms, is not inconsistent. Rather, the two articles must be construed together. LSA-C.C. Art. 17. Together, they mean that there is no parental liability without fault on the part of the child. Thus, if damage is caused by a minor child of the age of discernment, but without fault, the parent has no liability. Likewise, if damage is caused by a child too young for fault, the parent is not liable. These principles, in my opinion, are sound.

In *Toca v. Rojas*, *supra*, a fishhook held by defendant's fourteen-year-old son struck another youth in his eye. This Court found the evidence insufficient to establish that defendant's son was negligent, or at fault. In holding that the father was not liable, the Court stated:

'... While the law imputes the fault of the minor to the father, there must of necessity be some fault, actual or legal, in the act of the minor which caused the damage, before the father can be held liable in damages. Fathers and mothers are only made answerable for the offenses and quasi offenses committed by their children (C.C. 237), from which it follows that, if the act of the minor which caused the damage did not in law constitute an offense or quasi offense, there can be no paternal responsibility.'

In *Johnson v. Butterworth*, *supra*, a landmark decision making a thorough analysis of the history and meaning of the articles, this Court absolved the father of liability for the damage occasioned when his three-year-old child bit her nurse's arm. The Court held that parents are liable only for the damage of their minor children arising from offenses and quasi-offenses. Thus, parents are not liable for the damage caused by children too young to possess the reasoning power and discernment for fault.

There, this Court stated:

'In France, as we have said, the parental authority itself makes the parent responsible, for a tort committed by his minor child, unless the parent proves that he was unable to prevent the act that caused the damage. Because of that limitation on the responsibility of the parent for an injury done by his minor child, the age of the child is a matter of no importance in such a case. But, in Louisiana, the parent is responsible for a tort committed by his minor child, even though the parent could not have prevented the act that caused the injury. Because of that unqualified responsibility of the parent for a tort committed by his minor child, in Louisiana, the liability of the parent for an injury willfully inflicted by his minor child depends upon whether the child is old enough to be legally capable of committing a tort.'

In *Gott v. Scott*, *supra*, the Court formulated the principle of parental liability as follows:

'Articles 2318 and 237 of the Revised Civil Code must be read together and when that is done, it is made plain that the father is only liable for the damages caused by the offenses or quasi offenses of his minor daughter living with him.'

While relying upon French authorities, the majority announces a rule of liability for Louisiana parents far more stringent than that prevailing in France. There the parents have no liability if they prove that they could not prevent the act from which liability arises. French Civil Code Art. 1384; *Johnson v. Butterworth, supra*. The rule of liability is also more stringent than that prevailing in other states. In the common law, the parents had no vicarious liability even for the torts of a child. The child alone was resonsible. A number of states have enacted statutes imposing vicarious liability on parents. Most, if not all, of the statutes restrict liability to a child's intentional torts. They also fix a pecuniary limit on liability. Prosser, Law of Torts, (4th ed. 1971) § 123, p. 871; 55 Mich.L.Rev. 1205-1208.

Quite clearly, Louisiana's present rule ranks among the most liberal in the world for injured claimants. Parents are vicariously liable for the fault of their children in the full amount of the damage. Parents, of course, are individually liable for their own fault. I find no justification for extending parental liability or converting it into liability without fault.

Since I reject the rationale of the majority opinion, I express no opinion as to whether the six-year-old boy in the present case was capable of fault in the operation of his bicycle.

* * * * *

474

NOTES

1.   What is the liability imposed upon the parent of a non-discerning minor in *Turner*? Is it negligence? Vicarious liability? Strict liability? Absolute liability?

2.   Under La. C.C. Art. 2318 parents of a nondiscerning minor, who resides with them and who engages in conduct that would be tortious had the conduct been attributable to a discerning individual, will be held liable for the acts of that child. The legislature did not change this general principle.

3.   When combined with Article 2318, divorce of the parents and the implementation of joint custody plans raise interesting issues. If a joint custody plan provides that responsibility for the tortious conduct of the minor will rest with the parent who has physical custody of the minor at the time the tortious act is committed, will this plan provision defeat liability to third parties pursuant to La. C.C. Art 2318? *See, Henderson v. Sellers*, 815 So. 2d 853.

4.   In *Jones v. Cobb,* 834 So. 2d 13 (La.App. 2 Cir. 2002), a twelve year old batter in a sandlot softball game struck an eight year old child with a bat while swinging at a pitch. Using a risk-utility analysis, the Second Circuit determined the batter's conduct did not create an unreasonable risk of injury to the younger child, and therefore, there was no parental liability under La. C.C. Art. 2318.

5. The strict liability of a parent ends when the child reaches the age of 18. *Rhodus v. Lewis*, 193 So. 3d 215 (La.App. 1 Cir. 2016).

C.   CURATORS AND INSANE PERSONS

COMMENT

Prior to 2001, La. Civ. Code art. 2319 provided cryptically that "[t]he curators of insane persons are answerable for the damage occasioned by those under their care." The *Brady* case below was one of the few applications of that article. In 2000 the Legislature amended Article 2319 to provide as follows:

La. Civil Code Article 2319.   Acts of interdicts

Neither a curator nor an undercurator is personally responsible to a third person for a delictual obligation of the interdict in his charge solely by reason of his office.

Article 2319 appears to relieve curators and undercurators from delictual liability caused by those under their supervision. It does not prevent either the curator or undercurator from being found liable due to their independent fault. This newly enacted code article significantly changes the law regarding liability of curators and awaits judicial interpretation.

In order to clarify the liability of a curator or undercurator for conduct of an interdict, the legislature passed La. R.S. 9:2800.21. Such a person who performs duties without compensation is not personally liable for damage or loss caused by the interdict unless the loss was caused by gross negligence or willful and wanton misconduct by the curator or undercurator. This limitation of liability does not apply if there is insurance coverage, but recovery for damages or loss is limited to the amount of coverage.

BRADY
v.
STATE
525 So. 2d 102 (La.App. 3 Cir. 1988)

DOMENGEAUX, J.

Dora H. Brady and Stephen Brady commenced these proceedings to recover the damages they sustained as the result of an injury Dora Brady suffered while at a street dance sponsored by the Pinecrest State School for its residents. The Bradys named as the defendant, the State of Louisiana, in particular, the Department of Health and Human Resources, the state agency responsible for the Pinecrest School. The Trial Court rendered judgment in favor of the State, dismissing the Bradys' suit at their cost. The Court, in oral reasons, held that the State had not breached any duty imposed for the benefit of the Bradys and that it was, therefore, not negligent in its supervision of the street dance or the residents.

The Pinecrest State School is a controlled residential community administered by the State to provide living facilities for mentally handicapped individuals. The School, in November of 1984 when Brady suffered her injury, had approximately 1620 residents, of which eighty-six percent were profoundly or severely mentally handicapped and fourteen percent were moderately or mildly handicapped. Approximately 500 of the 1620 residents suffered from convulsive disorders which caused grand mal and petit mal seizures.

The premise underlying the administration of the Pinecrest School, as stated by Coats Stucky a Mental Retardation Facility Administrator IV, and the Superintendent of Pinecrest in November of '84, is to provide the residents with a protected living environment without totally restricting their activity. The residents live in cottage dormitories in groups not exceeding 24 persons. In accordance with Medi-cade requirements, three supervisory personnel, one Resident Training Specialist No. 2 (RTS-II) and two Resident Training Specialists (RTS's), are responsible for the residents around the clock.

On the evening of November 7, 1984, the residents of Pinecrest were enjoying their annual street dance on the school grounds. The event, which consisted of a band and concession booths or tables, was open to all Pinecrest residents, employees, both on and off-duty, and their families. Approximately 400 of the residents participated in the dance.

Dora Brady, the plaintiff, a clerk-typist-II at Pinecrest, was off-duty on the evening of November 7th and chose to participate in the festivities. Brady was injured about 6:35 or 6:45 that evening when she was unexpectedly struck from the rear by a person she described as a large light-skinned woman. Brady fell to the ground landing on her left foot causing it to break. The person who caused Brady to fall, a resident of Pinecrest, fell on top of her.

The resident who fell on Brady was Berdie Edwards. Edwards, a long time resident of Pinecrest, was a woman in her 60's. She was moderately mentally handicapped and was one of the many residents who experienced seizures.

Lemroy Culbert, Jr., an equipment operator at Pinecrest, was on duty the evening of the street dance and was responsible for patrolling the dance area. Culbert testified that he did not have an unobstructed view of the incident but, he did see Brady and Edwards fall to the ground. He testified that from his position in the crowd, approximately fifteen feet from the women, it appeared that Edwards either intentionally hit or involuntarily fell against the back of Brady's legs causing Brady to fall backwards.

Culbert, upon seeing the incident, went to the assistance of the women. He found both Brady and Edwards on the ground in an area partially paved and partially covered with gravel. Culbert testified that he permitted Edwards to lay on the ground for a short period of time because she was having a seizure. He was confident in his assessment that Edwards had experienced a seizure because her eyes were closed and she appeared as she had on the previous occasions when he had seen her experience seizures.

Culbert also testified that his instructions on the evening of the street dance were to return any resident who experienced one seizure to his or her dormitory room and that any resident who experienced three seizures was to be brought to the hospital. He did not state how many residents, if any, were brought to the hospital but, he did state that many residents experienced seizures.

The testimony of Paul Murphy, another employee of Pinecrest who assisted the women after their fall, was entered into the record by way of a stipulation. The parties stipulated that Murphy, who was approximately six to eight feet from the women, did not see what transpired, but did assist the women after the incident. The parties also stipulated that Murphy believed Edwards had experienced a seizure.

Hazel Paige, the RTS-II of Cottage 215, Edwards' cottage, testified that most of the twenty-one or twenty-three residents of Cottage 215 attended the dance. Paige stated that a short time before Brady was injured, Edwards, apparently because of a sense of insecurity, chose to stay close to another Pinecrest employee. Paige then told the Court that subsequent to the employee being called away to assist at a concession stand, Edwards chose to remain close to her (Paige). Paige stated that Edwards held her (Paige's) arm and that she assisted Edwards in the purchase of a sandwich and a drink. Paige then testified that Edwards, who was free to go about the facilities as she chose, let go of her arm and walked about fifty feet across the street from where the two of them were originally standing. Paige clearly explained that Edwards did not require one-on-one supervision and that she chose to remain close to her and the other Pinecrest employee entirely by her own choosing.

Paige testified that about two or three minutes after Edwards left she heard someone say that Edwards had experienced a seizure. When she arrived at the scene she saw Edwards, but did not believe that she had experienced a seizure. Paige, who was personally familiar with Edwards, stated that Edwards might not have a seizure for three or four months, but then could experience two in one month.

On appeal, the Bradys contend that the Trial Court erred in concluding that the State was not negligent. The Bradys, in essence, maintain that the law imposed on the State the duty of supervising the Pinecrest residents in a manner that would prevent them from injuring off-duty employees attending the street dance. The Bradys argue that the State breached its duty when it failed to prevent Edwards from injuring Dora Brady. The Bradys additionally maintain that the State should be found strictly liable in accordance with La.Civ.Code arts. 2317 (1870) and 2319 (1870). We conclude, as did the Trial Judge, that the State did not breach any duty imposed for the benefit of the Bradys and that it would be inappropriate to impose strict liability in this instance. We will, therefore, affirm the judgment of the District Court.

In Louisiana, in suits such as the instant case in which recovery is founded on allegations of negligence, the duty-risk analysis is utilized. The Louisiana Supreme Court in *Forest v. State, Louisiana Department of Transportation and Development,* 493 So. 2d 563 (La. 1986) recently restated the elements of the duty-risk analysis. The elements, as stated by the *Forest* Court, are: (1) Was the defendant's conduct a cause in fact of the plaintiff's injury? (2) Did the defendant owe the plaintiff a legal duty which encompassed the particular risk of harm to which the plaintiff was exposed? (3) Did the defendant breach its legal duty? and (4) Did the plaintiff sustain any damage? *See also,* La.Civ.Code art. 2315 (1870) (as amended); *Hill v. Lundin and Associates, Inc.,* 260 La. 542, 256 So. 2d 620 (1972); *Dixie Drive It Yourself System, Inc. v. American Beverage Co.,* 242 La. 471, 137 So. 2d 298 (1962).

We may immediately proceed to the question of the legal duty imposed because causation-in-fact is not at issue. We believe the issue is whether the State owed Dora Brady a duty to protect her from being unexpectedly knocked to the ground by a properly supervised moderately mentally handicapped resident experiencing a seizure, whose history of seizures reveals that they are infrequent and unpredictable. We do not believe the law imposed such a duty on the State.

In determining the scope of the State's duty, we surveyed the policy considerations announced in *Clomon v. Monroe City School Board,* 490 So. 2d 691 (La.App. 2 Cir. 1986). The Second Circuit in *Clomon* reviewed the following considerations: (1) the ease of association between the risk and the particular injury at issue; (2) the administrative burden that could result from recognizing the scope of the duty; (3) the economic ability of each party to liquidate the loss; (4) the moral culpability of each party; (5) the type, and the social and economic utility of the defendant's activity; and (6) the historical development of either or both the statutory law and the jurisprudence.

The evidence indicates that Edwards knocked Brady to the ground as the result of an involuntary seizure that could not have been predicted. Absent just short of sheltering Edwards away from all human contact, no amount of supervision could have prevented Brady's injury.

The fact that this incident occurred during the Pinecrest street dance is not significant. The two primary factors which combined to cause the injury were the fact that Brady was struck from the rear and the unpredictability of Edwards' seizures. Brady's injury, considering the contributing factors, could have easily occurred at any time.

The State, through its administration of the Pinecrest School, was performing a valuable and necessary function. The State's ability to provide this service should not be hampered by liability which in this case does not arise because the State was properly fulfilling its responsibilities.

The plaintiffs additionally maintain that should we decline to find for them on their negligence theory, we should render judgment for them based on the theory of strict liability. The Bradys urge that we review La.Civ.Code. arts. 2317 (1870) and 2319 (1870) and conclude that the circumstances which the State permitted to exist at the time of the incident created an unreasonable risk of harm dictating the imposition of strict liability.

Article 2317, Louisiana's statutory basis for imposing strict liability, provides:

> We are responsible, not only for the damage occasioned by our own act, but for that which is caused by the act of persons for whom we are answerable, or of the things which we have in our custody. This, however, is to be understood with the following modifications.

One of the modifications of art. 2317 is art. 2319, which provides, "[T]he curators of insane persons are answerable for the damage occasioned by those under their care."

The Louisiana Supreme Court in *Entrevia v. Hood,* 427 So. 2d 1146 (La. 1983), citing *Loescher v. Parr,* 324 So. 2d 441 (La. 1976), stated that the principal of fault underlying articles 2317 and 2322 (1870) was the same as that underlying article 2319. The Court then provided the following summarization on the theory of strict liability:

> When harm results from the conduct or defect of a person or thing which creates an unreasonable risk of harm to others, a person legally responsible under these code articles for the supervision, care, or guardianship of the person or thing may be held liable for the damage thus created, despite the fact that no personal negligent act or inattention on the former's part is provided. The liability arises from his legal relationship to the person or thing whose conduct or defect creates an unreasonable risk of injuries to others. The fault of the person thus liable is based upon his failure to prevent the person or thing for whom he is responsible from causing such unreasonable risk of injury to others. Thus, the person to whom society allots the supervision, care, or guardianship (custody) of the risk-creating person or thing bears the loss resulting from creation of the risk, rather than some innocent third person harmed as a consequence of his failure to prevent the risk. His fault rests upon his failure to prevent the risk-creating harm and upon his obligation to guard against the condition or activity (by the person or thing for which he is responsible) which creates the unreasonable risk of harm to others.

This jurisprudence recognized that the injured person must prove the vice (i.e., unreasonable risk of injury to another) in the person or thing whose act causes the damage, and that the damage resulted from this vice. Once this is proved, the owner or guardian responsible for the person or thing can escape liability only if he shows the harm was caused by the fault of the victim, by the fault of a third person, or by an irresistible force.

The legal fault thus arising from our code provisions has sometimes been referred to as strict liability. *Entrevia, supra* at 1148; quoting *Loescher, Id.* at 446-47.

The elements of a cause of action founded on strict liability, as adduced from articles 2317, 2319 and the interpretative jurisprudence, are: (1) the creation of an unreasonable risk of harm; (2) damage resulting from the risk of harm; and (3) a curatorship between the person which caused the damage and the party from whom the plaintiff is seeking recovery. Subsequent to our review of the record, we do not believe that the State in permitting Edwards to attend a street dance sponsored for the benefit of the Pinecrest residents created an unreasonable risk of harm. The facts and circumstances of this case do not warrant the application of strict liability. Our decision rests on the same moral, economic and social considerations discussed previously in this opinion. *See, Entrevia, supra*, (analysis of duty/risk in strict liability and negligence cases is essentially the same); *See also, Jacoby v. Louisiana,* 434 So. 2d 570 (La.App. 1 Cir. 1983).

For the above and foregoing reasons, the judgment of the District Court is affirmed. All costs of this appeal are assessed against the appellants, Dora H. Brady and Stephen Brady.

AFFIRMED.

NOTE

1. *Brady* was decided prior to the new C.C. Art 2319 and the related statute. How would the analysis change under the amendments?

D. ANIMALS

Prior to 1996, La. Civ. Code art. 2321 provided in relevant part that "(t)he owner of an animal is answerable for the damage he has caused...." In 1996, the article was amended to read as follows:

La. Civil Code Article 2321. Damage caused by animals

The owner of an animal is answerable for the damage caused by the animal. However, he is answerable for the damage only upon a showing that he knew or, in the exercise of reasonable care, should have known that his animal's behavior would cause damage, that the damage could have been prevented by the exercise of reasonable care, and that he failed to exercise such reasonable care. Nonetheless, the owner of a dog is strictly liable for damages for injuries to persons or property caused by the dog and which the owner could have prevented and which did not result from the injured person's provocation of the dog. Nothing in this Article shall preclude the court from the application of the doctrine of res ipsa loquitur in an appropriate case.

PEPPER
v.
TRIPLET
864 So. 2d 181 (La. 2004)

CALOGERO, C. J.

This dog-bites-man case represents the first time this court has considered the application of the legislature's 1996 revision of Louisiana Civil Code Article 2321 regarding the liability of an animal owner, particularly with respect to ownership of dogs. In pertinent part, Article 2321 as amended by Acts 1996, 1st Ex.Sess., No. 1, § 1, provides: "Nonetheless, the owner of a dog is strictly liable for damages for injuries to persons or property caused by the dog and which the owner could have prevented and which did not result from the injured person's provocation of the dog." While the legislature may have generally eliminated strict liability for owners of animals, it specifically continued strict liability for owners of dogs. In this process, however, the legislature limited the scope of that strict liability to situations in which (1) the dog owner could have prevented the injury and (2) the injury did not result from provocation of the dog by the injured party. We granted the writ application in this case to determine the parameters of Article 2321 governing strict liability for dog owners, as well as to review the finding of liability in this case by the trial court.

For the reasons explained below, we find that, to establish a claim in strict liability against a dog owner under La. Civ.Code art. 2321 as amended in 1996, the plaintiff must prove that his person or property was damaged by the owner's dog, that the injuries could have been prevented by the owner, and that the injuries did not result from the injured person's provocation of the dog. We hold that, to establish that the owner could have prevented the injuries under Article 2321, the plaintiff must show the dog presented an unreasonable risk of harm. Because the lower courts erred in requiring such a showing, we have reviewed the evidence *de novo* and have concluded that the defendant's dog under these facts did not present an unreasonable risk of injury to the plaintiff and, therefore, that the plaintiff has failed to establish a claim in strict liability under La. Civ.Code Art. 2321. Consequently, for the following reasons, we reverse the court of appeal's judgment.

I

The facts surrounding the dog bite in this case are fairly straightforward. The plaintiff, Dustin Pepper, is a thirty-year-old man who lives with his parents and has domiciliary custody of his two minor children. The defendant, Thomas Triplet, along with his wife and minor son, has lived next door to the Peppers for many years. About thirteen years prior to the incident which gave rise to this lawsuit, the defendant purchased a dog and named it Bandit. In his deposition, the defendant described the dog as a thirteen-year-old, Labrador/Huskie mixed breed. The defendant's backyard, where Bandit resided, was entirely fenced in. Along both sides of the defendant's backyard was a four-foot high hurricane or chain-link fence, which was topped by two feet of barbed wire on the side shared with the Peppers. The yard was bordered along the back by a wooden fence, described as being six or eight feet in height. The backyard could be accessed either through the defendant's home or through a six-foot wooden gate located on the Peppers' side of the Triplet home. There is no latch on the outside of this gate, and the defendant had placed a metal pipe across the gate on the inside to prevent the gate from being opened from outside and to prevent the dog from escaping. The defendant testified that Bandit early on "showed a tendency to guard his turf," and would bark and run along the fence when he saw someone in a neighboring yard.

Although they had been neighbors for many years, the plaintiff had never been invited into the defendant's house or backyard. Whenever children playing in the Peppers' yard would accidentally toss a ball over the fence into the Triplets' backyard, the custom, according to both parties, was for the child to knock on the Triplets' door, and either the defendant or his wife would go into the yard to retrieve the ball. The plaintiff's only contact with Bandit prior to the bite involved his petting the dog's nose through the chain-link fence separating the yards.

On November 11, 2000, the plaintiff was watching a football game with a friend and drinking beer. The plaintiff's son, who had been playing in the backyard, came in and told him that the ball had gone into the defendant's yard. The plaintiff instructed his daughter to knock on the Triplets' door and ask for the ball; she returned shortly thereafter and announced that the Triplets were not home. At this point, the plaintiff went into the Triplets' yard himself to retrieve his son's ball. The plaintiff testified that he did not want his son climbing the fence into the Triplets' yard and that he decided not to await the Triplets' return because this particular football was his son's favorite ball.

To gain access to the Triplets' backyard, the plaintiff testified that he "unlocked the gate and went in ... their yard." He explained that the gate was secured by a metal pipe that protruded through the fence into his yard and that he "shoved" the pipe, which allowed the gate to open. The plaintiff admitted that he had never been given permission to enter the yard and that he knew Bandit was "territorial." Nevertheless, he entered the yard, and was met by Bandit, who then followed him as he walked towards the ball. When the plaintiff reached down for the ball, Bandit bit him on the hand. The plaintiff pulled back his hand, and Bandit then bit him on the stomach. The plaintiff testified that Bandit let him go when he commanded the dog to stop. Thereafter, the plaintiff left the yard through the gate and replaced the metal pipe. After initially washing the wound with water, he was taken by a friend to the hospital, where he received treatment for his injuries.

This was not the dog's first biting incident. Some four to six weeks earlier, a boy visiting the plaintiff's children had used a ladder, apparently belonging to the Peppers, to climb the fence from the Peppers' backyard into the defendant's backyard. According to the defendant, the boy's mother informed him of the incident in verifying the health of the dog. The following day, the defendant checked his gate and fence to make sure they were secure, and he also discussed the incident with the plaintiff's mother, Mrs. Linda Pepper.

The plaintiff subsequently brought suit against the defendant and his insurer, Allstate Insurance Company. Following a one-day bench trial, the district court rendered a judgment in favor of the plaintiff, awarding him $37,623.92 in damages. After citing Frank L. Maraist, Thomas C. Galligan, *Louisiana Tort Law* (Michie 1996), the district court agreed with the authors that the "which the owner could have prevented" language in the newly revised La. Civ.Code art. 2321 with respect to dog owners was ambiguous. Nevertheless, the court found the defendant strictly liable because he could have prevented the injury and there was no evidence of provocation by the plaintiff. The court reasoned that the defendant could have prevented the injury, by warning the plaintiff and his family not to enter the yard, by placing a "beware of dog" sign on his fence, or by tying or otherwise restraining the dog inside the fence. The court further found no evidence of provocation.

The district court next rejected the defendant's argument that the plaintiff was a trespasser and that the defendant was entitled to an expectation of privacy. The court reasoned that the law regarding uninvited guests was not applicable; that, while the plaintiff was a trespasser, the parties were on friendly terms and the plaintiff had never been warned to stay out of the defendant's yard; and that, despite the defendant's right to privacy, the defendant had a duty and responsibility to the community to protect them from injury caused by his dog, because it was not uncommon for neighbors to enter the yards of other neighbors. The court apportioned 25% fault, however, to the plaintiff, reasoning that the plaintiff had taken some risk entering his neighbor's backyard with a dog he knew was never allowed out on the street, that the plaintiff could have waited until the defendant or his wife had returned home, and that entering the backyard was not the usual means by which the plaintiff or his children retrieved a stray ball in the neighbor's backyard.

As will be discussed in more detail below, a majority of the court of appeal affirmed. *Pepper v. Triplett,* 02-0022 (La.App. 1 Cir. 2002), 834 So. 2d 624.

II

A. Civil Code Article 2321 Liability Prior to 1996

Prior to the 1996 legislative changes, Article 2321 of the Civil Code provided in pertinent part that "[t]he owner of an animal is answerable for the damage he has caused...."[1] The two seminal cases addressing liability under former Article 2321 are *Holland v. Buckley,* 305 So. 2d 113 (La.1974), and *Boyer v. Seal,* 553 So. 2d 827, 832 (La.1989). In *Holland,* the plaintiff's German Shepherd was running loose in plaintiff's front yard when it bolted across the street and attacked the defendant's poodle walking on the opposite sidewalk. The defendant was bitten when he lifted his poodle out of the German Shepherd's reach. The *Holland* court found the defendant to be strictly liable for the plaintiff's injury. In *Boyer,* the plaintiff tripped over her daughter's house cat that had startled her when it rubbed against her leg while she was visiting in her daughter's home. The *Boyer* court declined to hold the daughter strictly liable for her mother's injury, finding that the cat had not posed an unreasonable risk of harm. The reasoning of both decisions will be discussed more fully below.

Early cases addressing Article 2321 liability against animal owners, such as *Montgomery v. Koester,* 35 La. Ann. 1091 (1883), for example, noted that French interpretations of French Civil Code Article 1385, essentially identical to Louisiana's Article 2321, had imposed strict liability upon the owner for harm caused by the animal, except in cases of force majeure or of contributory fault of the injured person, and regardless of whether the animal was vicious or whether the owner knew of its vicious character. *Holland v. Buckley,* 305 So. 2d at 116. The English rule, in contrast, was based on negligence, such that the owner was responsible for harm caused by his animal only if he knew the animal was dangerous and nevertheless allowed it to escape and thereupon do harm. *Holland,* 305 So. 2d at 116-17. And in *Delisle v. Bourriague,* 105 La. 77, 29 So. 731 (1901), the court characterized Article 2321 as

> founded upon the presumption that the fault is chargeable to the owner of the animal that caused the damage, or to the person in whose use or under whose care it was at the time of the accident; and that presumption can be made to give way only in the presence of proof either of an unforeseen event or by the imprudence of the one injured....

105 La. at 84-85, 29 So. at 734.

Around the turn of the Nineteenth Century, however, a line of jurisprudence in Louisiana interpreting Article 2321 began to adopt a standard of negligence that has been described as the "first bite" rule, in which the owner of a domestic animal owes no general duty to guard against harm to third persons until the animal has displayed dangerous propensities. *See* Frank L. Maraist, Thomas C. Galligan, *Louisiana Tort Law,* Sect. 14-7, p. 346 (Michie 1996) (hereinafter Maraist & Galligan); *see also Tripani v. Meraux,* 184 La. 66, 165 So. 453 (1936); *Martinez v. Bernhard,* 106 La. 368, 30 So. 901 (1901). The reasoning was that an owner who neither knew nor should have known that his animal posed some danger to others, perhaps by proving the previously gentle nature of the creature, could not have foreseen the "first bite," and thus would not be held responsible when the animal first caused damage. *Holland,* 305 So. 2d at 119; *see also* Frank L. Maraist, Thomas C. Galligan, Jr., *Burying Ceasar: Civil Justice Reform and the Changing Face of Louisiana Tort Law,* 71 Tul. L.Rev. 339, 352 (1996) (hereinafter *Burying Ceasar*).

According to *Holland,* three lines of cases developed after the appearance of the "first bite is free" approach in *Martinez v. Bernhard.* One line of cases allowed the victim to recover from the

---

[1] Civil Code Article 2321 had provided in full:
> The owner of an animal is answerable for the damage he has caused; but if the animal had been lost, or had strayed more than a day, he may discharge himself from this responsibility, by abandoning him to the person who has sustained the injury; except where the master has turned loose a dangerous or noxious animal, for then he must pay for all the harm done, without being allowed to make the abandonment.

owner upon proof of the dangerous propensities of the animal and the owner's presumed knowledge thereof. 305 So. 2d at 116-17. Though this approach was essentially what the *Holland* court would ultimately adopt, the court noted that the cases had reached their holdings with little or no consideration of Article 2321. *Id.* at 117. A second line of cases held that the harm caused by the animal created a presumption of fault on the part of its owner, which shifted the burden to the owner to show that he was free of even the slightest fault; however, the owner could exculpate himself from liability by showing that he himself did not contribute to the accident by some lack of care on his part, i.e., that he was not negligent. *Id.* at 117. The third line of cases required the victim to prove both the existence of a dangerous propensity of the animal and also the knowledge of such propensity on the part of the owner. *Id.* The *Holland* court noted that this approach placed a heavy burden upon the plaintiff and had no support in the text of Article 2321 or its legislative or jurisprudential history. *Id.*

The *Holland* court, rejecting any negligence based approach to liability for damages caused by animals, set forth what it held to be the correct interpretation of Article 2321:

> When a domesticated animal harms another, the master of the animal is presumed to be at fault. The fault so provided is in the nature of strict liability, as an exception to or in addition to any ground of recovery on the basis of negligence, Article 2316. The owner may exculpate himself from such presumed fault only by showing that the harm was caused by the fault of the victim, by the fault of a third person for whom he is not responsible, or by a fortuitous event.

> The chief difference between this view and that of the second line of cases cited above is that, therein, the owner was permitted to exculpate himself of fault by showing that he himself did not contribute to the accident by some lack of care on his part. Under our present holding, the owner can exculpate himself from the fault of having his animal hurt someone only by proving that the harm resulted from some independent cause not imputable to the defendant.

> The underlying reason for the owner's liability is that, as between him who created the risk of harm and the innocent victim thereby injured, the risk creator should bear the loss. He maintains the animal for his own use or pleasure.

Holland, 305 So. 2d at 119 (footnote omitted).

The *Holland* court observed that "[i]n the crowded society of today, the burden of harms caused by an animal should be borne by its master who keeps him for his own pleasure or use rather than by an innocent victim injured by the animal." *Holland*, 305 So. 2d at 119 and 120; *see also Boyer v. Seal*, 553 So. 2d at 832. As this court later explained, the injured person need not prove the negligence of the owner. *Howard v. Allstate Ins. Co.*, 520 So. 2d 715 (La. 1988). Liability arises solely from the legal relationship between the owner and the animal. *Rozell v. Louisiana Animal Breeders Co-op., Inc.*, 434 So. 2d 404 (La. 1983). Ultimately, the *Holland* court held the owner of the dog liable to the plaintiff whom the dog had bitten, because the owner did not rebut the presumption of fault created by the injury caused by the dog. *Id.* at 120.

A year later, this court decided *Loescher v. Parr*, 324 So. 2d 441 (La. 1975), a case involving a person's liability under La. Civ.Code art. 2317 for the damage caused by an inanimate thing over which he has garde.[2] The *Loescher* court adopted a variation of the French interpretation of Article

---

[2] La. Civ.Code. art. 2317 provides:
  We are responsible, not only for the damage occasioned by our own act, but for that which is caused by the act of persons for whom we are answerable, or of the things which we have in our custody. This, however, is to be understood with the following modifications.
  La. Civ.Code art. 2317.1, entitled:Damage caused by ruin, vice, or defect in things," and added by Acts 1996, 1st Ex.Sess., No. 1, § 1, eff. April 16, 1996, provides:
  The owner or custodian of a thing is answerable for damage occasioned by its ruin, vice, or defect, only upon a showing that he knew or, in the exercise of reasonable care, should have known of the ruin, vice, or defect which caused the damage, that the damage could have been prevented by the

1384 of the Code Napoleon, holding that, under La Civ.Code art. 2317, a guardian of a thing is liable when a plaintiff proves (a) that the thing which caused his damage was in the garde of the defendant, (b) that there was a defect or vice in the thing, i.e., an unreasonable risk of harm was created by it, and (c) that his damage occurred because of this defect or vice, unless the guardian can prove the damage was caused by the fault of the victim, by the fault of a third person, or by an irresistible force. *Loescher v. Parr,* 324 So. 2d at 449.

The *Loescher* decision, therefore, did two things: it not only applied a relational responsibility strict liability theory to Article 2317 damage claims, but it also set forth an analytical method for determining whether a thing possessed a defect or vice for which the guardian should be held strictly liable. As we noted in *Boyer,* the *Loescher* formula for determining a guardian's responsibility contained a "limitation" on strict liability not recognized by the French jurisprudence, i.e., the damage must have been caused by a vice or aspect of the thing that creates an unreasonable risk of harm to others.[3] *Boyer,* 553 So. 2d at 832. Nonetheless, in explaining the rationale for this analytical method, the court in *Loescher* described its previous interpretations of Civil Code articles 2318, 2320, 2321 and 2322 as logically consistent with such a method. 324 So. 2d at 446. The *Loescher* court then summarized the principles of legal fault underpinning these articles as follows:

> When harm results from the conduct or defect of a person or thing which creates an unreasonable risk of harm to others, a person legally responsible under these code articles for the supervision, care, or guardianship of the person or thing may be held liable for the damage thus caused, despite the fact that no personal negligent act or inattention on the former's part is proved. The liability arises from his legal relationship to the person or thing whose conduct or defect creates an unreasonable risk of injuries to others.

Loescher, 324 So. 2d at 446.

Subsequent to *Loescher,* this court in *Boyer* resolved any lingering question whether the injured plaintiff, in order to establish strict liability against the owner of an animal, as against the owner of a thing or building, must prove that the damage suffered by the plaintiff was caused by an animal that created an unreasonable risk of harm.[4] In *Boyer,* this court acknowledged the *Loescher* court's attempt to give manageable scope to strict liability and to harmonize its application by setting forth a coherent principle, i.e., "that the guardian of the person or thing should bear the cost of damage caused through unreasonable risks of harm that his charge creates." 553 So. 2d at 834. Accordingly, the court rejected "expand[ing] responsibility for animals into a rule of superstrict liability." *Id.* The *Boyer* court reasoned:

> There are various policies supporting the unreasonable risk principle: As *Loescher* observes, the person who has the guardianship and usually the enjoyment of the person or thing should bear the cost of damage caused by risks they create rather than the innocent victim. Further, it is thought that the guardian is in a better position to anticipate, detect, guard against, and insure against these risks, making him a better

___

exercise of reasonable care, and that he failed to exercise such reasonable care. Nothing in this Article shall preclude the court from the application of the doctrine of res ipsa loquitur in an appropriate case.

[3] *See Kent v. Gulf States Utilities Co.,* 418 So. 2d 493, 498, n. 6 (La. 1982); *id.* at 501, Dennis, J, concurring; Maraist & Galligan, *Burying Ceasar,* 71 Tul. L.Rev. at 344 ("[T]he Louisiana brand of strict liability--requiring a thing to have presented an unreasonable risk of harm, and presuming the custodian of the thing to have known of its defect- also was remarkably similar to some liability theories developed in American products--liability law. Thus, Louisiana's peculiar type of strict liability was a cross between civil law and American products-liability law. But, hybrid though it was, Louisiana's brand of strict liability was inspired, at least in part, by Louisiana's own civil-law tradition.") (footnote omitted).

[4] *See* Maraist & Galligan, Sect. 14-7, pp. 346-47; *see also Burying Ceasar,* 71 Tul. L.Rev. at 352.

risk spreader and more efficient conductor of the deterrent effects of civil liability. *A competing policy, however, is that the guardian should not be responsible for protecting against all risks; some risks are relatively too small to require him to protect others therefrom. Thus, if the unreasonable risk of harm principle were to be abolished in the cases involving liability for animals, these policies would tend to be defeated or at least not promoted and owners would be made insurers against loss from any risk, no matter how insignificant or socially tolerable the risk might be. We see no reason that animal owners should be treated less favorably than owners of buildings and guardians of inanimate things under strict liability conceptions of the Civil Code.* Moreover, it would appear that doing so might undermine the principle's application to strict liability under other delictual articles of the Code. Consequently, we conclude that the unreasonable risk of harm principle should be maintained in animal cases in the interest of the continued manageable and harmonious application of strict liability under the Civil Code.

Boyer v. Seal, 553 So. 2d at 834 (emphasis supplied). Essentially, then, *Boyer* applied the unreasonable risk of harm principle to animals in order to limit strict liability against their owners because of the competing social policy that the owner of an animal should not be required to insure against all risks and because the court had been applying the same or similar principle to things and buildings.

With the unreasonable risk of harm principle established as applicable to animal owners, the *Boyer* court determined that the cat in that case had not posed an unreasonable risk of harm. The method for determining whether a thing under garde poses an unreasonable risk of harm, the court noted, is similar to that of taking into account all of the social, moral, economic and other considerations as would a legislator regulating the matter, and the analysis is virtually identical to the risk-utility balancing test used in both negligence and products liability theories. 553 So. 2d at 834-36 (citing *inter alia Entrevia v. Hood,* 427 So. 2d 1146 (La. 1983), and *Bell v. Jet Wheel Blast,* 462 So. 2d 166 (La. 1985)).

To summarize, the *Holland* court, in applying Article 2321 to damages caused by animals, relied upon early Louisiana jurisprudence addressing Article 2321 and upon French commentators' interpretations of similar Article 1385 of the Code Napoleon. *Holland* thereupon rejected a "first bite is free" negligence approach in favor of a strict liability theory. The *Boyer* court later applied to animals the unreasonable risk of harm principle, a limitation on strict liability articulated in *Loescher,* to determine whether the owner of an animal should be held strictly liable for the damages caused by his animal.

B. Civil Code Article 2321 and the 1996 Tort Reform Act

In 1996, the legislature revised Civil Code Article 2321 regarding liability for damage caused by animals, which now reads:

The owner of an animal is answerable for the damage caused by the animal. However, he is answerable for the damage only upon a showing that he knew or, in the exercise of reasonable care, should have known that his animal's behavior would cause damage, that the damage could have been prevented by the exercise of reasonable care, and that he failed to exercise such reasonable care. *Nonetheless, the owner of a dog is strictly liable for damages for injuries to persons or property caused by the dog and which the owner could have prevented and which did not result from the injured person's provocation of the dog.* Nothing in this Article shall preclude the court from the application of the doctrine of res ipsa loquitur in an appropriate case.

Acts 1996, 1st Ex.Sess., No. 1, § 1, eff. April 16, 1996 (Emphasis supplied).

Our courts of appeal, as well as various commentators, have noted that the 1996 revision results in an ordinary negligence standard for owners of all animals except dogs, whose owners continue to be governed by a strict liability standard. *See* Maraist & Galligan, § 14-7; Comment (Joseph F. Piacun), *The Abolition of Strict Liability in Louisiana: A Return to a Fairer Standard or an Impossible Burden on Plaintiffs?,* 34 Loy. L.Rev. 215 (1997) (hereinafter *The Abolition of Strict Liability in Louisiana*). However, whether that standard remains the same as was articulated in *Loescher v. Parr* and explicitly made applicable to animal owners in *Boyer v. Seal* has, in light of increasing litigation under Article 2321, become a significant unresolved issue of law, in our view. Accordingly, we granted the defendants' writ application in this case to consider the 1996 changes to Article 2321 with respect to dogs and dog owners. *Pepper v. Triplet,* 03-0619 (La. 2003), 845 So. 2d 1074.

The first court to examine liability for dog owners under the new Article 2321 was *Allen v. State Farm Fire and Cas. Co.,* 36,377 (La.App. 2 Cir. 2002), 828 So. 2d 190, *writ denied,* 02-2577 (La. 2002), 833 So. 2d 343. The Second Circuit in *Allen,* affirming summary judgment for the plaintiff, asserted that the 1996 revision "effectively ended strict liability for all animal owners except dog owners." 828 So. 2d at 193 (citing *The Abolition of Strict Liability in Louisiana,* 34 Loy. L.Rev. at 231-34). With regard to dog owners, the court reasoned, the legislature had "retain[ed]" strict liability, yet "defin[ed] a three-part test" to determine liability under Article 2321:

> First, the dog must have actually caused the damage to the plaintiff's person or property. Second, the owner must have been able to prevent the damages, but failed to do so. Third, the damages must not have been caused by the injured person's provocation of the dog.

828 So. 2d at 193 (citing *The Abolition of Strict Liability in Louisiana,* 34 Loy. L.Rev. at 231-34).

The *Allen* court specifically rejected the defendants' argument that the plaintiff must still prove that the animal posed an unreasonable risk of harm under a balancing test, finding that the amended article does not require such a showing. *Id.* at 194. In applying the second part of the new test, the *Allen* court reasoned that the amended article "recognizes the obvious and great risk that a dog might bite someone," and therefore "imposes on the owner a duty to prevent dog bites." *Id.* Although the defendants in *Allen* maintained that their fence adequately prevented the dog from exiting the yard, the court found that the fence, which had a loose board through which the dog placed his head and bit the plaintiff, had failed to prevent the bite. The court reasoned that the defendants could have chained the dog or kept it indoors, and thus failed to prevent the damage to the plaintiff.

In the instant case, the First Circuit also addressed liability for dog owners under Article 2321. A majority of the appellate court affirmed the district court's judgment in favor of the plaintiff, though one judge dissented as to the fault allocation, believing that the plaintiff should have been assessed with 75% of the fault. The court of appeal stated that strict liability was replaced by a negligence standard for animals generally, but that the legislature retained strict liability for dog owners. The court then found that the amended article sets forth a three-part test for strict liability: A dog owner is liable if (1) the dog actually caused the damage to the plaintiff's person or property, (2) the owner could have prevented the damage, and (3) the dog was not provoked by the person suffering the damage. 02-0022, p. 5, 834 So. 2d at 628.

After noting that the defendant's dog had caused the damage, the court of appeal in the instant case turned to whether the defendant could have prevented the damage. The court rejected the defendant's argument that nothing the defendant could have done would have prevented damage to the plaintiff because the yard had been completely fenced and the gate secured, and the defendant had never given permission to the plaintiff to enter the yard. The court relied on *Allen, supra,* for the proposition that erecting a fence does not discharge the dog owner's duty to prevent dog bites and other damage. The court concluded that the district court had not manifestly erred in finding that the defendant could have prevented the injury by placing a "Beware of Dog" sign on the fence, by securing the gate by a more reliable means, or by chaining the dog. The court also found no error in the trial court's implicit finding that the defendant could have advised the plaintiff of the dog's propensity to bite, a fact of which the defendant had prior knowledge but which the plaintiff did not.

C. Defendant's Assignments of Error Nos. 1 and 2

In their first and second assignments of error, the defendants contend the lower courts erred in applying a standard of absolute liability, rather than strict liability, and failed to determine whether the defendant's dog posed an unreasonable risk of harm, an integral element of the strict liability standard called for by Article 2321. The defendants also assert the lower courts erred by literally interpreting the "could have prevented" language found in Article 2321. The defendants contend the fact-finder should continue to determine whether the dog posed an unreasonable risk of harm before imposing strict liability upon the owner, and they argue that the plaintiff failed to prove in this case that Bandit, enclosed within a secure fence, posed an unreasonable risk of harm to the trespassing plaintiff.

The defendants also argue that, although the codal article as revised expressly retains strict liability, it introduces "muddled" and ambiguous language in the form of the "could have prevented" phrase. The defendants maintain that the legislature intended to apply a modified form of strict liability to allow dog owners to exonerate themselves if they could not have prevented the damages or if the injured person has provoked the dog. The First Circuit, the defendants argue, applied this language too literally so that it results in imposition of absolute liability upon dog owners, contrary to the intent of the legislature, because in hindsight one may always envision some way by which the bite could have been avoided. The defendants assert that the "could have prevented" language should be read out of the article and the unreasonable risk of harm requirement maintained. Alternatively, the defendants call for a "reasonableness" standard to apply to what actions the dog owner must take to prevent injury to a third person.

D. Discussion

The issue before us, therefore, is whether the legislature in amending Article 1996 has negated the requirement, articulated in *Loescher v. Parr* and then applied to animals in *Boyer v. Seal,* that the plaintiff must show that the animal posed an unreasonable risk of harm before he may recover against the owner of the animal under the strict liability of the newly revised Article 2321. The Second Circuit in *Allen* has held that the plaintiff is no longer required to show that the dog posed an unreasonable risk of harm to permit recovery under this article, and the court of appeal in the instant case did not require such a showing before awarding the plaintiff recovery in strict liability under Article 2321. Whether a showing that the dog posed an unreasonable risk of harm remains necessary following the revision, however, cannot be decided without also addressing the language in the revised Article 2321 that the injury must be one that "the owner could have prevented." Maraist and Galligan have commented that the language is susceptible of different meanings that would render the language either superfluous or impose an absolute liability; instead, assuming the unreasonable risk of harm test will continue to determine strict liability for dog owners, they suggest the language "could have been prevented" might simply be ignored, as is similar language in La. Civ.Code art. 2322 regarding master and their servants. *Burying Ceasar,* 71 Tul. L.Rev. at 354-55. Another writer on the subject has suggested that the question of whether the owner could have prevented the injury should be answered by balancing the risks with the dog's utility. Comment, *The Abolition of Strict Liability in Louisiana,* 34 Loy. L.Rev. at 234 (citing *Entrevia v. Hood,* 427 So. 2d at 1149-50).

The function of statutory interpretation and the construction to be given to legislative acts rests with the judicial branch of the government. *Touchard v. Williams,* 617 So. 2d 885 (La. 1993). Under the general rules of statutory construction, courts begin with the premise that legislation is the solemn expression of legislative will and, therefore, the interpretation of a law involves, primarily, the search for the legislature's intent. La. Civ.Code art. 1; *Falgout v. Dealers Truck Equipment Co.,* 98-3150, p. 2 (La. 1999), 748 So. 2d 399, 401. When a law is clear and unambiguous and its application does not lead to absurd consequences, the law shall be applied as written and no further interpretation may be made in search of the intent of the legislature. La. Civ.Code art. 9; *Falgout,* 98-3150 at p. 2, 748 So. 2d at 401. Further, it is a well-recognized and long-established rule of statutory construction that statutory provisions should be construed along with the remainder of the statute, and all statutes on the same subject matter should be read together and interpreted as a whole to effect the legislative intent and should be construed in such a way as to reconcile, if possible, apparent inconsistencies or ambiguities so that each part is given effect. *Comm-Care Corp. v. Bishop,* 96-1711 (La. 1997), 696 So. 2d 969. Courts should give effect to all parts of a statute and should not give a statute an interpretation that makes any part superfluous or meaningless, if that result can be avoided. *In re Succession of Boyter,* 99- 0761, p. 9 (La. 2000), 756 So. 2d 1122, 1129. It is presumed that the intention of the legislative branch is to achieve a consistent body of law. *Boyter,* 99-0761 at p. 9, 756 So. 2d at 1130. The starting point for the interpretation of any statute, then, is the language of the statute itself. *Touchard v. Williams,* 617 So. 2d at 888.

As previously set forth, revised Article 2321 reads in pertinent part: "Nonetheless, the owner of a dog is strictly liable for damages for injuries to persons or property caused by the dog and which the owner could have prevented and which did not result from the injured person's provocation of the dog." Given the introductory clause of this provision, there can be no doubt, then, that the legislature intended to allow damage claims based upon strict liability against owners of dogs. The primary difference between ordinary negligence and strict liability is that, with the latter, the plaintiff need not prove the defendant's actual or constructive knowledge of the animal's dangerous propensities. *Kent v. Gulf States Utilities Co.,* 418 So. 2d at 497-98. Thus, the inability of a defendant to know or prevent the risk is not a defense in a strict liability case even though it precludes a finding of negligence. *Entrevia v. Hood,* 427 So. 2d at 1150. Given that Article 2317 and the first clause of former Article 2321, now the first sentence of revised Article 2321, seemingly impose liability without fault in all cases upon the owner or guardian of the defective thing or animal, the *Loescher* and *Boyer* cases effectively represented an attempt to limit the owner or guardian's strict liability under the rationale that the owner should not be required to insure against all injury however small the risk might be.

In this light, we do not see a practical change in how the courts should apply Article 2321 to dog claims with respect to the "which the owner could have prevented" language. We do not read that language as either superfluous or a new limitation on strict liability, nor do we read it as an expansion of liability toward a superstrict or absolute standard. Instead, we read that language as merely continuing to require that the plaintiff, in order to establish a claim in strict liability, show that the risk of injury outweighed the dog's utility such that it posed an unreasonable risk of harm. If the animal posed an unreasonable risk of harm, then the owner will be presumed to be at fault, because he failed to prevent an injury he could have prevented, and he will be held strictly liable for an injury caused by his dog, unless he can show that the injury was due solely to the fault of a third party unattributable to him or to a fortuitous event, or, as Article 2321 now provides, the plaintiff fails to establish that the injuries did not result from the injured person's provocation of the dog. Such a construction of the "could have prevented" clause, we believe, is supported by the historical jurisprudence discussed above and, more importantly, follows the language of the codal article as well as the intent of the legislature, which was to retain strict liability, as that legal doctrine has been applied in Louisiana, with regard to owners of dogs.[5]

---

[5] The legislative history shows that dogs were not originally an exception to the proposed requirement that the injured party must now establish fault or negligence on the part of the animal owner. During discussions of the Committee on Civil Law and Procedure, Representative Bowler expressed her concern that the liability of owners of animals would be decreased under the proposed bill. Professor Cheney Joseph proposed an amendment that would state that the owner of a dog would be strictly liable for injuries to person or properties caused by the dog which the owner could have prevented and which did not result from the injured person's provocation of the dog. Representative Bowler stated her concern was not with just dogs but all animals. Kimberly Wooten, the Governor's representative, explained that owners would still be answerable, but the plaintiff would have to prove that the owner knew or should have known that the animal would cause damage. The proposed amendment with respect to dog injuries was later adopted without further discussion. Minutes, H.B. No. 18, Civil Law and Procedure Committee, March 26, 1996.

Notably, an amendment to the bill that would include language "unless the vice or defect created an unreasonable risk of harm" was proposed in the same committee hearing, though not with respect to Article 2321, and then immediately rejected as possibly codifying the strict liability standard articulated by the Supreme Court. *See Id.* So the Committee, at least, understood that the concept of an unreasonable risk of harm was the standard to be used to determine strict liability in Louisiana. Therefore, in our view, we do not perceive any

We, therefore, disapprove of the holding of the Second Circuit in *Allen,* apparently relied upon by the First Circuit in the instant case, that the plaintiff is no longer required to show that the dog posed an unreasonable risk of harm in order to establish a claim of strict liability under Article 2321. We disagree with the Second Circuit's implicit finding that the legislature intended to impose upon owners of dogs a form of strict liability more stringent than that imposed upon them in *Holland* and *Boyer,* while at the same time eliminating strict liability against owners of all other animals, including, perhaps, wild animals. The legislature, as evidenced by the 1996 amendments to Louisiana tort law, was more concerned with the persons to whom strict liability would apply than the method for establishing a strict liability claim, if permitted. In *Holland,* itself a dog bite case, we recognized in the former Article 2321 that the owner of an animal could be strictly liable for injuries caused by his animal. Therefore, the legislature's 1996 amendment of Article 2321 simply changes the law to make *Holland* and the strict liability doctrine no longer applicable to animals other than dogs. Furthermore, as we explained in *Boyer,* the unreasonable risk of harm principle represented, in effect, a limitation, albeit perhaps a partially jurisprudential one, upon the reach of strict liability, so the owner of an animal is not required to insure against all risk or loss. We detect no legislative retreat from that principle in the 1996 amendment to Article 2321.

Accordingly, we hold that the method established in Louisiana for determining strict liability was continued by the legislature with regard to dog owners in La. Civ.Code art. 2321, and that, to ascertain whether the owner could have prevented the injury or damage, the plaintiff must establish that the dog posed an unreasonable risk of harm. Therefore, the lower courts erred when they held that plaintiffs are not required to establish that the defendant's dog posed an unreasonable risk of harm to the plaintiff before the plaintiff may recover under the strict liability provision directed to dog owners in revised Article 2321.

III

We next review the record *de novo* to determine whether the defendant's dog posed an unreasonable risk of harm to the plaintiff. In *Boyer v. Seal,* we stated that the criterion for determining whether a defendant has created or maintained an unreasonable risk of harm is a balancing of claims and interest, a weighing of the risk and gravity of harm, and a consideration of individual and societal rights and obligations. We have explained that the judicial process involved in deciding whether a risk is unreasonable is similar to that employed in determining whether a risk is unreasonable in a traditional negligence problem, and in deciding the scope of duty or legal cause under the duty risk analysis. *Entrevia v. Hood,* 427 So. 2d at 1149. The rationale is that in "both delictual areas the judge is called upon to decide questions of social utility that require him to consider the particular case in terms of moral, social and economic considerations, in the same way that the legislator finds the standards or patterns of utility and morals in the life of the community." *Id.*

With regard to the defendant and his dog, the record reveals that the dog was completely enclosed within a secure fence. On the plaintiff's side of the defendant's yard, there was a four-foot chain link fence with two feet of barbed wire above it. Thus, to enter the defendant's yard from the plaintiff's yard, one would have to scale this fence. Apparently, a child visiting the plaintiff's children had done so some four or six weeks prior to the incident involving the plaintiff. The facts surrounding the prior incident are not well known, except that the boy may have used a ladder belonging to the plaintiff or his parents to climb over the fence and that the boy was bitten. The severity of the bite or what happened when the boy dropped into the yard is not in evidence. However, the defendant was informed of the bite by the boy's mother, who wanted to verify that the dog was free of disease, and the next day, according to his uncontradicted testimony, the defendant went to the home of the plaintiff and spoke with the plaintiff's mother about the incident. Although the trial court could not say that the defendant had warned the plaintiff's mother not to allow children to go over the fence, it is certain that the plaintiff's mother was aware of the danger should any of her grandchildren or their friends go into the defendant's yard.

---

intent of the legislature either to increase or decrease the burden of a plaintiff in his pursuit of a strict liability claim against a dog owner, but to maintain the same standard, except with respect to provocation.

The defendant also verified that his fence was secure and that his gate, which led from a side yard to the backyard, was also secure. Generally then, the defendant's dog did not present an unreasonable risk of harm to anyone outside of the defendant's backyard. As the court in *Bell v. State Farm Fire & Cas. Co.,* 94-0460 (La.App. 4 Cir. 1994), 643 So. 2d 1262, *writ denied,* 94-1433 (La. 1994), 642 So. 2d 1289, reasoned "the presence of a dog within a fenced side yard in an urban neighborhood does not create an unreasonable risk of harm." However, given the prior bite, the trial judge was not without reason to warn the defendant that, should his dog escape from the backyard, there could be serious consequences. Nonetheless, the trial judge specifically stated that he could not find that the locking mechanism used on the defendant's gate was unreasonable, though he did opine that the defendant should consider a better means of preventing egress by the dog. The court of appeal suggested that the defendant could have tied or chained the dog within the yard or could have kept the dog inside the house. Yet, these steps were not necessary under the facts of this case to protect the innocent public from harm by the dog.

On the other hand, the plaintiff, an adult male, entered the defendant's yard without authorization by unlocking the gate from the defendant's side yard. As noted in *Entrevia v. Hood,* "the wholesale immunities from civil responsibility resulting from the common law classification of a person as a trespasser are not recognized by our law." 427 So. 2d at 1150 (citing *Cates v. Beauregard Elec. Co-op., Inc.,* 328 So. 2d 367 (La. 1976)). But the court in *Entrevia* did acknowledge that a criminal trespass under La.Rev.Stat. 14:63 is legally and morally reprehensible conduct and that "[a]n owner of property has valid economic and privacy interests which our law seeks to protect from intruders." *Id.* And in *Holland,* this court posed the question before it as: "When an innocent bystander is bitten by a dog, who shall bear the damages so caused? The bystander passing on the street, who did not provoke the attack? Or the owner of the dog, who created the risk by letting the dog go loose?" 305 So. 2d at 114.

The defendant argued that the trial court should have made a specific finding that the plaintiff had committed a trespass. While it is clear that the plaintiff intentionally entered the defendant's immovable property when he knew that his entry was unauthorized, the plaintiff may have had an affirmative defense to a criminal trespass charge under La.Rev.Stat. 14:63(C)(2), because the defendant's yard was not both fenced and posted with "no trespassing" signs as required by La.Rev.Stat. 14:63(E)(3). Nevertheless, the plaintiff's conduct does amount to a delict under La. Civ.Code art. 2315 in that he knowingly entered the defendant's property without his authorization. Article 2315 of the Civil Code provides in pertinent part that every act whatever of man that causes damage to another obliges him by whose fault it happened to repair it. A civil trespass is defined as the unlawful physical invasion of the property or possession of another. *Dickie's Sportsman's Centers, Inc. v. Department of Transp. and Development,* 477 So. 2d 744, 750 (La.App. 1 Cir. 1985), *writ denied,* 478 So. 2d 530 (La. 1985). And a trespasser has been defined as "one who goes upon the property of another without the other's consent." *Williams v. J.B. Levert Land Co., Inc.,* 1, 58 (La.App. 1 Cir. 1964), *writ refused,* 245 La. 1081, 162 So. 2d 574 (1964); *see also Britt Builders, Inc. v. Brister,* 618 So. 2d 899, 903 (La.App. 1 Cir. 1993). Under these facts, then, it is clear that the plaintiff committed a trespass.

The trial court opined, however, that it was foreseeable that balls would be accidentally tossed into the defendant's yard and that neighbors or children might enter the yard to retrieve the ball, such that the defendant could have posted signs warning of the dog or done something more to keep someone out of his yard. And the dissenting judge below reasoned that the defendant had a duty to protect from harm his neighbor and the community. However, the plaintiff's conduct in entering the yard was both intentional, in that he had never been given permission to enter the defendant's yard, and unforeseeable, in that the usual custom between the parties was to ask the defendant or his wife to retrieve the ball or, if they were not home, to await their return. As the dissenting judge acknowledged, a neighbor has no right to enter another's yard without express or tacit consent, and a fence indicates a desire to be free from intrusion, with the presence of a dog emphasizing that desire.

Under the facts of this case, until the plaintiff intentionally and knowingly entered the defendant's backyard without authority, the defendant's dog did not present an unreasonable risk of harm to the plaintiff or the public. Securing dogs in his or her yard is what is expected of a dog owner-

-it protects the dogs and it protects the innocent public. When a person who knows the security measures established by the owner, having abided by them in the past, nevertheless breaches that security, he eliminates the dog's isolated environment and, in essence, turns the dog loose upon himself. This is not a case of a dog running down the street unfettered to prey upon the public. The owner secured the dog against contact with outsiders by enclosing the dog within the fence and, with regard to his neighbors, by notice to the plaintiff's mother, an adult in that household, that the dog had previously bitten a child that had entered the defendant's yard through the plaintiff's yard. Secured, the dog posed no unreasonable risk of harm. Secured, the dog also was not subject to provocation. Secured, the dog was able to guard and protect his master's home with no undue risk of harm to the innocent public. By breaching the security that the dog's owner had created, the plaintiff negated that security. After balancing the various claims and interests, weighing the risk to the public and the gravity of harm, and considering individual and societal rights and obligations, we conclude that, under the facts of this case, the dog did not pose an unreasonable risk of harm. Accordingly, the plaintiff failed to establish a claim against the defendants in strict liability pursuant to Article 2321.

IV

We next turn to the defendant's assertion the trial court erred in assigning 75% fault to the defendant and only 25% fault to the plaintiff, a finding which the majority of the court of appeal affirmed.[6] The defendant also asserts he was not negligent and should be found to bear no fault for the plaintiff's injuries.

Under Article 2321, the "owner of an animal is answerable for the damage caused by the animal." However, as amended in 1996, the article further provides that the owner "is answerable for the damage only upon a showing that he knew or, in the exercise of reasonable care, should have known that his animal's behavior would cause damage, that the damage could have been prevented by the exercise of reasonable care, and that he failed to exercise such reasonable care." The defendant asserts he exercised reasonable care by enclosing the dog inside a fence with a secure gate. He argues there was nothing he could do to prevent the injury to the plaintiff who committed a trespass and entered the yard even though he knew a dog exhibiting territorial behavior was present, who had never been permitted in the yard, and who could have waited until the defendant or his wife returned to retrieve the ball as had been the custom between the parties for a number of years. The defendant argues that requiring him to do anything more than to ensure that the dog is enclosed within a secure fence would be unreasonable.

The plaintiff asserts the defendant knew or should have known of the dangerous propensities of his dog given the fact that the dog had some four weeks earlier bitten a child that had climbed over the defendant's fence using a ladder. The plaintiff also contends the defendant could have warned the plaintiff of the dog's propensity to bite either by telling him or posting signs on the fence, or by chaining or otherwise restraining the dog inside yard.

The lower courts did not apply a negligence standard to the plaintiff's claim, because they found the defendant to be strictly liable. However, as we noted above, that finding was legally incorrect because the lower courts had not imposed the requirement that the plaintiff establish that the defendant's dog posed an unreasonable risk of harm. However, the plaintiff did assert in his petition that the defendant was "on notice of the vicious propensities" of the dog because the dog "had bitten another individual within weeks" of the incident involving the instant plaintiff. Elsewhere, the plaintiff asserted that the defendant could have taken a number of actions that could have prevented his injuries, but the defendant failed to do so. Accordingly, we find that the plaintiff has asserted a claim in negligence under Article 2321. Because the lower courts erred in not considering this latter claim, we will review the matter *de novo.*

---

[6] Judge Downing dissented as to the fault allocation, believing that the plaintiff should have been assessed with 75% of the fault with the remainder to the defendant.

In order for liability in negligence to attach under our traditional duty/risk analysis, a plaintiff must prove five separate elements: (1) the defendant had a duty to conform his or her conduct to a specific standard of care (the duty element); (2) the defendant failed to conform his or her conduct to the appropriate standard (the breach of duty element); (3) the defendant's substandard conduct was a cause-in-fact of the plaintiff's injuries (the cause-in-fact element); (4) the defendant's substandard conduct was a legal cause of the plaintiff's injuries (the scope of liability or scope of protection element); and, (5) actual damages (the damages element). *Davis v. Witt*, 02-3102, 02-3110 (La. 2003), 851 So. 2d 1119. Under a duty/risk analysis, the court must view the defendant and plaintiff as individual and unique social actors, taking into account the conduct of each party and the peculiar circumstances of the case. *Socorro v. City of New Orleans*, 579 So. 2d 931, 938 (La. 1991).

Applying those principles to the instant case, we do not find that the plaintiff has sufficiently established the elements of a negligence claim against the defendant. Initially, we note that, while the defendant may have owed a general duty to protect the public and his neighbors from harm caused by his dog, such a duty is logically attenuated as regards a trespasser, particularly an adult male, even if that trespasser is a neighbor who may not possess criminal intent. While we agree with the lower courts that the status of the plaintiff as a trespasser is not alone determinative of the duty owed to him by the dog owner, that status, in light of the particular circumstances of the case, is surely relevant to the determination of the duty owed. *See, e.g., Cuevas v. City of New Orleans*, 99-2542 (La.App. 4 Cir. 2000), 769 So. 2d 82. At any rate, as we previously found, the plaintiff's behavior in entering the defendant's fenced yard without permission amounted to a trespass.

In this case, the plaintiff at trial answered affirmatively when his counsel asked him whether his behavior (presumably entering the defendant's yard without permission) would have been "altered" if he had known that the dog had bitten someone a month earlier. On the other hand, the defendant testified that, the day after he learned of the earlier incident in which a child who had been visiting at the plaintiff's home had scaled the fence and been bitten by the dog, he checked to make sure his fence and gate were secure. He also went over to the plaintiff's home and discussed the incident with the plaintiff's mother, Mrs. Pepper, the matriarch of the home. Although Mrs. Pepper could not recall when she had talked to the defendant, she could not dispute the defendant's testimony. Although the lower courts apparently reasoned that the defendant, who certainly was aware of the prior incident, should have told the plaintiff personally about the incident with the child, we cannot say that the defendant's conduct was deficient or negligent because he discussed the incident only with the plaintiff's mother, who was also the grandmother and part-time caretaker of the plaintiff's children and the matriarch of the household in which the plaintiff resided. We find that the defendant's action in discussing the incident with Mrs. Pepper was sufficiently dispositive of any responsibilities he may have owed to this plaintiff.

Furthermore, there is no indication that this plaintiff would have heeded a beware of dog sign, given that he knew the dog was present in the yard, it was territorial, it was never let out of the backyard, and the usual custom for retrieving stray balls was to await the defendants' return home. Not only was the defendant's property fenced, but barbed wire topped a portion of the fence, thus clearly indicating that the defendant wanted privacy and visitors, therefore, should keep out. Additionally, given that the plaintiff himself described his actions as "unlocking" the gate, we do not see how making the gate more secure would have deterred this plaintiff from entering the defendant's yard. Finally, the lower courts and the plaintiff posited that the defendant could have chained his dog within the fenced yard or could have kept the dog inside the home; however, we believe that such actions would not have been reasonable under the facts of this case. Accordingly, based on our review of the record, we conclude that the plaintiff did not carry his burden of proving that the defendant failed to exercise reasonable care in trying to prevent any damages to his neighbors that might be caused by his dog.

Conclusion

For these reasons, we find that, to establish a claim in strict liability against a dog owner under La. Civ.Code art. 2321 as amended in 1996, the plaintiff must prove that his person or property was damaged by the owner's dog, that the injuries could have been prevented by the owner, and that the injuries did not result from the injured person's provocation of the dog. We further hold that, to establish that the owner could have prevented the injuries under Article 2321, the plaintiff must show the dog presented an unreasonable risk of harm. Because the lower courts erred in requiring such a showing, we have reviewed the evidence *de novo* and have concluded that the defendant's dog under the facts of this case did not present an unreasonable risk of injury to the plaintiff and, therefore, that the plaintiff has failed to establish a claim in strict liability under La. Civ.Code art. 2321. Lastly, after reviewing the facts of this case, we conclude the plaintiff failed to carry his burden of proving that the defendant's conduct was negligent under Article 2321. Accordingly, the judgments of the district court and the court of appeal in favor of the plaintiff are reversed; judgment is granted in favor of the defendant and the plaintiff's claim for damages is dismissed with prejudice.

REVERSED.

NOTES

1.   In *Pepper v. Triplet* the owner of a dog, securely restrained inside a fenced yard, was not strictly liable for damages incurred by a neighbor who was bitten by the dog. Suppose an aggressive dog, restrained by its owner inside a fenced yard by a rope of sufficient length that allows the dog to reach the fence, bites a passing pedestrian. Is the dog's owner strictly liable pursuant to La. C.C. art. 2321 for the damages incurred by the pedestrian? *See, Becker v. Keasler,* 950 So. 2d 92 (La.App. 4 Cir. 2007).

2.   What must a plaintiff prove to establish ownership of a dog for purposes of La. C.C. Art. 2321? What if a defendant feeds a "stray" dog, but denies ownership of the dog, claiming never to have taken the stray to the veterinarian, never to have bought it anything, never to have walked it, never to have let it in his dwelling, and never to have told anyone that it was his. In contrast, defendant claims ownership of other dogs for which he did all of the foregoing things. Still, defendant admits that he has put food on his porch for his dogs, and he has known that for a long period of time the stray has eaten that food. Has the defendant become the owner of the stray dog? *See Terral v. Louisiana Farm Bureau Cas. Ins. Co.,* 892 So. 2d 732 (La. 2005). If the result is that one becomes an owner by virtue of knowing that a stray dog eats food put out at one's home, what conduct does such a result encourage? Why did the Louisiana Supreme Court reach the result that it did in *Terral*?

3.   What does the Art. 2321 language "…which did not result from the injured person's provocation of the dog" mean? Is this language intended to bar recovery or merely reduce it? Can provocation be imputed to animals as well as people? In *McCoy v. Lucius,* 839 So. 2d 1050, 1055 (La.App. 2 Cir. 2003), the Second Circuit stated, " La. C.C. art. 2321 speaks of "the injured *person's* provocation of the dog" (emphasis added). This raises the question of whether the defense of provocation may be raised in a case for damages to a dog. There are comparatively few "dog-bites-dog" cases in the jurisprudence, *see*, e.g., *Goldberg v. Ruckstuhl,* 408 So. 2d 374 (La.App. 1 Cir. 1981), and none since the revision of La. C.C. art. 2321. However, we find that provocation under La. C.C. art. 2321 may be imputed to animals as well as to people. The defendants clearly established through independent testimony that Jody was prone to be aggressive toward people and other dogs. A dog that aggressively charges another dog may provoke an aggressive response from the dog being charged, and that appears to be what occurred in this case."

4.   Does the 1996 amendment to La. C.C. Art. 2321 require plaintiffs injured by wild animals to prove that their owners were negligent in order to recover damages? Can absolute liability of wild animal owners be established under Article 2315?

5.   La. R.S. 3:2652 provides, "Any owner, harborer, or possessor of any dog that kills, harasses, or wounds livestock shall be liable to the owner of the livestock for the damages sustained, to be recovered before any court of competent jurisdiction." What is the nature of this liability?

6.   La. R.S. 3:2803 prohibits an owner of livestock from "knowingly, willfully, or negligently" allowing livestock to roam certain designated state highways. Parishes, through local option elections, may name additional "stock law" highways pursuant to La. R.S. 3:3001. In cases involving automobiles and livestock on "stock law" highways, these statutes have been interpreted to create a presumption of negligence, similar to that expressed in *Holland v. Buckley,* 305 So. 2d 113 (La. 1974), from which the livestock owner must exculpate herself from even the slightest degree of negligence. *See, Schexnider v.* Allstate *Insurance Company,* 304 So. 2d 825 (La.App. 3 Cir. 1974). Although La. C.C. art. 2321 was amended to eliminate the application of strict liability to animal owners other than dog owners; the legislation did not address the "stock law" statutes. Accordingly, courts continue to apply the strict liability concept of presumption of negligence in "stock law" cases. *See, Buller v. American National Property & Casualty Companies,* 838 So. 2d 67 (La.App. 3 Cir. 2003).

Additionally, owners of livestock may be subjected to civil liability through the application of *res ipsa loquitur* as provided in the last sentence of La. Civ. Code art. 2321. In *Honeycutt v. State Farm Fire & Casualty Co.,* 890 So. 2d 756 (La.App. 2 Cir. 2004), the appellate court affirmed the trial court's application of *res ipsa* stating that "(a)bsent negligence, a cow confined within fencing of proper height and maintenance will not wander into the center of the roadway in the middle of the night, endangering motorists."

E.   BUILDINGS

Prior to 1996, C.C. Article 2322 provided that "(t)he owner of a building is answerable for the damage occasioned by its ruin, when that is caused by neglect to repair it, or when it is the result of a vice in its original construction." The 1996 amendment produced the following version:

La. Civil Code Article 2322.   Damage caused by ruin of building

The owner of a building is answerable for the damage occasioned by its ruin, when this is caused by neglect to repair it, or when it is the result of a vice or defect in its original construction. However, he is answerable for damages only upon a showing that he knew or, in the exercise of reasonable care, should have known of the vice or defect which caused the damage, that the damage could have been prevented by the exercise of reasonable care, and that he failed to exercise such reasonable care. Nothing in this Article shall preclude the court from the application of the doctrine of res ipsa loquitur in an appropriate case.

COMMENT

The seminal interpretation of the pre-1996 version of La. Civ. Code art. is *Olsen v. Shell Oil Co.*, 365 So. 2d 1285 (La. 1978) which determined that a fixed drilling platform with its foundation in the soil is a "building" within the meaning of Article 2322 whether intended for habitation or not and which held the owner of a fixed drilling platform, to which movable living quarters had been attached thereby constituting an appurtenance, strictly liable for a defect in the living quarters although it did not own the living quarters.

The *Webre* case which follows is an application of the post-1996 version of Article 2322.

WEBRE
v.
ALTON OCHSNER MEDICAL FOUNDATION
759 So. 2d 146 (La.App. 5 Cir. 2000)

GOTHARD, J.

This is an action in negligence for injuries sustained by a patient of Ochsner Foundation Hospital (Ochsner). After a trial on the merits, the trial court found for plaintiff in the amount of $12,000.00. Defendant, Ochsner, has appealed the judgment. Plaintiff, Robert Webre, has filed an answer to the appeal. For reasons that follow, we reverse.

At trial, plaintiff, Robert Webre, testified that in February, 1997 his wife, Donna, began suffering severe headaches. She was also experiencing difficulty with speech and writing, and memory loss. On February 5, 1997 Mrs. Webre underwent a CAT scan at Ochsner Hospital, which revealed a brain tumor. She was admitted into the hospital and surgery to remove the tumor was performed on February 7, 1997. Mr. Webre and the couple's two daughters, Christy and Judy, were encouraged immediately after the surgery when Mrs. Webre came out of the surgery "feisty". Unfortunately, a subsequent biopsy resulted in the diagnosis of an incurable malignancy. The tragic news devastated the family members, who were now required to make heart-rending decisions on the best course of treatment for Mrs. Webre. Mrs. Webre elected to have radiation treatment, and was doing well for about one month after the surgery. During that period, Judy was helping her mother with personal hygiene needs.

On March 14, 1997, Mr. Webre noticed his wife seemed weaker than usual when he took her in for her daily radiation treatment. After the treatment the couple went to visit a friend in the hospital and drove home. Later that evening, Judy noticed that one side of Mrs. Webre's face was "quivering", and she seemed unable to speak. Later that evening, Mrs. Webre passed out and was brought to the hospital. Shortly after she arrived, she had a grand mal seizure and was taken into the emergency room for treatment. She was subsequently admitted to the hospital.

On March 16, 1997 she was sedated and resting comfortably. The next evening, she was awake and alert and discussing family matters with her daughters. According to Mr. Webre, it was the last time she was coherent. On the 17th Mrs. Webre began physical therapy. She was unable to carry on a conversation, but was responsive. The next day she was slightly improved.

Mr. Webre testified that he left the hospital at about 4:00 p.m. on March 18, 1997. Later that evening he received a telephone call from Dr. Laura Young who informed him that his wife had been struck in the head by a grate which fell from the ceiling of an elevator. Mrs. Webre was being transported from physical therapy back to her room when the incident occurred. Dr. Young called back shortly afterward to inform Mr. Webre that another CAT scan was being conducted on his wife.

When Mr. Webre returned to the hospital, his wife was unresponsive. He observed a bruise on the top of her head. She was released from the hospital on March 24th. Mr. Webre stated that his wife never returned to her "old self." Mrs. Webre died on June 13, 1997.

The court also heard testimony from Judy Webre Chaisson, who testified that she lived three doors down from her parents and visited her mother every day.... She arrived at the hospital in the evening after being informed of the accident. She found her mother asleep and unresponsive. From that time until her death on June 13th, Mrs. Webre did not recognize her family members. Mrs. Chaisson described her mother as "childlike." Mrs. Webre was unable to feed or dress herself, and required constant care. It was necessary for Mrs. Chaisson to bathe and groom her mother as she was unable to attend to basic hygiene needs herself.

When questioned about the injury her mother sustained from the falling grate, Mrs. Chaisson testified that she observed redness on the left side of the head above the surgical scar. She described the area as a large, bruised area.

* * * * *

The court also heard testimony from Marcus Campbell, who was employed by Ochsner Hospital on March 14, 1997. He testified that he was transporting Mrs. Webre from her room to physical therapy when the grate over the light fixture in the elevator fell and hit her on top of the head. She cried out in pain. Mr. Campbell rushed Mrs. Webre to the department of physical therapy and told the therapist, who checked the patient and wrote an incident report. Mr. Campbell testified that Mrs. Webre did not lose consciousness and was not cut in the incident. Mr. Campbell further stated that he transported Mrs. Webre before and after the incident and did not notice any change in her behavior as a result of the accident.

After reviewing all of the evidence the trial court rendered judgment in favor of plaintiff in the amount of $12,000.00 for loss of quality of life. It is clear from the judgment that the trial court made a factual finding that the accident which occurred while Mrs. Webre was under Ochsner's care was not an aggravating or contributing cause of her death.

LSA-C.C. art. 2322 provides as follows:

> The owner of a building is answerable for the damage occasioned by its ruin, when this is caused by neglect to repair it, or when it is the result of a vice or defect in its original construction. *However, he is answerable for damages only upon a showing that he knew or, in the exercise of reasonable care, should have known of the vice or defect* which caused the damage, that the damage could have been prevented by the exercise of reasonable care, and that he failed to exercise such reasonable care. Nothing in this Article shall preclude the court from the application of the doctrine of res ipsa loquitur in an appropriate case. (Emphasis added)

On appeal, Ochsner argues the doctrine of res ipsa loquitur does not apply, and the plaintiff failed in his burden of proof to show negligence. We agree. The above cited code article, which was in effect at the time of the injury, changed the law from the previous rule of strict liability to negligence. The law as applicable now requires a showing that the defendant knew or should have known of the defect. The mere showing that a defect existed which caused the injury is insufficient to carry the burden of proof.

The evidence offered at trial goes to causation and extent of damages. It does not address the essential element of knowledge of the defect. There was no showing at trial which would impact the knowledge requirement of the code article. Thus, an essential element necessary to find liability is absent. Accordingly, we must reverse the trial court.

Because we reverse the ruling and find for the defendant, we pretermit discussion of the issues presented by plaintiff's answer.

REVERSED.

* * * * *

NOTES

1.   What factors should be considered in determining whether attachments to a building can be considered part of a building in assessing liability under La. C.C. Art. 2322? *See Coulter v. Texaco*, 117 F.3d 909 (5th Cir. 1997).

2.   In cases involving a negligent plaintiff and a strictly liable defendant, the Louisiana Supreme Court has suggested that the judge or jury should compare causation. *See Howard v. Allstate Insurance Co.*, 520 So. 2d 715 (La. 1988). This may prove difficult, if not impossible. (Dennis, J. dissenting). *Id.* at 720. Note that La. Civ. Code art. 2323(B) requires the application of comparative fault. How should this be done?

CHAPTER 11

ABSOLUTE LIABILITY AND THE OBLIGATION OF NEIGHBORHOOD

A.   INTRODUCTION

COMMENT

Absolute liability generally is imposed in cases where harm is caused by an "ultrahazardous" thing or activity or an "unreasonably dangerous" thing or activity. Ultrahazardous activity is the formulation of the First Restatement of Torts; unreasonably dangerous is the construction of the Second Restatement. Both Restatements combine cases, which in Louisiana are regarded as "strict liability," with cases Louisiana law distinguishes as "absolute liability." This approach is followed by most commentators. *See* DAN DOBBS, THE LAW OF TORTS 941-68 (2000).

Both strict and absolute liability are often described as "liability without fault." *Id.*, at 941. However, this characterization is not accurate. *See* RICHARD EPSTEIN, TORTS 333-34 (1999). In truth, negligence, strict liability and absolute liability are theories of fault which operate in similar manners on quite different facts. *Cf. Langlois, supra.* Generally, negligence turns on determining (1) whether the defendant's response to the risks of harm in a given situation was reasonable, (2) in light of the extent and degree of harm possible. This is represented in the "Learned Hand formula" discussed in *Carroll Towing*. In strict liability cases, the risk and degree of harm are heightened.

Strict liability places the burden of any harm caused on the person who is in the best position to prevent the harm. Thus those persons who have "garde" under Civil Code Articles 2317 and 2322 have the incentive to take steps to reduce the risk of harm posed by the person or thing under their charge. When those steps are nullified by the defendant's behavior, strict liability generally does not apply. *See Kent v. Gulf States Utilities Company*, 418 So. 2d 493, 499 n. 9. Strict liability in Louisiana also includes harm caused by domestic animals. Another form of "strict liability," i.e., liability without fault, is vicarious liability (employer's responsibility for employee's behavior or parent's responsibility for his or her child). *See* Chapter 11.

Absolute liability is similar, but it involves cases of *significant risks of significant harm,* where the risks are not easily contained. Thus in most states absolute liability attaches when the harm is caused by things that cannot be controlled. Wild animals, for example, are always wild and thus likely to attack in unknown and very damaging ways; mining (with explosives) and pile driving are likely to cause damaging shockwaves that extend far and wide and result in difficult to anticipate damage to surrounding structures; storage of explosives or noxious and dangerous chemicals can be done with only limited reduction of the risk that an explosion or leak will cause harm to nearby people and things.

Negligence, strict liability, and absolute liability are distinguished mostly by the demands of proof on the plaintiff. To establish negligence, the plaintiff must show breach of duty and legal cause, but in an appropriate strict liability case, the plaintiff is required only to show that the thing over which the person has garde presented an unreasonable risk of harm and that the damages were legally caused by that thing. In absolute liability cases, the plaintiff need show only legal cause connecting the injuries to the unreasonably dangerous activity.

Fundamentally, the distinction between negligence, strict liability, and absolute liability turns on the characterization of the nature of the risks and danger posed by the activity in question. This is basically an allocation question which courts have tended to resolve in a particular way, with certain cases deemed strict liability and others absolute. This allocation function is, nevertheless, the kind of policy decision that legislatures are well suited to make. The Louisiana Legislature's 1996 modification to C.C. Art. 667 constitutes a reallocation of cases among the three categories, changing in Louisiana the basic determination of the risks in cases formerly deemed ultrahazardous.

The following case discusses the distinction between various theories of liability as it was applied prior to the 1996 tort reform.

KENT

v.

GULF STATES UTILITIES COMPANY
418 So. 2d 493 (La. 1982)

LEMMON, J.

This case of personal injury by contact with electrical lines involves an analysis of the respective duties and conduct of the electric utility company, of the executive officers of the construction company which was building a road that crossed under the electric lines, of the executive officers of the State Department of Highways, and of the electrocution victim who was a construction worker on the project.

The accident occurred when Keith Kent, an employee of Barber Brothers Contracting Company, was working on a highway department project to widen a roadway in the Baton Rouge area. The 30-foot aluminum pole he was using to texture the surface of the highway came in contact with a high voltage distribution line owned by Gulf States Utilities. Named as original defendants were Gulf States Utilities Company and the State of Louisiana Department of Highways. After the trial court determined plaintiff's exclusive remedy against the Department was for workmen's compensation benefits and dismissed that defendant, plaintiff named the Department's project engineer, W. L. Landon, Jr., and their project inspector, Killiam H. Kupper, as individual defendants. Also named defendants in their individual capacities were Barber's two executive officers.

After presentation of the evidence and closing arguments to the jury, the Barber defendants reached a settlement with plaintiff. The trial court's charge to the jury included instructions on the liability of the Barber defendants, and the jury returned a verdict in favor of plaintiff against Gulf States Utilities and Barber's two officers for $ 3,000,000. The trial court entered judgment following the verdict against Gulf States Utilities for $ 1,000,000, plus legal interest and one-third of the costs, as its share of the judgment. All other defendants were dismissed.

Plaintiff appealed, seeking reversal of the dismissal of Landon and Kupper and of the trial court's reduction of the judgment by two-thirds. Defendant Gulf States also appealed, reurging the defenses of contributory negligence and/or assumption of risk. The court of appeal held that Keith Kent's conduct barred his recovery and reversed the judgment against Gulf States, while affirming the dismissal of all other defendants. 398 So. 2d 560. We granted plaintiff's application for certiorari. 399 So. 2d 585.

Facts

Keith Kent began his employment with Barber shortly before the accident. At the time of his injury the 18-year old employee was making antihydroplaning grooves in the surface of the highway by pulling a metal rake, approximately five feet wide, across the surface of the freshly poured concrete.

The portion of the highway then under construction ran under three high voltage distribution lines, which intersected the highway at an angle. The uninsulated lines, located 25 feet 8 inches above the surface of the ground and 24 feet 8 inches above the surface of the slab, were clearly visible, and everyone on the construction site, including Keith Kent, was aware of them.

The metal rake used by the workers to create grooves had an aluminum handle, which had been extended to a length of 30 feet by screwing together several six-foot sections. That length was necessary because of the double width of the concrete roadway (two 13-foot widths) under construction.[2]

On the day of the accident Kent and his co-worker, David Jenkins, were using a walk bench bridge (a structure on wheels which straddled the slab) to transfer the rake from one side of the poured concrete to the other. The workers, after pulling the rake across the concrete, used the bench to slide the rake back across the slab to make the next pull. However, about two hours before the accident, a crew of Barber's concrete finishers needed the bench, and Kent and Jenkins relinquished it. They first tried to simply push the rake across and pull it back, but that procedure caused gouging. They then began using the "flip-flop" method to transfer the rake back and forth across the slab.[3] In using this method, Kent stood on one side of the slab and pulled the rake, creating the grooves across the concrete. He then returned the rake by holding onto the rake head, raising the handle in the air and letting the rake fall across the slab, where it was caught by Jenkins. Jenkins then pulled the rake across the surface and returned it to Kent in a similar manner.

Kent and Jenkins used this method until they came near the overhead lines. To avoid contact, they devised a method to walk away from the lines, to flip the rake, and then to return under the lines to rake across the surface. Kent and Jenkins had used this method without incident to work underneath and beyond the lines approximately eight or ten feet when the accident occurred.

None of the witnesses who testified at trial actually saw the rake handle contact the wire. David Jenkins testified that he and Kent had completed two pulls after crossing under the wires and that Kent was standing eight to ten feet from the point the wires intersected the highway at an angle. Suddenly "he [Kent] just went up in the air with it [the rake handle]". Jenkins described the handle as limber and wobbly.

Charles Smith, a cement finisher, testified that he walked over to Kent just before the accident to warn him of the lines. He stated that when he tapped Kent on the shoulder and pointed out the lines, Kent indicated he was aware of them and joked with Smith that the wires would get Jenkins, but not him. Smith testified he turned and walked about 20 feet when he heard the electrical boom caused by the handle's contact with the wire, and then he saw Kent slumped over motionless next to the slab.

It is therefore evident from the testimony that the accident occurred when Kent, while standing very near the overhead lines, raised the rake handle so that it made contact with one of the lines.

Liability of Gulf States

Plaintiff contends that Gulf States was negligent in failing to take reasonable measures to protect against the foreseeable risk that a person, in contact with the ground or with a grounded object, would come in contact with its wires in the construction area. Plaintiff further urges that we hold Gulf

---

[2] There was some testimony that grooving over a straight run of concrete pouring was usually accomplished by a machine and that hand raking was generally used only at intersections or for spot patching, when use of the machine was impractical. In such situations only a short-handled rake was usually required, because of the relatively short distance over which the rake had to be pulled. On the day of the accident the grooving machine was broken, and Barber's employees had to use the long-handled rake (which Barber had on the job) to create grooves on the 26-foot wide roadway.

[3] Testimony at trial conflicted as to how Kent and Jenkins came to use the flip-flop method. David Jenkins testified at trial that defendant Kupper instructed him and Kent, when they were about 50 feet from the wires, to give the bench to the cement finishers and to use the "flip-flop" method. In a statement given approximately six months after the accident, however, Jenkins was unable to say who instructed him and Kent to use that method. Defendant Kupper, on the other hand, denied having instructed the workers to use this method. In any event Kent and Jenkins used the flip-flop method for two hours in full view of the supervisors of both Barber and the Highway Department.

States under some form of absolute or strict liability, either as the custodian of a thing under C.C. Art. 2317 or as an enterpriser engaged in an ultrahazardous activity.

Negligence versus Strict Liability

C.C. Art. 2315 imposes delictual liability on a person whose *fault* causes damage to another. Since "fault" is a broader and more comprehensive term than "negligence", the codal scheme imposes responsibility on a person not only when his negligence causes damage, but also when the person has a legal relationship with a person, a thing, or an activity which causes damage. *Langlois v. Allied Chemical Corp.*, 258 La. 1067, 249 So. 2d 133 (1971). Liability is *strict* in the sense that it does not depend upon proof of personal negligence.

C.C. Art. 2317 provides:

"We are responsible, not only for the damages occasioned by our own act, but for that which is caused by the act of persons for whom we are answerable, or of the things which we have in our custody. This, however, is to be understood with the following modifications."

In *Loescher v. Parr*, 324 So. 2d 441 (La. 1975), this court interpreted Art. 2317 as imposing liability on the owner of a diseased tree which fell onto a neighbor's automobile, although the diseased condition of the tree was not apparent and the owner therefore could not be deemed *negligent* for failing to discover and correct the condition or to protect others from the risk resulting from that defective condition.   The court held that the tree's owner-guardian was liable for his *fault* in maintaining a defective tree and not preventing the thing from causing injury, unless he proved that the damage was caused by the fault of the victim, by the fault of a third person, or by an irresistible force.

Because the term "thing" encompasses a virtually unlimited range of subject matter, the *Loescher* decision has since been cited by innumerable litigants seeking to avoid the necessity of proving personal negligence in tort cases. The distinction between negligence cases and strict liability cases (such as *Loescher*) has largely been either misunderstood or completely disregarded. It is therefore appropriate for this court, in determining the applicability of Art. 2317, to review first the distinguishing effect of applying strict liability under that article.

In a typical negligence case against the owner of a thing (such as a tree) which is actively involved in the causation of injury, the claimant must prove that something about the thing created an unreasonable risk of injury that resulted in the damage, *that the owner knew or should have known of that risk*, and that the owner nevertheless failed to render the thing safe or to take adequate steps to prevent the damage caused by the thing. Under traditional negligence concepts, the knowledge (actual or constructive) gives rise to the duty to take reasonable steps to protect against injurious consequences resulting from the risk, and no responsibility is placed on the owner who acted reasonably but nevertheless failed to discover that the thing presented an unreasonable risk of harm.

In a strict liability case against the same owner, the claimant is relieved only of proving that the owner knew or should have known of the risk involved. The claimant must still prove that under the circumstances the thing presented an unreasonable risk of harm which resulted in the damage (or must prove, as some decisions have characterized this element of proof, that the thing was defective). The resulting liability is strict in the sense that the owner's duty to protect against injurious consequences resulting from the risk does not depend on actual or constructive knowledge of the risk, the factor which usually gives rise to a duty under negligence concepts. *Under strict liability concepts, the mere fact of the owner's relationship with and responsibility for the damage-causing thing gives rise to an absolute duty to discover the risks presented by the thing in custody.* If the owner breaches that absolute duty to discover, he is presumed to have discovered any risks presented by the thing in custody, and the owner accordingly will be held liable for failing to take steps to prevent injury resulting because the thing in his custody presented an unreasonable risk of injury to another.[5]

Thus, while the basis for determining the existence of the duty (to take reasonable steps to prevent injury as a result of the thing's presenting an unreasonable risk of harm) is different in C.C. Art. 2317 strict liability cases and in ordinary negligence cases, the duty which arises is the same. The extent of the duty (and the resulting degree of care necessary to fulfill the duty) depends upon the particular facts and circumstances of each case.

Accordingly, in a strict liability case in which the claimant asserts that the owner's damage-causing thing presented an unreasonable risk of harm, the *standard for determining liability* is to presume the owner's knowledge of the risk presented by the thing under his control and then to determine the reasonableness (according to traditional notions of blameworthiness) of the owner's conduct, in the light of that presumed knowledge.

Thus, in the *Loescher* case, the plaintiff did not have to prove the owner of the tree knew or should have known of the defect in the tree. Under strict liability concepts the owner was presumed to have knowledge of the tree's condition, and he was liable because a reasonable owner who had discovered the hazardous condition would not have maintained the thing as he did without correcting or minimizing the risk. As some torts scholars have observed, the test in strict liability cases, except for the element of the defendant's scienter, is virtually the same as that for negligence. *See* J. Wade, *Strict Tort Liability for Manufacturers*, 19 S.W.L.J. 5, 15 (1965).[6]

In the present case Gulf States knew that its lines were "hot" and were not wrapped with insulating material, a condition which presents a grave risk of harm to a person who comes in close proximity to the lines while in contact with the ground or a grounded object. (This risk was indeed a cause-in-fact of Kent's injury in this case.) Because of Gulf States' knowledge of the condition of its lines, it is unnecessary in this case to presume any knowledge of a risk of harm created by Gulf States' lines in this case, and C.C. Art. 2317's imposition of an absolute duty to discover the risks presented by the thing in its custody is not helpful to the determination of Gulf States' liability in this case. That liability as custodian of the thing depends on an analysis of the reasonableness of Gulf States' conduct in protecting persons against harm resulting from the risk of which Gulf States was well aware, which is essentially a negligence determination.

Strict Liability versus Absolute Liability

Liability for ultrahazardous activities, on the other hand, involves different considerations than liability under C.C. Art. 2317 for creating or maintaining a thing which presents an unreasonable risk of harm. There are some activities in which the risk may be altogether reasonable and still high enough that the party ought not undertake the activity without assuming the consequences. Such activities include pile driving, storage of toxic gas, blasting with explosives, crop dusting with airplanes, and the like, in which the activity can cause injury to others, even when conducted with the greatest prudence and care. 2 F. Harper and F. James, The Law of Torts, § 14.4 (1956); W. Prosser, The Law of Torts § 78 (4th ed. 1971).

---

[5] The theory is that the owner-guardian is regarded as the risk-creator because of his relationship with the thing which presents the risk. As between him and the faultless victim injured as a result of the risk, the owner-guardian theoretically should bear the loss, because he was in the best position to discover the risk and to prevent the injury.

[6] In products liability cases, the manufacturer is presumed to know the dangerous propensities of its product and is strictly liable for injuries resulting from the product's unreasonable risk of injury in normal use. The claimant nevertheless must prove that the product presented an unreasonable risk of injury in normal use (regardless of the manufacturer's knowledge), *thus in effect proving the manufacturer was negligent in placing the product in commerce with (presumed) knowledge of the danger*.

For these particular activities, Louisiana courts have imposed an *absolute* liability (as contrasted to the strict liability previously discussed), which virtually makes the enterpriser an insurer. The enterpriser, whether or not negligent in any respect, causes the damage, and the injured party recovers simply by proving damage and causation.

In these cases of absolute liability (or liability without proof of negligence or other fault), liability is imposed as a matter of policy when harm results from the risks inherent in the nature of the activity. The steps taken by the enterpriser to protect others from the inherent risks of the activity are not relevant to the determination of liability. The activity of driving piles, for example, is likely to cause damage, even when there is no substandard conduct on *anyone's* part. The activity, by its very nature, simply cannot be done without a high degree of risk of injury. On the other hand, the transmission of electricity over isolated high tension power lines is an everyday occurrence in every parish in this state and can be done without a high degree of risk of injury. And when the activity results in injury, it is almost always because of substandard conduct on the part of either the utility, the victim or a third party.[8]

The two activities of driving piles and of transmitting electricity are thus different from the point of view of a policy need to impose absolute liability irrespective of negligence or other fault. Indeed, we have not been directed to any decision from other states in which absolute liability has been imposed on the activity of transmitting electricity for public consumption. *See* 82 A.L.R. 3d 218 (1978).

We accordingly conclude that Gulf States should not be held absolutely liable, as an enterpriser engaged in ultrahazardous activities, when its activity of transmitting electricity is a cause-in-fact of injury to another, unless fault was proved on Gulf States' part.

Application to Gulf States

We now turn to the bottom line for resolving the issue of Gulf States' liability in this case and determine whether Gulf States took reasonable steps under the circumstances to protect against the risk that a person, in contact with the ground or with a grounded object, would come in contact with its electric lines in the construction area. Pointing out the provision in the National Electric Safety Code for a minimum vertical clearance of 20 feet over roads in urban and rural areas, Gulf States contends that its lines were "insulated by isolation", in that the lines were sufficiently isolated that contact was neither foreseeable nor likely. On the other hand, plaintiff contends that ... Gulf States could have installed temporary insulation or taken other simple protective measures, and should be held liable for failing to take any additional steps to reduce the risk.

* * * * *

A combination of unusual factors concurred to cause this accident. The breaking down of the road machine caused the need to use the rake over an unusually long distance and period of time. The double width of the roadway caused the need to use an exceptionally long handle. The appropriation of the bench to another use caused the need to utilize the flip-flop method (which the Barber executives and others testified they had never seen used with such a long handle). The progress of the grooving to the point of intersection with the wires caused the need to devise an alternative method of procedure under the wires. Finally, Kent's act of raising the handle into wires he had just been warned to avoid was necessary to complete the unfortunate scenario.

Under the overall circumstances, it is difficult to conclude that Gulf States acted unreasonably in failing to protect against these particular consequences. Gulf States' conduct at issue in this case is

---

[8] It is noteworthy that, in each of the activities placed in this special category by decisions of Louisiana courts, the enterpriser is almost invariably the sole cause of the damage and the victim seldom has the ability to protect himself. No decisions have placed in this category any activities in which the victim or a third person can reasonably be expected to be a contributing factor in the causation of damages with any degree of frequency.

its decision not to take additional precautions (such as installing rubber hose in the area of construction) beyond the precaution of insulating its lines by isolation, which was done in the original construction of the lines. We find that conduct not to be unreasonable. Furthermore, we find no ease of association between the risk presented by Gulf States' conduct under the overall circumstances and the injury which ultimately occurred. *Hill v. Lundin & Assoc., Inc.*, 260 La. 542, 256 So. 2d 620 (1972).

Liability of Kupper

Plaintiff contends that Kupper was in charge of the grooving project and, although aware of the wire, did not insure that Kent used proper tools and used a safe method to perform his work.

The duty to provide Kent with a safe place to work, including proper tools, equipment and methods for safely performing his duties, was primarily on his employer and the employer's executive officers. Kupper arguably could have prevented the accident by interjecting himself and demanding that Barber furnish Kent with a fiberglass rake, but he had no such duty to Kent, and is not liable for failing to do so. Furthermore, Kupper did not affirmatively create a hazardous situation by requiring Kent to use dangerous equipment or methods.

The judgment of the court of appeal is affirmed.

[Concurrences by Dixon, C.J., and Marcus, J., ommitted]

DENNIS, Justice, assigning additional concurring reasons.

I join in the majority opinion. Furthermore, in support of its thoughtful observations, I feel the following comments should be added.

I am convinced that this court in *Loescher v. Parr*, 324 So. 2d 441 (La. 1975), through use of the phrase "unreasonable risk of injury," intended to inject into the theory of liability under Article 2317, a balancing test closely analogous to that utilized in negligence actions.

The "unreasonable risk of injury" phrase is strikingly similar to language employed by many American courts, scholars, and law reform bodies in dealing with ordinary negligence and products liability law. *See* W. Prosser, Law of Torts § 31 (4th ed. 1971); Restatement of Torts § § 282 and 402A. The history of strict products liability in Louisiana indicates the requirement that a defective product must be "unreasonably dangerous" came into our jurisprudence due to the pervasive influence of section 402A of the Restatement of Torts after its publication in 1965. *DeBattista v. Argonaut-Southwest Ins.*, 403 So. 2d 26 (La. 1981); *Weber v. F. & C. Co.*, 259 La. 599, 250 So. 2d 754 (1971). *See* Andrus, 25 *La. B.J.* 105 (1977); Robertson, 50 Tul. L. Rev. 50 (1975). After using the "unreasonably dangerous" limitation in *Weber v. F. & C. Co.* as a condition to legal fault under Article 2315, the Louisiana Supreme Court employed a similar requirement in summarizing the principles of legal fault under Articles 2317, 2318, 2320, 2321 and 2322, by holding that strict liability results from the conduct or defect of a person or thing which creates an "unreasonable risk" of injury to others. *Loescher v. Parr, supra.*

All of these "unreasonable risk" tests imply a process of balancing the risk against the value of the interest which the defendant is seeking to protect, and the expedience of the course pursued. Prosser, at p. 149. This is the standard negligence test. In strict liability, except for the element of the defendant's knowledge, the test is the same as that for negligence. Wade, *On the Nature of Strict Tort Liability for Products*, 44 Miss. L.J. 825, 834-35 (1973); Wade, *Strict Tort Liability for Manufacturers*, 19 S.W.L.J. 5, 15 (1965). *Compare*, Comment, *Does Louisiana Really Have Strict Liability Under Civil Code Articles 2317, 2318, and 2321?*, 40 La. L. Rev. 207 (1979). In negligence, allowance is made for the risk apparent to the actor, for his capacity to meet it, and for the circumstances under which he must act. In strict liability, however, knowledge of the condition of the product is imputed to the defendant before the balancing test or negligence test is applied. In products liability, for example, a product is considered unreasonably dangerous when a reasonable seller would not sell the product if he knew of the risks involved or if the risks are greater than a reasonable buyer would expect. Thus, assuming that the defendant had knowledge of the condition of the product, would he then have been acting unreasonably in placing it on the market? This is another way of posing the question of whether the product presents an unreasonable risk of injury. And it may be the most useful way of presenting it. *See*, Wade, *Strict Tort Liability for Manufacturers*, 19 S.W.L.J. 5 (1965).

In the future, we may come to recognize that in the strict liability of *Loescher v. Parr*, except for the element of the knowledge of the custodian of the thing, the test is the same as that for negligence. Thus, assuming that the custodian of the thing had knowledge of its condition, would he then have been acting reasonably by maintaining it and exposing others to it? If this comes to be understood as the most useful way of presenting the *Loescher* test, then this type of strict liability will retain many of the characteristics of negligence law.

The *Loescher* strict liability bears little analogy to the common law doctrine of strict liability for abnormally dangerous conditions and activities with which it has sometimes been compared. *Dorry v. LaFleur*, 399 So. 2d 559 (La. 1981). Under the rule of *Rylands v. Fletcher*, the defendant will be liable when he damages another by a thing or activity *unduly dangerous and inappropriate to the place where it is maintained*, in the light of the character of that place and its surroundings. The conditions and activities to which the rule has been applied include water collected in quantity in a dangerous place, or allowed to percolate; explosives stored in quantity in a city; blasting and pile driving; and crop dusting, et al. Prosser, § 78, pp. 509-510. The Restatement of Torts has accepted this principle but has limited it to an "ultra hazardous activity" which "necessarily involves a risk of serious harm to the persons, land or chattels of others which cannot be eliminated by the exercise of the utmost care" and "is not a matter of common usage." Restatement of Torts, § § 519, 520. The *Loescher* doctrine is much broader since it covers all things, everywhere which create an unreasonable risk of injury to others. Most of the circumstances giving rise to strict liability under Act 2317 have been neither ultrahazardous nor unnatural to the locality. *See Dorry v. LaFleur, supra*; Malone, *Ruminations on Liability for the Acts of Things*, 42 La. L. Rev. 979 (1982).

The interpretation of *Loescher* suggested above preserves its worthy goals while providing the trier of fact with badly needed conceptual guidance and linkage with the familiar negligence network. The plaintiff must still prove, as part of his prima facie case, that his injury resulted from a thing in the defendant's custody presenting an unreasonable risk of injury to others. At the same time, the plaintiff is relieved of the burden of proving the custodian's knowledge of the thing's defective condition.[66] Although the custodian is presumed to have scienter, his conduct in failing to prevent the injury is judged, for the most part, according to negligence concepts with which laymen, jurors, and judges are comfortable and familiar. The custodian may still exculpate himself by proving that the injury resulted from the fault of the victim, the fault of a third person, or an irresistible force.

It would seem to follow that in cases such as the instant one, where the defendant clearly knew or should have known of the risk of injury to others by the thing in its care, the imputation of scienter afforded by *Loescher* is irrelevant. Applying the standard negligence test, I would agree with the author of the majority opinion that the plaintiff failed to prove that the power company acted negligently in causing Mr. Kent's injuries.

Part of the majority opinion does cause some concern, however. Although the transmission of high voltage electricity over uninsulated lines is not an ultrahazardous activity in most jurisdictions,

---

[66] The *Loescher* opinion has been criticized for discarding the traditional test of blameworthiness by imposing liability upon a defendant who had neither actual nor constructive knowledge of the defective condition of the thing in his custody. *See*, Malone, *Ruminations on Liability for the Acts of Things*, 42 LA. L. REV. 979 (1982). The perceived harshness of this result may be ameliorated, to a large degree, if the doctrine of comparative negligence is found to be applicable in 2317 actions. *See*, 1979 La. Acts. No. 431; Plant, *Comparative Negligence and Strict Tort Liability*, 40 LA. L. REV. 403 (1980); *Rodrigue v. Dixilyn Corp.*, 620 F.2d 537, 544 n. 11 (5th Cir. 1980); *Daly v. General Motors Corp.*, 20 Cal.3d 725, 144 Cal. Rptr. 380, 575 P.2d 1162 (1978).

see Annotation, *Applicability of Rule of Strict Liability to Injury From Electrical Current Escaping From Powerline*, 82 A.L.R.3d 218 (1978), this cannot be said so convincingly in Louisiana. Arguably, the conclusion that this activity is ultrahazardous could be reached through the same process by which this court decided, in *Langlois v. Allied Chemical Corp.*, 258 La. 1067, 249 So. 2d 133 (1971), that the storage of highly poisonous gas was an ultrahazardous activity:

> "We do not here establish a new standard for liability, but merely apply the standard set by law and applied repeatedly in our jurisprudence. The activities of man for which he may be liable without acting negligently are to be determined after a study of the law and customs, a balancing of claims and interests, a weighing of the risk and the gravity of harm, and a consideration of individual and societal rights and obligations. *See Yommer v. McKenzie*, 255 Md. 220, 257 A.2d 138 (1969)." 249 So. 2d at 140.

I find it unnecessary to contend with the argument at this time, however, because I find that the plaintiff's own fault would preclude him from recovering in this case even under a *Langlois* type of strict liability. Although it is a close question, as I appreciate the evidence, the plaintiff knowingly and unreasonably assumed the risk of electrocution by flip-flopping a metal pole near the defendant's power line.

WATSON, Justice, dissenting.

In view of the heavy construction activity in the vicinity, the transmission of deadly voltages of electricity over these uninsulated lines constituted an ultra-hazardous activity. Gulf States owed a high degree of care. Although the lines exceeded the safety code's minimum clearance by four feet, eight inches, this was insufficient. A dragline, which had been used at the site, also might "have got entangled" in the electric lines. (Tr. 476) Robert E. Briggs, an expert consultant in electrical engineering, testified that the hazard here could have been greatly reduced by the use of temporary insulation. According to Briggs, such an accident was "reasonably foreseeable". (Tr. 575) In Briggs' expert opinion, the National Electric Safety Code was violated by Gulf States. Gulf States had a duty to take further precautions against the risk of injury presented. The question of Gulf States' liability is a jury question. The jury's verdict against Gulf States should be affirmed. [citations ommited]

The jury did not give judgment against Kupper and apparently did not believe Jenkins' testimony that Kupper instructed them to use the flip-flop method. However, it is unlikely that Kent, a new, eighteen year old employee, devised that method himself. Because the long jointed pole was "clumsy up in the air" (Tr. 465), it came in contact with the electric lines.

I respectfully dissent.

NOTES

1.   The Common Law imposed liability without fault upon a landowner whose non-natural use of his or her land caused harm to neighbors. The doctrine evolved out of the famous case of *Rylands v. Fletcher*, L.R. 3 H.L. 330 (1868). Although Rylands was not generally adopted in the United States, the American Common Law gradually embraced a form of absolute liability for certain land use. The prevailing rule is embodied in Sections 519 and 520 of the Restatement (Second) of Torts, reproduced below.

§ 519 General Principle

(1) One who carries on an abnormally dangerous activity is subject to liability for harm to the person, land or chattels of another resulting from the activity, although he has exercised the utmost care to prevent the harm.

(2) This strict liability is limited to the kind of harm, the possibility of which makes the activity abnormally dangerous.

§ 520 Abnormally Dangerous Activities

In determining whether an activity is abnormally dangerous, the following factors are to be considered:

(A) existence of a high degree of risk of some harm to the person, land or chattels of others;

(B) likelihood that the harm that results from it will be great;
(C) inability to eliminate the risk by exercise of reasonable care;
(D) extent to which the activity is not a matter of common usage;
(E) inappropriateness of hte activity to the place where it is carried on; and
(F) extent to which its value to the community is outweighed by its dangerous attributes.

2.   The Restatement (Third) of Torts: Liability for Physical and Emotional Harm § 20 (2010) provides that:

(a) An actor who carries on an abnormally dangerous activity is subject to strict liability for physical harm resulting from the activity.
(b) An activity is abnormally dangerous if:
(1) the activity creates a foreseeable and highly significant risk of physical harm even when reasonable care is exercised by all actors; and
(2) the activity is not one of common usage.

Do you see any significant differences between the Second and Third Restatements?

3.   *Kent* holds that steps taken to protect against risk are irrelevant. What is the role of deterrence in absolute liability cases? Do these cases create a disincentive to take steps to protect against harm? Or, does this apparent paradox – disincentivizing precautionary behavior by creating liability because of the activity's inherent dangerousness – merely reflect the natural consequence of creating a liability system to deal with ultrahazardous activities?

4.   Generally, absolute liability is available in cases where the nature of the injury-causing activity is such that the plaintiff cannot protect himself from the risk of harm. For example, a homeowner whose walls are cracked by pile driving down the road cannot generally take steps to mitigate the harm even if he is aware of the risk to his home. Does this underlying characteristic of absolute liability mean that there cannot be comparative fault? *Kent*, 418 So. 2d 493, 499 n. 9. What of Justice Dennis' hope that the harshness of strict and absolute liability can be ameliorated by applying comparative fault to 2317 – is it realistic or is it inconsistent with the very notion of absolute liability?

LANGLOIS
v.
ALLIED CHEMICAL CORPORATION
258 La. 1067; 249 So. 2d 133 (1971)

[Plaintiff, a fireman, was overcome by gases leaked from defendant's chemical plant and sued for damages. The Court, in a detailed discussion, observed that Article 2315 sets "fault" as the basis for dilectual liability. In the following passages it discusses the basis for absolute liability as rooted in Article 2315 but drawing, by analogy, from the vicinage articles: Civil Code Articles 666-669.]

In general the early cases seem to rely upon an old common law treatise, [HORACE G WOOD, A PRACTICAL TREATISE ON THE LAW OF NUISANCES IN THEIR VARIOUS FORMS: INCLUDING REMEDIES THEREFOR AT LAW AND IN EQUITY, 2 vols. (3rd Ed. 1893)], as the basis for determining liability. In the late 1800's and the early 1900's a line of cases appeared which sometimes impliedly but other times expressly determined that liability was founded in tort law by analogy to codal standards of conduct defined in Articles 666, 667, 668, and 669. *Egan v. Hotel Grunewald Co.*, 129

La. 163, 55 So. 750 (1911) is sound jurisprudential authority that liability for dangerous and hazardous activities of man flows from Civil Code Article 2315 by analogy with other Civil Code Articles.[11]

In 1957 in *Gotreaux v. Gary*, 232 La. 373, 94 So. 2d 293, recovery was allowed against both the landowner and his contractor, a flying service, for crop damage from spraying operations. The court rejected negligence as a criterion for liability and looked to Civil Code Article 667 for the standard of conduct. Since Article 667 could not, of course, have literally afforded recovery against the contractor, the source for assigning responsibility for the act and to the parties must have been Civil Code Article 2315. See also *Jeanfreau v. Sanderson*, 239 La. 51, 117 So. 2d 907 (1960).

As recently as 1968 in *Craig v. Montelepre Realty Co.*, 252 La. 502, 211 So. 2d 627, this court allowed recovery for damage from pile driving. Although the court there applied Article 667, it specifically decided the action arose ex delicto and was prescribed by one year.[12]   The majority quoting from another case said: "... 'While negligence is an example of "fault" within the meaning of Article 2315, it is well settled that the obligation imposed upon proprietors by Article 667 is absolute and that proof of negligence is not required in order to recover for a violation or breach thereof.' *Gulf Insurance Co. v. Employers Liability Assur. Corp.*, La.App., 170 So. 2d 125, 127. Cf. 40 TUL.L.REV. 712; *Fontenot v. Magnolia Petroleum* Co., 227 La. 866, 80 So. 2d 845."

The storage of the dangerous, highly poisonous gas by Allied was an activity which, even when conducted with the greatest of care and prudence, could cause damage to others in the neighborhood. It was an ultra-hazardous activity, and the possible consequences of the gas escaping and causing harm were known or should have been known.

[The court then explained that the Fireman's Rule, which traditionally bars firefighters from recovering for injuries sustained while fighting a fire, did not apply. Plaintiff, the court noted, was overcome by the chemicals while on adjoining property and performing duties that were not his normal, truck driving duties. On this basis the court allowed recovery.] *See* Chapter 6, Sec. IV(c).

* * * * *

B.   The Vicinage Articles and 1996 Tort Reform

Prior to the 1996 amendments, the vicinage articles were quite broad.

---

[11] In that case the owner of the property and the contractor (who drove piling and sheet piling and conducted the excavation work) were both held for damage to an adjoining property owner. While the driving of the sheet piling into the footing of an adjoining building was the result of the negligence of the owner's architects and engineers in drawing the plans, the contractor was not negligent in following those plans. Furthermore, there was no finding of negligence, and indeed it would have been difficult to make a finding that the encountering of quicksand and the resulting seepage of water which caused damage to the adjacent property were the result of negligent conduct of the property owner or the contractor. The opinion cited Articles 667, 2315, 2316, and 2317, and cast the owner and the contractor as joint tort feasors for fault under Article 2315 by analogy with Article 667. Negligence under Article 2316 could be attributed to the owner in only one aspect.

[12] Compare with *Devoke v. Yazoo & M. V. R. Co.*, 211 La. 729, 30 So. 2d 816 (1947), where the court allowed recovery for damages occasioned by smoke, gases, soot, and cinders emanating from a roundhouse operated by the railroad. The court cited Articles 666, 667, 668, and 669 as authority for allowing recovery, stating: "Clearly, therefore, the plaintiffs' action is not one in tort, but, rather, one that springs from an obligation imposed upon property owners by the operation of law so that all may enjoy the maximum of liberty in the use and enjoyment of their respective properties." However, the court then discussed prescription and applied the one-year prescription for actions ex delicto as opposed to the 10-year prescription which would apply to a real action. See also *State ex rel. Violett et al. v. Judge*, 46 La.Ann. 78, 14 So. 423 (1894). The court there cited Civil Code Article 666, but allowed a lessee or tenant to recover. The landlord had not appealed, and this court specifically discussed the tenant's right to stand and recover in damages. Since the tenant's rights could not have arisen under the law of property, the recovery must have been granted under Article 2315.

Art. 667. Limitations on use of property

Although a proprietor may do with his estate whatever he pleases, still he cannot make any work on it, which may deprive his neighbor of the liberty of enjoying his own, or which may be the cause of any damage to him.

Art. 668. Inconvenience to neighbor

Although one be not at liberty to make any work by which his neighbor's buildings may be damaged, yet every one has the liberty of doing on his own ground whatsoever he pleases, although it should occasion some inconvenience to his neighbor.

Thus he who is not subject to any servitude originating from a particular agreement in that respect, may raise his house as high as he pleases, although by such elevation he should darken the lights of his neighbors's [neighbor's] house, because this act occasions only an inconvenience, but not a real damage.

Art. 669. Regulation of inconvenience

If the works or materials for any manufactory or other operation, cause an inconvenience to those in the same or in the neighboring houses, by diffusing smoke or nauseous smell, and there be no servitude established by which they are regulated, their sufferance must be determined by the rules of the police, or the customs of the place.

The articles listed above, the vicinage articles, deal with the relationship between neighbors. They are based on the Latin maxim *sic utere tuo, ut alienum nom laedas*, i.e., "use your own property in such a manner as not to injure that of another." They were the basis for a broad "absolute liability" prior to 1996 amendments. Professors Maraist and Galligan describe the problems of basing liability on these articles:

> The use of *sic utere* to impose absolute liability has generated some confusion, partly because of the antiquated language employed in the Code. One issue was whether absolute liability was a property claim or a tort action. Although *Langlois* did not specifically hold that the claim was firmly rooted either in tort law or property law, it did make clear that a violation of the vicinage articles could be fault for the purposes of Article 2315. Another issue was whether absolute liability could be imposed outside of the context of violation of the vicinage articles. Some courts indicated that the ultrahazardous activity had to relate to the use of land. A third issue was whether absolute liability was limited to the duty one landowner owed to a neighboring landowner. Absolute liability in Louisiana has not been so limited. Nonlandowners have recovered and nonlandowners, including lessees and contractors, have been held liable under the theory.

MARAIST & GALLIGAN, LOUISIANA TORT LAW § 16-3 at 16-6 – 16-7 (2d ed., Matthew Bender 2005) (citations omitted). In 1996 Article 667 was substantially amended adding the following, underlined language.

Art. 667 Limitations on use of property

Although a proprietor may do with his estate whatever he pleases, still he cannot make any work on it, which may deprive his neighbor of the liberty of enjoying his own, or which may be the cause of any damage to him. However, if the work he makes on his estate deprives his neighbor of enjoyment or causes damage to him, he is answerable for damages only upon a showing that he knew or, in the exercise of reasonable care, should have known that his works would cause damage, that the damage could have been prevented by the exercise of reasonable care, and that he failed to exercise such reasonable care. Nothing in this Article shall preclude the court from the application of the doctrine of res ipsa loquitur in an appropriate case. Nonetheless, the proprietor is answerable for damages without regard to his knowledge or his exercise of reasonable care, if the damage is caused by an ultrahazardous activity. An ultrahazardous activity as used in this Article is strictly limited to pile driving or blasting with explosives.

The new language was added to Article 667 to limit absolute liability to only two cases: pile driving or blasting with explosives. Thus, much of the material in this chapter is relevant only for pile driving and blasting. It remains relevant in other jurisdictions, however, where strict liability for ultrahazardous activities is similar to Louisiana's pre-1996 absolute liability.

NOTES

1.   What is blasting with explosives? Consider the long excerpt, below, from the recent Federal Fifth Circuit decision in *Roberts v. Cardinal Services, Inc.*, 266 F.3d 368 (5th Cir. 2001).

The *Roberts* court was required to decide whether use of a "wireline perforating gun" constituted "blasting" for the purposes of liability under arts. 2315 and 667. A wireline perforating gun is a tool used in oil drilling. The conical-shaped gun is filled with explosive charge and lowered into a well in order to facilitate drilling (by breaking obstructions or piercing a geological formation) or to seal and abandon a spent or otherwise unproductive well (the "p & a" procedure described in the case). In *Roberts*, a pressure sensitive trigger was set to fire the gun when lowered to a certain depth. However, the gun fired on the drilling platform, severely injuring the plaintiff, apparently because someone opened a valve releasing pressurized gas on the gun.

The court made the following observations:

C.   Use of Wireline Perforation Gun an Ultrahazardous Activity under Louisiana Law

The Plaintiffs appeal the district court's grant of summary judgment in favor of Kerr-McGee, dismissing their claims for vicarious and strict liability under Louisiana Civil Code arts. 2315 and 667. They assert that the district court erred when it determined that Kerr-McGee's independent contractor, Cardinal, was not engaged in an ultrahazardous activity while using the perforating gun in conducting the p&a job for Kerr-McGee. The Plaintiffs focus particularly on the district court's refusal to include wireline perforation within the ultrahazardous category of "blasting with explosives." Agreeing that wireline perforation is not congruent with "blasting with explosives" as that term is used in art. 667, and being convinced that wireline perforation does not satisfy Louisiana's broader jurisprudential test for ultrahazardous activities, we affirm the district court's grant of Kerr-McGee's summary judgment dismissing the Plaintiffs' claims under arts. 2315 and 667.

1. The Article 2315 Claim.

a. Framework

Before we proceed to analyze the Plaintiffs' negligence and vicarious liability claims against Kerr-McGee, an abbreviated review of the application of Louisiana's basic tort provision, art. 2315, appears to be in order. That article states that "[e]very act whatever of man that causes damage to another obliges him by whose fault it happened to repair it." Classically, a tort in Louisiana comprises art. 2315's four indispensable elements: act, damage, cause, and fault. The Louisiana Supreme Court observed in *Langlois v. Allied Chemical Corp.* that "[f]ault is the key word in art. 2315." In construing "fault" in art. 2315, *Langlois* further explained, the courts "[go] to the many other articles in our Code as well as statutes and other laws which deal with the responsibility of certain persons, the responsibility in certain relationships, and the responsibility which arises due to certain types of activities." In particular, noted the *Langlois* court, there is "sound jurisprudential authority that liability for dangerous and hazardous activities of man flows from Civil Code Article 2315 by analogy with other Civil Code Articles."

In our review of Louisiana law in *Perkins v. F.I.E. Corp.,* we took cognizance of the Louisiana courts' adherence to the structure established in Langlois, most notably, for purposes of the instant case, the imposition of liability for ultrahazardous activities under art. 2315 by analogy to art. 667. As we also noted in *Perkins*, however, the Louisiana Supreme Court, in *Kent v. Gulf States Utilities Co.,* later seemed to "cast liability for ultrahazardous activities directly upon art. 2315 alone, without relying, either directly or by analogy, on any other codal [sic] article."[55] Referred to as absolute liability, or liability without fault, this concept is perhaps more easily understood when viewed as "legal fault" or fault supplied by law. Thus, art. 2315's fault element is imputed, i.e., supplied by law, when designated persons elect to engage in particularly high-risk activities, even though they perform them lawfully, skillfully, and free of negligent or intentional fault in the usual sense. To date, the jurisprudential list of such activities includes only aerial crop dusting, storing hazardous materials, pile driving, and blasting with explosives.

b. Activities Ultrahazardous De Jure

Within this framework, the Plaintiffs' claims against Kerr-McGee must be analyzed against the backdrop of vicarious tort liability under Louisiana law. A well-established general rule under Louisiana law is that a principal is not liable for the delictual or quasi-delictual offenses (torts) committed by an agent who is an independent contractor in the course of performing its contractual duties. There are, however, two equally well-established exceptions to this rule: A principal may be liable (1) if it maintains operational control over the activity in question, or (2) if, even absent such control, the activity engaged in by the independent contractor is "ultrahazardous." Given the Plaintiffs' concession that Kerr-McGee did not retain the requisite operational control over Cardinal, Kerr-McGee could only be held liable in tort for damages caused to the Plaintiffs when Cardinal's wireline perforating gun discharged accidentally if that independent contractor's use of the device constituted an ultrahazardous activity and produced the injury. Thus, the dispositive question here is whether Cardinal's use of the wireline perforation gun in the p&a activity that it was performing for Kerr-McGee, being the activity that inflicted injury on Roberts, was ultrahazardous.[59]

Under Louisiana law, an activity may be ultrahazardous either as a matter of law or by classification under the test that has been created judicially. Again, activities that have been categorized in Louisiana as ultrahazardous as a matter of law are (1) storage of toxic gas, (2) crop dusting with airplanes, (3) pile driving, and (4) blasting with explosives. As the Louisiana Supreme Court observed in *Kent v. Gulf States Utilities*, each of these four undertakings is an activity that "can cause injury to others, even when conducted with the greatest prudence and care."

This concept is embodied in the jurisprudential test for ultrahazardous activities that we outlined in *Perkins v. F.I.E. Corp.* Under the *Perkins* test, an activity is ultrahazardous if it (1) relates to land or to other immovables; (2) causes the injury, and the defendant was directly engaged in the injury-producing activity; and (3) does not require the substandard conduct of a third party to cause injury.

The Plaintiffs insist that wireline perforation is a manifestation of "blasting with explosives," and should therefore be classified as an ultrahazardous activity as a matter of

---

[55] *Perkins*, 762 F.2d at 1261.

[59] We note Kerr-McGee's assertion that, in any case, it was not "directly engaged" in wireline perforation, as required by the test for imposing liability on the principal. As we join the district court in ruling that wireline perforation is not an ultrahazardous activity, we do not reach the question whether Kerr-McGee was engaged in the activity by virtue of its independent contractor's engagement in the activity.

law. We disagree. In *Fontenot v. Magnolia Petroleum Co.*,[64] the case that decreed "blasting with explosives" to be an ultrahazardous activity, the Louisiana Supreme Court reversed a judgment in favor of defendants whose geophysical exploration activities on the property of one owner caused damage to the plaintiffs' homes on adjoining land. The geophysical operations involved the intentional detonation of 10-pound charges of Nitramon "S" at a depth of approximately 70 feet below the surface, and the damage to the plaintiffs' homes (including cracks in walls and ceilings, and broken cement foundations) was alleged to have resulted from the "vibrations and concussions radiating in the soil from the point of the explosions conducted by defendants." The *Fontenot* court observed:

> It has been universally recognized that when, as here, the defendant, though without fault, is engaged in a lawful business, conducted according to modern and approved methods and with reasonable care, by such activities causes risk or peril to others, the doctrine of absolute liability is clearly applicable.

Stated differently, even though the blasting may have been conducted responsibly and according to the latest accepted methods, the defendants were nonetheless accountable for any unavoidable damage that flowed from the activity.

Subsequently, in *Schexnayder v. Bunge Corp.*,[67] we characterized *Fontenot* as involving "purposeful subterranean explosions in connection with oil exploration," and approved the trial court's jury instruction on ultrahazardous activities, which stated that "[a]n ultra-hazardous activity is an activity which [sic], even when conducted with the greatest of care and prudence, could cause a foreseeable harm or damage to those in the neighborhood." Thus, for over a quarter-century we have adhered to the Louisiana Supreme Court's reasoning in *Fontenot* for classifying the subsurface detonation of explosives as ultrahazardous: Foreseeably, such an activity could cause unavoidable collateral damage to neighbors, even if conducted with due care.

Lowering a perforation gun down a well on a wireline and firing it to pierce drill pipe or tubing in an oil and gas well simply does not fit within this rubric. In sharp contrast to the damage incurred by the neighbors in *Fontenot*, which was inflicted on structures located off the owners' premises by the inevitable, omni-directional underground shock waves produced by the intentional blasting on the owners' premises, the injuries incurred by Roberts were caused by the accidental detonation of the shaped-charge ammunition of the perforation gun, not downhole as intended but at the surface of the owner's premises, i.e., on the Kerr-McGee fixed platform. As we have noted, a perforation gun's shaped charges fire only in the direction toward which their open, conical ends are pointed. When conducted "according to modern and approved methods and with reasonable care," a perforating gun is lowered down a well to a predetermined depth, is fired in one or more predetermined directions, produces a force sufficient only to pierce the tubing or casing, and, at most, a matter of but several additional inches of the adjacent formation. The firing of the shaped charges causes virtually no incidental damage to the gun or the wellbore, and no collateral damage whatsoever by way of vibrations, even to the owner's premises, much less to adjoining property, no matter how proximate.

In the unfortunate occurrence that injured Roberts, the business end of the shaped charges--like the muzzle of a gun--happened to be pointed in his direction at a time when the gun was at the surface rather than downhole. His severe injuries were a direct, primary result of the gun's accidental firing, not collateral damage from shock waves or vibrations. And the unintentional firing of the gun was caused by an act of man, presumably the opening of the

---

[64] 227 La. 866, 80 So. 2d 845 (La. 1955).

[67] 508 F.2d 1069 (5th Cir. 1975).

valve, in turn causing a spike in pressure. We therefore reject the Plaintiffs' contention that the wireline perforation activity during which Roberts was injured is a variety of blasting with explosives and thus ultrahazardous as a matter of law.

c. Ultrahazardous De Facto

Wireline perforation also fails to meet at least one of the three conjunctive prongs of the broader *Perkins* test for ultrahazardousness under Louisiana law. The parties agree that wireline perforation of a well in connection with a p&a operation relates to land or to other immovables, and we shall assume arguendo that, through Cardinal, its independent contractor, Kerr-McGee was "directly engaged" in the wireline perforation activity even though the requisite control over Cardinal had not been retained by Kerr-McGee. Thus, we are concerned here only with the third prong of the Perkins test, whether wireline perforation is an activity that "can cause injury to others, even when conducted with the greatest prudence and care."[71] For essentially the same reasons that distinguish the perforation activity from blasting with explosives, we hold that the former is not a manifestation of the latter.

First, there is ample evidence in the record to support the contention that wireline perforation, whether employing electrically or pressure-activated firing heads to detonate the shaped charges, can be, and indeed generally is, safely performed thousands of times a year. There is further evidence suggesting that when the (infrequent) accident does occur in connection with wireline perforation, it is directly traceable to human error, either in the initial choice to employ a pressure-activated device in a particular well, or in the failure correctly to follow safety procedures. These features of wireline perforation are similar to the transmission of electricity over power lines which was the challenged activity in *Kent*. Regarding that activity, the *Kent* court stated that "the transmission of electricity over isolated high tension power lines is an everyday occurrence in every parish in this state and can be done without a high degree of risk of injury." The same can be said with equal certainty of wireline perforation of oil and gas wells. We therefore conclude that, unlike the stereotypical ultrahazardous activities recognized by statutes and courts of Louisiana, wireline perforation "is likely to cause damage only when there is substandard conduct on someone's part." None can dispute that this declaration is applicable to the sequence of events that transpired in the instant accident; it apparently occurred when someone opened the downhole valve, which increased the pressure, causing the perforation gun to fire while it was at the surface rather than hundreds of feet down the wellbore, as intended.

This position is consistent with our prior decisions. In *Ainsworth v. Shell Offshore, Inc.*,[74] we concluded that "drilling operations do not satisfy the third [element of the *Perkins* test]," holding that such activities were not ultrahazardous. As observed by the district court and reiterated above, wireline perforation is performed frequently in conjunction with both enhancing the flow of oil and gas in a well and plugging and abandoning particular strata or entire wells. This comports with the intermediate appellate court's observation in *Bergeron v. Blake Drilling & Workover Co., Inc.*[76] that "[a] well cannot produce oil or gas unless it is perforated. Thus, perforation is an internal and indispensable element of every well." Wireline perforation is therefore easily classifiable as a "drilling operation," and thus not ultrahazardous under *Ainsworth*.

We distinguish our holding today from the *Bergeron* court's holding which at first blush appears to be to the contrary. In *Bergeron*, a Louisiana court of appeal stated, "even if

---

[71] *Perkins v. F.I.E. Corp.*, 762 F.2d 1250, 1268 (5th Cir. 1985) (quoting *Kent v. Gulf States Utilities Co.*, 418 So. 2d 493, 498 (La. 1982)).

[74] 829 F.2d 548 (5th Cir. 1987).

[76] 599 So. 2d 827 (La.App. 1 Cir. 1992).

one found that perforating was not ultrahazardous[,] a finding that perforating is a[sic] inherently and intrinsically dangerous work is unavoidable." As the district court in the instant case correctly noted, however, the *Bergeron* court stopped short of classifying wireline perforation as an "ultrahazardous activity," characterizing it instead as "inherently dangerous," in the law of Louisiana a distinctly different term of art. Here, the district court continued:

> By holding Kerr-McGee liable under article 2315 for [an] "inherently dangerous" activity, this Court would be expanding the Louisiana Supreme Court's policy behind ultrahazardous activity as announced in [*Kent*]. In *Kent*, the Louisiana Supreme Court held that the ultrahazardous activity classification "was created for the rare instances in which the activity can cause injury to others, even when conducted with the greatest prudence and care." This Court does not find that an "inherently dangerous" activity fits within the "special category" of ultrahazardous liability.

We adopt this reasoning, adding only the observation that the perforating gun in *Bergeron* had a firing head that was activated by electricity, not by pressure as in the instant case. In contrast to electrical firing of some perforation guns, only the external application of sufficient psi of pressure can detonate a pressure-activated firing head like the one involved in Roberts's injury. Thus, the difference between an activity that is inherently dangerous and one that is ultrahazardous serves to distinguish *Bergeron* from the instant case, and the difference in the risk of accidental discharge between the firing devices involved in the two cases distinguishes them even further.

In summary, when we view the operable facts of the instant case in the light most favorable to the Plaintiffs as non-movants, we are satisfied that use of a wireline perforation gun in a p&a operation cannot be held to be an ultrahazardous activity, either de jure or de facto. Not only is such perforation factually distinguishable from "blasting with explosives," an actuality that would render such perforation an ultrahazardous activity as a matter of law were it not distinguishable; wireline perforation also fails to satisfy the third prong of the *Perkins* test, which requires the activity to be one that is likely to cause injury to others, even when conducted with the greatest prudence and care. This simply cannot be said of wireline perforation, which is conducted routinely in oilfield drilling, completing, producing, and plugging operations; and in which even the extremely infrequent accident is traceable to substandard human conduct.

The imposition of liability on a principal for acts of an independent contractor is permitted only in narrow circumstances. Like the district court before us, we are not willing to increase the range of circumstances when the courts and legislature of Louisiana have not seen fit to do so. Our pronouncement in *CNG Producing Co.* remains as true today as when it was uttered: "We would not subject this activity to strict liability without certain directions from the Louisiana courts" to which we would add, "or the Legislature."

2.   To what extent is the Fifth Circuit correct in its view that an alternative reading would supplant the legislature and expand the definition of blasting? What weight should be given the court's analysis in Louisiana courts, especially since the decision seems to rely heavily on the court's own prior opinion more than on any Louisiana decisions?

3.   Is *Roberts* explained on the simple ground that the wireline perforating gun was more like firing a gun (which is not ultrahazardous) than discharging explosives (which is)? How does one distinguish between firing a gun and blasting? Is firing a mortar or cannon more like firing a gun or blasting? Suppose it is a particularly large cannon? What if it is a black powder musket (especially one with flint- or wheelock or other, exposed triggering device)? Would it matter if it were an ancient cannon? Would it matter that it were firing an explosive charge rather than mere shot?

4.   The *Roberts* opinion maintains that there is a distinction between activities which are (1) ultrahazardous "as a matter of law," and (2) those classified as ultrahazardous under a judicially created test. Notice that the second test is not defined in any Louisiana decision, but is found instead in the Circuit's own decision, *Perkins*. Otherwise the court cites no authority for the distinction between these two bases for defining "ultrahazardous." Is the idea of judicially defined "ultrahazardous" activity consistent with the 1996 amendments which clearly limit ultrahazardous activity to pile driving and blasting? What relevance does it have, anyway, to the key question in *Roberts*, i.e., is use of the wireline perforation gun "blasting?" Why does the Circuit panel use this distinction?

5.   Is the court's "de facto" reading of ultrahazardous activity (the second prong, above) a compelling method for defining the limits of ultrahazardous activity and for distinguishing that activity from activities better analyzed under negligence?

C.   PROVING ABSOLUTE LIABILITY

HOLLAND
v.
KEAVENEY
306 So. 2d 838 (La.App. 4 Cir. 1975)

GULOTTA, J.

Defendant, a demolition contractor, appeals from a judgment in favor of plaintiffs in the sum of $1,500 for the loss of a rare Besenji dog which occurred on October 4, 1972, when a swarm of honey bees stung the dog to death after a wall in which their nests were located was leveled during the demolition of the old courthouse in St. John the Baptist Parish. The dog was caged in plaintiff's yard where they resided adjacent to the courthouse. Plaintiffs are tenants of the Parish School Board. The suit was dismissed as to the second defendant, St. John the Baptist Parish.

Recovery is sought not only for the loss of the dog but also for the mental anguish endured by Mrs. Holland while watching the dog suffer during the attack by the bees.

The defendant contractor's first specification of error is that the trial judge erred in finding him negligent. Keaveney claims he used care in the demolition of the building, and had no advance knowledge of the inordinately vast number of bees in the building. Defendant asserts that the formal bid for demolition contained no reference to the bees and that he had no duty to undertake the extermination of the insects. Moreover, according to the contractor, the police jury was aware of the large number of bees in the building and should have taken some precaution to afford protection to persons and animals in the area. Keaveney further seeks to exonerate himself from negligence by contending that the fact that the bees attacked and killed the dog is not within the realm of foreseeable risk.

The defendant contractor also claims that the strict liability responsibility of the owner under LSA-C.C.art. 667 does not apply to the contractor where a neighbor is injured. According to Keaveney, liability attaches to the contractor only after a finding of negligence. Keaveney, alternatively, argues that consistent with the holding in *D'Albora v. Tulane University*, 274 So. 2d 825 (La.App. 4 Cir. 1973), and with LSA-C.C.art. 667, St. John the Baptist Parish, the owner of the property, also should have been cast in judgment. Finally, defendant complains of the excessiveness of the award.

In response to defendant's specifications of error, plaintiffs contend the contractor was negligent because he knew of the presence of the large amount of bees; he complained about them to a member of the police jury and unsuccessfully sprayed roach powder in hopes of containing them. Therefore, under the circumstances, defendant was derelict in not taking proper action to have the bees exterminated.

Plaintiffs further take the position, as claimed by the defendant contractor, that based on Article 667 of the Civil Code, the owner of the property (the Parish) is strictly liable for the damage caused to the neighbor. Plaintiffs claim also the parish is not free from negligence since the police jury was aware of the presence of the bees and failed to remedy the hazard.

In response, the police jury argues that the parish cannot be cast in judgment because they did not own the bees since the insects were in their natural state and were not cultivated for commercial use. Furthermore, the parish claims that no liability attaches to it because it had no knowledge of the presence of the bees in the building.

We reject at the outset the finding of negligence by the trial court on the part of the contractor. The duty owed by defendant contractor was to demolish the building with the exercise of reasonable care. This duty included the risk of damage caused from the careless or negligent demolition of the building. However, we fail to find that the duty owed by the contractor included the risk of damage caused by the swarming of an unusually large amount of bees when a wall was demolished. If we assume the contractor failed to exercise proper care either to exterminate or to have the bees exterminated, we nevertheless cannot conclude that the death of the dog in a neighboring yard is within the foreseeable risk chargeable to this defendant. Under the circumstances, we do not agree with the trial court's finding that plaintiff is entitled to recovery against the contractor based on his negligence.

If liability attaches to the contractor in this case, it is through his relationship with the owner of the property, and is dependent on a theory of liability that an owner and his contractor are responsible for damages caused to a neighbor in accordance with a concept based on fault without negligence. *See* LSA-C.C.art. 667, art. 669 and art. 2315; *D'Albora v. Tulane University*, *supra*, and *Langlois v. Allied Chemical Corporation*, 258 La. 1067, 249 So. 2d 133 (1971).

In *D'Albora*, this court rendered judgment without a finding of negligence, against a subcontractor and owner in favor of a neighboring owner for damages caused as a result of pile driving activities on the owner's property. The court stated at page 829 of 274 So. 2d:

> "We conclude from our review of *Reymond, Chaney* and *Langlois* that the absence of negligence on a piling subcontractor's part is immaterial to his liability for damage caused by his pile-driving. Where causation is shown, the pile-driver's fault, in performing work he knows could damage neighbors, obliges him to repair the damage."[2]

In *Langlois*, *supra*, the court in citing with approval *Gotreaux v. Gary*, 232 La. 373, 94 So. 2d 293, stated that the court in *Gotreaux* looked to LSA-C.C.art. 667 as the required standard of conduct in a crop spraying case and rejected negligence as a criterion for liability to a neighbor. According to *Langlois*, the *Gotreaux* court relied on LSA-C.C.art. 667 as the required standard and permitted recovery against a contractor through LSA-C.C.art. 2315.

However, in the *D'Albora* and *Gotreaux* cases, the awards were in favor of neighboring property owners for damages to immovable property. Our case is different in that the claim is not by a neighboring property owner but by a lessee of a neighboring owner for damages caused from mental anguish suffered by the lessee and for loss of property (the dog) owned by the lessee. Because we are not concerned with immovable property of a neighboring landowner, the claim by the plaintiffs in the instant case is closer to the claim asserted in the *Langlois* case where the court, in a personal injury matter, allowed recovery against a property owner through the application of LSA-C.C.art. 669 and art. 2315. In *Langlois*, recovery was made to a fireman for injuries sustained by gas inhalation from escaping gas from adjacent property. The court stated at page 140 of 249 So. 2d:

---

[2] *Reymond v. State, Department of Highways*, 255 La. 425, 231 So. 2d 375 (1970); *Chaney v. Travelers Insurance Company*, 259 La. 1, 249 So. 2d 181 (1971); *Langlois v. Allied Chemical, supra.*

"Here we find that proof that the gas escaped is sufficient, and proof of lack of negligence and lack of imprudence will not exculpate the defendant. The defendant has injured this plaintiff by its fault as analogized from the conduct required under Civil Code Article 669 and others, and responsibility for the damage attaches to defendants under Civil Code Article 2315."

Implicit in the *Langlois* and *D'Albora* decisions is the concept that when one undertakes an ultrahazardous activity, one assumes responsibility for all anticipated and natural consequences of the performance of that activity. If one undertakes the driving of piles, he anticipates, and must by law, accept the responsibility for cracks in a neighbor's building which might result from that activity. When one undertakes to store poisonous gas, he is responsible for seepage of that gas as a natural consequence of that storage. Nevertheless, one may undertake these activities because the benefits which enure to him outweigh the possibility that he might incur liability should any damages result. By the same token, when damage and injury results from an occurrence not anticipated as a natural consequence of an ultrahazardous undertaking, liability does not attach to the owner and contractor.

In the instant case, we find that demolition was an ultrahazardous activity, but we cannot conclude that the death of the dog caused by a swarming of the bees was a natural and anticipated consequence of the performance of such activity. The contractor and the owner of the property could not have possibly anticipated that such a bizarre event would occur and cause the dog's death. In such instance, we cannot conclude that liability attaches to a demolition contractor or a landowner based on LSA-C.C.art. 667, art. 669 and art. 2315. Under these circumstances, plaintiffs are not entitled to recovery.

Accordingly, that part of the judgment dismissing plaintiff's suit against St. John the Baptist Parish is affirmed. That part of the judgment in favor of plaintiffs and against defendant contractor, Michael Keaveney, is reversed. Judgment is recast and is now rendered dismissing plaintiffs' suit against defendants, St. John the Baptist Parish and Michael Keaveney. Costs to be paid by plaintiffs-appellees.

AFFIRMED IN PART, REVERSED IN PART.

NOTES

1.   *Holland* sets out the elements of an absolute liability cause of action. It requires only proof of *cause* and *damages*. Does the court mean legal cause or some other formulation of cause such as direct cause or cause in fact? Does the use of legal cause interject into absolute liability an element of duty-risk analysis? How is absolute liability distinguished from negligence? *See* COMMENT, Section A, *supra*.

2.   Absolute liability had been applied in a number of areas: where pile driving on adjacent property caused damage, *D'Albora v. Tulane University*, 274 So. 2d 825 (La.App. 4 Cir. 1973); where a crop dusting service sprayed a pea field and the drift of the insecticides destroyed a neighboring cotton crop, *Gotreaux v. Gary*, 232 La. 373, 94 So. 2d 293 (1957); where use of explosive blasts while conducting geophysical observations damaged nearby homes, *Fontenot v. Magnolia Petroleum Co.*, 227 La. 866, 80 So. 2d 845, 848 (1955); where dredging destroyed oyster beds on the floor of a bay, *Butler v. Baber*, 529 So. 2d 374 (La. 1988); where noxious chemicals escaped and caused damage, *Langlois, supra. See also, Craig v. Montelpre Realty Co.*, 252 La. 502, 211 So. 2d 627 (1968) (pile driving); *Rosenblath v. Louisiana Bank and Trust Co.*, 432 So. 2d 285 (La.App. 2 Cir. 1983) (demolition of buildings); *Begeron v. Blake*, 599 So. 2d 827 (La.App. 1 Cir. 1992), *writs denied*, 605 So. 2d 1117, 1119 (1992) (perforating oil wells).

3.   The 1996 amendments to C.C. Art. 667 should not be applied retroactively. *Boudreaux v. State*, 815 So. 2d 7 (La. 2002). This means that cases previously governed by absolute liability and arising prior to 1996 might still be treated as absolute liability cases.

D. WILD ANIMALS

As noted in the previous chapter, *see Boyer v. Seal, supra*, harm caused by domestic animals has been traditionally distinguished from that brought on by wild animals. Louisiana cases hold that possessors of wild animals are absolutely liable for damages caused by those animals. *See Holland v. Buckley*, 305 So. 2d 113, 116 n. 4. *See also Vredenberg v. Behan*, 33 La. Ann. 627 (1881). This liability is based on Civil Code Art. 2321. As Art. 2321 was also amended in 1996, it is not clear whether absolute liability continues to exist for wild animals. The article now reads:

La. Civil Code Art. 2321 Damage caused by animals

The owner of an animal is answerable for the damage caused by the animal. However, he is answerable for the damage only upon a showing that he knew or, in the exercise of reasonable care, should have known that his animal's behavior would cause damage, that the damage could have been prevented by the exercise of reasonable care, and that he failed to exercise such reasonable care. Nonetheless, the owner of a dog is strictly liable for damages for injuries to persons or property caused by the dog and which the owner could have prevented and which did not result from the injured person's provocation of the dog. Nothing in this Article shall preclude the court from the application of the doctrine of res ipsa loquitur in an appropriate case.

The following case illustrates the application of absolute liability for harm caused by a wild animal owned by defendants. Notice the court dismisses evidence that the owner took all reasonable steps to prevent the animal's escape. Does revised Article 2321 now preclude recovery on the basis of absolute liability where the owner took reasonable steps?

BRILEY

v.

MITCHELL

238 La. 551, 115 So. 2d 851 (La. 1959)

SIMON, J.

Louis R. Briley, a police officer of the City of Natchitoches, Louisiana, instituted suit against Leon Mitchell and the Natchitoches Locker Plant, Inc., defendants herein, to recover damages for personal injuries sustained when the plaintiff was attempting, in line of his official duties, to recapture a wild, antlered deer which had escaped from the custody of the defendants, while kept on the latters' premises.

For answer the defendants pleaded the general issue, asserting their freedom of any degree of negligence. The action is also defended on first, the alternative ground of contributory negligence in that plaintiff knew or should have known of the potential danger in recapturing a wild deer and of it having heretofore injured other persons, thus demanding such care and caution as would have avoided the accidental injuries complained of; and, in the second alternative, that plaintiff assumed the risks by virtue of his acceptance of employment as a police officer with its inherently dangerous and perilous duties; that his injuries, if any, grow out of the performance of his official duties for which there can be no recovery.

The case, upon motion of the defendants, was tried by a jury which rendered a verdict and judgment in favor of the defendants, and which, on appeal to the Court of Appeal, Second Circuit, was affirmed. On plaintiff's application we granted writs of review.

The facts out of which this controversy arose are not seriously in dispute and may be substantially stated as follows:

On December 1, 1957, the defendant Mitchell, an officer and manager of the codefendant corporation, while travelling through Arkansas was attracted by a sixteen-point antlered deer staked out near the roadside. Concluding that this animal would be an entertaining contribution to the Natchitoches Christmas Festival and for the publicity of the Christmas program, arrangements were made and it was brought down to Natchitoches. The deer was unloaded at the Peoples Bank Drive-In, staked out in a small lawn, and was subsequently used in the parade and thereafter exhibited to the public. On the date of its escape, January 5, 1958, the wild animal was staked out on the premises of defendant corporation secured by an eighteen foot chain, with a swivel at each end, one swivel attached to a heavy leather collar around the deer's neck, the other attached to a three-quarter inch pipe driven five or six feet in the ground. Fearful of possible harm and as a safe-guard to persons who might tamper with or approach the deer, Mitchell requested the police headquarters for their cooperation by occasionally driving by the premises during their normal patrol. He concedes that these precautions were taken by him knowing that the wild deer was inherently dangerous to the public.

On the aforestated date of its escape plaintiff and two other police officers investigated a complaint that a wild antlered deer was roaming loose in a residential section of the city, threatening harm to the residents and their property. Upon arriving at the scene, the officers decided to attempt to capture the animal which still had the chain attached to his neck. As plaintiff approached the deer it suddenly attacked him, knocking him down. One of the antlers penetrated his right thigh, causing a deep wound and another caused a penetrating wound under the left armpit. Before the animal was finally brought under control by the other officers plaintiff also received numerous abrasions, contusions and lacerations of the chest, arm and legs. Plaintiff was hospitalized for eight days and thereafter was disabled for approximately two months.

In his submitted brief plaintiff relies upon the holding announced in the early case of *Vredenburg v. Behan*, 33 La.Ann. 627, which, after exhaustive research, is the only reported Louisiana decision dealing with the tort liability of a keeper or custodian of a wild animal.

On the other hand, defendants in their submitted brief invoke the reasoning and holding of the Court of Appeal in the instant case, wherein the Court ingenuously opined that the *Vredenburg* case, *supra*, was grounded upon liability by reason of fault and is not inconsistent with the many rulings in the several Court of Appeal cases which assess responsibility only where there exists fault or negligence before tort liability can be established. It is readily observed that the cases therein referred to and relied upon in each instance involve the injurious acts of domestic animals. Under the theory of these cases the defendant was held to be free from liability upon proof that he was not negligent and was without fault. *Willis v. Schuster*, La.App., 28 So. 2d 518; *Raziano v. T. J. James & Co., Inc.*, La.App., 57 So. 2d 251, with numerous cases therein cited; *Thomas v. Wright*, La.App., 75 So. 2d 559.

In the instant case the Court of Appeal concluded that the defendants exercised every reasonable care and precaution to prevent the animal's escape, and that the record did not suggest any additional safeguards which foreseeably would have prevented the unfortunate occurrence.

The pertinent parts of Article 2315 of the LSA-Civil Code provide: "Every act whatever of man that causes damage to another, obliges him by whose fault it happened to repair it;...."

Article 2316 of our LSA-Civil Code reads: "Every person is responsible for the damage he occasions not merely by his act, but by his negligence, his imprudence, or his want of skill."

Article 2317 of the Code also provides: "We are responsible, not only for the damage occasioned by our own act, but for that which is caused by the act of persons for whom we are answerable, or of the things which we have in our custody. This, however, is to be understood with the following modifications."

It is readily observed that in Articles 2315 and 2316, *supra*, liability, in the first instance, is provided for fault, and in the second instance, for negligence. Under the provisions of Article 2317 liability attaches for damages caused by "the things which we have in our custody." This obvious liability is, by its language, to be understood with modifications succeedingly set forth.

Article 2321 of our LSA-Civil Code is obviously couched in the most absolute terms: "The owner of an animal is answerable for the damage he has caused...." Its provisions necessarily are one of the modifications referred to in Article 2317, more particularly when it provides for stricter liability without reservation when damages are the result of a "dangerous or noxious" animal being loosed. It is therefore manifest that in dealing with the acts of domestic animals causing injuries or damages the courts have read into tort liability the requirement of fault or negligence, but have correctly drawn, we think, a clear distinction when dealing with wild animals, in which instance the doctrine of strict and absolute liability becomes an exception or modification (Article 2317) to the general doctrine of fault or negligence.

This distinction was concisely and unmistakably announced in the *Vredenburg* case, *supra*. It is the sole and last expression of this court in applying the doctrine of absolute tort liability towards keepers and custodians of wild animals, as contradistinguished from the doctrine of fault or negligence when dealing with domestic animals. We said:

> "... the responsibility attaching to those who own, control or keep animals ferae naturae, to which class a bear belongs, is of that strict and grave character, as not to be relieved or modified by considerations of the kind presented, nor to be measured by rules that apply to owners or keepers of domestic animals."

In the cited case we further observed that it is not sufficient that defendant has done everything possible to prevent the escape of the wild animal in his custody and it is of no consequence that a third party may have caused the release of the animal. In that case although the boy whose actions caused the bear to escape was an employee of plaintiff, defendant was still held liable for plaintiff's injuries on the theory that one who keeps wild animals does so at his own peril. The court in explaining its position said:

> "Animals of this kind, such as lions, tigers, bears, are universally recognized as dangerous. It is the duty of those who own or keep them, to keep them in such a manner as to prevent them from doing harm, under any circumstances, whether provoked, as they are liable to be, or not provoked. There must be security against them under all contingencies. DOMAT, p. 475; MERLIN, REPERTOIRE, tome 26, p. 242, verbo Quasi-Delit; MARCADE, tome 5, pp. 272, 273; 1 Law Repts., p. 263; 3 Law Repts., p. 330.

* * * * *

> "... the acts of the boy in provoking [the bear] cannot, for these reasons, affect [defendants'] liability."

In the instant case there is evidence that the wild deer may have, to some extent, assumed the appearance of a tame and domesticated animal prior to its attack upon plaintiff. The record discloses that the defendant Mitchell admitted knowing of the animal's dangerous propensities, sufficient unto itself to prompt him to call for police surveillance during their night and day patrols. In the cited case we further observed:

> "Nor does it matter that an animal of this kind may be to some extent tame and domesticated; the natural wildness and ferocity of his nature but sleeps, and is liable to be awakened at any moment, suddenly and unexpectedly, under some provocation, as was the case in this instance."

In regard to proof of negligence or fault on the part of a keeper or custodian of a wild animal as distinguished from that of domestic animals, and as to knowledge, if any, of its dangerous propensities, we further said:

"The owner of wild and savage beasts, such as lions, tigers, wolves, bears, etc., if he neglects to keep them properly secured, is liable for injuries committed by them according to their nature, without any evidence that he knew them to be ferocious, or that he was negligent in the mode of keeping them, since he is bound in ordinary prudence, to know that fact and to secure them from doing harm."

There can be no dispute over the dangers imposed on the public in the keeping of the wild deer. The record amply establishes this fact. Nor does the fact that this animal may not have freed himself by his own efforts relieve the defendants of liability. The fact that the captive wild deer escaped, no matter how, and thereafter caused injuries is sufficient to impose tort liability.

Our holding in the *Vredenburg* case, *supra*, is clearly in line with the law generally in other states. The general law pronounces that the owner of animals ferae naturae or of beasts of a dangerous or vicious class is liable under all circumstances for injuries done by them. The predicate of this rule of liability is the wrongful and unjustifiable conduct of the owner in keeping an animal of that species. Knowledge by the owner or custodian of its vicious nature need not be proved, as he is conclusively presumed to have had such knowledge. Security of the dangerous animal must be assured under all circumstances, for the gravamen of the tort liability is the keeping of the animal, and negligence, strictly speaking, is not an element of the owner's liability.

Generally any person has the undoubted right to keep a wild animal, and his right to exhibit it is of necessity judicially recognized, and such exhibitions are licensed everywhere. Being thus privileged, he assumes the obligations of an insurer to the public generally, and as such keeps it at his peril. 2 Cyc. 367; HALE ON TORTS, p. 459.

We are in agreement with the Court of Appeal in the instant case that the pleas of contributory negligence and the "doctrine of assumption of risk" [110 So. 2d 170] are without merit. The plea of contributory negligence has no legal foundation in this instance, and defendants do not seriously press the contention which is in effect that a police officer while in the performance of his official duties is not entitled to recover damages. In the performance of these duties it was proper and commendable to assist in the recapturing of the wild animal and thus prevent harm to the public. Whatever danger he was exposed to was an official risk peace officers must necessarily assume, and his right of recovery for damages, because of his official status should not be thus proscribed.

For the reasons assigned, it is ordered, adjudged and decreed that the judgment of the Court of Appeal be and the same is annulled and set aside.

It is further ordered that this cause be remanded to the Court of Appeal, Second Circuit, and that said Court proceed to determine and award the measure of damages to which plaintiff is entitled commensurate with the facts and circumstances presented in the record and in accordance with the views herein expressed.

All costs of this proceeding to be borne by the defendants.

COMMENT

Professor Frank L. Maraist and Dean Thomas Galligan have argued that, though the amendments to Article 2321 eliminate absolute liability for wild animals, it might be possible for courts to impose absolute liability in such cases by focusing on the inherent risks wild animals present.

> One might argue that there is some vestige of absolute liability for wild-animal owners in Article 2315 itself; however, the last time the supreme court considered the absolute liability of wild-animal owners, in *Briley v. Mitchell*, it relied principally upon Article 2321, not Article 2315. Interestingly, the court also relied, in part, upon the ancient civil-law doctrine of noxal surrender, which made "dangerous or noxious" animal owners liable "without reservation." Consequently, although there may be an argument that absolute liability for wild-animal owners continues under

Article 2315, which is unaffected by the amendment to Article 2321, Article 2321 is the more specific article, speaking directly to liability for animals, and it says nothing about absolute liability for wild-animal owners. Even assuming wild-animal owners are no longer absolutely liable, but must be negligent in order to be liable, the pragmatic effect still may be minimal. When the lion, tiger, or bear bites or maims (unless, perhaps, in a zoo), most courts or juries probably will somehow find negligence and impose liability.

Frank L. Maraist & Thomas C. Galligan, Jr., *Burying Cesar: Civil Justice Reform and the Changing Face of Louisiana Tort Law*, 71 TUL. L. REV. 339, 353-54 (1996) (citations omitted).

Might the significant risks presented by certain animals mean that the application of "negligence" produces an outcome indistinguishable from absolute liability, at least for those animals? In other words, perhaps it is not possible to take adequate steps to make certain animals safe? The concern here is on both of the risks present in a tort case: risk of the injury occurring and risk that the injury will be significant.

Consider, for example, the risk we might expect the owner of a Bengal tiger to anticipate. While he might take reasonable steps to prevent the tiger from escaping, any escape is likely to present a risk of very serious harm, since a Bengal tiger is one of the few animals known to eat humans. Suppose that he can show that he held the tiger in a "state of the art" cage; would this be adequate to bar liability?

Consider a different case. Suppose a hobbyist collects exotic fish as her hobby. She possesses a particular predatory fish that would do extreme damage to her state's fisheries if it got into the local ecosystem. Although she takes all the accepted steps to prevent the escape of the foreign fish, it nevertheless escapes and, over time, causes a severe reduction in the yields of the region's aquaculture businesses, even degrading the "sportsman's paradise."

These two cases are really the same. They each raise questions about the consequences of harm and the likelihood of that harm occurring. Can we identify cases, perhaps along the lines of these, where absolute liability is still implicated after the 1996 amendments because of the nature of the risks?

Even if a form of absolute liability can be read into Art. 2315, a substantial portion of pre-1996 absolute liability for wild animals is still lost. *Briley* held the possessor of a wild animal liable even if another person were to release it. As the court notes, one who possesses a wild animal does so at his peril under absolute liability. This portion of absolute liability is surely lost after 1996, isn't it? Would any court today hold the possessor of a wild animal liable where another person released it (absent an argument that that release was within the scope of the risk in negligence)?

E.   PROPERTY OWNERSHIP

The vicinage articles govern property relationships. Their use as the basis for tort liability was, until *Kent*, only through Article 2315. Now that the absolute liability has been drastically curtailed by the 1996 amendments, might there be a more prominent role for these articles, especially Article 669, as a basis for liability?

BARRETT
v.
T. L. JAMES, INC.
671 So. 2d 1186 (La.App. 2 Cir. 1996)

GASKINS, J.

[Plaintiffs sued, claiming a concrete crushing operation caused damages to their home and created unacceptable noise and dust. The appellate court upheld the district court's finding for the defendants on the ground that it was did not constitute manifest error. It described the obligations of vicinage after listing articles 667-669.]

The obligations of vicinage contained in these articles are legal servitudes imposed on the owner of property. These provisions embody a balancing of rights and obligations associated with the ownership of immovables. As a general rule, the landowner is free to exercise his rights of ownership in any manner he sees fit. He may even use his property in ways which occasion some inconvenience to his neighbor. However, his extensive rights do not allow him to do real damage to his neighbor. *Rodrigue v. Copeland*, 475 So. 2d 1071 (La. 1985); *Barras v. Hebert*, 602 So. 2d 186 (La.App. 3 Cir. 1992), *writ denied* 605 So. 2d 1367 (La. 1992).

La. C.C. Arts. 667-669 place limitations on the rights of owners by setting out principles of responsibility which require an owner to use his property in such a manner as not to injure another. La. C.C. Art. 667 prohibits uses which cause damage to neighbors or deprive them of the enjoyment of their property, while La. C.C. Art. 668 permits uses which merely cause neighbors some inconvenience. La. C.C. Art. 669 allows suppression of certain inconveniences if excessive under local ordinances or customs, and requires tolerance of lesser inconveniences. Together the three articles establish the following principles: No one may use his property so as to cause damage to another or to interfere substantially with the enjoyment of another's property. Landowners must necessarily be exposed to some inconveniences arising from the normal exercise of the right of ownership by a neighbor. Excessive inconveniences caused by the emission of industrial smoke, odors, noise, dust vapors, and the like need not be tolerated in the absence of a conventional servitude; whether an inconvenience is excessive or not is to be determined in the light of local ordinances and customs. *Inabnet v. Exxon Corporation*, 93-0681 (La. 1994), 642 So. 2d 1243; *Critney v. Goodyear Tire and Rubber Company*, 353 So. 2d 341 (La.App. 1 Cir. 1977).

We sometimes use the word nuisance in describing the type of conduct which violates the pronouncements embodied in La. C. C. Arts. 667-669. *Barras v. Hebert, supra*. While the owners of property are not required to suffer damage as a result of the works undertaken on their neighbor's property, the law has decreed that certain inconveniences must be tolerated. The extent of the inconvenience the property owner must tolerate without redress depends upon the circumstances. When the actions or work cease to be inconveniences and become damaging is a question of fact. *King v. Western Club, Inc.*, 587 So. 2d 122 (La.App. 2 Cir. 1991); *Hobson v. Walker*, 41 So. 2d 789 (La.App. 2 Cir. 1949).

The fact finder's decision in a nuisance case cannot be overturned in the absence of manifest error. *Barras v. Hebert, supra*. The determination is based upon the nature of the intrusion into the neighbor's property, plus the extent or degree of the damage. *Hero Lands v. Texaco, Inc.*, 310 So. 2d 93 (La. 1975).

In determining whether an activity or work occasions real damage or mere inconvenience, a court is required to determine the reasonableness of the conduct in light of the circumstances. This analysis requires consideration of factors such as the character of the neighborhood, the degree of intrusion and the effect of the activity on the health and safety of the neighbors. *Rodrigue v. Copeland, supra*; *Day v. Warren*, 524 So. 2d 1383 (La.App. 1 Cir. 1988).

While noise and dust do not necessarily constitute a nuisance, in some instances they may be so, depending upon the particular circumstances. *Hobson v. Walker, supra*; *King v. Western Club, Inc., supra*; *Codding v. Braswell Supply*, 54 So. 2d 852 (La.App. 2 Cir. 1951); *Day v. Warren, supra*.

* * * * *

BUTLER
v.
BABER
529 So. 2d 374 (La. 1988)

DIXON, J.

[Plaintiffs, holders of oyster leases, sued for damages to their oyster beds caused, they argued, by dredging of a canal for use in drilling an oil well. The court addressed their claims based on C.C. Art. 667 in detail:]

The development of C.C. 667 in this court indicates a trend in the direction of a broader interpretation of the language of the article. Prior to the translation of the French commentators by the Louisiana Law Institute and the subsequent commitment to the interpretation of the Civil Code without reference to common law doctrine, article 667 was interpreted in terms of common law nuisance, and distinctions were made between nuisance per se and nuisance in fact. Since the early 1970's, the direction has been to move away from nuisance theory.

In 1971 three cases dealing with C.C. 667 were considered by this court. *Robichaux v. Huppenbauer,* 258 La. 139, 245 So. 2d 385 (1971), involved the operation of a horse stable within a residential area of the City of New Orleans which was found to be not a nuisance per se but a nuisance in fact. Plaintiffs relied on C.C. 669 to support their claims. Although 667 and its companion articles 668-669 were referred to in the opinion, the court found the Civil Code articles did not deal explicitly with the standards to be followed and chose, therefore, to use these articles "together with the common law theory of nuisance to grant relief where a use of property causes inconvenience to a neighbor." *Robichaux v. Huppenbauer, supra* at 389. The court held that noxious smells, rats, flies and noise may be actionable nuisance although produced and carried on by a lawful business, where they result in material injury to neighboring property or interfere with its comfortable use and enjoyment by persons of ordinary sensibilities. The court remanded for a determination as to whether it was possible to maintain the stable free of complaints. Justice Barham concurred but was of the opinion that the result should have been reached solely by application of the civil law, more particularly article 669, without resort to common law authority or terminology. Barham felt that the language of 669 should be read as illustrative.

In *Chaney v. Travelers Insurance Co.,* 259 La. 1, 249 So. 2d 181 (1971), article 667 was found to be applicable to damage from construction incident to canal improvement by the parish. The adjoining property owner suffered cracks in the walls and ceilings of his home from the vibrations created by the use of heavy equipment within ten feet of the house. The court found that "work" includes "activity" as well as "structure," even though the proprietor's actions are prudent by usual standards. The majority also found the agents of the proprietor, such as contractors and representatives, are solidarily liable with the proprietor if his activity causes damage to a neighbor.

Hilliard v. Shuff, 260 La. 384, 256 So. 2d 127 (1971), the third case in 1971, dealt with four above ground fuel tanks on the property of a truck stop owner. The court found that when storage of fuels creates a substantial hazard, then use of the property runs counter to C.C. 667-669. There, 58,800 gallons of gasoline and diesel were found to prevent plaintiff from safely operating an auto, truck, tractor, or power mower within fifty feet of the fuel tanks. Since this threatened the physical security of plaintiff's family, it was held to be an enjoinable nuisance. The court remanded the case for evidence as to methods of correction.

Justice Barham would have granted a permanent injunction applying article 667 alone, because danger of fire and explosion is not a mere inconvenience under C.C. 668-669, but rather gave plaintiff a right under C.C. 667.

In 1973 the court rendered judgment in a case involving seventeen suits by one hundred nineteen plaintiffs claiming residential damages from construction and installation of an underground concrete drainage canal under a street. *Lombard v. Sewerage and Water Board of New Orleans,* 284

So. 2d 905 (La. 1973). In that case both the city and the Sewerage and Water Board were found to constitute "proprietors" under 667. Justice Barham in his concurrence objected to the majority's willingness to call anyone a "proprietor" in order to reach a result which broadens the base of liability for damages resulting from hazardous activities which cause damage even with the exercise of due care. The majority had again held that non-proprietors are solidarily liable under 667, and Barham felt that the court should use 2315, analogizing 667-669, or 2315 and 2317, to reach this result. He was of the opinion that parties other than proprietors are not made responsible for non-negligent acts under 667, whereas the majority did not cast liability under any other Code article. Barham felt that non-proprietors could only be cast for damages under the majority's theory of the case if they are negligent.

Lombard sets out the proper analysis for cases under C.C. 667. First, causation must be proved, but to be actionable cause need not be the sole cause, although it must be a cause in fact. In order to be a cause in fact in a legal contemplation, it must have a proximate relation to the harm which occurs, and it must be substantial in character. The court noted that certainty is generally unattainable from testimony produced in court. The law of evidence has long required that the testimony of witnesses be weighed by probabilities. Causation may also be proved by circumstantial evidence, which in many instances is the only evidence by which it can be proved. Circumstantial evidence must exclude other reasonable hypothesis with a fair amount of certainty, but this does not mean that it must negate all other possible causes. Also, saying that the plaintiff must establish a disputed fact by a preponderance of the evidence means that a plaintiff must prove that the existence of the disputed fact is more probable than its nonexistence. *Lombard v. Sewerage and Water Board of New Orleans, supra* at 913.

Salter v. B.W.S. Corporation, Inc., 290 So. 2d 821 (La. 1974), involved a situation in which a lessee had a legally cognizable interest and right of action under 667 to enjoin the defendant from using its neighboring property for disposal of chemical waste in underground trenches. The court found that the evidence established the probability that disposal without adequate precautions would pollute the well where plaintiff obtained water, posing a threat to health and safety. Although the operation could be conducted safely and in a manner not violative of the duties of vicinage, since the consequences of failure to exercise great care to prevent escape of poisonous materials were so serious, the court found a qualified injunction appropriate and remanded. The majority cited *State ex rel. Violett v. King*, 46 La.Ann. 78, 14 So. 423 (1894), which held that a tenant had a right of action to enjoin objectionable aspects of an operation conducted on neighboring property where that operation threatened the health and comfort of the tenant. Also the court noted in *Lombard, supra*, it was recognized that "proprietor" as used in 667 need not be limited to owners. Again Justice Barham concurred, with Justice Tate joining in the concurrence, and noted that 667 is designed to protect property from the abuse of right of ownership by the works made on a neighboring estate. According to Barham, lessees have only personal rights in immovable leases, and because art. 669 gives the lessee a personal right, the lessee had a right of action.

One of the major cases on this issue was decided in 1975 where damage and depreciation from construction of a gas pipeline was found to violate 667. *Hero Lands Company v. Texaco Inc.*, 310 So. 2d 93 (La. 1975). The hazardous, high pressure gas pipeline adjacent (within fifteen feet of the property line) gave rise to an action for damage caused by the proximity which impaired the market value and the full use of the neighboring estate. In this case the court noted that the circumstances of each case determine the applicability of article 667. This court contrasted article 2315 with article 667 and said that "recovery under Article 667 may be granted despite the reasonableness and prudence of the proprietor's conduct, when the work he erects on his estate causes damage to his neighbor." *Hero Lands Co. v. Texaco, supra* at 97. This decision also goes on to explain the nature of the circumstances which require redress:

"... But the extent of inconvenience the property owner must tolerate without redress depends upon the circumstances. When the actions or works cease to be inconveniences and become damaging is a question of fact. The problem is one which involves the nature of the intrusion into the neighbor's property, plus the extent or degree of damage. No principle of law confines this damage to physical invasion of the neighbor's premises--an extrinsic injury, as it were. The damage may well be intrinsic in nature, a combination of facts and conditions which, taken together, do not involve a physical invasion but which, under the circumstances, are nevertheless by their nature the very refinement of injury and damage." *Hero Lands Co. v. Texaco, supra* at 98.

The majority also said that violation of 667 is not a tort action in the sense that deliction in its usual connotation is a necessary element. A defendant under 667 must repair damage even though his actions are prudent by usual standards. It is not the manner in which the activity is carried on that is significant; it is the fact that the activity causes damage. Thus, 667 expresses the doctrine of strict liability which does not depend on deliction. Whereas, under 2315, "fault" must be proved, under 667, there is recovery despite reasonableness and prudence if the work causes damage.

Justice Tate concurred in this opinion but disagreed with what he regarded as the dicta that "fault" under 2315 need be distinguished from "fault" derived from 667. Justice Barham, in his concurrence, noted that in the jurisprudence "liability without fault" really means "liability without negligence," and therefore strict liability does not depend on negligence. He said that violation of 667 may constitute delictual action based on fault under 2315; it is fault which does not require proof of negligence. *See Langlois v. Allied Chemical Corp.*, 258 La. 1067, 249 So. 2d 133 (1971). Referring also to *Langlois*, Barham explained that 2315 "fault" is not limited to negligent acts and intentional misconduct, but also encompasses conduct which, because of its ultrahazardous nature, may cause harm even when the greatest care is exercised.

In 1976 this court dealt with the application of C.C. 667 to damages from chemical emissions from defendant's plant which killed or adversely affected trees on plaintiff's property. *Dean v. Hercules, Inc.*, 328 So. 2d 69 (La. 1976). After an analysis of the article's history, the court found a one year prescriptive period applicable to 667. The right of ownership is subject to limitations imposed by law, and 667 imposes such a limitation. 2 AUBRY ET RAU, DROIT CIVIL FRANCAIS, § 194 (7th ed. La. State Law Inst. tr. 1966). In prerevolutionary France, these limitations on the right of ownership were regarded as personal obligations founded on the quasi contract of vicinage. The court found that the codification of the *sic utere* doctrine deals with obligations much broader than the obligations arising from servitude. Yiannopoulos, *Civil Responsibility in the Framework of Vicinage: Articles 667-9 and 2315 of the Civil Code*, 48 TUL.L.REV. 195, 203 (1974). The court went on to say that an action for damages for a violation of article 667 is most closely associated with an action for damages based on article 2315. It can be said that a violation of article 667 constitutes fault within the meaning of article 2315. *Langlois v. Allied Chemical Corp., supra.* In footnote 4 the court notes that Professor Stone pointed out that such an approach finds favor among many of the French commentators. Stone, *Tort Doctrine in Louisiana: The Obligations of Neighborhood*, 40 TUL.L.REV. 701, 709 (1966). Also in *Langlois, supra*, article 667 is cited as an example of liability for fault which does not encompass negligence. Article 667 is not limited in its operation to damage to immovable property. The article seems to encompass liability for personal injuries as well as damage to movable property. Furthermore, in cases involving industrial pollutants, an act of man is required, and therefore no servitude can be acquired by the offending landowner by prescription. C.C. 727.

[The Court discussed the applicability of 667 liability to leaseholders, deciding it was appropriate to allow leaseholders to sue and be sued for 667-type violations.]

Liability under article 667 has been called strict liability, but strict liability is liability without negligence, not liability without fault. "Fault" in the sense of *Langlois* encompasses more than negligence, and violation of 667 constitutes fault. Fault under 667 is the damage done to neighboring property, and relief under 667 requires, therefore, only that damage and causation be proved.

The facts of this case clearly establish that the defendants' dredging operation caused damage to the plaintiffs' oyster beds and the oyster production from those beds. Despite the care and prudence exercised by defendants, plaintiffs are entitled to damages for their oyster leases.

* * * * *

NOTES

1.   In *Butler* the Court adroitly contrasts Art. 2315 and Art. 667, noting that a 667 action is not a tort action and that 667 liability can be established despite reasonable and prudent behavior by defendant. This is surely the kind of interpretation that the 1996 amendments are intended to reach. However, it is not clear that the amendment of Article 667 was meant to reach cases in nuisance and property, as opposed to delictual obligations. Also, the 1996 amendments did not change Article 669, which is an independent ground for nuisance-like liability.

In *Brown v. Olin Chemical*, 231 F.3d 197 (5th Cir. 2000), a panel of the United States Fifth Circuit affirmed a federal district court's grant of summary judgment in a claim against a chemical plant for injuries suffered by neighboring construction workers who were exposed to noxious fumes from the plant. The defendant, Olin Chemicals, argued that, because it had complied with state regulatory standards, it could not be liable. The plaintiffs, Horseshoe Casino and several workers hired to refurbish its casino-boat, claimed that they were not required to show negligence. The Circuit panel disagreed:

> Olin concedes that its plant emits sulfur dioxide and sulfuric acid but insists that it does so only within accepted regulatory limits. The evidence does not show that Olin exceeded acceptable emissions limits at any of the times at issue, nor was any evidence adduced showing that Olin exercised anything less than reasonable care in the operation of its plant. Horseshoe argues, however, that such proof is not necessary, contending that the applicable standard is strict liability pursuant to article 669 of the Louisiana Civil Code.[2]

> Horseshoe asserts that its claim under Article 669 does not require a showing of negligence, insisting that this article provides for liability without fault. We disagree. In 1996, the Louisiana Legislature amended Article 667 to require a showing of negligence in any claim for damages other than those caused by "pile driving" or "blasting with explosives."[3] Prior to this amendment, strict liability applied to all ultra-hazardous activities, which specifically included such endeavors as "pile driving, storage of toxic gas, blasting with explosives, and crop dusting with airplanes."[4] We are convinced that the 1996 amendment to Article 667 applies to Articles 668 and 669 as well, so that stating a claim under one or more of these articles now requires a showing of negligence. The Louisiana Supreme Court has consistently treated these three code articles (which together govern Louisiana's nuisance law) as a cohesive unit, uniformly interpreting them in pari materia.[5] As such, the 1996 amendment engrafted a standard of negligence on all three code articles and thus on nuisance law in Louisiana, leaving exceptions only for "pile driving" and "blasting with explosives" (neither of which were being undertaken by Olin's plant at the relevant times).[6]

---

[2] La. Civ. Code Ann. art. 669 (West 2000).

[3] *See* La. Civ. Code Ann. art. 667 (West 2000).

[4] *Bartlett v. Browning-Ferris Industries, Chemical Services, Inc.*, 683 So. 2d 1319, 1321 (La.App. 3 Cir. 1996).

[5] *See O'Neal v. Southern Carbon Co.*, 216 La. 96, 43 So. 2d 230 (La. 1949) (treating Articles 667-669 as a unit in deciding a case involving emissions from a manufacturing facility); *Dean v. Hercules, Inc.*, 328 So. 2d 69 (La. 1976); *McCastle v. Rollins Environmental Services of Louisiana, Inc.*, 456 So. 2d 612 (La. 1984); *Rodrigue v. Copeland*, 475 So. 2d 1071 (La. 1985); *Inabnett v. Exxon Corporation*, 642 So. 2d 1243 (La. 1994); *Ford v. Murphy Oil U.S.A., Inc.*, 703 So. 2d 542 (La. 1997) (declining to certify a class action against several petrochemical facilities and oil refineries for alleged emissions of airborne chemicals and assuming that the nuisance action arose under Articles 667-669 as a unit).

[6] *See* La. Civ. Code Ann. art. 667 (West 2000).

Is this reading of Art 669 compelling? Notice that, as in *Roberts v. Cardinal, supra*, the Fifth Circuit's opinions on Louisiana law are neither binding, nor necessarily compelling authority.

2.   Notwithstanding the 1996 amendments, injunctive relief might be appropriate under Arts. 667-669. Notice that in *Salter*, discussed in *Butler*, the court held that the *severe consequences* that might result if plaintiff's drinking water was contaminated by defendant's use of his land justified a limited injunction. *Salter*-like cases, where harm is unlikely if reasonable precautions are taken but severe when they do occur, might be said to justify some response. In *Salter* it justified a limited injunction. If such injunctions are available *before* the severe harm occurs, what argument supports barring damage actions *after* the severe harm has occurred?

3.   If the amendments to Article 667 do not reach nuisance cases under that article (or if the amendments are not applied to Art. 669), a version of absolute liability might be revived along the lines of *Butler* and *Street v. Equitable Petroleum Corp.*, 532 So. 2d 887 (La.App. 5 Cir. 1988). In *Street*, the panel held that a plaintiff was entitled to recover damages to her property upon showing of *causation* and *damages* from an oil spill from defendant's production facility and was not required to show that the defendant's activities were ultrahazardous activities.

Notice that the cause of action contemplated by *Butler* and *Street* is a nuisance action that is triggered by the factual showing demanded by the *Barrett* court. Once behavior is shown to be a nuisance, the nuisance can be abated or compensation paid. As *Butler* and *Street* noted, such a cause does not require a showing that the defendant's activity was either ultrahazardous or performed with want of due care.

Should courts continue to recognize nuisance actions after the 1996 amendments, they would be developing an already rich area of law. Nuisance actions have been allowed in diverse circumstances. In *King v. Western Club, Inc.*, 587 So. 2d 122 (La.App. 2 Cir. 1991), a lessee of a neighboring property was held to have deprived his neighbor of liberty of enjoyment of his property by loud noises emanating from the club run by the lessee. Where a dairy farmer's oxidation pond emitted noxious odors and overflowed onto plaintiff's property, the pond was determined to be a nuisance, entitling the plaintiff to recover damages. *Day v. Warren*, 524 So. 2d 1383 (La.App. 1 Cir. 1988). Property owners who said activity at a nearby airport caused injury and property damages could recover for nuisance, according to the Louisiana Fifth Circuit, even though the damage did not constitute a taking under state and federal law. *Ursin v. New Orleans Aviation Board*, 506 So. 2d 947 (La.App. 5 Cir. 1987). And, in *Acadian Heritage Realty, Inc. v. Lafayette*, 434 So. 2d 182 (La.App. 3 Cir. 1983), the Third Circuit found that proof of fault was not necessary to establish that a landfill was a nuisance diminishing the value of adjacent land and entitling the plaintiffs to damages.

4.   This jurisprudence is consistent with common law notions of nuisance. The Restatements distinguish between Public and Private Nuisance. A CONCISE RESTATEMENT OF TORTS, § 821, at 180-187 (2000). The vicinage articles in the Code are similar to Private Nuisance which the Restatements define as "a nontrespassory invasion of another's interest in the private use and enjoyment of land." *Id.*, at § 821D, at 182. Recovery for private nuisance is limited to "those to whom it causes significant harm, of a kind that would be suffered by a normal person in the community or property in normal condition and used for a normal purpose." *Id.* at § 821F, at 182.

Under the Restatements, however, recovery for private nuisance is much more limited than the pre-1996 Louisiana cases implying an Art. 667 or 669 action in cases of non-intentional, reasonable behavior which did not involve ultrahazardous activity. The Restatements limit recovery to either cases where the nuisance is both intentional *and* unreasonable, or to cases where the unintentional nuisance is negligent, reckless, or involves abnormally dangerous conditions or activities (i.e., ultrahazardous activities). *See* §§ 822 & 826.

5.   If Art. 669 is unaffected by the 1996 amendment to Art 667, it is important to note the key differences between the articles. Notice that Art. 669 is the more narrow, applying only when construction or works cause smoke, smells or other noxious elements to intrude on the plaintiff's nearby land. This distinction was crucial in *Stewart v. Pineville*, 511 So. 2d 26 (La. App. 3 Cir. 1987).

In *Stewart* the defendant town built a water pumping station on the lot adjacent to the plaintiff's home. Although the plaintiffs prevailed at trial, they were awarded only $1000.00 in damages, despite depreciation of the value of their home by almost $20,000.00. The panel upheld the award, noting that, generally, damages are not available for the mere depreciation of property owing to a neighbor's use of the land. *See Jeansonne v. Cox*, 233 La. 251, 96 So. 2d 557 (1957) (no depreciation damages for property where canal built in close proximity). Such damages were recognized under Article 667 only where the nearby land use causing the depreciation was an ultrahazardous activity. *See Hero Lands Co. v. Texaco, Inc.*, 310 So. 2d 93 (La. 1975) (recovery allowed for depreciation of land in close proximity to high pressure oil pipeline). Since the water pumping station was not ultrahazardous, Article 667 damages were not available. Therefore, recovery in *Stewart* could only be had for the noise and nuisance of the construction under Article 669, justifying the limited award of $1,000.00.

Notice that, with ultrahazardous activities now limited only to blasting and pile driving, it is unlikely that Article 667 will be a useful basis for nuisance actions. Rather, actions might be limited to Article 669, which requires at least that the damages be caused by a nuisance that comes onto the plaintiff's land, i.e., dust, smoke, smells, noise, etc.

6.   In *Yokum v. 615 Bourbon Street, L.L.C. d/b/a The Rock, Old Opera House, Inc.*, 977 So. 2d 859 (La. 2008), neighbors sued the owner of a French Quarter bar for loud noise emanating from a business operated by a lessee. The court held that under Art. 667, an owner is a "proprietor" and "work" includes activities such as operation of a loud establishment and that in a non-ultrahazardous activity case plaintiff must establish negligence.

CHAPTER 12

VICARIOUS LIABILITY
(Imputed Fault)

A.   GENERALLY

COMMENT

Vicarious liability, or imputed fault, imposes liability upon one person for the fault of another. The critical initial inquiry is whether the relationship between the at-fault actor and the person to whom her fault will be imputed is one justifying the imputation. The most common type of vicarious liability is that of an employer for the torts of an employee committed in the course and scope of the employer's business. Additionally, Louisiana law, but not common law, imposes liability upon the parent for the tort of a child above the age of discernment. The law sometimes imposes vicarious liability upon a partner for the torts of a partnership. The members of a joint venture also may be vicariously liable for the torts of the joint venture's members but creative efforts to turn groups into "joint ventures" have proven unsuccessful. *See also*, *Gabriel v. Hobbs*, 804 So. 2d 853 (La.App. 4 Cir. 2001) (a group of family members deciding to go on vacation in two vehicles is not a joint venture; there is no combination of property and no sufficient sharing or allocation of benefits, and the object is not for pecuniary gain). The current state of the Louisiana law of vicarious liability is explored below.

Another aspect of imputed fault is that the law will charge the fault of an at-fault actor to a plaintiff so as to bar or reduce the recovery of the plaintiff if the fault would have been imputed had plaintiff been sued for the at-fault actor's conduct. This is sometimes called imputed contributory negligence.

B.   EMPLOYER-EMPLOYEE

1.   Generally

COMMENT

An "employer" is vicariously liable for the torts of his "employee" committed in the course and scope of the employee's employment. There must be: (1) an employer/employee relationship; and (2) a tort committed by the employee in (3) the course and scope of the employee's work with the employer. The tort could be intentional or negligent but must be in the course and scope of employment. The traditional statutory source is CC Art. 2320. Read literally, the article appears to impose liability upon the employer only if the employer is personally negligent. However, that language has been ignored (*see, e.g.*, *Roger v. Dufrene*, 718 So. 2d 592 (La.App. 4 Cir. 1998); *Weaver v. W.L. Goulden Logging Co.*, 116 La. 468, 40 So. 798 (1906)), and Louisiana respondeat superior generally parallels the common law concept. Subsequent legislation, La. R.S. 9:3921, confirms the jurisprudence establishing employer vicarious liability (sometimes called "respondeat superior") in Louisiana law.

La. R.S. 9:3921 provides as follows:

> [E]very master or employer is answerable for the damage occasioned by his servant or employee in the exercise of the functions in which they are employed. Any remission, transaction, compromise, or other conventional discharge in favor of the employee, or any judgment rendered against him for such damage shall be valid as between the damaged creditor and the employee, and the employer shall have no right of contribution, division, or indemnification from the employee nor shall the employer be allowed to bring any incidental action under the provisions of Chapter 6 of Title I of Book II of the Louisiana Code of Civil Procedure against such employee.

There are two major issues:

(1) when is one an "employee," and

(2) when is the "employee" acting in the course and scope of his employment?

An employee who negligently causes personal injury to a third person is liable for damages for that injury, regardless of whether his employer also is liable under respondent superior. If the employer also is liable then there will be solidary liability for the employee's fault. However, a Louisiana appellate court held that if a plaintiff settles with the employer, the plaintiff cannot then sue the employee for the underlying tort, even if the settlement agreement with the employer expressly reserves rights against the employee. *See Nizzo v. Wallace*, 83 So. 3d 161 (La.App. 5 Cir. 2011), *writ denied*, 84 So. 3d 556 (La. 2012). The Fifth Circuit based this on the vicarious nature of the employer's liability:

> [T]he relationship between the employer and employee under Article 2320 is different in that the employer's liability does not arise from it being a tortfeasor; its liability is derivative and arises solely from its employment relationship with the tortfeasor employee. Thus, under most circumstances, unless the employer itself has been shown to be a tortfeasor, there are no virile shares; the employer is vicariously liable for the entirety of the damages owed to a victim as a result of the employee's tort.

Id. at 167.

Another characteristic of respondeat superior law in Louisiana is that an employer that satisfies a judgment for an employee's tort does not have a right of contribution or indemnification against the employee tortfeasor based upon Louisiana's anti-indemnity statute, La. R.S. 9:3921, reproduced *supra*.

In addition to being vicariously liable for the torts of an employee in the course and scope of employment, the employer may be negligent in hiring, training or retaining an employee. *See Roberts v. Benoit*, *supra* Chapter 6.D.12.

2.   The Employment Relationship

HICKMAN
v.
SOUTHERN PACIFIC TRANSPORT COMPANY
262 So. 2d 385 (La. 1972)

SUMMERS, J.

* * * * *

The legal relationship between Fowler and Southern Pacific Transport is to be determined from the contract between them and from their intentions in establishing and carrying out that relationship as manifested in its performance and the surrounding circumstances.

It is well understood by the courts of this State that the term independent contractor connotes a freedom of action and choice with respect to the undertaking in question and a legal responsibility on the part of the contractor in case the agreement is not fulfilled in accordance with its covenants. The relationship presupposes a contract between the parties, the independent nature of the contractor's business and the nonexclusive means the contractor may employ in accomplishing the work. Moreover, it should appear that the contract calls for specific piecework as a unit to be done according to the independent contractor's own methods, without being subject to the control and direction, in the performance of the service, of his employer, except as to the result of the services to be rendered. It must also appear that a specific price for the overall undertaking is agreed upon; that its duration is for a specific time and not subject to termination or discontinuance at the will of either side without a corresponding liability for its breach. *Amyx v. Henry & Hall*, 227 La. 364, 79 So. 2d 483 (1955).

The law further recognizes that inquiry to determine whether a relationship is that of independent contractor or that of mere servant requires, among other factors, the application of the principal test: the control over the work reserved by the employer. In applying this test it is not the supervision and control which is actually exercised which is significant, the important question is whether, from the nature of the relationship, the right to do so exists. *Amyx v. Henry & Hall, ibid.*

* * * * *

Another, and perhaps the most telling, fault in the contention that these facts present an independent contractor relationship is the stipulation that the contract between the parties could be terminated by either party upon written notice to the other, without incurring liability for breach; and the further stipulation that Southern Pacific Transport had the right to terminate the relationship at any time when Fowler's services "shall be unsatisfactory" to Southern Pacific Transport.

This right to terminate the relationship without cause, where no term of employment is prescribed, is characteristic of the master and servant or employer-employee relationship. The right is at the same time antagonistic to the independent contractor relationship. *See* La.Civil Code. art. 2746; *Pitcher v. United Oil & Gas Syndicate*, 174 La. 66, 139 So. 760 (1932); *Bell v. Albert Hanson Lumber Co., Ltd.*, 151 La. 824, 92 So. 350 (1922).

We hold, therefore, that Fowler was an employee of Southern Pacific Transport. As Fowler's employer, Southern Pacific Transport is responsible in solido with Fowler for damages caused by his negligent conduct in the course and scope of his employment. La. Civil Code arts. 176 and 2320.

NOTES

1. In *Doe v. Parauka*, 714 So. 2d 701 (La. 1998), involving the liability of a diocese for alleged child sexual abuse by a school church principal, the Court reiterated that "The single most important factor to consider in deciding whether the employer-employee relationship exists for the purposes of art. 2320 is the right of the employer to control the work of the employee.... The right of control necessarily encompasses supervision, selection and engagement, payment of wages or salary, and the power to dismiss."

2. While a principal normally is *not* vicariously liable for the torts of an independent contractor, there are exceptions. In Louisiana, a principal will be held liable for injuries resulting from negligent acts of an independent contractor if (1) the liability arises from ultrahazardous or inherently dangerous activities performed by the contractor on behalf of the principal (*see, e.g., Sims v. Cefolia*, 890 So. 2d 626 (La.App. 5 Cir. 2004), *writ denied*, 896 So. 2d 73 (La. 2005) (underground tunneling beneath an immovable structure is not inherently dangerous or ultrahazardous; thus the principal is not liable to third persons injured by the tunneling)), or (2) the principal retains operational control over the contractor's acts or expressly or impliedly authorizes those acts. *See Butler v. Boutan*, 168 So. 3d 501 (La.App. 1 Cir. 2014). Where the contract provides that contractor shall control the performance of the details of the work and shall be solely responsible for the condition of the injury-causing equipment, the principal does not have operational control (absent an express or implied order to the contractor to engage in the unsafe work practice leading to the injury) although the contract reserves to the principal the right to monitor the contractor's performance and the principal stations a "company man" on the premises who observes the contractor's activities, has the right to make safety recommendations to the contractor, and is obliged to report continuing unsafe work practices or conditions to principal. *Coulter v. Texaco, Inc.* 117 F.3d 909 (5th Cir. 1997). In *Anderson v. NOPSI*, 583 So. 2d 829 (La. 1991), the Supreme Court observed that the principal is subject to liability for the physical tortious conduct of an agent only if the principal has the power to control physical details of the agent's manner of his performance "which is characteristic of the relation of master and servant."

It concluded that the lower court erred in imputing to a mother the negligence of a person whom she asked to care for her child while the mother slept.

3.   Special statutes govern the respondeat superior liability of the state for its officials, officers or employees. See, e.g., R.S. 42:1441, 42:1441.2, 42:1441.3, 42:1441.4 and R.S. 13:5108.1. *See, also, Garrett v. Fleetwood*, 644 So. 2d 664 (La.App. 4 Cir. 1994), *writ denied,* 650 So. 2d 253 (La. 1995). R.S. 42:1441.3 provides factors for determining which political subdivision may be liable for the torts of a public employee. A political subdivision for this purpose includes local government units, district attorneys, sheriffs and all other elected parochial officials.

4.   When is a religious or charitable organization liable for the torts of a volunteer worker? *See Doe v. The Roman Catholic Church*, 615 So. 2d 410 (La.App. 4 Cir. 1992), *writ denied,* 618 So. 2d 412 (La. 1993).

5.   A principal also may be held liable for the torts of independent contractors if the principal has a non-delegable duty to see that the work is done. The leading case, *Maloney v. Rath*, 69 Cal. 2d 442, 1 Cal. Rptr. 897, 445 P. 2d 513 (1968), held that a car owner had a non-delegable duty to have operable brakes on her car and therefore was liable for the negligence of a brake (non)repair person. Why not just hold the owner strictly liable? Would that accomplish the same result? How would it be different? In a strict liability case plaintiff would not have to prove any negligence, would he?

6.   In Louisiana and elsewhere a most intellectually challenging issue arises in the borrowed servant context. Consider the next principal case.

MORGAN
v.
ABC MANUFACTURER
710 So. 2d 1077 (La. 1998)

KNOLL, J.

This case presents the issue of whether a general or lending employer who is in the business of hiring out temporary employees to other businesses is liable for its borrowed employee's tortious conduct while in the performance of his work with the borrowing employer. In *Lejeune v. Allstate Insurance Co.*, 365 So. 2d 471 (La. 1978), this Court determined that both the special and the general employer may be solidarily liable for the torts of a "borrowed" employee. This opinion revisits *Lejeune* in the context of a temporary agency providing industrial workers. We reaffirm our holding in *Lejeune*, and we further hold that where a general employer is engaged in the business of hiring out its employees under the supervision of another employer, the general employer remains liable for the torts of the "borrowed" employees.

Facts

On October 23, 1992, Edward Morgan, an employee of Goldin Industries of Louisiana, Inc. (Goldin), was cutting iron for scrap in the "burning field" of Goldin's yard in Harvey, Louisiana. Morgan was severely injured when he was struck by a large piece of scrap iron which fell free while being transported across the Goldin yard by a crane. Morgan alleged that the iron which struck him was negligently hooked to the crane by Daryl Hines, an employee of Worktec Temporaries, Inc. (Worktec), who was working in the Goldin yard that day as an industrial laborer.

Worktec is a temporary services provider, supplying technical employees such as engineers in addition to general laborers to its customers. In the instant case, Worktec entered into an agreement with Goldin to provide industrial laborers to work in Goldin's scrap yard in Harvey, Louisiana. In accordance with service standards submitted to Goldin, Worktec agreed to "recruit, screen, test, provide orientation, assign and continually monitor the performance" of the assigned employees. Worktec also agreed to provide workers compensation insurance, general liability insurance, and unemployment insurance for any assigned employee. Worktec handled all administration and clerical duties that were required, and it billed Goldin $7.65 per hour for the industrial laborers it provided.

Once assigned, Hines followed the instructions given him by Mark Harding, Goldin's operations manager, and Keith Templet, the operator of the crane at Goldin's facility. Any tools or equipment required were provided by Goldin. Although Goldin could dismiss Hines from its yard, only Worktec had the power to hire and fire Hines. At the end of each week, Hines would fill out a Worktec time sheet stating his hours worked and submit it to a Goldin supervisor for verification. Hines would then submit the verified time sheet to Worktec who would issue his paycheck. Worktec paid Hines an hourly wage of $5.00 from which it deducted Hines' state and federal payroll taxes.

There is no dispute that under the agreement, Hines at all times remained Worktec's payroll employee. The agreement provided that after a Worktec employee had been assigned for 12 weeks, Goldin could transfer that employee to its own payroll with no further obligation. However, the agreement provided that any Worktec employee hired away by Goldin during the first 12 weeks of an assignment would result in a "liquidation fee." Although Hines had been assigned to report to work in the Goldin yard for several months before the accident occurred, Goldin did not exercise its option to place Hines on its own payroll. Following the accident, Hines continued working for Worktec at the Goldin assignment as well as assignments with other Worktec customers. Additionally, as a result of the accident, Worktec required Hines to submit to a drug screening in accordance with Worktec personnel policies.

In addition to its assertions that Hines did not hook the load and that the accident was caused by the crane operator's negligence, Worktec maintained that it was not liable as Hines' employer because Hines had become the borrowed employee of Goldin. In support of its borrowed employee defense, Worktec submitted the following jury instruction, which was approved by the trial court and read to the jury: An employer, such as Worktec Temporaries, Inc., who lends its employees to another company is called a general or lending employer. The borrowing employer, such as Goldin Industries, is called the borrowing or special employer. If, after consideration of the ten factors listed above, you find that Worktec Temporaries was a lending employer, then Worktec is relieved of liability. The party who alleges that an employee has become a borrowed employee, in this case Worktec Temporaries, bears the burden of proving it by a preponderance of the evidence. In this matter, in order to escape liability, Worktec must prove that its employee, Darryl Hines, at some point became the borrowed employee of Goldin Industries, Inc. If you find that Darryl Hines was Worktec's employee, and not Goldin Industries' borrowed employee, then you may find Worktec liable for damages to Edward Morgan caused by Worktec's negligence, if any.

In its answer to a jury interrogatory, the jury found that Hines was the borrowed employee of Goldin. As instructed by the jury interrogatory, the jury then ended its deliberation and returned its verdict to the court. The trial court entered judgment in favor of Worktec, dismissing Morgan's suit with prejudice. The court of appeal affirmed. We granted writs to determine whether a general employer that operates as a temporary employment service agency can be held vicariously liable for the negligent conduct of its loaned employees.

Employer Liability for Borrowed Servant

In Louisiana, employers are vicariously liable for the torts of their employees under La.Civ.Code art. 2320, which provides:

> Masters and employers are answerable for the damage occasioned by their servants and overseers, in the exercise of the functions in which they are employed.

> Teachers and artisans are answerable for the damage caused by their scholars or apprentices, while under their superintendence.

In the above cases, responsibility only attaches, when the masters or employers, teachers and artisans, might have prevented the act which caused the damage, and have not done it.

The master is answerable for the offenses and quasi-offenses committed by his servants, according to the rules which are explained under the title: Of quasi-contracts, and of offenses and quasi-offenses.

Although Article 2320 provides that employers are only liable when they might have prevented the act which caused the damage, the courts of this state have consistently held that employers are vicariously liable for any torts occasioned by their employees. *Ermert v. Hartford Ins. Co.*, 559 So. 2d 467 (La. 1990). This judicial interpretation of La.Civ.Code art. 2320 has been codified by the legislature in La.R.S. 9:3921, which provides, in part: "every master or employer is answerable for the damage occasioned by his servant or employee in the exercise of the functions in which they are employed."

In the past, the courts of this state recognized that under certain circumstances, an employer, called the "general employer," who has relinquished control of his employee to another employer, known as the "special employer," may be legally absolved of liability for that employee's torts. This legal fiction, known as the "borrowed employee" defense was recognized by this Court in *Benoit v. Hunt Tool Co.*, 219 La. 380, 53 So. 2d 137 (1951). In *Benoit*, a welder in the general employ of Hunt Tool Company negligently injured two employees of his special employer, Morris and Meredith, Inc., a drilling company. The court stated:

> [I]t is often difficult where two possible masters are involved to determine which is liable for the tort, and to determine such liability we must look to the doctrine of the borrowed servant or employee pro hac vice. In determining liability under this doctrine, in some cases the courts have imposed liability on the person in whose business the employee was engaged at the time the tort was committed. In others the test has been the right of control over the servant at the time the tort was committed.

Benoit, supra at 389-90, 53 So. 2d 137.

The two prevailing tests for determining borrowed employee status can be summarized as follows. The "whose business" test inquires as to which employer's work was being performed at the time the accident occurred. The "right of control" test focuses on which employer had the right to control the specific acts of the employee at the time of the accident, the reasoning being that that employer is in the best position to prevent the injury. The two tests tend to overlap since an employer's right to control is generally coextensive with the scope of his business, and the tests are often used in a complimentary fashion by the courts in an attempt to determine which of the two employers should be liable. *Benoit, supra; The Standard Oil Company v. Anderson*, 212 U.S. 215, 29 S.Ct. 252, 53 L.Ed. 480 (1909).

In *Benoit*, the Court held that under the circumstances, Hunt was vicariously liable for the welder's tortious conduct based on a finding that he was not the borrowed servant of Morris and Meredith. This determination was based on the fact that Hunt retained almost complete control over its loaned employee. Hunt selected the welder, provided him with welding tools, paid his wages, and had the right to fire him. Morris and Meredith had no control over the methods employed by the welder in the performance of his job duties on the drilling rig.

Under the borrowed servant doctrine as it existed when Benoit was decided, the finding of borrowed servant status eliminated the possibility of vicarious liability on the part of the general employer. Liability was an "either or" issue: either the special employer was liable or the general employer was liable, but not both. The idea was that a servant could have only one master at a time, and a finding that a loaned employee was a borrowed servant meant that his relationship with the general employer was temporarily suspended, thus precluding liability.

Over the years, numerous courts and commentators expressed concern regarding the continuing applicability of the borrowed employee doctrine, especially considering the inconsistent results that the jurisprudential tests produced. The problem associated with the "right of control" test is that it is inconsistent with the premise of respondeat superior, namely, that direct fault of the employer need not be shown for the employer to be held liable. The test overlooks the fact that in a typical situation, the general employer retains broad control over its employees while the special employer has control over the details of the work. Since liability is based on the right of control, rather than actual control of the employee at the time of the accident, it is unreasonable to choose between the two employers when each shares the right to control the employee's actions. The same can be said of the "whose business" test; it is not unusual that the business of both the general and special employer is furthered at the same time by the employee's actions. Because the tests were so general, the outcome of many cases with parallel facts depended on which facts the courts chose to emphasize, creating inconsistent precedent. Courts holding general employers liable emphasized the general control those employers had over their employees. Similarly, courts finding against special employers focused on the special employer's right to supervise the employee at the time of the tort.

Dual Employers

Aware of these inconsistencies, this Court revisited the issue of the borrowed employee defense, and repudiated the "one master" rule of *Benoit* in favor of finding both the general employer and the special employer solidarily liable for the torts of the borrowed employee. In *Lejeune v. Allstate Insurance Co.*, 365 So. 2d 471 (La. 1978), a hearse driver loaned from Ardoin's Funeral Home of Ville Platte, Inc. to Ardoin's Funeral Home of Mamou, Inc. negligently failed to stop at a flashing red light during a funeral cortege. An employee of the special employer (Mamou) who was riding in the hearse was killed in the resulting collision between the hearse and an automobile with the right of way. Although the court found that the driver was the borrowed employee of the special employer, the court held the general employer liable, stating:

> Nevertheless, this [borrowed employee] determination should not relieve the general employer of his liability for his employee's negligent acts done in the pursuance of duties designated for him by his employer, in whose pay he continued and who had the sole right to discharge him. This is especially so in the present case, where the employee was loaned out to another in a continuing arrangement between the employers for their mutual benefit.

* * * * *

> A number of other jurisdictions have likewise held that both the general and special employer may be held solidarily liable for the employee's tort. We believe this to be the better rule and, accordingly, overrule expressions indicating to the contrary, as well as the two decisions of the intermediate courts (see footnote 11) which expressly held the general employer not liable to a third person for torts committed by his employee while loaned to a special employer.

> We conclude, therefore, that under the circumstances, Ville Platte, the general employer, is liable to the plaintiffs for the damages caused them by Lafleur while negligently driving the hearse for Mamou.

Lejeune, supra at 481-2. (Footnotes omitted).

The "dual employer" rule was recently reaffirmed by this court in *Blair v. Tynes*, 621 So. 2d 591 (La. 1993), wherein we held both a general and a special employer liable to a third party for damages caused through the negligence of five loaned sheriff's deputies. In *Blair*, we stated:

> Our jurisprudence has held that special and general employers may be solidarily liable in tort to third parties injured by the negligence of their employees. In *Lejeune v. Allstate Ins. Co.*, 365 So. 2d 471 (La. 1978), we addressed the issue of whether the

general employer of a negligent employee remained liable for its employee's tort despite the fact that the employee had been borrowed to perform services for a special employer at the time of an accident. We held that a general and special employer may be solidarily liable for injuries to a third party caused by an employee's negligence.

Blair, supra at 599.

As noted above, there is no legislative expression regarding the borrowed employee defense. It is a jurisprudential creation. The immunity provided to the general employer is in derogation of the general tort rights of victims. Thus the scope of the immunity must be strictly construed. See *Sewell v. Doctor's Hospital*, 600 So. 2d 577 (La. 1992). As we see it, the issue before this Court is not whether the scope of the borrowed employee defense should be restricted only to employers who exercise supervisory control over the borrowed employee. Rather, this Court must determine whether the borrowed employee defense extends to the circumstances of the instant case, namely, whether temporary agencies who are in the business of lending their employees under the supervision of others should receive the benefit of tort immunity. In short, Worktec asserts that its lack of supervisory control over its own employee should form the basis for its tort immunity. We are not persuaded by this argument.

This Court's limitation of the borrowed employee defense in Lejeune and Blair is supported by the continuing development in the law of employer liability or respondeat superior. While the borrowed servant defense focuses on which employer controlled the employee's actions, modern justification for employer liability is not based so much on the employer's control of the employee's actions, but on the concept of "enterprise liability." In *Ermert v. Hartford Ins. Co.*, 559 So. 2d 467 (La. 1990), this Court recently stated:

> The master's vicarious liability for the acts of its servant rests not so much on policy grounds consistent with the governing principles of tort law as in a deeply rooted sentiment that a business enterprise cannot justly disclaim responsibility for accidents which may fairly be said to be characteristic of its activities.

Ermert, supra at 476.

To a temporary services provider such as Worktec, loaned employees are its stock in trade. Though the essence of Worktec's business is to profit from its employee's labors, a significant feature of its business is to pass control of the details of the work to its customers. However, Worktec retains ultimate and overriding authority over its loaned workers. This makes the application of the traditional "right of control" test problematic. Additionally, Worktec only bills its customers for the hours its employees actually work for those customers. The loaned employees are furthering the business of Worktec at the identical time when they are also furthering the business of the special employer. Put simply, both employers had contemporaneous control over Hines, and both contemporaneously benefitted from his labor. It is therefore reasonable that considering the overlapping control and shared financial interest that they share liability. As noted by Professor Galligan:

> The two master rule is the more sensible rule, especially in cases where the general employer is engaged in the business of renting out people and equipment (or at least sometimes renting out people and equipment). In situations where the general employer's business is to rent out his or her employees and equipment to others, the general employer's business is being furthered even if he does not control the details of the actual work. Moreover, the special employer benefits: it is his work that is being done as well. In such situations, the relevant enterprise benefitted by the work consists of the combination of the general and special employers. The two master rule represents a triumph of function over (legal) fiction. Thomas C. Galligan, Jr., A Primer on the Patterns of Louisiana Workplace Torts, 55 Louisiana Law Review at 91 (1994).

The labor provided by Worktec is its product, and Worktec should bear the expenses and risks associated with its product, in addition to reaping the benefits derived therefrom. Since modern justification for employer liability is not based so much on the employer's control of the employee's actions, but on the concept of "enterprise liability," Worktec's failure to exercise direct supervisory control over Hines should not preclude its liability. We therefore hold that where, as here, a general employer is in the business of hiring its employees out under the supervision of others, the general employer remains liable for the "borrowed" employees' torts under La.Civ.Code art. 2320.

In the present case, plainly the jury instruction given by the trial court follows the "one master" rule and is inconsistent with the current law of the borrowed servant doctrine in Louisiana. The approved instruction provided: "[i]f after consideration of the ten factors listed above, you find that Worktec Temporaries was a lending employer, then Worktec is relieved of liability." *Lejeune* and *Blair, supra*, specifically repudiated the "one master" rule in favor of solidary liability among the general and the special employers. Put simply, a determination that Hines was the borrowed employee of Goldin does not preclude Worktec's liability. The trial court clearly erred as a matter of law in instructing the jury otherwise.

Accordingly, we find that the trial court committed legal error in instructing the jury that a finding that Hines was Goldin's borrowed employee would relieve Worktec of liability for his torts. When such a prejudicial error of law skews the trial court's finding of a material issue of fact and causes it to pretermit other issues, the appellate court is required, if it can, to render judgment on the record by applying the correct law and determining the essential material facts de novo. *Lasha v. Olin Corp.*, 625 So. 2d 1002 (La. 1993). Accordingly, for the foregoing reasons, we reverse and remand the case to the Fifth Circuit Court of Appeal for further consideration of the trial record and for a de novo decision on the merits.

NOTES

1.   Are both employers vicariously liable? Could a non-employee have held both Goldin and Worktec vicariously liable for Hines' tort? And, could Morgan? Could Hines recover indemnity from Worktec? Vice versa? What would that depend upon? Could Morgan sue Hines? What does Morgan recover from Goldin? If Morgan had negligently hurt Hines, could Hines recover in tort from Goldin? From Morgan? From Hines? Is all this more complicated than it has to be? How would you simplify it?

2.   Consider the case of a corporation that purchases another corporation and a tort claim arises from products sold before the sale by the purchased company. The purchased company is wholly absorbed by the purchaser company. Under what circumstances should a company, which simply acquires another company for growth purposes, be liable for earlier products released by the target, perhaps years before it makes the acquisition? Louisiana has not adopted the more liberal "continued product line" on successor liability. Thus when a corporation sells all of its assets to another, the latter is not responsible for the seller's debt or liabilities unless the purchaser assumes the obligation, or the purchaser is merely a continuation of the seller, or the transaction is entered into to escape liability. *Pichon v. Asbestos Defendants*, 52 So. 3d 240 (La.App. 4 Cir. 2010), *writ denied*, 57 So. 3d 317 (La. 2011).

3.   **Course and Scope of Employment**

REED

v.

HOUSE OF DECOR, INC.
468 So. 2d 1159 (La. 1985)

LEMMON, J.

We granted certiorari to determine whether the intermediate court erred in reversing a judgment which held that House of Decor, Inc. was vicariously liable for plaintiff's injuries caused by Chuck Williams, an alleged employee of House of Decor. The critical issue is whether Williams was an employee of the House of Decor in the course and scope of that employment at the time of the accident.

William Cusack and Steven Tomoletz, as individuals, leased certain immovable property in the Vieux Carré section of New Orleans. The lower floor of the main building on the property was used as a gift shop operated by the House of Decor, Inc., a corporation in which Cusack and Tomoletz were the sole shareholders. The two men resided on the upper floor of the main building.

The leased property also included slave quarters in the rear. Cusack and Tomoletz sublet the upper apartment in the slave quarters to Williams on a two-year lease for a monthly rental of $125, executing the sublease in their individual capacities and not as officers of the corporation. They used the lower floor of the slave quarters to store inventory for the House of Decor.

Shortly before the October 31, 1976 accident, Cusack and Tomoletz purchased immovable property in another location with the intention of moving their residence. They agreed with Chuck Williams that he was to close permanently when the lease ended in December, 1976.

The day before the accident, Cusack asked plaintiff, an employee of a hotel across the street from the House of Decor, to help move a refrigerator from Williams' upper apartment to the new residence. The accident occurred on a Sunday, before the hour that the gift shop opened. While Williams and plaintiff were attempting to move the refrigerator down the stairs of the slave quarters to Williams' truck, Williams lost his grip, and the refrigerator fell onto plaintiff's ankle.

Plaintiff filed suit against the House of Decor and Gulf Insurance Company as the corporation's liability carrier, alleging that the House of Decor was vicariously liable for the negligence of its "employee", Chuck Williams. Neither Cusack nor Tomoletz was ever named or served as an individual defendant, nor was any argument made to the jury that they were individually liable. Both sides restricted their opening and closing arguments to the jury (except for the issue of damages), to the issue of the House of Decor's vicarious liability for the negligence of Williams as a corporate employee.

* * * * *

Whether a party is liable for the act of a tortfeasor on the basis that the tortfeasor was the party's employee in the course and scope of employment depends upon the proof and assessment of several factors, including payment of wages by the employer, the employer's power of control, the employee's duty to perform the particular act, the time, place and purpose of the act in relation to service of the employer, the relationship between the employee's act and the employer's business, the benefits received by the employer from the act, the motivation of the employee for performing the act, and the reasonable expectation of the employer that the employee would perform the act.

* * * * *

In summary, Williams did not receive any wages from the House of Decor. The corporation had no power of control or power of discharge over his work activities.[67] The act of moving the refrigerator occurred at a time when the business operated by the corporation was closed and at a place away from the corporation's business premises. The moving of the refrigerator from an apartment occupied by Williams to another residence provided no apparent benefit to the corporation and had no relationship with the corporation's business. Indeed, the corporation was just about to close down the business permanently, and it is difficult to perceive any purpose in moving the refrigerator that was in any way related to the corporation.

Determination of the course and scope of employment is largely based on policy. The risks which are generated by an employee's activities while serving his employer's interests are properly allocated to the employer as a cost of engaging in the enterprise. However, when the party (the alleged employer) upon whom vicarious liability is sought to be imposed had only a marginal relationship with the act which generated the risk and did not benefit by it, the purpose of the policy falls, and the responsibility for preventing the risk is solely upon the tortfeasor who created the risk while performing the act.

In the present case, the jury found that Williams was an employee of the House of Decor. The evidence arguably supports this limited determination that he was an occasional employee.[68] If Williams were a regular employee of the small corporation, perhaps policy would dictate that he should be viewed as being in the course and scope of his employment when performing a task at the request of and for the personal benefit of the holder of 51% of the corporate shares in the two-shareholder corporation. However, there is no compelling policy reason for a similar conclusion in the case of someone who at best was an occasional employee.

We therefore conclude that Williams' act of moving the refrigerator, during the performance of which plaintiff was injured, was not performed by an employee of House of Decor in the course and scope of employment.

Accordingly, the judgment of the court of appeal is **AFFIRMED**.

Calogero and Dennis, JJ., dissent and assign reasons.

* * * * *

NOTE

Driver's "primary job" with the defendant newspaper was as an advertising account executive, but he also served as defendant's arts editor. He drove to New Orleans to attend a concert, and gained admission on a press card; "at an unsuspecting time he represented himself to be on newspaper business and his credentials were accepted by a disinterested third party." While he attended the concert for entertainment, "he was simultaneously obtaining information which furthered his employer's business interests." Although employee was operating his own auto at the time of the accident, this was only because his small size made company cars unavailable to him, and defendant paid for the gasoline used for the trip and "clearly benefitted from the journey." After the concert, employee made the decision -- "motivated by safety considerations" -- to stay the night with a friend;

---

[67] As landlords, Cusack and Tomoletz (the corporation's sole shareholders) could have legally terminated Williams' sublease for non-payment of rent. While this consideration may have explained Williams' motivation for performing uncompensated favors for the two men, there was no economic relationship between Williams and the corporation which the corporation had the power to control or terminate.

[68] On the undisputed evidence and the disputed evidence viewed mostly (sic) favorably to plaintiff (who was the prevailing party in the trial court). Williams was at best a marginal employee. However, the jury was not instructed on or questioned about the issue of course and scope of employment. Therefore, the reviewing court must determine that issue on the record, without deference to the jury's verdict on factual matters (although in this case there was no factual dispute pertinent to that issue).

while driving to the friend's house, he was involved in an accident. *Held*, driver's trip was "primarily 'employment-rooted'" and the decision of the trial court that driver was acting in the course of his employment at the time of the accident is not clearly wrong. *Austin v. Sherwood*, 446 So. 2d 274 (La. 1983).

MICHALESKI
v.
WESTERN PREFERRED CASUALTY COMPANY
472 So. 2d 18 (La. 1985)

WATSON, J.

Are defendants entitled to a summary judgment on the ground that Ricky Paul Leger was not in the course and scope of his employment on August 15, 1981, when he was involved in an automobile accident?

Facts

* * * * *

Leger, a resident of Church Point, Louisiana, was employed near Denham Springs, Louisiana, in Livingston Parish, as a motorman at an oil well workover. On August 14, Leger and the other employees set up the rig which had been brought in on trucks from Abbeville.[3] Leger had traveled in the last truck. The men finished work between 6:00 and 8:00 P.M. Leger had to leave his automobile in Abbeville and returned with one of the truck drivers to retrieve it. He was on the road most of the night bringing his car to the well site. Leger's crew of five started a shift the next morning, the day of the accident, at 6:00 A.M. Leger was working a twelve hour shift, "seven days on--seven days off." The time sheet showed that Ricky Leger worked twelve hours, from 6:00 A.M. to 6:00 P.M., on August 15, 1981. During their twelve hour shifts, the men ate on the run.

Leger received an hourly wage of $9.05. He also received $12 a day for food and gasoline from NL and a clothing allowance of $10 a day from Amoco. Both crews stayed in a trailer at the rig site. Leger said this was expected; the toolpusher said the men could sleep wherever they wished. As a practical matter, everyone slept at the well site. Each of the crew members had a separate bed. The company provided linens and the use of the kitchen. There was a disagreement about whether the stove and refrigerator in the crew trailer were operational when the accident occurred. Often the employees cook at the rig site, pooling their funds to buy groceries for the week. There was a grocery store approximately a mile and a half from the drilling site.

George Fritz, the rig supervisor or toolpusher for NL Well Service at the workover site, supervised ten men. Each crew of five included a driller, a derrick man, a motorman, and two floor hands. At the time of the accident, the "rigging up" had been finished and the crews were on a twelve hour schedule. In Fritz's opinion, NL provided trailers and a per diem allowance[4] because the hard physical work required adequate sleep and good eating habits. In an emergency or under extraordinary circumstances, Fritz might call one of the men who was off duty.

Leger's immediate superior was the driller for his crew. The two drillers work under the toolpusher. The drillers and the toolpusher had their transportation furnished by the company. There were three trailers on the site: one for the Amoco "company man", one for the toolpusher, and one for the two crews. The toolpusher was subject to call day and night. The final authority at the rig site was the Amoco company man.

---

[3] This was the third time Leger had worked on this particular rig.

[4] .... No food was available at the rig site.

On August 15, Leger and a co-worker, Joseph Matte, had driven five or six miles to eat dinner at the McDonald's in Denham Springs and were returning to the rig site. Leger was exhausted, closed his eyes momentarily, and opened them to see bright lights. Another car was coming out of a curve to Leger's right and he believed that both vehicles were over the center line. There was virtually a head-on collision between Leger's automobile and an automobile driven by Steven W. Michaleski carrying Sherri Michaleski, Arnold L. McLin, Jr., Debbie McLin, and Jaesa McLin as passengers.

Law

Generally, an employee is outside the course of employment until he reaches the employer's premises. However, payment of travel expenses can place an employee in employment status from the beginning of his travel until the end. *Samayoa v. Michel Lecler, Inc.*, 310 So. 2d 162 (La.App. 4 Cir. 1975), *writ den.*, 313 So. 2d 828 (La. 1975); *Pierre v. Gulf Janitorial Serv. of Baton Rouge, Inc.*, 277 So. 2d 509 (La.App. 1 Cir. 1973), *writ den.*, 279 So. 2d 689 (La. 1973).

An exception to the rule that employees are not in the course of employment going to and from work is recognized when transportation is furnished as an incident of employment, either through a vehicle, a conveyance and driver, or payment of expenses. *Griffin v. Catherine Sugar Co.*, 219 La. 846, 54 So. 2d 121 (1951); *Welch v. Travelers Insurance Company*, 225 So. 2d 623 (La.App. 1 Cir. 1969), *writ den.* 254 La. 852, 227 So. 2d 594 (1969); *Boutte v. Mudd Separators, Inc.*, 236 So. 2d 906 (La.App. 3 Cir. 1970), *writ den.* 256 La. 894, 240 So. 2d 231 (1970); *Prothro v. Louisiana Paving Co., Inc.*, 399 So. 2d 1229 (La.App. 3 Cir. 1981), *writ den.* 404 So. 2d 278 (La., 1981).[7] When an employer pays expenses and the trip in question is employment connected, an employee is in the course and scope of employment while away from his work place. *Austen v. Sherwood*, 446 So. 2d 274 (La. 1984); *Miller v. Keating*, 349 So. 2d 265 (La. 1977); *LeBrane v. Lewis*, 292 So. 2d 216 (La. 1974). *Also see Campbell v. Baker, Culpepper and Brunson*, 382 So. 2d 1046 (La.App. 2 Cir. 1980), *writ den.*, 385 So. 2d 793.

An employee is acting within the course and scope of his employment while on a job connected mission which the employer had reason to expect would be performed. *Stephens v. Justiss-Mears Oil Co.*, 312 So. 2d 293 (La. 1975); *St. Paul Fire & Marine Insurance Co. v. Roberts*, 331 So. 2d 529 (La.App. 1 Cir. 1976). When, at the time of an accident, "the employee is on a mission contemplated by employer and employee for which he is to be compensated, ... the employee is within the scope of his employment." *O'Brien v. Traders and General Insurance Company*, 136 So. 2d 852 at 864 (La.App. 1 Cir. 1961). Among the factors to be weighed in determining an employer's responsibility for the tort of an employee are: "the time, place and purpose of the act in relation to service of the employer, the relationship between the employee's act and the employer's business ... and the reasonable expectation of the employer that the employee would perform the act." *Reed v. House of Decor, Inc.*, 468 So. 2d 1159 at 1161 (La. 1985); LSA--C.C. art. 2320.

Conclusion

An oil company employee, working "seven days on" with living quarters and a food and gas allowance furnished by the employer, who is returning to the work place from a necessary trip for himself and a co-worker to eat is in the course of his employment. Such a journey is necessitated by the employment, since all the men had to leave the rig site to purchase groceries or a meal. *Compare Sellers v. Dixilyn Corporation*, 433 F.2d 446 (5 Cir. 1970) where plaintiff had completed his seven days on the rig and was not answerable to the call of duty as he drove home to commence his seven days on shore. Amoco's rig site here was not offshore. However, the very denomination of this employment indicates that Leger was at work during the "seven days on" at the rig site.

---

[7] *See also Willis v. Cloud*, 151 So. 2d 379 (La.App. 3 Cir. 1963), *writ den.* 244 La. 623, 153 So. 2d 415 (La. 1963), where an employee returning home in his own truck, which was used in performing job duties, was held to be in the course of employment, and *Shird v. Maricle*, 156 So. 2d 476 (La.App. 3 Cir. 1963).

Returning from a trip to buy food was an activity arising out of the nature of the employment. The employer anticipated the necessity of these temporary absences, because it compensated the employees with a per diem for their food and gasoline expenses. All of these employees were required to obtain meals or groceries away from the rig site and were furnished an allowance for that purpose. Leger did not deviate either in route or time on his errand. *See Wright v. Romano*, 279 So. 2d 735 (La.App. 1 Cir. 1973), *writ den.*, 281 So. 2d 757, 758.

Leger's negligence was the result of exhaustion, a foreseeable consequence of a hard twelve hour day. Since the risk of harm could reasonably be attributed to the employer's business, it cannot be said as a matter of law that Leger was not in the course and scope of his employment at the time of the automobile accident.

* * * * *

NOTES

1.   In *Winzer v. Richards*, 185 So. 3d 876 (La.App. 2 Cir. 2016), the Second Circuit held that a business was not liable for a rear-end collision by a former employee who was driving back to his home in Florida from the worksite in Texas. Although the former employer was paying travel expenses, the former employee was not in the course and scope of his employment. The court found the payment of expenses to be of no moment given that the driver no longer was an employee, he was driving his own vehicle home, his duties as a boilermaker did not involve use of a vehicle, at the time of the collision he was 600 miles from the worksite and the employer had no right or exercise of control over him, and he was not performing any mission or work for the employer's benefit. The employee could go home or anywhere else he chose by any route he chose. The risk of the employee's alleged negligent driving was not a risk fairly attributable to the employer's business.

2.   *Orgeron v. McDonald*, 639 So. 2d 224 (La. 1994) – Defendant supplied workers and equipment for catering services to the operators of offshore facilities; it dispatched workers to places designated by the customers, and the workers were transported to the work location by the customer. After its employee completed a 14-day shift and picked up his paycheck, defendant instructed him to begin a 7-day shift for another customer the following morning. Defendant did not provide employee with a travel allowance or reimburse him for travel expenses. Employee was involved in a auto accident while en route in his personal vehicle to the dock where he was to report to the customer. *Held*, "(t)he high degree of employer control and employer benefit in the specially ordered trip ... under the particular circumstances of this case brought the trip within the course and scope" of the employment, and thus employer is vicariously liable to a third person injured in the accident.

3.   In *Lorraine v. Nolty J. Theriot, Inc.*, 729 So. 2d 1160 (La.App. 1 Cir. 1999), *writ denied*, 745 So. 2d 30 (La. 1999), employer "interested itself" in employee's transportation to the worksites by providing transportation between the employer's office/warehouse and the worksites. However, employees were not paid wages for the time spent in traveling. *Held*, employee was in the course and scope of his employment when injured in an automobile accident between the office and the worksite; thus he was not covered under employer's policy, which excluded injuries sustained by employees in the course and scope of employment.

4.   In *Henly v. Phillips Abita Lumber Co., Inc.*, 971 So. 2d 1104 (La.App. 1 Cir. 2007), while riding together to work, employee's immediate supervisor exposed himself to employee and solicited her for sexual activity. The supervisor was found not to be in the course and scope of employment, and the employer was not exposed to vicarious liability.

TIMMONS
v.
SILMAN
761 So. 2d 507   (La. 2000)

KNOLL, J.

The writ before us concerns whether an employee's deviation from an employment related errand is so substantial as to render her deviation outside the course and scope of employment. During the deviation, a multi-vehicle accident occurred between Stacie Michelle Silman (Silman), Michael Timmons, and Bobby Hamilton (Hamilton) in the intersection of 18th Street and Stubbs Avenue in Monroe, Louisiana. In addition to filing suit against Silman and her motor vehicle insurer for injuries arising out of the accident, Michael Timmons and his wife, Wanda, (the Timmonses) filed suit against the insurer of Silman's employer, State Farm Fire and Casualty Insurance Company (State Farm), alleging that Silman's employer was vicariously liable for the damages arising out of Silman's fault. The trial court and court of appeal held that Silman's deviation was not in the course and scope of her employment, concluding that at the time of the accident she was on a personal errand unrelated to her employment. After a careful review of the record and applicable law, we conclude that the lower courts were correct in finding that Silman was not within the course and scope of her employment due to her substantial deviation from her employment duties. Accordingly, we affirm the lower courts.

Facts

Silman had been employed by attorney Catherine Stagg (Stagg) as a clerical assistant in Monroe, Louisiana for six months. As part of her duties as a clerical assistant, Silman ran errands, including traveling to the downtown post office to pick up the firm's mail and get postage for the firm's postage meter and also to the Central Bank located on the corner of North 18th Street and Stubbs Avenue to make firm deposits.

During an office Christmas luncheon on the day of the accident, Silman received her Christmas bonus check from Stagg. Shortly after returning to the office from lunch, Stagg instructed Silman to go to the post office and refill the firm's postage meter, and expected her to return with the filled meter. This task would require Silman to either walk or drive her car southwest four blocks to Monroe's downtown branch of the United States Post Office. Silman, using her personal vehicle to go to the post office, refilled the firm's postage meter and put it in her car. Rather than return to the firm, she then decided to embark on a personal errand and proceeded to the bank to cash her Christmas bonus check. On her way to the bank, she passed within one or two blocks of the firm without stopping to return the postage meter, and traveled northeast eighteen blocks beyond her place of employment. There was a branch of Central Bank located between the post office and her place of employment, but Silman was unaware of its location and did not use this branch bank. Before she reached the bank, Silman made a left turn in the path of an oncoming car in the intersection of North 18th Street and Stubbs Avenue and was thrust into Michael Timmons's car as he sat at the traffic light on Stubbs Avenue.

* * * * *

After the case was remanded and transferred to another division of the district court, the Timmonses moved for summary judgment on the same issue regarding whether Silman was in the course and scope of her employment with Stagg at the time of the accident. The trial court granted the Timmonses' motion and it was State Farm who then applied to the Second Circuit for relief. The appellate court granted State Farm the relief it requested, that is, a denial of the Timmonses' summary judgment motion, and remanded the case to the trial court for a trial on the merits.

After a bench trial, the court dismissed State Farm finding that Stagg was not vicariously liable as Silman was not in the course and scope of her employment at the time of the accident due to her personal deviation. The court of appeal affirmed. *Timmons v. State Farm Fire & Cas. Ins. Co.*, No. 30,036 (La.App. 2 Cir. 1997) (unpublished opinion). We granted certiorari to determine the correctness of the lower courts' judgments. *Timmons v. Silman*, 99-3264 (La. 2000), 753 So. 2d 842, 2000 La. LEXIS 380.

Law and Discussion

Under Louisiana law, an employer is answerable for the damage occasioned by its servants in the exercise of the functions in which the servant is employed. La. Civ.Code art. 2320. Specifically, an employer is liable for its employee's torts committed if, at the time, the employee was acting within the course and scope of his employment. *Baumeister v. Plunkett*, 95-2270 (La. 1996), 673 So. 2d 994, 996. An employee is acting within the course and scope of his employment when the employee's action is "of the kind that he is employed to perform, occurs substantially within the authorized limits of time and space, and is activated at least in part by a purpose to serve the employer." *Orgeron v. McDonald*, 93-1353 (La. 1994), 639 So. 2d 224, 226-27. An employee may be within the course and scope of his employment yet step out of that realm while engaging in a personal mission. *See* Denis Paul Juge, Louisiana Workers' Compensation § 8:8, at 8-59 (2nd ed. 1999).

The mere fact that an employee is performing a personal errand while on an employment related errand does not automatically compel the conclusion that the deviation removes the employee from the course and scope of employment. Generally, "[a]n identifiable deviation from a business trip for personal reasons takes the employee out of the course of employment until the employee returns to the route of the business trip, unless the deviation is so small as to be disregarded as insubstantial." 1 Larson's Workers' Compensation Law § 17-1 (emphasis added); *see also* Malone & Johnson, 13 Louisiana Civil Law Treatise, Workers' Compensation § 174, at 405 & n. 1.

Silman was clearly within the course and scope of her employment when she traveled to the post office to refill the firm's postage meter. This is not disputed. After the business errand was completed, Silman deviated from the business route to go to the bank, and, on her way to the bank, the accident in question occurred. In determining whether Silman's deviation to the bank was substantial or insubstantial, we will look at all the facts and circumstances of the deviation, including such illustrative factors as when and where, in relation to the business errand, the employee deviates from the employment related errand and commences with his personal errand, the temporal and spacial boundaries of the deviation, the nature of the employee's work, the additional risks created by the deviation, and the surrounding circumstances. *See* 1 Larson's Workers' Compensation Law § 17.06. This list of considerations is non-exhaustive, and a court should carefully consider all the facts unique to the case before it. When considering the foregoing factors, the trial court's findings of fact are entitled to great deference and should not be disturbed unless those findings are manifestly erroneous or clearly wrong. *Baumeister*, 673 So. 2d at 998.

In examining the when and where of a deviation, it is generally held that "[w]hen an employee deviates from the business route by taking a side-trip that is clearly identifiable as such, the employee is unquestionably beyond the course of employment while going away from the business route and toward the personal objective." 1 Larson's Workers' Compensation Law § 17.03[1], at 17-14 (emphasis added). In this case, Silman was on her way to the bank at the time of the accident, i.e., she was "going away from the business route and toward the personal objective." The Timmonses argue that because Silman retained the postage meter in her possession when she went to Central Bank, Silman had not completed her employment errand. Although we find this aspect of the deviation not controlling, it can be a persuasive factor if there is evidence of a linking relationship between the postage meter and the deviation. If not, then the mere presence of the postage meter in Silman's car could justify almost any deviation and in turn would untenably lead to the exposure of the employer to untold, unrelated risks of employment. To accept the Timmonses' argument would make an employer the insurer of all accidents arising out of an employee's personal errands absent a linking relationship. Here, Silman had completed her employment errand with the exception of returning to the office with the postage meter. Her deviation was only incidental to, and not as a result of or related to, the employment errand. The fact that Silman had completed her errand for her employer and passed up the place of employment to deviate for a personal errand weighs heavily against finding the deviation within the course and scope of employment.

In turning to the temporal aspect of the deviation, there is no evidence in the record as to the duration of the deviation. However, since we know that Silman was going out of her way for eighteen blocks in her automobile and there is nothing in the record to suggest any intervening occurrences, we assume that the time it took her to deviate to the bank would not have been an overly extended amount of time. This aspect would weigh in favor of Silman's deviation being within the course and scope of employment since the deviation was of relatively minor duration. However, more than a short duration for the personal errand is needed to justify a deviation falling within the course and scope of employment, i.e., weighing all of the factors that increase the risks of exposing the employer to vicarious liability.

Regarding the spacial element, Silman's deviation took her out of downtown Monroe and to an area approximately eighteen blocks away from her employment. These eighteen blocks were on the other side of her employment and in the opposite direction from the post office. She passed within a block or two of her employment on her way to Central Bank, and, instead of terminating her employment errand as expected by Stagg, she kept driving past the law office and on to her personal destination. The Timmonses argue, however, with some persuasion, that eighteen blocks is not a great distance. While we recognize that eighteen blocks is not a great distance, it is significantly farther than the post office, which was only four blocks away from the office. Having come so close to her place of employment, yet traveling eighteen blocks in the other direction, weighs against Silman's deviation being deemed insubstantial. Had Silman visited the branch of Central Bank located between her office and the post office, we would be presented with a closer set of facts favoring an insubstantial deviation regarding the temporal and spacial elements. There is no bright-line rule in determining what is a substantial or insubstantial deviation. *See* Malone & Johnson, 13 Louisiana Civil Law Treatise, Workers' Compensation § 174, at 406. This determination is a fact driven inquiry made on a case-by-case basis.

Focusing on the nature of the employee's work, part of Silman's employment duties included going to the post office and the bank for Stagg. However, on this particular occasion Silman was not instructed, or expected, to go to the bank for Stagg. Silman's motivation for going to the bank that day was purely personal, in that she unilaterally decided to cash her Christmas bonus check while on an errand to the post office for Stagg. The Timmonses argue that Silman's employment led her to the 18th Street branch of Central Bank as that was the bank where she took care of the firm's financial needs. Specifically, Silman had no checking account and knew of no other bank in the Monroe area where she could cash her check, save this one, and her knowledge of it arose from her employment. When she went to this bank on firm business, she would cash her payroll check at this time or, if she had no business banking that day, she would go to that branch after she got off work and cash her check. This was the first time she had made a special trip solely to cash her check. However, contrary to the Timmonses' assertions, the fact that she went to this branch of Central Bank to attend to firm business on a number of occasions is irrelevant. At the time of her deviation, Silman had no firm business to attend to at the bank. Instead, she traveled to the bank during her working hours for purely personal reasons without Stagg's permission, instruction, or knowledge, and beyond Stagg's expectations. Essentially, the Timmonses argue that since Silman was accustomed to using this bank because of her employment, this somehow makes her deviation employment related. We fail to see how familiarity with this particular bank through employment related errands, with nothing more, would cause this deviation for a personal reason to fall within the course and scope of employment.

"If the incidents of the deviation itself are operative to producing the accident, this in itself will weigh heavily on the side of non-compensability." 1 Larson's Workers' Compensation Law § 17.06[1], at 17-33. At oral arguments the parties spoke about the elevated risks inherent in the intersection at 18th Street and Stubbs Avenue, an intersection that Silman would not have traveled through had she returned to the office after filling the postage meter. However, since the parties failed to put on evidence regarding the additional risks created by the deviation, we are unable to consider this aspect of the deviation. Nonetheless, the record makes clear that at the time of this accident Silman had completed her employment related mission of refilling the meter and, instead of terminating the mission as her employer expected, she unilaterally decided to deviate on to a personal errand wholly unrelated to the business task. While the business errand required that Silman travel only four blocks, her personal errand required that she travel an additional eighteen blocks in the opposite direction. The accident occurred while she was attempting to cash her check. Clearly, her personal deviation dwarfed the business portion of the trip, such that it no longer can be said that it was a circumstance of her employment. Thus, the record supports the finding that it was the incidents of her personal deviation itself that were operative to producing this accident. As such, this factor weighs heavily against finding the deviation within the course and scope of the employment.

This case does not present this Court with a question of the reasonableness of Silman's unilateral decision to deviate to the bank. Stagg implied in her deposition that, although she ordinarily would not have minded, she "probably" would not have allowed Silman to cash her check on this day because the office was busy preparing to close for the Christmas holidays. However, that an employee would not have been fired, or even reprimanded, for their deviation is not the determinative factor. The focus of the Court is the determination of whether the deviation is substantial or insubstantial rather than whether it is reasonable. While the reasonableness of a deviation can have some bearing on this determination, it is not the controlling factor. A reasonable determination would militate against Silman's deviation being employment related, since it would have been more reasonable for her to have stopped at the bank branch that was located just off the route to the post office rather than to have traveled eighteen blocks past her place of employment.

In essence, Silman decided to deviate from her assigned errand of four blocks and unilaterally extended her trip eighteen blocks by going to the bank to cash her bonus check and thereby substantially increased the risk of exposing her employer to vicarious liability with no corresponding benefits received by her employer. We have examined numerous factors that demonstrate how this deviation was substantial in nature in relation to the employment related errand, and thereby elevated the risk of exposing Stagg to vicarious liability. The very nature of these factors being positively answered and showing a substantial deviation demonstrates that Silman exposed her employer to risks which were not inherent in her employment. Because Silman exposed her employer to the risk of liability as she unilaterally decided to perform a personal errand after she essentially completed her employment errand and came within a block or two of her place of employment, we find that Silman was not within the course and scope of her employment. Thus, we find no manifest error in the lower courts' finding of no vicarious liability on the part of Stagg. Accordingly, State Farm, as Stagg's insurer, has no responsibility to the Timmonses for their injuries arising out of the accident.

* * * * *

RICHARD
v.
HALL
874 So. 2d 131 (La. 2004)

KNOLL, J.

This is a wrongful death case that concerns a duck hunter who accidentally shot and killed another duck hunter. We are called upon to address two significant areas of tort law, namely, vicarious liability of an employer and the immunity afforded by Louisiana's Recreational Use Immunity Statutes.[1] Plaintiffs, the widow and child of the deceased, alleged the employer was vicariously liable and/or liable for its own negligence. The district court granted summary judgment in favor of the employer on both theories of tort liability. The majority of the court of appeal affirmed. We granted plaintiffs' application for a writ of certiorari to consider the correctness, *vel non,* of their decisions.

Facts and Procedural History

Screening Systems International, Inc., Louisiana Division (SSI)[2], a closely held corporation, entered into a duck hunting lease. SSI paid $10,000 to Loch Leven Plantation for hunting privileges

---

[1] La.Rev.Stat. 9:2791 and 9:2795.

[2] SSI is engaged in the business of manufacturing and selling traveling water screens.

that were to be utilized by three upper level management executives. The three executives authorized to enjoy SSI's duck hunting lease were Mr. Henry Watson, Jr., President, Mr. Michael Hall, Vice-President and General Manager, and Mr. George LeBlanc, Engineering Manager.

On January 2, 2000, Mr. Watson and Mr. Hall went to Loch Leven to hunt ducks. Also on that morning, John Richard was at Loch Leven to hunt as the guest of Todd Cavin; Mr. Cavin also held a duck lease at Loch Leven.[3] According to the customary practice, numbers were randomly drawn to determine the order in which blinds would be chosen by those who had purchased hunting rights. Todd Cavin drew the number "1" which meant he had first selection of a blind to use that day. Mr. Cavin chose a blind that could accommodate two more people than he had in his party; the location consisted of two sunken blinds abutting each other. Mr. Cavin asked Mr. Watson and Mr. Hall if they wanted to hunt with his party at the better blind. Mr. Watson and Mr. Hall accepted the invitation.

Mr. Watson, Mr. Hall and Mr. Richard occupied one of the blinds, with Mr. Richard seated in the middle. During the hunt, Mr. Hall accidentally and fatally shot Mr. Richard. Mr. Richard's widow, Karen Richard, subsequently filed suit against Michael Hall, SSI, Allstate Insurance Company (Hall's homeowner's insurance provider), and Empire Insurance Company (SSI's general liability insurer). Plaintiffs assert two bases for holding SSI liable: (1) vicarious liability for its employee's tortious conduct; and (2) direct liability for its failure to instruct authorized employees and their guests in the proper and safe use of firearms while hunting pursuant to SSI's duck lease.

Empire Insurance Company and SSI moved for summary judgment seeking to dismiss all of plaintiffs' claims. The district court signed a judgment on May 23, 2001, granting Empire's motion for summary judgment on the issue of vicarious liability. The court denied summary judgment on the negligence claim against SSI. Empire filed another motion for summary judgment in which it moved to dismiss plaintiffs' negligence claim against SSI, on the grounds that Louisiana's Recreational Use Immunity Statutes (RUS) afforded immunity to SSI. The district court granted the motion, holding the RUS barred plaintiffs' claim of negligence by SSI.[4]

Plaintiffs appealed the grant of summary judgments to the court of appeal. A majority of the appellate panel affirmed. *Richard v. Hall,* 02-0366 (La.App. 1 Cir. 2003), 843 So. 2d 433. The majority, relying upon our decision in *Ermert v. Hartford Ins. Co.,* 559 So. 2d 467 (La. 1990) (reh'g denied), held the trial judge did not err in granting summary judgment on the basis of the lack of vicarious liability on the part of SSI. The majority additionally found SSI was a lessee that qualified for the immunity afforded by the RUS, even though it was undisputed that Loch Leven was a recreational enterprise for profit. In dissent, Judge Pettigrew found duck hunting was a business

---

[3] Mr. Richard was also an employee of SSI. However, it was merely coincidental that he was hunting at Loch Leven that same day as Mr. Watson and Mr. Hall. There are no allegations by the plaintiffs that Mr. Richard's hunting trip was work related in any manner. In addition to Mr. Richard, Mr Cavin had three other guests join him that day.

[4] The district court actually rendered three judgments. On May 23, 2001, the court signed a judgment granting in part and denying in part Empire's motion for summary judgment. The court granted summary judgment dismissing plaintiffs' claim of vicarious liability on the part of SSI, Empire's insured. This judgment was not a final judgment and could be revised at any time prior to the rendition of the judgment adjudicating all the claims and the rights and liabilities of all the parties. La.Code Civ. Pro. art. 1915(B)(2); 1 Frank L. Maraist and Harry T. Lemmon, *Louisiana Civil Law Treatise--Civil Procedure,* § 12.1 (1999). At the time the judgment was signed, SSI's motion for summary judgment was pending before the court on this very issue. On September 10, 2001, the court heard argument on Empire's second motion for summary judgment, along with SSI's motion, concerning the issue of SSI's independent negligence. The court signed a second judgment on September 12, 2001, granting SSI's motion for summary judgment on the remaining negligence claim, dismissing all claims asserted against SSI. A Stipulated Amended Judgment was signed on September 21, 2001; this judgment noted that the parties agreed that the May 14, 2001 ruling should extend to SSI and be a part of the stipulated amended judgment. This third judgment vacated the September 12, 2001 judgment, and ordered that the motions for summary judgment filed by SSI and Empire be granted as to plaintiffs' remaining claim of independent negligence of SSI and further ordered that all claims against SSI and Empire be dismissed with prejudice.

activity of SSI thus precluding the application of the RUS. Judge Pettigrew found at a minimum there were material issues of fact in dispute as to whether it was a business activity and therefore summary judgment was improper. Additionally, he was of the opinion that the duck lease was not a lease at all, but a personal servitude of right of use, which would exclude the application of the RUS. We granted writs to address three issues: (1) whether plaintiffs had produced factual support sufficient to establish they would be able to satisfy their evidentiary burden of proof at trial that Mr. Hall's conduct was within the course and scope of his employment for purposes of vicarious liability; (2) whether SSI's "duck lease" was a lease or a personal servitude of right of use; and (3) whether the immunity afforded by the RUS applies where the owner[5] claiming the immunity is not using the premises principally for a commercial recreational enterprise for profit. *Richard v. Hall*, 03-1488 (La. 2003), 855 So. 2d 291.

Discussion

Summary Judgment

We will first address the initial summary judgment dismissing plaintiffs' claim against SSI on grounds of vicarious liability. Appellate courts review summary judgments *de novo,* using the same criteria that govern the trial court's consideration of whether summary judgment is appropriate. *Goins v. Wal-Mart Stores, Inc.,* 01-1136, p. 5 (La. 2001), 800 So. 2d 783, 788. Summary judgment shall be rendered if there is no genuine issue of material fact and the movant is entitled to judgment as a matter of law. La.Code Civ. Pro. art. 966(B); *Goins,* at p. 6, 800 So. 2d at 788. The movants, here SSI and Empire, have the burden of proof. La.Code Civ. Pro. art. 966(C)(2). However, if the movant will not bear the burden of proof at trial, its burden on the motion does not require it to negate all essential elements of the adverse party's action, but rather to point out to the court that there is an absence of factual support for one or more elements essential to the adverse party's claim. La.Code Civ. Pro. art. 966(C)(2). Thereafter, if the adverse party fails to produce factual support sufficient to establish they will be able to satisfy their evidentiary burden of proof at trial, there is no genuine issue of material fact. La.Code Civ. Pro. art. 966(C)(2). Because it is the applicable substantive law that determines materiality, whether a particular fact in dispute is "material" for summary judgment purposes can be seen only in light of the substantive law applicable to the case. *Dickerson v. Piccadilly Restaurants, Inc.,* 99-2633, p. 3-4 (La.App. 1 Cir. 2000), 785 So. 2d 842, 844; *Solomon v. Taylor Brokerage Services, Inc.,* 33,832, p. 4 (La.App. 2 Cir. 2000), 768 So. 2d 799, 801; *Harvey v. Francis,* 2000-1268, p. 5 (La.App. 4 Cir. 2001), 785 So. 2d 893, 897.

Vicarious Liability

The premise of vicarious liability is codified in La. Civ.Code art. 2320, which provides an employer is liable for the tortious acts of its "servants and overseers in the exercise of the functions in which they are employed." Vicarious liability rests in a deeply rooted sentiment that a business enterprise cannot justly disclaim responsibility for accidents which may fairly be said to be characteristic of its activities. *Ermert,* 559 So. 2d at 476, *citing Ira S. Bushey & Sons v. United States,* 398 F.2d 167, 171 (2d Cir. 1968); 2 M. Plainol & G. Ripert, Traité Élémentaire de Droit Civil No. 911 (La.St.L.Inst.Trans.1959); Douglas, *Vicarious Liability and the Administration of Risk I,* 38 Yale L.J. 584, 586 (1929). In determining whether a particular accident may be associated with the employer's business enterprise, the court must essentially decide whether the particular accident is a part of the more or less inevitable toll of a lawful enterprise. *Ermert,* 559 So. 2d at 476, *citing* 5 F. Harper, F. James & O. Gray, *The Law of Torts,* 26.7, at 28 (2d ed. 1986). When considering which risks the employer must bear under vicarious liability, the proper test bears resemblance to that which limits liability for workers' compensation, because the employer should be held to anticipate and allow for risks to the public that "arise out of and in the course of" his employment of labor. *Ermert,* 559 So. 2d at 476, *citations omitted.* While the course of employment test refers to time and place, the scope of employment test examines the employment-related risk of injury. *Russell v. Noullet,* 98-0816, p. 4 (La. 1998), 721 So. 2d 868, 871(*reh'g denied* 1999). The inquiry requires the trier of fact to determine

---

[5] We use the term "owner" here to include not only the landowner, but also a tenant, lessee, occupant or person in control of the premises, as defined in the RUS.

whether the employee's tortious conduct was so closely connected in time, place and causation to his employment-duties as to be regarded a risk of harm fairly attributable to the employer's business, as compared to conduct motivated by purely personal considerations entirely extraneous to the employer's interests. *Id.*

In *Ermert,* we addressed the determination of the scope of executive employment in a negligence case. There the plaintiffs alleged vicarious liability on the part of the corporation for the negligent acts of its servant, who was founder, majority stockholder, president and chief executive officer of the closely held corporation. We noted that the word "servant" does not exclusively denote a person rendering manual labor; rather it includes anyone who performs continuous service for another and whose physical movements are subject to the control or right to control of the other as to the manner of performing the service. While the rules for determining liability of the employer for the conduct of both superior servants and the humblest employees are the same, the application of these rules may differ due to the dissimilarity of their duties and responsibilities. *Ermert,* 559 So. 2d at 476, *citing Restatement (2d) of Agency* § 220 comment (a) (1958). The fact that the predominant motive of the servant is to benefit himself or a third person does not prevent the act from being within the scope of employment. *Ermert,* 559 So. 2d at 477, *citations omitted.* If the purpose of serving the master's business actuates the servant to any appreciable extent, the master is subject to liability if the act is otherwise within the service. *Id.* The scope of risks attributable to an employer increases with the amount of authority and freedom of action granted to the servant in performing his assigned tasks. *Id.*

The facts in *Ermert* involved an accidental shooting at a hunting camp. Karl F. Ermert, III, Kenneth Decareaux and others were present at the camp to build duck blinds for the upcoming duck season. Decareaux had picked up his shotgun to shoot a nutria to cook it for dinner. Decareaux, while loading his shotgun as he was walking inside the camphouse, accidentally shot Ermert in the foot. Decareaux was president of and majority stockholder in Nu-Arrow Fence Company. The trial court weighed the evidence and concluded that because Nu-Arrow derived economic benefit from Decareaux's activities at the camp, Nu- Arrow was vicariously liable. The court of appeal reversed, holding that Decareaux was engaged in a recreational pursuit in building the duck blinds. Upon reviewing the record and considering the principles of master-servant liability, we found the trial court's conclusion that Decareaux was within the scope of his employment was not clearly wrong. *Ermert,* 559 So. 2d at 478. He was acting within the scope of his employment because as chief executive and majority stockholder, he had established the practice of using the camp and his relationship with his hunting friends for the purpose of furthering his employer's business interests. *Ermert,* 559 So. 2d at 469. In our *ratio decidendi* we stated:

> While Decareaux used the camp partially for his own personal enjoyment and recreation, the record also indicates that he repeatedly and consistently used it for business purposes. Developing new business was a major part of Decareaux's employment with Nu-Arrow. Decareaux testified that he sold fences to almost every other member of the camp, and that the other members had all referred business to him. He had also taken a number of his preferred customers to the camp for entertainment, and these customers had likewise referred business to Nu-Arrow. Another important aspect of Decareaux's duties was dealing with employees. He testified that he had taken his employees to the camp on several occasions for picnics or entertainment, and he had also hosted his company-sponsored softball team at the camp. Considering this evidence, the finder of fact could reasonably conclude that one of Decareaux's motives for participating in the camp was to provide a place to entertain both customers and employees of Nu-Arrow. *Ermert,* 559 So. 2d at 478.

Because Decareaux had repeatedly and consistently used the hunting camp for business purposes, Nu-Arrow had made the risks associated with waterfowling (which are not normally characteristic of the activities of fence companies) a part of its business. The predominant motive of the servant to benefit himself or a third person does not prevent the act from being within the scope of employment. *Ermert,* 559 So. 2d at 477. If the purpose of serving the master's business actuates the servant to any appreciable extent, the master is subject to liability if the act is otherwise within the service. *Id.*

Our decision in *Ermert* reaffirmed and further explained the standards we previously enunciated in *Lebrane v. Lewis,* 292 So. 2d 216, 218 (La. 1974), and adapted those standards to the atypical master-servant problem that was before us. *Roberts v. Benoit,* 605 So. 2d 1032, 1041 (La. 1991). Under the *LeBrane* test, the determinative question is whether the employee's tortious conduct "was so closely connected in time, place and causation to his employment duties as to be regarded as a risk of harm fairly attributable to the employer's business, as compared with conduct motivated by purely personal considerations entirely extraneous to the employer's interest." *Id.* In a negligence case, as distinguished from an intentional tort case, the court need only determine whether the servant's general activities at the time of the tort were within the scope of employment. *Id.*

Defendants contend the facts in this case differ vastly from the facts in *Ermert.* Defendants argued the duck lease at Loch Leven was never used to entertain customers or for any business related purposes. In support of their motions for summary judgment on the issue of vicarious liability, defendants submitted deposition testimony which showed SSI never brought clients or customers to Loch Leven; no one from SSI ever conducted any business at Loch Leven; the only authorized users of SSI's duck lease at Loch Leven were the three executives; the expense was paid to provide a perk to upper management; there were no penalties or any other ramifications with respect to Mr. Hall's employment based upon whether or not he used the duck lease; and the duck lease was used purely for their social purposes.

In opposition to defendants' motion for summary judgment, plaintiffs contend SSI paid the $10,000 cost of the lease and treated this as a business expense, categorized as "business promotion," as testified to by SSI's comptroller in her deposition. Additionally, SSI did not record the duck lease as additional compensation on the IRS W-2 forms for the three executives. Mr. Hall testified in his deposition he believed the lease was officially for SSI's business and entertainment purposes. In a filing entitled "Response to Empire Insurance Company's List of Undisputed Facts" plaintiffs admit that no one ever took clients or customers to the lease, but argue the duck season was only in its third week at the time of the accident. Plaintiffs also admit Mr. Hall was not on the clock or getting paid while duck hunting on the day in question; however, plaintiffs counter this aspect is immaterial because Mr. Hall was not an hourly wage earner but a salaried executive. We find plaintiffs have failed to produce factual support sufficient to establish they can satisfy their evidentiary burden of proof at trial, namely, that in this negligence case, Mr. Hall's general activities at the time of the tort were within the scope of his employment. In *Ermert* we found vicarious liability because Decareaux had *repeatedly* and *consistently* used the camp for business purposes. The evidence supported a finding that the purpose of serving the business actuated him to an appreciable extent. In *Ermert* there was evidence Decareaux's hunting companions were also Nu Arrow's customers and referrers of business; that he had taken a number of preferred customers to the camp for entertainment; that he had taken Nu Arrow employees to the camp on several occasions; and he had hosted the company-sponsored softball team at the camp.

In the matter *sub judice,* the only factual support plaintiffs offered to support their allegation that Hall was within the course and scope of his employment at the time of the accident was the testimony of Hall and SSI's controller, that SSI intended the lease to be used for business purposes, and that it was treated as a business expense. Intent to utilize the recreational activity for business purposes and/or to entertain clients cannot transform the servant's activities to fall within the scope of employment. Where there is no evidence that any business related entertaining was ever done at the lease, that the servant had ever generated any business by his use of the lease, or that the servant was required to participate in the recreational activity, we cannot say his recreational activities were within the course and scope of his employment. Unlike the evidence in *Ermert,* SSI had not established the practice of using the recreational activity for the purpose of furthering its business interests.

In resolving this issue, our focus is on the servant and whether his activity at the time of the accident was within the scope of his employment. The servant must be motivated at least in part to serve the master's business. Despite our diligent research, we have been unable to find any jurisprudence from any jurisdiction in which an executive or servant was found to be in the scope of employment solely by the *intent* of the business to use the recreational activity for business purposes and/or to entertain clients, where the recreational activity had never been used for a business purpose, and was not being used for such purposes at the time of the incident giving rise to the litigation. A recreational activity cannot fairly be said to be characteristic of the business's activities merely upon the intent of the business to use the recreational activity for business purposes at an unspecified future time. Particularly relevant is that the servant, here Mr. Hall, for whose actions the plaintiffs are trying to hold the employer vicariously liable, never used the recreational activity for business purposes and was not actuated for purposes of serving the business at the time of the accident. Masters are broadly liable for torts of their servants but not liable for all their torts. Dan B. Dobbs, *The Law of Torts,* § 334 (2001). When the tort becomes uncharacteristic of the business, liability is not imposed. *Id.* Clearly, Mr. Hall's general activities at the time of this tragic accident were not within the scope of his employment. We find the appellate court was correct in affirming the trial court's grant of summary judgment on this issue.

* * * * *

Decree

For the foregoing reasons, the judgments of the district court and the appellate court are affirmed.

AFFIRMED.

NOTES

1. *See Samuels v. Southern Baptist Hospital*, 594 So. 2d 571 (La.App. 4 Cir. 1992), *writ denied,* 599 So. 2d 316 (La. 1992) – defendant hospital was not negligent in employing X as a nursing assistant in its psychiatric unit. Part of X's duties included "(t)aking care of the patient's well-being." X raped a patient in the unit while he was on duty and while the patient was "helpless in a locked environment." *Held*, hospital is vicariously liable to patient for damages resulting from the assault; "(t)he tortious conduct...was reasonably incidental to the performance of his duties....although totally unauthorized by the employer and motivated by the employee's personal interest.... (X's) actions were closely connected to his employment duties so that the risk of harm faced by the young ... victim was fairly attributable to his employer." *Compare Jackson v. Ferrand,* 658 So. 2d 691 (La.App. 4 Cir. 1994), *writ denied,* 659 So. 2d 496 (La. 1995), holding that an innkeeper is not liable for damages suffered by a guest at the hotel who was sexually molested by a hotel employee after the employee's work hours, at a location removed from the hotel premises, while the guest was on a "date" with the hotel employee. The fact that the employee "hatched" the plan to commit the tort and took affirmative steps toward carrying it out during the course and scope of his employment duties is an insufficient ground for imposing vicarious liability on the employer. *Compare Bertrand v. Bollich,* 695 So. 2d 1384 (La.App. 3 Cir. 1997), *writ denied,* 703 So. 2d 621 (La. 1997). There X, employed by defendant as a home health care nurse, took IV fluids to a home care patient near the end of her work day. There was no evidence establishing that the home delivery was an emergency. After completing the delivery, X did not return to the hospital but passed the hospital on her way home. She was involved in an auto accident about a half hour after her normal work shift ended, and seconds after she passed the hospital on her way home. *Held*, the jury did not err in finding that X was not in the course and scope of her employment.

2. In *Ermert v. Hartford Insurance Company*, 559 So. 2d 467 (La. 1990), the court did not find it necessary to determine if a member of an unincorporated association is vicariously liable for the torts of another member of the association in furtherance of the association's activities. Of course, a shareholder is not vicariously liable, i.e., his or her financial exposure ordinarily is limited to the value of his or her stock interest. In Louisiana, a partner is vicariously liable for his virile share of the debts of the partnership, but the creditors must look to the partnership first for payment of the debt. *See* CC Art. 2817. Recent legislation authorizes a "registered limited liability partnership" in which partners do not bear personal liability for the "errors, omissions, negligence, incompetence, or malfeasance committed in the course of partnership business by another partner or a representative of the partnership." *See* R.S. 9:3431-3. *See, e.g., Kelly v. Boh Bros. Constr. Co., Inc.,* 694 So. 2d 463 (La.App. 5 Cir. 1997), *writ denied,* 700 So. 2d 507 (La. 1997), holding that a joint venture is a

juridical entity in which the liability of the parties is determined by the law relating to partnerships. Under C.C. Art. 2817, if there is no agreement to the contrary, each joint venturer is liable for his virile share or equal portion. Other examples of vicarious liability include the "single business enterprise" theory.

Generally, a parent corporation is not liable for the torts of its subsidiary; however, the subsidiary may not operate as a separate corporation, and the "corporate veil" may be pierced to impose liability upon the parent corporation or the shareholders. *See also, Grayson v. R. B. Ammon and Associates, Inc.*, 778 So. 2d 1 (La.App. 1 Cir. 2000), *writ denied*, 782 So. 2d 1026 (La. 2001) (the principle that the corporation is a separate entity should be disregarded only in exceptional circumstances. Because the separateness of the corporate entity is disregarded in both the "single business enterprise" theory and the "piercing the corporate veil" theory, both theories are subject to the same burden of proof, i.e., clear and convincing evidence). *See, generally,* Morris and Holmes, Louisiana Civil Law Treatise, Business Organizations, pp. 50-101 (West Publ. Co., 1999 and Supp. 2005).

3.   A municipality is not vicariously liable for the tort of an off-duty, part-time police dispatcher committed in another parish solely on the basis that the dispatcher represented he was a police officer during the attack, where the representation was for the purpose of fleeing the scene of an aggravated battery in which he was involved and evading arrest by proper authorities. *Brasseaux v. The Town of Mamou*, 752 So. 2d 815 (La. 2000).

4.   In *Bell v. Hurstell*, 743 So. 2d 720 (La.App. 4 Cir. 1999), *writ denied,* 748 So. 2d 1165 (La. 1999), employee, after a meeting with a client at employer's office concluded about 7 p.m., went with the client to a lounge and then to a party given by another company with which employer had a business relationship. During that time, employee apparently became intoxicated. At about 11:20 p.m., employee, attempting to drive home, was involved in an accident. *Held*, employee was not in the course and scope of her employment at the time of the accident; "an accident that would not normally be considered as occurring during the course and scope of employment ... will not be considered as occurring during the course and scope of employment merely because alcohol, which may have contributed to the accident, was consumed (but not required to be consumed as a condition of employment) while the employee-tortfeasor was acting in the course and scope of employment."

5.   An employer is not vicariously liable for the actions of an employee in following an abusive patron into the parking lot and fighting with him, where the employee ignored two immediate and direct orders from his superior to remain behind the counter and not go outside. *Clark v. Burchard*, 802 So. 2d 824 (La.App. 4 Cir. 2001).

6.   The Second Circuit concluded that the employee's intentional act was not within the course and scope of employment when employee shot motorist, ostensibly to protect himself, after a minor collision while employee was driving employer's truck, *Culver v. Brown*, 803 So. 2d 242 (La.App. 2 Cir. 2001), or when employee struck plaintiff (a co-employee) after a confrontation in which employee told plaintiff that plaintiff's wife, also a fellow employee, was having an affair with a supervisor in the plant during working hours. *Wearrien v. Viverette*, 803 So. 2d 297 (La.App. 2 Cir. 2001).

7.   In *Cox v. Gaylord Container Corp.*, 897 So. 2d 1 (La.App. 1 Cir. 2005) (reh'g en banc), *writ denied,* 901 So. 2d 1102 (La. 2005), the court concluded that a child suffering negligently inflicted pre-natal injuries might have a cause of action against the mother who negligently operated a forklift at work. But when, because of federal law banning discrimination based on pregnancy, the employer had no choice but to allow mother to keep working, the employer was not vicariously liable under C.C. Art. 2320 for mother's alleged tort.

8.   Course and scope issues in intentional tort cases can be tricky because the misconduct often has very personal overtones. In *LeBrane v. Lewis*, 292 So. 2d 216 (La. 1974) the court held an employer vicariously liable where a supervisor knifed a former employee on company premises shortly after firing him. The court found the tort "employment rooted." In *Russell v. Noulet*, 721 So.

2d 868 (La. 1998), the court focused on (1) whether the employee's motivation for his general activities was "purely personal" and, if not, then (2) whether the specific activity which caused the harm was in furtherance of the employer's interests. Where sexual assault and/or harassment are involved, particularly troublesome issues arise under both state, *Baumeister v. Plunkett*, 673 So. 2d 994 (La. 1996), and federal law. William Corbett, *Faragher, Ellerth, and the Federal Law of Vicarious Liability for Sexual Harassment by Supervisors: Something Lost, Something Gained, and Something to Guard Against*, 7 Wm. & Mary Bill Rts. J. 801 (1999).

9.   *Drummond v. Fakouri*, 30 So. 3d 111 (La.App. 1 Cir. 2009). The owner and construction supervisor of a company took a loaded pistol from his work truck while it was being serviced and put it on his china cabinet in his home. His son accidentally shot a 17-year-old playmate with the gun. The corporation was not vicariously liable for storage of personal property in the employee's home several days after work-related activities ended.

COMMENT

Louisiana does not permit the awarding of punitive or exemplary damages unless specifically authorized by statute. Louisiana does have a few Civil Code articles authorizing the award of exemplary damages. *See* Chapter 8.F *supra*. Should an employer be held vicariously liable for punitive damages based on the conduct of an employee who was in the course and scope of employment? The Louisiana Supreme Court did not resolve the issue in *Berg v. Zummo*, 786 So. 2d 708 (La. 2001), *see* Chapter 6.D.7 *supra*. The Third Circuit decided that an employer should not be vicariously liable for exemplary damages in *Gillespie v. Calcasieu Parish School Bd.*, 179 So. 3d 966 (La.App. 3 Cir. 2015), *writ denied*, 187 So. 3d 470 (La. 2016). In *Gillespie*, a high school student and her parents recovered punitive damages under Article 2315.3 against a teacher for sexual conduct with a minor child. The court rejected the argument that the school board could be vicariously liable for punitive damages under Article 2320. Comparing the "damage occasioned by" language of Article 2320 with the language of Article 2324(A) ("damage caused by") imposing solidary liability on co-conspirators committing intentional torts, the court found guidance in a Louisiana Supreme Court decision regarding Article 2324. The Supreme Court has held that Article 2324 cannot be used to impose punitive damages on a party based on the acts of co-conspirators. *Gillespie*, 179 So. 3d at 971 (citing *Ross v. Conoco, Inc.*, 828 So. 2d 546, 553 (La. 2002)). Accordingly, the Third Circuit held that punitive damages could not be imposed under a theory of vicarious liability/respondeat superior.

C.   PARENT-CHILD

La. Civil Code Art. 2318.   Acts of minors

The father and the mother are responsible for the damage occasioned by their minor child, who resides with them or who has been placed by them under the care of other persons, reserving to them recourse against those persons. However, the father and mother are not responsible for the damage occasioned by their minor child who has been emancipated by marriage, by judgment of full emancipation, or by judgment of limited emancipation that expressly relieves the parents of liability for damages occasioned by their minor child.

The same responsibility attaches to the tutors of minors.

NOTES

1.   *See Turner v. Bucher, infra.* If the child is negligent, isn't the parents' liability under this article vicarious, instead of strict or absolute?

2.   A parent is liable for the torts of his or her minor child who "resides" with the parent. When the parents are divorced and there is joint custody, with whom does the child "reside"? The same problem surfaces as an insurance coverage issue, since most policies cover the named insured's relative who "resides" with him. The most instructive case thus far is *Gedward v. Sonnier*, 728 So. 2d 1265 (La. 1999). There, father, the insured, and mother exercised joint custody of victim pursuant to

a consent judgment under which father was free to exercise custodial privileges on alternating weekends. Father routinely exercised his custodial rights, and was exercising those rights when victim was injured on father's premises. The insurance policy provided that coverage for medical expenses did not apply to a "resident" of the insured's dwelling, but did not define the term "resident." *Held,* victim was a "resident" of the father's dwelling and excluded from coverage under the policy. "The judgment of joint custody, combined with the fact that (father) routinely exercised his custodial rights, convinces us that (victim) was in fact a resident of (father's) dwelling...[T]his is not a case where the parent having joint custody rarely, if ever, exercised his custodial privileges. We are not...holding as a matter of law that all minor dependent children of divorced parents subject to joint custody are necessarily residents of both parents' households."

3.   Paternal authority is the key to imposing tort liability on the father of a legitimate child. The father of an illegitimate minor child should be treated no differently than the father of a legitimate minor child. Where the illegitimate child does not reside with the father, the child is not subject to paternal authority, and the father is not subject to liability for the child's torts under CC Art. 2318. *Tippen v. Baker,* 718 So. 2d 617 (La.App. 2 Cir. 1998), *writ denied,* 730 So. 2d 464 (La. 1998).

4.   La. R.S. 9:335(A)(3), providing that a joint custody implementation order "shall allocate the legal authority and responsibility of the parents," relates to an allocation of responsibility between the parents and does not abrogate an individual parent's responsibility to third persons. Thus a joint custody implementation plan which shifts responsibility for the delictual act of their minor child to the parent who has physical custody of the child at the time the child commits the delictual act cannot defeat parental liability to third persons imposed by CC Art. 2318 for the acts of the minor child. *Henderson v. Sellers,* 861 So. 2d 923 (La App. 3 Cir. 2001).

5.   In *Wallmuth v. Rapides Parish School Board,* 813 So. 2d 341 (La. 2002), the Court observes that CC Art 2320 does not impose vicarious liability upon a School Board for the actions of its students; the article is not a true "vicarious liability" statute, as it requires independent fault on the part of the School Board (which "might have prevented the act"). Reaching this conclusion, the Supreme Court points out that although the language of article 2320 technically applies as well to the employer-employee relationship, Louisiana courts have not given effect to the "might have prevented" language in such a relationship since 1906, and the judicial interpretation of article 2320 as it applies to employers and employees has been codified by R.S. 9:3921. *But see Cox v. Gaylord Container Corp., supra.*

CHAPTER 13

NEGLIGENT PROVISION OF SERVICES

INTRODUCTION

A person who provides services to others for a fee may be liable in contract to the customer for damages caused by improper provision of those services. The provider may guarantee a certain result; if so, and the result is not achieved, the provider will be liable for breach of an express contractual provision.

In most cases, however, the provider does not guarantee a result. Nevertheless, the general rule under contract law is that the provider impliedly warrants that he or she will provide a workmanlike performance. This is sometimes called the warranty of workmanlike performance, i.e., the provider warrants (guarantees) that he or she possesses the skill ordinarily possessed by others providing the service for a fee, and that he or she will exercise that skill. Under a tort analysis, a provider of services may be negligent if he or she does not possess the skill ordinarily possessed by others who provide the service for a fee, or does not exercise that skill. Thus the contractual warranty of workmanlike performance and the negligent provision of services impose the same standard of care upon the provider. There are differences, however, such as the damages that are recoverable and the prescriptive periods that apply.

Some providers of services are deemed "professionals," and their wrongful provision of services is termed "malpractice." The materials in Section A focus primarily upon one of those providers – the healthcare provider. Section B presents some of the particular issues arising in other malpractice cases, such as legal and accounting malpractice.

A.   MEDICAL MALPRACTICE

1.   The Customary Standard of Care

La. R.S. 9:2794. Physicians and dentists; malpractice; burden of proof; jury charge

A.   In a malpractice action based on the negligence of a physician licensed under R.S. 37:1261 et seq., or a dentist licensed under R.S. 37:751 et seq., the plaintiff shall have the burden of proving:

(1)   The degree of knowledge or skill possessed or the degree of care ordinarily exercised by physicians or dentists licensed to practice in the state of Louisiana and actively practicing in a similar community or locale and under similar circumstances; and where the defendant practices in a particular specialty and where the alleged acts of medical negligence raise issues peculiar to the particular medical specialty involved, then the plaintiff has the burden of proving the degree of care ordinarily practiced by physicians or dentists within the involved medical specialty.

(2)   That the defendant either lacked this degree of knowledge or skill or failed to use reasonable care and diligence, along with his best judgment in the application of that skill, and

(3)   That as a proximate result of this lack of knowledge or skill or the failure to exercise this degree of care the plaintiff suffered injuries that would not otherwise have been incurred.

B.   Any party to the action will have the right to subpoena any physician or dentist either for a deposition and/or testimony for trial to establish the degree of knowledge or skill possessed or degree of care ordinarily exercised as described above without obtaining the consent of the physician or dentist who is going to be subpoenaed. The fee of the physician or dentist called for deposition and/or testimony under this Section will be set by the court.

C.   In medical malpractice actions the jury shall be instructed that the plaintiff has the burden of proving, by a preponderance of the evidence, the negligence of the physician or dentist. The jury shall be further instructed that injury alone does not raise a presumption of the physician's or dentist's negligence. The provisions of this Section shall not apply to situations where the doctrine of res ipsa loquitur is found by the court to be applicable.

D.   (1)   In a medical malpractice action against a physician, licensed to practice medicine by the Louisiana State Board of Medical Examiners under . . ., for injury to or death of a patient, a person may qualify as an expert witness on the issue of whether the physician departed from accepted standards of medical care only if the person is a physician who meets all of the following criteria:

(a) He is practicing medicine at the time such testimony is given or was practicing medicine at the time the claim arose.

(b) He has knowledge of accepted standards of medical care for the diagnosis, care, or treatment of the illness, injury, or condition involved in the claim.

(c) He is qualified on the basis of training or experience to offer an expert opinion regarding those accepted standards of care.

d) He is licensed to practice medicine by the Louisiana State Board of Medical Examiners . . . ., is licensed to practice medicine by any other jurisdiction in the United States, or is a graduate of a medical school accredited by the American Medical Association's Liaison Committee on Medical Education or the American Osteopathic Association.

(2)   For the purposes of this Subsection, "practicing medicine" or "medical practice" includes but is not limited to training residents or students at an accredited school of medicine or osteopathy or serving as a consulting physician to other physicians who provide direct patient care, upon the request of such other physicians.

(3)   In determining whether a witness is qualified on the basis of training or experience, the court shall consider whether, at the time the claim arose or at the time the testimony is given, the witness is board certified or has other substantial training or experience in an area of medical practice relevant to the claim and is actively practicing in that area.

(4)   The court shall apply the criteria specified in Paragraphs (1), (2), and (3) of this Subsection in determining whether a person is qualified to offer expert testimony on the issue of whether the physician departed from accepted standards of medical care.

(5)   Nothing in this Subsection shall be construed to prohibit a physician from qualifying as an expert solely because he is a defendant in a medical malpractice claim.

SHEELEY
v.
MEMORIAL HOSPITAL
710 A. 2d 161 (R. I. 1998)

GOLDBERG, J.

This case is before the court on the appeal of Joanne Sheeley (Sheeley) from the directed verdict entered against her in the underlying medical malpractice action. Specifically Sheeley asserts that the trial justice erred in excluding the testimony of her expert witness, which exclusion resulted in the entry of the directed verdict. For the reasons set forth below, we hold that the trial justice erred in excluding the testimony and reverse the judgment from which the appeal was taken. Furthermore, we take this opportunity to reexamine the proper standard of care to be applied in medical malpractice cases and, in so doing, abandon the "similar locality" rule, which previously governed the admissibility of expert testimony in such actions. The facts insofar as are pertinent to this appeal are as follows.

On May 19, 1987, Sheeley delivered a healthy child at Memorial Hospital (hospital) in Pawtucket, Rhode Island. At the time of the birth Sheeley was under the care of Mary Ryder, M.D. (Dr. Ryder), then a second-year family practice resident. Brian Jack, M.D. (Dr. Jack), was the faculty member responsible for the supervision of Dr. Ryder.

In conjunction with the delivery process Dr. Ryder performed an episiotomy on Sheeley. This procedure entails a cut into the perineum of the mother, the purpose being to prevent tearing during the delivery. After the baby had been delivered, Dr. Ryder performed a repair of the episiotomy, stitching the incision previously made into the perineum.

After her discharge from the hospital Sheeley developed complications in the area in which the episiotomy had been performed and ultimately developed a rectovaginal fistula. This condition, which consists of an opening between the vagina and the rectum, required corrective surgery. Notwithstanding the surgery, however, Sheeley continued to experience pain and discomfort at the site of the episiotomy. Sheeley, together with her husband Mark Sheeley, then filed suit against the hospital, Dr. Ryder, and Dr. Jack (collectively defendants), alleging that defendants were negligent in performing the episiotomy incision and repairing the same properly.

At the trial on the malpractice action, Sheeley sought to introduce the expert medical testimony of Stanley D. Leslie, M.D. (Dr. Leslie), a board certified obstetrician/gynecologist (OB/GYN). Doctor Leslie planned to testify about Dr. Ryder's alleged malpractice and the applicable standard of care as it relates to the performance of an episiotomy. The defendants objected and filed a motion in limine to exclude the testimony, arguing that Dr. Leslie, as an OB/GYN, was not qualified under G.L.1956 § 9-19-41[69] to testify against a family practice resident who was performing obstetric and gynecological care. A hearing on the motion was conducted, at which time it was disclosed that Dr. Leslie had been board certified in obstetrics and gynecology since 1961 and recertified in 1979. Doctor Leslie testified that board certification represents a level of achievement of skill and knowledge as established by a national standard in which the standard of care is uniform throughout the medical specialty. Doctor Leslie is currently a clinical professor of obstetrics and gynecology at the Hill-Science Center, State University, College of Medicine in Syracuse. He is a member of the New York Statewide Professional Standards Review Council, which reviews disputes between doctors and hospitals regarding diagnosis and management, and the Credentials and Certification Committee at the Crouse-Irving Hospital, where his responsibilities include drafting standards for family practice physicians. It was further revealed that Dr. Leslie has in the course of his career delivered approximately 4,000 babies and that even though he has been retired from the practice of obstetrics since 1975, he has maintained his familiarity with the standards and practices in the field of obstetrics through weekly conferences, active obstetric work, professorial responsibilities, and continuing education.

* * * * *

(D)efendants ... insist that Dr. Leslie is not qualified to testify. In essence defendants argue that Dr. Leslie is overqualified, stating that a board certified OB/GYN does not possess the same knowledge, skill, experience, training, or education as a second-year family practice resident performing obstetrics in Rhode Island. Furthermore defendants argue that because Dr. Leslie has not

---

[69] General Laws 1956 § 9-19-41 states:
   "In any legal action based upon a cause of action arising on or after January 1, 1987, for personal injury or wrongful death filed against a licensed physician, hospital, clinic, health maintenance organization, professional service corporation providing health care services, dentists or dental hygienist based on professional negligence, only those persons who by knowledge, skill, experience, training or education qualify as experts in the field of the alleged malpractice shall be permitted to give expert testimony as to the alleged malpractice."

actually practiced obstetrics since 1975, his experience in providing obstetrical care is "clearly outdated" and he is therefore not competent to testify concerning the appropriate standard of care as it applied to the performance of an episiotomy and the repair of the same--even while they acknowledge that the standard of care relative to the procedures involved in the alleged malpractice have changed little over the last thirty years. Finally defendants assert that pursuant to the limitations of the "similar locality" rule, Dr. Leslie must be disqualified because he lacks any direct knowledge about the applicable standard of care for a family practice resident providing obstetric care in Rhode Island. The defendants suggest that Dr. Leslie, although he has attended national conferences and studied medical journals and treatises in addition to his national certification, is not qualified to testify about the applicable *local* standard of care. In light of these arguments and with a view toward preventing any further confusion regarding the necessary qualifications of an expert testifying about the proper standard of care in medical malpractice actions, we take this opportunity to revisit our position on the appropriate standard of care.

For over three-quarters of a century this court has subscribed to the principle "that when a physician undertakes to treat or diagnose a patient, he or she is under a duty to exercise 'the same degree of diligence and skill which is commonly possessed by other members of the profession who are engaged in the same type of practice in similar localities having due regard for the state of scientific knowledge at the time of treatment....' " This "same or similar locality" rule is a somewhat expanded version of the "strict locality" rule, which requires that the expert testifying be from the same community as the defendant. *See Shilkret v. Annapolis Emergency Hospital Association,* 276 Md. 187, 349 A.2d 245, 248 (1975); *see, e.g., Moon v. United States,* 512 F.Supp. 140, 144 (D.Nev.1981); *Hoagland v. Kamp,* 155 A.D.2d 148, 552 N.Y.S.2d 978, 979 (1990). The rationale underlying the development of the "strict locality" rule was a recognition that opportunities, experience, and conditions may differ between densely and sparsely populated communities....

This restrictive rule, however, soon came under attack in that it legitimized a low standard of care in certain smaller communities and that it also failed to address or to compensate for the potential so-called conspiracy of silence in a plaintiff's locality that would preclude any possibility of obtaining expert testimony.... Furthermore, ... the locality rule is somewhat of an anachronism in view of "[m]odern systems of transportation and communication...." Thus many jurisdictions, including our own, adopted the "same or similar locality" rule, which allows for experts from similarly situated communities to testify concerning the appropriate standard of care. *Id....* Nevertheless, even with this somewhat expanded view, the medical malpractice bar has continually urged a narrow application of the rule, arguing the need for similar, if not identical, education, training, and experience.... The obvious result of such an application, however, is to reduce the pool of qualified experts to its lowest common denominator. This is a consequence that we have never intended.

The appropriate standard of care to be utilized in any given procedure should not be compartmentalized by a physician's area of professional specialization or certification. On the contrary, we believe the focus in any medical malpractice case should be the procedure performed and the question of whether it was executed in conformity with the recognized standard of care, the primary concern being whether the treatment was administered in a reasonable manner. Any doctor with knowledge of or familiarity with the procedure, acquired through experience, observation, association, or education, is competent to testify concerning the requisite standard of care and whether the care in any given case deviated from that standard. The resources available to a physician, his or her specific area of practice, or the length of time he or she has been practicing are all issues that should be considered by the trial justice in making his or her decision regarding the qualification of an expert. No one issue, however, should be determinative. Furthermore, except in extreme cases, a witness who has obtained board certification in a particular specialty related to the procedure in question, especially when that board certification reflects a national standard of training and qualification, should be presumptively qualified to render an opinion....

This court is of the opinion that whatever geographical impediments may previously have justified the need for a "similar locality" analysis are no longer applicable in view of the present-day realities of the medical profession. As the *Shilkret* court observed:

"The modern physician bears little resemblance to his predecessors. As we have indicated at length, the medical schools of yesterday could not possibly compare with the accredited institutions of today, many of which are associated with teaching hospitals. But the contrast merely begins at that point in the medical career: vastly superior postgraduate training, the dynamic impact of modern communications and transportation, the proliferation of medical literature, frequent seminars and conferences on a variety of professional subjects, and the growing availability of modern clinical facilities are but some of the developments in the medical profession which combine to produce contemporary standards that are not only much higher than they were just a few short years ago, but are also national in scope.

"In sum, the traditional locality rules no longer fit the present-day medical malpractice case." *Shilkret,* 349 A.2d at 252.

We agree. Furthermore, we note that in enacting § 9-19-41, the Legislature failed to employ any reference to the "similar locality" rule. We conclude that this omission was deliberate and constitutes a recognition of the national approach to the delivery of medical services, especially in the urban centers of this country, of which Rhode Island is certainly one.

Accordingly we join the growing number of jurisdictions that have repudiated the "same or similar" communities test in favor of a national standard and hold that a physician is under a duty to use the degree of care and skill that is expected of a reasonably competent practitioner in the same class to which he or she belongs, acting in the same or similar circumstances. In this case the alleged malpractice occurred in the field of obstetrics and involved a procedure and attendant standard of care that has remained constant for over thirty years. Doctor Leslie, as a board certified OB/GYN with over thirty years of experience, a clinical professor of obstetrics and gynecology at a major New York hospital, and a member of the New York Statewide Professional Standards Review Council, is undoubtedly qualified to testify regarding the appropriate standard of care.

* * * * *

NOTE

In evaluating a medical malpractice claim, the first issue may be whether a health care provider/patient relationship arose between the plaintiff and defendant. What if the defendant health care provider was rendering emergency services? Can a health care provider refuse to provide services? *See* the *Coleman* case, *infra.*

If a relationship did arise, the next issue may be whether the patient consented to the particular treatment. Because the law values highly the sanctity of a person's decisions affecting his body, the patient must give a consent to the treatment which must be informed. Much law has arisen surrounding that issue. The *Hondroulis* case and the following statute provide the present status of the law on that issue in Louisiana.

Where, as is usually the case, a health care provider/patient relationship arose and the patient consented to the particular treatment, the issue is whether that treatment was performed properly. Although their relationship arises out of contract, a health care provider's liability to the patient for performance of services usually is evaluated in terms of a tort concept, i.e., did the health care provider act as a reasonably prudent person? The plaintiff first must establish the standard of care which the health care provider was obligated to maintain; a breach of that standard which causes damage gives rise to a medical malpractice tort. The cases in this section explore that standard at common law and in Louisiana.

LEYVA
v.
IBERIA GENERAL HOSPITAL
643 So. 2d 1236 (La. 1994)

CALOGERO, C. J.

Plaintiff's medical malpractice case against the physician who performed on her a bilateral tubal ligation alleges that because of the physician's negligence during the first surgical procedure, she needlessly underwent subsequent surgeries. The jury trial resulted in a verdict and judgment in favor of the defendant.

We granted Plaintiff's writ application because it appeared that the district court and the court of appeal had erroneously applied the law when barring the testimony by plaintiff's expert witness, Dr. Jack Pruitt, causing material injustice. Supreme Court Rule 10, Section 1.(a) 4 (West 1994).

We now conclude that the courts below erred in excluding the testimony of Dr. Pruitt, an ob/gyn specialist whose proffered testimony indicates that he would have testified regarding the nationally applicable standard of care for performing the Parkland Procedure, the surgical procedure that plaintiff underwent.

Plaintiff, Jaqueline Dore Leyva, is a deaf-mute. Mrs. Leyva also has retinosa pigmentosa which has caused her eyesight to deteriorate. Chiefly, because of her physical condition, she chose to become sterile by having a lateral tubal litigation after the birth of her second child.

It was at Iberia General Hospital in New Iberia, Louisiana, on February 23, 1986, that she gave birth to a healthy son. Immediately after delivery, Dr. G.D. Sagrera performed the bilateral tubal litigation....

Dr. Emil Laga, a pathologist, examined the specimens. He testified that he was unable to identify the sample labeled "left fallopian tube" as part of a fallopian tube. Dr. Laga's supervisor, Dr. J.B. Pecot, also examined the specimens, and he too was unable to find any fallopian tube tissue in the left side specimen. After learning of the pathology findings, Dr. Sagrera told Ms. Nellian Dore, Ms. Leyva's mother. Ms. Dore than informed her daughter, Mrs. Leyva, of the dilemma.

* * * * *

About six weeks later, on April 4, 1986, a second surgical procedure was performed—called a laparotomy—in order to learn whether the left tube had been properly ligated during the first procedure, and should it be found that it had not been, to ligate the tube during this second procedure. Dr. Sagrera testified that in this second operation, he examined both tubes and concluded that they had been properly ligated in the first operation....

Thereafter, Mrs. Leyva underwent a third surgical procedure, an appendectomy. In a fourth operation, she had a cyst removed from an ovary. She filed this medical malpractice claim to recover damages arising from the second, third and fourth procedures. She asserts that the negligence which occurred in the first tubal ligation resulted in her having to undergo the subsequent surgeries....

At the trial Plaintiff called Dr. Jack Pruitt, an obstetrician/gynecologist practicing in Lake Jackson, Texas. Dr. Pruitt was tendered as an expert in obstetrics, including obstetrical surgery. Counsel for Dr. Sagrera objected on the grounds that Dr. Pruitt did not practice medicine in a locale similar to New Iberia, Louisiana, and that Dr. Pruitt is a specialist in obstetrics while Dr. Sagrera is only a general practitioner. After hearing arguments from both sides, outside the presence of the jury, the court barred Dr. Pruitt's testimony for the reason that Dr. Pruitt did not practice in a neighboring or similar community to New Iberia, Louisiana. This excluded testimony was nonetheless proffered. Later, without the benefit of Plaintiff's expert's testimony, the jury found Dr. Sagrera not negligent in his treatment of Mrs. Leyva.

* * * * *

The state of the law prior to 1975 was discussed by this Court in *Meyer v. St. Paul-Mercury Indemnity Co.*, 73 So. 2d 781 (La. 1953). In *Meyer*, we held that a physician, surgeon, or dentist had a duty to exercise the degree of skill ordinarily employed, under similar circumstances, by the members of his profession in good standing in the *same* community or locality, and to use reasonable care and diligence in the application of his skill.

In 1975, the Legislature passed Acts 1975, No. 807, § 1, ultimately designated as Louisiana Revised Statute 9:2794. This statute codified the holding in *Meyer* insofar as general practitioners were concerned. It also created for medical specialists a "uniform" standard of care based on standards existing within the specialty pursuant to national standards. In *Ardoin v. Hartford Acc. & Indem. Co.*, 360 So. 2d 1331, 1340 (La. 1978), this Court recognized the effect of the statute and *held*

> that a medical specialist is required by Louisiana Civil Code Articles 2315 and 2316, and Louisiana Revised Statute 9:2794, to exercise the degree of care and possess the degree of knowledge or skill ordinarily exercised and possessed by physicians within his medical specialty ...

Ardoin thus provided two standards: specialists were subject to a common standard to be discerned from within their specialty; general practitioners were only held to the standards prevailing within the community in which they practiced.

The test for general practitioners was legislatively altered in 1979, by an amendment to Louisiana Revised Statute 9:2794. This act substituted the phrase "in a **similar** community or locale and under similar circumstances" for the antecedent language which expressly limited the appropriate standard of care to that of general practitioners in the **same** community.

The legislative changes were recognized by this Court in *Sam v. XYZ Insurance Co. et al.*, 489 So. 2d 907 (La. 1986). In *Sam* a per curiam decision by this Court, we held that a doctor need not practice in the *same* community in order to be qualified to testify as an expert regarding the applicable standard of care. Rather, it is sufficient that the doctor practices in a "similar neighboring community." (Louisiana Revised Statute § 9:2794: "in a malpractice action based on the negligence of a non-specialist physician, the plaintiff has the burden of proving, among other elements, ... the degree of care ordinarily exercised by physicians ... in a similar community or locale and under similar circumstances ").

There have been no substantive changes in the law since 1979. This Court, however, has addressed its application in several opinions. In one such case, *McLean v. Hunter*, 495 So. 2d 1298 (La. 1986), we held that the testimony of a specialist with knowledge of the requisite subject matter was qualified to testify regarding the standard of care in a general practitioner's locale. This Court stated that a specialist was "no less a dentist because he engages in a specialty practice rather than a general dentistry practice" *Id.* at 1302.

The trial judge here, relying on *Sam*, found that Dr. Pruitt was not shown to have practiced in, or come from a similar or neighboring community (and, indeed, plaintiff did not attempt to present evidence which would have established the affinity between the two locales), and thus barred the testimony of Dr. Pruitt. Were this the controlling consideration, the trial judge's ruling would not be incorrect.

This case, however, presents a discrete circumstance as to which the controlling jurisprudence is *Piazza v. Behrman Chiropractic Clinic, Inc.*, 601 So. 2d 1378 (La. 1992). We held in *Piazza*, that where there is a uniform nationwide method for performing a particular medical procedure, an expert having knowledge of such method is qualified to testify, and that the testifying expert in this circumstance is not constrained by the need to have practiced in a similar community or locale and under similar circumstances. *Id.*

561

This case is governed by the foregoing principle. Dr. Sagrera's tubal ligation consisted of performing the "Parkland Procedure." This is a bilateral tubal ligation, a surgical procedure in which the patient is placed under general anesthesia and the physician enters the patient's abdomen and locates her fallopian tubes. The physician then takes a section out of each tube and ties the ends. After the tubes are cut, the egg is no longer able to travel from the ova and become fertilized. During the procedure, it is standard to remove a small section of each tube in order to verify that the appropriate organ has been subjected to the surgery.

Dr. Pruitt's proffered testimony evidences that he was familiar with the Parkland Procedure performed here. In fact, he stated that he had performed 500-600 of these procedures at the time of the trial. Dr. Pruitt also referred to the Parkland Procedure as a "modified Pomeroy" and stated that it is performed according to a common method regardless of where the procedure is done.

Also, the defendant himself, Dr. Sagrera, testified that he had no specific knowledge that the Parkland Procedure was performed according to a different technique elsewhere in the United States. When asked whether he had "ever hear [d] or read it's done differently anywhere else in the United States in 1986," Dr. Sagrera replied that he had not. It was also the testimony of both doctors that they participated in continuing medical education, and kept abreast of changes in the field.

Further, the testimony established that the Parkland Procedure was taught both doctors in medical school pursuant to the Williams Obstetrics textbook. In fact, Dr. Sagrera was presented with a Williams Obstetrics textbook at trial, and after reviewing a printed description of the Parkland Procedure, he stated that the text accurately described it.

Dr. Pruitt testified that he learned to perform the Parkland Procedure in medical school, and that he had performed 500-600 such procedures by 1986. By his testimony regarding his education, training, and experience, Dr. Pruitt established that he had knowledge of this procedure. He, therefore, should have been permitted to testify concerning it.

It is of no significance that Dr. Sagrera was not a specialist. He was accustomed to performing the procedure and did so on the plaintiff, the same Parkland Procedure (tubal ligation) that Dr. Pruitt had performed very frequently, a procedure which each had been taught in medical school, one governed by a common nationwide standard. Thus, we hold that the trial court erred in barring the testimony.

Because Dr. Pruitt's testimony, essential to plaintiff's case, was erroneously barred by the trial judge, the jury's pro-defense verdict is entitled to no deference. The court of appeal should therefore decide the case on the record without having to find first that the district court's judgement was clearly wrong. *Gonzales v. Xerox*, 320 So. 2d 163 (La.1975).

* * * * *

REVERSED; REMANDED TO THE COURT OF APPEAL.

NOTE

Generally, in medical malpractice cases, a plaintiff must present the testimony of a qualified expert that the conduct of the defendant breached the standard of care. If the plaintiff fails to produce such testimony, the plaintiff's case will be dismissed. There is an exception for cases in which the breach is so obvious that the fact finder does not need expert testimony. *See, e.g., Davis v. Women and Children's Hosp. Lake Charles*, 74 So. 3d 291 (La.App. 3 Cir. 2011), *writ denied*, 77 So. 3d 966 (La. 2012) (leaving sponge in patient during surgery; doctor has nondelegable duty regarding sponge count).

2. **Consent**

    a. **Obtaining Valid Consent**

La. R.S. 40:1159.4.   **Persons who may consent to surgical or medical treatment**

A.   In addition to such other persons as may be authorized and empowered, any one of the following persons in the following order of priority, if there is no person in a prior class who is reasonably available, willing, and competent to act, is authorized and empowered to consent, either orally or otherwise, to any surgical or medical treatment or procedures including autopsy not prohibited by law which may be suggested, recommended, prescribed, or directed by a duly licensed physician:

    (1)   Any adult, for himself.

    (2)   The judicially appointed tutor or curator of the patient, if one has been appointed.

    (3)   An agent acting pursuant to a valid mandate, specifically authorizing the agent to make health care decisions.

    (4)   The patient's spouse not judicially separated.

    (5)   An adult child of the patient.

    (6)   Any parent, whether adult or minor, for his child.

    (7)   The patient's sibling.

    (8)   The patient's other ascendants or descendants.

    (9)   Any person temporarily standing in loco parentis, whether formally serving or not, for the minor under his care and any guardian for his ward.

    (10)   A person chosen by the interdisciplinary team, as defined in R.S. 28:451.2, to make recommendations on behalf of an individual with a developmental disability, ... The interdisciplinary team shall exercise discretion in choosing, by majority vote, the family member, friend, or other person most familiar with the individual or most capable of making the decision at issue.

    (11)   A person chosen by an ad hoc team assembled by any interested person for the purpose of addressing the medical decision at issue for an individual with a developmental disability.

    (a) This team shall consist of at least three persons familiar with the circumstances and needs of the individual, and shall contain representatives from at least two different services, educational or advocacy agencies serving individuals with developmental disabilities.

    (b)   he team shall make decisions by majority vote, and no one agency shall provide a majority of the members.

    (c)   The team shall exercise discretion in choosing the family member, friend, or other person most familiar with the individual or most capable of making the decision at issue.

B.   If there is more than one person within the above named class in Paragraphs (A)(1) through (9), the consent for surgical or medical treatment shall be given by a majority of those members of the class available for consultation.

C. For an individual with a developmental disability, competency to act for the purpose of this Section shall be determined in accordance with principles set forth in R.S. 28:454.3, including capacity to consent and legally adequate consent.

D. Consent to surgical or medical treatment for an individual with a developmental disability will be implied where an emergency, as defined in R.S. 40:1159.5, exists.

La. R.S. 40:1159.5. Emergencies

A. In addition to any other instances in which a consent is excused or implied at law, a consent to surgical or medical treatment or procedures suggested, recommended, prescribed, or directed by a duly licensed physician will be implied where an emergency exists. For the purposes hereof, an emergency is defined as a situation wherein: (1) in competent medical judgment, the proposed surgical or medical treatment or procedures are reasonably necessary; and (2) a person authorized to consent under Section 1159.4 is not readily available, and any delay in treatment could reasonably be expected to jeopardize the life or health of the person affected, or could reasonably result in disfigurement or impair faculties.

B. For purposes of this Section, an emergency is also defined as a situation wherein: (1) a person transported to a hospital from a licensed health care facility is not in a condition to give consent; (2) a person authorized to give consent under 1159.4 is not readily available; and (3) any delay would be injurious to the health and well being of such person.

La. R.S. 40:1159.6. Construction of Subpart; general application

The provisions of this Part shall be liberally construed, and all relationships set forth herein shall include the marital, adoptive, foster and step-relations as well as the natural whole blood. A consent by one person so authorized and empowered shall be sufficient. Any person acting in good faith shall be justified in relying on the representations of any person purporting to give such a consent, including, but not limited to, his identity, his age, his marital status, his emancipation, and his relationship to any other person for whom the consent is purportedly given.

La. R.S. 40:1159.7. Right of adult to refuse treatment as to his own person not abridged

Nothing contained herein shall be construed to abridge any right of a person eighteen years of age or over to refuse to consent to medical or surgical treatment as to his own person.

PIZZALOTTO
v.
WILSON
437 So. 2d 859 (La. 1983)

DENNIS, J.

In this case the trial jury and the court of appeal, 411 So. 2d 1150, refused to hold a surgeon liable for removing a woman's reproductive organs without her consent. We reverse. The evidence presents no reasonable basis for finding that the woman consented either expressly or impliedly to a removal of her reproductive organs. Regardless of the reasonableness of the surgery or its eventual necessity, a physician may not act beyond his patient's authorization, except when a situation seriously threatens the health or life of the patient. There is no warrant in the record for a determination that the surgeon was forced by such a situation to remove the woman's female organs before obtaining her consent.

* * * * *

The decisive issues are whether the facts of this case justify the conclusion that the patient expressly or impliedly consented to the performance of the hysterectomy, or whether a life threatening emergency arose during surgery which authorized the doctor to act without his patient's consent.

Because we resolve these issues in the patient's favor, and because we agree with the court of appeal's exculpation of the physician from any breach of negligence or malpractice standards, the other issues considered by the previous courts are pretermitted.

The doctrine of consent to medical treatment is rooted in the idea that a person has the right to make major decisions regarding his own body. *See generally*, *Lacaze v. Collier*, 434 So. 2d 1039 (La. 1983). Justice Cardozo, when on the high court of New York, wrote "Every human being of adult years and sound mind has a right to determine what shall be done with his own body and a surgeon who performs an operation without his patient's consent commits an assault for which he is liable in damages." *Schloendorff v. Society of New York Hospitals*, 211 N.Y. 125, 105 N.E. 92, 93 (1914). A surgeon commits a battery on his patient when he undertakes a particular surgical procedure without the consent of the patient or an authorized person, except when an emergency requires immediate surgery for the preservation of life or health under circumstances when such consent cannot be practicably obtained.... An emergency is statutorily defined as a situation wherein, in competent medical judgment, the proposed surgical or medical treatment procedures are reasonably necessary, and a person authorized by statute to consent is not readily available, and any delay in treatment could reasonably be expected to jeopardize the life or health of the person affected or could reasonably result in disfigurement or impair faculties. La.R.S. 40:1299.54 [Redesignated as 40:1159.5]. Though a battery is generally manifested as an act of hostility, the basis of this battery is not the hostile intent of the physician, but rather the absence of consent on the part of the patient to a treatment that may in fact be beneficial.

Thus, an unauthorized operation that is skillfully performed still constitutes a battery. *Id.* Prosser, Law of Torts, 4th Ed. Ch. 2 § 9. The general rule prohibiting the performance of an operation extends to the performance of operations different in nature from that for which consent was given, and to operations involving risks and results not contemplated....

It is undisputed that Ms. Wilson did not expressly consent to the removal of her reproductive organs. Furthermore, the argument that she impliedly consented is also without merit. The surgery authorization form contained no mention of a hysterectomy or removal of her reproductive organs. She consented in writing only to a "laparotomy--lysis of adhesions, fulguration of endometrioma." A laparotomy is an exploratory and conservative operation to burn the adhesions which had entangled these organs. It does not entail the removal or destruction of reproductive organs. Ms. Wilson never said anything which signified her consent to a hysterectomy. Dr. Pizzalotto was aware of Ms. Wilson's strong desire to eventually have children. She had even read extensively on her diagnosed problems in order to more fully understand the nature and risks of the doctor's recommended treatment. Dr. Pizzalotto admitted that he never discussed with his patient the possible removal of her reproductive organs. The purpose of the operation which Dr. Pizzalotto performed was inimical to the aim of the surgery to which the patient consented. She agreed to a limited conservative operation calculated to save her reproductive organs but was instead subjected to a hysterectomy by which the organs were irrevocably removed. Neither Dr. Pizzalotto's belief that she was already sterile, nor his opinion that postponing removal would necessitate further surgery before she left the hospital fairly indicate that Ms. Wilson impliedly consented to the immediate removal of these organs.

That the physician may have complied with La. R.S. 40:1299.40 [Repealed by Acts 2012, §3, eff. June 12, 2012] insofar as a "laparotomy-lysis of adhesions, fulguration of endometrioma" is concerned, by informing her of the risks involved and obtaining her consent to these procedures, did not relieve him of his legal duty to inform her of the risks involved in a hysterectomy, which is a different procedure, and to obtain her consent thereto before it was performed. La.R.S. 40:1299.40 prescribes the legal duty of a physician to inform his patient of the known risks involved in the medical or surgical procedure he proposes to perform. If he fulfills this duty he cannot be held responsible for his failure to follow some different mode of giving notice of the risks involved in the medical or surgical procedure to be performed. However, his compliance with respect to a particular medical or surgical procedure is not a talisman before which all other legal duties disappear. If a physician only informs a patient of the risks of one operation and performs an entirely different surgical procedure, clearly he has not complied with his duty to inform the patient of the danger involved in the surgery actually performed.

The policy favoring patient consent to medical treatment must not impair a physician's ability to handle an emergency that immediately and seriously threatens a patient's health or life. However, this is not a case where the life or health of the patient was threatened by the failure to immediately remove her reproductive organs....

This evidence clearly establishes that the emergency exception is not applicable to Ms. Wilson's case. Her condition was not critical or life-threatening. Dr. Pizzalotto did not establish that the immediate further surgery was necessary. His testimony indicates only a possibility, or at most a probability, that additional surgery would be required before Ms. Wilson left the hospital. Drs. Jackson and Dickey testified that, despite the normal risks of further surgery, such as an additional exposure to the risks of anesthesia or infection, the hysterectomy or the bilateral salpingo-oophorectomy should not have been performed at that time without prior consent by Ms. Wilson. La.R.S. 40:1299.54 provides that an emergency which implies consent to a surgical procedure is one in which the procedure is reasonably necessary, a person authorized to consent is not available, *and* any delay in treatment could reasonably be expected to jeopardize the life or health of the person affected. The evidence conclusively shows that a delay of the total hysterectomy, at least until Ms. Wilson could decide the fate of her organs for herself, would not have jeopardized her life or her health.

By way of a further element of defense as to consent, it has come to our attention that Ms. Wilson signed a blanket authorization at the time of her admission to the hospital. The hospital's printed form authorized, inter alia, "the performance of operations and procedures in addition to or different from those now contemplated, whether or not arising from presently unforeseen conditions which the above named doctor or his associates or assistants may consider necessary or advisable in the course of the operation." However, as Judge Hardy observed of a similar blanket authorization in *Rogers v. Lumbermens Mutual Casualty Company, supra*, "the above so-called authorization is so ambiguous as to be almost completely worthless, and certainly, since it fails to designate the nature of the operation authorized, and for which consent was given, it can have no possible weight under the factual circumstances of the instant case". 119 So. 2d 652.

* * * * *

REVERSED and **REMANDED.**

* * * * *

NOTES & QUESTIONS

1.   Might it still be possible that a total failure of consent might still constitute a battery? Consider the discussion in the following cases questioning *Pizzalotto*.

In *Larche v. Rodriguez (In re Medical Review Panel for Larche)*, 714 So. 2d 56, 58 (La.App. 4 Cir. 1998), the court of appeal rejected the plaintiff's reliance on *Pizzalotto* for the proposition that, where the defendant performed a procedure in addition to the one for which he had consent, he committed a battery. The court in *Larche* agreed that

> ... liability in the *Pizzalotto* case ... was based on commission of a "battery" because the doctor did not obtain adequate consent from the patient for the procedures performed. However, the *Pizzalotto* decision on which this Court based its decision in *Baham* was rendered prior to the 1990 amendments to the Uniform Consent Law, LSA-R.S. 40:1299.40 [Repealed by Acts 2012, No. 759, §3, eff. June 12, 2012], which state the theory of recovery in lack of informed consent cases. Further, these decisions have been called into question by the recent decision of *Lugenbuhl v. Dowling*, 701 So. 2d 447 (La. 1997) wherein the Supreme Court clarified the use of the term "battery" in the *Pizzalotto* case.

The Fourth Circuit Panel had held that "Where the patient consents to operation A and the health care provider instead performs operation B, that is not medical malpractice, but is rather the intentional tort of medical battery and is not covered by the Medical Malpractice Act," *Baham v. Medical Center of Louisiana at New Orleans*, 674 So. 2d 458 (La.App. 4 Cir. 1996), but relied instead on the Louisiana Supreme Court's subsequent questioning of *Pizzalotto* in *Lugenbuhl* to deny recovery. The *Lugenbuhl* Court said of *Pizzalotto*:

> Liability in the *Pizzalotto* case was based on commission of a "battery" because the doctor, although obtaining consent to perform a laparotomy and to unbind the adhesions and fulgurate the endometrioma, performed other anticipated procedures for which he did not have consent. We deem it appropriate to clarify now the use of the term "battery" in the *Pizzalotto* case.
>
> While the early development of liability for failing to obtain informed consent was based on concepts of battery or unconsented touching, the imposition of liability in later cases has been based on breach of a duty imposed on the doctor to disclose material information in obtaining consent. Such a breach of duty by the doctor results in liability based on negligence or other fault. While perhaps the performance of a medical procedure without obtaining any kind of consent, in the absence of an emergency, technically constitutes a battery, liability issues involving inadequate consent are more appropriately analyzed under negligence or other fault concepts. *See* W. Page Keeton et al., Prosser and Keeton on the Law of Torts 190 (5th ed. 1984) ("Beginning around 1960, however, it began to be recognized that the matter was really one of the standard of professional conduct, and so negligence has now generally displaced battery as the basis for liability"); 1 Fowler v. Harper et al., The Law of Torts § 3.10 & nn.36-38 (3d ed. 1997) ("The problem of informed consent is essentially one of professional responsibility, not intentional wrongdoing, and can be handled more coherently within the framework of negligence law than as an aspect of battery."); 4 Stuart M. Speiser et al., The American Law of Torts § 15.71 n.21 (noting that "more and more courts have turned to the theory of negligence -- professional malpractice -- as the basis for suits predicated on lack of informed consent"); David W. Robertson et al., Cases and Materials on Torts 608 n.1 (1989) ("modern courts analyze the adequacy of consent as a question of negligence, not battery"); 3 David W. Louisell & Harold Williams, Medical Malpractice § 22.03[2] (1997); Frank L. Maraist & Thomas C. Galligan, Jr., Louisiana Tort Law § 2-9(a) (1996) ("most modern authorities now treat lack of informed consent as a negligence, i.e., malpractice matter"); *Natanson v. Kline*, 186 Kan. 393, 350 P.2d 1093 (1960); *Woolley v. Henderson*, 418 A.2d 1123 (Me. 1980).
>
> The Louisiana Legislature has also specified the theory of recovery in lack of informed consent claims as properly based on traditional fault theories, apparently to bring such claims under the Medical Malpractice Act. By La. Acts 1990, No. 1093, the Legislature amended La. Rev. Stat. 40:1299.40 [Repealed by Acts 2012, No. 759, §3, eff. June 12, 2012] to add Subsection E, which establishes the Louisiana Medical Disclosure Panel to determine the risks and hazards related to medical care and surgical procedures that must be disclosed to the patient....
>
> We therefore reject battery-based liability in lack of informed consent cases (which include no-consent cases) in favor of liability based on breach of the doctor's duty to provide the patient with material information concerning the medical procedure.

Lugenbuhl v. Dowling, 701 So. 2d 447, 452-53 (La. 1997).

Does *Lugenbuhl* mean that cases where there is no consent whatsoever must be viewed as negligence cases, or only cases where consent has been given but exceeded? Note that *Lugenbuhl* involved a plaintiff who consented to a hernia repair but insisted on having a nylon mesh inserted.

The defendant failed to insert the mesh, making it more likely that the repair would fail (as it did). Suppose the plaintiff has strong religious convictions and consents to a procedure only if no men are present? *See, Cohen v. Smith*, 648 N.E. 2d 329 (Ill. App. 3d 1995).

The Fourth Circuit held that an allegation of euthanasia is an allegation of an intentional tort that is not covered by the Medical Malpractice Act in *Lagasse v. Tenet Health Sys.*, 83 So. 3d 70 (La.App. 4 Cir. 2011).

2.   Assume that you represent a group of physicians. They fear liability because of *Pizzalotto*. What advice can you provide to minimize potential liability?

b.   The Doctrine of Informed Consent

The legislative response to *Hondroulis* was the adoption of the Medical Disclosure Panel, described in the following statute:

La. R.S. 40:1157.1   Consent to medical treatment; methods of obtaining consent

* * * * *

D.   In a suit against a physician or other health care provider involving a health care liability or medical malpractice claim which is based on the failure of the physician or other health care provider to disclose or adequately to disclose the risks and hazards involved in the medical care or surgical procedure rendered by the physician or other health care provider, the only theory on which recovery may be obtained is that of negligence in failing to disclose the risks or hazards that could have influenced a reasonable person in making a decision to give or withhold consent.

E.   Consent to medical treatment may be evidenced according to the provisions of Subsections A and C of this Section or, as an alternative, a physician or other health care provider may choose to avail himself of the lists established by the Louisiana Medical Disclosure Panel pursuant to the provisions of R.S. 40:1157.2 as another method by which to evidence a patient'sconsent to medical treatment.

* * * * *

J.   (1)   To the extent feasible, the panel shall identify and make a thorough examination of all medical treatments and surgical procedures in which physicians and other health care providers may be involved in order to determine which of those treatments and procedures do and do not require disclosure of the risks and hazards to the patient or person authorized to consent for the patient. The panel, initially, shall examine all existingmedical disclosure lists and update and repromulgate those lists under the authority vested in this Section. The dentist member of the panel shall participate only in the panel's deliberation, determination, and preparation of lists of dental treatments and procedures that do and do not require disclosure.

(2)   The panel shall prepare separate lists of those medical treatments and surgical procedures that do and do not require disclosure and for those treatments and procedures that do require disclosure shall establish the degree of disclosure required and the form in which the disclosure will be made.

(3)   Lists prepared pursuant to the provisions of this Section together with written explanations of the degree and form of disclosure shall be promulgated in accordance with the provisions of the Administrative Procedure Act. The form of the disclosure and manner in which such disclosure will be made shall be subject to legislative oversight by the House and Senate health and welfare committees.

K.   The lists compiled and published and rules promulgated relative to the form and manner of disclosure according to the provisions of this Section and evidence of such disclosures or failure to disclose by a physician or other health care provider as provided in this Section, shall be admissible in a health care liability suit or medical malpractice claim involving medical care rendered or a surgical procedure performed.

L. At least annually, or at such other period as the panel may determine, the panel shall identifyand examine anynewmedical treatments and surgical procedures that have been developed since its last determinations, shall assign them to the proper list, and shall establish the degree of disclosure required and the form in which the disclosure shall be made. The panel shall also review and examine such treatments and procedures for the purpose of revising lists previously published. These determinations shall be published in the same manner as described in Paragraph (J)(3) of this Section.

M. Before a patient or a person authorized to consent for a patient gives consent to any medical or surgical procedure that appears on the panel's list requiring disclosure, the physician or other health care provider shall disclose to the patient, or person authorized to consent for the patient, the risks and hazards involved in that kind of care or procedure. A physician or other health care provider may choose to utilize the lists prepared by the panel and shall be considered to have complied with the requirements of this Subsection if disclosure is made as provided in Subsection N of this Section.

N. Consent to medical care that appears on the panel's list requiring disclosure shall be considered effective pursuant to the provisions of this Section, if it is given in writing, signed by the patient or a person authorized to give the consent and by a competent witness, and if the written consent specifically states, in such terms and language that a layman would be expected to understand, the risks and hazards that are involved in the medical care or surgical procedure in the form and to the degree required by the panel pursuant to the provisions of this Section.

O. (1) All the following requirements shall apply in a suit against a physician or other health care provider involving a health care liability or medical malpractice claim that is based on the negligent failure of the physician or other health care provider to disclose or adequately to disclose the risks and hazards involved in the medical care or surgical procedure rendered by the physician or other health care provider:

(a) Both the disclosure made as provided in Subsection M of this Section and the failure to disclose based on inclusion of any medical care or surgical procedure on the panel's list forwhich disclosure is not required shall be admissible in evidence and shall create a rebuttable presumption that the requirements of Subsections M and N of this Section have been complied with and this presumption shall be included in the charge to the jury.

(b) The failure to disclose the risks and hazards involved in any medical care or surgical procedure required to be disclosed under Subsections M and N of this Section shall be admissible in evidence and shall create a rebuttable presumption of a negligent failure to conform to the duty of disclosure set forth in Subsections M and N of this Section, and this presumption shall be included in the charge to the jury. However, failure to disclose may be found not to be negligent, if there was an emergency as defined in R.S. 40:2113.6(C) or, if for some other reason, it was not medically feasible to make a disclosure of the kind that would otherwise have been negligence.

(2) If medical care is rendered or a surgical procedure performed with respect to which the panel has not made a determination regarding a duty of disclosure, the physician or other health care provider is under the general duty to disclose otherwise imposed by R.S. 40:1299.39.5.

P. In order to be covered by the provisions of this Section, the physician or other health care provider who will actually perform the contemplated medical or surgical procedure shall:

(1) Disclose the risks and hazards in the form and to the degree required by the panel.

(2) Disclose additional risks, if any, particular to a patient because of a complicating medical condition, either told to the physician or other health care provider by the patient or his

representative in a medical history of the patient or reasonably discoverable by such physician or other health care provider.

(3)   Disclose reasonable therapeutic alternatives and risks associated with such alternatives.

(4)   Relate that he is obtaining a consent to medical treatment pursuant to the lists formulated by the Louisiana Medical Disclosure Panel.

(5) Provide an opportunity to ask any questions about the contemplated medical or surgical procedure, risks, or alternatives and acknowledge in writing that he answered such questions, to the patient or other person authorized to give consent to medical treatment, receipt of which shall be acknowledged in writing.

HONDROULIS
v.
SCHUMACHER
553 So. 2d 398 (La. 1989)

(On Rehearing)

DENNIS, J.

Plaintiff, Viola Hondroulis, filed suit against John Schumacher, M.D., alleging the following facts: Mrs. Hondroulis consulted Dr. Schumacher in May, 1981, when she began to experience the spontaneous onset of pain in the lower back radiating down into her right hip and right leg. Dr. Schumacher treated her conservatively until June 24, 1981 when he performed a myelogram and lumbar laminectomy upon her. Subsequent to the surgery, plaintiff continued to experience pain in the lower back radiating down into the right hip and right leg and began to experience incontinency, constipation and numbness in her entire left leg. Before surgery, the plaintiff signed a consent form but was not properly informed by the doctor of the risk of losing the function of her organs, nerves or muscles, particularly with respect to those that control the use of her bladder. This risk was material and the doctor should have advised her of it. The plaintiff, as a reasonable person, would have refused the surgery had she been advised of the risk. The doctor failed to advise the plaintiff of alternative methods of treatment presenting smaller risks. The plaintiff did not know that a material risk of the operation was the loss of sphincter and bladder control and numbness in the left leg.

Defendant, Dr. Schumacher, filed a motion for summary judgment on the informed consent claim solely on the ground that the plaintiff signed a written consent to surgery stating that he understood all of the risks of the surgery and conforming with the statutory requirements of La. R.S. 40:1299.40. In the written consent form plaintiff Hondroulis consented to a lumbar laminectomy to remove a ruptured disc and acknowledged that "the following known risks are associated with this procedure including anesthesia: death; brain damage; disfiguring scars; paralysis; the loss of or loss of function of body organs; and the loss or loss of function of any arm or leg" and "further acknowledge[d] that all questions I have asked about the procedure have been answered in a satisfactory manner."

In opposition to the motion the plaintiff filed her deposition and her affidavit. In her affidavit she stated that Dr. Schumacher did not inform her prior to the operation of the risk of urinary incontinence or loss of use of her good left leg or give her an opportunity to ask questions about the surgical procedure or the alternative methods of treatment. In her deposition she testified that she had been admitted to the hospital for testing and that a myelogram had been performed. Without informing her of the results of the myelogram Dr. Schumacher came in to her room and said surgery would be necessary and that he would schedule her for the following day. He did not give her an opportunity to ask any questions. The nurse came in later and presented a form for Mrs. Hondroulis to sign telling her that it was the routine and to just sign it. She did not have an opportunity to ask questions at this time.

After a hearing, the trial court rendered summary judgment in favor of the doctor and against the plaintiff patient reasoning that a doctor does not have to inform a patient of all conceivable risks, that the consent form complied with R.S. 40:1299.40 [Repealed by Acts 2012, No. 759, §3, eff. June 12, 2012] and that plaintiff did not allege that the execution of the form was induced by misrepresentation of material facts.

Plaintiff appealed, and the court of appeal affirmed. 521 So. 2d 534 (La.App. 4 Cir. 1988). The opinion of the court signed by two judges held that the doctor's disclosure of the risk of "loss or loss of function of any organ or limb" fulfilled the requirement of informed consent under La. R.S. 40:1299.40(A) because this statutory language, coupled with the patient's right to ask questions, is sufficient to indicate informed consent, citing that court's decisions in *Madere v. Ochsner Foundation Hospital*, 505 So. 2d 146 (La.App. 4 Cir. l987) and *Leiva v. Nance*, 506 So. 2d 131 (La.App. 4 Cir. l987). Three judges of the court of appeal "reluctantly concur[red]", because the court of appeal, en banc, by a 6 to 6 deadlock, had refused to overturn the decisions relied upon by the two-judge lead opinion. In the absence of the precedent affirmed by deadlock, they would have held that the consent form's "loss of function of body organs" warning did not adequately disclose the material risk of "incontinence", and that to hold otherwise "leads to the absurd result that a physician [can] merely copy the language of the statute for every surgical procedure." 521 So. 2d at 538.

This court granted a writ to consider whether the trial and appellate courts correctly interpreted La. R.S. 40:1299.40 and its impact upon the informed consent doctrine as expressly and impliedly adopted by the courts of this state. 522 So. 2d 571 (La. 1988). The legislative enactment must, of course, be considered within the context of the jurisprudential development upon which its effect was intended to apply.

I

Informed Consent Doctrine Patient's Right - Doctor's Duty

The informed consent doctrine is based on the principle that every human being of adult years and sound mind has a right to determine what shall be done to his or her own body. *LaCaze v. Collier*, 434 So. 2d 1039 (La. 1983); *Canterbury v. Spence*, 464 F.2d 772 (D.C. Cir. 1972); *Schloendorff v. Society of New York Hospital*, 211 N.Y. 125, 105 N.E. 92 (1914). Surgeons and other doctors are thus required to provide their patients with sufficient information to permit the patient himself to make an informed and intelligent decision on whether to submit to a proposed course of treatment. Id. Prosser & Keeton on Torts §32 p.190 (5th ed. 1984) (citing authorities at n.61); Halligan, The Standard of Disclosure by Physicians to Patients: Competing Models of Informed Consent, 41 La.L.Rev. 9 (1980). Where circumstances permit, the patient should be told the nature of the pertinent ailment or condition, the general nature of the proposed treatment or procedure, the risks involved in the proposed treatment or procedure, the prospects of success, the risks of failing to undergo any treatment or procedure at all, and the risks of any alternate methods of treatment. *LaCaze v. Collier*, 434 So. 2d at 1043, 1045; *Canterbury v. Spence*, supra, at 789; Louiselle & Williams, Medical Malpractice, 1981, § 22.01 at 594.44; Prosser & Keeton, supra, p.190; *see Sard v. Hardy*, 281 Ma. 432, 379 A.2d 1014 (1977); *Crain v. Allison*, 443 A.2d 558 (D.C.App. 1982); *Miller v. Van Newkirk*, 628 P.2d 143 (Colo.App. 1981); *Truman v. Thomas*, 27 Cal.3d 285, 165 Cal.Rptr. 308, 611 P.2d 902 (1980).

Scope of Disclosure - Material Information

The doctor's duty is to disclose all risks which are "material". *LaCaze v. Collier*, 434 So. 2d at 1045-46; *Wheedon v. Madison*, 374 N.W.2d 367, 375 (S.D. l985)("Materiality is the cornerstone upon which the physician's duty to disclose is based."); *Canterbury v. Spence*, supra; *Crain v. Allison*, supra; *Klnkin v. Henpel*, 305 N.W.2d 589 (Minn. 1981); *see Borday v. Campbell*, 704 S.W.2d 8 (Tex. 1986); Prosser & Keeton, supra, p.191. In broad outline, a risk is material when a reasonable person in what the doctor knows or should know to be the patient's position, would be likely to attach significance to the risk or cluster of risks in deciding whether or not to forego the proposed therapy.

Canterbury v. Spence, supra, at 787; *LaCaze v. Collier, supra*, at 1045-46; *Harbeson v. Parke Davis, Inc.*, 746 F.2d 517 (9th Cir. 1984); Prosser & Keeton, *supra* at p.191.

The factors contributing significance to a medical risk are the incidence of injury and the degree of the harm threatened. If the harm threatened is great, the risk may be significant even though the statistical possibility of its taking effect is very small. But if the chance of harm is slight enough, and the potential benefits of the therapy or the detriments of the existing malady great enough, the risk involved may not be significant even though the harm threatened is very great. *Canterbury v. Spence, supra*, at 788 and authorities cited therein; *see Halligan, supra* at. p.28; *see generally*, Harper, James & Gray, § 16.9, p.469 et seq.

The determination of materiality is a two-step process. The first step is to define the existence and nature of the risk and the likelihood of its occurrence. "Some" expert testimony is necessary to establish this aspect of materiality because only a physician or other qualified expert is capable of judging what risk exists and the likelihood of occurrence. The second prong of the materiality test is for the trier of fact to decide whether the probability of that type harm is a risk which a reasonable patient would consider in deciding on treatment. The focus is on whether a reasonable person in the patient's position probably would attach significance to the specific risk. This determination of materiality does not require expert testimony. *Harbeson v. Parke Davis, Inc., supra*; *Canterbury* 464 F.2d at 786; *Adams v. Richland China, Inc.*, P.S. 37 Wash. App. 650, 681 P.2d 1305 (1984); *see* Shannon, 666 p.2d at 356; *Salgala v. Tavares*, 533 A.2d 165 (Pa. 1987).

Causation - Objective Standard

There must be a causal relationship between the doctor's failure to disclose material information and material risk of damage to the patient. *LaCaze v. Collier, supra*, at 1048; *Canterbury v. Spence, supra*, at 790; *see Fast v. United States*, 629 F.Supp. 682 (E.D.Mo. 1986); *Sard v. Hardy, supra*. Because of the likelihood of a patient's bias in testifying in hindsight on this hypothetical matter, this court and others have adopted an objective standard of causation: whether a reasonable patient in the plaintiff's position would have consented to the treatment or procedure had the material information and risks been disclosed. *LaCaze v. Collier, supra*, at 1048; *Canterbury v. Spence, supra*; *Hook v. Rothstein*, 281 S.C. 541, 316 S.E.2d 690 (1984); *Adams v. ElBash*, 388 S.E.2d 381 (W.Va. 1985); *Reikes v. Martin*, 471 So. 2d 385 (Miss. 1985); *Wheeldon v. Madison, supra*; *Barclay v. Campbell, supra*; *Cobbs v. Grant*, 8 Cal.3d 229, 104 Cal.Rptr. 505, 502 P.2d 1 (1972); *Harte v. Mcffelway*, 707 F.2d 1544 (D.C.Cir. 1983).

Exceptions - Doctor's Privilege Not to Disclose

The doctor is not required to disclose material risks or information when a genuine emergency arises because the patient is unconscious or otherwise incapable of consenting, and harm from a failure to treat is imminent and outweighs harm threatened by the proposed treatment. *Canterbury v. Spence, supra*, at 788; *see* Prosser & Keeton, *supra*, at p. 192, n. 77 ("*Compare Keogan v. Holy Family Hospital*, 1980, 95 Wa.2d 306, 622 P.2d 1246 (true emergency), with *Dewes v. Indian Health Service*, D.S.D. 1980, 504 F.Supp. 203 (inadequate emergency)".) In situations of that kind the physician should, however, attempt to secure a relative's consent if possible. But if time is too short to accommodate discussion, the doctor should proceed with treatment. *Canterbury v. Spence, supra*, at 789 and authorities cited therein. *See Allen v. Roark*, 625 S.W.2d 411 (Tex.App. 1981), modified, 633 S.W.2d 804; *see generally*, Boland, *The Doctrines of Lack of Consent and Lack of Informed Consent in Medical Procedures in Louisiana*, 45 La.L.Rev. 1, 17 (1984); Meisel, *The "Exceptions" to the Informed Consent Doctrine: Striking a Balance Between Competing Values in Medical Decision Making*, 1979 Wis.L.Rev. 413 (1979).

A doctor has a "therapeutic privilege" to withhold disclosure of a material risk when the physician reasonably foresees that disclosure will cause the patient to become ill or emotionally distraught so as to foreclose a rational decision, complicate or hinder treatment, or pose psychological damage to the patient. *Canterbury v. Spence, supra*, at 789; *see Meisel, Id.* This privilege must be carefully circumscribed, however, for otherwise it might devour the disclosure rule itself. Even in this kind of situation, the doctor should attempt to make disclosure to a close relative and obtain his consent. *Canterbury v. Spence, supra*, at 789 and authorities cited therein.

The physician is not required to disclose risks that are not reasonably foreseeable, *Hanks v. Drs. Ranson, Swan, and Birsch, Ltd.*, 359 So. 2d 1089 (La.App. 3 Cir. 1978); *Reiser v. Lohner*, 641 P.2d 93 (Utah 1982); *Koanda v. Houser-Norburg Medical Corp*, 419 N.E.2d 1024 (Ind.App. 1981), or not material, *Precourt v. Frederick*, 395 Mass. 689, 481 N.E.2d 1144 (1985); *Masquet v. Magure*, 638 P.2d 1105 (Oka. 1981); *Mcffinney v. Nash*, 120 Cal.App.3d 428, 174 Cal.Rptr. 624 (1981); *Henderson v. Milobsky*, 595 F.2d 654 (D.C. Cir. 1978). Risks that are commonly understood, obvious, or already known to the patient need not be disclosed by the doctor. *See* Prosser & Keeton, *supra*, at 192 and authorities cited therein.

Burden of Proof

In a trial on the merits of a suit claiming inadequate disclosure of risk information by a physician, the patient has the burden of going forward with evidence tending to establish prima facie the essential elements of the cause of action, and ultimately the burden of persuasion on those elements. *Canterbury v. Spence, supra*, at 791. *See also*, McCormick on Evidence (3rd ed. 1984) sections 336-338. The burden of going forward with evidence pertaining to a privilege not to disclose, however, rests properly with the physician. This is not only because the patient has made out a prima facie case before an issue on privilege is reached, but also because any evidence bearing on the privilege is usually in the hands of the physician alone. *Id. See* J. Wigmore, Evidence § 2486, 2488, 2489 (Chadbourn rev. 1981).

II

The Statute

The statute whose construction is involved in this case is La. R.S. 40:1299.40. [Repealed by Acts 2012, No. 759, §3, eff. June 12, 2012] It provides in pertinent part:

§ 1299.40.   Consent to Medical Treatment; Exception

   A.   Notwithstanding any other law to the contrary, written consent to medical treatment means a consent in writing to any medical or surgical procedure or course of procedures which (a) sets forth in general terms the nature and purpose of the procedure or procedures, together with the known risks, if any, of death, brain damage, quadriplegia, paraplegia, the loss or loss of function of any organ or limb, of disfiguring scars associated with such procedure or procedures, (b) acknowledges that such disclosure of information has been made and that all questions asked about the procedure or procedures have been answered in a satisfactory manner, and (c) is signed, by the patient for whom the procedure is to be performed, or if the patient for any reason lacks legal capacity to consent by a person who has legal authority to consent on behalf of such patient in such circumstances. Such consent shall be presumed to be valid and effective, in the absence of proof that execution of the consent was induced by misrepresentation of material facts.

   B.   Except as provided in Subsection A of this Section, no evidence shall be admissible to modify or limit the authorization for performance of the procedure or procedures set forth in such written consent.

   C.   Where consent to medical treatment from a patient, or from a person authorized by law to consent to medical treatment for such patient, is secured other than in accordance with Subsection A above, the explanation to the patient or to the person consenting for such patient shall include the matters set forth in Paragraph (a) of Subsection A above, and an opportunity shall be afforded for asking questions concerning the procedures to be performed which shall be answered in a satisfactory manner. Such consent shall be valid and effective and is subject to proof according to the rules of evidence in ordinary cases.

<h1 style="text-align:center">III</h1>

Considerations Preliminary to the Interpretation of the Statute

A. The Patient's Fundamental Right to decide whether to obtain or refuse medical treatment.

The United States Supreme Court's holdings regarding the right to privacy were succinctly set forth in *Carey v. Population Services International*, 431 U.S. 678, 684-685, 97 S.Ct. 2011, 2017, 52 L.Ed. 2d 675 (1977) Although "[t] he Constitution does not explicitly mention any right of privacy," the Court has recognized that one aspect of the "liberty" protected by the Due Process Clause of the Fourteenth Amendment is "a right of personal privacy, or a guarantee of certain areas or zones of privacy." *Roe v. Wade*, 410 U.S. 113, 152, 93 S.Ct. 705, 726, 35 L.Ed.2d 147 (1973). This right of personal privacy includes "the interest in independence in making certain kinds of important decisions." *Whalen v. Roe*, 429 U.S. 509, 599-600, 97 S.Ct. 069, 876, 51 L.Ed.2d 64 (1977). While the outer limits of this aspect of privacy have not been marked by the Court, it is clear that among the decisions that an individual may make without unjustified government interference are personal decisions "relating to marriage, *Loving v. Virginia*, 388 U.S. 1, 12 S.Ct. 1817, 1823, 18 L.Ed.2d 1010 (1967); procreation, *Skinner v. Oklahoma ex rel Williamson*, 316 U.S. 535, 541-42, 62 S.Ct. 1110, 1113-1114, 86 L.Ed. 1655 (1942); contraception, *Eisenstadt v. Baird*, 405 U.S. at 453454, 92 S.Ct. at 1042, 1043-1044 (White, J, concurring in result); family relationships, *Prince v. Massachusetts*, 321 U.S. 158, 166, 64 S.Ct. 438, 442, 88 L.Ed. 645 (1944); and child rearing and education, *Pierce v. Society of Sisters*, 268 U.S. 510, 535, 45 S.Ct. 571, 573, 69 L.Ed. 1070 (1925); *Meyer v. Nebraska* [262 U.S. 390, 399, 43 S.Ct. 625, 67 L.Ed. 1042 (1923)]." *Roe v. Wade, supra*, at 152-IS3, 93 S.Ct., at 726. *See also Cleveland Board of Education v. LaFleur*, 414 U.S. 632, 639-640, 94 S.Ct. 791, 796-797, 39 L.Ed.2d 52 (1974).

The decision to obtain or reject medical treatment clearly should be recognized as falling within this cluster of constitutionally protected choices. Although the highest court has yet to so hold, one lower federal court and numerous state courts have reasoned from Supreme Court decisions that the right to privacy is broad enough to grant an individual the right to chart his or her own medical treatment plan....

The choice of whether to undergo surgery or other medical treatment, no less than the decision to continue or terminate pregnancy, is, to an extraordinary degree, an intrinsically personal decision. The patient alone must live with his disorder, encounter the risks of therapy or reap the consequences of treatment. By the same token, the choice will profoundly affect his or her development or life. It may mean the difference between life and death, pain and pleasure, poverty and economic stability. *See Rasmussen by Mitchell v. Fleming, supra*; *Andrews v. Ballard, supra*.

Art. I, Section 5 of the 1974 Louisiana Constitution expressly guarantees that every person shall be secure in his person against unreasonable "invasions of privacy." This safeguard was intended to establish an affirmative right to privacy impacting non-criminal areas of law and establishing the principles of the Supreme Court decisions in explicit statement instead of depending on analogical development. *See* Hargrave, *Declaration of Rights*, 35 La.L.Rev. 1, 21 (1974); *see e.g. Roshto v. Hebert*, 439 So. 2d 428 (La. 1983); *Jaubert v. Crowley Post-Signal, Inc.*, 375 So. 2d 1386, 1387-88 fn.2 (La. 1979); *Easter Seal Society v. Playboy Enterprises*, 533 So. 2d 643, 646-647 (La.App. 4 Cir. 1988). Accordingly, we conclude that the Louisiana Constitution's right to privacy also provides for a right to decide whether to obtain or reject medical treatment.

* * * * *

That the constitutionally protected right to privacy extends to an individual's liberty to make medical treatment choices does not, however, automatically invalidate every state legislative regulation in this area. The practice of advising patients and obtaining their consent to treatment may be regulated in ways that do not infringe on protected individual choices. *See Carey v. Population Services Intern, supra.* And even a burdensome regulation may be validated by a sufficiently compelling state interest. In *Roe v. Wade*, for example, the Supreme Court cautioned that a woman's right to terminate her pregnancy is not absolute and that certain state interests may at some point "become sufficiently compelling to sustain regulation of the factors that govern the abortion decision. 410 U.S. at 154, 93 S.Ct. at 727. Thus, where a decision as fundamental as those included within the right of personal privacy is involved, regulations imposing a burden on it may be justified only by compelling state interests, and must be narrowly drawn to express only those interests, *Carey v. Population Services Intern.*, 431 U.S. at 685, 97 S.Ct. at 2016; *Roe v. Wade supra*; *cf. U.S. v. Robel*, 389 U.S. 258, 88 S.Ct. 419, 19 L.Ed.2d 508 (1967).

With these principles in mind we turn to the question whether the court of appeal was correct in its interpretation of La. R.S. 40:1299.40, the statute at issue in this case.

B. Constitutional Pitfalls of the Court of Appeal's Interpretation.

The court of appeal interpreted the statute as a rule of law decreeing that when a patient signs a written form which tracks the statute's language describing broad categories of damages that may result from medical treatment generally, i.e., "death, brain damage, quadriplegia, paraplegia, the loss or loss of function of any organ or limb, or disfiguring scars", she thereby gives "informed consent" to encounter every particular material risk involved in the surgery or treatment proposed by her physician that could result in the generally described kinds of damages. Although the court of appeal did not say that the statute establishes a conclusive or irrebuttable presumption of informed consent flowing from a patient's signature upon such a form, the substance and impact of its interpretation is to this effect. *See* Comment, The Irrebuttable Presumption Doctrine In The Supreme Court, 87 Harv.L.Rev. 1534, 1545 (1974).

If the Court of Appeal's statutory construction is correct, there can be little doubt that the statute is unconstitutional.

Under the Court of Appeal's view, the statute would impose a burden on or significantly interfere with the rights of patients to decide to obtain or reject medical treatment. Physicians would be encouraged by the law merely to present patients with a form copying the phraseology of the statute, rather than to fully inform each patient in layman's terms of the nature and severity of the particular material risks to be encountered in her case and the likelihood of their occurrence. Without pertinent case-specific information patients would lack the capacity to reason and make judgments on their own. They would therefore be deprived of the freedom to personally decide intelligently, voluntarily and without coercion whether to undergo the recommended treatment. The practical effect of the statute would be to deprive or burden an individual's right to decide to accept or forego medical treatment by substantially limiting access to information essential to a meaningful decision regarding the therapy proposed by the physician.

* * * * *

Because the court of appeal's interpretation of the statute would raise serious questions as to its constitutionality, we are called upon to determine whether there is another, equally reasonable and perhaps more appropriate, construction of the statute under which its validity may be clearly sustained. It is a basic rule of statutory interpretation that, if a statute is susceptible of two constructions, one of which will render it constitutional and the other of which will render it unconstitutional, or raise grave and doubtful constitutional questions, the court will adopt the interpretation of the statute which, without doing violence to its language, will maintain its constitutionality....

* * * * *

The statute may be interpreted reasonably as a modest amendment to the informed consent doctrine, rather than as a cryptic restatement of the whole body of law severely burdening or interfering with the rights of patients to make intelligent medical choices. Prior to this enactment our courts attached no particular legal significance to a medical consent merely because it happened to be in writing. (Apparently, only two American jurisdictions accorded any presumption of validity to a written consent by case law. *See Zaresky v. Jacobson* 126 So. 2d 757 (Fla.App. 1961); *Luna v. Nering*, 426 F.2d 95 (5th Cir. 1970) (Texas); *See* Meisel and Kabnick, Informed Consent To Medical Treatment: An Analysis of Recent Legislation, 41 U.Pitt.L.Rev. 407, 468 (1980) and authorities cited therein.) Consequently, a patient could introduce virtually any kind of relevant evidence to prove lack of consent or to rebut the doctor's evidence that the patient had consented to the therapy. Therefore, the statute may be viewed reasonably as having as its principal object a change in the law providing that, notwithstanding any other law to the contrary, a written consent to encounter the risks disclosed therein may not be rebutted except by a showing that consent was induced by misrepresentation.

* * * * *

(W)e conclude that, notwithstanding prior judicial expressions, the legislature by enacting La. R.S. 40:1299.40, did not intend to make substantive alterations in the informed consent doctrine. More particularly, the legislature did not intend to change the law with respect to major elements of the cause of action such as the doctor's duty to disclose material information (including reasonable alternative therapy) or the patient's burden to prove the materiality of any risk not disclosed. That the statute does not contain an express restatement of these principles is due simply to their being integral parts of the jurisprudential doctrine that the legislature tacitly accepted in accomplishing its limited purpose of regulating proof of lack of informed consent. Accordingly, we do not think the statute's reference to "known risks" indicates an intention to require physicians to inform patients of all known risks however slight or immaterial. It is more likely that the reference is to the general rule that the physician cannot be responsible for warning his patient of a hazard unless he either knew or, because of the state of knowledge in the medical profession, should have known of the particular risk.... The "known risk" qualification is actually a limitation upon the kind of material risk that the doctor must disclose; it does not expand his duty to require him to warn of nonmaterial risks. In a statute obviously designed to afford physicians some protection against frivolous claims and the susceptibility of claimants' testimony to modification based on hindsight it is highly unlikely that the legislature intended to enlarge doctors' potential liability so as to encompass responsibility for failure to warn of any known risk.

Similarly, it is a reasonable and constitutional interpretation of the statute that a physician must disclose all known material risks to his patient, but only if the risk foreseeably may result in "death, brain damage, quadriplegia, paraplegia, the loss or loss of function of any organ or limb, [or] disfiguring scars", in order to qualify the written consent for the presumption of validity. *See Hondroulis v. Schumacher*, 521 So. 2d 534, 535-536 (La.App. 4 Cir. 1988) (Lobrano, J., concurring). These undoubtedly are the most serious types of damage which may result from medical treatment or surgery. If the risk is one that cannot foreseeably result in damage of this type it does not fall within the ambit of the statute. Accordingly, these damage categories serve to mark the limits of the legislated law and were not intended to deprive patients of the concrete case-specific material information that is essential to an informed and intelligent decision as to proposed treatment.

V

Application Of Legal Precepts To This Case

In moving for summary judgment the defendant physician did not controvert the plaintiff's allegations that there was a risk of incontinence and loss of permanent bladder control associated with the surgery, that the risk was material, or that the risk materialized in her damage. The doctor moved exclusively on the ground that Mrs. Hondroulis was conclusively or irrebuttably presumed (or deemed by law) to have given informed consent to encounter every material risk associated with the surgery because she signed the consent form tracking the statutory language. We have concluded that the presumption created by the statute is not so broad, however, and that the patient is only presumed to consent to encounter whatever risks a reasonable person, in what the doctor knew or should have known to be the patient's position, would have apprehended from the written consent form. Consequently, the only issue presented by this case is whether the doctor carried his burden of showing there is no genuine issue that Mrs. Hondroulis, or a reasonable person in what the doctor should have known to be the plaintiff's position, was aware of the material risk of incontinence and loss of bladder control from the facts disclosed in the consent form so that her signature on the form was tantamount to informed consent.

Mrs. Hondroulis signed a written form in which she consented to the proposed surgery and acknowledged that she was aware that a risk of "loss of function of body organs" was associated with the procedure. Accordingly, it is presumed that she understood and consented to encounter whatever risk a reasonable lay person, in what the doctor knew or should have known to be her position, would have apprehended from this language. Mrs. Hondroulis does not contend that she can disprove the presumed fact by showing that her consent was induced by misrepresentation. (Ambiguous statements, which are reasonably capable of both a true and false meaning, however, will amount to misrepresentation if the false meaning is accepted, and is intended or known to be accepted. Prosser & Keeton on Torts § 106 (5th ed. 1984); Harper, James & Gray § 7.14 (1986); and authorities cited therein. So will nondisclosure where the parties stand in some confidential or fiduciary relation to one another. *Id.*)

On the other hand, in her papers opposing the motion for summary judgment, Mrs. Hondroulis averred and implied that the doctor knew that the surgery involved a risk that she would permanently lose control of her bladder and become incontinent, that this was a material risk because a reasonable person would have attached significance to it in deciding whether to undergo the surgery, that the doctor did not inform her of this risk, that the risk materialized in her injury and disability, and that the doctor's failure to adequately disclose the risk caused her damage because a reasonable person properly informed would have decided against the surgery.

A motion for summary judgment is properly granted only if the pleadings, depositions, answers to interrogatories, and admissions on file, together with the affidavits, if any, show that there is no genuine issue as to material fact, and that mover is entitled to judgment as a matter of law. La.C.C.P. art. 966. Because the mover has the burden of establishing no material factual issue exists, inferences to be drawn from the underlying facts contained in the materials before the court must be viewed in the light most favorable to the party opposing the motion.... *Vermillion Corp. v. Vaughn*, 397 So. 2d 490 (La. 1981); *Mashburn v. Collin*, 355 So. 2d 879 (La. 1977). To satisfy his burden the mover must meet a strict standard by a showing that it is quite clear what the truth is, and that excludes any real doubt as to the existence of any genuine issue of material fact.... The papers supporting movers position are closely scrutinized, while the opposing papers are indulgently treated, in determining whether the mover has satisfied his burden....

In order to apply these summary judgment precepts in an informed consent case it is essential to have a clear understanding of the two elements of the informed consent concept: information and consent.

With respect to the information element the general rule is that the physician is obliged to disclose all material risks of the therapy to the patient. The cases addressing this issue are legion, if not always uniform, *see Waltz* and *Scheuneman, supra* at 635, and we have discussed the question in some detail earlier in this opinion.

The cases have paid less attention to the consent element, *id.* at 643, but it is this component of the informed consent concept that is crucial to a correct resolution of the present case. Consent connotes the dual elements of awareness and assent. Restatement of Torts 2d §892 (1979). To establish consent to a risk, it must be shown both that the patient was aware of the risk and that he assented to encounter it. Restatement of Torts 2d §892A (1979). Therefore, it is obvious that a risk must have been understandably communicated before the element of awareness can be established. *Waltz* and *Schueneman, supra* at 643. It is for this reason that statements in standardized consent forms that the patient has been informed of "all" risks are unavailing; awareness requires that specific risks have been communicated in fact. *See, e.g. Rogers v. Lumbermen's Mut. Cas. Co.*, 119 So. 2d 649 (La. 1960)....

Communication involves the manner in which the physician must disclose risks – the vocabulary he must adopt and the degree of elaboration in which he must engage. Some courts have taken the approach that only the subjective state of mind of the patient should be considered in establishing the elements of awareness and consent.... This view has been criticized, because to require the physician, absolutely, to use language which his patient will in fact understand calls for clairvoyance. *Waltz* and *Schueneman, supra* at 644. Further, the subjective standard subjects the physician to unfair risks of liability due to a claimant's testimony being modified by hindsight or to the physician's reasonably mistaken belief that his patient understood and assented. *Id.* at 645.

We believe that La. R.S. 40:1299.40 was adopted in response to problems of this kind and that an objective test of awareness is therefore more appropriate in interpreting and applying the statute. Accordingly, the physician is required to disclose material risks in such terms as a reasonable doctor would believe a reasonable patient in the plaintiff's position would understand. Technical language will not ordinarily suffice to disclose a risk to an untutored layperson; *See, e.g., Corn v. French, supra*; and abstract or blanket terms may not be adequate to communicate specific dangers. *See, e.g., Petty v. United States*, 740 F.2d 1428 (8 Cir. 1984); *Rogers v. Lumberman's Mut. Cas. Co., supra*. In order for a reasonable patient to have awareness of a risk, she should be told in lay language the nature and severity of the risk and the likelihood of its occurrence. *See* Laufman, *Surgical Judgment*, in Christopher's Text Book of Surgery 1459, 1461 (9th ed. L. Davis 1968); *Waltz* and *Schueneman, supra* at 644.

Under the statute interpreted as adopting the objective test of consent, the patient is presumed to have been made aware of what a reasonable person should have apprehended from the doctor's disclosure, unless the physician should have known that something peculiar to the patient or her circumstances prevented her from having such an awareness. Professor Waltz and Mr. Scheuneman, *supra* at 645, succinctly explained the objective test as follows:

The basic issue in establishing consent is whether the physician was reasonable in proceeding after a risk was disclosed to the patient in a generally understandable manner. An objective test is therefore appropriate. The proper question is whether a reasonable man would conclude from the patient's behavior that he was aware of the risk and that he manifested a willingness to encounter it.

Drawing inferences from the facts contained in the summary judgment materials in the light most favorable to Mrs. Hondroulis, we conclude that there are genuine issues as to material fact and that the mover physician is not entitled to judgment as a matter of law. Assuming, as we must for purposes of the motion, that the doctor failed to inform Mrs. Hondroulis of the material risk of her loss of bladder control and incontinence that was associated with the surgery, that Mrs. Hondroulis was not aware of this particular hazard, that the materialization of the risk caused her loss of bladder control and incontinence, and that a reasonable patient in the plaintiff's position would have withheld consent to the surgery had the material risk been disclosed, the doctor would not be entitled to judgment because Mrs. Hondoulis should be allowed to recover as a matter of law.

An ordinary lay person would not gather from a warning that surgery involves a risk of "loss of function of body organs" that he or she is asked to assent to encounter the specific, material risk of being rendered permanently incontinent through loss of bladder control. The summary judgment materials do not show that Mrs. Hondroulis had any independent knowledge of this specific risk that was superior to that of an ordinary lay person. A bland statement as to a risk of "loss of function of body organs", particularly when not accompanied by any estimate of its frequency, does not amount to an understandable communication of any specific real risk. The average lay person is vaguely aware that any surgical operation involving anesthesia involves a slight chance of death and perhaps loss of body organ function that is no greater than the risk he or she assumes daily in driving an automobile, crossing a busy street or other activities causing non-material risks. Consequently, a notice of risk of "loss of function of body organs", without any description of the frequency of occurrence, the specific organ threatened or the cause of the damage involved, tends to de-emphasize the severity and frequency of the hazard. *See Petty v. United States, supra.* By requiring the doctor to set forth the material risks "in general terms" the statute demands that he describe the main elements of each risk rather than limited details, but it does not permit him to "generalize" in the sense of making vague or indefinite statements that do not understandably communicate the specific material risks to the patient. Any other interpretation of the statute would frustrate rather than promote intelligent self determination by patients and thereby undermine the informed consent doctrine and the patient's right to privacy.

* * * * *

MATTHIES
v.
MASTROMONACO, D.O
160 N.J. 26, 733 A.2d 456 (1999)

POLLOCK, J.

This appeal presents the question whether the doctrine of informed consent requires a physician to obtain the patient's consent before implementing a nonsurgical course of treatment. It questions also whether a physician, in addition to discussing with the patient treatment alternatives that the physician recommends, should discuss medically reasonable alternative courses of treatment that the physician does not recommend. We hold that to obtain a patient's informed consent to one of several alternative courses of treatment, the physician should explain medically reasonable invasive and noninvasive alternatives, including the risks and likely outcomes of those alternatives, even when the chosen course is noninvasive.

The Law Division concluded that plaintiff, Jean Matthies, could not assert a cause of action for breach of the duty of informed consent against defendant, Dr. Edward D. Mastromonaco. According to the court, a physician must secure a patient's informed consent only to invasive procedures, not to those that are noninvasive. Consequently, the court prevented Matthies from presenting evidence that Dr. Mastromonaco had not obtained her informed consent to use bed-rest treatment, which is noninvasive, instead of surgery. On the issue whether Dr. Mastromonaco had committed malpractice by failing to perform surgery on Matthies, the jury returned a verdict of no cause for action. The Appellate Division reversed, holding that the doctrine of informed consent applies even when the course of treatment implemented by the physician is noninvasive. 310 *N.J.Super.* 572, 709 *A.*2d 238 (App.Div.1998) We granted Dr. Mastromonaco's petition for certification, 156 *N.J.* 406, 719 *A.*2d 638 (1998), and now affirm.

I

In 1990, Matthies was eighty-one years old and living alone in the Bella Vista Apartments, a twenty-three-story senior citizen residence in Union City. On August 26, 1990, she fell in her apartment and fractured her right hip. For two days, she remained undiscovered. When found, she was suffering the consequences of a lack of prompt medical attention, including dehydration, distended bowels, and confusion. An emergency service transported her to Christ Hospital in Jersey City. She was treated in the emergency room and admitted to the intensive care unit.

One day after Matthies's admission, her initial treating physician called Dr. Mastromonaco, an osteopath and board-certified orthopedic surgeon, as a consultant. Dr. Mastromonaco reviewed Matthies's medical history, condition, and x-rays. He decided against pinning her hip, a procedure that would have involved the insertion of four steel screws, each approximately one- quarter inch thick and four inches long.

Dr. Mastromonaco reached that decision for several reasons. First, Matthies was elderly, frail, and in a weakened condition. Surgery involving the installation of screws would be risky. Second, Matthies suffered from osteoporosis, which led Dr. Mastromonaco to conclude that her bones were too porous to hold the screws. He anticipated that the screws probably would loosen, causing severe pain and necessitating a partial or total hip replacement. Third, forty years earlier, Matthies had suffered a stroke from a mismatched blood transfusion during surgery. The stroke had left her partially paralyzed on her right side. Consequently she had worn a brace and essentially used her right leg as a post while propelling herself forward with her left leg. After considering these factors, Dr. Mastromonaco decided that with bed rest, a course of treatment that he recognized as "controversial," Matthies's fracture could heal sufficiently to restore her right leg to its limited function. He prescribed a "bed-rest treatment," which consisted of complete restriction to bed for several days, followed by increasingly extended periods spent sitting in a chair and walking about the room.

Before her fall, Matthies had maintained an independent lifestyle. She had done her own grocery shopping, cooking, housework, and laundry. Her dentist of many years, Dr. Arthur Massarsky, testified that he often had observed Matthies climbing unassisted the two flights of stairs to his office. Matthies is now confined to a nursing home.

Matthies's expert, Dr. Hervey Sicherman, a board-certified orthopedic surgeon, testified that under the circumstances, bed rest was an inappropriate treatment. He maintained that bed rest alone is not advisable for a hip fracture unless the patient does not expect to regain the ability to walk. Essentially, he rejected bed rest except when the patient is terminally ill or in a vegetative state. Dr. Sicherman explained that unless accompanied by traction, the danger of treating a hip fracture with bed rest is that the fracture could dislocate. In fact, shortly after Matthies began her bed-rest treatment, the head of her right femur displaced. Her right leg shortened, and she has never regained the ability to walk. According to Dr. Sicherman, the weakness and porosity of Matthies's bones increased the likelihood of this bad outcome. Even defendant's expert, Dr. Ira Rochelle, another board-certified orthopedic surgeon, admitted that pinning Matthies's hip would have decreased the risk of displacement. He nonetheless agreed with Dr. Mastromonaco that Matthies's bones were probably too brittle to withstand insertion of the pins.

Dr. Mastromonaco's goal in conservatively treating Matthies was to help her "get through this with the least complication as possible and to maintain a lifestyle conducive to her disability." He believed that rather than continue living on her own, Matthies should live in a long-term care facility. He explained, "I'm not going to give her that leg she wanted. She wanted to live alone, but she couldn't live alone.... I wanted her to be at peace with herself in the confines of professional care, somebody to care for her. She could not live alone."

Matthies asserts that she would not have consented to bed rest if Dr. Mastromonaco had told her of the probable effect of the treatment on the quality of her life. She claims that Dr. Mastromonaco knew that without surgery, she never would walk again. He did not provide her, however, with the opportunity to choose between bed rest and the riskier, but potentially more successful, alternative of surgery. Dr. Mastromonaco maintained that bed rest did not foreclose surgery at a later date.

* * * * *

Matthies sued Dr. Mastromonaco on two theories. First, she claimed that he had deviated from standard medical care by failing to pin her hip at the time of her injury. Second, she asserted that he negligently had failed to obtain her informed consent to bed rest as a treatment alternative. Specifically, Matthies contended that Mastromonaco had failed to disclose the alternative of surgery.

Dr. Mastromonaco's counsel argued that informed consent was irrelevant in a case in which the treatment administered was noninvasive.

* * * * *

II

Choosing among medically reasonable treatment alternatives is a shared responsibility of physicians and patients. To discharge their responsibilities, patients should provide their physicians with the information necessary for them to make diagnoses and determine courses of treatment. Physicians, in turn, have a duty to evaluate the relevant information and disclose all courses of treatment that are medically reasonable under the circumstances. Generally, a physician will recommend a course of treatment. As a practical matter, a patient often decides to adopt the physician's recommendation. Still, the ultimate decision is for the patient.

We reject defendant's contention that informed consent applies only to invasive procedures. Historically, the failure to obtain a patient's informed consent to an invasive procedure, such as surgery, was treated as a battery. The physician's need to obtain the consent of the patient to surgery derived from the patient's right to reject a nonconsensual touching. Eventually, courts recognized that the need for the patient's consent is better understood as deriving from the right of self-determination. *Canesi v. Wilson,* 158 *N.J.* 490, 503-04, 730 *A.*2d 805 (1999); *Schloendorff v. Society of N.Y. Hosp.,* 211 *N.Y.* 125, 105 *N.E.* 92, 93 (1914). A shrinking minority of jurisdictions persist in limiting informed consent actions to invasive procedures. In those jurisdictions, battery survives as the appropriate cause of action. *See, e.g., Karlsons v. Guerinot,* 57 *A.D.*2d 73, 394 *N.Y.S.*2d 933, 939 (1977) (limiting application of informed consent to "those situations where the harm suffered arose from some affirmative violation of the patient's physical integrity such as surgical procedures, injections or invasive diagnostic tests"); *Morgan v. MacPhail,* 550 Pa. 202, 704 *A.*2d 617, 619 (1997) (stating that informed consent in Pennsylvania "has not been required in cases involving non-surgical procedures"). Most jurisdictions view the failure to obtain a patient's informed consent as an act of negligence or malpractice, not battery. *See, e.g.,* Joan P. Dailey, *The Two Schools of Thought and Informed Consent Doctrines in Pennsylvania: A Model For Integration,* 98 *Dick. L.Rev.* 713, 727-28 & n. 101 (stating battery basis recognized in only minority of jurisdictions, for example, Georgia, Pennsylvania, and Virginia); Paula Walter, *The Doctrine of Informed Consent: To Inform or Not To Inform?,* 71 *St. John's L.Rev.* 543, 543, 558-59 (1997) (noting that two 1980 cases moved informed consent doctrine of New York, one of few remaining battery jurisdictions, toward theory of negligence).

The rationale for basing an informed consent action on negligence rather than battery principles is that the physician's failure is better viewed as a breach of professional responsibility than as a nonconsensual touching. *Baird v. American Med. Optics,* 155 *N.J.* 54, 70-71, 713 A.2d 1019 (1998); *Largey v. Rothman,* 110 *N.J.* 204, 207-08, 540 *A.*2d 504 (1988). As we have stated, "Informed consent is a negligence concept predicated on the duty of a physician to disclose to a patient information that will enable him to 'evaluate knowledgeably the options available and the risks attendant upon each' before subjecting that patient to a course of treatment." *Perna v. Pirozzi,* 92 *N.J.* 446, 459, 457 A.2d 431 (1983); *see also Kaplan v. Haines,* 96 N.J.Super. 242, 257, 232 *A.*2d 840 (App.Div.1967), *aff'd o.b.,* 51 *N.J.* 404, 241 *A.*2d 235 (1968) (sanctioning negligence-view, lack-of-informed-consent tort twenty years prior to *Largey*). Analysis based on the principle of battery is generally restricted to cases in which a physician has not obtained any consent or has exceeded the scope of consent. 3 David W. Louisell & Harold Williams, *Medical Malpractice* §§ 22.02, 22.03 (1999). The essential difference in analyzing informed consent claims under negligence, rather than battery principles, is that the analysis focuses not on an unauthorized touching or invasion of the patient's body, but on the physician's deviation from a standard of care.

In informed consent analysis, the decisive factor is not whether a treatment alternative is invasive or noninvasive, but whether the physician adequately presents the material facts so that the patient can make an informed decision. That conclusion does not imply that a physician must explain in detail all treatment options in every case. For example, a physician need not recite all the risks and benefits of each potential appropriate antibiotic when writing a prescription for treatment of an upper respiratory infection. Conversely, a physician could be obligated, depending on the circumstances, to discuss a variety of treatment alternatives, such as chemotherapy, radiation, or surgery, with a patient diagnosed with cancer. Distinguishing the two situations are the limitations of the reasonable patient standard, which need not unduly burden the physician-patient relationship. The standard obligates the physician to disclose only that information material to a reasonable patient's informed decision. *Largey, supra,* 110 *N.J.* at 211-12; , 540 A.2d 504 3 Louisell & Williams, *supra,* § 22.03(2). Physicians thus remain obligated to inform patients of medically reasonable treatment alternatives and their attendant probable risks and outcomes. Otherwise, the patient, in selecting one alternative rather than another, cannot make a decision that is informed.

To the extent that *Parris v. Sands,* 21 Cal.App. 4th 187, 25 *Cal.Rptr.*2d 800 (Ct.App. 1993), on which Dr. Mastromonaco relies, would not require a physician to inform a patient of alternative treatments, we disagree with that decision. *Parris,* however, is distinguishable. It involved not the failure of a physician to inform a patient of a nonrecommended treatment alternative, but the alleged negligence of the physician in diagnosing the patient's pneumonia as viral rather than bacterial. *See* 3 Louisell & Williams, *supra,* § 22.04(3)(c) & n. 18. The extent to which the reasonable patient standard obligates physicians to disclose the details of alternative diagnoses, as distinguished from treatment alternatives, is not before us. In sum, physicians do not adequately discharge their responsibility by disclosing only treatment alternatives that they recommend.

To assure that the patient's consent is informed, the physician should describe, among other things, the material risks inherent in a procedure or course of treatment. *Largey, supra,* 110 *N.J.* at 210-13, 540 *A.*2d 504. The test for measuring the materiality of a risk is whether a reasonable patient in the patient's position would have considered the risk material. *Id.* at 211- 12, 540 A.2d 504. Although the test of materiality is objective, a "patient obviously has no complaint if he would have submitted to the therapy notwithstanding awareness that the risk was one of its perils." *Canterbury v. Spence,* 464 F.2d 772, 790 (D.C.Cir.), *cert. denied,* 409 *U.S.* 1064, 93 *S.Ct.* 560, 34 *L.Ed.*2d 518 (1972) (citation omitted). As the court stated in *Canterbury:*

> We think a technique which ties the factual conclusion on causation simply to the assessment of the patient's credibility is unsatisfactory.... [W]hen causality is explored at a postinjury trial with a professedly uninformed patient, the question whether he actually would have turned the treatment down if he had known the risks is purely hypothetical.... And the answer which the patient supplies hardly represents more than a guess, perhaps tinged by the circumstance that the uncommunicated hazard has in fact materialized. In our view, this method of dealing with the issue on causation comes in second- best.... Better it is, we believe, to resolve the causality issue on an objective basis: in terms of what a prudent person in the patient's position would have decided if suitably informed of all perils bearing significance. If adequate disclosure could reasonably be expected to have caused that person to decline the treatment because of the revelation of the kind of risk or danger that resulted in harm, causation is shown, but otherwise not. The patient's testimony is relevant on that score of course but it would not threaten to dominate the findings. And since that testimony would probably be appraised congruently with the factfinder's belief in its reasonableness, the case for a wholly objective standard for passing on causation is strengthened.

[*Id.* at 790-91....]

For consent to be informed, the patient must know not only of alternatives that the physician recommends, but of medically reasonable alternatives that the physician does not recommend. Otherwise, the physician, by not discussing these alternatives, effectively makes the choice for the patient. Accordingly, the physician should discuss the medically reasonable courses of treatment, including nontreatment....

Because the patient has a right to be fully informed about medically reasonable courses of treatment, we are unpersuaded that a cause of action predicated on the physician's breach of a standard of care adequately protects the patient's right to be informed of treatment alternatives. A physician may select a method of treatment that is medically reasonable, but not the one that the patient would have selected if informed of alternative methods. Like the deviation from a standard of care, the physician's failure to obtain informed consent is a form of medical negligence. *See Baird, supra,* 155 *N.J.* at 70, 713 *A.*2d 1019; *Teilhaber v. Greene,* 320 N.J.Super. 453, 457, 727 A.2d 518 (App.Div. 1999). Recognition of a separate duty emphasizes the physician's obligation to inform, as well as treat, the patient. The physician's selection of one of several medically reasonable alternatives may not violate a standard of care, but it may represent a choice that the patient would not make. Physicians may neither impose their values on their patients nor substitute their level of risk aversion for that of their patients. One patient may prefer to undergo a potentially risky procedure, such as surgery, to enjoy a better quality of life. Another patient may choose a more conservative course of treatment to secure reduced risk at the cost of a diminished lifestyle. The choice is not for the physician, but the patient in consultation with the physician. By not telling the patient of all medically reasonable alternatives, the physician breaches the patient's right to make an informed choice.

The physician's duty to inform the patient of alternatives is especially important when the alternatives are mutually exclusive. If, as a practical matter, the choice of one alternative precludes the choice of others, or even if it increases appreciably the risks attendant on the other alternatives, the patient's need for relevant information is critical. That need intensifies when the choice turns not so much on purely medical considerations as on the choice of one lifestyle or set of values over another.

* * * * *

The trial court, believing informed consent applied to invasive procedures only, precluded Matthies's attorney from cross-examining Dr. Mastromonaco on that issue. Several times during the trial, Matthies's counsel attempted to introduce testimony to refute Dr. Mastromonaco's assertion that he had discussed surgery as an option. Each time, the trial court barred the testimony. At the conclusion of the case, therefore, Dr. Mastromonaco had presented his side of the story on the issue of informed consent, but Matthies had been prevented from presenting her side. The trial court, moreover, refused to charge the jury on the issue of informed consent. Hence, the only issue submitted to the jury was whether Dr. Mastromonaco had breached a standard of care in selecting bed rest as a treatment alternative. Consequently, the jury did not have the opportunity to consider the issue that forms the basis of this appeal, whether Dr. Mastromonaco had obtained Matthies's informed consent to the treatment he recommended.

The issue of informed consent often intertwines with that of medical malpractice. *Baird, supra,* 155 *N.J.* at 70-71, 713 *A.*2d 1019. Because of the interrelationship between the malpractice and informed consent issues in the present case, the jury should consider both issues at the retrial.

The judgment of the Appellate Division is **AFFIRMED**.

3.   The Qualified Health Care Provider

In response to a perceived "medical malpractice crisis," some states have adopted statutes designed to decrease the financial impact upon the medical profession from a proliferation of medical malpractice suits. The statutes generally (1) place a "cap" upon the damages which may be recovered from a health care provider and (2) require that such claims first be "screened" through a medical review panel composed of health care providers and attorneys. In Louisiana, the "screening" process does not prevent the alleged victim from bringing suit, but he or she may not do so until the completion of the process. To benefit from these protections, the health care provider must "qualify" by obtaining liability insurance (or qualifying as a self-insured). The required liability insurance, and each health care provider's maximum liability, is $100,000. Additional damages, up to a $500,000 "cap," are paid by the Patient's Compensation Fund, a government agency funded primarily by the health care providers and their insurers. The Louisiana statutes and key jurisprudence governing this state's qualified health care provider procedures are discussed in this section.

La. R.S. 40:1231.1. Definitions and general applications

A.   As used in this Part:

* * * *

(9)   "Health care" means any act or treatment performed or furnished, or which should have been performed or furnished, by any health care provider for, to, or on behalf of a patient during

the patient's medical care, treatment, or confinement, or during or relating to or in connection with the procurement of human blood or blood components.

* * * * *

(10) "Health care provider" means a person, partnership, limited liability partnership, limited liability company, corporation, facility, or institution licensed or certified by this state to provide health care or professional services as a physician, hospital, nursing home, community blood center, tissue bank, dentist, registered or licensed practical nurse or certified nurse assistant, offshore health service provider, ambulance service under circumstances in which the provisions of R.S. 40:1299.39 are not applicable, certified registered nurse anesthetist, nurse midwife, licensed midwife, nurse practitioner, clinical nurse specialist, pharmacist, optometrist, podiatrist, chiropractor, physical therapist, occupational therapist, psychologist, social worker, licensed professional counselor, licensed perfusionist, licensed respiratory therapist, licensed radiologic technologist, licensed clinical laboratory scientist, or any nonprofit facility considered tax-exempt ... under Section 501(c)(3), Internal Revenue Code, pursuant to 26 U.S.C. 501(c)(3), for the diagnosis and treatment of cancer or cancer-related diseases, whether or not such a facility is required to be licensed by this state, or any professional corporation a health care provider is authorized to form under the provisions of Title 12 of the Louisiana Revised Statutes of 1950, or any partnership, limited liability partnership, limited liability company, management company, or corporation whose business is conducted principally by health care providers, or an officer, employee, partner, member, shareholder, or agent thereof acting in the course and scope of his employment.

* * * * *

13) "Malpractice" means any unintentional tort or any breach of contract based on health care or professional services rendered, or which should have been rendered, by a health care provider, to a patient, including failure to render services timely and the handling of a patient, including loading and unloading of a patient, and also includes all legal responsibility of a health care provider arising from acts or omissions during the procurement of blood or blood components, in the training or supervision of health care providers, or from defects in blood, tissue, transplants, drugs, and medicines, or from defects in or failures of prosthetic devices implanted in or used on or in the person of a patient.

* * * * *

(15) "Patient" means a natural person, including a donor of human blood or blood components and a nursing home resident who receives or should have received health care from a licensed health care provider, under contract, expressed or implied.

(16) "Physician" means a person with an unlimited license to practice medicine in this state.

La. R.S. 40:1231.2. Limitation of recovery

A. To be qualified under the provisions of this Part, a health care provider shall:

(1) Cause to be filed with the board proof of financial responsibility as provided by Subsection E of this Section.

(2) Pay the surcharge assessed by this Part on all health care providers according to R.S. 40:1299.44.

(3) For self-insured health care providers, initial qualification shall be effective upon acceptance of proof of financial responsibility by and payment of the surcharge to the board. Initial qualification shall be effective for all other health care providers at the time the malpractice insurer accepts payment of the surcharge.

B. (1) The total amount recoverable for all malpractice claims for injuries to or death of a patient, exclusive of future medical care and related benefits as provided in R.S. 40:1231.3, shall not exceed five hundred thousand dollars plus interest and cost.

(2) A health care provider qualified under this Part is not liable for an amount in excess of one hundred thousand dollars plus interest thereon accruing after April 1, 1991, and costs specifically provided for by this Paragraph for all malpractice claims because of injuries to or death of any one patient....

(3) (a) Any amount due from a judgment or settlement or from a final award in an arbitration proceeding which is in excess of the total liability of all liable health care providers, as provided in Paragraph (2) of this Subsection, shall be paid from the patient's compensation fund pursuant to the provisions of R.S. 40:1299.44(C).

(b) The total amounts paid in accordance with Paragraphs (2) and (3) of this Subsection shall not exceed the limitation as provided in Paragraph (1) of this Subsection.

* * * * *

E. (1) Financial responsibility of a health care provider under this Section may be established only by filing with the board proof that the health care provider is insured by a policy of malpractice liability insurance in the amount of at least one hundred thousand dollars per claim with qualification under this Section taking effect and following the same form as the policy of malpractice liability insurance of the health care provider, or in the event the health care provider is self-insured, proof of financial responsibility by depositing with the board one hundred twenty-five thousand dollars in money or represented by irrevocable letters of credit, federally insured certificates of deposit, bonds, securities, cash values of insurance, or any other security approved by the board. In the event any portion of said amount is seized pursuant to the judicial process, the self-insured health care provider shall have five days to deposit with the board the amounts so seized. The health care provider's failure to timely post said amounts with the board shall terminate his enrollment in the Patient's Compensation Fund.

(2) For the purposes of this Subsection, any group of self-insured health care providers organized to and actually practicing together or otherwise related by ownership, whether as a partnership, professional corporation or otherwise, shall be deemed a single health care provider and shall not be required to post more than one deposit. In the event any portion of the deposit of such a group is seized pursuant to judicial process, such group shall have five days to deposit with the board the amounts so seized. The group's failure to timely post said amounts with the board will terminate its enrollment and the enrollment of its members in the Patient's Compensation Fund.

La. R.S. 40:1231.3. Future medical care and related benefits

A. (1) In all malpractice claims filed with the board which proceed to trial, the jury shall be given a special interrogatory asking if the patient is in need of future medical care and related benefits that will be incurred after the date of the response to the special interrogatory, and the amount thereof.

(2) In actions upon malpractice claims tried by the court, the court's finding shall include a recitation that the patient is or is not in need of future medical care and related benefits that will be incurred after the date of the court's finding and the amount thereof.

(3) If the total amount is for the maximum amount recoverable, exclusive of the value of future medical care and related benefits that will be incurred after the date of the response to the special interrogatory by the jury or the court's finding, the cost of all future medical care and related benefits that will be incurred after the date of the response to the special interrogatory by the jury or the court's finding shall be paid in accordance with R.S. 40:1299.43(C).

(4)   If the total amount is for the maximum amount recoverable, including the value of the future medical care and related benefits, the amount of future medical care and related benefits that will be incurred after the date of the response to the special interrogatory by the jury or the court's finding shall be deducted from the total amount and shall be paid from the patient's compensation fund as incurred and presented for payment. The remaining portion of the judgment, including the amount of future medical care and related benefits incurred up to the date of the response to the special interrogatory by the jury or the court's finding shall be paid in accordance with R.S. 40:1231.4(A)(7) and R.S. 40:1231.4(B)(2)(a), (b), and (c).

(5)   In all cases where judgment is rendered for a total amount less than the maximum amount recoverable, including any amount awarded on future medical care and related benefits that will be incurred after the date of the response to the special interrogatory by the jury or the court's finding, payment shall be in accordance with R.S. 40:1231.4(A)(7) and R.S. 40:1231.4(B)(2)(a), (b), and (c).

(6)   The provisions of this Subsection shall be applicable to all malpractice claims.

B.   (1)   "Future medical care and related benefits" for the purpose of this Section means all of the following:

(a)   All reasonable medical, surgical, hospitalization, physical rehabilitation, and custodial services and includes drugs, prosthetic devices, and other similar materials reasonably necessary in the provision of such services, incurred after the date of the injury up to the date of the settlement, judgment, or arbitration award.

(b)   All reasonable medical, surgical, hospitalization, physical rehabilitation, and custodial services and includes drugs, prosthetic devices, and other similar materials reasonably necessary in the provisions of such services, after the date of the injury that will be incurred after the date of the settlement, judgment, or arbitration award.

(2)   "Future medical care and benefits" as used in this Section shall not be construed to mean non-essential specialty items or devices of convenience.

C.   Once a judgment is entered in favor of a patient who is found to be in need of future medical care and related benefits that will be incurred after the date of the response to the special interrogatory by the jury or the court's finding or a settlement is reached between a patient and the patient's compensation fund in which the provision of medical care and related benefits that will be incurred after the date of settlement is agreed upon and continuing as long as medical or surgical attention is reasonably necessary, the patient may make a claim to the patient's compensation fund through the board for all future medical care and related benefits directly or indirectly made necessary by the health care provider's malpractice unless the patient refuses to allow them to be furnished.

D.   Payments for medical care and related benefits shall be paid by the patient's compensation fund without regard to the five hundred thousand dollar limitation imposed in R.S. 40:1299.42.

E.   (1)   The district court from which final judgment issues shall have continuing jurisdiction in cases where medical care and related benefits are determined to be needed by the patient.

(2)   The court shall award reasonable attorney fees to the claimant's attorney if the court finds that the patient's compensation fund unreasonably fails to pay for medical care within thirty days after submission of a claim for payment of such benefits.

F.   Nothing in this Section shall be construed to prevent a patient and a health care provider and/or the patient's compensation fund from entering into a court-approved settlement agreement whereby medical care and related benefits shall be provided for a limited period of time only or to a limited degree.

G.   The patient's compensation fund shall be entitled to have a physical examination of the patient by a physician of the patient's compensation fund's choice from time to time for the purpose of determining the patient's continued need of future medical care and related benefits, ...

H.   If a patient fails or refuses to submit to examination in accordance with a notice and if the requirements of Subsection G of this Section have been satisfied, then the patient shall not be entitled to attorney fees in any action to enforce rights pursuant to Subsection E of this Section.

* * * * *

La. R.S. 40:1231.4. Patient's compensation fund

A.   (1)   a) All funds collected pursuant to the provisions hereof shall be considered self-generated revenues, promptly deposited by the Patient's Compensation Fund Oversight Board into a fund designated as the "Patient's Compensation Fund". The Patient's Compensation Fund Oversight Board is established and authorized pursuant to Subsection D of this Section. Neither the fund nor the board shall be a budget unit of the state. The assets of the fund shall not be state property, subject to appropriation by the legislature, or required to be deposited in the state treasury. The state recognizes and acknowledges that the fund and any income from it are not public monies, but rather are private monies which shall be held in trust as a private custodial fund by the board for the use, benefit, and protection of medical malpractice claimants and the fund's private health care provider members, and all of such funds and income earned from investing the private monies comprising the corpus of this fund shall be subject to use and disposition only as provided by this Section.

* * * * *

C.   If the insurer of a health care provider or a self-insured health care provider has agreed to settle its liability on a claim against its insured and claimant is demanding an amount in excess thereof from the patient's compensation fund for a complete and final release, then the following procedure must be followed:

(1)   A petition shall be filed by the claimant with the court in which the action is pending against the health care provider, if none is pending in the parish where plaintiff or defendant is domiciled seeking (a) approval of an agreed settlement, if any, and/or (b) demanding payment of damages from the patient's compensation fund.

(2)   A copy of the petition shall be served on the board, the health care provider and his insurer, at least ten days before filing and shall contain sufficient information to inform the other parties about the nature of the claim and the additional amount demanded.

(3)   The board and the insurer of the health care provider or the self-insured health care provider as the case may be, may agree to a settlement with the claimant from the patient's compensation fund, or the board and the insurer of the health care provider or the self-insured health care provider as the case may be, may file written objections to the payment of the amount demanded. The agreement or objections to the payment demanded shall be filed within twenty days after the petition is filed.

(4)   As soon as practicable after the petition is filed in the court the judge shall fix the date on which the petition seeking approval of the agreed settlement and/or demanding payment of damages from the fund shall be heard, and shall notify the claimant, the insurer of the health care provider or the self-insured health care provider as the case may be, and the board thereof as provided by   law.

(5)   (a)   At the hearing the board, the claimant, and the insurer of the health care provider or the self-insured health care provider, as the case may be, may introduce relevant evidence to enable the court to determine whether or not the petition should be approved if it

is submitted on agreement without objections. If the board, the insurer of the health care provider or the self-insured health care provider, as the case may be, and the claimant cannot agree on the amount, if any, to be paid out of the patient's compensation fund, then the trier of fact shall determine at a subsequent trial which shall take place only after the board shall have been given an adequate opportunity to conduct discovery, identify and retain expert witnesses, and prepare a defense, the amount of claimant's damages, if any, in excess of the amount already paid by the insurer of the health care provider or self-insured health care provider. The trier of fact shall determine the amount for which the fund is liable and render a finding and judgment accordingly. The board shall have a right to request trial by jury whether or not a jury trial has been requested by the claimant or by any health care provider.

(b)   The board shall not be entitled to file a suit or otherwise assert a claim against any qualified health care provider as defined in R.S. 40:1299.41(A) on the basis that the qualified health care provider failed to comply with the appropriate standard of care in treating or failing to treat any patient.

(c)   The board may apply the provisions of Civil Code Article 2323 or 2324, or both, to assert a credit or offset for the allocated percentage of negligence or fault of a qualified health care provider provided at least one of the following conditions is met:

(i) A payment has been made to the claimant by, in the name of, or on behalf of the qualified health care provider whose percentage of fault the board seeks to allocate.

(ii) A payment has been made to the claimant by, in the name of, or on behalf of another qualified health care provider in order to obtain a dismissal or release of liability of the qualified health care provider whose percentage of fault the board seeks to allocate, provided that there shall be no separate credit or offset for the fault of an employer or other vicariously liable entity who was not independently negligent or otherwise at fault and who makes a payment in order to obtain a dismissal or release of liability of a single qualified health care provider for whom the payor is vicariously liable.

(iii) All or a portion of a payment made by another qualified health care provider, by the insurer of another qualified health care provider, or by the employer of another qualified health care provider has been attributed to or allocated to the qualified health care provider whose percentage of fault the board seeks to allocate, provided that there shall be no separate credit or offset for the fault of an employer or other vicariously liable entity who was not independently negligent or otherwise at fault and who makes a payment in order to obtain a dismissal or release of liability of a single qualified health care provider for whom the payor is vicariously liable.

(iv) A medical review panel has determined that the qualified health care provider whose percentage of fault the board seeks to allocate failed to comply with the appropriate standard of care and that the failure was a cause of the damage or injury suffered by the patient, or a medical review panel has determined that there is a material issue of fact, not requiring expert opinion, bearing on liability of the qualified health care provider whose percentage of fault the board seeks to allocate for consideration by the trier of fact.

(v) The qualified health care provider does not object within thirty days after notice of the board's intention to allocate the health care provider's percentage of fault is delivered via certified mail to the plaintiff, the qualified health care provider, and the qualified health care provider's professional liability insurer or to their attorneys.

(vi) The court determines, after a hearing in which the qualified health care provider whose percentage of fault the board seeks to allocate shall be given an opportunity to appear and participate, that there has been collusion or other improper conduct between the defendant health care providers to the detriment of the interests of the fund.

(d)	Except where the sum of one hundred thousand dollars has been paid by, in the name of, or on behalf of the qualified health care provider whose percentage of fault the board seeks to allocate, in any case in which the board is entitled pursuant to the provisions of Civil Code Article 2323 or 2324, or both, to assert a credit or offset for the allocated percentage of negligence or fault of a qualified health care provider, the board shall have the burden of proving the negligence or fault of the qualified health care provider whose percentage of fault the board seeks to allocate.

(e)	In approving a settlement or determining the amount, if any, to be paid from the patient's compensation fund, the trier of fact shall consider the liability of the health care provider as admitted and established where the insurer has paid its policy limits of one hundred thousand dollars, or where the self-insured health care provider has paid one hundred thousand dollars.

(f)	In each instance in which a claimant seeks to recover any sum from the board, each qualified health care provider or insurer or employer of a qualified health care provider who has made or has agreed to make any payment, including any reimbursement of court costs, medical expenses, or other expenses, to the claimant, the claimant's attorney, or any other person or entity shall be required, not later than ten days after the filing of the petition for approval of the settlement, to file and serve upon the board an answer to the petition for approval of the settlement which sets forth a complete explanation of each such payment, to include the identity of each payee, the identity of each entity by or on whose behalf each payment has been or is to be made, each amount paid or to be paid directly or indirectly by, on behalf of, or which has been or is to be attributed or allocated to any qualified health care provider, the purpose of each such payment, and the precise nature of any collateral agreement which has been made or is to be made in connection with the proposed settlement.

(6)	Any settlement approved by the court shall not be appealed. Any judgment of the court fixing damages recoverable in any such contested proceeding shall be appealable pursuant to the rules governing appeals in any other civil court case tried by the court.

(7)	For the benefit of both the insured and the patient's compensation fund, the insurer of the health provider shall exercise good faith and reasonable care both in evaluating the plaintiff's claim and in considering and acting upon settlement thereof. A self-insured health care provider shall, for the benefit of the patient's compensation fund, also exercise good faith and reasonable care both in evaluating the plaintiff's claim and in considering and acting upon settlement thereof.

(8)	The parties may agree that any amounts due from the patient's compensation fund pursuant to R.S. 40:1231.4(B) be paid by annuity contract purchased by the patient's compensation fund for and on behalf of the claimant.

(9)	Notwithstanding any other provision of this Part, any self-insured health care provider who has agreed to settle its liability on a claim and has been released by the claimant for such claim or any other claim arising from the same cause of action shall be removed as a party to the petition, and his name shall be removed from any judgment that is rendered in the proceeding. Such release shall be filed with the clerk of court in the parish in which the petition is filed upon the filing of a properly executed, sworn release and settlement of claim.

* * * * *

Metcalf v. Christus Health Southwestern La., 33 So. 3d 939 (La.App. 3 Cir. 2010). La. R.S. 9:4753 requires that the lien of a health care provider against settlement of insurance proceeds or payment of a judgment requires that the lien be sent by certified mail and that it include the location of the health care provider. If it does not satisfy these requirements, the lien is invalid.

La. R.S. 40:1231.6. Malpractice coverage

A. (1) Only while malpractice liability insurance remains in force, or in the case of a self-insured health care provider, only while the security required by regulations of the insurance commissioner remains undiminished, are the health care provider and his insurer liable to a patient, or his representative, for malpractice to the extent and in the manner specified in this Part.

* * * * *

La. R.S. 40:1231.8. Medical review panel

A. (1) (a) All malpractice claims against health care providers covered by this Part, other than claims validly agreed for submission to a lawfully binding arbitration procedure, shall be reviewed by a medical review panel established as hereinafter provided for in this Section. The filing of a request for review by a medical review panel as provided for in this Section shall not be reportable by any health care provider, the Louisiana Patient's Compensation Fund, or any other entity to the Louisiana State Board of Medical Examiners, to any licensing authority, committee, or board of any other state, or to any credentialing or similar agency, committee, or board of any clinic, hospital, health insurer, or managed care company.

(b) A request for review of a malpractice claim or malpractice complaint shall contain, at a minimum, all of the following:

(i) A request for the formation of a medical review panel.

(ii) The name of the patient.

(iii) The names of the claimants.

(iv) The names of defendant health care providers.

(v) The dates of the alleged malpractice.

(vi) A brief description of the alleged malpractice as to each named defendant health care provider.

(vii) A brief description of alleged injuries.

(c) A claimant shall have forty-five days from the mailing date of the confirmation of receipt of the request for review in accordance with Subparagraph (3)(a) of this Subsection to pay to the board a filing fee in the amount of one hundred dollars per named defendant qualified under this Part.

(d) Such filing fee may be waived only upon receipt of one of the following:

(i) An affidavit of a physician holding a valid and unrestricted license to practice his specialty in the state of his residence certifying that adequate medical records have been obtained and reviewed and that the allegations of malpractice against each defendant health care provider named in the claim constitute a claim of a breach of the applicable standard of care as to each named defendant health care provider.

(ii) An in forma pauperis ruling issued in accordance with Louisiana Code of Civil Procedure Article 5181 et seq. by a district court in a venue in which the malpractice claim could properly be brought upon the conclusion of the medical review panel process.

(e)   Failure to comply with the provisions of Subparagraph (c) or (d) of this Paragraph within the specified forty-five day time frame in Subparagraph (c) of this Paragraph shall render the request for review of a malpractice claim invalid and without effect. Such an invalid request for review of a malpractice claim shall not suspend time within which suit must be instituted in Subparagraph (2)(a) of this Subsection.

(f)   All funds generated by such filing fees shall be private monies and shall be applied to the costs of the Patient's Compensation Fund Oversight Board incurred in the administration of claims.

(g)   The filing fee of one hundred dollars per named defendant qualified under this Part shall be applicable in the event that a claimant identifies additional qualified health care providers as defendants. The filing fee applicable to each identified qualified health care provider shall be due forty-five days from the mailing date of the confirmation of receipt of the request for review for the additional named defendants in accordance with R.S. 40:1231.8(A)(3)(a).

(2)   (a)   The filing of the request for a review of a claim shall suspend the time within which suit must be instituted, in accordance with this Part, until ninety days following notification, by certified mail, as provided in Subsection J of this Section, to the claimant or his attorney of the issuance of the opinion by the medical review panel, in the case of those health care providers covered by this Part, or in the case of a health care provider against whom a claim has been filed under the provisions of this Part, but who has not qualified under this Part, until ninety days following notification by certified mail to the claimant or his attorney by the board that the health care provider is not covered by this Part. The filing of a request for review of a claim shall suspend the running of prescription against all joint and solidary obligors, and all joint tortfeasors, including but not limited to health care providers, both qualified and not qualified, to the same extent that prescription is suspended against the party or parties that are the subject of the request for review. Filing a request for review of a malpractice claim as required by this Section with any agency or entity other than the division of administration shall not suspend or interrupt the running of prescription. All requests for review of a malpractice claim identifying additional health care providers shall also be filed with the division of administration.

(b)   The request for review of a malpractice claim under this Section shall be deemed filed on the date of receipt of the request stamped and certified by the division of administration or on the date of mailing of the request if mailed to the division of administration by certified or registered mail only upon timely compliance with the provisions of Subparagraph (1)(c) or (d) of this Subsection. Upon receipt of any request, the division of administration shall forward a copy of the request to the board within five days of receipt.

(c)   An attorney chairman for the medical review panel shall be appointed within one year from the date the request for review of the claim was filed. Upon appointment of the attorney chairman, the parties shall notify the board of the name and address of the attorney chairman. If the board has not received notice of the appointment of an attorney chairman within nine months from the date the request for review of the claim was filed, then the board shall send notice to the parties by certified or registered mail that the claim will be dismissed in ninety days unless an attorney chairman is appointed within one year from the date the request for review of the claim was filed. If the board has not received notice of the appointment of an attorney chairman within one year from the date the request for review of the claim was filed, then the board shall promptly send notice to the parties by certified or registered mail that the claim has been dismissed for failure to appoint an attorney chairman and the parties shall be deemed to have waived the use of the medical review panel. The filing of a request for a medical review panel shall suspend the time within which suit must be filed until ninety days after the claim has been dismissed in accordance with this Section.

(3)   It shall be the duty of the board within fifteen days of the receipt of the claim by the board to:

(a)   Confirm to the claimant by certified mail, return receipt requested, that the filing has been officially received and whether or not the named defendant or defendants have qualified under this Part.

(b)   In the confirmation to the claimant pursuant to Subparagraph (a) of this Paragraph, notify the claimant of the amount of the filing fee due and the time frame within which such fee is due to the board, and that upon failure to comply with the provisions of Subparagraph (1)(c) or (d) of this Subsection, the request for review of a malpractice claim is invalid and without effect and that the request shall not suspend the time within which suit must be instituted in Subparagraph (2)(a) of this Subsection.

(c)   Notify all named defendants by certified mail, return receipt requested, whether or not qualified under the provisions of this Part, that a filing has been made against them and request made for the formation of a medical review panel; and forward a copy of the proposed complaint to each named defendant at his last and usual place of residence or his office.

(4)   The board shall notify the claimant and all named defendants by certified mail, return receipt requested, of any of the following information:

(a)   The date of receipt of the filing fee.

(b)   That no filing was due because the claimant timely provided the affidavit set forth in Item (1)(d)(i) of this Subsection.

(c)   That the claimant has timely complied with the provisions of Item (1)(d)(ii) of this Subsection.

(d)   That the required filing fee was not timely paid pursuant to Subparagraph (1)(c) of this Subsection.

(5)   In the event that any notification by certified mail, return receipt requested, provided for in Paragraphs (3) and (4) of this Subsection is not claimed or is returned undeliverable, the board shall provide such notification by regular first class mail, which date of mailing shall have the effect of receipt of notice by certified mail.

B.   (1)   (a)   (i) No action against a health care provider covered by this Part, or his insurer, may be commenced in any court before the claimant's proposed complaint has been presented to a medical review panel established pursuant to this Section.

(ii) A certificate of enrollment issued by the board shall be admitted in evidence.

(b)   However, with respect to an act of malpractice which occurs after September 1, 1983, if an opinion is not rendered by the panel within twelve months after the date of notification of the selection of the attorney chairman by the executive director to the selected attorney and all other parties pursuant to Paragraph (1) of Subsection C of this Section, suit may be instituted against a health care provider covered by this Part. However, either party may petition a court of competent jurisdiction for an order extending the twelve month period provided in this Subsection for good cause shown. After the twelve month period provided for in this Subsection or any court-ordered extension thereof, the medical review panel established to review the claimant's complaint shall be dissolved without the necessity of obtaining a court order of dissolution.

        (c)   By agreement of all parties, the use of the medical review panel may be waived.

        (d)   By agreement of all parties and upon written request to the attorney chairman, an expedited medical review panel process may be selected. Unless otherwise specified in the provisions of Subsection N of this Section, the expedited process shall be governed by other provisions of this Section.

(2)   (a)   A health care provider, against whom a claim has been filed under the provisions of this Part, may raise any exception or defenses available pursuant to R.S. 9:5628 in a court of competent jurisdiction and proper venue at any time without need for completion of the review process by the medical review panel.

        (b)   If the court finds that the claim had prescribed or otherwise was perempted prior to being filed, the panel, if established, shall be dissolved.

(3)   Ninety days after the notification to all parties by certified mail by the attorney chairman of the board of the dissolution of the medical review panel or ninety days after the expiration of any court-ordered extension as authorized by Paragraph (1) of this Subsection, the suspension of the running of prescription with respect to a qualified health care provider shall cease.

C.   The medical review panel shall consist of three health care providers who hold unlimited licenses to practice their profession in Louisiana and one attorney. The parties may agree on the attorney member of the medical review panel. If no attorney for or representative of any health care provider named in the complaint has made an appearance in the proceedings or made written contact with the attorney for the plaintiff within forty-five days of the date of receipt of the notification to the health care provider and the insurer that the required filing fee has been received by the patient's compensation board as required by R.S. 40:1231.8(A)(1)(c), the attorney for the plaintiff may appoint the attorney member of the medical review panel for the purpose of convening the panel. Such notice to the health care provider and the insurer shall be sent by registered or certified mail, return receipt requested. If no agreement can be reached, then the attorney member of the medical review panel shall be selected in the following manner:

(1)   (a)   The office of the clerk of the Louisiana Supreme Court, upon receipt of notification from the board, shall draw five names at random from the list of attorneys who reside or maintain an office in the parish which would be proper venue for the action in a court of law. The names of judges, magistrates, district attorneys and assistant district attorneys shall be excluded if drawn and new names drawn in their place. After selection of the attorney names, the office of the clerk of the supreme court shall notify the board of the names so selected. It shall be the duty of the board to notify the parties of the attorney names from which the parties may choose the attorney member of the panel within five days. If no agreement can be reached within five days, the parties shall immediately initiate a procedure of selecting the attorney by each striking two names alternately, with the claimant striking first and so advising the health care provider of the name of the attorney so stricken; thereafter, the health care provider and the claimant shall alternately strike until both sides have stricken two names and the remaining name shall be the attorney member of the panel. If either the plaintiff or defendant fails to strike, the clerk of the Louisiana Supreme Court shall strike for that party within five additional days.

        (b)   After the striking, the office of the board shall notify the attorney and all other parties of the name of the selected attorney.

(2)   The attorney shall act as chairman of the panel and in an advisory capacity but shall have no vote. It is the duty of the chairman to expedite the selection of the other panel members, to convene the panel, and expedite the panel's review of the proposed complaint. The chairman shall establish a reasonable schedule for submission of evidence to the medical review panel but must allow sufficient time for the parties to make full and adequate presentation of related facts and authorities within ninety days following selection of the panel.

(3)   (a)   The plaintiff shall notify the attorney chairman and the named defendants of his choice of a health care provider member of the medical review panel within thirty days of the date of certification of his filing by the board.

        (b)   The named defendant shall then have fifteen days after notification by the plaintiff of the plaintiff's choice of his health care provider panelist to name the defendant's health care provider panelist.

        (c)   If either the plaintiff or defendant fails to make a selection of health care provider panelist within the time provided, the attorney chairman shall notify by certified mail the failing party to make such selection within five days of the receipt of the notice.

        (d)   If no selection is made within the five day period, then the chairman shall make the selection on behalf of the failing party. The two health care provider panel members selected by the parties or on their behalf shall be notified by the chairman to select the third health care provider panel member within fifteen days of their receipt of such notice.

        (e)   If the two health care provider panel members fail to make such selection within the fifteen day period allowed, the chairman shall then make the selection of the third panel member and thereby complete the panel.

        (f)   A physician who holds an unrestricted license to practice medicine by the Louisiana State Board of Medical Examiners and who is engaged in the active practice of medicine in this state, whether in the teaching profession or otherwise, shall be available for selection as a member of a medical review panel.

        (g)   Each party to the action shall have the right to select one health care provider and upon selection the health care provider shall be required to serve.

        (h)   When there are multiple plaintiffs or defendants, there shall be only one health care provider selected per side. The plaintiff, whether single or multiple, shall have the right to select one health care provider, and the defendant, whether single or multiple, shall have the right to select one health care provider.

        (i) A panelist so selected and the attorney member selected in accordance with this Subsection shall serve unless for good cause shown may be excused. To show good cause for relief from serving, the panelist shall present an affidavit to a judge of a court of competent jurisdiction and proper venue which shall set out the facts showing that service would constitute an unreasonable burden or undue hardship. A health care provider panelist may also be excused from serving by the attorney chairman if during the previous twelve-month period he has been appointed to four other medical review panels. In either such event, a replacement panelist shall be selected within fifteen days in the same manner as the excused panelist.

        (j)   If there is only one party defendant which is not a hospital, community blood center, tissue bank, or ambulance service, all panelists except the attorney shall be from the same class and specialty of practice of health care provider as the defendant. If there is only one party defendant which is a hospital, community blood center, tissue bank, or ambulance service, all panelists except the attorney shall be physicians. If there are claims against multiple defendants, one or more of whom are health care providers other than a hospital, community blood center, tissue bank, or ambulance service, the panelists selected in accordance with this Subsection may also be selected from health care providers who are from the same class and specialty of practice of health care providers as are any of the defendants other than a hospital, community blood center, tissue bank, or ambulance service.

(4) When the medical review panel is formed, the chairman shall within five days notify the board and the parties by registered or certified mail of the names and addresses of the panel members and the date on which the last member was selected.

* * * * *

G. The panel shall have the sole duty to express its expert opinion as to whether or not the evidence supports the conclusion that the defendant or defendants acted or failed to act within the appropriate standards of care. After reviewing all evidence and after any examination of the panel by counsel representing either party, the panel shall, within thirty days, render one or more of the following expert opinions, which shall be in writing and signed by the panelists, together with written reasons for their conclusions:

(1) The evidence supports the conclusion that the defendant or defendants failed to comply with the appropriate standard of care as charged in the complaint.

(2) The evidence does not support the conclusion that the defendant or defendants failed to meet the applicable standard of care as charged in the complaint.

(3) That there is a material issue of fact, not requiring expert opinion, bearing on liability for consideration by the court.

(4) When Paragraph (1) of this subsection is answered in the affirmative, that the conduct complained of was or was not a factor of the resultant damages. If such conduct was a factor, whether the plaintiff suffered: (a) any disability and the extent and duration of the disability, and (b) any permanent impairment and the percentage of the impairment.

H. Any report of the expert opinion reached by the medical review panel shall be admissible as evidence in any action subsequently brought by the claimant in a court of law, but such expert opinion shall not be conclusive and either party shall have the right to call, at his cost, any member of the medical review panel as a witness. If called, the witness shall be required to appear and testify. A panelist shall have absolute immunity from civil liability for all communications, findings, opinions and conclusions made in the course and scope of duties prescribed by this Part.

* * * * *

NOTE

The Louisiana Third Circuit held that the caps on damages were unconstitutional, but the Louisiana Supreme Court reversed on procedural grounds in *Taylor v. Clement*, 897 So. 2d 909 (La.App. 3 Cir. 2006), *vacated*, 947 So. 2d 732 (La. 2007). The Louisiana Supreme Court reversed the Third Circuit again in 2012 and again upheld the constitutionality of the damage caps in *Oliver v. Magnolia Clinic*, 85 So. 3d 39 (La. 2012).

COLEMAN
v.
DENO
813 So. 2d 303 (La. 2002)

LOBRANO, J. Pro Tempore.

We granted certiorari in this case primarily to determine whether the court of appeal erred in recognizing an intentional tort cause of action against an emergency room physician for improper transfer of a patient under general tort law, which is outside the scope of the limitations set forth in the Medical Malpractice Act, La. R.S. 40:1299.41, *et seq.* (MMA). After review of the evidence, we conclude that the plaintiff-patient's cause of action against the defendant-doctor is based solely on medical malpractice and thus the court of appeal's finding of an intentional tort of "patient dumping" is in error. With respect to the medical malpractice liability, we find no manifest error in the jury's finding of malpractice on the part of the defendant-doctor; however, we reallocate fault between the defendant-doctor and the non-party charity hospital. With respect to damages, we remand to the court of appeal for both a meaningful quantum review and a recasting of the ultimate judgment in accordance with the limitations of the MMA.

* * * * *

Intentional tort of improper transfer

While the trial court granted Dr. Deno's exception of no cause of action as to Coleman's "patient dumping" allegations, the court of appeal characterized the claim as an intentional tort of improper patient transfer based on Louisiana tort law, La. C.C. art. 2315. As such, the court reasoned that it was not "malpractice" under the MMA. In so holding, the appellate court concluded that Coleman plead two distinct causes of action: (1) negligent failure to treat-- malpractice, and (2) an intentional tort based on EMTALA for transfer to CHNO because of lack of funds-not malpractice. For the following reasons, we reverse the appellate court's conclusion that Dr. Deno was additionally at fault under general tort law for the intentional tort of "patient dumping."

The nature of the claim of improper transfer in this case is really a claim of failure to properly diagnose, failure to stabilize, or both. That is what the petition alleges, and that is what the evidence suggests to be the basis of Coleman's claim. The court of appeal, with little analysis and citing no authority, characterized such a claim as outside the scope of "malpractice" under the MMA and thus justified the entire $4,900,000 jury award. In so doing, we hold that the appellate court erred both procedurally and substantively.

Procedurally, neither Coleman's original nor amended petition alleges an intentional tort. The original petition alleges only medical malpractice; the amended petition alleges only negligence *per se* based on EMTALA. Nor were the pleadings expanded at trial, as provided for in La. C. Civ. P. art. 1154, to include such an alleged intentional tort. To the contrary, the effect of the trial court's granting of Dr. Deno's combined exception of no cause of action and motion in limine was to exclude any mention before the jury of either the financial reasons for the transfer or the EMTALA claim.[11] The court of appeal thus crafted an intentional tort that was not plead, not prayed for in relief, not argued, not tried, and not submitted to the jury.

Substantively, the court of appeal reasoned that "[t]he 'patient dumping' cause of action refers to an intentional tort where Dr. Deno directed plaintiff's transfer to Charity for lack of finances or insurance although it conflicted with JoEllen Smith Hospital's written policy." 99-2998 at p. 19, 787 So. 2d at 463. Acknowledging that neither EMTALA nor the Louisiana statutory counterpart provides

---

[11] The first mention by Coleman of an intentional tort was in this court where, in an attempt to support the appellate court's creation of this new tort, he contends that Dr. Deno made a "deliberate decision" to transfer based on non-medical reasons.

a private cause of action against a physician for patient dumping, the court reasoned that it could "find no express state law that excludes recovery under La. C.C. art. 2315, general tort law, or La. R.S. 40:2113.4-40:2113.6 [the Louisiana anti-dumping statute] against physicians for the *intentional* tort of patient dumping." *Id.* (emphasis added). Stated otherwise, the court reasoned that no statutory provision precludes a finding of liability under Louisiana tort law when a physician engages in the exact misconduct targeted by those anti-dumping statutes.

While the court of appeal reasoned that plaintiff's reference to anti-dumping statutes in his amended petition sufficed to state a cause of action under Article 2315, the issue before us is whether that characterization of plaintiff's assertions and the evidence in support thereof as outside the scope of "malpractice" under the MMA was correct. In resolving that issue, we begin by distinguishing this case from our prior two decisions in which we have addressed "patient dumping"[14] claims under the EMTALA and the Louisiana statutory counterpart. *Spradlin v. Acadia St. Landry Medical Foundation,* 98-1977 (La. 2000), 758 So. 2d 116; *Fleming v. HCA Health Services of Louisiana, Inc.,* 96-1968 (La. 1997), 691 So. 2d 1216. In both those prior cases the defendant was a hospital; the defendant in this case is an emergency room physician. The significance of this distinction is two-fold. First, the statutory duties imposed by EMTALA, and the Louisiana statutory counterpart, apply only to participating hospitals, not physicians.[15] Second, hospitals are distinct legal entities that do not, in the traditional sense of the term, "practice" medicine; whereas, physicians do "practice" their profession, and their negligence in providing such professional services is termed "malpractice." Frank L. Maraist & Thomas C. Galligan, Jr., *Louisiana Tort Law* § 21-2 (1996). The significance of the term "malpractice" is that it is used to differentiate professionals from nonprofessionals for purposes of applying certain statutory limitations of tort liability. *Id.* The limitation of tort liability at issue in this case is the MMA.

The MMA applies only to "malpractice;" all other tort liability on the part of a qualified heath care provider is governed by general tort law. *Spradlin, supra.* "Malpractice" is defined by La.Rev.Stat. 40:1231.1A(8) as follows:

> "Malpractice" means any *unintentional tort* or any breach of contract based on health care or professional services rendered, or which should have been rendered, by a health care provider, to a patient.... (Emphasis added).

---

[14] In *Spradlin v. Acadia St. Landry Medical Foundation,* 98-1977 at p. 1, n. 1 (La. 2000), 758 So. 2d 116, 117, we defined the term patient "dumping," noting that "[p]atient 'dumping' by a private hospital generally includes the refusal to treat patients with emergency medical conditions who are uninsured and cannot pay for medical treatment or the transfer of such patients to a public hospital."

[15] In *Spradlin,* we discussed the nature and purpose of both EMTALA and the Louisiana statutory counterpart and the relationship between those two "anti-dumping" statutes and the MMA. Simply stated, EMTALA imposes two statutory obligations on participating hospitals; to wit (i) to provide an appropriate medical screening, and (ii) to provide individuals who are found to have an "emergency medical condition" with treatment needed to "stabilize" that condition before transferring them to another hospital or back home. To ensure compliance with those obligations, EMTALA provides a private cause of action against participating hospitals for two distinct types of dumping claims: (i) failure to appropriately screen, and (ii) failure to stabilize an emergency medical condition. Attempts to imply a private cause of action against the physician have been rejected as inconsistent with EMTALA's congressional history. *Eberhardt v. City of Los Angeles,* 62 F.3d 1253 (9th Cir. 1995).

Similarly, the Louisiana "anti-dumping" statutory scheme, La. R.S. 40:2113.4-2113.6, establishes a duty on the part of certain hospitals to provide emergency treatment to all persons residing in the territorial area, regardless of the individual's indigence and lack of insurance. The purpose for this type state statutory scheme was to overcome the common law rule that hospitals had no duty to provide emergency treatment. Unlike EMTALA, the Louisiana "anti-dumping" statutory provisions contain no express private cause of action. On two prior occasions, we have left open the question of whether the Louisiana statutory scheme, which includes its own penalty provisions, can form the basis for a private cause of action under general tort law, La. C.C. art. 2315. *Spradlin, supra; Fleming v. HCA Health Services of Louisiana,* Inc., 96-1968 (La. 1997), 691 So. 2d 1216. Today, we decline for a third time to decide that issue, which factually is not before us given the defendant in this case is not a hospital, but a physician.

La.Rev.Stat. 40:1231.1 A(7) and (9) further define "tort" and "health care" as follows:

"Tort" means any breach of duty or any negligent act or omission proximately causing injury or damage to another. The standard of care required of every health care provider, except a hospital, in rendering professional services or health care to a patient, shall be to exercise the degree of skill ordinarily employed, under similar circumstances, by the members of his profession in good standing in the same community or locality, and to use reasonable care and diligence, along with his best judgment, in the application of his skill.

"Health care" means any act, or treatment performed or furnished, or which should have been performed or furnished, by any health care provider for, to, or on behalf of a patient during the patient's medical care, treatment or confinement.

Both statutory patient dumping claims and medical malpractice claims are simply particularized forms of torts that often overlap. However, even though all medical malpractice claims are personal injury claims, "the opposite is not true: every personal injury claim is not a medical malpractice claim." Scott E. Hamm, Note, *Power v. Arlington Hospital: A Federal Court End Run Around State Malpractice Limitations,* 7 B.Y.U. J. Pub.L., 335, 347-48 (1993). It follows then that the court of appeal in this case legally erred in characterizing a claim for patient "dumping" as always giving rise to an intentional tort and in reasoning that a bright line can be drawn between medical malpractice claims and patient "dumping" claims. Recognizing that the two claims can overlap, we determine in this case that Coleman's claim of "dumping"--improper transfer – is one of malpractice governed by the MMA.

Standard for defining a medical malpractice claim

In determining whether certain conduct by a qualified health care provider constitutes "malpractice" as defined under the MMA this court has utilized the following three factors:

"[1] whether the particular wrong is 'treatment related' or caused by a dereliction of professional skill,

[2] whether the wrong requires expert medical evidence to determine whether the appropriate standard of care was breached, and

[3] whether the pertinent act or omission involved assessment of the patient's condition."

Sewell v. Doctors Hospital, 600 So. 2d 577, 579 n. 3 (La. 1992)(quoting Holly P. Rockwell, Annotation, *What Patient Claims Against Doctor, Hospital, or Similar Health Care Provider Are Not Subject to Statutes Specifically Governing Actions and Damages for Medical Malpractice,* 89 A.L.R.4th 887 (1991)).[70] The latter annotation lists three additional factors that courts have considered, and we now add those to our *Sewell* list; to wit:

[4] whether an incident occurred in the context of a physician-patient relationship, or was within the scope of activities which a hospital is licensed to perform,

[5] whether the injury would have occurred if the patient had not sought treatment, and

---

[70] In several recent decisions by this court, we have classified various claims as outside the scope of the Act. In *Sewell, supra,* we concluded that a strict liability claim for the collapse of a bed was not malpractice. And, in *Hutchinson v. Patel,* 93-2156 (La. 1994), 637 So. 2d 415, we held that the claim of a patient's wife against a hospital and psychiatrist for their alleged failure to warn or to take other precautions to protect the wife against threats of violence communicated to the psychiatrist by the patient-husband were not malpractice.

[6] whether the tort alleged was intentional.

89 A.L.R.4th at 898.

Applying those six factors to the evidence in this case leads to the inescapable conclusion that Coleman's claim of improper transfer against Dr. Deno is within the scope of the MMA.

* * * * *

Damages

The most glaring error in the appellate court's analysis is in the treatment of damages, especially general damages. The entirety of the appellate court's review of the jury's $4,400,000 general damage award is a paragraph. In that paragraph, the court notes that while the trial court reviewed that part of the jury's award restricted by the MMA's cap, it did not review the part not restricted by the cap. The appellate court, without explanation, apparently allocated the entire award over the MMA's $500,000 cap--$4,400,000--to general damages. As to whether that was an excessive quantum award, the appellate court's reasoning was that it is the purpose of the jury to make the "very difficult" decision of the value of the loss of an arm. 99-2998 at p. 42, 787 So. 2d at 475.

The appellate court's one paragraph analysis of this sizeable general damage award was not sufficient to constitute a meaningful review of general damages. Indeed, the appellate court failed to make even the initial inquiry required for a meaningful review of a general damage award of "whether the particular effects of the particular injuries to the particular plaintiff are such that there has been an abuse of the 'much discretion' vested in the judge or jury." 1 Frank L. Maraist & Harry T. Lemmon, *Louisiana Civil Law Treatise: Civil Procedure* § 14.14 (1999).

Given our conclusion with respect to the quantum review, coupled with our reversal of the intentional tort (which the appellate court referred to as the part "that is not restricted by the Act's cap" 99-2998 at p. 42, 787 So. 2d at 475), we deem it necessary to remand. On remand, the court of appeal is instructed both to conduct a meaningful quantum review and to render judgment in accordance with the limitations of the MMA.

* * * * *

NOTE

The issue of whether certain acts constitute medical malpractice and thus come within the special protections of the Act has arisen in a number of cases, and the *Coleman* factors have been used to make that determination. *See, e.g., LaCoste v. Pendleton Methodist Hosp., L.L.C.*, 966 So. 2d 519 (La. 2007) (holding that decision to shelter in place during hurricane Katrina was not medical malpractice, but rather sounded in general negligence); *Jones v. Ruston La. Hosp. Co., LLC*, 71 So. 3d 1154 (La.App. 2 Cir. 2011), *writ denied*, 75 So. 3d 946 (La. 2011) (holding that failure to honor a "do not resuscitate order" was not medical malpractice); *Dupuy v. NMC Operating Co. L.L.C.*, 187 So. 3d 436 (La. 2016) (failure to sterilize equipment considered medical malpractice); *Billeaudeau v. Opelousas Gen. Hosp. Authority*, 218 So. 3d 513 (La. 2016) (negligent credentialing not considered medical malpractice).

B.   OTHER PROFESSIONALS

1.   Attorneys

Legal malpractice claims present the same general issues as medical malpractice claims. Did the attorney guarantee a result? If not, did the attorney possess and exercise the skill ordinarily possessed and exercised by other attorneys? In the same locality? What about attorneys who specialize?

The practice of law generally is regulated by canons of professional responsibility adopted by the appropriate lawgiver in each state, usually the state's highest court. Is a violation of one of these canons (rules) negligence per se, in the client's malpractice action against the attorney? Another issue is the scope of the risks, i.e., what if an attorney commits error in the defense of a criminal case, and his client, dejected after conviction, commits suicide?

Another important issue is the extent to which the attorney is responsible in tort to his client's opponent, or to third persons, for things said or done during the course of the client's litigation.

The resolution of all of these issues varies from state to state. Some of the relevant Louisiana jurisprudence appears in the notes that follow. The issues of breach and causation in legal malpractice are treated more fully in Chapter 5 part B, *supra*.

NOTES

1.   The Louisiana Constitution vests the Supreme Court with "exclusive original jurisdiction of disciplinary proceedings against a member of the bar." The Court has interpreted this provision as providing it with the power to define and regulate all facets of the practice of law, including the professional responsibility and conduct of lawyers and the client-attorney relationship. Thus the legislature cannot enact a law regulating the practice of law in any respect without the approval of the Court. *Succession of Wallace*, 574 So. 2d 348 (La. 1991).

2.   In *Herring v. Wainwright*, 742 So. 2d 120 (La.App. 2 Cir. 1999), *writ denied*, 752 So. 2d 865 (La. 2000), the court held that the "locality rule," and not a statewide standard, applies to a legal malpractice claim. Does this make sense? Don't all attorneys within a state pass the same general tests for qualifications (the state bar examination)?

3.   Cause in fact often is an issue in a legal malpractice case, particularly where the client's right which has been lost or damaged by the malpractice is of questionable validity. The traditional rule was that in such a case the client in his suit against his defalcating attorney must prove a "case within a case," i.e., that he would have won the case which the attorney allegedly botched. Is that the law in Louisiana? *See Jenkins v. St. Paul Fire & Marine Ins. Co.* in Chapter 5.

4.   A client's substandard conduct in dealing with the problem generated by the attorney's malpractice may reduce or bar his recovery on his malpractice claim. *See* Legal Malpractice; Negligence or Fault of Client as Defense, 10 ALR 5th 828 (1993).

5.   An attorney is not liable to the opposing party except for intentional tortious conduct. An adversary's tort action against an attorney acting on behalf of his client must allege facts showing specific malice or an intent to harm on the part of the attorney. *Penalber v. Blount*, 550 So. 2d 577 (La. 1989); *Monsalvo v. Sondes*, 637 So. 2d 127 (La. 1994).

6.   For the special prescriptive/peremptive statute governing legal malpractice claims, *see* Chapter 7.

2.   Accountants

The most frequent sources of accountant malpractice are failure to discover fraud, erroneous tax advice, and preparing or approving financial statements that inaccurately reflect the financial condition of the client. As to the latter, consider the exposure of an accounting firm which negligently approves a financial statement upon which hundreds of persons rely in purchasing the stock of the client? Should the scope of the risk extend to all reasonably foreseeable victims, or only to third persons of a particular class whom the accountant knew or should have known would rely upon the financial statement? Consider the Louisiana statute, reproduced below.

Accountant malpractice also is subject to a pre-suit review panel similar to that provided for medical malpractice claims (R.S. 37:101, et seq.) and also is subject to a special prescriptive/peremptive statute. (*See* Chapter 7.)

La. R.S. 37:91. Privity of Contract

* * * * *

B.   No action based on negligence brought against any licensee (certified public accountant), or any employee or principal of a licensee by any person or entity claiming to have been injured as a result of their justifiable reliance upon financial statements or other information examined, compiled, reviewed, certified, audited, or otherwise reported or opined on by the defendant licensee or in the course of an engagement to provide other services may be brought unless either of the following conditions exist:

(1)   The plaintiff is the issuer or successor of the issuer of the financial statements or other information examined, compiled, reviewed, certified, audited, or otherwise reported or opined on by the defendant, and has engaged the defendant licensee to examine, compile, review, certify, audit, or otherwise report or render an opinion on such financial statements or to provide other services.

(2)   The defendant licensee was aware at the time the engagement was undertaken that the financial statements or other information were to be made available for use in connection with a specified transaction by the plaintiff who was specifically identified to the defendant licensee, was aware that the plaintiff intended to rely upon such financial statements or other information in connection with the specified transaction, and had direct contact and communication with the plaintiff and expressed by words and conduct the defendant licensee's understanding of the reliance on such financial statements or other information.

3.   Architects

Faulty architecture can expose clients to financial disaster, but also can cause economic harm to contractors and physical injury to construction workers or ultimate users of the structure. Ideally, the architect would like to limit his responsibility in tort to those who are in privity of contract with him, but that is not the general rule. *See* 5 Am Jur 2d Architects, Secs. 2-3, 23-27 (1995).

4.   Clergy

Because of the constraints of the First Amendment (freedom of religion), clergy malpractice suits are seldom successful. Of course, the clergyman can act in a manner that is clearly outside any reasonable interpretation of religious belief (such as sex with a minor parishioner), and there have been a number of such cases in recent years. *See* 5 Am Jur 2d Sec. 66, Religious Societies, Sec. 28.

5.   Educational Malpractice

Generally, there is no recovery for educational malpractice. However, as with clergy, an educator can so far outstep the bounds of "academic freedom" as to become liable in tort, but successful suits based upon such instances apparently are rare. *See, e.g., Miller v. Loyola University of New Orleans*, 829 So. 2d 1057 (La.App. 4 Cir. 2002), *writ denied*, 839 So. 2d 38 (La. 2003) (Louisiana law does not recognize a cause of action for educational malpractice under contract or tort law).

CHAPTER 14

MISUSE OF THE LEGAL SYSTEM

INTRODUCTION

The legal system can be used in ways that cause injuries to people. For example, a person can be charged with a crime and prosecuted even though the person instigating the prosecution knows or should know that the defendant did not commit the crime. When a person is injured by another through misuse of the legal system, the injured person may seek relief. The torts of malicious prosecution and abuse of process address distinct injury-causing misuses of the legal system. The relatively new tort of spoliation, which is recognized in some jurisdictions, addresses another type.

Courts are reluctant to permit recovery for malicious prosecution. Their principal concern is that state constitutions guarantee open access to the courts, and liberally permitting recovery for malicious prosecution could chill exercise of a constitutional right. As the Louisiana Supreme Court explained in *Robinson v. Goudchaux's*, 307 So. 2d 287, 291 (La. 1975):

> Actions of this sort have never been favored, and, in order to sustain them, a clear case must be established, where the forms of justice have been perverted to the gratification of private malice and the willful oppression of the innocent. A relevant constitutional mandate provides that all courts shall be open, and every person for injury done him in his rights, lands, goods, person or reputation shall have adequate remedy by due process of law and justice administered without denial, partiality or unreasonable delay. La.Const. art. I, 6. Public policy requires that all persons shall fully resort to the courts for redress of wrongs and the law protects them when they act in good faith upon reasonable grounds in commencing either a civil or criminal proceeding.

A second reason for disfavoring tort lawsuits based on misuse of the legal system is that courts question whether more litigation is the best solution to remedy abusive use of the legal system. In some circumstances, other remedies are possible, such as an adverse presumption against a party that destroys (spoliates) evidence, or sanctions imposed on an attorney and/or the party that engages in improper conduct in litigation. An attorney's participation in misuse of the legal system also could involve the attorney's violation of the Rules of Professional Conduct and could subject the attorney to disciplinary action.

JONES
v.
SOILEAU
448 So. 2d 1268 (La. 1984)

DIXON, C. J.

Elsie Mae Jones filed suit to recover damages from Calvin Soileau for the latter's alleged malicious prosecution of Jones on four counts of issuing worthless checks. The trial court rendered judgment in her favor and awarded her $25,000 in damages. The court of appeal reversed, finding that there was probable cause to prosecute in the original case. We reverse.

Jones is elderly, disabled and has a seventh grade education. She lives in Ville Platte on Supplemental Security income ($208.00 per month) and food stamps ($33.00 per month). Soileau owns Cal's Grocery in Ville Platte. He is the city marshal, now in his third six year term. In October of 1979, Jones requested that Soileau allow her to buy groceries each month on credit. He agreed to do so if she would sign a counter check provided by him from a local bank for the amount of the purchase. Then, when Jones received her SSI check, he would cash it at the store, and hold out the balance due, and return the checks. Soileau testified that he told her he would institute criminal proceedings if she failed to pay at the first of the month. Soileau called these checks "hold checks." Soileau's wife, who managed the store, testified that this system, as well as Soileau's traditional use of an account book, were simply ways of accounting for the purchases and charges of each credit customer.

Both parties testified that the question of whether Jones had an account at the bank never arose. Neither Soileau nor his employees ever filled in the space provided in the checks for an account number. No one ever asked her for one.

This system worked satisfactorily for several months. In February, 1980, however, Jones' gas bill was $145.00, and she was ill and required medication. She also used her privilege on February 27 at Soileau's store to get $100.00. Soileau charged her $10.00 interest for the last two days of February. She did not pay her February bill.

Some weeks later, Soileau deposited the checks. They were returned; there was no account as drawn. In May, 1980, he sent her demand notices. These notices were pre-printed, containing blanks for a name, date, amount of check and the reason for it not being honored. They stated that criminal charges would be filed if she did not pay within ten days. Soileau filled in the blanks and signed each form "Cal Soileau, City Marshal." The total amount of the four checks was $315.78.

Soileau then went to see Jones. She offered to pay him $30.00 a month. He insisted on being paid in full. [At Soileau's insistence the district attorney filed a bill of information charging Jones with four counts of issuing worthless checks in violation of La. R.S. 14:71.].

Soileau's memory began to fail him when asked about his visits to first the city judge, then the district attorney, then his assistants. He remembered only that Pucheu told him that he had a good charge. Pucheu likewise had no recollection of the specifics of the meeting. Soileau testified that he would not have filed a formal complaint if he had not been told by the district attorney's office that the charge was a good one.

Trial was held some three weeks after the bill was filed. Counsel for Jones argued that the transaction involved an open account, not the issuing of worthless checks. The trial judge, however, ruled from the bench that the state had proved the elements of the crime beyond a reasonable doubt on three of the four counts. He dismissed one count because the check was signed by someone else "for Elsie Mae Jones." He sentenced Jones to ten days in jail on each of the three counts, the terms to run consecutively. In addition, he fined her $50.00 plus court costs. He suspended the sentence on the condition that she make restitution within ten days.

This court granted writs and reversed, finding the statute inapplicable because the transactions were in the nature of an open account. In addition, the court found insufficient proof of intent to defraud.

In the present suit, the record of the criminal case was introduced into evidence, and the trial judge heard the testimony of both parties, Soileau's wife, and Pucheu. In his reasons for judgment, he referred to the previous conviction and sentence and the reversal by this court. He found a "wanton and reckless disregard" of Jones' rights by Soileau and that Soileau "failed to exercise the caution and inquiry required by law before filing criminal charges." Finding all the elements for the action to be established by the record, he awarded her $25,000 in damages.

The court of appeal reversed, holding that it would be anomalous to find that Soileau had no probable cause to file a complaint when the trial judge found Jones guilty beyond a reasonable doubt on three of four counts.

The jurisprudence of the state recognizes a civil cause of action, based on fault under [Art. 2315], in favor of one "whose liberty has been interfered with in an unwarranted manner." F. Stone, 12 La.Civil Law Treatise, Tort Doctrine, §§ 200-01, at 264-66 (1977). Like any other delict under [Art. 2315], such an "interference" must be based on fault of the defendant which causes the damage complained of in order for the plaintiff to recover. In *Graf v. McCrory Corp.,* the defendant refused to drop criminal charges unless the plaintiff would release it from civil liability. The court emphasized that the unreasonableness of the defendant's actions under these circumstances is the key to determining fault in a malicious prosecution case just as in any other case based on [Arts. 2315-16].

Nevertheless, in *Eusant v. Unity Industrial Life Ins.*, the court, quoting from an encyclopedia, stated that the elements of a malicious prosecution action are: (1) the commencement or continuance of an original criminal or civil judicial proceeding; (2) its legal causation by the present defendant in the original proceeding; (3) its bona fide termination in favor of the present plaintiff; (4) the absence of probable cause for such proceeding; (5) the presence of malice therein; and (6) damage conforming to legal standards resulting to plaintiff. This test has been reaffirmed by this court on several occasions, most recently in *Hibernia National Bank v. Bolleter*.

The first three elements, the court of appeal found, are satisfied. The court of appeal reversed the trial court with respect to probable cause because of certain evidentiary presumptions which are controlling in other states. Citing an encyclopedia and the Restatement of Torts, it held that probable cause was conclusively established by the previous conviction unless fraud, perjury or other corrupt means are shown.

The applicable principles for determining probable cause were nevertheless correctly cited by the court of appeal from *Coleman v. The Kroger Co.*. The crucial determination is whether Soileau had an honest and reasonable belief in the guilt of Jones at the time he pressed charges. In applying these principles, a court may take into account events subsequent to the filing of the criminal charge. These are, however, simply additional pieces of evidence which comprise the entirety of the circumstances which it is the court's duty to review. A previous conviction is no more "conclusive" on this issue than is the subsequent reversal by this court or the subsequent finding of no probable cause by the trial court in the present proceeding.[71]

In this case, the trial judge had the record of the criminal proceeding before him. In addition, he heard the live testimony of the parties and of their witnesses. Except for the "presumptions" adopted by the court of appeal, there could be no claim that he failed to give proper evidentiary value to the record of the criminal case.

Soileau must have known that Jones had no bank account. He conceived the scheme to provide himself with a credible threat for collection purposes. The facts could not have given rise to an honest and reasonable belief in the guilt of Jones. When the threat proved to be insufficient to obtain payment in full (she did offer to pay $30.00 a month), he began to take steps to make good on the threat by going from first one official to another to see about filing charges.

Louisiana courts have, however, extended a qualified immunity to a defendant who files charges after seeking the advice of an attorney. The immunity operates, however, only when the advice of the attorney is based on full disclosure of all facts.

In the present case, the trial judge must have concluded that such a full disclosure was not made and that Soileau did not seek advice in good faith. Neither Soileau nor Pucheu remembered the substance of their conversations. [The district attorney] did testify that he knew that "hold checks" were not punishable under [La. R.S. 14:71]. He claimed, however, that a 1976 amendment to the statute would support a prosecution on the facts disclosed to him. The amendment (Acts 1976, No. 651) did away with the requirement of contemporaneous issuing of the check and delivery of the goods. The amendment, however, is irrelevant to the actual facts. In fact, the prosecutor in the criminal case established the contemporaneous signing of the "check" and the delivery of the goods or

---

[71] The potential arbitrariness of mechanically applied, formal presumptions is clearly illustrated in the present case. The trial judge in the criminal case dismissed one of the four counts against Jones because the state failed to prove the authorization of the person signing the check for Jones. The presumption of probable cause would not attach as to this count, and a court could then theoretically reach the issue of probable cause and find for Jones on this count alone.

cash. [The district attorney's] interpretation of the 1976 amendment, despite Jones' defense from the beginning that this was an open account transaction, was never made in the criminal case, either at trial or before this court.

In light of the sketchy recall of both Soileau and [the district attorney], the trial judge must have inferred that Soileau simply presented the three district attorneys with checks marked no account as drawn and asked if he could charge Jones with issuing worthless checks. Such an inference would be consistent with the theory which the state attempted to prove at trial. Therefore, the qualified immunity does not attach to Soileau's actions.

The fifth element is malice. It will be inferred when there is an absence of probable cause "... resulting from wanton and reckless disregard of the rights of the party sued, evincing absence of that caution and inquiry a party should employ before filing suit ..." Soileau knew that his ordinary civil remedies were of little value in attempting to collect from his customers who fell behind. So he created his own security device for the collection of debts on an open account. He signed the demand letters in his official capacity as city marshal. He then refused to negotiate with Jones and insisted on full payment. Such actions were clearly done with an intent to use the baseless criminal charge to collect from Jones. Under these circumstances, malice is inferred. Such an attempt to misuse an office of public trust for private ends, as well as to misuse the criminal process for the enforcement of civil claims, remains an intolerable abuse in this state.

The sixth element, damages, is also presumed when the other five elements are established. In the present case, the trial judge had "no doubt ... that plaintiff suffered extreme mental anguish, humiliation, embarrassment, etc. as she went through an entire criminal trial, resulting in a conviction and sentence, and that she is entitled to substantial damages for the malicious prosecution brought against her by the defendant." He then awarded her $25,000.

[Art. 1934(3)] gives the trial judge "much discretion" in assessing damages in the case of an offense or quasi offense. This court will not disturb an award absent a clear abuse of discretion under the particular circumstances of the case. Damage awards, however, in malicious prosecution suits should be compensatory only. There is no doubt that Jones suffered anguish and humiliation as a result of Soileau's actions. In an appropriate case, the trial judge's award would be proper. However, the record in this case does not support such an award. Much of the publicity apparently occurred when Jones filed this suit. No newspaper accounts or other documentation was introduced. Jones spent no time in jail and was never formally arrested. She testified that her blood sugar "acted up," but there was no other proof of this nor of any expenses which it may have caused. Her attorney's fees in the criminal action were not documented. In light of the record and the compensatory nature of the damage award in such cases, an award of $5,000 is adequate.

* * * * *

MARCUS, Justice (dissenting).

I agree with the majority view of the states that the conviction of the accused by a trial court, although reversed by an appellate tribunal, conclusively establishes the existence of probable cause unless the conviction was obtained by fraud, perjury or other corrupt means. Accordingly, I respectfully dissent.

NOTES

1. The standard for malicious prosecution cited in *Jones v. Soileau* has been employed by the Louisiana Supreme Court in numerous cases. *See, e.g., Eusant v. Unity Industrial Life Insurance Ass'n*, 195 La. 347, 196 So. 554 (1940); *Johnson v. Pearce*, 313 So. 2d 812 (La. 1975); *Hibernia National Bank v. Bolleter*, 390 So. 2d 842 (La. 1980); and *Miller v. East Baton Rouge Parish Sheriff's Dept.*, 511 So. 2d 446 (La. 1987).

2.　　　　Some jurisdictions distinguish between malicious prosecution (the basis for the tort claim is prior criminal prosecution) and wrongful or improper civil litigation. *See* Dan B. Dobbs, The Law of Torts § 436 (2000). Louisiana does not make this distinction, instead encompassing both within malicious prosecution. *See, e.g., MacFayden v. Lee*, 601 So. 2d 24 (La.App. 1 Cir. 1992) (malicious prosecution action predicated on prior civil action). Note that the first element of malicious prosecution in *Jones v. Soileau* is "the commencement or continuance of an original criminal or civil judicial proceeding."

3.　　　　Defendant police officers who neither initiated a complaint against plaintiff nor supported issuance of warrants by affidavits in the original proceeding are not liable for malicious prosecution despite having participated in the original proceeding after the initial complaint was made and an arrest warrant was issued. The officers were not a legal cause of commencement or continuation of the original proceeding against plaintiff. *Touchton v. Kroger Co.*, 512 So. 2d 520 (La.App. 3 Cir. 1987).

4.　　　　Malicious prosecution claims often can be combined with defamation claims. *See, e.g., MacFayden v. Lee*, 601 So. 2d 24 (La.App. 1 Cir. 1992). If a person is criminally prosecuted or civilly sued without probable cause, it is quite possible that false and damaging statements were made about him on which a defamation claim can be based.

5.　　　　Malicious prosecution and abuse of process are separate and distinct causes of action under Louisiana law. For a discussion of abuse of process, *see Waguespack, Seago and Carmichael v. Lincoln*, 768 So. 2d 287 (La.App. 1 Cir. 2000). The court explained that "the essential elements of an abuse of process claim: (1) the existence of an ulterior purpose; and (2) a willful act in the use of the process not proper in the regular prosecution of the proceeding ... Regular use of process cannot constitute abuse, even though the user was actuated by a wrongful motive, purpose, or intent, or by malice." *Id*. at 290-291. Whereas a malicious prosecution claim does not arise until the termination of the litigation on which it is based, an abuse of process claim is not so limited.

> Suppose the following scenario:
>
> Plaintiff sues two defendants. Plaintiff negotiates a settlement with one of the defendants, but does not want that settlement to leave the remaining defendant free to argue for an allocation of fault to the settling defendant. Consequently, plaintiff makes it a condition of the settlement that it will be implemented by the settling defendant filing a motion for summary judgment, which the plaintiff will not oppose. Defendant agrees, files the motion, and with no opposition from plaintiff, the court grants the motion and dismisses defendant from the case. The other defendant later discovers this arrangement.

Does the nonsettling defendant have a viable claim for abuse of process? Against whom?

6.　　　　Parties and attorneys that violate their obligations under Rule 11 of the Federal Rules of Civil Procedure and La. C.C.P. art. 863 can be sanctioned by courts. The obligations generally are that an attorney or party signing a pleading certifies that to the best of his knowledge, information and belief, formed after reasonable inquiry, the pleading is well grounded in fact and law and is not interposed for an improper purpose.

7.　　　　When evidence is destroyed or not preserved, a party to litigation who sought to use that evidence may have a claim for spoliation of evidence. This tort, which is recognized in some jurisdictions, originates in an evidence doctrine as explained by a Louisiana court:

> The tort of spoliation of evidence has its roots in the evidentiary doctrine of "adverse presumption," which allows a jury instruction for the presumption that the destroyed evidence contained information detrimental to the party who destroyed the evidence unless such destruction is adequately explained.

Pham v. Contico Int'l, Inc. 759 So. 2d 880, 882 (La.App. 5 Cir. 2000). The adverse presumption is based on the maxim, "All things are presumed against a spoliator." The adverse presumption may be an adequate remedy in a case in which the person destroying or not preserving the evidence is a party to the litigation. When the spoliator is not a party to the litigation, however, what remedy does the party that needed the evidence have?

The Louisiana Supreme Court held that Louisiana does not recognize the tort of negligent spoliation of evidence in *Reynolds v. Bordelon*, 172 So. 3d 589 (La. 2015), reproduced *supra* Chapter 1. The Court noted that there are alternative remedies for first-party negligent spoliation, such as discovery sanctions and criminal sanctions, as well as the availability of an adverse presumption against a litigant who had access to evidence and did not make it available or destroyed it.

The Louisiana Supreme Court has not ruled on whether Louisiana recognizes a cause of action for intentional spoliation. *See Rogers v. Averitt Express, Inc.*, 215 F.Supp. 3d 510 (M.D. La. 2017). However, a federal court has discerned ("*Erie* guess") that Louisiana does recognize such a cause of action. *Rogers*, 215 F.Supp. 3d at 515. Moreover, some Louisiana courts of appeal so hold. *See, e.g., Tomlinson v. Landmark American Ins. Co.*, 192 So. 3d 153, 159-60 (La.App. 4 Cir. 2016); *Pham v. Contico Int'l, Inc.*, 759 So. 2d 880, 882 (La.App. 5 Cir. 2000).

8.   *McClanahan v. McClanahan*, 27 So. 3d 862 (La.App. 5 Cir. 2009), *writ denied*, 25 So. 3d 833 (La. 2010). The claim for the tort of malicious prosecution is disfavored, and there must be strict compliance with all elements. The claim cannot be successfully urged by one who was not named as a party in the original action. In a later proceeding, the appellate court held that the defendant's reliance on advice of counsel negated malice or bad faith. *See McClanahan v. McClanahan*, 82 So. 3d 530, 537 (La.App. 5 Cir. 2011):

> [T]he Louisiana Supreme Court held: "Advice of counsel, even though erroneous, on questions of law, when accepted and acted on by the client in good faith, is a shield against charges of malice and bad faith." Therefore, the defense of advice of counsel does not depend on whether this Court found legal support lacking for the issues raised by Mr. Lowe in the partition appeal.

9.   The court considered a claim for abuse of process against attorneys who pleaded an incorrect procedural device seeking the return of their client's property from plaintiff in *Riccio v. Luminais*, 192 So. 3d 858 (La.App. 4 Cir. 2016). Use of an incorrect procedure was not a basis for a claim for abuse of process, and there was no evidence of malice on the part of the attorneys.

10.   Louisiana has a procedural device of a special motion to strike a cause of action against a person for an act in furtherance of that person's right of petition or free speech under the federal or state constitutions. La. C.C.P. Art. 971. A Louisiana court stated the following regarding that article:

> In response to the growing prevalence of such suits and recognizing that traditional legal remedies such as abuse of process or malicious prosecution claims and motions for summary judgment were inadequate tools to ameliorate the problem, states enacted legislation creating the special motion to strike. This extraordinary procedural remedy limits discovery, dismisses meritless claims quickly, and awards attorney's fees to the prevailing party.

Yount v. Handshoe, 171 So. 3d 381, 387 (La.App. 5 Cir. 2015).

CHAPTER 15

SOLIDARITY, INDEMNITY AND CONTRIBUTION

A. SOLIDARY TORT LIABILITY

COMMENT

Two or more debtors may be liable to the same creditor for the same debt. Where two or more debtors (obligors) are liable to the same creditor (obligee) for the same damages, they are called solidary obligors (in Louisiana) or joint and several debtors (at common law). In these kinds of cases, the creditor can require any one of the debtors to pay the full amount of the debt. The party paying the full amount may be able to recover all or part of what he or she has paid from the other persons who are solidarily liable, depending upon the nature of the obligation.

Solidary liability for tort damages may arise by contract (such as insurance, discussed *infra*). Solidary liability for tort damages also may arise by operation of law. Louisiana once recognized extensive solidary liability in tort by statute, but that is very limited now. One example is the vicariously liable employer and his tortfeasing employee (*see* Chapter 12). Another example is that, by statute, tortfeasors who conspire to commit an intentional tort are solidarily liable. Finally, the difficulty of determining causation may result in imposition of solidary liability where the faulty conduct of two or more persons coalesces to cause injury to the same victim. If the injuries are divisible, the parties are separate tortfeasors, and each owes only the amount of damage his tort has caused, unless the fault of the second tortfeasor is within the scope of the risks of the first tort. In that case, the first tortfeasor may owe all of the damages from both torts. The second tortfeasor should owe only those damages caused by his tortious conduct.

The most difficult problem has been how to allocate the damages among two or more tortfeasors whose fault coalesces to cause indivisible damages. As to intentional tortfeasors who conspire to cause harm, the answer is easy: each should be liable to the victim for the full amount of the damages, and thus they are solidary obligors. But what about the non-intentional tortfeasors whose fault coalesces to cause indivisible damages? Before the advent of comparative negligence, the law assumed that fault could not be quantified, and thus damages could not be allocated among these coalescing (concurrent) tortfeasors in that manner. However, requiring the victim to meet the impossible burden of proving which concurrent tortfeasor caused which damages would in effect deny the victim recovery. The law responded in two ways. Where the tortfeasors whose conduct caused the indivisible damages were not involved in the same trauma, the judicial system often required the judge or jury to divide the indivisible (except when the second accident was within the scope of the risks of the first, thus making the first liable for the full amount). *See, e.g., Hess v. Sports Publishing Co.*, 520 So. 2d 472 (La.App. 4 Cir. 1988); *Buccola v. Marchese*, 599 So. 2d 892 (La.App. 4 Cir. 1992) ("the damages must be apportioned if possible, although apportionment has some degree of arbitrariness inherent in the process"); *Jarreau v. Hirschey*, 650 So. 2d 1189 (La.App. 1 Cir. 1994) (apportionment should be made although it "necessarily contains an inherent degree of arbitrariness"). Where the tortfeasors' conduct was involved in the same accident or trauma, the law shifted the burden of proof to the concurrent tortfeasors, who also could not meet it; as a result, each was liable for the full amount of the damages. Thus the tortfeasors became solidary obligors. One who paid more than his "share" could recover from the other tortfeasor through contribution. However, he bore the risk that the other tortfeasor was insolvent, immune (such as the victim's employer) or unknown (i.e., a "phantom tortfeasor," such as the motorist who does not stop or the rapist who is not caught).

The law now permits the trier of fact to quantify fault among tortfeasors. After adoption of comparative fault, contribution among joint tortfeasors was based upon their percentages of fault. Thus, where all of the parties were known, solvent, and non-immune, each bore his share of the damages. Solidarity among tortfeasors was irrelevant, because if a tortfeasor paid more than his share, he recouped through contribution the excess from the tortfeasor whose share he paid. But what if one of the tortfeasors was immune, insolvent or unknown? Retention of solidarity among these tortfeasors would impose the risk upon the known, solvent, non-immune tortfeasor, and abolition of solidarity would impose the risk upon the victim. Louisiana's first "tort reform" response to this question was the 1979 version of CC Art. 2324, reproduced below.

La. Civil Code Article 2324.   **Liability as solidary or joint and divisible obligation**

A.   He who conspires with another person to commit an intentional or willful act is answerable, in solido, with that person, for the damage caused by such act.

B.   If liability is not solidary pursuant to Paragraph A, or as otherwise provided by law, then liability for damages caused by two or more persons shall be solidary only to the extent necessary for the person suffering injury, death, or loss to recover fifty percent of his recoverable damages; however, when the amount of recovery has been reduced in accordance with the preceding Article, a judgment debtor shall not be liable for more than the degree of his fault to a judgment creditor to whom a greater degree of fault has been attributed. Under the provisions of this Article, all parties shall enjoy their respective rights of indemnity and contribution. Except as described in Paragraph A of this Article, or as otherwise provided by law, and hereinabove, the liability for damages caused by two or more persons shall be a joint, divisible obligation, and a joint tortfeasor shall not be solidarily liable with any other person for damages attributable to the fault of such other person, including the person suffering injury, death, or loss, regardless of such other person's insolvency, ability to pay, degree of fault, or immunity by statute or otherwise.

C.   Interruption of prescription against one joint tortfeasor, whether the obligation is considered joint and divisible or solidary, is effective against all joint tortfeasors. Nothing in this Subsection shall be construed to affect in any manner the application of the provisions of R.S. 40:1299.41(G).

This extremely confusing 50% rule was subject to judicial application which the Legislature subsequently found undesirable. One application involved the actors whose fault would be quantified. If the fault of the immune tortfeasor (such as the employer) or the phantom was not quantified, and the plaintiff was not contributorily negligent, the non-immune tortfeasor still ended up paying 100%. The Supreme Court ultimately ruled that the fault of a non-party (such as an immune or phantom tortfeasor) could not be quantified. Another important application of the 50% rule was the issue of how many "below 50%" tortfeasors could be "bumped up" to 50%. *See Touchard v. Williams*, 716 So. 2d 885 (La. 1993); Thomas C. Galligan, Jr., *The Discombobulating State of Solidarity in Post-Tort Reform Louisiana*, 54 La. L. Rev. 551 (1994). If more than one could be "bumped up," then the plaintiff would recover 100% of the recoverable damages and would bear none of the risk of the insolvent or immune tortfeasor. One issue on which courts seemed to agree was that there was no solidary liability for punitive damages (at least in the absence of a conspiracy). *See, e.g., James v. Formose Plastic Corp. of La.*, 672 So. 2d 319 (La.App. 1 Cir. 1996). The Legislature's response to this state of solidary liability confusion was Act 3 of the 1996 Special session, which amended CC Article 2324B to read as follows:

> **B.**   If liability is not solidary pursuant to Paragraph A, then liability for damages caused by two or more persons shall be a joint and divisible obligation. A joint tortfeasor shall not be liable for more than his degree of fault and shall not be solidarily liable with any other person for damages attributable to the fault of such other person, including the person suffering injury, death or loss, regardless of such other person's insolvency, ability to pay, degree of fault, immunity by statute or otherwise, including but not limited to immunity as provided in R.S. 23:1032, or that the other person's identity is not known or reasonably ascertainable.
>
> **C.**   Interruption of prescription against one joint tortfeasor is effective against all joint tortfeasors.

In implementation of Act 3, Act 65 of the 1996 Special Session provided that in an action to recover damages for injury, death or loss, the court shall at the request of any party submit special written questions which include (1) whether a non-party was at fault and the degree of such fault, and

(2) the total amount of special damages and general damages and, when appropriate, exemplary damages. "(N)on-party means a person alleged by any party to be at fault, including but not limited to (I) a person who has obtained a release from liability from the person suffering injury, death, or loss, (ii) a person who exists but whose identity is unknown, or (iii) a person who may be immune from suit because of immunity granted by statute."

COMMENT

The "conspiring" joint tortfeasor's liability now is governed by Article 2324(A) and the concurrent ("coalescing") joint tortfeasor's liability is governed by Article 2324(B). It has been held that "the agreement between the actors involved in a conspiracy must be an agreement as to the intended <u>outcome</u> or <u>result</u> of their acts." *Walker v. American Honda Motor Company, Inc.*, 640 So. 2d 794 (La.App. 3 Cir. 1994), (emphasis by court). *See also, Chrysler Credit Corp. v. Whitney National Bank*, 51 F.3d 553 (5th Cir. 1995) (under C.C. Art. 2324A, a person who conspires with another to commit an intentional or willful act is liable in solido for damages caused by the act; *held*, a person "conspires" if he provides assistance or encouragement of such quality and character that a jury would be permitted to infer from it an underlying agreement and act that is the essence of the conspiracy).

The reaction of the lower courts to the amendments to CC Art. 2324 and the interpretations in *Keith* and *Aucoin* has been confusing. Some courts maintain that the *Veazey* approach remains viable. *See, e.g., McAvey v. Lee*, 58 F.Supp. 2d 724 (E.D. La. 1998) (if the intentional tortfeasor's conduct is within the ambit of protection encompassed by the duty owed by the negligent tortfeasor, it is inappropriate to instruct the jury to quantify the fault of the intentional tortfeasor. Only when the conduct of the intentional tortfeasor is outside the ambit of protection encompassed by the duty owed by the negligent tortfeasor, should the jury be instructed to quantify the fault of the intentional tortfeasor. *See, also, Pinsonneault v. Merchants & Farmers Bank & Trust Co.*, 738 So. 2d 172 (La.App. 3 Cir. 1999), *writ granted* and remanded for reconsideration in light of *Posecai*, 753 So. 2d 842 (2000). There, victim was shot and killed in 1992 by robbers as he attempted to use bank's night depository; bank was negligent in the placement of the depository. *Held:* (1) the fault of the robbers must be quantified, but (2) the bank's liability should not be reduced by the robbers' fault; "the scope of the bank's duty included the protection to the plaintiff against the very risk posed by the robbers.... The bank was . . . indisputable the legal cause of the injuries." The Louisiana Supreme Court later reversed, finding no breach by the bank. 816 So. 2d 270 (La. 2002).

Has that issue been laid rest by the decision in *Dumas v. State*, 828 So. 2d 130 (La. 2002), set forth *infra*?

Do *Keith* and *Aucoin* change the rule as to settling defendants? *See, e.g., Farbe v. Casualty Reciprocal Exchange*, 746 So. 2d 228 (La.App. 3 Cir. 1999). There, in a case arising out of a 1991 accident, plaintiff settled with one tortfeasor and went to trial against the other. The jury assessed the fault of the settling tortfeasor at 80% and the fault of the nonsettling tortfeasor at 20%. The appellate court ruled that under *Touchard v. Williams*, 617 So. 2d 885 (La. 1993), the non-settling tortfeasor was liable for 50% of the plaintiff's damages. The Supreme Court granted writs and reversed, holding that the non-settling tortfeasor is liable for only 20%. 755 So. 2d 890 (2000). *See also, Tremble v. Mid-Continent Ins. Co.*, 752 So. 2d 987 (La.App. 3 Cir. 1999), holding that in a 1997 accident, fault must be allocated between co-employees (the driver of a tractor trailer and the driver of an escort vehicle) for whom the employer is solidarily liable. The percentage of fault may affect the amount of the suspensive appeal bond and each party's ability to post such a bond.

In *Joseph v. Broussard Rice Mill, Inc.*, 772 So. 2d 94 (La. 2000) the court held that a defendant who urges the fault of a non-party bears the burden of providing evidence which preponderates that fault actually exists on the part of the non-party. To the same effect, *see Bradbury v. Thomas*, 757 So. 2d 666 (La.App. 1 Cir. 1999).

See generally, Maraist & Galligan, *Burying Caesar: Civil Justice Reform and the Changing Face of Louisiana Tort Law*, 71 Tul. L. Rev. 339 (1996).

B. ALLOCATION OF RISKS AMONG SOLIDARY OBLIGORS

COMMENT

Parties may allocate the risks of faulty conduct by contract. The most common, of course, is the insurance contract, in which one contracting party (the insurer) agrees to pay the tort damages which the other party (the insured) may become liable to pay to a third person. These "public indemnity" contracts are crucial to the tort system, and are heavily regulated by statute. Of course, insurance drives much of what happens in tort cases and the availability of insurance can create indemnity issues amongst insurers. For instance, in *Commercial Union Ins. Co. v. CBC Temporary Staffing Services, Inc.*, 897 So. 2d 647 (La.App. 1 Cir. 2004), where two insured entities were held to be a "single business enterprise" for the purpose of the underlying tort litigation; the insurer of one insured entity was allowed to seek indemnity or contribution from the other entity and its insurer. Characterizing the insured entities as members of a single business enterprise did not preclude a division of liability among the insurers. *See* Chapter 8. A non-insurer also may by contract agree to pay the damages which another party to the contract may become liable to pay to a third person. This generally is called contractual indemnity, and is discussed in Subsection 1 *infra*.

In the absence of a contractual agreement, the law nevertheless may impose upon one at-fault actor liability for a portion of the damages caused in part by another at-fault actor. The legal concepts through which this is achieved are called tort indemnity and tort contribution. These concepts are of waning importance in Louisiana law after the abolition of solidary liability; the general principles governing these concepts are set forth in Subsections 2 and 3, *infra*.

1. Contractual Indemnity

SOVEREIGN INSURANCE COMPANY
v.
THE TEXAS PIPE LINE COMPANY
488 So. 2d 982 (La. 1986)

DENNIS, J.

This court decided that a contract of indemnity whereby the indemnitee is indemnified against the consequences of his own negligence is strictly construed, and that such a contract will not be construed to indemnify an indemnitee against losses resulting to him through his own negligent acts, unless such an intention is expressed in unequivocal terms. *Polozola v. Garlock*, 343 So. 2d 1000 (La. 1977). The present case raises the question of whether a similar rule of contractual interpretation should be applied to determine if a contract provides indemnity against an indemnitee's strict liability under Civil Code article 2317 for damage to a third person caused by an unreasonably dangerous thing in the indemnitee's custody. The trial court decided that the instant contract did not afford indemnification against such a claim, and the Court of Appeal affirmed by an evenly divided en banc court. 470 So. 2d 969 (La.App. 1 Cir. 1985). We reverse. When a contract of indemnity makes no express provisions for indemnification against the consequences of the indemnitee's negligence, and an unequivocal intention to so indemnify cannot be found after interpreting each contractual provision in light of the whole contract and the general rules of contractual interpretation, the court will presume that the parties did not intend to hold the indemnitee harmless from such liability. On the other hand, this presumption does not apply to the question of whether the parties intended to indemnify against the indemnitee's strict liability under Civil Code article 2317. If the contract's provisions are doubtful or simply fail to address the question, the court may further interpret the contract on this point in light of everything that, by law, custom, usages or equity is considered as incidental or necessary to its effectuation.

Texas Pipeline Company leased a tract of land for purposes of operating a crude oil storage facility. On January 27, 1981, Texas entered into a contract with Atlas Construction Company, Inc. for the construction of three crude oil storage tank foundations. The contract provided that Atlas would indemnify Texas against any liability, cost, expense, damage or loss in connection with the contract, except that resulting solely from Texas' negligence.[72] On September 30, 1981, a roadbed on the leased premises collapsed, causing a cement truck owned by a subcontractor to overturn. The truck was a total loss except for its salvage value. The subcontractor's insurer, SOVEREIGN Insurance Company, paid most of the loss and received a conventional subrogation.

SOVEREIGN and the subcontractor sued Texas as custodian of the roadway, claiming strict liability based on Civil Code article 2317. Texas filed a third-party demand against Atlas for indemnity under the construction contract. The plaintiffs amended their petition to name Atlas and the landowner as defendants also.

After trial, the district court found that the damage was caused by a defective condition in the roadway on Texas' leased premises, held Texas strictly liable under Civil Code article 2317, rejected Texas' claim for indemnity under the contract, and dismissed all the other claims. The court of appeal, sitting en banc, affirmed by an evenly divided vote. An opinion subscribed to by a plurality reasoned that the strict construction rule of *Polozola v. Garlock* should be applied to decide whether the parties intended to indemnify the indemnitee against strict liability under Civil Code article 2317. We granted certiorari because incorrect results were reached below due to a failure to properly interpret the contract and a misunderstanding of the *Polozola v. Garlock* rule.

The general rules which govern the interpretation of other contracts apply in construing a contract of indemnity. *See Polozola v. Garlock, supra.* Interpretation of a contract is the determination of the common intent of the parties. *See* Civil Code arts. 1945, 1949, 1950 and 1956 (1870); Civil Code art. 2045 (1984).[73] When the words of a contract are clear and explicit and lead to no absurd consequences, no further interpretation may be made in search of the parties' intent. *See* Civil Code arts. 13 and 1945(3) (1870); *Maloney v. Oak Builders Inc.*, 256 La. 85, 235 So. 2d 386 (1970); Civil Code art. 2046 (1984). Each provision in a contract must be interpreted in light of the other provisions so that each is given the meaning suggested by the contract as a whole. Civil Code art. 1955 (1870); *see* Civil Code art. 2050 (1984). Although a contract is worded in general terms, it must be interpreted to cover only those things it appears the parties intended to include. Civil Code art. 1959 (1870); *see* Civil Code art. 2051 (1984). When the parties intend a contract to have a general scope, but particularly describe a specific situation to eliminate doubt, the interpretation of the contract must not restrict its scope to that specific situation. Civil Code art. 1962 (1870); Civil Code art. 2052 (1984). The obligation of contracts extends not only to what is expressly stipulated, but also to everything that, by law, equity or custom, is considered as incidental to the particular contract, or necessary to carry it into effect. Civil Code art. 1903 (1870).[74] Equity is based on the principles that

---

[72] The indemnity clause provided:

contractor [Atlas] shall fully defend, protect, indemnify and hold harmless the Company [Texas], its employees and agents from and against each and every claim, demand or cause of action and any liability, cost, expense (including but not limited to reasonable attorney's fees and expenses incurred in defense of the Company), damage or loss in connection therewith, which may be made or asserted by Contractor, Contractor's employees or agents, subcontractors, or any third parties, (including but not limited to Company's agents, servants or employees) on account of personal injury or death or property damage caused by, arising out of, or in any way incidental to, or in connection with the performance of the work hereunder, whether or not Company may have jointly caused or contributed to, by its own negligence, any such claim, demand, cause of action, liability, cost, expense, damage or loss, except such as may result solely from the Company's negligence.

[73] In the interests of clarity and conciseness, the language of 1984 La. Acts, No. 331, which revised titles III and IV of Book III of the Civil Code, is used herein whenever the modern version makes no change in the law.

[74] In the 1984 revision of the obligations articles, the substance of article 1903 was enlarged and reproduced in new article 2053 and converted from substantive law to an interpretative rule by Civil Code art. 2054 (1984).
Civil Code art. 2053 (1984) provides:
A doubtful provision must be interpreted in light of the nature of the contract, equity, usages, the conduct of the parties before and after the formation of the contract, and of other contracts of a like nature between the same parties.
Civil Code art. 2054 (1984) provides:

no one is allowed to take unfair advantage of another and that no one is allowed to enrich himself unjustly at the expense of another. Civil Code art. 1965 (1870); *see* Civil Code art. 2055 (1984).

Applying these interpretive rules to the contract in the present case, we conclude that the parties intended to provide for indemnity against Texas' strict liability to a third person under Civil Code art. 2317. The words of the contract are not clear and explicit regarding strict liability, so further interpretation may be made in search of the common intent. Although the contract provides that Atlas shall indemnify and hold Texas harmless against each and every claim, demand or cause of action and any liability, such general terms must be interpreted to cover only those things it appears the parties intended to include. When this provision is interpreted in light of the other provisions and the contract as a whole, however, it is evident that the parties intended to afford Texas indemnity against claims, causes of action and strict liability arising under Civil Code article 2317. In the other contractual provisions, Atlas represented that it had inspected the premises for hazardous conditions and had determined their nature and extent to its satisfaction; and Atlas promised to take any measures necessary to adequately protect all persons and property from injury or loss arising out of the work and to maintain all passageways for the protection of persons and property required by any local conditions. The contract excepts from the indemnity provision only claims, causes of action and liability resulting "solely from [Texas'] negligence."

The contract provides that Atlas is obliged to indemnify Texas "whether or not [Texas] may have jointly caused or contributed to, by its own negligence any such claim, demand, cause of action, liability ...." The parties described this specific situation to eliminate doubt, however, and did not intend to restrict the scope of the contract to that situation alone.

Considering the contract as a whole, it is clear that the parties adverted to the possibility of claims, causes of actions and judgments based upon strict liability for damage caused by premises hazards or defects. Accordingly, strict liability was within their contemplation when they agreed that indemnity should cover each and every claim, demand or cause of action, and liability, except for those resulting solely from Texas' negligence. Hence, the contract as a whole indicates an intention to provide indemnity against Texas' strict liability under article 2317 for damage caused by premises defects which arise out of the performance of the contract, and further interpretation of the agreement is not warranted because the meaning of its provision for indemnity against strict liability is not in doubt.

Because the rule of *Polozola v. Garlock* applies only in a case in which a contractual provision to indemnify against the indemnitee's negligence liability is still in doubt after a careful reading of the contract as a whole, the issues suggested by the plurality appellate opinion are not squarely presented in this case. In the interest of clarifying an area in which there is confusion, however, we will discuss the different contractual interpretation rules which apply to, first, a doubtful provision to indemnify against an indemnitee's strict liability under Civil Code article 2317 and, second, a doubtful provision to hold an indemnitee harmless from the consequences of his own negligence.

If the common intention of the parties as to strict liability is in doubt after applying the general rules and interpreting each provision in light of the contract as a whole, the court is called upon to interpret the contract further in light of everything that, by law, custom, usages, or equity, is considered as incidental to the particular contract or necessary to carry it into effect. *See* Civil Code arts. 1903, 1953, and 1965 (1870); *cf.* Civil Code arts. 2053, 2054 (1984). In such a case, these elements enter into every contract and may be shown for the purpose not only of elucidating it, but also of completing it. *Southern Bitulithic Co. v. Algiers Ry. & Lighting Co.*, 130 La. 830, 58 So. 588 (1912).

When the parties made no provision for a particular situation, it must be assumed that they intended to bind themselves not only to the express provisions of the contract, but also to whatever the law, equity, or usage regards as implied in a contract of that kind or necessary for the contract to achieve its purpose.

When there is doubt as to indemnification against an indemnitee's own negligence liability, however, usage, custom or equity may not be used to interpret a contract expansively in favor of the indemnitee. In such a case, if the provision is still in doubt after applying the general rules of construction and interpreting the provision in light of the contract as a whole, i.e., if the intention to indemnify against an indemnitee's liability for his negligence is equivocal, this court has established a presumption that the parties did not intend to indemnify an indemnitee against losses resulting from his own negligent act. *Polozola v Garlock, Inc., supra; see* Civil Code art. 2288 (1870); Civil Code art. 1852 (1984).

The rule or presumption of *Polozola v. Garlock, Inc.* is derived from the principles of equity. To impose on a person an obligation to indemnify another against the indemnitee's own negligence without the obligor's unambiguous consent is contrary to the principles of equity. Because of the obligor's lack of ability to evaluate, predict, or control the risk which may be created by the indemnitee's future conduct, enforcement of such a provision without clear evidence that the risk was bargained for and accepted may allow one to take unfair advantage of another and unjustly enrich himself at the other's expense. *See* Civil Code arts. 1964, 1965 and 1966 (1870); Civil Code art. 2055 (1984). Moreover, such an injustice may encourage antisocial acts and a relaxation of vigilance toward the rights of others by relieving the wrongdoer of liability for his conduct. *See Hyde v. Chevron*, 697 F.2d 614 (5th Cir. 1983); *Strickland v. Tesoro Drilling Co.*, 434 So. 2d 424 (La.App. 1 Cir. 1983); *Rodriguez v. Olin Corp.*, 780 F.2d 491 (5th Cir. 1986).

In the case of claims, causes of action and liability which may arise under Civil Code article 2317, the indemnitor usually is in as good a position as the indemnitee to evaluate and protect against the risk. Correlatively, indemnity against liability for the custodianship of dangerous things does not provide as great a disincentive to careful and prudent conduct as does indemnity against the consequences of the indemnitee's own negligence. Therefore, this court has not established a presumption of contractual intention in the instance of a doubtful provision regarding indemnity against strict liability under Civil Code article 2317.

For the reasons assigned, the judgment of the Court of Appeal is amended to render judgment in favor of third-party plaintiff, Texas Pipeline Company, and against third-party defendant, Atlas Construction Company, for full indemnity against the amounts Texas Pipeline was required to pay in judgment on the principal demands, with legal interest from the date of judicial demand until paid, all costs of these proceedings, and attorney's fees of $5000.00; otherwise the judgment of the Court of Appeal is affirmed.

AMENDED AND AFFIRMED.

* * * * *

LEMMON, Justice, dissenting.

The contract to build storage tanks on Texas' premises cannot reasonably be construed so as to conclude that Atlas intended to indemnify Texas for liability for latent premises defects in the roads on the premises when the defects were in existence prior to the commencement of Atlas' operations on the premises and were neither caused nor aggravated by those operations. Even more clearly, Atlas did not intend to indemnify Texas for liability for latent premises defects in areas other than the area in which Atlas was building the storage tanks. Moreover, Atlas was in no better position at the time of the execution of the contract to evaluate, predict or control the risks arising from latent defects on the premises for which Texas was responsible as custodian than it was to evaluate, predict or control the risks arising from Texas' negligence. Allowing indemnification to Texas under these circumstances discourages vigilance on the part of lessees to discover and remedy hazards on premises under their control.

La. R.S. 9:2780.   **Certain indemnification agreements invalid (the Louisiana Oilfield Anti-Indemnity Act)**

A.   The legislature finds that an inequity is foisted on certain contractors and their employees by the defense or indemnity provisions, either or both, contained in some agreements pertaining to wells for oil, gas, or water, or drilling for minerals which occur in a solid, liquid, gaseous, or other state, to the extent those provisions apply to death or bodily injury to persons. It is the intent of the legislature by this Section to declare null and void and against public policy of the state of Louisiana any provision in any agreement which requires defense and/or indemnification, for death or bodily injury to persons, where there is negligence or fault (strict liability) on the part of the indemnitee, or an agent or employee of the indemnitee, or an independent contractor who is directly responsible to the indemnitee.

B.   Any provision contained in, collateral to, or affecting an agreement pertaining to a well for oil, gas, or water, or drilling for minerals which occur in a solid, liquid, gaseous, or other state, is void and unenforceable to the extent that it purports to or does provide for defense or indemnity, or either, to the indemnitee against loss or liability for damages arising out of or resulting from death or bodily injury to persons, which is caused by or results from the sole or concurrent negligence or fault (strict liability) of the indemnitee, or an agent, employee, or an independent contractor who is directly responsible to the indemnitee.

C.   The term "agreement," as it pertains to a well for oil, gas, or water, or drilling for minerals which occur in a solid, liquid, gaseous, or other state, as used in this Section, means any agreement or understanding, written or oral, concerning any operations related to the exploration, development, production, or transportation of oil, gas, or water, or drilling for minerals which occur in a solid, liquid, gaseous, or other state, including but not limited to drilling, deepening, reworking, repairing, improving, testing, treating, perforating, acidizing, logging, conditioning, altering, plugging, or otherwise rendering services in or in connection with any well drilled for the purpose of producing or excavating, constructing, improving, or otherwise rendering services in connection with any mine shaft, drift, or other structure intended for use in the exploration for or production of any mineral, or an agreement to perform any portion of any such work or services or any act collateral thereto, including the furnishing or rental of equipment, incidental transportation, and other goods and services furnished in connection with any such service or operation.

(1) The provisions of this Section do not affect the validity of any insurance contract, except as otherwise provided in this Section, or any benefit conferred by the worker's compensation laws of this state, and do not deprive a full owner or usufructuary of a surface estate of the right to secure an indemnity from any lessee, operator, contractor, or other person conducting operations for the exploration or production of minerals on the owner's land.

* * * * *

G.   Any provision in any agreement arising out of the operations, services, or activities listed in Subsection C of this Section of the Louisiana Revised Statutes of 1950 which requires waivers of subrogation, additional named insured endorsements, or any other form of insurance protection which would frustrate or circumvent the prohibitions of this Section, shall be null and void and of no force and effect.

* * * * *

I.   This Act shall apply to certain provisions contained in, collateral to or affecting agreements in connection with the activities listed in Subsection C which are designed to provide indemnity to the indemnitee for all work performed between the indemnitor and the indemnitee in the future. This specifically includes what is commonly referred to in the oil industry as master or general service agreements or blanket contracts in whatever form and by whatever name. The provisions of this Act shall not apply to a contract providing indemnity to the indemnitee when such contract was executed before the effective date of this Act and which contract governs a specific terminable performance of a specific job or activity listed in Subsection C.

NOTES

1.   R.S. 9:2780 applies "if (but only if) the agreement (1) pertains to a well and (2) is related to exploration, development, production, or transportation of oil, gas or water.... (W)hether a contract pertains to a well or to drilling requires a fact intensive case-by-case analysis." There is no bright line standard for determining when natural gas no longer "pertains to a well"; in each situation there should be a reasonably determinable point at which the gas can no longer be identified with a particular well, or is so fundamentally changed in processing, commingling or preparation for distribution that it no longer "pertains to a well." *Transcontinental Gas v. Transportation Ins. Co.*, 953 F.2d 985 (5th Cir. 1992). *See also, Hanks v. Transcontinental Gas Pipe Corp.*, 935 F.2d 996 (5th Cir. 1992) – a contract for construction of an intermediate segment of an interstate gas transmission pipeline did not "pertain to a well" within the meaning of the Act. *See also, Broussard v. Conoco, Inc.*, 964 F.2d 1145 (5th Cir. 1992). In *Verdine v. Enasco Offshore Co.*, 225 F.3d 246 (5th Cir. 2001), the court, holding that the Louisiana Oilfield Anti-Indemnity Act applies to a contract to repair a dismantled fixed platform rig, observes that determination of the application of the act "requires a fact intensive case by case analysis," lists 10 non-exclusive factors relevant to the analysis, and further observes that the "decisive factor in most cases has been the functional nexus between an agreement and a well."

2.   In *Hutchins v. Hill Petroleum Co.*, a five-judge panel split 3-2, the majority holding that R.S. 9:2780 does not apply to a contract to provide labor service at an oil refinery. 609 So. 2d (La.App. 3 Cir. 1992).

3.   In *Meloy v. Conoco, Inc.*, 504 So. 2d 833 (La. 1987), the court ruled that the Oilfield Indemnity Act nullifies completely any provision in any agreement covered by the act that requires defense and/or indemnification where there is any negligence or fault on the part of the indemnitee. The court rejected the contention that the act bars indemnification only to the extent of the indemnitee's own fault but allows indemnification for the proportionate fault of the indemnitor. Since a cause of action for indemnification for cost of defense does not arise until the lawsuit is concluded and defense costs are paid, the allegations of the complaint against the indemnitee are irrelevant to the indemnitor's obligation to pay. "(T)he terms of the indemnity agreement...govern the obligations of the parties." Where R.S. 9:2780 applies, the indemnitor's obligation for cost of defense cannot be determined until there has been a judicial finding that the indemnitee is liable or that the charges against it were baseless. "If it is established at trial that there is no 'negligence or fault (strict liability) on the part of the indemnitee,' the Act does not prohibit indemnification for cost of defense."

4.   In *Griffin v. Tenneco Oil Co.*, 625 So. 2d 1090 (La.App. 4 Cir. 1993), the indemnity agreement extended to "sole negligence or gross negligence" but excluded injuries "intentionally caused by willful misconduct of employees...." *Held*, the indemnity agreement covers a claim for punitive damages under C.C. Art. 2315.3. The indemnity agreement excludes claims for intentional acts; the punitive damage claim is for conduct "falling somewhere between simple negligence and intentional wrong doing. Although it did not specially say so, it is highly probable that the legislature meant that conduct to be gross negligence...."

5.   Can the tort victim be a third party beneficiary to a contract of indemnity by which a third person agrees to indemnify the tortfeasor from damages caused by certain activities? If the third person is an insurer, the Louisiana Direct Action Statute, R.S. 22:655, produces the same result. What if the third person is not an insurer, but a private indemnitor? *See Dartez v. Dixon*, 502 So. 2d 1063 (La. 1987).

2. **Tort Indemnity**

R.S. 9:3921.   Remission, transaction, compromise, or other conventional discharge of obligations

A.   Notwithstanding any provision in Title Ill of Code Book Ill of Title 9 of the Louisiana Revised Statutes of 1950 to the contrary, every master or employer is answerable for the damage occasioned by his servant or employee in the exercise of the functions in which they are employed. Any remission, transaction, compromise, or other conventional discharge in favor of the employee, or any judgment rendered against him for such damages shall be valid as between the damaged creditor and the employee, and the employer shall have no right of contribution, division, or indemnification from the employee nor shall the employer be allowed to bring any incidental action under the provisions of Chapter 6 of Title I of Book II of the Louisiana Code of Civil Procedure against such employee.

B.   The provisions of this Section are remedial and shall be applied retrospectively and prospectively to any cause of action for damages arising prior to, on, or after the effective date of this Section.

NOTE

See Butler v. Intersouth Pipeline, 655 F.Supp. 587 (MD La. 1986), pointing out that in Louisiana tort indemnity, which has a statutory basis in C.C. Art. 1804, is available only when (1) the indemnitee is only vicariously liable, or (2) the indemnitee's liability is only strict, and the indemnitor's negligence created the unreasonably dangerous condition which made the indemnitee strictly liable. R.S. 9:3921, *supra*, speaks to the first kind of indemnity. With the demise of strict liability, the second type of indemnity is of waning importance.

3. **Contribution**

COMMENT

When tortfeasors are solidarily liable and one pays the share of another joint tortfeasor, he is entitled to recoup that payment through the Civil Codes article on subrogation. La. Civ. Code arts. 1804, et. seq., developed concept of tort contribution. In cases arising after the 1996 amendments, there is tort solidarity only in the case of conspiring intentional tortfeasors, so there will be few instances of tort contribution.

C.   EFFECT OF SETTLEMENT WITH ONE SOLIDARY OBLIGOR

La. Civil Code Article 1803.   Remission of debt to or transaction or compromise with one obligor

Remission of debt by the obligee in favor of one obligor, or a transaction or compromise between the obligee and one obligor, benefits the other solidary obligors in the amount of the portion of that obligor.

Surrender to one solidary obligor of the instrument evidencing the obligation gives rise to a presumption that the remission of debt was intended for the benefit of all the solidary obligors.

COMMENT

Where one of two or more joint tortfeasors settles with the tort victim, he may obtain from the victim a satisfaction of judgment. In that case, all of the tortfeasors are discharged, and the settling tortfeasor may have a claim for indemnity or contribution against the non-settling joint tortfeasors. Generally, however, the settling tortfeasor will obtain a partial release (releasing only the victim's claims against him), and the victim will reserve his rights against the non-settling tortfeasors. In such a case, the non-settling tortfeasors no longer have any right of contribution (subrogation) against the settling tortfeasor.

Where there is a settlement with one of the tortfeasors, evidence of his fault nevertheless is admissible to establish either (a) that the non-settling defendant was not at fault, or (b) the percentages of fault (and thus the liability of the non-settling defendant). A nonsettling defendant will attempt to prove a high percentage of fault by the settling defendant so that the allocation to the nonsettling defendant is smaller.

Since 1996 the only joint tortfeasors who are solidarily liable are those who conspire to commit an intentional or willful act. C.C. Art. 2324(A). It is not clear whether contribution is permitted between such tortfeasors. *See* Maraist & Galligan, Louisiana Tort Law (Lexis Nexis 2004 ed.), § 12.03. The Fifth Circuit held that fault should be allocated and there was a right of contribution if a solidarily liable intentional tortfeasor paid more than the virile share allocated to him in *Dileo v. Horn*, 189 So. 3d 1189 (La.App. 5 Cir. 2016). The court reasoned as follows:

> La. C.C. arts. 2323, 1917 and 1812 do not set forth an exception for solidary obligors with respect to the trial court's obligation to assign fault. Furthermore, while a solidary obligor is fully liable for the entire amount of damages awarded to the plaintiff, La. C.C. art. 1804 permits a solidary obligor who pays the entire award to seek contribution in the amount of the virile portion owed by each obligor. La. C.C. art. 1804 provides that the virile portion is determined from the fault assigned to each solidary obligor.

NOTES

1. The Louisiana approach of reducing the non-settling defendant's obligation to the plaintiff by the percentage of fault of the settling defendant did not find universal acceptance. Some jurisdictions give the non-settling defendant a "dollar for dollar" credit for the amount received by the plaintiff from the settling defendant, and preserve contribution rights among the defendants. *See, e.g., Federal Savings and Loan Insurance Corp. v. McGinnis, Juban, Bevan, Mullins & Patterson, PC*, 808 F. Supp. 1263 (ED La. 1992). Louisiana expressly rejected the "dollar-for-dollar" credit approach, both by the statutory language of CC Art. 1803 and by judicial decision. *See Taylor v. U.S.F. & G. Ins. Co.*, 630 So. 2d 237 (La. 1993).

2. Consider Louisiana Rule of Evidence 413: "Any amount paid in settlement...shall not be admitted into evidence unless the failure to make a settlement ... is an issue in the case."

3. Sometimes the settlement with a joint tortfeasor will not only release the settling tortfeasor but will also provide him with the opportunity to recoup part of what he has paid from the plaintiff's subsequent recovery from the non-settling tortfeasor. Such a Mary Carter agreement does not violate public policy. *Howard v. ICRR*, 709 So. 2d 1044 (La.App. 5 Cir. 1998). Important post-'96?

4. Settlement of a minor's claim is invalid unless court approval is obtained prior to confection of the settlement. Thus where the parties enter into a consent judgment in federal court before obtaining state court approval, the judgment is unenforceable, although the minor's guardian qualified as tutor before the consent judgment was entered, and the settlement funds have not been paid. *Carter v. Fenner*, 136 F.3d 1000 (5th Cir. 1998).

5. *Palmer v. Walker*, 31 So. 3d 443 (La.App. 5 Cir. 2010). After accident, driver of one vehicle signed release which stated that it released "all other persons, firms, and corporations from any and all claims ... arising out of ... [the] accident." The driver who signed the release did not realize that the other driver was in the course and scope of employment at the time of the accident. The driver's employer and insurer also were released by the compromise.

CHAPTER 16

PRODUCTS LIABILITY

A.   INTRODUCTORY NOTE

Products Liability is an area of tort law that defines the duties and obligations associated with the distribution of products. Tort law is not the only relevant area of substantive law. Because the distribution of products usually involves a sale, contract law or the law of obligations is also relevant. However, recovery in contract is usually limited to the value of the contract and to the parties to the contract. Individuals who were injured by defective products sought recovery of personal injury damages. Thus, jurisdictions have been forced to evaluate plaintiff's rights in a gray and hazy area somewhere between tort and contract.

Early cases often denied the injured plaintiff's claims because of the doctrine of "privity of contract." "Privity" required that the plaintiff be a party to the contract. Since the contract for sale usually was between the retailer and the purchaser plaintiff, the manufacturer was effectively shielded from liability. Similarly, many non-purchaser users or bystanders were denied recovery because they were not privies to the contract.[75]

Beginning with the landmark case of *McPherson v. Buick Motor Co.*, 217 N.Y. 382, 111 N.E. 1050 (Ct. of App., 1916), the doctrine of privity dramatically restricted and the area of "products liability," as a hybrid of tort and contract, took its place. Modern products liability is an amalgamation of contract law, negligence, strict liability, and doctrines designed exclusively for application to the distribution of products. Many jurisdictions, including Louisiana, have enacted statutes which replace the varied and somewhat inconsistent caselaw. However, the statutes leave some issues unanswered and raise new issues under the statutory language.

As you study products liability, keep several things in mind:

1.   Who is the defendant? Is the defendant a manufacturer, a retailer, or some other party in the chain of distribution? Different theories apply.

2.   Who is the plaintiff? Is the plaintiff a purchaser, user, bystander or some other party? Is the use foreseeable? Different theories and principles apply depending upon the nature of the plaintiff and the use of the product.

3.   What is the theory? Are you applying principles of contract, negligence, strict liability or a statutory theory?

In Louisiana, we must analyze products liability along several different theoretical lines. First, unlike many jurisdictions, the Louisiana law of obligations extended liability beyond the boundaries of the agreement to include the manufacturer. Second, Louisiana adopted the Louisiana Product Liability Act (LPLA) in 1988, but the statute applies prospectively only. However, most product liability cases are analyzed under the statute. Third, since the LPLA applies only to manufacturers and a few special non-manufacturer-sellers, most of the pre-Act law will apply to non-manufacturer defendants. Finally, many products are regulated and products liability attorneys must address the intersection between tort law and regulation.

---

[75] The doctrine of privity was not as important in Louisiana as in common law jurisdictions. *See* Section II. A. *infra*.

B.   PRE-LPLA LIABILITY

1.   Negligence and Redhibition

Prior to the passage of the Louisiana Product Liability Act (LPLA), a plaintiff could proceed against a manufacturer in negligence, redhibition (contract), or strict liability in tort. The plaintiff's negligence claim operated just like any other negligence claim. The plaintiff bore the burden of proving that the manufacturer or retailer failed to exercise reasonable care in preventing or correcting the risk. Lack of privity between the manufacturer and the plaintiff was not a defense.

In pre-LPLA cases, a plaintiff could also recover against the manufacturer by applying the law of obligations. The plaintiff's burden was to establish that the product had a "redhibitory vice." La. Civ. Code art. 2520. Under La. Civ. Code art. 2545, a seller who knows of a defect in his product and is in bad faith is liable for all damages which its product causes. Furthermore, a manufacturer is presumed to know the defects in the things it manufactures and thus is a bad faith seller. *George v. Shreveport Cotton Oil Co.*, 114 La. 498, 38 So. 432 (1905). Thus prior to 1988, the manufacturer of a defective product was liable in contract for personal injury damages. Privity between the manufacturer and the purchaser was not required, but there was some doubt concerning whether non-purchasers could bring an action for redhibition.

YOUNG
v.
FORD MOTOR COMPANY, INC.
595 So. 2d 1123 (La. 1992)

CALOGERO, C.J.

We granted a writ of review in this case to determine whether the purchaser of a defective or useless vehicle which has not caused physical injury can recover damages for emotional distress. For the reasons which follow, we conclude that such purchasers can recover mental anguish damages caused by purchase of the defective product even though the product is not unreasonably dangerous and they have not sustained physical injuries, but only if the requirements of Louisiana Civil Code articles 2545 and 1998 are satisfied. Article 2545 addresses the seller's liability for a product which contains a redhibitory defect, while Article 1998 concerns the availability of nonpecuniary damages in breach of contract cases.

* * * * *

In the present case, Iray Young, a forty-nine year old service station owner, purchased a 1988 Ford Supercab pickup truck from Bordelon Motors, Inc. on January 15, 1988 for use in connection with his service station and for recreation and pleasure. Within three days of the purchase, Young had returned to the dealer complaining about one of a number of major problems that surfaced with the truck and which subsequently prompted this redhibition action for rescission of the sale, attorney's fees, and damages for mental pain and anguish.

During this time, Young's medical doctor and friend, Dr. John Fruge, testified that the truck had caused Young problems with sleeping, concentrating, and even sex. He noted that Young became tense, angry and frustrated during this period and that this developed into depression for which Dr. Fruge prescribed a combination tranquilizer and antidepressant. The court of appeal stated that "the record supports the trial court's finding that plaintiff suffered emotional distress as a result of the hassels [sic] associated with this defective truck."

The case was tried to a jury which rendered a verdict casting Bordelon and Ford in solido for the sum of $19,910.07 (cost of the vehicle plus rental charges) and against Ford alone for $7,900.00 for plaintiff's attorney's fees, and the now disputed $3,750.00 in mental anguish damages. Although Bordelon Motors was not cast for any part of the $3,750, it joined Ford in the appeal which questioned only the $3,750 mental anguish damages.

This court has had no difficulty allowing mental anguish damages in cases where personal injury has resulted from defective products. For example, in *Philippe v. Browning Arms Co.*, 395 So. 2d 310, 319 (La. 1980), we held that "[t]he seller's (manufacturer's) act of delivering a defective thing, when he knows of the defect, gives rise to delictual, as well as contractual liability."[3] This court explained that in cases of injury by defective products, "the duty of the manufacturer is fixed by that part of the Civil Code dealing with sales, but that recovery for the injury arises under Article 2315."

However, this case presents a different issue than the ones just discussed. It involves the sale of a product containing a redhibitory vice that has not caused physical injury. Additionally, it involves a situation where the plaintiff seeks to have the sale rescinded under the redhibition articles of the Civil Code and to secure recovery of mental anguish damages incident thereto. We therefore look first to the redhibition articles and then to the obligations articles pertaining to damages recoverable in breach of contract cases.

Redhibition is defined in LSA-C.C. art. 2520:

> Redhibition is the avoidance of a sale on account of some vice or defect in the thing sold, which renders it either absolutely useless, or its use so inconvenient and imperfect, that it must be supposed that the buyer would not have purchased it, had he known of the vice.

Liability of the seller of a product which contains a redhibitory defect is set forth in Article 2545 (emphasis added):

> The seller who knows the vice of the thing he sells and omits to declare it, besides the restitution of price and repayment of the expenses, including reasonable attorneys' fees, is answerable to the buyer in damages.

In Louisiana, sellers are bound by an implied warranty that the thing sold is free of hidden defects and is reasonably fit for the buyer's intended use. *Rey v. Cuccia*, 298 So. 2d 840 (La. 1974). A buyer of an automobile who asserts a redhibition claim need not show the particular cause of the defects making the vehicle unfit for the intended purposes, but rather must simply prove the actual existence of such defects. *Crawford v. Abbott Automobile Co.*, 157 La. 59, 101 So. 871 (1924). Multiple defects can collectively form the basis of a redhibitory action even though many of the defects are minor or have been repaired. *Cangelosi v. McInnis Peterson Chevrolet, Inc.*, 373 So. 2d 1346 (La.App. 1 Cir. 1979); *Perrin v. Read Imports, Inc.*, 359 So. 2d 738 (La.App. 4 Cir. 1978). In situations where new vehicles present such defects as would render their use inconvenient and imperfect to the extent that the buyer would not have purchased the automobile had he or she known of the defects, the buyer is entitled to a rescission of the sale instead of merely a reduction in the price. *Davidson v. New Roads Motor Co., Inc.*, 385 So. 2d 319 (La.App. 1 Cir. 1980), *writ denied*, 391 So. 2d 454 (La. 1980).

* * * * *

There has been an abundance of discussion in the legal literature since the 1984 Obligations Revision, specifically regarding the Legislature's replacing former Article 1934(3) with current Article 1998.[9] This court has interpreted former Article 1934(3) in *Meador v. Toyota of Jefferson, Inc.*, 332

---

[3] *See infra,* note 5 and accompanying text for additional discussion regarding the jurisprudential principle of imputing knowledge of defects to manufacturers of the defective product.

[9] Former Article 1934(3) provided:
> Although the general rule is, that damages are the amount of the loss the creditor has sustained, or of the gain of which he has been deprived, yet there are cases in which damages may be assessed without calculating altogether on the pecuniary loss, or the privation of pecuniary gain to the party. Where the

So. 2d 433 (La. 1976), where an eighteen-year old plaintiff took her first car, damaged in a collision, to the car dealership for repair and did not get it back until seven months later. In that case, defendant contended that in order for plaintiff to recover nonpecuniary damages, the object of the contract must be exclusively intellectual enjoyment, rather than partially intellectual (now called nonpecuniary in the replacement article 1998) and partially physical (now called pecuniary). The court responded:

> This Court has never adopted a strict view but has reached results favoring the broader interpretation of Art. 1934(3).... The contract's object [in an analogous case regarding a contract for a wedding dress] was not purely intellectual, but rather entailed features both physical (her need for comfortable clothing), and intellectual (her preference for style, or "taste," and concern with her appearance on her wedding day ...).

Id. at 435-36 (citations omitted). The court cited two other cases where "there existed both intellectual and physical gratification" and then reviewed the origin of Article 1934(3) including its mistranslation from the French source provision into the 1825 Louisiana Civil Code. Id. at 436. After lengthy discussion, the court concluded that:

> While the foregoing interpretation does not allow nonpecuniary damages where the sole object is physical gratification, a proper interpretation of the entirety of Article 1934(3) does not in our view bar such damages in all instances where there exists as an object physical gratification. We believe that a contract can have "for its object" intellectual enjoyment, assuming that intellectual enjoyment is a principal object of the contract ...

> Thus, we would interpret Article 1934(3) as follows: Where an object, or the exclusive object, of a contract, is physical gratification (or anything other than intellectual gratification) nonpecuniary damages as a consequence of nonfulfillment of that object are not recoverable. On the other hand, where a principal or exclusive object of a contract is intellectual enjoyment, nonpecuniary damages resulting from the nonfulfillment of that intellectual object are recoverable. Damages in this event are recoverable for the loss of such intellectual enjoyment as well as for mental distress, aggravation, and inconvenience resulting from such loss, or denial of intellectual enjoyment.

Meador, 332 So. 2d at 437 (italics in original; bold emphasis added). Thus, in *Meador*, we determined that plaintiff was not entitled to recover mental anguish damages, but only because she did not prove that the intellectual enjoyment of which she was deprived while denied her car for seven months was "a principal object of the contract to have the car repaired." *Id.* (emphasis added).

* * * * *

Thus, under Article 1998, which is the controlling article for the type of damages referred to by the redhibition articles (specifically Article 2545), if it can be established that the obligee intended--and if the nature of the contract supports this contention--to gratify a significant nonpecuniary interest by way of the contract, and that the obligor either knew or should have known that failure to perform would cause nonpecuniary loss to the obligee, then the requirements for recovery of nonpecuniary damages are satisfied.

Although purchase of a new truck or car may be prompted by both the pecuniary interest of securing transportation and the nonpecuniary interest relating to enjoyment, taste, and personal

---

contract has for its object the gratification of some intellectual enjoyment, whether in religion, morality or taste, or some convenience or other legal gratification, although these are not appreciated in money by the parties, yet damages are due for their breach; a contract for a religious or charitable foundation, a promise of marriage, or an engagement for a work of some of the fine arts, are objects and examples of this rule.

preference of owning and driving the chosen vehicle, the nature of the contract is primarily pecuniary (unless other factors evidence a different conclusion).[19] Contrast the contract of purchase made in a standard new car sale with a contract for purchase of an antique car that, while it might be driven on the streets, represents the obligee's desire to own, and perhaps to show, a distinctive, unique automobile. Or, contrast the traditional new car purchase contract with a contract for purchase of a specially-designed, custom-built vehicle.

In this case, the nature of the contract does not make it evident, nor do the facts and circumstances surrounding the formation of the contract demonstrate that Young purchased the new pickup truck from Bordelon Motors, Inc. for a significant nonpecuniary purpose. Although he testified that he wanted a larger cab area so that he could lie down on trips if his back started to bother him, that desire seemed more incidental in nature than that which would constitute a significant nonpecuniary interest in purchasing the truck. The rest of his testimony concerned the need to use the truck in his service station business to haul tires or to transport customers while their cars were being fixed. Even his plans for recreational use of the vehicle (i.e., fishing trips) constituted the pecuniary interest of requiring suitable transportation to haul his fishing boat.

The jury cast defendant for $3,750, finding in answer to interrogatories propounded by the trial judge that Young had suffered "substantial and extreme emotional distress." However, the jury verdict was not returned following a charge elucidating the law as we have found and recited it herein. They simply determined in response to interrogatories that use of the vehicle by plaintiff caused him to suffer extreme emotional distress. Since they did not make the requisite determination that the plaintiff intended to gratify a significant nonpecuniary interest when he entered into the contract with Bordelon Motors, and because *Gonzales v. Xerox*, 320 So. 2d 163 (La. 1975) requires us to decide the case rather than remand it to the district court, we conclude from this record that Young did not make the requisite showing of having entered this contract with Bordelon Motors to gratify a significant nonpecuniary interest as Article 1998 requires for the recovery of mental anguish damages.

Decree

For the foregoing reasons, the judgment of the court of appeal denying plaintiff Iray Young's recovery of $3,750 in mental anguish damages is affirmed, for the reasons given in this opinion.

AFFIRMED.

NOTES AND QUESTIONS

1.   *Young* was decided in 1992, after the legislature enacted the LPLA. However, the LPLA is never mentioned. Why not?

2.   Does *Young* have any application following the adoption of the LPLA?   In what circumstances does it still apply?

---

[19] The use of the word "nonpecuniary" (and "pecuniary") flows from Article 1998, replacing the reference in former Article 1934(3) to "intellectual enjoyment". *See supra* notes 9 and 11 for more details regarding these terms. The term "physical" to represent the opposite of "intellectual enjoyment" was a jurisprudential creation. *See, e.g., Meador, supra* note 12.

2.   **Strict Liability**

WEBER

v.

FIDELITY & CAS. INS. CO. OF NEW YORK
259 So. 2d 599 (La. 1971)

TATE, J.

A customer claims damages from the manufacturer of cattle dip and its insurer. The dip had been bought from a local supplier, no longer a party. Application of the dip caused seven of the plaintiff's son's cattle to die shortly thereafter, and his two then-minor boys to become ill.

The court of appeal reversed a trial court judgment in favor of the plaintiff and his sons, now majors. 236 So. 2d 616 (La.App. 1 Cir. 1970) We granted certiorari, 256 La. 848, 239 So. 2d 356 (1970), to review the plaintiff's substantial contention that the court of appeal incorrectly denied recovery for damages resulting from the use of the manufacturer's product. The issue is whether the intermediate court erred in reversing the trial determination that the cattle dip was defective.

Both previous courts correctly found applicable the following legal principles:

> A manufacturer of a product which involves a risk of injury to the user is liable to any person, whether the purchaser or a third person, who without fault on his part, sustains an injury caused by a defect in the design, composition, or manufacture of the article, if the injury might reasonably have been anticipated. However, the plaintiff claiming injury has the burden of proving that the product was defective, i.e., unreasonably dangerous to normal use, and that the plaintiff's injuries were caused by reason of the defect.

> If the product is proven defective by reason of its hazard to normal use, the plaintiff need not prove any particular negligence by the maker in its manufacture or processing; for the manufacturer is presumed to know of the vices in the things he makes, whether or not he has actual knowledge of them.

In the present instance, as the previous courts found, the evidence clearly proves a causal relationship between the injuries sustained and the use of the product. The evidence shows that, as found by both of the previous courts, the seven cattle died, shortly after spraying, because of excessive amounts of arsenic in the spray solution containing the defendant's cattle dip product. Further, the plaintiff's two then-minor boys doing the spraying also became nauseated as the result of arsenical poisoning, due to such excessive arsenic.

* * * * *

Since the plaintiffs have established by circumstantial evidence that the most probable cause of their damages was the improper arsenic proportions and preparation of the dip by the manufacturer, we affirm the trial court's finding that the plaintiff has proved liability by a preponderance of the evidence.

Accordingly, for the reasons assigned, we reverse the judgment of the court of appeal which dismissed this suit, and we reinstate and affirm the judgment of the trial court awarding the plaintiffs damages in the amounts shown, with legal interest.

NOTE

Restatement (Second) of Torts § 402A in force at the time of *Weber* provided that:

(1)   One who sells any product in a defective condition unreasonably dangerous to the user or consumer or to his property is subject to liability for physical harm thereby caused to the ultimate user of consumer, or to his property, if

   (a)   the seller is engaged in the business of selling such a product, and

   (b)   it is expected to and does reach the user or consumer without substantial change in the condition in which it is sold.

(2)   The rule stated in subsection (1) applies although

   (a)   the seller has exercised all possible care in the preparation and sale of his product, and

      (b)   the use or consumer has not bought the product from or entered into any contractual relation with the seller.

Does Justice Tate adopt § 402A? If not, is the Weber standard similar to §402A? See if your analysis changes after you read the *Halphen* case below.

HALPHEN
v.
JOHNS-MANVILLE SALES CORPORATION
484 So. 2d 110 (La. 1986)

DENNIS, J.

A widow sued an asbestos products manufacturer in a United States District Court for the wrongful death of her husband caused by his exposure to asbestos.[1] She invoked Louisiana's strict products liability tort law under the court's diversity jurisdiction. Before trial the District Court excluded all evidence of whether the manufacturer knew or could have known of the dangers of asbestos on the grounds that such evidence is irrelevent to whether the product is unreasonably dangerous. After a trial, a jury found that the manufacturer's asbestos products were unreasonably dangerous and had been a proximate cause of the deceased's death. The District Court entered judgment awarding damages to the widow for her husband's illness and wrongful death.

The manufacturer appealed to the United States Court of Appeals. A divided three judge panel of that court affirmed. *Halphen v. Johns-Manville Sales Corp.*, 737 F.2d 462 (5th Cir. 1984). Acting en banc, however, the Court of Appeals recalled its decision and certified to us the following question:

---

[1] *See Halphen v. Johns-Manville Sales Corp.,* 755 F.2d 393 (5th Cir. 1985): "This is a strict products liability action for damages from wrongful death between Emma Jean Halphen, Plaintiff, and Johns-Manville Sales Corporation, Defendant, which was tried in the United States District Court for the Western District of Louisiana in Lake Charles, in January, 1982.
    "Plaintiff's husband, Samuel Halphen, died during the pendency of the lawsuit from a malignant pleural mesothelioma, a cancer of the lining of the lung. Plaintiff alleged that her husband had been exposed to asbestos-containing products sold by Johns-Manville, while working at a shipyard in Orange, Texas in 1945, and at various times during his career as a serviceman in the Air Force." *Id.* At 393-4.

Question Certified

In a strict products liability case, may a manufacturer be held liable for injuries caused by an unreasonably dangerous product if the manufacturer establishes that it did not know and reasonably could not have known of the inherent danger posed by its product? *Halphen v. Johns-Manville Sales Corp.*, 752 F.2d 124, 755 F.2d at 393 (5th Cir. 1985) (en banc).

Response to Certified Question

Having granted certification, we respond by (1) stating the legal precepts which govern the issues raised by the certified question, (2) answering the question specifically, and (3) elaborating the reasons for the precepts and answers.

1. Legal Precepts

There is general agreement upon the most basic principles of strict tort products liability. In order to recover from a manufacturer, the plaintiff must prove that the harm resulted from the condition of the product, that the condition made the product unreasonably dangerous to normal use, and that the condition existed at the time the product left the manufacturer's control. The plaintiff need not prove negligence by the maker in its manufacture or processing, since the manufacturer may be liable even though it exercised all possible care in the preparation and sale of its product. *Bell v. Jet Wheel Blast*, 462 So. 2d 166 (La. 1985); *Hebert v. Brazzel*, 403 So. 2d 1242 (La. 1981); *DeBattista v. Argonaut-Southwest Ins. Co.*, 403 So. 2d 26 (La. 1981); *Hunt v. City Stores*, 387 So. 2d 585 (La. 1980); *Chappuis v. Sears, Roebuck & Co.*, 358 So. 2d 926 (La. 1978); *Weber v. Fidelity & Casualty Ins. Co. of New York*, 259 La. 599, 250 So. 2d 754 (1971).

As strict products liability in tort was originally conceived, the manufacturer's ability to know of the danger of its product at the time of sale was immaterial. Under pure strict liability theory, the product is on trial, not the knowledge or conduct of the manufacturer. Subsequently, additional products liability theories developed which permit the plaintiff to recover when the manufacturer fails to give adequate warning or adopt an alternate design to make the product safer. Under these later theories, the knowledge available to the manufacturer when it designs, manufactures, and markets the product may be material. Accordingly, whether the knowledge of the danger in a product is material, relevant, or admissible depends on the particular theory of recovery under which the plaintiff tries his case.

An essential element of a plaintiff's case under each strict products liability theory of recovery is proof that the defendant's product was unreasonably dangerous to normal use. The method of proof of this element varies under each theory, however, and this is why the knowledge available to the manufacturer is material only with regard to certain theories. Because there is disagreement among jurisdictions as to the nature, the classification, and even the existence of some grounds of recovery, we will set forth the elements of each strict liability theory recognized by this court in order to explain whether knowledge available to the manufacturer is material under each theory.

In describing the theories of recovery, we use the classifications of unreasonably dangerous products recognized by most courts. Additionally, we recognize products which are "unreasonably dangerous per se" as a separate class of defective products. For products in this category liability may be imposed solely on the basis of the intrinsic characteristics of the product irrespective of the manufacturer's intent, knowledge or conduct. This category should be acknowledged as giving rise to the purest form of strict liability and clearly distinguished from other theories in which the manufacturer's knowledge or conduct is an issue.

A product is unreasonably dangerous per se if a reasonable person would conclude that the danger-in-fact of the product, whether foreseeable or not, outweighs the utility of the product.[2] *Hunt*

---

[2] This test is known as the risk-utility or danger-utility test. Other tests may have their own merits in different contexts, *see DeBattista v. Argonaut-Southwest Ins. Co. Supra; Herbert v. Brazzell, supra; Welch v. Outboard*

v. City Stores, Inc., 387 So. 2d 585 (La. 1980); *cf. Entrevia v. Hood*, 427 So. 2d 1146 (La. 1983); *Langlois v. Allied Chemical Corp.*, 258 La. 1067, 249 So. 2d 133, 140 (1971). This theory considers the product's danger-in-fact, not whether the manufacturer perceived or could have perceived the danger, because the theory's purpose is to evaluate the product itself, not the manufacturer's conduct. Likewise, the benefits are those actually found to flow from the use of the product, rather than as perceived at the time the product was designed and marketed. The fact that a risk or hazard related to the use of a product was not discoverable under existing technology or that the benefits appeared greater than they actually were are both irrelevant. . Under this theory, the plaintiff is not entitled to impugn the conduct of the manufacturer for its failure to adopt an alternative design or affix a warning or instruction to the product. A warning or other feature actually incorporated in the product when it leaves the manufacturer's control, however, may reduce the danger-in-fact. If a plaintiff proves that the product is unreasonably dangerous per se, it is not material that the case could have been tried as a design defect case or other type defect case.

A product is unreasonably dangerous in construction or composition if at the time it leaves the control of its manufacturer it contains an unintended abnormality or condition which makes the product more dangerous than it was designed to be. *See Weber v. Fidelity & Casualty Ins. Co., N.Y., supra* (cattle dip arsenic content exceeded intended specifications); *MacPherson v. Buick Motors*, 217 N.Y. 382, 111 N.E. 1050 (1916); Prosser and Keeton on Torts, p. 695 (5th ed. 1984); A manufacturer or supplier who sells a product with a construction or composition flaw is subject to liability without proof that there was any negligence on its part in creating or failing to discover the flaw. Evidence of what knowledge was available to the manufacturer has no relevance in such cases because the product, by definition, failed to conform to the manufacturer's own standards.

Although a product is not unreasonably dangerous per se or flawed by a construction defect, it may still be an unreasonably dangerous product if the manufacturer fails to adequately warn about a danger related to the way the product is designed. A manufacturer is required to provide an adequate warning of any danger inherent in the normal use of its product which is not within the knowledge of or obvious to the ordinary user. In performing this duty a manufacturer is held to the knowledge and skill of an expert. It must keep abreast of scientific knowledge, discoveries, and advances and is presumed to know what is imparted thereby. A manufacturer also has a duty to test and inspect its product, and the extent of research and experiment must be commensurate with the dangers involved. Under the failure to warn theory evidence as to the knowledge and skill of an expert may be admissible in determining whether the manufacturer breached its duty.

A product may be unreasonably dangerous because of its design for any one of three reasons: (1) A reasonable person would conclude that the danger-in-fact, whether foreseeable or not, outweighs the utility of the product. This is the same danger-utility test applied in determining whether a product is unreasonably dangerous per se. This first reason for concluding that a design is defective is governed by the same criteria for deciding whether a product is unreasonably dangerous per se. The overlap in categories makes it unnecessary to decide whether a product's defect is one of design or of another kind if the product is proven to be unreasonably dangerous per se. (2) Although balancing under the risk-utility test leads to the conclusion that the product is not unreasonably dangerous per se, alternative products were available to serve the same needs or desires with less risk of harm; or, (3) Although the utility of the product outweighs its danger-in- fact, there was a feasible way to design the product with less harmful consequences. In regard to the failure to use alternative products or designs, as in the duty to warn, the standard of knowledge, skill and care is that of an expert, including the duty to test, inspect, research and experiment commensurate with the danger. Accordingly, evidence as to whether the manufacturer, held to the standard and skill of an expert, could know of and feasibly avoid the danger is admissible under a theory of recovery based on alleged alternative designs or alternative products. Such evidence is not admissible, however, in a suit based on the first design defect theory, which is governed by the same criteria as proof that a product is unreasonably dangerous per se.

Marine Corp., 481 F.2d 252 (5th Cir. 1973). We are convinced, however, that the risk utility test is best for determining whether a product is unreasonably dangerous per se.

The plaintiff may elect to try his case upon any or all of the theories of recovery. If he decides to pursue more than one, he is entitled to an instruction that evidence which is admissible exclusively under one theory may be considered only for that purpose.

2. Answer to Certified Question

In a strict products liability case, if the plaintiff proves that the product was unreasonably dangerous per se (whether because of defective design or another kind of defect) or unreasonably dangerous in construction or composition, a manufacturer may be held liable for injuries caused by an unreasonably dangerous product, although the manufacturer did not know and reasonably could not have known of the danger.

3. Reasons for Precepts and Answer

Strict products liability evolved from principles of public order, and its contours should be shaped according to the purposes it serves within the framework of our civil code. *See Bell v. Jet Wheel Blast*, 462 So. 2d 166, 170 (La. 1985); *Langlois v. Allied Chemical Corp.*, 258 La. 1067, 249 So. 2d 133 (1971); Planiol, Civil Law Treatise, Vol. 2, Part 1, Nos. 806, 807 (LSLI translation 1939). Accordingly, we have relied on analogy to the codal principle of legal fault or strict liability as well as empirical elements in reaching our conclusions.

A. Codal Principle of Legal Fault or Strict Liability

A principle of legal fault or strict liability underlies articles 2317- 22 of the Civil Code: When harm results from the conduct of a person or defect of a thing which creates an unreasonable risk of harm to others, a person legally responsible under these code articles for the supervision, care, or guardianship of the person or thing may be held liable for the damage thus caused, despite the fact that no personal negligent act or inattention on the former's part is proved. The injured person must prove the vice (i.e., unreasonable risk of injury to another) in the person or thing whose act causes the damage, and that the damage resulted from this vice. Once this is proved the owner or guardian responsible for the person or thing can escape liability only if he shows the harm was caused by the fault of the victim, by the fault of a third person, or by an irresistible force. *Loescher v. Parr*, 324 So. 2d 441 (La. 1975).

The strict liability or legal fault thus arising from our code provisions is more than a rebuttable presumption of negligence. The owner or guardian cannot be absolved from his strict liability even if he proves that he did not know and could not have known of the unreasonable risk of harm to others. *See Loescher v. Parr, supra*. (A tree owner is responsible for damage caused by the tree's fall although he could not reasonably have known of its internally diseased condition. C.C. Article 2317); *Holland v. Buckley*, 305 So. 2d. 113 (La. 1974). (A dog owner is strictly liable for injury done by the animal's first bite even if he could not have known of the dog's harm- causing characteristic. C.C. 2321); *Turner v. Bucher*, 308 So. 2d 270 (La. 1975). (A parent is strictly liable for damage caused by his child's defective conduct regardless of the fact that the parent could not have prevented the child's act. C.C. 2318); *Olsen v. Shell Oil Corp.*, 365 So. 2d 1285 (La. 1979) (A building owner is strictly liable for damage caused by the defective condition of the premises regardless of whether he is ignorant of the condition and reasonably could not have detected it. C.C. Art. 2322).

The underlying reason for the owner's or guardian's strict liability is that the person to whom society allots the supervision, care or guardianship (custody) of the risk-creating person or thing should bear the loss resulting from creation of the risk, rather than some innocent third person harmed as a consequence of his failure to prevent the risk. *Loescher v. Parr, supra*; *see Olsen v. Shell Oil Corp., supra* n. 13;

The principle of strict products liability is analogous to the principle of legal fault or strict liability underlying civil code articles 2317-22. The manufacturer who places an unreasonably dangerous product on the market that causes injury to innocent victims is subject to strict liability even if he has not been guilty of any negligence. The liability arises from his legal relationship to the product and is based on the product's unreasonably dangerous condition. One of the reasons for strict products liability is similar to that underlying the codal strict liability: The person to whom society allots the supervision, care, or guardianship (custody) of the risk-creating thing bears the loss resulting from creation of the risk, rather than some innocent third person harmed as a consequence of its defective condition. Although the manufacturer usually does not have custody of the product when the injury occurs, in order for strict product liability to arise, the plaintiff must prove that the product's unreasonably dangerous condition arose or existed while it was in the manufacturer's control, that the condition existed at the time the product left the control of the manufacturer, and that the product reached the user in substantially that same defective condition. Another underlying reason for strict products liability affords grounds for holding the manufacturer even more strictly liable than the owner or custodian for damage caused by his risk-creating product: Manufacturers typically are better able than owners or custodians to spread the cost of strict liability through pricing and liability insurance.

Because of the close resemblance between the two forms of strict liability and the reasons for them, reliance on analogy to the civil code indicates that the manufacturer who places an unreasonably dangerous product on the market that causes injury to innocent victims should not be permitted to escape liability by showing that he did not know and could not have known of the danger. Otherwise, the liability of a manufacturer who distributes large numbers of unreasonably dangerous products causing multiple injuries and deaths would be less strict than that of an ordinary homeowner for the act or defect of his child, animal or tree.

An injured person cannot recover under the codal theory of strict liability if he fails to prove there was an unreasonable risk of injury inherent in the thing which caused his damage. Failing in his attempt to prove a vice in the thing, the injured person cannot rely on strict liability but must pursue a theory of recovery instead which requires him to impugn the conduct of the defendant. Analogy to the product liability field indicates, therefore, that an injured consumer who fails to prove that the product is unreasonably dangerous per se or has a construction defect must pursue a less strict theory of recovery which impugns the conduct of the manufacturer, such as an action for failure to warn or for failure to adopt an alternative design.

The parties urge contradictory arguments based on different parts of this court's opinion in *Weber v. Fidelity & Casualty Ins. Co. of New York, supra.* Plaintiff contends that one passage in that opinion indicates that the manufacturer is absolutely and conclusively presumed to know of the defects in its products under all theories of products liability recovery, including the failure to warn theory. Defendant argues that another passage imposes a general requirement that the particular danger which results in the user's injury must have been foreseeable by the manufacturer for it to be held strictly liable. But, in *Weber* the manufacturer was held liable under a theory that the product was unreasonably dangerous because of a manufacturing flaw or construction defect, viz., an excessive amount of arsenic in cattle dip not made in accordance with the producer's intended specifications. Thus, the difficult issues presented by scientifically unknowable dangers or liability for failure to warn were not raised, and we do not attribute to the *Weber* court any intention to decide these issues prematurely.

Even if we were to agree with one of the parties' interpretations, we would still answer the certified question as we have. *Weber* is this court's landmark opinion on strict products liability, and we continue to be guided by its basic holding and its spirit. Nevertheless, this court has viewed strict products liability as an instrument of public order based on both codal principles and empirical considerations, not as a purely judicial creation. Accordingly, the principle of strict liability has developed since *Weber*, and its shape will continue to be molded by its purpose within our codal framework. *See*, e.g., *Bell v. Jet Wheel Blast, supra*; *Hunt v. City Stores, Inc., supra*; *Chappuis v. Sears, Roebuck & Co., supra*; cf. *Kent v. Gulf States Utilities Co.*, 418 So. 2d 493 (La. 1982); *Entrevia v. Hood, supra.*

B. Empirical Elements

Strict products liability and accident law in general pursue four primary goals: (1) reduction of the total cost of accidents by deterring activity causing accidents, (2) reduction of the societal cost of accidents by spreading the loss among large numbers, (3) reducing the cost of administering accident cases, and (4) achieving these goals by methods consistent with justice. Since these goals are not fully consistent with one another, the overall aim is to strive for the best combination of cost reduction in all these categories in a just way. *See Bell v. Jet Wheel Blast, supra*; *DeBattista v. Argonaut-Southwest Ins. Co., supra*; *Turner v. NOPSI*, 476 So. 2d 800, 806 (La. 1985) (concurring opinion); G. Calabresi, The Costs of Accidents, (Yale University 1979).

To further these goals within the framework of our civil code, we have concluded that as between an innocent consumer injured by a product which is unreasonably dangerous per se, i.e., too dangerous to be placed on the market, and the manufacturer who puts the product into commerce without being aware or able to know of its danger, the manufacturer must bear the cost of the damage caused by its product. On the other hand, if the consumer fails to prove that the product is unreasonably dangerous per se and seeks to prove his case by impugning the manufacturer's conduct, e.g., by contending that the manufacturer failed to warn or to adopt feasible alternative designs, in fairness the manufacturer should be permitted to introduce evidence and present argument as to the standard of knowledge and conduct by which its conduct is to be judged.

The scientific inability to avoid occasional flaws in products due to miscarriages in the construction process has never altered the fact that an impure or flawed product is defective if the product proves to be more dangerous than it was intended to be. Similarly, when a plaintiff proves that a product is bad and defective because its utility is outweighed by its danger-in-fact, i.e., unreasonably dangerous per se, and the plaintiff proves this theory of recovery without impugning the conduct of the manufacturer, the producer should be held strictly liable regardless of scientific inability to know or to avoid the danger.

On balance, a rule of law requiring the manufacturer to assume the cost of accidents caused by products which are unreasonably dangerous per se, regardless of whether the danger was foreseeable, will provide an effective incentive to eliminate all possible dangers before putting products on the market. *Cf. Bell v. Jet Wheel Blast, supra*; moreover, any discouragement to produce new products or to discover safety improvements will be mitigated by the manufacturer's ability to defend failure to warn cases, alternative design cases and alternative product cases on the basis of scientific unknowability and inability. We conclude that recognizing an unreasonably dangerous per se category as a form of "pure" strict liability along with construction or manufacturing defects will provide even greater incentives to produce safe products.

Reducing the societal cost of accidents by spreading the loss among large groups would not be promoted by leaving part of the cost of accidents, diseases and deaths caused by unreasonably dangerous products on consumers. Insurance specifically designed to cover such losses would be unavailable to consumers as a practical matter. Of course, some losses from scientifically unknowable dangers may prove to be uninsurable for producers also. Manufacturers as a class, however, are still in a better position than consumers to analyze and take action to avoid the risk, to negotiate for broader insurance coverage, and to pass losses on in the form of price increases. Furthermore, the rule we have adopted does not prevent the manufacturer from introducing evidence of scientific knowledge, or the lack thereof, in cases where such knowledge is material, such as in duty-to-warn cases. If the cost of accidents caused by products which are unreasonably dangerous per se and are defective because of construction flaws is placed on manufacturers, a much greater portion of the cost of such accidents may be spread among consumers and manufacturers rather than placed on individual accident victims.

The costs of administering the unreasonably dangerous per se category of products liability cases will be reduced by eliminating litigation over the date when a product's danger became scientifically knowable. In unreasonably dangerous per se cases, as in construction defect cases now, the parties should not be forced to produce experts in the history of science and technology to speculate, and possibly confuse jurors, as to what knowledge was available and what improvements were feasible in a given year.

Further, a sense of justice also requires that a manufacturer not be permitted to subsidize its production of a product which is unreasonably dangerous per se at the expense of innocent accident victims. Just as our civil code requires that a custodian of a dangerous thing compensate a victim for the unforeseen harm it causes, so should a manufacturer bear the unforeseen costs that its product inflicts on the helpless user. Moreover, great injustice will result if a manufacturer who knew that a product was unreasonably dangerous per se before it was marketed escapes liability because the plaintiff cannot carry the difficult burden of proving when scientific knowledge was available to the manufacturer. Finally, equality in treatment of like cases which is at the heart of our received notions of justice demands that the manufacturer of a product which is unreasonably dangerous per se should not be allowed a defense which is unavailable to the maker of a product that happens to have a construction flaw, or to the custodian of an animal, child or thing. Each of these defendants is strictly liable in tort for injuries caused by the product, person or thing for which he is responsible, even though the defect or dangerous characteristic was not discoverable prior to the time of the injury. Justice and consistency dictate that the manufacturer of a product that is unreasonably dangerous per se be treated in the same manner.

Conclusion

Accordingly, we answer the certified question as set forth in this opinion. Pursuant to Rule XII, Supreme Court of Louisiana, the judgment rendered by this court upon the question certified shall be sent by the clerk of this court under its seal to the United States Court of Appeals for the Fifth Circuit and to the parties.

CERTIFIED QUESTION ANSWERED.

NOTES

1. Applying *Halphen*, the Fifth Circuit concluded that asbestos was unreasonably dangerous per se. *Halphen v. Johns-Manville Sales Corp.*, 788 F.2d 275 (5th Cir. 1986).

2. How does *Halphen* alter the *Weber* test? How do you determine if *Halphen* applies in a given case?

3. How would you apply *Halphen* to the following products: cigarettes *(Gilboy v. American Tobacco Co.*, 582 So. 2d 1263 (La. 1991)), escalators *(Brown v. Sears, Roebuck & Co.*, 514 So. 2d 439 (La. 1987)), three-wheel ATVs *(Antley v. Yamaha Motor Corp. USA*, 539 So. 2d 696 (La.App. 3 Cir. 1989)), shotguns *(Cappo v. Savsage Indus., Inc.*, 691 So. 2d 876 (La.App. 2 Cir. 1997)).

4. In response to *Halphen*, the Louisiana legislature enacted the Louisiana Products Liability Act. Note therein how the legislature changed the product liability analysis.

C.   LOUISIANA PRODUCTS LIABILITY ACT

La. R.S. 9:2800.52.   Scope of this Chapter

This Chapter establishes the exclusive theories of liability for manufacturers for damage caused by their products. A claimant may not recover from a manufacturer for damage caused by a product on the basis of any theory of liability that is not set forth in this Chapter. Conduct or circumstances that result in liability under this Chapter are "fault" within the meaning of Civil Code Article 2315. This Chapter does not apply to the rights of an employee or his personal representatives, dependents or relations against a manufacturer who is the employee's employer or against any principal or any officer, director, stockholder, partner or employee of such manufacturer or principal as limited by R.S. 23:1032, or to the rights of a claimant against the following, unless they assume the status of a manufacturer as defined in R.S. 9:2800.53(1):

(1) Providers of professional services, even if the service results in a product.

(2) Providers of nonprofessional services where the essence of the service is the furnishing of judgment or skill, even if the service results in a product.

(3) Producers of natural fruits and other raw products in their natural state that are derived from animals, fowl, aquatic life, or invertebrates, including but not limited to milk, eggs, honey, and wool.

(4) Farmers and other producers of agricultural plants in their natural state.

(5) Ranchers and other producers of animals, fowl, aquatic life, or invertebrates in their natural state.

(6) Harvesters and other producers of fish, crawfish, oysters, crabs, mollusks, or other aquatic animals in their natural state.

La. R.S. 9:2800.53.   Definitions

The following terms have the following meanings for the purpose of this Chapter:

[handwritten: → Focus on professional nature for purposes of LPLA]

(1)   "Manufacturer" means a person or entity who is in the business of manufacturing a product for placement into trade or commerce. "Manufacturing a product" means producing, making, fabricating, constructing, designing, remanufacturing, reconditioning or refurbishing a product. "Manufacturer" also means:

(a) A person or entity who labels a product as his own or who otherwise holds himself out to be the manufacturer of the product.

[handwritten: #making product DOESN'T nece mean create from scratch]

(b) A seller of a product who exercises control over or influences a characteristic of the design, construction or quality of the product that causes damage.

(c) A manufacturer of a product who incorporates into the product a component or part manufactured by another manufacturer. *[handwritten: → doesn't usually apply to sellers]*

[handwritten: #walmart not liable under LPLA for selling something # ↓ BUT if labeled as own, then it may be liable as manufacturer]

(d) A seller of a product of an alien manufacturer if the seller is in the business of importing or distributing the product for resale and the seller is the alter ego of the alien manufacturer. The court shall take into consideration the following in determining whether the seller is the alien manufacturer's alter ego: whether the seller is affiliated with the alien manufacturer by way of common ownership or control; whether the seller assumes or administers product warranty obligations of the alien manufacturer; whether the seller prepares or modifies the product for distribution; or any other relevant evidence. A "product of an alien manufacturer" is a product that is manufactured outside the United States by a manufacturer who is a citizen of another country or who is organized under the laws of another country.

(2)   "Seller" means a person or entity who is not a manufacturer and who is in the business of conveying title to or possession of a product to another person or entity in exchange for anything of value.

(3)   "Product" means a corporeal movable that is manufactured for placement into trade or commerce, including a product that forms a component part of or that is subsequently incorporated into another product or an immovable. "Product" does not mean human blood, blood components, human organs, human tissue or approved animal tissue to the extent such are governed by R.S. 9:2797.

(4)   "Claimant" means a person or entity who asserts a claim under this Chapter against the manufacturer of a product or his insurer for damage caused by the product.

[handwritten: → Exclusive Theory But → exception: rehibition claim (in notes)]

(5)   "Damage" means all damage caused by a product, including survival and wrongful death damages, for which Civil Code Articles 2315, 2315.1 and 2315.2 allow recovery. "Damage" includes damage to the product itself and economic loss arising from a deficiency in or loss of use of the product only to the extent that Chapter 9 of Title VII of Book III of the Civil Code, entitled "Redhibition," does not allow recovery for such damage or economic loss. Attorneys' fees are not recoverable under this Chapter.

(6)   "Express warranty" means a representation, statement of alleged fact or promise about a product or its nature, material or workmanship that represents, affirms or promises that the product or its nature, material or workmanship possesses specified characteristics or qualities or will meet a specified level of performance. "Express warranty" does not mean a general opinion about or general praise of a product. A sample or model of a product is an express warranty.

(7)   "Reasonably anticipated use" means a use or handling of a product that the product's manufacturer should reasonably expect of an ordinary person in the same or similar circumstances.

(8)   "Reasonably anticipated alteration or modification" means a change in a product that the product's manufacturer should reasonably expect to be made by an ordinary person in the same or similar circumstances, and also means a change arising from ordinary wear and tear. "Reasonably anticipated alteration or modification" does not mean the following:

(a) Alteration, modification or removal of an otherwise adequate warning provided about a product.

(b) The failure of a person or entity, other than the manufacturer of a product, reasonably to provide to the product user or handler an adequate warning that the manufacturer provided about the product, when the manufacturer has satisfied his obligation to use reasonable care to provide the adequate warning by providing it to such person or entity rather than to the product user or handler.

(c) Changes to or in a product or its operation because the product does not receive reasonable care and maintenance.

(9)   "Adequate warning" means a warning or instruction that would lead an ordinary reasonable user or handler of a product to contemplate the danger in using or handling the product and either to decline to use or handle the product or, if possible, to use or handle the product in such a manner as to avoid the damage for which the claim is made.

La. R.S. 9:2800.54.   Manufacturer responsibility and burden of proof

[handwritten: → "foreseeably" caused]

A.   The manufacturer of a product shall be liable to a claimant for damage proximately caused by a characteristic of the product that renders the product unreasonably dangerous when such damage arose from a reasonably anticipated use of the product by the claimant or another person or entity.

B.   A product is unreasonably dangerous if and only if: [handwritten: ✳ 4 theories P can recover from ✳]

(1)   The product is unreasonably dangerous in construction or composition as provided in R.S. 9:2800.55; [handwritten: ✳ BAD BATCH theory ✳ → just about the batch, NOT the design]

(2)   The product is unreasonably dangerous in design as provided in R.S. 9:2800.56;

(3)   The product is unreasonably dangerous because an adequate warning about the product has not been provided as provided in R.S. 9:2800.57; or

635

(4)   The product is unreasonably dangerous because it does not conform to an express warranty of the manufacturer about the product as provided in R.S. 9:2800.58.

C.   The characteristic of the product that renders it unreasonably dangerous under R.S. 9:2800.55 must exist at the time the product left the control of its manufacturer. The characteristic of the product that renders it unreasonably dangerous under R.S. 9:2800.56 or 9:2800.57 must exist at the time the product left the control of its manufacturer or result from a reasonably anticipated alteration or modification of the product.

D.   The claimant has the burden of proving the elements of Subsections A, B and C of this Section.

La. R.S. 9:2800.55.   Unreasonably dangerous in construction or composition

Did product deviate in material way from when it left control of manufacturer?

A product is unreasonably dangerous in construction or composition if, at the time the product left its manufacturer's control, the product deviated in a material way from the manufacturer's specifications or performance standards for the product or from otherwise identical products manufactured by the same manufacturer.

La. R.S. 9:2800.56. Unreasonably dangerous in design

A product is unreasonably dangerous in design if, at the time the product left its manufacturer's control:

cost/burden analysis

(1)   There existed an alternative design for the product that was capable of preventing the claimant's damage; and

risk/utility balancing kinda

(2)   The likelihood that the product's design would cause the claimant's damage and the gravity of that damage outweighed the burden on the manufacturer of adopting such alternative design and the adverse effect, if any, of such alternative design on the utility of the product. An adequate warning about a product shall be considered in evaluating the likelihood of damage when the manufacturer has used reasonable care to provide the adequate warning to users and handlers of the product.

Failure to warn claim

La. R.S. 9:2800.57.   Unreasonably dangerous because of inadequate warning

A.   A product is unreasonably dangerous because an adequate warning about the product has not been provided if, at the time the product left its manufacturer's control, the product possessed a characteristic that may cause damage and the manufacturer failed to use reasonable care to provide an adequate warning of such characteristic and its danger to users and handlers of the product.

B.   A manufacturer is not required to provide an adequate warning about his product when:

(1)   The product is not dangerous to an extent beyond that which would be contemplated by the ordinary user or handler of the product, with the ordinary knowledge common to the community as to the product's characteristics; or

(2)   The user or handler of the product already knows or reasonably should be expected to know of the characteristic of the product that may cause damage and the danger of such characteristic.

C.   A manufacturer of a product who, after the product has left his control, acquires knowledge of a characteristic of the product that may cause damage and the danger of such characteristic, or who would have acquired such knowledge had he acted as a reasonably prudent manufacturer, is liable for damage caused by his subsequent failure to use reasonable care to provide an adequate warning of such characteristic and its danger to users and handlers of the product.

After-the-fact warning duty

636

La. R.S. 9:2800.58. **Unreasonably dangerous because of nonconformity to express warranty**

A product is unreasonably dangerous when it does not conform to an express warranty made at any time by the manufacturer about the product if the express warranty has induced the claimant or another person or entity to use the product and the claimant's damage was proximately caused because the express warranty was untrue.

La. R.S. 9:2800.59. **Manufacturer knowledge, design feasibility and burden of proof**

A. Notwithstanding R.S. 9:2800.56, a manufacturer of a product shall not be liable for damage proximately caused by a characteristic of the product's design if the manufacturer proves that, at the time the product left his control:

(1) He did not know and, in light of then-existing reasonably available scientific and technological knowledge, could not have known of the design characteristic that caused the damage or the danger of such characteristic; or

(2) He did not know and, in light of then-existing reasonably available scientific and technological knowledge, could not have known of the alternative design identified by the claimant under R.S. 9:2800.56(1); or

(3) The alternative design identified by the claimant under R.S. 9:2800.56(1) was not feasible, in light of then-existing reasonably available scientific and technological knowledge or then-existing economic practicality.

B. Notwithstanding R.S. 9:2800.57(A) or (B), a manufacturer of a product shall not be liable for damage proximately caused by a characteristic of the product if the manufacturer proves that, at the time the product left his control, he did not know and, in light of then-existing reasonably available scientific and technological knowledge, could not have known of the characteristic that caused the damage or the danger of such characteristic.

La. R.S. 9:2800.60. Liability of manufacturers and sellers of firearms

A. The legislature finds and declares that the Louisiana Products Liability Act1 was not designed to impose liability on a manufacturer or seller for the improper use of a properly designed and manufactured product. The legislature further finds and declares that the manufacture and sale of firearms and ammunition by manufacturers and dealers, duly licensed by the appropriate federal and state authorities, is lawful activity and is not unreasonably dangerous.

B. No firearm manufacturer or seller shall be liable for any injury, damage, or death resulting from any shooting injury by any other person unless the claimant proves and shows that such injury, damage, or death was proximately caused by the unreasonably dangerous construction or composition of the product as provided in R.S. 9:2800.55.

C. Notwithstanding any other provision of law to the contrary, no manufacturer or seller of a firearm who has transferred that firearm in compliance with federal and state law shall incur any liability for any action of any person who uses a firearm in a manner which is unlawful, negligent, or otherwise inconsistent with the purposes for which it was intended.

D. The failure of a manufacturer or seller to insure that a firearm has a device which would: make the firearm useable only by the lawful owner or authorized user of the firearm; indicate to users that a cartridge is in the chamber of the firearm; or prevent the firearm from firing if the ammunition magazine is removed, shall not make the firearm unreasonably dangerous, unless such device is required by federal or state statute or regulation.

E. (1) For the purposes of this Chapter, the potential of a firearm to cause serious injury, damage, or death as a result of normal function does not constitute a firearm malfunction due to defect in design or manufacture.

(2) A firearm may not be deemed defective in design or manufacture on the basis of its potential to cause serious bodily injury, property damage, or death when discharged legally or illegally.

F. Notwithstanding any provision of law to the contrary, no manufacturer or seller of a firearm shall incur any liability for failing to warn users of the risk that:

(1) A firearm has the potential to cause serious bodily injury, property damage, or death when discharged legally or illegally.

(2) An unauthorized person could gain access to the firearm.

(3) A cartridge may be in the chamber of the firearm.

(4) The firearm is capable of being fired even with the ammunition magazine removed.

G. The provisions of this Section shall not apply to assault weapons manufactured in violation of 18 U.S.C. § 922(v).

NOTES AND QUESTIONS

1. Pursuant to R.S. 9:2800.52, the LPLA provides the exclusive theories of liability for manufacturers. However, Louisiana courts continue to allow redhibition claims for economic loss. What language in the LPLA allows such a claim to continue to be viable? *See Draden v. Winn-Dixie of La, Inc.*, 652 S0. 2d 675 (La.App. 1 Cir. 1995).

2. The LPLA exludes claims of negligence against manufacturers. What is the purpose of this exclusion? Two of your authors have argued that the elimination of negligence may be "ill-founded and ill-advised." Frank L. Maraist and Thomas C. Galligan, Louisiana Tort Law §15-5 (1996 and Supp. 2002).

3. The statute requires that an "unreasonably dangerous" characteristic of the product "proximately" cause the injury. The statute also requires that the damage arise out of a "reasonably-anticipated use" of the product. What is the relationship between these two inquiries?

4. The LPLA is not retroactive. *Gilboy v. American Tobacco Co.*, 528 So. 2d 1263 (La. 1991). It applies only to causes of action accruing on or after Sept. 1, 1988. For purposes of the LPLA, a cause of action accrues when the claimant suffers damage. *Brown v. R.J. Reynolds Tobacco Co.*, 52 F.3d 524 (5th Cir. 1995) (smoker who produces no evidence that he suffered damages or bodily injury before the effective date of the Act cannot recover under the *Haphen* "unreasonably dangerous per se theory). But *see Pitre v. GAF Corp.*, 705 So. 2d 1149 (La.App. 1 Cir. 1997) (declining to follow *Brown v. Reynolds Tobacco*; in long-latent product liability claim, governing law is law in effect when the victim is significantly exposed to the product).

5. There are some statutes that apply to specific products. For example, the Protection of Lawful Commerce in Arms Act, 15 U.S.C. §§ 7901-7903, generally bars any civil action in federal or state court by any person against a manufacturer or seller of a firearm or ammunition for damages or other remedy resulting from the criminal or unlawful misuse of such a product by the person or third party.

6. For useful primers on the LPLA, *see* Thomas C. Galligan, Jr., The Louisiana Products Liability Act: Making Sense of It All, 49 La.L.Rev. 323 (1991); John N. Kennedy, A Primer on the Louisiana Products Liability Act, 49 La.L.Rev. 565 (1989).

7.   *Allstate Ins. Co. v. Fred's, Inc.*, 33 So. 3d 976 (La.App. 2 Cir. 2010), *writ denied*, 38 So. 3d 33 (La. 2010).   Under La. R.S. 9:2800.53(1) (a), a seller is a manufacturer if he "labels a product as his own."   Seller was held to be a manufacturer where label stated that it was "distributed by" seller, label stated that the product was made in China, product was sold in seller's retail store, and the product bore no other party's label.

8.   For a case regarding the common law doctrine of apparent manufacturer, *see Chevron USA, Inc. v. Aker Maritime, Inc.*, 604 F.3d 888 (5th Cir. 2010).   The court described the following facts, which constituted sufficient evidence of apparent manufacturer status:

> The jury heard evidence that Lone Star was "well-known" as a bolt manufacturer.   Chevron's agent, Aker, dealt directly and exclusively with Lone Star in purchasing bolts, and Lone Star did nothing to inform Aker that the bolts it sold were not its own. Instead, it shipped the bolts in Lone Star-labeled boxes and included a packing slip indicating that Lone Star possibly manufactured the bolts in question. It is true that the bolts had small "OF" markings on their heads. Although a bolt purchaser might have reasonably understood that the marking suggested someone other than Lone Star likely manufactured the bolts, the Oceaneering employee who photographed the bolts upon receipt was left with the impression that the bolts were Lone Star bolts, not Oriental Fastener bolts.... When considered in the context of the other evidence that Lone Star held itself out as a manufacturer, this one piece of evidence will not cause us to reverse the jury's interpretation of the facts before it.

9.   The economic loss rule denies recovery where a product fails to meet the plaintiff's economic expectations, as distinguished from products which pose an unreasonable risk of harm to the plaintiff's property and health.   Louisiana does not recognize the rule, but, as we have noted, tort damages for economic losses may be recoverable to a plaintiff under laws unique to Louisiana.   For one thing, a plaintiff may have a remedy for economic losses under Louisiana redhibition laws. In *Re Chinese Manufactured Drywall Products*, 680 F. Supp 2d 780 (ED La. 2010).

10.   In comparison to product liability in a traditional common law jurisdiction, the LPLA is a model of clarity.   Most common law jurisdictions apply Restatement (Second) Torts §402A. (Section 402A is produced following *Weber* at section B.2 of this Chapter).   Section 402A has been interpreted as applying strict liability for a "product in a defective condition unreasonably dangerous."   While the law varies, there are some common issues.   First, what does strict liability mean?   Some jurisdictions apply what appears to be absolute liability while others apply strict liability akin to the standard for construction or composition claims under the LPLA.

Second, some jurisdictions apply strict liability to all actors in the chain of distribution while others limit strict liability to manufacturers.

Third, many jurisdictions consider a product "unreasonably dangerous" if it is more dangerous than a reasonable consumer would expect.   In contrast to this consumer expectation test, other jurisdictions apply a risk-utility balancing test like that utilized for design defect claims under the LPLA.

There are many other difficult and important issues that common law courts or legislatures must resolve, and the resolution of those issues is far from uniform.

11.   In response to the uncertainty surrounding Restatement (Second §402A, the American Law Institute released the Restatement (Third) of Torts: Products Liability.   One of the more controversial features of the Restatement (Third) is that it eliminates the consumer expectation test.   Does eliminating the consumer expectation test favor plaintiffs or defendants?   Why?

D. APPLICATION OF THE STATUTE

BERNARD

v.

FERRELLGAS, INC.

689 So. 2d 554 (La.App. 3 Cir. 1997)

WOODARD, J.

Plaintiff appeals trial court's granting of a directed verdict in favor of defendant in this products liability action. We reverse.

Facts

On October 16, 1992, Russell Bernard, husband of plaintiff Jennifer Bernard (Bernard), died at the Swifty Food Store in Carenco, Louisiana. At the time of the accident, Russell was working at Swifty as a butcher and was responsible for operating the outdoor meat smoker. Two to three times a week, Russell Bernard would load the smoker with meat and light the gas burner under the wood. The smoker was custom-made, that is, it was not mass produced. While there was some discussion at trial as to whether the smoker was considered an indoor or outdoor one, the facts indicate that the smoker was located in a screened area outside the store. It was fueled by propane gas and required manual operation to start the flow of gas and light the burner. The propane delivery system for the smoker was built and installed by the defendant, Ferrellgas. The system consisted of tubing and valves running from the propane tank, through a "T" fitting, to the burner. To light the burner, Russell Bernard had to open two valves, one running from the "T" connector which started the flow of gas (the first valve), and then one closer to the burner to allow the gas into the burner (the second valve). The second valve was close to ground level. Russell Bernard was instructed to open the first valve, but not to open the second valve, until he had lit some kind of a striker to ignite the gas. If both valves were open with no flame to ignite the gas, the propane, being heavier than air, would accumulate in the bottom of the smoker, thereby causing an explosion when ignited.

Apparently, when the smoker was lit, it exploded, causing Russell Bernard to suffer massive head injuries causing instant death. Jennifer Bernard filed suit against Ferrellgas, asserting that the propane delivery system was defective because it did not have a thermocouple or other "safety shut-off" device to reduce the probability of this type of accident. In response, Ferrellgas claimed that Russell Bernard's own negligence in opening both valves was the cause of the injury. A jury trial was held January 10-16, 1996. At the close of Bernard's case, Ferrellgas moved for a directed verdict, contending that Bernard had failed to prove a prima facie case. In particular, Ferrellgas asserted that Bernard failed to show a breach of any legal duty Ferrellgas may have owed to Russell Bernard, or prove that a breach was the legal cause, or cause-in-fact of Russell Bernard's death. The trial court granted the directed verdict. Bernard now appeals this decision.

* * * * *

The Louisiana Products Liability Act (LPLA) establishes the exclusive theories of recovery against manufacturers for damage caused by their products. La.R.S. 9:2800.54 reads in pertinent part:

> A.   The manufacturer of a product shall be liable to a claimant for damage proximately caused by a characteristic of the product that renders the product unreasonably dangerous when such damage arose from a reasonably anticipated use of the product by the claimant or another person or entity.

> B.   A product is unreasonably dangerous if and only if:

> (1)   The product is unreasonably dangerous in construction or composition as provided in R.S. 9:2800.55;

640

        (2)   The product is unreasonably dangerous in design as provided in R.S. 9:2800.56;

C.   The characteristic of the product that renders it unreasonably dangerous under R.S. 9:2800.55 must exist at the time the product left the control of the manufacturer.   The characteristic of the product that renders it unreasonably dangerous under R.S. 9:2800.56 or 9:2800.57 must exist at the time the product left the control of the manufacturer or result from a reasonably anticipated alteration or modification of the product.

D.   The claimant has the burden of proving the elements of Subsections A, B and C of this Section.

Thus, any plaintiff asserting liability for damage caused by a product must prove that: (1) the defendant manufactured the product, (2) the product was unreasonably dangerous for reasonably anticipated use, and (3) the dangerous characteristic of the product existed at the time the product left the manufacturer's control, or was the result of a reasonably anticipated alteration or modification. At trial, Laress Landry, a Ferrellgas employee, testified that he installed the gas supply system and was aware of the availability of alternative safety devices such as pilot lights and automatic shutoff systems. Weston Kilchrist, a former manager at Ferrellgas, also testified that he had knowledge of alternative products, such as pilot lights and automatic shut-off systems. Uncontroverted evidence at trial established that the product was not altered or modified in any way. Thus, Bernard has shown that Ferrellgas manufactured the product, that alternative products existed at the time the gas supply system was manufactured and left Ferrellgas' control, and that the product was not altered or modified in any way. This leaves the court to determine if the second
requirement, whether the product is unreasonably dangerous, has been met. La.R.S. 9:2800.56 provides that:

A product is unreasonably dangerous in design if, at the time the product left its manufacturer's control:

        (1)   There existed an alternative design for the product that was capable of preventing the claimant's damage; and

        (2)   The likelihood that the product's design would cause the claimant's damage and the gravity of that damage outweighed the burden on the manufacturer of adopting such alternative design and the adverse effect, if any, of such alternative design on the utility of the product. An adequate warning about a product shall be considered in evaluating the likelihood of damage when the manufacturer has used reasonable care to provide the adequate warning to users and handlers of the product.

This section requires a dual showing. First, the plaintiff must show that: (1) an alternative design existed for the product at the time it left the manufacturer's control, and (2) the alternative design was capable of preventing the claimant's damage. However, even if there existed an alternative product capable of preventing the damage, a plaintiff must also meet the second requirement, the so called "risk-utility" analysis, in which the utility of the product is weighed against the risk of harm. We shall analyze these requirements in turn.

Existence of an Alternative Design

The first requirement is that there existed an alternative design for the product that was capable of preventing the claimant's damage. It has already been established through testimony that alternative products existed. We must, however, determine whether those products might have prevented Russell Bernard's injuries. A cause of action under the LPLA, while differing from general tort law in some areas, is premised upon tort principles. Bernard is asserting that Ferrellgas was negligent in its design of the gas supply system and that this omission caused Russell Bernard's

641

injuries. If there was no alternative way to make the product safer, Ferrellgas could not have prevented the decedent's injuries and therefore, is not liable.

Another way to answer this question is through a cause-in-fact analysis. "Courts which have evaluated cause in fact ... have applied the 'but for' and substantial factor tests alternately and in combination to determine cause in fact." *Quick v. Murphy Oil Co.*, 93-2267, p. 8 (La.App. 4 Cir. 9/20/94); 643 So. 2d 1291, 1295, *writ denied*, 94-2583 (La. 1/6/95); 648 So. 2d 923. "Conduct is a cause in fact of harm to another if it was a substantial factor in bringing about that harm." *Thomas v. Missouri Pacific Railroad Co.*, 466 So. 2d 1280, 1285 (La. 1985). The requirement that an alternative design be capable of preventing the injury essentially asks whether Ferrellgas' failure to equip the gas supply system with a pilot light or other safety device was a substantial factor in bringing about Russell Bernard's injuries. That is, whether Russell Bernard's death would have been prevented "but for" Ferrellgas' failure to adopt an alternative design.

* * * * *

In the present case, Bernard asserts that even if Russell Bernard opened both valves before lighting the burner, there was testimony that a pilot light or other safety shut-off system would have significantly reduced the chances of an explosion resulting from such inadvertence. Furthermore, Dr. Pesuit testified that, based on the location of the second valve so close to the ground, a person could inadvertently open the valve with his or her foot, causing gas to escape. Further, based on tests of the valve in question, Dr. Pesuit opined that the valve did not need to be completely opened in order for gas to escape. Thus, Bernard has presented a factual scenario with which reasonable persons could agree; namely, that Russell Bernard unknowingly opened the second valve with his foot or lower leg, even slightly, and then lit the accumulated gas. Based upon this evidence we conclude that reasonable jurors could find Ferrellgas' failure to equip the smoker with a safety device was a significant factor in causing Russell Bernard's injuries.

Duty/Risk

It has already been determined that there existed an alternative design for the gas supply system. We must determine, however, whether the lack of some alternative safety device rendered the product unreasonably dangerous.

A product may be unreasonably dangerous because of its design for one of the following reasons: (1) a reasonable person would conclude that the danger-in- fact, whether foreseeable or not, outweighs the utility of the product; (2) although balancing under the risk-utility test leads to the conclusion that the product is not unreasonably dangerous per se, alternative products were available to serve the same needs and desires with less risk of harm; or (3) although the utility of the product outweighs its danger-in-fact, there was a feasible way to design the product with less harmful consequences.

* * * * *

Like the initial determination as to whether there existed an alternative design capable of preventing the claimant's harm, the second requirement, the so called "risk utility" requirement, is also based on general tort principles. Once the defect in design is found to be the cause-in-fact of the injury, the court must determine whether the manufacturer had a duty to design the product differently. Thus, the "risk utility" test asks whether, based on the alternative designs available, the manufacturer breached its duty of care in adopting the particular design in question....

The first determination to be made is what risk, if any, the product in question created. In assessing this risk, this court may also consider any effect an adequate warning may have had on the likelihood of damage. In the present case, evidence overwhelmingly established that the gas supply system was very dangerous if not used properly....

The next determination is whether a reasonable person would conclude that the danger-in-fact, whether foreseeable or not, outweighs the utility of the product. In the present case, Ferrellgas contends that the product was not unreasonably dangerous and that the explosion was caused solely by Russell Bernard's negligence. Ferrellgas further argues that Russell Bernard was well aware of the dangers of the system and, in fact, had trained others on its safe use. Russell Bernard's deliberate opening of both valves, however, was not the only possible cause of this accident. As was shown above, Dr. Pesuit testified that the second valve was close to the ground and could have been inadvertently opened by someone's foot, allowing gas to escape. Based upon this testimony, we find that a reasonable juror could reach a contrary verdict.

* * * * *

Conclusion

The judgment of the trial court is reversed, and this case is remanded. Costs of this appeal are to be determined upon outcome of the trial.

NOTES & QUESTIONS

1. How would the analysis in *Bernard* change if *Halphen* were still valid?

2. How does *Bernard* differ from a typical negligence case?

3. What are the requirements of a failure to warn theory? Consider the following case.

KRUMMEL
v.
BOMBARDIER CORPORATION
206 F.3d 548 (5th Cir. 2000)

DUHÉ, J.

Robert Krummel and his wife, Patricia Krummel, brought an admiralty and maritime claim under Fed.R.Civ.P. 9(h) against Bombardier Corp. and Bombardier, Inc. ("Bombardier") for damages resulting from Robert Krummel's injuries while using a Bombardier personal watercraft.[2] They alleged that the watercraft was unreasonably dangerous and Bombardier failed to warn them of these dangers. After a bench trial, the district court held that Bombardier did not defectively design the watercraft; however, Bombardier failed to provide warnings regarding use of the watercraft. The court awarded damages. Bombardier appeals arguing that the district court erred in finding it had a duty to warn. We agree and reverse.

Background

The Krummels in 1994 purchased two 1994 Bombardier Sea-Doo GTX watercraft ("watercraft"). Bombardier, Inc. manufactured the watercraft and Bombardier Corp. distributed it. The watercraft is designed to carry one operator and two passengers. The watercraft's footwells are approximately five and one-half inches wide and 11 inches high at the area where an operator places his or her feet. These footwells slope and therefore are not as high at the spot where the rear passenger places his or her feet. Prior to the accident, Robert Krummel read all of Bombardier's instruction manuals and watched a video. None of these materials warned him of the potential for his leg to become trapped when the vehicle tipped over. Bombardier's promotional material called falling overboard an expected part of the fun.

---

[2] The Appellees pled causes of action only under the Louisiana Products Liability Act and the Restatement (Third) of Products Liability.

On August 27, 1994, Robert Krummel operated his watercraft on the Tchefuncte River, a navigable body of water located in St. Tammany Parish, Louisiana. Riding with him were Patricia Krummel, seated behind him, and their daughter, seated in front of him. While Robert Krummel was waiting on the watercraft at an idle speed for his son, using the other watercraft, to catch up, a wake struck the starboard side of the watercraft, causing the Krummels to tip to the port side. As he began to fall, Robert Krummel intentionally buried his left foot into the footwell in an attempt to brace himself and keep from falling off. His wife, who had her arms wrapped around her husband, pulled on him as she fell off. Robert Krummel's foot remained in the footwell as his body continued to move to the left. His tibia and fibula snapped, and the break occurred at between eight and 11 inches up the leg.

* * * * *

The court held that the entrapment caused by the high footwell was the sole and proximate cause of Mr. Krummel's injury. The court then made two important legal conclusions. First it determined that the 11-inch footwells did not render the product defective in design under the Restatement (Third) of Product Liability § 2(b) and the Louisiana Products Liability Act ("LPLA") La.Rev.Stat. Ann. § 9:2800.56. Second, the court held Bombardier liable for failing to warn Krummel regarding the risks posed by the height of the footwell. The court determined liability under both the Restatement (Third) of Products Liability § 2(c) and the LPLA, La.Rev.Stat. Ann. § 9:2800.57(A).

Standard of Review

In admiralty cases tried by the district court without a jury, we review the district court's legal conclusions de novo and its factual findings for clear error.

Discussion

Under the LPLA, a product is unreasonably dangerous because of an inadequate warning, "if, at the time the product left its manufacturer's control, the product possessed a characteristic that may cause damage and the manufacturer failed to use reasonable care to provide an adequate warning of such characteristic and its danger to users and handlers of the product." La.Rev.Stat. Ann. § 9:2800.57(A). Courts applying the LPLA have noted that even when a product is not defective, a manufacturer may have a duty to instruct reasonably foreseeable users of the product's safe use. "A manufacturer must anticipate foreseeable misuse and also consider the particular hazard. When a product presents a serious risk of harm, the manufacturer must warn in a manner likely to catch the user's attention."

Based on the evidence presented at trial, the district court concluded that under the LPLA the watercraft was unreasonably dangerous because Bombardier provided no warnings regarding the risk of foot entrapment. The court said this failure to warn amounted to a lack of reasonable care by Bombardier. Therefore, the watercraft was dangerous to an extent beyond that which an ordinary user would have or should have contemplated.

We find that the district court erred in articulating the proper legal standard under the LPLA. State and federal courts applying the LPLA have established a detailed analysis for determining liability in both design defect and failure to warn cases. *See*, e.g., *McCarthy v. Danek Medical, Inc.*, 65 F.Supp.2d 410, 412 (E.D.La. 1999) ("Louisiana law does not allow a fact finder to presume an unreasonably dangerous design solely from the fact that injury occurred.") In both defective design and failure to warn cases courts have applied a risk-utility analysis to determine liability. A court must first determine what risk, if any, the product created. A court must then determine whether a reasonable person would conclude that the danger- in-fact, whether foreseeable or not, outweighs the utility of the product. *Bernard v. Ferrellgas*, 689 So. 2d 554, 560-61 (La.App. 3 Cir. 1997) (applying risk-utility analysis to La.Rev.Stat. Ann. § 9:2800.56 (design defect) and § 9:2800.57). In applying the risk-utility analysis, we have said that a plaintiff must show evidence "concerning the frequency of accidents like his own, the economic costs entailed by those accidents, or the extent of the reduction in frequency of those accidents that would have followed on the use of his proposed alternative design."

Lavespere v. Niagara Machine & Tool Works, Inc., 910 F.2d 167, 183 (5th Cir. 1990) (applying the risk-utility analysis to a design defect claim under La.Rev.Stat. Ann. § 9:2800.56).[4]

In this case, the district court found liability based solely on the fact that an injury occurred but did not properly apply the risk-utility analysis. The court heard no expert testimony regarding the risk the product created. Dr. Jacobson testified regarding forces necessary for bone fractures, not the quantum of risk inherent in the watercraft design. Moreover, other than Ms. Lester's two accidents, Krummel provided no evidence as to the frequency of such accidents. Price testified that Bombardier considered foot entrapment when designing the footwells; however, such consideration does not amount to a showing that Bombardier used unreasonable care. Even if Bombardier kept poor accident records, Krummel must provide evidence regarding the frequency of the accidents. Without evidence showing the severity of the risk created by the footwells or the frequency of foot entrapment, it cannot be shown Bombardier failed to use reasonable care. Therefore, Bombardier cannot be held liable for failure to warn under the LPLA.

The Restatement (Third) of Products Liability § 2(c) requires a similar risk-utility analysis. This provision says: "A product is defective because of inadequate instructions or warnings when the foreseeable risks of harm posed by the product could have been reduced or avoided by the provision of reasonable instructions or warnings by the seller...." Applying the Restatement, the district court determined that Robert Krummel could have reduced his chance of injury if Bombardier had warned him regarding the risk of foot entrapment.

The district court again erred in applying the proper legal standard. Like the LPLA, the Restatement requires more extensive evidence in order to find liability. The comments to the Restatement (Third) of Product Liability § 2 note that in design defect cases and inadequate warning cases "some sort of independent assessment of advantages and disadvantages, to which some attach the label 'risk-utility balancing,' is necessary." *See id.* at cmt. a. *See also Whitted v. General Motors Corp.*, 58 F.3d 1200, 1206-7 (7th Cir. 1995) (finding that for liability for failure to warn under Indiana product liability law and citing to then-proposed Restatement (Third) of Products Liability § 2(c) a plaintiff must present evidence, via statistics or other means, to illustrate that there is a possibility the product may cause injury). The district court again failed to apply the risk-utility analysis. In this case, the evidence showed an injury occurred because of foot entrapment, but no evidence shed light on whether Bombardier should have foreseen--either by a pattern of similar accidents or a design defect--the probability and risk of such an injury. Because the district court failed to make this inquiry, we find Bombardier did not have a duty to warn under the Third Restatement of Products Liability § 2(c).

Conclusion

For these reasons, we reverse and render judgment for Appellants.

DENNIS, Circuit Judge, dissenting:

The majority, by either confusion or judicial legerdemain, purports to amend the Louisiana Products Liability Act, La.R.S. 9:2800.51 et. seq. (LPLA), so that a claimant, to recover for harm caused by a manufacturer's failure to warn, must prove essentially the same elements necessary to recover for harm caused by a manufacturer's defective design of its product. The majority's decision should not be considered a valid precedent, however, because it radically departs from the LPLA, the

---

[4] A plaintiff may not need to detail and to quantify the risk and utility of a product where the product or the design feature in question is "relatively uncomplicated and 'must be such that a layman could readily grasp them.'" *Lavespere*, 910 F.2d at 184. In this case, the district court heard testimony that footwell height and width impacted many aspects of the watercraft, including ease of entry and exit, steering, support for the body, comfort, and buoyancy. This being so, a layperson obviously could not have grasped the adequacy of the footwell design and the need, if any, for warnings.

Louisiana jurisprudence, the Restatement (Third) Of Torts, and the virtually unanimous view of all other courts and legal scholars.

* * * * *

As a practical matter, if expert and prior accident evidence are not required in every LPLA alternative design theory case, it makes no sense impose such a substantive requirement in the much less complex failure to adequately warn cases. Inadequate warning actions do not involve the complex comparisons of the costs/benefits and risks/utilities of two different product designs that are required in design defect actions. Indeed, the majority vaguely acknowledges in its fourth footnote that even a design defect claimant need not detail and quantify the risk and utility of the product or the design feature at issue where they are relatively uncomplicated and can be readily grasped by laymen. However, the majority errs in pointing to the various design aspects of the footwell and gunnel to conclude that "a layperson obviously could not have grasped the adequacy of the footwell design and the need, if any, for warnings." A district court judge is perfectly capable of relying upon his common sense and the background knowledge gleaned from evidence presented at trial to "fill in the gaps" of the plaintiff's case, if any, in estimating the extent of the risk involved in the design of a footwell on a personal watercraft. The footwell at issue is approximately five and one-half inches wide at the bottom, 11 inches high, and sloping slightly outward so as to be wider at the top. Certainly this design feature is relatively uncomplicated and lends itself to a non-scientific determination of the extent of the risk of "foot entrapment" and the extent of risk reduction to be gained by an appropriate warning of the danger. Furthermore, if the present failure to warn case is too complex for a district court judge to understand, without adding the testimony of even more experts to those whose testimony is in the record, it is doubtful that any case will be simple enough to be tried without voluminous expert testimony or evidence of the frequency of similar accidents. (How many and what kinds of experts does the majority want?) Only very wealthy plaintiffs will be able to afford to bring an action under the majority's revised version of the LPLA.

* * * * *

Thus, the majority erred not only in concluding that expert testimony was required by the LPLA in this failure to warn case, but also in concluding that the district court based liability solely upon the fact of the injury and without sufficient evidence of a risk of harm to find that Bombardier owed a duty of care to the Krummels to warn against the risk of foot entrapment.

For the foregoing reasons, I respectfully but emphatically dissent.

NOTES AND QUESTIONS

1.   Both the "design defect" and "inadequate warning" cases require a form of risk-utility balancing. How is the balance similar to the Hand Formula balance from *U.S. v. Carroll Towing*, *supra*? How is it distinct?

2.   The requirement that a plaintiff show an alternative design has been criticized on the ground that some products may be so dangerous that they should not be marketed at all. *See* Galligan, *supra* note 5, following the LPLA, *supra*. The obvious intent of the legislature was to eliminate the *Halphen* "unreasonably dangerous perse" category of products. *Halphen* is reprinted in Section B of this chapter.

3.   One of the most vexing questions in the LPLA is the interplay of the design defect balance and the state of the art defense. More particularly, the question is who bears the burden of proof concerning state of the art. Under La. Rev. Stat. 9:2800.56(1), the plaintiff must establish that an alternative design existed at the time the product left the manufacturer's control. La. Rev. Stat. 9:2800.59 (A)(2) creates an affirmative defense based on the manufacturer's inability to know about the alternative design at the time the product left the manufacturer's control. But why would the defendant ever need to present evidence of the state of the art if the plaintiff fails to prove its case in

chief? *See*, Frank Maraist and Thomas Galligan, Louisiana Torts Law §15.10[2]-[5] (2d. ed., Matthew Bender 2005).

4.   Notice that the court uses the Restatement (Third) of Product Liability to determine the standard applicable to a failure to warn case even though the LPLA is quite specific.

5.   The LPLA requires that the plaintiff's injury result from a "reasonably anticipated use" of the product. Consider the following case discussing the reasonably anticipated use requirement.

MATTHEWS
v.
REMINGTON ARMS, INC.
641 F.3d 635 (5th Cir. 2011)

BARKSDALE, C J.

Following a bench trial, judgment was rendered against Jerry Matthews' claim under the Louisiana Products Liability Act (LPLA), LA.REV.STAT. ANN. § 9:2800.51–.59 (1988), for his injuries that resulted from his firing a Remington Model 710 rifle. When Matthews fired it, the bolt head, which was designed to be connected to the bolt body by a bolt-assembly pin, did not lock with the barrel, allowing an uncontained explosion.

At issue are the district court's findings that: the bolt-assembly pin was missing, rather than out-of-specification, when Matthews fired the rifle; and, pursuant to LPLA, manufacturer Remington Arms Company, Inc., did not "reasonably anticipate" a user would fire its rifle after someone had removed, but failed to reinstall, that pin. Concerning that reasonably-anticipated-use finding, primarily at issue is whether the district court erred by concluding that, for purposes of LPLA, the scope of Matthews' "use" of the rifle included such removal and failure to reinstall; that is, whether his "use" was firing the rifle with the bolt-assembly pin missing, as opposed to only firing it. AFFIRMED.

I

Following the bench trial in June 2009, the district court rendered findings of fact and conclusions of law. The only contested finding is that, prior to Matthews' firing the rifle, the bolt-assembly pin had been removed but not reinstalled, as opposed to its' being in the rifle but out-of-specification or not functioning. In 2000, Remington introduced its Model 710 bolt-action rifle. Instead of using a solid bolt, that model was manufactured with a two-piece bolt assembly: the bolt head is attached to the bolt body with a bolt-assembly pin. The bolt handle is attached to the bolt body. When the bolt handle and, therefore, the bolt body, is rotated downward, the bolt head (if the bolt-assembly pin is installed) simultaneously rotates downward and locks the "lugs" on the bolt head into the mating locking recesses in the receiving barrel interface (rifle receiver): the firing position. In such an instance, the rifle is "in battery." Only when the rifle is in battery will it fire properly.

The bolt-assembly pin, a cylinder, is not of insignificant size; it is .685" long and .247" in diameter. It is made from low-strength, unhardened steel. The pin is essential to the simultaneous downward rotation of the bolt head and body. If the bolt-assembly pin is missing or malfunctioning, it is possible for the bolt handle and body to be rotated into locked position without the bolt head also rotating into locked position. In that situation, the lugs on the bolt head will not lock into the mating locking recesses in the rifle receiver, resulting in inadequate engagement between the bolt-head lugs and their locking recesses. In this situation, the rifle is "out of battery". If the trigger is pulled while a round is chambered and the rifle is out of battery, the rifle will either misfire or, as happened to Matthews, have an uncontained explosion.

Under normal conditions (in battery), the bolt-assembly pin does not contain the pressure from the cartridge's being fired; the bolt head contains the pressure with the seal that is created when the locking lugs are engaged with their mating recesses in the rifle receiver—that engagement is critical to pressure containment. Accordingly, the rifle can be fired without the pin in place if the bolt head is locked in place—the pin is not the critical pressure containment device.

The Model 710's owner's manual instructs users to disassemble the bolt assembly, including removing the bolt-assembly pin, for cleaning; and to reassemble the bolt assembly, by reinserting the bolt-assembly pin. Remington also instructs its factory assembly workers to keep a finger beneath the bolt-assembly-pin hole on the bolt body to prevent the bolt-assembly pin from falling out during assembly; however, this instruction is not included in the owner's manual. The owner's manual does not include any warnings of potential hazards if the bolt-assembly pin is not properly installed. Matthews, who borrowed, instead of owned, the rifle, testified he neither received, nor read, the owner's manual prior to the accident.

As of this action's being filed in August 2007, Remington had sold nearly 500,000 Model 710 rifles; but, it had not received a report of a user firing a Model 710 rifle without an installed bolt-assembly pin. Following the district court's ruling in favor of Remington in September 2009, however, Matthews moved unsuccessfully, pursuant to Federal Rule of Civil Procedure 60, for a new trial or to have the judgment altered or amended, based on newly discovered evidence of an October 2008 incident for which a Remington customer reported to Remington that his Model 770 rifle (part of the Model 710 series and also employing a two-piece bolt assembly) came apart when he tried to open the bolt to eject a cartridge. The district court ruled that this newly discovered evidence did not change the trial result and would not have provided Remington with notice of any problem when the rifle fired by Matthews was manufactured in September 2001.

When the rifle fired by Matthews left Remington's control in 2001, it contained a bolt-assembly pin manufactured to specifications. Matthews' mother-in-law, Margaret Minchew, purchased the rifle from her nephew in 2006. It had been owned by several persons before she purchased it; but, when she acquired it, she did not receive the owner's manual.

Before the date of the accident, Matthews and others fired the rifle without incident; but, prior to Matthews' accident, someone disassembled the rifle and the bolt assembly and failed to reinstall the bolt-assembly pin. (As noted supra, this critical finding of fact by the district court is contested by Matthews; he maintains that, when he fired the rifle, the bolt-assembly pin was either defective or malfunctioning, rather than missing.)

Approximately two to four weeks before the accident, Margaret Minchew loaned the rifle to her daughter, Amanda Minchew. She and the man with whom she was living, Nicholas Glass, lived next door to Matthews and his wife, another of Margaret Minchew's daughters.

Matthews borrowed the rifle from Amanda Minchew on the morning of the accident in October 2006; the bolt handle appeared to be closed. Matthews took the rifle to his house to obtain ammunition, and then proceeded to another's to "sight" the scope that had been installed recently on the rifle by Nicholas Glass.

In preparing to fire the rifle, Matthews rotated the bolt handle upward; pulled it back in order to load a shell; loaded it; pushed the bolt handle forward; and rotated it downward into what appeared to be the closed position. When he pulled the trigger, the shell did not fire (misfired). He again rotated the bolt handle; pulled it back slowly (because he knew there could be compression); and removed the shell. Observing nothing wrong with the shell, Matthews reloaded a shell; pushed the bolt handle forward; rotated it downward into what appeared to be the closed position; and pulled the trigger. The rifle fired. Upon its doing so, an uncontained explosion occurred, sending portions of the bolt assembly into Matthews' head, causing serious injuries, including the loss of an eye.

The accident resulted from the absence of the bolt-assembly pin: the bolt handle and body had rotated downward, but the bolt head had not. Therefore, the locking lugs on the bolt head failed to engage the locking mating recesses in the rifle receiver, and the rifle was out of battery. Matthews knew it would be dangerous to fire the rifle if either the bolt-assembly pin was missing or the bolt handle was not closing properly.

In district court, Matthews contended, inter alia: firing the rifle out of battery (due to the absence of the bolt-assembly pin) was a "reasonably anticipated use" under LPLA because the rifle appeared to operate normally and a failure to reinstall the bolt-assembly pin was foreseeable to Remington; and the rifle was "unreasonably dangerous" in construction and design and lacked an adequate warning. Remington disputed this and also contended, inter alia, that Matthews' use of the rifle was "obviously dangerous", claiming he knew the bolt would not close properly prior to firing the rifle.

The district court's findings of fact were, inter alia: Matthews' use of the rifle was not "obviously dangerous"; "[a]t some point prior to the accident, however, someone disassembled the bolt assembly and failed to reinstall the bolt assembly pin"; and his using it in an "out of battery" condition—the bolt-assembly pin missing—was not "reasonably anticipated" by Remington. Concerning the latter finding, the court concluded that, absent special circumstances not present in this action, Remington was entitled to expect an ordinary user to reassemble the rifle with all its parts, including the bolt-assembly pin. Having found no "reasonably anticipated use", which, as discussed infra, is the threshold LPLA element, the district court ruled in favor of Remington and declined to address the remaining LPLA elements at issue.

In denying Matthews' motion for a new trial, and in regard to the bolt-assembly pin, the district court found: trial evidence established that the pin was not defective, but was removed prior to the accident; and "Remington's expert testified that the bolt assembly pin was manufactured to specifications and that the accident was caused by a missing, not broken, bolt assembly pin."

II

Louisiana law controls for this diversity action. *See generally Erie R.R. Co. v. Tompkins*, 304 U.S. 64, 58 S.Ct. 817, 82 L.Ed. 1188 (1938). LPLA "establishes the exclusive theories of liability for manufacturers for damage caused by their products." LA.REV.STAT. ANN. § 9:2800.52. A claimant under LPLA must prove: (1) "damage proximately caused by a characteristic of the product that renders [it] unreasonably dangerous when such damage arose from a reasonably anticipated use of the product by the claimant or another person or entity"; (2) the product was "unreasonably dangerous" either in construction, design, or warning; and (3) the characteristic rendering the product unreasonably dangerous either "exist[ed] at the time the product left the control of its manufacturer or result[ed] from a reasonably anticipated alteration or modification of the product" (depending on the type of defect claimed). *Id*. at § 9:2800.54 (emphasis added).[1]

Because "reasonably anticipated use" is the threshold LPLA element, and the district court limited its analysis to that element, our review does not reach whether the rifle is "unreasonably dangerous" because, inter alia, its design permitted it to be fired with the bolt-assembly pin missing— out of battery. The LPLA section at issue provides: "The manufacturer of a product shall be liable to a

---

[1] Section 9:2800.54 provides:
   A. The manufacturer of a product shall be liable to a claimant for damage proximately caused by a characteristic of the product that renders the product unreasonably dangerous when such damage arose from a reasonably anticipated use of the product by the claimant or another person or entity.
   B. A product is unreasonably dangerous if and only if:
      (1) The product is unreasonably dangerous in construction or composition as provided in R.S. 9:2800.55;
      (2) The product is unreasonably dangerous in design as provided in R.S. 9:2800.56;
      (3) The product is unreasonably dangerous because an adequate warning about the product has not been provided as provided in R.S. 9:2800.57; or
      (4) The product is unreasonably dangerous because it does not conform to an express warranty of the manufacturer about the product as provided in R.S. 9:2800.58.
   C. The characteristic of the product that renders it unreasonably dangerous under R.S. 9:2800.55 must exist at the time the product left the control of its manufacturer. The characteristic of the product that renders it unreasonably dangerous under R.S. 9:2800.56 or 9:2800.57 must exist at the time the product left the control of its manufacturer or result from a reasonably anticipated alteration or modification of the product.

claimant for damage proximately caused by a characteristic of the product that renders the product unreasonably dangerous when such damage arose from a reasonably anticipated use of the product by the claimant or another person or entity". LA.REV.STAT. ANN. § 9:2800.54(A) (emphasis added). "The availability of an alternative design is relevant only if the user was engaged in a 'reasonably anticipated use' of the product, for unless that threshold element is satisfied, a manufacturer does not have a legal duty to design its product to prevent such use." *Butz v. Lynch*, 762 So. 2d 1214, 1217–18 (La.App. 1 Cir. 2000); *see also Kampen v. Am. Isuzu Motors*, 157 F.3d 306, 309 (5th Cir. 1998) (en banc) ("If a plaintiff's damages did not arise from a reasonably anticipated use of the product, then the 'unreasonably dangerous' question need not be reached.") (citing *Johnson v. Black & Decker U.S., Inc.*, 701 So. 2d 1360, 1366 (La.App. 2 Cir. 1997)). Accordingly, our analysis is limited to the question of reasonably anticipated use.

As noted, Remington maintained in district court that Matthews' use of the rifle was obviously dangerous, asserting he knew, prior to the accident, that the bolt would not close properly. Insofar as Remington makes this contention here, it has failed to adequately brief, and has, therefore, waived, it. E.g., *Procter & Gamble Co. v. Amway Corp.*, 376 F.3d 496, 499 n. 1 (5th Cir. 2004) ("Failure adequately to brief an issue on appeal constitutes waiver of that argument."); FED. R.APP. P. 28(a)(9)(A). The same failure-to-brief waiver applies insofar as Matthews contends the district court erred for any rulings on motions in limine, including by not considering evidence of other incidents of claimed out of battery firings.

Bench-trial findings of fact are reviewed for clear error; legal conclusions, de novo. E.g., *Kleinman v. City of San Marcos*, 597 F.3d 323, 325 (5th Cir. 2010). A question of statutory interpretation is, of course, reviewed de novo. E.g., *Great Am. Ins. Co. v. AFS/IBEX Fin. Servs.*, Inc., 612 F.3d 800, 809 (5th Cir. 2010). The establishment of each LPLA element is a question of fact, reviewed for clear error. *Ellis v. Weasler Eng'g, Inc.*, 258 F.3d 326, 331–32 (5th Cir. 2001); *Johnson*, 701 So. 2d at 1363 (each product liability case is resolved primarily on its own particular facts). A finding of fact is clearly erroneous only if, "although there is evidence to support it, the reviewing court on the entire evidence is left with the definite and firm conviction that a mistake has been committed". *United States v. U.S. Gypsum Co.*, 333 U.S. 364, 395, 68 S.Ct. 525, 92 L.Ed. 746 (1948); *see*, e.g., *Mumblow v. Monroe Broad., Inc.*, 401 F.3d 616, 622 (5th Cir. 2005).

Therefore, at issue are whether the district court clearly erred by finding that: when Matthews fired the rifle, the bolt-assembly pin was missing, rather than out-of-specification; and such "use" should not have been "reasonably anticipated" by Remington. Regarding that use, at issue is whether the court erred in concluding that it was not merely firing the rifle, but firing it after someone had removed, and failed to reinstall, the bolt-assembly pin. " 'Reasonably anticipated use' means a use or handling of a product that the product's manufacturer should reasonably expect of an ordinary person in the same or similar circumstances." LA.REV.STAT. ANN. § 9:2800.53(7).

A

* * * * *

[The court examined the evidence relevant to the question of whether the bolt assembly pin was in the rifle or not when Matthews fired it and concluded that the district court was not clearly erroneous in finding that it was missing.]

B

In the light of our not finding clearly erroneous the district court's missing-pin finding of fact, next at issue are: the district court's conclusion of law for the applicable LPLA scope-of-use; and its finding of fact, based on that scope-of-use, that Matthews' use of the rifle (with a missing bolt-assembly pin) was not reasonably anticipated by Remington. The district court did not err in its scope-of-use conclusion; and we can not say that its not-reasonably-anticipated-use finding of fact was clearly erroneous.

For obvious reasons, "the level of generality at which a plaintiff's 'use' of a product is defined will bear directly on whether [he] satisfies the LPLA's reasonably anticipated use requirement". *Kampen*, 157 F.3d at 310. Again, a critical issue is whether Matthews' "use" of the Model 710 rifle is limited to his firing it or includes the removal of, but failure to reinstall, the bolt-assembly pin. As discussed, the district court interpreted "use" at a level of generality that included firing the rifle without the bolt-assembly pin, as opposed to firing it. Again, this interpretation included someone's removal of, and failure to reinstall, the bolt-assembly pin prior to Matthews' firing the rifle. And as noted, because the scope-of-use inquiry requires interpreting LPLA, our review is de novo. A scope-of-use decision is premised on "the apparent purpose of the reasonably anticipated use requirement[:] ... 'to express the types of product uses and misuses by a consumer that a manufacturer must take into account when he designs a product [and] drafts instructions for its use ... in order that the product not be unreasonably dangerous.' " *Kampen*, 157 F.3d at 310–11 (citation and internal quotation marks omitted) (quoting John Kennedy, A Primer on the Louisiana Products Liability Act, 49 LA. L.REV. 65, 584 (1989)) (Kennedy was a co-drafter of LPLA). For that LPLA action against the manufacturer of a vehicle jack, our en banc court in *Kampen held*: the scope of use included not only claimant's jacking up the vehicle, but also, while the vehicle was in that position, crawling under it. *Id.* at 312.

For the scope-of-use inquiry, *Kampen* held: "We thus define [plaintiff's] 'use' of the jack at a level of generality that will take into account the risks [the manufacturer] must (or should) have reasonably contemplated when designing the jack...." *Id.* at 311. Consistent with the warnings not to do so, provided in the owner's manual and in the vehicle's spare-tire compartment, those risks were that the claimant would not only jack up the vehicle, but also, after doing so, crawl under it. *Kampen* further held: "[I]f we consider that *Kampen*'s 'use' of the jack includes his jacking up the car and nothing else, then the question of reasonably anticipated use answers itself: a manufacturer quite reasonably anticipates his jack to be used for jacking!" *Id.* at 310. Similarly, it is obvious that firing a rifle, with all of its parts in place, is reasonably anticipated.

In reaching the holding that defendant did not reasonably anticipate this expanded use (jack-up and crawl-under), *id.* at 312, *Kampen* provided a detailed analysis of Louisiana cases interpreting LPLA's reasonably-anticipated-use element, including which conduct constituted a "use". *See id.* at 310–12. Louisiana courts have interpreted "use" to include interactions with the product prior to the claimant's injury. *See Johnson*, 701 So. 2d at 1365 (affirming jury's finding that using a saw after either claimant, or another, had removed the manufacturer's guard was not a "reasonably anticipated use"); *Delphen v. Dep't of Transp. & Dev.*, 657 So. 2d 328, 334 (La.App. 4 Cir. 1995) (holding claimant's "use" was borrowing and riding an obviously dangerous racing bicycle without obtaining additional instructions regarding use and knowing the wheel had previously become loose). As reflected in our en-banc opinion in *Kampen*, our court has applied the Louisiana-state-court LPLA interpretation. E.g., *Broussard v. Procter & Gamble Co.*, 517 F.3d 767, 769–70 (5th Cir. 2008) (holding "use" of heatwrap in contravention of warning not "reasonably anticipated") (citing *Kampen*, 157 F.3d at 314); Ellis, 258 F.3d at 337–38 (holding "reasonably anticipated use" of pecan harvester included walking between tractor and harvester to inspect harvester while running); *Hunter v. Knoll Rig & Equip. Mfg. Co.*, 70 F.3d 803, 810 (5th Cir. 1995) (holding racking pipes against a racking board in an uncommon and "obviously dangerous" manner was not a "reasonably anticipated use"); see LA.REV.STAT. ANN. § 9:2800.53(7) (" 'Reasonably anticipated use' means a use or handling of a product that the product's manufacturer should reasonably expect of an ordinary person in the same or similar circumstances."); *Kampen*, 157 F.3d at 311 ("[W]e observe that 'reasonably anticipated use' is defined [in § 9:2800.53(7)] in terms of a 'use or handling' of the product".) (emphasis in original).

Again, the LPLA section at issue provides: "The manufacturer of a product shall be liable to a claimant for damage proximately caused by a characteristic of the product that renders the product unreasonably dangerous when such damage arose from a reasonably anticipated use of the product by the claimant or another person or entity". LA.REV.STAT. ANN. § 9:2800.54(A) (emphasis added). "[U]se of the product by [Matthews] or another person" is linked, of course, to the district court's above-discussed finding of fact, which we can not say is clearly erroneous, that, "[a]t some point prior to the accident, ... someone disassembled the bolt assembly and failed to reinstall the bolt assembly pin". In the light of its scope-of-use conclusion, the district court was not required to find whether that "someone" was Matthews or another person.

As noted, in *Johnson*, the Louisiana appellate court affirmed the jury's finding that using a saw after the manufacturer's guard had been removed was not a "reasonably anticipated use". 701 So. 2d at 1365. In so doing, the court found it was unclear whether the guard had been removed by the claimant or by another. Id. at 1362, 1364. In *Hunter*, our court found the manner in which pipes were leaned against a racking board was not reasonably anticipated. 70 F.3d at 810. In that case, it was not only the claimant's interaction with the product, but also those by other experienced workers, that resulted in the pipes being racked improperly. *Id.* at 805, 810. These decisions demonstrate, inter alia, that, consistent with LPLA § 9:2800.54(A) (defining "use" to include "use of the product by the claimant or another person or entity" (emphasis added)), "use" of a product is determined by examining overall interactions with a product—including another person's handling it.

Accordingly, "use" under LPLA includes interactions with the product by Matthews and others. The scope of the "use" included the removal of, and failure to reinstall, the bolt-assembly pin prior to Matthews' firing the rifle because, in order to be held liable under LPLA, that is the "use" Remington had to have "reasonably anticipated" ("expect[ed]"). *See* LA.REV.STAT. ANN. § 9:2800.53(7) (" 'Reasonably anticipated use' means a use or handling of a product that the product's manufacturer should reasonably expect of an ordinary person in the same or similar circumstances.").

2

Therefore, in the light of this scope-of-use, at issue is whether it was "reasonably anticipated" by Remington that someone would fail to reinstall the bolt-assembly pin and that the rifle would be fired in that condition. As discussed, the establishment of each LPLA element is a question of fact, reviewed for clear error. Ellis, 258 F.3d at 331–32; Johnson, 701 So. 2d at 1366.[13] Again, " '[r]easonably anticipated use' means a use or handling of a product that the product's manufacturer should reasonably expect of an ordinary person in the same or similar circumstances". LA.REV.STAT. ANN. § 9:2800.53(7) (emphasis added). "This objective inquiry requires us to ascertain what uses of its product the manufacturer should have reasonably expected at the time of manufacture." *Kampen*, 157 F.3d at 309 (emphasis added) (citing *Myers v. Am. Seating Co.*, 637 So. 2d 771, 775 (La.App. 1 Cir.1994)). Accordingly, at issue is whether the district court clearly erred by finding that Remington, at the time of manufacture, should not have reasonably expected Matthews' "use": firing a Model 710 rifle after someone had removed, but failed to reinstall, the bolt-assembly pin. *See Butz*, 762 So. 2d at 1218; *Hunter*, 70 F.3d at 806–07, 810.

" '[R]easonably anticipated use' is more restrictive than the broader, [pre-LPLA] standard of 'normal use' ", and it does not suggest manufacturer liability "for every conceivable foreseeable use of a product". *Delphen*, 657 So. 2d at 333–34; *see also Lockart v. Kobe Steel Ltd. Constr. Mach. Div.*, 989 F.2d 864, 868 (5th Cir. 1993). "The LPLA's 'reasonably anticipated use' standard should be contrasted with the pre–LPLA 'normal use' standard; 'normal use' included 'all intended uses, as well as all reasonably foreseeable uses and misuses of the product.' " Kampen, 157 F.3d at 309 (citing *Hale Farms, Inc. v. Am. Cyanamid Co.*, 580 So. 2d 684, 688 (La.App. 2 Cir. 1991)). " 'Normal use' also included 'reasonably foreseeable misuse that is contrary to the manufacturer's instructions.' " *Id.* (emphasis removed) (citing *Hale Farms*, 580 So. 2d at 688).

Under LPLA, whether a use is reasonably anticipated is an objective standard ascertained from the manufacturer's viewpoint at the time of manufacture. *Payne v. Gardner*, 56 So.3d 229, 231–32 (La. 2011); *Green v. BDI Pharm.*, 803 So. 2d 68, 75 (La.App. 2 Cir. 2001); *Hunter*, 70 F.3d at 809 n. 7; *Daigle v. Audi of Am., Inc.*, 598 So. 2d 1304, 1307 (La.App. 3 Cir. 1992) (quotation omitted). "It is clear that by adopting the reasonably anticipated use standard, the Louisiana Legislature intended to narrow the range of product uses for which a manufacturer would be responsible." *Kampen*, 157 F.3d at 309 (citing *Delphen*, 657 So. 2d at 333; *Myers*, 637 So. 2d at 775).

We can not say that the district court clearly erred in finding that Remington should not have reasonably anticipated (reasonably expected) the rifle to be fired after someone had removed, but failed to reinstall, the bolt-assembly pin. This is evidenced by the instructions in Remington's Model 710 owner's manual to reinstall the bolt-assembly pin when reassembling the bolt assembly. Of course, it was "reasonably foreseeable" that a user might drop the bolt-assembly pin during reassembly, as evidenced by the instruction from Remington to its assembly workers to keep a finger beneath the bolt-assembly-pin hole during the initial assembly; however, that is not the LPLA standard. The standard is: at the time of manufacture, how did the manufacturer reasonably expect its product to be used by an ordinary person.

"[T]he LPLA requires a link between damages and reasonably anticipated use.... [I]f damages are linked to a product misuse (i.e., one that is not reasonably anticipated), then those damages are not recoverable under the Act". Kampen, 157 F.3d at 316; see also Payne, 56 So.3d 229, 231–32. Here, the damages incurred by Matthews are directly caused by his firing the rifle after someone had removed the bolt-assembly pin and failed to reinstall it. For the reasons that follow, and in the light of the trial evidence, we can not say that the district court clearly erred in finding that such "use" was not "reasonably anticipated" by Remington.

Matthews failed to prove Remington, at the time of manufacture of the rifle at issue, was aware of a single other incident where a Model 710 rifle, or any rifle using a similar two-piece bolt assembly, was fired without a properly installed and functioning bolt-assembly pin. The district court found:

> Remington anticipated that a user would disassemble the Model 710 bolt assembly for cleaning and remove the bolt assembly pin, but Mr. and Mrs. Matthews have not presented persuasive evidence that Remington also should have anticipated that users would fail to reinstall the bolt assembly pin. Both lay and expert witnesses testified that an ordinary firearm user knows and understands that reassembly of a firearm with all its parts is critical to safe operation. The Court, therefore, finds that Remington was entitled to expect that an ordinary user would reassemble the rifle with all its parts, absent special circumstances not present in this case.

Acknowledging again that the district court is in a superior position to appraise and weigh the evidence, "the force and effect of the testimony, considered as a whole", does not convince us "that the findings are so against the great preponderance of the credible testimony that they do not reflect or represent the truth and right of the case". Mumblow, 401 F.3d at 622 (citation omitted). Under LPLA, what a manufacturer should reasonably anticipate is determined by how the manufacturer expected the product to be used by an ordinary person. Again, we can not say the district court clearly erred by finding Remington should not have expected a Model 710 rifle to be fired after someone had removed, but failed to reinstall, the bolt-assembly pin.[2]

---

[2] The dissent does not challenge the two above-discussed critical findings of fact that we can not say are clearly erroneous: the bolt-assembly pin was not in the rifle when Matthews fired it; and Remington should not have expected the rifle to be fired after *someone* had removed, but failed to reinstall, that pin. (Therefore, the dissent's statements of fact at 2–3, note 3, including about the sale of extra bolt-assembly pins, are of no moment.) The dissent instead challenges only our holding, on *de novo* review, that the applicable LPLA reasonably-anticipated scope-of-use was not just Matthews' firing the rifle; it was his firing it with the missing bolt-assembly pin.

In advancing a theory not urged by Matthews, the dissent maintains the missing-pin aspect can not, as a matter of law, be attributed to Matthews, akin to his being an innocent bystander. As discussed *supra*, however, the district court did not find Matthews was not the "someone" who removed, and failed to reinstall, the pin because it was not necessary to do so. Therefore, the dissent repeatedly errs in stating someone other than Matthews did so.

In any event, who did so is irrelevant; what is relevant is the use Remington could "reasonably anticipate[ ] ... by the claimant [Matthews] or another person or entity". LA.REV.STAT. ANN. § 9:2800.54(A). In short, for the reasons presented *supra,* it matters not when the pin was removed and not re-installed and, assuming he was not the person who did so, whether it was outside Matthews' presence. Again, what is relevant, pursuant to the plain language of the LPLA, is the reasonably anticipated use of the product, whether by Matthews or another, including the reason for the missing bolt-assembly pin. Therefore, the dissent's fundamental error is asserting that the applicable scope-of-use should be limited to Matthews' firing the rifle (or, as the dissent erroneously phrases it: "*his* reasonably anticipated use", Dissent at 649 (emphasis added); and "his

III

For the foregoing reasons, the judgment is **AFFIRMED**.

DENNIS, Circuit Judge, dissenting:

I respectfully dissent. The undisputed, concrete facts of this fully tried case show that the damage to the claimant, Jerry Matthews, arose from his own use of the rifle to shoot at a target, a use that an objective rifle manufacturer should reasonably expect of an ordinary person in the same or similar circumstances as Matthews'. Matthews did not allege or attempt to show that his damage arose from the use of the rifle by another person or entity. Thus, both the district court and the majority of this panel erred in misinterpreting and misapplying the Louisiana Products Liability Act (LPLA or "the Act") as if it required Matthews to show that his damage arose from a reasonably expected use of the rifle by another person or entity. The LPLA does not place such an additional and greater burden upon a claimant at the threshold reasonably-anticipated-use stage of a products liability case. Therefore, their dismissal of Matthews' claim on the ground that he failed to demonstrate that his damages arose from his reasonably anticipated use of the rifle was legal error. It may be that Matthews' case ultimately might have failed on the merits of his design and warning claims, but under the LPLA he should not have been poured out of court at the threshold reasonably-anticipated-use stage, because he obviously used the rifle as a manufacturer should reasonably have anticipated, and did not use the rifle in an irrational or abnormal way.

I

... Under the plain language of the Act, a plaintiff asserting a products liability action against a manufacturer has a threshold burden of showing that his damages arose from a reasonably anticipated use of the product. *See* La.Rev.Stat. § 9:2800.54(D); *Kampen v. Am. Isuzu Motors, Inc.*, 157 F.3d 306, 314 (5th Cir. 1998) (en banc). The LPLA defines a reasonably anticipated use as "a use or handling of the product that the product's manufacturer should reasonably expect of an ordinary person in the same or similar circumstances." La.Rev.Stat. § 9:2800.53(7). When the claimant asserts that his damages arose from a reasonably anticipated use of the product by the claimant himself, "in the same or similar circumstances" plainly refers to the same or similar circumstances as the claimant's use. *Id.*; *see also id.* § 9:2800.54(A). This is an "objective inquiry," requiring a court to ascertain whether the use of the product, from which the plaintiff's damages arose, is a use that a manufacturer such as the defendant should have reasonably expected at the time of manufacture. *Kampen*, 157 F.3d at 309.

Applying the objective inquiry to the undisputed facts, it is self-evident that Matthews' damages arose from a use or handling of the rifle that a manufacturer such as Remington should have reasonably expected at the time of the manufacture. Matthews was using the rifle to shoot at a target while sighting in a new telescope on the rifle when his damages arose. This use obviously falls within the core purpose for which Remington designed and made the rifle, viz., to fire a bullet at a target. Moreover, Matthews was found by the district court to have used the rifle as an ordinary user would have under the circumstances; he was not found to be negligent or at fault in his use of the rifle. Thus, Remington, as a rifle manufacturer, reasonably should have anticipated that the rifle would be used just as Matthews did for that purpose.

The LPLA does not require a claimant at the threshold stage to prove that his damages were also proximately caused by a characteristic of the product that renders the product unreasonably dangerous. Nor does it require a claimant at the threshold stage to prove that a third person's conduct was not a contributing or proximate cause of his damages. Those are additional burdens that a claimant must face only if he satisfies the initial threshold burden of showing that his damages arose from his use of the product that a manufacturer reasonably should have anticipated. Further, those are

---

own personal use", *id.* at 654). That analysis writes "or another person or entity" out of the LPLA and converts it from imposing product, to imposing absolute, liability.

issues that the district court should have given plenary consideration to as part of a full merits trial inquiry into unsafe design, inadequate warning, and/or comparative fault, and should not have adverted to at the threshold reasonably anticipated-use stage of the case.

* * * * *

Therefore, in my view, the district court committed several clear legal errors in interpreting and applying the LPLA by: (1) failing to recognize that Matthews had carried his threshold burden of showing that his damages arose from his own use of the rifle and that his use was one that a manufacturer reasonably should have anticipated; (2) failing to proceed to consider and decide the merits issues of whether the rifle product was unreasonably dangerous in design or whether an adequate warning about the product's dangerous characteristic was given; (3) undertaking, at the threshold stage of the case, an anomalous inquiry into whether the accident was proximately caused by a defective pin or by an unknown previous user's failure to properly replace the pin upon reassembling the rifle; (4) establishing a legal presumption that Remington is entitled to presume that no user of its rifles will ever fail to replace a bolt assembly pin, although it is undisputed that the rifle can give the appearance of operating properly without such a pin; and (5) rejecting Matthews' claims because he failed to adduce sufficient contrary evidence of Remington's subjective expectations to overcome this apparently irrebuttable legal presumption.

II

... The majority stretches and distorts the statutory words, "use of the product by ... another person or entity," to have them apply to the unknown person whom the district court found had left out the missing pin. But the legislature clearly did not intend for them to have that meaning or interpretation. Those words plainly were meant to apply when a claimant's damage arises from a use of a product by another person or entity: for example, when an innocent bystander is injured by a characteristic of a product such as a lawn mower, automobile or other mechanical device while it is being used by another person or entity in a manner that a manufacturer should reasonably expect of an ordinary person in the same or similar circumstances as the user. The majority's interpretation and application of the statutory words, "use of the product by ... another person or entity," differently from the plain, straightforward manner used and intended by the legislature, is therefore unwarranted; to apply those words as the majority does here distorts the "clear and unambiguous" words of the law, which should be applied "as written" to the undisputed concrete facts, without "further interpretation in search of the intent of the legislature." La. Civ.Code art. 9. Matthews alleged and sought to prove that his damage arose from his own use of the rifle, not from the use of the rifle by another person or entity. Thus, the only reasonably anticipated use question presented is whether the use of the rifle by Matthews, the claimant, was a reasonably anticipated use. This case fits squarely within the plainly relevant LPLA legislated rules, viz., the reasonably anticipated use definition at § 9:2800.53(7) and the claimant's assertion that his injuries arose from his own use of the rifle, La.Rev.Stat. § 9:2800.54(A); therefore, the majority is not authorized to formulate a new rule to decide the case by resorting to its own judicial conceptions of "equity, ... justice, reason, and prevailing usages." La. Civ.Code art. 4.

* * * * *

The majority alleges and argues that because someone, unknown to Matthews, removed the bolt-assembly pin from the rifle before Matthews fired it and was injured, Matthews' use of the rifle should not have been reasonably anticipated by Remington. The majority's reasoning depends on the premise that the LPLA requires a claimant to prove not only that his use was reasonably anticipated, but also that all prior users' uses of the product were reasonably anticipated. That interpretation of the clear and unambiguous words of the law is incorrect. If the claimant asserts that he was the user of the product when he was injured, as Matthews does, the LPLA requires that he prove only that his own personal use was reasonably anticipated in order to fulfill the reasonably anticipated use requirement.[4]

---

[4] Of course, if a claimant contends that he was injured by another person's or entity's use of the product he must prove that the other's use was reasonably anticipated. Here, Matthews contends and has clearly shown that his

Thus, I respectfully but emphatically disagree with the majority's unorthodox interpretation of the LPLA, which in effect (1) makes the LPLA's definition of "reasonably anticipated use" become a useless appendage whenever a third person's prior use may have affected the product, although the claimant alleges and proves that his damage arose from his own use of the product, which the manufacturer reasonably should have anticipated; (2) distorts the LPLA's "use of the product by ... another person or entity" proviso (that was intended to expand, not narrow, protections for victims of unsafe products) into an additional manufacturer's defense not explicitly legislated or intended; (3) creates an additional hurdle and burden for claimants that the legislature did not expressly provide for; and (4) is contrary to this court's en banc interpretation of the LPLA in *Kampen*, because it makes the reasonably anticipated use of the product by another person or entity proviso "do the work that comparative fault is intended to do" under Louisiana law. *See Kampen*, 157 F.3d at 316 (citing, *inter alia, Bell v. Jet Wheel Blast, Div. of Ervin Indus.*, 462 So. 2d 166 (La. 1985)) ("[C]omparative fault" still has a place in "Louisiana products liability law" because "[a] plaintiff's negligent conduct which does not remove his use of the product from the realm of reasonably anticipated uses may nevertheless contribute to cause his injuries. Such negligence will lessen a plaintiff's recovery without barring his right to recover altogether."); *see also Bell*, 462 So. 2d at 170 (explaining that in a negligence action, "a plaintiff's claim for damages [cannot] be barred totally because of his negligence. At most his claim may be reduced in proportion to his fault.").

* * * * *

E.   LIABILITY OF THE NON-MANUFACTURER SELLER

The focus of this chapter is the responsibility of a product manufacturer. However, the manufacturer is only the first link in a chain of wholesalers, retailers and even transporters who get the product into the hands of the ultimate consumer. It is possible that an injured plaintiff may recover against other participants in the distribution chain by applying several theories.

First, to the extent that the plaintiff's contract is with the retailer/seller, the plaintiff should have the full range of actions that exist under the law of contracts or obligations. *See*, e.g., *Young v. Ford Motor Company*, reprinted in Section (B), *supra*.

Second, negligence is always available. You should note, however, that the analysis of duty changes depending upon the role of the distributor/wholesaler/retailer. For example, a retailer may have a duty to remove products from the shelves when it knows or should know of a risk to consumers. In *Alexander v. Toyota Motor Sales, U.S.A.*, 123 So. 3d 712 (La. 2013), the Court held that a car dealer, as a non-manufacturing seller, did not have a duty under either a federal regulation or Louisiana law to replace a car's airbag warning with a revised warning label. The Court stated, "[P]laintiffs produced no evidentiary support to show that the lack of the 1997 revised airbag warning labels in the plaintiff's 1995 vehicle rendered the car unreasonably dangerous under the cited definition." *Id.* at 715.[1]

---

injuries arose from his own use of the rifle to shoot at a target and that that use reasonably should have been anticipated by the manufacturer. He did not contend that he was injured by the use of the product by another person or entity. Remington is not entitled to amend Matthews' pleadings or presentation of his case so as to require him to prove that his injuries arose from a reasonably anticipated use of the rifle by another person or entity.

[1] In a pre-LPLA case, a fuel supplier provided fuel which was tainted by mixture with the residue of another type of fuel. The Supreme Court imposes strict liability upon the supplier, observing that "a commercial supplier who sells a product in a defective and unreasonably dangerous condition is strictly liable for harm caused by the defect, even if the supplier was not negligent." *Guidry v. Frank Guidry Oil Co., Inc.*, 579 So. 2d 947 (La. 1991).

Third, as a variation on negligence, a retailer may be under a duty to provide operating instructions or warnings to the purchaser. If a non-manufacturer retailer is under a duty to provide warnings, how does that affect the manufacturer's duty under the LPLA?

Finally, what about the responsibility of an injured worker's employer? *See*, e.g., *Guidry v. Frank Guidry Oil Company*, 579 So. 2d 947 (La. 1991).

F.   FEDERAL PREEMPTION

CIPOLLONE
v.
LIGGETT GROUP, INC.
505 U.S. 504 (1992)

Justice **STEVENS** delivered the opinion of the Court, except as to Parts V and VI.

"WARNING: THE SURGEON GENERAL HAS DETERMINED THAT CIGARETTE SMOKING IS DANGEROUS TO YOUR HEALTH." A federal statute enacted in 1969 requires that warning (or a variation thereof) to appear in a conspicuous place on every package of cigarettes sold in the United States. The questions presented to us by this case are whether that statute, or its 1965 predecessor which required a less alarming label, pre-empted petitioner's common-law claims against respondent cigarette manufacturers.

Petitioner is the son of Rose Cipollone, who began smoking in 1942 and who died of lung cancer in 1984. He claims that respondents are responsible for Rose Cipollone's death because they breached express warranties contained in their advertising, because they failed to warn consumers about the hazards of smoking, because they fraudulently misrepresented those hazards to consumers, and because they conspired to deprive the public of medical and scientific information about smoking. The Court of Appeals held that petitioner's state- law claims were pre-empted by federal statutes, 893 F.2d 541 (CA3 1990), and other courts have agreed with that analysis. The highest court of the State of New Jersey, however, has held that the federal statutes did not pre-empt similar common-law claims. Because of the manifest importance of the issue, we granted certiorari to resolve the conflict. We now reverse in part and affirm in part.

I

On August 1, 1983, Rose Cipollone and her husband filed a complaint invoking the diversity jurisdiction of the Federal District Court. Their complaint alleged that Rose Cipollone developed lung cancer because she smoked cigarettes manufactured and sold by the three respondents. After her death in 1984, her husband filed an amended complaint. After trial, he also died; their son, executor of both estates, now maintains this action. Petitioner's third amended complaint alleges several different bases of recovery, relying on theories of strict liability, negligence, express warranty, and intentional tort. These claims, all based on New Jersey law, divide into five categories.

The "design defect claims" allege that respondents' cigarettes were defective because respondents failed to use a safer alternative design for their products and because the social value of their product was outweighed by the dangers it created. The "failure to warn claims" allege both that the product was "defective as a result of [respondents'] failure to provide adequate warnings of the health consequences of cigarette smoking" and that respondents "were negligent in the manner [that] they tested, researched, sold, promoted and advertised" their cigarettes. The "express warranty claims" allege that respondents had "expressly warranted that smoking the cigarettes which they manufactured and sold did not present any significant health consequences". The "fraudulent misrepresentation claims" allege that respondents had willfully, "through their advertising, attempted to neutralize the [federally mandated] warnin[g]" labels, and that they had possessed, but had "ignored and failed to act upon" medical, and scientific data indicating that "cigarettes were hazardous to the health of consumers". Finally, the "conspiracy to defraud claims" allege that respondents conspired to deprive the public of such medical and scientific data.

As one of their defenses, respondents contended that the Federal Cigarette Labeling and Advertising Act, enacted in 1965, and its successor, the Public Health Cigarette Smoking Act of 1969, protected them from any liability based on their conduct after 1965. In a pretrial ruling, the District Court concluded that the federal statutes were intended to establish a uniform warning that would prevail throughout the country and that would protect cigarette manufacturers from being "subjected to varying requirements from state to state," *Cipollone v. Liggett Group, Inc.*, 593 F.Supp. 1146, 1148 (N.J.1984), but that the statutes did not pre-empt common-law actions. Accordingly, the court granted a motion to strike the pre-emption defense entirely.

The Court of Appeals accepted an interlocutory appeal pursuant to 28 U.S.C. § 1292(b), and reversed. *Cipollone v. Liggett Group, Inc.*, 789 F.2d 181 (CA3 1986). The court rejected respondents' contention that the federal Acts expressly pre-empted common-law actions, but accepted their contention that such actions would conflict with federal law. Relying on the statement of purpose in the statutes,[5] the court concluded that Congress' "carefully drawn balance between the purposes of warning the public of the hazards of cigarette smoking and protecting the interests of national economy" would be upset by state-law damages actions based on noncompliance with "warning, advertisement, and promotion obligations other than those prescribed in the [federal] Act." . Accordingly, the court *held*:

> "[T]he Act preempts those state law damage[s] actions relating to smoking and health that challenge either the adequacy of the warning on cigarette packages or the propriety of a party's actions with respect to the advertising and promotion of cigarettes. [W]here the success of a state law damage[s] claim necessarily depends on the assertion that a party bore the duty to provide a warning to consumers in addition to the warning Congress has required on cigarette packages, such claims are preempted as conflicting with the Act." Ibid. (footnote omitted).

The court did not, however, identify the specific claims asserted by petitioner that were pre-empted by the Act.

This Court denied a petition for certiorari, 479 U.S. 1043, 107 S.Ct. 907, 93 L.Ed.2d 857 (1987), and the case returned to the District Court for trial. Complying with the Court of Appeals' mandate, the District Court held that the failure-to-warn, express-warranty, fraudulent-misrepresentation, and conspiracy-to-defraud claims were barred to the extent that they relied on respondents' advertising, promotional, and public relations activities after January 1, 1966 (the effective date of the 1965 Act). 649 F.Supp. 664, 669, 673-675 (N.J.1986). The court also ruled that while the design defect claims were not pre-empted by federal law, those claims were barred on other grounds. Following extensive discovery and a 4-month trial, the jury answered a series of special interrogatories and awarded $400,000 in damages to Rose Cipollone's husband. In brief, it rejected all of the fraudulent-misrepresentation and conspiracy claims, but found that respondent Liggett had breached its duty to warn and its express warranties before 1966. It found, however, that Rose Cipollone had " 'voluntarily and unreasonably encounter[ed] a known danger by smoking cigarettes' " and that 80% of the responsibility for her injuries was attributable to her. For that reason, no damages were awarded to her estate. However, the jury awarded damages to compensate her husband for losses caused by respondents' breach of express warranty.

---

[5] It is the policy of the Congress, and the purpose of this chapter, to establish a comprehensive Federal program to deal with cigarette labeling and advertising with respect to any relationship between smoking and health, whereby—

"(1) the public may be adequately informed that cigarette smoking maybe hazardous to health by inclusion of a warning to that effect on each package of ciarettes; and

"(2) commerce and the national economy may be (A) protected to the maximum extent consistent with this declared policy and (B) not impeded by diverse, nonuniform, and confusing cigarette labeling and advertising regulations with respect to any relationship between smoking and health." 15 U.S.C.§ 1331 (1982 ed.).

On cross-appeals from the final judgment, the Court of Appeals affirmed the District Court's pre-emption rulings but remanded for a new trial on several issues not relevant to our decision. We granted the petition for certiorari to consider the pre-emptive effect of the federal statutes.

II

Although physicians had suspected a link between smoking and illness for centuries, the first medical studies of that connection did not appear until the 1920's. *See* U.S. Dept. of Health and Human Services, Report of the Surgeon General, Reducing the Health Consequences of Smoking: 25 Years of Progress 5 (1989). The ensuing decades saw a wide range of epidemiologic and laboratory studies on the health hazards of smoking. Thus, by the time the Surgeon General convened an advisory committee to examine the issue in 1962, there were more than 7,000 publications examining the relationship between smoking and health.

In 1964, the advisory committee issued its report, which stated as its central conclusion: "Cigarette smoking is a health hazard of sufficient importance in the United States to warrant appropriate remedial action." U.S. Dept. of Health, Education, and Welfare, U.S. Surgeon General's Advisory Committee, Smoking and Health 33 (1964). Relying in part on that report, the Federal Trade Commission (FTC), which had long regulated unfair and deceptive advertising practices in the cigarette industry, promulgated a new trade regulation rule. That rule, which was to take effect January 1, 1965, established that it would be a violation of the Federal Trade Commission Act "to fail to disclose, clearly and prominently, in all advertising and on every pack, box, carton, or container [of cigarettes] that cigarette smoking is dangerous to health and may cause death from cancer and other diseases." 29 Fed.Reg. 8325 (1964). Several States also moved to regulate the advertising and labeling of cigarettes. *See*, e.g., 1965 N.Y.Laws, ch. 470; see also 111 Cong.Rec. 13900-13902 (1965) (statement of Sen. Moss). Upon a congressional request, the FTC postponed enforcement of its new regulation for six months. In July 1965, Congress enacted the Federal Cigarette Labeling and Advertising Act (1965 Act or Act). The 1965 Act effectively adopted half of the FTC's regulation: the Act mandated warnings on cigarette packages (§ 5(a)), but barred the requirement of such warnings in cigarette advertising (§ 5(b)).

Section 2 of the Act declares the statute's two purposes: (1) adequately informing the public that cigarette smoking may be hazardous to health, and (2) protecting the national economy from the burden imposed by diverse, nonuniform, and confusing cigarette labeling and advertising regulations. In furtherance of the first purpose, § 4 of the Act made it unlawful to sell or distribute any cigarettes in the United States unless the package bore a conspicuous label stating: "Caution: Cigarette Smoking May Be Hazardous to Your Health." In furtherance of the second purpose, § 5, captioned "Preemption," provided in part:

> "(a) No statement relating to smoking and health, other than the statement required by section 4 of this Act, shall be required on any cigarette package.

> "(b) No statement relating to smoking and health shall be required in the advertising of any cigarettes the packages of which are labeled in conformity with the provisions of this Act."

Although the Act took effect January 1, 1966, § 10 of the Act provided that its provisions affecting the regulation of advertising would terminate on July 1, 1969.

As that termination date approached, federal authorities prepared to issue further regulations on cigarette advertising. The FTC announced the reinstitution of its 1964 proceedings concerning a warning requirement for cigarette advertisements. 34 Fed.Reg. 7917 (1969). The Federal Communications Commission (FCC) announced that it would consider "a proposed rule which would ban the broadcast of cigarette commercials by radio and television stations." *Id.*, at 1959. State authorities also prepared to take actions regulating cigarette advertisements.

It was in this context that Congress enacted the Public Health Cigarette Smoking Act of 1969 (1969 Act or Act), which amended the 1965 Act in several ways. First, the 1969 Act strengthened the warning label, in part by requiring a statement that cigarette smoking "is dangerous" rather than that it "may be hazardous." Second, the 1969 Act banned cigarette advertising in "any medium of electronic communication subject to [FCC] jurisdiction." Third, and related, the 1969 Act modified the pre-emption provision by replacing the original § 5(b) with a provision that reads:

> "(b) No requirement or prohibition based on smoking and health shall be imposed under State law with respect to the advertising or promotion of any cigarettes the packages of which are labeled in conformity with the provisions of this Act."

Although the Act also directed the FTC not to "take any action before July 1, 1971, with respect to its pending trade regulation rule proceeding relating to cigarette advertising," the narrowing of the pre-emption provision to prohibit only restrictions "imposed under State law" cleared the way for the FTC to extend the warning-label requirement to print advertisements for cigarettes. The FTC did so in 1972. *See In re Lorillard*, 80 F.T.C. 455 (1972).

III

Article VI of the Constitution provides that the laws of the United States "shall be the supreme Law of the Land; ... any Thing in the Constitution or Laws of any state to the Contrary notwithstanding." Art. VI, cl. 2. Thus, since our decision in *M'Culloch v. Maryland*, 17 U.S. (4 Wheat.) 316, 427, 4 L.Ed. 579 (1819), it has been settled that state law that conflicts with federal law is "without effect." *Maryland v. Louisiana*, 451 U.S. 725, 746, 101 S.Ct. 2114, 2128, 68 L.Ed.2d 576 (1981). Consideration of issues arising under the Supremacy Clause "start[s] with the assumption that the historic police powers of the States [are] not to be superseded by ... Federal Act unless that [is] the clear and manifest purpose of Congress." Accordingly, " '[t]he purpose of Congress is the ultimate touchstone' " of pre-emption analysis.

Congress' intent may be "explicitly stated in the statute's language or implicitly contained in its structure and purpose." In the absence of an express congressional command, state law is pre-empted if that law actually conflicts with federal law, *see* Pacific Gas & Elec. Co. v. State Energy Resources Conservation and Development Comm'n, 461 U.S. 190, 204, 103 S.Ct. 1713, 1722, 75 L.Ed.2d 752 (1983), or if federal law so thoroughly occupies a legislative field " 'as to make reasonable the inference that Congress left no room for the States to supplement it.' "

The Court of Appeals was not persuaded that the pre-emption provision in the 1969 Act encompassed state common-law claims. It was also not persuaded that the labeling obligation imposed by both the 1965 and 1969 Acts revealed a congressional intent to exert exclusive federal control over every aspect of the relationship between cigarettes and health. Nevertheless, reading the statute as a whole in the light of the statement of purpose in § 2, and considering the potential regulatory effect of state common-law actions on the federal interest in uniformity, the Court of Appeals concluded that Congress had impliedly pre-empted petitioner's claims challenging the adequacy of the warnings on labels or in advertising or the propriety of respondents' advertising and promotional activities.

In our opinion, the pre-emptive scope of the 1965 Act and the 1969 Act is governed entirely by the express language in § 5 of each Act. When Congress has considered the issue of pre-emption and has included in the enacted legislation a provision explicitly addressing that issue, and when that provision provides a "reliable indicium of congressional intent with respect to state authority," *Malone v. White Motor Corp.*, 435 U.S., at 505, 98 S.Ct., at 1190, "there is no need to infer congressional intent to pre-empt state laws from the substantive provisions" of the legislation. *California Federal Savings & Loan Assn. v. Guerra*, 479 U.S. 272, 282, 107 S.Ct. 683, 690, 93 L.Ed.2d 613 (1987) (opinion of Marshall, J.). Such reasoning is a variant of the familiar principle of expression unius est exclusio alterius: Congress' enactment of a provision defining the pre-emptive reach of a statute implies that matters beyond that reach are not pre-empted. In this case, the other provisions of the 1965 and 1969 Acts offer no cause to look beyond § 5 of each Act. Therefore, we need only identify the domain expressly pre-empted by each of those sections. As the 1965 and 1969 provisions differ substantially, we consider each in turn.

IV

In the 1965 pre-emption provision regarding advertising (§ 5(b)), Congress spoke precisely and narrowly: "No statement relating to smoking and health shall be required in the advertising of [properly labeled] cigarettes." Section 5(a) used the same phrase ("No statement relating to smoking and health") with regard to cigarette labeling. As § 5(a) made clear, that phrase referred to the sort of warning provided for in § 4, which set forth verbatim the warning Congress determined to be appropriate. Thus, on their face, these provisions merely prohibited state and federal rulemaking bodies from mandating particular cautionary statements on cigarette labels (§ 5(a)) or in cigarette advertisements (§ 5(b)).

Beyond the precise words of these provisions, this reading is appropriate for several reasons. First, as discussed above, we must construe these provisions in light of the presumption against the pre-emption of state police power regulations. This presumption reinforces the appropriateness of a narrow reading of § 5. Second, the warning required in § 4 does not by its own effect foreclose additional obligations imposed under state law. That Congress requires a particular warning label does not automatically pre-empt a regulatory field. *See McDermott v. Wisconsin*, 228 U.S. 115, 131-132, 33 S.Ct. 431, 434-435, 57 L.Ed. 754 (1913). Third, there is no general, inherent conflict between federal pre-emption of state warning requirements and the continued vitality of state common-law damages actions. For example, in the Comprehensive Smokeless Tobacco Health Education Act of 1986, Congress expressly pre-empted state or local imposition of a "statement relating to the use of smokeless tobacco products and health" but, at the same time, preserved state-law damages actions based on those products. *See* 15 U.S.C. § 4406. All of these considerations indicate that § 5 is best read as having superseded only positive enactments by legislatures or administrative agencies that mandate particular warning labels.

This reading comports with the 1965 Act's statement of purpose, which expressed an intent to avoid "diverse, nonuniform, and confusing cigarette labeling and advertising regulations with respect to any relationship between smoking and health." Read against the backdrop of regulatory activity undertaken by state legislatures and federal agencies in response to the Surgeon General's report, the term "regulation" most naturally refers to positive enactments by those bodies, not to common-law damages actions.

The regulatory context of the 1965 Act also supports such a reading. As noted above, a warning requirement promulgated by the FTC and other requirements under consideration by the States were the catalyst for passage of the 1965 Act. These regulatory actions animated the passage of § 5, which reflected Congress' efforts to prevent "a multiplicity of State and local regulations pertaining to labeling of cigarette packages," H.R.Rep. No. 449, 89th Cong., 1st Sess., 4 (1965), and to "preemp[t] all Federal, State, and local authorities from requiring any statement relating to smoking and health in the advertising of cigarettes." *Id.*, at 5 (emphasis supplied).

For these reasons, we conclude that § 5 of the 1965 Act only pre-empted state and federal rulemaking bodies from mandating particular cautionary statements and did not pre-empt state-law damages actions.

V

Compared to its predecessor in the 1965 Act, the plain language of the pre-emption provision in the 1969 Act is much broader. First, the later Act bars not simply "statement[s]" but rather "requirement[s] or prohibition[s] ... imposed under State law." Second, the later Act reaches beyond statements "in the advertising" to obligations "with respect to the advertising or promotion" of cigarettes.

Notwithstanding these substantial differences in language, both petitioner and respondents contend that the 1969 Act did not materially alter the pre-emptive scope of federal law. Their primary support for this contention is a sentence in a Committee Report which states that the 1969 amendment "clarified" the 1965 version of § 5(b). S.Rep. No. 91-566, p. 12 (1969). We reject the parties' reading as incompatible with the language and origins of the amendments. As we noted in another context, "[i]nferences from legislative history cannot rest on so slender a reed. Moreover, the views of a subsequent Congress form a hazardous basis for inferring the intent of an earlier one." *United States v. Price*, 361 U.S. 304, 313, 80 S.Ct. 326, 332, 4 L.Ed.2d 334 (1960). The 1969 Act worked substantial changes in the law: rewriting the label warning, banning broadcast advertising, and allowing the FTC to regulate print advertising. In the context of such revisions and in light of the substantial changes in wording, we cannot accept the parties' claim that the 1969 Act did not alter the reach of § 5(b).

Petitioner next contends that § 5(b), however broadened by the 1969 Act, does not pre-empt common-law actions. He offers two theories for limiting the reach of the amended § 5(b). First, he argues that common-law damages actions do not impose "requirement[s] or prohibition[s]" and that Congress intended only to trump "state statute[s], injunction[s], or executive pronouncement [s]." We disagree; such an analysis is at odds both with the plain words of the 1969 Act and with the general understanding of common-law damages actions. The phrase "[n]o requirement or prohibition" sweeps broadly and suggests no distinction between positive enactments and common law; to the contrary, those words easily encompass obligations that take the form of common-law rules. As we noted in another context, "[state] regulation can be as effectively exerted through an award of damages as through some form of preventive relief. The obligation to pay compensation can be, indeed is designed to be, a potent method of governing conduct and controlling policy." *San Diego Building Trades Council v. Garmon*, 359 U.S. 236, 247, 79 S.Ct. 773, 780, 3 L.Ed.2d 775 (1959).

Although portions of the legislative history of the 1969 Act suggest that Congress was primarily concerned with positive enactments by States and localities, see S.Rep. No. 91-566, p. 12, the language of the Act plainly reaches beyond such enactments. "We must give effect to this plain language unless there is good reason to believe Congress intended the language to have some more restrictive meaning." In this case there is no "good reason to believe" that Congress meant less than what it said; indeed, in light of the narrowness of the 1965 Act, there is "good reason to believe" that Congress meant precisely what it said in amending that Act.

Moreover, common-law damages actions of the sort raised by petitioner are premised on the existence of a legal duty, and it is difficult to say that such actions do not impose "requirements or prohibitions." It is in this way that the 1969 version of § 5(b) differs from its predecessor: Whereas the common law would not normally require a vendor to use any specific statement on its packages or in its advertisements, it is the essence of the common law to enforce duties that are either affirmative requirements or negative prohibitions. We therefore reject petitioner's argument that the phrase "requirement or prohibition" limits the 1969 Act's pre-emptive scope to positive enactments by legislatures and agencies.

* * * * *

We consider each category of damages actions in turn. In doing so, we express no opinion on whether these actions are viable claims as a matter of state law; we assume, arguendo, that they are.

Failure to Warn

To establish liability for a failure to warn, petitioner must show that "a warning is necessary to make a product ... reasonably safe, suitable and fit for its intended use," that respondents failed to provide such a warning, and that that failure was a proximate cause of petitioner's injury. In this case, petitioner offered two closely related theories concerning the failure to warn: first, that respondents "were negligent in the manner [that] they tested, researched, sold, promoted, and advertised" their cigarettes; and second, that respondents failed to provide "adequate warnings of the health consequences of cigarette smoking."

Petitioner's claims are pre-empted to the extent that they rely on a state- law "requirement or prohibition ... with respect to ... advertising or promotion." Thus, insofar as claims under either failure-to-warn theory require a showing that respondents' post-1969 advertising or promotions should have included additional, or more clearly stated, warnings, those claims are pre-empted. The Act does not, however, pre-empt petitioner's claims that rely solely on respondents' testing or research practices or other actions unrelated to advertising or promotion.

Breach of Express Warranty

Petitioner's claim for breach of an express warranty arises under N.J.Stat.Ann. § 12A:2-313(1)(a) (West 1962), which provides:

> "Any affirmation of fact or promise made by the seller to the buyer which relates to the goods and becomes part of the basis of the bargain creates an express warranty that the goods shall conform to the affirmation or promise."

Petitioner's evidence of an express warranty consists largely of statements made in respondents' advertising. *See* 893 F. 2d, at 574, 576; 683 F. Supp. 1487, 1497 (N.J.1988). Applying the Court of Appeals' ruling that Congress pre-empted "damage[s] actions ... that challenge ... the propriety of a party's actions with respect to the advertising and promotion of cigarettes," 789 F.2d, at 187, the District Court ruled that this claim "inevitably brings into question [respondents'] advertising and promotional activities, and is therefore pre-empted" after 1965. 649 F.Supp., at 675. As demonstrated above, however, the 1969 Act does not sweep so broadly: The appropriate inquiry is not whether a claim challenges the "propriety" of advertising and promotion, but whether the claim would require the imposition under state law of a requirement or prohibition based on smoking and health with respect to advertising or promotion.

A manufacturer's liability for breach of an express warranty derives from, and is measured by, the terms of that warranty. Accordingly, the "requirement[s]" imposed by an express warranty claim are not "imposed under State law," but rather imposed by the warrantor. If, for example, a manufacturer expressly promised to pay a smoker's medical bills if she contracted emphysema, the duty to honor that promise could not fairly be said to be "imposed under state law," but rather is best understood as undertaken by the manufacturer itself. While the general duty not to breach warranties arises under state law, the particular "requirement ... based on smoking and health ... with respect to the advertising or promotion [of] cigarettes" in an express warranty claim arises from the manufacturer's statements in its advertisements. In short, a common-law remedy for a contractual commitment voluntarily undertaken should not be regarded as a "requirement ... imposed under State law " within the meaning of § 5(b).

That the terms of the warranty may have been set forth in advertisements rather than in separate documents is irrelevant to the pre-emption issue (though possibly not to the state law issue of whether the alleged warranty is valid and enforceable) because, although the breach of warranty claim is made "with respect ... to advertising," it does not rest on a duty imposed under state law. Accordingly, to the extent that petitioner has a viable claim for breach of express warranties made by respondents, that claim is not pre-empted by the 1969 Act.

Fraudulent Misrepresentation

Petitioner alleges two theories of fraudulent misrepresentation. First, petitioner alleges that respondents, through their advertising, neutralized the effect of federally mandated warning labels. Such a claim is predicated on a state-law prohibition against statements in advertising and promotional materials that tend to minimize the health hazards associated with smoking. Such a prohibition, however, is merely the converse of a state-law requirement that warnings be included in advertising and promotional materials. Section 5(b) of the 1969 Act pre-empts both requirements and prohibitions; it therefore supersedes petitioner's first fraudulent- misrepresentation theory.

663

Regulators have long recognized the relationship between prohibitions on advertising that downplays the dangers of smoking and requirements for warnings in advertisements. For example, the FTC, in promulgating its initial trade regulation rule in 1964, criticized advertising that "associated cigarette smoking with such positive attributes as contentment, glamour, romance, youth, happiness ... at the same time suggesting that smoking is an activity at least consistent with physical health and well-being." The Commission concluded:

> "To avoid giving a false impression that smoking [is] innocuous, the cigarette manufacturer who represents the alleged pleasures or satisfactions of cigarette smoking in his advertising must also disclose the serious risks to life that smoking involves." 29 Fed.Reg. 8356 (1964).

Longstanding regulations of the Food and Drug Administration express a similar understanding of the relationship between required warnings and advertising that "negates or disclaims" those warnings: "A hazardous substance shall not be deemed to have met [federal labeling] requirements if there appears in or on the label ... statements, designs, or other graphic material that in any manner negates or disclaims [the required warning]." 21 CFR § 191.102 (1965). In this light it seems quite clear that petitioner's first theory of fraudulent misrepresentation is inextricably related to petitioner's first failure-to-warn theory, a theory that we have already concluded is largely pre-empted by § 5(b).

Petitioner's second theory, as construed by the District Court, alleges intentional fraud and misrepresentation both by "false representation of a material fact [and by] conceal[ment of] a material fact." Tr. 12727. The predicate of this claim is a state-law duty not to make false statements of material fact or to conceal such facts. Our pre-emption analysis requires us to determine whether such a duty is the sort of requirement or prohibition proscribed by § 5(b).

Section 5(b) pre-empts only the imposition of state-law obligations "with respect to the advertising or promotion" of cigarettes. Petitioner's claims that respondents concealed material facts are therefore not pre-empted insofar as those claims rely on a state-law duty to disclose such facts through channels of communication other than advertising or promotion. Thus, for example, if state law obliged respondents to disclose material facts about smoking and health to an administrative agency, § 5(b) would not pre-empt a state-law claim based on a failure to fulfill that obligation.

Moreover, petitioner's fraudulent-misrepresentation claims that do arise with respect to advertising and promotions (most notably claims based on allegedly false statements of material fact made in advertisements) are not pre-empted by § 5(b). Such claims are predicated not on a duty "based on smoking and health" but rather on a more general obligation the duty not to deceive. This understanding of fraud by intentional misstatement is appropriate for several reasons. First, in the 1969 Act, Congress offered no sign that it wished to insulate cigarette manufacturers from longstanding rules governing fraud. To the contrary, both the 1965 and the 1969 Acts explicitly reserved the FTC's authority to identify and punish deceptive advertising practices--an authority that the FTC had long exercised and continues to exercise. *See* § 5(c) of the 1965 Act; § 7(b) of the 1969 Act; *see also* nn. 7, 9, *supra*. This indicates that Congress intended the phrase "relating to smoking and health" (which was essentially unchanged by the 1969 Act) to be construed narrowly, so as not to proscribe the regulation of deceptive advertising.

Moreover, this reading of "based on smoking and health" is wholly consistent with the purposes of the 1969 Act. State-law prohibitions on false statements of material fact do not create "diverse, nonuniform, and confusing" standards. Unlike state-law obligations concerning the warning necessary to render a product "reasonably safe," state-law proscriptions on intentional fraud rely only on a single, uniform standard: falsity. Thus, we conclude that the phrase "based on smoking and health" fairly but narrowly construed does not encompass the more general duty not to make fraudulent statements. Accordingly, petitioner's claim based on allegedly fraudulent statements made in respondents' advertisements is not pre-empted by § 5(b) of the 1969 Act.

Conspiracy to Misrepresent or Conceal Material Facts

Petitioner's final claim alleges a conspiracy among respondents to misrepresent or conceal material facts concerning the health hazards of smoking. The predicate duty underlying this claim is a duty not to conspire to commit fraud. For the reasons stated in our analysis of petitioner's intentional fraud claim, this duty is not pre-empted by § 5(b) for it is not a prohibition "based on smoking and health" as that phrase is properly construed. Accordingly, we conclude that the 1969 Act does not pre-empt petitioner's conspiracy claim.

VI

To summarize our holding: The 1965 Act did not pre-empt state law damages actions; the 1969 Act pre-empts petitioner's claims based on a failure to warn and the neutralization of federally mandated warnings to the extent that those claims rely on omissions or inclusions in respondents' advertising or promotions; the 1969 Act does not pre-empt petitioner's claims based on express warranty, intentional fraud and misrepresentation, or conspiracy.

The judgment of the Court of Appeals is accordingly reversed in part and affirmed in part, and the case is remanded for further proceedings consistent with this opinion.

NOTES

1.   Prior to *Cipollone*, courts routinely rejected preemption arguments by manufacturers. *See*, e.g., *Ferebee v. Chevron Chem. Co.*, 736 F.2d 1529 (D.C. Cir. 1984); *Abbott v. American Cyanamid Co.*, 844 F.2d 1108, 1112 n. 1 (4th Cir. 1988) (FDA-approved labeling of DPT vaccine: "The overwhelming majority of courts considering federal preemption of state law as regards vaccines have found no preemption."). Since *Cipollone*, preemption is frequently raised in products liability litigation.

2.   Preemption issues have been raised pursuant to the Federal Insecticide, Fungicide, and Rodenticide Act (FIFRA), 7 U.S. §§ 136-136y, *King v. E.I. Dupon De Nemouis & Co.*, 996 F 2d 1346 (2d 1993) (failure to warn claim preempted), the Medical Device Amendments of 1976 (MDA), 21 U.S.C. §§ 360c-3601, *Kennedy v. Collagen Corp.*, 67 F.3d 1453 (9th Cir. 1996) (negligence, strict liability, and breach of warranty claims related to Zyderm Collagen Implant not preempted), and the Consumer Product Safety Act (CPSA), 15 U.S.C. §§ 2051-2084, *Moe v. MTD Products, Inc.*, 73 F.3d 179 (8th Cir. 1995) (regulation requiring blade-control system and warning requirement preempts warning claim but not design claim).

3.   In March 2009 the Supreme Court held in *Wyeth v. Levine*, 555 U.S. 555 (2009), that federal law does not preempt personal injury lawsuits against name brand drug manufacturers for failing to adequately warn about the serious side effects of their drug.

However, generic drug manufacturers Actavis and Pliva recently argued that federal law preempts state-based personal injury claims for failing to warn of the dangers resulting from generic drugs. In June of 2011, in the case *Pliva, Inc., et al. v. Mensing*, 564 U.S. 604 (2011), the Supreme Court concluded that federal drug regulations applicable to generic drug manufacturers directly conflict with, and thus pre-empt, state law claims. Because federal regulations covers drug labeling for generic drugs, the manufacturers of generic drugs cannot be sued for damages under state laws for failing to warn of possible risks.

CHAPTER 17

REPUTATIONAL AND PRIVACY TORTS

INTRODUCTORY NOTE

The torts of defamation and invasion of privacy are, for the most part,[76] torts involving communication of an alleged fact concerning the plaintiff to a third party. The information communicated must be false for defamation to apply; falsity is not necessarily required for invasion of privacy. In either case, the communicative nature of the torts implicates the First Amendment guarantees of freedom of speech and the press.

The common law and the Louisiana civil code initially both imposed absolute liability on the communicator of untruthful defamatory words. In several cases discussed later in this chapter, the United States Supreme Court ruled that a higher degree of fault is required in some cases to protect First Amendment values. Although it is not crystal clear which cases are subjected to First Amendment scrutiny, you should ask the following questions:

1. *Who is the plaintiff?* Is the plaintiff a public figure or a purely private citizen? If the plaintiff has received publicity, has the plaintiff made a choice to be public or has the publicity been "thrust upon him?"

2. *Who is the defendant?* Is the defendant a media defendant?

3. *What is the subject matter of the communication?* Is this a matter of public or private concern?

In those cases where the First Amendment applies, state courts and legislatures may not apply strict, absolute or "mere negligence" standards to the speech. Rather, the plaintiff must show that the defendant behaved with "actual malice," defined as "knowledge of the false nature of the statement or reckless disregard for the truth or falsity of the communication."

Invasion of Privacy is a very recent tort, and its contours are still forming. First Amendment values are applied to protect some speech which might otherwise constitute an invasion of privacy but the "actual malice" standard can not be applied literally because invasion of privacy can involve disclosure of a true fact. In most invasion of privacy cases, the issue is whether the plaintiff's reasonable expectation of privacy or investment-backed publicity right outweighs the public's right-to-know or right-to-use the allegedly private fact.

Invasion of privacy is a tort that has been implicated in much recent litigation in relation to computers and electronic communication.

---

[76] The exceptions are intrusion on seclusion and the right of publicity.

KENNEDY
v.
SHERIFF OF EAST BATON ROUGE
935 So. 2d 669 (La. 2006)

WEIMER, J.

This case arises out of a claim for defamation brought by a private individual against a fast food restaurant. The allegedly defamatory statements were made by employees of the restaurant when they contacted police to report that an occupant in a vehicle in the drive-through lane of the restaurant had attempted to buy food with a counterfeit one hundred dollar bill. The district court granted summary judgment in favor of the restaurant, but the court of appeal reversed. We granted certiorari primarily to consider whether a private individual is entitled to a conditional or qualified privilege when the individual reports suspected criminal activity to the police, and if so, whether the privilege was abused in this case. Finding that the report to police of suspected criminal activity was conditionally privileged, and that the plaintiff failed to submit evidence sufficient to demonstrate that he will be able to meet his burden of proof at trial that the privilege was abused, we reverse the judgment of the court of appeal and reinstate the summary judgment in favor of the restaurant.

Facts and Procedural History

Shortly after midnight on December 7, 2001, Alfred Kennedy, III, accompanied by four female companions, entered the drive-through lane of a Jack in the Box restaurant in Baton Rouge, Louisiana. After confirming with the attendant on duty that the restaurant would accept one hundred dollar bills, the party placed an order for food and drinks. Kennedy tendered a 1974 series one hundred dollar bill in payment of the order. Suspecting the bill was counterfeit, the restaurant employee who received the bill notified local law enforcement. East Baton Rouge Parish sheriff's deputies arrived on the scene in minutes. Upon examining the bill and determining that it looked "suspicious," one of the deputies approached the vehicle, which was still in the drive-through lane, and motioned for the driver to move her car from the line. After the car was parked, and identification obtained from each of the occupants, the deputies proceeded to ascertain who in the vehicle had tendered the one hundred dollar bill. When Kennedy identified himself as the owner of the currency, he was asked to exit the car, whereupon he was handcuffed and transported to a nearby sheriff's substation to await investigation into the bill's authenticity.

While Kennedy waited at the substation, one of the deputies obtained a counterfeit detection marker from a nearby business. The bill was ultimately determined to be legitimate, and Kennedy was released and his money returned.

On June 26, 2002, Kennedy filed suit against both the Sheriff of East Baton Rouge Parish ("Sheriff") and Jack in the Box[1] seeking damages. Answers were filed by both defendants, following which the Sheriff moved for summary judgment. Jack in the Box filed an exception of no cause of action, and alternative motion for summary judgment. The matter was heard on December 8, 2003. At the conclusion of the hearing, the district court denied Jack in the Box's exception of no cause of action, but granted both motions for summary judgment. With respect to the claims against the Sheriff, the district court ruled that the deputies had probable cause to effect an arrest of Kennedy. As to the claims against Jack in the Box, the court found no evidence to indicate that Jack in the Box or any of its employees detained Kennedy, and thus no evidence sufficient to support a claim for wrongful arrest. In addition, the court found that "[t]he record is also void of any showing of malice to support any kind of claim for defamation." A judgment dismissing the claims against the Sheriff and Jack in the Box was signed by the district court on December 16, 2003.

---

[1] Although plaintiff named "Jack in the Box Eastern Division L.P. d/b/a Jack in the Box Restaurant" as defendant, an answer was filed in the name of "Jack in the Box, Inc." (hereinafter "Jack in the Box").

Kennedy appealed the adverse judgment. Jack in the Box answered the appeal seeking damages for frivolous appeal. On March 24, 2005, the Court of Appeal, First Circuit, handed down its opinion in this matter. *Kennedy v. Sheriff of East Baton Rouge,* 04-0574 (La.App. 1 Cir. 2005), 899 So. 2d 682. After conducting a de novo review of the materials submitted in connection with the summary judgment motions, the court of appeal concluded as a matter of law that the "defendants failed to show that they acted reasonably or without a reckless disregard for Mr. Kennedy's rights when a criminal investigation was instituted because the bill he presented merely looked unusual." *Kennedy,* 04-0574 at 11, 899 So. 2d at 689. The court found that defendants failed to offer any evidence to indicate that their employees received any training or possessed any specialized knowledge with respect to identifying counterfeit currency, thereby raising factual questions as to the reasonableness of their conduct. Accordingly, the court of appeal vacated the district court judgment granting summary judgment in favor of defendants and remanded the matter for further proceedings.

Upon Jack in the Box's application,[2] we granted certiorari primarily to address the defamation claim, and more particularly, whether Jack in the Box's employees enjoyed a qualified privilege in reporting suspected criminal activity to law enforcement officials; and if so, whether sufficient evidence was offered of an abuse of the privilege to defeat Jack in the Box's motion for summary judgment. *Kennedy v. Sheriff of East Baton Rouge,* 05-1418 (La. 2006), 920 So. 2d 217.

Law and Discussion

We most recently addressed the tort of defamation in *Costello v. Hardy,* 03-1146 (La. 2004), 864 So. 2d 129. Therein, we noted that defamation is a tort involving the invasion of a person's interest in his or her reputation and good name. *Costello,* 03-1146 at 12, 864 So. 2d at 139. Four elements are necessary to establish a claim for defamation: (1) a false and defamatory statement concerning another; (2) an unprivileged publication to a third party; (3) fault (negligence or greater) on the part of the publisher; and (4) resulting injury. *Id., quoting Trentecosta v. Beck,* 96-2388, p. 10 (La. 1997), 703 So. 2d 552, 559; Restatement (Second) of Torts § 558 (1977). The fault requirement is generally referred to in the jurisprudence as malice, actual or implied. *Costello,* 03-1146 at 12, 864 So. 2d at 139.

By definition, a statement is defamatory if it tends to harm the reputation of another so as to lower the person in the estimation of the community, deter others from associating or dealing with the person, or otherwise expose the person to contempt or ridicule. *Costello,* 03-1146 at 13, 864 So. 2d at 140; *Trentecosta,* 96-2388 at 10, 703 So. 2d at 559 (*citing* Restatement (Second) of Torts § 559 cmt. e (1977)). In Louisiana, defamatory words have traditionally been divided into two categories: those that are defamatory per se and those that are susceptible of a defamatory meaning. *Costello,* 03-1146 at 13, 864 So. 2d at 140; *Madison v. Bolton,* 234 La. 997, 102 So. 2d 433, 438 (La. 1958). Words which expressly or implicitly accuse another of criminal conduct, or which by their very nature tend to injure one's personal or professional reputation, without considering extrinsic facts or circumstances, are considered defamatory per se. *Costello,* 03-1146 at 13-14, 864 So. 2d at 140; *Cangelosi v. Schwegmann Brothers. Giant Super Markets,* 390 So. 2d 196, 198 (La. 1980). When a plaintiff proves publication of words that are defamatory per se, falsity and malice (or fault) are presumed, but may be rebutted by the defendant. *Costello,* 03-1146 at 14, 864 So. 2d at 140. Injury may also be presumed. *Id.* When the words at issue are not defamatory per se, a plaintiff must prove, in addition to defamatory meaning and publication, falsity, malice (or fault) and injury. *Id.*

In the instant case, plaintiff's petition alleges that "Jack in the Box employee(s) made the false allegation to law enforcement officers that the plaintiff had passed counterfeit or unlawful tender at its restaurant." Such an allegation could be construed as Jack in the Box employees falsely accusing the plaintiff of the crime of monetary instrument abuse, LSA-R.S. 14:72.2. Under Louisiana's traditional defamation rules, such a statement would be considered defamatory per se, and the elements of falsity

---

[2] The Sheriff did not seek supervisory relief in this court; therefore, we will not discuss any issues respecting the wrongful arrest claim pending against the Sheriff.

and malice (or fault) would, as a result, be presumed, shifting the burden of proof to defendant to rebut the adverse presumption.

Constitutional Requirements

Since the seminal decision of the United States Supreme Court in *New York Times Co. v. Sullivan,* 376 U.S. 254, 84 S.Ct. 710, 11 L.Ed.2d 686 (1964), the tort of defamation has been subject to the constraints of the First Amendment to the Constitution and its prohibition against any law abridging freedom of speech or of the press. In *New York Times*, the Supreme Court held that the First Amendment prohibits a public official from recovering damages arising from a defamatory falsehood published in relation to his or her official conduct unless the public official proves that statement was made with "actual malice"--that is, with knowledge that it was false or with reckless disregard of whether it was false or not. *New York Times,* 376 U.S. at 279-280, 84 S.Ct. at 726. The Supreme Court granted the protection to speech concerning public officials because of its perception that the common law rules of defamation, which imposed strict liability on the publisher of a defamatory statement that later proved to be false, regardless of whether the publisher had exercised due care to check the accuracy of the statement and reasonably believed it to be true, would have a chilling effect on constitutionally valuable speech. *Id.,* 376 U.S. at 277-80, 84 S.Ct. at 723-725.[3] Thus, the *New York Times* decision not only imposed the requirement of a high degree of fault in defamation actions brought by public officials, but also shifted the burden of proof of fault to the public official and imposed a heightened burden. *Trentecosta,* 96-2388 at 12, 703 So. 2d at 560.

In *Curtis Publishing Co. v. Butts,* 388 U.S. 130, 87 S.Ct. 1975, 18 L.Ed.2d 1094 (1967), this constitutional protection was subsequently extended to "public figures"[4] when the defamatory statements related to issues of public concern, and in *Rosenbloom v. Metromedia, Inc.,* 403 U.S. 29, 91 S.Ct. 1811, 29 L.Ed.2d 296 (1971), to all "communication involving matters of public or general concern without regard to whether the persons involved are famous or anonymous." *Id.,* 403 U.S. at 44, 91 S.Ct. at 1820.

Rosenbloom, a plurality opinion, marked the farthest extension of the free speech protections of the First Amendment to defamation law. However, the decision was not without its detractors, as the dissenting justices in *Rosenbloom* expressed concern that the holding of the case would unfairly abridge the rights of private individuals to protect their reputations. The tensions between those competing interests came fully to light in *Gertz v. Robert Welch, Inc.,* 418 U.S. 323, 94 S.Ct. 2997, 41 L.Ed.2d 789 (1974).

Gertz involved a private individual suing a media defendant for defamation on an issue of public concern. The Supreme Court recognized that a state's interest in compensating injury to the reputation of individuals is greater in the case of private individuals than for public officials and public figures, because private individuals characteristically have less access to channels of effective communication to counteract false statements than do public officials and public figures. Additionally, private individuals have not, by placing themselves in the public eye, voluntarily exposed themselves to increased risk of injury from defamatory falsehoods. The Supreme Court held that a private plaintiff need not prove "actual malice" under *New York Times* in order to recover actual damages in a defamation action. Rather, the Supreme Court in *Gertz* left to the states the freedom to establish their own standards of liability for a publisher or broadcaster of a defamatory falsehood injurious to a private individual, so long as the states do not impose liability without fault. *Gertz,* 418 U.S. at 344-347, 94 S.Ct. at 3009-3010.

---

[3] The Supreme Court pointed out that "debate on public issues should be uninhibited, robust, and wide-open, and that it may well include vehement, caustic, and sometimes unpleasantly sharp attacks on government and public officials." *New York Times,* 376 U.S. at 270, 84 S.Ct. at 721.

[4] A "public figure" is a non-public official who is intimately involved in the resolution of important public questions or who, by reason of his or her fame, shapes events in areas of concern to society at large. *Butts,* 388 U.S. at 164, 87 S.Ct. at 1996 (Warren, C.J., concurring in result).

In *Philapelphia Newspapers, Inc. v. Hepps,* 475 U.S. 767, 106 S.Ct. 1558, 89 L.Ed.2d 783 (1986), the Supreme Court expanded its decision in *Gertz* by holding that the First Amendment requires placement of the burden of proving falsity, as well as fault, on the plaintiff in a defamation action by a private individual against a media defendant on a matter of public concern.[5]

Rosenbloom, Gertz, and *Philadelphia* Newspapers represent a series of decisions in which the Supreme Court attempted to define the reach of the First Amendment to defamation actions, like the one before us, brought by private individuals. The legacy of these cases is that, while the states remain free to establish their own standards of liability for a publisher of defamatory falsehoods injurious to a private individual, the protections afforded by the First Amendment supercede the common law presumptions of fault, falsity, and damages with respect to speech involving matters of public concern, at least insofar as media defendants are concerned.

The instant case involves a private, non-public figure plaintiff (a college student attempting to purchase food at a local restaurant) and speech of public concern: the report to law enforcement officers of suspected criminal activity involving the distribution of counterfeit currency in the community.[6] The defendant, however, is a private, non-media entity. Whether First Amendment restraints supercede the presumptions of falsity, malice (or fault), and injury that would ordinarily obtain under Louisiana law when a statement is defamatory per se depends upon whether the constitutional protections extended to media defendants in *Gertz* and *Philadelphia Newspapers* obtain where the defendant is a private, non-media defendant, a question the Supreme Court has not squarely answered.[7] It is therefore left to this court to determine whether the principles enunciated by the Supreme Court in *Gertz* and *Philadelphia Newspapers* should logically extend to include non-media defendants, and whether, in any event, this court should so hold as a matter of state law.

* * * * *

Like the First Amendment to the United States Constitution, Article I, § 7 of the Louisiana Constitution, quoted *infra,* prohibits any law curtailing or restraining freedom of speech as well as

---

[5] Any discussion of the impact of the First Amendment on defamation law would not be complete without also mentioning the Supreme Court's plurality decision in *Dunn & Bradstreet, Inc. v. Greenmoss Builders, Inc.,* 472 U.S. 749, 105 S.Ct. 2939, 86 L.Ed.2d 593 (1985). In contrast to the Supreme Court's earlier decisions, *Dunn & Bradstreet* involved a private-figure plaintiff suing a non-media defendant over speech of purely private concern. In such a scenario, a plurality of the Supreme Court held that, in light of the reduced constitutional value of speech involving matters of purely private concern as opposed to speech on matters of public concern, the state interest in compensating private individuals for injury to their reputation adequately supports awards of presumed and punitive damages--even absent a showing of "actual malice." *Dunn & Bradstreet,* 472 U.S. at 761, 105 S.Ct. at 2946. In other words, the Supreme Court ruled that when the plaintiff is a private individual and the speech is of private concern, the First Amendment does not necessarily force any change in at least some of the features of the common law of defamation.
Our decision in *Costello*, *supra,* which involved a private plaintiff, a non-media defendant, and speech of purely private concern, was guided by the ruling in *Dunn & Bradstreet.*

[6] The Supreme Court has described speech on matters of public concern as speech "relating to any matter of political, social, or other concern to the community." *Connick v. Myers,* 461 U.S. 138, 146, 103 S.Ct. 1684, 1690, 75 L.Ed.2d 708 (1983). Whether speech addresses a matter of public concern must be determined by the content, form, and context of a given statement, as revealed by the entire record. *Id.,* 461 U.S. at 147-148, 103 S.Ct. at 1690. Clearly, a report to law enforcement regarding the suspected distribution of counterfeit currency in the community is a matter of public concern, as it is an issue about which information is appropriate and needed, and in which the public, and particularly the business community, may reasonably be expected to have a legitimate interest.

[7] It is clear that the holding in *Gertz* was limited to media expression. Not only was the defendant in that case a member of the media, but the opinion itself is replete with references to "the news media," "publishers and broadcasters," and "the press and broadcast media.." *Gertz,* 418 U.S. at 341, 348, 94 S.Ct. at 3007, 3011. The opinion in *Philadelphia Newspapers* similarly confines itself to media expression. *Philadelphia Newspapers,* 475 U.S. at 779 n. 4, 106 S.Ct. at 1565 n. 4.

freedom of the press. Therefore, apart from any future Supreme Court holding based on constitutional grounds, we conclude as a matter of state law that the *Gertz* and *Philadelphia Newspapers* holdings should apply to media and non-media defendants alike. Such a holding has previously been adopted in at least one appellate court decision from this state. *Wattigny v. Lambert,* 408 So. 2d 1126, 1130-1131 (La.App. 3 Cir.), *writ denied,* 410 So. 2d 760 (1981), *cert. denied,* 457 U.S. 1132, 102 S.Ct. 2957, 73 L.Ed.2d 1349 (1982). Courts in other states, applying a similar rationale, have adopted a similar holding. *Jacron Sales Co., Inc. v. Sindorf,* 276 Md. 580, 350 A.2d 688 (1976); *Bryan v. Brown,* 339 So. 2d 577 (Ala.1976); *Ryder Truck Rentals, Inc., v. Latham,* 593 S.W.2d 334 (Tex.Civ.App. El Paso, 11/14/79).

Fault

Having concluded that the rules announced in *Gertz* and *Philadelphia Newspapers* apply to non-media defendants, and hence to the present case, we must next decide the standard of liability that should govern in a case, such as this one, in which a private individual is allegedly injured by a defamatory communication by a non-media defendant about a matter of public concern, a question we expressly left unresolved in *Trentecosta,* 96-2388 at 13, 703 So. 2d at 561.

In holding that "so long as they do not impose liability without fault, the states may define for themselves the appropriate standard of liability"[8] for a publisher of a defamatory falsehood injurious to a private individual, the Supreme Court in *Gertz* effectively sanctioned a simple negligence standard as complying with the minimum requirements of the First and Fourteenth Amendments.[9] Nevertheless, under *Gertz,* the states remain free to adopt stricter standards of liability than negligence, and at least one current and one former member of this court have urged that we do so. *Trentecosta,* 96-2388 at 1, 703 So. 2d at 565 (Johnson, J., dissenting); *Romero v. Thomson Newspapers (Wisconsin), Inc.,* 94-1105, p. 1 (La. 1995), 648 So. 2d 866, 871 (Dennis, J., concurring). However, for the reasons expressed below, we decline the invitation to adopt a *New York Times* standard of liability in cases involving private individuals and matters of public concern, and instead adopt the negligence standard set forth in the Restatement (Second) of Torts § 580B. Our reasons for doing so are fourfold.

First, the considerations which prompted the Supreme Court to adopt an actual malice standard of liability in defamation actions involving public officials and public figures do not, as the Supreme Court recognized in *Gertz,* apply with equal force when private individuals are involved. The First Amendment interest in vigorous reporting of the activities of public officials is clearly more compelling than the interest in reporting activities of private individuals because "[c]riticism of government is at the very center of the constitutionally protected area of free discussion." *Rosenblatt v. Baer,* 383 U.S. 75, 85, 86 S.Ct. 669, 675-676, 15 L.Ed.2d 597 (1966). Further, the extension of *New York Times* to public figures may be justified on the grounds that a state has a less substantial interest in protecting persons who have voluntarily exposed themselves to increased risk of injury from defamatory falsehoods. *Gertz,* 418 U.S. at 345, 94 S.Ct. at 3010. By contrast, private individuals are less likely to seek public attention and comment, and typically have less access to channels of effective communication to counteract false statements. *Id.* They are at once both more vulnerable to injury and more deserving of protection and recovery. *Id.*

---

[8] *Gertz,* 418 U.S. at 347, 94 S.Ct. at 3010.

[9] At one point in its discussion, the Supreme Court noted: "Our inquiry would involve considerations somewhat different from those discussed above if a State purported to condition civil liability on a factual misstatement whose content did not warn a reasonably prudent editor or broadcaster of its defamatory potential." *Gertz,* 418 U.S. at 348, 94 S.Ct. at 3011. Elsewhere, in holding that the states may not permit recovery of presumed or punitive damages when liability is not based on a showing of knowledge of falsity or reckless disregard for the truth, the *Gertz* court explained that "punitive damages are wholly irrelevant to the state interest that justifies a negligence standard for private defamation actions." *Gertz,* 418 U.S. at 350, 94 S.Ct. at 3012. Finally, in his concurring opinion, Justice Blackmun frankly explains that "the Court now conditions a libel action by a private person upon a showing of negligence." *Id.,* 418 U.S. at 353, 94 S.Ct. at 3014.

Second, Louisiana's interest in protecting the reputations of private individuals is clearly expressed and preserved in our constitution. Louisiana Constitution art. I, § 7 provides:

> No law shall curtail or restrain the freedom of speech or of the press. Every person may speak, write, and publish his sentiments on any subject, **but is responsible for abuse of that freedom.** [Emphasis added.]

Our constitution has expressly balanced the right of free speech with the responsibility for abuse of that right. This concern for the abuse of free speech is not explicitly found in the United States Constitution. Courts in other states with similar clauses in their constitutions have interpreted the proviso against abuse as evidencing an express concern for injury to reputation that justifies adoption of a negligence standard for private plaintiffs in defamation actions. *Jones v. Palmer Communications, Inc.,* 440 N.W.2d 884, 896 (Iowa 1989); *Troman v. Wood,* 62 Ill.2d 184, 340 N.E.2d 292 (1975); *McCall v. Courier-Journal and Louisiville Times Company,* 623 S.W.2d 882 (Ky. 1981); *Martin v. Griffin Television, Inc.,* 549 P.2d 85 (Okl.1976). We agree with this line of cases and will not ignore the express concern for injury to reputation found in the Louisiana Constitution.

Third, adoption of a negligence standard promotes simplicity and consistency in the law of defamation, at least insofar as private individuals are concerned. In our recent decision in *Costello v. Hardy, supra,* a case involving a private individual injured by a defamatory falsehood in a matter of purely private concern, we held that the malice, or fault, necessary to establish an action in defamation is a lack of reasonable belief in the truth of the statement giving rise to the defamation. Citing the RESTATEMENT (SECOND) OF TORTS § 580B, we explained that "[m]alice in this sense is more akin to negligence with respect to the truth than to spite or improper motive." *Costello,* 03-1146 at 18-19, 864 So. 2d at 143. We thereby endorsed the negligence standard of liability in actions by private individuals involving matters of private concern.[10] Adopting the same standard of liability for private individuals respecting matters of public concern simplifies the law in what has, admittedly, become a complex area.

Finally, a review of the relevant jurisprudence reveals that in the wake of *Gertz*, a majority of states to consider the issue have adopted negligence as the standard of liability in defamation actions by private individuals....

We join that majority today and hold that the standard of negligence set forth in the RESTATEMENT (SECOND) OF TORTS § 580B is to be applied in cases such as the present one, involving a private individual allegedly injured by a defamatory falsehood in a matter of public concern. Section 580B states:

> One who publishes a false and defamatory communication concerning a private person, or concerning a public official or public figure in relation to a purely private matter not affecting his conduct, fitness or role in his public capacity, is subject to liability, if, but only if, he
>
> (a) knows that the statement is false and that it defames the other,
> (b) acts in reckless disregard of these matters, or
> (c) acts negligently in failing to ascertain them.

Based on the foregoing, to prevail on his claim against Jack in the Box[11] in the present case, Kennedy bears the burden of affirmatively proving (1) a false and defamatory statement; (2) an

---

[10] It must be pointed out that *Costello* did not involve words that were defamatory per se; therefore, the presumptions of falsity, malice (or fault), and injury did not apply, and the burden of proving each of those elements remained with the plaintiff.

[11] While defamation is an individual tort which, as a general rule, does not give rise to solidary liability, when the defamatory statements are made by an employee in the course and scope of his or her employment, liability is nevertheless attributable to the employer under vicarious liability principles. *Trentecosta,* 96-2388 at 8-10, 703

unprivileged publication to a third party; (3) negligence (as set forth in the RESTATEMENT (SECOND) OF TORTS § 580B) on the part of Jack in the Box's employees; and (4) resulting injury. If even one of these required elements is found lacking, the cause of action fails. *Costello,* 03-1146 at 12, 864 So. 2d at 140.

Conditional or Qualified Privilege

In Louisiana, privilege is a defense to a defamation action. *Costello,* 03-1146 at 15, 864 So. 2d at 141. The doctrine of privilege rests upon the notion that sometimes, as a matter of public policy, in order to encourage the free communication of views in certain defined instances, one is justified in communicating defamatory information to others without incurring liability. *Toomer v. Breaux,* 146 So. 2d 723, 725 (La.App. 3 Cir. 1962). Privileged communications are divided into two general classes: (1) absolute; and (2) conditional or qualified. *Madison v. Bolton,* 234 La. 997, 102 So. 2d 433, 439 n. 7 (1958). An absolute privilege exists in a limited number of situations, such as statements by judges and legislators in judicial and legislative proceedings. *Id.* A conditional or qualified privilege arises in a broader number of instances. *Id.* In fact, there are a variety of situations in which the interest that an individual is seeking to vindicate or to further is regarded as sufficiently important to justify some latitude for making mistakes so that publication of defamatory statements is deemed to be conditionally or qualifiedly privileged. *Trentecosta,* 96-2388 at 18, 703 So. 2d at 563. It is impossible to reduce the scope of a conditional or qualified privilege to any precise formula. *Id.* Nevertheless, the elements of the conditional privilege have been described as "good faith, an interest to be upheld and a statement limited in scope to this purpose, a proper occasion, and publication in the proper manner and to proper parties only." *Madison,* 102 So. 2d at 439 n. 7. The privilege, it has been held, "arises from the social necessity of permitting full and unrestricted communication concerning a matter in which the parties have an interest or duty, without inhibiting free communication in such instances by the fear that the communicating party will be held liable in damages if the good faith communication later turns out to be inaccurate." *Toomer,* 146 So. 2d at 725.

Early appellate court decisions in Louisiana characterized the conditional or qualified privilege as applying "if the communication is made (a) in good faith, (b) on any subject matter in which the person communicating has an interest or in reference to which he has a duty, (c) to a person having a corresponding interest or duty." *Toomer,* 146 So. 2d at 725; *Elmer v. Coplin,* 485 So. 2d 171, 176 (La.App. 2 Cir.), *writ denied,* 489 So. 2d 246 (1986). Under this formulation, which finds its genesis in Madison's citation of a passage from an encyclopedia,[12] courts typically focused on the requirements of good faith and proper publication to determine in the first instance if the privilege applied.

In *Smith v. Our Lady of the Lake Hospital, Inc.,* 93-2512 (La. 1994), 639 So. 2d 730, we eschewed that approach, holding that the analysis for determining whether a conditional privilege exists involves a two-step process. *Smith,* 93-2512 at 18, 639 So. 2d at 745.[13] First, it must be determined whether the attending circumstances of a communication occasion a qualified privilege. *Id.* The second step of the analysis is a determination of whether the privilege was abused, which requires that the grounds for abuse--malice or lack of good faith--be examined. *Id.* "While the first step is generally determined by the court as a matter of law, the second step of determining abuse of a conditional privilege or malice is generally a fact question for the jury '[u]nless only one conclusion can be drawn from the evidence.' "*Id., quoting* W. KEETON ET AL., PROSSER & KEETON ON TORTS § 115 at 835 (5th ed.1984).

So. 2d at 558-559. Jack in the Box does not contend that the employee who reported the suspicious currency to police was not acting in the course and scope of her employment.

[12] *Madison,* 102 So. 2d at 439 n. 7, cites 33 Am.Jur. *Verbo Libel and Slander* § 124--126 at123-126 as authority for this particular formulation of the privilege.

[13] While the precise issue before this court in *Smith* was the construction to be given LSA-R.S. 13:3715.3(C), granting qualified immunity to peer review committees, we expressly drew on the jurisprudence regarding the conditional or qualified privilege to interpret the statutory provision.

Following this analysis, we note that in the present case, Jack in the Box asserted the affirmative defense of qualified or conditional privilege in answer to the petition filed by Kennedy, alleging that such a privilege obtains when a report of a possible crime is communicated to the proper authorities for investigation. The existence of the privilege, and the lack of evidence of abuse of the privilege (and hence the absence of a factual dispute), was the focus of Jack in the Box's motion for summary judgment.

The essence of the qualified or conditional privilege claimed by Jack in the Box in the present case is that its employees were simply communicating suspected wrongful acts to officials authorized to protect the public from such acts, which, if substantiated, would implicate important community interests. The RESTATEMENT (SECOND) OF TORTS § 598 describes the public interest privilege as follows:

> An occasion makes a publication conditionally privileged if the circumstances induce a correct or reasonable belief that
>
> (a) there is information that affects a sufficiently important public interest, and
>
> (b) the public interest requires the communication of the defamatory matter to a public officer or a private citizen who is authorized or privileged to take action if the defamatory matter is true.

Comment (d) to Section 598 states that the privilege is applicable "when any recognized interest of the public is in danger, including the interest in the prevention of crime and the apprehension of criminals." Louisiana courts have similarly recognized that the public has an interest in possible criminal activity being brought to the attention of the proper authorities, and have extended a qualified privilege to remarks made in good faith. *Simon v. Variety Wholesalers, Inc.,* 2000-0452 (La.App. 1 Cir. 2001), 788 So. 2d 544, *writ denied,* 01-2371 (La. 2001), 802 So. 2d 617; *Jones v. Wesley,* 424 So. 2d 1109(La.App. 1 Cir. 1982); *Crump v. Crump,* 393 So. 2d 337 (La.App. 1 Cir. 1980). The public policy reasons supporting the extension of such a privilege are succinctly stated in *Arellano v. Henley,* 357 So. 2d 846, 849 (La.App. 4 Cir. 1978):

> It would be self-defeating for society to impose civil liability on a citizen for inaccurately reporting criminal conduct with no intent to mislead. If the risks to the citizen are too high, a fertile field for criminal suppression will have disappeared.

In other words, the qualified or conditional privilege extended to the communication of alleged wrongful acts to the officials authorized to protect the public from such acts is founded on a strong public policy consideration: vital to our system of justice is that there be the ability to communicate to police officers the alleged wrongful acts of others without fear of civil action for honest mistakes.

The privilege clearly applies in the present case, as the employees of Jack in the Box reported circumstances involving a matter affecting the public interest--the possible commission of a crime (counterfeiting or "[m]onetary instrument abuse")--to the police, who had a duty to take action should the allegations prove to be true. It is the second step of the privilege analysis-- the determination of whether the privilege was abused--on which the resolution of this case ultimately hinges.

The practical effect of the assertion of the conditional or qualified privilege is to rebut the plaintiff's (Kennedy's) allegations of malice (or fault, which in this case amounts to negligence) and to place the burden of proof on the plaintiff to establish abuse of the privilege. *Smith,* 93-2512 at p. 20, 639 So. 2d at 746. In order to resolve the motion for summary judgment at issue in this case it is critical to define the circumstances that constitute an abuse of the conditional privilege.

Historically, courts in Louisiana ruled that the conditional privilege was defeated by proof that the defamatory statements were made with malice in fact, *i.e.,* that the defendant was actuated by motives of personal spite or ill will, independent of the occasion on which the communication was made. *Berot v. Porte,* 144 La. 805, 81 So. 323 (1919). At least since the decision of this court in *Madison v. Bolton, supra,* courts have held that the conditional privilege is defeated by proof that the defamatory statements were not made in good faith, or more precisely, with reasonable grounds for believing the statements to be true. According to the courts, it is "[o]nly when lack of such reasonable grounds is found can it be said that the person uttering the statement is actuated by malice or ill will." *Elmer,* 485 So. 2d at 177, *citing Ward v. Sears Roebuck & Company,* 339 So. 2d 1255 (La.App. 1 Cir. 1976). *See also, Smith,* 93-2512 at p. 17, 639 So. 2d at 744-745, in which we reviewed Louisiana jurisprudence on the qualified or conditional privilege and noted that, in Louisiana, the most commonly cited ways in which the conditional privilege can be abused are when the defendant's remarks are made with malice or without good faith or for a purpose outside of the scope of the privilege. We affirmed that in this context, "good faith" is synonymous with "without malice," and means having reasonable grounds for believing that the statement is correct. *Id.,* 93-2512 at 23-24, 639 So. 2d at 749.

A few years subsequent to our decision in *Smith v. Our Lady of the Lake Hospital, Inc., supra,* we had occasion to once again examine the qualified or conditional privilege in the context of a defamation action. *Trentecosta, supra,* presented a defamation claim by the owner of a bingo hall against three police officers and the Louisiana Department of Public Safety and Corrections seeking damages arising from statements made by one officer to the press that plaintiff was operating an illegal bingo hall which had bilked charities out of thousands of dollars. We granted certiorari in that case "primarily to address the question of whether the law enforcement officers enjoyed a qualified privilege in reporting on an investigation and a resulting arrest, and whether they abused the privilege." *Trentecosta,* 96-2388 at 7, 703 So. 2d at 558. In the course of our examination, we noted that the constitutional restraints imposed on the tort of defamation by virtue of the *New York Times* decision have called into question the continued viability of the conditional or qualified privilege. We explained:

> [U]nder the jurisprudence engendered by *Sullivan* and *Gertz* which requires some defamation plaintiffs to prove actual malice with regard to the falsity of the statement, such proof also proves the lack of any reasonable grounds for belief in the truth of the statement, which is the equivalent of proving the defendant's abuse of any privilege urged as a defense.

> Arguably, conditional privileges therefore have lost their significance under the current state of the law which requires the offended person to prove the publisher's fault with regard to the falsity of the statement, at least when proof of actual malice is required as an element of the cause of action.

Trentecosta, 96-2388 at 7, 703 So. 2d at 562-563. Rather than reject the conditional privilege analysis as superfluous in light of the *New York Times* and *Gertz* requirements, we instead adopted the approach of the RESTATEMENT (SECOND) OF TORTS §§ 599-600; we held that, at least insofar as the privilege respecting reports of governmental proceedings and activities is concerned, the privilege is abused if the publisher (a) knows the matter to be false, or (b) acts in reckless disregard as to its truth or falsity. *Trentecosta,* 96-2388 at 20 n. 16, 703 So. 2d at 564 n. 16. In other words, since *Trentecosta,* mere negligence as to falsity (or lack of reasonable grounds for believing the statement to be true) is no longer sufficient to prove abuse of the conditional privilege. Instead, knowledge or reckless disregard as to falsity is necessary for this purpose.

While *Trentecosta,* in fact, concerned a different privilege (the privilege respecting reports of governmental proceedings and activities) than that asserted in this case, we perceive no reason that its holding should not be extended to the privilege for the communication of alleged wrongful acts to an official authorized to protect the public from such acts. Our reasons for making this determination are as follows.

First, adopting the approach of the RESTATEMENT (SECOND) OF TORTS § 600 in this instance acknowledges the changes in defamation law that have been wrought by the Supreme Court's interpretation of the First Amendment, and adjusts to the evolving law in this area. Since *Gertz*, it is apparent that there is an inherent conflict between the constitutional fault (negligence or greater) that a plaintiff bears the burden of proving in certain situations and the lack of reasonable grounds for belief in the truth of the statement (basically, negligence as to the truth) which has traditionally formed a basis for abuse of the privilege in Louisiana. If a plaintiff proves the required constitutional fault (negligence or greater) in order to have a cause of action, he has by that action proved the abuse of any conditional privilege that might apply, and rendered the conditional privilege analysis irrelevant. RESTATEMENT (SECOND) OF TORTS, Special Note on Conditional Privileges and the Constitutional Requirement of Fault at 259-260.

Nevertheless, privileges continue to serve an important function in our law. A conditional privilege is one of the methods utilized for balancing the interest of the defamed person in the protection of his or her reputation against the interests of the publisher, of third persons, and of the public in having the publications take place. The latter interests are not strong enough under the circumstances to create an absolute privilege but they are of sufficient significance to relax the usual standard of liability. RESTATEMENT (SECOND) OF TORTS § 598 cmt. b. Adopting the actual malice standard (knowing falsity or reckless disregard for the truth) of the RESTATEMENT allows courts to continue to balance these competing interests in accordance with the particular facts of each case, and in the process, to retain the hierarchy of specially protected types of speech that we have traditionally recognized.[14]

Second, since the decision in *New York Times*, courts in a growing number of jurisdictions have held that knowing falsity or reckless disregard for the truth on the part of the defendant must be shown to defeat a qualified privilege. *Barreca v. Nickolas*, 683 N.W.2d 111 (Iowa 2004); *Marchesi v. Franchino*, 283 Md. 131, 387 A.2d 1129 (1978); *Rice v. Hodapp*, 919 S.W.2d 240 (Mo. 1996); *Dun & Bradstreet, Inc. v. O'Neil*, 456 S.W.2d 896 (Tex. 1970); *Bender v. City of Seattle*, 99 Wash.2d 582, 664 P.2d 492 (1983). The shift to this standard is prompted in no small part by the desire to simplify and create consistency between constitutional law and state law definitions of fault and malice as respects the tort of defamation, a goal we endorse herein.[15]

Finally, adoption of the knowing falsity or reckless disregard for the truth standard of abuse in this case, which involves a report to law enforcement officers of suspected criminal activity, strikes a necessary and appropriate balance between a person's interest in protecting his or her reputation and the need to encourage individuals to report suspected criminal activity to the proper authorities without fear of being exposed to civil liability for honest mistakes. Unless such protection is extended, fear of being exposed to civil liability could discourage individuals from alerting police to suspicious activity, thereby enabling criminals to escape detection and endangering other potential victims. Individuals who engage in behavior beneficial to society should not be penalized by facing exposure to civil liability for mistakes in judgment attributable to simple negligence.

Consistent with our decision in *Trentecosta*, we hold that knowledge of falsity or reckless disregard for truth, the standard adopted in the RESTATEMENT (SECOND) OF TORTS § 600, is the standard by which abuse of the conditional privilege asserted in this case is to be determined.

---

[14] Adopting the knowing or reckless disregard for the truth standard in this particular case honors the heightened protection that we have recognized should be accorded to speech on matters of public concern. *See, Romero*, 648 So. 2d at 869.

[15] In Louisiana, defamation is a delict governed by LSA-C.C. art. 2315. *Miller v. Holstein*, 16 La. 389, *on reh'g.*, 16 La. 395 (La. 1840). Nevertheless, in examining the parameters of the tort, Louisiana courts have drawn on and borrowed from the common law terminology. *See e.g., Madison v. Bolton, supra.*

In light of the foregoing principles, we turn now to an examination of Jack in the Box's motion for summary judgment and the court of appeal's decision reversing the district court judgment in favor of Jack in the Box.

As a preliminary matter, we note that because of the chilling effect on the exercise of free speech, defamation actions have been found particularly susceptible to summary judgment. Summary adjudication, we have recognized, is a useful procedural tool and an effective screening device for avoiding the unnecessary harassment of defendants by unmeritorious actions which threaten the free exercise of rights of speech and press. *Mashburn v. Collin,* 355 So. 2d 879, 890-891 (La.1977).[16]

In this case, Jack in the Box asserted the affirmative defense of conditional privilege in its answer. Its motion for summary judgment was based on the contention that the actions of its employees were protected by the conditional or qualified privilege and that there was no evidence of abuse, and hence a lack of factual dispute, entitling it to judgment as a matter of law. In connection with the motion, Jack in the Box submitted the affidavits of Deputy Eric Jones and Lieutenant Richard Harris of the East Baton Rouge Parish Sheriff's Office. The affidavits, which are virtually identical, recite in pertinent part that an employee of Jack in the Box called the East Baton Rouge Parish Sheriff's Office on December 7, 2001, and reported that someone had attempted to buy food with a counterfeit one hundred dollar bill. Deputy Jones and Lieutenant Harris were dispatched to the location, where Deputy Jones was informed by two restaurant employees that an occupant of a vehicle in the drive-through lane had attempted to make a food purchase with a counterfeit one hundred dollar bill. The employees presented the bill to Deputy Jones. Both Deputy Jones and Lieutenant Harris examined the bill and confirmed that it "looked suspicious ... as the bill appeared to be short and dark in color and the size of Benjamin Franklin's head looked small." The officers both noted that, at the time of the incident, there had been many cases of counterfeit bills being used at Circle K and Exxon stores in the area. The Jack in the Box employees pointed out the vehicle from which the one hundred dollar bill was tendered, which was still in the drive-through lane. At that point, the involvement of Jack in the Box's employees ceased, and the East Baton Rouge Parish officers took over.

The affidavits submitted by Jack in the Box confirm the existence of the conditional or qualified privilege. They establish that employees of Jack in the Box reported a matter affecting the public interest-- the possible commission of a crime--to police, who have the duty to take action should the allegations prove true.[17] As noted earlier, the effect of the assertion of the conditional or qualified privilege is to rebut the plaintiff's allegations of fault and shift the burden to plaintiff to establish abuse of the privilege. *Smith,* 93-2512 at 20, 639 So. 2d at 746. In other words, once the privilege is established, it becomes incumbent on the plaintiff to come forward with rebuttal evidence establishing abuse. Required proof of abuse in this particular case is proof that the defendant/publisher knew the defamatory statement to be false, or acted in reckless disregard as to its truth or falsity.[18]

---

[16] In *Sassone v. Elder,* 626 So. 2d 345 (La. 1993), we held that the summary judgment standard is different in defamation cases than in other cases; in order to survive a motion for summary judgment, a defamation plaintiff must produce evidence of sufficient quality and quantity to demonstrate that he likely will be able to meet his burden of proof at trial.

Since our decision in *Sassone,* the legislature has amended the summary judgment articles, 1996 La. Acts, 1st Ex.Sess., No. 9, with the result that summary judgment is now favored, thereby eliminating the need for courts to impose a different summary judgment standard in defamation cases. Nevertheless, the considerations that make defamation actions particularly susceptible to summary judgment remain the same.

[17] In fact, the allegations of Kennedy's petition confirm the circumstances giving rise to the privilege, as the petition avers that "Jack in the Box employee(s) made the false allegation to law enforcement officers that the plaintiff had passed counterfeit or unlawful tender at its restaurant, causing the plaintiff's arrest on a false complaint." There is no allegation in any pleading that the communication was made to anyone other than the appropriate law enforcement personnel.

[18] We note, incidentally, that in a case such as this one, where a conditional privilege is found to exist, the negligence standard that is part of plaintiff's prima facie case is logically subsumed in the higher standard for

In the present case, there is no allegation and certainly no evidence to support a contention that the Jack in the Box employees who alerted Sheriff's deputies to the suspected counterfeit currency knew their statements were false. In fact, Kennedy's petition alleges only negligence on the part of Jack in the Box and its employees. Therefore, to meet his evidentiary burden in this case, plaintiff must establish that the statements of the Jack in the Box employees were made with reckless disregard for whether they were true or false.

While "reckless disregard" cannot be fully encompassed in one definition, the courts have provided some guidance on application of the standard. *Trentecosta,* 96-2388 at 14, 703 So. 2d at 561, *citing St. Amant v. Thompson,* 390 U.S. 727,730, 88 S.Ct. 1323, 1325, 20 L.Ed.2d 262 (1968). For example, in *Garrison v. Louisiana,* 379 U.S. 64, 74, 85 S.Ct. 209, 216, 13 L.Ed.2d 125 (1964), the Supreme Court explained that only those false statements made with a high degree of awareness of their probable falsity meet the reckless disregard standard. In *Curtis Publishing Co. v. Butts,* 388 U.S. 130, 87 S.Ct. 1975, 18 L.Ed.2d 1094 (1967), the Supreme Court reiterated that reckless disregard requires a plaintiff to "prove that the publication was deliberately falsified, or published despite the publisher's awareness of probable falsity." *Id.,* 388 U.S. at 153, 87 S.Ct. at 1991. Finally, in *St. Amant v. Thompson, supra,* the Supreme Court explained that "[t]here must be sufficient evidence to permit the conclusion that the defendant in fact entertained serious doubts as to the truth of his publication." *St. Amant,* 390 U.S. at 731, 88 S.Ct. at 1325. Under this standard, even proof of gross negligence in the publication of a false statement is insufficient to prove reckless disregard. *Davis v. Borsky,* 94-2399, p. 10 (La. 1995), 660 So. 2d 17, 23, *citing Masson v. New Yorker Magazine, Inc.,* 501 U.S. 496, 510, 111 S.Ct. 2419, 2429, 115 L.Ed.2d 447 (1991). Rather, there must be evidence that the defendant was highly aware that the statements were probably false. *Id.*

In opposing Jack in the Box's motion for summary judgment, plaintiff submitted his own affidavit, which simply recites that he tendered payment of a 1974 series one hundred dollar bill to a Jack in the Box employee "while unknown to affiant, the Jack in the Box employee communicated to law enforcement officers that someone in Affiant's party had attempted to purchase food and drink with a counterfeit $100 bill." No other allegations appear with respect to the conduct of the Jack in the Box employees. In opposing the Sheriff's separate motion for summary judgment, plaintiff also submitted the Sheriff's responses to interrogatories propounded by the plaintiff. In those responses, the Sheriff indicated that the *deputies* had received no formal training or instruction in detecting counterfeit currency.

In its decision reversing the district court's summary judgment in favor of Jack in the Box, the court of appeal examined this evidence and concluded that "questions of fact remain as to whether the defendants took action to set a criminal investigation in motion on the basis of unfounded suspicion and conjecture." *Kennedy,* 04-0574 at 11, 899 So. 2d at 689. According to the court of appeal, "[t]he type of reasonable and trustworthy information sufficient to justify a man of average caution in the belief that a person has tendered a counterfeit bill would seem to require some knowledge or training in the detection of counterfeit bills to constitute probable cause." *Id.* Because there was no showing by either defendant that its employees were provided with instruction, training, or procedures to address suspicions of counterfeit money, or with counterfeit detection markers, the court of appeal concluded that defendants failed to show that they acted reasonably or without a reckless disregard for Kennedy's rights when a criminal investigation was instituted because the bill looked unusual. *Id.*

With all due respect to the court of appeal, its judgment reflects an erroneous application of the law. First, as explained above, it was not defendant's burden to establish that its employees acted without knowledge of falsity or reckless disregard for the truth; once the privilege was established, it was plaintiff's burden to demonstrate abuse. Further, as we explained in *Trentecosta,* conduct which would constitute reckless disregard is typically found where a story is fabricated by the defendant, is

---

proving knowing falsity or reckless disregard as to truth or falsity. Therefore, the negligence analysis drops out of the case, for if the plaintiff is incapable of proving the knowing falsity or reckless disregard as to truth or falsity necessary to overcome the privilege, it is of no consequence that he or she might be able to prove the lesser standard of negligence.

the product of his imagination, or is so inherently improbable that only a reckless man would have put it in circulation. *Trentecosta,* 96-2388 at 15, 703 So. 2d at 561- 562, *quoting St. Amant,* 390 U.S. at 732, 88 S.Ct. at 1326. In the instant case, there was absolutely no evidence offered to demonstrate such conduct on the part of any employee of Jack in the Box. In fact, if anything, the suspicions of the Jack in the Box employees that the bill was counterfeit were shown to have a basis in fact, as evidenced by the affidavits of the two Sheriff's deputies, attesting to the fact that the bill looked "suspicious" because it "appeared to be short and dark in color and the size of Benjamin Franklin's head looked small."

The crux of the court of appeal decision appears to be its conclusion that Jack in the Box's employees failed to take reasonable measures to verify the authenticity of the bill before reporting their suspicions to police. However, it is quite clear that mere negligence as to falsity is not sufficient to amount of abuse of a conditional or qualified privilege. RESTATEMENT (SECOND) OF TORTS § 600 cmt. b. As we have noted, failure to investigate does not present a jury question on whether a statement was published with reckless disregard for the truth. *Romero,* 648 So. 2d at 869. In this instance, the suspicions of the Jack in the Box employees clearly were not arbitrary, as the bill does not resemble modern currency. While it might have been more reasonable for the employees to have had training in the identification of counterfeit currency or a counterfeit detection marker, the plaintiff cannot show reckless disregard for the truth by demonstrating only that the defendant acted negligently and failed to investigate fully before contacting police. *Davis,* 94-2399 at 13, 660 So. 2d at 24-25; *Romero,* 648 So. 2d at 869. The failure of Jack in the Box employees to receive training in the detection of counterfeit currency or to investigate further before contacting police is insufficient to establish reckless disregard for the truth.

Given the failure of plaintiff to make any factual showing of knowing falsity or reckless disregard for the truth on the part of defendant's employees, reasonable minds, viewing the evidence in Kennedy's favor, must inevitably conclude that defendant's defamatory statements were privileged and that the privilege was not abused. Because plaintiff failed to submit evidence sufficient to show that he will be able to meet his burden of proof at trial that defendant abused the conditional or qualified privilege, summary judgment on Kennedy's defamation claim was properly granted by the district court. The court of appeal erred in reversing that summary judgment.

Summary judgment was also properly granted by the district court on Kennedy's claim against Jack in the Box for wrongful arrest. Wrongful arrest, or the tort of false imprisonment, occurs when one arrests and restrains another against his will and without statutory authority. *Kyle v. City of New Orleans,* 353 So. 2d 969 (La.1977). The tort of false imprisonment consists of the following two essential elements: (1) detention of the person; and (2) the unlawfulness of the detention. *Tabora v. City of Kenner,* 94-613, p. 8 (La.App. 5 Cir. 1995), 650 So. 2d 319, 322, *writ denied,* 95-0402 (La. 1995), 651 So. 2d 843. In the instant case, the district court found that there are no facts in the record to show detention of the plaintiff by Jack in the Box or any of its employees, and the court of appeal did not disturb this finding. Our review of the record confirms the correctness of the district court's determination in this regard. The affidavit of Kennedy, submitted in opposition to the Jack in the Box motion for summary judgment, confirms that, after placing his order and tendering payment, Kennedy simply waited in line for his food. There is no allegation that any employee of Jack in the Box restrained him or prevented him from leaving. Kennedy was detained only when Sheriff's deputies asked him to leave the drive through lane and to exit the car, whereupon he was handcuffed and transported to a nearby substation. There is thus no factual support for an essential element of plaintiff's cause of action. Summary judgment was appropriate as to the false imprisonment claim against Jack in the Box.[19]

---

[19] In brief, Kennedy argues that there is a "parallel" between his claim for defamation and an action for malicious prosecution. To the extent that this argument belatedly attempts to assert that plaintiff has stated a claim for malicious prosecution that should not have been dismissed on summary judgment, we find it to be without merit.

The elements necessary to support a claim for malicious prosecution are: (1) the commencement or continuance of an original criminal or civil judicial proceeding; (2) its legal causation by the present defendant against plaintiff who was defendant in the original proceeding; (3) its bona fide termination in favor of the present plaintiff; (4) the absence of probable cause for such proceeding; (5) the presence of malice therein; and

Conclusion

For the reasons expressed above, we find that the report to law enforcement officers of suspected criminal activity by Jack in the Box employees was conditionally privileged, and that plaintiff failed to submit evidence sufficient to show that he will be able to meet his burden of proof at trial that defendant abused the conditional privilege. Because plaintiff cannot produce factual support for an essential element of his cause of action--proof of an unprivileged communication to a third party--summary judgment was properly granted by the district court. The decision of the court of appeal with respect to defendant Jack in the Box is reversed and the judgment of the district court granting summary judgment in favor of defendant Jack in the Box is reinstated.

REVERSED.

NOTE

In *Costello v. Hardy*, 864 So. 2d 129 (La. 2004), attorneys claimed that a former client defamed them when she sued them for malpractice in drafting a will. Because the allegation was merely that the attorneys' behavior was negligent, the words were capable of defamatory meaning but were not defamatory per se, the attorneys were required to show "malice," defined as the "lack of reasonable belief in the truth of the statement giving rise to the defamation." Such malice was lacking.

The court noted that "[m]alice," in this context, is to be distinguished from "actual malice," or publication that a statement is false or with reckless disregard for its truth, which is constitutionally required in certain cases; for example, those in which a public official or figure sues a media defendant." The "malice" standard in *Costello* referred to the requirement of showing fault unless the statement was defamatory per se. The "actual malice" standard did not apply because the dispute was between private individuals and involved a purely private matter.

---

(6) damage conforming to legal standards resulting to plaintiff. *Miller v. East Baton Rouge Parish Sheriff's Dept.,* 511 So. 2d 446, 452 (La. 1987); *Jones v. Soileau,* 448 So. 2d 1268, 1271 (La.1984). Never favored in our law, a malicious prosecution action must clearly establish that the forms of justice have been perverted to the gratification of private malice and the willful oppression of the innocent. *Johnson v. Pearce,* 313 So. 2d 812, 816 (La. 1975).

In this case, it is clear that plaintiff has failed to produce factual support sufficient to show that he will be able to meet his burden of proof at trial as to the second element of the malicious prosecution claim: legal causation by Jack in the Box. The affidavits of Deputy Jones and Lieutenant Harris, introduced in support of the Jack in the Box motion for summary judgment, establish that the employees of Jack in the Box merely reported their suspicions of counterfeit currency to the Sheriff's Office. When the deputies arrived at the restaurant, Jack in the Box employees pointed out the vehicle from which the one hundred dollar bill had been tendered and handed over the suspect currency. At that point, the involvement of Jack in the Box employees ceased, and the East Baton Rouge Parish officers took over, conducting their own examination of the currency before approaching the plaintiff. Given these facts, which were not controverted by plaintiff, it is clear that any chain of causation regarding plaintiff's subsequent detention was broken. The decision to detain plaintiff was made by the independent actions and investigation of the Sheriff's Office. *See, Banks v. Brookshire Brothers Inc.,* 93-1616 (La.App. 3 Cir. 1994), 640 So. 2d 680. Therefore, because plaintiff cannot establish that he will be able to provide factual support sufficient to satisfy his burden of proving legal causation, an essential element of a malicious prosecution action, that claim (to the extent it was stated) was properly dismissed.

HUSTLER MAGAZINE
v.
FALWELL
485 U.S. 46 (1988)

Chief Justice **REHNQUIST** delivered the opinion of the Court.

Petitioner Hustler Magazine, Inc., is a magazine of nationwide circulation. Respondent Jerry Falwell, a nationally known minister who has been active as a commentator on politics and public affairs, sued petitioner and its publisher, petitioner Larry Flynt, to recover damages for invasion of privacy, libel, and intentional infliction of emotional distress. The District Court directed a verdict against respondent on the privacy claim, and submitted the other two claims to a jury. The jury found for petitioners on the defamation claim, but found for respondent on the claim for intentional infliction of emotional distress and awarded damages. We now consider whether this award is consistent with the First and Fourteenth Amendments of the United States Constitution.

The inside front cover of the November 1983 issue of Hustler Magazine featured a "parody" of an advertisement for Campari Liqueur that contained the name and picture of respondent and was entitled "Jerry Falwell talks about his first time." This parody was modeled after actual Campari ads that included interviews with various celebrities about their "first times." Although it was apparent by the end of each interview that this meant the first time they sampled Campari, the ads clearly played on the sexual double entendre of the general subject of "first times." Copying the form and layout of these Campari ads, Hustler's editors chose respondent as the featured celebrity and drafted an alleged "interview" with him in which he states that his "first time" was during a drunken incestuous rendezvous with his mother in an outhouse. The Hustler parody portrays respondent and his mother as drunk and immoral, and suggests that respondent is a hypocrite who preaches only when he is drunk. In small print at the bottom of the page, the ad contains the disclaimer, "ad parody--not to be taken seriously." The magazine's table of contents also lists the ad as "Fiction; Ad and Personality Parody."

* * * * *

[Falwell sued alleging defamation, intentional infliction of emotional distress, and invasion of privacy. The defendants were granted a directed verdict on the invasion of privacy claim and a jury found for defendants on the defamation claim, specifically finding that the ad parody could not "reasonably be understood as describing actual facts about [Falwell] or actual events in which he participated." Jury found for Falwell on the IIED claim and awarded $100,000 compensatory damages and $50,000 punitive damages. The Fourth Circuit affirmed.]

This case presents us with a novel question involving First Amendment limitations upon a State's authority to protect its citizens from the intentional infliction of emotional distress. We must decide whether a public figure may recover damages for emotional harm caused by the publication of an ad parody offensive to him, and doubtless gross and repugnant in the eyes of most. Respondent would have us find that a State's interest in protecting public figures from emotional distress is sufficient to deny First Amendment protection to speech that is patently offensive and is intended to inflict emotional injury, even when that speech could not reasonably have been interpreted as stating actual facts about the public figure involved. This we decline to do.

At the heart of the First Amendment is the recognition of the fundamental importance of the free flow of ideas and opinions on matters of public interest and concern. "[T]he freedom to speak one's mind is not only an aspect of individual liberty--and thus a good unto itself--but also is essential to the common quest for truth and the vitality of society as a whole. We have therefore been particularly vigilant to ensure that individual expressions of ideas remain free from governmentally imposed sanctions. The First Amendment recognizes no such thing as a "false" idea. *Gertz v. Robert Welch, Inc.,* 418 U.S. 323, 339, 94 S.Ct. 2997, 3007, 41 L.Ed.2d 789 (1974). As Justice Holmes wrote, "when men have realized that time has upset many fighting faiths, they may come to believe even more than they believe the very foundations of their own conduct that the ultimate good desired is better reached by free trade in ideas--that the best test of truth is the power of the thought to get itself accepted in the competition of the market....

* * * * *

Of course, this does not mean that *any* speech about a public figure is immune from sanction in the form of damages. Since *New York Times Co. v. Sullivan,* 376 U.S. 254, 84 S.Ct. 710, 11 L.Ed.2d 686 (1964), we have consistently ruled that a public figure may hold a speaker liable for the damage to reputation caused by publication of a defamatory falsehood, but only if the statement was made "with knowledge that it was false or with reckless disregard of whether it was false or not." *Id.,* 376 U.S., at 279-280, 84 S.Ct., at 726. False statements of fact are particularly valueless; they interfere with the truth-seeking function of the marketplace of ideas, and they cause damage to an individual's reputation that cannot easily be repaired by counterspeech, however persuasive or effective. *See Gertz,* 418 U.S., at 340, 344, n. 9, 94 S.Ct., at 3007, 3009, n. 9. But even though falsehoods have little value in and of themselves, they are "nevertheless inevitable in free debate," *id.,* at 340, 94 S.Ct., at 3007, and a rule that would impose strict liability on a publisher for false factual assertions would have an undoubted "chilling" effect on speech relating to public figures that does have constitutional value. "Freedoms of expression require 'breathing space.' " *Philadelphia Newspapers, Inc. v. Hepps,* 475 U.S. 767, 772, 106 S.Ct. 1558, 1561, 89 L.Ed.2d 783 (1986) (quoting *New York Times, supra,* 376 U.S., at 272, 84 S.Ct., at 721). This breathing space is provided by a constitutional rule that allows public figures to recover for libel or defamation only when they can prove *both* that the statement was false and that the statement was made with the requisite level of culpability.

Respondent argues, however, that a different standard should apply in this case because here the State seeks to prevent not reputational damage, but the severe emotional distress suffered by the person who is the subject of an offensive publication. *Cf. Zacchini v. Scripps-Howard Broadcasting Co.,* 433 U.S. 562, 97 S.Ct. 2849, 53 L.Ed.2d 965 (1977) (ruling that the "actual malice" standard does not apply to the tort of appropriation of a right of publicity). In respondent's view, and in the view of the Court of Appeals, so long as the utterance was intended to inflict emotional distress, was outrageous, and did in fact inflict serious emotional distress, it is of no constitutional import whether the statement was a fact or an opinion, or whether it was true or false. It is the intent to cause injury that is the gravamen of the tort, and the State's interest in preventing emotional harm simply outweighs whatever interest a speaker may have in speech of this type.

Generally speaking the law does not regard the intent to inflict emotional distress as one which should receive much solicitude, and it is quite understandable that most if not all jurisdictions have chosen to make it civilly culpable where the conduct in question is sufficiently "outrageous." But in the world of debate about public affairs, many things done with motives that are less than admirable are protected by the First Amendment.

In *Garrison v. Louisiana,* 379 U.S. 64, 85 S.Ct. 209, 13 L.Ed.2d 125 (1964), we held that even when a speaker or writer is motivated by hatred or ill will his expression was protected by the First Amendment:

> "Debate on public issues will not be uninhibited if the speaker must run the risk that it will be proved in court that he spoke out of hatred; even if he did speak out of hatred, utterances honestly believed contribute to the free interchange of ideas and the ascertainment of truth." *Id.,* at 73, 85 S.Ct., at 215.

Thus while such a bad motive may be deemed controlling for purposes of tort liability in other areas of the law, we think the First Amendment prohibits such a result in the area of public debate about public figures.

Were we to hold otherwise, there can be little doubt that political cartoonists and satirists would be subjected to damages awards without any showing that their work falsely defamed its subject. Webster's defines a caricature as "the deliberately distorted picturing or imitating of a person, literary style, etc. by exaggerating features or mannerisms for satirical effect." Webster's New Unabridged Twentieth Century Dictionary of the English Language 275 (2d ed. 1979). The appeal of the political cartoon or caricature is often based on exploitation of unfortunate physical traits or politically embarrassing events--an exploitation often calculated to injure the feelings of the subject of the portrayal. The art of the cartoonist is often not reasoned or evenhanded, but slashing and one-sided. One cartoonist expressed the nature of the art in these words:

> "The political cartoon is a weapon of attack, of scorn and ridicule and satire; it is least effective when it tries to pat some politician on the back. It is usually as welcome as a bee sting and is always controversial in some quarters." Long, The Political Cartoon: Journalism's Strongest Weapon, The Quill 56, 57 (Nov. 1962).

* * * * *

We conclude that public figures and public officials may not recover for the tort of intentional infliction of emotional distress by reason of publications such as the one here at issue without showing in addition that the publication contains a false statement of fact which was made with "actual malice," *i.e.,* with knowledge that the statement was false or with reckless disregard as to whether or not it was true. This is not merely a "blind application" of the *New York Times* standard, *see Time, Inc. v. Hill,* 385 U.S. 374, 390, 87 S.Ct. 534, 543, 17 L.Ed.2d 456 (1967), it reflects our considered judgment that such a standard is necessary to give adequate "breathing space" to the freedoms protected by the First Amendment.

Here it is clear that respondent Falwell is a "public figure" for purposes of First Amendment law. The jury found against respondent on his libel claim when it decided that the Hustler ad parody could not "reasonably be understood as describing actual facts about [respondent] or actual events in which [he] participated." App. to Pet. for Cert. C1. The Court of Appeals interpreted the jury's finding to be that the ad parody "was not reasonably believable," 797 F.2d, at 1278, and in accordance with our custom we accept this finding. Respondent is thus relegated to his claim for damages awarded by the jury for the intentional infliction of emotional distress by "outrageous" conduct. But for reasons heretofore stated this claim cannot, consistently with the First Amendment, form a basis for the award of damages when the conduct in question is the publication of a caricature such as the ad parody involved here. The judgment of the Court of Appeals is accordingly.

REVERSED.

NOTES AND QUESTIONS

1.   Note the interaction of constitutional limitations on the tort of intentional infliction of emotional distress as well as defamation.

2.   In *Hahn v. City of Kenner*, 984 F.Supp. 436 (E.D. La. 1997), a radio commentator made comments about plaintiff's failed confirmation for a public position, and the plaintiff called the commentator and engaged in an on-the-air dialogue. The plaintiff suggested the commentator talk to a third party. The radio commentator called the third party who then allegedly defamed the plaintiff during an on-the-air conversation. The court found that the plaintiff is a "limited public figure," at least for the purposes of the third party's comments.

3.   The issue of whether a corporation is a "public figure" for defamation should be made on a case-by-case basis, examining all relevant circumstances including (1) "the notoriety of the corporation to the average individual in the relevant geographic area," (2) the nature of the corporation's business (prominent consumer goods makers or merchants and consumer service corporations are much more likely to attain public figure status), and (3) the frequency and intensity of media scrutiny that a corporation normally receives (even a small corporation that does not deal with consumers might attain notoriety if it engages in frequent corporate takeovers that become widely publicized). *Snead v. Redland Aggregates Ltd.*, 5 F.3d 1493 (5th Cir. 1993), *cert. dismissed*, 511 U.S. 1050 (1994).

4.   There are some privileges applicable to the defamation action. An absolute privilege (which cannot be lost) applies in limited circumstances, such as a judge in a judicial proceeding or a legislator in a legislative proceeding. *See Kennedy, supra.* A non-litigant witness is entitled to absolute immunity from a defamation action based on his "in court" statements. *Spellman v. Desselles* 596 So. 2d 843 (La.App. 4 Cir. 1992), *writ denied*, 605 So. 2d 1080 (La. 1992). Louisiana does not follow the law of many other jurisdictions regarding an absolute privilege for defamatory statements in pleadings: "The Louisiana rule is unique. In Louisiana, alone, relevant written allegations in judicial proceedings can form the basis for a libel action, if false, malicious and made without probable cause." *Lyons v. Knight*, 65 So. 3d 257, 262 (La.App. 3 Cir. 2011), *writ denied*, 74 So. 3d 215 (La. 2011).

The most commonly asserted privilege in defamation and invasion of privacy cases is referred to as the "qualified" or "conditional" privilege. As the name suggests, it is a privilege that can be lost. The two requirements for application of the privilege are 1) the existence of a an interest or duty on the part of both parties to the communication; and 2) the party communicating the information is acting in good faith, meaning he has reasonable grounds for believing the truth of the information. *See, e.g., Kennedy, supra; Hines v. Arkansas Louisiana Gas Co.*, 613 So. 2d 646 (La.App. 2 Cir. 1993), *writ denied*, 617 So. 2d 932 (La. 1993); *Cook v. American Gateway Bank*, 49 So. 3d 23 (La.App. 1 Cir. 2010).

The director of public safety at the convention center alerted staff to deny admission to plaintiff who had been involved in a fight at the center while working for a contractor and was fired. Plaintiff's photo and name also were posted at various security and access points. Plaintiff sued for defamation. The Fourth Circuit held that the state recognizes defamation by implication or innuendo for posting photographs in which the context in which the photo appears provides the implication. *Williams v. New Orleans Ernest N. Morial Convention Center*, 92 So. 3d 572 (La.App. 4 Cir. 2012). However, the Supreme Court held that the qualified privilege applied, and plaintiff could not prove malice or lack of good faith to defeat the privilege. *Williams v. New Orleans Ernest N. Morial Convention Center* , 98 So. 3d 299 (La. 2012).

An employer communicating the reason for an employee's termination to the Office of Employment Security is covered by the qualified privilege. *Watson v. Willis-Knighton Med. Ctr.*, 93 So. 3d 855 (La.App. 2 Cir. 2012).

5.   A Louisiana court rejected liability for defamation in a case in which a news broadcast used the name of a crime suspect in a news report, holding that there is no case law or statutory authority prohibiting publication of the name of an alleged suspect or the facts surrounding investigation of a crime. *See Johnston v. NOE Corp.*, LLC, 81 So. 3d 735 (La.App. 2 Cir. 2011), *writ denied*, 84 So. 3d 532 (La. 2012).

6.   La. Code Civ. Pro. Article 971 provides for a special motion to strike a claim in furtherance of the right of petition or free speech regarding a public issue. The motion, which provides a vehicle for early dismissal of defamation and invasion of privacy claims, requires a two-part burden of proof. The moving party must first prove that the subject cause of action arises from an act in the exercise of his right of free speech regarding a public issue. If the moving party satisfies this initial burden of proof, then the burden shifts to the plaintiff to show a probability of success on his claim. *Ahearn v. City of Alexandria*, 191 So. 3d 689 (La.App. 3 Cir. 2016).

7.   It is very common for defamation and invasion of privacy theories to be asserted based on the same facts. *See, e.g., Johnston v. NOE, supra.*

B. INVASION OF PRIVACY

COMMENT

Defined as the right to be left alone, invasion of privacy is a relatively recent addition to the field of tort law. Although common law decisions prior to 1890 appear to have embraced certain aspects of the right to privacy, invasion of privacy had its genesis in a law review article by Samuel D. Warren and Louis Brandeis, *The Right to Privacy,* 4 Harv. L. Rev. 193 (1890). Today the tort of invasion of privacy is recognized by Louisiana and a large majority of common law jurisdictions. Comprised of four distinct invasions of privacy, the tort protects an individual from (a) unreasonable intrusion upon an individual's seclusion or solitude; (b) unreasonable appropriation of an individual's name or likeness for the use or benefit of the appropriator; (c) publicity that unreasonably places an individual in false light before the public; or (d) unreasonable publicity of embarrassing facts of an individual's private life. Most defenses applicable in defamation actions also apply in invasion of privacy cases.

JAUBERT
v.
CROWLEY POST-SIGNAL, INC.
375 So. 2d 1386 (La. 1979)

DIXON, J.

In August, 1977 Mr. and Mrs. James Jaubert returned from a brief business trip to discover that a photograph of their family home had been published on the front page of the Crowley Post-Signal, the local newspaper. The photograph was one of a series of at least six scenes of Crowley and its environs, all taken by the newspaper's photographer on the same day and published within a period of about two weeks. In the photograph, the Jauberts' home appeared framed by the branches of an oak tree; the caption under the picture read, "One of Crowley's stately homes, a bit weatherworn and unkempt, stands in the shadow of a spreading oak." Although neither the street address nor the names of the owners appeared in the newspaper, some residents of Crowley recognized the home as the Jauberts' and commiserated with them about the unwelcome publicity. The Jauberts sued the newspaper for invasion of privacy, seeking $15,000 each in damages for mental suffering, embarrassment, and humiliation. The trial court entered judgment for the plaintiffs and awarded each spouse $500. The judgment was affirmed by the Third Circuit Court of Appeal, which held that the publication was not privileged as newsworthy, and that an action for invasion of privacy was precluded neither by the fact that the publication did not identify the owners of the house nor by the fact that the photograph depicted the house as it was visible from a public street. We reverse.

In 1890 Samuel D. Warren and Louis D. Brandeis published an article[1] tracing the development and advocating the recognition of a right to protection against invasion of privacy.[2] Even

---

[1] The Right to Privacy, 4 Harv.L.Rev. 193 (1890).

[2] The right to privacy under discussion here is one which protects the individual against private action and is grounded in tort. It should be distinguished from the constitutional right to privacy which the United States Supreme Court, in a line of cases, has found to emanate from certain provisions of the Bill of Rights and to protect, from governmental invasion only, those personal rights which are deemed fundamental or implicit in the concept of ordered liberty. Schopler, Annotation, The Supreme Court's Views as to the Federal Legal Aspects of the Right to Privacy, 43 L.Ed.2d 871 (1975).

The Louisiana Constitution of 1974, Art. I, § 5, entitled "Right to Privacy," provides in pertinent part: "Every person shall be secure in his person, property, communications, houses, papers, and effects against unreasonable searches, seizures, or invasions of privacy." This section's reference to a right to privacy represents a change from the language of earlier constitutions. A review of Records of the Louisiana Constitutional Convention of 1973: Convention Transcripts leaves open the question of whether the section was intended to provide constitutional protection against private conduct. Generally, the provision seems to have been drafted as a counterpart to the United States Constitution's Fourth Amendment prohibition against governmental searches and seizures and other forms of "authoritarian intrusion." Transcripts, Vol. VI, 1072. However, in The

earlier, the existence of such a right had been implicit in the remedies afforded by certain courts: in *Denis v. Leclerc*, 1 Mart. (O.S.) 297 (1811), the Louisiana Supreme Court upheld an injunction of publication of the plaintiff's private letter written to a third party by finding that the writer had an exclusive property right in the letter. A 1905 Georgia decision, *Pavesich v. New England Mut. Life Ins. Co.*, 122 Ga. 190, 50 S.E. 68, is considered the first case to expressly affirm the principle of a right to privacy. Also in 1905, this court declared in *Itzkovitch v. Whitaker*, 115 La. 479, 482, 39 So. 499, 500, that: "Every one who does not violate the law can insist upon being let alone (the right of privacy). In such a case the right of privacy is absolute."

By 1978, the right of privacy was recognized by the courts of all but three states.[3] The right of privacy embraces four different interests, each of which may be invaded in a distinct fashion; *Cox Broadcasting Corp. v. Cohn*, 420 U.S. 469, 95 S.Ct. 1029, 43 L.Ed.2d 328 (1975); Prosser, Law of Torts, 4th ed. (1971); Prosser, Privacy, 48 Calif.L.Rev. 383 (1960); Restatement Second of the Law of Torts (1959). One type of invasion takes the form of the appropriation of an individual's name or likeness, for the use or benefit of the defendant. While it is not necessary that the use or benefit be commercial or pecuniary in nature, the mere fact that a newspaper is published for sale does not constitute such use or benefit on the part of the publisher. Another type of invasion occurs when the defendant unreasonably intrudes upon the plaintiff's physical solitude or seclusion. Because the situation or activity which is intruded upon must be private, an invasion does not occur when an individual makes a photograph of a public sight which any one is free to see; Prosser, Law of Torts, 809. A third type of invasion consists of publicity which unreasonably places the plaintiff in a false light before the public. While the publicity need not be defamatory in nature, but only objectionable to a reasonable person under the circumstances, it must contain either falsity or fiction. A fourth type of invasion is represented by unreasonable public disclosure of embarrassing private facts. With reference to this category, Prosser states that "(i)t seems to be generally agreed that anything visible in a public place can be recorded and given circulation by means of a photograph, to the same extent as by a written description, since this amounts to nothing more than giving publicity to what is already public and what anyone present would be free to see." Law of Torts, 811. Similarly, the Restatement Second of the Law of Torts indicates that "there is no liability for giving further publicity to what the plaintiff himself leaves open to the public eye." *Supra* at 386.

In Louisiana jurisprudence, the right to privacy has been variously defined as "the right to be let alone" and "the right to an 'inviolate personality.' " *Pack v. Wise*, 155 So. 2d 909, 913 (La.App. 3 Cir. 1963), quoting *Hamilton v. Lumbermen's Mut. Cas. Co.*, 82 So. 2d 61, 63 (La.App. 1 Cir. 1955), *writ denied* 1955. Where an individual has such a right, in the form of one of the interests outlined above, other members of society have a corresponding duty not to violate that right. A violation constitutes a breach of duty, or fault, and may be actionable under C.C. 2315, which provides that "(e)very act whatever of man that causes damage to another obliges him by whose fault it happened to repair it." *Pack v. Wise, supra; Tuyes v. Chambers*, 144 La. 723, 81 So. 265 (1919). Where no such right to privacy exists, however, a person's conduct may be the cause of another person's embarrassment, discomfiture, or monetary loss, but it will not constitute a "legal cause," because no duty has been breached.

Declaration of Rights of the Louisiana Constitution of 1974, 35 La.L.Rev. 1 (1974), Professor Hargrave concluded that the protection afforded by this provision is not limited to state action because the phrase "no law shall ..." is conspicuously absent and because the provision does not appear among those sections dealing with procedural rights in criminal cases. He predicted that the provision would be a fertile field for future developments in the law of torts. At least one delegate was also of the opinion that "this proposal protects a person not only from state action but also from private action." Transcripts, Vol. VI, 1076.

    In *Trahan v. Larivee*, 365 So. 2d 294 (La.App. 3 Cir. 1978), *writ denied* 1979, the court found that Art. I, § 5 would prohibit the disclosure of certain city employee performance reports; but in that case the reports were in the custody of the City of Lafayette, so that disclosure might have been seen as state action.

[3] These states were Nebraska, Rhode Island and Wisconsin. First Amendment Rights to Free Speech and a Free Press: Change and Continuity, 12 Akron L.Rev. 228 (1978).

Even where a right to privacy is found to exist, Louisiana courts have distinguished between invasions of that right which are actionable and those which are not. An actionable invasion of privacy occurs only when the defendant's conduct is unreasonable[4] and seriously interferes with the plaintiff's privacy interest. Comment, The Right of Privacy in Louisiana, 28 La.L.Rev. 469 (1968). For an invasion to be actionable, it is not necessary that there be malicious intent on the part of the defendant. *Lucas v.Ludwig*, 313 So. 2d 12 (La.App. 4 Cir. 1975), *writ denied* 1975. The reasonableness of the defendant's conduct is determined by balancing the conflicting interests at stake; the plaintiff's interest in protecting his privacy from serious invasions, and the defendant's interest in pursuing his course of conduct. Thus, it was found reasonable for a school board, during the war effort, to inquire into teachers' use of their afterschool time, *Reed v. Orleans Parish School Board*, 21 So. 2d 895 (La.App.Orl. Cir. 1945), and for a school board to require that its employees undergo medical examinations and that the results be disclosed to school officers. *Pitcher v. Iberia Parish School Board*, 280 So. 2d 603 (La.App. 3 Cir. 1973), *writ denied* 1973, *cert. denied* 416 U.S. 904, 94 S.Ct. 1608, 40 L.Ed.2d 109 (1974). On the other hand, it was held unreasonable for a private employer to utilize medical photographs of an employee's work-related injury, in its safety campaign, without obtaining the employee's consent or withholding his name. *Lambert v. Dow Chemical Co.*, 215 So. 2d 673 (La.App. 1 Cir. 1968).

Only a few Louisiana cases have addressed the situation in which an individual's right to privacy must be weighed against the freedom of the press guaranteed by the First Amendment of the United States Constitution and by Art. I, § 7 of the Louisiana Constitution of 1974.[5] It should be noted, however, that this court indicated in *Mashburn v. Collin*, 355 So. 2d 879, 891 (La. 1977), that "(s)ince the (United States) Supreme Court decisions from *New York Times* through *Gertz* and *Firestone* establish only minimum safeguards for the freedom of speech and the freedom of press under the First Amendment, it is permissible and perhaps appropriate for a state to grant broader protection of these important rights under its own constitution or laws."[6] In an early decision in this

---

[4] Article I, § 5 of the 1974 Constitution provides protection against Unreasonable searches, seizures, or invasions of privacy. *See* note 2, *supra*.

[5] Article I, § 7 of the 1974 Constitution provides: "No law shall curtail or restrain the freedom of speech or of the press. Every person may speak, write, and publish his sentiments on any subject, but is responsible for abuse of that freedom." This section is essentially identical to the corresponding provision of the 1921 Constitution. The "abuse of freedom" wording was retained in order to explicitly bring actions for libel, slander, and defamation under the scope of C.C. 2315. One delegate to the 1973 convention noted the possibility of conflicts between certain rights guaranteed in the proposed Declaration of Rights, citing as an example the conflict between the right to privacy and the right to take photographs. Records of the Louisiana Constitutional Convention of 1973: Convention Transcripts, Vol. VI, 1114.

[6] In actions for defamation, involving injury to reputation instead of injury to a privacy interest, the United States Supreme Court has held that the plaintiff must show actual malice, i. e. that the publication was knowingly false or circulated with reckless disregard for its truth or falsity where the plaintiff is a public official, *New York Times Co. v. Sullivan*, 376 U.S. 254, 84 S.Ct. 710, 11 L.Ed.2d 686 (1964), or a public figure, *Curtis Publishing Co. v. Butts*, 388 U.S. 130, 87 S.Ct. 1975, 18 L.Ed.2d 1094 (1967). Where the plaintiff in a defamation action is a private individual and the content of the factual misstatement should have warned a reasonably prudent editor of its defamatory potential, the Court has held that "so long as they do not impose liability without fault, the States may define for themselves the appropriate standard of liability." *Gertz v. Robert Welch, Inc.*, 418 U.S. 323, 347, 94 S.Ct. 2997, 3010, 41 L.Ed.2d 789, 809 (1974) (emphasis added).
In actions for the "false light" form of invasion of privacy, the Court has held that the actual malice showing is required where the material is assertedly private but a matter of public interest. *Time, Inc. v. Hill*, 385 U.S. 374, 87 S.Ct. 534, 17 L.Ed.2d 456 (1967). But in *Cantrell v. Forest City Publishing Co.*, 419 U.S. 245, 95 S.Ct. 465, 42 L.Ed.2d 419 (1974), the Court noted that it had not yet addressed the issue of whether the actual malice standard is constitutionally required in all "false light" invasion of privacy cases, where the plaintiff is a private individual.
Cox Broadcasting Corp. v. Cohn, 420 U.S. 469, 95 S.Ct. 1029, 43 L.Ed.2d 328 (1975), involved an action based on the public disclosure theory of invasion of privacy, in which the published material is true but embarrassing or painful to the plaintiff. The Court declined to hold broadly that the press may never be made liable for publication of accurate material, no matter how damaging it may be to a plaintiff's sensibilities or reputation. Instead, the Court found that the material published formed part of the public records and was therefore not private. Justice Powell, concurring, was of the opinion that, under *Gertz v. Robert Welch, Inc.*,

area, *Martin v. The Picayune*, 115 La. 979, 986, 40 So. 376, 378 (1906), this court observed that words may be actionable, even if not defamatory, under the principle of the right to privacy, but that the right "has considerable limitations." In that case, on facts that would now constitute a "false light" form of invasion of privacy, the court found the invasion to be actionable because both malice and injury had been alleged. In *Schwartz v. Edrington*, 133 La. 235, 62 So. 660 (1913), this court upheld the injunction of publication of a petition for village incorporation because some of the individuals who had signed the petition had subsequently repudiated it. The court found that the Louisiana Constitution of 1898 protected the publication of one's own sentiments but did not protect the unauthorized use of the purported sentiments of others.[7] In *Norris v. King*, 355 So. 2d 21 (La.App. 3 Cir. 1978), *writ denied* 1978, U.S. *cert. denied*, the appellate court affirmed a damage award against a private individual for unreasonably harassing acts of public disclosure. However, the court distinguished that case, involving publication by a private individual in which no public interest was served by the defendant's conduct, from cases involving the privileges and responsibilities of the news media. In *Mahaffey v. Official Detective Stories, Inc.*, 210 F.Supp. 251 (W.D.La.1962), plaintiffs sought damages for a magazine's publication of an accurate story about the murder of their son. Applying Louisiana law, the United States District Court held that plaintiffs could not recover for libel because the published material was true, and that there could be no recovery for invasion of privacy because the material was of public, newsworthy interest and because "(r)ecovery for invasion of a right of privacy is only available when the plaintiff's private affairs have been given unauthorized exposure." 210 F.Supp. 251, 253.

In deciding the case before us, it is not necessary that we reach the broad question of the extent to which freedom of the press may be limited by an ordinary citizen's right to privacy. Instead, it is only necessary that we determine the form of privacy violation which plaintiffs allege and the kind of privacy interest which they assert.

Plaintiffs have not alleged that the publication placed them, or their home, in a false light; and the record shows that the photograph was not retouched and that the property was indeed in need of repairs. It is also clear that there was no physical intrusion upon the plaintiffs' seclusion; the photograph was taken from the middle of a public street. Finally, this is not a case in which defendant has appropriated an aspect of plaintiffs' personality for its own use or benefit, since mere publication for profit may not be interpreted in this light. Plaintiffs' claim for relief must therefore be based upon the theory of public disclosure of private facts, as in *Mahaffey v. Official Detective Stories, Inc., supra*.

We have already indicated that, according to established principles of the law of privacy, no right to privacy attaches to material in the public view. The only question before this court is thus whether the photograph and words of description depicted a matter which was actually within the plaintiffs' protected zone of privacy. It is clear from the record that the Jauberts' home was plainly visible from the public street, and that passersby were presented with a view of the property which was identical to that published by the defendant. Therefore, plaintiffs had no right to privacy, regarding the house and its condition; defendant committed no fault, and the judgments of the lower courts are reversed; there is now judgment for the defendant, Crowley Post- Signal, Inc., rejecting the demands of the plaintiffs, at their cost.

---

supra, truth is a complete defense not only to a defamation suit by a private individual but also to an invasion of privacy action where the interests to be protected are similar to those considered in *Gertz*.

[7] Article 3 of the 1898 Constitution provided: "No law shall ever be passed to curtail or restrain the liberty of speech or of the press; any person may speak, write and publish his sentiments on all subjects, being responsible for the abuse of that liberty."

ROSHTO
v.
HEBERT
439 So. 2d 428 (La. 1983)

LEMMON, J.

This is an action to recover damages for invasion of privacy arising out of defendants' publication in *The Iberville South,* a local weekly newspaper, of an article which allegedly concerned plaintiffs' private lives. The issue is whether a newspaper's verbatim reproduction, as part of a regular feature, of the original front page of a randomly selected 25-year old edition, constitutes invasion of a person's right to privacy, when the reproduced article accurately describes the details of a local criminal conviction for which the person was subsequently pardoned.

The Iberville South for many years had reproduced the front page of randomly selected prior editions in a regular feature called "Page from Our Past." In 1973, the *South* reproduced the front page of the April 4, 1952 edition, which contained an article about the cattle theft trial of Carlysle, Alfred and E.R. Roshto, three brothers who are the plaintiffs in the instant litigation. Four years later, in 1977, the *South* reproduced the front page of the November 14, 1952 edition, which contained another article about the Roshto brothers, this time concerning the fact that they had been sentenced to prison after their convictions had been affirmed on appeal. Plaintiffs' names were not blocked out in either reproduction.

Plaintiffs then filed the present action, which asserted that the 1977 publication invaded their privacy, since the 25-year old matter was no longer of public concern. They further contended that they had served their term of imprisonment, had been law-abiding and hard working citizens of the community, and had ultimately received full pardons. Because each plaintiff admitted the truth of the articles at the trial on the merits, the trial judge rendered judgment for defendants on the basis that truth was an absolute defense. The court of appeal set aside that judgment, holding that truth is not a defense to an action for invasion of privacy. The court further held that defendants' action constituted an invasion of privacy for which each plaintiff was entitled to $35,000 in damages. 413 So. 2d 927. We granted certiorari. 420 So. 2d 439.

The right of privacy involves the basic right of a person to be let alone in his private affairs. S. Warren and L. Brandeis, The Right to Privacy, 4 Harv.L.Rev. 193 (1890). Unwarranted invasion of a person's right of privacy may give rise to liability for the resulting harm. *Jaubert v. Crowley Post-Signal, Inc.,* 375 So. 2d 1386 (La. 1979); W. Prosser, Law of Torts §117 (4th ed. 1971); 3 Restatement of Torts 2d § 652 A (1977). One of the ways in which a person may subject himself to liability for damages for invasion of privacy is by giving publicity to a matter concerning the private life of another, when the publicized matter would be highly offensive to a reasonable person and is not of legitimate concern to the public. 3 Restatement of Torts 2d § 652 D (1977). The determination of whether a person's conduct constitutes the tort of invasion of privacy depends on the facts and circumstances of each case.

The particular form of invasion of privacy in this case is complicated by the implication of federal constitutional guarantees under the First Amendment of freedom of speech and of the press.[1] In *Cox Broadcasting Corp. v. Cohn,* 420 U.S. 469, 95 S.Ct. 1029, 43 L.Ed.2d 328 (1975), the Court addressed the constitutional guarantee in the context of publication of true statements of fact concerning a person's private life.

The *Cox Broadcasting* decision involved the television report of the name of a rape victim, despite a Georgia statute making it unlawful to publish a rape victim's name. The father of the victim who had been killed in the course of the crime sued the television station for damages, claiming that

---

[1] La. Const. Art. I, § 7 (1974) provides a similar guarantee. However, La. Const. Art. I, § 5 (1974) also guarantees every person security against unreasonable invasions of privacy.

his right of privacy had been invaded by the broadcast. The Court held that a state may not impose sanctions on the accurate publication of a rape victim's name obtained from records of a public criminal proceeding in which the official court documents were open for public inspection.[2] The Court expressly declined to address the question of whether truthful publications may *ever* be constitutionally subjected to civil or criminal liability; instead, the Court focused on the "narrower interface between press and privacy that this case presents, namely, whether the State may impose sanctions on the accurate publication of the name of a rape victim obtained from public records--more specifically, from judicial records which are maintained in connection with a public prosecution and which themselves are open to public inspection."[3]

To the extent that the *Cox Broadcasting* opinion dealt with a current prosecution, that decision is not controlling in the present case.[4] On the other hand, the passage of a considerable length of time after the pertinent event does not of itself convert a public matter into a private one. Lapse of time is merely one of the factors to be considered in determining liability for damages for invasion of privacy by publication of an offensive but truthful matter which was once one of public concern and is still of public record. The circumstances surrounding the publication may also give rise to important factors to be considered.

For example, when a person convicted of a crime has served his sentence, changed his name, moved to a faraway city, concealed his identity, and led an obscure, respectable and useful life for 20 years, a newspaper reporter who institutes an investigation of the little-known citizen's past history and reveals the conviction in a newspaper published in the citizen's new community (far from the site of the crime), the reporter possibly may be liable for damages for invasion of privacy, even though the information is true and is contained in the public records.[5] The intentional nature of the disclosure (which likely involves an element of malice), the lack of the legitimate public interest in an ancient crime committed in a faraway town, and the disclosure of the private facts regarding the criminal's new name and address (after his concerted efforts to conceal his identity and maintain obscurity) are all pertinent factors in determining whether liability should be imposed for damages under the circumstances.[6]

The court of appeal relied on *Briscoe v. Reader's Digest Ass'n,* 4 Cal.3d 529, 93 Cal.Rptr. 866, 483 P.2d 34 (1971), in which the defendant published an article on hijacking and deliberately included plaintiff's name as a convicted hijacker, although plaintiff had since reformed and taken a place in respectable society. In the present case, however, the fact of defendants' convictions was publicized inadvertently as part of the publication of a randomly selected front page, which contained a number of articles. No one deliberately pointed the finger of blame at plaintiffs. There was no attempt to highlight the matter or to relate plaintiffs' past history to their present life and place of residence. There was also no suggestion of intentional behavior or malice on the part of the editor,

---

[2] The Georgia statute only provided a criminal sanction. However, civil liability is often determined by analogy to criminal statutes, when the court sets the standard of care and imposes the duty of maintaining that standard. *See Pierre v. Allstate Ins. Co.,* 257 La. 471, 242 So. 2d 821 (1970).

[3] Justice Powell concurred, stating his view that truth is a complete defense in those invasion of privacy actions in which the interests sought to be protected are similar to those interests protected in defamation actions based on falsehoods injurious to a private individual.

[4] The court of appeal believed *Cox* inapposite, largely because it dealt with the publication of information of a current nature, whereas the information about the Roshto brothers was 25 years old. The court stated the Roshto story "had absolutely no value as a newsworthy item". 413 So. 2d at 933.

[5] *See* Illustration 26 in Chapter 28A of Restatement, above.

[6] Indeed, under the postulated circumstances, the reporter may be liable for damages for intentional infliction of mental anguish.

who testified that he did not even know the Roshto brothers.[7] Moreover, the convictions had occurred in the community in which the newspaper was published, and the information was a matter of public record there. Finally, the community information contained on randomly selected front pages of former editions of a newspaper, when viewed collectively, is certainly a matter of legitimate public interest, in the absence of extenuating circumstances regarding the publication.

The intermediate court was apparently concerned that newspapers are possibly being accorded a tremendous amount of freedom without being required to exercise a corresponding degree of responsibility, and arguably a balancing of rights and responsibilities should be required. When the published information is accurate and true and a matter of public record, this fact weighs heavily in such a balancing process, but a newspaper cannot be allowed unrestricted freedom to publish any true statement of public record, regardless of the purpose or manner of publication or of the temporal and proximal relationship of the published fact to the present situation.[8] This case, however, does not reveal any abuse in the purpose or manner of publication.

Defendants were arguably insensitive or careless in reproducing a former front page for publication without checking for information that might be currently offensive to some members of the community. However, more than insensitivity or simple carelessness is required for the imposition of liability for damages when the publication is truthful, accurate and non- malicious. Plaintiffs in the present case simply did not establish additional factors and circumstances to warrant the imposition of damages.

Accordingly, the judgment of the court of appeal is reversed, and the judgment of the district court is reinstated.

DIXON, C.J., concurs.

WATSON, J., concurs in the result.

CALOGERO, Justice, concurring.

I respectfully concur, agreeing that the plaintiffs have not proven an actionable invasion of privacy. While the defendant's conduct need not be malicious, it must at least be injurious and highly offensive to the reasonable man, reckless in its disregard for its offensiveness, and without any independent justification for revealing the plaintiffs' identity. In this case, the plaintiffs have simply failed to show it.

NOTES

1.   Is the unauthorized display of high quality photos of an unidentified infant in a photographer's studio an actionable invasion of privacy? *See, Slocum v. Sears Roebuck and Co.,* 542 So. 2d 777 (La.App. 3 Cir. 1989).

2.   Do volunteer participants in a videotaped parade have a cause of action for invasion of privacy when portions of the video appear as background scenery in an x-rated movie? *See, Easter Seal Society v. Playboy Enterprises, Inc.,* 530 So. 2d 643 (La.App. 4 Cir. 1988), *writ denied*, 532 So. 2d 1390 (La. 1988). Do allegations that a former police cadet had been expelled for using steroids

---

[7] Plaintiffs claim, however, that E.R. Roshto, after the publication of the first article, went to the newspaper's office and requested that no more articles concerning their conviction for cattle theft be published. Mr. Roshto testified that he was assured by a man who identified himself as the editor that the Roshto name would be blocked out if any more such articles were published.

The trial judge, by finding there was neither actual or *implied* malice, apparently concluded that defendant editor did not receive a complaint about the first publication.

[8] Even if the *Cox Broadcasting* decision stands for the proposition that a newspaper has the right to publish true facts obtained from court records which are open for public inspection, there can be an abuse of that right.

give rise to an action of invasion of privacy? *See, Fourcade v. City of Gretna,* 598 So. 2d 415 (La.App. 5 Cir. 1992).

3.   Does the expectation of privacy extend to a trash bin? *See, Camp, Dresser & McKee, Inc. v. Steimle and Associates, Inc.,* 652 So. 2d 44 (La.App. 5 Cir. 1995).

4.   Louisiana courts have not allowed claims for attempted invasion of privacy. In *Meche v. Wal-Mart Stores, Inc.,* 692 So. 2d 544 (La.App. 3 Cir. 1997), *writ denied,* 693 So. 2d 760 (La. 1997), *cert. denied,* 522 U.S. 1002 (1997), female employees sued their employer because a camera had been installed in a restroom. Although a jury found an abuse of rights by defendant, no invasion of privacy occurred because the camera could not receive pictures.

5.   The rise of computers, the internet, and electronic communications has increased the volume of litigation of privacy issues. The tort of invasion of privacy is implicated in many cases. Other sources of law relevant in some cases are the Omnibus Crime Control and Safe Streets Act of 1968, as amended (including the Electronic Communications Privacy Act and the Stored Communications Act) (federal law); the Computer Fraud and Abuse Act (federal law); the Fourth Amendment to the U.S. Constitution; and various state laws.

6.   When employees have sued their employers for invasions of privacy based on computer monitoring, they usually have lost because courts conclude that they have no expectation of privacy on an employer-owned computer. *See, e.g., TBG Ins. Services Corp. v. Superior Court,* 96 Cal.App.4th 443, 117 Cal.Rptr.2d 155 (Cal. App. 2d Dist. 2002); *Smyth v. Pillsbury Co.,* 914 F.Supp. 97 (E.D. Pa. 1996). Most employers today disseminate computer use policies, restricting use to business purposes and reserving the right to monitor and inspect.

CPSIA information can be obtained
at www.ICGtesting.com
Printed in the USA
LVHW101456050719
623280LV00002B/24/P